HANDBOOK OF REHABILITATION PSYCHOLOGY

SECOND EDITION

HANDBOOK OF REHABILITATION PSYCHOLOGY

SECOND EDITION

EDITED BY
Robert G. Frank
Mitchell Rosenthal
Bruce Caplan

AMERICAN PSYCHOLOGICAL ASSOCIATION
WASHINGTON, DC

Published by
American Psychological Association
750 First Street, NE
Washington, DC 20002
www.apa.org

To order
APA Order Department
P.O. Box 92984
Washington, DC 20090-2984
Tel: (800) 374-2721; Direct: (202) 336-5510
Fax: (202) 336-5502; TDD/TTY: (202) 336-6123
Online: www.apa.org/books/
E-mail: order@apa.org

In the U.K., Europe, Africa, and the Middle East, copies may be ordered from
American Psychological Association
3 Henrietta Street
Covent Garden, London
WC2E 8LU England

Typeset in Berkeley by Circle Graphics, Columbia, MD

Printer: Edwards Brothers, Inc., Ann Arbor, MI
Cover Designer: Berg Design, Albany, NY
Technical/Production Editor: Emily Welsh

The opinions and statements published are the responsibility of the authors, and such opinions and statements do not necessarily represent the policies of the American Psychological Association.

Library of Congress Cataloging-in-Publication Data

Handbook of rehabilitation psychology / edited by Robert G. Frank, Mitchell Rosenthal, and Bruce Caplan. — 2nd ed.
      p. cm.
    Includes bibliographical references and index.
    ISBN-13: 978-1-4338-0444-1
    ISBN-10: 1-4338-0444-1
  1. Clinical health psychology—Handbooks, manuals, etc. 2. Medical rehabilitation—Psychological aspects—Handbooks, manuals, etc. I. Frank, Robert G., 1952- II. Rosenthal, Mitchell, 1949- III. Caplan, Bruce.

    R726.7.H366 2010
    616.001'9—dc22
                                   2009010002

British Library Cataloguing-in-Publication Data
A CIP record is available from the British Library.

Printed in the United States of America
Second Edition

Bringing to fruition the second edition of the *Handbook of Rehabilitation Psychology* required more than 3 years of concerted, but enjoyable, collaborative effort among the coeditors and diligent work by our many contributors. In May of 2007, tragedy struck when our close friend and colleague, Mitch Rosenthal, died unexpectedly. The impact of Mitch's death on this book and the field of rehabilitation psychology defies description. As an editor of this volume, Mitch provided the same leadership, scholarship, passion, and humor he shared with rehabilitation psychologists and other specialists for more than 30 years. The shock and sadness that spread across the country—indeed, the world—as colleagues learned of Mitch's death reflected not only his significant intellectual contributions to all things rehabilitation but also his unique and wonderful capacity to form fruitful friendships with so many people. We dedicate the *Handbook of Rehabilitation Psychology, Second Edition,* to the memory of Mitch Rosenthal. Our dedication serves as a lasting tribute to his many and varied contributions to the fields of rehabilitation psychology and rehabilitation medicine and his extraordinary and enduring personal and professional impact on all of us.

Contents

Contributors   xi
Acknowledgments.   xv
Introduction.   3
    Robert G. Frank and Bruce Caplan

Part I. Clinical Conditions   7

Chapter 1. Spinal Cord Injury.   9
       J. Scott Richards, Donald G. Kewman, Elizabeth Richardson,
       and Paul Kennedy
Chapter 2. Limb Amputation   29
       Bruce Rybarczyk, Jay Behel, and Lynda Szymanski
Chapter 3. Traumatic Brain Injury in Adults   43
       Joseph H. Ricker
Chapter 4. Rehabilitation Psychology and Neuropsychology
       With Stroke Survivors.   63
       Bruce Caplan
Chapter 5. Psychological Assessment and Practice in Geriatric Rehabilitation   95
       Peter A. Lichtenberg and Brooke C. Schneider
Chapter 6. Psychological Rehabilitation in Burn Injuries.   107
       Shelley Wiechman Askay and David Patterson
Chapter 7. Chronic Pain   119
       Michael E. Robinson and Erin M. O'Brien
Chapter 8. Cognition and Multiple Sclerosis: Assessment and Treatment.   133
       Nancy D. Chiaravalloti and John DeLuca

Part II. Assessment   145

Chapter 9. Functional Status and Quality-of-Life Measures.   147
       Allen W. Heinemann and Trudy Mallinson
Chapter 10. Neuropsychological Practice in Rehabilitation   165
       Thomas A. Novack, Mark Sherer, and Suzanne Penna
Chapter 11. Forensic Psychological Evaluation in Rehabilitation   179
       Brick Johnstone, Laura H. Schopp, Cheryl L. Shigaki,
       and Kelly Lora Franklin

Chapter 12. Assessment of Personality and Psychopathology 195
 Douglas Johnson-Greene and Pegah Touradji
Chapter 13. Neuroimaging 213
 Erin D. Bigler

Part III. Clinical Interventions 239

Chapter 14. Alcohol and Other Drug Use in Traumatic Disability 241
 Charles H. Bombardier and Aaron P. Turner
Chapter 15. Psychotherapeutic Interventions 259
 Michele J. Rusin and Jay M. Uomoto
Chapter 16. Assistive Technology for Cognition and Behavior 273
 Ned L. Kirsch and Marcia J. Scherer
Chapter 17. Cognitive Rehabilitation 285
 Tessa Hart
Chapter 18. Evidence-Based Practice With Family Caregivers:
 Decision-Making Strategies Based on Research and Clinical Data 301
 Kathleen Chwalisz and Stephanie Clancy Dollinger

Part IV. Pediatrics 313

Chapter 19. Pediatric Neuropsychology in Medical Rehabilitation Settings 315
 *Janet E. Farmer, Stephen M. Kanne, Maureen O. Grissom,
 and Sally Kemp*
Chapter 20. Neurodevelopmental Conditions in Children 329
 Seth Warschausky and Jacqueline Kaufman
Chapter 21. Rehabilitation in Pediatric Chronic Illness:
 Juvenile Rheumatic Diseases as an Exemplar 337
 Janelle Wagner, Kevin A. Hommel, Larry L. Mullins, and John M. Chaney
Chapter 22. Family, School, and Community:
 Their Role in the Rehabilitation of Children 345
 Shari L. Wade and Nicolay Chertkoff Walz

Part V. Emerging Topics for Rehabilitation Psychology 355

Chapter 23. Vocational Rehabilitation 357
 Robert T. Fraser and Kurt Johnson
Chapter 24. Spirituality and Rehabilitation 365
 Kathie J. Albright, Martin Forchheimer, and Denise G. Tate
Chapter 25. Women's Experience of Disability 371
 Margaret A. Nosek
Chapter 26. The Social Psychology of Disability 379
 Dana S. Dunn
Chapter 27. Central Nervous System Plasticity and Rehabilitation 391
 *Gitendra Uswatte, Edward Taub, Victor W. Mark, Christi Perkins,
 and Lynne Gauthier*
Chapter 28. Prevention, Assessment, and Management of Work-Related
 Injury and Disability 407
 Stephen T. Wegener and William Stiers

Chapter 29. Application of Positive Psychology to Rehabilitation Psychology 417
    Dawn M. Ehde

Part VI. Professional Issues 425

Chapter 30. Ethics.. 427
    Stephanie L. Hanson and Thomas R. Kerkhoff
Chapter 31. Health Policy 101: Fundamental Issues in Health Care Reform 439
    Glenn S. Ashkanazi, Kristofer J. Hagglund, Andrea Lee, Zoe Swaine,
    and Robert G. Frank
Chapter 32. The Rehabilitation Team 451
    Lester Butt and Bruce Caplan
Chapter 33. Rehabilitating the Health Care Organization:
    Administering Psychology's Opportunity 459
    Charles D. Callahan
Chapter 34. Competencies of a Rehabilitation Psychologist...................... 467
    Mary R. Hibbard and David R. Cox

Afterword: Of Bins and Arrows 477
    John D. Corrigan
Index 483
About the Editors.. 503

Contributors

Kathie J. Albright, PhD, University of Michigan Health System, Ann Arbor

Glenn S. Ashkanazi, PhD, University of Florida, Gainesville

Shelley Wiechman Askay, PhD, University of Washington School of Medicine, Seattle

Jay Behel, PhD, Rush University Medical Center, Chicago, IL

Erin D. Bigler, PhD, Brigham Young University, Provo, UT

Charles H. Bombardier, PhD, University of Washington School of Medicine, Seattle

Lester Butt, PhD, ABPP (Rp), Craig Hospital, Englewood, CO

Charles D. Callahan, PhD, ABPP, Memorial Medical System, Springfield, IL

Bruce Caplan, PhD, Rp, CN, Independent Practice, Wynnewood, PA

John M. Chaney, PhD, Oklahoma State University, Stillwater

Nancy D. Chiaravalloti, PhD, Kessler Medical Rehabilitation Research and Education Center, West Orange, NJ

Kathleen Chwalisz, PhD, Southern Illinois University, Carbondale

John D. Corrigan, PhD, Ohio State University, Columbus

David R. Cox, PhD, ABPP, Neuropsychology & Rehabilitation Consultants, P.C., Chapel Hill, NC

John DeLuca, PhD, ABPP, Kessler Medical Rehabilitation Research and Education Center, University of Medicine and Dentistry of New Jersey, West Orange

Stephanie Clancy Dollinger, Southern Illinois University, Carbondale

Dana S. Dunn, PhD, Moravian College, Bethlehem, PA

Dawn M. Ehde, PhD, University of Washington School of Medicine, Seattle

Janet E. Farmer, PhD, ABPP, University of Missouri, Columbia

Martin Forchheimer, MPP, University of Michigan Health System, Ann Arbor

Robert G. Frank, PhD, Kent State University, Kent, OH

Kelly Lora Franklin, PhD, Colmery O'Neil VA Medical Center, Topeka, KS

Robert T. Fraser, PhD, CRC, University of Washington, Seattle

Lynne Gauthier, University of Alabama at Birmingham

Maureen O. Grissom, PhD, University of Missouri, Columbia

Kristofer J. Hagglund, PhD, ABPP, University of Missouri, Columbia

Stephanie L. Hanson, PhD, ABPP, University of Florida, Gainesville

Tessa Hart, PhD, Moss Rehabilitation Research Institute, Elkins Park, PA

Allen W. Heinemann, PhD, ABPP (Rp), FACRM, Feinberg School of Medicine Northwestern University, Rehabilitation Institute of Chicago, Chicago, IL

Mary R. Hibbard, PhD, ABPP, Department of Rehabilitation Medicine, Mount Sinai Hospital, New York, NY

Kevin A. Hommel, PhD, Cincinnati Children's Hospital Medical Center, Cincinnati, OH

Douglas Johnson-Greene, PhD, MPH, ABPP (Cn, Rp, Cp), Johns Hopkins University School of Medicine, Baltimore, MD

Kurt Johnson, PhD, CRC, University of Washington, Seattle

Brick Johnstone, PhD, University of Missouri, Columbia

Stephen M. Kanne, PhD, ABPP, University of Missouri, Columbia

Jacqueline Kaufman, PhD, University of Michigan, Ann Arbor

Sally Kemp, PhD, Neuropsychoeducational Consultative Services, Camdenton, MO; University of Missouri, Columbia

Paul Kennedy, DPhil, FBPS, University of Oxford, Headington, Oxford, England

Thomas R. Kerkhoff, PhD, ABPP, University of Florida, Gainesville

Donald G. Kewman, PhD, ABPP, Nevada City, CA

Ned L. Kirsch, PhD, University of Michigan Health System, Ann Arbor

Andrea Lee, University of Florida, Gainesville

Peter A. Lichtenberg, PhD, Wayne State University Institute of Gerontology, Detroit, MI

Trudy Mallinson, PhD, OTR/L, Rehabilitation Institute of Chicago, Chicago, IL

Victor W. Mark, MD, University of Alabama at Birmingham

Larry L. Mullins, PhD, Oklahoma State University, Stillwater

Margaret A. Nosek, PhD, Baylor College of Medicine, Houston, TX

Thomas A. Novack, PhD, University of Alabama at Birmingham

Erin M. O'Brien, MS, Brown University Medical School, Providence, RI

David Patterson, PhD, ABPP, Harborview Medical Center, Seattle, WA

Suzanne Penna, PhD, Atlanta VA Medical Center, Atlanta, GA

Christi Perkins, University of Alabama at Birmingham

J. Scott Richards, PhD, ABPP, University of Alabama at Birmingham

Elizabeth Richardson, PhD, University of Alabama at Birmingham

Joseph H. Ricker, PhD, University of Pittsburgh, Pittsburgh, PA

Michael E. Robinson, PhD, University of Florida, Gainesville

Mitchell Rosenthal, PhD, Kessler Medical Research and Education Corporation, West Orange, NJ

Michele J. Rusin, PhD, ABPP (Rp), Independent Practice, Atlanta, GA

Bruce Rybarczyk, PhD, ABPP, Virginia Commonwealth University, Richmond

Marcia J. Scherer, PhD, MPH, FACRM, Institute for Matching Person & Technology, Inc., University of Rochester Medical Center, Webster, NY

Brooke C. Schneider, Wayne State University Institute of Gerontology, Detroit, MI

Laura H. Schopp, PhD, University of Missouri, Columbia

Mark Sherer, PhD, TIRR Memorial Hermann, Houston, TX

Cheryl L. Shigaki, PhD, ABPP, University of Missouri, Columbia

William Stiers, PhD, ABPP, Johns Hopkins University School of Medicine, Baltimore, MD

Zoe Swaine, MS, University of Florida, Gainesville

Lynda Szymanski, PhD, The College of St. Catherine, St. Paul, MN

Denise G. Tate, PhD, ABPP, FACRM, University of Michigan Health System, Ann Arbor

Edward Taub, PhD, University of Alabama at Birmingham

Pegah Touradji, PhD, Johns Hopkins University School of Medicine, Baltimore, MD

Aaron P. Turner, PhD, University of Washington School of Medicine, Seattle

Jay M. Uomoto, PhD, University of Washington School of Medicine, Seattle

Gitendra Uswatte, PhD, University of Alabama at Birmingham

Shari L. Wade, PhD, Cincinnati Children's Hospital Medical Center, Cincinnati, OH

Janelle Wagner, PhD, Medical University of South Carolina, Charleston

Nicolay Chertkoff Walz, PhD, Cincinnati Children's Hospital Medical Center, Cincinnati, OH

Seth Warschausky, PhD, University of Michigan Health System, Ann Arbor

Stephen T. Wegener, PhD, ABPP, Johns Hopkins University School of Medicine, Baltimore, MD

Acknowledgments

Robert G. Frank: Janet, Daniel, and Brian provide the juice of life; their support makes the sky bluer, the mountains taller, and the sun warmer.

Bruce Caplan: Thanks to my father, Jerome Caplan, who taught me the difference between being "smart" and being "wise," and also taught me to be kind, because everyone you meet is fighting a hard battle. Thanks, also, to my endlessly patient and forgiving wife and best friend, Judy Shechter, whose tolerance knows no limits and whose love means everything.

With extraordinary grace and good humor, Robbie Eller at the University of Florida and Patty Schiffhauer-Pearlberg at Kent State University each provided outstanding organizational and administrative skills that kept the project on track. We both thank them.

Handbook of
Rehabilitation
Psychology

SECOND EDITION

Introduction

Robert G. Frank and Bruce Caplan

The demand for rehabilitation psychology expertise increases daily. People across the age spectrum with chronic health conditions, children with developmental disorders, and soldiers injured in battle are just a few of the growing populations needing rehabilitation intervention. The emotional distress caused by injury or illness can be considerable, affecting both patients and caregivers. Disability-induced emotional turmoil can be disabling in its own right, compounding the already considerable obstacles faced by rehabilitation patients. Furthermore, for those whose disability includes cognitive impairment, such as survivors of stroke or traumatic brain injury, neuropsychological assessment and intervention are critical elements of a successful rehabilitation program. Clearly, to treat the full spectrum of emotional, cognitive, familial, social, and vocational consequences of disability encountered in consumers of rehabilitation services, psychological expertise is required.

Historically, rehabilitation psychologists have served an unusually wide variety of populations, making it difficult to formulate a concise definition of the field. However, a recent work by Scherer et al. (in press) captures the essential elements:

> Rehabilitation Psychology is a specialty area within psychology that focuses on the study and application of psychological knowledge and skills on behalf of individuals with disabilities and chronic health conditions in order to maximize health and welfare, independence and choice, functional abilities, and social role participation. Rehabilitation Psychologists are uniquely trained and specialized to engage in a broad range of activities including clinical practice, consultation, program development, service provision, research, teaching and education, training, administration, development of public policy and advocacy related to persons with disability and chronic health conditions.

This second edition of the *Handbook of Rehabilitation Psychology* provides an up-to-date, comprehensive overview of the issues related to rehabilitation psychology. The remainder of this chapter discusses the history of rehabilitation psychology, the new features of this second-edition *Handbook,* as well as the structure of the volume.

A BRIEF HISTORY OF REHABILITATION PSYCHOLOGY

Rehabilitation psychology emerged as a recognizable specialty following World War II in parallel with the flowering of rehabilitation medicine in the United States. Advances in treatment on the battlefield yielded increased survival rates and a concomitant substantial incidence of disabling conditions among those survivors. Driven by the return of soldiers with complex injuries, multidisciplinary rehabilitation treatment achieved outcomes exceeding those of one-dimensional medical models (Rusk, 1969). Rehabilitation psychologists made important contributions to these efforts by developing and implementing a multifactorial model of adjustment, one that took into consideration the reciprocally interacting influences of the injured person and multiple aspects of his or her environment (Wright, 1960). This early emergence of what could be considered the first of the "biopsychosocial models" remained relatively unique to rehabilitation psychology, with little recognition by other specialties. Starting after World War II with the treatment of survivors of spinal cord injury, rehabilitation programs recognized the need for comprehensive, multidisciplinary interventions addressing medical, psychological, and ambulatory concerns (see chap. 32, this volume, for a comprehensive discussion of the rehabilitation team). Despite these innovative contributions, the field then struggled for definition and broad respectability through the next 25 years, sustained by a small group of individuals dedicated to concepts, practices, and patient populations that were not yet in vogue.

Between 1970 and the mid-1990s, rehabilitation psychology benefited from several interrelated developments. In the 1970s, the National Institute of Disability and Rehabilitation Research (NIDRR) funded a series of "Model Systems" of care designed to demonstrate the effectiveness of coordinated, comprehensive rehabilitation for persons with spinal cord injury. These Model Systems were usually implemented in academic health centers, most of which were Level 1 Trauma Centers, designed to provide rapid, comprehensive treatment for trauma victims. Psychologists were viewed as core participants on Model Systems rehabilitation teams.

In the 1980s, scientist–clinicians at the Rusk Institute of Rehabilitation Medicine in New York began widespread dissemination of their methods of neuropsychological rehabilitation for persons with stroke and traumatic brain injury. Leonard Diller, Yehuda Ben-Yishay, Joseph Weinberg, and colleagues developed and refined treatments for unilateral neglect and other neurobehavioral dysfunctions (Diller & Gordon, 1981). Previously, individuals with higher-cortical dysfunctions were viewed as unlikely to benefit from rehabilitation in the psychological and neuropsychological domains. Now, however, a subsequent generation of clinicians was inspired to formulate and evaluate interventions for a wide range of such dysfunctions. In part because of these efforts, the Model Systems approach was extended to traumatic brain injury.

During this same period, the behavioral model of rehabilitation of persons with chronic pain, articulated by Wilbert Fordyce (1976), gained wide recog-

nition, with rehabilitation psychologists serving as core members of the pain treatment team. A third set of Model Systems was created—this time devoted to burn care emphasizing pain management, in which rehabilitation psychologists played a vital role in both research and clinical care (Patterson, 2007).

In 1995, leaders in Division 22 (Rehabilitation Psychology) of the American Psychological Association (APA) issued the first training guidelines for rehabilitation psychologists (Patterson & Hanson, 1995). In the same year, the American Board of Rehabilitation Psychology (ABRP) was established as an independent body, aligning in 1997 with the American Board of Professional Psychology as its 11th designated specialty. The Academy of Rehabilitation Psychology, the educational arm of ABRP, is beginning to emerge as a group responsible for high-quality continuing education for rehabilitation psychologists to ensure that competence is maintained by all practitioners—both diplomates (i.e., individuals recognized by the ABRP for having demonstrated specialist practice skills) and nondiplomates.

The beginning of the 21st century is witnessing another wave of injured soldiers returning from conflicts, this time in the Middle East. Once again, advances in combat medicine and rapid treatment have resulted in a growing cohort of soldiers presenting with disabling symptoms. In this instance, there has been mounting public awareness of the high incidence of multitrauma among returning soldiers, with special emphasis on posttraumatic stress disorder and traumatic brain injury (Hoge et al., 2008) but also including a host of other injuries such as amputations and burns; these conditions demand psychological and neuropsychological assessment and intervention (Sayer et al., 2008). The confluence of these multisystem war injuries, combined with the aging of the American population, may well herald a new wave of demand for rehabilitation psychology skills and services.

NEW FEATURES OF THE SECOND-EDITION *HANDBOOK*

In 2000, APA published the first edition of the *Handbook of Rehabilitation Psychology*. Fueled by the growth of the discipline (as reflected in the increasing number of individuals acquiring diplomate status from ABRP), as well as by recognition by related specialties (e.g., health psychology, clinical neuropsychology) of rehabilitation psychology's considerable relevance to their own work, the *Handbook* gained recognition as the most influential text in the field (Ryan & Tree, 2004).

New developments in the field now warrant this revised edition of the *Handbook*. This second edition includes 34 chapters, more than one-third of which cover new topics such as assistive technology, family caregivers, health care administration, positive psychology, and spirituality. An entirely new section on pediatrics has been added, with chapters on important developmental issues and risk factors for children with severe illness or injures. The remaining chapters offer substantive updates of the relevant principles and practices of rehabilitation psychology.

Space limitations dictated that several topics could not be carried over from the first edition. After much consideration, we elected to eliminate topics for which a lesser degree of change and development had occurred in the interim. Of course, the exclusion of a topic from the second edition should not be considered to reflect negatively on the importance of the area to the field. Interested readers may well find the material in the earlier edition still pertinent to their practice.

ORGANIZATION OF THIS VOLUME

The second edition of the *Handbook* is divided into six sections. Part I, Clinical Conditions, provides rehabilitation practitioners with current research and practice guidelines for the most common rehabilitation conditions, including spinal cord injury, limb amputation, traumatic brain injury, stoke, geriatrics, burns, chronic pain, and multiple sclerosis.

Part II, Assessment, focuses on common methods to evaluate relevant psychosocial and neurobehavioral factors. This section includes chapters on functional status and quality-of-life measurement, neuropsychological and forensic evaluation in rehabilitation, as well as personality and psychopathology assessment and new developments in neuroimaging.

Part III, Clinical Interventions, reviews a variety of psychological intervention strategies, such as treatment for alcohol and other substance misuse in traumatic disability, a common problem for people with severe illness or injuries. Chapters also address psychotherapeutic strategies with individuals in rehabilitation, emerging models of psychological treatment and cognitive rehabilitation, the use of assistive technology for those with cognitive impairments, and the treatment of family members of injured individuals.

Part IV, Pediatrics, includes four chapters examining issues specific to children requiring rehabilitation. Neuropsychology, neurodevelopment, juvenile rheumatoid arthritis, and the vital roles of school, family, and community are explored.

Part V, Emerging Topics for Rehabilitation Psychology, addresses several new areas that affect rehabilitation outcome: vocational rehabilitation, spirituality, women's unique experiences in rehabilitation, concepts in social psychology, central nervous system plasticity, the role of work-related injuries, and the emerging perspective of positive psychology.

The last section, Part VI, Professional Issues, considers the impact of rehabilitation psychology's interests on national agendas. Readers will find an updated review of ethics as applied to rehabilitation cases, a consideration of the role of federal health policy in rehabilitation psychology and issues faced by rehabilitation teams and roles of the rehabilitation psychologist therein, administration of inpatient rehabilitation teams, and the notion of competences in this field. The chapter on competences outlines the process whereby an individual can seek diplomate status through ABRP.

We view this volume as a useful sourcebook for the growing ranks of rehabilitation psychologists, as well as researchers and practitioners in the many related health fields—medicine, nursing, psychiatry, physical therapy, occupational therapy, speech and language therapy, health care administration, education, and family therapy, to name a few. Meeting the needs of persons with disabilities and chronic health conditions requires a multidisciplinary approach, and this volume demonstrates the important role of psychology in that effort. We hope that readers will find herein the requisite knowledge to contribute to the further evolution of rehabilitation psychology.

References

Diller, L., & Gordon, W. (1981). Rehabilitation and clinical neuropsychology. In S. Filskov & T. Boll (Eds.), *Handbook of clinical neuropsychology* (pp. 702–733). New York: Wiley.

Fordyce, W. (1976). *Behavioral methods in chronic pain and illness.* St. Louis, MO: Mosby.

Hoge, C. W., McGurk, D., Thomas, J. L., Cox, A. L., Engel, C. C., & Castro, C. A. (2008). Mild traumatic brain injury in U.S. soldiers returning from Iraq. *The New England Journal of Medicine, 358,* 453–463.

Patterson, D. R. (2007). The NIDRR burn injury rehabilitation model system program: Selected findings. *Archives of Physical Medicine and Rehabilitation, 88*(12, Suppl. 2), S1–S2.

Patterson, D. R., & Hanson, S. L. (1995). Joint Division 22 and ACRM guidelines for postdoctoral training in rehabilitation psychology. *Rehabilitation Psychology, 40,* 299–310.

Rusk, H. A. (1969). The growth and development of rehabilitation medicine. *Archives of Physical Medicine and Rehabilitation, 50,* 463–466.

Ryan, J. J., & Tree, H. A. (2004). Essential readings in rehabilitation psychology. *Teaching of Psychology, 31,* 138–140.

Sayer, N. A., Chiros, C. E., Sigford, B., Scott, S., Clothier, B., Pickett, T., & Lew, H. L. (2008). Characteristics and rehabilitation outcomes among patients with blast and other injuries sustained during the Global War on Terror. *Archives of Physical Medicine and Rehabilitation, 89,* 163–170.

Scherer, M., Blair, K., Bost, R., Hanson, S., Hough, S., Kurylo, M., et al. (in press). Rehabilitation psychology. In I. B. Weiner & W. E. Craighead (Eds.), *The concise Corsini encyclopedia of psychology and behavioral science* (4th ed.). Hoboken, NJ: Wiley.

Wright, B. (1960). Physical disability: A psychological approach. New York: Harper & Row.

Part I

CLINICAL CONDITIONS

CHAPTER 1

SPINAL CORD INJURY

J. Scott Richards, Donald G. Kewman, Elizabeth Richardson, and Paul Kennedy

Spinal cord injury (SCI) resulting from trauma imposes major and permanent life changes. Although improvements in medical care over recent years have improved life expectancy, social, attitudinal, and architectural integration have often lagged behind. In this chapter, we review the changing demographics of this population. Activities unique to SCI for the practice of rehabilitation psychology are also discussed. Finally, we address the importance of environmental factors with regard to long-term adjustment and coping.

INJURY CHARACTERISTICS

Functional outcomes post-SCI depend on the neurological level and extent of the injury. Injury classification is determined by conducting a neurological assessment of sensory and motor functioning using standards endorsed by the American Spinal Injury Association (2006) whereby specific groups of muscles (myotomes) and sensory regions (dermatomes) are assessed. The neurological level of injury is defined by the lowest segment of the cord corresponding to normal feeling and movement. Persons with SCIs are classified as having tetraplegia or paraplegia. *Tetraplegia* is characterized by sensory and/or motor loss throughout the body, including the upper limbs, resulting from cord injury within the cervical vertebrae. *Paraplegia* denotes cord injury located at the first thoracic vertebra or below and is usually characterized by sensory and/or motor loss in the lower limbs and/or lower portions of the trunk with preserved function in the upper limbs. An additional factor affecting the extent of spared

sensation and movement is the completeness of the injury. In *complete* injuries, sensory and motor function are absent below the level of injury. *Incomplete* injuries, however, may result in varied degrees of residual function ranging from sensation without movement to minimal deficits below the level of injury.

Depending on the location of the lesion within the cord, incomplete injuries may be further classified into one of several syndromes. Rarely do injuries neatly fall within the circumscribed areas with which these syndromes correspond. It is more common to observe varying degrees of symptoms that are characteristic of the syndrome, or additional symptoms that may not exactly correspond to the ascribed syndrome.

Ventral (anterior) cord syndrome results from damage to anterior sections of the cord, which comprise most of the efferent motor neurons controlling body movement, efferent autonomic neurons facilitating bladder control, and afferent pain and temperature sensory neurons. Individuals with ventral cord syndrome, depending on the extent of damage, experience varying degrees of paralysis, urinary incontinence, and an inability to sense pain and temperature bilaterally below the level of the lesion (Woolsey & Martin, 2003). Because afferent posterior columns are spared, proprioception (i.e., position sense) and touch sensation are typically preserved.

Brown-Sequard's syndrome, also known as *lateral cord syndrome*, is associated with hemisection or damage to one side of the spinal cord (Connolly, 2003; Woolsey & Martin, 2003). The unilateral involvement of the posterior column and anterior tracts is associated with paralysis or muscle weakness and loss of proprioception and touch sensation on the side of the body corresponding to the side of the lesion in the cord. Because only one side of the efferent neurons affecting continence is damaged, bladder control may be spared. A hallmark feature of Brown-Sequard's syndrome, however, is the contralateral loss of pain and temperature relative to the side of the lesion beginning at one to two dermatomes below the level of injury. This contralateral deficit is a result of decussation (i.e., crossing over) of the ascending pain and temperature fibers shortly after these fibers enter the spinal canal.

Central cord syndrome is commonly localized within the cervical regions and is characterized by a lesion in the most medial and central aspects of the cord. Because of the somatotopic arrangement of laminae (i.e., sacral fibers lie laterally; cervical fibers mostly medially), individuals with central cord syndrome experience disproportionate motor impairment in the upper and lower extremities with greater paralysis or weakness in the arms and hands and little or no impairment in the legs (Woolsey & Martin, 2003). Depending on the extent of the lesion, bladder dysfunction and sensory deficits below the level of injury may also be present.

ETIOLOGY AND DEMOGRAPHICS

A great deal of what we know about the demographics and etiology of SCI comes from the collaborative database derived from the Model SCI System of Care program funded by the National Institute on Disability and Rehabilitation Research. From that source, we know that more than half of all injuries occur in the 16–30-year-old group and that men make up about 80% of the cases (Go, DeVivo, & Richards, 1995; Jackson, Dijkers, DeVivo, & Poczatek, 2004). This percentage has changed little in the more than 30 years since the database has been in operation (Stover & Fine, 1986).

The ethnic makeup of the SCI population does not appear to correspond to that of the general population. In 1990, the proportion of Caucasians in the Model Systems database was 70.1% (Go, DeVivo, & Richards, 1995), but that figure has decreased to

62.9% for those injured since 2000 (National Spinal Cord Injury Statistical Center [NSCISC], 2005). Both figures are considerably lower than the 75.1% of Caucasians found in the 2000 national census. In addition, since 2000, those with SCIs who are of either African American or Hispanic origin represent a larger proportion of the Model Systems database relative to the general population (22% and 12.6%, respectively; NSCISC, 2005). Because true population-based figures do not exist, it is unclear whether the trends reported from the NSCISC reflect true racial and ethnic differences or other factors as well, such as referral patterns for the Model Systems and/or changes in locations of the Model Systems over time.

The educational level of persons with SCIs tends to be lower than that of the population in general, even when taking the median age of this population into consideration. For instance, 59.4% of persons with SCIs ages 18–21 are at least high school graduates (Meade, Lewis, Jackson, & Hess, 2004), whereas for the same age group in the general population the figure is 80.4%. Most persons with SCIs are single (i.e., never married) at the time of injury; for the national database, this figure is 51.85% (NSCISC, 2005). This is congruent with the relatively young age at which most injuries occur.

Motor vehicle crashes account for 47.5% of cases reported to the NSCISC since 2000 (NSCISC, 2005). The next most common causes of SCI are falls, acts of violence, and recreational sporting activities (NSCISC, 2005). There has been a relative increase in falls over time as a cause of injury, with a concomitant decrease in injuries acquired in sports activities (Jackson et al., 2004). SCI epidemiology varies across different countries, reflecting differences in risk and exposure factors (Ackery, Tator, & Krassioukov, 2004).

ASSESSMENT AND TREATMENT ISSUES

Many psychologists hired to work on rehabilitation units have not had formal training in rehabilitation psychology, despite the existence of board specialization in that specialty. In addition, a number of factors make a literal translation of practice patterns from traditional clinical psychology settings to the rehabilitation setting problematic. Accordingly, in the following section, emphasis is placed on empirically derived theories, assessment approaches, and interventions specific to rehabilitation settings so as to guide the reader in his or her own work.

Psychological Adjustment to Spinal Cord Injury

Much of the early literature on adjustment following SCI used a stage model of that process in which individuals are expected to move through certain stages in a sequential fashion leading to an endpoint of acceptance. Such models implied that negative affective states such as anger and hostility were not only common but also essentially necessary and that if one did not "work through" these stages, an adequate level of adjustment could not be attained. Trieschmann (1988) summarized the deficits and lack of supporting evidence for such models, emphasizing the need for the field to embrace more recent theoretical formulations that focus on a coping and/or adjustment model reflecting the individual variability that can occur within the adjustment process. Moreover, the course of coping and adjustment is dynamic, fluctuating across the life span as a function of intrapersonal, environmental, and biological factors.

SCI is, nonetheless, a life-changing event, and significant emotional reactions can occur over time as people learn about and attempt to cope with consequent changes. Depressive and anxiety disorders can occur and need to be evaluated and addressed by the treatment team. In this chapter, we review the literature on these disorders in the context of SCI, as well as discuss outcome studies of intervention techniques. We also discuss factors that might negatively affect coping and adjustment, such as concomitant cognitive disorders, pain, and substance abuse. Important related topics are also reviewed, including sexuality, vocation, educational issues, and specific concerns regarding the pediatric SCI population. Interventions both direct (e.g., psychotherapy outcome trials) and indirect (e.g., peer counseling) are addressed.

Depression. Depression is one of the most commonly reported and psychologically researched aspects of SCI. Severe depression can limit a person's

functioning and quality of life and place a strain on health resources. In a rehabilitation setting, people who also experience depression tend to require longer hospitalizations and have less functional independence and mobility when discharged (Umlauf & Frank, 1983). Depression has also been associated with the occurrence of preventable secondary complications, such as pressure sores and urinary tract infections (Herrick, Elliott, & Crow, 1994). Persons with SCIs residing in the community who have high levels of depressive behavior spend more days in bed, have fewer days out of the home, use more paid attendants, and incur increased overall medical expenses (Tate, Forchheimer, Maynard, & Dijkers, 1994). Kennedy and Rogers (2000) examined the prevalence of depression from onset of injury until 2 years postdischarge, using a self-report measure of depressive symptom severity among 104 patients admitted to a national spinal injury center. They found that levels of depression increased the longer patients were in hospital, and mean scores for the cohort exceeded the clinical cutoff point for significant depressive symptoms. After discharge, levels decreased and were below the cutoff point for the remaining 2 years of the study. Bombardier, Richards, Krause, Tulsky, and Tate (2004) found an 11.4% prevalence of major depression in a community-dwelling sample of persons with SCIs, using a screening measure for depression that correlates highly with the *Diagnostic and Statistical Manual of Mental Disorders* (4th ed.; American Psychiatric Association, 1994) criteria. Major depression was not associated with demographic or injury characteristics; however, it was associated with poorer subjective health, lower satisfaction with life, and more difficulty in daily role functioning.

When assessing depression in people with SCIs, it is important to use appropriate diagnostic criteria (Elliott & Frank, 1996). Depressed mood alone, which may be a common consequence of trauma, does not constitute diagnosable depression; diagnoses other than major depression may be more appropriate (e.g., dysthymic disorder, depressive disorder not otherwise specified, a disorder of the bipolar spectrum).

A number of personal factors may contribute to depression in people with SCIs. People with premorbid histories of maladjustment, psychological disorders, and alcohol or substance use are often prone to depressive behavior following SCI (Dryden et al., 2005; Judd, Stone, Webber, Brown, & Burrows, 1989; Tate, 1993). In general, difficulty coping with life prior to the injury portends difficulty in dealing with SCI. Conversely, good problem-solving skills are associated with lower depression scores (Elliott, Godshall, Herrick, Witty, & Spruell, 1991). Hope and a strong desire to achieve goals are also associated with lower distress (Elliott, Witty, Herrick, & Hoffman, 1991). Other protective factors for depression include employment, high quality social support, and engagement in wheelchair sports (Sipski & Richards, 2006).

Despite the extensive literature on the correlates and concomitants of depression among persons with SCIs, little attention has been given to its effective treatment. Elliott and Kennedy (2004) extensively reviewed the published literature on the treatment of depression post-SCI and found only nine studies that matched inclusion criteria. Of these, only three were psychological interventions and none included truly randomized control groups. There is an unmet need for randomized controlled trials for the treatment of depression post-SCI. Therefore, clinicians who would like to practice evidence-based techniques, at least for now, will have to use approaches that do not yet meet Level I criteria in the SCI literature or that have met those criteria but in different intervention populations.

Pharmacotherapy for the treatment of clinical depression in people with SCIs should be efficacious. However, the lack of outcome studies requires the clinician to extrapolate to determine the most appropriate medication on the basis of non-SCI outcome studies. Tricyclic antidepressants often produce side effects that could be especially problematic for people with SCIs. Consequently, selective serotonin reuptake inhibitors and other nontricyclic antidepressants are more typically the treatment of choice. Because of the paucity of research and possible deleterious side effects of antidepressant medications, the psychologist's role in medication management is to consult regarding the need for antidepressants and to help monitor efficacy and side effects. Because side effect profiles have not been established in the

SCI population, the psychologist must be alert for unanticipated effects.

Some individuals with SCIs may consider suicide when setbacks interfere with their quality of life. Suicide can take the form of overt action, self-neglect, or refusal of required care (Dijkers, Abela, Gans, & Gordon, 1995). Suicides as a percentage of all deaths for people with SCIs are reported at 5% to 10% (Charlifue & Gerhart, 1991; DeVivo, Kartus, Stover, Rutt, & Fine, 1989; Geisler, Jousse, Wynne-Jones, & Breithaupt, 1983; Nyquist & Bors, 1967). The suicide rate for the population as a whole is only 1.4% of all deaths. The suggested risk factors for suicide in people with SCIs are alcohol and drug abuse, psychiatric history, criminal history, family dysfunction, and suicide attempts prior to the injury or during hospitalization (Charlifue & Gerhart, 1991). Dijkers et al. (1995) found that the suicide rate for people with SCIs was highest among young adults, males, and Caucasians. Suicide rates were highest for people with incomplete paraplegia. In addition, the authors found that the rate of suicide diminishes by year postinjury, dropping off considerably after the 5th year. There is also increasing focus on investigating factors that contribute to the perceived positive benefits consequent to SCI, such as increased family closeness and sense of compassion (McMillen & Loveland Cook, 2003). Developing programs targeting the first few years postdischarge for not only monitoring and decreasing risk but also enhancing protective factors may aid in reducing the prevalence of suicide to that of the general population norms.

Anxiety disorders. Anxiety disorders have not been studied as thoroughly as depression among people with SCIs. Therefore, their incidence and prevalence are uncertain. Anxiety is a logical possibility considering the traumatic circumstances often associated with the onset of SCI and the physical and psychological sequelae associated with acute care, rehabilitation, and community reentry, which can also induce distress (Radnitz et al., 1995).

Hancock, Craig, Dickson, Chang, and Martin (1993) found that over the 1st year postinjury, anxiety levels were significantly higher for people with SCIs than were those for a control group. In their sample, 25% of people with SCIs scored one standard deviation above the cutoff score for their anxiety measure as compared with 5% of control subjects. In addition, anxiety did not decrease over the course of the year. Looking at the same subjects after a 2-year period, Craig, Hancock, and Dickson (1994) found that anxiety levels were still elevated compared with control subjects and had not decreased. Frank, Elliott, Buckelew, and Haut (1988) found that age was not related to level of general anxiety, but anxiety was related to the amount of life stress their sample of persons with SCIs had endured.

Social anxiety and social phobia can develop in persons with SCIs. Dunn (1977) analyzed anxiety and avoidance in social situations on the basis of age, type of injury (i.e., paraplegia vs. tetraplegia), and time since injury. He found that social anxiety was related to age but not to type of injury or time since injury. Specifically, regardless of type of injury or time since injury, older subjects endorsed more social discomfort than did younger subjects. Dunn, Van Horn, and Herman (1981) evaluated techniques and materials for development of social skills in persons with SCIs that can reduce social discomfort and avoidance.

Posttraumatic stress disorder.   The traumatic nature of SCI would appear to place such individuals at risk of posttraumatic stress disorder (PTSD). Radnitz et al. (1995) assessed the current and life-time diagnosis of PTSD in a group of veterans with SCIs. Using a PTSD scale and a structured interview based on *Diagnostic and Statistical Manual of Mental Disorders* (3rd ed., rev.; American Psychiatric Association, 1987) criteria, they found a current diagnosis rate of 14.3% to 16.7% and a lifetime diagnosis rate of 33.6% to 34.9%, depending on the instrument used. The authors reported that these rates were similar to those of other traumatized groups. Lude, Kennedy, Evans, Lude, and Beedie (2005) examined 156 Europeans with SCIs for PTSD symptomatology, depression, and coping. They too found that between 10% and 20% scored above the clinical cutoff for PTSD. Regression analysis indicated that the coping strategies of "focusing and venting emotions" and "not accepting" predicted 31% of the variance in intrusion scores.

Adaptation.   Using structural equation modeling, Martz, Livneh, Priebe, Wuermser, and Ottomanelli (2005) examined the influence of disability-related medical and psychological variables on psychosocial adaptation to SCI. They developed a model of adaptation that showed a moderate fit for data derived from 213 participants with SCIs. These researchers concluded that negative emotional reactions (e.g., depression, anxiety), disengagement-type coping, and the severity and impact of injury were related to lower levels of adaptation.

Kennedy, Taylor, and Duff (2005) explored the characteristics of people who showed benefit from a group-based intervention aimed at improving psychological adjustment. Results from this study found that age, level of injury, gender, and coping strategies were not associated with treatment benefit; however, self-perception and time since injury were. This most likely captures the inherent dynamic nature of both coping and adjustment: Neither are unitary events per se, but processes that unfold over time. The injured person's appraisals, emotional responses, and coping behaviors change and develop according to the changing situation during acute medical care, rehabilitation, and reintegration into the community.

For people living with SCIs in the community, quality of life improves with time (Krause, 1998). Most people gradually accommodate to the injury and adapt to a lifestyle that they find satisfying. The coping strategies people mobilize in response to the consequences of a SCI are important in determining the extent of the psychological distress experienced. There is a growing body of evidence that highlights the strong predictive relationship between the coping strategies used and the level of psychological distress. Depression and anxiety are often the consequences of escape-avoidance strategies, whereas positive affective states are associated with coping strategies such as acceptance, positive reappraisal, and problem solving (Kennedy et al., 2000; Martz et al., 2005; Reidy, Caplan, & Shawaryn, 1991). Duff and Kennedy (2003) developed a post-SCI adjustment model, emphasizing the importance of considering preinjury factors such as emotional history and previous vulnerabilities, as well as the beliefs that the individual has about disability and his or her capacity to cope. Through a process of primary and secondary appraisal, the individual will either mobilize approach-focused coping or avoidance-focused coping. *Approach-focused coping* will result in a sense of mastery, self-efficacy, and posttraumatic growth. Conversely, *avoidance-focused coping* can lead to anxiety, depression, self-neglect, and substance abuse problems. Primary and secondary appraisal processes made throughout the early stages of the injury influence the selection of approach- or avoidance-focused strategies. Kennedy et al. identified a number of coping strategies that were associated with positive adjustment, which included accepting the reality of the injury having occurred, availability of high quality social support, the capacity to engage in positive reappraisal, and engagement in planned problem solving. Maladaptive coping strategies associated with poor adjustment included behavioral and mental disengagement, alcohol and drug use ideation, denial, escape-avoidant coping strategies, focusing on and venting of emotions, and low social support.

Cognitive Deficits

Because rehabilitation involves relearning or new learning following SCI, it is important to ascertain that the person with SCI has sufficient cognitive capacity to learn and retain what is required for effective and healthy postrehabilitation living. Assessment of cognitive difficulties in this population has been given considerable focus in the literature, much of that focus being directed toward the identification of possible concomitant traumatic brain injury (TBI). Given that traumatic-onset SCI, by definition, occurs most often via a rapid deceleration event (e.g., motor vehicle crash, diving injury, falls) and, in other instances, may be associated with a period of anoxia (e.g., surgical complications, cardiopulmonary arrest at onset), the possibility of concomitant cognitive deficits has been well-recognized (Davidoff, Roth, & Richards, 1992). In addition to injury-related events that could compromise cognitive functioning, preinjury events likewise can lead to lingering cognitive difficulties. For example, persons may have prior histories of TBI, learning disability, or prolonged alcohol or drug abuse. A number of postinjury factors could also compromise neuropsychological test performance, suggesting cognitive deficits that may or may not be significant.

For example, depression, preoccupation with the impact of injury, pain, medications, or lack of cooperation with testing may present as "cognitive deficits." If low intellectual ability and educational achievement are also present, it can be quite problematic in the individual case to draw unequivocal inferences about possible traumatic brain injury that may have occurred at the time of the SCI.

However, the importance of moderate to severe TBI with respect to lingering cognitive and behavioral difficulties has been well-explicated (Dikmen, Machamer, Winn, & Temkin, 1995). Almost 50% of persons with SCIs experience loss of consciousness or significant posttraumatic amnesia associated with their injury (Davidoff et al., 1992; Dowler et al., 1997; Richards, Brown, Hagglund, Bua, & Reeder, 1988). The presence of such findings should raise the suspicion of a concomitant TBI and encourage the psychologist to pursue evaluation of cognitive abilities and deficits. Such deficits, if present, are likely to be diffuse rather than focal if the SCI was the result of a rapid deceleration event such as a motor vehicle accident in an individual without a prior history of cortical insult (Gennarelli, 1993).

Individuals who sustain both SCI and TBI show fewer functional gains in a similar period of time during acute rehabilitation compared with those with SCI only (Macciocchi, Bowman, Coker, Apple, & Leslie, 2004). Given the importance of learning ability in rehabilitation, the rehabilitation psychologist working on the SCI unit is well-advised to routinely carry out at least some rudimentary assessment of cognitive ability, with more in-depth formal neuropsychological evaluations considered for those who show evidence of significant impairment. Because much of the information presented in rehabilitation is presented verbally and less in written format, some assessment of verbal learning ability (e.g., California Verbal Learning Test-II; Delis, Kramer, Kaplan, & Ober, 2000) is helpful. Limited hand function in persons with tetraplegia precludes the use of many neuropsychological tests that assume intact motor function. Several authors have devised comprehensive neuropsychological test batteries that do not require hand function and can be considered when more in-depth evaluation is indicated (Dowler et al., 1997; Richards et al., 1988). Once an individual's level of cognitive functioning and ability is better understood, the rehabilitation protocols can be tailored to the individual to maximize functional outcome. For example, simple one-step instructions, use of visual cuing, avoiding overstimulation, and providing ample time for an individual with concomitant TBI to process information may be required to facilitate progress (Sommer & Witkiewicz, 2004). Because cognitive capacity may change over time (Richards et al., 1988), continual monitoring can aid in adjustments in acute care protocols and determining long-term care needs. Although mild concomitant TBI may have few long-term implications, more moderate and severe cases may have persisting cognitive and behavioral difficulties, with significant implications for personal and social functioning of the person with SCI in the interpersonal context (Dowler et al., 1997; Richards et al., 1991).

Pain

Pain following SCI is a vexing complication with widely discrepant prevalence estimates ranging from 48% to 94% (Ragnarsson, 1997). Variations in prevalence estimates are likely a function of differences in sample populations and pain assessment methods (Richards, 1992). It is not clear why some individuals develop this problem and others do not (Richards; Rintala, Holmes, Fiess, Courtade, & Loubser, 2005; Yezierski, 1996). Whereas post-SCI pain is receiving appropriate increased attention with respect to biomedical theories of its origin (Yezierski, 1996), patients with SCIs who have to cope with this complication on a day-to-day basis experience pain as an "insult added to injury." Chronic pain has been frequently correlated with lower quality of life (Barrett, McClelland, Rutkowski, & Siddall, 2003; Donnelly & Eng, 2005; Lundquist, Siösteen, Blomstrand, Lind, & Sullivan, 1991). Therefore, although biomedical approaches to understanding and treating pain following SCI are needed and hopefully will be fruitful, those experiencing pain daily can benefit from psychological assessment and assistance with management of this complication.

Many different SCI pain classification schemes have been proposed (Richards, 1992) with no uniform agreement as to subtypes and their definitions.

However, there have been recent attempts by the scientific community to refine and adopt a single taxonomy (Bryce, Dijkers, Ragnarsson, Stein, & Chen, 2006; Siddall, Yezierski, & Loeser, 2000). Most authorities would agree that the major subtypes of pain, cutting across different classification schemes, include overuse or mechanical pain and at-level and below-level neuropathic pain. Some have proposed other subtypes, such as visceral and referred pain. It is important for a psychologist working with this population to realize that pain can be *referred*; that is, experienced in one body part but originating elsewhere (e.g., ruptured appendix experienced as shoulder pain) and that pain can reflect correctable (e.g., over-use, unstable fracture) and dangerous conditions (e.g., ascending syrinx). The importance of working with a competent physician in the evaluation of these complaints cannot be overstated. In some cases, post-SCI pain becomes a chronic condition that does not yield easily to physical, medical, or surgical intervention.

Although it is always difficult to determine causation, psychosocial factors are inextricably linked with chronic pain in this population, as in others. Persons injured by gunshot are more likely to develop post-SCI pain (Richards, Stover, & Jaworski, 1990) and also are more likely to be of minority status from lower socioeconomic levels (Go et al., 1995). Substance abuse is a factor in the onset of many SCIs, and a return to substance abuse after rehabilitation is also frequent (Heinemann, Mamott, & Schnoll, 1990). The potential for abuse of narcotics or other medications with abuse potential (e.g., Valium) is high in this population. "Self-medication" for pain via alcohol use or abuse is also a risk that needs to be monitored.

Cognitive–behavioral and operant strategies for assessing SCI pain have been developed and treatment approaches broadly outlined (Umlauf, 1992) and, in some cases, implemented (Budh, Kowalski, & Lundeberg, 2006). Most authors suggest a multiaxial assessment approach involving self-report pain measures (e.g., visual analog scale, McGill Pain Questionnaire; Melzack, 1975), coping scales (e.g., Rosenstiel & Keefe, 1982), structured clinical interview (e.g., Kerns, Turk, & Rudy, 1985), and/or personality measures. A comprehensive assessment should be used to select treatment approaches (Wegener & Elliott, 1992) so that patients with SCI pain who are also depressed, for example, receive different interventions than do those with an ongoing substance abuse problem, family stress, or secondary gain component. A comprehensive, evidence-based review of the recent literature on SCI pain (Sipski & Richards, 2006) revealed some evidence that anti-seizure medications, such as gabapentin or its successor pregabalin, may be helpful for neuropathic SCI pain. Less methodologically sound studies have indicated some benefit from a variety of other medications, forms of exercise and stretching, surgery, acupuncture, and cognitive–behavioral interventions (Sipski & Richards, 2006; Budh et al.). One nonrandomized, controlled investigation of the impact of a combined educational, cognitive and behavioral intervention for SCI neuropathic pain demonstrated efficacy at 12 months follow-up (Budh et al.). However, in the absence of Level I outcome studies of treatment effectiveness, the clinician is left with attempts to use techniques proven efficacious with other chronic pain populations with appropriate modifications for persons with SCIs. Operant learning techniques aimed at modifying reinforcement contingencies in the environment, cognitive–behavioral and pharmacologic treatment of depression and or anxiety, family therapy, relaxation training, biofeedback, and hypnosis can be helpful. Goal setting, problem solving, assertiveness and other skills training, substance abuse treatment, even treatment of sexual dysfunction, and general counseling regarding adjustment and future plans may also be helpful in individual cases in which chronic pain is problematic.

Alcohol and Substance Abuse

Alcohol abuse is often a vexing problem for persons with SCIs negatively impacting a variety of outcomes such as pain (Tate, Forchheimer, Krause, Meade, & Bombardier, 2004), development of pressure sores (Elliott, Kurylo, Chen, & Hicken, 2002), functional improvement during inpatient rehabilitation (Bombardier, Stroud, Esselman, & Rimmele, 2004), and risk of subsequent injuries (Krause, 2004). The prevalence of alcohol abuse has been estimated to be 21% among community-residing individuals with SCIs (Young, Rintala, Rossi, Hart, & Fuhrer, 1995).

This increased rate, however, may be reflective of problematic drinking predating the injury, as studies indicate that 35% to 57% showed evidence of alcohol abuse before the injury (Bombardier & Rimmele, 1998; Bombardier, Stroud, et al., 2004; Kolakowsky-Hayner et al., 1999), a factor that may have contributed to sustaining the SCI (Heinemann et al., 1990; McKinley, Kolakowsky, & Kreutzer, 1999). Thus, acute postinjury care and rehabilitation hospitalization may often become a de facto detoxification program. Most SCI rehabilitation programs address substance abuse individually and in psychoeducational groups; however, patient receptivity may be variable. On the one hand, there may be overt denial of problem drinking, or the patient may feel that he or she does not need treatment because he or she has been abstinent for several weeks. On the other hand, realization of the grave consequences of his or her behavior and experiencing greater alcohol-related life problems overall may lead to a greater readiness to change in the days following the injury (Bombardier & Rimmele, 1998). Motivational interviewing, an intervention technique designed to promote motivation at these various stages of change, has shown evidence of efficacy in other disability groups (Bombardier, 1995). Moreover, the brevity of this particular approach may prove more practical than formal treatment approaches in the increasingly short and compacted rehabilitation stays. Issues regarding assessment and treatment are discussed in more detail in chapter 14 of this volume.

Assessing for substance abuse is difficult because information derived from self-report or questionnaire data, in the absence of confirming or denying data from a well-informed other, has questionable reliability. As such, less is known about illicit drug use and abuse among persons with SCIs, although some studies indicate an increased prevalence (Heinemann et al., 1990; Kolakowsky-Hayner et al., 2002). Many of the commonly used substance abuse screening instruments have obvious item content (e.g., Michigan Alcoholism Screening Test; Selser, 1971) and are thereby subject to potential sources of self-report bias. Scales with more subtle content and/or questioning in the context of established trust and rapport may be more beneficial in gathering accurate data.

In addition to pre- and post-injury illicit substance abuse, the clinician needs to be alert to the potential for prescription drug abuse. Such medications as Valium (often prescribed for spasticity), narcotic-based analgesics for pain, anxiolytics, and other psychotropic medications have the potential for abuse. Given the absence of a highly effective treatment for central pain, treating physicians are often faced with continuous pressure from patients to prescribe strong narcotics. If this occurs, some of these individuals can develop tolerance and may eventually require detoxification.

Sexuality

Perhaps because of the predominance of men in the SCI population, more has been written about sexuality for men with SCIs than for women, although that trend is changing (e.g., Krotoski, Nosek, & Turk, 1996; Sipski & Arenas, 2006). SCI, depending on the level of the neurologic deficit and extent, can have a profound impact on sexual physiology or the "mechanics" of sexuality. The goal of assessment and treatment in this important arena of life functioning, as in other aspects of rehabilitation, is optimal adaptation or accommodation to changes in the physical as well as psychological aspects of sexuality.

For men, impairment in obtaining psychogenic erections (i.e., erections solely triggered by mental or nontactile stimulation) following SCI is probable. In a large case series, Bors and Comarr (1960) found a relationship between upper and lower motor neuron status and the likelihood of reflex or psychogenic erections. Patients with complete upper motor neuron lesions are likely to have reflex erections (i.e., automatic erections typically stimulated by contact that can occur in the absence of arousal). These may not be sufficiently firm, however, or last long enough for intercourse. Ejaculation and psychogenic erection are unlikely in this group. Men with complete lower motor neuron injuries (i.e., one out of four) are somewhat more likely to have psychogenic erections and much less likely to have reflex erections. About one in five are able to ejaculate. The ability of clinicians to predict erectile response and ejaculation becomes far less certain for men with incomplete lesions. Fertility remains problematic: If ejaculation can occur during intercourse, the viability and quality of sperm are often low. Some success has occurred with the use of electroejaculation (Heruti, Katz, & Menashe, 2001) and externally applied vibration (Bird, Brackett, & Lynne, 2001) to extract semen and produce pregnancy through artificial insemination. Penile prostheses, both fixed and inflatable, were the major recourse to improve erectile dysfunction in the 1960s and 1970s. Recently, externally applied vacuum devices and injections have become available, as has the use of systemic medications applied orally, intraurethrally, or transdermally (DeForge et al., 2006). Recent reviews have suggested that treating physicians tend to use oral medications as the first approach and only resort to more invasive approaches, such as injections and implants, when the former have failed (DeForge et al.). Few studies have focused on sexual satisfaction and behavior following these interventions, although data do exist that support their effectiveness in those domains as well (Richards, Lloyd, James, & Brown, 1992). Sipski, Alexander, and Gomez-Marin (2006) conducted laboratory-based evaluations of the sexual response in men with SCIs. They found physiological changes in heart rate and blood pressure as a function of sexual stimulation similar to those occurring in able-bodied men. They also found self-reported orgasm to be more frequently reported in those with incomplete injuries and less frequently reported in those with lower motor neuron injuries. The work of these researchers to date has indicated that orgasm in men with SCIs may be more feasible than what was previously believed and that orgasm can occur without frank ejaculation.

For women, changes in sexual physiology equivalent to those of men are thought to be lubrication (parallel to erection) and uterine and vaginal contractions (parallel to ejaculation; Sipski & Alexander, 1992). Sipski, Alexander, and Rosen (1995) demonstrated in unique laboratory settings that women with SCIs are capable of achieving orgasm and that some, but not all, of the physiological changes that occur in able-bodied women also occur in women with SCIs (Sipski, Alexander, & Rosen, 2001). However, the work of Jackson, Wadley, Richards, and DeVivo (1995), as well as that of others (Ferreiro-Velasco et al., 2005), suggested that participation in sexual intercourse diminishes somewhat postinjury for women and that self-reported orgasm decreases markedly. These two lines of research suggest the possibility, untested yet in controlled studies, that a substantial proportion of women post-SCI could be taught stimulation techniques (self or other) that would substantially improve sexual response and/or experience. The same is likely true for post-SCI men.

Temporary disruption in hormonal and menstrual cycles in women post-SCI is common, and the need for appropriate birth control counseling should therefore be emphasized. In the absence of information to the contrary, and in the absence of pelvic sensation and early postinjury menstruation, some women post-SCI may conclude erroneously that they are not capable of becoming pregnant again. Successful pregnancies do occur, but the possibility of unique complications argues for careful follow-up during pregnancy and delivery by an obstetrician familiar with SCI (Jackson, 1995).

The role of the psychologist with regard to sexual dysfunction can range from education to active sex therapy. The role of sex educator, however, can be assumed by several different professionals in the rehabilitation setting. The rehabilitation psychologist should be familiar and comfortable with the topic so that it can be addressed directly when the topic is broached. One particular area in which psychologist involvement in education could be productive is the prevention of sexually transmitted diseases (STDs). Because discomfort, a common symptom of STDs, may not be felt by the person with SCI, the presence of an STD may go undetected in men or women. In addition to education, persons with SCIs may need specific suggestions regarding exploration and renewal of their sexuality. Sensate focus activities coupled with a prohibition of attempts at intercourse are an effective method for couples to reduce performance anxiety and learn to focus on sexual communication and mutual pleasuring. Social skills training may be helpful so that the person with SCI is more comfortable initiating contact with others. Proper assessment and treatment of other psychosocial problems that may impede sexual readjustment are also in order (e.g., depression, substance abuse, proper hygiene, bowel and bladder accidents).

Sexuality post-SCI has been widely explored, and there are numerous excellent written and audio-

visual resources to help the rehabilitation psychologist become more knowledgeable and effective in this arena (e.g., Ducharme & Gill, 1996; Sipski & Alexander, 1997; Tepper, 1997). Formal training in sex counseling and therapy is also available (e.g., with the American Association of Sex Educators, Counselors and Therapists).

INTERVENTION STRATEGIES

There is not sufficient space in this chapter to describe all of the possible intervention approaches that have been used with persons with SCIs. Trieschmann (1988) and, more recently, McAweeney, Tate, and McAweeney (1997) summarized the available intervention literature for this population. We briefly describe unique characteristics and issues that occur when providing intervention services in the rehabilitation environment for persons with SCIs and suggest approaches that have been successful.

The clinician may experience a general resistance or reluctance to engage actively in psychotherapeutic interventions by many persons with acute onset SCIs. From the patient's perspective, his or her primary reason for being in a rehabilitation hospital is not for "mental health purposes" but to achieve maximal physical independence. Compounding this reality is the fact that many men who acquire SCIs are not typically introspective individuals (Rohe & Krause, 1993). For many of these individuals, being seen by a psychologist, particularly when such a service is not requested, may have a stigmatizing effect. To address this stigma, it is useful to develop alternative service delivery models, such as routinely referring all inpatients to the psychologist. Psychological services are therefore presented as part of the overall "rehabilitation package." A routine referral can help destigmatize the process and reduce resistance. Traditional, insight-oriented psychotherapy, either on an individual or group basis, is not routinely practiced in rehabilitation settings.

Psychoeducational Approaches

A structured psychoeducational group experience for acutely injured persons with SCIs is frequently offered. Descriptions of such approaches can be found in Trieschmann (1988). In these approaches, each group session, rather than being unstructured, or insight- and/or affect-oriented, addresses topics reflective of the new realities with which the person with SCI must cope. Information is presented in a didactic fashion with group discussion afterward. In the context of a peer-coping model, the presence of an experienced individual with SCI often facilitates discussion. Family members are invited to attend as well, and sessions are often led by the members of the rehabilitation team. The psychologist's role consists of organizing the group schedule, facilitating discussion, and presenting information for one or more sessions. With the reduction in the length of inpatient rehabilitation in recent years, the number of sessions needs to be limited, with constant recycling. A list of topics could include such issues as the search for a cure for SCI, sexuality and fertility, social skills and assertiveness, disability legislation, architectural and attitudinal barriers, travel, recreational opportunities, managing personal care attendants, bowel and bladder functioning, diet, skin care, medication use and abuse, and substance abuse.

Reasonable goals for the psychologist during the initial rehabilitation phase should be focused on assessment of history, personality and behavioral style, development of rapport, and participation in the psychoeducational process outlined earlier. If these goals are accomplished, the individual with SCI and/or family member may be more likely to contact the psychologist postdischarge if difficulties develop. This could allow more in-depth individual work with that psychologist or permit a referral to an independent living center or mental health resource in the patient's community.

Indirect intervention also occurs through consultation with the rehabilitation team members. They typically spend much more time with the individual with SCI and his or her family members and are therefore more likely to confront behavioral or emotional difficulties that limit progress. Guiding the team in terms of behavioral management techniques and providing guidance about responding to emotionally difficult reactions or situations are important, albeit typically (unfortunately) non-reimbursed, activities for the psychologist.

Coping and Cognitive–Behavioral Interventions

Cognitive–behavioral therapies (CBTs) are common psychological interventions for the management of a range of emotional disorders, including depression, anxiety, and adjustment disorders. SCIs result in many new situations that precipitate considerable uncertainty and fear about the future. If the individual has a belief that a situation can be managed, he or she is more likely to adopt a problem-focused solution that facilitates coping and adjustment. Individuals who appraise their SCIs as unmanageable have a low expectation of coping, which may impair adaptation. Tirch and Radnitz (2000) suggested six categories of cognitive distortions following SCI. These include the following: (a) an overly negative view of the self and others, (b) negative appraisals about self-worth following injury, (c) expectations of rejection from others and inadequacy, (d) the expectation of consistent failure, (e) development of a sense of excessive personal entitlement, and (f) an overdeveloped sense of vulnerability.

Craig, Hancock, and Dickson (1999) advocated the provision of group-based CBT to ameliorate the emotional concerns of people with SCIs. They found that with the use of a nonrandomized convenience control, those who received a group-based CBT program during rehabilitation had significantly fewer hospital admissions and higher self-reported adjustment than controls. Kennedy, Duff, Evans, and Beedie (2003) evaluated a group-based coping effectiveness training program aimed at improving adjustment and enhancing adaptive coping post-SCI. The intervention involved guided group discussions, practical problem-solving exercises, and appraisal training. It consisted of seven 70 to 75 minute sessions run twice a week with between six and nine people. In matched controlled trials with 85 participants, the intervention group showed a significant reduction in depression and anxiety, although there was no evidence of change in the pattern of coping. Improvements were understood on the basis of changing participants' negative appraisals about the consequence of the injury and increased and socially validated (i.e., by peers) perception of manageability.

Peer Counseling

Exposure to peers or persons with a similar injury has been considered beneficial to adjustment to SCI through modeling and emotional support. Such exposure may take place informally by receiving rehabilitation in a setting with other persons who have an SCI. More formal interaction with a peer who provides information or counseling is often integrated into the rehabilitation process as part of a purposefully designed program (Tate, Rasmussen, & Maynard, 1992). This is sometimes done in a group format with experienced peers leading a discussion of a topic related to independent living. Group learning for adults with SCIs in rehabilitation facilities has the advantage of providing peer support and opportunities to share problems, reducing isolation, and increasing motivation (Payne, 1995). However, one-to-one counseling by a peer may be the most frequently used delivery model for such services. Often these services are obtained through a community-based independent living center from peers who have received some orientation and training to become a peer counselor.

The timing of peer counseling is another subject of interest. Psychologists may be involved in deciding the best timing for introducing a peer counselor. In some settings, the psychologist may brief and/or debrief the peer counselor to optimize this kind of intervention and better coordinate psychological care.

VOCATIONAL AND EDUCATIONAL ISSUES

For young people, going to school is an important social role. Following graduation from school, entering the workforce becomes a preeminent social role. Participation in these roles is associated with superior psychosocial adjustment for adults with SCIs compared with those who were either non-students or unemployed (Krause & Anson, 1997). However, not all studies have demonstrated a clear relationship between psychological functioning and employment in SCI (e.g., Fox, 2000).

Most children with SCIs attend school. Because of federal legislation (most notably, P.L. 94–142, and Section 504 of the Rehabilitation Act of 1973), many are mainstreamed in regular classrooms, with various accommodations and additional services provided where needed. Psychologists can serve as advocates for children with SCIs and their families by educating them regarding the special education process and applicable laws. In addition, psychologists may offer recommendations to the school regarding academic accommodations and social reintegration issues. Psychologists sometimes discuss with a teacher methods for reintroducing the child back into the social environment of the classroom, such as having the teacher or child discuss aspects of SCI in a matter-of-fact way.

Children with SCIs generally perform well academically. In one study (Massagli, Dudgeon, & Ross, 1996), teachers and students rated the academic performance of students with SCIs at or above the level of their peers. Their mean grade point average was 3.05 on a 4.0-point scale; 45% of students were in the top quartile and 18% were in each of the other quartiles. Of high school graduates with SCIs, 82% entered college as compared with 56% of their peers without disabilities. This is of particular significance relative to employment data from the same study that found 71% of college graduates with an SCI were employed; however, no youngsters with a high school education or less were employed (Massagli et al.). These rates of post-high school education for those injured as children appear to be much higher than for those persons injured as adults, estimated as 22% in one study (Kewman & Forchheimer, 1997). Students with SCIs had an average of 23 absences per year.

Being Caucasian, younger at injury, having lived more years with SCI, having a less severe injury, and more years of education are all predictive of being employed following SCI (Krause et al., 1999). Education is consistently one of the strongest predictors of employment, and post-high school training has been shown to be critical in boosting the chances of employment following SCI (Hedrick, Pape, Heinemann, Ruddell, & Reis, 2006; Kewman & Forchheimer, 1997). A study using a large national sample (Dijkers et al., 1995) found employment reached a peak of 32% 10 years after injury for men and 33% 11 years after injury for women. Racial minorities generally have lower rates of employment compared with Caucasians (Krause & Anson, 1996; Meade et al., 2004).

Crewe (2000) found that vocational counseling, early work experiences, and a strong ethic that valued work contributed to high rates of employment after SCI. Completion of a vocational education program may increase the likelihood of employment. Unfortunately, however, few youngsters with SCIs receive vocational planning, vocational education, or part-time community work experiences during their schooling. Moreover, implementing accommodations aimed solely at the completion of school may not be sufficient for the demands of the competitive workplace (Massagli et al., 1996). For adults, the number of persons in one study receiving state vocational rehabilitation services at discharge from inpatient rehabilitation was 45% and declined thereafter (Dijkers et al., 1995).

Psychologists working in SCI care frequently do vocational interest testing and discuss options for acquiring needed skills. In part, this preliminary vocational counseling serves to convey and validate the message that working after an SCI is a viable goal (Crewe, 2000). To some degree, the effort to promote post-high school education and vocational productivity may be affected by specific psychological characteristics of persons with SCIs. Chapin and Kewman (2001) found that key psychological factors associated with employment were optimism, self-esteem, achievement orientation, and use of role models. Key environmental factors were monetary incentives, disincentives, access, and accommodation. Schonherr, Groothoff, Mulder, Schoppen, and Eisma (2004) also demonstrated that positive expectations regarding resumption of work are associated with employment after SCI. Compared with the general population, men with SCIs have been shown to be more introverted and interested in working in "blue-collar" compared with "white-collar" jobs that involve fewer concrete tasks and increased interpersonal relations (Rohe & Athelstan, 1982). This interest pattern is at odds with the majority of jobs that may be available to persons with physical limitations such as SCIs and emphasizes the need for careful educational and career planning to maximize the chances of a successful vocational placement.

The use of a supported employment approach (Targett, Wehman, McKinley, & Young, 2004) and on-the-job assistive technology (Inge, Strobel,

Wehman, Todd, & Targett, 2000) have been shown to overcome some of the barriers to employment for persons with SCIs and are important for job success (Hedrick et al., 2006). Assistive technology is discussed in more depth in chapter 16 of this volume. Job retention services, such as identification of at-risk workers, and employee preparation to make accommodation requests, may be particularly useful (Roessler, 2001). Chapin and Kewman (2001) suggested that the development of increased optimism might promote employment for persons with SCIs, whose perception of employment barriers as insurmountable needs to be decreased. Policies that promote return to work with former employers are likely to improve employment rates for persons with SCIs. A more intensive job-exploration process using job shadowing of peers and positive peer models may also improve employment after SCI.

PEDIATRICS

There is an equal distribution of males and females who sustain SCIs before 5 years of age, followed by increased percentages of males injured with advancing age (DeVivo & Vogel, 2004). Compared with adults, a greater proportion of youth, ages 0 to 16, are injured in vehicular accidents, and this percentage has increased from 1973 to the present. Sports, violence, and medical complications as causes of SCI are higher for adolescents (ages 13–21) compared with adults. DeVivo and Vogel also found a greater percentage of paraplegia and complete lesions in children injured before 13 years of age. However, in older adolescents, vehicular crashes more often resulted in cervical level injuries. In those injured before age 19, the most frequent causes of death after SCI were respiratory (21%), injury (13%), heart disease (10%), and suicide (9%; Anderson & DeVivo, 2004).

Risk factors for adjustment problems are probably similar to those for the general population of children with chronic illness and disability. These risk factors include preinjury psychological status, parents' psychological status, family stress, and low cohesion (Warschausky, Engel, Kewman, & Nelson, 1996).

Consistent with the general literature for children with disability and chronic disease, and based on a qualitative study of children with SCIs, Parnell (1991) suggested several buffers to psychological difficulties. These include family support, intrafamily strengths and adaptive coping styles, healthy preinjury personality style, positive preinjury peer relations, good preinjury school performance, financial resources, ability to provide essential equipment, community acceptance and support, preinjury recreation choices, ability to maintain educational level in the hospital and return to the classroom setting, and contact with friends during hospitalization. As an example, the degree of posttraumatic stress among family members has been shown to mediate functional independence in the pediatric SCI population (Boyer, Hitelman, Knolls, & Kafkalas, 2003). The importance of social and environmental factors as determinants of quality of life outcomes has also been demonstrated for ventilator-assisted children with SCIs (Nelson, Dixon, & Warschausky, 2004).

There has also been speculation that impaired mobility of children growing up with an SCI may negatively affect curiosity and initiation (Johnson, Berry, Goldeen, & Wicker, 1991; Zejdlik, 1992). Of adolescents with SCIs, 24% reported feeling infantilized and overprotected by parents (Iannaccone, 1994). Lollar (1994) assessed cognitive function in 145 children and adolescents (mean age 15.9) with SCIs. Although they presented stronger overall intellectual functioning and better mental flexibility, their social awareness and judgment were poorer. Warschausky, Kewman, Bradley, and Dixon (2003) discussed how children with SCIs may be at risk of social integration difficulties because of social stigma. Despite these obstacles, 32% of adults injured before age 18 had a college degree, 57% were employed, 65% were living independently, and 20% were married (Anderson, Vogel, Betz, & Willis, 2004).

Psychological intervention aimed at teaching and promoting specific social skills, such as how to enter peer interactions and positively coping with teasing or avoidance by peers, is an important therapeutic goal. Behavioral interventions have also been used to address additional issues facing children with SCIs, including noncompliance (Gorski, Slifer, Townsend, Kelly-Suttka, & Amari, 2005) and anxiety (Warzak, Engel, Bischoff, & Stefans, 1991). Self-injury has also been treated using behavior therapy (Colville

& Mok, 2003) and anticonvulsants because self-injury may be secondary to dysesthesia (Vogel & Anderson, 2002).

CONCLUSION

Traditionally trained psychologists who become involved in rehabilitation of persons with SCIs will have opportunities to use all of the assessment and therapy skills at their command as well as acquired knowledge and skills specific to the rehabilitation setting. Problems encountered in the general mental health field, such as depression, anxiety, suicide, and substance abuse, will also be encountered in the SCI population. However, skills unique to practice with persons who have sustained an SCI need to be developed as well, such as assessment and treatment of chronic pain (see chap. 7, this volume), neurologically based sexual dysfunction, and secondary conditions. The psychologist also needs to remain mindful that he or she may not always be the best source of therapeutic intervention. Peer counselors or independent living centers may be important adjunct or primary sources of help. Perhaps more than in traditional mental health fields, adjusting to SCI should be considered a lifelong process with issues and interventions changing as a function of time postinjury and age.

Changes in health care reimbursement and delivery can be seen as both a threat and an opportunity (see chap. 31, this volume). The threat is associated with decreased lengths of stay in the hospital, and a seemingly endless stream of services (including psychological services) that are either no longer covered by third party payers or that are reimbursed at low rates and with limits that make adequate service delivery impossible via traditional venues. The challenge will be in actively coping with these trends by designing assessment and intervention approaches that are demonstrably valid, clearly articulated, and cost-effective enough so as to be transmittable to other clinicians. Using nontraditional and low-cost providers under the direction of a clinical psychologist and moving into the community via telehealth and other technologies for remote service delivery are directions to explore. In a related way, a psychologist identifying him or herself more strongly with behavioral medicine than with traditional mental health service delivery is consistent with the continuing need for creative and effective ways to prevent and treat the secondary conditions that compromise quality of life and the need for better ways to maintain wellness once it is achieved.

Although the need continues for effective, well-trained clinicians who can work with persons with SCIs, there is an even greater need for clinicians–researchers. Psychologists have lagged behind in attempts to rigorously evaluate the efficacy of their interventions. In an era of increasing scrutiny of health care practice and outcomes, those who design health care plans can marginalize a profession without a substantial research base documenting the efficacy of its interventions. Psychologists are better equipped than most, if not all, of their rehabilitation team colleagues to carry out such research. The complexity of such endeavors notwithstanding, clinical intervention research by psychologists must be undertaken with rigor and urgency to preserve our place in the rewarding arena of rehabilitation and lifelong care of persons with SCIs.

References

Ackery, A., Tator, C., & Krassioukov, A. (2004). A global perspective on spinal cord injury epidemiology. *Journal of Neurotrauma, 21,* 1355–1370.

American Psychiatric Association. (1987). *Diagnostic and statistical manual of mental disorders* (3rd ed., rev.). Washington, DC: Author.

American Psychiatric Association. (1994). *Diagnostic and statistical manual of mental disorders* (4th ed.). Washington, DC: Author.

American Spinal Injury Association. (2006). *Standard neurological classification of spinal cord injury.* Retrieved November 14, 2006, from http://www.asia-spinalinjury.org/publications/2006_Classif_worksheet.pdf

Anderson, C. J., & DeVivo, M. (2004). Mortality in pediatric spinal cord injury [Abstract]. *Journal of Spinal Cord Medicine, 27*(Suppl. 1), S113–114.

Anderson, C. J., Vogel, L. C., Betz, R. R., & Willis, K. M. (2004). Overview of adult outcomes in pediatric-onset spinal cord injuries: Implications for transition to adulthood. *Journal of Spinal Cord Medicine, 27*(Suppl. 1), S98–106.

Barrett, H., McClelland, J. M., Rutkowski, S. B., & Siddall, P. J. (2003). Pain complications in patients admitted to hospital with complications after spinal cord injury. *Archives of Physical Medicine and Rehabilitation, 84,* 789–795.

Bird, V. G., Brackett, N. L., & Lynne, C. M. (2001). Reflexes and somatic responses as predictors of ejaculation by penile vibratory stimulation in men with spinal cord injury. *Spinal Cord, 39,* 514–519.

Bombardier, C. (1995). Alcohol use and traumatic brain injury. *Western Journal of Medicine, 162,* 150–151.

Bombardier, C. H., Richards, J. S., Krause, J. S., Tulsky, D., & Tate, D. G. (2004). Symptoms of major depression in people with spinal cord injury: Implications for screening. *Archives of Physical Medicine and Rehabilitation, 85,* 1749–1755.

Bombardier, C. H., & Rimmele, C. T. (1998). Alcohol use and readiness to change after spinal cord injury. *Archives of Physical Medicine and Rehabilitation, 79,* 1110–1115.

Bombardier, C. H., Stroud, M. W., Esselman, P. C., & Rimmele, C. T. (2004). Do preinjury alcohol problems predict poorer rehabilitation progress in persons with spinal cord injury? *Archives of Physical Medicine and Rehabilitation, 85,* 1488–1492.

Bors, E., & Comarr, A. E. (1960). Neurological disturbances of sexual function with special reference to 529 patients with spinal cord injury. *Urologic Surveys, 10,* 191–197.

Boyer, B. A., Hitelman, J. S., Knolls, M. L., Kafkalas, C. M. (2003). Posttraumatic stress and family functioning in pediatric spinal cord injuries: Moderation or mediation? *American Journal of Family Therapy, 31*(1), 23–37.

Bryce, T. N., Dijkers, P. J. M., Ragnarsson, K. T., Stein, A. B., & Chen, B. (2006). Reliability of the Bryce/Ragnarsson spinal cord injury pain taxonomy. *Journal of Spinal Cord Medicine, 29,* 1–15.

Budh, C. N., Kowalski, J., & Lundeberg, T. (2006). A comprehensive pain management programme comprising educational, cognitive and behavioral interventions for neuropathic pain following spinal cord injury. *Journal of Rehabilitation Medicine, 38,* 172–180.

Chapin, M. H., & Kewman, D. G. (2001). Factors affecting employment following spinal cord injury: A qualitative study. *Rehabilitation Psychology, 46,* 400–416.

Charlifue, S. W., & Gerhart, K. A. (1991). Behavioral and demographic predictors of suicide after traumatic spinal cord injury. *Paraplegia, 72,* 488–492.

Colville, G. A., & Mok, Q. (2003). Psychological management of two cases of self injury on the paediatric intensive care unit. *Archives of Disease in Childhood, 88,* 335–336.

Connolly, P. J. (2003). Factors affecting surgical decision making. In V. W. Lin et al. (Eds.), *Spinal cord medicine: Principles and practice* (pp. 125–130). New York: Demos.

Craig, A., Hancock, K., & Dickson, H. (1999). Improving the long-term adjustment of spinal cord injured persons. *Spinal Cord, 37,* 345–350.

Craig, A. R., Hancock, K. M., & Dickson, H. G. (1994). A longitudinal investigation into anxiety and depression in the first 2 years following a spinal cord injury. *Paraplegia, 32,* 675–679.

Crewe, N. M. (2000). A 20-year longitudinal perspective on the vocational experiences of persons with spinal cord injury. *Rehabilitation Counseling Bulletin, 43,* 122–133.

Davidoff, G. N., Roth, E. J., & Richards, J. S. (1992). Cognitive deficits in spinal cord injury: Epidemiology and outcome. *Archives of Physical Medicine and Rehabilitation, 73,* 275–284.

DeForge, D. D., Blackmer, J., Garritty, C., Yazdi, F., Cronin, V., Barrowman, N., et al. (2006). Male erectile dysfunction following spinal cord injury: A systematic review. *Spinal Cord, 44,* 465–473.

Delis, D. C., Kramer, J. H., Kaplan, E. & Ober, B. A. (2000). *The California Verbal Learning Test—Second edition.* San Antonio, TX: Psychological Corporation.

DeVivo, M. J., Kartus, P. L., Stover, S. L., Rutt, R. D., & Fine, P. R. (1989). Cause of death in patients with spinal cord injuries. *Archives of Internal Medicine, 149,* 1761–1766.

DeVivo, M. J., & Vogel, L. C. (2004). Epidemiology of spinal cord injury in children and adolescents. *Journal of Spinal Cord Medicine, 27*(Suppl. 1), S4–S10.

Dijkers, M. P., Abela, M., Gans, B., & Gordon, W. A. (1995). The aftermath of spinal cord injury. In S. L. Stover, J. A. DeLisa, & G. G. Whiteneck (Eds.), *Spinal cord injury: Clinical outcomes from the Model Systems* (pp.185–212). Gaithersberg, MD: Aspen Publishers.

Dikmen, S. S., Machamer, J. E., Winn, H. R., & Temkin, N. R. (1995). Neuropsychological outcome at 1 year postinjury. *Neuropsychology, 9,* 80–90.

Donnelly, C., & Eng, J. J. (2005). Pain following spinal cord injury: The impact on community reintegration. *Spinal Cord, 43,* 278–282.

Dowler, R. N., Herrington, D. L., Haaland, K. Y., Swanda, R. M., Fee, F., & Fiedler, K. (1997). Profiles of cognitive functioning and chronic spinal cord injury and the role of moderating variables. *Journal of the International Neuropsychological Society, 3,* 464–472.

Dryden, D. M., Saunders, L. D., Rowe, B. H., May, L. A., Yiannakoulias, N., Svenson, L. W., et al. (2005). Depression following traumatic spinal cord injury. *Neuroepidemiology, 25*(2), 55–61.

Ducharme, S. H., & Gill, K. M. (1996). *Sexuality after spinal cord injury.* Baltimore: Brookes Publishing.

Duff, J., & Kennedy, P. (2003). Spinal cord injury. In S. Llewelyn & P. Kennedy (Eds.), *Handbook of clinical health psychology* (pp. 251–278). Chichester, England: Wiley.

Dunn, M. (1977). Social discomfort in the patient with spinal cord injury. *Archives of Physical Medicine and Rehabilitation, 58,* 257–260.

Dunn, M., Van Horn, E., & Herman, S. H. (1981). Social skills and spinal cord injury: A comparison of three training procedures. *Behavior Therapy, 12,* 153–164.

Elliott, T. R., & Frank, R. G. (1996). Depression following spinal cord injury. *Archives of Physical Medicine and Rehabilitation, 77,* 816–823.

Elliott, T. R., Godshall, F., Herrick, S., Witty, T., & Spruell, M. (1991). Problem-solving appraisal and psychological adjustment following spinal cord injury. *Cognitive Therapy Research, 15,* 387–398.

Elliott, T. R., & Kennedy, P. (2004). Treatment of depression following spinal cord injury: An evidence-based review. *Rehabilitation Psychology, 49,* 134–139.

Elliott, T. R., Kurylo, M., Chen, Y., & Hicken, B. (2002). Alcohol abuse history and adjustment following spinal cord injury. *Rehabilitation Psychology, 47,* 278–290.

Elliott, T. R., Witty, T., Herrick, S., & Hoffman, J. (1991). Negotiating reality after physical loss: Hope, depression, and disability. *Journal of Personality and Social Psychology, 61,* 608–613.

Ferreiro-Velasco, M. E., Barca-Buyo, A., de la Barrera, S. S., Montoto-Marques, A., Vazquez, X. M., Rodriguez-Sotillo, A. (2005). Sexual issues in a sample of women with spinal cord injury. *Spinal Cord, 43,* 51–55.

Fox, A. J. (2000). The assessment of independence and personality in adults with spina bifida and spinal cord injury. *Dissertation abstracts international: Section B: Sciences and engineering, 60*(7–B), 3562.

Frank, R. G., Elliott, T. R., Buckelew, S. P., & Haut, A. E. (1988). Age as a factor in response to spinal cord injury. *American Journal of Physical Medicine and Rehabilitation, 67,* 128–131.

Geisler, W., Jousse, A., Wynne-Jones, M., & Breithaupt, D. (1983). Survival in traumatic spinal cord injury. *Paraplegia, 21,* 364–373.

Gennarelli, T. A. (1993). Cerebral concussion and diffuse brain damage. In T. R. Cooper (Ed.), *Head injury* (3rd ed., pp. 137–158). Baltimore: Williams & Wilkins.

Go, B. K., DeVivo, M. J., & Richards, J. S. (1995). The epidemiology of spinal cord injury. In S. L. Stover, J. A. DeLisa, & G. G. Whiteneck (Eds.), *Spinal cord injury: Clinical outcomes from the model systems* (pp. 21–55). Gaithersburg, MD: Aspen Publishers.

Gorski, J. A., Slifer, K. J., Townsend, V., Kelly-Suttka, J., & Amari, A. (2005). Behavioural treatment of non-compliance in adolescents with newly acquired spinal cord injuries. *Pediatric Rehabilitation, 8,* 187–198.

Hancock, F. M., Craig, A. R., Dickson, H. G., Chang, E., & Martin, J. (1993). Anxiety and depression over the first year of spinal cord injury: A longitudinal study. *Paraplegia, 31,* 349–357.

Hedrick, B., Pape, T. L., Heinemann, A. W., Ruddell, J. L., & Reis, J. (2006). Employment issues and assistive technology use for persons with spinal cord injury. *Journal of Rehabilitation Research and Development, 43,* 185–198.

Heinemann, A. W., Mamott, B. D., & Schnoll, S. (1990). Substance use by persons with recent spinal cord injuries. *Rehabilitation Psychology, 35,* 217–228.

Herrick, S., Elliott, T. R., & Crow, F. (1994). Social support and the prediction of health complications among persons with spinal cord injuries. *Rehabilitation Psychology, 39,* 231–250.

Heruti, R. J., Katz, H., & Menashe, Y. (2001). Treatment of male infertility due to spinal cord injury using rectal probe ejaculation: The Israeli experience. *Spinal Cord, 39,* 168–175.

Iannaccone, S. T. (1994). Pediatric aspects of spinal rehabilitation. *Journal of Neurologic Rehabilitation, 8*(1), 41–46.

Inge, K., Strobel, W., Wehman, P., Todd, J., & Targett, P. (2000). Vocational outcomes for persons with severe physical disabilities: Design and implementation of workplace supports. *NeuroRehabilitation, 15,* 175–187.

Jackson, A. J. (1995). Obstetrical outcomes in women with spinal cord injury. *Journal of Spinal Cord Medicine, 18,* 140.

Jackson, A. J., Dijkers, M., DeVivo, M. J., & Poczatek, R. B. (2004). A demographic profile of new traumatic spinal cord injuries: Change and stability over 30 years. *Archives of Physical Medicine and Rehabilitation, 85,* 1740–1748.

Jackson, A. J., Wadley, V. G., Richards, J. S., & DeVivo, M. J. (1995). Sexual behavior and function among spinal cord injured women. *Journal of Spinal Cord Medicine, 18,* 141.

Johnson, K. M. S., Berry, E. T., Goldeen, R. A., & Wicker, E. (1991). Growing up with a spinal cord injury. *Spinal Cord Injury Nursing, 8,* 11–19.

Judd, F. K., Stone, J., Webber, J. E., Brown, D. J., & Burrows, G. D. (1989). Depression following spinal cord injury: A prospective in-patient study. *British Journal of Psychiatry, 154,* 668–671.

Kennedy, P., Duff, J., Evans, M., & Beedie, A. (2003). Coping effectiveness training reduces depression and anxiety following traumatic spinal cord injuries. *British Journal of Clinical Psychology, 42,* 41–52.

Kennedy, P., Marsh, N., Lowe, R., Grey, N., Short, E., & Rogers, B. (2000). A longitudinal analysis of psychological impact and coping strategies following spinal cord injury. *British Journal of Health Psychology, 5,* 157–172.

Kennedy, P., & Rogers, B. A. (2000). Anxiety and depression after spinal cord injury: A longitudinal analysis. *Archives of Physical Medicine and Rehabilitation, 81,* 932–937.

Kennedy, P., Taylor, N., & Duff, J. (2005). Characteristics predicting effective outcomes after coping effectiveness training for people with spinal cord injuries. *Journal of Clinical Psychology in Medical Settings, 12,* 93–100.

Kerns, R. D., Turk, D., & Rudy, T. (1985). The West Haven-Yale multidimensional pain inventory (WHYMPI). *Pain, 23,* 345–56.

Kewman, D. G., & Forchheimer, M. (1997, September). *Factors predicting return to work 3 to 6 years following spinal cord injury.* Poster session presented at the annual meeting of the American Association of Spinal Cord Injury Psychologists and Social Workers, Las Vegas, NV.

Kolakowsky-Hayner, S. A., Gourley, E. V., Kreutzer, J. S., Marwitz, J. H., Cifu, D. X., & McKinley, W. O. (1999). Preinjury substance abuse among persons with brain injury and persons with spinal cord injury. *Brain Injury, 13,* 571–581.

Kolakowsky-Hayner, S. A., Gourley, E. V., Kreutzer, J. S., Marwitz, J. H., Meade, M. A., & Cifu, D. X. (2002). Postinjury substance abuse among persons with brain injury and persons with spinal cord injury. *Brain Injury, 16,* 583–592.

Krause, J. S. (1998). Aging and life adjustment after spinal cord injury. *Spinal Cord, 36,* 320–328.

Krause, J. S. (2004). Factors associated with risk for subsequent injuries after traumatic spinal cord injury. *Archives of Physical Medicine and Rehabilitation, 85,* 1503–1508.

Krause, J. S., & Anson, C. A. (1996). Employment after spinal cord injury: Relation to selected participant characteristics. *Archives of Physical Medicine and Rehabilitation, 77,* 737–43.

Krause, J. S., & Anson, C. A. (1997). Adjustment after spinal cord injury: Relationship to participation in employment or educational activities. *Rehabilitation Counseling Bulletin, 40,* 202–214.

Krause, J. S., Kewman, D., DeVivo, M. J., Maynard, F., Coker, J., Roach, M. J., & Ducharme, S. (1999). Employment after spinal cord injury: An analysis of cases from the Model Spinal Cord Injury Systems.

Archives of Physical Medicine and Rehabilitation, 80, 1492–1500.

Krotoski, D., Nosek, M., & Turk, M. (1996). *Women with physical disabilities.* Baltimore: Brookes Publishing.

Lollar, D. J. (1994). Psychological characteristics of children and adolescents with spinal cord injury. *SCI Psychosocial Process, 7,* 55–59.

Lude, P., Kennedy, P., Evans, M., Lude, Y., & Beedie, A. (2005). Posttraumatic distress symptoms following spinal cord injury: A comparative review of European samples. *Spinal Cord, 43,* 102–108.

Lundquist, C., Siösteen, A., Blomstrand, C., Lind, B., & Sullivan, M. (1991). Spinal cord injuries: Clinical, functional, and emotional status. *Spine, 16,* 78–83.

Macciocchi, S. N., Bowman, B., Coker, J., Apple, D., & Leslie, D. (2004). Effect of co-morbid traumatic brain injury on functional outcome of persons with spinal cord injuries. *American Journal of Physical Medicine and Rehabilitation, 83,* 22–26.

Martz, E., Livneh, H., Priebe, M., Wuermser, L. A., & Ottomanelli, L. (2005). Predictors of psychosocial adaptation among people with spinal cord injury or disorder. *Archives of Physical Medicine and Rehabilitation, 86,* 1182–1192.

Massagli, T. L., Dudgeon, B. J., & Ross, B. W. (1996). Educational performance and vocational participation after spinal cord injury in childhood. *Archives of Physical Medicine and Rehabilitation, 77,* 995–999.

McAweeney, M. J., Tate, D. G., & McAweeney, W. (1997). Psychosocial interventions in the rehabilitation of people with spinal cord injury: A comprehensive methodological inquiry. *SCI Psychosocial Process, 78,* 58–66.

McKinley, W. O., Kolakowsky, S. A., & Kreutzer, J. S. (1999). Substance abuse, violence, and outcome after traumatic spinal cord injury. *American Journal of Physical Medicine and Rehabilitation, 78,* 306–312.

McMillen, J. C., & Loveland Cook, C. (2003). The positive by-products of spinal cord injury and their correlates. *Rehabilitation Psychology, 48,* 77–85.

Meade, M. A., Lewis, A., Jackson, M. N., & Hess, D. W. (2004). Race, employment, and spinal cord injury. *Archives of Physical Medicine and Rehabilitation, 85,* 1782–1792.

Melzack, R. (1975). The McGill pain questionnaire: Major properties and scoring methods. *Pain, 1,* 277–299.

National Spinal Cord Injury Statistical Center. (2005). Spinal cord injury: Facts and figures at a glance. *Journal of Spinal Cord Medicine, 28,* 379–380.

Nelson, V. S., Dixon, P. J., & Warschausky, S. A. (2004). Long-term outcome of children with high tetraplegia and ventilator dependence. *Journal of Spinal Cord Medicine, 27*(Suppl. 1), S93–S97.

Nyquist, R., & Bors, E. (1967). Mortality and survival in traumatic myelopathy during 19 years from 1946–1965. *Paraplegia, 5,* 22–48.

Parnell, M. A. (1991). When a child is physically disabled: Impact on the child and family. *SCI Psychosocial Process, 4*(1), 16–21.

Payne, J. A. (1995). Group learning for adults with disabilities or chronic disease. *Rehabilitation Nursing, 20,* 268–272.

Radnitz, C. L., Schlein, I. S., Walczak, S., Broderick, C. P., Binks, M., Tirch, D. D., et al. (1995). The prevalence of posttraumatic stress disorder in veterans with spinal cord injury. *SCI Psychological Process, 8,* 145–149.

Ragnarsson, K. T. (1997). Management of pain in persons with spinal cord injury. *The Journal of Spinal Cord Medicine, 20,* 186–199.

Reidy, K., Caplan, B., & Shawaryn, M. (1991). *Coping strategies following spinal cord injury: Accommodation to trauma and disability.* Paper presented at the 68th Annual Meeting of the American Congress of Rehabilitation Medicine, Washington, DC.

Richards, J. S. (1992). Chronic pain and spinal cord injury: Review and comment. *The Clinical Journal of Pain, 8,* 119–122.

Richards, J. S., Brown, L., Hagglund, K., Bua, G., & Reeder, K. (1988). Spinal cord injury and concomitant traumatic brain injury: Results of a longitudinal investigation. *American Journal of Physical Medicine and Rehabilitation, 67,* 211–216.

Richards, J. S., Lloyd, L. K., James, J. W., & Brown, J. (1992). Treatment of erectile dysfunction secondary to spinal cord injury: Sexual and psychosocial impact on couples. *Rehabilitation Psychology, 37,* 205–213.

Richards, J. S., Osuna, F. J., Jaworski, T. M., Novack, T. A., Leli, D. A., & Boll, T. J. (1991). The effectiveness of different methods of defining traumatic brain injury in predicting postdischarge adjustment in a spinal cord injury population. *Archives of Physical Medicine and Rehabilitation, 72,* 275–279.

Richards, J. S., Stover, S. L., & Jaworski, T. (1990). Effect of bullet removal or subsequent pain in persons with spinal cord injury secondary to gunshot wound. *Journal of Neurosurgery, 73,* 401–404.

Rintala, D. H., Holmes, S. A., Fiess, R. N., Courtade, D., & Loubser, P. G. (2005). Prevalence and characteristics of chronic pain in veterans with spinal cord injury. *Journal of Rehabilitation Research & Development, 42,* 573–583.

Roessler, R. T. (2001). Job retention services for employees with spinal cord injuries: A critical need in vocational rehabilitation. *Journal of Applied Rehabilitation Counseling, 32*(1), 3–9.

Rohe, D. E., & Athelstan, G. T. (1982). Vocational interests of persons with spinal cord injury. *Journal of Counseling Psychology, 29*, 283–291.

Rohe, D. E., & Krause, J. S. (1993). *The five factor model of personality: Findings among males with spinal cord injury*. Paper presented at the convention of the American Psychological Association, Toronto, Ontario, Canada.

Rosenstiel, A. K., & Keefe, F. J. (1983). The use of coping strategies in chronic low back pain patients: Relationship to patient characteristics and current adjustment. *Pain, 17*, 33–44.

Schonherr, M. C., Groothoff, J. W., Mulder, G. A., Schoppen, T., & Eisma, W. H. (2004). Vocational reintegration following spinal cord injury: Expectation, participation, and interventions. *Spinal Cord, 42*, 177–184.

Selser, M. L. (1971). The Michigan Alcoholism Screening Test (MAST): The quest for a new diagnostic instrument. *American Journal of Psychiatry, 3*, 176–181.

Siddall, P. J. U., Yezierski, R. P., & Loeser, J. D. (2000). Pain following spinal cord injury: Clinical features, prevalence, and taxonomy. *IASP Newsletter, 3*, 3–7.

Sipski, M. L., & Alexander, C. J. (1992). Sexual function and dysfunction after spinal cord injury. *Physical Medicine and Rehabilitation Clinics of North America, 3*, 811–828.

Sipski, M. L., & Alexander, C. J. (1997). *Sexual function in people with disability and chronic illness: A health professional's guide*. Gaithersburg, MD: Aspen Publishers.

Sipski, M. L., Alexander, C. J., & Gomez-Marin, O. (2006). Effects of level and degree of spinal cord injury on male orgasm. *Spinal Cord, 44*, 798–804.

Sipski, M. L., Alexander, C. J., & Rosen, R. C. (1995). Physiologic responses associated with orgasm in SCI women. *Journal of Spinal Cord Medicine, 18*, 140.

Sipski, M. L., Alexander, C. J., & Rosen, R. C. (2001). The neurologic basis of sexual arousal and orgasm in women: Effects of spinal cord injury. *Annals of Neurology, 49*, 35–44.

Sipski, M. L., & Arenas, A. (2006). Female sexual function after spinal cord injury. *Progress in Brain Research, 152*, 441–447.

Sipski, M. L., & Richards, J. S. (2006). Spinal cord injury rehabilitation: A state of the science review. *American Journal of Physical Medicine and Rehabilitation, 85*, 310–342.

Sommer, J. L., & Witkiewicz, P. M. (2004). The therapeutic challenges of dual diagnosis: TBI/SCI. *Brain Injury, 18*, 1297–1308.

Stover, S. L., & Fine, P. R. (1986). *Spinal cord injury: The facts and figures*. Birmingham: University of Alabama at Birmingham.

Targett, P. S., Wehman, P. H., McKinley, W. O., & Young, C. L. (2004). Successful work supports for persons with SCI: Focus on job retention. *Journal of Vocational Rehabilitation, 21*(1), 19–26.

Tate, D. G. (1993). Alcohol use among spinal cord injured patients. *American Journal of Physical Medicine and Rehabilitation, 72*, 192–195.

Tate, D. G., Forchheimer, M. B., Krause, J. S., Meade, M. A., & Bombardier, C. H. (2004). Patterns of alcohol and substance use and abuse in persons with spinal cord injury: Risk factors and correlates. *Archives of Physical Medicine and Rehabilitation, 85*, 1837–1847.

Tate, D. G., Forchheimer, M., Maynard, F., & Dijkers, M. (1994). Predicting depression and psychological distress in persons with spinal cord injury based on indicators of handicap. *American Journal of Physical Medicine and Rehabilitation, 73*, 175–183.

Tate, D. G., Rasmussen, L., & Maynard, F. (1992). Hospital to community: A collaborative medical rehabilitation and independent living program. *Journal of Applied Rehabilitation Counseling, 23*, 18–21.

Tepper, M. C. (1997). *Providing comprehensive sexual health care in spinal cord injury rehabilitation*. Huntington, CT: Sexual Health Network.

Tirch, D. D., & Radnitz, C. L. (2000). Spinal cord injury. In C. L. Radnitz (Ed.), *Cognitive–behaviour therapy for persons with disabilities*. Northvale, NJ: Jason Aronson.

Trieschmann, R. B. (1988). *Spinal cord injuries: Psychological, social, and vocational rehabilitation* (2nd ed.). New York: Demos.

Umlauf, R. L. (1992). Psychological interventions for chronic pain following spinal cord injury. *The Clinical Journal of Pain, 8*, 111–118.

Umlauf, R. L., & Frank, R. G. (1983). A cluster-analytic description of patient subgroups in the rehabilitation setting. *Rehabilitation Psychology, 28*, 157–167.

Vogel, L. C., & Anderson, C. J. (2002). Self-injurious behavior in children and adolescents with spinal cord injuries. *Spinal Cord, 40*, 666–8.

Warschausky, S., Engel, L., Kewman, D., Nelson, V. S. (1996). Psychosocial factors in rehabilitation of the child with a spinal cord injury. In R. R. Betz & M. J. Mulcahey (Eds.), *The child with a spinal cord injury* (pp. 471–482). Rosemont, IL: American Academy of Orthopaedic Surgeons.

Warschausky, S. A., Kewman, D. G., Bradley, A., Dixon, P. (2003). Pediatric neurological conditions: Brain and spinal cord injury, muscular dystrophy. In M. Roberts (Ed.), *Handbook of pediatric psychology* (3rd ed., pp. 375–391). New York: Guilford Press.

Warzak, W. J., Engel, L. E., Bischoff, L. G., & Stefans, V. A. (1991). Developing anxiety-reduction procedures for a ventilator-dependent pediatric patient. *Archives of Physical Medicine and Rehabilitation, 72,* 503–507.

Wegener, S. T., & Elliott, T. R. (1992). Pain assessment in spinal cord injury. *The Clinical Journal of Pain, 8,* 93–101.

Woolsey, R. M., & Martin, D. S. (2003). Acute nontraumatic myelopathies. In V. W. Lin et al. (Eds.), *Spinal cord medicine: Principles and practice* (pp. 407–417). New York: Demos.

Yezierski, R. (1996). Pain following spinal cord injury: The clinical problem and experimental studies. *Pain, 68,* 185–194.

Young, M. E., Rintala, D. H., Rossi, C. D., Hart, K. A., & Fuhrer, M. J. (1995). Alcohol and marijuana use in a community-based sample of persons with spinal cord injury. *Archives of Physical Medicine and Rehabilitation, 76,* 525–532.

Zejdlic, C. P. (1992). *Management of spinal cord injury.* Boston: Jones & Bartlett.

CHAPTER 2

LIMB AMPUTATION

Bruce Rybarczyk, Jay Behel, and Lynda Szymanski

Although limb amputation is one of the most prevalent disabilities, it has been largely invisible to the general public due to advances in prosthetic technology in the United States over the past 50 years, allowing concealment from the general public to become the norm. Nonetheless, a recent dramatic rise in amputations (Rowley & Bezold, 2005) will likely serve to increase the public visibility of the amputation experience. In fact, public awareness of this disability already appears to be increasing due, in part, to greater media coverage of advances in prosthetic technology and the postamputation rehabilitation experience of injured American military personnel. The percentage of amputations to date among American military personnel in the Iraq war has been double that of any of our past military conflicts (Glasser, 2006).

According to the most recent estimate, there are 1.9 million adults in the United States living with a limb loss (Wegener & Ephraim, 2006). Approximately 90% of amputations are of a lower extremity, and the most common etiology for lower limb amputation is peripheral vascular disease (PVD), most often caused by Type 2 diabetes, which accounted for 82,000 amputations in the year 2000 (Dillingham, Pezzin, & MacKenzie, 2002). In the United States, the incidence of diabetes and consequent PVD-related amputations is expected to double or even triple by 2025 due to the growing, aging population and the obesity epidemic (Rowley & Bezold, 2005). Already, the majority of amputations are performed on individuals age 65 and older, but in the future this

disability will be even more closely linked with late life.

There is a high mortality rate among individuals with an amputation, with 40% to 60% of lower extremity amputees dying within 2 years of their surgery (Cutson & Bongiorni, 1996). Most of the deaths occur in older adults with multiple medical illnesses and are secondary to cardiac complications. In addition, the risk of losing the contralateral leg following a unilateral amputation is 15% to 20% 2 years after the amputation and approximately 40% 4 years after that (Cutson & Bongiorni).

Until recently, the lack of attention to amputation, in spite of the large numbers, had extended to the rehabilitation psychology literature. Ironically, one of the first studies in the emerging field of rehabilitation psychology addressed adjustment to amputation among war veterans (Dembo, Leviton, & Wright, 1956). The relatively limited amount of scholarly work on the amputation experience was likely related to national research funding priorities and medical center-based investigators' limited experience with this population. After the initial hospitalization and inpatient rehabilitation, most individuals with amputations receive amputation-related services from an outpatient prosthetic clinic. Fortunately, in the past 10 years a broad range of international studies, both theory-driven quantitative studies as well as hypothesis-generating qualitative studies, addressing psychological adjustment and pain issues have emerged. This chapter emphasizes developments that have occurred since 2000.

PSYCHOLOGICAL ADJUSTMENT AMONG INDIVIDUALS WITH AMPUTATIONS

Although trauma in its various forms would seem to be the inevitable response to an amputation, the actual responses range from profound psychological distress to little or no adjustment difficulty. In fact, over time, the majority of individuals with amputations make a successful adjustment and their amputation becomes just one of many life challenges rather than a defining characteristic.

Nonetheless, it is well-documented that a significant subset of individuals with amputations experience symptoms of emotional distress, with estimates of depression ranging from 21% to 35% (Rybarczyk et al., 2000). A recent stratified telephone survey (Darnall et al., 2005), with the largest and most representative sample to date, found that 28.7% of 914 participants with amputations reported significant depressive symptoms. These rates of depression are two to three times greater than those reported in the general population but comparable to rates in outpatient samples of individuals with a range of chronic conditions (Darnall et al.).

Clinical observation and the fact that anxiety has been less-studied by investigators (Horgan & MacLachlan, 2004) suggest that anxiety disorder is less common than depression following an amputation. One recent survey of older British veterans with longstanding amputations found that 16% had moderate or severe levels of anxiety (Desmond & MacLachlan, 2006a). Clearly, the prevalence of anxiety symptoms should be assessed in future survey studies.

Even individuals who do not develop clinically significant depression or anxiety often experience an initial period of adjustment accompanied by feelings of loss and vulnerability. One study of individuals with recent amputations found high rates of sadness (62%), anxiety (53%), crying spells (53%), and insomnia (47%; Shukla, Sahu, Tripathi, & Gupta, 1982), emotions and responses that appear to be normal reactions to any loss and physical change of this magnitude.

Factors in Adjustment to an Amputation

It is difficult to predict individual responses to an amputation, but a number of factors have value in predicting and understanding adjustment reactions. Table 2.1 identifies and categorizes these individual factors in adjustment and provides a rating of the level of empirical support for each factor. Notable in these findings is the fact that with a few exceptions (i.e., pain, traumatic etiology, activity restriction) the physical factors of the amputation are much less influential in the adaptation process than the psychological and social context in which such adaptation occurs. To paraphrase a medical maxim, "What disability a person has is less important than what person a disability has." The following sections provide a more in-depth and nuanced look at some of these factors.

Amputation-related factors. One variable that would seem to be important in psychological adjustment is the length of time since the amputation. The popular wisdom, supported by limited research only (e.g., Heinemann, Bulka, & Smetak, 1988), is that coping after any acquired disability improves with the passage of time. Yet, studies examining this variable do not find a significant relation between adjustment and time since an amputation (Frank et al., 1984; Rybarczyk et al., 1992; Rybarczyk, Nyenhuis, Nicholas, Cash, & Kaiser, 1995). Similarly, a recent national survey (Darnall et al., 2005) indicated that time since amputation had no significant effect on level of depressive symptoms when other factors were controlled.

In our clinical work, we encountered a significant subset of individuals who exhibit an initial sense of relief at the time of the amputation and only later experience grief over their losses. That is consistent with a retrospective study of older adults with amputations (MacBride, Rogers, Whylie, & Freeman, 1980), which found that only 23% of participants reported that the initial period following their amputation was the most distressing time. These authors note that many older adults have the opportunity for "anticipatory grief" during the period preceding an amputation as the possibility of losing a leg increases. Sometimes the most negative response comes when the individual is fitted with a prosthesis and subsequently discovers that it does not function as effectively as he or she had hoped or expected.

TABLE 2.1

Potential Factors That Influence Depression Among Individuals With Amputations

Factor	Research evidence	Studies with supporting evidence	Notes
Medical:			
Cause of amputation	Moderate	Darnall et al., 2005	Traumatic amputation leads to increased
		Livneh, Antonak, & Gerhardt, 1999	risk relative to other causes.
Time since amputation	Minimal	Katz, 1992; Pell, Donnan, Fowkes, &	Several studies found support for
Phantom limb pain	Strong	Ruckley, 1993; Gallagher, Allen, &	increased adjustment problems
Residual limb pain	Moderate	MacLachlan, 2001	closer to the time of the amputation
Back pain	Strong	Darnall et al., 2005	but studies with stronger controls
Medical comorbidities	Moderate	Darnall et al., 2005	did not.
Disability:			
Level and number of amputations	None		Activity restriction = restrictions as a
Activity restriction	Moderate	Williamson, Schulz, Bridges, &	result of the amputation in self-care,
		Behan, 1994	other care, work, recreation and/or
			friendships.
Demographic:			
Children versus adolescents	Moderate	Atala & Carter, 1992	Children adjust better than adolescents
			in case studies.
Older adults versus younger adults	Moderate	Dunn, 1997; Frank et al., 1984; Livneh	Older adults had fewer body image dis-
		et al., 1999; Williamson et al., 1994	turbances, less anxiety and depres-
			sion in these studies.
Gender:	Minimal	Kashani, Frank, Kashani, &	Men were found to have less depression
		Wonderlich, 1983	than women in one study.
Marital status	Moderate	Darnall et al., 2005	Divorced or separated at greater risk.
Education level	Moderate	Darnall et al., 2005	Lower education at greater risk.
Poverty status	Moderate	Darnall et al., 2005	"Near poor" at greater risk than poor or
			not poor.
Interpersonal:			
Perceived social stigma	Moderate	Rybarczyk, Nyenhuis, Nicholas, Cash,	
		& Kaiser, 1995	
Perceived vulnerability	Moderate	Behel, Rybarczyk, Elliott, Nicholas, &	
		Nyenhuis, 2002	
Perceived social support	Moderate	Rybarczyk et al., 1992; Rybarczyk	
		et al., 1995	
Amputation-related body image and public self-consciousness	Strong	Rybarczyk et al., 1992; Rybarczyk et al., 1995; Williamson, 1995	
Positive coping			
Problem-solving	Strong	Desmond & MacLachlan, 2006b;	
		Livneh et al., 1999	
Finding positive meaning	Strong	Gallagher et al., 2001; Dunn, 1997	
Optimism	Moderate	Dunn, 1997; Schulz, 1992	

Note. The rating given for the strength of the research evidence was qualitative in nature, based on the number of studies supporting the finding as well as the amount of variance explained in these studies.

Another factor that would presumably play a role in adjustment is the medical cause of amputation (i.e., congenital condition, cancer, diabetes, vascular disease, wartime injury, or trauma). Although several studies have found that no particular cause stands out as a predictor of poor adjustment (Rybarczyk et al., 1992; Rybarczyk et al., 1995), a survey by Darnall et al. (2005) found that individuals with trauma-related amputations were more likely to report symptoms of depression. Similarly, individuals with recent amputations caused by trauma had high levels of posttraumatic stress disorder (PTSD), whereas those with nontraumatic amputations had no such elevations (Cavanagh, Shin, Karamouz, & Rauch, 2006). The authors speculated that the PTSD may have been a response to emotional stress surrounding the accident rather than the amputation per se.

In the case of a vascular-related amputation, quality of life can actually improve following amputation, especially when an individual has experienced years of vascular-related chronic pain or undergone repeated surgical attempts to save the leg. Nonsurgical attempts to treat foot ulcerations secondary to diabetes often require months of decreased weight bearing and prolonged bed rest, which can lead to a sense of helplessness and despair. Indeed, a study of diabetic patients with amputations found that they were better adjusted than a matched group of diabetic patients with chronic foot ulcerations (Carrington, Mawdsley, Morley, Kincey, & Boulton, 1996).

Pain factors. Pain, a near universal aspect of the postamputation experience, can take the form of pain in the amputated limb (i.e, phantom limb pain), incision pain, muscle spasms and other forms of discomfort in the stump (i.e., residual limb pain), and pain in other parts of the body, such as in the back or contralateral limb that is often caused by the strain of postamputation mobility. In a national survey of 914 people with amputations, Ephraim, Wegener, MacKenzie, Dillingham and Pezzin (2005), for example, found that 95% of participants experienced pain, with more than half reporting more than one type.

The relation between phantom limb pain (PLP) and postamputation adjustment difficulties has been studied at length (Darnall et al., 2005; Katz, 1992; Pell, Donnan, Fowkes, & Ruckley, 1993). PLP is the experience of pain in the amputated limb; its prevalence ranges from 60% to 90% (Buchanan & Mandel, 1986; Edhe et al., 2000; Kooijman, Dijkstra, Geertzen, Elzinga, & van der Schans, 2000; Sherman & Sherman, 1983; Wartan, Hamann, Wedley, & McColl, 1997). The quality of PLP varies but most commonly is described as intermittent cramping or burning (Krane & Heller, 1995). PLP in adults can be continuous or episodic, is most frequently experienced during the first 6 months postsurgery (Jensen, Krebs, Nielsen, & Rasmussen, 1984; Krane & Heller, 1995; Sherman, 1997) and often decreases in frequency and intensity during that time (Jensen

et al., 1984). PLP lasting longer than 6 months often becomes chronic and is particularly difficult to treat.

Although the pathophysiology of PLP is not fully understood, promising information about the role of cortical reorganization in PLP has emerged in the 1990s (e.g., Birbaumer et al., 1997; Kaas, 1995). Specifically, studies have demonstrated that for many people significant reorganization of the somatosensory cortex occurs after an amputation. Essentially, the cortical "space" previously occupied by a lost limb is reallocated to other parts of the body. Subsequent studies demonstrated considerable individual difference in degree of reorganization observed. Although early researchers (e.g., Katz, 1992) assumed that greater neural plasticity would translate into lower levels of PLP, subsequent investigations (e.g., Flor et al., 1995) have consistently found higher levels of cortical reorganization associated with more severe PLP. Based on this finding, Birbaumer and colleagues hypothesized that PLP and cortical reorganization may be the products of a shared underlying process and that interventions that target cortical reorganization may evolve as an important avenue for treatment.

A number of medical and psychosocial risk factors for and correlates of PLP, particularly chronic PLP, have been identified. Dijkstra, Geertzen, Stewart, and van der Schans (2002) observed that increased risk of PLP was associated with (a) preamputation pain, (b) persistent stump pain, (c) bilateral amputations, and (d) lower limb amputation. It has also been noted that PLP is more frequent in patients who had the amputation secondary to blood clots (Weiss & Lindell, 1996).

Gerhards, Florin, and Knapp (1984) found that patients with more social support had less PLP than those with fewer social resources. However, Hanley et al. (2004) have observed that the form that social support takes is important. Specifically, they noted that good, general social support at 1-month postamputation predicted good adjustment and relatively low pain interference at 1- and 2-year follow-ups. However, individuals receiving solicitous, pain-focused support had poorer adjustment and more pain interference at follow-up.

Predictably, depression is a significant emotional consequence of PLP. Darnall et al. (2005) found that rates of depression were nearly three times as high among amputation patients who were "somewhat bothered" or "extremely bothered" by PLP as those "not bothered" by PLP. Back pain and residual limb pain were associated with depression as well. Van der Schans, Geertzen, Schoppen, & Dijkstra (2002) found that health-related quality of life (i.e., a construct with individual scales such as health perception, physical functioning, social functioning, and role limitations) was poorer among participants with persistent PLP than those with little or no PLP. In an interesting counterpoint, Whyte and Niven (2001) found that level of depressive symptoms in participants with amputations was more attributable to pain-related disability than to pain per se. Furthermore, Whyte and Carroll (2004) found a strong relation between catastrophizing thoughts and disability among participants with persistent PLP.

Disability factors. One common assumption is that more physical impairment leads to poorer psychological adjustment. However, whereas the degree of impairment is substantially less with a below-knee amputation compared with an above-knee amputation (Medhat, Huber, & Medhat, 1990) and even less compared with bilateral amputations, several studies (Darnall et al., 2005; Rybarczyk et al., 1995; Williamson, Schulz, Bridges, & Behan, 1994) have found no connection between the level of amputation and emotional adjustment. In contrast, Williamson and Schulz (1994) tested the relation between a self-rated measure of "activity restriction" and adjustment to an amputation. They found that the extent to which an individual reports activity restrictions was significantly correlated with depression. In contrast, several other measures that provided an approximate measure of impairment (e.g., level of amputation) had no direct relation to adjustment. According to their theory, when activities that are essential to an individual's identity and self-worth (i.e., self-care, other-care, work, recreation, friendships) are threatened, the individual may feel demoralized and is at much greater risk of depression.

Developmental factors. The specific psychosocial issues faced at each stage of development are affected in different ways by the added task of adjusting to an amputation. Developmental challenges can be amplified or sometimes minimized when occurring in the context of the greater challenge of adjusting to an acquired disability. The developmental stages that have been examined most closely in terms of unique amputation experiences include childhood, adolescence, and older adulthood.

Children and adolescents. Nearly one third of amputations secondary to trauma in the United States occur in children and adolescents (Hostetler, Schwartz, Shields, Xiang, & Smith, 2005). Between 1990 and 2002, approximately 111,600 children and adolescents were treated in emergency departments in the United States for injuries that required amputations (Hostetler et al., 2005). However, the decrease in trauma-related amputations over the 13-year period of study may be related to a renewed public health focus on accident prevention. The majority of partial amputations (e.g., removal of part of a finger) occurred in children younger than two (43.8%), whereas the majority of complete amputations (e.g., removal of a limb) occurred in adolescents (70.2%).

Overall, research indicates that young children cope fairly well with the loss of a limb (Atala & Carter, 1992) and that adaptation becomes more difficult as age increases (Tebbi & Mallon, 1987). In a review article, Tyc (1992) identified several psychosocial factors that can contribute to a child's positive adjustment to a limb amputation, including family cohesion, good social support, and low levels of family conflict. In addition, high daily stressors, parental depression, and medical problems predicted poor adjustment (Tyc).

Adolescents often have unique concerns affecting their adjustment to amputation. At a critical point in development, they are striving for independence while growing increasingly dependent on their parents because of their disability. More than half of adolescents and young adults who underwent amputations thought their parents were being overprotective yet also identified their parents as a primary source of social support (Tebbi & Mallon, 1987). Body image concerns are often salient during adolescence. Varni and Setoguchi (1991, 1996) have identified many factors that predict how adolescents with an amputation perceive their physical appearance. These factors include social support from parents, teachers, and classmates; peer acceptance; thriving in academics or sports; few daily hassles; and low levels of marital conflict among parents. Those who have a positive perception of their physical appearance tend to have higher self-esteem and fewer symptoms of depression.

Several studies have disputed the common misperception that children and adolescents rarely experience phantom limb sensations and pain (Krane & Heller, 1995). Krane and Heller reported phantom limb sensation in 100% and PLP in approximately 83% of the children and adolescent patients who underwent amputations. Their study demonstrated that PLP in children and adolescents tends to decrease in frequency and intensity over time, more so than in adults. In addition, this study suggested that health professionals underreport phantom experiences. Phantom sensations and pain were documented in medical charts in only half of those who retrospectively reported the experiences. Another study found that 42% of children and adolescents with amputations experienced phantom limb sensations and 29% experienced PLP (Wilkins, McGrath, Finley, & Katz, 1998). Notably, those who had a surgical amputation due to injury, cancer, or other medical problem had significantly more phantom sensations and pain than those who had a congenital limb deficiency. Wilkins et al. reported that the primary strategies used by children and adolescents for dealing with PLP included ignoring it (79%) and massaging the stump (29%).

Older adults. Several studies indicate that older adults often do not use their prostheses within months of rehabilitation training because of the high physical demands (e.g., Cutson & Bongiorni, 1996). Thus, when older adults undergo an amputation it often is complicated by other coping issues related to physical frailty and chronic illness. Indeed, medical comorbidities have been shown to be a risk factor for depression in individuals with amputations (Darnall et al., 2005).

Comorbid conditions notwithstanding, it has been hypothesized that older adults may be more effective at coping with illness and disability because of accumulated coping experiences and the fact that they are more likely to view losses and changes in functioning as an undesirable but relatively "on-time"

event (i.e., common for their age). Three studies found limited support for the hypothesis that older adults (age 65 and older) with amputations are less prone to psychological adjustment problems compared with younger adults (Dunn, 1994; Frank et al., 1984; Williamson et al., 1994), but other investigators did not (Darnall et al., 2005; Rybarczyk et al., 1992; Rybarczyk et al., 1995).

Body image factors. Acquired disabilities demand that individuals make complex adjustments to internal representations and evaluations of their physical selves (i.e., body image), both in their body's static appearance and in how they move and how their body looks in motion (i.e., kinetic body image; Rybarczyk & Behel, 2002). Individuals with amputations also are called on to adapt their body image to their appearance with and without a prosthesis. Although many people manage this intricate transformation of self-concept with only mild, transient distress, some develop negative attitudes about themselves as a result of their altered body and consequent disability. Individuals with amputations may express embarrassment, shame, or even revulsion (Rybarczyk et al., 1995); others report that they feel positive when wearing a prosthesis but prefer not to see themselves without the prosthesis or look at their prosthesis when not wearing it.

Negative body image has been shown to be a predictor of depression (Rybarczyk et al., 1992; Rybarczyk et al., 1995), lower ratings of adjustment by the professional who provides the individual with prosthetic services (Rybarczyk et al., 1995), lower activity level (Wetterhahn, Hanson, & Levy, 2002), and lower overall quality of life (Rybarczyk et al., 1995). Similarly, Williamson (1995) found greater self-consciousness in public situations to be correlated with activity restriction among older adults with amputations. Because of the growing body of research supporting the importance of body image in the adjustment process, the Amputation Body Image Scale has been developed and further validated (Gallagher, Horgan, Franchignoni, Giordano, & MacLachlan, 2007).

Interpersonal factors. The most common interpersonal problem described by individuals with amputations is that others view them as globally disabled and/or assume that individuals who undergo an amputation see it as a tragic event. Being aware of common negative biases and learning not to personalize these biases is often promoted as a healthy approach for individuals with disabilities (e.g., Winchell, 1995). In one of the earliest adjustment studies, Chaiklin and Warfield (1973) found that those who denied the existence of any kind of a social stigma were less likely to make good progress in rehabilitation, but no psychological measures of adjustment were included. The authors suggested that awareness is a first step toward "managing" or "neutralizing" stigma.

Although this popular notion suggests that it is adaptive to be aware of discrimination and stigma, our research found that individuals who reported being more stigmatized were more likely to be depressed (Rybarczyk et al., 1995) and to have poorer overall adjustment, as rated by the participants' prosthetist. In effect, this study seemed to suggest that it was adaptive to be less attuned to the negative biases that others might hold, regardless of whether these biases were taken personally. An alternative explanation is that these respondents accurately perceived greater bias from others because individuals with disabilities who have depression elicit stronger negative stereotypes and reactions from nondisabled persons (Elliott & Frank, 1990). If this is the case, then it is important for psychologists and other professionals to help these individuals differentiate between the negative responses they are getting in relation to their mood from those they are getting in response to their amputation.

A sense of vulnerability to victimization would appear to be another interpersonal factor in adjustment to amputation. It has been noted that individuals with physical disabilities often present to rehabilitation professionals with issues related to fears regarding violence, property crime, and sexual victimization (Goodwin & Holmes, 1988). In particular, individuals with amputations frequently report a heightened sense of vulnerability to personal crime (Williamson, 1995). They either report a specific concern (e.g., about being mugged) or a global sense of fear about "being taken advantage of." Some individuals experience a realistic concern that leads them to take appropriate precautions whereas others have

an exaggerated concern that results in excessive avoidant behaviors, a diminished quality of life, and poorer health (Ross, 1993). Behel, Rybarczyk, Elliott, Nicholas, and Nyenhuis (2002) found that individuals with recent amputations who reported feeling more "vulnerable to becoming a crime victim" and feeling "less able to defend [them]self" had significantly higher depression scores, greater social isolation, lower ratings of adjustment by their prosthetist, and an overall lower quality of life than those not feeling vulnerable. Likewise, Williamson showed that feelings of vulnerability among older adults with amputations were strongly related to activity restriction and not feeling comfortable in public.

Coping strategy factors.   Recent investigations have demonstrated that certain coping strategies foster more positive adjustment to amputation. Livneh, Antonak, and Gerhardt (1999) found active problem-solving to be negatively associated with depression and internalized anger and positively associated with adjustment and acceptance of disability. Desmond and MacLachlan (2006b) surveyed 796 individuals with amputations in the United Kingdom and also found that problem solving was negatively associated with depression and anxiety whereas avoidance was positively associated with psychological distress. Dunn (1997) found that individuals who were predisposed to optimism were more positively adjusted to their amputation.

Recent studies have addressed positive psychological factors in adjustment to amputation. Dunn (1997) investigated the issue of finding positive meaning among a sample of predominantly well-educated male members of an amputee golf league. He found that the 77% of the 138 study participants who reported that something positive happened as a result of their amputation had a lower rate of depression than those who reported that nothing positive happened. Similarly, Gallagher and MacLachlan (2000) reported that 48% of individuals with amputations were able to find positive meaning and reported that something good had come about as a result of their amputation, including increased independence, viewing the experience as character building, having a different attitude toward life, improved coping abilities, financial benefits, elimination of pain, experiencing a better way of life, and meeting new people as a result. Another qualitative study of 12 individuals with good adjustment to their amputation (Oaksford, Frude, & Cuddihy, 2005) confirmed earlier case study observations (Rybarczyk, Nicholas, & Nyenhuis, 1997) that two frequently used and effective coping strategies are humor about the amputation (e.g., stories about a prosthesis falling off in public) and downward comparison (e.g., "At least I have one leg. I can't imagine losing both legs.").

ADJUSTMENT TO ARM OR HAND AMPUTATION

Whereas the majority of research has focused on adjustment to lower limb amputation, reflecting that upwards of 90% of all amputations in the United States and the United Kingdom are of the lower limb, there have been some recent investigations of individuals with arm and hand amputations. This growing interest is important because of emerging evidence that arm and hand amputations appear to produce qualitatively different experiences than lower limb amputations for several reasons. First, arm and hand function is central to many activities of daily living, including personal hygiene and food preparation, and carrying out some of these tasks can become quite challenging. Second, the arms and hands play a crucial role in nonverbal dimensions of social communication and interaction through actions such as gesturing and physical contact. Third, because a missing arm or prosthetic hand is much more difficult to conceal than a leg or foot prosthesis, the amputation is much more noticeable to others, increasing the likelihood that the person with an upper extremity amputation might feel scrutinized and self-conscious (Cheung, Alvaro, & Colotla, 2003). Visible disabilities may present a more challenging psychological adjustment than conditions that are perhaps equally disabling but are better masked. Fourth, the prosthetic devices available for hands, although advancing greatly in recent years, are not nearly as functional as those for lower limb amputations (Esquenazi, 2004). Finally, most upper limb amputations occur from trauma (e.g., work-related injuries, war) and occur at younger ages than lower limb amputations (Esquenazi).

A retrospective chart review conducted by Cheung et al. (2003) investigated symptoms of depression and PTSD in those who experienced traumatic upper or lower limb amputations from industrial accidents. Predictably, those with upper limb amputations had significantly more symptoms of depression and PTSD than those with lower limb amputations, although the groups did not differ in their reports of stump pain or PLP. The authors concluded that those undergoing upper limb amputations are at significant risk of depression and PTSD and that psychological services should be provided following upper limb amputations to facilitate coping and to prevent emotional sequelae. Similarly, Fukunishi (1999) found that 18.5% of individuals who experienced digital amputation had PTSD during the first 2 years postamputation.

In contrast, Demet, Martinet, Guillemin, Paysant, and Andre (2003) found that those experiencing upper limb amputation had significantly better health-related quality of life than those experiencing lower limb amputations. Specifically, those who had their arm(s) amputated reported better quality of life scores on measures of physical disability, pain, energy, emotional reaction, and sleep compared with those who had undergone leg amputation. The two groups did not differ significantly on the social isolation factor.

The use of prosthetic devices in upper limb amputation presents many challenges. Dudkiewicz, Gabrielov, Seiv-Ner, Zelig, and Heim (2004) studied prosthetic use in 45 patients with upper limb amputation and found that more than 70% reported difficulty with their prosthetic device. Some reasons given included the weight of the device, excessive sweating, displeasure with its appearance or its functionality, and the experience of PLP. It is interesting that significantly more people consistently used a cosmetic prosthesis (55%) compared with a functional prosthetic device (40%). This finding speaks to both the concerns related to body image in those living with an upper limb amputation and the limitations of functionality in most upper limb prostheses.

INTERVENTION ISSUES

Many of the psychological experiences outlined earlier are not shared with family members, friends, or health care providers; they are experienced privately.

Individuals with amputations can "pass" in the non-disabled world because of the effectiveness of prosthetic technology. Therefore, it often falls to clinicians to begin a dialogue about the adjustment process, helping to normalize the feelings and experiences of individuals with amputations.

Normalization is often accomplished by meeting and talking with others who have a similar disability to see how others find positive meaning in their amputation experience. Even though there are more than a million individuals with leg amputations in the United States, they are largely "hidden" from each other because of the aforementioned prosthetic technology. The Internet and national organizations that maintain a strong presence on the Internet, such as the Amputation Coalition of America (ACA), are an important bridge to finding others in a similar situation. Individuals who use amputation support groups sponsored by the ACA report a high level of satisfaction with these groups (Wegener & Ephraim, 2006), but some people who need them have trouble finding a support group, especially in smaller communities. In one sample (Rybarczyk et al., 1995), 50% of the patients who had significant levels of depression were not in a support group even though they reported a desire to be in one and support groups were abundant in the area. Also, some individuals avoid support groups because the divergent medical and demographic characteristics and psychological responses of individuals with amputations can limit the amount of "common ground" in a group. As such, Internet communities and self-help literature (e.g. Winchell, 1995) are vital alternatives to support groups.

When clinically significant levels of depression or anxiety are present, mental health services beyond support groups and self-help are needed. The recent national survey (Darnall et al., 2005) revealed a mixed picture of mental health treatment for individuals with amputations. Almost 22% of the sample reported receiving some mental health services and 44.6% of those with significant depressive symptoms had received mental health service in the previous year. On the negative side, more than half of the depressed individuals who received care reported that they needed more than they received and 32.9% of individuals with depressive symptoms received no care

at all. Cost (27.7%) and not knowing where to go (19.2%) were the two most common barriers to care. Thus, much progress needs to be made to improve detection of depression and to facilitate referrals by clinicians as well as to improve insurance coverage for mental health services.

One promising cost-effective approach for prevention and treatment of psychological adjustment problems is group psychoeducational interventions, particularly those targeting individuals with empirically identified risk factors (e.g., traumatic etiology). A randomized clinical trial (Wegener & Ephraim, 2006) compared a standard support group with an eight-session group intervention: the Promoting Amputee Life Skills (PALS) program. The PALS program was modeled after other successful self-management programs for chronic conditions (e.g., Lorig & Holman, 1993) and covered topics such as cognitive–behavioral approaches to managing pain, anxiety and depression, problem solving, effective communication, and health information on such topics as exercise, nutrition, sleep, and amputation-related skin care. Consistent with the recent emphasis on consumer-driven intervention programs for individuals with disabilities, one leader for each PALS class was an individual with an amputation. At the 6-month follow-up, the PALS participants ($n = 275$) demonstrated significantly increased self-efficacy and positive mood and reduced limitations in function compared with control participants in a standard support group ($n = 223$; Wegener & Ephraim, 2006). Among PALS participants, 77% rated the intervention as more effective than support groups in which they had participated previously. The most significant outcomes for the PALS intervention were obtained among individuals who were fewer than 3 years postamputation. These findings led to the initiation of a second PALS randomized clinical trial with several refinements: targeting individuals with recent amputations, matching each participant with a peer mentor, and using motivational interviewing for recruitment (Wegener & Ephraim, 2006).

Another pragmatic approach would be to implement intervention strategies at prosthetic clinics, which often become the primary care settings for any amputation-related health issues. Individuals involved in self-help organizations such as the ACA may tend to be better adjusted and more proactive to begin with than the general amputation population. Accordingly, intervention programs need to be proactive in eliminating barriers to participation and acceptance by those who are most in need.

Phantom Limb Pain

Although psychosomatic explanations are no longer central in PLP, psychologists continue to play a critical role in its treatment. This role remains important in part because no single treatment modality has been shown to be consistent and reliable in relieving PLP. Gevirtz (2005) briefly outlined six broad categories of PLP treatment: prophylactic (i.e., presurgical) analgesia, pharmacologic treatment, physical treatments, mirror box techniques, psychological and surgical interventions. In assessing their efficacy, he noted that mirror box techniques, an imagery technique in which the patient learns to manage involuntary muscle spasms in the amputated limb, and cognitive–behavioral interventions have been somewhat effective. Evidence for the benefit of prophylactic analgesia and pharmacological treatments is equivocal. Anecdotally, physical techniques, such as acupuncture and heat and cold, provide some relief, but more scientifically rigorous studies are needed. Surgical techniques have been largely abandoned. In short, although substantial progress in understanding PLP has been made and many different approaches have been tried, much work, particularly randomized prospective trials for existing treatments, remains.

Hanley, Ehde, Campbell, Osborn, & Smith (2006) examined the treatment experiences of 255 individuals with lower extremity amputations of whom 72% reported ongoing PLP. Of those with PLP, 47% had never pursued treatment for their pain, including 38% of those with severe pain. Among those who were treated, most rated the 18 listed treatments as only minimally or somewhat effective. Only chiropractic treatment and opioid medications were rated as moderately or extremely helpful by more than half of the respondents. The authors concluded that although better treatments are needed, barriers to treatment provision and treatment acceptance must also be investigated and eliminated.

As with all chronic pain conditions, concurrent treatment of depression should be universal. The national amputation survey by Ephriam et al. (2005) found that the presence of depressive symptomatology was a key predictor of pain intensity and "bothersomeness." The authors argued that any effective pain management strategy will include frequent assessment for and aggressive treatment of any mood disturbance.

Sexual Functioning

Although a critical aspect of health and well-being, postamputation sexuality is frequently overlooked by rehabilitation professionals. Williamson and Walters (1996) found that only 9% of their sample was given any information or opportunities to ask questions about sexual functioning after an amputation. Although the absence of a clear medical link between amputation and sexual functioning may account for some of this unfortunate oversight, culturally enforced discomfort with sexual discussions certainly plays a part as well. In a study of Japanese participants with amputations (Ide, Watanabe, & Toyonaga, 2002), 60% reported that they continued to engage in intercourse, but 42.4% also acknowledged a postamputation change in sexuality. Ide (2004) noted that although this rate of sexual activity is higher than is typically seen among people with spinal cord injury and other acquired disabilities, little is genuinely understood about the nature of postamputation changes in sexuality or the subjective quality of the sexual lives of people with amputations. Current interventions aimed at decreasing the impact of an acquired disability on sexuality typically provide instruction on how to remain sexually active within the limitations of a disability and how to initiate a dialogue with a partner. Increasing the comfort level of the health care provider is another vitally important target for intervention.

FUTURE DIRECTIONS IN CLINICAL RESEARCH

In spite of excellent progress in the past 10 years, there is still much to be learned about the process of adjusting to an amputation. For example, all but one study (Edhe et al., 2004) in Table 2.1 are cross-sectional in design. Many have small numbers of participants and highly selective convenience samples.

Only one study obtained a sample that was representative of the U.S. amputation population (Darnall et al., 2005). Furthermore, investigators and funding agencies should begin to work together to design and fund well-controlled clinical intervention studies targeting at-risk groups. Cognitive–behavioral interventions would appear to be highly appropriate for this population, given the cognitive processes (e.g., self-evaluation, perceptions of others) that have been linked to positive adjustment. Although it is encouraging that children and adolescents seem to cope well with amputations, further research is also necessary to determine factors that promote resiliency, identify risk factors for less-than-optimal functioning, and generate strategies to optimize psychological adjustment.

A specialized but important future area of research will be to examine the adjustment issues among military personnel related to amputations that occur in the context of polytrauma (i.e., multiple injuries in conjunction with a brain injury). Such injuries have become common in recent military actions and are likely to continue. Improvised explosive devices, blasts, and landmines now account for 65% of combat injuries (Department of Veterans Affairs, 2005), and these injuries often include a combination of brain injury, multiple amputations, and PTSD. Future studies need to investigate how rehabilitation psychologists can best address the multiple psychological and neuropsychological needs of these individuals.

Finally, it should be emphasized that the majority of individuals with amputations are well-adjusted and have come to see their amputation not as a defining characteristic but as one of many challenges faced in their lives. Accordingly, future research should continue to focus on the positive coping used by individuals who experience an amputation. Longitudinal studies that focus on the process by which most individuals return to their "set point" of self-esteem, life satisfaction, and happiness would be of particular value.

References

Atala, K. D., & Carter, B. D. (1992). Pediatric limb amputation: Aspects of coping and psychotherapeutic intervention. *Child Psychiatry and Human Development, 23,* 117–130.

Behel, J., Rybarczyk, B., Elliott, T., Nicholas, J. J., & Nyenhuis, D. (2002). The role of perceived vulnerability in adjustment to lower extremity amputation: A preliminary investigation. *Rehabilitation Psychology, 47,* 92–105.

Birbaumer, N., Lutzenberger, W., Montoya, P., Larbig, W., Unertl, K., Topfner, S., et al. (1997). Effects of regional anesthesia on phantom limb pain are mirrored in changes in cortical reorganization. *Journal of Neuroscience, 17,* 5503–5508.

Buchanan, D. C., & Mandel, A. R. (1986). The prevalence of phantom limb experiences in amputees. *Rehabilitation Psychology, 31,* 183–188.

Carrington, A. L., Mawdsley, S. K. V., Morley, M., Kincey, J., & Boulton, A. J. M. (1996). Psychological status of diabetic people with or without lower limb disability. *Diabetes Research and Clinical Practice, 32,* 19–25.

Cavanagh, S. R., Shin, L. M., Karamouz, N., & Rauch, S. L. (2006). Psychiatric and emotional sequelae of surgical amputation. *Psychosomatics, 47,* 459–64.

Chaiklin, H., & Warfield, M. (1973). Stigma management and amputee rehabilitation. *Rehabilitation Literature, 34,* 162–167.

Cheung, E., Alvaro, R., & Colotla, V. A. (2003). Psychological distress in workers with traumatic upper or lower limb amputations following industrial injuries. *Rehabilitation Psychology, 48,* 109–112.

Cutson, T. M., & Bongiorni, D. R. (1996). Rehabilitation of the older lower limb amputee: A brief review. *Journal of the American Geriatric Society, 44,* 1388–1393.

Darnall, B. D., Ephraim, P., Wegener, S. T., Dillingham, T., Pezzin, L., Rossbach, P., & MacKenzie, E. J. (2005). Depressive symptoms and mental health service utilization among persons with limb loss: Results of a national survey. *Archives of Physical Medicine and Rehabilitation, 86,* 650–658.

Dembo, T., Leviton, G. L., & Wright, B. A. (1975). Adjustment to misfortune: A problem of social–psychological rehabilitation. *Rehabilitation Psychology, 22,* 1–100. (Reprinted from *Artificial Limbs, 3,* 4–62, 1956)

Demet, K., Martinet, N., Guillemin, F., Paysant, J., & Andre, J. (2003). Health related quality of and related factors in 539 persons with amputation of upper and lower limb. *Disability and Rehabilitation, 25,* 480–486.

Department of Veterans Affairs. (2005, June 8). *Polytrauma Rehabilitation Centers* (VHA Directive 2005–024). Washington, DC: Veterans Health Administration.

Desmond, D. M., & MacLachlan, M. (2006a). Affective distress and amputation-related pain among older men with long-term, traumatic limb amputations. *Journal of Pain and Symptom Management, 31,* 362–368.

Desmond, D. M., & MacLachlan, M. (2006b). Coping strategies as predictors of psychosocial adaptation in a sample of elderly veterans with acquired lower limb amputations. *Social Science and Medicine, 62,* 208–16.

Dijkstra, P. U., Geertzen, J. H., Stewart, R., & van der Schans, C. P. (2002). Phantom pain and risk factors: A multivariate analysis. *Journal of Pain and Symptom Management, 24,* 578–585.

Dillingham, T. R., Pezzin, L. E., & MacKenzie, E. J. (2002). Limb amputation and limb deficiency: Epidemiology and recent trends in the United States. *Southern Medical Journal, 95,* 875–883.

Dudkiewicz, I., Gabrielov, R., Seiv-Ner, I., Zelig, G., & Heim, M. (2004). Evaluation of prosthetic usage in upper limb amputees. *Disability and Rehabilitation, 26,* 60–63.

Dunn, D. S. (1994). Positive meaning and illusion following disability: Reality negotiation, normative interpretation, and value change. *Journal of Social Behavior and Personality, 9,* 123–138.

Dunn, D. S. (1997). Well-being following amputation: Salutary effects of positive meaning, optimism, and control. *Rehabilitation Psychology, 41,* 285–302.

Ehde, D. M., Czerniecki, J. M., Smith, D. G., Campbell, K., Edwards, W., Jensen, M., & Robinson, L. (2000). Chronic phantom sensations, phantom pain, residual limb pain, and other regional pain after lower limb amputation. *Archives of Physical Medicine and Rehabilitation, 81,* 1039–1044.

Elliott, T., & Frank, R. (1990). Social and interpersonal responses to depression and disability. *Rehabilitation Psychology, 35,* 135–147.

Ephraim, P. L., Wegener, S. T., MacKenzie, E. J., Dillingham, T. R., & Pezzin, L. E. (2005). Phantom pain, residual limb pain, and back pain in amputees: Results of a national survey. *Archives of Physical Medicine and Rehabilitation, 86,* 1910–1919.

Esquenazi, A. (2004). Amputation rehabilitation and prosthetic restoration. From surgery to community reintegration. *Disability and Rehabilitation, 26,* 831–836.

Flor, H., Elbert, T., Knecht, S., Wienbruch, C., Pantev, C., Birbaumer, N., et al. (1995). Phantom-limb pain as a perceptual correlate of cortical reorganization following arm amputation. *Nature, 357,* 482–484.

Frank, R. G., Kashani, J. H., Kashani, S. R., Wonderlich, S. A., Umlauf, R. L., & Ashkanazi, G. S. (1984). Psychological response to amputation as a function of age and time since amputation. *British Journal of Psychiatry, 144,* 493–497.

Fukunishi, I. (1999). Relationship of cosmetic disfigurement to the severity of posttraumatic stress disorder in burn injury or digital amputation. *Psychotherapy and Psychosomatics, 68,* 82–86.

Gallagher, P., Allen, D., & MacLachlan, M. (2001). Phantom limb pain and stump pain: A comparative analysis. *Disability and Rehabilitation, 23,* 522–530.

Gallagher, P., Horgan, O., Franchignoni, F., Giordano, A., & MacLachlan, M. (2007). Body image in people with lower limb amputation: A Rasch analysis of the Amputee Body-Image Scale (ABIS). *American Journal of Physical Medicine and Rehabilitation, 86*(3), 205–215.

Gallagher, P., & MacLachlan, M. (2000). Positive meaning in amputation and thoughts about the amputated limb. *Prosthetics and Orthotics International, 24,* 196–204.

Gerhards, F., Florin, I., & Knapp, T. (1984). The impact of medical, reeducational, and psychological variables on rehabilitation outcome in amputees. *International Journal of Rehabilitation Research, 7,* 379–388.

Geviritz, C. (2005). Update on the treatment of phantom pain. *Topics in Pain Management, 20,* 1–6.

Glasser, R. J. (2006). *Wounded: From Vietnam to Iraq.* New York: Braziller.

Goodwin, L. R., & Holmes, G. E. (1988). Counseling the crime victim: A guide for rehabilitation counselors. *Journal of Applied Rehabilitation Counseling, 19,* 42–47.

Hanley, M. A., Ehde, D. M., Campbell, K. M., Osborn, B., & Smith, D. G. (2006). Self-reported treatments used for lower-limb phantom limb pain: Descriptive findings. *Archives of Physical Medicine & Rehabilitation, 87,* 270–277.

Hanley, M. A., Jensen, M. P., Ehde, D. M., Hoffman, A. J., Patterson, D. R., & Robinson, L. R. (2004). Psychosocial predictors of long-term adjustment to lower limb amputation and phantom limb pain. *Disability and Rehabilitation, 26,* 882–893.

Heinemann, A. W., Bulka, M., & Smetak, S. (1988). Attributions and disability acceptance following traumatic injury: A replication and extension. *Rehabilitation Psychology, 33,* 195–199.

Horgan, O., & MacLachlan, M. (2004). Psychosocial adjustment to lower limb amputation: A review. *Disability & Rehabilitation, 26,* 837–850.

Hostetler, S. G., Schwartz, L., Shields, B. J., Xiang, H., & Smith, G. A. (2005). Characteristics of pediatric traumatic amputations treated in hospital emergency departments: United States, 1990–2002. *Pediatrics, 116,* 667–674.

Ide, M. (2004). Sexuality in persons with limb amputation: A meaningful discussion of re-integration. *Disability and Rehabilitation, 26,* 939–943.

Ide, M., Watanabe, T., & Toyonaga, T. (2002). Sexuality in persons with limb amputation. *Prosthetics and Orthotics International, 26,* 189–194.

Jensen, T. S., Krebs, B., Nielsen, J., & Rasmussen, P. (1984). Nonpainful phantom limb phenomena in amputees: Incidence, clinical characteristics and temporal course. *Acta Neurologica Scandinavia, 70,* 407–414.

Kaas, J. H. (1995). The reorganization of sensory and motor maps in adult mammals. In M. S. Gazzaniga (Ed.), *The cognitive neurosciences* (pp. 51–71). Cambridge, MA: MIT Press.

Kashani, J. H., Frank, R. G., Kashani, S. R., & Wonderlich, S. A. (1983). Depression among amputees. *Journal of Clinical Psychiatry, 44,* 256–258.

Katz, J. (1992). Psychophysiological contributions to phantom limb. *Canadian Journal of Psychiatry, 37,* 282–298.

Kooijman, C. M., Dijkstra, P. U., Geertzen, J. H., Elzinga, A., & van der Schans, C. P. (2000). Phantom pain and phantom sensations in upper limb amputees: An epidemiological study. *Pain, 87,* 33–41.

Krane, E. J., & Heller, L. B. (1995). The prevalence of phantom sensation and pain in pediatric amputees. *Journal of Pain and Symptom Management, 10,* 21–29.

Livneh, H., Antonak, R. F., & Gerhardt, J. (1999). Psychosocial adaptation to amputation: The role of sociodemographic variables, disability-related factors, and coping strategies. *International Journal of Rehabilitation Research, 22,* 21–31.

Lorig, K., & Holman, H. R. (1993). Arthritis self-management studies: A 12-year review. *Health Education Quarterly, 20,* 17–28.

MacBride, A., Rogers, J., Whylie, B., & Freeman, S. J. J. (1980). Psychosocial factors in the rehabilitation of elderly amputees. *Psychosomatics, 21,* 258–265.

Medhat, A., Huber, P. M., & Medhat, M. A. (1990). Factors that influence the level of activities in persons with lower extremity amputation. *Rehabilitation Nursing, 15,* 13–18.

Oaksford, K., Frude, N., & Cuddihy, R. (2005). Positive coping and stress-related psychological growth following lower limb amputation. *Rehabilitation Psychology, 50*(3), 266–284.

Pell, J. P., Donnan, P. T., Fowkes, F. G. R., & Ruckley, C. V. (1993). Quality of life following lower limb amputation for peripheral arterial disease. *European Journal of Vascular Surgery, 7,* 448–451.

Ross, C. E. (1993). Fear of victimization and health. *Journal of Quantitative Criminology and Health, 9,* 159–175.

Rowley, W. R., & Bezold, C. (2005). *Diabetes forecasts to 2025 and beyond: The looming crisis demands change.* Retrieved January 26, 2007, from the Institute for Alternative Futures Web site: http://www.altfutures.com/foresight/IAF%20Diabetes%20Looming%20Crisis%20Forecasts%20Nov%202005.pdf

Rybarczyk, B. D., & Behel, J. M. (2002). Rehabilitation medicine and body image. In T. F. Cash & T. Pruzinsky (Eds.), *Body image.* New York: Guilford Press.

Rybarczyk, B., Nicholas, J. J., & Nyenhuis, D. (1997). Coping with a leg amputation: Integrating research and clinical practice. *Rehabilitation Psychology, 42,* 241–256.

Rybarczyk, B., Nyenhuis, D. L., Nicholas, J. J., Cash, S., & Kaiser, J. (1995). Body image, perceived social stigma, and the prediction of psychosocial adjustment to leg amputation. *Rehabilitation Psychology, 40,* 95–110.

Rybarczyk, B., Szymanski, L., & Nicholas, J. J. (2000). Psychological adjustment to a limb amputation. In R. Frank & T. Elliott (Eds.), *Handbook of rehabilitation psychology* (pp. 29–47). Washington, DC: American Psychological Association.

Rybarczyk, B. D., Nyenhuis, D. L., Nicholas, J. J., Schulz, R., Alioto, R. J., & Blair, C. (1992). Social discomfort and depression in a sample of adults with leg amputations. *Archives of Physical Medicine and Rehabilitation, 73,* 1169–1173.

Sherman, R., & Sherman, C. (1983). Prevalence and characteristics of chronic phantom limb pain among American veterans: Results of a trial survey. *American Journal of Physical Medicine, 62,* 227–238.

Sherman, R. A. (1997). *Phantom pain.* New York: Plenum Press.

Shukla, G. D., Sahu, S. C., Tripathi, R. P., & Gupta, D. K. (1982). A psychiatric study of amputees. *British Journal of Psychiatry, 141,* 50–53.

Tebbi, C. K., & Mallon, J. C. (1987). Long-term psychosocial outcome among cancer amputees in adolescence and early adulthood. *Journal of Psychosocial Oncology, 5,* 69–82.

Tyc, V. L. (1992). Psychosocial adaptation of children and adolescents with limb deficiencies: A review. *Clinical Psychology Review, 12,* 275–291.

van der Schans, C. P., Geertzen, J. H. B., Schoppen, T., & Dijkstra, P. U. (2002). Phantom pain and health-related quality of life in lower limb amputation. *Journal of Pain and Symptom Management, 24,* 429–436.

Varni, J. W., & Setoguchi, Y. (1991). Correlates of perceived physical appearance in children with congenital/acquired limb deficiencies. *Journal of Developmental and Behavioral Pediatrics, 12,* 171–176.

Varni, J. W., & Setoguchi, Y. (1996). Perceived physical appearance and adjustment of adolescents with congenital/acquired limb deficiencies. *Journal of Clinical Child Psychology, 25,* 201–208.

Wartan, S. W., Hamann, W., Wedley, J. R., & McColl, I. (1997). Phantom pain and sensation among British veteran amputees. *British Journal of Anesthesiology, 78,* 652–659.

Wegener, S. T., & Ephraim, P. (2006, June). Epidemiological techniques and health interventions in limb loss. Paper presented at the American Association of Health and Disability and National Center for Birth Defects and Developmental Disability Conference, Ames, IA.

Weiss, S. A., & Lindell, B. (1996). Phantom limb pain and etiology of amputation in unilateral lower extremity amputees. *Journal of Pain and Symptom Management, 11,* 3–17.

Wetterhahn, K. A., Hanson, C., & Levy, C. (2002). Effect of participation in physical activity on body image of amputees. *American Journal of Physical Medicine and Rehabilitation, 81,* 194–201.

Whyte, A., & Carroll, L. J. (2004). The relationship between catastrophizing and disability in amputees experiencing phantom pain. *Disability and Rehabilitation, 26,* 649–54.

Whyte, A. S., & Niven, C. A. (2001). Psychological distress in amputees with phantom limb pain. *Journal of Pain Symptom Management, 22,* 938–946.

Wilkins, K. L., McGrath, P. J., Finley, G. A., & Katz, J. (1998). Phantom limb sensations and phantom limb pain in child and adolescent amputees. *Pain, 78,* 7–12.

Williamson, G. M. (1995). Restriction of normal activities among older adult amputees: The role of public self-consciousness. *Journal of Clinical Geropsychology, 1,* 229–242.

Williamson, G. M., & Schulz, R. (1994). Activity restriction mediates the association between pain and depressed affect: A study of younger and older adult cancer patients. *Psychology and Aging, 10,* 369–378.

Williamson, G. M., Schulz, R., Bridges, M. W., & Behan, A. M. (1994). Social and psychological factors in adjustment to limb amputation. *Journal of Social Behavior and Personality, 9,* 249–268.

Williamson, G. M., & Walters, A. S. (1996). Perceived impact of limb amputation on sexual activity: A study of adult amputees. *The Journal of Sex Research, 33,* 221–230.

Winchell, E. (1995). *Coping with limb loss.* Garden City Park, NY: Avery Publishing.

CHAPTER 3

TRAUMATIC BRAIN INJURY IN ADULTS

Joseph H. Ricker

Over the past 30 years, traumatic brain injury (TBI) has emerged as a primary diagnostic group in medical rehabilitation facilities. Though they serve less than 10% of the inpatient rehabilitation population, specialized brain injury rehabilitation programs at the inpatient and post-acute stage are far more numerous than are other accredited rehabilitation programs, such as those for persons with spinal cord injury or chronic pain (Commission on Accreditation of Rehabilitation Facilities, 2006). Given the high incidence of TBI and the neurobehavioral, cognitive, and psychosocial disabilities that may result, it is essential that rehabilitation psychologists be critically involved in the evaluation and treatment of this multifaceted disability.

The present chapter provides a broad overview of TBI relevant to the practice of rehabilitation psychology. It reviews epidemiology and injury factors, including basics of TBI pathophysiology and acute medical issues; clinical assessment, with particular emphasis on tools likely to be used by rehabilitation psychologists; multiple modalities of intervention, including psychological, pharmacological, and cognitive therapies; and a variety of outcome and long-term rehabilitation issues, such as prediction of outcome, community reintegration, vocational and academic outcomes, and standards of care.

EPIDEMIOLOGY OF TRAUMATIC BRAIN INJURY

The research literature describing the epidemiology of TBI is somewhat confusing, in part due to differing definitions of TBI. In this chapter, *traumatic brain injury* is defined as it is in the Traumatic Brain Injury Model Systems of Care National Database (Harrison-Felix, Newton, Hall, & Kreutzer, 1998) as follows:

> Damage to brain tissue caused by an external mechanical force, as evidenced by loss of consciousness due to brain trauma, posttraumatic amnesia, skull fracture, or objective neurological findings that can be reasonably be attributed to TBI on physical examination or mental status examination. (p. 2)

In the past decade, the estimated incidence of brain injury has ranged from below 100 to nearly 400 per 100,000 of the U.S. population (Kraus & McArthur, 1998). Analysis of the National Hospital Ambulatory Medical Care Survey data indicate that approximately 1 million Americans sustain a brain injury each year, with approximately 80,000 persons annually experiencing TBI-related disability (Guerreo, Thurman, & Sniezek, 2000). Of hospitalized cases of TBI, 19% are classified as severe, 21% as moderate, and 52% as mild (Thurman, Coronado, & Selassie, 2007). Despite the magnitude of these numbers, the Centers for Disease Control and Injury Prevention (CDC; Langlois, Kegler, & Butler, 2003) suggest that the overall incidence rate of inpatient hospitalization for TBI has greatly decreased to fewer than 70 per 100,000 hospital discharges, possibly due to the trend for individuals with very mild injuries to be seen in emergency rooms and released without being hospitalized. Given the pressures in recent years to decrease inpatient bed use, this trend is likely to continue. Another factor in the decreased incidence is the increased use of seat belts, airbags, child car seat restraints, bicycle helmets, and other protective devices (Thurman et al.).

TBI is related to a variety of key demographic and etiologic factors. Recent CDC studies have confirmed two peak age ranges for TBI: between 15 and 24 (145 per 100,000) and over 75 years (191 per 100,000) of age (Thurman & Guerrero, 1999). Approximately twice as many men as women sustain TBIs. Some studies have reported a significantly greater incidence of TBI in ethnic minority populations, particularly within lower socioeconomic strata (Langlois et al., 2003). Primary etiologies for TBI include motor vehicle crashes, assaults, falls, and sports or recreation-related injuries.

Individuals who experience a TBI are not representative of the general population in certain ways. First, the incidence of positive blood alcohol findings (found to exceed 50% in most studies and often significantly beyond the legal intoxication limit) in motor vehicle crashes and violence-related TBI represents an important risk factor (Kraus & McArthur, 1998). This observation is likely as relevant in cases of illicit drug use. Second, it appears that a high proportion of individuals who sustain TBI have a criminal history. For example, Kreutzer, Marwitz, and Witol (1996) found that 19.5% of 327 consecutive admissions for TBI had a preinjury criminal record. In addition, studies have demonstrated that persons with TBI often had preinjury learning disabilities, emotional problems, and attentional deficits (Woodward et al., 1999).

NATURE AND PATHOLOGY OF INJURIES

Ultimately, it is not the role of the rehabilitation psychologist or neuropsychologist to make neuropathological inferences. There are no neuropsychological tests or patterns that are specific to any particular neuropathology following TBI. Rather, the psychologist may incorporate neuropathologic data or hypotheses in the overall determination of functional status and potential for recovery or restoration of function. Thus, psychologists working with survivors of TBI must have a basic understanding of the potential neurobiological mediators and

consequences of TBI. For a more comprehensive review of the neuropathology of TBI, the reader is referred to Kochanek, Clark, and Jenkins (2007) and Povlishock and Katz (2005).

The neuropathological effects of TBI can be grossly classified as anatomic or biochemical. This distinction may not be useful clinically, however, because anatomic and biochemical changes routinely coexist and interact. Thus, it may be more useful clinically to conceptualize neuropathological events as primary or secondary.

Primary Injuries

Primary injuries are those injuries that occur at the time that mechanical forces act upon the head. In general, the human brain is well protected from everyday mechanical forces, suspended within cerebrospinal fluid, surrounded by three layers of meninges (i.e., pia, arachnoid, and dura), and encased in the skull. Mechanical trauma to the head can, however, cause lasting injury. This can occur from the skull and brain being penetrated, for example, by a gunshot wound or assault with an object such as a screwdriver, or from blunt trauma that results in displacement of the skull into brain tissue. Penetrating injuries typically exert their greatest neurobehavioral effects in a manner consistent with their anatomic focus, but widespread effects are possible.

In addition to penetration or fracture of the skull, the mechanical forces to which the brain may be subjected during a fall, assault, or motor vehicle accident may lead to structural damage to the brain. Sufficient inertial loading (i.e., the speed at which the head—and therefore the brain—is moving; often referred to as *acceleration*) combined with a sudden stop (i.e., head impact or abrupt change in the direction of the head's movement; often referred to as *deceleration*), may cause the brain to come into abrupt contact with one or more internal surfaces of the skull. The anterior portions of the brain (i.e., the frontal poles, orbitofrontal cortex, and anterior temporal lobes) are more vulnerable to this effect as compared with posterior brain regions, and may become contused against the bony prominence of the skull (e.g., sphenoid wing, temporal fossa).

Secondary Injuries

Secondary injuries are injuries that result from delayed physiological responses and occur much later in time after the initial mechanical injury. Focal lesions and cortical contusions may not represent the most debilitating mechanism of TBI. The brain can move within the skull, which may result in twisting or stretching of ascending and descending axonal pathways. Furthermore, commissural fibers (e.g., corpus callosum) and other fiber tracts (e.g., fornices) may also become stretched as the result of differential deceleration of the brain within the skull case. This mechanical disruption of axonal tracts may lead to later biochemical responses. The potential disruption of axons has historically been referred to as *diffuse axonal injury* (DAI). Earlier conceptualizations of DAI (e.g., Strich, 1961) assumed that axonal injuries were immediate and were the sole result of direct mechanical forces that would tear or shear axons. It has been demonstrated that the permanent neuropathology of DAI occurs many hours to days following the event as the result of biochemical cascades (Chung et al., 2005; Smith, Meany, & Shull, 2003). DAI may mediate many of the long-term neurobehavioral consequences of moderate and severe brain injury by causing widespread disconnection of brain regions. In addition, although often referred to as a diffuse process, more recent conceptualizations of axonal injury encourage the use of the term *traumatic axonal injury* (Kochanek et al., 2007).

Edema, a frequent secondary complication of moderate and severe brain injuries, occurs when there is an increase in water concentration within cells, between cells, or both. It may be caused by direct mechanical trauma, or it may be the result of altered vascular permeability. Consequently, increased intracranial pressure can result, which may lead to further cerebral disruption and damage.

Additional Complications

Cardiac and respiratory changes can also result from either TBI, or other aspects of trauma that resulted in TBI. For example, blunt force to the chest during a motor vehicle accident may result in cardiac or pulmonary contusions, possibly leading to cardiac arrest, hypoxia, or respiratory complications.

Infection may follow a head injury, often as the result of septic skull penetration. Metabolic and endocrine changes may also occur, either from mechanical trauma to the stalk of the pituitary or secondary to posttraumatic changes in cortisol and thyroid hormones.

Seizures may follow focal contusions or penetrating injuries; they are not known to be caused by axonal injury alone. Seizure vulnerability and prophylaxis are frequently discussed in TBI care, and occurrence varies with severity of injury. Although it appears that most persons sustaining severe TBI are given antiseizure medications for several days or up to weeks after injury, the impact of such a practice on the prevention of later seizures remains unproven and controversial (Benardo, 2003). In a population-based study, 5-year cumulative probabilities for seizure following brain injury are as follows: after severe brain injury, 10.0%; after moderate brain injury, 1.2%; after mild brain injury, 0.7% (Annegers, Hauser, Coan, & Rocca, 1998).

Consciousness and Coma

Loss of consciousness is typical in significant TBI. Exceptions occur, of course, in instances of focal injuries, and, conversely, loss of consciousness does not always occur in penetrating injuries, Nevertheless, although the formal term *coma*, defined as absence of eye opening, not following commands, and not speaking intelligibly and defined as well by a Glasgow Coma Scale score of 8 or less, need not be present in TBI, the depth of disrupted consciousness is a generally accepted indicator of brain injury severity, particularly in cases of suspected diffuse cerebral injury. The use of length of coma and duration of unconsciousness in predicting outcome are discussed in a later section of this chapter.

Vegetative and minimally conscious states.

About 20% of severely injured TBI survivors remain unresponsive at 30 days postinjury (Jennett, 2005). Although the term *coma* is used in the popular parlance, true coma can only last for several weeks. An individual who has spontaneous sleep–wake cycles but no apparent level of conscious awareness is typically in a persistent vegetative state (PVS). The fact that persons in coma usually maintain relatively normal sleep–wake patterns may be particularly troubling for family members who observe that the patient appears awake but does not interact. Because of this wakefulness, family members may also be susceptible to inferring that a person in a PVS is attending to the environment and behaving in a goal-directed manner. Persons sustaining TBI may also emerge into a minimally conscious state, demonstrating objective evidence of consciousness, although these behaviors have been observed inconsistently (Giacino et al., 2002).

Posttraumatic amnesia. *Posttraumatic amnesia* (PTA) refers to a confusional state following head trauma during which an individual demonstrates impaired temporal orientation, decreased ability to form continuous memories, and, possibly, agitation (Sherer, Nakase-Thompson, Yablon, & Gontkovsky, 2005). Recent research suggests that a more accurate characterization of PTA would be as a form of delirium (i.e., a posttraumatic confusional state; Nakase, Sherer, Yablon, Nick, & Trzepacz, 2004; Stuss et al., 1999). Length of PTA is a very useful clinical indicator of outcome, in combination with immediate injury severity variables (Levin, Benton, & Grossman, 1982; Zafonte et al., 1997). Although PTA is useful when properly measured and tracked regularly during the course of recovery (e.g., using the Galveston Orientation and Amnesia Test; Levin, O'Donnell, & Grossman, 1979), retrospective estimates of PTA by patients or clinicians may be unreliable (Gronwall & Wrightson, 1981). Many factors independent of brain injury can interfere with measurement or estimation of PTA (e.g., alcohol or other substances at the time of injury, pain or effects of other injuries, emotional trauma from the accident, inaccurate retelling of events with incorporation of what has been told by others).

COURSE OF RECOVERY AND MEDICAL COMPLICATIONS

Although the primary injury in TBI is typically the brain injury itself, many additional medical problems often co-occur. Such comorbid complications can not only exacerbate the primary brain injury

(e.g., pulmonary contusion or cardiac arrest leading to hypoxia) but may also interfere with goal attainment in the rehabilitation process (e.g., sensory or motor impairments may interfere with full participation in critical aspects of rehabilitation). (For more information, see Hammond & McDeavitt, 1999; Zafonte, Elovic, O'Dell, Mysiw, & Watanabe, 1999; Zygun, Kortbeek, Fick, Laupland, & Doig, 2005.)

Given the differing etiologies and multifaceted nature of possible brain and systemic dysfunction following a given TBI, it is difficult to predict the specific neuropsychological sequelae for a given individual. In general, the following cognitive impairments are often observed following TBI: deficits in arousal, attention, memory, capacity for new learning; problems in initiating, maintaining, organizing, or engaging in goal-directed behavior; self-monitoring and awareness of deficits; impaired language and/or communication; visuoperceptual deficits; and emotional and/or behavioral problems such as agitation, aggression, disinhibition, and depression (Whyte, Hart, Laborde, & Rosenthal, 2005). The nature, severity, and chronicity of these deficits are highly variable across individuals and are mediated by the interactions among a variety of factors, including the nature of the brain dysfunction, time since injury, gender, preinjury neuropsychological and psychological status, family support, financial and physical access to services, and receptivity of the physical, psychological, and social environments (Hanks, Ricker, & Millis, 2004). A challenge for psychologists in TBI rehabilitation is to select those measures that are not only sensitive and specific to the effects of TBI but that also demonstrate the greatest predictive relations with acute and long-term outcomes.

MEASUREMENT IN REHABILITATION

The psychologist working in brain injury must be familiar with several scales and measures, even though he or she may not have the responsibility for their application. Nonetheless, having a working knowledge of each is critical in order to provide valid and clinically meaningful interpretations and predictions of functional status and future outcome.

The Glasgow Coma Scale (GCS; Teasdale & Jennett, 1974) is an ordinal scale that assesses a patient's behavioral responses in the domains of eye movement, motor functions, and vocalization. The total score ranges from 3 to 15, with lower scores representing increased depth of unconsciousness. Clinically, scores of 13 to 15 are considered to reflect mild injury, scores from 9 to 12 indicate moderate injuries, and scores of 8 and below represent severe brain injuries. Historically, the GCS has been viewed as an adequate though gross predictor of outcome at 6-months postinjury (Jennett & Teasdale, 1981). There is some variability in the predictive power of the GCS when used alone (Udekwu, Kromhout-Schiro, Vaslef, Baker, & Oller, 2004). For example, individuals with an initial GCS in the 13 to 15 range who also demonstrate focal lesions on neuroimaging (i.e., complicated mild) often have outcomes comparable with those of patients with GCS totals in the 9 to 12 range (Williams, Levin, & Eisenberg, 1990). Furthermore, an initial GCS may be lowered by factors other than the primary brain injury (e.g., the presence of significant amounts of alcohol in one's system at the time of injury; an acute medical crisis; Sperry et al., 2006; Zafonte, Hammond, & Peterson, 1996).

A modification to the GCS, the Glasgow-Liege Score, has been used to improve outcome prediction on the basis of initial presentation (Born, Albert, Hans, & Bonnal, 1985). The Glasgow-Liege assesses several brainstem reflexes in addition to gross verbal, motor, and eye opening responses, and can be useful in prediction of outcome (Born, 1988).

The Rancho Los Amigos Levels of Cognitive Functioning Scale (RLAS; Hagen, Malkmus, & Durham, 1972) is an ordinal scale with anchor points reflecting levels of behavior and gross cognition. The RLAS ranges from Level I (*no response*) to Level VIII (*purposeful and appropriate behavior*). This scale is based on multiple behavioral observations and is not as useful in clinical prediction as other measures. This scale is qualitative rather than truly quantitative, and it is possible for an individual to be at one RLAS level for one domain of functioning while at another level on another domain.

The Galveston Orientation and Amnesia Test (GOAT; Levin et al., 1979) was designed to be an objective way of measuring presence and depth of PTA. The GOAT assesses temporal orientation (i.e., day, date, place, time of day) and recall of the trauma including events immediately before and following its onset. More recently, a briefer instrument has been developed: the Orientation Log (O-LOG; Jackson, Novack, & Dowler, 1998), which is more amenable to serial evaluations of orientation.

The Glasgow Outcome Scale (GOS; Jennett & Bond, 1975) is an ordinal scale that provides a global evaluation of outcome. Patients are rated on a 1 to 5 scale: 1 = *Death,* 2 = *Persistent Vegetative State,* 3 = *Severe Disability,* 4 = *Moderate Disability,* 5 = *Good Recovery.* The GOS is widely used and is related to GCS and PTA in terms of outcome prediction (Jennett & Teasdale, 1981). An Extended Glasgow Outcome Scale (GOS-E; Wilson, Pettigrew, & Teasdale, 1998) addresses several of the limitations of the GOS by dividing the last three categories into lower and upper levels, increasing the number of outcome categories to eight (Levin et al., 2001).

The Disability Rating Scale (DRS; Rappaport, Hall, Hopkins, Belleza, & Cope, 1982) was developed for the purpose of assessing disability across the continuum of care from coma to community. It correlates with the GOS (Rappaport et al.), although the DRS has a greater psychometric range than the GOS and has been demonstrated to have interrater reliabilities between 0.97 and 0.98 (Gouvier, Blanton, Laporte, & Nepomuceno, 1987). This scale is widely used in rehabilitation research and has been used extensively in outcome studies of persons with TBI (Frankel et al., 2006).

The Functional Independence Measure (FIM; Hamilton, Granger, Sherwin, Zielzny, & Tashman, 1987) was originally an 18-item ordinal scale designed to provide a standard measure of functional independence, regardless of specific disability. The FIM can be divided into two subscales: motor (i.e., self-care, sphincter control, mobility) and cognition (i.e., communication, psychosocial adjustment, cognitive function). Twelve items composing the Functional Assessment Measure (FAM) were added to the FIM to address reading, writing, speech, community access, and additional cognitive issues (e.g., orientation, attention, safety judgment). The FIM has been validated for use in the TBI population (Corrigan, Smith-Knapp, & Granger, 1997). However, even with the addition of new items, the FIM/FAM might not be specific enough to discern cognitive or other neurobehavioral changes, particularly beyond the inpatient rehabilitation phase of recovery from TBI (Hawley, Taylor, Hellawell, & Pentland, 1999).

The Community Integration Questionnaire (CIQ; Willer, Rosenthal, Kreutzer, Gordon, & Rempel, 1993) was developed to assess the degree of handicap experienced by an individual with a TBI upon return to community living. Its 15 items form three subscales: Home Integration, Social Integration, and Productivity. The CIQ has proven useful as a measure of quality of life and level of social and vocational functioning, although it has received some criticism as to its psychometric properties, sensitivity to change over time, and reliability for individuals with severe cognitive deficits (Dijkers, 1997). Additional participation activities have been added to a revised CIQ (Johnston, Goverover, & Dijkers, 2005).

LEVELS OF BRAIN INJURY SEVERITY AND CORRESPONDING PRESENTATIONS

A brain injury that is classified as *severe* does not invariably result in total and permanent disability. Of note is the degree of variability in outcome. For example, a severe brain injury (i.e., GCS of 8 or less) may result in death but also may eventually lead to surprisingly good recovery. Prolonged impairments in consciousness, from coma through posttraumatic confusion, are common following severe TBI. Approximately 30% to 50% of individuals who sustain severe TBI die; of those who survive severe TBI, about 20% remain in an unresponsive state 30 days postinjury (Rutland-Brown, Langlois, Thomas, & Xi, 2006). The initial recovery process may be prolonged, and individuals may not be amenable to extensive psychometric assessment or higher level interventions during acute rehabilitation.

Individuals who sustain brain injuries of moderate initial severity may show a great deal of variability in their presentation and sometimes are difficult to differentiate functionally from persons with more severe initial injuries (Colantonio et al., 2004); most studies generally do not make a sharp distinction

between moderate and severe TBI. In addition, some persons who sustain relatively mild brain injuries in terms of GCS score but who also have focal lesions (e.g., from a discrete penetrating injury, such as a screwdriver) are often classified in research as having sustained *moderate* TBI (Williams et al., 1990). Clinically, however, such persons are usually described as having sustained *complicated mild* injuries (Kennedy et al., 2006).

Mild brain injury has been of tremendous interest to clinicians and researchers, as well as the subject of some controversy. This has no doubt been prompted by some inconsistencies in research findings, increased numbers of outpatient brain injury rehabilitation programs, and escalation of personal injury litigation after mild TBI. Reviews using meta-analysis (Binder, Rohling, & Larrabee, 1997; Frencham, Fox, & Mayberry, 2005) suggest the effects of mild TBI on neuropsychological functioning are minimal, mainly involving attention, working memory, and speed of processing and achieve statistical significance only in the acute stage following injury. A small number of individuals continue to report symptoms and disability for months, or even years following mild head trauma. Iverson's (2005) comprehensive review of the literature in mild TBI concluded that many factors beyond injury to the brain might serve to maintain the cognitive and emotional symptoms that persist beyond a few weeks or months among persons with mild TBI.

A real-world model for the prospective study of the natural history of mild head injury is that of persons examined before and after sports-related concussion. The CDC reports that approximately 300,000 sport-related concussions occur in the United States each year (Thurman, Branche, & Sniezek, 1998). During the acute stage (i.e., from immediately to within 1 week after injury; Echemendia & Julian, 2001), neuropsychological impairment is detectable through traditional paper-and-pencil testing as well as with computerized testing (Lovell & Collins, 2002). Practice guidelines suggest that athletes who sustain a concussion not return to play until they are completely asymptomatic (American Academy of Neurology, 1997; Cantu, 2001). Although acute cognitive impairments are not unusual, as a group, persons with sports-related concussion do not demonstrate neuropsychological deficits at any greater level than controls at 90 days postinjury (McCrea et al., 2003).

ASSESSMENT AND INTERVENTION

As an integral part of the rehabilitation team, psychologists are often called on to provide psychological assessment and intervention. These assessments and interventions may occur at various times in the rehabilitation process and can involve a variety of neuropsychological, behavioral, and psychosocial techniques.

Role of the Psychologist at the Acute Stage

At the acute stage of recovery, the primary focus of care is on sustaining life and addressing very early medical issues and initial consultations and referrals. Nevertheless, rehabilitation psychologists can play an important role. Psychologists utilize early assessment instruments (e.g., GOAT: Levin et al., 1979; Coma-Near-Coma Scale: Rappaport, Dougherty, & Kelting, 1992; Coma Recovery Scale-Revised: Giacino, Kalmar, & Whyte, 2004; Agitated Behavior Scale: Corrigan, 1989) to assist other health care professionals in making realistic early treatment plans. Psychologists can also be a resource for family education and support during the acute stage of brain injury (see chap. 18, this volume). Early rehabilitation intervention is the standard of care in the National Institute on Disability and Rehabilitation Research (NIDRR) TBI Model Systems of Care (described later in this chapter), but studies demonstrating the efficacy of early intervention by psychology (or any other discipline) are lacking.

Role of the Psychologist at the Postacute Stage

Psychologists have multiple roles in the successful rehabilitation of individuals with TBI. Heinemann, Hamilton, Linacre, Wright, and Granger (1995) analyzed outcome data from 140 patients with TBI and 106 patients with spinal cord injury contributed by eight hospitals participating in the Uniform Data System for Medical Rehabilitation. Patients were enrolled in comprehensive multidisciplinary reha-

bilitation programs, but the intensities of physical therapy, occupational therapy, or speech therapy were not associated with changes in functional outcome, even after controlling for factors such as age, admission status, and length of stay. Only intensity of psychological services had any relation to functional improvement. This finding appeared to be specific to cognitive functioning among patients with brain injury. Other studies have demonstrated the predictive value of neuropsychological testing during inpatient rehabilitation in relation to longer term outcome (Boake et al., 2001; Sherer et al., 2002).

Neuropsychological assessment. In the context of rehabilitation, neuropsychological assessment can provide a wealth of information to the treating team, patient, and family. In rehabilitation, neuropsychological assessment is rarely purely diagnostic, because the primary diagnosis is already established. Rather, neuropsychological assessment can assess the level of disability, as well as assist in formulating realistic rehabilitation goals, assessing changes in status, and making discharge plans. Neuropsychological assessment can help target methods of rehabilitation intervention that will lead to more successful outcomes of treatment. For example, understanding limitations in verbal or visual processing may suggest different methodologies of rehabilitation learning and adaptation. To meet these objectives, neuropsychological assessment in rehabilitation is usually of the "flexible" (i.e., as opposed to "fixed battery") variety (see chap. 10, this volume).

The NIDRR TBI Model Systems of Care (Ragnarsson, Thomas, & Zasler, 1993) adopted a battery of neuropsychological tests that were studied during both inpatient and outpatient rehabilitation from 1989 until 2002. This battery included the following: the GOAT (Levin et al., 1979), Symbol Digit Modalities Test (Smith, 1991), the Token Test (Benton, Hamsher, & Sivan, 1994), Wechsler Memory Scale-Revised Logical Memory I & II (Wechsler, 1987), Wechsler Adult Intelligence Scale-Revised Digit Span and Block Design (Wechsler, 1981), Grooved Pegboard (Matthews & Klove, 1964), Visual Form Discrimination test (Benton, Hamsher, Varney, & Spreen, 1983), Controlled Oral Word Association test (Benton et al., 1994), Rey Auditory

Verbal Learning Test (Rey, 1964), Trail Making Test (Army Individual Test Battery, 1941), and the Wisconsin Card Sorting Test (Grant & Berg, 1948). At 1-year follow-up, improvements in neuropsychological functioning were noted in the majority of these formal tests, with the most improvement noted on tests of attention, concentration, and verbal learning (Kreutzer, Gordon, Rosenthal, & Marwitz, 1993). At 5 years after injury, impairments remained in most persons (62%) with moderate and severe TBI, although a significant subset of persons (22%) demonstrated substantial recovery for several years after injury (Millis et al., 2001). This battery has recently been revised and updated to reflect new versions of tests and newer conceptualizations of cognition after TBI. See chapter 10, this volume, for more information about neuropsychological assessment.

Behavior management. Persons sustaining TBI often have behavioral disturbances such as disinhibition and agitation. Some aspects of their behavior may be related to nonbehavioral factors (e.g., biologically mediated agitation), although other issues may be at least partially addressed through the application of behavior modification and other environmental approaches (Lombard & Zafonte, 2005). It must be noted, however, that traditional approaches to behavior modification are based on learning theory, and learning is typically impaired among TBI survivors. Thus, successful behavior management with TBI survivors may need to focus more on stimulus control (i.e., environmental factors) than operant learning (i.e., explicitly recalling contingencies between behaviors and their consequences). Several useful manuals have been published that detail the application of behavior management techniques and practical behavioral recommendations when providing services to persons with TBI (Jacobs, 1993; Matthies, Kreutzer, & West, 1997; Rusin & Jongsma, 2001).

Patient and family education and support. Rehabilitation psychologists working in TBI rehabilitation are frequently called on to provide education and support to patients and/or their families. Survivors of TBI tend to become more dependent on family members (Struchen, Atchison, Roebuck, Caroselli, & Sander, 2002), and this burden may not decrease as time passes (Brooks, Campsie, Symington, Beattie, & McKinlay, 1987; Sander et al., 2003). Patient and family education may occur through a variety of approaches, ranging from formal interdisciplinary family conferences and educational groups to supportive counseling and formal family therapy (Aiteken et al., 2005; Leith, Phillips, & Sample, 2004; Muir, Rosenthal, & Diehl, 1990). Internet-based approaches are also emerging as a means of providing support and education (Ricker et al., 2002; Rotondi, Sinkule, & Spring, 2005). For more information about treating family caregivers, see chapter 18, this volume.

Psychopharmacological management. The vast majority of psychologists do not prescribe medications, although this scope of practice has become a reality on a very limited basis. However, it is important to have familiarity with the drugs used in the treatment and management of TBI. Many applications are off-label and based on case reports or small samples (Parton, Coulthard, & Husain, 2005), but there is a growing and promising literature.

Psychostimulants such as methylphenidate (i.e., Ritalin), amantadine, and bromocriptine are often used with TBI patients in the treatment of diminished attention or arousal. Much clinical experience, prompted by intriguing basic science research (Feeney & Sutton, 1987), has resulted in widespread use of psychostimulants in the TBI population. Supporting human literature, however, is quite limited and based mostly on unblended small-sample studies (Gordon et al., 2006). Randomized controlled trials of methylphenidate (Whyte et al., 1997; Whyte et al., 2004) and bromocriptine (McDowell, Whyte, & D'Esposito, 1998) have suggested small but clinically significant positive effects on attention after TBI. Amantadine has also shown a favorable trend in treatment of cognitive symptoms after TBI, but additional research is needed (Leone & Polsonetti, 2005).

Antiseizure medications are, of course, used as seizure prophylaxis or to control a known seizure disorder. These medications are also used in some TBI patients to manage agitation (Lombard &

Zafonte, 2005). Despite relatively widespread use, substantial evidence for their value is lacking (Fleminger, Greenwood, & Oliver, 2003). As in non-TBI populations, antiseizure medications are also used in TBI populations as a primary or adjunctive treatment for mood disorders (e.g., bipolar disorder).

Antipsychotic medications are often used to control agitated behavior in non-TBI populations. Their use with TBI survivors is more controversial, however, and may exacerbate the neurobehavioral symptoms of TBI, thus interfering with the rehabilitation process (Mysiw et al., 2006). Of note, however, are the newer atypical antipsychotics, the properties of which may be of benefit for management of some TBI symptoms (Elovic, Langsang, Li, & Ricker, 2003).

Cognitive rehabilitation. Cognitive rehabilitation is dealt with comprehensively in chapter 18 of this volume. In brief, however, it must be noted that cognitive rehabilitation has received much interest and attention for persons with TBI, given the age groups and, thus, the great number of potential productive years, in which TBI is most likely to occur. Until quite recently, most literature on cognitive rehabilitation was anecdotal or based on highly variable inclusion criteria and methods. Cicerone and colleagues (2000, 2005) have analyzed the literature on cognitive rehabilitation using a priori criteria derived from evidence-based practice standards. This work group has concluded that there now exists substantial evidence in support of cognitive rehabilitation for persons with TBI. Effective approaches include strategy training for impaired attention and memory, and structured interventions to improve functional communication.

Prognostication of long-term outcome. Empirical prediction of long-term outcome poses several challenges in the TBI population. The first issue is that of identifying those variables one wishes to use for prediction. Length of coma is a good predictor of outcome, but length of PTA appears to be the best acute predictor of most outcome endpoints at 1 year (Brown et al., 2005).

Return to work has frequently been used as a dependent variable in outcome prediction studies. For example, data from the TBI Model Systems of

Care indicated that those with less severe levels of injury (i.e., as measured by GCS, length of coma, and length of posttraumatic amnesia), physical functioning (i.e., indexed with the FIM and DRS), cognitive functioning (i.e., delayed verbal recall), and behavioral functioning (i.e., indexed with the RLAS) were more likely to return to work at 1-year post TBI (Cifu, Keyser-Marcus, et al., 1997). Using a multivariate model to predict return to work at 1 to 2 years postinjury, Dikmen et al. (1994) found that relatively accurate predictions could be made based on education, preinjury work history, severity of brain injury, neuropsychological functioning (i.e., as measured with the Halstead-Reitan Neuropsychological Test Battery; Reitan & Wolfson, 1993), and severity of other (nonhead) injuries. More recently, Sherer et al. (2002) demonstrated that early neuropsychological test results are very predictive of return to work at 1-year postinjury.

There is still much that is not known about long-term outcome following brain injury; for example, improvement is not uncommon beyond the general clinically accepted cutoff of 12 to 18 months. More studies also need to be conducted on predicting long-term outcome based on multivariate models of acute factors. Furthermore, the critical role of preinjury medical, educational, and psychosocial variables needs further investigation.

Facilitation of other post-acute rehabilitation services. In addition to providing direct services to the patient or family, psychologists can facilitate transition to other services. Following acute neurorehabilitation, a variety of treatment options are available to an individual with a traumatic brain injury, depending on severity and type of disability, financial resources, access to transportation, and family support. In addition, though there are numerous brain injury programs in the United States, certain types are not equally distributed in urban or rural areas and in certain parts of the country. Given the decreasing length of stay in acute inpatient rehabilitation hospitals (Hoffman et al., 2003), access to postacute rehabilitative services is becoming increasingly important to optimize long-term outcome for persons with a brain injury and their families.

Salcido, Moore, Schleenbaker, and Klim (1996) defined *subacute rehabilitation* (SR) as the following:

> A level of rehabilitation care designed to meet the needs of patients who medically and physically are too frail to participate in the rigors of a conventional inpatient physical rehabilitation program (i.e. 3 hours or more of daily therapy). SR also may be appropriate for patients who do not require intense multiple therapies but may have medical comorbidities and complicating factors that require the medical supervision of a physiatrist. (p. 60)

Patients receive the same types of rehabilitation services as in acute rehabilitation (i.e., physical, occupational, and speech therapy), but with lesser intensity, and care is often provided by paraprofessionals or health care workers with less specialized experience. Psychologists typically provide services in subacute brain injury rehabilitation programs, but often as consultants (see Ricker, 2004). For patients who are deemed "slow-to-recover" (i.e., remaining in a minimally responsive state for weeks or months after injury or individuals making very slow progress in rehabilitation therapy), SR is often recommended either immediately after acute neurotrauma care or after comprehensive inpatient rehabilitation has been completed. For low-level patients, a focus of rehabilitative therapy is on sensory stimulation and continual assessment of the patient's responsiveness to the environment. SR may also be viewed as a more cost-effective alternative for older adults with TBI who are capable of significant gain in functional outcome but may require more time to achieve such gains due to comorbidities and reduced capacities in speed of learning (Cifu et al., 1996; Reeder, Rosenthal, Lichtenberg, & Wood, 1996). Although studies on individuals who have sustained hip fractures and stroke suggest similar outcomes following acute rehabilitation or SR (Deutsch et al., 2006), this finding has not been systematically investigated with the TBI population. The lack of research on this critical issue, given the complexity of rehabilitation needs of individuals with TBI, marks an important opportunity.

Some individuals who are minimally responsive after acute rehabilitation require a chronic treatment program, usually located in a nursing home, which provides primarily medical, nursing and custodial care with therapy to maintain function and prevent further physical deterioration. Again, there is a lack of empirical research on program by level of injury in this sector.

Perhaps the most pervasive forms of postacute rehabilitation are outpatient therapy and day treatment. *Outpatient therapy* can consist of a single or combination of treatments (e.g., physical therapy, occupational therapy, speech-language therapy, psychotherapy) at a rehabilitation center or specialized brain injury rehabilitation program. In all but the mildest of cases, a period of outpatient therapy is recommended after inpatient rehabilitation to assist the person with a TBI in reaching their highest level of physical and psychological functioning. This is often accompanied by periodic medical monitoring, usually by a physiatrist, and follow-up neuropsychological evaluation after 6 months or longer to assess level of recovery and residual impairments and plan for community reintegration. *Day treatment*, encompassing a full array of outpatient services, may be available to individuals who typically attend 3 to 5 days per week, 4 to 6 hours per day, for 3 to 6 months. These programs, which are often accredited by the Commission on Accreditation of Rehabilitation Facilities (CARF) as "community-integrated programs," provide the standard array of rehabilitation services with ongoing medical supervision, cognitive rehabilitation, case management, vocational rehabilitation services, and individual, family, and group psychotherapy. Many of these programs are psychologist-led or managed and are termed *holistic* or *neuropsychological rehabilitation* programs and have produced impressive outcomes (see Gordon et al., 2006).

Transitional living programs are designed for medically stable, higher functioning individuals who are ready to learn independent living skills in a community setting. Usually, transitional living programs are located in single or multifamily dwellings in the community, staffed by counselors or therapists who may be affiliated with a brain injury rehabilitation program. Because of a variety of cognitive and/or behavioral problems, residents in a transitional living program need some training to develop or regain skills in community mobility, shopping, managing personal finance, job seeking, use of leisure time, and developing interpersonal relationships.

For individuals with chronic, severe behavior problems, a *neurobehavioral residential treatment* program is often a desired placement. This type of program may be hospital-based with a high degree of structure, systematic use of behavioral management, physical management, and/or psychopharmacology. Individuals who exhibit severe disinhibition, agitation (i.e., beyond the acute phase of recovery), and antisocial behavior (i.e., including the threat of potential harm to self or others) are likely candidates for treatment in these settings.

Family reintegration.   Families are often characterized as the "second victim" of a traumatic brain injury. The catastrophic nature of the injury and its persisting sequelae, accompanied by the circumstances surrounding it (often a motor vehicle crash or violent encounter) creates obstacles to accepting and coping with "life after brain injury." Yet, the family is a critical element in efforts to achieve successful community integration. The typical adult with brain injury is unmarried and living alone prior to the injury. Quite often, they return to the family of origin, which assumes the primary role of caregiver. This poses a considerable burden on family members, who are unaccustomed to their new roles and experience a great deal of "burden" that may even increase over the years postinjury (Sander et al., 2003). In other cases, a person with a TBI returns to a spouse, who may quite accurately perceive their partner as a significantly different person or even as a "child." This can create tremendous stress on the caregiving spouse, and in some cases, a parent–child relationship supplants the marital one. As Serio, Kreutzer, and Gervasio (1995) found in their study of family needs following brain injury, the need for emotional support is most frequently unmet, in comparison with needs for medical information, professional support, and instrumental support. For more information on working with family caregivers, see chapter 18, this volume.

Vocational reintegration.   For many survivors of brain injury, the process of re-entering competitive employment is one of the greatest obstacles to regaining a sense of quality of life. Despite the catastrophic nature of TBI, many survivors have sufficiently recovered basic physical and cognitive skills within 6 to 12 months postinjury to begin the process of vocational rehabilitation (Malec & Degiorgio, 2002). Receiving appropriate vocational rehabilitation services may, in fact, be more critical in returning to work than injury characteristics, severity, medical factors, or survivor demographics (Johnstone, Mount, & Schopp, 2003).

The first step in vocational rehabilitation is usually a referral from the rehabilitation facility to the state vocational rehabilitation agency. Many state offices have counselors who specialize in traumatic brain injury. After establishing eligibility for services, an individualized written rehabilitation plan may be established consisting of the following: (a) a comprehensive extended evaluation, which may include up-to-date medical, neuropsychological, and vocational interest/aptitude examinations; (b) referral to a specialized brain injury rehabilitation program which has a vocational rehabilitation component; (c) contact with the preinjury employer to assist the client to return in the same or, more typically, modified or reduced job; (d) referral to a supported employment program, which may be administered by the state agency, a vocational rehabilitation company, or brain injury rehabilitation program. In the supported employment model, which is known as a *place–train* model, clients are placed in a competitive work setting with a job coach who works alongside the employee until the employee no longer needs cueing or guidance (Wehman, Targett, West, & Kregel, 2005). For more information on vocational rehabilitation, see chapter 23, this volume.

Academic reintegration.   For children or young adults who sustain a TBI, an important goal is resumption of school or academic activities. In the past decade, the federal and state education agencies have recognized traumatic brain injury as a distinct entity. Children and adolescents who experience a TBI are eligible to receive special education services under the Individuals with Disabilities Education Act (2006). In some rehabilitation programs, educational tutoring is initiated during the inpatient hospitalization. As discharge approaches, the rehabilitation team (frequently the psychologist or social worker) often works directly with the individual's local school district to develop a transition plan to reestablish an educational program. An individualized educational plan is developed, which may include homebound tutoring, part-time schedule, use of compensatory strategies or devices, modified curriculum, assistive technology, special transportation, and similar services. This plan is subject to review on a yearly basis, or more often, as needed. Some large school districts even have a designated special education expert, knowledgeable about traumatic brain injury, who oversees the educational programming of children with TBI. For young adults in their college years, many universities offer services for students with disabilities. For more information on the role of schools in the rehabilitation of children, see chapter 22, this volume.

Sexuality

The combination of physical, neuropsychological, and behavioral sequelae of TBI result in a variety of social disabilities, including the challenges of reestablishing meaningful social relationships, particularly of an intimate nature. Self-image is often significantly impaired following TBI, even in cases where changes in physical appearance may be minor. Problems in accurately perceiving and expressing emotion, as well as physical limitations, can pose obstacles for individuals attempting to engage in sexual behavior. On a more basic level, feelings of unattractiveness or change in sexual role may impede the capacity to establish satisfying intimate relationships (Schopp, Good, Barker, Mazurek, & Hathaway, 2006). In addition, poor impulse control might interfere with a TBI survivor's ability to respect limits with a partner (Hibbard, Gordon, Flanagan, Haddad, & Labinsky, 2000). Sexual education, assertiveness training, and couples counseling are some techniques to assist the person with TBI to resume their identity as a "sexual being" (Simpson & Long, 2004).

Substance Abuse

A major risk factor that may interfere with successful community reintegration following TBI is the use and abuse of alcohol and/or drugs (Bombardier, Temkin, Machamer, & Dikmen, 2003; Horner et al., 2005). One study from the TBI Model Systems of Care that examined cross-sectional ($n = 322$) and longitudinal samples ($n = 73$) up to 4 years postinjury (Kreutzer et al., 1996) found that those who used alcohol excessively prior to the injury remained heavy drinkers at follow-up several years postinjury; this finding has been replicated in more recent studies (Bogner, Corrigan, Mysiw, Clinchot, & Fugate, 2001). Other investigators have identified substance abuse as a major impediment to participation in supported employment programs and job retention (Wehman et al., 2005). Community-based models have been shown to increase productivity and decrease the level of substance use in persons with severe traumatic brain injury (Corrigan & Bogner, 2007). Though many rehabilitation psychologists do not have advanced training in substance abuse treatment, it is important to utilize screening measures, such as the Brief Michigan Alcoholism Screening Test (Pokorney, Miller, & Kaplan, 1972) or the CAGE (Ewing, 1984) to identify those who used substances excessively and may be at risk of abuse following discharge into the community. It is also important for the rehabilitation psychologist to identify, educate, and/or refer to community providers who can treat substance abuse problems in persons with traumatic brain injury. For more information about substance abuse in traumatic disability, see chapter 14, this volume.

MODELS AND STANDARDS OF CARE

The only widely accepted standards of care for traumatic brain injury are those promulgated by CARF (2006). These standards were originally developed by the Brain Injury Special Interest Group of the American Congress of Rehabilitation Medicine and later adopted by CARF in 1985. The initial standards were only intended to cover comprehensive inpatient rehabilitation, but in 1988 regulations were developed for the rapidly expanding field of postacute brain injury rehabilitation. The standards were termed *community integrative* and intended to include programs that provided a structured brain injury rehabilitation program in an outpatient, day treatment, or residential setting. Of note is that psychological services, such as neuropsychological assessment, cognitive rehabilitation, behavioral management, and patient and family counseling, are identified in the standards as integral to brain injury rehabilitation service delivery.

From a consumer protection standpoint, the adoption of standards of care was an important development in providing persons with brain injury and families a guide for selection and evaluation of program quality. The addition of specific "ethical standards" to the brain injury rehabilitation standards in the early 1990s was, in part, a response to the many allegations of fraud and abuse among brain injury service providers (Kerr, 1992). Despite these safeguards, the existence of such standards of care cannot prevent unscrupulous providers from engaging in misleading or deceptive practices or providing exorbitantly expensive, unnecessary, or ineffective treatment (Banja, 2005). The CARF standards are in a continuous state of evolution, being revised every 3 years. Psychologists have been instrumental in the promulgation and refinement of CARF standards. In recent years, the role of team members, including, perhaps even explicitly, the rehabilitation psychologist as a compulsory member of the rehabilitation team, has been challenged. To date, the importance of psychological factors in medical rehabilitation and the position of the rehabilitation psychologist as a member of the core rehabilitation team have been successfully maintained. Yet, as the essential characteristics of comprehensive rehabilitation and identifying which patients should receive such services continue to be questioned, rehabilitation psychologists must be vigilant to these potential threats and provide sufficient evidence to document their contributions to optimal rehabilitation outcomes.

In 1987, shortly after the development of CARF standards, NIDRR announced funding for a new program of service demonstration and research: TBI Model Systems of Care, modeled after the existing Spinal Cord Injury (SCI) Model Systems of Care, which was initiated in 1971. Ragnaarson et al. (1993) described a model system of care as a system of ser-

vice delivery that provides "an entire spectrum of care—emergency evacuation and advanced life support at the accident scene, intensive care, comprehensive physical and psychosocial rehabilitation and long-term community follow-up" (p. 3). There are currently 16 such centers nationwide. The overall objectives of the TBI Model Systems of Care program are to (a) develop and demonstrate a model system of care for persons with TBI, stressing continuity and comprehensiveness of care; and (b) develop and maintain a standardized national database for innovative analyses of TBI treatments and outcomes (Harrison-Felix et al., 1996; Ragnaarson et al., 1993). The major issues addressed in this project include the following: (a) demographics of the population; (b) causes of injury; (c) nature of diagnoses, including severity, level of impairment, disability, and handicap; (d) types of services or treatment; (e) the costs of treatment; and (f) measurement and prediction of outcome. Psychologists serve as principal investigators or coprincipal investigators on the majority of these grants.

In addition, the following priorities were established: (a) to investigate the efficacy of alternative methods of service delivery intervention after inpatient rehabilitation discharge and other post-acute pathways; (b) to identify and evaluate interventions, including those using emerging technology, that can improve vocational outcomes and community integration; (c) to develop key predictors of rehabilitation outcome, including subjective well-being at hospital discharge and at long-term follow-up; (d) to determine relations between cost of care, specific treatment interventions, and functional outcomes; (e) to examine the implications of violence as a cause of TBI on treatment interventions, rehabilitation costs, and long-term outcomes; and (f) to investigate the outcome of alternative pathways of post-acute treatment, such as skilled nursing facilities, subacute rehabilitation facilities and home care (Bushnik, 2003). The model systems have emphasized outcomes measurement. Studies have assessed the reliability and validity of well-known measures such as the DRS and the FIM, as well as more recent instruments such as the CIQ. To date, over 6,500 persons with TBI have been enrolled into the TBI model systems since 1988.

ECONOMIC ISSUES FOLLOWING TRAUMATIC BRAIN INJURY

In addition to personal disruption in the areas of cognition, vocation, and family, survivors of disabling TBI can encounter significant financial burdens. One obvious cost is that of medical rehabilitation care. For severe TBI, High et al. (1996) reported that the average cost to provide initial inpatient rehabilitation care and services to one individual may exceed $85,000. Financial costs are not limited to medical rehabilitation, however. TBI survivors may also incur costs related to lost wages, along with loss of future financial security for families. Almost 20 years ago it was estimated that the total lifetime expense for head injuries resulted in a cost of $44 billion in United States, with only $4.5 billion attributable to direct treatment costs (Max, MacKenzie, & Rice, 1991). In addition, it has also been estimated that brain injury-related work loss and disability result in a total cost of $20.6 billion.

Given these economic issues, as well as concerns in recent years about fraud and abuse in the head injury rehabilitation industry, it is reasonable to ask whether TBI rehabilitation is truly worth the cost. Several investigations of cost-effectiveness have supported the provision of comprehensive rehabilitation for persons with TBI, particularly for earlier services to persons with severe brain injury (Aronow, 1987; Cope, Cole, Hall, & Barkan, 1991; Johnston & Lewis, 1991). In general, rehabilitation decreases the need for later care, with more acutely treated cases demonstrating greater benefit. Similar findings were found in the United Kingdom, suggesting that the effects are related to rehabilitation and not solely related to system of care (Turner-Stokes, Paul, & William, 2006).

Although it appears that TBI rehabilitation works and that intensive early rehabilitation increases its efficacy, increased amounts of rehabilitation do not necessarily lead to improved outcome. Johnston (1991) conducted a follow-up evaluation with the patients reported in the previously discussed Johnston and Lewis study (1991). He found no difference in longer-term outcome between patients who had received a few months of residential rehabilitation versus those who had received years of similar treat-

ment. The amount spent on treatment also does not necessarily correlate with outcome (Putnam & Adams, 1992). Ricker (1998) reviewed the empirical literature regarding TBI rehabilitation, with specific attention given to cost issues. His conclusion to the question "TBI rehabilitation: Is it worth the cost?" was "Yes! However . . . ." Although it was clear that TBI rehabilitation could improve functional outcome by reducing need for supervision, improving vocational reintegration, and increasing the ability to perform activities of daily living, at the time of the review, there was essentially no empirical research that directly addressed the issue of cost–benefit, or potentially the lack thereof, specifically for clinical neuropsychological or rehabilitation psychology services in TBI rehabilitation. Sherer and Novack (2003) recently addressed the topic of cost outcomes in the context of neuropsychological services for brain injury rehabilitation. They concluded that although no new data exist that would specifically address the cost–benefit of such services, such studies would be feasible if conducted from the standpoint of diminished caregiver burden and reduction of future care costs.

SUMMARY AND CONCLUSIONS

This chapter has provided a brief overview of the nature of TBI and its short- and long-term physical, cognitive, and neurobehavioral consequences. A framework has been provided for understanding the multiple roles of psychologists in assessing and managing the deficits and the rehabilitation process, both for the survivor with brain injury and significant others. Within the past 3 decades, TBI has become a central component of most rehabilitation programs in the United States and has received increasing interest in the international community. Psychologists have been instrumental in establishing innovations in clinical practice and in conducting critical research to establish the validity of new assessment techniques and rehabilitative interventions. In addition, psychologists have been actively involved in treatment efficacy research, which has become of increased salience in the era of health care reform and managed care. Psychologists have also been at the forefront in the growth of model systems of care for persons with TBI and in developing standards of care. Future developments in the art and science of brain injury rehabilitation will likely continue to be dependent, in large measure, on the substantial contributions of psychologists committed to the concerns of persons with brain injury and their families.

References

Aiteken, M. E., Korehbandi, P., Parnell, D., Parker, J. G., Stefans, V., Tompkins, E., & Schulz, E. G. (2005). Experiences from the development of a comprehensive family support program for pediatric trauma and rehabilitation patients. *Archives of Physical Medicine and Rehabilitation, 86,* 175–179.

American Academy of Neurology. (1997). Practice parameter: The management of concussion in sports (summary statement). *Neurology, 48,* 585.

Annegers, J. F., Hauser, W. A., Coan, S. P., & Rocca, W. A. (1998). A population-based study of seizures after traumatic brain injuries. *The New England Journal of Medicine, 338,* 20–24.

Army Individual Test Battery. (1941). *The trail making test.* Washington, DC: Department of Defense.

Aronow, H. U. (1987). Rehabilitation effectiveness with severe brain injury: Translating research into policy. *Journal of Head Trauma Rehabilitation, 2,* 24–36.

Banja, J. (2005). *The persons served: Ethical perspectives on CARF's accreditation standards and guidelines.* Tucson, AZ: Commission on Accreditation of Rehabilitation Facilities.

Benardo, L. S. (2003). Prevention of epilepsy after head trauma: Do we need new drugs or a new approach. *Epilepsia, 44*(Suppl. 10), 27–33.

Benton, A. L., Hamsher, K. de S., & Sivan, A. B. (1994). Multilingual aphasia examination (3rd ed.). Iowa City, IA: AJA Associates.

Benton, A. L., Hamsher, K. de S., Varney, N. R., & Spreen, O. (1983). *Contributions to neuropsychological assessment.* New York: Oxford University Press.

Binder, L. M., Rohling, M. L., & Larrabee, G. J. (1997). A review of mild head trauma. Part I: Meta-analytic review of neuropsychological studies. *Journal of Clinical and Experimental Neuropsychology, 19,* 421–431.

Boake, C., Millis, S. R., High, W. M., Delmonico, R. L., Kreutzer, J. S., Rosenthal, M., et al. (2001). Using early neuropsychological testing to predict long-term productivity outcome from traumatic brain injury. *Archives of Physical Medicine and Rehabilitation, 82,* 761–768.

Bogner, J. A., Corrigan, J. D., Mysiw, W. J., Clinchot, D., & Fugate, L. (2001). A comparison of substance abuse and violence in the prediction of long-term rehabilitation outcomes after traumatic brain injury. *Archives of Physical Medicine and Rehabilitation, 82,* 571–577.

Bombardier, C. H., Temkin, N. R., Machamer, J., & Dikmen, S. S. (2003). The natural history of drinking and alcohol-related problems after traumatic brain injury. *Archives of Physical Medicine and Rehabilitation, 84,* 185–191.

Born, J. D. (1988). The Glasgow-Liege Scale. Prognostic value and evolution of motor response and brain stem reflexes after severe head injury. *Acta Neurochirgica, 91*(1–2), 1–11.

Born, J. D., Albert, A., Hans, P., & Bonnal, J. (1985). Relative prognostic value of best motor response and brain stem reflexes in patients with severe head injury. *Neurosurgery, 16,* 595–600.

Brooks, N., Campsie, L., Symington, C., Beattie, A., & McKinlay, W. (1986). The 5-year outcome of severe blunt head injury: A relative's view. *Journal of Neurology, Neurosurgery and Psychiatry, 49,* 764–770.

Brown, A. W., Malec, J. F., McClelland, R. L., Diehl, N. N., Englander, J., & Cifu, D. X. (2005). Clinical elements that predict outcome after traumatic brain injury: A prospective multicenter recursive partitioning (decision-tree) analysis. *Journal of Neurotrauma, 22,* 1040–1051.

Bushnik, T. (2003). Introduction: The Traumatic Brain Injury Model Systems of care. *Archives of Physical Medicine and Rehabilitation, 84,* 151–152.

Cantu, R. C. (2001). Posttraumatic retrograde and anterograde amnesia: Pathophysiology and implications in grading and return safe to play. *Journal of Athletic Training, 36,* 244–248.

Chung, R. S., Staal, J. A., McCormack, G. H., Dickson, T. C., Cozens, M. A., Chuckowree, J. A., et al. (2005). Mild axonal stretch injury in vitro induces a progressive series of neurofilament alterations ultimately leading to delayed axotomy. *Journal of Neurotrauma, 22,* 1081–1091.

Cicerone, K. D., Dahlberg, C., Kalmar, K., Langenbahn, D. M., Malec, J. F., Bergquist, T. F., et al. (2000). Evidence-based cognitive rehabilitation: Recommendations for clinical practice. *Archives of Physical Medicine & Rehabilitation, 81,* 1596–1615.

Cicerone, K. D., Dahlberg, C., Malec, J. F., Langenbahn, D. M., Felicetti, T., Kneipp, S., et al. (2005). Evidence-based cognitive rehabilitation: Updated review of the literature from 1998 through 2002. *Archives of Physical Medicine and Rehabilitation, 86,* 1681–1692.

Cifu, D. X., Keyser-Marcus, L., Lopez, E., Wehman, P., Kreutzer, J. S., Englander, J., & High, W. (1997). Acute predictors of successful return to work 1 year after traumatic brain injury: A multicenter analysis. *Archives of Physical Medicine and Rehabilitation, 78,* 125–131.

Cifu, D. X., Kreutzer, J. S., Marwitz, J. H., Rosenthal, M., Englander, J., & High, W. (1997). Functional outcomes of older adults with traumatic brain injury: A prospective, multicenter analysis. *Archives of Physical Medicine and Rehabilitation, 78,* 125–131.

Colantonio, A., Ratcliff, G., Chase, S., Kelsey, S., Escobar, M., & Vernich, L. (2004). Long-term outcomes after moderate to severe traumatic brain injury. *Disability and Rehabilitation, 26,* 253–261.

Commission on Accreditation of Rehabilitation Facilities. (2006). *Standards for medical rehabilitation programs.* Tucson, AZ: Author.

Cope, D. N., Cole, J. R., Hall, J. M., & Barkan, H. (1991). Brain injury: Analysis of outcome in a post-acute rehabilitation system. Part I: General analysis. *Brain Injury, 5,* 111–125.

Corrigan, J. D. (1989). Development of a scale for assessment of agitation following traumatic brain injury. *Journal of Clinical and Experimental Neuropsychology, 11,* 261–277.

Corrigan, J. D., & Bogner, J. (2007). Interventions to promote retention in substance abuse treatment. *Brain Injury, 21,* 343–356.

Corrigan, J. D., Smith-Knapp, K., & Granger, C. V. (1997). Validity of the Functional Independence Measure for persons with traumatic brain injury. *Archives of Physical Medicine and Rehabilitation, 78,* 828–834.

Deutsch, A., Granger, C. V., Heinemann, A. W., Fiedler, R. C., DeJong, G., Kane, R. L., et al. (2006). Poststroke rehabilitation: Outcomes and reimbursement of inpatient rehabilitation facilities and subacute rehabilitation programs. *Stroke, 37,* 1477–1482.

Dijkers, M. (1997). Measuring the long-term outcomes of traumatic brain injury: A review of the Community Integration Questionnaire. *Journal of Head Trauma Rehabilitation, 12*(6), 74–91.

Dikmen, S. S., Temkin, N. R., Machamer, J. E., Holubkov, A. L., Fraser, R. T., & Winn, R. (1994). Employment following traumatic head injuries. *Archives of Neurology, 51,* 177–186.

Echemendia, R. J., & Julian, L. J. (2001). Mild traumatic brain injury in sports: Neuropsychology's contribution to a developing field. *Neuropsychology Review, 11*(2), 69–88.

Elovic, E. P., Lansang, R., Li, Y., & Ricker, J. H. (2003). The use of atypical antipsychotics in traumatic brain injury. *Journal of Head Trauma Rehabilitation, 18*(2), 177–195.

Ewing, J. A. (1984). Detecting alcoholism: The CAGE Questionnaire. *JAMA, 252,* 27.

Feeney, D. M., & Sutton, R. L. (1987). Pharmacotherapy for recovery of function after brain injury. *Critical Reviews in Neurobiology, 3,* 135–197.

Fleminger, S., Greenwood, R. J., & Oliver, D. L. (2003). Pharmacological management for agitation and aggression in people with acquired brain injury. Cochrane Database System *of Systematic Reviews, 2003*(1), Article CD0032992005. Retrieved November 11, 2008, from the Cochrane Library Database, http://www.cochrane.org/reviews/en/ab003299.html

Frankel, J. E., Marwitz, J. H., Cifu, D. X., Kreutzer, J. S., Englander, J., & Rosenthal, M. (2006). A follow-up study of older adults with traumatic brain injury: Taking into account decreasing length of stay. *Archives of Physical Medicine and Rehabilitation, 87,* 57–62.

Frencham, K., Fox, A., & Mayberry, M. (2005). Neuropsychological studies of mild traumatic brain injury: A meta-analytic review of research since 1995. *Journal of Clinical and Experimental Neuropsychology, 27,* 334–351.

Giacino, J. T., Ashwal, S., Childs, N., Cranford, R., Jennett, B., Katz, D. I., et al. (2002). The minimally conscious state: Definition and diagnostic criteria. *Neurology, 58,* 349–353.

Giacino, J. T., Kalmar, K., & Whyte, J. (2004). The JFK Coma Recovery Scale-Revised: Measurement characteristics and diagnostic utility. *Archives of Physical Medicine and Rehabilitation, 85,* 2020–2029.

Gordon, W. A., Zafonte, R., Cicerone, K., Cantor, J., Brown, M., Lombard, L., et al. (2006). Traumatic brain injury rehabilitation: State of the science. *American Journal of Physical Medicine & Rehabilitation, 85,* 343–382.

Gouvier, W. D., Blanton, P., Laporte, K., & Nepomuceno, C. (1987). Reliability and validity of the Disability Rating Scale and the Levels of Cognitive Functioning Scale in monitoring recovery from severe head injury. *Archives of Physical Medicine and Rehabilitation, 68,* 94–97.

Grant, D. A., & Berg, E. A. (1948). A behavioral analysis of the degree of reinforcement and ease of shifting to new responses in a Weigl-type card sorting problem. *Journal of Experimental Psychology, 38,* 404–411.

Guerreo, J. L., Thurman, D. J., & Sniezek, J. E. (2000). Emergency department visits associated with traumatic brain injury. *Brain Injury, 14,* 181–186.

Hagen, C., Malkmus, D., & Durham, P. (1972). *Levels of cognitive functioning.* Downey, CA: Rancho Los Amigos Hospital.

Hamilton, B. B., Granger, C. V., Sherwin, F. S., Zielzny, M., & Tashman, J. S. (1987). A uniform national data system for medical rehabilitation. In M. Fuhrer (Ed.),

Rehabilitation outcome analysis and measurement. Baltimore: Brookes Publishing.

Hammond, F. M., & McDeavitt, J. T. (1999). Medical and orthopedic complications. In M. Rosenthal, J. S. Kreutzer, E. R. Griffith, & B. Pentland (Eds.), *Rehabilitation of the adult and child with traumatic brain injury* (3rd ed., pp. 53–73). Philadelphia: F. A. Davis.

Hanks, R. A., Ricker, J. H., & Millis, S. R. (2004). Empirical evidence in the neuropsychological assessment of moderate and severe traumatic brain injury. In J. H. Ricker (Ed.), *Differential diagnosis in adult neuropsychological assessment* (pp. 218–242). New York: Springer Publishing Company.

Harrison-Felix, C., Newton, N., Hall, K. M., Kreutzer, J. S. (1996). Descriptive findings from the traumatic brain injury model systems national database. *Journal of Head Trauma Rehabilitation, 11*(5), 1–14.

Hawley, C. A., Taylor, R., Hellawell, D. J., & Pentland, B. (1999). FIM+FAM in head injury rehabilitation: A psychometric analysis. *Journal of Neurology, Neurosurgery, and Psychiatry, 67,* 749–754.

Heinemann, A. W., Hamilton, B., Linacre, J. M., Wright, B. D., & Granger, C. (1995). Functional status and therapeutic intensity during inpatient rehabilitation. *American Journal of Physical Medicine and Rehabilitation, 74,* 315–326.

Hibbard, M. R., Gordon, W. A., Flanagan, S., Haddad, L., & Labinsky, E. (2000). Sexual dysfunction after traumatic brain injury. *NeuroRehabilitation, 15,* 107–120.

High, W. M., Hall, K. M., Rosenthal, M., Mann, N., Zafonte, R., Cifu, D. X., et al. (1996). Factors affecting hospital length of stay and charges following traumatic brain injury. *Journal of Head Trauma Rehabilitation, 11*(5), 85–96.

Hoffman, J. M., Doctor, J. N., Chan, L., Whyte, J., Jha, A., & Dikmen, S. (2003). Potential impact of the new Medicare prospective payment system on reimbursement for traumatic brain injury inpatient rehabilitation. *Archives of Physical Medicine and Rehabilitation, 84,* 1165–1172.

Horner, M. D., Ferguson, P. L., Selassie, A. W., Labbate, L. A., Kniele, K., & Corrigan, J. D. (2005). Patterns of alcohol use 1 year after traumatic brain injury: A population-based, epidemiological study. *Journal of the International Neuropsychological Society, 11,* 322–330.

Individuals With Disabilities Education Act. (2006, August 14). *Federal Register, 71*(156; FR Doc 06–6656, pp. 46539–46845). Washington, DC: U.S. Government Printing Office.

Iverson, G. L. (2005). Outcome from mild traumatic brain injury. *Current Opinion in Psychiatry, 18,* 301–317.

Jackson, W. T., Novack, T. A., & Dowler, R. N. (1998). Effective serial measurement of cognitive orientation in rehabilitation: The Orientation Log. *Archives of Physical Medicine and Rehabilitation, 79,* 718–20.

Jacobs, H. E. (1993). *Behavior analysis guidelines and brain injury rehabilitation: People, principles and programs.* Gaithersburg, MD: Aspen Publishers.

Jennett, B. (2005). Thirty years of the vegetative state: Clinical, ethical, and legal problems. *Progress in Brain Research, 150,* 537–543.

Jennett, B., & Bond, M. R. (1975). Assessment of outcome in severe brain damage: A practical scale. *The Lancet, 1,* 480–484.

Jennett, B., & Teasdale, G. (1981). *Management of head injuries.* Philadelphia: F. A. Davis.

Johnston, M. V. (1991). Outcomes of community re-entry programmes for brain injury survivors. Part 1: Independent living and productive activities. *Brain Injury, 5,* 141–154.

Johnston, M. V., Goverover, Y., Dijkers, M. (2005). Community activities and individuals' satisfaction with them: Quality of life in the first year after traumatic brain injury. *Archives of Physical Medicine & Rehabilitation, 86,* 735–745.

Johnston, M. V., & Lewis, F. D. (1991). Outcomes of community re-entry programmes for brain injury survivors. Part 2: Further investigations. *Brain Injury, 5,* 155–168.

Johnstone, B., Mount, D., & Schopp, L. H. (2003). Financial and vocational outcomes 1 year after traumatic brain injury. *Archives of Physical Medicine and Rehabilitation, 84,* 238–241.

Kennedy, R. E., Livingston, L., Marwitz, J. H., Gueck, S., Kreutzer, J. S., & Sander, A. M. (2006). Complicated mild traumatic brain injury on the inpatient rehabilitation unit: A multicenter analysis. *Journal of Head Trauma Rehabilitation, 21,* 260–271.

Kerr, P. (1992, March 16). Centers for head injury accused of earning millions for neglect. *New York Times,* p. 1.

Kochanek, P., Clark, R. S. B., & Jenkins, L. (2007). TBI pathobiology. In N. Zasler, D. Katz, R. D. Zafonte (Eds.), *Brain injury medicine: Principles and practice* (pp. 81–96). New York: Demos.

Kraus, J. S., & McArthur, D. L. (1998). Incidence and Prevalence of traumatic brain injury. In M. Rosenthal, E. Griffith, J. Kreutzer, & B. Pentland (Eds.), *Rehabilitation of the adult and child with traumatic brain injury* (3rd ed., pp. 3–18). Philadelphia: F. A. Davis.

Kreutzer, J. S., Gordon, W. A., Rosenthal, M., & Marwitz, J. (1993). Neuropsychological characteristics of patients with brain injury: Preliminary findings from a multicenter investigation. *Journal of Head Trauma Rehabilitation, 8,* 47–59.

Kreutzer, J. S., Marwitz, J. H., & Witol, A. D. (1995). Interrelationships between crime, substance abuse, and aggressive behaviors among persons with traumatic brain injury. *Brain Injury, 9,* 757–768.

Kreutzer, J. S., Witol, A. D., Sander, A. M., Cifu, D. X., Marwitz, J. H., & Delmonico, R. (1996). A prospective longitudinal multicenter analysis of alcohol use patterns among persons with traumatic brain injury. *Journal of Head Trauma Rehabilitation, 11*(5), 58–69.

Langlois, J. A., Kegler, S. R., & Butler, J. A. (2003). Traumatic brain injury related hospital discharges: Results from a 14-state surveillance system. *Morbidity and Mortality Weekly Reports, 52*(4), 1–20.

Leith, K. H., Phillips, L., & Sample, P. L. (2004). Exploring the service needs and experiences of persons with TBI and their families: The South Carolina experience. *Brain Injury, 18,* 1191–1208.

Leone, H., & Polsonetti, B. W. (2005). Amantadine for traumatic brain injury: Does it improve cognition and reduce agitation? *Journal of Clinical Pharmacy and Therapeutics, 30,* 101–104.

Levin, H. S., Benton, A. L., & Grossman, R. G. (1982). Neurobehavioral consequences of closed head injury. New York: Oxford University Press.

Levin, H. S., Boake, C., Song, J., McCauley, S., Contant, C., Diaz-Marchan, P., et al. (2001). Validity and sensitivity to change of the extended Glasgow Outcome Scale in mild to moderate traumatic brain injury. *Journal of Neurotrauma, 18,* 575–584.

Levin, H. S., O'Donnell, V. M., & Grossman, R. G. (1979). The Galveston Orientation and Amnesia Test: A practical scale to assess cognition after head injury. *Journal of Nervous and Mental Diseases, 167,* 675.

Lombard, L. A., & Zafonte, R. D. (2005). Agitation after traumatic brain injury: Considerations and treatment options. *American Journal of Physical Medicine and Rehabilitation, 84,* 797–812.

Lovell, M. R., & Collins, M. W. (2002). New developments in the management of sports concussion. *Current Sports Medicine Reports, 1,* 287–292.

Malec, J. F., & Degiorgio, L. (2002). Characteristics of successful and unsuccessful completers of 3 post-acute brain injury rehabilitation pathways. *Archives of Physical Medicine & Rehabilitation, 83,* 1759–1764.

Matthews, C. G., & Klove, H. (1964). *Instruction manual for the Adult Neuropsychology Test Battery.* Madison, WI: University of Wisconsin Medical School.

Matthies, B. K., Kreutzer, J. S., West, D. D. (1997). *The behavior management handbook: A practical approach to patients with neurological disorders.* San Antonio, TX: Therapy Skill Builders.

Max, W., MacKenzie, E. J., & Rice, D. P. (1991). Head injuries: Costs and consequences. *Journal of Head Trauma Rehabilitation, 6*(2), 76–941.

McCrea, M., Guskiewicz, K. M., Marshall, S. W., Barr, W., Randolph, C., Cantu, R. C., et al. (2003). Acute effects and recovery time following concussion in collegiate football players: The NCAA Concussion Study. *JAMA, 290*(19), 2556–2563.

McDowell, S., Whyte, J., & D'Esposito, M. (1998). Differential effect of a dopaminergic agonist on prefrontal function in traumatic brain injury patients. *Brain, 121,* 1155–1164.

Millis, S. R., Rosenthal, M., Novack, T. A., Sherer, M., Nick, T. G., Kreutzer, J. S., et al. (2001). Long-term neuropsychological outcome after traumatic brain injury. *Journal of Head Trauma Rehabilitation, 16,* 343–355.

Muir, C. A., Rosenthal, M., & Diehl, L. N. (1990). Methods of family intervention. In M. Rosenthal, E. R. Griffith, M. R. Bond, & J. D. Miller (Eds.), *Rehabilitation of the adult and child with traumatic brain injury,* (2nd ed., pp. 433–448). Philadelphia: F. A. Davis.

Mysiw, W. J., Bogner, J. A., Corrigan, J. D., Fugate, L. P., Clinchot, D. M., & Kadyan, V. (2006). The impact of acute care medications on rehabilitation outcome after traumatic brain injury. *Brain Injury, 20,* 905–911.

Nakase-Thompson, R., Sherer, M., Yablon, S. A., Nick, T. G., & Trzepacz, P. T. (2004). Acute confusion following traumatic brain injury. *Brain Injury, 18,* 131–142.

Parton, A., Coulthard, E., & Husain, M. (2005). Neuropharmacological modulation of cognitive deficits after brain damage. *Current Opinion in Neurology, 18,* 675–680.

Pokorney, A. D., Miller, B. A., & Kaplan, H. B. (1972). The Brief MAST: A shortened version of the Michigan Alcoholism Screening Test. *American Journal of Psychiatry, 129,* 342.

Povlishock, J. T., & Katz, D. I. (2005). Update of neuropathology and neurological recovery after traumatic brain injury. *Journal of Head Trauma Rehabilitation, 20*(1), 76–94.

Putnam, S. H., & Adams, K. M. (1992). Regression-based prediction of long-term outcome following multi-disciplinary rehabilitation for traumatic brain injury. *The Clinical Neuropsychologist, 6,* 383–405.

Ragnarsson, K. T., Thomas, J. P., & Zasler, N. D. (1993). Model systems of care for individuals with traumatic brain injury. *Journal of Head Trauma Rehabilitation, 8,* 1–11.

Rappaport, M., Dougherty, A., & Kelting, D. (1992). Evaluation of coma and the vegetative states. *Archives of Physical Medicine and Rehabilitation, 73,* 628–634.

Rappaport, M., Hall, K. M., Hopkins, H. K., Belleza, T., & Cope, D. N. (1982). Disability rating scale for severe head trauma: Coma to community. *Archives of Physical Medicine and Rehabilitation, 63,* 118–123.

Reeder, K., Rosenthal, M., Lichtenberg, P., & Wood, D. (1996). Impact of age on functional outcome following traumatic brain injury. *Journal of Head Trauma Rehabilitation, 11*(3), 22–31.

Reitan, R. M., & Wolfson, D. (1993). *Halstead-Reitan Neuropsychological Test Battery.* Tucson, AZ: Neuropsychology Press.

Rey, A. (1964). *L'examen clinique en psychologie.* Paris: Presses Universitaires de France.

Ricker, J. H. (1998). Traumatic brain injury rehabilitation: Is it worth the cost? *Applied Neuropsychology, 5*(4), 184–193.

Ricker, J. H. (2004). Traumatic brain injury and stroke. In G. S. Kolt & M. B Anderson (Eds.), *Psychology in the physical and manual therapies* (pp. 183–206). Edinburgh, Scotland: Churchill Livingstone.

Ricker, J. H., Rosenthal, M., Garay, E., DeLuca, J., Germain, A., Abraham-Fuchs, K., & Schmidt, K. U. (2002). Telerehabilitation needs: A survey of persons with acquired brain injury. *Journal of Head Trauma Rehabilitation, 17,* 242–250.

Rotondi, A. J., Sinkule, J., & Spring, M. (2005). An interactive Web-based intervention for persons with TBI and their families: Use and evaluation by female significant others. *Journal of Head Trauma Rehabilitation, 20,* 173–185.

Rusin, M. J., & Jongsma, A. E. (2001). *The rehabilitation psychology treatment planner.* Hoboken, NJ: Wiley.

Rutland-Brown, W., Langlois, J. A., Thomas, K. E., & Xi, Y. L. (2006). Incidence of traumatic brain injury in the United States, 2003. *Journal of Head Trauma Rehabilitation, 21,* 544–548.

Salcido, R., Moore, R. W., Schleenbaker, R. E., & Klim, G. (1996). The physiatrist and subacute rehabilitation. *Physical Medicine Clinics of North America, 7*(1), 55–81.

Sander, A. M., Kreutzer, J. S., Rosenthal, M., Delmonico, R., & Young, M. E. (1996). A multicenter longitudinal investigation of return to work and community integration following traumatic brain injury. *Journal of Head Trauma Rehabilitation, 11*(5), 70–84.

Sander, A. M., Sherer, M., Malec, J. F., High, W. M. Jr., Thompson, R. N., Moessner, A. M., & Josey, J. (2003). Preinjury emotional and family functioning in caregivers of persons with traumatic brain injury. *Archives of Physical Medicine and Rehabilitation, 84,* 197–203.

Schopp, L. H., Good, G. E., Barker, K. B., Mazurek, M. O., & Hathaway, S. L. (2006). Masculine role adherence and outcomes among men with traumatic brain injury. *Brain Injury, 20,* 1155–1162.

Serio, C. D., Kreutzer, J. S., Gervasio, A. H. (1995). Predicting family needs after brain injury:

Implications for intervention. *Journal of Head Trauma Rehabilitation, 10,* 32–45.

Sherer, M., Nakase-Thompson, R., Yablon, S. A., & Gontkovsky, S. T. (2005). Multidimensional assessment of acute confusion after traumatic brain injury. *Archives of Physical Medicine and Rehabilitation, 86,* 896–904.

Sherer, M., & Novack, T. A. (2003). Neuropsychological assessment after traumatic brain injury in adults. In G. P. Prigatano & N. H. Pliskin (Eds.), *Clinical neuropsychology and cost outcome research* (pp. 39–60). New York: Taylor & Francis.

Sherer, M., Sander, A. M., Nick, T. G., High, W. M. Jr., Malec, J. F., & Rosenthal, M. (2002). Early cognitive status and productivity outcome after traumatic brain injury: Findings from the TBI model systems. *Archives of Physical Medicine and Rehabilitation, 83,* 183–192.

Simpson, G., & Long, E. (2004). An evaluation of sex education and information resources and their provision to adults with traumatic brain injury. *Journal of Head Trauma Rehabilitation, 19,* 413–428.

Smith, A. (1991). *Symbol Digit Modalities Test.* Los Angeles: Western Psychological Services.

Smith, D. H., Meaney, D. F., & Shull, W. H. (2003). Diffuse axonal injury in head trauma. *Journal of Head Trauma Rehabilitation, 18,* 307–316.

Sohlberg, M. M., & Mateer, C. A. (1989). Introduction to cognitive rehabilitation: Theory and practice. New York: Guilford Press.

Sperry, J. L., Gentilello, L. M., Minei, J. P., Diaz-Arrastia, R. R., Friese, R. S., & Shafi, S. (2006). Waiting for the patient to "sober up": Effect of alcohol intoxication on Glasgow Coma Scale score of brain injured patients. *Journal of Trauma, 61,* 1305–1311.

Spreen, O., & Strauss, E. (2006). *A compendium of neuropsychological tests* (3rd ed.). New York: Oxford University Press.

Strich, S. (1961). Shearing of nerve fibres as a cause of brain damage due to head injury. *The Lancet, 2,* 443–448.

Struchen, M. A., Atchison, T. B., Roebuck, T. M., Caroselli, J. S., & Sander, A. M. (2002). A multidimensional measure of caregiving appraisal: Validation of the Caregiver Appraisal Scale in traumatic brain injury. *Journal of Head Trauma Rehabilitation, 17,* 132–154.

Stuss, D. T., Binns, M. A., Carruth, F. G., Levine, B., Brandys, C. E., Moulton, R. J., et al. (1999). The acute period of recovery from traumatic brain injury: Posttraumatic amnesia or posttraumatic confusional state? *Journal of Neurosurgery, 90,* 635–643.

Teasdale, G., & Jennett, B. (1974). Assessment of coma and impaired consciousness. *The Lancet, 2,* 81–84.

Thurman, D. J., Branche, C. M., & Sniezek, J. E. (1998). The epidemiology of sports-related traumatic brain injuries in the United States: Recent developments. *Journal of Head Trauma Rehabilitation, 13*(2), 1–8.

Thurman, D. J., Coronado, V., & Selassie, A. (2007). The epidemiology of TBI: Implications for public health. In N. Zasler, D. Katz, & R. D. Zafonte (Eds.), *Brain injury medicine: Principles and practice* (pp. 45–55). New York: Demos.

Thurman, D. J., & Guerrero, J. L. (1999). Trends in hospitalization associated with traumatic brain injury. *JAMA, 282,* 954–957.

Turner-Stokes, L., Paul, S., & Williams, H. (2006). Efficiency of specialist rehabilitation in reducing dependency and costs of continuing care for adults with complex acquired brain injuries. *Journal of Neurology, Neurosurgery, & Psychiatry, 77,* 634–639.

Udekwu, P., Kromhout-Schiro, S., Vaslef, S., Baker, C., & Oller, D. (2004). Glasgow Coma Scale score, mortality, and functional outcome in head-injured patients. *Journal of Trauma, 56,* 1084–1089.

Wechsler, D. (1981). *Wechsler Adult Intelligence Scale-Revised.* San Antonio, TX: Psychological Corporation.

Wechsler, D. (1987). *Wechsler Memory Scale-Revised.* San Antonio, TX: Psychological Corporation.

Wehman, P., Targett, P., West, M., & Kregel, J. (2005). Productive work and employment for persons with traumatic brain injury: What have we learned after 20 years? *Journal of Head Trauma Rehabilitation, 20*(2), 115–127.

Weinberg, J., Diller, L., Gordon, W. A., Gerstman, L. J., Lieberman, A., Lakin, P., et al. (1977). Visual scanning training effect on reading-related tasks in acquired right brain damage. *Archives of Physical Medicine and Rehabilitation, 58,* 479–486.

Weinberg, J., Diller, L., Gordon, W. A., Gerstman, L. J., Lieberman, A., Lakin, P., et al. (1979). Training sensory awareness and spatial organization in people with right brain damage. *Archives of Physical Medicine and Rehabilitation, 58,* 491–496.

Whyte, J., Hart, T., Laborde, A., & Rosenthal, M. (2005). Rehabilitation issues in traumatic brain injury. In J. A. DeLisa et al. (Eds.), *Physical medicine & rehabilitation: Principles and practice* (4th ed., pp. 1677–1713). Philadelphia: Lippincott Williams & Wilkins.

Whyte, J., Hart, T., Schuster, K., Fleming, M., Polansky, M., & Coslett, H. B. (1997). The effects of methylphenidate on attentional function after traumatic brain injury: A randomized, placebo-controlled trial. *American Journal of Physical Medicine and Rehabilitation, 76,* 440–450.

Whyte, J., Hart, T., Vaccaro, M., Grieb-Neff, P., Risser, A., Polansky, M., & Coslett, H. B. (2004). Effects of methylphenidate on attention deficits after traumatic brain injury: A multidimensional, randomized, controlled trial. *American Journal of Physical Medicine and Rehabilitation, 83,* 401–420.

Willer, B., Rosenthal, M., Kreutzer, J. S., Gordon, W. A., & Rempel, R. (1993). Assessment of community integration following rehabilitation for traumatic brain injury. *Journal of Head Trauma Rehabilitation, 8*(2), 75–87.

Williams, D. H., Levin, H. S., & Eisenberg, H. M. (1990). Mild head injury classification. *Neurosurgery, 27,* 422–428.

Wilson, J. T. L., Pettigrew, L. E. L., & Teasdale, G. M. (1998). Structured interviews for the Glasgow Outcome Scale and the Extended Glasgow Outcome Scale: Guidelines for their use. *Journal of Neurotrauma, 15,* 573–585.

Woodward, H., Winterbalther, K., Donders, J., Hackbarth, R., Kuldanek, A., & Sanfilippo, D. (1999). Prediction of neurobehavioral outcome 1–5 years postpediatric traumatic head injury. *Journal of Head Trauma and Rehabilitation, 14,* 351–359.

Zafonte, R. D., Elovic, E., O'Dell, M., Mysiw, W. J., & Watanabe, T. (1999). Pharmacology in traumatic brain injury: Fundamentals and treatment strategies. In M. Rosenthal, J. S. Kreutzer, E. R. Griffith, & B. Pentland (Eds.), *Rehabilitation of the adult and child with traumatic brain injury* (3rd ed., pp. 536–555). Philadelphia: F. A. Davis.

Zafonte, R. D., Hammond, F. M., & Peterson, J. (1996). Predicting outcome in the slow to respond traumatically brain injured patient: Acute and subacute parameters. *NeuroRehabilitation, 6,* 19–32.

Zafonte, R. D., Mann, N. R., Millis, S. R., Black, K. L., Wood, D. L., & Hammond, F. (1997). Posttraumatic amnesia: Its relation to functional outcome. *Archives of Physical Medicine and Rehabilitation, 78,* 1103–1106.

Zygun, D. A., Kortbeek, J. B., Fick, G. H., Laupland, K. B., & Doig, C. J. (2005). Nonneurologic organ dysfunction in severe traumatic brain injury. *Critical Care Medicine, 33,* 654–660

CHAPTER 4

REHABILITATION PSYCHOLOGY AND NEUROPSYCHOLOGY WITH STROKE SURVIVORS

Bruce Caplan

Stroke constitutes the third leading cause of death in Western countries, and with more than two thirds of stroke patients having major functional limitations (Baum, 1982), stroke is the primary cause of adult disability in the United States (Centers for Disease Control, 2003; Dobkin, 2005; Kelly, Pangilinan, & Rodriguez, 2007). As "stroke is more disabling than lethal" (de Freitas, Bezerra, Maulaz, & Bogousslavsky, 2005, p. 1), stroke survivors represent the largest diagnostic category of referrals to rehabilitation hospitals (Granger, Hamilton, & Gresham, 1988). With the accelerated "graying" of the U.S. population, stroke will remain a public health problem with major personal, societal, and economic implications. Even the "oldest old" may be reasonable candidates for rehabilitation after stroke (Lieberman & Lieberman, 2005). Furthermore, advances in thrombolytic and neuroprotective treatments after stroke (Goldberg, 2007; Hemmen & Lyden, 2007; Romero, Babikian, Katz, & Finklestein, 2006) and stem cell research (Haas, Weidner, & Winkler, 2005) may elevate to "rehabilitatable" status some who previously would not have been able to benefit, although the status of and prospects for these strategies remain controversial (Diener et al., 2008; Hussain & Shuaib, 2008; Rother, 2008; Sacchetti, 2008; Savitz & Schabitz, 2008).

Rehabilitation services are typically provided to those in the middle range of impairment. Individuals with milder strokes are often discharged directly to their homes, perhaps with recommendations for outpatient therapies or a home program. More severely affected individuals who cannot tolerate, or are judged unlikely to benefit from, inpatient rehabilitation tend to be discharged to a nursing home or skilled care facility, some of which offer modest therapeutic services.

Rehabilitation psychological and neuropsychological assessment and intervention with stroke survivors demand a broad range of knowledge and skills reflecting the multiple consequences precipitated by the neurological event. *Stroke psychologists* must be well versed in both neuropsychology and traditional rehabilitation psychology to assist patients, family members, and the treating team in dealing with the cognitive, emotional, physical, social, sexual, and vocational ramifications of stroke. In addition, familiarity with principles and practices (e.g., treatment adherence, stress management) of what has traditionally been considered health psychology is advisable.

This chapter reviews, necessarily to a relatively superficial extent, the facts and abilities rehabilitation psychologists need so as to work effectively with stroke survivors. Interested readers should consult related works (e.g., Cullum, Rilling, Saine, & Samson, 2008; Festa, Lazar, & Marshall, 2008; Lazar, 2008; Macciocchi, Alderson, & Schara, 2005; Robinson, 2006) for discussion of particular topics in greater depth. An overview of epidemiological factors, economic impact, types of stroke, and the characteristics of particular regional syndromes is followed by discussions of selected issues of phenomenology, assessment, and treatment of stroke as they typically arise in the acute medical, acute rehabilitation, and postacute phases, respectively.

Bruce Caplan

OVERVIEW

Stroke is "an acute neurological dysfunction of vascular origin with sudden (within seconds) or at least rapid (within hours) occurrence of symptoms and signs corresponding to the involvement of focal areas of the brain" (World Health Organization, 1989, p. 1412). For public education purposes, stroke has also been called a "brain attack" to draw the etiological parallel between stroke and heart attack, both of which often result from atherosclerotic processes (Caramata, Heros, & Latchaw, 1994).

It is important to distinguish stroke from related terms. *Transient ischemic attacks* (TIAs) are ischemia-based episodes of focal neurologic dysfunction that typically last 2 to 15 minutes and resolve fully within 24 hours. *Reversible ischemic neurologic deficits* (RINDs) are symptomatically similar to TIAs but of longer duration: 24 hours to 1 to 3 weeks. (There has, however, been controversy about the uniqueness of this entity. For more information, see Yatsu, Grotta, & Pettigrew, 1995.) When symptoms persist beyond 3 weeks, the term *stroke* unequivocally applies. So-called silent strokes (Vermeer, Koudstaal, Oudkerk, Hofman, & Breteler, 2002) produce no overt symptoms and generally go undetected until a later, more florid event. However, Royall (2004) argued that the term is inaccurate because the lesions may disrupt prefrontal-subcortical pathways and cause subtle behavioral deficits. In this regard, it is worth noting the study by Vernooij et al. (2007), which found asymptomatic brain infarcts in 7.2% of 2,000 participants from the Dutch general population. Notably, the incidence increased with age, rising from 4% for those aged 45 to 59 years to more than 18% among those 75 years and older. Recently, the term *whispering stroke* has been proposed to refer to events that produce symptoms (e.g., weakness, language difficulty) that are apparently slight enough that no diagnosis of stroke is assigned (Howard et al., 2007). Subtle cognitive decline resulting from undetected hypertension-induced vascular compromise may be a harbinger of a clinically significant event (Wadley et al., 2007).

Historically, the public has had an inadequate understanding of stroke (Pancioli et al., 1998). Schneider et al. (2003) found that 70% of their tele-

phone survey respondents could identify one of five established warning signs of stroke (i.e., unilateral weakness or paralysis, sudden onset of blurred vision, difficulty speaking, dizziness or loss of balance and coordination, severe headache) versus 57% in the 1998 study. However, there was little change in the number that could name one stroke risk factor (68% vs. 72%), and those at greatest risk (i.e., older people, men, African Americans) continued to be the least well informed. Williams, Bruno, Rouch, and Marriott (1997) reported that only 25% of their consecutive sample of stroke patients correctly interpreted their symptoms, but this did not result in earlier presentation for treatment. This finding is buttressed by the report of Koenig et al. (2007) that more than half of their sample of stroke rehabilitation inpatients could not name any stroke risk factors or warning signs, thus increasing the risk of recurrence.

There is some evidence that community stroke screening programs may improve lay knowledge, at least in the short term, but it is not known whether this affects health-related behavior (DeLemos, Atkinson, Croopnick, Wentworth, & Akins, 2003). Some studies of the impact of public education campaigns on public awareness found minimal effects (Silver, Rubini, Black, & Hodgson, 2003), but a statewide effort in Michigan produced a doubling in the proportion of individuals who could name three warning signs of stroke (Reeves, Rafferty, Aranha, & Theisen, 2008). Furthermore, even intermittent television advertising produced significant improvements in stroke-related knowledge (Hodgson, Lindsay, & Rubini, 2007).

An inventive approach was taken by Kleindorfer et al. (2008), who educated beauticians in two urban areas about stroke risk factors, warning signs, and proper emergency action; these individuals, in turn, educated their clients during their appointments. Although knowledge of risk factors did not change, awareness of warning signs improved, as did recognition that one should call 911 for help. A recent study from the Czech Republic, however, suggested that merely knowing the warning signs is not sufficient to trigger effective action. Mikulik et al. (2008) found that those who understood stroke to be both a serious condi-

64

tion and treatable were more likely to call 911; mere knowledge of stroke symptoms was not enough to prompt a call for help.

EPIDEMIOLOGY

Recent statistics suggest an estimated annual incidence of about 600,000 first and 180,000 recurrent strokes (American Heart Association, 2008). Broad population values are somewhat misleading, however, because the incidence of stroke varies substantially as a function of age, type of stroke, gender, and ethnic group. For instance, stroke incidence increases with age (Terent, 1993), and men have higher incidence rates than do women at younger, but not older, ages. African Americans have nearly double the risk of stroke compared with White Americans (Broderick et al., 1998).

Studies of stroke prevalence reveal that over 3 million Americans are disabled because of stroke (Terent, 1993). According to Bonita and Beaglehole (1993), men have a higher death rate than women (i.e., 42 vs. 33 per 100,000). Although the stroke mortality rate is declining in most industrialized countries because of both decreasing incidence and increased survival, stroke remains the third most common cause of death in the developed world, trailing only heart disease and cancer (Elkind, 2003).

ECONOMIC IMPACT

Stroke has a huge economic impact on the individual and family, the medical community, and society. Estimates of annual stroke-related costs, both direct and indirect, have risen from approximately $7 billion in 1976 (Adelman, 1981) to $65.5 billion in 2008 (American Heart Association, 2008). The lifetime cost of stroke per person varies considerably by stroke type: subarachnoid hemorrhage = $228,030; intracranial hemorrhage = $123,565; ischemic stroke = $90,981 (Taylor et al., 1996). Such long-term costs can be reduced by preventing initial or recurrent stroke (i.e., by modification of risk factors, discussed later), limiting secondary complications (Goldberg & Berger, 1988), and providing multidisciplinary rehabilitation (Dobkin, 1995).

RISK FACTORS

Some stroke risk factors (Strauss, Majumdar, & McAlister, 2002) are modifiable (e.g., hypertension, diabetes mellitus, atrial fibrillation, alcohol use, smoking), whereas others are not (e.g., prior stroke, age, sex, race or ethnicity, family history). Manipulation of modifiable risk factors may have dramatic effects on the incidence, prevalence, and economic and personal costs of stroke; Devasenapathy and Hachinski (2004) maintained that up to 75% of all strokes are preventable. Gorelick (1994) estimated that 378,500 strokes could be prevented each year through treatment of hypertension, cigarette smoking, atrial fibrillation, and heavy alcohol consumption. Therefore, it is discouraging that Swedish investigators reported low rates of implementation of secondary preventive measures (e.g., pharmacologic treatment of hypertension and high cholesterol, weight loss) among stroke survivors (Li, Engstrom, & Hedblad, 2008). Intriguing recent reports citing depression as a possible risk factor suggest another avenue of prophylaxis (Salaycik et al., 2007; Williams, 2005).

TYPES OF STROKE

Stroke is not a single condition but a collection of cerebrovascular disorders. The two major categories are (a) cerebral infarction or ischemic stroke caused by thrombosis or embolism (accounting for over 80% of first strokes) and (b) hemorrhage, either intracerebral or subarachnoid (accounting for 11% and 6% of first strokes, respectively; Williams, Jiang, Matachar, & Samsa, 1999). These conditions stand in stark opposition: The former results from insufficient blood reaching the brain, whereas the latter is produced by excessive blood in the cranium. Early identification of the responsible mechanism is vital because treatments are substantially different. Recently developed interventions for acute ischemia (e.g., tissue plasminogen activator; Kaste, 2005) that seek to enhance blood flow are clearly contraindicated in hemorrhagic conditions (Ocava, Singh, Malhotra, & Rosenbaum, 2006).

The two categories of stroke differ in incidence and early mortality, but less so in long-term outcome.

In general, hemorrhage is more likely to be fatal in the short term (Ropper & Brown, 2005); one study reported a 30-day case fatality rate of 45% for subarachnoid hemorrhage, 52% for intracerebral hemorrhage (ICH), and about 10% for thrombotic-embolic stroke (Bamford, Dennis, Sandercock, Burn, & Warlow, 1990). Rehabilitation patients with ICH had worse functional status at admission than did those with ischemic stroke, but those differences disappeared by discharge (Kelly et al., 2003). Self-perceived quality of life (de Haan, Limburg, Van der Meulen, Jacobs, & Aaronson, 1995), as well as neurologic and functional outcome, does not differ between groups with hemorrhage or infarction, but the former may improve at a more rapid rate (Chae, Zorowitz, & Johnston, 1996).

Ischemic Stroke

Cerebral ischemia occurs when blood flow is reduced to a level insufficient to maintain the physiological requirements of the nerve cell; infarction results when diminished blood flow causes cell death (Welch & Levine, 1991). Initially, areas surrounding the damaged tissue are rendered temporarily inactive but still may be viable. Damage to this *ischemic penumbra* (Heiss, 2000) will likely become permanent without intervention, but reperfusion is thought to promote recovery of function (Kalra & Ratan, 2006).

The most common cause of ischemia and subsequent infarction is atherosclerosis, a noninflammatory, progressive disease beginning in childhood and peaking between the ages of 50 and 70 that may affect any artery in the body. Fatty deposits accumulate on the arterial wall, producing a thrombus that gradually narrows the arterial passage until the vessel becomes sufficiently occluded to produce stroke. With complete deprivation of blood flow beyond several minutes, permanent damage generally ensues (Welch & Levine, 1991). Because plaque buildup occurs slowly, compensatory blood flow through collateral vessels may be adequate to delay onset and/or diminish severity of symptoms. Another type of ischemic event, lacunar stroke, occurs when small penetrating branches of the major cerebral arteries become clogged, resulting in thrombotic infarction (Ropper & Brown, 2005), frequently affecting the basal ganglia, internal capsule, thalamus, and pons.

Location-specific syndromes may result from lacunar infarcts, including pure motor or sensory stroke, dysarthric stroke, and hemiparesis with ataxia.

Embolic stroke is produced by abrupt interruption of blood supply by bits of thrombus that have broken loose and lodged in a "downstream" vessel. This mechanism causes rapid onset of (usually focal) symptoms with little opportunity for compensation via collateral blood supply. Once the embolus becomes lodged in an arterial vessel, ischemic factors similar to those in thrombotic stroke begin to operate.

Hemorrhagic Stroke

Hemorrhagic stroke (Carhuapoma & Hanley, 2002) occurs when a cerebral blood vessel ruptures, frequently resulting in dramatic onset of symptoms. Hemorrhagic strokes are typically classified according to the anatomical locus of the bleeding (i.e., extradural, subdural, subarachnoid, inter- or intracerebral, cerebellar). I briefly consider two primary mechanisms of hemorrhage: primary intracerebral and subarachnoid.

Primary intracerebral hemorrhage, the third most common cause of stroke, following thrombotic and embolic stroke (Ropper & Brown, 2005), results from degeneration and rupture of a penetrating cerebral artery, often because of hypertension. In this type of hemorrhage, the blood rarely reaches the surface of the cortex but enters the cerebrospinal fluid in about 90% of cases (Ropper & Brown). Significant compression of brainstem structures may prove fatal.

The fourth most common cause of stroke is *subarachnoid hemorrhage* (SAH) resulting from ruptured saccular aneurysm. An aneurysm is a small ballooning of the arterial wall that weakens the vessel, leaving it prone to rupture and hemorrhage. In SAH, blood leaks into the subarachnoid space (i.e., between the external surface of the brain and the arachnoid meningeal layer). Hemorrhagic stroke may announce itself in either an acute or gradual fashion according, in large part, to the size of the affected vessel and that of the rupture itself. With rapid onset, the consequences are often severe. Dramatic elevation in intracranial pressure resulting from the outpouring of blood into the brain is the primary life-threatening process.

Regional Syndromes

The neurobehavioral effects of stroke are substantially determined by the location and size of the lesion, and these, in turn, depend on the artery that is involved (see Bogousslavsky & Caplan, 2001). Individual differences in cerebral organization of functions produce some unpredictability, as does the existence and extent of temporarily dysfunctional, but potentially viable, regions (i.e., the ischemic penumbra; Hakim, 1998). Cramer (2004) listed a variety of other premorbid and stroke-related factors that modify the behavioral expression of poststroke behavior. Nonetheless, certain symptoms tend to accompany damage to particular cortical regions. What follows is a brief overview of cerebral vasculature and the most common deficits following stroke affecting major anatomical landmarks.

Anterior cerebral artery stroke.   Arising from the ends of the anterior communicating artery, the left and right anterior cerebral arteries (ACA) supply the anterior-medial aspects of each cerebral hemisphere. This distribution includes cortical regions such as the medial orbital divisions of the frontal lobe and the frontal pole, and subcortical territory including anterior portions of the corpus callosum, internal capsule, caudate nucleus, and globus pallidus. Lesions limited to the ACA are relatively rare; they most often co-occur with middle cerebral artery (MCA) infarction. Typically, there is contralateral lower extremity motor impairment, with relative sparing of upper extremities. Other effects may include incontinence, motor aphasia, and affective and behavioral changes associated with orbital and medial frontal lobe damage (e.g., poor decision making, personality change, affective lability, loss of initiative and spontaneity; see DeLuca & Chiaravalloti, 2002).

Middle cerebral artery stroke.   The left and right MCA have the largest distributions of any cerebral artery, supplying the lateral aspects of their respective hemispheres. This distribution includes the cortical and subcortical portions of the lateral frontal lobe and parietal lobe, as well as the superior aspects of the temporal lobe and insula. The penetrating branches of the MCA also irrigate the basal ganglia.

The classic picture of total MCA occlusion is contralateral hemiplegia of face, arms, and legs; hemisensory deficits; and loss of vision in the field contralateral to the lesion. Various forms of aphasia follow occlusion of particular left MCA branches, whereas right MCA stroke may cause deficits in visual spatial, constructional, and attentional processes (especially unilateral neglect), as well as anosognosia (i.e., unawareness of deficits) and aprosodia (i.e., impaired understanding or expression of the emotional components of language). Contralateral visual field defects, including superior quadrantanopia and homonymous hemianopsia, occur following infarction of either hemisphere.

Internal carotid artery stroke.   The internal carotid artery (ICA), along with the external carotid, arises from the common carotid artery and is the primary conduit for blood to the anterior and MCAs. Although one might expect severe consequences to follow carotid stroke because of the breadth of blood distribution that may be disrupted, this is not necessarily the case. Cerebral vasculature redundancy permits blood flow to be maintained to tributaries of the ICA, thereby limiting the functional consequences.

At greatest risk are the border-zone (i.e., watershed) regions between areas of arterial perfusion (i.e., at the border of the superior parietal and superior frontal lobe and within the deep portions of each hemisphere). The behavioral effects of ICA stroke depend on the aspect of the middle cerebral, anterior cerebral, or deep penetrating branches that is most affected. Consequences similar to those seen in MCA infarction are common.

Posterior cerebral artery stroke.   The vertebral arteries join at the level of the brainstem to form the basilar artery. Branches of the vertebrobasilar circulation irrigate the medulla, pons, midbrain, and cerebellum; thus, stroke in this region can be life threatening. Beyond the brainstem level, the basilar artery bifurcates into left and right posterior cerebral arteries (PCAs) that feed the inferomedial and medial temporal regions, the primary and secondary visual cortices, and much of the thalamus, substantia nigra, and midbrain.

PCA stroke that affects thalamic regions can cause a variety of deficits, but severe sensory loss across all modalities may be most the most problematic. Other deficits associated with subcortical damage include oculomotor palsy and cerebellar ataxia. Cortical infarcts of the posterior cerebral artery may result in hemianopia, achromatopsia, tunnel vision (i.e., inability to see objects not centrally located), alexia without agraphia, and memory impairment.

Readers interested in the medical aspects of stroke should consult Bogousslavsky and Caplan (2001) or Ropper and Brown (2005). I now consider the neurobehavioral phenomenology and management of stroke as manifested in various phases of recovery.

PSYCHOLOGICAL ASSESSMENT AND INTERVENTION

The importance of psychological assessment and treatment in stroke was shown some time ago by the Framingham study finding that psychosocial disabilities were more common than physical ones following stroke (Gresham et al., 1975). Stroke psychologists assess cognitive and emotional functioning, contribute to judgments about patients' suitability for rehabilitation, monitor and treat psychological and social factors that affect recovery, advise other members of the treating team about neurobehavioral matters, educate patients and relatives, and offer referrals and recommendations for postdischarge living. The following section describes the "what" and "how" of "stroke psychology" in the acute medical, acute rehabilitation, and postacute periods.

Acute Medical Assessment and Treatment

The first encounter with a stroke patient may occur in the intensive care unit. Some hospitals use designated *stroke units* operating according to a detailed treatment protocol or *critical pathway* (Wentworth & Atkinson, 1996). The value of such special units has been generally supported (e.g., Cochrane Database, 2000; Govan, Weir, & Langhorne, 2008; Stroke Unit Trialists' Collaboration, 1997) though not for all outcome variables (Kwan & Sandercock, 2003). Also, it is not clear whether patients maintain gains over time (Dijkerman, Wood, & Hewer, 1996). Furthermore, stroke units have idiosyncratic features that affect processes and outcomes (Bernhardt, Chitravas, Meslo, Thrift, & Indredavik, 2008).

The rehabilitation psychologist's contributions to stroke patient care at this point can include preliminary cognitive and emotional assessment, counseling of patient and family, and consultation to staff. Patients in such circumstances may be poorly responsive because of direct effects of the stroke (e.g., depressed arousal, aphasia) and/or secondary consequences (e.g., medication effects, sleep deprivation). Although formal evaluation may be difficult, some attempt should be made to assess the patient's neurobehavioral status, even if all that can be concluded is that he or she is "not yet testable." Several brief cognitive screening measures are available (see Ruchinskas & Curyto, 2003), but all lack depth and detail and permit only tentative inferences and/or development of hypotheses rather than conclusive diagnostic or prognostic statements.

Two instruments mentioned in the Post-Stroke Rehabilitation Guideline (Agency for Health Care Policy and Research [AHCPR]: Gresham et al., 1995) are the Mini-Mental State Examination (MMSE; Folstein, Folstein, & McHugh, 1975) and the Neurobehavioral Cognitive Status Examination (NCSE; Kiernan, Mueller, Langston, & Van Dyke, 1987), now marketed as Cognistat. The MMSE is heavily weighted with language-based tasks, rendering it of limited applicability with aphasic patients. Also, only a single summary score is derived. An expanded version of the MMSE (Modified MMSE, or 3MS; Teng & Chui, 1987) has greater sensitivity and a lower false-negative rate than the original version and also better predictive value for functional outcome. Cognistat briefly samples a broad array of cognitive functions, yielding separate scores for individual domains. However, it has been sparsely used in controlled investigations of stroke and failed to distinguish between patients with left and right hemisphere lesions (Osmon, Smet, Winegarden, & Gandhavadi, 1992). Moreover, as both tests show education effects, they may underestimate impairment in well-educated people and overestimate deficits in those with lesser schooling.

The Repeatable Battery for Assessment of Neuropsychological Status (RBANS; Randolph, 1998) is a recent promising addition with parallel forms and demonstrated construct validity for stroke populations (Wilde, 2006). Larson et al., (2003) found that certain RBANS scores, especially the Visuospatial/

Constructional index, obtained during inpatient rehabilitation correlated with measures of functional impairment administered by telephone interview 6 months later. A 12-month follow-up study by these same authors (Larson, Kirschner, Bode, Heinemann, & Goodman, 2005) confirmed these findings.

Strokes tend to affect older individuals, many of whom have preexisting medical problems that can compromise cognition; intellectual decline, therefore, may have already begun, creating a fragile baseline on which stroke-related cognitive deficits will be superimposed. For example, Phillips and Mate-Kole (1997) found neuropsychological impairments in patients with peripheral vascular disease that were highly similar to those exhibited by persons with cerebral infarcts. Henon et al. (1997) reported a 16% incidence of prestroke dementia (as assessed by informant questionnaire) in 202 consecutive patients, virtually none of who had been formally diagnosed as demented. In one study, nearly 40% of those diagnosed with poststroke dementia had experienced cognitive loss before stroke onset (Pohjasvaara, Erkinjuntti, Vataja, & Kaste, 1997).

It should be noted that the concept of "vascular dementia" has recently been criticized by, among others, Paul, Garrett, and Cohen (2003), who argued that certain "myths" (e.g., stepwise decline) plague diagnostic efforts. Devasenapathy and Hachinski (2004) presented the case for the term *vascular cognitive impairment* (VCI), a clinical syndrome with a spectrum of levels of impairment from *at risk* to *severe dementia*. This is a rapidly evolving area with respect to terminology, etiology, and clinical correlates, as entities labeled *cognitive impairment, no dementia* and *mild cognitive impairment* have recently achieved prominence and the "overlap and potential synergy" (Gorelick & Bowler, 2008) between VCI and Alzheimer's disease has been noted.

Psychological evaluation at this stage must address rehabilitation potential. Assessment of memory is particularly relevant because much of rehabilitation requires learning new ways to manage daily life activities. Some inferential caution is dictated, however, by the fact that the type of "procedural memory" most relevant to physical and occupational therapy may well be distinct from the semantic memory processes tapped by typical neuropsychological tests. Percep-

tual deficits such as unilateral neglect must be detected because they have profound implications for treatment and outcome (e.g., Jehkonen, Laihosalo, & Kettunen, 2006).

Because of the emotional stress produced by stroke, supportive and educational counseling of patient and family is an important function of the rehabilitation psychologist. It may not be possible to evaluate the affective state of an acutely ill cognitively impaired stroke patient who cannot understand or reliably respond to interview questions. Furthermore, behaviors or symptoms (e.g., sleep disturbance, poor appetite) that might signify depression, anxiety, and so forth in healthy individuals may not have the same diagnostic meaning in a hospitalized stroke patient (Woessner & Caplan, 1996). Although effective psychological counseling of the patient may not be feasible under these constraints, frequent visits will make the psychologist a "familiar face," building a foundation for future intervention and easing the transition into rehabilitation.

The psychologist's interactions with the patient's relatives are of great importance as well. An acute-onset illness such as stroke may disrupt long-standing familial equilibrium, eliciting anxiety about the uncertain future. A spouse may feel anger at the patient for having failed to modify at-risk behaviors or may feel guilt about having provoked an argument that he or she fears caused the stroke. Such worries and misconceptions often diminish with brief discussion about the causes and consequences of stroke and preparation concerning prognosis, even if, as is likely, these cannot yet be determined (Woldag et al., 2006). Family members can be advised about the factors that complicate early prediction and the time frame within which prognosis may become clearer. Relatives can be relieved to hear explanations of such peculiar and troubling phenomena as neglect, aphasia, or aprosodia.

Many individuals benefit from reassurance that the range of "normal" emotional reactions (their own and those of their affected relative) is vast; in addition to struggling with the primary distress caused by this frightening event, they should not be further burdened with worrying whether their reactions are "appropriate." They can be also made aware of the existence of support groups for stroke survivors and their relatives. Some may find value in selected reading material by professionals (Lezak, 1978; Stein, 2004) or first person accounts of survivors (e.g., chap. 6 in Kapur, 1997; O'Kelly, 2005).

Acute Rehabilitation Assessment and Treatment

Transfer to the rehabilitation unit may produce problematic emotional and cognitive responses. McCaffery and Fisher (1987) described the constellation of losses (e.g., privacy, dignity, self-efficacy, self-reliance, financial independence) and fears (e.g., death, dependence, recurrent stroke) that may then become apparent to the stroke survivor, engendering strong emotional reactions. Constant confrontation with the disabilities of others on the unit may be demoralizing as well. In light of the importance of psychological care in rehabilitation, it is discouraging to note Lewinter and Mikkelsen's (1995) finding that patients from an experimental stroke rehabilitation unit reported that treatment of non-physical factors (e.g., psychological, social, sexual phenomena) received insufficient attention.

The psychologist's activity now accelerates, as more extensive evaluations of cognitive functioning and emotional status are generally possible. However, the patient's productive time is likely to be limited by fatigue (Ingles, Eskes, & Phillips, 1999; Stulemeijer, Fasotti, & Bleijenberg, 2006), medical fragility, and the competing demands of other staff members. Multiple brief (30 minute) sessions may be required.

The AHCPR Guideline (Gresham et al., 1995) asserts that those patients who exhibit evidence of cognitive or emotional problems should be given tests that "sample key cognitive, emotional, behavioral, and motivational domains. Cognitive elements include attention, orientation, memory, language, reasoning, judgment, spatial skills, motor coordination, and social skills" (p. 91). Patients should be evaluated for the presence of depression, anxiety, extent of awareness of deficits and their implications, and level of motivation for rehabilitation. The guideline also requires a complete neuropsychological examination in those instances "when more precise understanding of deficits will facilitate treatment" (p. 91). This probably applies to the great majority of stroke survivors seen in rehabilitation

units, given the incidence of higher cognitive deficits and emotional distress. Findings should be routinely shared with other members of the treating team.

In addition to the importance of psychological and neuropsychological data for shaping treatment (Caplan, 1982), there is considerable empirical support for its predictive value (Barker-Collo & Feigin, 2006). In particular, depression (Angeleri, Angeleri, Foschi, Giaquinto, & Nolfe, 1993; Morris, Robinson, Andrzejewski, Samuels, & Price, 1993; Robinson, Starr, Lipsey, Rao, & Price, 1984) and unilateral neglect (Paolucci et al., 1996) are negative prognostic indicators, unless successfully treated (Gonzalez-Torrecillas, Mendlewicz, & Lobo, 1995).

Space does not permit an extensive treatment of the common neuropsychological deficits and emotional reactions demonstrated by stroke patients. I briefly discuss several of the more common problems in this chapter. Table 4.1 contains brief definitions of many pertinent disorders. Interested readers should consult Lazar (2009) and Lezak (2004) for valuable discussions of the phenomena and pertinent assessment methods.

Neuropsychological Disorders

Because stroke tends to be a focal phenomenon, the accompanying deficits of higher cognitive function may be exquisitely selective. Indeed, the growing enterprise of cognitive neuropsychology has devoted substantial effort to the fractionation of cognitive functions via intensive single-case or small group studies of individuals with cognitive deficits, often following stroke. Lateralized lesions tend to produce predictable symptoms, left hemisphere damage compromising language skills but leaving spatial-perceptual abilities relatively intact, whereas right hemisphere lesions result in the opposite pattern (Jordan & Hillis, 2005).

Intrahemispheric localization is relevant as well. For example, anterior left hemisphere injury generally produces nonfluent aphasia characterized by effortful, halting, agrammatic speech that contains a preponderance of "high information" words (i.e., so-called telegraphic speech); comprehension is better-preserved than expression. Posterior lesions of the left hemisphere, in contrast, are accompanied by

TABLE 4.1

Neuropsychological Disorders Secondary to Stroke

Syndrome	Structure involved
Dominant hemisphere syndromes	
Aphasia. Impairment of language comprehension or production.	LH
■ *Broca's (expressive) aphasia.* Nonfluent output characterized by poor articulation but adequate comprehension.	Left FL, IFG
■ *Wernicke's (receptive) aphasia.* Fluent output with poverty of content and poor comprehension.	Left posterior TL, STG
■ *Conduction aphasia.* Fluent output and adequate comprehension with poor repetition and difficulty with auditory–verbal memory span.	PL, SMG
■ *Global aphasia.* Significant impairment of both expressive and receptive language functions.	LH
■ *Anomic aphasia.* Deficit in word finding with fluent language and good comprehension and repetition.	LH
Pure alexia. Deficit in reading. May be acquired or developmental in nature and may occur with or without writing difficulty (agraphia).	Posterior LH
Agraphia. Disorders of writing and spelling. May be limited to writing and spelling or include deficits in reading (i.e., alexia with agraphia).	Posterior LH AG
Apraxia. Inability to correctly perform skilled movements that is not a result of weakness, sensory loss, or tremor.	LH
■ *Ideomotor apraxia.* Difficulty in performing overlearned actions, particularly when asked to pantomime them.	Anterior CC, Left PL, PM
■ *Ideational apraxia.* Difficulty in performing sequences of actions to achieve a goal.	Left PL
Acalculia. Impairment in the ability to calculate arithmetic problems.	Left PL, AG, MG
Perceptual and attentional syndromes	
Agnosia. Partial or complete inability to recognize sensory stimuli, not explainable by defects in basic sensation or diminished alertness.	LH
■ *Visual.* Impairment of visual object recognition.	Left or right OT
■ *Auditory.* Inability to recognize sounds in the presence of otherwise intact hearing.	Left or right TL
■ *Somatosensory.* Difficulty perceiving objects through tactile stimulation, despite otherwise intact somatosensory capacity.	PL
Visuospatial and constructional disorders. Impairment in using the spatial properties of objects (location, orientation, space relationships).	RH
■ *Disorders of perception.* Difficulty in localizing, describing, and using relationships among objects in space.	Right PL
■ *Constructional apraxia.* Inability to copy drawings or three-dimensional structures secondary to visuoperceptual impairment.	Right PL
Body perception disturbances. Impairment in knowledge about the arrangement of body parts and their spatial relationship to objects in the environment.	PL
■ *Right-left disorientation.* Difficulty recognizing the right and left sides of the patient's or another person's body.	Left PL
■ *Autotopagnosia.* Inability to localize and name the parts of one's own body or on another person's body.	Left posterior PL
■ *Finger agnosia.* Inability to identify one's own fingers or those of another person.	Left and right PL
Neglect. Failure of a patient to report, respond, or orient to stimuli presented contralateral to a lesion.	Right IPL, FL, SC
■ *Sensory neglect.* Failure to detect sensory stimuli presented on the side contralateral to a lesion.	Right IPL
■ *Spatial neglect.* Difficulty orienting one's body in space or solving problems with a spatial component as a result of neglect of one side of space.	Right IPL

(continued)

TABLE 4.1 *(cont.)*

Syndrome	Structure involved
Anosognosia. Unawareness of neurological deficits or illness.	Right PL
Memory disturbances	
Working memory disturbance. Difficulty holding information in short-term memory while engaging in other cognitive tasks.	DLPFC
Amnestic syndromes. Impairment in the ability to learn or recall information.	MTL, BF, TH
Frontal-lobe syndromes	
Disinhibition syndrome. Disinhibition in social and sexual activity with dramatic changes in affect or impaired judgment and insight.	OFL
Executive function syndrome. Deficiency in planning, initiating, monitoring, and maintaining flexibility in behavior.	DLPFC
Apathetic syndromes. Generalized apathy in motivation and spontaneous actions with indifference.	ML
Disturbances of emotional functioning	
Emotional disorders. Alteration in emotional functioning.	RH
Poststroke depression. Appearance of symptoms of depression secondary to stroke that are primarily attributed to the location of the damage and only partially as reaction to injury.	Anterior LH, BG, Anterior RH
Aprosodia. Difficulty in producing and comprehending the affective components of language.	RH, IFG, IPL, STG

Note. AG = angular gyrus; BF = basal forebrain; BG = basal ganglia; CC = corpus callosum; DLPFC = dorsolateral prefrontal cortex; FL = frontal lobe; IFG = inferior frontal gyrus; IPL = inferior parietal lobe; LH = left hemisphere; MG = marginal gyrus; MTL = medial temporal lobe; OFL = orbital frontal lobe; OT = occipital temporal region; PL = parietal lobe; PM = premotor cortex; RH = right hemisphere; SC = subcortical structures; STG = superior temporal gyrus; TL = temporal lobe; TH = thalamus; SMG = supramarginal gyrus. For more information, see Feinberg and Farah (1997), Filley (1995), Kolb and Whishaw (1990), and Williams (1993). From *Handbook of Rehabilitation Psychology* (pp. 86–87), edited by R. G. Frank and T. R. Elliott, 2000, Washington, DC: American Psychological Association. Copyright 2000 by the American Psychological Association.

fluent prosodic speech, albeit of impoverished content, but impaired comprehension.

Certain phenomena may occur, although with dissimilar frequencies, following damage to either hemisphere, but the phenomena take different forms and show varying associated features, depending on the involved side. For instance, constructional apraxia has been viewed as primarily a perceptual impairment in cases of right hemisphere lesions but as a dysexecutive deficit when it follows left hemisphere damage (Kirk & Kertesz, 1989). Also, although contralateral neglect occurs far more frequently with right than left hemisphere cortical involvement (and also with subcortical lesions), the accompanying reading disorders (i.e., alexia) may differ. Right hemisphere patients fail to read material on the left side of the page (or even the left-sided portion of individual words) and commit other perceptual errors; individuals with left hemisphere

lesions may omit right-sided material but also commit other alexic errors that parallel their spontaneous speech (Caplan, 1987; Coslett, 1997).

Of special note is the area of executive functions (e.g., self-regulation, planning and goal setting, use of feedback, "set switching"). Pohjasvaara et al. (2002) reported a 40.6% incidence of executive dysfunction (ED) at 3 months after onset. Those with ED tended to be older, less educated, more dependent and depressed, and more cognitively impaired than those without ED. Zinn, Bosworth, Hoenig, and Swartzwelder (2007) found high rates of impairment on most tests in this domain among acute stroke patients as well as with a group with TIA and another with only stroke risk factors. The striking incidences in the last two groups suggest prestroke decline in executive abilities on which would be superimposed the further handicapping effects of the stroke itself. Because executive dysfunction is associated with worse functional outcome after stroke (Pohjasvaara et al., 2002), further development of assessment and intervention methods is warranted.

The logistics of the contemporary rehabilitation unit—where psychological and neuropsychological evaluation and treatment constitute only one arm of the armamentarium of services—encourage adoption of the "flexible" or "hypothesis testing" approach (Kaplan, 1988). That patients are typically "available" (i.e., physically and mentally) for, at most, 1 hour at a time allows one to administer a few tests, review the results, and consider what the day's findings dictate for the next day's session.

In the initial contact with the patient (and visiting relatives or friends), rehabilitation psychologists should identify themselves as members of the treating team and note that referral for psychological services is routine. The emotional stress of acute illness and hospitalization should be acknowledged and "normalized," followed by a brief description of the brain basis of neuropsychological functions and how these might have been affected by the stroke. The psychologist should explain the importance of identifying any deficits so that these can be considered in planning the rehabilitation program and so that the patient will be aware of and participate in learning to compensate for them.

A broad distinction can be drawn between those individuals who require a lower-level screening (e.g., RBANS: Randolph, 1998; Cognistat: Kiernan, Mueller, & Langston, 1995) and those who can tackle more challenging tasks. In the latter instance, one might begin with several short, multifactorial tasks (e.g., Trail Making Test: Reitan & Wolfson, 1993; Symbol Digit Modalities: Smith, 1982) coupled with selected subtests of the Wechsler scales (e.g., Information, Digit Span, Similarities; Wechsler, 1997) and brief measures of reading (because of its association with premorbid intellect and sensitivity to visual neglect) and memory (because of its previously noted central role in rehabilitation). Preliminary results dictate the selection of subsequent measures. In each session, tests on which success is anticipated are mixed with those that are expected to reveal the patient's deficits; an evaluation that only documents areas of difficulty will simply frustrate and demoralize the patient. Depending on the length of stay,

selective retesting may be valuable to quantify progress and to support, with current information, recommendations for postdischarge activities. For further descriptions of the process of neuropsychological evaluation in rehabilitation, see Caplan and Shechter (1995) and chapter 10 of this volume.

There is considerable merit in supplementing one's experience of the patient's performance during formal testing with observation of their behavior, achievements, and difficulties in other therapies and on the nursing unit. Salient differences in environments (e.g., lighting, noise, presence of others), motivation, and task complexity may lead to varying levels of behavioral adequacy, the early recognition of which permits adjustment of the treatment program to foster higher-level performance. Given the multiple roles of the stroke psychologist, it is advisable to complete the bulk of testing as quickly as possible. The emphasis can then shift to the affective, behavioral, familial, and vocational realms where indicated, and (assuming need, expertise, and resources) to neuropsychological rehabilitation.

The historically pessimistic view of the permanence of neurologically based cognitive deficits began to give way in the 1980s to a more adventurous, interventionist posture (see Diller & Gordon, 1981). Among the specific targets of treatment have been deficits in attention, memory, visual scanning, and executive functions.

There has been debate about the necessity of a theoretical basis for interventions, and some vital practical lessons have been learned (Wilson, 1997; also see Barrett et al., 2006, for a review concerning neglect). For example, one cannot assume that training effects will do more than improve performance on tests (Bowen & Lincoln, 2007); rather, one must plan for and train toward generalization to real-world activities. Also, rote drill alone is of limited usefulness. Multimodal intervention is desirable, as is psychological counseling, especially when the patient's diminished awareness of deficits (see the following discussion) is a limiting factor.

The practice of neuropsychological rehabilitation continues to expand, the literature proliferates, and professional training and practice guidelines emerge (Cappa et al., 2005; Cicerone, et al., 2005). New techniques such as virtual reality (Katz et al., 2005; Kim et al., 2007; Schultheis & Rizzo, 2001) and the use of prismatic lenses (Frassinetti, Angeli, Meneghello, Avanzi, & Ladavas, 2002; Keane, Turner, Sherrington, & Beard, 2006; Luaute, Halligan, Rode, Courtois, & Boisson, 2006) for treatment of neglect offer promise. Web-based interventions (e.g., Kirsch et al., 2004) may prove valuable for ameliorating a variety of deficits, although they have thus far only been used in cases of traumatic brain injury. See chapters 16 and 17 of this volume for a detailed treatment of this topic as well as volumes by Eslinger (2002) and Prigatano (1999).

I now proceed to a consideration of diminished awareness, which constitutes a suitable segue between discussions of neuropsychological and affective phenomena, as this has been viewed both as an emotional response to illness (i.e., psychological denial) and as a manifestation of higher cortical dysfunction (i.e., anosognosia).

Impaired Awareness

The phenomenon of impaired awareness (i.e., anosognosia) has a long, vexing, but nonetheless edifying history (Kortte & Wegener, 2004). Several facts now seem clear. First, unawareness may involve a variety of deficits, including, but not limited to, hemiplegia, sensory deficits, and various cognitive abilities (Vallar & Ronchi, 2006). The term *denial* in isolation carries little meaning because global denial is rare; failure to identify what is being denied leads to misinterpretation, misunderstanding, and, possibly, mistreatment. Furthermore, patients may be selectively anosognosic, oblivious to hemiplegia but distressed by other disabling consequences. Berti, Ladavas, and Della Corte (1996) reported dissociations for awareness of upper and lower limb weakness within the same patient and also for verbal and behavioral indicators of awareness.

Unawareness occurs more often with right (especially parietal and basal ganglia) than left hemisphere dysfunction and, as such, is often, though not invariably, found in association with unilateral neglect (e.g., Ellis & Small, 1997). Cutting (1978) reported an incidence of 58% among right hemisphere lesion patients and 14% in the left hemisphere group. Cognitive impairment may coexist with anosognosia (Levine, Calvanio, & Rinn, 1991), but it is not a requisite (Small & Ellis, 1996). Starkstein, Federoff, Price, Leiguarda, and Robinson (1992) found mild, moderate, and severe anosognosia in 10%, 11%, and 13%, respectively, of their series. Anosognosia is more common and of greater intensity in the early phase and tends to moderate over time (Weinstein, 1991); what begins as florid denial may evolve to acknowledgement of the existence of the impairment but denial or minimization of the implications of the condition (i.e., anosodiaphoria). Persistent anosognosia may be more common in those with severe hemisensory deficit, spatial neglect, and intellectual deficits (Levine et al., 1991).

The contributions of both neurological and psychological factors must be explored in individual cases. Although there should be a high index of suspicion for patients with right hemisphere lesions (because of the neurological injury), one should also seek to identify any psychological component by asking relatives or knowledgeable others about the individual's habitual coping strategies, which may have included denial, avoidance, or some related tactic. Structured interviews (Starkstein et al., 1992) and other measures (Anderson & Tranel, 1989) have been offered to assist in establishing degree and content of anosognosia.

Staff must be sensitive to the conflict patients face by relinquishing, or emerging from, denial and having to acknowledge either neurological or psychological defects. The former may be less amenable to treatment, but the latter connote a sort of character flaw, immaturity, or other undesirable trait. Another "no-win" situation confronting the stroke survivor is the implicit choice between depression and denial: If one does not appear depressed, one must be "in denial," and when one is no longer in denial, one must necessarily become depressed. Here again, the situation is more complicated and variable. Denial does not immunize against depression (Starkstein et al., 1992), and signs of depression may be interspersed among assertions of unrealistic expectations that staff interpret as denial.

In considering how best to manage anosognosia, one must recognize the distinction between verbal denial and behavioral denial. It is generally preferable for staff to finesse direct confrontation of patients' overt verbal denial as long as they are engaging in therapies, for this participation reflects some degree of awareness of deficits that require treatment. Attacking denial and forcing patients and families to accept a grim prognosis may yield a pointless "victory" for staff. Those whose unawareness creates a consistent barrier to participation in therapy, however, may require repeated gentle demonstrations of the functional consequences of their difficulties, coupled with discussion of available interventions and the promise of the therapist's best efforts. Nonetheless, it must be recognized that for some individuals, unawareness may preclude optimal rehabilitation. Readers are directed to the work of Langer and Padrone (1992) and Crosson et al. (1989) for interventions derived from particular conceptualizations of awareness.

Emotional Disorders

A variety of forms of emotional distress have been identified in stroke survivors (Angelelli et al., 2004). Two of the most common are now considered in some detail.

Depression. Investigations of poststroke depression (PSD) have proliferated in the past 20 years, spurred in large measure by the work of Robinson and his colleagues (Robinson, 2006). PSD may derive from: (a) structural alterations to the brain, (b) the patient's emotional response to sudden and disabling illness, or (c) a combination of (a) and (b). Researchers have examined the incidence, course, associated symptoms, cerebral lateralization and localization, and treatment of PSD. Gordon and Hibbard (1997) found reported prevalences to range from 25% to 79%, but Desmond et al. (2003) found a much lower rate—11%. Pooled estimates encompassing a variety of settings and poststroke durations have suggested that roughly one third of survivors display symptoms of depression at some point after stroke (Hackett, Yapa, Parag, & Anderson, 2005). Depression may also occur in association with other emotional or behavioral disorders, including irritability, aggression, and anxiety (Chan, Campayo, Moser, Arndt, & Robinson, 2006).

Debate continues about whether depression is more common with damage to one or the other hemisphere. Some have reported the highest incidence of PSD among patients with left anterior or left basal ganglia lesions (Morris, Robinson, Raphael, & Hopwood, 1996); others have found more frequent depression among individuals with right hemisphere lesions (Schwartz et al., 1993), whereas still others (Gainotti, Azzoni, Gasparini, Marra, & Razzano, 1997) have found nonsignificant differences between the two laterality groups. Some reviews (Carson et al., 2000; Narushima, Kosier, & Robinson, 2003) and meta-analyses were inconclusive.

There are also conflicting findings regarding the causes, characteristics, and course of PSD (Tateno, Kimura, & Robinson, 2002). One review (Ouimet, Primeau, & Cole, 2001) identified the following factors as most consistently associated with PSD: history of psychiatric condition (including depression), dysphasia, functional disability, living alone, and social isolation. The underlying causes might differ as a function of chronicity, acute depression being attributable to biologic factors (e.g., location of lesion, depletion of norepinephrine and/or serotonin), whereas depression during rehabilitation might stem from growing awareness of functional limitations, with chronic phase depression deriving from the socially handicapping consequences of stroke. Consensus is also lacking regarding the relevance of somatic symptoms in the diagnosis of PSD; specifically, whether these may simply be natural consequences of the stroke and therefore not true symptoms of depression (Paradiso, Ohkubo, & Robinson, 1997; Stein, Sliwinski, Gordon, & Hibbard, 1996).

A further point of dispute involves the impact of PSD on cognitive functioning, with some (Robinson, Bolla-Wilson, Kaplan, Lipsey, & Price, 1986) arguing for a dementia syndrome of depression in stroke survivors and others (House, Dennis, Warlow, Hawton, & Molyneux, 1990) finding, at most, only a weak association between depression and higher cognitive deficit. Hackett and Anderson (2005) concluded from their review that cognitive impairment was one of only three factors associated with PSD, the others being stroke severity and physical disability.

Studies have suggested that PSD prolongs hospitalization, hampers participation in therapies, limits the ultimate level of functional recovery, increases use of medical services after discharge, and compromises social reintegration and quality of life (e.g., Brodaty, Withall, Altendorf, & Sachdev, 2007; Cully et al., 2005; Ghose, Williams, & Swindle, 2004; Lenze et al., 2004; Lo et al., 2008; Ramasubbu, Robinson, Flint, Kosier, & Price, 1998; Sturm et al., 2004; Zalewski, Keller, Bowers, Miske, & Gradman, 1994). There is also the alarming finding that depression is associated with increased mortality (House, Knapp, Bamford, & Vail, 2001; Williams, Ghose, & Swindle, 2004). The suicide rate in this population is roughly twice that of the general population (Teasdale & Engberg, 2001), with women and those under 60 years of age being particularly vulnerable (Stenager, Madsen, Stenager, & Boldsen, 1998). Thomas and Lincoln (2006) reported impaired communication and external locus of control to be the strongest predictors of persistent depression, which may result in direct or indirect self-destructive behavior.

Assessment of emotional state in this population is fraught with hazards, as most diagnostic instruments were not constructed for the assessment of stroke patients. Although several measures (e.g., observer rating scales and a self-report instrument with stylized happy and sad faces at opposite ends of a line) have been developed for use with neurologically compromised individuals (e.g., Nelson, Mitrushina, Satz, Sowa, & Cohen, 1993; Quaranta, Marra, & Gainotti, 2008; Rybarczyk, Winemiller, Lazarus, Haut, & Hartman, 1996; Stern & Bachman, 1991), these have not been widely adopted. Furthermore, aphasic patients may not be able to communicate their emotional state; indeed, the common practice of excluding many, if not most, aphasic patients from studies of PSD clearly limits the generalizability of the findings. (However, see Thomas & Lincoln, 2008, for a recent study that included persons with aphasia and used a visual analogue self-esteem scale that correlates well with measures of mood.) The Patient Health Questionnaire-9 has shown some diagnostic promise (Williams et al., 2005), and a recent report suggested that response to a single yes–no question may offer a reasonably accurate screen for PSD (Watkins et al., 2007).

Affective information provided by stroke survivors may be unreliable (Toedter et al., 1995) due to fatigue, confusion, cognitive problems, lowered arousal level with consequent impaired perception

of emotional state, or impaired awareness (Spencer, Tompkins, & Schulz, 1997). In addition, patients whose speech is aprosodic (i.e., uninflected, lacking rhythm and "melody") may be mistakenly viewed as depressed because they "sound sad," even if their words and behavior do not conform to that diagnosis (Ross, 1997). Clinicians must determine the most reliable source of information, often a difficult choice. Klinedinst, Clark, Blanton, and Wolf (2007) reported poor congruence between patient and caregiver with respect to the former's symptoms of depression, and Hochstenbach, Prigatano, and Mulder (2005) found low levels of agreement between patient and relative reports across a range of cognitive, affective, and behavioral domains.

In light of the obvious complexities, it seems reasonable to conceptualize PSD as a biopsychosocial phenomenon and to take a multimodal approach to assessment (Hibbard, Gordon, Stein, Grober, & Sliwinski, 1993) using some combination of standardized self- and observer-report instruments (i.e., with awareness of the caveats for interpretation offered by Woessner & Caplan, 1996), interview of both patient and family members, and behavioral observations by multiple staff in multiple contexts. Clinicians should also note the suggestions of Ross and Rush (1981), who argued that depression in stroke (and head injury) patients might be signified by poor or erratic recovery, noncompliance with the rehabilitation program, "management difficulties," and deterioration from a previously stable level. It should also be noted that historically depressed individuals sustain strokes, and that premorbid depression has been associated with greater likelihood of discharge to an institution rather than home (Nuyen, Spreeuwenberg, Groenewegen, van den Bos, & Schellevis, 2008).

There is remarkably little research on the efficacy of psychological treatments for PSD. This may be due, in part, to the enduring view of poststroke depression as a natural, unavoidable (even necessary or desirable) response, a regrettable consequence of the now largely discredited stage theory of adjustment; as a result, referrals for treatment may have been infrequent. Nonetheless, one early, unpublished study (Latow, 1983) suggested that individual psychotherapy during rehabilitation could be effective.

Grober, Hibbard, Gordon, Stein, and Freeman (1993) described some success with adaptations of cognitive–behavioral therapy (CBT) techniques (see especially their Table 11-2 for detailed treatment strategies), but Lincoln and Flannaghan (2003) found CBT to be no more effective than standard care or an attention placebo condition. Clearly, this remains an area with much research potential (Kneebone & Dunmore, 2000).

Pharmacologic treatment of PSD has met with greater, albeit not uniform, success. Following a report of a positive impact of nortriptyline (Lipsey, Robinson, Pearlson, Rao, & Price, 1984), investigators described encouraging results with other tricyclics such as imipramine (Lauritzen et al., 1994) and amitriptyline as well as selective serotonin reuptake inhibitors (Andersen, Vestergaard, & Lauritzen, 1994; Choi-Kwon, Choi, Kwon, Kang, & Kim, 2008). Narushima, Chan, Kosier, and Robinson (2003) even found cognitive improvement in some depressed patients treated with antidepressants. Although a systematic review (Hackett, Anderson, & House, 2005) reached a pessimistic conclusion regarding the efficacy of antidepressant treatment of PSD, a recent randomized controlled trial (Williams et al., 2007) of an intervention combining patient and family education, medication, and close monitoring offers some basis for optimism.

One study (Rasmussen et al., 2003) found those stroke survivors who received a 12-month course of prophylactic administration of Zoloft had roughly one third the incidence of depression as those who were given placebo. More recently, Robinson and colleagues (2008) compared groups of stroke survivors who received "preventive intervention" of either Lexapro or problem-solving therapy with a placebo control group. Those who received placebo were 4.5 times more likely to become depressed during 1-year follow-up than those in the drug group and 2.2 times more likely that those who received the psychological intervention.

Stimulant treatment (Kraus, 1995), once thought to be useful for PSD, has largely been replaced by use of the newer antidepressants. Electroconvulsive therapy, felt to be effective in severe refractory depression (Currier, Murray, & Welch, 1992), is rarely used (Paranthaman & Baldwin, 2006). A less intrusive approach to treatment of PSD involves therapeutic exercise, which may enhance both mood and perceived quality of life (Lai et al., 2006) as well as helping to combat the effects of fatigue (Glader, Stegmayr, & Asplund, 2002).

Anxiety.   Most studies have found poststroke anxiety to be less common than poststroke depression but disabling, nonetheless. Starkstein et al. (1990) identified generalized anxiety disorder (GAD) in 24% of acute stroke patients, most of whom also showed evidence of major depression; only 6% had GAD alone. Shimoda and Robinson (1998) found that GAD in association with major depression delayed recovery from depression and also compromised resumption of social functioning and activities of daily living; the presence of GAD alone, however, did not have the same disabling impact. Barker-Collo (2007) reported nearly equivalent incidences of anxiety and depression (21.1% and 22.8%, respectively) in individuals at 3 months after onset. Left hemisphere locus was associated with anxiety. There is some evidence that being female and of younger age increases the likelihood of poststroke anxiety (Morrison, Johnston, & Walter, 2000; Schultz, Castillo, Kosier, & Robinson, 1997). In a longitudinal study, Astrom (1996) identified 20 cases of GAD among 71 acute stroke patients (28%), 11 of whom also had a diagnosis of major depression. Prevalence remained high at 3 months (31%), 1 year (24%), 2 years (25%), and 3 years (19%), and in each instance, more than half had comorbid depression.

Three studies (Burvill et al., 1995; O'Rourke, MacHale, Signorini, & Dennis, 1998; Sharpe et al., 1990) found agoraphobia to be the most common subtype of anxiety disorder, although the actual incidence was only about 7% to 8% for stroke survivors. Burvill et al. found women to be four times as likely as men to be diagnosed as agoraphobic. Burvill and colleagues (1995) noted that, whereas depression is generally held to result from the experience of loss, anxiety is more often produced by threat (e.g., fear of additional strokes, physical vulnerability, financial troubles). There is often associated fear of recurrent stroke or of falling while away from home and being stranded (Sharpe et al.). It would be of interest to investigate the perspectives of stroke survivors on perceived losses and threats accompanying their condition and the association of these views with symptoms of depression or anxiety.

When anxiety stems from exaggerated fears about imagined postdischarge problems, frank and specific problem-focused counseling may alleviate the condition. Pharmacotherapy and behavioral treatment both appear to be effective, although the former seems to produce greater impact (Pinquart & Duberstein, 2007). Nortriptyline has been reported to be especially valuable in treating comorbid anxiety and depression after stroke (Kimura, Tateno, & Robinson, 2003).

Apathy.   The presence of apathy might seem to be an exclusionary criterion for admission to rehabilitation, as one would not expect apathetic patients to exhibit the requisite motivation for therapy. However, patients may be admitted primarily for the purpose of training family members who will provide care at home. Also, one must be cautious not to conclude that an aprosodic individual is "apathetic."

Starkstein, Federoff, Price, Leiguarda, and Robinson (1993) reported a 22.5% incidence of apathy within 10 days after stroke. Half of these also showed (primarily major) depression, but the others exhibited apathy alone; the latter group had a high frequency of lesions affecting the posterior portion of the internal capsule. Apathetic patients without depression were also more cognitively impaired and functionally disabled. Given the widespread belief that the *indifference reaction* is associated with right hemisphere injury (e.g., Gainotti, 1972), it is notable that no hemispheric differences were reported. Okada, Kobayashi, Yamasati, Takahashi, and Yamaguchi (1997) found a 50% incidence of apathy among patients with subcortical infarction, 40% of whom also exhibited depression. Okada et al. opined that poststroke apathy results from cortical serotonergic deficits and that dopaminergic and serotonergic agents might be effective treatments. In this regard, it is of interest that Marin, Fogel, Hawkins, Duffy, and Krupp (1995) described a series of seven apathetic patients (four with vascular etiology) who were successfully treated pharmacologically, several with stimulants.

Other forms of emotional disorder may follow stroke, such as mania, atypical psychosis, delusional behavior, and pathological emotionalism (see Robinson, 2006, for further discussion). Although various forms of emotional distress are certainly quite common, especially in the early poststroke phase, in the longer term, some survivors identify positive consequences including increases in social relations and altruism, personal growth, and improved health awareness (Gillen, 2005). Stroke psychologists may be able to facilitate these perspectives and insights.

Concerns with family and staff.   The rehabilitation psychologist can assist in managing the sometimes fractious relations that develop between staff and patient and/or his or her family, fostering better communication and understanding of the other "team's" stresses, motivations, concerns, and behavior (Caplan & Reidy, 1996). Simply reframing or rephrasing certain comments or actions may be sufficient. For example, staff can be advised to view "intrusive" family members as "concerned" and "involved," albeit perhaps overwhelmed (see Caplan & Shechter, 1993, for discussion of terminology in rehabilitation).

The rehabilitation psychologist also plays a significant role in discharge planning, whatever the destination. Although transfer to a nursing home or assisted living facility may, in fact, be a permanent move, it is often not a certainty at the time. Thus, one can say, without being misleading, that what is being decided is simply where the individual should go next, emphasizing that improvement need not end with rehabilitation discharge. Neurological recovery and functional recovery are not invariably parallel processes. Furthermore, one must distinguish between "recovery" at the levels of impairment, disability, and handicap. Certainly, a stable neurologic deficit does not preclude further reduction of disability or improvement in social functioning (Roth et al., 1998).

Palmer and Glass (2003) offered a useful discussion of the vital role of families in stroke recovery from a family systems perspective, reviewing positive factors such as family availability, problem-solving skills, and empathy as well as counter-productive ones, such as over-protection. Palmer, Glass, Palmer, Loo, and Wegener (2004) described their use of a single-session intervention for stroke survivors and caregivers that incorporates education and cognitive–behavioral strategies within a crisis intervention framework. They argued that this inoculates against development of problems such as depression, excessive caregiver burden, and social isolation that may arise after discharge.

Postacute Assessment and Treatment

Increasing numbers of stroke survivors are being discharged from rehabilitation units before they have "plateaued," thus creating a continuum between inpatient and outpatient treatment. Although some discharges are no doubt driven by cost concerns, there are benefits to limited inpatient stays, including regaining the physical comforts of home, the opportunity to implement therapy lessons in the real world, and the resumption of aspects of control of one's life and activities. Von Koch, Wottrich, and Holmqvist (1998) found that patients receiving home therapy showed greater initiative than those undergoing hospital-based treatment, but it should also be noted that stress on the caregiver may increase (Donnelly, Power, Russell, & Fullerton, 2004). It is also at this point that "emotional and psychosocial rehabilitation" assumes paramount importance, as survivors and their families struggle with reestablishing their lives, taking into account the survivor's residual limitations and continuing needs. They must confront the "new normal."

Of the many topics relevant to this phase, four are discussed as follows—driving, sexual functioning, caregiver burden, and vocational prospects—for which psychological expertise may be sought. Other equally meritorious subjects could have been included. For example, the problem of persisting pain after stroke has recently come to notice, but there is as yet sparse literature. Jonsson, Lindgren, Hallstrom, Norving, and Lindgren (2006) found moderate to severe pain in 32% of stroke patients at 4 months after onset, decreasing to 21% at 16 months. This is an area in need of further investigation, as persistent pain can result in depression, disrupted sleep, and limited activity level.

Driving. As the ability to drive represents freedom and independence, loss of this privilege can be devastating for one's self-image and also because of the social, recreational, and vocational limitations that follow. Restrictions should not be imposed lightly, nor should approval be given in a cavalier fashion. Many common consequences of stroke (e.g., hemianopia, neglect, hemiplegia, sensory loss, aphasia) might be expected to compromise safe driving, and formal testing may indeed identify such profound levels of deficit (e.g., gross distractibility, severe unilateral neglect) that a road test would be ill advised. However, the AHCPR Guideline (Gresham et al., 1995) cites studies demonstrating that poor performance on formal testing does not necessarily translate to impaired behavior behind the wheel (e.g., Brooke, Questad, Patterson, & Valois, 1992). More recent investigations (e.g., Akinwuntan et al., 2006; Whelihan, DiCarlo, & Paul, 2005) have scarcely been more encouraging with respect to the value of formal testing. Despite the apparent importance of intact language functioning (e.g., for reading street signs, speedometers), two early studies (Golper, Rau, & Marshall, 1980; Lebrun, Leleux, Fery, Doms, & Buyssens, 1978) found that language ability alone did not predict driving performance in aphasics. A recent potentially valuable development is the availability of the "driving scenes" subtest of the Neuropsychological Assessment Battery (Brown et al., 2005), which correlated .55 with on-road driving performance in a mixed sample of older persons with mild dementia and healthy controls (Brown et al., 2005).

Resumption of driving may be a moot issue for most stroke survivors. Legh-Smith, Wade, and Hewer (1986) found that two thirds of their sample had stopped driving before their illness and, of the remainder, 58% did not resume afterward. Fisk, Owsley, and Pulley (1997) reported that only 30% of prestroke drivers resumed driving after discharge. However, Legh-Smith et al. found nondrivers to be less socially active and, perhaps as a result, more depressed than more mobile peers. Given the age of these studies, this is an area in need of further investigation.

Some rehabilitation facilities have driving specialists that conduct detailed evaluations including on-road tests, but these are relatively rare; only 5% of the sample of Fisk et al. (1997) had undergone a road test. In the absence of such services, the team and family may look to the rehabilitation psychologist for guidance. Nonetheless, the final decision on an individual's license to drive resides with the State Department of Motor Vehicles. Psychologists should know their obligations under state law to report individuals with conditions that might compromise their ability to operate a vehicle in a safe manner. Regardless of state law, one could argue that patients should be advised to undergo evaluation and possibly even retake their state's examination for their own protection and peace of mind. Given the potential financial risks if they are involved in an accident, the imprimatur of a professional driver-evaluator and/or a passing grade on the state examination would clearly be advantageous.

Sexual functioning. Sexual dysfunction is common in both men and women following stroke (Kimura, Murata, Shimoda, & Robinson, 2001), but clinicians often fail to address the issue because of simple oversight, discomfort with the topic, or stereotypic notions about the asexual elderly. Although sexual activity may well decline with age, the status and wishes of each individual and their partner should be evaluated. Fugl-Meyer and Jaasko (1980) found that 83% of their subjects had been sexually active prior to stroke, but at 1-year follow-up, about one third were completely inactive, one third reported decreased frequency, and the remainder had returned to prestroke levels. Monga, Lawson, and Inglis (1986) found that incidences of sexual inactivity increased from 11% to 64% in men and 29% to 54% in women after stroke onset.

Little longitudinal work has been conducted on this topic, but Hawton (1984) provided some encouraging findings, noting return of libido at about 6 months after onset in the majority of his sample that had been premorbidly sexually active. Erectile ability returned at approximately 7 weeks, and intercourse resumed at an average of 11 weeks. Aloni and colleagues reported on small groups of male (Aloni, Ring, Rozenthul, & Schwartz, 1997) and female (Aloni, Schwartz, & Ring, 1994) stroke patients at admission and 6 to 12 months later. For neither sex

was any particular pattern identified, although more dysfunction tended to be reported among those with nondominant hemisphere lesions. Buzzelli, di Francesco, Giaquinto, and Nolfe (1997) studied 139 consecutive patients 1 month after stroke and about half of them again at 1 year. Although decline in sexual activity was quite common (83.3% incidence), no association was found with age, depression, or level of disability.

Causes of poststroke sexual disturbances are multiple, including physiological dysfunctions such as diminished erectile capacity in men or lubrication in women, comorbid diseases (e.g., diabetes), reduced sensory or motor function, and the impact of medications. One must also consider factors such as loss of self-esteem, depression, reduced level of desire, fear of precipitating another stroke, role shifts, concern about the partner's response, performance anxiety, limited mobility, communication difficulties, and cognitive deficits (Good, 1997). Psychological barriers to resumption of an active sex life after stroke appear to be at least as important as physical limitations (Buzzelli et al., 1997; Korpelainen, Nieminen, & Myllyla, 1999).

Ducharme (1987) outlined the rehabilitation psychologist's role in sexual counseling, using the PLISSIT model (Permission, Limited Information, Specific Suggestions, and Intensive Therapy; Annon, 1974). At a minimum, during rehabilitation, the first two components (i.e., Permission, Limited Information) should be completed. Simply raising the topic, thereby legitimizing discussion (i.e., giving permission) and offering a few basic facts does an immense service. Although virtually all team members should be capable of handling these two steps, many, perhaps most, staff members receive no training in this area (McLaughlin & Cregan, 2005), so sexual counseling often becomes the psychologist's responsibility by default. As requested by the patient and his or her partner, specific suggestions may be given regarding adaptive techniques, and audiovisual resources may be recommended. Intensive therapy should be provided only by those with specific training. I urge clinicians to keep in mind the distinction drawn by Trieschmann (1980) regarding sex drives, sex acts, and sexuality. This typology is useful in identifying the locus of dysfunction and determining suitable interventions.

Caregiver burden.   In recent years, the multiple burdens that accompany the caregiving role have begun to receive attention (see chap. 18, this volume). However, synthesizing the findings of empirical studies is made difficult by the existence of a plethora of partially overlapping measures (i.e., 45 in Visser-Meily, Post, Riphagen, & Lindeman, 2004). Given the shift toward outpatient care, it is vital to attend to the needs of the person who may be the linchpin of the stroke survivor's posthospital life— the spouse (although children may be called on as well); the best discharge plan will fail if the primary caregiver's health deteriorates.

The physical burdens are obvious, especially for those with health problems of their own: providing assistance with transfers, pushing the wheelchair, monitoring ambulation, and so forth. At least as taxing are the emotional strains: dealing with a spouse who may have been "characterologically altered" (Lezak, 1978) by the stroke, who exhibits cognitive deficits (especially impaired language; Blonder, Langer, Pettigrew, & Garrity, 2007) or behavioral change, who cannot fulfill the same social roles, make financial decisions, share driving, and so on. Caregivers have greater difficulty dealing with these cognitive–behavioral consequences of stroke than the physical ones (Anderson, Linto, & Stewart-Wynne, 1995). The result can be a deteriorating spiral of social isolation, emotional distress, and functional decline for both partners. Indeed, Rochette, Desrosiers, Bravo, Tribble, and Bourget (2007) reported sizable reductions for caregivers of stroke survivors in the domains of personal relationships, employment, and recreation. It should not be surprising, therefore, that Grant, Elliott, Giger, and Bartolucci (2001) found social support to be the best predictor of caregiver satisfaction with life.

Caregiving is associated with troubling levels of anxiety, depression, frustration, and social isolation as well as disruption of lifestyle (Berg, Palomaki, Lonnqvist, Lehtihalmes, & Kaste, 2005; Han & Haley, 1999) and possibly an increased susceptibility to accidents (Hartke, Heinemann, King, & Semik, 2006). Stein, Berger, Hibbard, and Gordon

(1993) provided a good overview of the problem and discussed some possible interventions. One potentially important tactic is suggested by the finding of Williamson et al. (2005) that caregivers are less distressed by the care recipient's difficult behaviors that they attribute to the illness rather than to the person, that is, when the behaviors are viewed as outside the individual's control. Education of family members about the neurological basis of such consequences as disinhibition and depression may help to minimize misattributions.

Respite care programs or day hospitals may provide some relief, but caregivers often must be reassured that using these resources does not constitute abandonment. Caregivers must be reminded to take adequate care of themselves so that they may continue to attend to their affected partner (Lezak, 1978). Once again, "giving permission" is an important psychological service.

Vocational functioning.   Although stroke primarily afflicts older persons, a significant proportion (i.e., roughly 15%–20%) of survivors are of traditional working age (e.g., Becker et al., 1986; Macaden, 2005). One study found that 41% of their sample had returned to work at follow-up (Vestling, Tufvesson, & Iwarsson, 2003), although a range of 21% to 73% has been reported (Wozniak et al., 1999). Furthermore, as more older workers remain on the job, either from necessity, given the uncertainties surrounding the future of the Social Security system in the United States, or by choice, the possibility of return to work will need to be considered for more survivors of stroke. Unfortunately, few studies exist of poststroke vocational restoration, and those that do are difficult to compare because of methodological differences, including the fundamental one of variable definitions of *work* (see Wozniak & Kittner, 2002, for a review). Indeed, the author of a vocational rehabilitation chapter in a recent textbook on stroke recovery acknowledged that the content drew on the traumatic brain injury literature because of the paucity of evidence from stroke (Macaden, 2005).

McMahon and Slowinski Crown (1998), noting that reported rates of return to work after stroke have varied dramatically from 3% to 84%, listed several potentially explanatory factors, including the state of the economy, severity of impairment, and geographic location. They also called attention to the useful distinction between *fixed* (e.g., age, work history, educational level) and *modifiable* (e.g., motivation, cognitive deficits, availability of transportation) variables, the latter being potentially susceptible to intervention. In their study of 200 stroke survivors, those with left hemisphere strokes and aphasia were most likely to return to work and those with right hemisphere strokes accompanied by cognitive and/or perceptual deficits were least likely to do so. This contrasts with the findings of Wozniak et al. (1999), who reported no association of lesion location with return to work. Another relevant limiting factor is emotional distress (Glozier, Hackett, Parag, & Anderson, 2008).

Weisbroth, Esibill, and Zuger (1971) reported that over one third of their sample under age 65 returned to work, albeit some at a lesser level; women were more likely to return to work, although age and education had little effect. Smolkin and Cohen (1974), however, discovered that those who did not complete high school were less likely to resume work than were high school graduates, especially if they were women. Professionals had a higher return-to-work rate than did less skilled workers, a conclusion also reached by Howard, Till, Matthews, and Truscott (1985) and by Vestling et al. (2003). Gresham, Phillips, and Wolf (1979) reported that "decreased vocational function" was the most prevalent functional limitation at 6 months or more postonset, but removing the influence of comorbid conditions (e.g., arthritis) reduced the incidence of vocational impairment from 65% to 38%, thereby demonstrating the more limited vocational impact of stroke per se.

Many stroke patients considering returning to work can benefit from a comprehensive neuropsychological evaluation (Caplan & Shechter, 1991). Merceier et al. (1991) found neuropsychological test performance to have the best predictive value for return to work of all factors they considered. Test results should be conveyed to the patient and family as well as to vocational counselors, and possible "reasonable accommodations" to the workplace may be discussed. Black-Schaffer and Lemieux (1994)

noted that most accommodations fall into one of five categories: physical access to the work facility, use of technological equipment or modifications, personal assistance services, flexible scheduling, and restructuring of responsibilities.

Few programs exist whose purpose is vocational restoration of the stroke survivor. Kempers (1994) and Black-Schaffer and Lemieux (1994) described services at the Rehabilitation Institute of Chicago and New England Rehabilitation Hospital, respectively. The former is considered "prevocational," whereas the latter appears more comprehensive. Data on inpatient treatment show that about half of their clients returned to some form of productive activity. Aphasia, substance use (i.e., alcohol, smoking) and inability to drive were associated with lesser likelihood of return to work (Black-Schaffer & Osberg, 1990). The efficacy of "supported employment" procedures (i.e., job-site strategies implemented by professional staff such as employer education, performance feedback to the client, task-specific cognitive rehabilitation) used with individuals with traumatic brain injury and other disabilities (e.g., Wehman et al., 1989) should be examined in stroke survivors.

SUMMARY AND FUTURE DIRECTIONS

The term *stroke* is aptly onomatopoetic in its connotation of a rapid-onset event, one that affects multiple domains of functioning at individual, familial, and societal levels. Although rapid treatment of acute stroke may improve outcome for some individuals, the ever-increasing number of aging persons virtually guarantees the expanding need for stroke rehabilitation services. In addition to continuing to fulfill the roles outlined in this chapter, rehabilitation psychologists can contribute to the refinement of stroke treatment in a number of ways. This section notes several relevant aims and activities.

Psychologists can assist public education, both large-scale and at the individual client level, about the risk factors and early warning signs of stroke. Behavioral management strategies, pioneered by health psychologists, can assist in reducing such modifiable risk factors as smoking and alcohol consumption and also in promoting adherence to treatment of conditions such as diabetes and hypertension that are associated with stroke.

Numerous areas in need of research can be identified, including efficacy of psychological counseling, in alleviating poststroke emotional distress, nature of coping strategies used by stroke survivors (Donnellan, Hickey, & O'Neill, 2006), and the relation between treatment intensity and outcome. Also, there would be great value in more precise determination of the predictive validity of neuropsychological measures to assist in establishing early prognosis and guiding treatment. The value of the algorithm for postdischarge placement suggested by Ween et al. (1996) might well be improved by the addition of neuropsychological data.

Equally important is the need for documenting the ecological validity of testing for recommendations about such postdischarge activities as driving, handling finances, and return to work. This area warrants major attention, as payers are increasingly unwilling to fund services that are not demonstrably cost-efficient. Instruments such as the Money Management Survey (Hoskin, Jackson, & Crowe, 2005) and the Rivermead tests of neglect and of memory developed by Wilson and her colleagues (Wilson, Cockburn, & Baddeley, 1985; Wilson, Cockburn, & Halligan, 1987) represent an encouraging step in the right direction. Similarly, proponents of neuropsychological rehabilitation must redouble their efforts to demonstrate meaningful impact on daily life activities. Further, collaboration with colleagues in neuroradiology who are using modern dynamic imaging techniques (Orr, Rodriguez, & Cramer, 2007) may help elucidate mechanisms of recovery following stroke. For more information on neuroimaging, see chapter 13 of this volume.

The findings of Lewinter and Mikkelsen (1995) suggest a troubling level of patient dissatisfaction with the extent to which emotional needs are addressed during stroke rehabilitation. As my earlier discussion showed, accurate assessment of the stroke survivor's emotional state can present multiple challenges, but this should inspire creative approaches, not resignation. Reliable and valid behavioral indicators need to be identified and new assessment tools evaluated in depth. Rehabilitation

psychologists must serve as advocates for treatment of depression, anxiety, and other forms of emotional disturbance that are too often viewed by staff as "understandable" or "expected" and therefore ignored. There are regrettably few formal investigations of the efficacy of psychological treatments of poststroke distress in either individual or group formats; given the multiple ways in which emotional distress can sabotage rehabilitation, persistent depression, anxiety, and so forth must be recognized and addressed.

The trend toward limiting inpatient stays and emphasizing rehabilitation in outpatient settings has become firmly established. Rehabilitation psychologists need to ensure that their expertise is recognized and applied in this venue. Many of the strategies proposed by Stiers and Kewman (1997) remain pertinent, including serving as case managers, supervising paraprofessionals, developing treatment protocols, advocating for provision of services guaranteed under the Americans With Disabilities Act, conducting or consulting in research, and lobbying for enlightened public policy on issues affecting persons with disabilities. Callahan (chap. 33, this volume) presents a strong case for psychologists serving in a less familiar capacity as administrators.

The Model Systems approach that has succeeded with spinal cord injury and traumatic brain injury could be extended to stroke. Recently, a task force of the American Stroke Association released "Recommendations for the Establishment of Stroke Systems of Care" (Schwamm et al., 2005) that explicitly recognize the place of neuropsychologists on the stroke rehabilitation team. The U.S. Department of Veterans Affairs and the U.S. Department of Defense have also published a clinical practice guideline for adult stroke rehabilitation (Bates et al., 2005; Duncan et al., 2005), noting the importance of evaluation of psychosocial and cognitive status and including the psychologist as a core member of the treating team. In an ever-tightening health care market, rehabilitation psychologists must continually reinforce their position as providers of essential services.

Finally, rehabilitation psychologists must work to influence various agencies that accredit health care organizations. These agencies no longer tend to designate a "core team" with specific members; rather, the trend is toward flexibility in team composition, depending on the needs of the particular person served. There is an urgent need for rehabilitation psychologists to garner evidence that their skills and knowledge are essential to the rehabilitation enterprise; these must encompass more than testimonials and anecdotes. Empirical studies must demonstrate the following: (a) that psychological testing enhances the specificity of development and execution of rehabilitation interventions and identifies emotional problems that can sabotage patient motivation and participation; (b) that psychological counseling helps to ameliorate, for example, depression and anxiety, making patients more receptive to treatment; (c) that intervention with distressed families facilitates their involvement in their loved one's rehabilitation and planning for postdischarge life; (d) that advising and educating other therapists about management of difficult patient behaviors increases the value of those treatments; and (e) that the development and refinement of assessment and outcome measures must ensure that these have sound psychometric properties, a task for which psychologists are ideally suited. Such achievements should enhance the likelihood that psychologists will function as members of the de facto "core" team.

References

Adelman, S. M. (1981). National survey of stroke: Economic impact. *Stroke, 12* (Suppl. 1), I-69–I-88.

Akinwuntan, A., Feys, H., DeWeerdt, W., Baten, G., Arno, P., & Kiekens, C. (2006). Prediction of driving after stroke: A prospective study. *Neurorehabilitation and Neural Repair, 20,* 417–423.

Aloni, R., Ring, H., Rozenthul, N., & Schwartz, J. (1997). Sexual function in male patients after stroke: A follow up study. *Sexuality and Disability, 11,* 121–128.

Aloni, R., Schwartz, J., & Ring, H. (1994). Sexual function in poststroke female patients. *Sexuality and Disability, 12,* 191–199.

American Heart Association. (2008). *Heart disease and stroke statistics.* Retrieved January 7, 2009, from http://www.americanheart.org/presenter.jhtml? identifier=3037327

Andersen, G., Vestergaard, K., & Lauritzen, L. (1994). Effective treatment of poststroke depression with selective serotonin reuptake inhibitor citalopram. *Stroke, 25,* 1099–1104.

Anderson, G., Linto, J., & Stewart-Wynne, E. (1995). A population-based assessment of the impact and burden of caregiving for long-term stroke survivors. *Stroke, 26,* 843–849.

Anderson, S., & Tranel D. (1989). Awareness of disease states following cerebral infarction, dementia, and head trauma: Standardized assessment. *The Clinical Neuropsychologist,* 327–339.

Angelelli, P., Paolucci, S., Bivona, U., Piccardi, L., Ciurli, P., Cantagallo, A., et al. (2004). Development of neuropsychiatric symptoms in poststroke patients: A cross-sectional study. *Acta Psychiatrica Scandinavica, 110,* 55–63.

Angeleri, F., Angeleri, V. A., Foschi, N., Giaquinto, S., Nolfe, G. (1993). The influence of depression, social activity, and family stress on functional outcome after stroke. *Stroke, 24,* 1478–1483.

Annon, J. (1974). *The behavioral treatment of sexual problems.* Honolulu, HI: Enabling Systems.

Astrom, M. (1996). Generalized anxiety disorder in stroke patients: A 3-year longitudinal study. *Stroke, 27,* 270–275.

Bamford, J., Dennis, M., Sandercock, P., Burn, J., & Warlow, C. (1990). The frequency, causes and timing of death within 30 days of stroke: The Oxfordshire community stroke project. *Journal of Neurology, Neurosurgery, and Psychiatry, 53,* 824–829.

Barker-Collo, S., & Feigin, V. (2006). The impact of neuropsychological deficits on functional stroke outcomes. *Neuropsychology Review, 16,* 53–64.

Barker-Collo, S. L. (2007). Depression and anxiety 3-months poststroke: Prevalence and correlates. *Archives of Clinical Neuropsychology, 22,* 519–531.

Barrett, A., Buxbaum, L., Coslett, H., Edwards, E., Heilman, K., Hillis, A., et al. (2006). Cognitive rehabilitation interventions for neglect and related disorders: Moving from bench to bedside in stroke patients. *Journal of Cognitive Neuroscience, 18,* 1223–1236.

Bates, B., Choi, J. Y., Duncan, P. W., Glasberg, J. J., Graham, G. D., Katz, R. C., et al. (2005). Veterans Affairs/Department of Defense clinical practice guideline for the management of adult stroke rehabilitation care. *Stroke, 36,* 2049–2056.

Baum, H. (1982). Stroke prevalence: An analysis of data from the 1977 National Health Interview survey. *Public Health Reports, 97,* 24–30.

Becker, C., Howard, G., McLeroy, K. R., Yatsu, F. M., Toole, J. F., Coull, B., et al. (1986). Community hospital-based stroke programs: North Carolina, Oregon, and New York. II. Description of Study Population. *Stroke, 17,* 285–293.

Berg, A., Palomaki, H., Lonnqvist, J., Lehtihalmes, M., & Kaste, M. (2005). Depression among caregivers of stroke survivors. *Stroke, 36,* 639–643.

Bernhardt, J., Chitravas, N., Meslo, I. L., Thrift, A. G., & Indredavik, B. (2008). A comparison of physical activity patterns in Melbourne, Australia and Trondheim, Norway. *Stroke, 39,* 2059–2065.

Berti, A., Ladavas, E., & Della Corte, M. (1996). Anosognosia for hemiplegia, neglect dyslexia, and drawing neglect: Clinical findings and theoretical considerations. *Journal of the International Neuropsychological Society, 2,* 426–440.

Black-Shaffer, R. M., & Lemieux, L. (1994). Vocational outcome after stroke. *Topics in Stroke Rehabilitation, 1,* 74–86.

Black-Shaffer, R. M., & Osberg, J. (1990). Return to work after stroke: Development of a predictive model. *Archives of Physical Medicine and Rehabilitation, 71,* 285–290.

Blonder, L. X., Langer, S. L., Pettigrew, L. C., & Garrity, T. F. (2007). The effects of stroke disability on spousal caregivers. *NeuroRehabilitation, 22,* 85–92.

Bogousslavsky, J., & Caplan, L. (2001). Part II. Vascular topographic syndromes. In J. Bogousslavsky & L. Caplan (Eds.), *Stroke syndromes* (2nd ed., pp. 34–48). Cambridge, England: Cambridge University Press.

Bonita, R., & Beaglehole, R. (1993). Stroke mortality. In J. P. Whisnant (Ed.), *Stroke: Populations, cohorts, and clinical trials* (pp. 59–79). Boston: Butterworth-Heineman.

Bowen, A., & Lincoln, N. (2007). Cognitive rehabilitation for spatial neglect following stroke (Article Number CD003586. DOI: 10.1002/14651858.CD003586. pub2). *Cochrane Database of Systematic Reviews, 2.* Retrieved November 15, 2008, from http://www.cochrane.org/reviews/en/ab003586.html

Brodaty, H., Withall, A., Altendorf, A., & Sachdev, P. S. (2007, June). Rates of depression at 3 and 15 months poststroke and their relationship with cognitive decline: The Syndey stroke study. *American Journal of Geriatric Psychiatry, 15,* 477–486.

Broderick, J., Brott, T., Kothari, R., Miller, R., Khoury, J., Pancioli, A., et al. (1998). The greater Cincinnati/Northern Kentucky stroke study: Preliminary first-ever and total incidence rates of stroke among blacks. *Stroke, 29,* 415–421.

Brooke, M., Questad, K., Patterson, D., & Valois, T. (1992). Driving evaluation after traumatic brain injury. *American Journal of Physical Medicine and Rehabilitation, 71,* 177–182.

Brown, L. B., Stern, R. A., Cahn-Weiner, D. A., Rogers, B., Messer, M. A., Lannon, M. C., et al. (2005). Driving Scenes test of the Neuropsychological Assessment Battery (NAB) and on-road driving performance in aging and very mild dementia. *Archives of Clinical Neuropsychology, 20,* 209–215.

Burvill, P. W., Johnson, G. A., Jamrozik, K. D., Anderson, C. S., Stewart-Wynne, E. G., & Chakera, T. M. H. (1995). Anxiety disorders after stroke: Results from the Perth Community Stroke Study. *British Journal of Psychiatry, 166,* 328–332.

Buzzelli, S., di Francesco, L., Giaquinto, S., & Nolfe, G. (1997). Psychological and medical aspects of sexuality following stroke. *Sexuality and Disability, 15,* 261–270.

Caplan, B. (1982). Neuropsychology in rehabilitation: Its role in evaluation and intervention. *Archives of Physical Medicine and Rehabilitation, 63,* 362–366.

Caplan, B. (1987). Assessment of unilateral neglect: A new reading test. *Journal of Clinical and Experimental Neuropsychology, 9,* 359–364.

Caplan, B., & Reidy, K. (1996). Staff–patient–family conflicts in rehabilitation: Sources and solutions. *Topics in Spinal Cord Injury, 2,* 21–33.

Caplan, B., & Shechter, J. A. (1991). Vocational capacity with cognitive impairment. In S. J. Scheer (Ed.), *Medical perspectives in vocational assessment of impaired workers* (pp. 149–172). Gaithersburg, MD: Aspen Publishers.

Caplan, B., & Shechter, J. (1993). Reflections on the "depressed," "unrealistic," "inappropriate," "manipulative," "unmotivated," "noncompliant," "denying," "maladjusted," "regressed," etc. patient. *Archives of Physical Medicine and Rehabilitation, 74,* 1123–1124.

Caplan, B., & Shechter, J. (1995). The role of neuropsychological assessment in rehabilitation: History, rationale, and examples. In L. A. Cushman & M. J. Scherer (Eds.), *Psychological assessment in medical rehabilitation* (pp. 359–391). Washington, DC: American Psychological Association.

Cappa, S. F., Benke, T., Clarke, S., Rossi, B., Stemmer, B., van Heugten, C. M., et al. (2005, September). EFNS guidelines on cognitive rehabilitation: Report of an EFNS task force. *European Journal of Neurology, 12,* 665–680.

Caramata, P. J., Heros, R. C., & Latchaw, R. E. (1994). "Brain attack": The rationale for treating stroke as a medical emergency. *Neurosurgery, 34,* 144–157.

Carhuapoma, J. R., & Hanley, D. F. (2002). Intracerebral hemorrhage. In A. K. Asbury, G. M. McKhann, & W. I. McDonald. (Eds.), *Diseases of the nervous system* (2nd ed., pp. 1383–1391). Cambridge, England: Cambridge University Press.

Carson, A., MacHale, S. Allen, K., Lawrie, S., Dennis, M., House, A., & Sharpe, M. (2000). Depression after stroke and lesion location: A systematic review. *The Lancet, 356,* 122–126.

Centers for Disease Control. (2003). Hospitalizations for stroke among adults aged over 65 years—United States, 2000. *JAMA, 290,* 1023–1024.

Chae, J., Zorowitz, R. D., & Johnston, M. V. (1996). Functional outcome of hemorrhagic and nonhemorrhagic stroke patients after in-patient rehabilitation. *American Journal of Physical Medicine and Rehabilitation, 75,* 177–182.

Chan, K. L., Campayo, A., Moser, D. J., Arndt, S., & Robinson, R. G. (2006). Aggressive behavior in patients with stroke: Association with psychopathology and results of antidepressant treatment on aggression. *Archives of Physical Medicine and Rehabilitation, 87,* 793–798.

Choi-Kwon, S., Choi, J., Kwon, S. U., Kang, D. W., & Kim, J. S. (2008). Fluoxetine improves the quality of life in patients with poststroke emotional disturbances. *Cerebrovascular Diseases, 26,* 266–271.

Cicerone, K. D., Dahlberg, C., Malec, J. F., Langenbahn, D. M., Felicetti, T., Kneipp, S., et al. (2005). Evidence-based cognitive rehabilitation: Updated review of the literature from 1998 through 2002. *Archives of Physical Medicine and Rehabilitation, 86,* 1681–1692.

Coslett, H. B. (1997). Acquired dyslexia. In T. E. Feinberg & M. J. Farah (Eds.), *Behavioral neurology and neuropsychology* (pp. 197–208). New York: McGraw-Hill.

Cramer, S. (2004). Functional imaging in stroke recovery. *Stroke, 35,* 2695–2698.

Crosson, B., Barco, P. P., Velozo, C. A., Bolesta, M. M., Cooper, P. V., Werts, D., & Brobeck, T. C. (1989). Awareness and compensation in postacute head injury rehabilitation. *Journal of Head Trauma Rehabilitation, 4,* 46–54.

Cullum, C., Rilling, L., Saine, K., & Samson, D. (2008). Intracranial hemorrhage, vascular malformations, cerebral aneurysms, and subarachnoid hemorrhage. In J. Morgan & J. Ricker (Eds.), *Textbook of clinical neuropsychology* (pp. 392–410). New York: Taylor & Francis.

Cully, J. A., Gfeller, J. D., Heise, R. A., Ross, M. J., Teal, C. R., & Kunik, M. E. (2005, December). Geriatric depression, medical diagnosis, and functional recovery during acute rehabilitation. *Archives of Physical Medicine and Rehabilitation, 86,* 2256–2260.

Currier, M. B., Murray, G. B., & Welch, C. C. (1992). Electroconvulsive therapy for poststroke depressed geriatric patients. *Journal of Neuropsychiatry and Clinical Neurosciences, 4,* 140–144.

Cutting, J. (1978). Study of anosognosia. *Journal of Neurology, Neurosurgery, and Psychiatry, 41,* 48–555.

De Freitas, G., Bezerra, D., Maulaz, A., & Bogousslavsky, J. (2005). Stroke: Background, epidemiology, etiology, and avoiding recurrence. In M. Barnes, B. Dobkin, & J. Bogousslavsky (Eds.), *Recovery after stroke* (pp. 1–46). New York: Cambridge University Press.

de Haan, R. J., Limburg, M., Van der Meulen, J. H., Jacobs, H. M., & Aaronson, N. K. (1995). Quality of life after stroke. Impact of stroke type and lesion location. *Stroke, 26,* 402–408.

DeLemos, C. D., Atkinson, R. P., Croopnick, S. L., Wentworth, D. A., & Akins, P. T. (2003). How effective are "community" stroke screening programs at improving stroke knowledge and prevention practices? Results of a 3-month follow-up study. *Stroke, 34,* E247–E249.

DeLuca, J., & Chiaravalloti, N. D. (2002). The neuropsychological consequences of ruptured aneurysms of the anterior communicating artery. In J. E. Harrison & A. M. Owen (Eds.), *Cognitive deficits in brain disorders* (pp. 17–36). London: Martin Dunitz.

Desmond, D. W., Remien, R. H., Moroney, J. T., Stern, Y., Sano, M., & Williams, J. B. W. (2003). Ischemic stroke and depression. *Journal of the International Neuropsychological Society, 9,* 429–439.

Devasenapathy, A., & Hachinski, V. (2004). Cerebrovascular disease. In M. Rizzo & P. J. Eslinger (Eds.), *Principles and practice of behavioral neurology and neuropsychology* (pp. 597–613). Philadelphia: W. B. Saunders Company.

Diener, H. C., Lees, K. R., Lyden, P., Grotta, J., Davalos, A., Davis, S. M., et al. (2008). NXY-059 for the treatment of acute stroke: Pooled analysis of the SAINT I and II trials. *Stroke, 39,* 1751–1758.

Dijkerman, H., Wood, V., & Hewer, R. L. (1996). Long-term outcome after discharge from a stroke rehabilitation unit. *Journal of the Royal College of Physicians of London, 30,* 538–546.

Diller, L., & Gordon, W. A. (1981). Rehabilitation and clinical neuropsychology. In S. B. Filskov & T. J. Boll (Eds.), *Handbook of clinical neuropsychology* (pp. 702–733). New York: Wiley.

Dobkin, B. D. (1995). The economic impact of stroke. *Neurology, 45*(Suppl. 1), S6–S9.

Dobkin, B. D. (2005). Rehabilitation after stroke. *New England Journal of Medicine, 352,* 1677–1684.

Donnellan, C., Hevey, D., Hickey, A., & O'Neill, D. (2006). Defining and quantifying coping strategies after stroke: A review. *Journal of Neurology, Neurosurgery, and Psychiatry, 77,* 1208–1218.

Donnelly, M., Power, M., Russell, M., & Fullerton, K. (2004). Randomized controlled trial of an early discharge rehabilitation service: The Belfast Community Stroke Trial. *Stroke, 35,* 27–33.

Ducharme, S. (1987). Sexuality and physical disability. In B. Caplan (Ed.), *Rehabilitation psychology desk refer-*

ence (pp. 419–435). Gaithersburg, MD: Aspen Publishers.

Duncan, P., Zorowitz, R., Bates, B., Choi, J. Y., Glasberg, J. J., Graham, G. D., et al. (2005). Management of adult stroke rehabilitation care. *Stroke, 36,* e100.

Elkind, M. (2003). Stroke in the elderly. *Mount Sinai Journal of Medicine, 70*(1), 27–37.

Ellis, S., & Small, M. (1997). Localization of lesion in denial of hemiplegia after acute stroke. *Stroke, 28,* 67–71.

Eslinger, P. (Ed.). (2002). *Neuropsychological interventions.* New York: Guilford Press.

Festa, J., Lazar, R., & Marshall, R. (2008). Ischemic stroke and aphasic disorders. In J. Morgan & J. Ricker (Eds.), *Textbook of clinical neuropsychology,* (pp. 363–383). New York: Taylor & Francis.

Fisk, G. D., Owsley, C., & Pulley, L. V. (1997). Driving after stroke: Driving, exposure, advice, and evaluations. *Archives of Physical Medicine and Rehabilitation, 78,* 1338–1345.

Folstein, M. F., Folstein, S. E., & McHugh, P. R. (1975). Mini-Mental State. *Journal of Psychiatric Research, 12,* 189–198.

Frassinetti, F., Angeli, V., Meneghello, F., Avanzi, S., & Ladavas, E. (2002) Long-lasting amelioration of visuospatial neglect by prism adaptation. *Brain, 125,* 608–623.

Fugl-Meyer, A., & Jaasko, L. (1980). Poststroke hemiplegia and sexual intercourse. *Scandinavian Journal of Rehabilitation Medicine, 7*(Suppl.), 158–165.

Gainotti, G. (1972). Emotional behavior and hemispheric side of lesion. *Cortex, 8,* 41–55.

Gainotti, G., Azzoni, A., Gasparini, F., Marra, C., & Razzano, C. (1997). Relation of lesion location to verbal and nonverbal mood measures in stroke patients. *Stroke, 28,* 2145–2149.

Ghose, S., Williams, L., & Swindle, R. (2004). Depression and other mental health diagnoses after stroke increase inpatient and outpatient medical utilization 3-years poststroke. *Medical Care, 43,* 1259–1264.

Gillen, G. (2005). Positive consequences of surviving a stroke. *American Journal of Occupational Therapy, 59*(3), 346–350.

Glader, E. L., Stegmayr, B., & Asplund, K. (2002). Post-stroke fatigue: A 2-year follow-up study of stroke patients in Sweden. *Stroke, 33,* 1327–1333.

Glozier, N., Hackett, M. L., Parag, V., & Anderson, C. S. (2008). The influence of psychiatric morbidity on return to paid work after stroke in younger adults. *Stroke, 39,* 1526–1532.

Goldberg, G., & Berger, G. G. (1988). Secondary prevention in stroke: A primary rehabilitation concern.

Archives of Physical Medicine and Rehabilitation, 69, 32–40.

Goldberg, M. (2007). New approaches to clinical trials in neuroprotection. *Stroke, 38,* 789–790.

Golper, L., Rau, M., & Marshall, R. (1980). Aphasic adults and their decisions on driving: An evaluation. *Archives of Physical Medicine and Rehabilitation, 61,* 34–40.

Gonzalez-Torrecillas, J. L., Mendlewicz, J., & Lobo, A. (1995). Effects of early treatment of poststroke depression on neuropsychological rehabilitation. *International Psychogeriatrics, 7,* 547–560.

Good, D. (1997). Sexual dysfunction following stroke. In M. Aisen (Ed.), *Sexual and reproductive neurorehabilitation* (pp. 145–167). Totowa, NJ: Humana.

Gordon, W. A., & Hibbard, M. R. (1997). Poststroke depression: An examination of the literature. *Archives of Physical Medicine and Rehabilitation, 78,* 658–663.

Gorelick, P., & Bowler, J. (2008). Advances in vascular cognitive impairment 2007. *Stroke, 39,* 279–282.

Gorelick, P. B. (1994). Stroke prevention: An opportunity for efficient utilization of health care resources during the coming decade. *Stroke, 25,* 220–224.

Govan, L., Weir, C. J., & Langhorne, P. (2008). Organized inpatient (stroke unit) care for stroke. *Stroke, 39,* 2402.

Granger, C., Hamilton, B., & Gresham, G. (1988). Stroke rehabilitation outcome study—Part 1: General description. *Archives of Physical Medicine and Rehabilitation, 68,* 506–509.

Grant, J. S., Elliott, T. R., Giger, J. N., & Bartolucci, A. A. (2001). Social problem-solving abilities, social support, and adjustment among family caregivers of individuals with a stroke. *Rehabilitation Psychology, 46*(1), 44–57.

Gresham, G. E., Duncan, P. W., Stason, W. B., Adams, H. P., Adelman, A. M., Alexander, D. N., et al. (1995). *Clinical Practice Guideline Number 16: Post-Stroke Rehabilitation* (AHCPR Publication 95-0662). Rockville, MD: U.S. Department of Health and Human Services. Public Health Service, Agency for Health Care Policy and Research.

Gresham, G. E., Fitzpatrick, T. E., Wolf, P. A., McNamara, P. M., Kannel, W. B., & Dawber, T. R. (1975). Residual disability in survivors of stroke—The Framingham Study. *New England Journal of Medicine, 293,* 954–956.

Gresham, G., Phillips, T., & Wolf, P. (1979). Epidemiologic profile of long-term stroke disability: The Framingham study. *Archives of Physical Medicine and Rehabilitation, 60,* 487–491.

Grober, S., Hibbard, M., Gordon, W., Stein, P., & Freeman, A. (1993). The psychotherapeutic treatment of poststroke depression with cognitive–behavioral therapy. In W. A. Gordon (Ed.), *Advances in stroke rehabilitation*. Andover, MA: Andover Medical.

Haas, S., Weidner, N., & Winkler, J. (2007). Adult stem cell therapy in stroke. *Current Opinion in Neurology, 18*, 59–64.

Hackett, M. L., & Anderson, C. S. (2005). Predictors of depression after stroke: A systematic review of observational studies. *Stroke, 36*, 2296–2301.

Hackett, M. L., Anderson, C. S., & House, A. H. (2005). Management of depression after stroke: A systematic review of pharmacological therapies. *Stroke, 36*, 1092.

Hackett, M. L., Yapa, C., Parag, V., & Anderson, C. S. (2005). Frequency of depression after stroke. *Stroke, 36*, 1330.

Hakim, A. M. (1998). Ischemic penumbra: The therapeutic window. *Neurology, 51*(Suppl. 3), S44–S46.

Han, B., & Haley, W. E. (1999). Family caregiving for patients with stroke: Review and analysis. *Stroke, 30*, 1478–1485.

Hartke, R., Heinemann, A., King, R., & Semik, P. (2006). Accidents in caregivers of persons surviving stroke and their relation to caregiver stress. *Rehabilitation Psychology, 51*, 150–156.

Hawton, K. (1984). Sexual adjustment of men who have had strokes. *Journal of Psychosomatic Research, 28*, 243–249.

Heiss, W. D. (2000). Ischemic penumbra: Evidence from functional imaging in man. *Journal of Cerebral Blood Flow and Metabolism, 20*, 1276–1293.

Hemmen, T., & Lyden, P. (2007). Induced hypothermia for acute stroke. *Stroke, 38*, 794–799.

Henon, H., Pasquier, F., Durieu, I., Godefroy, O., Lucas, C., Lebert, F., & Leys, D. (1997). Preexisting dementia in stroke patients: Baseline frequency, associated factors, and outcome. *Stroke, 28*, 2429–2436.

Hibbard, M., Gordon, W., Stein, P., Grober, E., & Sliwinski, M. (1993). A multimodal approach to the diagnosis of poststroke depression. In W. Gordon (Ed.), *Advances in stroke rehabilitation* (pp. 185–214). Andover, MA: Andover Medical.

Hochenstenbach, J., Prigatano, G., & Mulder, T. (2005). Patients' and relatives' reports of disturbances 9 months after stroke: Subjective changes in physical functioning, cognition, emotion, and behavior. *Archives of Physical Medicine and Rehabilitation, 86*, 1587–1593.

Hodgson, C., Lindsay, P., & Rubini, F. (2007). Can mass media influence emergency department visits for stroke? *Stroke, 38*, 2115–2122.

Hoskin, K. M., Jackson, M., & Crowe, S. F. (2005). Money management after acquired brain dysfunction: The

validity of neuropsychological assessment. *Rehabilitation Psychology, 50*, 355–365.

House, A., Dennis, M., Warlow, C., Hawton, K., & Molyneux, A. (1990). The relationship between intellectual impairment and mood disorder in the first year after stroke. *Psychological Medicine, 20*, 805–814.

House, A., Knapp, P., Bamford, J., & Vail, A. (2001). Mortality at 12 and 24 months after stroke may be associated with depressive symptoms at 1 month. *Stroke, 32*, 696.

Howard, G., Safford, M., Meschia, J., Moy, C., Howard, V., Pulley, L., et al. (2007). Stroke symptoms in individuals reporting no prior stroke or transient ischemic attack are associated with a decrease in indices of mental and physical functioning. *Stroke, 38*, 2446–2452.

Howard, G., Till, J., Toole, J., Matthews, C., & Truscott, L. (1985). Factors influencing return to work following cerebral infarction. *JAMA, 253*, 226–232.

Hussain, M. S., & Shuaib, A. (2008). Research into neuroprotection must continue . . . but with a different approach. *Stroke, 39*, 521–522.

Ingles, J. L., Eskes, G. A., & Phillips, S. J. (1999). Fatigue after stroke. *Archives of Physical Medicine and Rehabilitation, 80*, 173–178.

Jehkonen, M., Laihosalo, M., & Kettunen, J. (2006). Impact of neglect on functional outcome after stroke: A review of methodological issues and recent research findings. *Restorative Neurology and Neuroscience, 24*, 209–215.

Jonsson, A. C., Lindgren, I., Hallstrom, B., Norving, B., & Lindgren, A. (2006). Prevalence and intensity of pain after stroke: A population based study focusing on patients' perspectives. *Journal of Neurology, Neurosurgery, & Psychiatry, 77*, 590–595.

Jordan, L. C., & Hillis, A. E. (2005). Aphasia and right hemisphere syndromes in stroke. *Current Neurology and Neuroscience Reports, 5*, 458–464.

Kalra, L., & Ratan, R. (2006). Recent advances in stroke rehabilitation 2006. *Stroke, 38*, 235–237.

Kaplan, E. (1988). A process approach to neuropsychological assessment. In T. Boll & B. Bryant (Eds.), *Clinical neuropsychology and brain function: Research, measurement, and practice* (pp. 125–168). Washington, DC: American Psychological Association.

Kapur, N. (Ed.). (1997). *Injured brains of medical minds: Views from within*. New York: Oxford University Press.

Kaste, M. (2005). Thrombolysis: What more does it take? *Stroke, 36*, 200–202.

Katz, N., Ring, H., Naveh, Y., Kizony, R., Feintuch, U., & Weiss, P. (2005). Interactive virtual environment training for safe street crossing of right hemisphere stroke patients with unilateral spatial neglect. *Disability and Rehabilitation, 27*, 1235–1243.

Keane, S., Turner, C., Sherrington, C., & Beard, J. R. (2006). Use of Fresnel prism glasses to treat stroke patients with hemispatial neglect. *Archives of Physical Medicine and Rehabilitation, 87*, 1668–1672.

Kelly, P. J., Furie, K. L., Shafqat, S., Rallis, K., Chang, Y., & Stein, J. (2003, July). Functional recovery following rehabilitation after hemorrhagic and ischemic stroke. *Archives of Physical Medicine and Rehabilitation, 84*, 968–972.

Kelly, B., Pangilinan, P., & Rodriguez, G. (2007). The stroke rehabilitation paradigm. *Physical Medicine and Rehabilitation Clinics of North America, 18*, 631–650.

Kempers, E. (1994). Preparing the young stroke survivor for return to work. *Topics in Stroke Rehabilitation, 1*, 65–73.

Kiernan, R., Mueller, J., & Langston, W. J. (1995). *COGNI-STAT (Neurobehavioral Cognitive Status Examination).* Lutz, FL: Psychological Assessment Resources.

Kiernan, R. J., Mueller, J., Langston, J. W., & Van Dyke, C. (1987). The Neurobehavioral Cognitive Status Examination: A brief but quantitative approach to cognitive assessment. *Annals of Internal Medicine, 107*, 481–485.

Kim, J., Kim, K., Kim, D. Y., Chang, W. H., Park, C., Ohn, S. H., et al. (2007, February). Virtual environment training system for rehabilitation of stroke patients with unilateral neglect: Crossing the virtual street. *CyberPsychology & Behavior, 10*, 7–15.

Kimura, M., Murata, Y., Shimoda, K., & Robinson, R. (2001). Sexual dysfunction following stroke. *Comprehensive Psychiatry, 42*, 217–222.

Kimura, M., Tateno, A., & Robinson, R. G. (2003). Treatment of poststroke generalized anxiety disorder comorbid with poststroke depression. *American Journal of Geriatric Psychiatry, 11*, 320–327.

Kirk, A., & Kertesz, A. (1989). Hemispheric contributions to drawing. *Neuropsychologia, 27*, 881–886.

Kirsch, N. L., Shenton, M., Spirl, E., Rowan, J., Simpson, R., Schreckenghost, D., et al. (2004). Web-based assistive technology interventions for cognitive impairments after traumatic brain injury: A selective review and two case studies. *Rehabilitation Psychology, 49*, 200–212.

Kleindorfer, D., Miller, R., Sailor-Smith, S., Moomaw, C. J., Khoury, J., & Frankel, M. (2008). The challenges of community-based research. *Stroke, 39*, 2331–2335.

Klinedinst, N. J., Clark, P. C., Blanton, S., & Wolf, S. L. (2007). Congruence of depressive symptom appraisal between persons with stroke and their caregivers. *Rehabilitation Psychology, 52*, 215–225.

Kneebone, I. I., & Dunmore, E. (2000). Psychological management of poststroke depression. *British Journal of Clinical Psychology, 39*(1), 53–65.

Koenig, K. L., Whyte, E. M., Munin, M. C., O'Donnell, L., Skidmore, E. R., Penrod, L. E., et al. (2007). Stroke-related knowledge and health behaviors among post-stroke patients in inpatient rehabilitation. *Archives of Physical Medicine and Rehabilitation, 88*, 1214–1216.

Korpelainen, J. T., Nieminen, P., & Myllyla, V. V. (1999). Sexual functioning among stroke patients and their spouses. *Stroke, 30*, 715–719.

Kortte, K., & Wegener, S. (2004). Denial of illness in medical rehabilitation populations: Theory, research, and definitions. *Rehabilitation Psychology, 49*, 187–199.

Kraus, M. F. (1995). Neuropsychiatric sequelae of stroke and traumatic brain injury: The role of psychostimulants. *International Journal of Psychiatry in Medicine, 25*, 39–51.

Kwan, J., & Sandercock, P. (2003). In-hospital care pathways for stroke: A Cochrane systematic review. *Stroke, 34*, 587–588.

Lai, S. M., Studenski, S., Richards, L., Perera, S., Reker, D., Rigler, S., et al. (2006). Therapeutic exercise and depressive symptoms after stroke. *Journal of the American Geriatrics Society, 54*, 240–247.

Langer, K. G., & Padrone, F. J. (1992). Psychotherapeutic treatment of awareness in acute rehabilitation of traumatic brain injury. *Neuropsychological Rehabilitation, 2*, 59–70.

Larson, E. B., Kirschner, K., Bode, R. K., Heinemann, A. W., Clorfene, J., & Goodman, R. (2003). Brief cognitive assessment and prediction of functional outcome in stroke. *Topics in Stroke Rehabilitation, 9*(4), 10–21.

Larson, E. B., Kirschner, K., Bode, R., Heinemann, A., & Goodman, R. (2005). Construct and predictive validity of the Repeatable Battery for the Assessment of Neuropsychological Status in the evaluation of stroke patients. *Journal of Clinical and Experimental Neuropsychology, 27*(1), 16–32.

Latow, J. (1983, August). Effectiveness of psychotherapy for stroke victims during rehabilitation. Paper presented at the meeting of the American Psychological Association, Los Angeles.

Lauritzen, L., Bjerg Bendsen, B., Vilmar, T., Bjerg Bendsen, E., Lunde, M., & Bech, P. (1994). Post-stroke depression: Combined treatment with imipramine or desipramine and mianserin. *Psychopharmacology, 114*, 119–122.

Lazar, R. (Ed.). (2008). *Neurovascular neuropsychology.* New York: Springer Publishing Company.

Lebrun, Y., Leleux, C., Fery, C., Doms, M., & Buyssens. E. (1978). Aphasia and fitness to drive. *Clinical Aphasiology Conference Proceedings.* Minneapolis, MN: BRK.

Legh-Smith, J., Wade, D. T., & Hewer, R. L. (1986). Driving after stroke. *Royal Society of Medicine, 79,* 200–203.

Lenze, E. J., Munin, M. C., Quear, T., Dewe, M. A., Rogers, J. C., Begley, A. E., et al. (2004). Significance of poor patient participation in physical and occupational therapy for functional outcome and length of stay. *Archives of Physical Medicine and Rehabilitation, 85,* 1599–1601.

Levine, D. N., Calvanio, R., & Rinn, W. E. (1991). The pathogenesis of anosognosia for hemiplegia. *Neurology, 41,* 1770–1781.

Lewinter, M., & Mikkelsen, S. (1995). Patients' experience of rehabilitation after stroke. *Disability and Rehabilitation, 17,* 3–9.

Lezak, M. D. (1978). Living with the characterologically altered brain-injured patient. *Journal of Clinical Psychiatry, 39,* 592–598.

Lezak, M. D. (2004). *Neuropsychological assessment* (4th ed.). New York: Oxford University Press.

Li, C., Engstrom, G., Janzon, L., & Hedblad, B. (2008). Long-term stroke prognosis in relation to medical prevention and lifestyle factors: A prospective population-based study. *Cerebrovascular Diseases, 25,* 526–532.

Lieberman, D., & Lieberman, D. (2005). Rehabilitation following stroke in patients aged 85 and above. *Journal of Rehabilitation Research & Development, 42*(1), 47–54.

Lincoln, N. B., & Flannaghan, T. (2003). Cognitive behavioral psychotherapy for depression following stroke: A randomized controlled trial. *Stroke, 34,* 111–115.

Lipsey, J. R., Robinson, R. G., Pearlson, G. D., Rao, K., & Price, T. (1984). Nortriptyline treatment for post-stroke depression: A double-blind trial. *The Lancet, 1,* 297–300.

Lo, R. S., Cheng, J. O., Wong, E. M., Tang, W. K., Wong, L. K., Woo, J., & Kwok, T. (2008). Handicap and its determinants of change in stroke survivors. *Stroke, 39,* 148–153.

Luaute, J., Halligan, P., Rode, G., Courtois, S., & Boisson, D. (2006). Prism adaptation first among equals in alleviating left neglect: A review. *Restorative Neurology and Neuroscience, 24,* 409–418.

Macaden, A. (2005). Vocational rehabilitation. In M. Barnes, B. Dobkin, & J. Bogousslavsky (Eds.), *Recovery after stroke* (pp. 623–636). New York: Cambridge University Press.

Macciocchi, S. N., Alderson, A. L., & Schara, S. L. (2005). Cerebrovascular disorders: Neurocognitive and neurobehavioral features. In S. S. Bush & T. A. Martin (Eds.), *Geriatric neuropsychology* (pp. 219–242). New York: Taylor & Francis.

Marin, R. S., Fogel, B. S., Hawkins, J., Duffy, J., & Krupp, B. (1995). Apathy: A treatable syndrome. *Journal of Neuropsychiatry and Clinical Neurosciences, 7,* 23–30.

McCaffrey, R. J., & Fisher, J. M. (1987). Cognitive, behavioral and psychosocial sequelae of cerebrovascular accidents and closed head injuries in older adults. In L. L. Carstensen & B. A. Edelstein (Eds.), *Handbook of clinical gerontology* (pp. 277–288). New York: Pergamon Press.

McLaughlin, J., & Cregan, A. (2005). Sexuality in stroke: A neglected quality of life issue in stroke rehabilitation: A pilot study. *Sexuality and Disability, 23,* 213–226.

McMahon, R., & Slowinski Crown, D. (1998, Summer). Return to work factors following a stroke. *Topics in Stroke Rehabilitation, 5*(2), 54–60.

Merceier, P., LeGall, D., Aubin, G., Joseph, P., Alhayek, G., & Guy, G. (1991). Value of the neuropsychological evaluation in cerebral arterial aneurysms surgically treated. *Neurochirurgie, 37,* 32–39.

Mikulik, R., Bunt, L., Hrdlieka, D., Dusek, L., Vaclavik, D., & Kryza, J. (2008). Calling 911 in response to stroke: A nationwide study assessing definitive individual behavior. *Stroke, 39,* 1844–1849.

Monga, T., Lawson, J., & Inglis, J. (1986). Sexual dysfunction in stroke patients. *Archives of Physical Medicine and Rehabilitation, 67,* 19–22.

Morris, P. L. P., Robinson, R. G., Andrzejewski, P., Samuels, J., & Price, T. R. (1993). Association of depression with 10-year poststroke mortality. *American Journal of Psychiatry, 150,* 124–129.

Morris, P. L. P., Robinson, R. G., Raphael, B., & Hopwood, M. J. (1996). Lesion location and poststroke depression. *Journal of Neuropsychiatry and Clinical Neurosciences, 8,* 399–403.

Morrison, V., Johnston, M., & Walter, R. M. (2000). Predictors of distress following an acute stroke: Disability, control cognitions, and satisfaction with care. *Psychology and Health, 15,* 395–407.

Narushima, K., Chan, K., Kosier, J., & Robinson, R. (2003). Does cognitive recovery after treatment of poststroke depression last? A 2-year follow-up of cognitive function associated with poststroke depression. *American Journal of Psychiatry, 160,* 1157–1162.

Narushima, K., Kosier, J., & Robinson, R. (2003). A reappraisal of post-stroke depression, intra- and interhemispheric lesion location using meta-analysis. *Journal of Neuropsychiatry and Clinical Neuroscience, 14,* 422–430.

Nelson, L., Mitrushina, M., Satz, P., Sowa, M., & Cohen, S. (1993). Cross-validation of the neuropsychology behavior and affect profile in stroke patients. *Psychological Assessment, 5,* 374–376.

Nuyen, J., Spreeuwenberg, P. M., Groenewegen, P. P., van den Bos, G. A., & Schellevis, F. G. (2008). Impact of preexisting depression on length of stay and discharge destination among patients hospitalized for acute stroke. *Stroke, 39,* 132.

Ocava, L. C., Singh, M., Malhotra, S., & Rosenbaum, D. M. (2006). Antithrombotic and thrombotic therapy for ischemic stroke. *Clinics in Geriatric Medicine, 22*(1), 135–154.

Okada, K., Kobayashi, S., Yamagati, S., Takahashi, K., & Yamaguchi, S. (1997). Poststroke apathy and regional cerebral blood flow. *Stroke, 28,* 2437–2441.

O'Kelly, D. (2005). A patient's perspective. In M. Barnes, B. Dobkin, & J. Bogousslavsky (Eds.), *Recovery after stroke* (pp. 637–645). New York: Cambridge University Press.

O'Rourke, S., MacHale, S., Signorini, D., & Dennis, M. (1998). Detecting psychiatric morbidity after stroke. *Stroke, 29,* 980–985.

Orr, E., Rodriguez, R., & Cramer, S. (2007). Functional neuroimaging in recovery from stroke. In J. DeLuca & F. Hillary (Eds.), *Functional imaging in clinical populations.* New York: Guilford Press.

Osmon, D. C., Smet, I. C., Winegarden, B., & Gandhavadi, B. (1992). Neurobehavioral cognitive status examination: Its use with unilateral stroke patients in a rehabilitation setting. *Archives of Physical Medicine and Rehabilitation, 73,* 414–418.

Oumet, M., Primeau, M., & Cole, M. (2001). Psychosocial risk factors in poststroke depression: A systematic review. *Canadian Journal of Psychiatry, 48,* 819–828.

Palmer, S., & Glass, T. A. (2003). Family function and stroke recovery: A review. *Rehabilitation Psychology, 48,* 255–265.

Palmer, S., Glass, T. A., Palmer, J. B., Loo, S., & Wegener, S. T. (2004). Crisis intervention with individuals and their families following stroke: A model for psychosocial service during inpatient rehabilitation. *Rehabilitation Psychology, 49,* 338–343.

Pancioli, A. M., Broderick, J., Kothari, R., Brott, T., Tuchfarber, A., Miller, R., et al. (1998). Public perception of stroke warning signs and knowledge of potential risk factors. *JAMA, 279,* 1288–1292.

Paolucci, S., Antonucci, G., Gialloretti, L. E., Traballesi, M., Lubich, S., Pratesi, L., & Palombi, L. (1996). Predicting stroke inpatient rehabilitation outcome: The prominent role of neuropsychological disorders. *European Neurology, 36,* 385–390.

Paradiso, S., Ohkubo, T., & Robinson, R. (1997). Vegetative and psychological symptoms associated with depressed mood over the first two years after stroke. *International Journal of Psychiatry in Medicine, 27,* 137–157.

Paranthaman, R., & Baldwin, R. (2006). Treatment of psychiatric syndromes due to cerebrovascular disease. *International Review of Psychiatry, 18,* 453–470.

Paul, R., Garret, K., & Cohen, R. (2003). Vascular dementia: A conundrum for the clinical neuropsychologist. *Applied Neuropsychology, 10,* 129–136.

Phillips, N. A., & Mate-Kole, C. C. (1997). Cognitive deficits in peripheral vascular disease: A comparison of mild stroke patients and normal control subjects. *Stroke, 28,* 777–784.

Pinquart, M., & Duberstein, P. R. (2007). Treatment of anxiety disorders in older adults: A meta-analytic comparison of behavioral and pharmacological interventions. *American Journal of Geriatric Psychiatry, 15,* 639–651.

Pohjasvaara, T., Erkinjuntti, T., Vataja, R., & Kaste, M. (1997). Dementia three months after stroke: Baseline frequency and effect of different definitions of dementia in the Helsinki Stroke Aging Memory Study (SAM) cohort. *Stroke, 28,* 785–792.

Pohjasvaara, T., Leskela, M., Vataja, R., Kalska, H., Ylikoski, R., Hietanen, M., et al. (2002). Poststroke depression, executive dysfunction and functional outcome. *European Journal of Neurology, 9,* 269–275.

Prigatano, G. (1999). *Principles of neuropsychological rehabilitation.* New York: Cambridge University Press.

Quaranta, D., Marra, C., & Gainotti, G. (2008). Mood disorders after stroke: Diagnostic validation of the poststroke depression rating scale. *Cerebrovascular Diseases, 26,* 237–243.

Ramasubbu, R., Robinson, R. G., Flint, A. J., Kosier, T., & Price, T. R. (1998). Functional impairment associated with acute poststroke depression: The stroke data bank study. *Journal of Neuropsychiatry and Clinical Neurosciences, 10,* 26–33.

Randolph, C. (1998). *The repeatable battery for assessment of neuropsychological status.* New York: Psychological Corporation.

Rasmussen, A., Lunde, M., Poulsen, D. L., Sorensen, K., Qvitzau, S., & Bech, P. (2003). A double-blind placebo-controlled study of Sertraline in the prevention of depression in stroke patients. *Psychosomatics, 44,* 216–221.

Reeves, M. J., Rafferty, A. P., Aranha, A. A., & Theisen, V. (2008). Changes in knowledge of stroke risk factors and warning signs among Michigan adults. *Cerebrovascular Diseases, 25,* 385–391.

Reitan, R., & Wolfson, D. (1993). *The Halstead-Reitan neuropsychological test battery: Theory and clinical applications* (2nd ed.). Tucson, AZ: Neuropsychology Press.

Robinson, R. G. (2006). *The clinical neuropsychiatry of stroke: Cognitive, behavioral, and emotional disorders following vascular brain injury.* New York: Cambridge University Press.

Robinson, R. G., Bolla-Wilson, K., Kaplan, E., Lipsey, J., & Price, T. (1986). Depression influences intellectual impairment in stroke patients. *British Journal of Psychiatry, 148,* 541–547.

Robinson, R. G., Jorge, R. E., Moser, D. J., Acion, L., Solodkin, A., Small, S. L., et al. (2008). Escitalopram and problem-solving therapy for prevention of poststroke depression. *JAMA, 299,* 2391–2400.

Robinson, R. G., Starr, L. B., Lipsey, J. R., Rao, K., & Price, T. (1984). A 2-year longitudinal study of poststroke mood disorders: Dynamic changes in associated variables over the first 6 months of follow-up. *Stroke, 15,* 510–517.

Rochette, A., Desrosiers, J., Bravo, G., Tribble, D. S., & Bourget, A. (2007). Changes in participation level after spouse's first stroke and relationship to burden and depressive symptoms. *Cerebrovascular Diseases, 24,* 255–260.

Romero, J. R., Babikian, V. L., Katz, D. I., & Finklestein, S. P. (2006). Neuroprotection and stroke rehabilitation: Modulation and enhancement of recovery. *Behavioural Neurology, 17*(1), 17–24.

Ropper, A. H., & Brown, R. H. (2005). *Adams and Victor's principles of neurology* (8th ed.). New York: McGraw-Hill.

Ross, E. (1997). The aprosodias. In T. Feinberg & M. Farah (Eds.), *Behavioral neurology and neuropsychology* (pp. 699–709). New York: McGraw-Hill.

Ross, E., & Rush, A. (1981). Diagnosis and neuroanatomical correlates of depression in brain-damaged patients. *Archives of General Psychiatry, 38,* 1345–1354.

Roth, E. J., Heinemann, A. W., Lovell, L. L., Harvey, R. L., McGuire, J. R., & Diaz, S. (1998). Impairment and disability: Their relation during stroke rehabilitation. *Archives of Physical Medicine and Rehabilitation, 79,* 329–335.

Rother, J. (2008). Neuroprotection does not work! *Stroke, 39,* 523–524.

Royall, D. R. (2004). "Silent stroke": An oxymoron meaning "dementia." *Seminars in Cerebrovascular Diseases and Stroke, 4*(2), 97–101.

Ruchinskas, R. A., & Curyto, K. J. (2003). Cognitive screening in geriatric rehabilitation. *Rehabilitation Psychology, 48,* 14–22.

Rybarczyk, B., Winemiller, D. R., Lazarus, L. W., Haut, A., & Hartman, C. (1996). Validation of a depression screening measure for stroke inpatients. *American Journal of Geriatric Psychiatry, 4,* 131–139.

Sacchetti, M. L. (2008). Is it time to definitely abandon neuroprotection in acute ischemic stroke? *Stroke, 39,* 1659–1660.

Salaycik, K., Kelly-Hayes, M., Beiser, A., Nguyen, A., Brady, S., Kase, C., & Wolf, P. (2006). Depressive symptoms and risk of stroke: The Framingham study. *Stroke, 38,* 16–21.

Savitz, S. I., & Schabitz, W. R. (2008). A critique of SAINT II: Wishful thinking, dashed hopes, and the future of neuroprotection for acute stroke. *Stroke, 39,* 1389–1391.

Schneider, A. T., Pancioli, A. M., Khoury, J. C., Rademacher, E., Tuchfarber, A., Miller, R., et al. (2003, January). Trends in community knowledge of the warning signs and risk factors for stroke. *JAMA, 289,* 343–346.

Schultheis, M., & Rizzo, A. (2001). The application of virtual reality technology for rehabilitation. *Rehabilitation Psychology, 46,* 1–16.

Schultz, S. K., Castillo, C. S., Kosier, J. T., & Robinson, R. G. (1997). Generalized anxiety and depression: Assessment over 2 years after stroke. *American Journal of Geriatric Psychiatry, 5,* 229–237.

Schwamm, L. H., Pancioli, A., Acker, J. E., III, Goldstein, L. B., Zorowitz, R. D., Shephard, T. J., et al. (2005). Recommendations for the establishment of stroke systems of care: Recommendations from the American Stroke Association's Task Force on the Development of Stroke Systems. *Stroke, 36,* 690–703.

Schwartz, J. A., Speed, N. M., Brunberg, J. A., Brewer, T. L., Brown, M., & Greden, J. F. (1993). Depression in stroke rehabilitation. *Biological Psychiatry, 33,* 694–699.

Sharpe, M., Hawton, K., House, A., Molyneux, A., Sandercock, P., Bamford, J., & Warlow, C. (1990). Mood disorders in long-term survivors of stroke: Associations with brain lesion location and volume. *Psychological Medicine, 20,* 815–828.

Shimoda, K., & Robinson, R. G. (1998). Effect of anxiety disorder on impairment and recovery from stroke. *Journal of Neuropsychiatry and Clinical Neurosciences, 10,* 34–40.

Silver, F. L., Rubini, F., Black, D., & Hodgson, C. S. (2003). Advertising strategies to increase public knowledge of the warning signs of stroke. *Stroke, 34,* 1965–1968.

Small, M., & Ellis, S. (1996). Denial of hemiplegia: An investigation into the theories of causation. *European Neurology, 36,* 353–363.

Smith, A. (1982). *Symbol Digit Modalities Test (SDMT) manual* (rev. ed.). Los Angeles: Western Psychological Services.

Smolkin, C., & Cohen, B. (1974). Socioeconomic factors affecting the vocational success of stroke patients. *Archives of Physical Medicine and Rehabilitation, 55,* 269–271.

Spencer, K. A., Tompkins, C. A., & Schulz, R. (1997). Assessment of depression in patients with brain pathology: The case of stroke. *Psychological Bulletin, 122,* 132–152.

Starkstein, S. E., Cohen, B. S., Federoff, P., Parikh, R. M., Price, T. R., & Robinson, R. G. (1990). Relationship between anxiety disorders and depressive disorders in patients with cerebrovascular injury. *Archives of General Psychiatry, 47,* 246–251.

Starkstein, S. E., Federoff, J. P., Price, T. R., Leiguarda, R., & Robinson, R. G. (1992). Anosognosia in patients with cerebrovascular lesions: A study of causative factors. *Stroke, 23,* 1446–1453.

Starkstein, S. E., Federoff, J. P., Price, R., Leiguarda, R., & Robinson, R. G. (1993). Apathy following cerebrovascular lesions. *Stroke, 24,* 1625–1630.

Stein, J. (2004). *Stroke and the family: A new guide.* Cambridge, MA: Harvard University Press.

Stein, P., Berger, A., Hibbard, M., & Gordon, W. (1993). Interventions with the spouses of stroke survivors. In W. Gordon (Ed.), *Advances in stroke rehabilitation* (pp. 242–257). Andover, MA: Andover Medical.

Stein, P., Sliwinski, M., Gordon, W., & Hibbard, M. (1996). The discriminative properties of somatic and nonsomatic symptoms for poststroke depression. *The Clinical Neuropsychologist, 10,* 141–148.

Stenager, E. N., Madsen, C., Stenager, E., & Boldsen, J. (1998). Suicide in patients with stroke: Epidemiological study. *British Medical Journal, 316,* 1206–1210.

Stern, R. A., & Bachman, D. L. (1991). Depressive symptoms following stroke. *American Journal of Psychiatry, 148,* 351–356.

Stiers, W., & Kewman, D. (1997). Psychology and medical rehabilitation: Moving toward a consumer driven health care system. *Journal of Clinical Psychology in Medical Settings, 4,* 167–179.

Straus, S. E., Majumdar, S. R., & McAlister, F. A. (2002). New evidence for stroke prevention: Scientific review. *JAMA, 288,* 1388–1395.

Stroke Unit Trialists' Collaboration. (1997). How do stroke units improve patient outcomes? A collaborative systematic review of the randomized trials. *Stroke, 28,* 2139–2144.

Stroke Unit Trialists' Collaboration. (2007). Organised inpatient (stroke unit) care for stroke. *Cochrane Database of Systematic Reviews, 4,* Article CD000197. DOI: 10.1002/14651858.CD000197.pub2. Retrieved November 15, 2008, from http://www.mrw.interscience.wiley.com/cochrane/clsysrev/articles/CD000197/frame.html

Stulemeijer, M., Fasotti, L., & Bleijenberg, G. (2007). Fatigue after stroke. In J. DeLuca (Ed.), *Fatigue as a window on the brain* (pp. 73–87). Cambridge, MA: MIT Press.

Sturm, J. W., Donnan, G. A., Dewey, H. M., Macdonell, R. A. L., Gilligan, A. K., & Thrift, A. G. (2004). Determinants of handicap after stroke: The North East Melbourne Stroke Incidence Study (NEMESIS). *Stroke, 35,* 715–720.

Tateno, A., Kimura, M., & Robinson, R. G. (2002). Phenomenological characteristics of poststroke depression. *American Journal of Geriatric Psychiatry, 10,* 575–582.

Taylor, T. N., Davis, P. H., Turner, J. C., Holmes, J., Meyer, J. W., & Jacobson, M. F. (1996). Lifetime cost of stroke in the United States. *Stroke, 27,* 1459–1466.

Teasdale, T. W., & Engberg, A. W. (2001). Suicide after a stroke: A population study. *Journal of Epidemiology and Community Health, 55,* 863–866.

Teng, E. L., & Chui, H. C. (1987). The Modified Mini-Mental State (3MS) examination. *Journal of Clinical Psychiatry, 48,* 314–318.

Terent, A. (1993). Stroke morbidity. In J. P. Whisnant (Ed.), *Stroke: Populations, cohorts, and clinical trials* (pp. 37–58). Boston: Butterworth-Heineman.

Thomas, S. A., & Lincoln, N. B. (2006). Factors relating to depression after stroke. *British Journal of Clinical Psychology, 45*(1), 49–61.

Thomas, S. A., & Lincoln, N. B. (2008). Predictors of emotional distress after stroke. *Stroke, 39,* 1240–1245.

Toedter, L. J., Reese, C. A., Berk, S. N., Schall, R. R., Hyland, D. T., & Dunn, D. S. (1995). The reliability of psychological measures in the assessment of stroke patients: Caveat inquisitor? *Archives of Physical Medicine and Rehabilitation, 76,* 719–725.

Trieschmann, R. B. (1980). *Spinal cord injuries.* New York: Pergamon Press.

Vallar, G., & Ronchi, R. (2006). Anosognosia for motor and sensory deficits after unilateral brain damage: A review. *Restorative Neurology and Neuroscience, 24,* 247–257.

Vermeer, S. E., Koudstaal, P. J., Oudkerk, M., Hofman, A., & Breteler, M. M. B. (2002). Prevalence and risk factors of silent brain infarcts in the population-based Rotterdam Scan Study. *Stroke, 33,* 21–25.

Vernooij, M. W., Ikram, M. A., Tanghe, H. L., Vincent, A. J., Hofman, A., Krestin, G. P., et al. (2007). Incidental findings on brain MRI in the general population. *New England Journal of Medicine, 357,* 1821–1828.

Vestling, M., Tufvesson, B., & Iwarsson, S. (2003). Indicators for return to work after stroke and the importance of work for subjective well-being and life satisfaction. *Journal of Rehabilitation Medicine, 35,* 127–131.

Visser-Meily, J. M. A., Post, M. W., Riphagen, I. I., & Lindeman, E. (2004). Measures used to assess burden among caregivers of stroke patients: A review. *Clinical Rehabilitation, 18,* 601–623.

von Koch, L., Wottrich, A. W., & Holmqvist, L. W. (1998). Rehabilitation in the home versus the hospital: The importance of context. *Disability and Rehabilitation, 20,* 367–372.

Wadley, V., McClure, L., Howard, V., Unverzagt, F., Go, R., Moy, C., et al. (2007). Cognitive status, stroke symptom reports and modifiable risk factors among individuals with no diagnosis of stroke or transient ischemic attack in the Reasons for Geographic and Racial Differences in Stroke (REGARDS) study. *Stroke, 28*, 143–114.

Watkins, C. L., Lightbody, C. E., Sutton, C. J., Holcroft, L., Jack, C. I., Dickinson, H. A., et al. (2007). Evaluation of a single-item screening tool for depression after stroke: A cohort study. *Clinical Rehabilitation, 21*, 846–852.

Wechsler, D. (1997). *Wechsler Adult intelligence Scale III.* San Antonio, TX: The Psychological Corporation.

Ween, J. E., Alexander, M. P., D'Esposito, M., & Roberts, M. (1996). Factors predictive of stroke rehabilitation outcome in a rehabilitation setting. *Neurology, 47*, 388–392.

Wehman, P., West, M., Fry, R., Sherron, P., Groah, C., Kreutzer, J., & Sale, P. (1989). Effect of supported employment on the vocational outcomes of persons with traumatic brain injury. *Journal of Applied Behavior Analysis, 22*, 395–405.

Weinstein, E. (1991). Anosognosia and denial of illness. In G. Prigatano & D. Schacter (Eds.), *Awareness of deficit after brain injury* (pp. 240–257). New York: Oxford University Press.

Weisbroth, S., Esibill, N., & Zuger, R. (1971). Factors in the vocational success of hemiplegic patients. *Archives of Physical Medicine and Rehabilitation, 52*, 441–446.

Welch, K., & Levine, S. (1991). Focal brain ischemia: Pathophysiology and acid-base status. In R. Bornstein & G. Brown (Eds.), *Neurobehavioral aspects of cerebrovascular disease* (pp. 17–38). New York: Oxford University Press.

Wentworth, D., & Atkinson, R. (1996). Implementation of an acute stroke program decreases hospitalization costs and length of stay. *Stroke, 27*, 1040–1043.

Whelihan, W. M., DiCarlo, M. A., & Paul, R. H. (2005). The relationship of neuropsychological functioning to driving competence in older persons with early cognitive decline. *Archives of Clinical Neuropsychology, 20*, 217–228.

Wilde, M. C. (2006). The validity of the Repeatable Battery of Neuropsychological Status in acute stroke. *Clinical Neuropsychologist, 20*, 702–715.

Williams, G., Jiang, J., Matachar, D., & Samsa, G. (1999). Incidence and occurrence on total (first-ever and recurrent) stroke. *Stroke, 30*, 2523–2528.

Williams, L., Brizendine, E., Plue, L., Bakas, T., Tu, W., Hendrie, H., & Kroenke, K. (2005). Performance of the PHQ-9 as a screening tool for poststroke depression. *Stroke, 36*, 635–638.

Williams, L., Ghose, S., & Swindle, R. (2004). Depression and other mental health diagnoses increase mortality risk after ischemic stroke. *American Journal of Psychiatry, 161*, 1090–1095.

Williams, L. S. (2005). Depression and stroke: Cause or consequence? *Seminars in Neurology, 25*, 396–409.

Williams, L. S., Bruno, A., Rouch, D., & Marriott, D. J. (1997). Stroke patients' knowledge of stroke. *Stroke, 28*, 912–915.

Williams, L. S., Kroenke, K., Bakas, T., Plue, L. D., Brizendine, E., Tu, W., et al. (2007). Care management of poststroke depression: A randomized, controlled trial. *Stroke, 38*, 998.

Williamson, G., Martin-Cook, K., Weiner, M., Svetlik, D., Saine, K., Hynan, L., et al. (2005). Caregiver resentment: Explaining why care recipients exhibit problem behavior. *Rehabilitation Psychology, 50*, 215–223.

Wilson, B. (1997). Cognitive rehabilitation: How it is and how it might be. *Journal of the International Neuropsychological Society, 3*, 487–496.

Wilson, B. A., Cockburn, J., & Baddeley, A. D. (1985). *Rivermead Behavioural Memory Test.* Flempton, England: Thames Valley Test Company.

Wilson, B. A., Cockburn, J., & Halligan, P. (1987). *Behavioural Inattention Test.* Flempton, England: Thames Valley Test Company.

Woessner, R., & Caplan, B. (1996). Emotional distress following stroke: Interpretive limitations of the SCL-90-R. *Assessment, 3*, 291–305.

Woldag, H., Gerhold, L. L., De Groot, M., Wohlfart, K., Wagner, A., & Hummelsheim, H. (2006). Early prediction of functional outcome after stroke. *Brain Injury, 20*, 1047–1052.

World Health Organization. (1989). Stroke 1989: Recommendations on stroke prevention, diagnosis, and therapy. *Stroke, 20*, 1407–1431.

Wozniak, M., & Kittner, S. (2002). Return to work after ischemic stroke: A methodological review. *Neuroepidemiology, 21*, 159–166.

Wozniak, M. A., Kittner, S. J., Price, T. R., Hebel, J. R., Sloan, M. A., & Gardner, J. F. (1999). Stroke location is not associated with return to work after first ischemic stroke. *Stroke, 30*, 2568–2573.

Yatsu, F., Grotta, J., & Pettigrew, L. (1995). *Stroke: 100 Maxims.* St. Louis, MN: Mosby, Inc.

Zalewski, C., Keller, B., Bowers, C., Miske, P., & Gradman, T. (1994). Depressive symptomatology and poststroke rehabilitation outcome. *Clinical Gerontologist, 14*, 52–67.

Zinn, S., Bosworth, H. B., Hoenig, H. M., & Swartzwelder, H. S. (2007). Executive function deficits in acute stroke. *Archives of Physical Medicine and Rehabilitation, 88*, 173–180.

CHAPTER 5

PSYCHOLOGICAL ASSESSMENT AND PRACTICE IN GERIATRIC REHABILITATION

Peter A. Lichtenberg and Brooke C. Schneider

America is clearly graying in a dramatic fashion. According to the Federal Interagency Forum on Aging-Related Statistics (2000), during the 20th century, the population of adults over the age of 65 grew from 3 million to 35 million. Today, hovering around 40 million, this cohort is expected to reach 70 million individuals by 2030. Perhaps even more dramatic, and more relevant to geriatric rehabilitation psychology, is the demography concerning the older old (i.e., those over age 85). This population, which numbered only 100,000 in 1900, grew to over 4 million in 2000 and is projected to reach over 21 million by 2030. Sensory impairments, memory difficulties, and impaired mobility are twice as common in the older old as they are in those 65 to 84 years. These rates of disability and impairment highlight their considerable need for rehabilitation services.

Changes caused by aging alone are fairly straightforward, but the interactions among age changes, gender, and racial and ethnic composition add complexity. Whereas the non-Hispanic White population currently accounts for over 80% of older individuals, this proportion is expected to decline to 60% by 2050 (Federal Interagency Forum on Aging-Related Statistics, 2000). The increases in Hispanic, Black, and Asian elders will lead to increased diversity of our older population. Black and Hispanic elders have higher rates of chronic disease, obesity, cognitive impairment, and disability than do White or Asian elders. These conditions have been linked to education, poverty, and neighborhood differences, as well as to disparity in health care services, even when access is not a problem. Due to these demographic trends, a sizeable proportion of the population can be expected to be growing older and sicker.

The most significant trend is that although life expectancy is increasing across the life span, it is not because of the elimination of chronic disease. In 1900, a person 65 years of age could expect to live another 10 to 12 years; he or she can now expect to live another 20 years. In 1900, a person age 85 who was expected to live 2.5 years now has a life expectancy nearly three times as long. Deaths due to heart disease (and to a lesser extent stroke) have dropped considerably, but the prevalence of heart disease has remained stable (Federal Interagency Forum on Aging-Related Statistics, 2000). Therefore, rehabilitation psychologists are likely for the foreseeable future to treat a growing population of older patients with complicated medical conditions and disorders.

Working with older adults in rehabilitation requires rehabilitation psychologists to understand geriatric issues from a broad perspective and to clearly identify their roles in enhancing quality of life for older rehabilitation patients. The remainder of this chapter consists of three sections. The first focuses on core geriatric concepts such as disability, comorbidity, and frailty and how these produce the path to disability; the next section considers major clinical issues for rehabilitation psychologists, namely depression and cognitive disorders; and the final section focuses on the broadening role of rehabilitation psychology with older adults, including treatment of sleep disorders, alcohol abuse, and pain.

GERIATRIC CONCEPTS: DISABILITY, COMORBIDITY, AND FRAILTY

Once used synonymously, disability, comorbidity, and frailty are now understood as distinct, although overlapping and related, conditions, which have significant implications for rehabilitation psychology. Perhaps the most familiar concept is *disability*, defined as difficulty or dependency in carrying out activities essential to independent living. Impairments affecting lower extremity mobility, for example, may curtail a person's independence in transportation and locomotion. In community settings, 20% to 30% of people over age 70 demonstrate disability (Fried, Ferrucci, Darer, Williamson, & Anderson, 2004). The third of older adults with the greatest disability demonstrate high rates of problems with walking two to three blocks, bathing and meal preparation, as well as having a high prevalence of vision impairment. In geriatric rehabilitation, disability increases directly with age (Lichtenberg, 1998). Independence with mobility dropped from 30% for rehabilitation patients in their 60s to 3% for those ages 80 to 95. Similarly, independence with toileting was 65% in the 60-year-old group and dropped to 40% in those 80 to 95 years (Lichtenberg, 1998).

Frailty describes an aggregate risk of complications for an older patient. Its early definition centered on the presence of more than one system (e.g., heart, lung, kidney, brain) compromised by disease and disability. More recently, frailty has become more clearly defined in its symptoms and effects on rehabilitation outcomes. Fried et al. (2004) summarized her group's definition as a syndrome with the following elements: decreased appetite and weight loss, gait disturbance and falling, and declining cognition. Some cases also have significant respiratory distress. This constellation of symptoms has an unclear etiology, and rather, represents multiple system failure. Frailty has been linked to significantly increased rates of nursing home placement and mortality (Ferrucci et al., 2002). In the rehabilitation setting, frailty is related to older age of the patient (Hanks & Lichtenberg, 1996). Discharge from rehabilitation to a dependent situation increased from 35% in those 60 to 79 years to near 50% in those 80

to 95 years. More specifically, discharge to a nursing home increased from 5% of those ages 60 to 69 to 25% of those 80 to 95.

Comorbidity refers to the presence of two or more medically diagnosed diseases in a given individual. Community-dwelling older adults most commonly suffer from arthritis (48%), hypertension (36%), and heart disease (27%); the prevalence of these conditions increases with age (Federal Interagency Forum on Aging-Related Statistics, 2000). This relation often does not hold in rehabilitation settings. That is to say that although there is a clear relation between disability and patient age, there is no clear relation between comorbidity and age. In our studies (Lichtenberg, 1999), those ages 60 to 69 had 1.4 comorbidities, those 70 to 79 had 1.6 comorbidities, and those 80 to 95 had 1.3 comorbidities. The lack of a relation between age and comorbidity was further supported in a 3-year mortality study in which age was not related to mortality but comorbidity was. In this study (Arfken, Lichtenberg, & Kuiken, 2000), 36% of the sample died within 3 years of discharge from rehabilitation, with equal proportions of deaths coming from the 60 to 69, 70 to 79, and 80 to 95 age groups.

The overlap between and distinctions among disability, frailty, and comorbidity in older individuals has specific implications for rehabilitation psychology. Disability is inversely related to strength, coordination, and muscle mass, all characteristics associated with younger versus older ages. Frailty is a specific and extreme expression of the multisystem failures that occur when diseases interact with age-related deficiencies. Thus, in rehabilitation, no matter what the primary diagnosis, one finds that younger patients are stronger, suffer less disability, and return more easily to independent living compared with the oldest patients. Comorbidity issues stand in contrast, however, as younger individuals have amounts of comorbid disease equal to those of the oldest patients. In fact, the finding that mortality does not differ among age groups indicates that perhaps the younger and older sets of geriatric rehabilitation patients represent different populations. The younger group (i.e., ages 60–79) present with much more extreme disease and disability than their community-based peers, whereas the older group more closely resembles their community cohort. It may well be that significant numbers of the young–old cohort never make it to the oldest-old age groups.

Research has identified several precursors to disability in the elderly, including arthritis, cognitive decline, greater illness burden, and unhealthy lifestyle behaviors. The identification of pathways to disability has become increasingly important as nearly 30% of community-dwelling older adults over the age of 70 reports a disability in mobility or difficulty with tasks of household management (Fried et al., 2004). Declines in functional status are associated with higher rates of mortality, morbidity (Gill, Richardson, & Tinetti, 1995), and negative outcomes, such as hospitalization (Ostir, Volpato, Kasper, Ferrucci, & Guralnik, 2001). Therefore, early identification and treatment of individuals at risk for disability may help to delay its onset and decrease health care costs. Although several risk factors for disability have been identified, a great deal of heterogeneity exists in patterns of decline; not all individuals will experience disability onset in the same manner.

Cognitive decline has consistently been linked to disability onset (Tabbarah, Crimmins, & Seeman, 2002). Declines in cognitive functioning are associated with slower gait on performance-based measures of disability (Rosano et al., 2005) and greater difficulty performing activities of daily living (ADLs; Wang, van Belle, Kukull, & Larson, 2002). More specifically, deficits in executive functioning limit an older adult's ability to carry out more complex tasks, such as those that require planning and integration of multiple cognitive processes (Sheridan, Solomont, Kowall, & Hausdorff, 2003). Thus, although an older adult may be physically capable of carrying out a particular complex ADL (e.g., balance a checkbook), cognitive deficits may limit his or her ability to actually do so (Grigsby, Kaye, Baxter, Shetterly, & Hamman, 1998).

Illness burden, the impact of comorbid chronic and acute medical conditions, reduces an individual's normal activity level, placing him or her at a greater risk of disease and disability. Diseases appear to work in a synergistic manner in older adults as risk of disability increases along with the number of reported diseases. Conversely, positive health behaviors (e.g., exercise, proper nutrition, sleep) delay the onset of disability and improve the functional ability of those who are already disabled (Phelan, Williams, Pennix, LoGerfo, & Leveille, 2004). Positive health behaviors, specifically aerobic exercise, have been shown to account for differences in disability independent of SES and illness burden (Seeman et al., 1995). An important point is that positive health behaviors are modifiable risk factors that adults may alter in later life to decrease risk of disability.

Arthritis is a leading cause of disability. For example, the risk of disability resulting from osteoarthritis of the knee is greater than that attributable to any other medical condition in older adults (Guccione et al., 1994). With prevalence rates at approximately 30% to 60% (Dunlop et al., 2005), arthritis leads to increased dependence and activity limitations in at least 10% of adults (Centers for Disease Control and Prevention, 2005; Stang et al., 2006). Rates of functional decline associated with arthritis tend to be greatest for women, African Americans, and Hispanics (Dunlop et al., 2005). It is of interest to note that a recent study by Kauppi, Hartikainen, Kautiainen, Laiho, & Sulkava (2005) found no difference between older adults with and without arthritis in their capacity to carry out ADLs. However, in this study, there was a higher rate of disability in the arthritis sample, with the most severe levels of disability associated with dementia. This suggests that although arthritis may act as a risk factor for disability, it tends to have the greatest effect in individuals who have other disease processes. These findings support previous studies showing that levels of physical limitation and disability increase when arthritis occurs in the presence of other disease states (Fried, Bandeen-Roche, Kasper, & Guralnik, 1999). In addition to comorbidity, research has shown that lack of physical activity, a modifiable risk factor, is associated with more rapid decline in older adults with arthritis (Jette & Keysor, 2003; Dunlop et al., 2005). Therefore, interventions have increasingly focused on promoting physical activity as well as developing methods to reduce the synergistic effects of diseases co-occurring with arthritis.

CLINICAL ISSUES FOR PSYCHOLOGISTS IN GERIATRIC REHABILITATION

We focus on two areas for which assessments are most often requested: (a) cognitive evaluation and discharge planning, and (b) depression evaluation and treatment planning. Rehabilitation for older adults is taking place primarily in short stay (i.e., 7–10 days) inpatient rehabilitation hospitals and in skilled nursing facilities. Although clinical psychologists are often in the rehabilitation hospital on a daily basis, they are usually outside consultants to skilled nursing facilities, typically spending parts of 1 to 2 days per week in those settings. Skilled nursing facilities usually have a longer length of stay for older adults (i.e., an average of around 20 days) than do the inpatient hospitals. The changing lengths of stay for inpatient rehabilitation psychology practice necessitate that psychologists emphasize assessment, identification of disorders, and relation of the disorder to function, independence and decision-making most particularly. Thus, cognitive impairment, depression, and capacity are the main areas of focus for rehabilitation psychologists.

Cognitive Impairment

Dementias such as Alzheimer's disease are strongly related to advancing age (Riley, 1999). Indeed, the prevalence of dementia doubles every 5 years beginning at age 60 and is estimated to affect 30% to 45% of persons over the age of 85 (Turner, 2003). In our experience, dementia among rehabilitation patients can frequently go undetected (Lichtenberg, 1998). Possible reasons for this include a focus on basic cognitive functions, such as following commands, and rudimentary safety behaviors, as well as an assumption that persons with dementia are screened out before they come to rehabilitation. Because many geriatric rehabilitation patients live alone, there may thus be few, if any, informants who can give accurate information about the patient's memory and functional abilities. Therefore, given the high risk of dementia in this population, it is critical that the rehabilitation psychologist be familiar with cognitive assessment for older adults.

Geriatric neuropsychology has a rich 25-year tradition in the United States. With the creation of the

Alzheimer's disease research centers in the late 1970s, sophisticated cognitive evaluation became an integral part of dementia evaluation and care. As described earlier, older patients often come to rehabilitation with cognitive changes already occurring. Gauging risk of cognitive decline solely from the primary rehabilitation diagnosis can lead to many undetected cases of dementia because cognitive impairment equally affects those with a stroke and those with a lower extremity fracture (Mast, MacNeill, & Lichtenberg, 1999). Dementia is twice as common in young-old medical rehabilitation patients (i.e., ages 60–79; Lichtenberg, 1998) as in young-old community-dwelling elders (Evans et al., 1989), placing rehabilitation patients at risk of institutionalization, loss of independence, and poor social outcome. In their inpatient practices, rehabilitation psychologists often have to determine who is in most need of an evaluation. They must quickly triage cases, deciding who gets an immediate evaluation and who may better be served by an outpatient evaluation or no full evaluation at all.

Screening processes serve dual purposes: to detect cognitive impairment and to determine priority of services. In our practice, we link patient and family interview data with brief cognitive and depression screening. The Mundt interview provides a systematic and quantitative approach to the caregiver or collateral report of symptoms common in cognitive dysfunction (Mundt, Freed, & Greist, 2000). Memory items include repeating questions, forgetting appointments, and needing reminders for basic chores. Personality and mood items include being sad, losing interest in things, irritability or suspiciousness; functional items include trouble with driving, managing affairs, and basic self-care. The 11-item questionnaire has a cutoff score of 4, and is a useful screening tool for an in-person or phone interview.

Metacognition is another useful factor to assess in determining the needs of patient and family, although the several available excellent in-depth instruments are quite time consuming. Anderson and Tranel (1989) suggested asking patients to rate the severity of their problems in several domains (e.g., language, attention, memory, visuospatial, executive functioning) from *no problems* to *significant problems* and then comparing these ratings with empirical test results to assess patients' accuracy. Awareness of deficit is related not only to cognitive function but also to functional abilities (LaBuda & Lichtenberg, 1999). Lack of awareness was associated with decreased performance-based instrumental ADLs even when cognition was controlled for.

Brief performance-based cognitive measures are also important and should be integrated with the environmental demands. MacNeill and Lichtenberg (2000) detailed a series of questions that allow one to determine the priority of a cognitive evaluation for immediate treatment planning needs. The questions focus on awareness of cognitive deficits by patient and caregiver, the need for the patient to perform advanced and/or basic self-care skills without supervision, and whether the patient lives alone. The last is a key variable because nearly 40% of older rehabilitation patients live alone (Lichtenberg, 1998).

Ruchinskas and Curyto (2003) listed a number of validated cognitive measures for brief screening needs. These included the Mini-Mental State Examination (MMSE; Folstein, Folstein, & McHugh, 1975), Dementia Rating Scale (Mattis, 1988), Neurobehavioral Cognitive Status Examination

(Cognistat; Kiernan, Mueller, Langston, & Van Dyke, 1987), Clock Drawing (Sunderland et al., 1989), the Repeatable Battery for the Assessment of Neuropsychological Status (RBANS; Randolph, 1998) and the Cambridge Examination for Mental Disorders in the Elderly (CAMCOG; Blessed, Black, Butler, & Kay, 1991). The characteristics of each test with regard to items covered, administration time, and some general comments can be found in Table 5.1. The MMSE is the most common screening measure used in clinical practices. The 30-item test consists of general orientation questions, memory and language questions, as well as a simple praxis task. The authors pointed out that demographic variables (i.e., age and education, primarily) should be factored into test interpretation. Indeed, this is the biggest challenge for all cognitive screening tests; age and education influences often lead to overestimates of cognitive impairment in geriatric rehabilitation patients. Thus, care needs to be taken to use appropriate norms for patients who are either very old (i.e., over 85), poorly educated (i.e., below 8 years), or both.

A newer alternative to cognitive screening includes the use of computer- or Internet-based assessments.

TABLE 5.1

Characteristics of Common Cognitive Screening Measures

Test	Items covered	Time to administer	Comments
Mini-Mental State Examination (MMSE; Folstein, Folstein, & McHugh, 1975)	Orientation, language, memory, simple copying	10 minutes	Most widely used screening test for dementia across medical settings
MacNeill-Lichtenberg Decision Tree (MLDT; MacNeill & Lichtenberg, 2000)	Orientation, fluency	5 minutes	Does not require good vision or use of hands
Neurobehavioral Cognitive Status Examination (Cognistat; Kiernan, Mueller, Langston, & Van Dyke, 1987)	Orientation, memory, calculation, attention, reasoning	5–15 minutes	Uses a single item in each domain as an initial screen
Dementia Rating Scale (DRS; Mattis, 1988)	Orientation, initiation, memory, visuospatial skills, abstract reasoning	20–45 minutes	Less of a floor effect than other screening instruments
Repeatable Battery for the Assessment of Neuropsychological Status (RBANS; Randolph, 1998)	Immediate and delayed memory, language, attention, visuospatial skills	30 minutes	Created to characterize abnormal cognitive decline in older adults
Cambridge Examination for Mental Disorders in the Elderly (CAMCOG; Blessed, Black, Butler, & Kay, 1991)	Orientation, memory, initiation, reasoning, visuospatial skills	30–45 minutes	Created for use with older adults

These assessment instruments generally do not demand any level of computer expertise, usually requiring the use of only the number and/or arrow keys. Our research group has been involved in the validation of the Cognitive Screening Test (Lichtenberg et al., 2006), an Internet-based screening test. The Cognitive Screening Test is voice automated and consists of three tasks that take 8 to 10 minutes in total. The first task simply familiarizes the older person with the number and arrow keys of the keypad. The other tasks involve selective reminding (i.e., tests of learning 10 items in specific locations in a cabinet across three trials). There is a delayed recall portion of this test as well. The executive functioning test assesses individuals' abilities to inhibit learned responses and exhibit new responses. The first task has the patient hit the identical number key (1 or 2) that is shown. The next task has the patient reverse the number key (e.g., press the 2 key when a 1 is shown). Measures of both speed and accuracy are taken. In a study of 102 geriatric medical patients, the Cognitive Screening Test demonstrated a sensitivity of .80 and specificity of .88 compared with physician diagnoses made blind to CST results. These clinical utility indices were 15 points better than the MMSE, even when age and education were integrated into the screening. The advantages of the computerized assessments include standard administration of tests, but more particularly, the ability to use age and education in interpreting screening test results.

Depression

Several national databases have found extremely high rates of mental health problems in older medical patients, paramount among which is depression, with estimated prevalence rates ranging from 30% to 44%. Depression is twice as prevalent in medical rehabilitation patients as in community-dwelling elders. Studies have found that 30% to 40% of older medical rehabilitation patients suffer from significant depression (Lichtenberg, 1998; Diamond, Holroyd, Macciocchi, & Felsenthal, 1995), whereas the community estimate was 15% (Blazer, 2003). Depression in medical rehabilitation patients is unrelated to demographic variables but significantly related to functional abilities.

Depression is becoming recognized as a chronic condition best treated through multiple modalities, many of which are extremely relevant to the rehabilitation process and methods. Several etiologies of depression have been described; the treatments based on these etiologies are briefly presented.

The most common etiology of depression involves the neurotransmitter model, particularly some disruption of norepinephrine, dopamine, and/or serotonin. In the past decade the selective serotonin reuptake inhibitors (SSRIs) have become the medication of choice to treat depression; however, their popularity may be greater than their effectiveness. A review of the studies that were used in the U.S. Food and Drug Administration approval process for the SSRIs found efficacy essentially identical to that of the tricyclic antidepressants (i.e., 35%–40% of persons improved significantly), but the SSRIs had a much lower discontinuation rate because of side effects (Newhouse, 1996). Antidepressant medications can clearly be useful in treating depression, but it would be unwise to routinely use medications alone without other modalities of treatment.

A second etiology is based on activity limitation theory. Briefly, the presence of a disease is linked to depression only when the disease limits the desired activity of the individual (Franks, Lichtenberg, MacNeill, & Bank, 2003). Franks et al. found strong relations between advanced ADLs and depressive symptoms in a geriatric rehabilitation population. Accordingly, treatments to improve strength and conditioning (e.g., aerobic and resistance exercise), thereby increasing activity level, have shown promising results in reducing depression (Singh, Clements, & Singh, 2001). Rehabilitation psychologists should work closely with their colleagues in medicine and physical and occupational therapy before determining a specific exercise intervention for frail elders. It will be the rare exception when exercise is not appropriate for the patient.

A third etiology, based on neuron degeneration, is the Vascular Depression Hypothesis (Alexopoulos, 1997). This view postulates that depression is more likely to occur in those who have vascular risk, purportedly through microvascular changes in white matter. Mast, MacNeill, and Lichtenberg (2004) examined rates of depression in three groups of geriatric rehabilitation patients: those with stroke, those without stroke but with vascular risk factors (e.g., atrial fibrillation, diabetes, hypertension), and those without either stroke or vascular risk factors. The prevalence of depressive symptoms did not differ among the three groups (i.e., they were essentially at 30% for each), but when a threshold model was used (i.e., more than two risk factors), depression prevalence significantly increased from 30% to 47% in the nonstroke, vascular risk group. The authors viewed this finding as evidence for "vascular burden." The vascular burden theory was further supported in a 4-year study (Krishnan, Mast, Ficker, Lawhorne, & Lichtenberg, 2005) of older adults without stroke, which found that depression, in the presence of vascular burden, accounted for the most variance in predicting occurrence of a stroke. Whereas 58% of those with depression had a first stroke during the follow-up period, only 4% of those without depression did so. The authors wondered whether depression in the face of vascular burden is a strong warning signal of imminent stroke. Rehabilitation psychologists can play valuable roles by assessing adherence to medical advice aimed at reducing vascular risk factors and by educating or intervening with noncompliant patients.

A fourth etiology, the cognitive–behavioral approach, is a better known psychological theory of depression. Although initiating a cognitively oriented therapeutic approach in a rehabilitation setting may be difficult, incorporating behavioral treatments tends to be easier. Lichtenberg et al. (1998) and others (Sood, Cisek, Zimmerman, Zaleski, & Fillmore, 2003) have provided preliminary evidence for the efficacy of depression treatment using behavioral techniques. This method is based on classic Lewinsohnian theory (Lewinsohn & Graf, 1973) that suggests mood is variable (i.e., largely determined by a person's daily experiences) and modifiable. The rehabilitation process, therefore, is structured to incorporate pleasant events into the patient's treatment day in an effort to decrease patients' focus on unpleasant events and thereby improve mood.

A fifth etiology of depression involves reaction to loss and grief, such as the effects of loss in widow-

hood. In the Health and Retirement Survey (Turvey, Carney, Arndt, Wallace, & Herzog, 1999), depression rates after 3 years were three times higher in those who had been widowed than they were in non-widowed individuals. Symptoms of depression and normal grief share considerable overlap in early grief (e.g., trouble concentrating, poor sleep, crying, poor appetite), with 30% of the widowed sample reporting these in the 1st month after grief. After a year, depression prevalence decreased to 12% for the widowed individuals and remained steady for the following 2 years. Worden (1991) referred to depression that lasts well into the grief process as a common factor in complicated grief. The healing process of grief becomes stymied by the presence of depression, making it imperative to treat the depression.

In sum, depression in late life can have multiple etiologies and influences, and it can be treated through numerous modalities, including medical, psychological, and physical approaches. It is clear that depression in late life puts an older adult at higher risk of mortality and morbidity, as well as a significantly lower quality of life, underscoring the importance of treatment of depression in older adults.

EMERGING ROLES FOR REHABILITATION PSYCHOLOGISTS

Despite the heavy emphasis on depression and dementia, other important behavioral health issues arise in the daily work of rehabilitation psychologists. Although these behavioral health issues are commonly seen in younger rehabilitation populations, it is only in the past 10 years that they have been noticed in and applied to and tailored for older adults.

Pain

Tait (1999) and Yonan and Wegener (2003) discussed pain assessment and treatments in geriatric rehabilitation. Tait provided examples of simple instruments to assess pain severity and impact, including visual analog scales, a pain diary, and the Pain Attitude Scale, which assesses a behavioral feature critical to successful coping with pain. Finally, the Pain Disability Index is provided to assist clinicians in understanding the influence of pain on self-care and other important functional skills. Yonan and

Wegener provided guidelines for the treatment of pain in older adults.

Cognitive–behavioral theory underlies pain interventions by rehabilitation psychologists. Pain beliefs and expectancies about treatment effectiveness are important to evaluate and address because they have important implications for success of treatment. Patients who believe their pain is intractable and uncontrollable can benefit from education about pain and its response to treatments. Those willing to engage in cognitive–behavioral treatment can be helped to identify coping strategies such as diverting attention away from pain, and reinterpreting pain sensations. Patient self-monitoring for adherence to treatment as well as involvement of caregivers will increase the effectiveness of treatment (see chap. 7, this volume).

Sleep Disturbance

Sleep disorders represent another syndrome in which behavioral aspects of coping greatly influence treatment outcomes. Trevorrow (1999) documented common sleep changes associated with aging, and Stepanski, Rybarczyk, Lopez, & Steven (2003) discussed the high prevalence of sleep problems in older adults, noting that sleepiness affects the quality of both mental and motor performance. These authors provided an interview schedule with which to evaluate sleep disorders. As with virtually all geriatric conditions, a multimodal approach is needed for optimal assessment and treatment. Underlying medical conditions can be primary or contributing causes of sleep disorders (Treverrow, 1999). Although these problems may not be unique to older adults, it is only recently that sleep disorders have been regularly recognized and treated in older adults.

There are three main psychological approaches to sleep disorder interventions: stimulus control, sleep restriction, and cognitive–behavioral approaches. The first two arise from behavioral paradigms specific for sleep, whereas the last applies cognitive–behavioral therapy approaches to sleep problems. *Stimulus control* refers to ways that sleep is better tied to a bedroom. Watching television, reading in bed, and lounging in bed are strongly discouraged so that the bedroom is linked more tightly to sleep preparation and sleep itself. Sleep restriction is a more intense technique that actually schedules a sleep debt for people by making them stay up later and yet wake up at the same time. This partial sleep deprivation strengthens the person's sleep system. Finally, cognitive–behavioral therapies help prevent patients' catastrophizing about their sleep problems, reduce their fears regarding sleep, and improve their ability to cope, thereby influencing the quality of sleep.

Substance Abuse

Alcohol and other substance misuse and abuse is another emerging area for geriatric rehabilitation psychological assessment and intervention. Alcohol use disorders include the clinical problems of alcohol abuse and dependence. (For criteria, see the *Diagnostic and Statistical Manual of Mental Disorders,* 4th ed.; American Psychiatric Association, 1994). The field has come to recognize an additional category of alcohol problems, *at-risk use,* which refers to an amount of drinking in older adults that puts them at risk of problems. As a person ages, much less alcohol is required to produce an elevated blood alcohol level and thus more than seven drinks per week is classified as putting a person at risk (Lawton Barry & Blow, 1999). *Alcohol abuse* refers to a level of use that has directly contributed to negative medical, social, or psychological conditions. Brief assessment tools (Lawton Barry & Blow, 1999) include the Geriatric version of the Michigan Alcohol Screening Test (MAST-G; Blow et al., 1992), both short and long version, the CAGE (Ewing, 1984) questions, and the Alcohol Use Disorders Identification Test (AUDIT; Fleming, Barry, & MacDonald, 1991).

Although more severe problems with alcohol require specialized techniques, a range of interventions, including brief motivational interviewing, can reduce at-risk drinking in older people (Blow & Lawton Barry, 2000). These authors found a significant reduction in both quantity of drinking and episodes of binge drinking for those who underwent brief interventions. Research on alcohol abuse in older rehabilitation patients is scarce, however. Lichtenberg (1998) demonstrated a high prevalence of self-reported drinking problems among the young-old (i.e., ages 60–79) in an urban population, but no treatment protocols have been evaluated.

Despite the scarcity of research on the topic, it remains a central clinical issue for older patients.

SUMMARY AND CONCLUSIONS

Older adults, particularly the older-old (i.e., those over age 85), will soon comprise the majority of medical rehabilitation patients. Rehabilitation psychologists must thus be familiar with basic geriatric syndromes and be able to integrate the principles and practices of geropsychology into their daily work. The recent geropsychology guidelines of the American Psychological Association (APA, 2004) should be a sine qua non of rehabilitation psychology training. Rehabilitation psychologists should also become familiar with the major geriatric syndromes of disability, frailty, and comorbidity. Although overlapping, these syndromes are not synonymous. Frailty describes an advanced process of multisystem failure, whereas disability includes both minor and major changes in functioning with preserved ability to perform valued roles. Comorbidity is related to the other concepts but it refers to the presence of several disease conditions (e.g., diabetes, arthritis, depression). These syndromes interact with age and age-related changes in different ways. Whereas both disability and frailty are directly related to age in medical rehabilitation patients, comorbidity is not. Younger-old medical rehabilitation patients typically suffer from the same number of disease conditions, as do older-old patients. Thus, uncontrolled comorbid disease states likely lead to premature death for many younger-old rehabilitation patients. The import for rehabilitation psychologists of geriatric notions such as disability, frailty, and comorbidity lies in their relation to comorbid mental health disorders and implications for discharge planning.

Rehabilitation teams rely on rehabilitation psychologists for the detection of cognitive disorders and for an assessment of how these disorders affect discharge planning. Detection of dementia requires an understanding of normal aging patterns, the early behavioral and personality markers of disorders such as Alzheimer's disease, and training in cognitive assessment. Cognitive assessment no longer serves simply to establish a diagnosis. It is now para-mount that cases with suspected dementia are prioritized correctly and that test results are linked to discharge planning and functional skills of the patient. Several brief cognitive screening tests, validated for use in older adults, can be valuable tools for the rehabilitation psychologist. Novel, computer-based cognitive screening tests are also becoming more available.

The detection and treatment of depression represent a second essential role for rehabilitation psychologists working with older adults. We recommend a broad multimodal view of both etiology and treatment of late life depression. In particular, an advanced understanding of vascular depression is forcing rehabilitation psychologists to reconceptualize their views of depression. The effects of vascular disease and burden (i.e., prestroke) on late-life depression and comorbid executive dysfunction are well documented and suggest that chronic disease management, along with cognitive–behavioral and other treatment techniques, are important in the treatment of late life depression. Etiologies such as neurotransmitter disturbances, grief and loss, major life stress, and activity limitation are other important aspects of late life depression.

Clinical research in geropsychology has resulted in improved tools for assessment of cognitive, depressive, and other behavioral disorders. APA (2004) published guidelines for psychological practice with older adults that encourage psychologists to be aware of ageism and ageist attitudes. The guidelines also direct psychologists to be familiar with psychological factors and psychopathologies unique to older adults and to appreciate the importance of collaborating with other members of the interdisciplinary health care team. The APA guidelines contain excellent citations of critical information for assessment and intervention related to older adults. Rehabilitation psychologists, although generally skilled in understanding many medical disorders, may need to improve their knowledge of specific abilities relative to the assessment and treatment of the aging.

The changing demography, with increases in the oldest-old population, coupled with the better distinctions among geriatric syndromes, will bring new types of patient problems to the attention of rehabilitation psychology. Understanding the relation of cognitive disorders or mental health to issues of frailty will require further studies. The past decade has witnessed expanded knowledge in the areas of cognitive assessment, depression treatment, and behavioral health with older adults. The number and types of services available from rehabilitation psychologists is growing steadily. In the future, rehabilitation psychologists are likely to find more opportunities for clinical interventions and assessment with older adults.

References

Alexopoulos, G. S., Meyers, B. S., Young, R. C., Kakuma, T., Silbersweig, D., & Charlson, M. (1997). Clinically defined vascular depression. *American Journal of Psychiatry, 154,* 562–565.

American Psychiatric Association. (1994). *Diagnostic and statistical manual of mental disorders* (4th ed.). Washington, DC: Author.

American Psychological Association. (2004). Guidelines for psychological practice with older adults. *American Psychologist, 59,* 236–260.

Anderson, S., & Tranel, D. (1989). Awareness of disease states following cerebral infarction, dementia and head trauma: Standardized assessment. *The Clinical Neuropsychologist, 3,* 327–339.

Arfken, C. L., Lichtenberg, P. A., & Kuiken, T. (1998). Importance of comorbid illnesses in predicting mortality for geriatric rehabilitation. *Topics in Geriatric Rehabilitation, 13,* 69–76.

Blazer, D. (2003). Depression in late life: Review and commentary. *Journal of Gerontology: Medical Sciences, 58A,* 249–265.

Blessed, G., Black, S., Butler, T., & Kay, D. (1991). The diagnosis of dementia in the elderly: A comparison of CAMCOG, the AGECAT program, the MMSE, and some short rating scales. *British Journal of Psychiatry, 159,* 193–198.

Blow, F. C., Brower, K. J., Schulenberg, J. E., Demo-Dannaberg, L. M., Young, J. P., & Beresford, T. P. (1992). The Michigan Alcohol Screening Test-Geriatric Version (MAST-G): A new elderly specific screening. *Alcoholism: Clinical and Experimental Research, 19,* 372.

Blow, F. C., & Lawton Barry, K. (2000). Advances in alcohol screening and brief intervention with older adults. *Advances in Medical Psychotherapy, 10,* 107–124.

Centers for Disease Control and Prevention. (2005). *Physical activity and good nutrition: Essential elements to prevent chronic diseases and obesity 2005.* Retrieved August 30, 2005, from http://www.cdc.gov/nchs/hdi.htm

Diamond, P. T., Holroyd, S., Macciocchi, S. N., & Felsenthal, G. (1995). Prevalence of depression and outcome on the geriatric rehabilitation unit. *American Journal of Physical Medicine & Rehabilitation, 74,* 214–217.

Dunlop, D. D., Semanik, P., Song, J., Manheim, L. M., Shih, V., & Chang, R. W. (2005). Risk factors for functional decline in older adults with arthritis. *Arthritis and Rheumatism, 52,* 1274–1282.

Evans, D. A., Funkenstein, H., Albert, M. S., Scherr, P. A., Cook, N. R., Chown, M. J., et al. (1989). Prevalence of Alzheimer's disease in a community population of older persons. *Journal of the American Medical Association, 262,* 2551–2556.

Ewing, J. A. (1984). Detecting alcoholism: The CAGE Questionnaire. *Journal of the American Medical Association, 252,* 27.

Federal Interagency Forum on Aging-Related Statistics. (2000). Older Americans 2000: Key indicators of well-being. Retrieved May 25, 2004, from http://www.agingstats.gov

Ferrucci, L., Guralnik, J. M., Simonsick, E., Salive, M. E., Corti, C., & Langlois, J. (1996). Progressive versus catastrophic disability: A longitudinal view of the disablement process. *Journals of Gerontology Series A: Biological Sciences and Medical Sciences, 51A*(3), M123–M130.

Fleming, M., Barry K. L., & MacDonald, R. (1991). The Alcohol Use Disorders Identification Test. *International Journal of Addiction, 26,* 1173–1185.

Folstein, M. F., Folstein, S. E., & McHugh, P. R. (1975). Mini-mental state. *Journal of Psychiatric Research, 12,* 189–198.

Franks, M. M., Lichtenberg, P. A., MacNeill, S. E., & Bank, A. L. (2003). Activity limitations and depression: Perspectives of older African American women and their close companions. *Rehabilitation Psychology, 48,* 50–55.

Fried, L. P., Bandeen-Roche, K., Kasper, J. D., & Guralnik, J. M. (1999). Association of comorbidity with disability in older women: The Women's Health and Aging Study. *Journal of Clinical Epidemiology, 52,* 27–37.

Fried, L. P., Ferrucci, L., Darer, J., Williamson, J. D., & Anderson, G. (2004). Untangling the concepts of disability, frailty, and cormorbidity: Implications for improved targeting and care. *Journals of Gerontology: Medical Sciences, 59,* 255–263.

Gill, T. M., Richardson, E. D., & Tinetti, M. E. (1995). Evaluating the risk of dependence in activities of daily living among community-living older adults with mild to moderate cognitive impairment.

Journals of Gerontology Series A: Biological Sciences and Medical Sciences, 50A(5), M235–M241.

Grigsby, J., Kaye, K., Baxter, J., Shetterly, S. M., & Hamman, R. F. (1998). Executive cognitive abilities and functional status among community-dwelling older persons in the San Luis Valley Health and Aging Study. *Journal of the American Geriatrics Society, 46,* 590–596.

Guccione, A. A., Felson, D. T., Anderson, J. J., Anthony, J. M., Zhang, Y., Wilson, P. W., et al. (1994). The effects of specific medical conditions on the functional limitations of elders in the Framingham Study. *American Journal of Public Health, 84,* 351–358.

Hanks, R. A., & Lichtenberg, P. A. (1996). Physical, psychological and social outcomes in geriatric rehabilitation patients. *Archives of Physical Medicine and Rehabilitation, 77,* 783–792.

Jette, A. M., & Keyser, J. J. (2003). Disability models: Implications for arthritis, exercise, and physical activity interventions. *Arthritis and Rheumatism, 49,* 114–120.

Kauppi, M., Hartikainen, S., Kautiainen, H., Laiho, K., & Sulkava, R. (2005). Capability for daily activities in old people with rheumatoid arthritis: A population based study. *Annals of Rheumatic Diseases, 64,* 56–58.

Kiernan, R. J., Mueller, J., Langston, J. W., & Van Dyke, C. (1987). The Neurobehavioral Cognitive Status Examination: A brief but quantitative approach to cognitive assessment. *Annals of Internal Medicine, 107,* 481–485.

Krishnan, M. S., Mast, B. T., Ficker, L. J., Lawhorne, L., & Lichtenberg, P. A. (2005). The effects of preexisting depression on cerebrovascular health outcomes in geriatric continuing care. *Journal of Gerontology: Medical Sciences, 60A,* 915–919.

LaBuda, J., & Lichtenberg, P. A. (1999). The role of cognition, depression, and awareness of deficit in predicting geriatric rehabilitation patients' IADL performance. *The Clinical Neuropsychologist, 13,* 258–267.

Lawton Barry, K., & Blow, F. C. (1999). Screening and assessment of alcohol problems in older adults. In P. A. Lichtenberg (Ed.), *Handbook of Assessment in Clinical Gerontology* (pp. 243–269). New York: Wiley.

Lewinsohn, P. M., & Graf, M. (1973). Pleasant activities and depression. *Journal of Consulting and Clinical Psychology, 41,* 261–268.

Lichtenberg, P. A. (1998). *Mental health practice in geriatric health care settings.* New York: Haworth Press.

Lichtenberg, P. A., Johnson, A. S., Erlanger, D. M., Kaushik, T., Maddens, M. E., Imam, K., et al. (2006). Enhancing cognitive screening in geriatric care: Use of an internet-

based system. *International Journal of Healthcare Information Systems and Informatics, 1,* 47–57.

Lichtenberg, P. A., Kimbarow, M. L., Wall, J. R., Roth, R. E., & MacNeill, S. E. (1998). *Depression in geriatric medical and nursing home patients: A treatment manual.* Detroit, MI: Wayne State University Press.

MacNeill, S. E., & Lichtenberg, P. A. (2000). The MacNeill-Lichtenberg Decision Tree: A unique method of triaging mental health problems in older medical rehabilitation patients. *Archives of Physical Medicine and Rehabilitation, 81,* 618–622.

Mast, B. T., MacNeill, S. E., & Lichtenberg, P. A. (1999). Geropsychological problems in medical rehabilitation: Dementia and depression among stroke and lower extremity fracture patients. *Journal of Gerontology: Medical Sciences, 54A,* M607–M612.

Mast, B. T., MacNeill, S. E., & Lichtenberg, P. A. (2004). Post stroke and vascular depression in geriatric rehabilitation patients. *American Journal of Geriatric Psychiatry, 12,* 84–92.

Mattis, S. (1988). *Dementia Rating Scale (DRS).* Odessa, FL: Psychological Assessment Resources.

Mundt, J. C., Freed, D. M., & Greist, J. H. (2000). Lay person-based screening for early detection of Alzheimer's disease: Development and validation of an instrument. *Journal of Gerontology: Psychological Science, 55B*(3), 163–170.

Newhouse, P. A. (1996). Use of serotonin selective reuptake inhibitors in geriatric depression. *Journal of Clinical Psychiatry, 57,* 12–22.

Ostir, G. V., Volpato, S., Kasper, J. D., Ferrucci, L., & Guralnik, J. M. (2001). Summarizing amount of difficulty in ADLs: A refined characterization of disability. Results from the women's health and aging study. *Aging, 13*(6), 465–472.

Phelan, E. A., Williams, B., Pennix, B. W., LoGerfo, J. P., & Leveille, S. G. (2004). Activities of daily living function and disability in older adults in a randomized trial of the health enhancement program. *Journals of Gerontology Series A: Biological Sciences and Medical Sciences, 59,* 838–843.

Randolph, C. (1998). *The repeatable battery for assessment of neuropsychological status.* New York: The Psychological Corporation.

Riley, K. P. (1999). Assessment of dementia in the older adult. In P. A. Lichtenberg (Ed.), *Handbook of assessment in clinical gerontology* (pp. 134–166). New York: Wiley.

Rosano, C., Simonsick, E. M., Harris, T. B., Kritchevsky, S. B., Brach, J., Yaffe, K., et al. (2005). Association between physical and cognitive function in healthy elderly: The health, aging and body composition study. *Neuroepidemiology, 24,* 8–14.

Ruchinskas, R. A., & Curyto, K. J. (2003). Cognitive screening in geriatric rehabilitation. *Rehabilitation Psychology, 48,* 14–22.

Seeman, T. E., Berkman, L. F., Charpentier, P. A., Blazer, D. G., Albert, M. S., & Tinetti, M. E. (1995). Behavioral and psychosocial predictors of physical performance: MacArthur studies of successful aging. *Journals of Gerontology Series A: Biological Sciences and Medical Sciences, 50,* M177–M183.

Sheridan, P. L., Solomont, J., Kowall, N., & Hausdorff, J. M. (2003). Influence of executive function on locomotor function: Divided attention increases gait variability in Alzheimer's disease. *Journal of the American Geriatrics Society, 51,* 1633–1637.

Singh, N. A., Clements, K. M., & Singh, M. A. (2001). The efficacy of exercise as a long-term antidepressant in elderly subjects. A randomized controlled trial. *Journal of Gerontology: Medical Sciences, 56A,* M497–M504.

Sood, J. R., Cisek, E., Zimmerman, J., Zaleski, E. H., & Fillmore, H. H. (2003). Treatment of depressive symptoms during short-term rehabilitation: An attempted replication of the DOUR project. *Rehabilitation Psychology, 48,* 44–49.

Stang, P. E., Brandenburg, N. A., Lane, M. C., Merikangas, K. R., Von Korff, M. R., & Kessler, R. C. (2006). Mental and physical comorbid conditions and days in role among persons with arthritis. *Psychosomatic Medicine, 68,* 152–158.

Stepanski, E., Rybarczyk, B., Lopez, M., & Steven, S. (2003). Assessment and treatment of sleep disorders in older adults: A review for rehabilitation psychologists. *Rehabilitation Psychology, 48,* 23–36.

Sunderland, T., Hill, J. L., Mellow, A. M., Lawlor, B. A., Gundersheimer, J., Newhouse, P. A., & Grafman, J. H. (1989). Clock drawing in Alzheimer's disease: A novel measure of dementia severity. *Journal of the American Geriatrics Society, 37,* 725–729.

Tabbarah, M., Crimmins, E. M., & Seeman, T. E. (2002). The relationship between cognitive and physical performance: MacArthur studies of successful aging. *Journals of Gerontology Series A: Biological Sciences and Medical Sciences, 57,* M228–M235.

Tait, R. (1999). Assessment of pain and response to treatment in older adults. In P. A. Lichtenberg (Ed.), *Handbook of assessment in clinical gerontology* (pp. 555–584). New York: Wiley.

Trevverow, T. (1999). Assessing sleep functioning in older adults. In P. A. Lichtenberg (Ed.), *Handbook of assessment in clinical gerontology* (pp. 331–350). New York: Wiley.

Turner, R. S. (2003). Neurologic aspects of Alzheimer's disease. In P. A. Lichtenberg, D. L. Murman, & A. M. Mellow (Eds.), *Handbook of dementia: Psychological, neurological, & psychiatric perspectives* (pp. 1–25). Hoboken, NJ: Wiley.

Turvey, C., Carney, C., Arndt, S., Wallace, R., & Herzog, R. (1999). Conjugal loss and syndromal depression in a sample of elders aged 70 years or older. *American Journal of Psychiatry, 156,* 1596–1601.

Wang, L., van Belle, G., Kukull, W. B., & Larson, E. B. (2002). Predictors of functional change: A longitudinal study of nondemented people aged 65 and older. *Journal of the American Geriatrics Society, 50*(9), 1525–1534.

Worden, J. W. (1991). *Grief counseling and grief therapy.* New York: Springer Publishing Company.

Yonan, C. A., & Wegener, S. T. (2003). Assessment and management of pain in the older adult. *Rehabilitation Psychology, 48,* 4–13.

CHAPTER 6

PSYCHOLOGICAL REHABILITATION IN BURN INJURIES

Shelley Wiechman Askay and David Patterson

This chapter begins by addressing the demographics of people with burn injuries and moves on to a brief description of the physical rehabilitation that a person with a burn injury must endure. We then discuss rehabilitation models relevant to burn care and the various stages of psychosocial recovery that burn survivors encounter. We conclude by discussing various other topics relevant to burn care.

Patients with burn injuries are surviving after increasingly large and severe injuries and are consequently posing unique physical and psychological rehabilitation challenges, such as scarring, contractures, amputations, pain, and poor psychological adjustment. Most of the literature on burn injuries is devoted to the acute phase of hospitalization, particularly resuscitation efforts and surgical interventions. Because of the relative infancy of the field of burn rehabilitation, there is little research on effective interventions that can help with the long-term challenges, such as pain, depression, and posttraumatic stress disorder (PTSD) that these survivors face once they are discharged from the hospital.

DEMOGRAPHICS AND TRENDS

Although published demographics from burn centers in the United States are almost a decade old, they nonetheless provide insight into the occurrence, etiology, and trends of burn injuries. Burn injuries account for an estimated 70,000 hospitalizations annually (40,000 of these hospitalizations are children or adolescents), and 5,500 deaths in the United States alone (Brigham & McLoughlin, 1996; Rutan, 1998). The etiology of a burn injury is related to age. The most common cause of burns is hot water scalds, with children, older people, and people with disabilities being most prone to this type of injury. Male adolescents typically suffer burn injuries resulting from risk-taking behavior such as playing with fireworks or gasoline. People in certain occupations are at greater risk of burn injuries, including electricians and workers in the food service, chemical, and fuel industries (Rutan, 1998). The overwhelming majority of people who sustain burn injuries are men between the ages of 20 and 40.

The severity of burn injury is determined by the total body surface area of the burn and the depth of the burn. First degree or superficial burn injuries extend only into the epidermis. These burns rarely blister, are painful, and get better in 3 to 4 days without scarring. Partial thickness burns extend through the epidermis and into the dermis. Burns in this category are harder to classify initially; they may or may not require grafting and if left to heal on their own, will likely cause scarring. These burns are typically quite painful. Full thickness burns extend all the way through the dermis and into the subcutaneous fat. These burns will need to be excised and grafted so that they might heal.

This material is based in part on work supported by Grant R01 GM42725–09A1 (National Institutes of Health) and Grant H133A020103 (National Institute on Disability and Rehabilitation Research).

Moderate to severe burn injuries are almost always treated in surgical units and preferably in multidisciplinary burn centers verified by the American Burn Association (i.e., at least in the United States and Canada). The mission of most burn care, put simply, is to promote the healing of any open wound. As such, the practice of many burn centers is to debride burned skin on a daily or twice-daily basis to avoid infection and promote healing. This process involves scraping off the dead skin and washing the area. Burn injuries that lack the potential to heal on their own are typically treated with skin grafts. Such wound cleaning and grafting procedures are frequently painful for weeks. Resulting pain can be worse than that experienced with the initial burn injury and can wear on the best of a patient's coping mechanisms.

Over the past several years, there have been improvements in burn care, such as the development of comprehensive burn centers, advances in resuscitation, and surgical management of patients with large burns, that have resulted in improved survival rates for this population. There has even been federal funding from the National Institute on Disability Rehabilitation Research for model systems of care for burn injuries for both the acute phases of the burn as well as long-term management. Between 1985 and 1995, the age-adjusted death rate for burn injuries declined by 33% (Esselman, Thombs, Fauerbach, Magyar-Russell, & Price, 2005). For the psychologist, this means that a much larger population of burn survivors face the unique challenges of life after a burn injury.

PHYSICAL REHABILITATION PROBLEMS WITH BURNS

Individuals who survive large burn injuries, or even sustain small burn injuries over joints or other problematic areas, potentially have complex and long-term physical rehabilitation needs because of such secondary conditions as hypertrophic scarring, contractures, amputations, neuropathies, heterotropic ossification, and pain. Therefore, rehabilitation team members such as physical, occupational, and speech therapists, and rehabilitation psychologists are ideally incorporated into the multidisciplinary burn

team. At the conclusion of the acute phase of burn care, many patients will require a more intensive, inpatient rehabilitation program and continue to be followed in rehabilitation medicine, as well as in the surgery clinics. Treatment to prevent these complications includes aggressive range of motion exercises, pressure garments, and splints, and can be painful or uncomfortable for patients, making treatment adherence a challenge. Although we know that the incidence of hypertrophic scarring, contractures, neuropathies, and ongoing pain can be quite high, few randomized controlled trials have examined the efficacy of treatment for these conditions once they occur (Esselman et al., 2005).

PSYCHOLOGICAL REHABILITATION PROBLEMS WITH BURNS

Assumptions in the literature about the extent and nature of negative psychological reactions after a burn injury have mirrored those related to many other types of disabilities (Wright, 1959). Specifically, in early studies (Patterson et al., 1993), there was an inherent assumption that depression or other forms of psychopathology were almost universal reactions to a severe burn injury (Bernstein, 1976). Such studies viewed outcome in terms of psychiatric symptoms and listed high rates of them. Also characteristic of early reports on burn injuries were univariate, one-to-one causality models for predictor variables and outcome. Perhaps the most salient example of this was burn size. Medically driven reports automatically assumed (and often still do) that the larger the burn injury, the more severe the accompanying psychopathology. Furthermore, substantial disfigurement was believed to doom survivors to poor psychological outcome. Psychoanalytically driven models postulated that even if a patient appeared to present well psychologically, he or she was only masking the inevitable conflicts between the patient's self-worth and a society that values appearance and attractiveness (Bernstein, 1976).

Distress (rather than psychopathology) is an almost universal reaction to burn injuries, and societal response to disfigurement is a frequent challenge for survivors. However, early conceptualizations failed to explain observations of clinicians working in burn care and the findings of repeated, better designed studies; specifically, some survivors with massive burn areas (e.g., 80% of the body surface area) seemed to go through life largely untouched psychologically by their cosmetic and physical changes. This was the case both with adults (Patterson et al., 1993) and children with massive area burn injuries (Blakeney et al., 1993; Blakeney et al., 1998; Tarnowski, Rasnake, Linscheid, & Mulick, 1989). In contrast, people with small areas of scarred skin, even in areas that were largely hidden to the general public, were occasionally observed to be psychologically devastated by their injuries. Four decades of reports on the psychological outcome of burn survivors did little to explain such phenomena.

Research by rehabilitation psychologists proved to be useful in understanding these reactions to burns and in understanding that the adjustment of burn survivors was similar to that of people with other forms of disabilities, such as spinal cord injuries and amputations. Useful concepts from this literature were the "requirement of mourning," often assumed by an outsider (Wright, 1983), or the projections of health care workers on the patients. With regard to the latter point, Wright pointed out that people observe people with disabilities from an outsider's perspective. They assume that the person with a disability is adjusting to it as they would were they to be put in the same circumstances. As such, it was not surprising that burn team members rated patients' levels of depression higher and optimism lower than did the patients themselves (Adcock, Goldberg, Patterson, & Brown, 2000). Clinical writings erroneously assumed that patients underwent an orderly stage of psychological reactions in adjusting to their injuries (Wortman & Silver, 1989), whereas well-designed studies found that people with burn injuries, like those with any type of disability, do not traverse predictable stages of psychological recovery.

Predictions of suffering from burn injuries have been generated from studies that use biopsychosocial models of burn outcome (Fauerbach, Spence, & Patterson, 2006; Patterson et al., 1993). It is important that the influence of preinjury factors is often ignored in attempting to determine burn

psychological outcome, and such variables may be the most powerfully predictive (Patterson et al., 2003; Patterson & Jensen, 2003). Also often ignored are variables such as resiliency and hardiness in coping with trauma. Furthermore, the burn literature often fails substantially to acknowledge the interplay among preinjury variables, the nature of a burn injury and its care, patient coping skills, and social support, and the dynamic interplay between these factors and secondary complications (i.e., contractures, additional surgeries). When all factors are considered, it becomes more understandable that the size of a burn injury does little to predict how survivors will adjust. It is much more a matter of who the person is that sustains the injury, their environment and social support, and how these factors play out with the nature of burn rehabilitation over time.

PREINJURY FACTORS FOR PSYCHOLOGICAL RECOVERY

Several studies focus on the issue of premorbid psychopathology in people presenting at hospitals for burn care, and it may be useful to describe what such problems are as well as treatment implications. The available research largely supports the impression that individuals with burns severe enough to warrant hospital care often have preexisting chaos and dysfunction in their lives. Several reviews of the literature found that the incidence of mental illness and personality disorders was higher in burn unit patients than the general population (Kolman, 1983; Patterson et al., 1993; Patterson & Jensen, 2003). For example, Patterson et al. (1993) estimated that the presence of premorbid psychiatric disorders ranged between 28% and 75%, higher than expected in the general population. These disorders include depression, personality disorders, and substance abuse. Another study by Patterson et al. (2003) found patients with burn injuries scored higher on premorbid levels of psychological distress, anxiety, depression, and loss of behavioral and emotional control when compared with a national normative sample. These studies also found that individuals with preexisting psychopathology often cope with hospitalization through previously established, dysfunctional, and often disruptive, patterns. Such dysfunctional coping styles, in turn, had an adverse impact on hospital course that increased length of stay and led to more serious psychopathology on discharge. As an example, a burn injury and its subsequent treatment can often exacerbate depression in previously depressed patients, and treatment should obviously be offered through burn care.

Patients with personality disorders often cause great difficulty for the staff. Burn team members need to be educated about the personality disorder and understand that a person with a burn injury will not be "cured" of his or her personality disorder while on the burn unit. Psychologists or appropriately trained professionals in mental health should be consulted to devise behavior plans and to train staff in managing these disorders.

Often patients with substance abuse problems will have a strong reliance on the pharmacological management of pain. Depending on their drug of choice, they may have a lower pain tolerance or display more pain behaviors. Specialists, such as a pain relief service, may need to be consulted. Patients with substance abuse problems should still be offered nonpharmacological approaches and should be encouraged to use them. Medicating sufficiently for their acute pain through a regular medication schedule (i.e., vs. prn) will also help in managing pain for these patients. In the instance of premorbid anxiety and chronic pain problems, patients should be encouraged to use whatever coping techniques they have used effectively in the past. If they have not been exposed to nonpharmacological coping strategies, this may be an optimal time for patients to learn them; they may be more motivated to learn that these strategies can be useful in treating their preexisting problems. (See the discussion that follows on nonpharmacological approaches to pain management, such as hypnosis and distraction, for more details on this issue.)

Finally, although research on resiliency and posttraumatic growth is lacking in the burn field, clinical experience has shown that those who had effective coping skills and strong social support prior to the burn rely on these adaptive strategies to adjust to a burn injury. Although they should still be screened

for depression and anxiety and treated accordingly, they are much less likely to develop these disorders and, if they do, the disorders are less severe and usually temporary reactions.

Adjustment to a burn injury appears to involve a complex interplay between the preinjury characteristics of the survivor, the moderating environmental factors, and the nature of the injury and ensuing medical care. Actual rates of Axis I disorders, such as major depressive disorder and PTSD (*Diagnostic and Statistical Manual of Mental Disorders*, 4th ed. [*DSM–IV*]; American Psychiatric Association, 1994) are hard to pinpoint because of discrepancies in the literature. These discrepancies are likely caused by the use of different assessment tools and measurement at different time points, as well as by various methodological problems. For most people with burns large enough to require hospitalization, symptoms of depression and PTSD are common and considered to be in the realm of normal adjustment (Difede et al., 2002; Ehde, Patterson, Wiechman, & Wilson, 1999; Fauerbach et al., 1997). For the majority of people, the symptoms will subside over time with no treatment and will not develop into a diagnosable disorder. However, for a certain group of people, symptoms do not subside over time and may develop into an Axis I disorder. Also, patients may be so distressed by their symptoms that it affects their quality of life. For this reason, we recommend screening for these symptoms both during inpatient hospitalization and again during outpatient clinic visits and treating as indicated. We recommend a thorough psychological intake that includes a brief history and an assessment of pain level, quality of sleep, and symptoms of depression and PTSD. We have also found success in using brief screening tools such as the Patient Health Questionnaire, 9-item (PHQ-9; Spitzer, Williams, Kroenke, Hornyak, & McMurray, 2000) to supplement the intake.

PHASES OF REHABILITATION

Hospitalization for burn injuries may vary in length from less than 1 week to several months, depending on the severity of the burn and the presence of other medical complications. Although not to be taken literally as a "stage theory," the physical and emotional recovery of patients often differs according to their phase of care. The recovery period can usually be broken down into three phases: (a) the *resuscitative* or *critical phase,* typically spent in the intensive care unit (ICU); (b) the *acute phase,* when the patient is medically stable and able to begin rehabilitation; and (c) the *outpatient phase,* after the patient has been discharged from the hospital but continues in outpatient rehabilitation therapies. Although each phase represents a major milestone of recovery, each also comes with an expectation of an increase in independence, which can increase anxiety for the patient. The transition to each phase can be initially challenging, and the patient making the transition should be warned of the increase in independence and decreased level of nursing care. Each phase and the recommended corresponding treatments are described in the next section.

Critical Phase

Patients are usually treated in the ICU during both the resuscitative and critical phase and may stay there for weeks. Characteristics of the resuscitative phase include uncertainty regarding outcome and a struggle for survival, particularly if the burn is severe. During this phase, patients typically undergo repeated medical procedures and must contend with severe physiological stressors, including electrolyte imbalance, infections, anoxia, and edema. The environment of the ICU can be both overstimulating with its bright lights, machines, and multiple health care providers, yet also extremely monotonous, as patients are forced to lie in a hospital bed, often immobile for weeks at a time (Steiner & Clark, 1977). Coping with this environment is affected by a patient's cognitive changes, such as extreme drowsiness, confusion, disorientation, and delirium. These cognitive changes may be symptoms of infections, alcohol withdrawal, metabolic complications, or effects of high doses of medications (Perry & Blank, 1984).

Psychological intervention that extends beyond helping the patient feel safe and comfortable during this phase is of minimal value. Even if patients do become more alert, focusing on past or future con-

cerns may be counterproductive. The patient's primary task now is physical recovery, if not survival. Patients should be encouraged to cope with the frighteningly unusual circumstances of the ICU through whatever defenses are available to them, even primitive strategies such as denial and repression. Supportive psychological interventions should focus on immediate concerns, such as sleep, pain control, and protecting the coping strategies being used by the patient. Nonpharmacological approaches to pain controls, such as hypnosis and relaxation, can be effective during this time.

The medical staff can also effectively intervene psychologically during this early phase of recovery by working with the patient's family members. Understandably, family members may be anxious and distressed while observing the patient undergo painful treatment. The patient's coping ability is often influenced by cues from significant others. As family members express high levels of anxiety and stress, the patient may detect these cues and behave accordingly. It is important to help family members understand this process and encourage them to convey a sense of hope and calm that may be transmitted to the patient.

Acute Phase

The acute phase of recovery focuses on restorative care, such as nutritional support, excision and grafting, and topical wound care. Although patients are moved off the ICU to an environment that is more consistent and less intrusive, they still must undergo painful treatments. As cognition improves and patients become more alert during this phase, they face these painful procedures and physical therapy with less sedation. Consequently, symptoms of anxiety, depression, and grief may become more apparent, and pain and sleep disturbance will need to be addressed.

During this phase, when patients usually have the cognitive clarity to understand the impact of their trauma, medication management for anxiety, sleep, and depression should be considered. Brief counseling and psychoeducation may also be an option. Nonpharmacological approaches to pain management, such as relaxation, imagery, hypnosis, and virtual reality, become effective at this phase of recovery. During this phase, it can also be useful to provide brief interventions for alcohol and drug abuse. Hospitalization presents a window in which patients are receptive to evaluating the impact that such destructive habits may be having on their lives.

Outpatient Phase

The long-term phase of recovery typically begins when patients leave the hospital and are challenged to reintegrate into society. For patients with severe burn injuries, this phase likely involves continued physical rehabilitation on an outpatient basis, along with possible continuation of procedures such as dressing changes and cosmetic surgery. Patients may encounter daily pain during rehabilitation, and they may also be forced to confront cosmetic or other existential changes that have occurred as a result of their injury. This is a period when patients slowly regain a sense of competence while adjusting to the practical limitations of a burn injury. Studies have shown that the first year after hospitalization is a psychologically unique period of high distress (Patterson et al., 1993).

It can be helpful to make follow-up phone calls to patients after discharge or to continue to see them in the outpatient clinic to screen for symptoms of distress and to provide psychotherapy. It is likely that patients who have symptoms of distress in the months or years following discharge will need some sort of intervention, obviously matched to their symptoms. Because there have been few randomized controlled clinical trials specific to patients with burn injuries, treatments should be used that have been effective for nonburn patients with these psychological problems. For example, depressed burn survivors may benefit from a combination of medication, cognitive–behavior therapy, and exercise. Exposure therapy may be effective for burn survivors with PTSD (Foa, 1995). A multidisciplinary team approach should also be used because patients can benefit from support from a vocational or rehabilitation counselor to address issues related to return to work. Social workers will also be needed to assist with a variety of matters, including financial resources. Support groups and

peer counseling visitation may also be useful if carefully monitored by trained professionals (Williams et al., 2002).

NONPHARMACOLOGICAL APPROACHES TO PAIN MANAGEMENT

Both pharmacological and nonpharmacological (e.g., relaxation, distraction, imagery, hypnosis) treatments are necessary to control pain in the burn patient. There is considerable empirical evidence for the efficacy of nonpharmacological treatments, particularly when used as an adjunct to opioid medications (Frenay, Faymonville, Devlieger, Albert, & Vanderkelen, 2001; Hoffman, Doctor, Patterson, Carrougher, & Furness, 2000; Hoffman, Patterson, Carrougher, & Sharar, 2001; Patterson & Ptacek, 1997). The impact of anxiety on pain is often underestimated and its treatment overlooked. Because anxiety greatly exacerbates pain, it is important to begin nonpharmacological treatments as early as possible in the patient's stay so as to help mitigate anticipatory anxiety and the subsequent anxiety–pain cycle (Patterson, Ptacek, Carrougher, & Sharar, 1997). Rehabilitation psychologists with unique expertise in the nonpharmacological approaches to pain management can implement the intervention themselves or teach other staff to use some of these techniques.

COPING STRATEGIES

Thurber, Martin-Herz, and Patterson (2000) described coping strategies of burn patients in the form of a continuum based on control. Patient responses in these circumstances lie on a continuum ranging from turning over control to the health care professional and desiring little information to seeking as much information as possible and participating in the procedures. Patients who wish to give up control have a tendency toward cognitive avoidance and will use and benefit from various types of distraction techniques to avoid the painful stimuli. These patients are said to have more of an *avoidant* coping style. In contrast, patients who seek information about the procedure and like to participate as much as they can may find distraction techniques distressing, as they have to give up too much control. They are said to have more of an *approach* coping style (Martin-Herz, Thurber, & Patterson, 2000). It is important to note that both coping styles can be adaptive, and it is best for the burn team to identify and support an individual's coping style rather than try to change their natural response. Health care professionals may also find that patients may change their coping style depending on the procedure. For example, a patient may find it is easier to use distraction techniques for short procedures such as receiving injections, whereas they are more comfortable attending to details of their long wound care sessions and participating whenever appropriate. Patients may also alter their coping style as they become more familiar and comfortable with the environment. A person's coping style needs to be assessed prior to choosing a nonpharmacological pain management technique. This can best be done by asking a patient how he or she typically responds

to stressful medical procedures, such as going to the dentist or getting shots.

The approach–avoidance coping continuum and the interventions that fall along this continuum are illustrated in Figure 6.1. Although techniques such as imagery or hypnosis may fall into various categories on the continuum, depending on the outcome goals and script, the continuum is a useful heuristic to guide clinicians in choosing an appropriate technique. Details of the various interventions listed are beyond the scope of this chapter, but many resources are available to assist in mastering these skills (Bensen, 1975; Gawain, 1978; Kabat-Zinn, 1990).

BODY IMAGE DISSATISFACTION

Burn injuries can cause significant changes in appearance, whether from scarring, contractures, changes in skin pigmentation, or amputations. The impact that these physical changes have on self-esteem and body

---

Control Coping Continuum

Psychologically distant
from burn wound care

	Avoidance	Hypnotic analgesia Guided imagery Distraction Virtual reality
	Relaxation	Deep breathing Muscle relaxation Positive reinforcement
	Operant Techniques	Quota system Preparation for surgery
	Information	Preparation for wound care Preparation for discharge
	Cognitive Restructuring	Thought stopping Reappraisal Regulate the pace of wound care
	Participation	Help staff perform wound care Perform own wound care

Psychologically close
to burn wound care

FIGURE 6.1. Control coping continuum. From "Psychological principles of burn wound pain in children. I: Theoretical framework," by C. A. Thurber, S. P. Martin-Herz, & D. R. Patterson, 2002, *Journal of Burn Care Rehabilitation, 21,* 376–387. Copyright 2002 by Lippincott Williams & Wilkins. Used with permission.

image has only recently been studied (Fauerbach et al., 2002). Several studies of risk factors for the development of poor body image found that burn characteristics, such as the visibility of the scar, depression, female gender, and coping style, best predicted body image dissatisfaction (Abdullah et al., 1994; Fauerbach et al., 2002; Lawrence, Fauerbach, Heinberg, & Doctor, 2004). An additional predictor of body image dissatisfaction is the importance that a patient placed on their appearance before the burn injury. In other words, if a person did not place much importance on his or her appearance before the burn, he or she tends to be much less distressed by the consequences of disfigurement (Fauerbach et al., 2002).

A variety of approaches have been used to address cosmetic concerns in those who present in the treatment setting (Fauerbach et al., 2006; Pruzinsky & Cash, 1990). Surprisingly, there have been no published studies on the efficacy of these various treatments. Most treatments focus on cognitive–behavioral strategies to address a person's appraisal of his or her appearance, to teach adaptive coping strategies, and to introduce social skills that enhance self esteem and improve social competence. One program designed to enhance self-esteem is the Changing Faces program in Great Britain (Partridge, 1997), which includes a hospital-based image enhancement and social skills program, along with a series of publications for patients dealing with aspects of facial disfigurement. The program, based on a cognitive–behavioral model developed jointly by a burn survivor and psychologists, allows people to explore their internal reactions to the response of others toward their disfigurement and also to access a number of adaptive behaviors in response to the inevitable negative societal responses to disfigurement. Fauerbach et al. (2002) found that adult burn survivors who used approach and avoidant coping (both of which are emotion-focused strategies) during acute hospitalization had higher levels of body image dissatisfaction at 2 months postdischarge than those who used only one strategy or an alternative coping method. As a result, they proposed using a motivational model of adjustment to assess a person's ambivalence about coping strategies and to teach adaptive coping skills that could potentially prevent future body image dissatisfaction.

SELF-INJURY

Burn units must often manage patients with self-inflicted burns; rates of admission for self-inflicted burn injuries range from 1% to 9% (Daniels, Fenley, Powers, & Cruse, 1991; Scully & Hutcherson, 1983) of the total of such admissions. Although a small percentage, these patients are often difficult to manage and require considerable staffing resources. Often, they have a diagnosis of borderline personality disorder characterized by a pervasive pattern of instability in interpersonal relationships and affect, as well as marked impulsivity across many contexts according to *DSM–IV*. The nurturing environment of medical inpatient units, such as a burn unit, may be quite appealing while the long length of hospitalization and the relationships that are formed with nurses and therapists set the stage for intense, interpersonal conflict with patients with this disorder.

Several behavioral management strategies can minimize frustration and conflict with these patients (Wiechman, Ehde, Wilson, & Patterson, 2000). First, they should be treated on an outpatient basis whenever possible. If hospitalization is needed, consider admitting them to an inpatient psychiatric unit and offering burn nursing support for dressing changes. The lower intensity of the outpatient setting and the inpatient psychiatric unit will be less rewarding for these patients. If an inpatient admission to a burn unit is necessary, it is usually important to consult hospital psychology or psychiatric services. These services may be willing to provide staff training on managing these patients. However, with repeated admissions, it may actually be disadvantageous to have mental health professionals involved, as the goal is often to not reward admissions for self-harm with any more attention than is necessary. Finally, having primary nurses when possible and having a designated burn team member to discuss the treatment plan and pain medication management will lead to better communication, less confusion, and may reduce attempts to "split" staff (Wiechman et al., 2000).

MOTIVATIONAL ISSUES

Patients are often reluctant to participate in their burn care and therapies. We believe that this is often because they are exhibiting learned helplessness in response to the overwhelming nature of burn care. They may regard repeated dressing changes as a form of punishment. In addition, they may have to undergo a number of blood draws and medical procedures, aggressive therapies, and wound care over the course of a day. To overcome these obstacles, we suggest motivational interviewing (MI), a technique for changing addictive behavior that allows people to recognize the value of change in their own internal processing. MI relies substantially on reflective listening. The clinician interacts with the patient based on the FRAMES acronym (i.e., *feedback, responsibility, advice, menu of options, empathy, self-efficacy*; Miller & Rollnick, 1991). The elements of the therapeutic approach are used interchangeably and certainly not in the order in which they are listed. We can illustrate this with a patient who has burn scarring in his axilla (i.e., armpit) and is refusing to do his range of motion exercises.

For *feedback,* the patient is given normative-based, nonjudgmental information about the consequences of his injury, such as, "You have scarred tissue in your armpit. As this tissue matures it will become increasingly tight. If you do not work actively to keep it flexible, your arm will eventually contract and become barely usable unless we do a surgical release." *Responsibility* suggests the locus of change is in the patient: "It is totally up to you as to whether and how you do your exercises. No one can make you do them." *Advice* is acceptable using this model, but it should be done after asking the patient in a noncoercive manner, "Do you mind if I give you some advice? I think that this is an overwhelming time for you, and you haven't really been able to realize that doing physical therapy is a lot better option for you than a surgical release." The *menu of options* is a series of suggestions for the patient that allows him or her to choose but provides new ideas and a series of potential choices. For example, one might say, "There are several ways you could make therapy more agreeable," and then list them. *Empathy* is the most critical component of the MI approach and yet the most difficult one for clinicians to grasp and implement. Empathy is expressed largely through reflective listening, such as, "So it sounds like you really do want to avoid surgery but the prospect of doing exercises on your arm every

day seems absolutely overwhelming to you." The object here is to have the patient do most of the talking and to allow him to express his ambivalence. Reflective listening that is done effectively will allow the patient to voice reasons for change and become the source of motivation for change. *Self-efficacy* instills in the patient a sense that he or she can perform the behavior and that it will lead to effective results: "I know that this all seems very difficult, but I have seen patients with even worse injuries that suddenly find that the therapies are not only worth doing but are also much easier to do than they ever imagined. I am confident that you can avoid surgery."

The quota system is another technique that we have found useful in motivating patients on the burn unit who require long-term physical therapy. This system is an operant technique often used by physical and occupational therapists to promote a sense of mastery among patients undergoing painful and difficult physical therapies. It was originally designed for use with chronic pain; Ehde, Patterson, and Fordyce (1998) described its use among burn patients. Staff are encouraged to lower their demands to be more consistent with what is within the individual's level of tolerance by taking baseline measurements for each task that needs to be performed, gradually increasing the demands on each task (i.e., by 5% per day). Rest is used as the reinforcement for performing these predetermined tasks. Goals for each task are determined based on what was done the previous day, and patients are expected to work until the goal is accomplished, rather than until they feel pain or fatigue. This technique puts more control in the hands of the patient, preventing a syndrome of learned helplessness that can often develop as a result of painful therapies. It also avoids reinforcing pain behaviors. The quota system is based on the notion that physical therapies after a burn injury will be painful, but this pain is not damaging.

To illustrate, a patient with leg burns may find it too painful to walk. A therapist using the quota system would have the patient walk to a point of fatigue or pain for three baseline sessions. For the purposes of this example, we might assess the distance as 150, 100, and 50 ft over the three sessions. Eighty percent of the average (i.e., 100 ft) of these

3 days, or 80 ft, would be the patient's starting point. Walking would be limited to an increase of about 5% a day, or 5 ft. Even if the patient still feels like continuing, activity is stopped when he or she meets the quota. This rewards increased activity with rest and avoids the underexertion that often follows overexertion interchanged with underactivity.

SLEEP

Burn injuries are highly disruptive to sleep, both in the hospital and during the postdischarge follow-up phase. A number of factors understandably interfere with a burn survivor's sleep, including pain, medications, anxiety, pruritus (i.e., itching), and the disruption of the hospital setting. Sleep problems that develop specifically in patients with burn injuries and how to treat them are reviewed by Jaffe and Patterson (2004). It is preferable to intervene with sleep problems using behavioral methods first such as stimulus conditioning (e.g., going to bed only when tired and awakening at a consistent time), avoiding naps, avoiding caffeine after 3 p.m., and removing TVs from the bedroom. Some patients will require pharmacologic interventions in addition to behavioral ones. The current treatment of choice appears to be the mixed agonist agents such as zolpidem and zaliplon. Such drugs can cause dependency and should be prescribed only for limited periods of time. If the patient has a history of depression or does not do well with the aforementioned agents, then trazadone may be a desirable option. Trazadone is a tricyclic antidepressant that has been found to promote sustained sleep but is less addicting than the agonist–antagonist agents described earlier (Jaffe & Patterson, 2004).

PRURITUS

Pruritus can be a terrible problem for burn patients and is a common occurrence as wounds begin to heal. Unfortunately, there is no good body of studies regarding medications for postburn itching. Possibilities include antihistamines and topical agents (Esselman et al., 2005). A particularly good application of hypnosis with burn survivors is to reduce itching, with or without medications.

CONCLUSION

Fifty years ago, there was far less of a role for rehabilitation psychologists in burn rehabilitation; the concept was almost unknown to the field. Small burns healed with no major rehabilitative or psychological concerns, and patients with large burns usually did not survive. The situation is dramatically different now, as patients commonly survive with burn injuries as large as 80% to 90% of their body surface areas. This patient population brings a unique set of rehabilitation concerns, even to those well-versed in rehabilitation psychology. Patients may require the strengthening and conditioning typically needed by those with an acquired disability. Burn injury rehabilitation is unique largely because of the magnitude of cosmetic concerns shown by many survivors, as well as the extreme pain caused by treatment (as well as the injury itself). The treatment milieu is also atypical for general medical settings (although characteristic of rehabilitation units), with professionals often tightly bound in multidisciplinary teams. Effective psychological treatment involves being acculturated into such treatment teams.

Treatment interventions borne out of traditional clinical and neuropsychological practices have become increasingly important as greater numbers of patients survive severe burns. We emphasized in this chapter how the patients' preinjury status plays a large role in the etiology of their burn, as well as in how they recover. Knowledge of substance abuse treatment, as well as management of *DSM–IV* Axis II personality disorders, is particularly useful in this regard. Neuropsychology skills can be important with patients who have inhalation injuries, electrocution, or comorbid traumatic brain injuries.

Basic psychology has an important role in burn rehabilitation, and the skills of rehabilitation psychologists are particularly relevant. Theories from this specialty area present salient examples. Burn injuries are typically treated in surgical units, where biopsychosocial models of recovery are often poorly grasped by the staff. For this and other reasons, simplistic models of psychological recovery after burn injuries have flourished, with assumptions that the size or nature of the injury determines outcome. We have learned that such recovery is a far more complex and dynamic process, and a knowledge of the patient's history, support systems, coping style, secondary complications, and the nature of burn care will be necessary to appreciate and facilitate it.

The most effective clinicians working with burn injuries will combine their training in clinical psychology with knowledge and interventions from rehabilitation psychology. Traditional psychiatric diagnosis has a role in burn care, particularly in the area of depression, anxiety, and stress disorders. Much can be borrowed from treatment of patients who have such diagnoses and have not been burned or otherwise traumatized. However, burn survivors often experience a tremendous amount of distress that may not fit formal diagnostic criteria. Severe pain, disfigurement, sleep disruption, and itching can be primary sources of such distress. The unique problems faced by a burn survivor are ones that a rehabilitation psychologist will be well trained to treat.

References

Abdullah, A., Blakeney, P., Hunt, R., Broemeling, L., Phillips, L., Herndon, D. N., et al. (1994). Visible scars and self-esteem in pediatric patients with burns. *Journal of Burn Care & Rehabilitation, 15,* 164–168.

Adcock, R., Goldberg, M., Patterson, D., & Brown, P. (2000). Staff perceptions of emotional distress in patients with burn trauma. *Rehabilitation Psychology, 45,* 179–192.

American Psychiatric Association. (1994). *Diagnostic and statistical manual of mental disorders* (4th ed.). Washington, DC: Author.

Bensen, H. (1975). *The relaxation response.* New York: Morrow.

Bernstein, N. R. (1976). *Emotional care of the facially burned and disfigured.* Boston: Little, Brown.

Blakeney, P., Meyer, W., Moore, P., Murphy, L., Broemeling, L., Robson, M., et al. (1993). Psychosocial sequela of pediatric burns involving 80% or greater total body surface area. *Journal of Burn Care & Rehabilitation, 14,* 684–689.

Blakeney, P., Meyer, W., III, Robert, R., Manubhai, D., Wolf, S., & Herndon, D. (1998). Long-term psychosocial adaptation of children who survive burns involving 80% or greater total body surface area. *The Journal of Trauma: Injury, Infection, and Critical Care, 44,* 625–634.

Brigham, P. A., & McLoughlin, E. (1996). Burn incidence and medical care use in the United States: Estimates, trends and data sources. *Journal of Burn Care & Rehabilitation, 17,* 95–107.

Daniels, S. M., Fenley, J. D., Powers, P. S., & Cruse, C. W. (1991). Self-inflicted burns: A 10-year retrospective study. *Journal of Burn Care & Rehabilitation, 12,* 144–147.

Difede, J., Ptacek, J. T., Roberts, J., Barocas, D., Rives, W., Apfeldorf, W., et al. (2002). Acute stress disorder after burn injury: A predictor of posttraumatic stress disorder? *Psychosomatic Medicine, 64,* 826–834.

Ehde, D. M., Patterson, D. R., & Fordyce, W. E. (1998). The quota system in burn rehabilitation. *Journal of Burn Care & Rehabilitation, 19,* 436–439.

Ehde, D. M., Patterson, D. R., Wiechman, S. A., & Wilson, L. G. (1999). Posttraumatic stress symptoms and distress following acute burn injury. *Burns, 25,* 587–592.

Esselman, P., Thombs, B., Fauerbach, J., Magyar-Russell, G., & Price, M. (2005). *Burn state of the science review.* Seattle, WA: National Institutes of Health.

Fauerbach, J. A., Heinberg, L. J., Lawrence, J. W., Bryant, A. G., Richter, L., & Spence, R. J. (2002). Coping with body image changes following a disfiguring burn injury. *Health Psychology, 21,* 115–121.

Fauerbach, J., Lawrence, J., Haythornthwaite, J., Richter, D., McGuire, M., & Schmidt, C. (1997). Psychiatric history affects post trauma morbidity in a burn injured adult sample. *Psychosomatics, 38,* 374–385.

Fauerbach, J., Spence, R., & Patterson, D. (Eds.). (2006). *Adult burn injury.* Philadelphia: Lippincott Williams & Wilkins.

Foa, E. B. (Ed.). (1995). *PDS (Posttraumatic Stress Diagnostic Scale) manual.* Minneapolis, MN: National Computer Systems.

Frenay, M. C., Faymonville, M. E., Devlieger, S., Albert, A., & Vanderkelen, A. (2001). Psychological approaches during dressing changes of burned patients: A prospective randomised study comparing hypnosis against stress reducing strategy. *Burns, 27,* 793–799.

Gawain, S. (1978). *Creative visualization.* New York: Bantam Books.

Hoffman, H. G., Doctor, J. N., Patterson, D. R., Carrougher, G. J., & Furness, T. A., III. (2000). Use of virtual reality as an adjunctive treatment of adolescent burn pain during wound care: A case report. *Pain, 85,* 305–309.

Hoffman, H. G., Patterson, D. R., Carrougher, G. J., & Sharar, S. R. (2001). Effectiveness of virtual reality-based pain control with multiple treatments. *Clinical Journal of Pain, 17,* 229–235.

Jaffe, S. E., & Patterson, D. R. (2004). Treating sleep problems in patients with burn injuries: Practical considerations. *Journal of Burn Care Rehabilitation, 25,* 294–305.

Kabat-Zinn, J. (1990). *Full catastrophe living: Using the wisdom of your body and mind ot face stress, pain, and illness.* New York: Delta.

Kolman, P. B. R. (1983). The incidence of psycholopathology in burned adult patients: A critical review. *Journal of Burn Care & Rehabilitation, 4,* 430–436.

Lawrence, J. W., Fauerbach, J. A., Heinberg, L., & Doctor, M. (2004). Visible versus hidden scars and their relation to body esteem. *Journal of Burn Care & Rehabilitation, 25,* 25–32.

Martin-Herz, S. P., Thurber, C. A., & Patterson, D. R. (2000). Psychological principles of burn wound pain in children. II: Treatment applications. *Journal of Burn Care & Rehabilitation, 21,* 458–472.

Miller, W. R., & Rollnick, S. (1991). *Motivational interviewing: Preparing people to change addictive behavior.* New York: Guilford Press.

Partridge, J. (1997). *When burns affect the way you look.* London: Changing Faces.

Patterson, D., Everett, J., Bombardier, C., Questad, K., Lee, V., & Marvin, J. (1993). Psychological effects of severe burn injuries. *Psychological Bulletin, 113,* 362–378.

Patterson, D. R., Finch, C. P., Wiechman, S. A., Bonsack, R., Gibran, N., & Heimbach, D. (2003). Premorbid mental health status of adult burn patients: Comparison with a normative sample. *Journal of Burn Care & Rehabilitation, 24,* 347–350.

Patterson, D., & Jensen, M. (2003). Hypnosis and clinical pain. *Psychological Bulletin, 129,* 495–521.

Patterson, D. R., & Ptacek, J. T. (1997). Baseline pain as a moderator of hypnotic analgesia for burn injury treatment. *Journal of Consulting and Clinical Psychology, 65,* 60–67.

Patterson, D. R., Ptacek, J. T., Carrougher, G. J., & Sharar, S. (1997). Lorazepam as an adjunct to opioid analgesics in the treatment of burn pain. *Pain, 72,* 367–374.

Perry, S., & Blank, K. (1984). Relationship of psychological processes during delirium to outcome. *American Journal of Psychiatry, 141,* 843–847.

Pruzinsky, T., & Cash, T. F. (1990). Integrative themes in body-image development, deviance, and change.

In T. F. Cash & T. Pruzinsky (Eds.), *Body images: Development, deviance, and change* (pp. 337–349). New York: Guilford Press.

Rutan, R. L. (1998). Physiologic response to cutaneous burn injury. In G. Carrougher (Ed.), *Burn care and therapy* (pp. 1–33). St. Louis, MO: Mosby.

Scully, J., & Hutcherson, R. (1983). Suicide by burning. *American Journal of Psychology, 140,* 905–906.

Spitzer, R. L., Williams, J. B., Kroenke, K., Hornyak, R., & McMurray, J. (2000). Validity and utility of the PRIME-MD patient health questionnaire in assessment of 3000 obstetric-gynecologic patients: The PRIME-MD Patient Health Questionnaire Obstetrics-Gynecology Study. *American Journal of Obstetrics and Gynecology, 183,* 759–769.

Steiner, H., & Clark, W. R. (1977). Psychiatric complications of burned adults: A classification. *Journal of Trauma, 17,* 134–143.

Tarnowski, K. J., Rasnake, L. K., Linscheid, T. R., & Mulick, J. A. (1989). Behavioral adjustment of pediatric burn victims. *Journal of Pediatric Psychology, 14,* 607–615.

Thurber, C. A., Martin-Herz, S. P., & Patterson, D. R. (2000). Psychological principles of burn wound pain in children. I: Theoretical framework. *Journal of Burn Care & Rehabilitation, 21,* 376–387.

Wiechman, S. A., Ehde, D. M., Wilson, B. L., & Patterson, D. R. (2000). The management of self-inflicted burn injuries and disruptive behavior for patients with borderline personality disorder. *Journal of Burn Care & Rehabilitation, 21,* 310–317.

Williams, R. M., Patterson, D. R., Schwenn, C., Day, J., Bartman, M., & Engrav, L. H. (2002). Evaluation of a peer consultation program for burn inpatients. *Journal of Burn Care & Rehabilitation, 23,* 449–453.

Wortman, C. B., & Silver, R. C. (1989). The myths of coping with loss. *Journal of Consulting and Clinical Psychology, 57,* 349–357.

Wright, B. (1983). *Physical disability: A psychological approach* (2nd ed.). New York: Beatrice A. Wright.

Wright, B. A. (1959). *Psychology and rehabilitation.* Washington, DC: American Psychological Association.

Chapter 7

CHRONIC PAIN

Michael E. Robinson and Erin M. O'Brien

This chapter describes the multidimensional nature of chronic pain, including both the sensory and affective components of the pain experience and the prevalence of pain in populations commonly seen in rehabilitation settings. Issues related to assessment and treatment of chronic pain are presented following this introduction, with the final sections presenting current challenges involved in the management of chronic pain, specifically issues related to placebo and central sensitization.

THE MULTIDIMENSIONAL NATURE OF PAIN

The International Association for the Study of Pain defines *pain* as "an unpleasant sensory and emotional experience associated with actual or potential tissue damage, or described in terms of such damage" (p. 210; Merskey & Bogduk, 1994). While this definition acknowledges the multidimensional nature of pain (i.e., that pain includes both a sensory and an emotional component), it does not reflect current evidence that negative emotion is an essential part of the pain experience. Further, it does not recognize that many patients are unable to describe their sensations in terms of tissue damage. A definition by Price (1999) incorporates the involvement of negative emotion into the experience of pain and highlights the role of threat and pain quality in the pain experience. Price defined pain as "a somatic perception containing (1) a bodily sensation with qualities like those reported during tissue-damaging stimulation, (2) an experienced threat associated with this sensation, and (3) a feeling of unpleasantness or

other negative emotion based on this experienced threat" (pp. 1–2). Studies have demonstrated that pain sensation intensity and pain unpleasantness can be reliably differentiated as components of an individual's pain experience (e.g., Gallez, Albanese, Rainville, & Duncan, 2005; Price, 1999; Rainville, Carrier, Hofbauer, Bushnell, & Duncan, 1999). This is further supported by evidence from brain imaging studies that have demonstrated that pain intensity and pain unpleasantness can be differentiated (Gallez et al., 2005; Rainville et al., 1999) and different areas of the brain also appear to modulate each of these separate characteristics of the pain experience (Rainville, 2002; Rainville, Duncan, Price, Carrier, & Bushnell, 1997).

In addition to being consistent with clinical experience and making theoretical sense, much empirical research has supported the conception of chronic pain as being multidimensional in nature. Robinson and Riley (1999) summarized the extensive literature regarding emotion and pain. Across many studies, patients with chronic pain demonstrated higher levels of depression and anxiety compared with individuals who were pain free, and also obtained higher scores on a measure of state anger than published norms (Robinson & Riley, 1999). Furthermore, negative affect was found to predict treatment outcome, health care costs, and chronicity among chronic pain patients; there was also evidence to indicate that negative affect may mediate the relationship between pain and disability in these patients. Various biological and psychological factors, such as somatization, catastrophizing, interpersonal factors, and degree of life control or interference by pain, have been postulated as potential mediators between pain and negative mood. Although there has been some support for the role of each of these variables, no conclusions can yet be drawn regarding the relative importance of any one of these factors in the relationship between pain and negative affect in this population.

PAIN IN TRADITIONAL REHABILITATION POPULATIONS

Pain is frequently a presenting problem, or a concomitant condition, among many populations commonly treated in rehabilitation settings. The following section reviews the prevalence of pain among some of the most commonly encountered rehabilitation patient populations as well as existing evidence for how the presence of pain can impact patients' functional outcomes.

Spinal Cord Injury

Chronic pain has been noted to be prevalent among patients who have suffered a spinal cord injury (SCI; e.g., Bonica, 1991; Mariano, 1992; Nashold, 1991). A review by Siddall and Loeser (2001) reported an average prevalence of pain in 65% of people with SCI across studies. Further, these authors reported that approximately one third of these individuals rated their level of pain as severe, highlighting the importance of addressing the problem of pain in SCI populations. Mariano (1992) concluded that chronic pain is a significant challenge facing SCI populations and is associated with substantial psychosocial impairment, necessitating a multidisciplinary treatment approach for optimal outcomes. For more information on spinal cord injuries, see chapter 1 of this volume.

Traumatic Brain Injury

Pain is a common occurrence following traumatic brain injuries (TBIs), although exact prevalence rates have not yet been clearly established. A review by Walker (2004) reported that the most common type of pain experienced following TBI is posttraumatic headache (PTHA) with incidence reports ranging from 18% to 93% (e.g., Beetar, Guilmette, & Sparadeo, 1996; Lahz & Bryant, 1996; Uomoto & Esselman, 1993) following an

injury (Martelli, Grayson, & Zasler, 1999; Walker, 2004) and estimates of 44% for chronic PTHA lasting more than 6 months after an injury (Martelli et al., 2004). PTHA may be more common in patients with mild TBI, in comparison with moderate or severe TBI, although this association requires further study. Sustaining a TBI can lead to a new onset of pain, as well as exacerbate any preexisting pain disorders (Branca & Lake, 2004). Post-TBI pain can be particularly problematic in rehabilitation populations because pain may make several common postbrain injury behaviors worse (e.g., inattention, sleep disturbances), as well as exacerbate behavioral noncompliance due to patients resisting activities that increase their level of pain (Walker, 2004). Several investigations have also discussed the importance of examining the complex relationships among pain, sleep disturbances, and cognitive dysfunctions observed in TBI populations (e.g., Beetar et al., 1996; Richter, Cowan, & Kaschalk, 1995, 1997). In conclusion, the convergence of factors present in patients following TBI is likely to reduce the overall benefit that they derive from rehabilitative therapies and may lead to poorer functional outcomes for these individuals. For more information on TBIs, see chapter 3 of this volume.

Stroke

Stroke is a prevalent neurological condition that can lead to significant morbidity and mortality. Pain is a frequently reported symptom following stroke, although the nature and impact of poststroke pain have received limited study, perhaps because of the complex nature of poststroke pain. Hemiplegic shoulder pain has been noted as the most common pain condition following stroke, with studies reporting an incidence ranging from 38% to 84% for this condition (Kong, Woon, & Yang, 2004). Central poststroke pain is another relatively common pain condition reported in stroke populations, with research indicating an incidence rate of 2% to 8% for this condition (e.g., Andersen, Vestergaard, Ingeman-Nielsen, & Jensen, 1995; Bowsher, 1995; Leijon, Boivie, & Johansson, 1989).

While there have been conflicting reports regarding the impact of poststroke pain on patients' quality of life (Jonsson, Lindgren, Hallstrom, Norrving, & Lindgren, 2006; Kong et al., 2004), research has demonstrated its relationship to patients' rehabilitation (e.g., Bowsher, 1995; Leijon et al., 1989). There is no consistent time frame for the occurrence of pain following stroke; pain can occur immediately or at some point during the weeks or months following stroke (e.g., Leijon et al., 1989). Studies have reported results indicating that a substantial proportion of patients reporting poststroke pain indicate that their pain is of at least moderate severity (e.g., Jonsson et al., 2006) and is present continuously or nearly continuously (e.g., Jonsson et al., 2006; Widar, Samuelsson, Karlsson-Tivenius, & Ahlstrom, 2002). For more information on stroke, see chapter 4 of this volume.

Orthopedic and Musculoskeletal Conditions

Several reviews have reported decreases in pain and improvement in functioning following arthroplasty for joint conditions (Bryant et al., 2005; Jones, Beaupre, Johnston, & Suarez-Almazor, 2005), as well as some initial positive findings (i.e., improvements in pain and disability ratings) for the use of arthroplasty in the treatment of degenerative spinal conditions (Gamradt & Wang, 2005). Of note, heterogeneity in the results found across studies limits confidence in the consistency of these findings, and arthroplasty is still considered an experimental procedure for back pain. Studies have also demonstrated more rapid improvement in levels of joint pain, compared with functional status, during the postsurgical period, as reviewed in Jones et al. Although overall results for arthroplasty for joint replacement have been encouraging, as many as 15% to 30% of patients undergoing these procedures report little or no improvement following surgery or are unsatisfied with the results a few months following surgery (as reviewed in Jones et al.). Because it remains unclear what factors may predict poor functional and pain-related outcomes following surgery in this population, more recent investigations have begun to focus on psychological factors as possible predictors (Jones et al., 2005). Some initial work has reported that psychological factors, such as self-efficacy and expectancy about surgical outcomes, contribute

more to the prediction of postsurgical pain and functional outcomes than do other medical and baseline variables (Brander et al., 2003; Sharma et al., 1996).

ASSESSMENT OF CHRONIC PAIN

A comprehensive pain assessment should include a thorough evaluation of the patient's pain experience and the impact of pain on his or her functioning. Thus, it is important to assess pain in a manner that captures both the sensory and affective dimensions of the pain experience and to also assess mood, coping, and behavioral dimensions that may also have an important role in patients' functioning.

Pain Measurement

The assessment of pain has become a vital part of routine patient care. In fact, the American Pain Society coined the phrase "Pain: The Fifth Vital Sign" (Campbell, 1995) to encourage improved awareness of the need for effective assessment and treatment of pain among health care professionals. In addition, the Joint Commission on Accreditation of Health Care Organizations and the Commission on Accreditation of Research Facilities have identified accurate and timely pain assessment and management as an important patient care initiative. Along these lines, it is important to discuss the various methodologies for the assessment of pain, as well as pain-related sequelae. Due to the subjective nature of pain, patients' self-reports provide the most valid assessment of their pain experience (Melzack & Katz, 2001). Since pain can only be measured indirectly, the accurate assessment of pain is a challenging goal as well as an important topic for discussion and research.

Patient self-report is one of the most common ways of assessing pain and includes a number of different techniques, ranging from the use of questionnaires, to asking patients to report a numerical value for their current/average/worst pain, to the use of visual analog scales for assessing different aspects of the pain experience (e.g., intensity and unpleasantness). Visual analog scales (VAS) and numerical rating scales (NRS) are among the most frequently used self-report measures used to assess pain intensity. VAS have been shown to be valid measures of pain intensity that are sensitive to treatment effects (Jensen & Karoly, 2001). In addition, a significant advantage to the use of VAS is that they appear to demonstrate ratio scale properties, which is lacking in other types of measurement instruments (Price, Harkins, & Baker, 1987). This is an important issue given the emphasis of providers and health care agencies on "percentage improvement" in pain or other outcome scores. Only a ratio level measurement allows for true percentage improvement outcomes. However, it is important to note that the use of VAS may be somewhat more difficult for patients to understand, making them a less than ideal assessment instrument with certain populations (e.g. cognitively impaired patients; Jensen & Karoly, 2001). However, our experience indicates that with appropriate training and instructions, the vast majority of patients are able to successfully use VAS.

Another frequently used assessment instrument for pain intensity is the NRS, which also has been shown to be a valid measure that is sensitive to treatment effects. An additional benefit of the NRS is that it is easier to understand and administer, enabling its use with a greater variety of patients (Jensen & Karoly, 2001). However, unlike the VAS, the NRS does not appear to have to have ratio measurement properties, and this is its most notable weakness (Jensen & Karoly, 2001).

The McGill Pain Questionnaire (MPQ), which was developed by Melzack and colleagues in the 1970s, is the first assessment instrument designed to measure the three components of pain postulated by the gate control theory, that is, the sensory, affective, and evaluative dimensions of pain (Turk & Melzack, 2001a). Three major indices can be obtained from administration of the MPQ: the Pain Rating Index, which is based on the rank values of the words in each of the three categories; the total number of words chosen; and the Present Pain Intensity index, which is the number–word combination chosen as the indicator of overall pain intensity at the time the questionnaire was administered (Melzack & Katz, 2001). Research has demonstrated that the MPQ meets the requirements of being a valid, reliable, consistent, and useful instrument for measuring the subjective pain experience. Further, the MPQ appears to provide some insight into the quality of pain that is experienced by

patients with different pain conditions, as patients with the same condition demonstrate remarkable consistency in their choice of words to describe their pain (Melzack & Katz, 2001). A short-form version of the MPQ has also been developed, which has also demonstrated validity, sensitivity to treatment effects, and the ability to discriminate between different chronic pain populations, consistent with findings for the full MPQ (Melzack & Katz, 2001).

Psychophysical testing procedures have also been used in the assessment of pain. Typically, psychophysical methods have involved one of several procedures. One procedure involves assessing individuals' pain threshold levels and subsequent changes in those levels. A second method asks individuals to rate the pain intensity they experienced in response to an experimental stimulus on an ordinal scale involving numerical or verbal scaling intervals. A third method asks individuals to make judgments regarding pain intensity or unpleasantness of a given sensation on a VAS (Price, Riley, & Wade, 2001). Research has shown that the ratio of pain intensity to pain unpleasantness differs systematically for different types of experimental pain (Rainville et al., 1992) and for different types of clinical pain (Price et al., 1987).

As advanced imaging procedures, such as single-photon emission tomography and functional magnetic resonance imaging, have developed, they have begun to provide new insights into the processing of nociceptive information in the brain (Turk & Melzack, 2001b). Research has shown that many different areas of the brain respond to the same noxious stimuli, which supports the view that the pain experience is a distributive process and results from interaction among a number of distinct brain regions. Although great strides are being made in the understanding of pain processing in the brain, there are no current clinical applications of functional imaging of pain.

Negative Affect

The nature of chronic pain allows for a potentially greater role for psychological factors in an individual's subjective experience of pain, as well as in his or her response to and report about pain, necessitating the assessment of psychological factors in patients with chronic pain (Turk & Melzack, 2001a). An important and well-researched predictor of pain, as well as of pain-related outcomes, is catastrophizing. *Catastrophizing* is defined as "an exaggerated negative orientation toward pain stimuli and pain experience" (p. 253; Sullivan, Stanish, Waite, Sullivan, & Tripp, 1998), and has been reported to account for between 7% and 31% of the variance in individual's pain ratings (e.g., Geisser, Robinson, Keefe, & Weiner, 1994; Sullivan et al., 2001). Furthermore, catastrophizing has been found to be related to greater disability, increased use of health care services, increased use of pain medications, increased pain behaviors, and increased recovery time during postsurgical rehabilitation (Boothby, Thorn, Stroud, & Jensen, 1999; Keefe, Rumble, Scipio, Giordano, & Perri, 2004). Traditional methods of assessing negative affect are applicable to the rehabilitation and pain populations and are beyond the scope of this review. However, it should be noted that a good understanding of the expected physical symptoms associated with the primary medical conditions is critical for the interpretation of scores on mood inventories.

A recent addition to the understanding of chronic pain is the fear-avoidance model described by Vlaeyen, Kole-Snijders, Boeren, and van Eek (1995). This model proposes that, following an injury, individuals' prior pain experiences and beliefs, current level of stress, pain behavior, and specific personality traits, can lead to the development of elevated fear-avoidance beliefs (Vlaeyen et al., 1995). These fear-avoidance beliefs, in turn, lead the individual to engage in avoidance behavior, which can culminate in a state of chronic disability (Lethem, Slade, Troup, & Bentley, 1983; Vlaeyen & Linton, 2000). It was further suggested that fear-avoidance beliefs influenced sensory input, such that elevated fear-avoidance beliefs were related to increased pain sensitivity via the development of an exaggerated pain perception (Lethem et al., 1983; Vlaeyen & Linton, 2000). Research has produced broad empirical support for this model of chronic pain, with clinical and experimental studies demonstrating that pain-related fear and anxiety are predictive of individuals' adaptation to persistent pain (Vlaeyen & Linton, 2000). Using the conceptual framework of the fear-avoidance model, Boersma and Linton (2006) were able to identify distinct profiles of pain-related fear and depression that were meaningfully related to patients' subsequent dis-

ability. A study by George, Wittmer, Fillingim, and Robinson (2006) also reported that fear-avoidance beliefs, along with temporal summation from thermal quantitative sensory testing procedures, significantly predicted pain-related disability in a group of chronic low-back pain patients. In addition, the applicability of the fear-avoidance model to different chronic pain populations has been assessed. The fear-avoidance model was found to be broadly consistent across three different age groups of adults with chronic pain, although pain-related fear was found to be a stronger mediator for older adults in structural equation modeling analyses (Cook, Brawer, & Vowles, 2006). Elevated ratings of pain-related fear and anxiety have been associated not only with higher ratings of pain but also with increased attention to pain sensations, higher self-reported disability and depression, increased pain behaviors, and decreased coping (Keefe et al., 2004).

As part of a comprehensive pain assessment, it is important to evaluate the pain behaviors that an individual with chronic pain is exhibiting, as well as the responses of others to these pain behaviors. While pain is a subjective experience, individuals are able to communicate that they are in pain via verbal and nonverbal pain behaviors (Fordyce, 1976). Pain behaviors are an important component within a behavioral perspective on the chronic pain experience, and these formulations often focus considerable attention on the influence of social learning in the development and maintenance of pain behaviors (Keefe, Williams, & Smith, 2001). Rehabilitation settings often offer a rich environment in which to observe and rate or quantify pain behavior in the context of social interactions with staff, other patients, and family members. Formal assessment of pain behavior or informal observation can both yield important information about operant features of a patient's pain behavior that can be addressed in rehabilitation (Keefe et al., 2001).

The phrase *coping with chronic pain* refers to an individual's attempts, either adaptive or maladaptive, to resolve pain-related problems, and these attempts are strongly influenced by patients' beliefs about pain (DeGood & Tait, 2001). Studies have demonstrated that variations in pain coping are related to pain, psychological distress, pain behaviors, and physical functioning (Boothby et al., 1999; Keefe et al., 2004).

Research involving the Vanderbilt Pain Management Inventory (Brown & Nicassio, 1987), which assesses active and passive coping strategies specific to chronic pain, has demonstrated associations between active coping and increased levels of activity and positive affect. Conversely, passive coping strategies have been linked to higher pain ratings and greater levels of disability and psychological distress (Boothby et al., 1999). The more recently revised Vanderbilt Multidimensional Pain Coping Inventory has been found to demonstrate improved predictive ability in assessing physical and psychological function (Smith, Wallston, Dwyer, & Dowdy, 1997). The Coping Strategies Questionnaire-Revised (CSQ-R; Robinson et al., 1997) retains 27 items from the original Coping Strategies Questionnaire (CSQ; Rosenstiel & Keefe, 1983) and assesses cognitive and behavioral coping strategies in chronic pain populations, including catastrophizing. Catastrophizing is a maladaptive coping strategy identified by both the CSQ and CSQ-R, as well as other coping measures (i.e., the Pain Catastrophizing Scale; Sullivan, Bishop, & Pivik, 1995), that has been linked to higher pain ratings, increased disability, and poorer psychological functioning in a large number of studies (Boothby et al.; Keefe et al., 2004). The assessment of coping allows the clinician to target specific maladaptive coping strategies for elimination and adaptive strategies for therapeutic intervention.

McCracken, Carson, Eccleston, and Keefe (2004) proposed an alternative approach to the treatment of chronic pain that has garnered some empirical support, requiring assessment of the "acceptance" of pain. Rather than placing the focus on patients learning how to "cope" with their chronic pain condition, they suggested that it may be more adaptive for many patients to develop an attitude of "acceptance" toward their pain. The rationale behind this approach was that the most common psychological treatments for pain, which typically involve learning cognitive and behavioral strategies to reduce one's experience of pain, may become problematic in many circumstances and may actually serve to exacerbate the problem. These researchers proposed that, rather than avoiding or trying to control unwanted (i.e., painful) experiences, an alternative approach is to accept their occurrence; they further noted that

scientific evidence is growing for the use of acceptance-based approaches (e.g., Hayes, Strosahl, & Wilson, 1999; Hayes, Wilson, Gifford, Follette, & Strosahl, 1996). Within the context of chronic pain, McCracken et al. defined *acceptance* as "an active willingness to engage in meaningful activities in life regardless of pain-related sensations, thoughts, and other related feelings that might otherwise hinder that engagement" (p. 6). In studies comparing coping versus acceptance in relation to pain and pain-related outcomes (e.g., disability, psychological functioning), acceptance has been reported to have stronger beneficial relationships to pain, disability, negative mood, and work status (McCracken, 1998; McCracken & Eccleston, 2003, 2005, 2006). The majority of studies examining the impact of acceptance in chronic pain have used a measure called the Chronic Pain Acceptance Questionnaire (McCracken, 1998). Overall, findings have suggested that acceptance is an important predictor of negative affect (i.e., depression, pain-related anxiety) as well as physical and psychosocial disability, even when controlling for pain intensity (e.g., McCracken; McCracken & Eccleston, 2003).

TREATMENT OF CHRONIC PAIN

Just as the assessment of pain has evolved and become more comprehensive, so has treatment for chronic pain. The following section reviews various methods for treating chronic pain and provides the available evidence to support these different treatments.

Medication

The efficacy of opioid medications for the treatment chronic nonmalignant pain has been the subject of considerable debate. Numerous surveys and uncontrolled studies have demonstrated that a large proportion of patients with chronic nonmalignant pain experience various degrees of pain reduction in response to treatment with opioid analgesics (e.g., France, Urban, & Keefe, 1984; Haythornthwaite, Menefee, Quatrano-Piacentini, & Pappagallo, 1998; Zenz, Strumpf, & Tryba, 1992), whereas controlled trials have suggested generally favorable outcomes in terms of pain reduction overall (e.g., Hale et al.,

1999; Jamison, Raymond, Slawsby, Nedeljkovic, & Katz, 1998; Schnitzer, Gray, Paster, & Kamin, 2000). A systematic review of opioid trials in patients with nonmalignant pain produced mixed results (Kalso, Edwards, Moore, & McQuay, 2004), although only 18 studies met the inclusion criteria and there was considerable variability observed in endpoints, placebo blinding, and outcome measures. In trials reporting a positive outcome, there was a reduction in pain of approximately 30%; however, only 44% of patients remained on opioids in studies that included follow-on open label trials. Lack of opioid efficacy and adverse side effects were the most frequently reported reasons for discontinuation of opioid medication. These studies focused primarily, or exclusively, on pain reduction, without regard to functional outcomes. Several studies have examined the relationship between pain reduction and functional improvement (e.g., Haythornthwaite et al., 1998; Jamison et al., 1998; Schnitzer et al., 2000; Zenz et al., 1992), but mixed results have been reported, with half reporting increased functioning and half reporting no change in functioning. This inconsistency indicates that additional research, using performance-based measures of function in addition to self-report measures, is needed to determine whether opioid therapy improves functioning in patients with chronic pain.

Similarly, although muscle relaxants are widely used in the management of low-back pain, this practice is considered to be controversial in light of the available evidence. A review by van Tulder, Touray, Furlan, Solway, and Bouter (2003) reported that there is evidence to support the effectiveness of muscle relaxants for short-term pain relief among low-back pain patients. However, the utility of muscle relaxants for long-term pain management in this population and the relative effectiveness of these medications compared with analgesics or nonsteroidal anti-inflammatory drugs have not yet been demonstrated. In addition, this review noted a high incidence of adverse effects from the use of muscle relaxants, and the authors stressed that this must be considered when determining whether to prescribe these medications for individual patients (van Tulder et al., 2003).

Regional analgesia techniques attempt to reduce pain by directly blocking neural impulses using local anesthetic compounds (Bonica & Buckley, 1990). One application of this technique is the use of local anesthetic, either alone or in combination with steroids or saline solution, for repeated trigger point injections. Local anesthetic has been used for successful reduction of myofascial pain (e.g., Simons, 1988). However, while local anesthetic blockade of the sympathetic nervous system is widely used to treat complex regional pain syndrome, a recent review was unable to draw any conclusions regarding the effectiveness of this procedure and reported that there is little evidence to support the use of this treatment as a gold standard for this condition (Cepeda, Carr, & Lau, 2005). Several studies have examined the use of epidural injections of steroids with or without a local anesthetic for the treatment of low-back pain, with an average success rate of approximately 60% reported at 3 to 6 months follow-up (e.g., Lindholm & Salenius, 1964). It is important to note that success rates have declined over time for these procedures (e.g., Cappio, 1957). Similarly, the use of intraspinal narcotics has received limited support for the treatment of chronic nonmalignant pain (Ready, 1990), although intramuscular injection of lidocaine was reported to be an effective treatment for mechanical neck pain in a recent review (Peloso et al., 2007).

Spinal Cord Stimulation

Spinal cord stimulation (SCS) for the treatment of certain types of chronic pain involves the delivery of pulses by an implantable electrical generator to a targeted spinal cord area. The exact mechanism of action of SCS is poorly understood. A review of the available evidence was conducted by Mailis-Gagnon, Furlan, Sandoval, and Taylor (2004); only two randomized controlled trials of this intervention were found in the literature. One of these trials studied the effects of SCS for failed back surgery syndrome (FBSS), whereas the other trial involved a group of patients with complex regional pain syndrome type 1 (i.e., reflex sympathetic dystrophy; CRPS 1). The authors of this review concluded that, although SCS might be effective for certain patients, little evidence is currently available to sufficiently assess the benefits and harms of this treatment (Mailis-Gagnon et al., 2004). Turner, Loeser, Deyo, and Sanders (2004) noted that SCS provided modest improvement in pain for patients with CRPS and FBSS, although pain relief appeared to decrease over time. In addition, this review found no significant improvement in functioning following SCS and noted adverse events among 34% of the patients included in the studies reviewed. Current evidence indicates that additional data from more methodologically rigorous studies are needed before recommendations regarding the use of SCS as a treatment for chronic pain can be made (Carter, 2004; Mailis-Gagnon et al., 2004; Turner et al., 2004).

Prolotherapy

Prolotherapy is a treatment for chronic low-back pain that uses injections to strengthen weakened ligaments. Prolotherapy protocols usually include cointerventions, such as manipulation, exercises, and injections into tender muscles to enhance the effectiveness of the injections. Dagenais, Yelland, Del Mar, & Schoene (2007) reviewed four studies examining the effect of prolotherapy injections on 344 patients with low-back pain of at least a 3-month duration. They concluded that the evidence regarding the efficacy of prolotherapy is conflicting because of the frequent presence of cointerventions as well as the considerable heterogeneity among the studies examined. Overall, prolotherapy injections alone were not found to be more effective than control injections alone; however, in the presence of co-interventions, prolotherapy injections were more effective than control injections (Dagenais et al., 2007).

Radiofrequency Denervation

One potential cause of ongoing neck or back pain can be a joint or a damaged disc between two vertebral joints, and injections that block these specific joint nerves can determine whether this is the source of an individual's pain. Radiofrequency denervation is a technique that aims to deactivate the pain-causing nerve by applying electric current to cauterize it (i.e., damage with heat). A review of selected trials by Niemisto, Kalso, Malmivaara, Seitsalo, and Hurri (2003) concluded that there is limited evidence for radiofrequency denervation offering short-term relief for chronic neck pain of zygapophyseal joint origin and for chronic cervicobrachial pain. However, this review further concluded that there is conflicting evidence on the short-term effect of this treatment for

pain and disability in chronic low-back pain of zygapophyseal joint origin and limited evidence to suggest that intradiscal radiofrequency thermocoagulation is not effective for chronic discogenic low-back pain. No conclusions could be drawn regarding the long-term effects of radiofrequency denervation because of the current lack of data. The authors also noted that randomized controlled trials are needed to examine the effectiveness of this technique in nonspinal indications because of its current use in these instances without any scientific evidence to support such applications (Niemisto et al., 2003).

Transcutaneous Electrical Nerve Stimulation

The technique of transcutaneous electrical nerve stimulation (TENS) was introduced more than 30 years ago as a nonpharmacological method for the management of pain. It is currently widely used as a treatment for patients with chronic low-back pain, but its use continues to be controversial. Khadilkar and colleagues (2008) undertook a systematic review of randomized controlled trials (i.e., two trials, 175 patients) to examine the effectiveness of TENS in treating chronic low-back pain. They reported that there is limited and inconsistent evidence regarding the use of TENS as an isolated treatment modality for this condition (Khadilkar et al., 2008). Similarly, a review by Brosseau and colleagues (2002) reported no significant differences between patients receiving active TENS treatment compared with placebo. These researchers concluded that there is currently no evidence to support the use of TENS among chronic low-back pain populations and that additional well-designed studies are needed to examine this treatment (Brosseau et al., 2002).

Psychological Interventions

By far, the interventions with the most consistent empirical support for the treatment of chronic pain involve behavioral and cognitive–behavioral therapies. Behavioral and cognitive–behavioral therapies for chronic pain aim to identify maladaptive ways of thinking and behaving related to pain and to help patients learn more adaptive ways of perceiving their pain and interacting with the environment, including other people (Turk, 2003). Rather than trying to "cure" one's pain, which is often not possible, these treatments emphasize the restoration of functioning. A large body of research supports the effectiveness of these treatments in chronic pain populations.

Meta-analyses have examined the effectiveness of these psychological interventions for chronic pain, both as stand-alone treatments and as part of a multidisciplinary treatment approach. When compared with a treatment-as-usual or minimal care condition or a wait-list control group, cognitive–behavioral treatments for chronic pain have been shown to lead to improvements in pain (Linton, Boersma, Jansson, Svard, & Botvalde, 2005; Nash, Park, Walker, Gordon, & Nicholson, 2004; Turner, Mancl, & Aaron, 2006), reduced pain-related interference with activity (Puder, 1988; Turner, Mancl, & Aaron, 2005; Turner et al., 2006; Turner-Stokes et al., 2003), improvements in coping and perceived control over pain (Puder; Turner et al., 2005, 2006; Turner-Stokes et al., 2003), improvements in mood (Turner et al., 2006; Turner-Stokes et al., 2003), fewer absences from work at 1 year (Linton & Andersson, 2000; Linton et al., 2005), reduced use of medications and/or health care services (Linton & Andersson, 2000; Linton et al., 2005; Nash et al., 2004), and improved quality of life (Nash et al., 2004).

A meta-analysis by Flor, Fydrich, and Turk (1992) examined the outcomes of multidisciplinary treatments for patients with chronic back pain, compared with single-discipline treatments and control groups. The multidisciplinary treatments had significantly greater overall effectiveness with stable results over time. In addition to the reductions noted for pain and level of interference, the multidisciplinary treatments demonstrated beneficial effects on a number of additional outcome measures, including patients' mood, ability to return to work, and health care utilization (Flor et al., 1992). Similarly, a recent meta-analysis by Hoffman, Papas, Chatkoff, and Kerns (2007) found evidence for the effectiveness of psychological interventions, whether as an individual treatment or as a component of a multidisciplinary treatment package, for chronic low back pain patients. The effect size for this result was noted to be small but robust, and moderate effect sizes were noted when psychological interventions were compared with

wait-list control conditions for pain intensity and health-related quality of life. In comparison with active control conditions (e.g., treatment as usual, physiotherapy), psychological interventions were noted to have moderate effects for reducing work-related disability and small effects for reduction of pain interference. Overall, psychological interventions were demonstrated to have a robust effect on pain intensity across all control group comparisons.

Importantly, whereas demographic and physical finding variables have not demonstrated reliable relationships to outcomes in behavior or cognitive–behavioral treatments for chronic pain (McCracken & Turk, 2002), studies have revealed certain significant behavioral or psychological predictors and outcomes from these types of treatments in chronic pain patients. Specifically, chronic pain patients who have stronger beliefs in control over pain use less negative thinking in response to pain (e.g., catastrophizing), and experience less anxiety and depression regarding their pain tend to have more favorable outcomes from behavioral and cognitive–behavioral treatments (McCracken & Turk, 2002). Patients who report expectancies for successful treatment outcome also tend to experience more favorable outcomes from these interventions (Goossens, Vlaeyen, Hidding, Kole-Snijders, & Evers, 2005; Milling, Reardon, & Carosella, 2006). These findings suggest that these factors should be considered when making treatment decisions for chronic pain populations.

Placebo

Recent work on understanding the nature of placebo (Vase, Price, Verne, & Robinson, 2004) has illustrated the importance of patients' expectations and desire for pain relief in the context of the relationship to the provider and analgesia. Evidence that the placebo effect is a complex, powerful, physiologically and psychologically active phenomenon is mounting. Brain imaging studies from a number of labs have demonstrated that placebo interventions influence well-known brain areas associated with pain processing. Furthermore, certain placebo interventions appear to have an endogenous opioid mechanism, whereas other forms have still unknown mechanisms (Vase, Robinson, Verne, & Price, 2005). Simple changes in the instructions about a drug can produce profound analgesic effects in clinical pain, even when no drug is given (Vase, Robinson, Verne, & Price, 2003). The recent work on placebo highlights the importance of the placebo effect and patient expectations in all forms of treatment. Every intervention with a patient involves a placebo effect. While considerable controversy remains regarding the use of inactive agents as placebos, clinicians should give careful consideration to how they can enhance patients' expectations for success from existing, well-validated interventions.

Central Sensitization

There is growing evidence that many chronic pain conditions are characterized by *hyperalgesia,* thought to be the result of central sensitization (Staud et al., 2003). The behavioral phenomenon, sometimes termed *temporal summation* or *windup,* is characterized by an increasing perception of pain upon repeated stimulation, even though neural activity at the receptor and peripheral nerves is not increasing. The exact nature of the mechanism continues to be explored and is beyond the scope of this review. However, the existence of the phenomenon in clinical populations and the relationship of central sensitization to psychological factors (Robinson, Wise, Gagnon, Fillingim, & Price, 2004) are of relevance to psychologists working with people in pain. This phenomenon illustrates one mechanism whereby changing patient negative affect (particularly anxiety) can directly affect pain processing. Furthermore, early pain intervention, whether by pharmacological, surgical, physical, or psychological methods, has the potential for inhibiting the development of central sensitization and perhaps avoiding the development of long-term treatment resistant pain conditions.

SUMMARY

In this chapter, the definition and components of chronic pain have been reviewed, along with the relevant literature highlighting the high prevalence and importance of pain in traditional rehabilitation populations. An attempt has also been made to emphasize that the treatment of chronic pain in nontraditional rehabilitation conditions, such as chronic low-back pain, constitutes rehabilitation, and many of the issues found in traditional settings and disorders

(e.g., stroke, TBI) are relevant to these patients. This chapter has also reviewed the literature showing that psychologists and cognitive–behavioral interventions for chronic pain conditions have strong empirical support, stronger in fact, than other more traditional medical interventions for pain. Finally, issues and mechanisms that may underpin the behavioral and psychological interventions that have been shown to be successful in treating chronic pain have been highlighted.

References

Andersen, G., Vestergaard, K., Ingeman-Nielsen, M., & Jensen, T. S. (1995). Incidence of central poststroke pain. *Pain, 61,* 187–193.

Beetar, J. T., Guilmette, T. J., & Sparadeo, F. R. (1996). Sleep and pain complaints in symptomatic traumatic brain injury and neurologic populations. *Archives of Physical Medicine and Rehabilitation, 77,* 1298–1302.

Boersma, K., & Linton, S. J. (2006). Psychological processes underlying the development of a chronic pain problem: A prospective study of the relationship between profiles of psychological variables in the fear-avoidance model and disability. *Clinical Journal of Pain, 22,* 160–166.

Bonica, J. J. (1991). Introduction: Semantic, epidemiologic, and educational issues. In K. L. Casey (Ed.), *Pain and central nervous system disease: The central pain syndromes* (pp. 13–29). New York: Raven Press.

Bonica, J. J., & Buckley, P. (1990). Regional anesthesia with local anesthetics. In J. J. Bonica (Ed.), *The management of pain: Vol. 2.* (2nd ed., pp. 1883–1966). Philadelphia: Lea & Febiger.

Boothby, J. L., Thorn, B. E., Stroud, M. W., & Jensen, M. P. (1999). Coping with pain. In R. J. Gatchel & D. C. Turk (Eds.), *Psychosocial factors in pain: Clinical perspectives* (pp. 343–359). New York: Guilford Press.

Bowsher, D. (1995). The management of central poststroke pain. *Postgraduate Medical Journal, 71,* 598–604.

Branca, B., & Lake, A. E. (2004). Psychological and neuropsychological integration in multidisciplinary pain management after TBI. *Journal of Head Trauma Rehabilitation, 19*(1), 40–57.

Brander, V. A., Stulberg, S. D., Adams, A. D., Harden, R. N., Bruehl, S., Stanos, S. P., et al. (2003). Predicting total knee replacement pain: A prospective, observational study. *Clinical Orthopaedics and Related Research, 416,* 27–36.

Brosseau, L., Milne, S., Robinson, V., Marchand, S., Shea, B., Wells, G., et al. (2002). Efficacy of the transcutaneous electrical nerve stimulation for the treatment of chronic low back pain: a meta-analysis. *Spine, 27,* 596–603.

Brown, G. K., & Nicassio, P. M. (1987). The development of a questionnaire for the assessment of active and passive coping strategies in chronic pain patients. *Pain, 31,* 53–65.

Bryant, D., Litchfield, R., Sandow, M., Gartsman, G. M., Guyatt, G., & Kirkley, A. (2005). A comparison of pain, strength, range of motion, and functional outcomes after hemiarthroplasty and total shoulder arthroplasty in patients with osteoarthritis of the shoulder. A systematic review and meta-analysis. *Journal of Bone and Joint Surgery, 87,* 1947–1956.

Campbell, J. (1995, December). *Presidential Address.* Paper presented at the American Pain Society, Los Angeles, CA.

Cappio, M. (1957). Sacral epidural administration of hydrocortisone in therapy of lumbar sciatica: Study of 80 cases. *Reumatismo, 9*(1), 60–70.

Carter, M. L. (2004). Spinal cord stimulation in chronic pain: A review of the evidence. *Anaesthesia and Intensive Care, 32*(1), 11–21.

Cepeda, M. S., Carr, D. B., & Lau, J. (2005). Local anesthetic sympathetic blockade for complex regional pain syndrome (Article Number CD004598). *Cochrane Database of Systematic Reviews, 4.* Retrieved June 6, 2007 from http://www.ncbi.nlm.nih.gov/pubmed/16235369

Cook, A. J., Brawer, P. A., & Vowles, K. E. (2006). The fear-avoidance model of chronic pain:Validation and age analysis using structural equation modeling. *Pain, 121,* 195–206.

Dagenais, S., Yelland, M. J., Del Mar, C., & Schoene, M. L. (2007). Prolotherapy injections for chronic low-back pain (Article Number CD004059). *Cochrane Database of Systematic Reviews, 2.* Retrieved June 6, 2007 from http://www.ncbi.nlm.nih.gov/pubmed/17443537

DeGood, D. E., & Tait, R. C. (2001). Assessment of pain beliefs and pain coping. In D. C. Turk & R. Melzack (Eds.), *Handbook of pain assessment* (pp. 320–345). New York: Guilford Press.

Flor, H., Fydrich, T., & Turk, D. C. (1992). Efficacy of multidisciplinary pain treatment centers: A meta-analytic review. *Pain, 49,* 221–230.

Fordyce, W. E. (1976). *Behavioral methods for chronic pain and illness.* St. Louis, MO: Mosby.

France, R. D., Urban, B. J., & Keefe, F. J. (1984). Long-term use of narcotic analgesics in chronic pain. *Social Science and Medicine, 19,* 1379–1382.

Gallez, A., Albanese, M. C., Rainville, P., & Duncan, G. H. (2005). Attenuation of sensory and affective responses to heat pain: Evidence for contralateral mechanisms. *Journal of Neurophysiology, 94,* 3509–3515.

Gamradt, S. C., & Wang, J. C. (2005). Lumbar disc arthroplasty. *The Spine Journal, 5*(1), 95–103.

Geisser, M. E., Robinson, M. E., Keefe, F. J., & Weiner, M. L. (1994). Catastrophizing, depression and the sensory, affective and evaluative aspects of chronic pain. *Pain, 59,* 79–83.

George, S. Z., Wittmer, V. T., Fillingim, R. B., & Robinson, M. E. (2006). Fear-avoidance beliefs and temporal summation of evoked thermal pain influence self-report of disability in patients with chronic low back pain. *Journal of Occupational Rehabilitation, 16*(1), 95–108.

Goossens, M. E., Vlaeyen, J. W., Hidding, A., Kole-Snijders, A., & Evers, S. M. (2005). Treatment expectancy affects the outcome of cognitive–behavioral interventions in chronic pain. *Clinical Journal of Pain, 21,* 18–26.

Hale, M. E., Fleischmann, R., Salzman, R., Wild, J., Iwan, T., Swanton, R. E., et al. (1999). Efficacy and safety of controlled-release versus immediate-release oxycodone: Randomized, double-blind evaluation in patients with chronic back pain. *Clinical Journal of Pain, 15,* 179–183.

Hayes, S. C., Strosahl, K., & Wilson, K. G. (1999). *Acceptance and commitment therapy: An experiential approach to behavior change.* New York: Guilford Press.

Hayes, S. C., Wilson, K. G., Gifford, E. V., Follette, V. M., & Strosahl, K. (1996). Experimental avoidance and behavioral disorders: A functional dimensional approach to diagnosis and treatment. *Journal of Consulting and Clinical Psychology, 64,* 1152–1168.

Haythornthwaite, J. A., Menefee, L. A., Quatrano-Piacentini, A. L., & Pappagallo, M. (1998). Outcome of chronic opioid therapy for non-cancer pain. *Journal of Pain Symptom Management, 15,* 185–194.

Hoffman, B. M., Papas, R. K., Chatkoff, D. K., & Kerns, R. D. (2007). Meta-analysis of psychological interventions for chronic low back pain. *Health Psychology, 26*(1), 1–9.

Jamison, R. N., Raymond, S. A., Slawsby, E. A., Nedeljkovic, S. S., & Katz, N. P. (1998). Opioid therapy for chronic noncancer back pain. A randomized prospective study. *Spine, 23,* 2591–2600.

Jensen, M. P., & Karoly, P. (2001). Self-report scales and procedures for assessing pain in adults. In D. C. Turk & R. Melzack (Eds.), *Handbook of pain assessment* (pp. 15–34). New York: Guilford Press.

Jones, C. A., Beaupre, L. A., Johnston, D. W., & Suarez-Almazor, M. E. (2005). Total joint arthroplasties: Current concepts of patient outcomes after surgery. *Clinics in Geriatric Medicine, 21,* 527–541.

Jonsson, A. C., Lindgren, I., Hallstrom, B., Norrving, B., & Lindgren, A. (2006). Prevalence and intensity of pain after stroke: A population-based study focusing on patients' perspectives. *Journal of Neurology, Neurosurgery, and Psychiatry, 77,* 590–595.

Kalso, E., Edwards, J. E., Moore, R. A., & McQuay, H. J. (2004). Opioids in chronic noncancer pain: Systematic review of efficacy and safety. *Pain, 112,* 372–380.

Keefe, F. J., Rumble, M. E., Scipio, C. D., Giordano, L. A., & Perri, L. M. (2004). Psychological aspects of persistent pain: Current state of the science. *Journal of Pain, 5,* 195–211.

Keefe, F. J., Williams, D. A., & Smith, S. J. (2001). Assessment of pain behaviors. In D. C. Turk & R. Melzack (Eds.), *Handbook of pain assessment* (pp. 170–187). New York: Guilford Press.

Khadilkar, A., Odebiyi, D. O., Brosseau, L., & Wells, G. A. (2008). Transcutaneous electrical nerve stimulation (TENS) versus placebo for chronic low-back pain (Article Number CD003008). *Cochrane Database of Systematic Reviews, 4.* Retrieved November 9, 2008 from http://www.ncbi.nlm.nih.gov/pubmed/18843638

Kong, K. H., Woon, V. C., & Yang, S. Y. (2004). Prevalence of chronic pain and its impact on health-related quality of life in stroke survivors. *Archives of Physical Medicine Rehabilitation, 85,* 35–40.

Lahz, S., & Bryant, R. A. (1996). Incidence of chronic pain following traumatic brain injury. *Archives of Physical Medicine and Rehabilitation, 77,* 889–891.

Leijon, G., Boivie, J., & Johansson, I. (1989). Central poststroke pain: Neurological symptoms and pain characteristics. *Pain, 36,* 13–25.

Lethem, J., Slade, P. D., Troup, J. D., & Bentley, G. (1983). Outline of a fear-avoidance model of exaggerated pain perception. I. *Behavior Research and Therapy, 21,* 401–408.

Lindholm, R., & Salenius, P. (1964). Caudal, epidural administration of anaesthetics and corticoids in the treatment of low-back pain. *Acta Orthopaedica Scandinavica, 34,* 114–116.

Linton, S. J., & Andersson, T. (2000). Can chronic disability be prevented? A randomized trial of a cognitive–behavior intervention and two forms of information for patients with spinal pain. *Spine, 25,* 2825–2831.

Linton, S. J., Boersma, K., Jansson, M., Svard, L., & Botvalde, M. (2005). The effects of cognitive–behavioral and physical therapy preventive interventions on pain-related sick leave: a randomized controlled trial. *Clinical Journal of Pain, 21,* 109–119.

Mailis-Gagnon, A., Furlan, A. D., Sandoval, J. A., & Taylor, R. (2004). Spinal cord stimulation for chronic pain (Article Number CD003783). *Cochrane Database System of Reviews, 3.* Retrieved June 6, 2007 from http://www.ncbi.nlm.nih.gov/pubmed/15266501

Mariano, A. J. (1992). Chronic pain and spinal cord injury. *Clinical Journal of Pain, 8,* 87–92.

Martelli, M. F., Grayson, R. L., & Zasler, N. D. (1999). Posttraumatic headache: Neuropsychological and psychological effects and treatment implications. *Journal of Head Trauma Rehabilitation, 14*(1), 49–69.

McCracken, L. M. (1998). Learning to live with the pain: Acceptance of pain predicts adjustment in persons with chronic pain. *Pain, 74,* 21–27.

McCracken, L. M., Carson, J. W., Eccleston, C., & Keefe, F. J. (2004). Acceptance and change in the context of chronic pain. *Pain, 109,* 4–7.

McCracken, L. M., & Eccleston, C. (2003). Coping or acceptance: What to do about chronic pain? *Pain, 105,* 197–204.

McCracken, L. M., & Eccleston, C. (2005). A prospective study of acceptance of pain and patient functioning with chronic pain. *Pain, 118,* 164–169.

McCracken, L. M., & Eccleston, C. (2006). A comparison of the relative utility of coping and acceptance-based measures in a sample of chronic pain sufferers. *European Journal of Pain, 10*(1), 23–29.

McCracken, L. M., & Turk, D. C. (2002). Behavioral and cognitive–behavioral treatment for chronic pain: Outcome, predictors of outcome, and treatment process. *Spine, 27,* 2564–2573.

Melzack, R., & Katz, J. (2001). The McGill Pain Questionnaire: Appraisal and current status. In D. C. Turk & R. Melzack (Eds.), *Handbook of pain assessment* (pp. 35–52). New York: Guilford Press.

Merskey, H., & Bogduk, N. (Eds.). (1994). *Classification of chronic pain: Descriptions of chronic pain syndromes and definitions of pain terms* (2nd ed.). Seattle, WA: IASP Press.

Milling, L. S., Reardon, J. M., & Carosella, G. M. (2006). Mediation and moderation of psychological pain treatments: Response expectancies and hypnotic suggestibility. *Journal of Consulting and Clinical Psychology, 74,* 253–262.

Nash, J. M., Park, E. R., Walker, B. B., Gordon, N., & Nicholson, R. A. (2004). Cognitive–behavioral group treatment for disabling headache. *Pain Medicine, 5,* 178–186.

Nashold, B. S. (1991). Paraplegia and pain. In B. S. Nashold & J. Ovelmen-Levitt (Eds.), *Deafferentation pain syndromes: Pathophysiology and treatment* (pp. 301–319). New York: Raven Press.

Niemisto, L., Kalso, E., Malmivaara, A., Seitsalo, S., & Hurri, H. (2003). Radiofrequency denervation for neck and back pain: A systematic review within the framework of the cochrane collaboration back review group. *Spine, 28,* 1877–1888.

Peloso, P. M. J., Gross, A., Haines, T., Trinh, K., Goldsmith, C. H., Burnie, S. J., & Cervical Overview Group. (2007). Medicinal and injection therapies for mechanical neck disorders (Article Number CD000319). *Cochrane Database System of Reviews, 3.* Retrieved June 6, 2007 from http://www.ncbi.nlm.nih.gov/pubmed/17636629

Price, D. D. (1999). *The phenomenon of pain: Vol. 15. Psychological mechanisms of pain and analgesia. Progress in Pain Research and Management* (pp. 3–14). Seattle, WA: IASP Press.

Price, D. D., Harkins, S. W., & Baker, C. (1987). Sensory–affective relationships among different types of clinical and experimental pain. *Pain, 28,* 297–307.

Price, D. D., Riley, J. L., III, & Wade, J. B. (2001). Psychophysical approaches to measurement of the dimensions and stages of pain. In D. C. Turk & R. Melzack (Eds.), *Handbook of pain assessment* (pp. 53–76). New York: Guilford Press.

Puder, R. S. (1988). Age analysis of cognitive–behavioral group therapy for chronic pain outpatients. *Psychology and Aging, 3,* 204–207.

Rainville, P. (2002). Brain mechanisms of pain affect and pain modulation. *Current Opinion in Neurobiology, 12,* 195–204.

Rainville, P., Carrier, B., Hofbauer, R. K., Bushnell, M. C., & Duncan, G. H. (1999). Dissociation of sensory and affective dimensions of pain using hypnotic modulation. *Pain, 82,* 159–171.

Rainville, P., Duncan, G. H., Price, D. D., Carrier, B., & Bushnell, M. C. (1997). Pain affect encoded in human anterior cingulate but not somatosensory cortex. *Science, 277,* 968–971.

Rainville, P., Feine, J. S., Bushnell, M. C., & Duncan, G. H. (1992). A psychophysical comparison of sensory and affective responses to four modalities of experimental pain. *Somatosensory and Motor Research, 9,* 265–277.

Ready, L. B. (1990). Regional analgesia with intraspinal opioids. In J. J. Bonica (Ed.), *The management of pain: Vol. 2* (2nd ed., pp. 1967–1979). Philadelphia: Lea & Febiger.

Richter, K. J., Cowan, D. W., & Kaschalk, S. M. (1995). A protocol for managing pain, sleep disorders, and associate psychological sequelae of presumed mild head injury. *Journal of Head Trauma Rehabilitation, 10,* 7–15.

Richter, K. J., Cowan, D. W., & Kaschalk, S. M. (1997). Sleep and pain complaints in TBI. *Archives of Physical Medicine and Rehabilitation, 78,* 451.

Robinson, M. E., & Riley, J. L., III (1999). The role of emotion in pain. In R. J. Gatchel & D. C. Turk (Eds.), *Psychosocial factors in pain* (pp. 74–88). New York: Guilford Press.

Robinson, M. E., Riley, J. L., III, Myers, C. D., Sadler, I. J., Kvaal, S. A., Geisser, M. E., et al. (1997). The Coping Strategies Questionnaire: A large sample, item level factor analysis. *Clinical Journal of Pain, 13*(1), 43–49.

Robinson, M. E., Wise, E. A., Gagnon, C., Fillingim, R. B., & Price, D. D. (2004). Influences of gender role and anxiety on sex differences in temporal summation of pain. *Journal of Pain, 5,* 77–82.

Rosenstiel, A. K., & Keefe, F. J. (1983). The use of coping strategies in chronic low back pain patients: Relationship to patient characteristics and current adjustment. *Pain, 17,* 33–44.

Schnitzer, T. J., Gray, W. L., Paster, R. Z., & Kamin, M. (2000). Efficacy of tramadol in treatment of chronic low back pain. *Journal of Rheumatology, 27,* 772–778.

Sharma, L., Sinacore, J., Daugherty, C., Kuesis, D. T., Stulberg, S. D., Lewis, M., et al. (1996). Prognostic factors for functional outcome of total knee replacement: A prospective study. *Journals of Gerontology, Series A: Biological Sciences and Medical Sciences, 51,* M152–M157.

Siddall, P. J., & Loeser, J. D. (2001). Pain following spinal cord injury. *Spinal Cord, 39*(2), 63–73.

Simons, D. G. (Ed.). (1988). *Myofascial pain syndromes of head, neck and low back.* New York: Elsevier.

Smith, C. A., Wallston, K. A., Dwyer, K. A., & Dowdy, S. W. (1997). Beyond good and bad coping: A multidimensional examination of coping with pain in persons with rheumatoid arthritis. *Annals of Behavioral Medicine, 19,* 11–21.

Staud, R., Cannon, R. C., Mauderli, A. P., Robinson, M. E., Price, D. D., & Vierck, C. J., Jr. (2003). Temporal summation of pain from mechanical stimulation of muscle tissue in normal controls and subjects with fibromyalgia syndrome. *Pain, 102,* 87–95.

Sullivan, M. J. L., Bishop, S. R., & Pivik, J. (1995). The Pain Catastrophizing Scale: Development and validation. *Psychological Assessment, 7,* 524–532.

Sullivan, M. J., Stanish, W., Waite, H., Sullivan, M., & Tripp, D. A. (1998). Catastrophizing, pain, and disability in patients with soft-tissue injuries. *Pain, 77,* 253–260.

Sullivan, M. J., Thorn, B., Haythornthwaite, J. A., Keefe, F., Martin, M., Bradley, L. A., et al. (2001). Theoretical perspectives on the relation between catastrophizing and pain. *Clinical Journal of Pain, 17,* 52–64.

Turk, D. C. (2003). Cognitive–behavioral approach to the treatment of chronic pain patients. *Regional Anesthesia and Pain Medicine, 28,* 573–579.

Turk, D. C., & Melzack, R. (2001a). The measurement of pain and the assessment of people experiencing pain. In D. C. Turk & R. Melzack (Eds.), *Handbook of pain assessment* (pp. 3–14). New York: Guilford Press.

Turk, D. C., & Melzack, R. (2001b). Trends and future directions in human pain assessment. In D. C. Turk & R. Melzack (Eds.), *Handbook of pain assessment* (pp. 707–715). New York: Guilford Press.

Turner, J. A., Loeser, J. D., Deyo, R. A., & Sanders, S. B. (2004). Spinal cord stimulation for patients with failed back surgery syndrome or complex regional pain syndrome: A systematic review of effectiveness and complications. *Pain, 108,* 137–147.

Turner, J. A., Mancl, L., & Aaron, L. A. (2005). Brief cognitive–behavioral therapy for temporomandibular disorder pain: Effects on daily electronic outcome and process measures. *Pain, 117,* 377–387.

Turner, J. A., Mancl, L., & Aaron, L. A. (2006). Short- and long-term efficacy of brief cognitive–behavioral therapy for patients with chronic temporomandibular disorder pain: A randomized, controlled trial. *Pain, 121,* 181–194.

Turner-Stokes, L., Erkeller-Yuksel, F., Miles, A., Pincus, T., Shipley, M., & Pearce, S. (2003). Outpatient cognitive–behavioral pain management programs: A randomized comparison of a group-based multidisciplinary versus an individual therapy model. *Archives of Physical Medicine and Rehabilitation, 84,* 781–788.

Uomoto, J. M., & Esselman, P. C. (1993). Traumatic brain injury and chronic pain: Differential types and rates by head injury severity. *Archives of Physical Medicine and Rehabilitation, 74,* 61–64.

van Tulder, M. W., Touray, T., Furlan, A. D., Solway, S., & Bouter, L. M. (2003). Muscle relaxants for non-specific low-back pain (Article Number CD004252. DOI: 10.1002/14651858.CD004252CD004252). *Cochrane Database of Systematic Reviews, 4.* Retrieved June 6, 2007 from http://www.cochrane.org/reviews/en/ab004252.html

Vase, L., Price, D. D., Verne, G. N., & Robinson, M. E. (2004). The contribution of changes in expected pain levels and desire for relief to placebo analgesia. In D. D. Price & M. C. Bushnell (Eds.), *Psychological methods of pain control: Basic science and clinical perspectives* (pp. 207–234). Seattle, WA: IASP Press.

Vase, L., Robinson, M. E., Verne, G. N., & Price, D. D. (2003). The contributions of suggestion, desire, and expectation to placebo effects in irritable bowel syndrome patients. An empirical investigation. *Pain, 105,* 17–25.

Vase, L., Robinson, M. E., Verne, G. N., & Price, D. D. (2005). Increased placebo analgesia over time in irritable bowel syndrome (IBS) patients is associated with desire and expectation but not endogenous opioid mechanisms. *Pain, 115,* 338–347.

Vlaeyen, J. W., Kole-Snijders, A. M., Boeren, R. G., & van Eek, H. (1995). Fear of movement/(re)injury in chronic low back pain and its relation to behavioral performance. *Pain, 62,* 363–372.

Vlaeyen, J. W., & Linton, S. J. (2000). Fear-avoidance and its consequences in chronic musculoskeletal pain: A state of the art. *Pain, 85,* 317–332.

Walker, W. C. (2004). Pain pathoetiology after TBI: Neural and nonneural mechanisms. *Journal of Head Trauma Rehabilitation, 19*(1), 72–81.

Widar, M., Samuelsson, L., Karlsson-Tivenius, S., & Ahlstrom, G. (2002). Long-term pain conditions after a stroke. *Journal of Rehabilitation Medicine, 34*(4), 165–170.

Zenz, M., Strumpf, M., & Tryba, M. (1992). Long-term oral opioid therapy in patients with chronic non-malignant pain. *Journal of Pain Symptom Management, 7*(2), 69–77.

CHAPTER 8

COGNITION AND MULTIPLE SCLEROSIS: ASSESSMENT AND TREATMENT

Nancy D. Chiaravalloti and John DeLuca

Multiple sclerosis (MS) is a progressive disease of the central nervous system (CNS) characterized by widespread lesions, or plaques, in the myelin sheath of the CNS, which is vital to the normal transmission of nerve impulses (Rumrill, Kaleta, & Battersby, 1996). The widespread nature of these plaques results in a wide array of motor, cognitive and neuropsychiatric symptoms, with vast individual differences in symptoms and disease course (Brassington & Marsh, 1998). Common symptoms include motor and sensory impairment, bowel and bladder difficulty, vision problems, alterations in sexual functioning, fatigue, and cognitive deficits (Kurtze et al., 1972). Women are approximately twice as likely as men to suffer from MS (Kraft, 1981), and MS is significantly more prevalent in specific geographic regions (Rumrill et al.). It is estimated that MS affects at least 400,000 Americans and 2.5 million people worldwide, with diagnosis typically occurring between the ages of 20 and 50 (National Multiple Sclerosis Society, 2008). Although the exact cause of MS remains elusive, it is currently thought to be the result of immunologic, genetic, and viral factors (Rumrill et al., 1996).

The current chapter focuses on cognition and its relation to other factors (e.g., everyday life functioning, quality of life [QoL], emotional symptomatology, fatigue) as well as the assessment and treatment of cognitive deficits in MS. We also discuss recent imaging findings in MS.

PREVALENCE AND EFFECTS OF COGNITIVE IMPAIRMENT IN MULTIPLE SCLEROSIS

Cognitive impairment is a common concomitant of many neurological illnesses and injuries. However, for years the cognitive impairment associated with MS has been minimized. It is only in the past few decades that cognition has been afforded the appropriate attention in the MS population.

Prevalence

Cognitive impairment is common in MS, with estimated prevalence rates ranging from 43% to 70% (Peyser, Rao, LaRocca, & Kaplan, 1990; Rao, Leo, Bernardin, & Unverzagt, 1991). MS negatively affects various aspects of cognitive functioning, including attention (Litvan, Grafman, Vendrell, & Martinez, 1988), working memory (WM; Lengenfelder, Chiaravalloti, & DeLuca, 2003), information processing speed (e.g., DeLuca, Chelune, Tulsky, Lengenfelder, & Chiaravalloti, 2004), executive functioning (Arnett et al., 1997), visuospatial processing (Rao, Leo, Bernardin, & Unverzagt, 1991), and episodic memory (e.g., DeLuca, Barbieri-Berger, & Johnson, 1994).

Although MS compromises various aspects of cognitive functioning, impairments of information processing speed and WM as well as episodic memory have received the majority of recent attention. Although frequently cited as distinct areas of deficit, difficulties with WM and information pro-

133

cessing speed have both often been documented in individuals with MS (e.g., Archibald & Fisk, 2000; Lengenfelder et al., 2003) and may be interrelated. Deficits in both the maintenance (Litvan et al., 1988) and manipulation (Rao et al., 1993) of information in WM have been reported. Studies suggest that slowed information processing speed appears to be the more fundamental deficit (DeLuca et al., 2004; Demaree, DeLuca, Guadino, & Diamond, 1999; Lengenfelder et al., 2006), as it appears to limit the ability of persons with MS to learn new information and to perform higher level cognitive functions (DeLuca et al., 1994; Gaudino, Chiaravalloti, DeLuca, & Diamond, 2001; Thornton & Raz, 1997).

Episodic memory is one of the most frequently impaired functions identified in persons with MS, evident in up to 65% of patients (Rao et al., 1993). The early literature on memory impairment in MS suggested that retrieval failure was the primary cause of the memory deficit (Rao, 1986; Rao, Leo, & St. Aubin-Faubert, 1989). However, more recent research has demonstrated that when equated on the amount of information initially acquired, persons with MS perform within normal limits in the recall or recognition of newly learned information (DeLuca et al., 1994; DeLuca, Gaudino, Diamond, Christodoulou, & Engel, 1998; Thornton & Raz, 1997). This suggests that the memory deficit in MS is one of acquisition of new information, not retrieval from long-term storage, an important distinction for rehabilitation, as discussed as follows.

Effects on Everyday Life Functioning and Emotions

The most significant impact of impaired cognition on the everyday lives of individuals with MS is the low employment rate (Roessler & Rumrill, 2003). Individuals with MS have identified slowed information processing speed and episodic memory deficits as significant obstacles to maintaining meaningful employment (Roessler & Rumrill, 1995). Those who rarely experience cognitive problems report a 53% unemployment rate, whereas those with frequent cognitive problems report one of 86% (Edgley, Sullivan, & Dehoux, 1991).

Cognitive dysfunction is also closely related to daily life functional status in persons with MS

(Beatty, Blanco, Wilbanks, Paul, & Hames, 1995), causing difficulty with a variety of daily tasks, including shopping, doing housework, washing clothes, ironing, and cooking. Cognition also affects driving abilities, assessed by actual driving performance (Schultheis, Garay, & DeLuca, 2001) or a computer-simulated driving test (Shawaryn, Schultheis, Garay, & DeLuca, 2002). Rao, Leo, Ellington, et al. (1991) found that cognitively impaired individuals with MS, as opposed to those with a purely physical disability, were less likely to be employed, engaged in fewer social and vocational activities, had greater difficulties carrying out routine household tasks, and were more vulnerable to psychiatric illness. Clearly, physical disability alone cannot account for the extent of difficulties individuals with MS experience with many everyday activities, particularly those with a significant cognitive load. For more information on functional status measures, see chapter 9 of this volume. Although functional abilities in cognitively impaired populations have traditionally been assessed with self-report measures, subjective reports do not always mirror objective measures (e.g., Goverover et al., 2005). It is worth noting that Goverover et al. found self-report correlated not with performance in everyday life but with emotional distress.

Recent research shows a rather clear link between emotional symptoms and cognitive functions in many neurological populations, including MS (Goverover, Chiaravalloti, & DeLuca, 2005). Depression and anxiety are common symptoms in MS that can interfere considerably with both cognitive and noncognitive activities (Schwid, 2003). Lifetime prevalence rates for depression in individuals with MS greatly exceed those seen in healthy individuals, falling between 37% and 54% (Minden & Schiffer, 1991). Specifically, depression level is associated with neuropsychological functioning in MS; depressed individuals with MS are significantly more impaired on cognitive tasks than their nondepressed counterparts, evident in WM functions (e.g., Arnett et al., 1999), processing speed (Arnett et al., 1999), memory performance, and nonverbal intelligence measures (e.g., Ravens Progressive Matrices; Gilchrist & Creed, 1994). Although anxiety has been less of a focus of MS research, it is often comorbid with depression and has been shown to have a prevalence rate of approximately 8% in an MS sample (Joffe, Lippert, Gray, Sawa, & Horvath, 1987).

Evidence exists that by treating the cognitive deficits associated with MS, emotional symptoms are alleviated. This has been noted following both behavioral interventions (e.g., Jonsson, Korfitzen, Heltberg, Ravnborg, & Byskov-Ottosen, 1993) and psychopharmacological treatment (Greene et al., 2000). These findings highlight the delicate relation between cognitive and emotional symptoms in persons with MS.

Effects on Quality of Life

There is a substantial body of literature indicating that QoL is decreased in individuals with MS (Grima et al., 2000) and that the degree of decrement in QoL correlates with deficits in cognitive functioning (Cutajar et al., 2000); depressive symptomatology (e.g., Wang, Reimer, Metz, & Patten, 2000); increased disability (Henriksson, Fredrikson, Masterman, & Jönsson, 2001); duration, severity, and progression of the disease (Pfennings et al., 1999); decreased cerebral integrity on magnetic resonance imaging (MRI; Janardhan & Bakshi, 2000); and diminished capacity to carry out activities of daily living (Gulick, 1997). QoL is also lower during periods of relapse (Henriksson et al., 2001) and correlates with neurological disability (Barker-Collo, 2006). Multiple studies have also clearly demonstrated that cognitive deficits are detrimental to QoL and productivity in MS (Cutajar et al., 2000; Rao, Leo, Bernardin, & Unverzagt, 1991), with such deficits demonstrating a significant relationship with QoL in MS (Plohmann et al., 1998).

MS groups show significantly lower health-related QoL than others with chronic medical conditions and neurological illnesses (Hermann et al., 1996; The Canadian Burden of Illness Study Group, 1998). Researchers have also identified lower QoL scores in the presence of more severe and advanced MS, with a longer disease duration (e.g., Pfennings et al., 1999). Factors found to be associated with increased QoL in MS include living with a spouse, being employed, reduced pain (Gulick, 1997), better cognitive functioning (Cutajar et al., 2000), and diminished depression (Wang et al., 2000).

Because patients with diseases such as MS may survive for many years, the goal of health care is often to maximize health-related QoL. Rehabilitative treatments (e.g., T'ai chi, Husted, Pham, Hekking, & Niederman, 1999; training in coping skills, Schwartz, 1999; cognitive rehabilitation, Jonsson, Korfitzen, Heltberg, Ravnborg, & Byskov-Ottosen, 1996) can improve QoL in MS, as can comprehensive rehabilitation (Jonsson et al., 1996).

Effects on Fatigue

Fatigue is one of the most common symptoms in MS, yet it remains poorly understood and difficult to manage (Krupp, Christodoulou, & Schombert, 2005). Currently, the primary approach to measuring fatigue is by patient subjective report (e.g., Krupp et al.), but this correlates poorly with actual physical performance or measures of disease activity (e.g., lesion load; DeLuca, 2005). Even measures of physiological fatigue (e.g., muscle metabolism) do not correlate with subjective reports (Tartaglia et al., 2004).

Not surprisingly, little relationship has been found between subjective fatigue in MS and cognitive dysfunction, such as decline in WM (Johnson, Lange, DeLuca, Korn, & Natelson, 1997), short-term memory (Johnson, DeLuca, Diamond, & Natelson, 1998), executive function or complex attention (Krupp & Elkins, 2000; Rao, Leo, Bernardin, & Unverzagt, 1991), vigilance (Paul, Beatty, Schneider, Blanco, & Hames, 1998), verbal fluency (Rao, Leo, Bernardin, & Unverzagt, 1991), or verbal memory (Krupp & Elkins, 2000). Cognitive fatigue can be thought of as decreased performance over a prolonged period of time (e.g., during the course of a day) or during acute but sustained mental effort. To date, it appears that although prolonged effort cognitive activity produces an increase in the subjective experience of fatigue in clinical samples, this does not necessarily translate into observable cognitive performance deficits. Studies examining the effect of fatigue on acute but sustained mental effort have demonstrated diminished performance over the course of sustained work (Krupp & Elkins, 2000; Bryant, Chiaravalloti, & DeLuca, 2004), though not consistently correlating with self-report. Decreased performance over time during sustained mental effort may represent a useful objective measure of cognitive fatigue.

ASSESSMENT OF COGNITION AND QUALITY OF LIFE IN MULTIPLE SCLEROSIS

Given the substantial evidence highlighting deficits in cognition in persons with MS, as well as their reduced QoL, it should not be surprising that significant efforts have been dedicated to determining the optimal means of identifying such difficulties when they exist. Although the diversity of the patient population in terms of specific symptomology presents an obstacle to the identification of the most reliable and valid means of assessment of these areas, much progress has been made to date.

Cognition

Although the current gold standard for the identification of cognitive deficits is the neuropsychological evaluation, these procedures have been criticized for having only limited ecological validity, as well as being costly and time consuming. Therefore, MS researchers have recently focused on developing brief screening tools for cognitive deficits in MS. These include the Brief Neuropsychological Battery (Rao, Leo, Bernardin, & Unverzagt, 1991), the Screening Examination for Cognitive Impairment (Beatty, Paul, et al., 1995), and the Basso Screening Battery (Basso, Beason-Hazen, Lynn, Rammohan, & Bornstein, 1996; see Benedict et al., 2002, for a complete review). Because of the tradeoff between brevity and comprehensiveness, such screening batteries fail to assess important areas of cognition (Benedict et al., 2002). To address this limitation, the Minimal Assessment of Cognitive Functioning

in Multiple Sclerosis (MACFIMS; Benedict et al., 2002) was developed by a group of experienced MS neuropsychologists. The MACFIMS assesses aspects of cognition typically affected by MS, including processing speed and WM, learning and memory, executive functions, visuospatial processing, and language functions (see Table 8.1). Two tests are included to measure each domain. Administration of the full battery requires approximately 90 minutes (see Benedict et al., 2002, for a complete review).

To potentially triage patients who will later require neuropsychological assessment, Benedict et al. (2003) developed the Multiple Sclerosis Neuropsychology Questionnaire (MSNQ), a 15-item self-report instrument addressing attention, processing speed, and memory. The MSNQ has both a self-report and an informant report form. The self-report form (MSNQ-S) correlates inconsistently with measures of neuropsychological outcome, but consistently with measures of depression, whereas the informant form (MSNQ-I) demonstrates significant correlations with neuropsychological functioning and depression, with difficulty differentiating between the cognitive impairment and depression (Benedict et al., 2003). Reports on the sensitivity and specificity of the MSNQ-I and MSNQ-S have been variable thus far (Benedict et al., 2003, 2004).

Quality of Life

Researchers and clinicians use both generic measures of QoL, such as the SF-36 (e.g., Vickrey, Hays, Genovese, Myers, & Ellison, 1997) and the Farmer QoL Index (Rudick, Miller, Clough, Gragg, &

TABLE 8.1

Tests Included in the Minimal Assessment of Cognitive Function in Multiple Sclerosis (MACFIMS)

Domain	Test	Reference
Processing speed and working memory	Paced Auditory Serial Addition Test	Rao, Leo, Ellington, et al., 1991
	Symbol Digit Modalities Test	Rao, Leo, Bernardin, & Unverzagt, 1991
Learning and memory	California Verbal Learning Test–II	Delis, Kramer, Kaplan, & Ober, 2000
	Brief Visuospatial Memory Test–Revised	Benedict, 1997
Executive functioning	Delis Kaplan Executive Functioning System–Sorting Test	Delis, Kaplan, & Kramer, 2000
Visual perception and spatial processing	Judgment of Line Orientation Test	Benton, Sivan, Hamsher, Varney, & Spreen, 1994
Language/other	Controlled Oral Word Association Test	Lezak, 2004

Farmer, 1992), and measures specifically developed to examine QoL in persons with MS, such as the Quality of Life Index–MS Version (Ferrans & Powers, 1985), the Leeds Multiple Sclerosis Quality of Life Scale (Ford et al., 2001), the Hamburg Quality of Life Questionnaire in Multiple Sclerosis (Gold et al., 2001), and the Functional Assessment of Multiple Sclerosis (Cella et al., 1996). The Multiple Sclerosis Quality of Life Inventory (MSQLI; Consortium of Multiple Sclerosis Centers Health Services Research Subcommittee, 1997) was designed to be specific to MS while also allowing comparisons with other patient populations. Hence, the MSQLI comprises 10 scales, both generic and MS-specific. Although the authors recommend that the MSQLI be administered in its entirety, each scale can each be used in isolation (Fischer, Rudick, Cutter, & Reingold, 1999). For more information about QoL measures, see chapter 9 of this volume.

ROLE OF NEUROIMAGING IN ASSESSING MULTIPLE SCLEROSIS

The rapid development of technology has revolutionized the study of cognition. Both structural and functional neuroimaging techniques have been applied to clinical populations over the last few decades in an effort to increase our understanding of how the brain responds to injury and illness in terms of both structure and function. MS is no exception, and the surge of research using imaging techniques with persons with MS is rapidly advancing our understanding of the disease itself as well as its impact on cognition.

Structural Neuroimaging

MRI has been widely used in MS for diagnosis and measurement of disease severity. An MRI lesion severity score has been shown to be related to functional impairment (Edwards, Farlow, & Stevens, 1986), immunologic function (Oger, Kastrukoff, Li, & Paty, 1988), visual psychophysical deficits (Caruana et al., 2000), and QoL (Janardhan & Bakshi, 2000). Unique attempts to analyze lesion burden include measurement of ventricular diameter (Berg, Maurer, Warmuth-Metz, Rieckmann, & Becker, 2000) and the creation of whole-brain

quantitative diffusion histograms (Wilson, Morgan, Lin, Turner, & Blumhardt, 2001).

In recent years, a number of studies have attempted to relate imaging evidence of lesion location and lesion burden to cognitive dysfunction in MS. Using MRI, Swirsky-Sacchetti et al. (1992) found total lesion area to be the best predictor of cognitive test performance, supporting an earlier finding by Rao, Leo, Haughton, St Aubin-Faubert, and Bernardin (1989). Frontal region lesions were the most significant predictors of impairment on nearly 50% of the cognitive tasks administered. Regional MRI studies have shown that the greatest representation of lesion volume in subjects with MS is in the frontal regions, consistently observable over 4 years in the same sample (Sperling et al., 2001). Furthermore, a correlation has been noted between total, frontal, and parietal lesion burden and cognitive performance on tasks assessing WM and new learning (Sperling et al., 2001). Anatomical studies have demonstrated that poor performance on tests of WM, processing speed, and verbal memory was associated with frontal, parietal, and total lesion burden but not with lesions in the temporal, occipital, brainstem, or cerebellar regions (Sperling et al., 2001). Some investigators have reported that atrophy demonstrates a stronger relationship with cognitive performance in MS than does other MRI variables (e.g., Benedict, Weinstock-Guttman, et al., 2004). For more information on structural neuroimaging, see chapter 13 of this volume.

Functional Neuroimaging

Functional neuroimaging studies have also provided valuable information about the integrity of brain structure and function. Functional MRI (fMRI) studies of the motor system in MS have focused on fine finger movements, showing significant differences in patterns of cortical activation during motor tasks when compared with healthy controls (e.g., Filippi et al., 2004; Lee et al., 2000; Reddy et al., 2002; Rocca et al., 2003). Specifically, MS participants show both increased contralateral and ipsilateral activation of the sensorimotor cortex compared with healthy controls (e.g., Rocca et al., 2002, 2003), suggesting that the motor tasks are recruiting additional cortical resources.

The limited number of existing studies examining cognition in MS using functional neuroimaging has focused on attention, executive functions, and WM. Studies using functional MRI (fMRI) to examine attention have shown a more diffuse pattern of cortical activation in persons with MS than in healthy controls (Penner, Rausch, Kappos, Opwis, & Radu, 2003). However, studies of executive functioning have not revealed differences (Lazeron, Rombouts, Scheltens, Polman, & Barkhof, 2004). More studies are needed before any definitive conclusions can be drawn about the neuroanatomical underpinnings of attention and executive control in MS.

In the study of WM in MS, two general patterns of cortical activation have been observed with fMRI. First, in contrast to healthy control participants, who tend to show more focal left frontal activation, MS participants exhibit bilateral frontal activation (Audoin et al., 2003, 2005; Chiaravalloti et al., 2005; Mainero et al., 2004). Second, compared with healthy control participants, MS groups show significantly greater activation dispersed throughout the entire brain. Some authors have noted differences in patterns of cerebral activation in MS participants with impaired WM versus those without impaired WM (Chiaravalloti et al., 2005), whereas others have not (Audoin et al., 2005; Mainero et al., 2004); fMRI studies using other WM tasks suggest that the pattern of activation between the MS participants and healthy controls does not differ when performance is similar (e.g., Sweet, Rao, Primeau, Mayer, & Cohen, 2004). However, the level of activation within the activated regions has been found to be significantly greater in MS as compared with the healthy control participants (e.g., Hillary et al., 2003; Sweet et al., 2004). In regard to the cerebellum, a significant decrease in the number of voxels activated in the right and left cerebellar hemispheres has been noted in MS as compared with healthy control participants on a WM task (Li et al., 2004).

The effect of fatigue on brain activity in MS has also been examined using functional neuroimaging, with neurofunctional differences reported between persons with MS who complain of fatigue and those who do not (e.g., Fillipi et al., 2002; Roelcke et al., 1997). Although the pathophysiology of fatigue in MS is still unclear, these neuroimaging studies demonstrated greater activation in persons with MS not reporting fatigue as compared with those reporting fatigue in the ipsilateral cerebellar hemisphere, inferior frontal region, parietal cortex, contralateral middle frontal gyrus, and thalamus. In contrast, the MS group with fatigue showed increased activation in the cingulate motor area. However, more studies are needed to elucidate the cause of fatigue in MS and explain such neuroimaging correlates.

Of the various explanations put forth for the differing levels and patterns of cerebral activation in MS, the most common one involves cerebral reorganization (Filippi & Rocca, 2004; Mainero et al., 2004), an attempt to recruit additional cortical regions as a compensatory mechanism to decrease the effects of MS-related motor and cognitive impairments (Rocca et al., 2002). However, alternative explanations stress the impact of the level of task demand for a given individual and neuronal integrity (Voelbel, Chiaravalloti, & DeLuca, 2007). For more information on functional neuroimaging, see chapter 13 of this volume.

TREATMENT OF COGNITIVE IMPAIRMENTS IN MULTIPLE SCLEROSIS

The treatment of cognitive deficits in MS has received little attention. Cognitive rehabilitation studies with MS have shown encouraging results for the treatment of attention (Plohmann et al., 1998), executive dysfunction (Birnboim & Miller, 2004), communication skills (Foley et al., 1994), and episodic memory (Allen, Goldstein, Heyman, & Rondinelli, 1998). In addition, studies examining the effectiveness of multimodal treatment protocols (Lincoln, Dent, & Harding, 2003) as well as neuropsychologic counseling (Benedict et al., 2000) have shown some positive results in MS.

In contrast, a lack of support for various forms of cognitive rehabilitation in MS has also been reported (Solari et al., 2004). Unfortunately, methodological limitations often limit the conclusions that can be drawn. Specifically, much of the cognitive rehabilitation research in MS suffers from such methodological flaws as limited length of follow-up, lack of a control group, small sample sizes, or lack of randomization, as well as failure to look at the generalization of treatment effects to everyday life or the impact of treatment on QoL. Future studies need to take these methodological factors into account to advance rehabilitative care in MS.

MS researchers have attempted to apply novel approaches for improving new learning and memory in individuals with MS, including the repetition effect (Chiaravalloti, Demaree, Gaudino, & DeLuca, 2003) and the generation effect (Chiaravalloti & DeLuca, 2002). Simple repetition of information is insufficient to improve new learning and memory, but Chiaravalloti and DeLuca showed that persons with MS could benefit from self-generation when learning new information. A follow-up study found significant improvement from self-generation on memory for functional tasks (e.g., cooking, managing finances) in persons with MS (Goverover, Chiaravalloti, & DeLuca, 2008). These findings suggest that persons with MS can improve everyday memory function through the application of self-generation to everyday tasks.

Although the research is limited, some studies have noted beneficial effects of cognition-enhancing medications such as donepezil (Aricept; e.g., Krupp et al., 2004), amantadine (Symmetrel; Cohen & Fisher, 1989), and modafinil (Provigil; Rammohan, Rosenberg, Lynn, Pollak, & Nagaraja, 2002). Other studies, however, have failed to find improvement (Geisler et al., 1996; Krupp, 2003). Immuno-modulating medications are used extensively to lessen the effect of MS-related symptoms and potentially slow disease progression, yet few studies have examined the impact of these medications on cognition. Betaseron has been shown to produce mild improvement of visual memory and attention (Pliskin et al., 1996), whereas Avonex modestly improved memory, information processing, visuospatial skills, and executive functions in relapsing-remitting MS (Fisher et al., 1998). Copaxone has not yet shown cognitive-enhancing effects (Weinstein et al., 1999).

CONCLUSIONS AND FUTURE DIRECTIONS

The examination of cognition in MS has expanded considerably over the past 20 years and researchers are now beginning to understand that MS negatively affects various aspects of cognitive functioning, including working memory, information processing speed, executive functioning, and episodic memory. Fatigue is one of the most common symptoms in MS, yet little relationship has been found between subjective fatigue in MS and cognitive dysfunction. Cognitive dysfunction has been shown to be closely related to daily life functional status; physical disability alone cannot account for the extent of difficulties individuals with MS experience with many everyday activities. Recent advancements in neuroimaging have allowed us to increase our understanding of cognitive deficits in MS and better relate our understanding to the structure and function of the brain. We expect imaging to continue to increase our understanding of MS in the coming years. Despite the identification of the pervasive and influential nature of cognitive deficits in MS, little attention has been paid to identifying effective treatments for cognitive impairment in MS, and much of the existing research is methodologically flawed. Future research should focus on identifying effective means of improving cognitive functioning in MS with the goal of increasing functional status and overall QoL.

References

Allen, D. D., Goldstein, G., Heyman, R. A., & Rondinelli, T. (1998). Teaching memory strategies to persons with multiple sclerosis. *Journal of Rehabilitation Research and Development, 35,* 405–410.

Archibald, C. J., & Fisk, J. D. (2000). Information processing efficiency in patients with multiple sclerosis. *Journal of Clinical and Experimental Neuropsychology, 22,* 686–701.

Arnett, P. A., Higgonson, C. I., Voss, W. D., Bender, W. I., Wurst, J. M., & Tippin, J. M. (1999). Depression in multiple sclerosis: Relationship to working memory capacity. *Neuropsychology, 13,* 546–556.

Arnett, P. A., Rao, S. M., Grafman, J., Bernardin, L., Luchetta, T., Binder, J. R., & Lobeck, L. (1997). Executive functions in multiple sclerosis: An analysis of temporal ordering, semantic encoding, and planning abilities. *Neuropsychology, 11,* 535–544.

Audoin, B., Au Duong, M. V., Ranjeva, J. P., Ibarrola, D., Malikova, I., Confort-Gouny, S., et al. (2005). Magnetic resonance study of the influence of tissue damage and cortical reorganization on PASAT performance at the earliest stage of multiple sclerosis. *Human Brain Mapping, 24,* 216–228.

Audoin, B., Ibarrola, D., Ranjeva, J. P., Confort-Gouny, S., Malikova, I., Ali-Cherif, A., et al. (2003). Compensatory cortical activation observed by fMRI during a cognitive task at the earliest stage of MS. *Human Brain Mapping, 20,* 51–58.

Barker-Collo, S. L. (2006). Quality of life in multiple sclerosis: Does information processing speed have an independent effect? *Archives of Clinical Neuropsychology, 21,* 167–174.

Basso, M. R., Beason-Hazen, S., Lynn, J., Rammohan, K., & Bornstein, R. A. (1996). Screening for cognitive dysfunction in multiple sclerosis. *Archives of Neurology, 53,* 980–984.

Beatty, W. W., Blanco, C. R., Wilbanks, S. L., Paul, R. H., & Hames, K. A. (1995). Demographic, clinical, and cognitive characteristics of multiple sclerosis patients who continue to work. *Journal of Neuro-Rehabilitation, 9,* 167–173.

Beatty, W. W., Paul, R. H., Wilbanks, S. L., Hames, K. A., Blanco, C. R., & Goodkin, D. E. (1995). Identifying multiple sclerosis patients with mild or global cognitive impairment using the Screening Examination for Cognitive Impairment (SEFCI). *Neurology, 45,* 718–723.

Benedict, R. H. B. (1997). *Brief Visuospatial Memory Test-Revised: Professional manual.* Odessa, FL: Psychological Assessment Resources.

Benedict, R. H. B., Cox, D., Thompson, L. L., Foley, F. W., Weinstock-Guttman, B., & Munschauer, F. (2004). Reliable screening for neuropsychological impairment in MS. *Multiple Sclerosis, 10,* 675–678.

Benedict, R. H. B., Fischer, J. S., Archibald, C. J., Arnett, P. A., Beatty, W. W., Bobholz, J., et al. (2002). Minimal neuropsychological assessment of MS patients: A consensus approach. *The Clinical Neuropsychologist, 16,* 381–397.

Benedict, R. H. B., Munschauer, F. E., Linn, R., Miller, C., Foley, F. W., & Jacobs, L. D. (2003). Screening for multiple sclerosis cognitive impairment using a self-administered 15-item questionnaire. *Multiple Sclerosis, 9,* 95–100.

Benedict, R. H., Shapiro, A., Priore, R., Miller, C., Munschauer, F., & Jacobs, L. (2000). Neuropsychological counseling improves social behavior in cognitively impaired multiple sclerosis patients. *Multiple Sclerosis, 6,* 391–396.

Benedict, R. H., Weinstock-Guttman, B., Fishman, I., Sharma, J., Tjoa, C. W., & Bakshi, R. (2004). Prediction of neuropsychological impairment in multiple sclerosis: Comparison of conventional magnetic resonance imaging measures of atrophy and lesion burden. *Archives of Neurology, 61,* 226–230.

Benton, A. L., Sivan, A. B., Hamsher, K., Varney, N. R., & Spreen, O. (1994). *Contributions to neuropsychological assessment* (2nd ed.). New York: Oxford University Press.

Berg, D., Maurer, M., Warmuth-Metz, M., Rieckmann, P., & Becker, G. (2000). The correlation between ventricular diameter measured by transcranial sonography and clinical disability and cognitive dysfunction in patients with multiple sclerosis. *Archives of Neurology, 57,* 1289–1292.

Birnboim, S., & Miller, A. (2004). Cognitive rehabilitation for multiple sclerosis patients with executive dysfunction. *Journal of Cognitive Rehabilitation, 22*(4), 11–18.

Brassington, J. C., & Marsh, N. V. (1998). Neuropsychological aspects of multiple sclerosis. *Neuropsychology Review, 8*(2), 43–77.

Bryant, D., Chiaravalloti, N. D., & DeLuca, J. (2004). Objective measurement of cognitive fatigue in multiple sclerosis. *Rehabilitation Psychology, 49,* 114–122.

The Canadian Burden of Illness Study Group. (1998). Burden of illness of multiple sclerosis. Part II: Quality of life. *Canadian Journal of Neurological Science, 25,* 31–38.

Caruana, P. A., Davies, M. B., Weatherby, S. J. M., Williams, R., Haq, N., Foster, D. H., & Hawkins, C. P. (2000). Correlation of MRI lesions with visual psychophysical deficit in secondary progressive multiple sclerosis. *Brain, 123,* 1471–1480.

Cella, D. F., Dineen, K., Arnason, B., Reder, A., Webster, K. A., Karabatsos, G., et al. (1996). Validation of the functional assessment of multiple sclerosis quality of life instrument. *Neurology, 47*(1), 129–39.

Chiaravalloti, N. D., & DeLuca, J. (2002). Self-generation as a means of maximizing learning in multiple sclerosis: An application of the generation effect. *Archives of Physical Medicine and Rehabilitation, 83,* 1070–1079.

Chiaravalloti, N. D., Demaree, H., Gaudino, E., & DeLuca, J. (2003). Can the repetition effect maximize learning in multiple sclerosis? *Clinical Rehabilitation, 17,* 58–68.

Chiaravalloti, N. D., Hillary, F. G., DeLuca, J., Ricker, J. H., Liu, W. C., & Kalnin, A. J. (2005). Cerebral activation patterns during working memory performance in multiple sclerosis using fMRI. *Journal of Clinical and Experimental Neuropsychology, 27,* 33–54.

Cohen, R. A., & Fisher, M. (1989). Amantadine treatment of fatigue associated with multiple sclerosis. *Archives of Neurology, 46,* 676–680.

Consortium of Multiple Sclerosis Centers Health Services Research Subcommittee. (1997). *Multiple Sclerosis Quality of Life Inventory: A user's manual.* New York: The National Multiple Sclerosis Society.

Cutajar, R., Ferriani, E., Scandellari, C., Sabattini, L., Trocino, C., Marchello, L. P., et al. (2000). Cognitive function and quality of life in multiple sclerosis patients. *Journal of Neurovirology, 6*(Suppl. 2), S186–S190.

Delis, D. C., Kaplan, E., & Kramer, J. H. (2000). *Delis-Kaplan Executive Function System.* San Antonio, TX: Psychological Corporation.

Delis, D. C., Kramer, J. H., Kaplan, E., & Ober, B. A. (2000). *California Verbal Learning Test* (2nd ed.). San Antonio, TX: Psychological Corporation.

DeLuca, J. (2005). Fatigue, cognition, and mental effort. In J. DeLuca (Ed.), *Fatigue as a window to the brain.* Cambridge, MA: MIT Press.

DeLuca, J., Barbieri-Berger, S., & Johnson, S. K. (1994). The nature of memory impairment in multiple sclerosis: Acquisition versus retrieval. *Journal of Clinical and Experimental Neuropsychology, 16,* 183–189.

DeLuca, J., Chelune, G., Tulsky, D., Lengenfelder, J., & Chiaravalloti, N. D. (2004). Is speed of processing or working memory the primary information processing deficit in multiple sclerosis? *Journal of Clinical and Experimental Neuropsychology, 26,* 550–562.

DeLuca, J., Gaudino, E. A., Diamond, B. J., Christodoulou, C., & Engel, R. A. (1998). Acquisition and storage deficits in multiple sclerosis. *Journal of Clinical and Experimental Neuropsychology, 20,* 376–90.

Demaree, H. A., DeLuca, J., Guadino, E. A., & Diamond, B. J. (1999). Speed of information processing as a key deficit in multiple sclerosis: Implications for rehabilitation. *Journal of Neurology, Neurosurgery, and Psychiatry, 67,* 661–663.

Edgley, K., Sullivan, M. J., & Dehoux, E. (1991). A survey of multiple sclerosis: Part 2. Determinants of employment status. *Canadian Journal of Rehabilitation, 4,* 127–132.

Edwards, M. K., Farlow, M. R., & Stevens, J. C. (1986). Multiple sclerosis: MRI and clinical correlation. *American Journal of Roentgenology, 147,* 571–574.

Ferrans, C., & Powers, M. (1985). Quality of life index: Development and psychometric properties. *Advances in Nursing Science, 8,* 15–24.

Filippi, M., & Rocca, M. A. (2004). Cortical reorganization in patients with MS. *Journal of Neurology Neurosurgery and Psychiatry, 75,* 1087–1089.

Filippi, M., Rocca, M. A., Mezzapesa, D. M., Falini, A., Colombo, B., Scotti, G., & Comi, G. (2004). A functional MRI study of cortical activations associated with object manipulation in patients with MS. *NeuroImage, 21,* 1147–1154.

Fischer, J. S., Rudick, R. A., Cutter, G. R., & Reingold, S. (1999). The Multiple Sclerosis Functional Composite Measure (MSFC): An integrated approach to MS clinical outcome assessment. *Multiple Sclerosis, 5,* 244–250.

Fisher, J. S., Priore, R. L., Jacobs, L. D., Cookfair, D. L., Rudick, R. A., Herndon, R. M., et al. (1998). Neuropsychological effects of Interferon B-1a in relapsing multiple sclerosis. *Annals of Neurology, 48,* 885–892.

Foley, F. W., Dince, W. M., LaRocca, N. G., Kalb, R., Carusso, L. S., Smith, C. R., et al. (1994). Psycho-remediation of communication skills for cognitively impaired persons with multiple sclerosis. *Journal of Neurological Rehabilitation, 8,* 165–176.

Ford, H. L., Gerry, E., Tennant, A., Whalley, D., Haigh, R., & Johnson, M. H. (2001). Developing a disease-specific quality of life measure for people with multiple sclerosis. *Clinical Rehabilitation, 15,* 247–258.

Gaudino, E., Chiaravalloti, N. D., DeLuca, J., & Diamond, B. J. (2001). A comparison of memory performance in relapsing-remitting, primary-progressive and secondary progressive multiple sclerosis. *Neuropsychiatry, Neuropsychology, and Behavioral Neurology, 14,* 32–44.

Geisler, M. W., Sliwinski, M., Coyle, P. K., Masur, D. M., Dosher, C., & Krupp, L. B. (1996). The effects of amantadine and pemoline on cognitive functioning in multiple sclerosis. *Archives of Neurology, 53,* 185–188.

Gilchrist, A. C., & Creed, F. H. (1994). Depression, cognitive impairment, and social stress in multiple sclerosis. *Journal of Psychosomatic Research, 38,* 193–201.

Gold, S. M., Heesen, C., Schulz, H., Guder, U., Monch, A., Gbadamosi, J., et al. (2001). Disease specific quality of life instruments in multiple sclerosis: Validation of the Hamburg Quality of Life Questionnaire in Multiple Sclerosis (HAQUAMS). *Multiple Sclerosis, 7,* 119–130.

Goverover, Y., Chiaravalloti, N. D., & DeLuca, J. (2005). The relationship between self-awareness of neurobehavioral symptoms, cognitive functioning, and emotional symptoms in multiple sclerosis. *Multiple Sclerosis, 11,* 203–212.

Goverover, Y., Chiaravalloti, N. D., & DeLuca, J. (2008). *Self-generation to improve learning and memory of functional activities in multiple sclerosis: Meal preparation and managing finances.* Manuscript submitted for publication.

Goverover, Y., Kalmar, J., Gaudino-Goering, E., Shawaryn, M., Moore, N. B., Halper, J., & DeLuca, J. (2005). The relation between subjective and objective measures of everyday life activities in persons with multiple sclerosis. *Archives of Physical Medicine and Rehabilitation, 86,* 2303–2308.

Greene, Y. M., Tariot, P. N., Wishart, H., Cox, C., Holt, C. J., Schwid, S., & Noviasky, J. (2000). A 12-week, open trial of donepezil hydrochloride in patients with multiple sclerosis and associated cognitive impairments. *Journal of Clinical Psychopharmacology, 20,* 350–356.

Grima, D. T., Torrance, G. W., Francis, G., Rice, G., Rosner, A. J., & Lafortune, L. (2000). Cost and health related quality of life consequences of multiple sclerosis. *Multiple Sclerosis, 6,* 91–98.

Gulick, E. E. (1997). Correlates of quality of life among persons with multiple sclerosis. *Nursing Research, 46,* 305.

Henriksson, F., Fredrikson, S., Masterman, T., & Jönsson, B. (2001). Costs, quality of life, and disease severity in multiple sclerosis: A cross-sectional study in Sweden. *European Journal of Neurology, 8,* 27–35.

Hermann, B. P., Vickrey, B., Hays, R. D., Cramer, J., Devinsky, O., Meador, K., et al. (1996). A comparison of health-related quality of life in patients with epilepsy, diabetes, and multiple sclerosis. *Epilepsy Research, 25,* 113–118.

Hillary, F. G., Chiaravalloti, N. D., DeLuca, J., Ricker, J. H., Liu, W. C., & Kalnin, A. J. (2003). An investigation of working memory rehearsal in multiple sclerosis using fMRI. *Journal of Clinical and Experimental Neuropsychology, 25,* 965–978.

Husted, C., Pham, L., Hekking, A., & Niederman, R. (1999, September). Improving quality of life for people with chronic conditions: The example of t'ai chi and multiple sclerosis. *Alternative Therapies in Health & Medicine, 5,* 70–74.

Janardhan, V., & Bakshi, R. (2000). Quality of life and its relationship to brain lesions and atrophy on magnetic resonance images in 60 patients with multiple sclerosis. *Archives of Neurology, 57,* 1485–1491.

Joffe, R. T., Lippert, G. P., Gray, T. A., Sawa, G., & Horvath, R. N. (1987). Mood disorder and multiple sclerosis. *Archives of Neurology, 44,* 376–378.

Johnson, S. K., DeLuca, J., Diamond, B. J., & Natelson, B. H. (1998). Memory dysfunction in fatiguing illness: Examining interference and distraction in short-term memory. *Cognitive Neuropsychiatry, 3,* 269–285.

Johnson, S. K., Lange, G., DeLuca, J., Korn, L. R., & Natelson, B. H. (1997). The effects of fatigue on neuropsychological performance in patients with chronic fatigue syndrome, multiple sclerosis, and depression. *Applied Neuropsychology, 4,* 145–153.

Jonsson, A., Korfitzen, E. M., Heltberg, A., Ravnborg, M. H., & Byskov-Ottosen, E. (1993). Effects of neuropsychological treatment in patients with multiple sclerosis. *Acta Neurologica Scandinavica, 88,* 394–400.

Kraft, G. I. (1981). Multiple sclerosis. In W. C. Stolov & M. R. Cloers (Eds.), *Handbook of severe disability* (pp. 111–118). Washington, DC: United States Department of Education and Rehabilitation Services Administration.

Krupp, L. B. (2003). Fatigue in multiple sclerosis: Definition, pathophysiology, and treatment. *CNS Drugs, 17*(4), 225–234.

Krupp, L. B., Christodoulou, C., Melville, P., Scherl, W. F., MacAllister, W. S., & Elkins, L. E. (2004). Donezepil improved memory in multiple sclerosis in a randomized clinical trial. *Neurology, 63,* 1579–1585.

Krupp, L. B., Christodoulou, C., & Schombert, H. (2005). Multiple sclerosis and fatigue. In J. DeLuca (Ed.), *Fatigue as a window to the brain.* Cambridge, MA: MIT Press.

Krupp, L. B., & Elkins, L. E. (2000). Fatigue and declines in cognitive functioning in multiple sclerosis. *Neurology, 55,* 934–939.

Kurtze, J. F., Beebe, G. W., Nagler, B., Auth, T. L., Kurland, L. T., & Nefzger, M. D. (1972). Studies on the natural history of multiple sclerosis. *Acta Neurologica Scandinavica, 48,* 19–46.

Lazeron, R. H., Rombouts, S. A., Scheltens, P., Polman, C. H., & Barkhof, F. (2004). An fMRI study of planning-related brain activity in patients with moderately advanced multiple sclerosis. *Multiple Sclerosis, 10,* 549–555.

Lee, M., Reddy, H., Johansen-Berg, H., Pendlebury, S. T., Jenkinson, M., Smith, S., et al. (2000). The motor cortex shows adaptive functional changes to brain injury from multiple sclerosis. *Annals of Neurology, 47,* 606–613.

Lengenfelder, J., Bryant, D., Diamond, B. J., Kalmar, J. H., Moore, N. B., & DeLuca, J. (2006). Processing speed interacts with working memory efficiency in multiple sclerosis. *Archives of Clinical Neuropsychology, 21,* 229–238.

Lengenfelder, J., Chiaravalloti, N. D., & DeLuca, J. (2003). Deciphering components of impaired working memory in multiple sclerosis. *Cognitive and Behavioral Neurology, 16*(1), 28–39.

Lezak, M. D. (2004). *Neuropsychological Assessment* (4th ed.). New York: Oxford University Press.

Li, Y., Chiaravalloti, N. D., Hillary, F. G., DeLuca, J., Liu, W-C., Kalnin, A. J., & Ricker, J. H. (2004). Differential cerebellar activation on fMRI during working memory performance in individuals with multiple sclerosis. *Archives of Physical Medicine and Rehabilitation, 85,* 635–639.

Lincoln, N. B., Dent, A., & Harding, J. (2003). Treatment of cognitive problems for people with multiple sclerosis. *International Journal of Therapeutic Rehabilitation, 10,* 412–416.

Litvan, I., Grafman, J., Vendrell, P., & Martinez, J. M. (1988). Slowed information processing in multiple sclerosis. *Archives of Neurology, 45,* 281–285.

Mainero, C., Caramia, F., Pozzilli, C., Pisani, A., Pestalozza, I., Borriello, G., et al. (2004). fMRI evidence of brain reorganization during attention and memory tasks in multiple sclerosis. *NeuroImage, 21,* 858–867.

Minden, S. L., & Schiffer, R. B. (1991). Depression and mood disorders in multiple sclerosis. *Neuropsychiatry, Neuropsychology and Behavioral Neurology, 4,* 62–77.

National Multiple Sclerosis Society. (2008). *Who gets MS?* Retrieved November 11, 2008, from http://www.nationalmssociety.org/about-multiple-sclerosis/who-gets-ms/index.aspx

Oger, J., Kastrukoff, L. F., Li, D. K., & Paty, D. W. (1988). Multiple sclerosis: In relapsing patients, immune functions vary with disease activity as assessed by MRI. *Neurology, 38,* 1739–1744.

Paul, R. H., Beatty, W. W., Schneider, R., Blanco, C., & Hames, K. (1998). Impairments of attention in individuals with multiple sclerosis. *Multiple Sclerosis, 4,* 433–439.

Penner, I. K., Rausch, M., Kappos, L., Opwis, K., & Radu, E. W. (2003). Analysis of impairment related functional architecture in MS patients during performance of different attention tasks. *Journal of Neurology, 250,* 461–472.

Peyser, J. M., Rao, S. M., LaRocca, N. G., & Kaplan, E. (1990). Guidelines for neuropsychological research in multiple sclerosis. *Archives of Neurology, 47,* 94–97.

Pfennings, L., Cohen, L., Ader, H., Polman, C., Lankhorst, G., Smits, R., & van der Ploeg, H. (1999). Exploring differences between subgroups of multiple sclerosis patients in health-related quality of life. *Journal of Neurology, 246,* 587–591.

Pliskin, N. H., Hamer, D. P., Goldstein, D. S., Towle, V. L., Reder, A. T., Noronha, A., & Arnason, B. G. W. (1996). Improved delayed visual reproduction test performance in multiple sclerosis patients receiving interferon β-1b. *Neurology, 47,* 1463–1468.

Plohmann, A. M., Kappos, L., Ammann, W., Thordai, A., Wittwer, A., Huber, S., et al. (1998). Computer assisted retraining of attentional impairments in patients with multiple sclerosis. *Journal of Neurology, Neurosurgery, and Psychiatry, 64,* 455–462.

Rammohan, K. W., Rosenberg, J. H., Lynn, D. J., Blumenfeld, A. M., Pollak, C. P., & Nagaraja, H. N. (2002). Efficacy and safety of modafinil (Provigil) for the treatment of fatigue in multiple sclerosis: A two centre phase 2 study. *Journal of Neurology, Neurosurgery, and Psychiatry, 72,* 179–183.

Rao, S. M. (1986). Neuropsychology of multiple sclerosis: A critical review. *Journal of Clinical and Experimental Neuropsychology, 8,* 503–542.

Rao, S. M., Grafman, J., DiGuilio, D., Mittenberg, W., Bernardin, L., Leo, G. J., et al. (1993). Memory dysfunction in multiple sclerosis: Its relation to working memory, semantic encoding, and implicit learning. *Neuropsychology, 7,* 364–374.

Rao, S. M., Leo, G. J., Bernardin, L., & Unverzagt, F. (1991). Cognitive dysfunction in multiple sclerosis: Frequency, patterns, and prediction. *Neurology, 41,* 685–691.

Rao, S. M., Leo, G. J., Ellington, L., Nauertz, T., Bernardin, L., & Unverzagt, F. (1991). Cognitive dysfunction in multiple sclerosis: II. Impact on employment and social functioning. *Neurology, 41,* 692–696.

Rao, S. M., Leo, G. J., Haughton, V. M., St. Aubin-Faubert, P., & Bernardin, L. (1989). Correlation of magnetic resonance imaging with neuropsychological testing in multiple sclerosis. *Neurology, 39,* 161–166.

Rao, S. M., Leo, G. J., & St. Aubin-Faubert, P. (1989). On the nature of memory disturbance in multiple sclerosis. *Journal of Clinical and Experimental Neuropsychology, 11,* 699–712.

Reddy, H., Narayanan, S., Woolrich, M., Mitsumori, T., Lapierre, Y., Arnold, D. L., & Matthews, P. M. (2002). Functional brain reorganization for hand movement in patients with multiple sclerosis: Defining distinct effects of injury and disability. *Brain, 125,* 2646–2657.

Rocca, M. A., Falini, A., Colombo, B., Scotti, G., Comi, G., & Filippi, M. (2002). Adaptive functional changes in cerebral cortex of patients with nondisabling multiple sclerosis correlate with the extent of brain structural damage. *Annals of Neurology, 51,* 330–339.

Rocca, M. A., Mezzapesa, D. M., Falini, A., Ghezzi, A., Martinelli, V., Scotti, G., et al. (2003). Evidence for axonal pathology and adaptive cortical reorganization in patients at presentation with clinically isolated syndromes suggestive of multiple sclerosis. *Neuroimage, 18,* 847–855.

Roelcke, U., Kappos, L., Lechner-Scott, J., Brunnschweiler, H., Huber, S., Ammann, W., et al. (1997). Reduced glucose metabolism in the frontal cortex and basal ganglia of multiple sclerosis patients with fatigue: A 18F-fluorodeoxyglucose positron emission tomography study. *Neurology, 48,* 1566–1571.

Roessler, R. T., & Rumrill, P. D., Jr. (1995). The relationship of perceived worksite barriers to job mastery and job satisfaction for employed people with multiple sclerosis. *Rehabilitation Counseling Bulletin, 39*(1), 2–14.

Roessler, R. T., & Rumrill, P. D. (2003). Multiple sclerosis and employment barriers: A systemic perspective on diagnosis and intervention. *Work, 21*(1), 17–23.

Rudick, R. A., Miller, D., Clough, J. D., Gragg, L. A., & Farmer, R. G. (1992). Quality of life in multiple sclerosis. Comparison with inflammatory bowel disease and rheumatoid arthritis. *Archives of Neurology, 49,* 1237–1242.

Rumrill, P. D., Kaleta, D. A., & Battersby, J. C. (1996). Etiology, incidence, and prevalence. In P. D. Rumrill (Ed.), *Employment issues and multiple sclerosis.* New York: Demos.

Schultheis, M., Garay, E., & DeLuca, J. (2001). The influence of cognitive impairment on driving performance in multiple sclerosis. *Neurology, 56*, 1089–1094.

Schwartz, C. E. (1999). Teaching coping skills enhances quality of life more than peer support: Results of a randomized trial with multiple sclerosis patients. *Health Psychology, 18*, 211–220.

Schwid, S. R. (2003). Management of cognitive impairment in multiple sclerosis. In R. A. Rudick & J. A. Cohen (Eds.), *Multiple sclerosis therapeutics* (2nd ed.). London: Martin Dunitz.

Shawaryn, M. A., Schultheis, M., Garay, E., & DeLuca, J. (2002). Assessing functional status: Exploring the relationship between the Multiple Sclerosis Functional Composite and driving. *Archives of Physical Medicine and Rehabilitation, 83*, 1123–1129.

Solari, A., Motta, A., Mendozzi, L., Pucci, E., Forni, M., Mancardi, G., et al. (2004). Computer-aided retraining of memory and attention in people with multiple sclerosis: A randomized, double-blind controlled trial. *Journal of the Neurological Sciences, 222*(1–2), 99–104.

Sperling, R., Guttmann, C., Hohol, M., Warfield, S., Jacab, M., Parente, M., et al. (2001). Regional magnetic resonance imaging lesion burden and cognitive function in multiple sclerosis. *Archives of Neurology, 58*, 115–121.

Sweet, L. H., Rao, S. M., Primeau, M., Mayer, A. R., & Cohen, R. A. (2004). Functional magnetic resonance imaging of working memory among multiple sclerosis patients. *Journal of Neuroimaging, 14*, 150–157.

Swirsky-Sacchetti, T., Mitchell, D. R., Seward, J., Gonzales, C., Lublin, F., Knobler, R., et al. (1992). Neuropsychological and structural brain lesions in multiple sclerosis: A regional analysis. *Neurology, 42*, 1291–1295.

Tartaglia, M. C., Narayanan, S., Francis, S. J., Santos, A. C., DeStefano, N., Lapierre, Y., & Arnold, D. L. (2004). The relationship between diffuse axonal damage and fatigue in multiple sclerosis. *Archives of Neurology, 61*, 176–177.

Thornton, A. E., & Raz, N. (1997). Memory impairment in multiple sclerosis: A quantitative review. *Neuropsychology, 11*, 357–366.

Vickrey, B. G., Hays, R. D., Genovese, B. J., Myers, L. W., & Ellison, G. W. (1997). Comparison of a generic to disease-targeted health-related quality-of-life measures for multiple sclerosis. *Journal of Clinical Epidemiology, 50*, 557–569.

Voelbel, G. T., Chiaravalloti, N. D., & DeLuca, J. (2007). Functional neuroimaging in multiple sclerosis. In J. DeLuca & F. G. Hillary (Eds.), *Functional neuroimaging in clinical populations* (pp. 277–300). New York: Guilford Press.

Wang, J. L., Reimer, M. A., Metz, L. M., & Patten, S. B. (2000). Major depression and quality of life in individuals with multiple sclerosis. *International Journal of Psychiatry in Medicine, 30*, 309–317.

Weinstein, A., Schwid, S. R., Schiffer, R. B., McDermott, M. P., Giang, D. W., & Goodman, A. D. (1999). Neuropsychological status in multiple sclerosis after treatment with glatiramer acetate (Copaxone). *Archives of Neurology, 56*, 319–324.

Wilson, M., Morgan, X., Lin, X., Turner, B. P., & Blumhardt, L. D. (2001). Quantitative diffusion weighted magnetic resonance imaging, cerebral atrophy, and disability in multiple sclerosis. *Journal of Neurology, Neurosurgery, and Psychiatry, 70*, 318–322.

PART II

ASSESSMENT

CHAPTER 9

FUNCTIONAL STATUS AND QUALITY-OF-LIFE MEASURES

Allen W. Heinemann and Trudy Mallinson

Health care and rehabilitation in the United States are undergoing major transitions. Administrators are consolidating and integrating delivery systems, providers are assuming financial risk for patient outcomes, and patients' satisfaction with care received and outcomes obtained are of increasing importance. In particular, the last decade witnessed a move toward prospective payment by both public and private payers. Although there are various approaches to prospective payment, these strategies generally reimburse health care providers at fixed rates based on patient severity regardless of services received. In rehabilitation, functional status is an important measure of severity, so measuring function has become of increasing importance in recent years. A major criticism of prospective payment systems is that they create a disincentive for providers to ensure quality care because reimbursement will be the same regardless of the care provided. In response to these criticisms, pay for performance, often referred to as P4P, is becoming an integral part of health care reimbursement (Bodenheimer, May, Berenson, & Coughlan, 2005). In P4P, providers receive additional payment for achieving better-than-average patient outcomes. Thus, effectively measuring patient health outcomes is becoming increasingly important and will be an important driving force in the development and refinement of outcome measures in the coming decade.

The purpose of this chapter is to summarize the work of rehabilitation psychologists and other clinical investigators related to measurement of functional status and quality of life, and relate it to the practice and research endeavors of rehabilitation psychologists. In this chapter, we provide an overview of conceptual approaches to defining and measuring quality of life and functional status measures, provide an overview of instruments, describe applications to rehabilitation and chronic illness populations, describe issues in the selection and use of these instruments, and discuss future trends.

TERMINOLOGY

Two of the most important outcomes in rehabilitation are the client's functional status and quality of life. Broadly, *function* refers to the performance of everyday activities, and *quality of life* (QoL) refers to individuals' perceptions of their health in relation to their expectations. Medical rehabilitation attempts to maximize QoL, emphasizing functional, psychological, and social restoration, as well as adjustment to residual disability. The World Health Organization's (WHO) model of disablement provides a useful structure for thinking about measurement of function and QoL (WHO, 2001).

Disablement is conceptualized as involving complex relationships between health conditions and

Funding for this work was provided by a Health Services Research Disability and Rehabilitation Research Project on Medical Rehabilitation (H133A030807) and a Rehabilitation Research and Training Center on Measuring Rehabilitation Outcomes and Effectiveness (H133B040032) awarded by the National Institute on Disability and Rehabilitation Research to the Rehabilitation Institute of Chicago (Allen W. Heinemann, PI).

contextual factors, both environmental and personal; the relationships are potentially two-directional. Disablement, which occurs as a product of this interaction between the health condition and the environment, can be manifested by impairment, activity limitations, or restrictions in participation. *Impairment* is defined as "problems in body function or structure, such as a significant deviation or loss." (WHO, 2001, p. 10). Level and completeness of spinal cord injury are examples of impairments. In interaction with contextual factors, impairments may result in *activity limitations,* defined as "difficulties an individual may have in executing activities" (WHO, p. 10). In turn, impairment or activity limitations may interact with contextual factors to result in *participation restrictions,* "problems an individual may experience in involvement in life situations" (WHO, p. 10). The inability to resume social roles such as worker, homemaker, student, and community member is an example of restrictions in participation.

Assessments of function typically are focused at the level of activity limitation and participation dimensions. However, these assessments generally do not consider how the environment contributes to activity limitations. For example, a typical item on functional scales is bathing. Whether a person is independent or needs assistance may have much to do with whether the bath itself is designed to be accessible. A person may be independent in bathing in the hospital, where there are an accessible bath and tap fittings, but dependent in his or her home bath, where the tub will not allow easy access and he or she cannot turn the faucets. The term *disability* as frequently used in the current literature and as measured with many current assessments of function, views disability as residing entirely within the person. Under the International Classification of Functioning, Disability and Health (ICF), disability is a process, an interaction between the person and the environment.

QoL is no less complicated. WHO defines QoL as "individuals' perception of their position in life in the context of the culture and value systems in which they live and in relation to their goals, expectations, standards and concerns" (WHOQoL Group, 1995, p. 1405). Yet, there is continued definitional confusion that reflects the fact that QoL means many things to different people. Material possessions, wealth,

body functioning, social relationships, life satisfaction, emotional well-being, and spiritual wholeness are aspects of QoL many people describe when asked to provide a definition. One central distinction in QoL concerns the perspective one takes (Dijkers, 1997). *Subjective* approaches define QoL in terms of congruence between aspirations and achievements as judged by the person. *Objective* approaches focus on observable characteristics such as income, neighborhood, poverty level, life span, education, and disorders. *Health-related QoL,* the focus of this chapter, concerns those aspects of life, which may be affected by health; these characteristics typically include functional status, energy level, pain, participation in social and daily activities, and ability to leave one's home. The importance of assessing both subjective and objective measures of disability and QoL is recognized widely (Ferrucci et al., 2004; Wood-Dauphinee et al., 2002). QoL evaluation has a long tradition as a focus of research in the chronic illness (Kane, 1995) and cancer literature (Cella, Lloyd, & Wright, 1996), but it has only more recently become a central concern of rehabilitation clinicians and researchers (Deyo et al., 1998; Duncan et al., 2005).

As this review illustrates, functional status is often viewed in the general health care literature as a component of QoL. For example, the Short Form-36 (SF-36; Ware, 1993) includes a physical function subscale composed of 10 items, which are summed separately or as part of a total score. This is a different perspective from rehabilitation professionals who usually think of functional status as an aspect of disablement. Both conceptual models are useful, though one must clarify the framework an author is using in order to communicate clearly. The confidence with which one can sum items from diverse conceptual domains and obtain coherent, unitary measures has been evaluated adequately with only a few instruments.

The relationship between disability, at least as defined by the ICF, and QoL, is not always clear. Many studies purport to measure both disability and QoL, yet, as we have seen from the definitions provided earlier, there is a good deal of overlap in the dimensions that define these two concepts. Function is not simply a subdomain of QoL. For example, in examining the relationship between content of health-related QoL (HRQoL) instruments and the ICF, Cieza and Stucki (2005) found that a number of concepts in HRQoL measures had no parallel under the ICF classification, yet significant ICF concepts such as mobility and the environment are rarely addressed by HRQoL measures. In general, the WHO ICF model ascribes cause for disability to a person–environment interaction. QoL models typically ascribe no cause or relate it primarily to the health condition (Hays, Hahn, & Marshall, 2002). Many of our current measures of function, then, are more aligned with a QoL perspective because most do not capture function as a person–environment interaction. In many ways, our measurement of function has yet to catch up with our definition. This is hardly an esoteric issue. When we use measures of function, we create definitions of individuals. In addition, we ascribe meanings to the data these measures produce and use them to assign resources and interventions; we need to be clear that the data mean what we think or intend them to mean.

REHABILITATION PSYCHOLOGISTS' ROLE IN MEASURING FUNCTIONAL STATUS AND QUALITY OF LIFE

Rehabilitation professionals generally, and rehabilitation psychologists specifically, must deal on a daily basis with patients' concerns related to function and HRQoL. Rehabilitation psychologists, given their expertise in clinical measurement, have key roles in selecting assessments to guide patient care planning and in assisting rehabilitation team members to select and use assessment measures for program evaluation and research purposes.

The growth of rehabilitation professionals' interest in QoL is illustrated by the absence of QoL index listings in Marcus Fuhrer's landmark 1987 textbook (Fuhrer, 1987), whereas his 1997 textbook has extensive listings (Fuhrer, 1997). Rehabilitation psychology's fundamental concern with the experiences of people with chronic illness and disability allows for relative ease in grasping the vocabulary of the QoL literature (Livneh & Antonak, 1997).

As part of the rehabilitation team, psychologists bring unique expertise to patient care in areas such as identifying mood and other mental health dis-

orders, examining and intervening in how patients adapt following disability onset, understanding learning and acquisition of new skills, and assessing mental health and cognition. Assessment of function and QoL cuts across rehabilitation disciplines, and each profession brings a unique set of skills to understanding these concerns.

Conceptualizing Function

Functional status covers a range of daily activities, including personal and instrumental activities of daily living. *Personal activities of daily living* (PADLs) include activities such as bathing or showering, dressing, and eating meals. These activities occur on a regular daily basis and are considered important to rehabilitation because difficulty completing them affects one's ability to live independently, or at least increases one's need for assistance. *Instrumental activities of daily living* (IADLs) are higher level everyday activities, which are generally more complex and may involve care and support of others or engagement outside the home. IADLs include activities such as laundry, meal preparation, grocery shopping, and yard work.

The classification of an activity as a PADL or IADL can be arbitrary. In addition, although PADLs and IADLS are considered distinct from productive, educational, and leisure activities, how an activity is classified for a given individual is less clear. For example, one individual may perform grooming, home maintenance, and child care activities as part of self-maintenance, whereas another individual may perform these as vocational activities.

In general, the items on functional status assessments reflect only a small number of PADLs and IADLs and are commonly referred to as *limited data sets*. Often, for reasons of time, cost, and efficiency, the number of items included is kept to a minimum, and the items focus only on those activities that are not influenced by societal gender roles and that can be observed in a variety of health care settings. Functional status instruments are frequently designed to meet pragmatic goals, such as assessing the outcomes of treatment programs, to predict successful living in a home or community setting, need for assistance, or the need for nursing home care as well as to evaluate the impact of impairments on daily life.

Conceptualizing Quality of Life

A plethora of definitions and terms abound in the QoL literature. One of the most authoritative compendiums of QoL measures asserts that there is no agreement on the number and types of QoL components (Spilker, 1996). Various levels of QoL components are sometimes viewed in a hierarchical fashion in which multiple, specific components comprise a bottom level, broad domains comprise a higher level, and an overall appraisal of well-being comprises the top level. Domains generally referenced include (a) physical status and functional abilities, (b) psychological status and well-being, (c) social interactions, (d) economic and vocational status and factors, and (e) religious and spiritual status. Spilker categorized the foci of instruments designed to assess QoL into five realms: (a) universally agreed on aspects of health-related QoL applicable to everyone, (b) components of HRQoL applicable to everyone, (c) components of HRQoL applicable to persons with specific conditions, (d) components sometimes viewed as an aspect of HRQoL that are usually classified as clinical measures (e.g., depression, pain, cognition), and (e) tangential aspects of QoL that are used occasionally. Schipper, Clinch, and Olweny (1996) asserted that QoL is a multifactorial construct, subjectively appraised and related to a concept of reintegration to normal living. It reflects the "net consequences of disease and its treatment on the patient's perception of his ability to live a useful and fulfilling life" (Schipper et al., p. 15).

Accompanying this increased interest in health care outcomes generally, and QoL specifically, dozens of instruments have been promoted. However, their psychometric properties and clinical utility vary widely (Coons, Rao, Keininger, & Hays, 2000; Hickey, Barker, McGee, & O'Boyle, 2005; Willke, Burke, & Erickson, 2004). Commonly used instruments include the Short-Form 36 (SF-36; Ware, 1993), EuroQol (Szende, Oppe, & Devlin, 2007), WHOQoL (WHOQoL Group, 1998a, 1998b), Satisfaction with Life Questionnaire (Diener, Emmons, Larsen, & Griffin, 1985), and Functional Assessment of Chronic Illness Therapy (FACT-G; Cella, Eton, Lai, Peterman, & Merkel, 1993). However, there is no gold standard QoL instrument given the needs of various users, divergent scaling

properties, experiences of different clinical populations, and the high level of sophistication needed to understand and interpret these instruments. For example, instrument developers have promoted item sets for use in such diverse undertakings as multicenter clinical trials, monitoring of outcomes in various clinical practices (Clark et al., 1997; Epstein & Sherwood, 1996; Werner & Kessler, 1996), "severity" or "risk-adjusting" outcomes (Iezzoni, 1994), and development of care protocols (U.S. Department of Health and Human Services, 1995).

Because rehabilitation psychologists use QoL measures in both clinical practice with individual clients and for evaluating wide groups of patients, such as program evaluation research, an important distinction is made between generic and disease-specific approaches to QoL. *Generic approaches* do not consider the impact of particular disease sequelae on QoL and focus on general domains and concerns. For example, physical appearance may be of particular concern in evaluating QoL in individuals with burns but does not appear as an issue in most generic QoL instruments. Generic approaches to QoL are advantageous in that they allow comparison across multiple groups of individuals. *Disease-specific* approaches are advantageous in that they consider issues important to individuals with particular conditions that might be overlooked in a generic approach. Which approach a rehabilitation psychologist chooses to use will depend in large part on the goal of the assessment. This is discussed in more detail later in this chapter.

Proponents of both generic and disease-specific measures seek instruments with a minimum number of items, a high level of precision, clinical relevance, and sensitivity. Aggregating scores across individuals or programs and comparing outcomes over time are typical applications. Applicability to people with a variety of chronic illnesses and disabilities is also valued although it is often at odds with the need to assess disability-specific characteristics.

Review of Functional Status Instruments

In this section, we present a brief review of some of the most commonly used measures of function. Whole texts are dedicated to this topic (e.g., Kane & Kane, 2004; McDowell, 2006), and readers are referred to these for greater detail. The goals of this section are to introduce instruments that are likely to be encountered in clinical practice and to address issues with their use. We begin by reviewing important dimensions of functional assessment, namely, the kinds of rating scales encountered, the mode of administration, generic versus disease-specific instruments, and the role of technology in functional assessment. This is followed by a review of assessments of function in common use that highlights the issues just discussed.

Dimensions of Functional Assessment

Many factors influence the choice of an assessment instrument. The following represent some of the more common concerns that can influence the kind of data one can expect to produce and the ease with which it might be collected.

Type of rating scale.   A wide range of rating scales are used to score functional status items. For example, rating scales may ask about difficulty performing a task, need for assistance to complete a task, or frequency or importance of completing a task. Need for assistance might be an important outcome of rehabilitation programs in which planning for community discharge is required. Difficulty with task performance might be important in outpatient settings in which, for example, matching a person's performance with the vocational demands of a job is required. When selecting functional status measures, it is important to be clear about how data will be used once collected, because doing so can avoid a good deal of frustration. For example, are the data to be used for developing treatment plans or for evaluating the outcomes of a program? Because it is unlikely that one instrument can serve both purposes, it is important to identify the goal so as to ensure the utility of the data. Too often, an outcome instrument is selected when the goal is treatment planning. Outcome measures seldom serve the purpose of treatment planning because they do not provide information about the underlying cause of the disability and therefore are of little help in directing treatment.

Outcome-focused instruments provide a picture of the person's overall level of functional ability, as, for example, does the Functional Independence Measure (FIM; Guide for the Uniform Data Set for Medical Rehabilitation, 1997), arguably the most widely used functional assessment measure and the foundation of Medicare's prospective payment system for inpatient rehabilitation. Such a picture can be useful for goal setting (i.e., a reasonable level for the person to achieve by discharge) and for outcomes evaluation (i.e., whether the person achieved this functional goal). However, such an instrument is of little use in treatment planning because it does not provide information about why the person cannot complete a task. Instruments such as the Assessment of Motor and Process Skills (AMPS; Fisher, 2003) that clearly describe where task performance breaks down or those that describe dynamic assessment strategies identifying how context influences task performance are more appropriate for treatment planning.

Mode of administration.   An important distinction in functional assessment is the mode of administration. This is generally distinguished as self-report or performance-based (Coman & Richardson, 2006). In self-report, as the name implies, the person reports on his or her ability to complete the activities. In performance-based or observational assessments, the person is observed completing functional tasks, and completion of the task or components of the task performance is rated. Each approach has strengths and limitations. Sometimes the comparison of these two approaches is unhelpful, as in the distinction of self-report as "subjective" and performance-based as "objective"; both approaches require a personal judgment, so neither is truly more "objective" than the other. In addition, "subjective" carries a notion of lack of validity or credibility, which is far from the case in functional assessments in which individuals themselves might indeed be much better judges of their ability under a variety of circumstances than a clinician who has only observed the person once or twice. Perhaps a more helpful framework for considering these approaches can be borrowed from the field of qualitative and anthropologic research, that of emic/cultural and etic/universal perspectives (Schalock et al., 2005). An *emic/cultural perspective* is one that describes behavior in a way that is meaningful to the actor, whereas an *etic/universal perspective* is one that describes behavior in a way that is meaningful to the observer or across the wider community. Such a view avoids the pejorative stand inherent within subjective–objective or insider–outsider dichotomies and recognizes that both perspectives have value in understanding functional status.

Generic versus disease-specific instruments. Functional status instruments cover a gamut from generic to disease-specific. Generic instruments can be applied across wide groups of individuals and have been demonstrated to maintain adequate reliability and validity regardless of a person's diagnosis. Generic instruments can be very useful for comparison across large populations, such as Medicare patients, or in epidemiologic studies in the U.S. adult population, such as the National Health Interview Survey or the National Health and Nutrition Examination Survey. Generic instruments designed to measure function in clinical populations include instruments such as the FIM (Guide for the Uniform Data Set for Medical Rehabilitation, 1997), Barthel Index (Malhoney & Barthel, 1965), Instrumental Activities of Daily Living Scale (Lawton & Brody, 1969), and the Minimum Data Set (MDS; Hawes et al., 1995). Disease-specific instruments are used when it is important to understand function within the context of a specific set of symptoms or conditions that occur with a particular diagnosis. For example, the Western Ontario and McMaster Osteoarthritis Index (WOMAC 3.1; Bellamy, Buchanan, Goldsmith, Campbell, & Stitt, 1988) evaluates function from the perspective of individuals with lower extremity osteoarthritis who complete activities with pain and have limited range of motion in their hips and/or knees (Bellamy, 1995). The Parkinson's Disease Activities of Daily Living Scale includes items that reflect activities that are most likely to be of concern for persons experiencing the tremor and rigidity of movement that accompanies this condition (Hobson, Edwards, & Meara, 2001). Selection of disease-specific or generic instruments depends largely on how the data will be used and whether the appropriate comparison group is the general population or others with a similar condition.

Assessment technology. Functional assessment is undergoing considerable change as technology influences how assessments can be administered. Computer adaptive testing (CAT) provides opportunities to present to the patient only those items that are most relevant to the person (Haley, Ni, Hambleton, Slavin, & Jette, 2006). For example, a person who can walk 100 yards easily is unlikely to have difficulty with easy items such as eating. Presenting only items that are closely targeted to a person's level of ability both decreases testing time and increases the precision with which a person's functional status is measured (Haley et al., 2006). Jette and colleagues are undertaking preliminary work for CAT of rehabilitation patients. The goal of their work is to develop a single measure that can be used effectively across the range of postacute settings, the Activity Measure for PostAcute Care (AM-PAC; Haley, Coster, et al., 2004; Haley et al., 2006; Jette & Haley, 2005; Jette et al., 2007).

Similar technology is helping to overcome the problem of comparing persons measured using different instruments. With so many functional assessments available, it may be difficult to compare individuals if the same items are not used in each study. Instrument equating, which uses the same psychometric technology as CAT (i.e., item response theory [IRT]), enables clinicians and researchers to overcome this problem. For example, Fisher and colleagues equated 13 motor function items from the FIM (Guide for the Uniform Data Set for Medical Rehabilitation, 1997) and 22 from the Patient Evaluation Conference System (PECS; Fisher, Harvey, Taylor, Kilgore, & Kelly, 1995). Equating provided a crosswalk between patients' scores on the more widely used FIM with the locally used PECS. McHorney (2002) linked three sets of functional status items from the Asset and Health Dynamics among the oldest-old data set that is used to track functional status in community-living older adults. Linking respondents measured in different rounds of the survey on partially different item sets allowed them to be compared in a common metric. This technology will play a vital role in rehabilitation psychologists' future assessment practices because it is now being adopted in large, federally funded projects, such as the National Institute of Neurological Disorders and Stroke Neurology Quality of Life project and the National Institute of Aging Toolbox for

Assessment of Neurological and Behavioral Function (http://www.neuroqol.org/default.aspx; http://www.nihtoolbox.org/default.aspx).

Functional status instruments. This section presents a sampling of commonly used functional assessments. It is not intended to be exhaustive but to highlight different approaches to measuring function.

Early instruments. The Barthel Index (Mahoney & Barthel, 1965) is one of the earliest measures of function and is still widely used, particularly outside the United States. In its original form, it consists of 10 items of everyday self-care activities. Not every item has the same number of rating scale steps. For example, grooming is rated on a dichotomous scale and transfers are rated on a 4-point scale. The steps of the ratings scales are specifically defined for each item. In addition, the items are weighted so that being independent in bathing earns 5 points, whereas independence in toilet transfers earns 10 points. The instrument has been shown to have good reliability and validity (Wade & Collin, 1988). The Barthel Index is most notable because it has served as the basis for many newer ADL instruments.

The IADL scale, first published by Lawton and Brody (1969), is an eight-item assessment of activities such as shopping, doing laundry, using a telephone, preparing food, and managing finances. Each item is rated on a 3- or 4-point scale. Like the Barthel Index, the rating scale steps are defined uniquely for each item. It recognizes that function in older adults extends beyond basic self-care activities. Still frequently used in research studies, this instrument is notable as a precursor to many others.

Administrative assessments. Because function is recognized as an important outcome of rehabilitation and also a predictor of functional recovery, payers of rehabilitation services have long been interested in capturing this dimension. As one of the largest payers of rehabilitation services, the Centers for Medicare and Medicaid (CMS) have invested heavily in the development of instruments that can be used to both evaluate the outcomes of rehabilitation programs and to determine payment. Each of the Medicare assessment systems used in postacute care includes a measure of functional status. Inpatient

rehabilitation facilities use the Patient Assessment Instrument, skilled nursing facilities use the Minimum Data Set (MDS; http://www.cms.hhs.gov/nursinghomequalityinits/25_nhqimds30.asp) and home health agencies use the Outcome and Assessment Information Set (http://www.cms.hhs.gov/oasis/). Each instrument is mandated by CMS and forms the basis for establishing reimbursement under each of the postacute care prospective payments systems. The MDS includes 11 ADL items covering tasks such as bed mobility and transfers, mobility, dressing, eating, toilet use, and hygiene. Each item is rated on two rating scales: a 5-point self-performance scale and a 4-point support scale. The MDS version 2.0 has demonstrated reliability and validity (Hawes et al., 1995). An update to the MDS, version 3.0, is under development; the function items are revised and use a single 8-point rating scale of need for assistance.

New and innovative assessments. The Assessment of Motor and Process Skills (AMPS; Fisher, 2003) represents a significant innovation in the measurement of function both in how function is conceptualized and how it is implemented. The AMPS is an observational assessment of instrumental activities of daily living. Patients are observed completing two IADL tasks and then rated on 16 motor and 20 process skill items. A key aspect of the AMPS is that patients select which tasks they wish to complete in consultation with the assessor, so that the patient is carrying out familiar, meaningful tasks. A unique feature of the AMPS is the skills (or items) on which performance is rated. Process skills include such abilities as selecting, interacting with, and using tools and materials, carrying out individual actions and steps, and modifying performance when problems are encountered. Motor skills include abilities such as transporting items, reaching for items, and positioning one's body in relation to the task. Because the AMPS rates skill components, patient performance indicates when and how task completion breaks down, making the AMPS an ideal tool for intervention planning.

The AMPS is administered by a certified rater who observes and scores the patient during the tasks. After scoring, the AMPS software (an application of a many-faceted Rasch model) converts raw score data to equal-interval measures. It also accounts for differences in rater severity (Fisher, 2003). The AMPS has demonstrated reliability and validity in both home and clinic settings and across diagnostic groups (Nygard, Bernspang, Fisher, & Winblad, 1994; Park, Fisher, & Velozo, 1994).

The ability to order each of the motor and process skills, and to order the activities performed in order from hardest to easiest, makes the AMPS an invaluable treatment-planning tool because therapists can determine the "just-right" challenge to be worked on in the next rehabilitation session. Use of the AMPS is limited because of the extensive training required and the need for computer software for scoring.

The Activity Measure for Postacute Care (AM-PAC; Haley et al., 2006; Haley, Andres, et al., 2004; Jette & Haley, 2005; Jette et al., 2007) is based on the ICF and includes 233 items in three activity domains of movement, personal, and cognitive factors. A computer-scoring algorithm presents items to patients based on their response to the previous item. Each person is presented with an average of six items for the movement domain, seven items for the personal domain, and eight for the cognitive domain (Haley et al., 2006).

CAT administration is efficient and precise because it enables a large domain to be tapped with only a few items. This instrument has strong psychometric properties and, although new, has a growing body of literature to support its reliability and validity. Because it uses CAT methodology, the AM-PAC is restricted to rehabilitation facilities with sophisticated information technology infrastructure. AM-PAC short forms are available (Haley, Andres, et al., 2004). In addition, the AM-PAC is formatted as self-report, which may limit its use with some rehabilitation patients.

Review of Quality of Life Instruments

The wealth of QoL instruments makes the selection of representative instruments daunting. Interested readers are directed to the excellent guides of McDowell (2006), McDowell and Newell (1996), Spilker (1996), and Bowling (1995, 1997), as well as to the official journal of the International Society for Quality of Life Research, *Quality of Life Research*.

This section summarizes information about widely used QoL measures, the SF-36, the Functional Assessment of Chronic Illness Therapy (FACIT; http://www.facit.org/) family of instruments, and a National Institutes of Health (NIH) initiative to develop patient reported outcome measures.

Short form-36 health survey. John Ware and the Rand Corporation developed the SF-36 for use in the Health Insurance Study Experiment/Medical Outcomes Study (1993). Their intent was to develop a generic measure of subjective health status that could be applied widely to persons with a variety of conditions. The SF-36 evolved from a factor analysis of responses from over 22,000 persons to 149 items. The instrument was distributed initially by the Rand Corporation and by the Health Outcomes Institute; the Medical Outcomes Trust of the Health Institute at the New England Medical Center is the distributor of a slightly revised version. Rand distributes the original survey, now called the Rand 36-Item Health Survey, as does the Health Outcomes Institute; the latter version is called the Health Status Questionnaire (Bowling, 1997). An online version with sample scoring is available at http://www.qualitymetric.com/demos/ from QualityMetric. The 36 items measure eight dimensions: physical functioning, social functioning, role limitations because of physical problems, role limitations because of emotional problems, mental health, energy and vitality, pain, and general health perceptions. A ninth category addresses perceptions of health changes over the past year. Separate versions allow assessment of health perceptions over the past 4 weeks and past week.

A variety of response formats are used, including a dichotomous, "yes/no," format as well as 3, 5, and 6 category rating scales that indicate frequency of problems, extent of limitations, severity of pain, and extent of agreement with various statements. The eight subscale scores are the product of summing item responses; raw subscale scores are transformed algebraically into a 0 (*poor health*) to 100 (*good health*) continuum by computing where an individual's score resides in the possible raw score continuum. Evidence for reliability and validity is good across a variety of health conditions; it appears sensitive to changes in health status over time. Floor and ceiling effects may be a problem in specific samples.

Haley, McHorney, and Ware (1994) reported a rating scale analysis of the 10 physical function (PF-10) items from the SF-36. They examined the hierarchical order of the items, unidimensionality of the item set, and reproducibility of item calibrations. Their results support the unidimensionality of the PF-10 for most patient groups and the reproducibility of item calibrations across patient groups and repeated assessments. Their results support the content validity of the PF-10 as a measure of physical functioning. Their subsequent publication (McHorney, Haley, & Ware, 1997) evaluated the relative precision of raw scores and linear measures. Differences between raw scores and linear measures were attributed to the logarithmic nature of the linear measures, the uneven distribution of the PF-10 item calibrations, and reduction of within-group variance. The explicit, but perhaps unintended, weighting of items with more response categories could also have contributed to their findings. They found that the linear measures discriminated better than raw scores between patients who differed in disease severity. In all comparisons, differences between raw scores and linear measures were most apparent in clinical groups with extreme scores.

Bode (1997) extended the rating scale analysis of Haley by evaluating the fit of all 36 items to an underlying construct of health status in a sample of 526 adults with intermittent claudication, a condition that results from atherosclerosis of the leg arteries and often limits walking (Feinglass, McCarthy, Slavensky, Manheim, & Martin, 2000). The items cohered to define a unidimensional construct of health status and measured four strata of health (i.e., excellent, good, fair, poor). Rescoring several items and designating "pivot points" between good and poor health improved reliability by increasing the spread of item difficulties. The hierarchy of item difficulties made clinical sense such that persons with relatively good health reported few activity limitations, infrequent mood disruption, minimal pain, and a perception that their health was stable. In contrast, persons with relatively poor health reported several activity limitations, frequent mood disruption, pain disruption, and an overall percep-

tion that their health was declining. These results supported the utility of the SF-36, provided a measure that is sensitive to change, provided measures with known measurement error, and helped identify individuals whose responses do not fit the underlying construct.

The functional assessment of chronic illness therapy family of instruments.   The FACIT Measurement System (http://www.facit.org) is a set of HRQoL instruments that are designed to facilitate the management of persons with chronic illness. The measurement system began with the creation of a generic questionnaire called the Functional Assessment of Cancer Therapy-General (FACT-G) in 1987 (Cella, et al., 1993). The current version (4) of the FACT-G is a 27-item set of questions that assess four domains of well-being: physical, social and family, emotional, and functional (Webster, Odom, Peterman, Lent, & Cella, 1999). The FACT-G is designed for use with patients with any form of cancer; extensions have been used and validated in samples with other chronic illness conditions, including HIV/AIDS, multiple sclerosis, Parkinson's disease, and rheumatoid arthritis, as well as in the general population. The FACIT Measurement System has been translated into more than 45 languages. Assessments can be tailored to individual patients so that only the most relevant of the over 400 available questions are administered. Tailoring is accomplished by the selection of subscales for specific QoL domains and with CAT. FACIT questionnaires are administered by self-report (paper or computer), face-to-face, or by telephone interview. Assessment time is usually less than 15 minutes. Scoring information and normative data are available from the developer (http://www.facit.org).

The patient-reported outcomes measurement information system network.   NIH implemented a trans-NIH initiative called the Patient-Reported Outcomes Measurement Information System (PROMIS; http://www.nihpromis.org/default.aspx) network with the aim of developing ways to measure patient-reported symptoms such as pain and fatigue and aspects of HRQoL across a wide variety of chronic diseases and conditions (see http://www.

nihpromis.org/default.aspx). The PROMIS network aims to revolutionize the way patient-reported outcome instruments are selected and used in clinical research and practice evaluation and to establish a national resource for accurate and efficient measurement of patient-reported symptoms and other health outcomes in clinical practice.

The objectives of the PROMIS initiative are to (a) develop and test a large bank of items measuring patient-reported outcomes, (b) create a CAT system that allows for efficient, psychometrically robust assessment of patient-reported outcomes in clinical research involving a wide range of chronic diseases, and (c) create a publicly available system that can be added to and modified periodically and that allows clinical researchers to access a common repository of items and computerized adaptive tests. Data analyses are based on item-response theory and developed with extensive input from a team of co-investigators and consultants. Consensus on domain framework and priority domains for bank development was achieved using a modified Delphi approach. Qualitative item review began with expert classification and review of existing questions, followed by individual interviews and focus groups with patients.

The consensus-developing process resulted in selection of the World Health Organization domains. From these domains, pain, fatigue, emotional distress, physical functioning, and social role participation were selected, along with general health perceptions, around which to develop measures. Consensus definitions of each concept were developed and IRT analyses to evaluate item quality are applied to existing data sets. When needed, new items are written to ensure the content of each of the five selected domains is adequately represented. Further information is available at http://www.nihpromis.org/default.aspx.

Three measurement domains guide PROMIS activities: (a) physical, (b) mental, and (c) social health. Pain and fatigue are the two symptoms measured in the physical function domain. The domain of mental health focuses on emotional distress. Emotional distress refers to unpleasant emotions or thoughts that interfere with the ability to cope with a disease, its physical symptoms, and treatment. The social health domain is defined as perceived well-being regarding social activities and relationships, including the ability to relate to individuals, groups, communities, and society as a whole. Components of social health, or functioning, include understanding and communication, getting along with people, participating in society and performing social roles. Social role participation and social support are viewed as distinct aspects of social health. Social role participation is defined as involvement in, and satisfaction with, usual social roles in life situations and activities.

QUALITY OF LIFE AND FUNCTIONAL STATUS AS MEASURES OF HEALTH CARE QUALITY

Functional status and QoL measures provide a means of comparing (a) changes within an individual over time, (b) groups of individuals defined on the basis of disability or illness, or (c) organizations that provide rehabilitation or health care. Measures of functional status and QoL have varied according to whether the recipient, provider, payer, or purchaser was the intended user of the information. The development of functional status and QoL measures allows us to assess (a) functional, psychological, and social improvements experienced by persons with impairments; (b) the structure and processes of provider organizations; and (c) the relative value of services received. The history described below focuses on the utility of functional status and QoL measures as they serve the need to describe health care outcomes.

Donabedian (1966), the father of health care quality monitoring, distinguished three components for measuring health care quality: (a) structure (i.e., the settings in which health care is provided, the adequacy of facilities and equipment, qualifications of staff), (b) process (i.e., information obtained from patients, technical competence of staff, extent of preventive management, coordination and continuity of care); and (c) outcomes (i.e., recovery, restoration of function, survival). Early attempts to evaluate health care focused on structure and process because this information was the most readily available. More recently, researchers have argued that outcomes should be the focus of our attention because good outcomes are the product that medical care is seeking. Accreditation bodies have added outcome measurement to their traditional focus on structure and process. However, an exclusive focus on outcomes denies the power of organizational attributes and is unable to provide direction for quality improvement. A comprehensive quality measurement system must include indicators of structure, process, and outcome.

There is considerable evidence of variation in use and outcomes of rehabilitation services (Buntin et al., 2005; Kane, Lin, & Blewett, 2002; Liu, Gage, Harvell, Stevenson, & Brennan, 1999). In medical rehabilitation, variations in outcomes are evident to inpatient rehabilitation subscribers to eRehabData (http://www.erehabdata.com) and the Uniform Data System for Medical Rehabilitation (http://www.udsmr.org); subscribers receive comparative outcome information nationally and by region. The current movement toward clinical guidelines or protocols is based on the assumption that greater standardization of practice will result in greater quality at less cost and help reduce practice variations. Empirical demonstration of variation in practice and an explanation for why it exists are entirely another matter. Clinicians and researchers are just now achieving consensus about how best to treat certain illnesses or conditions, due in part to the work of Patient Outcomes Research Teams, clinical guidelines funded by the Agency for Healthcare Quality and Research, the NIH PROMIS initiative, and accrediting organizations. Current efforts to identify "best practices" reflect the belief that clinical processes are related to outcomes.

A BRIEF HISTORY OF INSTRUMENTS DESIGNED TO MEASURE QUALITY IN HEALTH CARE

We can distinguish three generations of health-related measurement. In the first generation, information was collected to improve the quality of acute care hospital processes and outcomes. The Health Care Financing Administration inaugurated a hospital-specific mortality report to monitor and improve surgical outcomes in the mid-1980s (U.S. Department of Health and Human Services, 1986). The Joint Commission on Accreditation of Healthcare Organi-

zations (Nadzam, Turpin, Hanold, & White, 1993; Turpin et al., 1996) and the Maryland Hospital Association (Kazandjian, Lawthers, Cernak, & Pipesh, 1993) subsequently developed indicator monitoring systems that were designed to improve quality of patient care. In medical rehabilitation, the Uniform Data System for Medical Rehabilitation (Hamilton, Granger, Sherwin, Zielezny, & Tashman, 1987) and the Medical Outcome System (Formations in Health Care, 1998) were developed to provide rehabilitation facilities with a comparative outcomes database for program improvement. The Commission on Accreditation of Rehabilitation Facilities (CARF) Strategic Outcome Initiative will increase its focus on performance-based information for postacute care (Wilkerson, 1997).

Outcome measure development moved from acute hospitals to a variety of settings in the second generation as payers and purchasers came to realize the value of outcomes information in selecting provider groups based on cost-effectiveness. The Health Plan Employer Data and Information Set (HEDIS) initiative by the National Committee for Quality Assurance (NCQA; Morrissey, 1996b) exemplifies this shift in focus. HEDIS is a set of standardized performance measures that were designed to provide purchasers and consumers with information to compare the performance of managed health care plans. HEDIS performance measures target conditions such as cancer, heart disease, smoking, asthma, and diabetes, and focuses on performance in terms of customer service, access to care and claims processing (http://www.ahrq.gov/qual/tools/toolsria2.htm). Large provider groups, such as Columbia/HCA Healthcare Corporation (Greene, 1996) and United HealthCare Corporation (McGlynn, 1993), promoted the value of comparative data in marketing to purchasers. A variety of purchaser coalitions continue to support accountability in health care by emphasizing purchasing decisions based on outcomes.

The third generation is characterized by consumer groups' interest in outcomes. The Foundation for Accountability published summaries of performance measures to help patients select providers based on access and quality (Modern Healthcare, 1995; Morrissey, 1996a). Health Pages provides consumer-oriented comparative information in specific markets (see http://www.thehealthpages.com). Improved functional status, shortened lengths of stay and minimized costs, efficient gains in functional status, and home discharge are the types of rehabilitation outcomes considered by CARF in its development of performance indicators. In recent years, Medicare has begun paying close attention to the quality of the services it purchases for beneficiaries. To help Medicare beneficiaries be more informed about the quality of services, CMS has developed a range of quality information websites. These sites provide information on quality indicators, comparing a particular facility's performance to those in the same state and a cross the country. Two of the sites with which rehabilitation psychologists should be familiar are Nursing Home Compare (http://www.medicare.gov/NHCompare/home.asp) and Home Health Compare (http://www.medicare.gov/HHCompare/home.asp).

Measurement Issues

Measurement is crucial to the advancement of rehabilitation practice. Recent changes in rehabilitation organization and service delivery have important implications for the science and practice of functional assessment. What we measure, how we measure, and how well these measures predict functional outcomes, use, and care setting are of great importance to consumers, providers, and payers, although each has specific concerns in regard to these data. Summarized as follows are fundamental issues in how we measure functional status and QoL.

We have come to realize that the summed scores are ordinal in nature and should not be used in parametric statistical comparisons. A measurement procedure that can be used to develop interval-scaled measures from ordinal scores is rating scale, or Rasch, analysis (Rasch, 1980), named after the Danish mathematician whose work in the 1950s and 1960s has been widely applied in educational testing. Transforming ordinal raw scores to interval measures allows one to quantify an individual's level of functional status or QoL along an equal-interval continuum, to make quantitative comparisons within an individual across time, or to compare individuals or groups. Rating scale analysis helps evaluate the

extent to which responses to a set of items are dominated by one dimension. This procedure defines items along a continuum that ranges from *easy-to-perform* (or endorse) to *difficult-to-perform* (or endorse). Rating scale analysis provides clinicians and researchers with a method of describing extent of functional status and QoL in persons undergoing rehabilitation, of extending scales across a continuum of settings, of identifying persons for whom a common scale is not useful, and of identifying items that do not work well to define a unidimensional construct.

Applications to Rehabilitation and Chronic Health Conditions

A critical question that one must consider in test selection is, Will the test provide the required information? A satisfactory answer requires that one must state in advance what one wants to measure in order to select an appropriate test. Testing for the sake of testing is unlikely to yield useful information. In addition, assessment is expensive, so the resulting data must be useful and informative if it is to be cost effective. Choosing an instrument involves pragmatic issues, such as what plans to measure and who can administer the test; psychometric issues, such as test reliability and validity; and usability issues such as test targeting and sensitivity to change.

Choosing Instruments

This section describes a range of issues related to selecting functional and QoL instruments. This review is not intended to be an exhaustive list but to act as a guide to thinking about how instrument selection can influence the process of data collection, the kind of data collected, and the interpretations of the data that can be made.

Administrative requirements. There are often pragmatic issues involved in test selection. For example, the AMPS is innovative but requires a sophisticated testing environment. How an assessment can be implemented practically in a clinical setting should not be overlooked; the most elegant of studies will never produce data if the assessments cannot be practically implemented. Questions to consider include the following: Who can use and/or complete the test? Does the administrator need training? If it is a self-report test, can a proxy complete the test? What is the format of the test and is it suitable for the intended population? What is the method of administration? How long does it take to complete? Is the test acceptable to patients? Is it suitable to one's purpose? How relevant and sensible is the instrument?

Issues of interpretability.   Although it is tempting to adopt an instrument described in a journal because it seems to address a concern similar to one you have been attempting to understand, serious consideration must be given to how the test was designed and how results can be interpreted. Often, researchers develop an instrument to meet the need of a particular study that may not be related to clinical needs. Important questions to consider include the following: How were the items selected? What populations have been sampled? How is it scored? Are normal values available or is there a cutoff score? Are there distinct subscores? How does the purpose for which the test was designed relate to the purpose for which the test will be used?

Interpretability also relates to selection of generic versus disease-specific instruments. Generic instruments have value in that they enable comparison across a wide range of clinical populations. Yet, how well they inform understanding about a particular group of patients may be limited because the items do not address issues that are salient to the experience of patients with a specific condition.

Reliability.   *Reliability* concerns the issue of how consistently a score is obtained. Measurement error can affect repeated measures across time or situation or between raters. Reliability theory distinguishes two components of any score: that which is true and that which is due to error. Noise or imprecision in measurement creates error. Reliability of measurement is defined as the ratio of true variation to observed variance. Internal consistency of tests evaluates how well a set of items coheres. Cronbach's alpha and Kuder-Richardson's formula are traditional ways of assessing internal consistency. As noted earlier, newer psychometric approaches built on Georg Rasch's rating scale model extends these ideas by distinguishing item and

person fit characteristics (Wright & Masters, 1982; Wright & Stone, 1979).

Validity.   *Validity* concerns the meaning of scores derived from an instrument; it is commonly defined as the extent to which a test measures what it purports to measure. A more general definition of validity focuses on the range of interpretations that can be appropriately placed on a score, that is, its meaning. Related concepts are sensitivity and specificity. *Sensitivity* pertains to how well a test identifies persons with a certain condition; *specificity* reflects the extent to which a test identifies only those persons with that condition. Validity can be assessed in several ways. Content validation is a usual first step. Comprehensiveness or adequacy of sampling is the domain of interest with content validity. Relevance of items to the concept being measured is considered in determining content validity. Sensibility is a related concept in that it refers to the clinical appropriateness of the measure. Critical reviews by patients or experts in the field are ways to assess content validity.

Criterion validity assesses how well a new instrument is related to a gold standard that measures the same construct. Criterion validity is often divided into concurrent and predictive validity, reflecting an interest in contemporaneous versus future relationships. Sensitivity and specificity may reflect a variety of patient background factors, such as gender and education in the case of QoL appraisals.

Construct validity emerges when sufficient evidence is collected that allows test users to evaluate how well a test measures its intended construct. Correlational evidence (i.e., that the new test correlates with similar established tests but not with dissimilar ones) is useful for such an appraisal. Clearly stated hypotheses about the relationship of a test to other tests are required to evaluate the construct validity of a test.

Level of measurement.   A classical distinction in measurement defines four levels that reflect the properties of the test (Stevens, 1951). *Nominal* scales distinguish presence or absence of a condition, or ability or inability to complete a task. *Ordinal* scales provide for rank ordering of a condition or phenomenon from more to less, such as severity of symptoms or disruption of function. *Interval* level of measurement is defined by equal spacing of responses; physical measures of length, pressure, and weight in terms of centimeters, millimeters of mercury, and kilograms. *Ratio* level of measurement extends interval measurement with the addition of an absolute zero point; temperature in degrees Kelvin is such an example. Most rating scales of functional status and QoL provide only ordinal data. Assumptions about severity of impairment based on sums of item values are limited because the extent of a condition is unknown.

Sensitivity to change.   An important issue for outcomes assessment is how well the instrument can detect differences in the sample of patients to which it is applied. This is often referred to as *sensitivity to change,* and, although change is certainly one aspect, this obfuscates the fact that an instrument that does a poor job of detecting differences in an individual's performance over time probably does not do a good job of detecting differences among individuals either. However, how much change should an instrument be able to detect? How sensitive should a measure be? An important new concept in clinical outcomes research is that of *clinically important difference* and the related term, *minimally clinically important difference* (MCID). MCID is the smallest amount of change that it makes clinical sense to detect (Cella, Eton, Lai, Peterman, & Merkel, 2002). In a comparison of two means, a statistically significant difference can sometimes be found, although the actual difference between the two groups in real terms of the construct being measured is so small as to be meaningless. This is because statistically significant differences are, in part, a function of sample size. The larger the two samples that are being compared, the smaller the difference that is needed to be statistically significant. Conversely, in small clinical samples, clinically meaningful change may have occurred in patients though the result appears miniscule because there is insufficient power to detect change.

Targeting.   An important aspect of instrument selection is ensuring that the items of the test cover the range of the construct to be measured that is appropriate for the intended group of patients. For

example, an assessment of function that only included simple ADL tasks would most likely not be appropriate for community living adults because most of the items would not be challenging. This is often referred to as a *ceiling effect;* that is, too many individuals with maximum scores on the test. The opposite problem, a *floor effect,* occurs when the test is too hard for the sample. This is a problem for function and QoL assessments. Unlike a math test, in which many people may get 100% of the items correct, indicating that those individuals have all acquired a particular amount of math knowledge, function and QoL assessments are administered to detect differences among individuals. If too many individuals score the maximum on a function test, we cannot tell whether they differ in functional level. We suspect they do, but we cannot detect the difference with the instrument. Choosing a well-targeted test requires maximizing the amount of variance that is detected in a sample.

Developmental level must also be considered in selecting instruments. For example, the pediatric version of the Functional Independence Measure, the Wee-FIM (Msall et al., 1994), has modified item definitions that consider developmental expectations. Similarly, the Pediatric Evaluation of Disability Inventory (Haley, Coster, Ludlow, Haltiwanger, & Andrellos, 1992) was developed to assess children's functional status. As described, cocalibration of items from different instruments can equate performance level of individuals, regardless of age, when the items cohere in defining a common construct.

CONCLUSION AND FUTURE DIRECTIONS

Rehabilitation psychologists are well-qualified to evaluate functional status and QoL measures, given a shared scientist–practitioner background and exposure to measurement basics. The literature on functional status and QoL can be evaluated with skills acquired in graduate training. The basics of rating scale analysis can be acquired through textbooks cited here, or through on-line resources, such as the following:

- Institute for Objective Measurement (http://www.rasch.org)

- Australian Council for Educational Research (http://www.acer.edu.au)
- Jean Piaget Society (http://www.piaget.org/links.html)
- Assessment Systems, Corp. (http://www.assess.com)
- Information Technology for the Social and Behavioral Sciences (http://www.gamma.rug.nl)
- QualityMetric, Inc. (http://www.qualitymetric.com/demos)
- NIH PROMIS (http://www.nihpromis.org)

The application of sophisticated psychometric methods has allowed us to conceptualize more clearly what we mean by functional status and QoL. In turn, we have benefited from measuring these constructs with improved reliability, validity, and sensitivity. We have only begun to cocalibrate items from different instruments and explore the pattern of misfitting items and persons to measurement models. Cocalibrated instruments will allow clinicians and researchers to describe QoL using different instruments. Understanding patterns of person misfit to measurement models will allow us to make more informed choices of instruments. Better generic and condition-specific measures will be developed, and the characteristics of specific impairments and of persons that affect QoL perceptions will be understood better. Better QoL measures can, in turn, be used to improve the utilities or values assigned to outcomes by patients in cost-effectiveness and decision analysis research that use quality-adjusted life years. Continued growth in measurement technology should continue to benefit the users of functional status and QoL measures, and ultimately the health of persons with whom these instruments are used.

The increasing prominence of chronic diseases in the health literature, changing population demography, and growing cost containment concerns all converge to support functional status and QoL as a major focus in rehabilitation. The development of prospective payment for medical rehabilitation and the utility of functional status in providing a basis for prospective payment underscore the need to understand and apply functional status concepts. In addition, continuing efforts to develop indica-

tors of health providers' performance by the Joint Commission on Accreditation of Healthcare Organizations and CARF, as well as managed care organizations' performance by NCQA, rely heavily on functional status and QoL concepts. A clear understanding of how functional status and QoL as outcomes of rehabilitation are connected to clinical practices (i.e., process) and provider organizations (i.e., structure) is a prerequisite to improving quality of services. The current focus of health care debates on accountability and quality improvement requires that rehabilitation providers collect and report information about their programs' outcomes so that consumers can make comparative evaluations. Rehabilitation psychologists' skills in assessment, familiarity with disablement concepts, and exposure to measurement processes prepare them to be sophisticated developers and users of functional status and QoL measures.

References

Bellamy, N. (1995). *WOMAC Osteoarthritis Index. A user's guide.* London, Ontario, Canada: University of Western Ontario.

Bellamy, N., Buchanan, W. W., Goldsmith, C. H., Campbell, J., & Stitt, L. W. (1988). Validation study of WOMAC: A health status instrument for measuring clinically important patient relevant outcomes to antirheumatic drug therapy in patients with osteoarthritis of the hip or knee. *Journal of Rheumatology, 15,* 1833–1840.

Bode, R. (1997). Pivoting items for construct definition. *Rasch Measurement Transactions, 11,* 576–577.

Bodenheimer, T., May, J. H., Berenson, R. A., & Coughlan, J. (2005, December). Can money buy quality? Physician response to pay for performance. *Issue Brief of the Center for the Study of Health System Change, 102,* 1–4.

Bowling, A. (1995). *Measuring disease.* Philadelphia: Open University Press.

Bowling, A. (1997). *Measuring health: A review of quality of life measurement scales* (2nd ed.). Philadelphia: Open University Press.

Buntin, M. B., Garten, A. D., Paddock, S., Saliba, D., Totten, M., & Escarce, J. J. (2005). How much is postacute care use affected by its availability? *Health Services Research, 40,* 413–434.

Cella, D., Eton, D. T., Lai, J. S., Peterman, A. H., & Merkel, D. E. (2002). Combining anchor and distribution-based methods to derive minimal clinically important differences on the Functional Assessment of Cancer Therapy (FACT) anemia and fatigue scales. *Journal of Pain and Symptom Management, 24,* 547–561.

Cella, D. F., Lloyd, S. R., & Wright, B. D. (1996). Cross-cultural instrument equating: Current research and future directions. In B. Spilker (Ed.), *Quality of life and pharmacoeconomics in clinical trials* (2nd ed., pp. 707–716). Philadelphia: Lippincott-Raven.

Cella, D. F., Tulsky, D. S., Gray, G., Sarafian, B., Linn, E., Bonomi, A., et al. (1993). The Functional Assessment of Cancer Therapy scale: Development and validation of the general measure. *Journal of Clinical Oncology, 11,* 570–579.

Cella, D. F., Tulsky, D. S., Gray, G., Sarafian, B., Lloyd, S., Linn, E., et al. (1993). The Functional Assessment of Cancer Therapy (FACT) scale: Development and validation of the general measure. *Journal of Clinical Oncology, 11,* 570–579.

Cieza, A., & Stucki, G. (2005). Content comparison of health-related quality of life (HRQOL) instruments based on the international classification of functioning, disability and health (ICF). *Quality of Life Research, 14,* 1225–1237.

Clark, F., Azen, S. P., Zemke, R., Jackson, J., Carlson, M., Mandel, D., et al. (1997). Occupational therapy for independent-living older adults. *JAMA, 278,* 1321–1326.

Coman, L., & Richardson, J. (2006). Relationship between self-report and performance measures of function: A systematic review. *Canadian Journal of Aging, 25,* 253–270.

Coons, S. J., Rao, S., Keininger, D. L., & Hays, R. D. (2000). A comparative review of generic quality-of-life instruments. *Pharmacoeconomics, 17,* 13–35.

Deyo, R. A., Battie, M., Beurskens, A. J., Bombardier, C., Croft, P., Koes, B., et al. (1998). Outcome measures for low back pain research. A proposal for standardized use. *Spine, 23,* 2003–2013.

Diener, E., Emmons, R. A., Larsen, R. J., & Griffin, S. (1985). The Satisfaction with Life Scale. *Journal of Personality Assessment, 49,* 71–75.

Dijkers, M. (1997). Quality of life after spinal cord injury: A meta-analysis of the effects of disablement components. *Spinal Cord, 35,* 829–840.

Donabedian, A. (1966). Evaluating the quality of medical care. *Millbank Memorial Fund Quarterly, 44,* 166–206.

Duncan, P. W., Zorowitz, R., Bates, B., Choi, J. Y., Glasberg, J. J., Graham, G. D., et al. (2005). Management of adult stroke rehabilitation care: A clinical practice guideline. *Stroke, 36,* e100–e143.

Epstein, R. S., & Sherwood, L. M. (1996). From outcomes research to disease management: A guide for the perplexed. *Annals of Internal Medicine, 124,* 838–842.

Feinglass, J., McCarthy, W. J., Slavensky, R., Manheim, L. M., & Martin, G. J. (2000). Functional status and walking ability after lower extremity bypass grafting or angioplasty for intermittent claudication: Results from a prospective outcomes study. *Journal of Vascular Surgery, 31,* 93–103.

Ferrucci, L., Guralnik, J. M., Studenski, S., Fried, L. P., Cutler, G. B., Jr., & Walston, J. D. (2004). Designing randomized, controlled trials aimed at preventing or delaying functional decline and disability in frail, older persons: A consensus report. *Journal of the American Geriatric Society, 52,* 625–634.

Fisher, A. G. (2003). *Assessment of motor and process skills: Volume 1. Development, standardization, and administration manual* (5th ed.). Fort Collins, CO: Three Star Press.

Fisher, W. P., Jr., Harvey, R. F., Taylor, P., Kilgore, K. M., & Kelly, C. K. (1995). Rehabits: A common language of functional assessment. *Archives of Physical Medicine and Rehabilitation, 76,* 113–122.

Formations in Health Care. (1998). *Medical outcome system.* Chicago: Author.

Fuhrer, M. J. (Ed.). (1987). *Rehabilitation outcomes: Analysis and measurement.* Baltimore: Brookes Publishing.

Fuhrer, M. J. (Ed.). (1997). *Assessing medical rehabilitation practices: The promise of outcomes research.* Baltimore: Brookes Publishing.

Greene J. (1996). Columbia starts quality comparisons. *Modern Healthcare, 66,* 6.

Guide for the Uniform Data Set for Medical Rehabilitation (including the FIM™ instrument; Version 5.1; 1997) [Computer software]. Buffalo, NY: State University of New York at Buffalo.

Haley, S. M., Andres, P. L., Coster, W. J., Kosinski, M., Ni, P., & Jette, A. M. (2004). Short-form activity measure for postacute care. *Archives of Physical Medicine and Rehabilitation, 85,* 649–660.

Haley, S. M., Coster, W. J., Ludlow, L., Haltiwanger, J., & Andrellos, P. (1992). *Pediatric Evaluation of Disability Inventory (PEDI).* Boston: Boston University Center for Rehabilitation Effectiveness.

Haley, S. M., Coster, W. J., Andres, P. L., Ludlow, L. H., Ni, P., Bond, T. L., Sinclair, S. J., & Jette, A. M. (2004). Activity outcome measurement for postacute care. *Medical Care, 42*(Suppl. 1), I49–I61.

Haley, S. M., McHorney, C. A., & Ware, J. E., Jr. (1994). Evaluation of the MOS SF-36 physical functioning scale (PF-10): I. Unidimensionality and reproducibility of the Rasch item scale. *Journal of Clinical Epidemiology, 47,* 671–684.

Haley, S. M., Ni, P., Hambleton, R. K., Slavin, M. D., & Jette, A. M. (2006). Computer adaptive testing improved accuracy and precision of scores over random item selection in a physical functioning item bank. *Journal of Clinical Epidemiology, 59,* 1174–1182.

Hamilton, B. B., Granger, C. V., Sherwin, F. S., Zielezny, M., & Tashman, J. S. (1987). A uniform national data system for medical rehabilitation. In M. J. Fuhrer (Ed.), *Rehabilitation outcomes: Analysis and measurement*. Baltimore: Brookes Publishing.

Hawes, C., Morris, J. N., Phillips, C. D., Mor, V., Fries, B. E., & Nonemaker, S. (1995). Reliability estimates for the Minimum Data Set for nursing home resident assessment and care screening (MDS). *Gerontologist, 35,* 172–178.

Hays, R. D., Hahn, H., & Marshall, G. (2002). Use of the SF-36 and other health-related quality of life measures to assess persons with disabilities. *Archives of Physical Medicine and Rehabilitation, 83*(12, Suppl. 2), S4–9.

Hickey, A., Barker, M., McGee, H., & O'Boyle, C. (2005). Measuring health-related quality of life in older patient populations: A review of current approaches. *Pharmacoeconomics, 23,* 971–993.

Hobson, J. P., Edwards, N. I., & Meara, R. J. (2001). The Parkinson's disease Activities of Daily Living Scale: A new simple and brief subjective measure of disability in Parkinson's disease. *Clinical Rehabilitation, 15,* 241–246.

Iezzoni, L. (Ed.). (1994). *Risk adjustment for measuring health care outcomes*. Ann Arbor, MI: Health Administration Press.

Jette, A. M., & Haley, S. M. (2005). Contemporary measurement techniques for rehabilitation outcomes assessment. *Journal of Rehabilitation Medicine, 37,* 339–345.

Jette, A. M., Haley, S. M., Tao, W., Ni, P., Moed, R., Meyers, D., et al. (2007). Prospective evaluation of the AM-PAC-CAT in outpatient rehabilitation settings. *Physical Therapy, 87,* 385–398.

Kane, R. L. (1995). Improving the quality of long-term care. *JAMA, 273,* 1376–1380.

Kane, R. L., & Kane, R. A. (Eds.). (2004). *Assessing older persons: Measures, meaning, and practical applications*. New York: Oxford University Press.

Kane, R. L., Lin, W. C., & Blewett, L. A. (2002). Geographic variation in the use of postacute care. *Health Services Research, 37,* 667–682.

Kazandjian, V. A., Lawthers, J., Cernak, C. M., & Pipesh, F. C. (1993). Relating outcomes to processes of care. *Journal of Quality Improvement, 19,* 530–538.

Lawton, M. P., & Brody, E. M. (1969). Assessment of older people: Self-maintaining and instrumental activities of daily living. *Gerontologist, 9,* 179–186.

Liu, K., Gage, B., Harvell, J., Stevenson, D., & Brennan, N. (1999). Medicare's postacute care benefit: Background, trends, and issues to be faced. *Report to the Department of Health and Human Services*. Retrieved November 17, 2008, from http://aspe.hhs.gov/daltcp/reports/mpacb.htm

Livneh, H., & Antonak, R. F. (1997). *Psychosocial adaptation to chronic illness and disability*. Gaithersburg, MD: Aspen Publishers.

Mahoney, F. I., & Barthel, D. (1965). Functional evaluation: The Barthel Index. *Maryland State Medical Journal, 14,* 56–61.

McDowell, I. (2006). *Measuring health: A guide to rating scales and questionnaires* (3rd ed.). New York: Oxford University Press.

McDowell, I., & Newell, C. (1996). *Measuring health: A guide to rating scales and questionnaires* (2nd ed.). New York: Oxford University Press.

McGlynn, E. A. (1993). Gathering systematic information on health plans: An interview with Sheila Leatherman. *Journal on Quality Improvement, 19,* 266–271.

McHorney, C. A. (2002). Use of item response theory to link three modules of functional status items from the Asset and Health Dynamics Among the Oldest-Old study. *Archives of Physical Medicine and Rehabilitation, 83,* 383–394.

McHorney, C. A., Haley, S. M., & Ware, J. E., Jr. (1997). Evaluation of the MOS SF-36 Physical Functioning Scale (PF-10): II. Comparison of relative precision using Likert and Rasch scoring methods. *Journal of Clinical Epidemiology, 50,* 451–461.

Morrissey, J. (1996a). Alliance prepares to roll out proposed performance measures. *Modern Healthcare, 25,* 54.

Morrissey, J. (1996b). NCQA database to allow quick HMO comparisons. *Modern Healthcare, 25,* 50.

Msall, M. E., DiGaudio, K., Rogers, B. T., LaForest, S., Catanzaro, N. L., Campbell, J., et al. (1994). The Functional Independence Measure for Children (WeeFIM). Conceptual basis and pilot use in children with developmental disabilities. *Clinical Pediatrics, 33,* 421–430.

Nadzam, D. M., Turpin, R., Hanold, L. S., & White, R. E. (1993). Data-driven performance improvement in health care: The Joint Commission's Indicator Measurement System. *Journal of Quality Improvement, 19,* 492–500.

Nygard, L., Bernspang, B., Fisher, A. G., & Winblad, B. (1994). Comparing motor and process ability of persons with suspected dementia in home and clinic settings. *American Journal of Occupational Therapy, 48,* 689–696.

Park, S., Fisher, A. G., & Velozo, C. A. (1994). Using the assessment of motor and process skills to compare occupational performance between clinic and home settings. *American Journal of Occupational Therapy, 48,* 697–709.

Rasch, G. (1980). *Probabilistic models for some intelligence and attainment tests.* Chicago: University of Chicago Press. (Original work published 1960)

Schalock, R. L., Verdugo, M. A., Jenaro, C., Wang, M., Wehmeyer, M., Jiancheng, X., et al. (2005). Cross-cultural study of quality of life indicators. *American Journal on Mental Retardation, 110,* 298–311.

Schipper, H., Clinch, J. J., & Olweny, C. L. M. (1996). Quality of life studies: Definitions and conceptual issues. In B. Spilker (Ed.), *Quality of life and pharmaco-economics in clinical trials* (2nd ed., pp. 11–24). Philadelphia: Lippincott-Raven.

Spilker, B. (1996). *Quality of life and pharmacoeconomics in clinical trials* (2nd ed.). Philadelphia: Lippincott-Raven.

Stevens, S. S. (1951). *Handbook of experimental psychology.* New York: Wiley.

Szende, A., Oppe, M., & Devlin, N. J. (2007). EQ-5D value sets: Inventory, comparative review, and user guide. London: Springer Publishing Company.

Turpin, R. S., Darcy, L. A., Koss, R., McMahill, C., Meyne, K., Morton, D., et al. (1996). A model to assess the usefulness of performance indicators. *International Journal for Quality in Health Care, 8,* 321–329.

U.S. Department of Health and Human Services (1995). *Post-stroke rehabilitation* (AHCPR Publication No. 95–0662). Washington, DC: Author.

Wade, D. T., & Collin, C. (1988). The Barthel ADL Index: A standard measure of physical disability? *International Disabilities Studies, 10,* 64–7.

Ware, J. E. (1993). *SF-36 Health Survey: Manual and interpretation guide.* Boston: The Health Institute, New England Medical Center.

Webster, K., Odom, L., Peterman, A., Lent, L., & Cella, D. (1999). The Functional Assessment of Chronic Illness Therapy (FACIT) measurement system: Validation of version 4 of the core questionnaire. *Quality of Life Research, 8,* 604.

Werner, R. A., & Kessler, S. (1996). Effectiveness of an intensive outpatient rehabilitation program for postacute stroke patients. *American Journal of Physical Medicine and Rehabilitation, 75,* 114–120.

WHOQoL Group. (1995). The World Health Organization Quality of Life assessment (WHOQoL): Position paper from the World Health Organization. *Social Science Medicine, 41,* 1403–9.

WHOQoL Group. (1998a). Development of the World Health Organization: WHOQoL-BREF quality of life assessment. *Psychological Medicine, 28,* 551–558.

WHOQoL Group. (1998b). The World Health Organization Quality of Life Assessment (WHOQoL): Development and general psychometric properties. *Social Science and Medicine, 46,* 1569–85.

Wilkerson, D. L. (1997). Accreditation and the use of outcomes-oriented information systems. *Archives of Physical Medicine and Rehabilitation, 78,* S31–S35.

Willke, R. J., Burke, L. B., & Erickson, P. (2004). Measuring treatment impact: A review of patient-reported outcomes and other efficacy endpoints in approved product labels. *Controlled Clinical Trials, 25,* 535–552.

Wood-Dauphinee, S., Exner, G., Bostanci, B., Exner, G., Glass, C., Jochheim, K. A., et al. (2002). Quality of life in patients with spinal cord injury: Basic issues, assessment, and recommendations. *Restorative Neurology and Neuroscience, 20*(3–4), 135–149.

World Health Organization. (2001). *The International Classification of Functioning, Disability, and Health.* Retrieved November 17, 2008, from http://www3.who.int/icf/onlinebrowser/icf.cfm

Wright, B. D., & Masters, G. (1982). *Rating scale analysis: Rasch measurement.* Chicago: MESA Press.

Wright, B. D., & Stone, M. H. (1979). *Best test design.* Chicago: MESA Press.

CHAPTER 10

NEUROPSYCHOLOGICAL PRACTICE IN REHABILITATION

Thomas A. Novack, Mark Sherer, and Suzanne Penna

The incidence of brain disorder, such as that due to traumatic brain injury and stroke, necessitates among those providing rehabilitation services an awareness of neuropsychological principles and practice. This chapter describes the contribution of neuropsychology to inpatient and outpatient rehabilitation services and the value of information derived from neuropsychological assessment in predicting outcome.

DEFINITION OF *NEUROPSYCHOLOGY*

The practice of neuropsychology in a rehabilitation setting requires a broad knowledge base encompassing neuroanatomy, psychological and neuropsychological testing, clinical neurological syndromes, psychotherapy, and neuroimaging. These specialized skills and knowledge are complementary to the interdisciplinary rehabilitation team, which is composed of a variety of professional health care disciplines. The rehabilitation-oriented neuropsychologist offers a unique contribution to the rehabilitation effort by relating an understanding of the nature of brain-behavior sequelae of injury or illness and their long-term consequences to the potential impact on daily living skills, such as driving, living independently, and participating in one's community. This chapter highlights those unique contributions.

REHABILITATION NEUROPSYCHOLOGICAL PRACTICE IN THE INPATIENT SETTING

Neuropsychologists have been integrated into most inpatient rehabilitation programs because of the emphasis on treating people with brain disorders.

Neuropsychologists may offer a unique perspective that complements contributions from other team members.

Contributing to the Team Effort

A neuropsychologist practicing in an inpatient rehabilitation setting can assist the treatment team in several ways. First, the neuropsychologist helps by focusing attention on cognitive and behavioral barriers (e.g., memory disorder, impulsivity, executive deficits) to patient discharge to ensure that clinical interventions are targeted efficiently. Neuropsychological findings are best communicated during patient rounds and staff meetings. Creation of a written report is necessary, but not sufficient, if the information is to benefit the patient.

In addition to identifying the problems, the neuropsychologist can assist in developing a treatment approach, including advising therapists about ways to maximize patient participation. Evaluation of progress, a major issue in rehabilitation, is an area of strength for neuropsychologists, who generally have training in scale development and application, as well as in commonly used outcome measures. Because of their grasp of behavioral, cognitive, and emotional difficulties associated with brain disorders, neuropsychologists are well suited to contribute to discharge planning, which includes issues such as the patient's ability to return to community activities (e.g., independent living, driving, employment, school, managing finances). In this role, neuropsychologists can counsel patients and caregivers, educating them about the effects of brain disorders and about what to expect in the future. In many settings, neuropsychologists also direct research programs, consistent with their training in research methodology and statistics. In fulfilling these roles, it is essential that neuropsychologists function as part of the rehabilitation team.

Patient History

Obtaining a thorough patient history can be a major contribution of a neuropsychologist, particularly on teams that do not have a clinical psychologist. Neuropsychologists take a broad view, supplementing the medical history by focusing on social history (particularly education and employment), substance use, daily activities, psychiatric background, coping capacity, and family history. It is important that family members and caregivers are interviewed in addition to the patient, as this contact allows confirmation (or refutation) of information given by the patient and also prepares the way for family counseling, if needed, and later discussions about recovery and discharge planning.

Cognitive Assessment

Practicing neuropsychology in a rehabilitation setting presents multiple challenges. The rehabilitation neuropsychologist must be prepared to evaluate patients at all levels of functioning, ranging from coma to full responsiveness. The neuropsychologist should be facile with instruments validated for assessing patients with disorders of consciousness, such as the Glasgow Coma Scale (Teasdale & Jennett, 1974), Coma-Near Coma Scale (Rappaport, Dougherty, & Kelting, 1992), and Coma Recovery Scale-Revised (Giacino, Kalmar, & Whyte, 2004). In some cases, inpatients are fully responsive and capable of participating in a comprehensive neuropsychological evaluation. This may be particularly true of patients who are doing well physically and are admitted because of cognitive and behavioral problems affecting safety. Even those with severe brain disorder may be capable of completing a brief evaluation within a month of onset (Dikmen, McLean, Temkin, & Wyler, 1986; Pastorek, Hannay, & Contant, 2004). Testing completed during this time span (or inability to participate in testing) predicts outcome following traumatic brain injury (TBI; Boake et al., 2001; Pastorek et al., 2004).

However, a comprehensive neuropsychological assessment is premature for many in inpatient rehabilitation who are involved in several hours of therapy a day and subject to fatigue. For these individuals, the most effective approach is to use repetitive, short screens to monitor cognitive and behavioral improvement occurring in the initial stages of recovery from a brain disorder. Initially, patients may exhibit an acute confusional state (Stuss et al., 1999) that has characteristics of delirium (Nakase-Thompson, Sherer, Yablon, Nick, & Trzepacz, 2004), necessitating careful monitoring and medical management. Several scales are available to evaluate patients in the midst of a confusional state. The Galveston Orientation and Amnesia Test (Levin, O'Donnell, & Grossman, 1979) is a well-established instrument for TBI. Recently, scales that can be applied to a broader population of patients with acquired brain disorder have been developed. For instance, the Orientation Log (O-Log; Jackson, Novack, & Dowler, 1998) can be used with any patient population. Although brief (i.e., 10 questions, 5 minutes to administer), the O-Log predicts rehabilitation outcome and cognitive outcome following discharge (Alderson & Novack, 2002). An accompanying scale, the Cognitive Log (Alderson & Novack, 2003), tracks changes in concentration and memory skills and is also predictive of rehabilitation outcome and status 1 year following TBI. The Mississippi Aphasia Screening Test (MAST; Nakase-Thompson et al., 2005) assesses language skills at bedside. Such scales allow neuropsychologists to track recovery using a brief bedside assessment administered on a daily basis, if indicated.

A broader, but still brief, assessment of cognition can be accomplished with scales focusing on mental status (see Ruchinskas & Curyto, 2003; Wagner, Nayak, & Fink, 1995, for reviews), the most widely used of which is the Mini-Mental State Examination (MMSE; Folstein, Folstein, & McHugh, 1975), which has established reliability and validity. This scale can be somewhat cumbersome to use because of the need for the administrator and the patient to manipulate materials, but it does provide assessment of multiple cognitive domains. There is only a global score, so interpretation of domain-specific performance must be qualitative. However, scores have been tied to community activities, at least for the Alzheimer's population (Galasko et al., 1997). The Cognistat (Kiernan, Mueller, Langston, & Van Dyke, 1987) has also developed a following in rehabilitation settings. Domain specific scores are provided, but there has been only cursory attention to establishing their validity. This is best administered in an office rather than at bedside. The Repeatable Battery for the Assessment of Neuropsychological Status (RBANS; Randolph, Tierney, Mohr, & Chase, 1998) is also gaining in popularity, as it is a more comprehensive assessment than provided by the MMSE or Cognistat and requires about 30 minutes. Parallel versions of the test and domain-specific scores make the RBANS appealing for the rehabilitation population. For cases of dementia, the Dementia Rating Scale-2 (Jurica, Leitten, & Mattis, 2001) is well-normed and provides both global and domain-specific scores. The Confusion Assessment Protocol (Sherer, Nakase-Thompson, Yablon, & Gontkovsky, 2005) is a recent addition specifically intended for patients in the midst of an acute confusional state, such as during the early phase of recovery from TBI.

There are also unique areas of cognitive deficit that warrant attention in a rehabilitation setting. For instance, diminished awareness of difficulties caused by the brain disorder is a common problem that can compromise rehabilitation outcome (Giacino & Cicerone, 1998). Poor awareness, not only of the existence of deficits but also in understanding their impact on everyday life, may be evident. Several scales measure self-awareness in this population (Sherer, Hart, & Nick, 2003). In general, patients are more aware of physical than cognitive deficits (Hart, Sherer, Whyte, Plansky, & Novack, 2004), which is a major challenge because cognitive deficits may have more impact on return to independent living, at least for those experiencing TBI. Executive deficits in general (including self-awareness) affect safety, such as risk of falls (Rapport, Hanks, Millis, & Deshpande, 1998) and return to daily independent activities (Sherer, Bergloff, Boake, High, & Levin, 1998).

Behavioral and Emotional Assessment

Members of the rehabilitation team often need consultation for assessment and treatment of inappropriate behavior associated with brain disorder. In the inpatient setting, the major focus is on behavior that presents a potential risk of injury, such as restlessness, impulsivity, and agitation. Such behavior can best be understood in light of existing cognitive deficits, such as limited self-awareness, executive difficulties, and memory disturbance. Thus, an assessment of behavior needs to be coupled with evaluation of cognitive status. One of the most widely recognized instruments to evaluate behavioral difficulties in the rehabilitation setting is the Agitated Behavior Scale (ABS; Corrigan, 1989). Agitated behavior, as assessed by the ABS, has been tied to changes in cognition (Corrigan & Mysiw, 1988), and the ABS can be used serially to judge the effectiveness of interventions (Novack & Penrod, 1993). With regard to emotional status of inpatients, emphasis should be placed on regular contact, interview, and observation. People with acquired brain disorder may present with alteration in affect during acute recovery, often being described as "blunted" or "flattened" or, conversely, as "emotionally labile." Emotions at this level of recovery are often shallow and transient. Again, the influence of cognitive deficits needs to be emphasized. The neuropsychologist may focus on interventions to lessen emotional lability, including instituting a controlled environment and consulting regarding treatment with medications.

Intervention

A neuropsychologist can assist staff in generating interventions for the cognitive, emotional, and behavioral problems accompanying acquired brain disorder. Cognitive remediation is widely used, even though some interventions lack definitive evidence of effectiveness (see Cicerone et al., 2005, for a review; see also chap. 17, this volume). Cognitive interventions are provided in speech therapy and occupational therapy in most settings, but neuropsychologists may assist in the process. In some cases, group intervention has proven helpful, for example, with regard to orientation and awareness (Corrigan, Arnett, Houck, & Jackson, 1985; Youngjohn & Altman, 1989). Psychotherapy for emotional distress can be implemented in some cases, but the duration of inpatient rehabilitation is often insufficient to complete treatment, and the presence of cognitive difficulties may preclude such intervention. Neuropsychologists can assist the team in identifying medications to treat emotional distress as well as behavioral issues. In many cases, the role of the neuropsychologist as an educator is essential, for example, in assisting staff to understand the relation between the patient's behavior and brain disorder. This is particularly true for conditions that result in unusual or bizarre behavior, such as the misidentification syndromes (Feinberg & Roane, 1997), agnosia (Bauer & Demery, 2003), and sensory neglect (Heilman, Watson, & Valenstein, 2003).

REHABILITATION NEUROPSYCHOLOGICAL PRACTICE IN THE OUTPATIENT SETTING

In the best of situations, there is a continuation of neuropsychological services from the inpatient to outpatient settings. Improvement in cognitive functioning can be documented based on comparison with earlier assessment, and interventions can be continued and modified as progress warrants. The neuropsychologist working in an outpatient rehabilitation setting must still be capable of assessing patients exhibiting varying levels of responsiveness, but in most cases more challenging and comprehensive assessments can now be administered. The issues addressed during outpatient assessments shift as the patient improves. The initial focus on guiding cognitive remediation and need for supervision yields to concerns about capacity to return to community activities such as school, work, and driving. The neuropsychologist does not dictate resumption of such activities independent of the opinions of other health care providers, but the contribution of the neuropsychologist to these judgments is essential. In many cases the involvement of the neuropsychologist extends for months, and sometimes years, after discharge.

Follow-up Assessment

There is no established standard for follow-up intervals for neuropsychological evaluation. This is problematic because it is impossible then to compare a patient's performance with a sample of similar cases to determine whether he or she is progressing as expected. Follow-up is often dictated by the expectation that most recovery after acquired brain injury occurs during the first year after onset, within 6 to 12 months after a severe head injury, and over a shorter period for stroke, aneurysm, or a less severe TBI (Clifton, Hayes, Levin, Michel, & Choi, 1992; Levin, 1993). However, recovery may continue for several years, and serial neuropsychological assessment may detect meaningful changes in cognitive, behavioral, or emotional status (Millis et al., 2001). In most cases of acquired brain injury, follow-up 3 to 6 months after onset is important because it is during this interval that issues of independence are often raised. In the case of TBI, repeat neuropsychological assessments have been suggested at 3 to 6 months, 1 year, and 2 years postinjury (Sherer & Novack, 2003), but clinicians may alter these time frames depending on individual patient needs.

Basing follow-up assessments on tests administered early in recovery is a double-edged sword. "Practice effects" can muddy the identification of improvement in a particular cognitive domain although these may be minimal in severely impaired patients. Substituting equivalent tests or using alternate forms of the same test and lengthening the interval between evaluations can reduce practice effects. Recognizing that some improvement on certain neuropsychological measures may be due to practice effects, one should attempt to obtain corroborating evidence of improvement (or lack thereof) from family reports (see Beglinger et al., 2005; McCaffrey & Westervelt, 1995, for a review of these issues). As with inpatient assessment, it is important to assess a broad range of cognitive domains, focusing on areas that have previously appeared impaired. The neuropsychologist should also consider the need for symptom validity testing (i.e., for detection of malingering), especially when issues of secondary gain are evident (see Bush et al., 2005, for a review in this area).

In structuring a comprehensive evaluation, the neuropsychologist confronts several issues of test selection, the most fundamental of which is the choice of a flexible versus fixed battery approach (Levin, 1994). Traditional fixed batteries, such as the Halstead-Reitan (Reitan & Wolfson, 1993), have some appeal, given their years of use and large normative databases, but the tests often do not lead to clear inferences about everyday functioning that are important in rehabilitation settings. In practice, the Halstead-Reitan battery is often supplemented with other tests, particularly of memory, which renders it no longer a "fixed" battery. To address the issue of inference to everyday functioning, Barbara Wilson and others have developed tests intended to be ecologically valid in that the tasks are similar to those required in daily living (Robertson, Ward, Ridgeway, & Nimmo-Smith, 1994; Wilson, 1985; Wilson, Cockburn, & Halligan, 1987), but these tests (e.g., Rivermead Behavioural Memory Test, Wilson, Cockburn, & Baddeley, 1986; Test of Everyday Attention, Robertson et al., 1994) have not yet taken a strong hold in American neuropsychology, although they represent an important emerging trend.

Many neuropsychologists use a flexible battery of tests that can be tailored to the specific deficits of the patient or to the referral question. Fortunately, there are many tests that exhibit adequate validity and reliability for this purpose. The emphasis is not on particular tests but rather on ensuring that important areas of cognitive functioning are assessed, such as attention and concentration, language skills, spatial and constructional abilities, memory for new information, executive abilities, academic skills, and intelligence. The drawback to using a flexible battery is that even though the normative sampling may have been excellent, each test has an independent normative sample, meaning that comparison of performance across tests must be done with caution. This concern has led to a trend of norming several instruments at once, such as was done with the Wechsler Adult Intelligence Scale-III and the Wechsler Memory Scale-III, which were normed simultaneously on the same population (Wechsler, 1997). This means that standard scores can be directly compared, allowing the clinician greater certainty in identifying strengths and weaknesses in the cognitive profile.

History Taking

Assessment should include an interview of the patient and preferably a family member or caregiver. The interview of the patient should establish their view of their functional gains since the last contact

(e.g., independence in ADLs; participation in household activities, such as parenting, cooking, or paying bills; return to major activities, such as driving or work). Resumption of important relationships in the community and with relatives should be examined in detail. The interview should address the patient's perspective on physical recovery (including motor and sensory functioning), cognitive status, and emotional and behavioral status. Their understanding of what medications are prescribed, as well as why and when they are taken, is an important window on self-awareness and independence. Substance use should also be addressed.

It is important to obtain collateral information from family members whenever possible. Family members may provide a markedly different report than patients, who may overstate their recovery. The interview also allows the family to discuss their experience as caregivers and the accompanying frustrations and challenges. Just having the opportunity to talk about these issues can be beneficial for a caregiver's perceived level of stress.

Treatment Planning

It is important to tailor the neuropsychological evaluation with a view toward functional outcomes. Informing a patient and family members of cognitive deficits such as memory disorder is not valuable unless tied to some understanding of the impact on daily functioning, what can be done by way of management, and the outcome that is anticipated. The follow-up evaluation can address the effectiveness of cognitive remediation and readiness for vocational rehabilitation or specialized school programs. A thorough understanding of such rehabilitation programs is essential for the rehabilitation neuropsychologist, as is the ability to work closely with teachers and vocational counselors in program implementation.

A neuropsychological assessment can also assess the impact of medication. Although limited information exists regarding the effectiveness of psychoactive medications following acquired brain injury, there is increasing understanding of biochemical mechanisms involved in brain injury and recovery, leading to logical inferences regarding the potential benefit of medications such as cholinesterase inhibitors, selective serotonin reuptake inhibitors, and dopamine agonists. Pharmacological treatment of acquired brain injury has changed significantly over the past 20 years, but empirical evidence of its effectiveness is sparse (Glenn & Wroblewski, 2005). Neuropsychological assessment provides an important gauge of the effectiveness of these substances at an individual and group level.

Sensitivity to Evolving Difficulties

During recovery, difficulties may develop that were not present during acute hospitalization. Although cognitive abilities almost invariably improve during the early months of recovery, emotional and behavioral difficulties may appear, persist, or worsen. With cognitive recovery also comes greater awareness of the injury and consequent functional limitations on one's lifestyle, which can lead to dysphoria and depression (Ownsworth & Oei, 1998). Posttraumatic stress disorder can also follow brain injury, particularly when the event was violent (e.g., car crash, assault), and there is recall of events surrounding the injury (Bryant, 2001). Behavioral difficulties may be similar to those seen in an inpatient setting (e.g., impulsivity, agitation, mood lability), but these may be more problematic because of increased physical recovery and mobility. Difficult behaviors are important to address in a neuropsychological assessment because of the effect on community functioning, particularly return to work, as well as the strain generated on caregivers (Lezak, 1988).

Patient and Family Education

Education of the patient and family members is an essential component of any follow-up assessment. This may involve much repetition of what was presented during the acute hospitalization, but it is important to highlight changes as well. A patient's emotional and behavioral functioning, as well as cognitive deficits, is strongly associated with the perceived burden of the primary caregiver, usually to a greater extent than the patient's physical limitations (Groom, Shaw, O'Conner, Howard, & Pickens, 1998). To reduce this burden, or at least normalize it, objective information regarding brain injury in general, and applied to the specific case, is of value. Personalized information about TBI and

rehabilitation progress increases satisfaction with rehabilitation and functional outcome (Pegg et al., 2005). A primary goal of feedback is to increase the injured person's awareness regarding the extent of injury, the associated deficits, and their impact on daily life. Impaired awareness makes it difficult for the person to see the need to invest effort in rehabilitation and is a major obstacle to resumption of community activities (Trudel, Tryon, & Purdum, 1998). Neuropsychologists often play a pivotal role in holistic programs focusing on increasing awareness of strengths and deficits as community reintegration is achieved (Prigatano, 1999). For successful functioning, it is essential that the injured person understand the implications of deficits on daily life beyond simply acknowledging the existence of the deficits, which is often a focus during acute rehabilitation.

Assessment of Behavioral and Emotional Status

Just as important as cognitive evaluation is assessment of emotional and behavioral functioning, which may be more distressing to family and more of a hindrance in returning to premorbid functioning than are cognitive deficits (Lezak, 1988). Depression and anxiety are common emotional difficulties following brain injury (Hibbard, Uysal, Kepler, Bogdany, & Silver, 1998; Rosenthal, Christensen, & Ross, 1998), which can be reflected in mood lability or, conversely, flattened affect and lack of emotional response. Behaviors associated with these symptoms are agitation, temper outbursts, or impulsivity. Family members may become frustrated when the injured person is not socially engaged because of behavioral and emotional problems.

The best way to assess these areas is through comparison of family and self-report. Unfortunately, most assessment instruments have not been independently normed for those with acquired brain injury, and this may create problems in interpretation. Measures of depression, for instance, often include items relating to vegetative or cognitive symptoms that can be caused by brain disorder independent of emotional distress. Several instruments measuring behavior and affect were developed specifically for those with brain disorders, including the Neurobehavioral Rating Scale

(Levin et al., 1987), Neurobehavioral Functioning Inventory-Revised (Kreutzer, Marwitz, Seel, & Serio, 1996), Neuropsychology Behavior and Affect Profile (Nelson, Satz, & D'Elia, 1994), and Poststroke Depression Rating Scale (Gainotti et al., 1997). Several scales that assess behavioral difficulties associated with frontal involvement (e.g., Frontal Systems Behavior Scale: Grace & Malloy, 2001; Dysexecutive Questionnaire: Bennett, Ong, & Ponsford, 2005) can be particularly helpful because cognitive testing may not be informative in such cases.

ASSOCIATION OF TEST RESULTS WITH OUTCOME

Some have questioned the ecological validity of neuropsychological testing, arguing that it only measures a subset of the abilities needed for real world functioning and that findings obtained in the quiet, controlled setting of the testing room do not translate to predictions about functioning in the intense, stimulus-rich environments of the workplace or other community settings (Hart & Hayden, 1986). However, recent literature supports the utility of cognitive test findings in predicting functioning in daily life (Chaytor & Schmitter-Edgecombe, 2003). Although results from neuropsychological assessments alone may not dictate definitive recommendations regarding personal independence and return to work for persons with brain impairments, such findings can make an important contribution to these recommendations. Brief reviews of the relevance of neuropsychological test findings are provided for: (a) decision making capacity, (b) return to work, (c) need for supervision, and (d) return to driving.

Decision-Making Capacity

The ability to make one's own decisions may be evaluated in a number of contexts, including capacity to consent to medical care, to participate in research, and to manage finances. Determination of decision-making capacity is a clinical judgment based on examination of the patient, consideration of collateral reports, behavioral observations, and knowledge of the patient's clinical condition. In contrast, a conclusion about competency is a legal decision made by a judge (Marson & Hebert, 2005).

Determination of medical or research decision-making capacity may pose an ethical dilemma for rehabilitation professionals (Blackmer, 2003; Venesy, 1994). In the role of care provider, the clinician may hold a strong opinion as to the appropriate course of treatment. Patient refusal might then be interpreted (fairly or not) as prima facie evidence of impaired decision-making capacity. Similarly, the rehabilitation researcher may encounter family members willing to consent to a patient's participation in a study, though the patient refuses. This may create an incentive for the investigator to conclude that the patient has impaired decision-making capacity and that the relative's position should take precedence. Kirschner, Stocking, Wagner, Foye, and Siegler (2001) found that determination of decision-making capacity was the third most common ethical issue identified by rehabilitation clinicians.

Decision-making capacity is determined by evaluating the patient's ability to: (a) communicate a choice, (b) appreciate the consequences of the choice, (c) reason about the choice or provide a rational explanation of the choice, and (d) understand the context in which the choice was made as well as risk and benefits of the choice made and the alternatives (Appelbaum & Grisso, 1995; Marson & Hebert, 2005). There has been some limited investigation of decision-making capacity in patient groups seen in rehabilitation settings, including TBI (Marson et al., 2005) and stroke (Deiner & Bischof-Rosarioz, 2004). Unlike persons with dementia, loss of decision-making capacity may be temporary in patients with TBI or stroke. Marson et al., for instance, found that medical decision-making capacity following TBI was impaired, but improved over a span of 6 months, although not reaching the same level as exhibited by noninjured controls, on average.

In a clinical assessment of decision-making capacity, the initial step of determining the patient's ability to communicate a choice may be a substantial barrier for patients with aphasia (Deiner & Bischof-Rosarioz, 2004) or for those in the minimally conscious state (Coughlan, Rix, & Neumann, 2005). Certain neuropsychological tests have been used to assist in determining decision-making capacity. Persons with capacity have differed from those lacking capacity on measures of intelligence (Sutto,

Clare, Holland, & Watson, 2005) and attention and speed of visual scanning (Bassett, 1999). The abilities to provide a rational explanation for one's choice and to appreciate the consequences of one's decision are best predicted by measures of verbal fluency (Marson, Chatterjee, Ingram, & Harrell, 1996; Marson, Cody, Ingram, & Harrell, 1995), whereas ability to understand the context, risks, and benefits of one's choice is best predicted by measures of conceptualization and confrontation naming.

Although standard neuropsychological tests are useful in evaluating decision-making capacity, special instruments have been developed just for this purpose. Commonly used instruments include the MacArthur Competence Assessment Tool (Appelbaum & Grisso, 1995) and the Capacity to Consent to Treatment Instrument (Marson et al., 1995), both of which involve evaluation of four legal standards (enumerated earlier) essential to providing consent to treatment. Scores are derived on the basis of subject responses to vignettes describing medical problems.

Return to Work

Because of financial need and the value placed on employment in American culture, decisions regarding return to work are of particular importance to persons with disabilities and their families. An extensive literature shows that neuropsychological test findings are useful in predicting return to work in patients with TBI (Sherer, Novack, et al., 2002). In a study of 293 patients with TBI, Boake et al. (2001) showed that 10 of 15 neuropsychological measures obtained during inpatient rehabilitation predicted employment outcome at 1 to 4 years postinjury. Patients with impaired auditory comprehension, cognitive processing speed, visual analysis, and verbal memory were markedly less likely to be employed at follow-up than patients with intact abilities in these areas. Sherer, Sander, et al. (2002) studied 667 patients with TBI and found that a global index of cognitive status (obtained by combining scores from several neuropsychological measures collected during inpatient rehabilitation) predicted employment status at 1-year postinjury. This held even after adjustment for other predictors of employment outcome including age, education

level, injury severity, and preinjury employment status. Finally, Novack, Bush, Meythaler, and Canupp (2001) showed that early neuropsychological test performance has a greater effect on employment outcome than do premorbid functioning, injury severity, or postinjury emotional adjustment.

The literatures on neuropsychological assessment and employment outcomes for other patient populations are less extensive than that for TBI. Stroke location has only a limited relation to eventual return to work in patients with stroke (Wozniak et al., 1999), highlighting the need for other predictors of stroke outcome. In a study of 134 persons with stroke, Vilkki et al. (2004) found that neuropsychological tests of verbal concept formation and executive functions predicted return to work.

Need for Supervision

Supervision of persons with acquired brain injury may become burdensome to caregivers and disheartening for patients. Recommendations regarding the amount of supervision needed by patients are generally given at discharge from inpatient rehabilitation and revised at follow-up assessments. Neuropsychological test findings have been shown to predict patients' supervision needs and, thus, are helpful in these recommendations. In a study of 452 persons with TBI, Hart et al. (2003) found that a wide range of neuropsychological test findings were predictive of the degree of supervision that patients received. Measures that predicted level of supervision included tests of orientation, auditory comprehension, verbal fluency, memory, attention, fine motor dexterity, cognitive processing speed, visual search, visual construction skills, and executive functions. After adjustment for other potential contributing factors, a measure of cognitive speed and visual search was the best predictor of level of supervision.

Predictors of functional independence at rehabilitation discharge differ depending on stroke location. Novack, Haban, Graham, and Satterfield (1987) found that measures of motor persistence, visual construction skills, and memory best predicted functional independence for patients with right hemisphere stroke, whereas measures of memory, sensory suppressions, motor persistence, and verbal fluency best predicted degree of independence for patients with left hemisphere stroke.

Risk of falls is a major factor in determining supervision needs for patients in rehabilitation, as falls carry significant risk of additional injury. In a study of a heterogeneous group of 90 rehabilitation inpatients with brain, orthopedic, and spinal injuries, Rapport and colleagues (1998) found that measures of executive functioning predicted patient falls.

Return to Driving

Recommendations regarding return to driving are particularly challenging, given the potential liability involved. Rehabilitation professionals tend to be conservative in releasing persons with acquired brain injuries to return to driving, whereas patients are generally eager to regain the independence symbolized by driving. There is general agreement that an actual road test is the gold standard for judgments about return to driving, but cognitive testing can also play a role.

In a study of 71 persons with TBI, Coleman et al. (2002) found that neuropsychological measures of working memory, sustained visual attention, and abstract reasoning predicted driving status. These results are similar to findings from investigations of persons with early dementia where executive functioning and visual attention have been shown to predict driving safety (Whelihan, DiCarlo, & Paul, 2005). As in other areas of community functioning, executive abilities appear to play an important role in the capacity to return to driving following brain injury (Bryer, Rapport, & Hanks, 2006). Virtual reality programs may have a great deal to offer in this area in the future, but they remain largely untested, with the exception of a study by Lengenfelder, Schultheis, Al-Shihabi, Mourant, and DeLuca (2002). Standard neuropsychological assessment and tests such as the Useful Field of View, which has recently been applied to people with acquired brain injury (Calvanio et al., 2004; Novack et al., 2006), still have merit in assisting with driving decisions.

Although cognitive test findings provide important information to assist persons with disabilities, their caregivers, and health care providers in judging capacity to return to work, personal independence, and driving, many other factors must be considered when decisions are made regarding a specific person in a specific set of life circumstances. For example, determinations regarding such capacity should consider psychiatric status in addition to cognitive capability. Decisions concerning return to work must take account of previous work history and the degree of support available at the job site, along with cognitive status. Architectural characteristics of the home (e.g., stairs vs. no stairs) as well as the community setting (e.g., busy urban street vs. quiet suburban cul-de-sac) may influence decisions regarding intensity of supervision needed after hospital discharge. Factors such as preinjury driving record and the availability (or lack) of alternative means of transportation may influence decisions regarding timing of release for driving. Rehabilitation providers must consider a staggering array of factors when making specific recommendations regarding personal independence and community participation issues for persons with disability. Neuropsychological findings regarding the person's cognitive capabilities are one important source of guidance in making these recommendations.

CONCLUSIONS

Neuropsychologists have a great deal to offer in a rehabilitation setting. Although not specifically focusing on rehabilitation neuropsychologists, the value of neuropsychology in medical settings has been documented. Bishop, Temple, Tremont, Westervelt, and Stern (2003) noted that for 100 patients receiving a neuropsychological evaluation, discharge summaries referred to the assessment in 78 cases with regard to diagnosis and reported the recommendations of the neuropsychologist in 68 instances, indicating a reliance on neuropsychologists to assist in patient management. The combination of clinical psychology and clinical neurology may be of growing importance as the intricacies of the central nervous system are unraveled, leading to better understanding of behavior, emotion, and thought. This is a complex undertaking in which comprehension of biological and biochemical processes will be paramount. Neuropsychologists are in a unique position to bridge the gap between such basic scientific information and the application to everyday existence.

The contribution of neuropsychologists to understanding neurobehavioral mechanisms is already being demonstrated with respect to neuroimaging, including studies involving functional magnetic resonance imaging and other cutting edge imaging techniques (see chap. 13, this volume).

Helping patients, family members, and staff understand mechanisms of injury and recovery in everyday terms is a continuing contribution of rehabilitation neuropsychology. Development of increasingly specific tests relating to resumption of community functioning can be anticipated. This is already occurring with respect to capacity to make decisions, such as decisions regarding medical care. These tests will not supplant, but rather supplement, conventional tests. In the future, neuropsychological testing will likely focus more on specific questions of competency and perhaps be briefer as a result. In some cases a brief, valid cognitive screening may be sufficient to address referral questions (and may be all that can be obtained, given time constraints and the responsiveness of the patient). Finally, with the increasing emphasis on the biological and biochemical processes underpinning recovery from brain injury, there will be increasingly sophisticated interventions to guide the process of recovery. Use of neurostimulatory medications combined with focused cognitive and behavioral remediation programs can be anticipated, including the use of virtual reality paradigms (Rizzo, Buckwalter, & Neumann, 1997). Neuropsychologists will certainly contribute to trials assessing the effectiveness of such interventions in terms of basic cognitive and behavioral abilities, as well as community outcome.

Neuropsychology, like rehabilitation psychology as a whole, will be challenged in a future of diminishing resources to justify the time, effort, and expense of psychological assessment and intervention. Initial steps have been taken to address the cost effectiveness of neuropsychology services (Prigatano & Pliskin, 2003), but more information will be needed to satisfy the health care community. Documentation that neuropsychologists are providing services important to patients, family members, and health care providers is essential, along with an ongoing scientific contribution to understanding the nature of brain injury and recovery.

References

Alderson, A. L., & Novack, T. A. (2002). Measuring recovery of orientation during acute rehabilitation for traumatic brain injury: Value and expectations of recovery. *Journal of Head Trauma Rehabilitation, 17,* 210–219.

Alderson, A. L., & Novack, T. A. (2003). Reliable serial measurement of cognitive processes in rehabilitation: The Cognitive-Log. *Archives of Physical Medicine and Rehabilitation, 84,* 668–672.

Appelbaum, P., & Grisso, T. (1995). The MacArthur Treatment Competent Study. I: Mental illness and competence to consent to treatment. *Law and Human Behavior, 19,* 105–126.

Bassett, S. S. (1999). Attention: Neuropsychological predictor of competency in Alzheimer's disease. *Journal of Geriatric Psychiatry and Neurology, 12,* 200–205.

Bauer, R. M., & Demery, J. A. (2003). Agnosia. In K. M. Heilman & E. Valenstein (Eds.), *Clinical neuropsychology* (4th ed., pp. 236–295). New York: Oxford University Press.

Beglinger, L. J., Gaydos, B., Tangphao-Daniels, O., Duff, K., Kareken, D. A., Crawford, J., et al. (2005). Practice effects and the use of alternate forms in serial neuropsychological testing. *Archives of Clinical Neuropsychology, 20,* 517–529.

Bennett, P. C., Ong, B., & Ponsford, J. (2005). Measuring executive dysfunction in an acute rehabilitation setting: Using the dysexecutive questionnaire (DEX). *Journal of the International Neuropsychological Society, 11,* 376–385.

Bishop, C. L., Temple, R. O., Tremont, G., Westervelt, H. J., & Stern, R. A. (2003). Utility of the neuropsychological evaluation in an acute hospital setting. *The Clinical Neuropsychologist, 21,* 371–382.

Blackmer, J. (2003). The unique ethical challenges of conducting research in a rehabilitation medical population. *BMC Medical Ethics, 4,* E2.

Boake, C., Millis, S. R., High, W. M., Jr., Delmonico, R. L., Kreutzer, J. S., Rosenthal, M., et al. (2001). Using early neuropsychologic testing to predict long-term productivity outcome from traumatic brain injury. *Archives of Physical Medicine and Rehabilitation, 82,* 761–768.

Bryant, R. A. (2001). Posttraumatic stress disorder and traumatic brain injury: Can they coexist? *Clinical Psychology Review, 21,* 931–948.

Bryer, R. C., Rapport, L. J., & Hanks, R. A. (2006). Determining fitness to drive: Neuropsychological and psychological considerations. In J. M. Pellerito, Jr. (Ed.), *Driver rehabilitation and community mobility principles and practice* (pp. 165–184). St. Louis, MO: Mosby.

Bush, S. S., Ruff, R. M., Troster, A. I., Barth, J. T., Koffler, S. P., Pliskin, N. H., et al. (2005). Symptom validity assessment: Practice issues and medical necessity. NAN policy & planning committee. *Archives of Clinical Neuropsychology, 20,* 419–26.

Calvanio, R., Williams, R., Burke, D. T., Mello, J., Lepak, P., Al-Adawi, S., & Shah, M. K. (2004). Acquired brain injury, visual attention, and the useful field of view test: A pilot study. *Archives of Physical Medicine & Rehabilitation, 85*(3), 474–478.

Chaytor, N., & Schmitter-Edgecombe, M. (2003). The ecological validity of neuropsychological tests: A review of the literature on everyday cognitive skills. *Neuropsychology Review, 13,* 181–187.

Cicerone, K. D., Dahlberg, C., Malec, J. F., Langenbahn, D. M., Felicetti, T., Kneipp, S., et al. (2005). Evidence-based cognitive rehabilitation: Updated review of the literature from 1998 through 2002. *Archives of Physical Medicine and Rehabilitation, 86,* 1681–1692.

Clifton, G. L., Hayes, R. L., Levin, H. S., Michel, M. E., & Choi, S. E. (1992). Outcomes measures in clinical trials involving traumatically brain-injured patients: Report of a conference. *Neurosurgery, 31,* 975–978.

Coleman, R. D., Rapport, L. J., Ergh, T. C., Hanks, R. A., Ricker, J. H., & Millis, S. R. (2002). Predictors of driving outcome after traumatic brain injury. *Archives of Physical Medicine and Rehabilitation, 83,* 1415–1422.

Corrigan, J. D. (1989). Development of a scale for assessment of agitation following traumatic brain injury. *Journal of Clinical and Experimental Neuropsychology, 11,* 261–277.

Corrigan, J. D., Arnett, J. A., Houck, L. J., & Jackson, R. D. (1985). Reality orientation for brain injured patients: Group treatment and monitoring recovery. *Archives of Physical Medicine &Rehabilitation, 66,* 626–630.

Corrigan, J. D., & Mysiw, W. J. (1988). Agitation following traumatic head injury: Equivocal evidence for a discrete stage of cognitive recovery. *Archives of Physical Medicine & Rehabilitation, 69,* 487–492.

Coughlan, A. K., Rix, K. J., & Neumann, V. (2005). Assessing decision-making capacity in minimally aware patients. *Medical Science and Law, 45,* 249–255.

Diener, B. L., & Bischof-Rosarioz, J. A. (2004). Determining decision-making capacity in individuals with severe communication impairments after stroke: The role of augmentative-alternative communication (AAC). *Topics in Stroke Rehabilitation, 11,* 84–88.

Dikmen, S., McLean, A., Temkin, N. R., & Wyler, A. R. (1986). Neuropsychologic outcome at 1-month postinjury. *Archives of Physical Medicine & Rehabilitation, 67,* 507–513.

Feinberg, T. E., & Roane, D. M. (1997). Misidentification syndromes. In T. E. Feinberg & M. J. Farah (Eds.), *Behavioral neurology and neuropsychology* (pp. 391–397). New York: McGraw-Hill.

Folstein, M. F., Folstein, S. E., & McHugh, P. R. (1975). "Mini-Mental State." A practical method for grading the cognitive state of patients for the clinician. *Journal of Psychiatric Research, 12,* 189–198.

Galasko, D., Bennett, D., Sano, M., Ernesto, C., Thomas, R., Gundman, M., & Ferris, S. (1997). An inventory to assess activities of daily living for clinical trials in Alzheimer's disease. *Alzheimer Disease & Associated Disorders, 11*(Suppl. 2), 533–539.

Giacino, J. T., & Cicerone, K. D. (1998). Varieties of deficit unawareness after TBI. *Journal of Head Trauma Rehabilitation, 13*(5), 1–15.

Giacino, J. T., Kalmar, K., & Whyte, J. (2004). The JFK Coma Recovery Scale-Revised: Measurement characteristics and diagnostic utility. *Archives of Physical Medicine & Rehabilitation, 85,* 2020–2029.

Gianotti, G., Azzoni, A., Razzano, C., Lanzillotta, M., Marra, C., & Gasparini, F. (1997). The Poststroke Depression Rating Scale: A test specifically devised to investigate affective disorders of stroke patients. *Journal of Clinical & Experimental Neuropsychology, 19,* 340–356.

Glenn, M. B., & Wroblewski, B. (2005). Twenty years of pharmacology. *Journal of Head Trauma Rehabilitation, 20,* 51–61.

Grace, J., & Malloy, P. F. (2001). *Frontal Systems Behavior Scale Professional Manual.* Lutz, FL: Psychological Assessment Resources.

Groom, K. N., Shaw T. G., O'Conner, M. E., Howard, N. I., & Pickens, A. (1998). Neurobehavioral symptoms and family functioning in traumatically brain injured adults. *Archives of Clinical Neuropsychology, 13,* 695–711.

Hart, T., & Hayden, M. E. (1986). The ecological validity of neuropsychological assessment and remediation. In B. P. Uzzell & Y. Gross (Eds.), *Clinical neuropsychology of intervention* (pp. 21–50). Boston: Martinus Nijhoff.

Hart, T., Millis, S., Novack, T., Englander, J., Fidler-Shephard, R., & Bell, K. R. (2003). The relationship of neuropsychologic function and level of caregiver supervision at 1 year after traumatic brain injury. *Archives of Physical Medicine and Rehabilitation, 84,* 221–230.

Hart, T., Sherer, M., Whyte, J., Plansky, M., & Novack, T. A. (2004). Awareness of behavioral, cognitive, and physical deficits in acute traumatic brain injury. *Archives of Physical Medicine and Rehabilitation, 85,* 1450–1456.

Heilman, K. M., Watson, R. T., & Valenstein, E. (2003). Neglect and related disorders. In K. M. Heilman & E. Valenstein (Eds.), *Clinical neuropsychology* (4th ed., pp. 296–346). New York: Oxford University Press.

Hibbard, M. R., Uysal, S., Kepler, K., Bogdany, J., & Silver, J. (1998). Axis I psychopathology in individuals with traumatic brain injury. *Journal of Head Trauma Rehabilitation, 13*(4), 24–39.

Jackson, W. T., Novack, T. A., & Dowler, R. N. (1998). Effective serial measurement of cognitive orientation in rehabilitation: Reliability of the orientation log. *Archives of Physical Medicine and Rehabilitation, 79,* 718–20.

Jurica, P. J., Leitten, C. L., & Mattis, S. (2001). *DRS-2 Dementia Rating Scale-2 Professional Manual.* Lutz, FL: Psychological Assessment Resources.

Kiernan, R. J., Mueller, J., Langston, J. W., & Van Dyke, C. (1987). The Neurobehavioral Cognitive Status Examination: A brief but differentiated approach to cognitive assessment. *Annals of Internal Medicine, 107,* 481–485.

Kirschner, K. L., Stocking, C., Wagner, L. B., Foye, S. J., & Siegler, M. (2001). Ethical issues identified by rehabilitation clinicians. *Archives of Physical Medicine and Rehabilitation, 82,* 52–58.

Kreutzer, J. S., Marwitz, J. H., Seel, R., & Serio, C. D. (1996). Validation of a neurobehavioral functioning inventory for adults with traumatic brain injury. *Archives of Physical Medicine & Rehabilitation, 77*(2), 116–124.

Lengenfelder, J., Schultheis, M. T., Al-Shihabi, T., Mourant, R., & DeLuca, J. (2002). Divided attention and driving: A pilot study using virtual reality technology. *Journal of Head Trauma Rehabilitation, 17,* 26–37.

Levin, H. S. (1990). Predicting the neurobiological sequelae of closed head injury. In R. L. Wood (Ed.), *Neurobehavioral sequelae of traumatic brain injury* (pp. 89–109). Philadelphia: Taylor & Francis.

Levin, H. S. (1994). A guide to clinical neuropsychological testing. *Archives of Neurology, 51,* 854–859.

Levin, H. S., High, W. M., Goethe, K. E., Sisson, R. A., Overall, J. E., Rhoades, H. M., et al. (1987). The neurobehavioral rating scale: Assessment of the behavioral sequelae of head injury by the clinician. *Journal of Neurology, Neurosurgery, and Psychiatry, 50,* 183–193.

Levin, H. S., O'Donnell, V. M., & Grossman, R. G. (1979). The Galveston Orientation and Amnesia Test a practical scale to assess cognition after head injury. *Journal of Nervous and Mental Disease, 167,* 675–684.

Lezak, M. D. (1988). Brain damage is a family affair. *Journal of Clinical & Experimental Neuropsychology, 10,* 111–123.

Marson, D. C., Chatterjee, A., Ingram, K. K., & Harrell, L. E. (1996). Toward a neurologic model of competency: Cognitive predictors of capacity to consent in Alzheimer's disease using three different legal standards. *Neurology, 46,* 666–672.

Marson, D. C., Cody, H. A., Ingram, K. K., & Harrell, L. E. (1995). Neuropsychological predictors of competency in Alzheimer's disease using a rational reasons legal standard. *Archives of Neurology, 52,* 955–959.

Marson, D. C., Dreer, L. E., Krzywanski, S., Huthwaite, J. S., DeVivo, M. J., & Novack, T. A. (2005). Impairment and partial recovery of medical decision-making capacity in traumatic brain injury: A 6-month longitudinal study. *Archives of Physical Medicine and Rehabilitation, 86,* 889–895.

Marson, D. C., & Hebert, K. (2005). Assessing civil competencies in older adults with dementia: Consent capacity, financial capacity, and testamentary capacity. In G. Larrabee (Ed.), *Forensic neuropsychology: A scientific approach* (pp. 334–377). New York: Oxford.

McCaffrey, R. J., & Westervelt, H. J. (1995). Issues associated with repeated neuropsychological assessments. *Neuropsychology Review, 5,* 203–221.

Millis, S. R., Rosenthal, M., Novack, T. A., Sherer, M., Nick, T. G., Kreutzer, J. S., et al. (2001). Long-term neuropsychological outcome after traumatic brain injury. *Journal of Head Trauma Rehabilitation, 16,* 343–355.

Nakase-Thompson, R., Manning, E., Sherer, M., Yablon, S. A., Gontkovsky, S. L. T., & Vickery, C. (2005). Brief assessment of severe language impairments: Initial validation of the Mississippi Aphasia Screening Test. *Brain Injury, 19,* 685–691.

Nakase-Thompson, R., Sherer, M., Yablon, S. A., Nick, T. G., & Trzepacz, P. T. (2004). Acute confusion following traumatic brain injury. *Brain Injury, 18,* 131–142.

Nelson, L. D., Satz, P., & D'Elia L. F. (1994). *Neuropsychology behavior and affect profile.* Palo Alto, CA: Mind Garden.

Novack, T. A., Baños, J. H., Alderson, A. L., Schneider, J. J., Weed, W. Blankenship, J., & Salisbury, D. (2006). UFOV performance and driving ability following traumatic brain injury. *Brain Injury, 20,* 455–461.

Novack, T. A., Bush, B. A., Meythaler, J. D., & Canupp, K. (2001). Outcome after traumatic brain injury: Pathway analysis of contribution from premorbid, injury severity, and recovery variables. *Archives of Physical Medicine and Rehabilitation, 82,* 300–305.

Novack, T. A., Haban, G., Graham, K., & Satterfield, W. T. (1987). Prediction of stroke rehabilitation outcome from psychologic screening. *Archives of Physical Medicine and Rehabilitation, 68,* 729–734.

Novack T. A., & Penrod, L. (1993). Using the Agitated Behavior Scale to evaluate restlessness/agitation following traumatic brain injury: A case example. *NeuroRehabilitation, 3,* 79–82.

Ownsworth, T. L., & Oei, T. P. S. (1998). Depression after traumatic brain injury: Conceptualization and treatment considerations. *Brain Injury, 12,* 735–752.

Pastorek, N. J., Hannay, H. J., & Contant, C. S. (2004). Prediction of global outcome with acute neuropsychological testing following closed-head injury. *Journal of the International Neuropsychological Society, 10,* 807–817.

Pegg, P. O., Jr., Auerbach, S. M., Seel, R. T., Buenaver, L. F., Kiesler, D. J., & Plybon, L. E. (2005). The Impact of patient-centered information on patients' treatment satisfaction and outcomes in traumatic brain injury rehabilitation. *Rehabilitation Psychology, 50,* 366–374.

Prigatano, G. P. (1999). *Principles of neuropsychological rehabilitation.* New York: Oxford University Press.

Prigatano, G. P., & Pliskin, N. H. (2003). *Clinical neuropsychology and cost outcome research.* New York: Taylor & Francis.

Randolph, C., Tierney, M. C., Mohr, E., & Chase, T. N. (1998). The Repeatable Battery for the Assessment of Neuropsychological Status (RBANS): Preliminary clinical validity. *Journal of Clinical and Experimental Neuropsychology, 20,* 310–319.

Rappaport, M., Dougherty, A. M., & Kelting, D. L. (1992). Evaluation of coma and vegetative states. *Archives of Physical Medicine & Rehabilitation, 73,* 628–634.

Rapport, L. J., Hanks, R. A., Millis, S. R., & Deshpande, B. A. (1998). Executive functioning and predictors of falls in the rehabilitation settings. *Archives of Physical Medicine and Rehabilitation, 79,* 629–633.

Reitan, R. M., & Wolfson, D. (1993). *The Halstead-Reitan Neuropsychological Test Battery: Theory and clinical interpretation* (2nd ed.). Tucson, AZ: Neuropsychology Press.

Robertson, I. H., Ward, T., Ridgeway, V., & Nimmo-Smith, I. (1994). *Test of everyday attention.* London: Thames Valley Test Company.

Rizzo, A. A., Buckwalter, J. G., & Neumann, U. (1997). Virtual reality and cognitive rehabilitation: A brief review of the future. *Journal of Head Trauma Rehabilitation, 12*(6), 1–15.

Rosenthal, M., Christensen, B. K., & Ross, T. P. (1998). Depression following traumatic brain injury. *Archives of Physical Medicine and Rehabilitation, 79,* 90–103.

Ruchinskas, R. A., & Curyto, K. J. (2003). Cognitive screening in geriatric rehabilitation. *Rehabilitation Psychology, 48,* 14–22.

Sherer, M., Bergloff, P., Boake, C., High, W., Jr., & Levin, E. (1998). The Awareness Questionnaire: Factor structure and internal consistency. *Brain Injury, 12,* 63–68.

Sherer, M., Hart, T., & Nick, T. G. (2003). Measurement of impaired self-awareness after traumatic brain injury: A comparison of the Patient Competency Rating Scale and the Awareness Questionnaire. *Brain Injury, 17,* 25–37.

Sherer, M., Nakase-Thompson, R., Yablon, S. A., & Gontkovsky, S. T. (2005). Multidimensional assessment of acute confusion after traumatic brain injury. *Archives of Physical Medicine & Rehabilitation, 86,* 896–904.

Sherer, M., & Novack, T. A. (2003). Neuropsychological assessment after traumatic brain injury in adults. In G. P. Prigatano & N. H. Pliskin (Eds.), *Neuropsychology and cost outcome research: A beginning* (39–60). New York: Psychology Press.

Sherer, M., Novack, T. A., Sander, A. M., Struchen, M. A., Alderson, A., & Thompson, R. N. (2002). Neuropsychological assessment and employment outcome after traumatic brain injury: A review. *The Clinical Neuropsychologist, 16,* 157–178.

Sherer, M., Sander, A. M., Nick, T. G., High, W. M., Jr., Malec, J. F., & Rosenthal, M. (2002). Early cognitive status and productivity outcome following traumatic brain injury: Findings from the TBI Model Systems. *Archives of Physical Medicine and Rehabilitation, 83,* 183–192.

Stuss, D. T., Binns, M. A., Carruth, F. G., Levine, B., Brandys, C. E., Moulton, R. J., et al. (1999). The acute period of recovery from traumatic brain injury: Posttraumatic amnesia or posttraumatic confusional state? *Journal of Neurosurgery, 90,* 635–643.

Sutto, W. M. I., Clare, C. H., Holland, A. J., & Watson, P. C. (2005). Capacity to make financial decisions among people with mild intellectual disabilities. *Journal of Intellectual Disability Research, 49,* 199–209.

Teasdale, G., & Jennett, B. (1974). Assessment of coma and impaired consciousness: A practical scale. *The Lancet, 2,* 81–84.

Trudel, T. M., Tryon, W. W., & Purdum, C. M. (1998). Awareness of disability and long-term outcome after traumatic brain injury. *Rehabilitation Psychology, 43,* 267–281.

Venesy, B. A. (1994). A clinician's guide to decision-making capacity and ethically sounds medical decisions. *American Journal of Physical Medicine and Rehabilitation, 73,* 219–226.

Vilkki, J. S., Juvela, S., Siironen, J., Ilvonen, T., Varis, J., & Porras, M. (2004). Relationship of local infarctions to cognitive and psychosocial impairments after aneurismal subarachnoid hemorrhage. *Neurosurgery, 55,* 790–803.

Wagner, M. T., Nayak, M., & Fink, C. (1995). Bedside screening of neurocognitive functioning. In L. A. Cushman & M. J. Scherer (Eds.), *Psychological assessment in medical rehabilitation* (pp. 145–198). Washington, DC: American Psychological Association.

Wechsler, D. (1997). *Wechsler Adult Intelligence Scale III/Wechsler Memory Scale, third edition technical manual.* San Antonio, TX: Psychological Corporation.

Whelihan, W. M., DiCarlo, M. A., & Paul, R. H. (2005). The relationship of neuropsychological functioning to driving competence in older persons with early cognitive decline. *Archives of Clinical Neuropsychology, 20,* 217–228.

Wilson, B. (1985). Adapting "portage" for neurological patients. *International Rehabilitation Medicine, 7*(1), 6–8.

Wilson, B., Cockburn, J., & Baddeley, A. (1986). *The Rivermead Behavioural Memory Test (RBMT).* London: Thames Valley Test Company.

Wilson, B., Cockburn, J., & Halligan, P. (1987). Development of a behavioral test of visuospatial neglect. *Archives of Physical Medicine & Rehabilitation, 68*(2), 98–102.

Wozniak, M. A., Kittner, S. J., Price, T. R., Hebel, J. R., Sloan, M. A., & Gardner, J. F. (1999). Stroke location is not located with return to work after first ischemic stroke. *Stroke, 30,* 2568–2573.

Youngjohn, J. R., & Altman, I. M. (1989). A performance-based group approach to the treatment of anosognosia and denial. *Rehabilitation Psychology, 34,* 217–222.

CHAPTER 11

FORENSIC PSYCHOLOGICAL EVALUATION IN REHABILITATION

Brick Johnstone, Laura H. Schopp, Cheryl L. Shigaki, and Kelly Lora Franklin

Psychologists working in rehabilitation settings are increasingly participating in the legal arena as experts on psychological impairments associated with physical and mental disabilities. Historically, rehabilitation psychologists have been primarily concerned with direct patient care, such as diagnosing and treating psychological disorders associated with disabilities. However, because many individuals with physical and mental disabilities are involved in litigation related to the cause of their disability, it is essential for rehabilitation psychologists to be knowledgeable about the legal system and their role in forensic evaluation. Although psychologists in rehabilitation are interested primarily in improving individuals' adaptation to disability, attorneys are interested primarily in advocating for their clients. Therefore, psychologists' testimony is frequently shaped not by clinical data, but rather by the attorney's strategic decisions about how to best present facts in support of their case. Given psychologists' increasing involvement in litigation (and their active promotion of their services to attorneys), psychologists must be prepared to interact with attorneys, disability boards, and the courts. Indeed, the American Psychological Association's (APA's) Committee on Ethical Guidelines for Forensic Psychologists (1991) clearly suggested that any psychologist who evaluates or treats a client with an injury-related problem should assume that information from such an evaluation would become part of a legal action.

This chapter focuses specifically on forensic evaluation in cases of traumatic brain injury (TBI) because it is the injury most commonly involved in litigation.

However, rehabilitation psychologists certainly deal with other trauma-related physical conditions (e.g., spinal cord injuries, musculoskeletal disorders) and may be called to testify about their psychological and social impact.

GROWTH OF FORENSIC PSYCHOLOGICAL EVALUATION IN REHABILITATION

The growing need for forensic psychological evaluations of individuals with disabilities caused by TBI comes from several factors, including increased understanding of brain injury, higher survival rates of individuals with brain injuries and their associated chronic disabilities, recognition of psychology's unique role in evaluating brain injury, and growth of civil litigation involving brain injuries. Highlighting the substantial use of psychological evaluation in the legal arena that started over 2 decades ago, Puente (1987) reported that 41% of all applications for Social Security assistance (i.e., nearly 150,000 individuals) had a diagnosis of organic brain syndromes or related disorders.

In TBI (especially mild cases), structural injury may occur at a microscopic level and is not always visualized by modern neurodiagnostic techniques. Some patients, therefore, show disrupted cognitive and behavioral functioning in the absence of clear evidence of structural damage (Belanger, Vanderploeg, Curtiss, & Warden, 2007; Borg et al., 2004). As neuropsychological research began to suggest that long-standing impairments in these domains might occasionally follow even mild brain injury (e.g., Raskin, Mateer, & Tweeten, 1998; Sorenson &

Krause, 1991), psychologists were increasingly drawn into the courtroom (Laing & Fisher, 1997; Puente & Gillespie, 1991).

Although statistics are not available regarding the forensic practice of rehabilitation psychologists, Guilmette, Faust, Hart, and Arkes (1990) reported that of 449 psychologists who reported offering neuropsychological services, 50% had testified at least once in forensic neuropsychology cases and nearly 20% had testified more than 10 times. Similarly, Putnam, DeLuca, and Anderson (1994) reported on a survey of APA Division 40 (Clinical Neuropsychology) members and revealed that 51% of respondents reported some involvement in forensic activities. Essig, Mittenberg, Petersen, Strauman, and Cooper (2001) surveyed members of the National Academy of Neuropsychology (NAN) and established that approximately 94% of responding neuropsychologists stated that some portion of their practice involved personal injury evaluations of brain injury claims, up from a decade earlier when 68% of surveyed members of APA Division 40 reported receiving forensic personal injury referrals (Essig et al.; Putnam et al., 1994). More recently, Sweet, Nelson, and Moberg (2006) surveyed doctoral-level members of Division 40 and other neuropsychologists via a Web-based survey company. Results indicated that pediatric neuropsychologists were less involved in forensic activities per week, devoted more hours to a forensic evaluation, and charged a higher hourly fee (Sweet et al., 2006). Those who were identified as pediatric neuropsychologists spent an average of 5.8% of their practice in forensic work. Volunteers who identified as adult only, pediatric/adult, and no identity devoted an average of 12.0%, 20.8%, and 20.5%, respectively, to forensic practice. For the full sample, forensic involvement had a mean of 4.5 hours per week and a mean practice percentage of 14.3. Results also indicated that forensic practice involvement was positively correlated with income (Sweet et al., 2006).

HISTORY OF PSYCHOLOGY IN THE LEGAL SYSTEM

During the early 1900s, both experimental psychologists (e.g., Munsterberg, 1908) and clinical psychiatrists (e.g., Freud, 1906) discussed psychology's potential for assisting lawyers seeking to establish the truth (Kurke, 1986). One of the first indicators of the developing relationship between psychology and law was the establishment of a psychological clinic attached to the juvenile court in Chicago in the early 1900s (Kurke, 1986), which provided data from the courts for psychological research (Healy, 1915).

Further collaboration between psychology and law was initially slow to develop. In 1921, a psychologist from West Virginia served as an expert witness in the courtroom (*State v. Driver,* 1921), although his testimony was ultimately rejected (Giuliano, Barth, Hawk, & Ryan, 1997). In 1962, the District of Columbia Court of Appeals (*Jenkins v. United States,* 1962) held that a lower federal court had erred in excluding psychological testimony and ruled that psychologists could provide expert testimony about criminal responsibility, despite their lack of a medical degree (Giuliano et al., 1997). Since that time, both legislation and court decisions generally have affirmed and expanded the role of psychologists as expert witnesses within their field of expertise (Barth, Ryan, & Hawk, 1992).

The seminal forensic testimony of a neuropsychologist occurred in 1974 (Puente, 1997), when Ralph Reitan testified in a brain injury case (*Indianapolis Union Railway v. Walker,* 1974). Although Reitan's original testimony was not considered admissible because he was not a physician, the decision was eventually overturned in the Indiana Court of Appeals because of the value that the neuropsychological evidence provided. Similarly, in the mid-1980s, Antonio Puente's testimony on brain injury in *Horne v. Goodson Logging Company* (1986) was originally ruled inadmissible on the grounds that Puente was not a physician. However, that ruling, too, was reversed on appeal in light of the sensitivity of neuropsychological testing to neurocognitive deficits (Puente, 1997). By the end of the 1970s, the relationship between psychology and law gained significant momentum. Interdisciplinary groups such as the American Psychology-Law Society and the American Board of Forensic Psychology were established, with the latter offering board certification in the specialty (Kurke, 1986).

ADMISSIBILITY OF FORENSIC PSYCHOLOGICAL TESTIMONY

Given the surge of forensic activity in psychology, the validity and reliability of psychological assessment—indeed, the admissibility of psychological input—has been attacked in the legal arena based on questions about its scientific merit, or lack thereof (Bigler, 2007; Hom, 2003; Lees-Haley & Fox, 2001; Matarazzo, 1987). It has been argued by a minority of psychologists that the discipline "has not reached the state of scientific development or knowledge that permits legal questions to be answered with reasonable certainty" (Faust, Ziskin, & Hiers, 1991, p. 2). Nonetheless, neuropsychological testing procedures have become more forensically respectable (Gilandas & Touyz, 1983) and have been generally accepted as a viable adjunct or alternative to medical testimony in disability determinations and personal injury litigation (Anchor, Rogers, Solomon, Barth, & Peacock, 1983; Zasler & Martelli, 2003). It is evident that the courts are aware of the scientific limitations within the behavioral health fields (and other scientific disciplines), and yet continue to seek out and welcome testimony from psychologists (Barth et al., 1992).

The Federal Rules of Evidence 702 through 705, which govern admissibility of opinions and expert testimony, permit the admission of a qualified expert's opinion into evidence if it is based on specialized knowledge and will assist the judge or the jury (Federal Rule of Evidence, 702; Green, Nesson, & Murray, 1997). The Federal Rules do not require perfection of scientific evidence and expert opinion, and clearly frame the question of admissibility as one of incremental rather than absolute validity (Green et al., 1997; Melton, 1994). Experts are expected to be open about the bases of their evaluations, limitations of their data, and uncertainty in their opinions (Guilmette & Giuliano, 1991; Hawk & Benedek, 1989). In turn, the law relies on cross-examination (Federal Rules of Evidence, 705) to illuminate the strengths and weaknesses of opinion evidence and on the capacity of the jury to perceive and weigh it fairly (Green et al., 1997; Melton, 1994).

Prior to the Federal Rules of Evidence, admissibility of expert opinion and scientific evidence was based on the *Frye* standard (Broun et al., 1992),

which was adopted in 1923 by the United States Court of Appeals for the District of Columbia Circuit, and which required that to be admissible, such evidence had to be "sufficiently established to have gained general acceptance in the particular field to which it belongs" (*Frye v. United States*, 1923, p. 1014). In 1993, however, the U.S. Supreme Court superseded *Frye* (regarding federal law) in favor of the *Daubert* standard for the admissibility of scientific evidence that was more consistent with the Federal Rules (Cohen, 1996; Hom, 2003; Livingood, 1994). *Daubert* was concerned with the admissibility of unpublished research indicating that Bendectin could cause birth defects. In *Daubert*, the Supreme Court suggested factors for the lower courts to consider in their review of scientific evidence, including the "general acceptance" concept of *Frye* but also the concepts of empirical substantiveness of the techniques used, including error rates and use of controls in the technique's operation (Lally, 2003; Reed, 1996). Most jurisdictions follow the *Daubert* standard, although 23 states still use *Frye*, a unique standard, or have not yet ruled on the matter (*Phillips v. Industrial Machine*, 1999). According to Reed, the circuit courts are divided as to whether the *Daubert* standard should be applied to scientific knowledge only or whether it should extend to expert testimony based on specialized knowledge. The relevance of whether a test or technique has general acceptance within a field determines whether a court will permit expert testimony based on the test (American Psychology-Law Society, 2001).

Although *Daubert* broadens admissibility by permitting scientifically derived but unpublished data, it has been speculated that *Daubert* would lead to stricter scrutiny of scientific evidence in courts (Laing & Fisher, 1997). In fact, the *Daubert* standard has been applied to neuropsychological evidence in this manner in *Chapple v. Ganger* (1994), a case with important implications for the practice of forensic psychologists. In *Chapple*, results from three neuropsychological batteries were offered in the case of a brain injury sustained by a child in an automobile accident. In considering the conflicting interpretations of these neuropsychological assessments, the court chose to accept "fixed" or standardized battery results in toto, but not "flexible" (i.e., nonstandardized) battery results. Thus, *Chapple* set a precedent favoring fixed-battery assessments. However, it is important to note that in *Chapple* the court also accepted some of the individual tests used in the flexible batteries (and/or as supplements to the fixed battery) as meeting the *Daubert* requirements of scientific validity, reliability, methodology, and procedure (Reed, 1996). Indeed, Hom (2003) stated that the Halstead-Reitan Neuropsychological Battery (HRB) is the most well-validated and comprehensively researched neuropsychological battery in use. Bigler (2007) suggested that Hom's publication in Archives of Clinical Neuropsychology has been used by attorneys to argue that only a fixed-battery approach (i.e., HRB) complies with the Daubert criteria. Bigler concluded that "the so-called fixed battery . . . certainly cannot be considered the only reliable method in assessment of cognitive and behavioral deficits associated with neurological impairment" (p. 50).

In addition, it is important to note that the *Chapple* decision does not question the admissibility of neuropsychological evidence in and of itself. In fact, Richardson and Adams (1992) reviewed nearly 200 appellate case decisions regarding the use of clinical psychologists and neuropsychologists as expert witnesses concerning brain damage since 1980. They reported that of all cases reviewed, the courts have supported the right of neuropsychologists to testify concerning the presence of brain dysfunction. However, the courts have been divided regarding the admissibility of neuropsychological testimony regarding the cause of brain damage or dysfunction. For example, Florida and Ohio appellate courts have held that etiology of brain damage is a medical issue and, therefore, only physicians are qualified to testify regarding causality (Richardson & Adams, 1992). Although little is available to determine eligibility of neuropsychologists to testify regarding prognosis of a patient following brain injury, these authors have speculated that jurisdictions are most likely to follow the precedents set on the causality issue.

WHAT TO EXPECT IN COURTROOM TESTIMONY

It is essential for psychologists working in the legal system to be aware of the norms, orientation, goals, and procedures of the legal system and how these differ from traditional psychological practice. The purpose of legal proceedings can appear unfamiliar and strange to the rehabilitation psychologist, who is primarily concerned with promoting optimal adjustment and functioning of patients and families.

The primary role of the forensic rehabilitation psychologist as expert witness is to provide information or specialized knowledge that assists the trier of fact (i.e., the jury or the judge) in its deliberations (Melton, 1994). The psychologist as expert witness may be called on to make what seem to be unduly dichotomous distinctions between "organic" and "psychological" influences on outcome. Faced with such different demand characteristics and role expectations, the psychologist may be tempted either to qualify remarks excessively or to overstate findings. Either extreme can be problematic and can increase the likelihood of clinician judgment errors (Wedding, 1991). Finally, there may be minimal scientific evidence that pertains directly to the concerns of the court, and psychologists may be forced to extrapolate from studies that are only partially relevant to the legal question at hand (Faust, 1991).

The rehabilitation psychologist entering the forensic setting also faces potentially conflicting demands on the scope of his or her concern. The psychologist is permitted under Rule 704 of the Federal Rules of Evidence to offer opinions on "ultimate issue" questions, such as dangerousness, specific prognosis of the individual in question, and so forth. However, the dictates of professional ethics discourage such speculation, leaving it to the trier of fact to decide these matters (Melton, 1994). The APA's Committee on Ethical Guidelines for Forensic Psychologists (1991) further suggested that psychologists withhold testimony on questions outside their realm of specialized knowledge. Although it is desirable both in clinical and legal settings to avoid broad speculation and to limit conclusions to those drawn from the data at hand, the line is drawn even more sharply in the forensic context. Thus, psychologists must be vigilant about role constraints because nonscientific conjecture can carry especially serious consequences for a litigant's independence, finances, and reputation.

Sweet, Grote, and van Gorp (2002) provided a unique examination of ethical aspects in forensic neuropsychology. More specifically, the authors addressed ethical conflicts that frequently occur in forensic work. For instance, Sweet et al. indicated that role differences (i.e., fact vs. expert witness); limitations of confidentiality; billing issues; competency; objectivity; balancing expectations, legal rules, and ethical responsibilities; and legitimate versus pseudocredentials (e.g., vanity boards) are ethical issues with which forensic neuropsychologists frequently come into contact and should be familiar.

Although practicing psychologists are accustomed to providing a rationale for the conclusions they reach, few are routinely called on to withstand rigorous cross-examination about their findings. Aggressive questioning is rarely personal in nature (Adams & Rankin, 1996), but it can challenge the psychologist to maintain composure and avoid argument. Fortunately, there are some excellent guides for the rehabilitation psychologist working with pragmatic strategies to cope with personal injury, disability determination, worker's compensation (Barth, Ryan, Schear, & Puente, 1992), direct and cross-examination (Adams & Rankin, 1996), and common pitfalls in testimony (Brodsky, 1991, 1999; Guilmette & Giuliano, 1991). Also available are updates on case law, descriptions of forensic publications (Schwartz, 1991), and discussions of reliability, validity, and standard error of measurement as they pertain to psychological testimony (Matarazzo, 1987). Expert witnesses in rehabilitation psychology are also well-advised to become familiar with works challenging neuropsychological testimony (Faust, 1991; Wedding, 1991) and publications written for attorneys, especially those that pertain to challenging neuropsychological testimony (Faust, Ziskin, & Hiers, 1991; Sbordone & Saul, 2000).

The types of cases most relevant to the rehabilitation psychologist include personal injury, malpractice, competency, and disability determination cases. Therefore, psychologists must be aware of litigation procedures, common mistakes, and testimony skills that will help them articulate an expert opinion and prevent their views from being misrepresented or misconstrued. Several excellent and specific guides to the legal process are available, covering steps from initial telephone contact with the attorney through the deposition and trial phases (see Adams & Rankin, 1996; Greiffenstein & Cohen, 2005).

In the *preassessment* and *assessment phases*, the psychologist must communicate clearly and honestly with the attorney about how psychological testimony may be helpful or damaging to the plaintiff or defendant's case. This phase involves communication about the nature of the case, fees, expectations, and testing procedures.

In the *deposition* or *"discovery" phase,* the psychologist gives information under oath that offers the attorneys for all sides a view of both the content of the psychologist's opinions and conclusions as well as their skill in presenting their position. Anything the psychologist says, as well as any written materials used during the deposition, may be used in court. The deposition may be videotaped. Although most cases settle out of court (Adams & Rankin, 1996), some do proceed to trial, where the psychologist is subject to direct examination, cross-examination, and redirect and re-cross-examination.

The attorney employing the psychologist calls on the psychologist for testimony during *direct examination,* beginning with questions qualifying the psychologist as an expert. The attorney will portray the psychologist as favorably as possible, and will present aspects of the psychological evaluation that support that attorney's case. In brain injury litigation, the psychologist is usually asked to provide, within a reasonable degree of psychological certainty, an opinion as to whether the client suffered brain damage as a result of the incident in question, and the extent to which that injury is likely to affect the patient's daily life functioning, including their vocational prospects. The direct examination represents the period of explication of the case under sympathetic questioning.

In contrast, the *cross-examination* by the opposing attorney seeks to cast doubt on the psychologist's testimony, often by use of debunking tactics. For example, the opposing attorney may try to reveal the psychologist's lack of knowledge about obscure facts or studies, use a yes/no question format that cannot be answered in a simple manner, criticize the psychologist's credibility by accusing the psychologist of operating as a "hired gun," question the psychometric properties of widely used instruments, and other such strategies (Adams & Rankin, 1996). The psychologist is well advised to become familiar with these ploys and with strategies to cope with them before entering the courtroom (Adams & Rankin, 1996; Brodsky, 1991, 1999). The *redirect* and *re-cross-examination* phases are attempts by the employing and opposing attorneys, respectively, to undo damage done by the opposite side and to recast testimony in the light most favorable to their own purposes.

In civil cases, the plaintiff must prove the case based on a preponderance of evidence, which means that those deciding the case find the allegation more likely to be true than not true. The standard for the expert witness psychologist is one of "reasonable certainty," based on expertise derived from training and clinical experience.

Those charged with deciding cases may be swayed by skilled attorney cross-examination that undermines a psychologist's testimony. Psychologists are vulnerable to such attack because of the lack of a universal assessment standard, poor correlation between training and experience and diagnostic accuracy, limited ecological validity of neuropsychological tests, inability to rule out malingering definitively, and fallibility of clinical judgment even in the face of relevant information (Matarazzo, 1987; Wedding, 1983; Ziskin & Faust, 1988). Psychologists need to be aware of the actual and apparent vulnerabilities of their testimony and should prepare to be confronted on these matters by the opposing attorney. One potential problem area includes failure to obtain and review all relevant educational, medical, and psychological records, which may lead to the possibility of missing information suggestive of preinjury medical and psychological disorders and/or low level of functioning. Several recently published volumes on forensic neuropsychology review important considerations for psychologists working in the forensic arena as well as specific case examples of forensic cases, issues, and testimony (Bush and Drexler, 2002; Heilbronner, 2005; Hom, 2003; Larrabee, 2005a; Sweet, 1999).

SALIENT CONTENT AREAS FOR FORENSIC REHABILITATION PSYCHOLOGY

For rehabilitation psychologists to be most effective in forensic settings, it is incumbent on them to be aware of the most salient clinical practice and legal issues. In general, these include being knowledgeable regarding the following: assessment measures that are most commonly accepted, different methods of estimating preinjury cognitive abilities, issues related to perceived bias of experts, neurodevelopmental issues and course of injury recovery, malingering, and issues related to overdiagnosis of impairment.

Accepted Assessment Measures

As previously stated, *Chapple v. Ganger* (1994) set a precedent of preference for fixed-battery approaches in civil litigation, and Russell (1998) and Russell, Russell, and Hill (2005) articulated a corresponding position in the professional literature. However, Greiffenstein and Cohen (2005) argued that the flexible-battery approach (i.e., a core set of measures supplemented by others, depending on particulars of the case) is the most appropriate, and they indicated that even most proponents of the fixed-battery approach conduct flexible evaluations by including measures that are not part of the standard battery, such as the Wechsler Memory Scale. In fact, Lees-Haley, Smith, Williams, and Dunn (1996) suggested that the flexible-battery approach is the preference of the majority of neuropsychologists. For example, Lees-Haley et al. reviewed the forensic neuropsychological reports of 100 examiners in over 20 states and found that, on average, 11.73 (*SD* = 6.70) tests were administered per assessment. The five most frequently administered tests were the Wechsler Adult Intelligence Scale-Revised (WAIS-R; Wechsler, 1981; 76% of evaluations), the Minnesota Multiphasic Personality Inventory (MMPI; Hathaway & McKinley, 1940) and MMPI-2 (Hathaway et al., 1989; 68%), the Wechsler Memory Scale-Revised (Wechsler, 1987; 51%), and the Trail Making Test parts A and B (Army Individual Test Battery, 1944; 48% and 47%, respectively). Ten percent of evaluations included part or all of the Luria-Nebraska Neuropsychological

Battery (Moses, Golden, Ariel, & Gustavson, 1983). Although Halstead-Reitan Neuropsychological Test Battery (HRNB; Reitan & Wolfson, 1985) subtests were found to be pervasive, few clinicians used the entire battery. Batteries characterized by examiners as the HRNB varied from five to eight or more of the procedures described by Reitan and Wolfson. It is not surprising that these authors found that few neuropsychologists used precisely the same battery as any other neuropsychologist.

Most recently, Rabin, Barr, and Burton (2005) surveyed test use patterns among 747 clinical neuropsychologists associated with Division 40 of APA, NAN, or the International Neuropsychological Society. These authors reported that respondents used an average of 12 different tests in an assessment battery. Commensurate with findings of other surveys (e.g., Lees-Haley, 1997; Sweet, Moberg, & Suchy, 2000), most participants (68%) favored a flexible-battery approach, with 11% preferring a standardized battery. The most frequently used instruments were the WAIS-III (Wechsler, 1997a; 63.1%), WMS-III (Wechsler, 1997b; 42.7%), Trail Making Test (Army Individual Test Battery, 1944; 17.6%), California Verbal Learning Test (CVLT-II; Delis, Kramer, Kaplan, & Ober, 1987; 17.3%), Wechsler Intelligence Scale for Children-III (WISC-III; Wechsler, 1991; 15.9%), and the HRNB (Reitan & Wolfson, 1985; 15.5%). When using different tests and batteries to evaluate brain dysfunction, psychologists need to be cognizant of those tests most likely to be permitted as evidence in trial, with examples of previous cases in which these tests were used.

Reed (1996) and Hom (2003) suggested that only commercially available fixed batteries, such as the Halstead-Reitan, would survive a *Daubert* challenge and that flexible batteries would not be admissible, a view that has been further supported by Reitan and Wolfson (2002). Conversely, Bigler (2007) and Greiffensten and Cohen (2005) suggested that fixed and flexible batteries have both been generally accepted as valid in forensic cases and cite a case study (McKinzey & Ziegler, 1999) that indicated that a judge ruled that a flexible-battery approach was valid because of the doctrine of general acceptance.

Estimation of Premorbid Functioning

One of the hallmarks of personal injury litigation is the need to establish that the plaintiff has sustained a decrement in physical, vocational, neuropsychological, academic, or social abilities associated with injury. Assessment of functional decline necessitates a comparison of current abilities with an estimate of premorbid level, and this presupposes an adequate standard for estimating previous abilities. To document decline, psychologists must correctly differentiate preexisting developmental weaknesses from actual injury-related decline, and do so based on intraindividual comparisons and comparisons with others in relevant population subgroups.

If possible, psychologists should obtain pre-injury testing or examples of premorbid level of functioning, including intelligence and academic tests, standardized educational testing (often available in school transcripts), work evaluations, and so forth. If this information is not available, as is often the case, it is necessary to use alternate means to estimate premorbid levels of functioning. Several strategies to estimate pre-injury functioning have been proposed in the literature, with the most common being level of education, current reading ability, and demographically based regression equations. Education is assumed to be a good estimate of premorbid intelligence, given the high correlation between these factors (Lezak, 2004). Reading ability is also believed to be a reliable indicator of premorbid abilities based on the assumption that it is an overlearned ability and is therefore relatively spared following brain injury (e.g., Crawford, Besson, & Parker, 1988; Johnstone & Wilhelm, 1996; Ryan & Paolo, 1992). Others have argued that demographic prediction equations, such as the Barona Index (Barona, Reynolds, & Chastain, 1984) and its variants such as the Oklahoma Premorbid Intelligence Estimate (Scott, Krull, Williamson, Adams, & Iverson, 1997), are the best predictors of premorbid skills. A special issue of *Archives of Clinical Neuropsychology* (1997) presented a valuable series of articles on the most common methods to estimate premorbid functions, and Franzen, Burgess, and Smith-Seemiller (1997) provided an excellent review of methods of estimating premorbid functioning.

Perceived Clinician Bias

Opinions based on neuropsychological data are used in forensic arenas because of the nomothetic approach, which provides the foundation for objectively categorizing an individual's performances on standardized tests (van Gorp & Kalechstein, 2005). Reliable and valid testimony rests on the objectivity of the examiner. If the judge or jury perceives the expert witness as biased, either because of a strong advocacy role or because the psychologist is a "hired gun," both the client and the profession suffer. Several tactics may reduce expert witness bias. Adhering strictly to available scientific evidence will introduce a corrective tendency because of the scientific method's disconfirmation bias. A disciplined approach of attending to all relevant data (e.g., past history, medication effects, alternative explanations for dysfunction) will also attenuate clinician bias. Limiting one's exposure to others' impressions of the case has resulted in less confirmatory bias, and deliberately challenging hypotheses about possible causes of poor test performance other than "brain damage" may lessen clinicians' susceptibility to such confirmatory bias (Williams, 1997).

Developmental Issues and Injury Outcome

Expert witnesses help a jury assess the extent to which injury will affect future functioning, and damages are awarded, in part, on the basis of a life-care plan detailing an individual's future needs. The importance of accurate projection of the course of disability and recovery becomes especially acute in cases involving children, in that costs related to both care and diminished future educational and vocational opportunities are anticipated.

In the past, brain injury at an earlier age was believed to carry a more favorable prognosis than similar injuries sustained at a later age because of the brain's early plasticity. However, there is mounting evidence that this may not be the case. For example, recent research suggests that damage sustained in the first year of life is associated with more severe deficits than damage sustained later, due largely to arrested neuroanatomical development during the first year (Kolb & Fantie, 1997). Also, children's deficits may not be evident until later years, when more complex skills fail to develop because of a compromised sub-

strate (Kolb & Fantie, 1997). These issues are complex, and the rehabilitation psychologist must help the judge and jury to anticipate the appearance and course of future deficits based on limited current information. Such speculation could place the psychologist on uncertain ground. It is difficult to predict a client's ultimate level of recovery at any point, especially so during the first year after injury. Fortunately, few cases involving brain injury go to trial so quickly, and the psychologist is thereby able to delay prognostic statements until a client's neuropsychological functioning has better stabilized. Repeat assessment closer to the trial date is often needed.

Malingering

Malingering is defined as the deliberate presentation of "false or grossly exaggerated physical or psychological symptoms" (American Psychiatric Association, 2000, p. 739) to achieve secondary gain, often for external incentive (e.g., money, drugs, avoiding work or punishment). A key role of the rehabilitation psychologist as expert witness involves detection of malingering, a challenging task that has become increasingly important as more psychologists are called to offer expert testimony (McCaffrey, O'Bryant, Ashendorf, & Fisher, 2003; Mittenberg, Patton, Canyock, & Condit, 2002; Slick, Sherman, & Iverson, 1999; Tombaugh, 2002). Several researchers suggest that neuropsychological impairment can be faked successfully by individuals (including children) instructed to present as brain-injured (e.g., Bernard, 1990; Faust, Hart, & Guilmette, 1988; Faust, Hart, Guilmette, & Arkes, 1988; Heaton, Smith, Lehman, & Vogt, 1978). To be fully aware of current research and professional issues related to malingering and feigned cognitive deficit, psychologists are encouraged to review recently published volumes by Boone (2007) and Larrabee (2007).

Lees-Haley (1997) suggested that approximately 20% to 30% of plaintiffs should be considered possible malingerers, and Greiffenstein, Baker, and Gola (1994) estimated that nearly 41% of civil litigants referred for neuropsychological evaluation were probably malingering. Rogers (1997) reported that the incidence of malingering varies by context, ranging from 5.6% in posttraumatic stress disorder assessments (Resnick, 1997) to 15.7% in forensic settings

(Clark, 1997). Whenever the psychologist evaluates a litigant in a civil suit, financial and other incentives should be investigated and the possibility of malingering should be considered.

Several well-known indicators are suggestive of malingering, including history of antisocial personality disorder, recent substance abuse (American Psychiatric Association, 2000), brief tenure on the job in which one was allegedly injured (Adams & Rankin, 1996), and potential for financial gain. Other red flags include a wide discrepancy between physical findings and functional impairment, reporting bizarre and unrelated symptoms, and obvious response bias of endorsing virtually any symptom about which one is questioned. Other unusual features noted in clinical interview, such as a course inconsistent with that expected from the injury, as well as patterns of equal decline across all areas, should arouse the evaluator's concern. Larrabee (2005b) suggested a four-component consistency analysis to help detect possible malingering:

1. Are the data consistent within and between neuropsychological domains?
2. Is the neuropsychological profile consistent with the suspected etiology?
3. Are the neuropsychological data consistent with the documented severity of injury?
4. Are the neuropsychological data consistent with the individual's behavioral presentation?

It is now common for objective testing to be administered to help detect possible malingering, although this is difficult, given the absence of ideal measures. Most measures err on the conservative side, which suggests that malingering is more likely to go undetected than to be overdiagnosed (Etcoff & Kampfer, 1996; Rogers, 1997; Youngjohn, Burrows, & Erdal, 1995). However, some psychologists are reluctant even to raise the specter of malingering (Pankratz & Erickson, 1990) because it is not at all clear that psychologists make those determinations of intent more accurately than do others. However, these and other professional criticisms aside, malingering is an issue of significant legal interest, and psychologists should be prepared to address the question of secondary gain when providing testimony.

Bordini, Chaknis, Ekman-Turner, and Perna (2002) provided a useful overview of advances in the detection of malingering in neuropsychological assessment. One of the most prevalent strategies for assessment of malingering of intellectual and neuropsychological abilities has been forced-choice testing or symptom validity testing (Hurley & Deal, 2006; Pankratz & Binder, 1997). In the forced-choice approach, an examinee's performance using a two-choice option is compared with chance performance or an empirically derived cutoff score determined to distinguish between persons with and without brain impairment. Performance that is significantly below chance (i.e., 50% correct) strongly suggests that the examinee has deliberately chosen incorrect responses (Hurley & Deal, 2006; Pankratz & Binder, 1997); scores below an established cutoff provide somewhat weaker support for this conclusion. Forced-choice instruments include the Test of Memory Malingering (TOMM; Tombaugh, 1996), Portland Digit Recognition Test (Binder, 1993), the Hiscock Digit Recognition Test (Hiscock & Hiscock, 1989), and Recognition Memory Test (Warrington, 1984).

Sharland and Gfeller (2007) conducted a recent survey of neuropsychologists' beliefs and practices with regard to measurement of effort. The authors surveyed NAN professional members and fellows and found that 56% of respondents indicated that they often or always included a measure of effort in their evaluation. According to Sharland and Gfeller, the most frequently used measures of effort were the TOMM (Tombaugh, 1996; 75.3% often use, 63% always use), MMPI-2 F-K ratio (Butcher, Dahlstrom, Graham, Tellegen, & Kaemmer, 1989; 76.5% often use, 46% always use), MMPI-2 FBS scale (Butcher et al.; 75.1% often use, 43% always use), the Rey 15-item test (Rey, 1964; 74.4% often use, 42% always use), and the CVLT-II (Delis et al., 1987; 63.1% often use, 43% always use).

Malingering of emotional and psychiatric symptoms is also a concern for forensic psychologists (McCaffrey, O'Bryant, Ashendorf, & Fisher, 2003). The MMPI-2 (Hathaway et al., 1989) is one of the most commonly administered tests by psychologists (Grillo, Brown, Hilsabeck, Price, & Lees-Haley, 1994; Lees-Haley, 1997), with research indicating that the F scale can discriminate between individuals who do and do not malinger (Aribisi & Ben-Porath, 1998). Recent reviews on malingering have been conducted, including a meta-analysis of malingering on the MMPI-2 by Rogers, Sewell, and Salekin (1994) and by Reznek (2005), who completed a meta-analysis on the 15-Item Memory Test. In addition, Nelson, Sweet, and Demakis (2006) conducted a meta-analysis of the MMPI-2 Fake Bad Scale (FBS; Butcher et al., 1989), which is being increasingly used as a measure of possible malingering, and reported that the FBS performs as well as, if not better than, other MMPI-2 validity scales in discriminating between populations who do and do not overreport symptoms.

Other reviews of methods used to evaluate symptom exaggeration and malingering outline legal standards for various malingering tests (Etcoff & Kampfer, 1996; Hom & Denney, 2002a, 2002b). Citing Rogers's (1988) work, Etcoff and colleagues outlined five levels of certainty of malingering. A *definite* standard of malingering is defined as one in which 90% of individuals are correctly classified as malingering or nonmalingering on the basis of a broad body of research. *Probable* methods correctly classify at least 75% of individuals, and *tentative* methods have some empirical support but may not be useful in classifying particular individuals.

More recently, Slick et al. (1999) proposed a set of diagnostic criteria of malingering of neurocognitive dysfunction (MND). The authors defined MND as "the volitional exaggeration or fabrication of cognitive dysfunction for the purpose of obtaining substantial material gain, or avoiding or escaping formal duty or responsibility" (p. 552). A definite MND was characterized as the "presence of clear evidence of volitional exaggeration or fabrication of cognitive dysfunction and the absence of plausible alternative explanations (i.e., presence of a substantial external incentive, definite negative response bias)" (p. 552). A probable MND would be indicated by the presence of evidence strongly suggesting volitional exaggeration or fabrication and the absence of plausible alternative explanations (i.e., presence of a substantial external incentive, two or more types of evidence from neuropsychological testing, excluding definite negative response bias). A possible MND would be "indicated by the presence of evidence suggesting

volitional exaggeration or fabrication of cognitive dysfunction and the absence of plausible alternative explanations (i.e., presence of a substantial external incentive, evidence from self-report)" (p. 553). The research methods for measuring malingering in laboratory settings have been debated in the scholarly literature. However, leaving aside arguments about whether individuals instructed to "fake bad" in the lab actually do so in a way that is similar to actual malingering, these levels of certainty offer at least some guidance for the clinician in evaluating tests of malingering against a broad, if somewhat vague, standard.

Using this framework, symptom validity tests have been rated according to level of certainty. Only a few tests met criteria for definite, including the Hiscock Digit Recognition Test (72-item version and 36-item version; Hiscock & Hiscock, 1989); the Portland Digit Recognition Test (full 72-item version and 54-item version with conservative scoring; Binder, 1993); the MMPI-2 F scale and F minus K index (Butcher et al., 1989); WAIS-R age-corrected scaled scores of less than 4 on the Digit Span subtest (Wechsler, 1997); and an error score of 24 or more on the Speech Sounds Perception Test (Etcoff & Kampfer, 1996). The authors emphasized that even in using measures that have empirical support, clinicians should not rely solely on one instrument to make definitive statements regarding malingering or symptom exaggeration. Indeed, a recent review of practices by members of the American Board of Clinical Neuropsychology (Mittenberg, Aguila-Puentes, Patton, Canyock, & Heilbronner, 2002) indicated that board-certified neuropsychologists generally rely on multiple methods for assessment of the probability of malingering or symptom exaggeration.

Overdiagnosis of Impairment

It has been argued that neuropsychological impairment and brain injuries are frequently overdiagnosed in the forensic setting (Larrabee, 2005b), as all individuals have neuropsychological weaknesses that may be inappropriately concluded to be related to cerebral injury rather than to longstanding developmental weaknesses or other nonneurologic disorders. For example, Iverson (2006) surveyed individuals diagnosed with depression (and no history of brain injury) and reported that nearly 9 of 10 individuals met liberal criteria for diagnosis of postconcussion syndrome and that more than 5 in 10 met conservative diagnostic criteria for postconcussion syndrome. It is therefore important for rehabilitation psychologists to be aware that complaints of symptoms commonly experienced following brain injury are not necessarily indicative of a brain injury or neurologic etiology.

It is also important for psychologists to be aware of weaknesses in published normative data. McCaffrey, Palav, O'Bryant, and Labarge's (2003) volume provides information on the base rates of symptoms across diverse disorders (e.g., individuals with AIDS, arthritis, chronic fatigue syndrome, chronic pain, diabetes, cerebrovascular accident, fetal alcohol syndrome). Indication of an "abnormal" test score according to published norms is not necessarily indicative of brain injury and is actually not uncommon in nonclinical samples. For example, Heaton, Grant, and Matthews's (1991) original normative data program is frequently used to identify neuropsychological impairments, although only 10% of their normative sample had no scores in the abnormal range, the median number of abnormal scores was 4 (out of 40), and 45% of the sample had between 5 and 20 test scores in the abnormal range. Clearly, the presence of an abnormal test score is not automatically indicative of cerebral injury or dysfunction.

SUMMARY

It is incumbent on the rehabilitation psychologist to develop a familiarity with forensic issues and the legal system, largely because of the increasing probability of injury cases entering the legal system for redress. It is also important for psychologists to understand the different roles psychologists play in legal versus clinical settings, to know what to expect in depositions and courtroom testimony, and how best to present clinically relevant information to judges, juries, and attorneys. A familiarity with diagnostic problems, psychometric properties of instruments, symptom courses and recovery curves, and questions of secondary gain is the sine qua non of ethical forensic rehabilitation practice.

References

Adams, R. L., & Rankin, E. J. (1996). A practical guide to forensic neuropsychological evaluations and testimony. In R. L. Adams, O. A. Parsons, J. L. Culbertson, & S. J. Nixon (Eds.), *Neuropsychology for clinical practice* (pp. 455–487). Washington, DC: American Psychological Association.

American Psychiatric Association. (2000). *Diagnostic and statistical manual of mental disorders* (4th ed., text rev.). Washington, DC: American Psychiatric Association.

American Psychological Association. (1991). Specialty guidelines for forensic psychologists. *Law and Human Behavior, 15,* 655–665.

American Psychology-Law Society. (2001). *American Psychology–Law Society News, 21*(1), 1–26.

Anchor, K. N., Rogers, J. P., Solomon, G. S., Barth, J. T., & Peacock, C. (1983). Alternatives to medical testimony in determining vocational and industrial disability. *American Journal of Trial Advocacy, 6,* 443–480.

Arbisi, P. A., & Ben-Porath, Y. S. (1988). The ability of the Minnesota Multiphasic Personality Inventory-2 validity scales to detect fake-bad responses in psychiatric inpatients. *Psychological Assessment, 10,* 221–228.

Army Individual Test Battery. (1944). *Manual of directions and scoring.* Washington, DC: War Department, Adjutant General's Office.

Barona, A., Reynolds, C. R., & Chastain, R. (1984). A demographically based index of premorbid intelligence for the WAIS-R. *Journal of Consulting and Clinical Psychology, 52,* 885–887.

Barth, J. T., Ryan, T. V., & Hawk, G. L. (1992). Forensic neuropsychology: A reply to the method skeptics. *Neuropsychology Review, 2,* 251–266.

Barth, J. T., Ryan, T. V., Schear, J. M., & Puente, A. E. (1992). Forensic assessment and expert testimony in neuropsychology. In S. L. Hanson & D. M. Tucker (Eds.), *Physical medicine & rehabilitation, 6, state of the art reviews: Neuropsychological assessment,* (pp. 531–546). Philadelphia: Hanley & Belfus.

Belanger, H. G., Vanderploeg, R. D., Curtiss, G., & Warden, D. L. (2007). Recent neuroimaging techniques in mild traumatic brain injury. *The Journal of Neuropsychiatry and Clinical Neurosciences, 19,* 5–20.

Bernard, L. C. (1990). Prospects for faking believable memory deficits on neuropsychological tests and the use of incentives in simulation research. *Journal of Clinical and Experimental Psychology, 12,* 715–728.

Bigler, E. D. (2007). A motion to exclude and the "fixed" versus "flexible" battery in "forensic" neuropsychology: Challenges to the practice of clinical neuropsychology. *Archives of Clinical Neuropsychology, 22,* 45–51.

Binder, L. M. (1993). An abbreviated form of the Portland Digit Recognition Test. *The Clinical Neuropsychologist, 7,* 104–107.

Boone, K. B. (Ed.). (2007). *Assessment of feigned cognitive impairment: A neuropsychological perspective.* New York: Guilford Press.

Bordini, E. J., Chaknis, M. M., Ekman-Turner, R. M., & Perna, R. B. (2002). Advances and issues in the diagnostic differential of malingering versus brain injury. *NeuroRehabilitation, 17,* 93–104.

Borg, J., Holm, L., Cassidy, J. D., Peloso, P. M., Carroll, L. J., von Holst, H., et al. (2004). Diagnostic procedures in mild traumatic brain injury: Results of the World Health Organization Collaborating Centre Task Force on mild traumatic brain injury. *Journal of Rehabilitation Medicine, 43,* S61–75.

Brodsky, S. L. (1991). *Testifying in court: Guidelines and maxims for the expert witness.* Washington, DC: American Psychological Association.

Brodsky, S. L. (1999). *The expert witness.* Washington, DC: American Psychological Association.

Broun, K. S., Dix, G. E., Graham, M. H., Kaye, D. H., Mosteller, R. P., & Roberts, E. F. (Eds.). (1992). *McCormick on evidence* (4th ed.). St. Paul, MN: West.

Bush, S. S., & Drexler, M. L. (Eds.). (2002). *Ethical issues in clinical neuropsychology.* Lisse, Netherlands: Swets & Zeitlinger.

Butcher, J. N., Dahlstrom, W. G., Graham, J. R., Tellegen, A. M., & Kaemmer, B. (1989). *Minnesota Multiphasic Personality Inventory-2 (MMPI-2): Manual for administration and scoring.* Minneapolis, MN: University of Minnesota Press.

Chapple v. Ganger, 851 F. Supp. 1481 (E.D. Wash. 1994).

Cohen, L. E. (1996). The Daubert decision: Gatekeeper or executioner? *Trial, 32,* 52.

Clark, C. R. (1997). Sociopathy, malingering, and defensiveness. In R. Rogers (Ed.), *Clinical assessment of malingering and deception* (pp. 68–84). New York: Guilford Press.

Crawford, J. R., Besson, J. A. O., & Parker, D. M. (1988). Estimation of premorbid intelligence in organic conditions. *British Journal of Psychiatry, 153,* 178–181.

Daubert v. Merrell Dow Pharmaceuticals, 113 S. Ct. 2786 (1993).

Delis, D. C., Kramer, J., Kaplan, E., & Ober, B. A. (1987). *California Verbal Learning Test (CVLT) Manual.* San Antonio, TX: Psychological Corporation.

Essig, S. M., Mittenberg, W., Petersen, R. S., Strauman, S., & Cooper, J. T. (2001). Practices of forensic neuropsychology: Perspectives of neuropsychologists and trial attorneys. *Archives of Clinical Neuropsychology, 16,* 271–291.

Etcoff, L. M., & Kampfer, K. M. (1996). Practical guidelines in the use of symptom validity and other psychological tests to measure malingering and symptom exaggeration in traumatic brain injury cases. *Neuropsychology Review, 6,* 171–201.

Faust, D. (1991). Forensic neuropsychology: The art of practicing a science that does not yet exist. *Neuropsychology Review, 2,* 205–231.

Faust, D., Hart, K., J., & Guilmette, T. J. (1988). Pediatric malingering: The capacity of children to fake believable deficits on psychological testing. *Journal of Consulting and Clinical Psychology, 36,* 578–582.

Faust, D., Hart, K., Guilmette, T. J., & Arkes, H. R. (1988). Neuropsychologists' capacity to detect adolescent malingerers. *Professional Psychology: Research and Practice, 19,* 508–515.

Faust, D., Ziskin, J., & Hiers, J. B. (1991). *Brain damage claims: Coping with neuropsychological evidence. Vols. I & II.* Los Angeles: Law & Psychology Press.

Franzen, M. D., Burgess, E. J., & Smith-Seemiller, L. (1997). Methods of estimating premorbid functioning. *Archives of Clinical Neuropsychology, 12,* 711–738.

Freud, S. (1906/1959). Psycho-analysis and the ascertaining of truth in courts of law. *Clinical Papers and Papers on Technique, Collected Papers: Vol. 2* (pp. 13–24). New York: Basic Books.

Frye v. United States, 293 Fed. 1013 (D.C. Cir. 1923).

Gilandas, A. J., & Touyz, S. W. (1983). Forensic neuropsychology: A selective introduction. *Journal of Forensic Sciences, 28,* 713–723.

Giuliano, A. J., Barth, J. T., Hawk, G. L., & Ryan, T. V. (1997). The forensic neuropsychologists: Precedents, roles, and problems. In R. J. McCaffrey, A. D. Williams, J. M. Fisher, & L. C. Laing (Eds.), *The practice of forensic neuropsychology: Meeting challenges in the courtroom* (pp. 1–35). New York: Plenum Press.

Green, E. D., Nesson, C. R., & Murray, P. L. (1997). *Federal Rules of Evidence: With selected legislative history, California evidence code, and case supplement.* New York: Aspen Law & Business.

Greiffenstein, M. F., Baker, W. J., & Gola, T. (1994). *Validation of malingered amnesia measures with a large clinical sample.* Odessa, FL: Psychological Assessment Resources.

Greiffenstein, M. F., & Cohen, L. (2005). Neuropsychology and the law: Principles of productive attorney–neuropsychologist relations. In G. Larrabee (Ed.), *Forensic neuropsychology: A scientific approach* (pp. 29–91). New York: Oxford University Press.

Grillo, J., Brown, R. S., Hilsabeck, R., Price, R. J., & Lees-Haley, P. R. (1994). Raising doubts about claims of malingering: Implications of relationships between MCMI-II and MMPI-2 performances. *Journal of Clinical Psychology, 40,* 651–655.

Guilmette, T. J., Faust, D., Hart, K., & Arkes, H. R. (1990). A national survey of psychologists who offer neuropsychological services. *Archives of Clinical Neuropsychology, 5,* 373–392.

Guilmette, T. J., & Giuliano, A. J. (1991). Taking the stand: Issues and strategies in forensic neuropsychology. *Clinical Neuropsychologist, 5,* 197–219.

Hathaway, S. R., & McKinley, J. C. (1940). *The MMPI manual.* New York: Psychological Corporation.

Hathaway, S. R., McKinley, J. C., Butcher, J. N., Dahlstrom, W. G., Graham, J. R., Tellegen, A., & Kacmmer, B. (1989). *Minnesota Multiphasic Personality Inventory 2: Manual for administration and scoring.* Minneapolis, MN: University of Minnesota Press.

Hawk, G., & Benedek, E. P. (1989). The forensic evaluation in the criminal justice system. In R. Michels (Ed.), *Psychiatry* (pp. 1–15). Philadelphia: Lippincott Williams & Wilkins.

Healy, W. (1915). *Honesty: A study of the causes and treatment of dishonesty among children.* Indianapolis, IN: Bobbs-Merrill.

Heaton, R. K., Grant, I., & Matthews, C. G. (1991). *Comprehensive norms for an expanded Halstead-Reitan Battery: Demographic corrections, research findings, and clinical applications.* Odessa, FL: Psychological Assessment Resources.

Heaton, R. K., Smith, H. H., Lehman, R. A., & Vogt, A. T. (1978). Prospects for faking believable deficits on neuropsychological testing. *Journal of Consulting and Clinical Psychology, 46,* 892–900.

Heilbronner, R. L. (2005). *Forensic neuropsychology casebook.* New York: Guilford Press.

Hiscock, M., & Hiscock, C. K. (1989). Refining the forced-choice method for the detection of malingering. *Journal of Clinical and Experimental Neuropsychology, 11,* 967–974.

Hom, J. (2003). Forensic neuropsychology: Are we there yet? *Archives of Clinical Neuropsychology, 18,* 827–845.

Hom, J., & Denney, R. L. (Eds.). (2002a). Detection of response bias in forensic neuropsychology. Part I. *Journal of Forensic Neuropsychology, 2,* 1–166.

Hom, J., & Denney, R. L. (Eds.). (2002b). Detection of response bias in forensic neuropsychology. Part II. *Journal of Forensic Neuropsychology, 2,* 167–314.

Horne v. Goodson Logging Company, 349 S. E. 2d 293 (North Carolina Court of Appeals 1986).

Hurley, K. E., & Deal, W. P. (2006). Assessment instruments measuring malingering used with individuals who have mental retardation: Potential problems and issues. *Mental Retardation, 44,* 112–119.

Indianapolis Union Railway v. Walker, (1974, November 12). Court of Appeals of Indiana, First District, 578–590.

Iverson, G. L. (2006). Misdiagnosis of the persistent post-concussion syndrome in patients with depression. *Archives of Clinical Neuropsychology, 21,* 303–310.

Jenkins v. United States, 113 U.S. App. D.C. 300, 307 F.2d 637 (1962).

Johnstone, B., & Wilhelm, K. L. (1996). The longitudinal stability of the WRAT-R reading subtest: Is it an appropriate estimate of premorbid intelligence? *JINS, 2,* 282–285.

Kolb, B., & Fantie, B. (1997). Development of the child's brain and behavior. In C. R. Reynolds & E. Fletcher-Janzen (Eds.), *Handbook of clinical child neuropsychology* (2nd ed., pp. 17–41). New York: Plenum Press.

Kurke, M. I. (1986). Anatomy of product liability/personal injury litigation. In M. I. Kurke & R. G. Meyer (Eds.), *Psychology in product liability and personal injury litigation* (pp. 3–15). Washington, DC: Hemisphere Publication Services.

Laing, L. C., & Fisher, J. M. (1997). Neuropsychology in civil proceedings. In R. J. McCaffrey, A. D. Williams, J. M. Fisher, & L. C. Laing (Eds.), *The practice of forensic neuropsychology: Meeting challenges in the courtroom* (pp. 117–133). New York: Plenum Press.

Lally, S. J. (2003). What tests are acceptable for use in forensic evaluations? A survey of experts. *Professional Psychology: Research and Practice, 34,* 491–498.

Larrabee, G. J. (Ed.). (2005a). *Forensic neuropsychology: A scientific approach.* New York: Oxford University Press.

Larrabee, G. J. (2005b). A scientific approach to forensic neuropsychology. In G. J. Larrabee (Ed.), *Forensic neuropsychology: A scientific approach* (pp. 3–28). New York: Oxford University Press.

Larrabee, G. J. (Ed.). (2007). *Assessment of malingered neuropsychological deficits.* New York: Oxford University Press.

Lees-Haley, P. R. (1997). MMPI-2 base rates for 492 personal injury plaintiffs: Implications and challenges for forensic assessment. *Journal of Clinical Psychology, 53,* 745–755.

Lees-Haley, P. R., & Fox, D. D. (2001). Isn't everything in forensic neuropsychology controversial? *NeuroRehabilitation, 16,* 267–273.

Lees-Haley, P. R., Smith, H. H., Williams, C. W., & Dunn, J. T. (1996). Forensic neuropsychological test usage: An empirical study. *Archives of Clinical Neuropsychology, 11,* 45–51.

Lezak, M. D. (2004). *Neuropsychological Assessment* (4th ed.). New York: Oxford University Press.

Livingood, J. A. (1994). Admissibility and reliability of expert scientific testimony after Daubert. *Defense Counsel Journal, 61,* 19–21.

Matarazzo, J. D. (1987). Validity of psychological assessment: From the clinic to the courtroom. *The Clinical Neuropsychologist, 1,* 307–314.

McCaffrey, R. J., O'Bryant, S. E., Ashendorf, S., & Fisher, J. M. (2003). Correlations among the TOMM, Rey-15 item, and MMPI-2 validity scales in a sample of TBI litigants. *Journal of Forensic Neuropsychology, 3,* 45–53.

McCaffrey, R. J., Palav, A. A., O'Bryant, S. E., & Labarge, A. S. (Eds.). (2003). *Practitioner's guide to symptom base rates in clinical neuropsychology.* New York: Kluwer Academic.

McKinzey, R. K., & Ziegler, T. G. (1999). Challenging a flexible neuropsychological battery under *Kelly/Frye:* A case study. *Behavioral Sciences and Law, 17,* 543–551.

Melton, G. B. (1994). Expert opinions: "Not for cosmic understanding." In B. D. Sales & G. R. VandenBos (Eds.), *Psychology in litigation and legislation: Master lectures in psychology* (pp. 59–99). Washington, DC: American Psychological Association.

Mittenberg, W., Aguila-Puentes, G., Patton, C., Canyock, E. M., & Heilbronner, R. L. (2002). Neuropsychological profiling of symptom exaggeration and malingering. *Journal of Forensic Neuropsychology, 3,* 225–240.

Mittenberg, W., Patton, C., Canyock, E. M., & Condit, D. C. (2002). Base rates of malingering and symptom exaggeration. *Journal of Clinical and Experimental Neuropsychology, 8,* 1094–1102.

Moses, J. A., Jr., Golden, C. J., Ariel, R., & Gustavson, J. L. (1983). *Interpretation of the Luria-Nebraska Neuropsychological Battery. Volume 1.* New York: Grune & Stratton.

Munsterberg, H. (1908). *On the witness stand.* New York: Doubleday.

Nelson, N. W., Sweet, J. J., & Demakis, G. J. (2006). Meta-analysis of the MMPI-2 Fake Bad Scale: Utility in forensic practice. *The Clinical Neuropsychologist, 20,* 39–58.

Pankratz, L., & Binder, L. M. (1997). Malingering on intellectual and neuropsychological measures. In R. Rogers (Ed.), *Clinical assessment of malingering and deception* (pp. 223–236). New York: Guilford Press.

Pankratz, L., & Erickson, R. C. (1990). Two views of malingering. *The Clinical Neuropsychologist, 4,* 379–389.

Phillips v. Industrial Machine, 597 N.W.2d 377 (1999).

Puente, A. (1987). Social security disability and clinical neuropsychological assessment. *The Clinical Neuropsychologist, 1,* 353–363.

Puente, A. E. (1997). Forensic clinical neuropsychology as a paradigm for clinical neuropsychological assessment: Basic and emerging issues. In R. J. McCaffrey, A. D.

Williams, J. M. Fisher, & L. C. Laing (Eds.), *The practice of forensic neuropsychology: Meeting challenges in the courtroom* (pp. 165–175). New York: Plenum Press.

Puente, A. E., & Gillespie, J. B. (1991). Workers' compensation and clinical neuropsychological assessment. In J. Dywan, R. D. Kaplan, & F. J. Pirozzolo (Eds.), *Neuropsychology and the law* (pp. 39–63). New York: Springer-Verlag.

Putnam, S. H., DeLuca, J. W., & Anderson, C. (1994). The second TCN salary survey: A survey of neuropsychologists. Part II. *The Clinical Neuropsychologist, 8,* 245–282.

Rabin, L. A., Barr, W. B., & Burton, L. A. (2005). Assessment practices of clinical neuropsychologists in the United States and Canada: A survey of INS, NAN, and APA Division 40 members. *Archives of Clinical Neuropsychology, 20,* 33–65.

Raskin, S. A., Mateer, C. A., & Tweeten, R. (1998). Neuropsychological assessment of individuals with mild traumatic brain injury. *The Clinical Neuropsychologist, 12,* 21–30.

Reed, J. E. (1996). Fixed vs. flexible neuropsychological test batteries under the Daubert Standard for the admissibility of scientific evidence. *Behavioral Sciences and the Law, 14,* 315–322.

Reitan, R. M., & Wolfson, D. (1985). *The Halstead-Reitan Neuropsychological Test Battery.* Tucson, AZ: Neuropsychology Press.

Reitan, R. M., & Wolfson, D. (2002). Detection of malingering and invalid test results using the Halstead-Reitan Battery. *Journal of Forensic Neuropsychology, 3,* 275–314.

Resnick, P. J. (1997). Malingering of posttraumatic disorders. In R. Rogers (Ed.), *Clinical Assessment of malingering and deception* (pp. 130–152). New York: Guilford Press.

Rey, A. (1964). *L'examen clinique en psychologie.* Paris: Presses Universitaires de France.

Reznek, L. (2005). The Rey-15 item test for malingering: A meta-analysis. *Brain Injury, 19,* 539–543.

Richardson, R. E., & Adams, R. L. (1992). Neuropsychologists as expert witnesses: Issues of admissibility. *The Clinical Neuropsychologist, 6,* 295–308.

Rogers, R. (1988). Introduction. In R. Rogers (Ed.), *Clinical assessment of malingering and deception* (p. 19). New York: Guilford Press.

Rogers, R. (1997). Introduction. In R. Rogers (Ed.), *Clinical assessment of malingering and deception* (pp. 1–22). New York: Guilford Press.

Rogers, R., Sewell, K. W., & Salekin, R. T. (1994). A meta-analysis of malingering on the MMPI-2. *Assessment, 1,* 227–237.

Russell, E. W. (1998). In defense of the Halstead-Reitan Battery: A critique of Lezak's review. *Archives of Clinical Neuropsychology, 13,* 365–381.

Russell, E. W., Russell, S. L. K., & Hill, B. D. (2005). The fundamental psychometric status of neuropsychological batteries. *Archives of Clinical Neuropsychology, 20,* 785–794.

Ryan, J. J., & Paolo, A. M. (1992). A screening procedure for estimating premorbid intelligence in the elderly. *The Clinical Neuropsychologist, 6,* 53–62.

Sbordone, R. J., & Saul, R. E. (2000). *Neuropsychology for health care professionals and attorneys.* Boca Raton, FL: CRC Press.

Schwartz, M. L. (1991). Sometimes safe, sometimes out: Umpire gives split decision. *The Clinical Neuropsychologist, 5,* 89–99.

Scott, J. G., Krull, K. R., Williamson, D. J. G., Adams, R. L., & Iverson, G. L. (1997). Oklahoma Premorbid Intelligence Estimate (OPIE): Utilization in clinical samples. *The Clinical Neuropsychologist, 11,* 146–154.

Sharland, M. J., & Gfeller, J. D. (2007). A survey of neuropsychologists beliefs and practices with respect to the assessment of effort. *Archives of Clinical Neuropsychology, 22,* 213–223.

Slick, D. J., Sherman, E., & Iverson, G. L. (1999). Diagnostic criteria for malingered neurocognitive dysfunction: Proposed standards for clinical practice and research. *The Clinical Neuropsychologist, 13,* 545–561.

Sorenson, S., & Krause, J. F. (1991). Occurrence, severity, and outcomes of brain injury. *Journal of Head Trauma Rehabilitation, 6,* 1–10.

State v. Driver, 88 W.Va. 479, 107 S.E. 189 (1921).

Sweet, J. J. (1999). *Forensic neuropsychology: Fundamentals and practice.* Washington, DC: Psychology Press.

Sweet, J. J., Grote, C., & van Gorp, W. G. (2002). Ethical issues in forensic neuropsychology. In S. Bush & M. L. Drexler (Eds.), *Ethical issues in clinical neuropsychology* (pp. 103–133). Lisse, Netherlands: Swets & Zeitlinger.

Sweet, J. J., Moberg, P. J., & Suchy, Y. (2000). Ten-year follow-up survey of clinical neuropsychologists. Part I: Practices and beliefs. *The Clinical Neuropsychologist, 14,* 18–37.

Sweet, J. J., Nelson, N. W., & Moberg, P. J. (2006). The TCN/AACN 2005 "Salary Survey": Professional practices, beliefs, and incomes of U.S. neuropsychologists. *The Clinical Neuropsychologist, 20,* 325–364.

Tombaugh, T. N. (1996). *Test of memory malingering.* Toronto, Ontario: Multi-Health Systems.

Tombaugh, T. N. (2002). The test of memory malingering (TOMM) in forensic psychology. *Journal of Forensic Neuropsychology, 2,* 69–96.

van Gorp, W. G., & Kalechstein, A. (2005). Threats to the validity of the interpretation and conveyance of forensic neuropsychological results. *Journal of Forensic Neuropsychology, 4*(3), 67–77.

Warrington, E. K. (1984). *Recognition Memory Test.* Windsor, UK: NFER-Nelson.

Wechsler, D. (1981). *Manual for the Wechsler Adult Intelligence Scale-Revised.* New York: Psychological Corporation.

Wechsler, D. (1987). *Manual for the Wechsler Memory Scale-Revised.* San Antonio, TX: Psychological Corporation.

Wechsler, D. (1991). *Manual for the Wechsler Intelligence Scale for Children* (WISC-III; 3rd ed.). San Antonio, TX: Psychological Corporation.

Wechsler, D. (1997a). *WAIS-III administration and scoring manual.* San Antonio, TX: Psychological Corporation.

Wechsler, D. (1997b). *WMS-III administration and scoring manual.* San Antonio, TX: Psychological Corporation.

Wedding, D. (1983). Clinical and statistical prediction in neuropsychology. *Clinical Neuropsychology, 5,* 49–55.

Wedding, D. (1991). Clinical judgment in forensic neuropsychology: A comment on the risks of claiming more than can be delivered. *Neuropsychology Review, 2,* 223–239.

Williams, A. D. (1997). The forensic evaluation of adult traumatic brain injury. In R. J. McCaffrey, A. D. Williams, J. M. Fisher, & L. C. Craig (Eds.), *The practice of forensic neuropsychology* (pp. 37–56). New York: Plenum Press.

Youngjohn, J. R., Burrows, L., & Erdal, K. (1995). Brain damage or compensation neurosis? The controversial postconcussion syndrome. *Clinical Neuropsychologist, 9,* 112–123.

Zasler, N. D., & Martelli, M. F. (2003). Mild traumatic brain injury: Impairment and disability assessment caveats. *Neuropsychological Rehabilitation, 12,* 31–41.

Ziskin, J., & Faust, D. (1988). Challenging clinical judgement. In J. Ziskin & D. Faust (Eds.), *Coping with psychiatric and psychological testimony:* Vol. 1. (4th ed., pp. 220–295). Marina del Rey, CA: Law & Psychology Press.

CHAPTER 12

ASSESSMENT OF PERSONALITY AND PSYCHOPATHOLOGY

Douglas Johnson-Greene and Pegah Touradji

Optimal adjustment to chronic health conditions requires the capacity to cope with multiple stressors and adapt to new life demands (Elliott, Bush, & Chen, 2006), processes that are heavily influenced by the individual's personality attributes and psychopathology (premorbid or reactive). Experienced clinicians recognize that accurate understanding of these factors is integral to optimal rehabilitation planning. Psychologists make an important contribution by tailoring assessment and intervention to account for individual characteristics, thus increasing the likelihood of positive rehabilitation outcomes. Though it can be difficult to tease apart the unique contributions of personality and psychological factors to long-term adjustment to disability or illness, these factors most certainly affect rehabilitation participation and outcome.

Individuals arrive at the onset of injury or illness with differing capacities for enduring stressful events, and their capacities and characteristics may change for the worse as a function of their illness (e.g., brain injury causing loss of inhibition, low frustration tolerance). Although personality characteristics may influence reactions to medical illness and trauma, early rehabilitation psychologists showed the importance of other psychosocial variables, such as the physical environment and societal expectations, in shaping behaviors and outcomes (Dembo, Leviton, & Wright, 1956; Wright, 1983). This suggests an important interplay between individual characteristics and other psychosocial variables. In other words, individuals may not respond in specific or predictable ways, despite the presumed

relative stability of their personality traits (Wortman & Silver, 1989).

Rehabilitation theorists propose a dynamic interaction of enduring personality characteristics (e.g., injury and illness-related consequences, demographic factors, emotional functioning, environmental and social factors, sociopolitical influences) in the determination of rehabilitation outcomes and adjustment to disability (Elliott, 2002; Olkin & Pledger, 2003). The biopsychosocial model incorporates recognition of the multidimensional nature of impairments and disability and the interplay between personal attributes and environmental factors (Trieschmann, 1980). In this model, disease and illness occur not in isolation but rather within a milieu in which psychosocial factors, including personality and psychopathology, influence the severity of impairment and an individual's adjustment. Thus, psychological variables play a key role in determining responses to disability and level of adaptation (Dembo et al., 1956; Wright, 1983). The interplay of personality characteristics with social and environmental factors in determining adjustment to disability is a useful theoretical model that can assist psychologists in conceptualizing and planning effective interventions.

In this chapter, we provide an overview of the interface between personality factors and psychopathology in rehabilitation by discussing theoretical premises, characteristics associated with positive and negative coping, neurologically-based "personality" changes, assessment and diagnostic considerations, and common assessment measures. Our intent is not to provide a detailed examination of personality theory and psychopathology, or all of the possible instruments available in a psychologist's arsenal, but rather to provide an overview of basic premises and the role that personality and psychopathology may play in influencing rehabilitation outcomes and adjustment to disability and chronic illness.

DEFINITIONS AND THEORETICAL DIMENSIONS OF PERSONALITY

According to the *Diagnostic and Statistical Manual of Mental Disorders* ([*DSM–IV–TR*] 4th ed., text rev.; American Psychiatric Association, 2000), *personality* is "enduring patterns of perceiving, relating to, or thinking about the environment or oneself that are exhibited in a wide range of social and personal contexts" (p. 630). Our personality shapes our perceptions of ourselves and our environment and that, in turn, influences how we behave and are likely to interact with others. Unfortunately, there is a lack of common nomenclature. *Traits, dispositions,* and *coping styles* are terms used to describe personality that are often used interchangeably and are poorly defined. Further complicating matters, there are a multitude of factors that have influenced personality theory.

It is important to understand that there are as many definitions and constructs of personality as there are theories and theorists who have attempted to describe it. For example, at last count, there were at least 18 different proposals for a dimensional model of personality disorders (Widiger & Simonsen, 2005). Nonetheless, there are several broad vectors that are useful to consider when defining *personality theory*. One aspect is simply whether the theory focuses solely on abnormal personality functioning or attempts to describe general personality structure. Another closely related concept is whether the model is a *categorical model,* such as can be found with diagnostic categories that define seemingly unitary personality disorders, or whether it is a dimensional model of personality. *Dimensional models* avoid describing personality functioning along a single parameter and instead use multidimensional profile descriptions to describe personality structure (Widiger & Samuel, 2005).

Some of the differences in definitions and theories of personality reflected in the literature are a result of the heterogeneity of studying groups of people and the criteria that are used in empirical investigations. *Nomothetic* criterion approaches are used to develop common units (i.e., constructs) to describe groups of people. However, the utility of nomothetic information has been problematic in clinical settings and has tended to take a back seat to *idiographic* criterion approaches aimed at describing individual characteristics or *polythetic* criterion approaches that account for the existence of problematic heterogeneity by requiring individuals to have only an overlap, as opposed to a perfect match, with the component parts of a personality construct (e.g., borderline personality disorder). Even the stability of personality characteristics has become controversial (Skodol et al., 2005; Zanarini, Frankenburg, Hennen, Reich, & Silk, 2005), representing a direct challenge to the long-held belief that personality comprises relatively enduring features. If situations mainly control how people behave, then the existence or relevance of traits is questionable, or at least minimized.

Differences also exist in the literature based on the knowledge domain being studied. Classic Freudian and neo-Freudian personality theories can be conceptualized within the *intrapsychic domain,* which is largely based on mental mechanisms of unconscious dispositions, defenses, and motives. A *dispositional domain* is more concerned with fundamental dispositions (closely linked in earlier research on temperaments) and the ways in which individuals differ from one another, such as the degree to which individuals can be described as having characteristics of openness or neuroticism. Last, the *adjustment domain* is concerned with how personality plays a key role in how people cope, adapt, and adjust to events in daily life and has been linked to health outcomes. It is this last domain that is more intimately linked to the positive psychology movement and interventions aimed at fostering positive coping and resilience (Anson & Ponsford, 2006).

Most clinicians associate pathology with *DSM–IV–TR*. With regard to the area of abnormal personality, *DSM–IV–TR* uses a categorical model of abnormal personality functioning that contains a classification and diagnostic scheme for 10 personality disorders. However, there are dimensional classification systems that have been reported in the literature, and it has been suggested that these models would be more appropriate for describing disorders of personality (Widiger & Trull, 2007). The most researched dimensional model of personality is the five-factor personality model (FFM; Costa & McCrae, 1992; McCrae & Costa, 1999). The FFM suggests that personality comprises the following key dimensions: (a) neuroticism (or emotional stability), (b) extroversion (or surgency), (c) openness (or intellect, imagination, and unconventionality), (d) agreeableness, and (e) and conscientiousness (or constraint). The five factors were derived from factor analyses of self and peer reports using adjectives and questionnaire items. Unfortunately, there are several potential shortcomings to the model: (a) Many adjectives correlate with more than one dimension, so it would be incorrect to assume that the five factors are isomorphic; (b) subsequent studies have revealed a number of subfacets (30 in all) with more explanatory power for certain subgroups and pathologies, which obviously diminishes the simplicity of the five factor model; (c) the dimensions cannot be equated with the more durable "traits" common to personality theory, and a person can have fluctuating dimensions depending on circumstances; and (d) thus far, there has been limited clinical utility associated with the FFM. Studies have found that the FFM also accounts for a relatively small percentage of the variance of personality adjectives, which has prompted other dimensional models that include additional factors such as religiosity, honesty, deceptiveness, conservativeness, conceit, thrift, humorousness, sensuality, and masculinity-femininity.

RELATIONSHIP BETWEEN PERSONALITY AND REHABILITATION

Three general themes emerge from the literature on personality and rehabilitation, all of which appear to seek to identify the origin of "new" personality traits: (a) personality that emerges from specific neurological illness or injury (e.g., temporal lobe personality), (b) exacerbation of premorbid personality, and (c) a reaction to an acquired disability.

Despite considerable ad hoc clinical observations, there is limited empirical evidence in support of these models. Similarly, little is known about factors leading to reports of personality change or causal attributions regarding personality modification. On the whole, families can be more accurate than patients about personality changes, though these seem to be predominantly anchored to specific adverse or stressful events such as trauma resulting in physical injury (Alfano, Neilson, & Fink, 1994; Dodwell, 1988), which would seem to bring into question the validity of the overwhelming majority of the literature that has relied on retrospective patient self-report. However, this appears to be an unsettled issue because at least one study has found reasonable convergence between patient and significant other reports (Rush, Malec, Brown, & Moessner, 2006).

Even in the absence of a specific personality disorder, disadvantageous personality "traits" can interfere with positive coping and adaptation. McCrae and Costa (1990) defined *personality traits* as "dimensions of individual differences in tendencies to show consistent patterns of thoughts, feelings, and actions" (p. 23). Personality traits are manifested in motives, habits, and attitudes that can affect behavior. They are not necessarily predicted from behaviors but should be viewed as dispositions inferred from patterns of thoughts, feelings, and actions (McCrae & Costa, 1995). The vast majority of the literature has focused on the multidimensional FFM.

Both negative and positive traits have been associated with the adaptation process, though the primary focus has been on the former. Factors that have been shown to foster maladaptive coping include higher levels of neuroticism and negative emotions (Krause & Rohe, 1998), the use of avoidance coping strategies (Hanson, Buckelew, Hewett, & O'Neal, 1993; Kennedy et al., 2000), catastrophizing that includes exaggerated negative expectations and focus (Buer & Linton, 2002; Turner, Jensen, Warms, & Cardenas, 2002), poor frustration tolerance (Weinryb, Gustavsson, & Barber, 2003), ineffective problem-solving abilities (Elliott et al., 2006), a low level of hope (Snyder, Lehman, Kluck, & Monsson, 2006), and avoidance and self-blame (Victorson, Farmer, Burnett, Ouellette, &

Barocas, 2005). Ambivalent coping, or vacillating between the use of venting emotions and mental distancing rather than the consistent use of either coping strategy, was shown to be associated with persistent symptoms of negative mood after traumatic injury (Fauerbach, Lawrence, Bryant, & Smith, 2002).

Although disability research is often focused on maladaptive coping strategies, it should not be assumed that disability in itself would result in poor coping or negative traits. The tendency to emphasize negative attributes and traits and their relation to adverse outcomes is consistent with the medical model. As a result, the literature is overly focused on the characteristics of maladaptive coping, though there is now a gradual shift toward positive coping attributes in rehabilitation research (Dunn & Dougherty, 2005). The emerging areas of positive psychology and resilience have redirected attention toward healthy psychological traits of the person and the teaching of more effective coping strategies (King & Kennedy, 1999). These approaches depart from the traditional medical model as they recognize the importance of social, contextual, and behavioral cues in shaping individual responses. In this way, they comport with the long-standing rehabilitation psychology paradigm.

Positive psychology "explores factors that make life worth living and the human strengths that enable individuals to confront challenges, appreciate others, and regard daily experiences as meaningful" (Dunn & Dougherty, 2005, p. 305). Positive coping as reflected in mood and life satisfaction ratings has been attributed to greater levels of hope (Elliott, Kurylo, & Rivera, 2002; Elliott, Witty, Herrick, & Hoffman, 1991), lower levels of neuroticism (Krause & Rohe, 1998), higher levels of agreeableness (Elliott, Kurylo, & Rivera, 2002), and an internal locus of control (Frank, Elliott, Corcoran, & Wonderlich, 1987). Individuals who preferentially seek control over their responses rather than rely on external events (Heckhausen & Schulz, 1995), look for positive aspects of their experiences (Tennen & Affleck, 2002), use optimism and positive appraisal (Taylor & Armor, 1996), or who rate highly on the dimension of hope (Snyder, Irving, & Anderson, 1991) report less subjective distress and more posi-

tive adaptation to disabling illness. There is a need to adopt models and practice patterns that accommodate positive psychological factors to facilitate adjustment and coping following physical trauma or illness (Elliott et al., 2002). Some of the leading individual coping models that have been postulated include the *crisis-coping model,* which postulates three styles of responding to situations including emotional-focused, problem-focused, and avoidant (Lindemann, 1994), the *behavioral model* (Kazdin, 2000), and the *social model* of disability (Olkin, 1999).

Theories related to adjustment to illness and disability have long emphasized the importance of appraisals in dealing with life stressors, and they suggest an association between personality traits and psychopathology. For example, *attributional style* refers to the characteristic way in which an individual explains causes of events. This has especially been associated with concepts of learned helplessness (Abramson, Seligman, & Teasdale, 1978) and the hopelessness theory of depression (Abramson, Metalsky, & Alloy, 1989). Research consistently shows that depressed individuals are shown to attribute negative outcomes or experiences to internal, stable, and global causes, whereas positive outcomes are attributed to external, unstable causes (Seligman, Abramson, Semmel, & von Baeyer, 1979).

NEUROLOGICALLY BASED PERSONALITY CHANGE

Personality changes are frequently reported among those with acquired injuries and illness such as traumatic brain injuries (TBIs), multiple sclerosis (Nelson Elder, Tehrani, & Groot, 2003), dementia (e.g., Jacomb et al., 2000), epilepsy (Gromov, Eroshina, & Mikhailov, 2006), and stroke (e.g., Stone et al., 2004). However, there is limited empirical evidence that neurocognitive disorders alter premorbid personality traits (Malec, Brown, & Moessner, 2004; Rush, Malec, Moessner, & Brown, 2004). Furthermore, studies have found limited support to suggest that pre-injury personality factors are associated with barriers to rehabilitation (Rush et al., 2004); premorbid personality has been proven difficult to assess, in part, because cognitive deficits may interfere with the capacity of the patient to provide an accurate and reliable self-assessment (Roche, Fleming, & Shum, 2002). Studies also show that patients rate themselves as more "normal" on personality inventories than do informants (Kurtz & Putnam, 2006). Another potential source of bias is associated with over-reliance on informant ratings. For example, hospital staff may minimize a patient's emotional distress, or more often, overestimate the degree of patient distress or psychopathology (Gans, 1981). Last, compromised mental health (e.g., depression, anxiety) among informants has been associated with increased perception of personality disruptions in patients (Jacomb et al., 2000; Stone et al., 2004).

Prigatano (1992) suggested that central nervous system injury can have both direct and indirect influences on personality disturbance. The former may result from damage to neuroanatomical structures associated with affective functioning (e.g., limbic system), neuropsychological deficits that affect personality and the emotional response (e.g., executive functions), neurotransmitter disturbances, and/or electrophysiological abnormalities (Dunn & Dougherty, 2005; Prigatano, 1992). Neurocognitive deficits can also indirectly affect psychological well-being by, for instance, limiting an individual's ability to participate in social and occupational roles, thus contributing to social isolation and depression (Prigatano, 1992).

Common behavioral and emotional changes associated with neurological illness or injury include irritability, emotional lability, lack of spontaneity, depression, and anxiety (Prigatano, 1992). Those with mild head injuries and those involved in litigation tend to have more elevated (i.e., pathological) profiles on personality measures than those with more severe head injuries and those not pursuing litigation (Youngjohn, Davis, & Wolf, 1997), which are widely believed to reflect preexisting personality traits and disorders. However, some studies have not found an association between personality traits and development of behavioral and emotional changes, despite theories that neurological illness may exacerbate premorbid personality characteristics (Tate, 1998).

In a longitudinal study with a random sample of elderly persons, there was a higher incidence of reported dysphoria, apathy, and suspiciousness in those with dementia compared with controls

(Jacomb et al., 2000). Personality changes were associated with the incidence of dementia and its progression; the addition of symptoms of stroke increased the likelihood of reported personality changes. Personality changes associated with stroke include reduced patience and confidence, increased frustration, more dissatisfaction, and a less easy-going nature (Stone et al., 2004), which the authors conceded may reflect features of depression, a common disturbance affecting as much as one half of patients with stroke (Kotila et al., 1998). Studies using personality inventories have yielded inconsistent results with regard to personality changes following the onset of a disability. In one study using monozygotic twins, no significant differences were found on the Neuroticism-Extroversion-Openness Personality Inventory, Revised (NEO-PI-R) between those with spinal cord injury (SCI) and their non-injured twin, suggesting that personality traits are robust even after a traumatic injury. It has been suggested that assessment of premorbid personality traits is helpful in predicting response to illness or injury. For instance, informant rated premorbid neuroticism on the NEO-PI-R was a significant predictor of depression for stroke patients (Storor & Byrne, 2006).

Depression is a major clinical problem in rehabilitation and is associated with decreased participation in rehabilitation therapies (Gillen, Tennen, McKee, Gernert-Dott, & Affleck, 2001), disruption in family relationships (Angeleri, Angeleri, Foschi, Giaquinto, & Nolfe, 1993), and increased risk of comorbid conditions. It is therefore important for the psychologist to differentiate between clinically significant depression, which would warrant treatment with medications or psychotherapy, and sadness or feelings of grief, which are situation appropriate and do not necessarily require intervention.

INFLUENCE ON INTERPERSONAL INTERACTIONS AND REHABILITATION SERVICES

In the acute rehabilitation setting, an individual's personality characteristics may shape the rehabilitation team's perception of the individual, influence the team's willingness to work with the individual, and/or interact with personality factors of their care providers to affect interaction style and quality. For instance, personality characteristics that are viewed by team members as negative (e.g., pessimism, catastrophic thinking) may result in the individual being perceived as unmotivated and unwilling to participate (Caplan & Shechter, 1993), thus resulting in alterations in rehabilitative care and possible early discharge from the acute setting.

Social support, particularly family social support, has been shown to be instrumental to the rehabilitation process. Rehabilitation outcome and adjustment to disability may depend not only on personality or psychological factors but also on their interaction with the level of external support (Kendell, Saxby, Farrow, & Naisby, 2001). Personality characteristics may influence the extent to which an individual will self-advocate and require enhanced structure and social supports. Those with personality styles that are proactive and resilient may cope more effectively with illness and be less reliant on external supports. However, even for those who face disability with resilience and growth, social barriers such as stigma, limited resources, or poor accessibility may threaten adjustment to disability, for instance, by hindering community reintegration. Thus, even for those persons with adaptive personality styles, psychological interventions must exist at multiple levels, including the individual, social (i.e., family, treatment team), societal, and political levels (Olkin & Pledger, 2003). In addition, following onset of disability, social–environmental factors may shape the individual's personality (e.g., affecting optimism) and psychological or personal characteristics, such as resilience, hope, and personal values (Olkin & Pledger, 2003).

PSYCHOPATHOLOGY AND REHABILITATION

Psychopathology has an even greater potential than personality traits for interfering with rehabilitation activities. Major psychiatric illness (e.g., affective, anxiety, somatoform disorders) can influence both responses to physical disability and one's ability to cope with psychosocial and physical changes. Schizophrenia and other psychotic disorders are associated with poor insight, judgment, and perception, as well as the possibility of diminished cognitive functioning that would impede learning of new skills and behaviors. Persons with psychotic disorders may not fully understand the limitations or new needs imposed by a physical illness or disability or may have diminished motivation, and are therefore at greater risk of noncompliance, unsafe behavior, medical complications, and diminished benefit from rehabilitation. Problems with emotional regulation and thought disturbances associated with psychotic disorders can also affect communication with staff and compromise engagement in the rehabilitation process. As previously stated, disability may carry a greater risk of psychological distress, though disability should not be viewed as synonymous with psychopathology. We first consider personality disorders and then Axis I psychopathology.

The *DSM–IV–TR* defines a *personality disorder* as an "inner experience and behavior that deviates markedly from the expectations of the individual's culture, is pervasive and inflexible, has an onset in adolescence or early adulthood, is stable over time, and leads to distress or impairment" (p. 630). Inherent in this definition is the nature of inflexible or maladaptive beliefs, attitudes, and perceptions that adversely affect our functional abilities or cause us significant personal distress. The disturbance must be consistent across a broad range of situations, be stable and of long duration, and cannot be due to another mental illness, medical condition, or the direct physiological effects of a substance. The *DSM–IV–TR* has several shortcomings. It is atheoretical, fails to account for subclinical characteristics, and does not describe personality except to infer the presence of personality disorders in persons who experience adverse impact because of their behavior. The greatest contribution of the *DSM–IV–TR* is that it has become an efficient method for communication among clinicians and third-party payers.

In addition to personality disorders, some individuals with rehabilitation needs have other types of psychopathology. Although the prevalence of mood and cognitive comorbidities in rehabilitation populations is often advanced as the rationale for inclusion of psychological care in rehabilitation, clinicians must be aware that (a) many individuals with physical impairments do not develop mood disturbances or other psychological symptoms, (b) most do not develop major psychiatric disorders, and (c) professionals are likely to overestimate the level of mood disturbances in persons with disability (Frank et al., 1987). The rates of these symptoms and conditions vary depending on the sample and criteria used, though they are higher in rehabilitation populations than the general population.

Common symptoms and their prevalence rates include depression (10%–61%) and anxiety (5%–30%) following stroke (Carson et al., 2000; Warlow et al., 2001); depression (22%–40%) and anxiety disorders (25%–60%; Elliott & Frank, 1996; Fullerton, Harvey, Klein, & Howell, 1981; Kennedy & Rogers, 2000) following SCI; depression after lower extremity amputation (20%–35%; Kashani, Frank, Kashani, Wonderlich, & Reid, 1983; Rybarczyk et al., 1992); and psychiatric symptomatology, including depression, anxiety, and behavioral disturbance following TBI (30%–80%; Fann et al., 2004; Jorge et al., 2004). These rates reflect a range of psychological distress responses and are not indicative of the percentage of individuals who would meet the diagnostic criteria for the formal disorder.

Substance abuse is a significant problem in persons with TBI and SCI (Fann et al., 2004; Heinemann, Schnoll, Brandt, Maltz, & Keen, 1988). Psychological distress and disorders are often accompanied by cognitive impairments of varying severity, reflecting that both affect and intellect are subserved by brain integrity. Cognitive impairments are found in 24% to 60% of patients with stroke (Desmond, Moroney, Sano, & Stern, 2002) and 25% to 60% of patients with acute traumatic SCI (Davidoff, Roth, & Richards, 1992; Roth et al., 1989).

Somatization occurs when psychological distress is expressed in the form of physical symptoms (Lipowski, 1987). Somatoform disorders often arise in the rehabilitation setting, including somatization disorder, conversion disorder, hypochondriasis, and body dysmorphic disorder. These conditions all present with an alteration or loss of a physical function suggestive of a medical disorder, but by definition the symptoms cannot be fully explained physiologically or traced to a specific physical cause. Conversion disorder is a specific form of somatization in which the patient presents with symptoms and signs that are confined to the central nervous system; thus, the somatoform disorder is most frequently seen in rehabilitation settings (Lazare, 1981). By definition, symptoms in a conversion reaction are related to severe stress, emotional conflict, and/or an associated psychiatric disorder. Many studies confirm high incidence of depression and anxiety in patients with conversion disorder and as many as half of these patients have comorbid personality disorders (Guze, Woodruff, & Clayton, 1971; Lipowski, 1990). The degree of impairment in these disorders is often significant and interferes with daily activities. Prolonged loss of function may produce complications such as muscle atrophy or joint contractures (Mace & Trimble, 1996).

ASSESSMENT OF PERSONALITY FUNCTIONING AND PSYCHOPATHOLOGY

Information about the patient's psychological characteristics, both premorbid and postmorbid, is a critical part of the rehabilitation psychology assessment and integral to planning interventions. No information is more important than the clinical interview because of its utility in identifying relevant history and subtle changes in behavior that are most noticeable to the patient and their family members. The patient's history can be collected from a number of sources. If available, the patient's medical chart may provide important clues about issues pertaining to personality and psychopathology. For example, repeated notations about patient–staff conflicts are common when these issues are present (Caplan & Reidy, 1996). Certain aspects of the patient's history are best collected from the patient through a structured interview that includes specific questions regarding his or her psychiatric history; previous experience with stressful life events; and relationships with friends, family members, and health care providers. The quality of the information collected from the patient depends on his or her reliability. Patients with cognitive impairments, apathy, poor motivation, denial, or unawareness of deficits are less likely to be reliable informants (Prigatano & Klonoff, 1998; Roche et al., 2002). Because many factors could affect a patient's self-reported history, collateral sources, particularly the patient's past psychiatric history, should be used whenever they are available as alternative sources of information. Collateral sources are also frequently the only source of information concerning possible changes in psychological functioning or personality.

Behavioral observations are another important source of information about a patient's functioning. Indicators of insight, judgment, reasoning, and affective regulation can all provide evidence of psychosis and/or psychopathology. The interaction style with the examiner and reports about themes of conflict with others, especially family members and care providers, can provide important indications about personality disorders, affective disorders, and/or behavioral problems secondary to neurocognitive impairments. In sum, behavioral data provide an important context for evaluating objective information and can serve as an important ancillary source of qualitative information about personality functioning and psychopathology.

A prerequisite for interpreting assessment data is a high degree of confidence that the patient was not feigning or exaggerating his or her complaints and was putting forth his or her best effort. It is important to note that diminished motivation does not necessarily reflect intentional misrepresentation but may stem from pain, fatigue, depression, or other factors. Assessment of effort is also important for differential diagnosis because neurologically based impairments may resemble unmotivated performance. Several standardized neuropsychological instruments designed specifically for assessing motivation are now routinely administered as a means of identifying dissimulation across a broad range of nonneuropsychological domains, such as pain and chronic fatigue. Some examples include the Word Memory Test (Green, Iverson, & Allen, 1999), Test of Memory Malingering (Tombaugh, 1996), and the Victoria Symptom Validity Test (Slick, Hopp, Strauss, & Spellacy, 1995).

One of the major goals of the clinical interview and history is to assess the consistency of the available information. Specifically, a provider should evaluate consistency between the patient's presenting complaints and (a) the clinician or another health care provider's behavioral observations, (b) observations from family members or other collateral sources,

(c) performance on standardized psychological and neuropsychological measures, (d) characteristics that are typical of the presumed etiology, (e) impairment in activities of daily living, and (f) temporal consistency in presentation and complaints over time. When discrepancies arise, it is important to determine the magnitude of those discrepancies and their putative cause. Impaired awareness due to cognitive deficits and/or neurological insults and distorted perceptions associated with personality disorders or other forms of mental illness are common explanatory factors.

INTERPRETIVE ISSUES IN REHABILITATION POPULATIONS

As previously described, assessment of premorbid adaptation and personality can assist the clinician in identifying an individual's level of risk of psychosocial problems and poor health outcomes, as well as in identifying adaptive traits (e.g., coping styles) that can be useful in promoting positive coping and adjustment. It is assumed that psychologists will use instruments with established psychometric properties and normative data critical for interpretation; however, there are a number of caveats and shortcomings common to all measures of personality and psychopathology that can influence interpretation of assessment measures in rehabilitation populations.

First of all, emotional states can affect test results and should therefore be assessed as part of a psychological or neuropsychological evaluation. Assessment of premorbid emotional disorders allows one to consider their impact on test interpretation, especially because emotional states have been consistently linked to increased distractibility and fatigue that may influence test performance or responding. Another issue pertains to the construct and population-specific validity of the measure with the population being assessed. The available normative data may need to be applied with caution when evaluating individuals with various physical and/or neurological disabilities because the data may not be population-specific. There have been limited validation studies using most common measures of personality and psychopathology with rehabilitation populations. Although a number of measures may be useful for assessing personality and psycho-pathology in normative populations, they may be of more limited value in rehabilitation settings or with persons with disabilities, both in terms of their validation for the purpose for which the measure was intended and in terms of the availability of normative data representative of the population being evaluated. With rehabilitation populations, threats to validity can be caused by an excessive length of administration and the potential impact of fatigue, the self-report nature of most measures and their interaction with cognitive impairments such as memory difficulty or diminished insight, and the invalidity caused by administering the measure to persons with physical and sensory impairments (i.e., nearly all measures are validated using populations with intact sensory and motor abilities).

Last, content validity may also be lacking for rehabilitation populations. Some studies have shown elevations on specific scales among those with various physical and cognitive disabilities, but these elevations may reflect the significant physical or neurological impairments these patients face rather than a pathological response or change in personality traits. As evidence of this concern, many inventories contain physical and cognitive items that are presumed to reflect psychopathology but that are also associated with various medical conditions. A patient's endorsement of these items may carry a different diagnostic meaning than would be the case for physically healthy individuals (Woessner & Caplan, 1996). This can result in artificially inflated estimates of incidence and severity of psychopathology (Nyenhuis et al., 1995). Thus, available normative data may need to be applied with caution to individuals with various physical or other disabilities because of the potential for "overpathologizing" some patient populations.

COMMON ASSESSMENT MEASURES

A description of commonly used measures of personality and psychopathology are summarized in the remainder of the text and are listed in Table 12.1. We have made no attempt to be exhaustive with regard to the tests we have listed or the plethora of validation issues that have been raised about each.

Rather, we have attempted to provide the reader with a sampling of some of the personality, depression, and anxiety and somatic functioning measures in common use and to highlight some of the psychometric issues that have been reported in the literature.

Personality Measures

The Millon Clinical Multiaxial Inventory-III (MCMI-III; Millon, Millon, & Davis, 1997) is a self-report measure designed primarily to assess personality disorders (i.e., maladaptive patterns of personality traits and behavior). The MCMI-III consists of 175 true/false items making up 24 clinical scales and 3 "modifier" scales (i.e., disclosure, desirability, debasement) aimed at patients' tendencies to distort the truth. It is relatively brief, can be completed in 20 to 30 minutes, and requires only an 8th-grade reading level. Although the MCMI-III is designed to provide diagnostic information consistent with the *Diagnostic and Statistical Manual of Mental Disorders* (4th ed.; American Psychiatric Association, 1994) criteria for Axis I and Axis II disorders, it may have limited utility in a rehabilitation setting because of its emphasis on psychopathology as opposed to normal personality variants and the relative neglect of adaptive patterns of coping. In addition, there have been few validation studies using the MCMI-III with rehabilitation populations; a search revealed no literature published since 2000 using the MCMI-II with rehabilitation populations. Thus, although it remains popular as a research tool among those studying psychopathology and a useful tool for evaluating known or suspected Axis II disorders, it has limited utility for other patient populations.

The Minnesota Multiphasic Personality Inventory-2 (MMPI-2; Butcher, Dahlstrom, Graham, Tellegen, & Kaemer, 1989) is a self-report measure used primarily for the identification of psychopathology, but it has been applied in the analysis of normal personality patterns as well as patterns of behavior and coping relevant to specific conditions, such as chronic pain. The MMPI-2 consists of 567 true or false items written at about a 7th-grade reading level, which make up 10 clinical scales as well as 3 validity scales. The short form comprises the first 370 items and provides information for those who would like the results of primary clinical scales but are willing to

TABLE 12.1

Common Measures for Personality and Psychopathological Conditions

Type of measure	Common measures	Strengths	Weaknesses	Recent examples of populations studied
Personality and psychopathology	MCMI-III	Rapid and easy administration; useful diagnostic tool for psychopathology; superior for assessing personality disorders	Lack of norms for persons with disabilities; questionable utility in rehabilitation setting	None applicable since 2000
	MMPI-2	Extensively researched; useful for assessing personality, psychopathology, and validity of symptom reports	Limited norms for persons with disabilities; very lengthy; administration limitations; questionable utility with neurological samples	Pain (Fishbain et al., 2006) MS (Nelson, Elder, Tehrani, & Groot, 2003) TBI (Lachapelle & Alfano, 2005) SCI (Barncord & Wanlass, 2000)
	PAI	Valid for assessment of psychopathology symptoms, personality traits, interpersonal problems	Long; lack of norms for rehabilitation populations	Pain (Karlin et al., 2005) TBI (Demakis et al., 2007)
	NEO-PI	Measures broad categories of maladaptive and adaptive personality types	Limited clinical utility	TBI (Rush, Malec, Brown, & Moessner, 2006) SCI (Krause & Rohe, 1998)
	16PF	Measures both maladaptive and adaptive personality traits	Utility of theoretical dimensions in rehabilitation populations are not well studied	None applicable since 2000
Depression	BDI-II	Brief screening for depression	Confusing for those with cognitive impairments; somatic complaints may be attributed to depression	Pain (Poole, Bramwell, & Murphy, 2006)
	CES-D	Brief screening for depression	Confusing for those with cognitive impairments; somatic complaints may be attributed to depression	TBI (McCauley et al., 2006) Arthritis (Martens et al., 2006)
	GDS	Brief screening for depression; yes and no format; devoid of somatic and sexual functioning items	Response bias possible	Stroke (Creed, Swanwick, & O'Neill, 2004) Pain (Mossey & Gallagher, 2004) Amputation (Schubert, Burns, Paras, & Sioson, 1992)
	SIDI	Brief measure of depression; validated for stroke population; yes and no format	Primarily applicable to hospitalized patients with acute stroke, limited validation	Stroke (Rybarczyk et al., 1996)
Anxiety and somatic functioning	BAI	Brief screening for anxiety	Somatic complaints attributed to anxiety	None Applicable Since 2000
	SCL-90-R	Relatively short; particularly well-suited for somatoform disorders	Limited capacity to detect exaggeration; may view somatic symptoms as pathological	SCI (Tate, Kewman, & Maynard, 1990) TBI (Palav & McCaffrey, 2001)
	BSI	Useful for identifying level of distress and quality of life	Limited capacity to detect exaggeration; may view somatic symptoms as pathological	SCI (Tate et al., 1990) (Scherer & Cushman, 2001) Pain (Geisser, Perna, Kirsch, & Bachman,1998)

Note. BAI = Beck Anxiety Inventory; BDI-II = Beck Depression Inventory-II; BSI = Brief Symptom Inventory; CES-D = Center for Epidemiologic Studies Depression Scale; GDS = Geriatric Depression Scale; MCMI-III = Millon Clinical Multiaxial Inventory-III; MMPI-II = Minnesota Multiphasic Personality Inventory-2; NEO-PI = Neuroticism, Extroversion, and Openness Personality Inventory; PAI = Personality Assessment Inventory; SCL-90-R = Symptoms Check List-90-R; SIDI = Stroke Inpatient Depression Inventory; 16PF= Sixteen Personality Factor Questionnaire.

forgo the many available specialty subscales. The measure was developed using a rational empirical scale construction strategy that involved identification of items sensitive to specific clinical populations. Administration time is quite variable but often takes up to several hours. Although well-established, the MMPI-2 is quite lengthy and difficult to adapt for people with physical or sensory impairments, although an audiotaped version exists for those who are unable to read the test questions. For those with physical or neurological disabilities, spurious elevations can occur on scales that have items reflecting somatic complaints and neurologically relevant responses (Gass, 1996). Several authors have developed correction procedures that have been examined in an attempt to improve the validity of the MMPI-2 for use with persons with disabilities, including those with neurological conditions (Barncord & Wanlass, 2000; Gass, 1996). The MMPI-2 does have the advantage of having been studied and validated with a number of special populations, including groups thought of as traditional rehabilitation populations, such as patients with chronic pain (Fishbain et al., 2006), multiple sclerosis (Nelson et al., 2003), TBI (Lachapelle & Alfano, 2005), and SCI (Barncord & Wanlass, 2000).

The Personality Assessment Inventory (PAI; Morey, 1991) is a self-report measure of personality and psychopathology similar to the MMPI-2. The PAI consists of 344 items measuring 22 scales that assess a range of psychopathology symptoms, personality traits, interpersonal problems, and treatment indicators. It also includes validity scales. This self-administered instrument takes about 40 to 50 minutes to complete and demands only a 6th-grade reading level. Items are rated on a 4-point scale from *false* to *very true*. A short form consists of the first 160 items of the longer form. Although there have been limited studies using the PAI within a rehabilitation setting, there is some evidence that the factor structure found in initial development studies is robust, for instance, in those with chronic pain (Karlin et al., 2005) and TBI (Demakis et al., 2007). Similar to the MMPI-2, elevations occur on clinical scales of the PAI (e.g., Somatic Complaints, Depression) reflecting behavioral and cognitive symptoms common in patients with varying TBI

severity but that do not necessarily reflect psychopathology. For example, questions about fatigue may represent a physiological characteristic as opposed to symptoms of depression in a person with recent TBI.

The Neuroticism, Extroversion, and Openness Personality Inventory (NEO-PI; Costa & McCrae, 1992) and Sixteen Personality Factor Questionnaire (16PF; Castillo, Starkstein, Fedoroff, Price, & Robinson, 1993) measure both maladaptive and adaptive personality traits, which have particular relevance to rehabilitation given the interest in positive and adaptive traits and coping. The NEO-PI consists of 181 items rated on a 5-point scale (i.e., *strongly disagree* to *strongly agree*) that measure trait aspects of personality based on the FFM (i.e., extroversion, neuroticism, openness to experience, conscientiousness, agreeableness). Unlike measures designed to assess only pathology states, this instrument can assist in identifying personality factors that may predict how well an individual will cope with a stressful event. For instance, *neuroticism* refers to a disposition consistent with emotional instability, negative affectivity, and maladaptive coping, whereas *extroversion* refers more to a propensity for positive affectivity, interpersonal interaction, and stimulation.

The 16PF consists of 128 forced-choice response items measuring 16 primary normal personality characteristics and 5 second-order dimensions similar to the NEO-PI FFM. Although the 16PF has been shown to be psychometrically adequate for use with persons with various physical disabilities, the utility of theoretical dimensions of the instrument in rehabilitation populations has not been well studied.

Depression Measures

In addition to the clinical interview, several inventories can assist the psychologist in the diagnosis of depression. These include the Beck Depression Inventory-II (BDI-II; Beck, Steer & Brown, 1996), the Center for Epidemiological Studies Depression Scale (CES-D; Radloff, 1977); and the Geriatric Depression Scale (GDS; Jamison & Scogin, 1992), which is designed specifically for older adults. The Stroke Inpatient Depression Inventory (SIDI; Rybarczyk, Winemiller, Lazarus, Haut, & Hartman,

1996) was designed specifically to assess depressive symptoms in stroke patients. These paper and pencil tests can be self-administered or presented by an examiner orally. All of these measures are relatively brief, they have the ability to quickly and efficiently screen for depressive and anxiety symptoms, and can be included in a standard clinical evaluation with ease.

However, there are several significant limitations of which one should be aware in working with depression inventories, which are probably more aptly conceptualized as depression screening measures. First, many of the measures use a multipoint rating scale that allows for qualitative ratings, which can be difficult for cognitively impaired patients to complete (Bedard et al., 2003). The GDS and SIDI use a yes and no format, which greatly simplifies the communicative and cognitive demands. Secondly, these measures are prone to response biases, such as minimization or exaggeration of symptoms (Hunt, Auriemma, & Cashara, 2003). Finally, as previously described, spurious ratings can be obtained because many contain somatic symptoms (e.g., fatigue, sleep disturbance, loss of interest) that are common in both patients with depression and those with medical conditions (Callahan, Kaplan, & Pincus, 1991; Turk & Okifuji, 1994), which may cause overestimates of depression (Buckley, Parker, & Heggie, 2001). Support for the importance of somatic items on depression measures comes from a recent factor analysis of four common depression measures, the Beck, CES-D, Hamilton (1960), and Zung (1965) by Shafer (2006), who found two factors across measures: a general depression severity factor and a somatic factor. The implication is that the depression severity factor is likely to have greater validity in many medical populations than the somatic factor.

Anxiety and Somatic Functioning Measures

Anxiety is a common reaction to new onset impairments and hospitalization. Early identification and treatment of anxiety is important for ensuring maximal benefit from rehabilitation efforts, and avoiding unnecessary suffering. Several brief tests for assessing anxiety include the Beck Anxiety Inventory (Beck & Steer, 1990) and the Anxiety subscales of the Symptoms Check List-90-R (SCL-90-R; Derogatis, 1992; Derogatis, Lipman, & Covi, 1973) and the

Brief Symptom Inventory (BSI; Derogatis & Melisaratos, 1983). In addition, there are measures that assess psychological distress across a variety of dimensions. The SCL-90-R consists of 90 items (rated on a 5-point scale for symptoms) and 9 clinical scales measuring a variety of symptom clusters, including somatization, obsessive–compulsive tendencies, interpersonal sensitivity, depression, anxiety, hostility, phobic anxiety, paranoid ideation, and psychoticism. Three measures of global distress based on overall item responses reflect the breadth and severity of the problems reported. The BSI is an abbreviated 53-item version that measures the same 9 subscales as the SCL-90-R. BSI norms for persons with SCI have been developed (Scherer & Cushman, 2001). An even shorter version of the BSI, with only 18 items (BSI-18) has recently been used to measure distress in medical patients (Derogatis, 1993). However, BSI may not be an equivalent abbreviation of the SCL-90, as reports of psychological distress were significantly different on these two measures among SCI patients (Tate, Kewman, & Maynard, 1990).

These measures suffer from many of the same flaws as other measures of personality and psychopathology, namely, their lack of validation with a wide array of rehabilitation populations and their inability to differentiate symptoms (e.g., somatic ills) associated with psychopathology from those that are common in disabling medical conditions. For example, it may be expected for a patient with TBI to have occasional headaches, but some measures may interpret reports of headaches as an indication of anxiety or difficulties managing stress.

SUMMARY

Personality factors and psychopathology play an important role in rehabilitation, and there exists empirical support linking these factors with quality of life and positive health outcomes following injury and illness. Understanding the structure and manifestations of an individual's personality, and assessing psychopathology, are vital parts of rehabilitation psychology assessments and are likely to result in more successful interventions through identification of both assets and challenges faced by patients.

There are a variety of objective measures available for assessment of personality constructs and psychopathology. However, although they are objective in how they are administered and scored, they are not objective in the way they are interpreted. Each measure is associated with strengths but also with weaknesses, such as limited validation with rehabilitation populations. Qualitative measures, such as behavioral observations and clinical interviews with patients and family members, have their place and can provide useful information. Future efforts in this area may find it fruitful to focus more on standardized assessments for family member informants. History gathering to include the use of collateral sources, behavioral observations, and the use of objective and standardized measures should be considered a standard of care for any comprehensive assessment. The primary goal is always to obtain a consensus among these diverse pieces of data or to explain why a coherent picture is lacking.

The limitations of unidimensional diagnostic categories have been apparent for some time, and there has been a greater appreciation in recent years for a multidimensional approach to describing personality and psychopathology. Despite decades of research, relatively little is known about the clinical implications of personality and psychopathology for patients and their family members during rehabilitation. It seems clear that we are in need of translational research that focuses on the clinical implications of personality and psychopathology data and their potential for tailoring treatment programs to optimize rehabilitation outcomes.

References

Abramson, L. Y., Metalsky, F. L., & Alloy, L. B. (1989). Hopelessness depression: A theory-based subtype of depression. *Psychological Review, 96,* 358–372.

Abramson, L. Y., Seligman, M. E. P., & Teasdale, J. D. (1978). Learned helplessness in humans: Critique and reformulation. *Journal of Abnormal Psychology, 87,* 32–48.

Alfano, D. P., Neilson, P. M., & Fink, M. P. (1994). Sources of stress in family members following head or spinal cord injury. *Applied Neuropsychology, 1,* 57–62.

American Psychiatric Association. (1994). *Diagnostic and statistical manual of mental disorders* (4th ed.). Washington, DC: Author.

American Psychiatric Association. (2000). *Diagnostic and statistical manual of mental disorders* (4th ed., text rev.). Washington, DC: Author.

Angeleri, F., Angeleri, V. A., Foschi, N., Giaquinto, S., & Nolfe, G. (1993). The influence of depression, social activity, and family stress on functional outcome after stroke. *Stroke, 24,* 1478–1483.

Anson, K., & Ponsford, J. (2006). Coping and emotional adjustment following traumatic brain injury. *Journal of Head Trauma Rehabilitation, 21,* 248–259.

Barncord, S., & Wanlass, R. (2000). A correction procedure for the Minnesota Multiphasic Personality Inventory-2 for persons with spinal cord injury. *Archives of Physical Medicine and Rehabilitation, 81,* 1185–1190.

Beck, A. T., & Steer, R. (1990). *Beck Anxiety Inventory manual.* San Antonio, TX: Psychological Corporation.

Beck, A. T., Steer, R. A., & Brown, G. K. (1996). *Manual for the Beck Depression Inventory* (2nd ed.). San Antonio, TX: Psychological Corporation.

Bedard, M., Malloy, D. W., Squire, L., Mithorn-Biggs, M. D., Dubois, S., Lever, J. A., & O'Donnell, M. (2003). Validity of self-reports in dementia research: The Geriatric Depression Scale. *Clinical Gerontologist, 26,* 155–163.

Buckley, T. C., Parker, J. D., & Heggie, J. (2001). A psychometric evaluation of the BDI-II in treatment-seeking substance abusers. *Journal of Substance Abuse Treatment, 20,* 197–204.

Buer, N., & Linton, S. J. (2002). Fear-avoidance beliefs and catastrophizing: Occurrence and risk factor in back pain and ADL in the general population. *Pain, 99,* 485–491.

Butcher, J. N., Dahlstrom, W. G., Graham, J. R., Tellegen, A., & Kaemmer, B. (1989). *The Minnesota Multiphasic Personality Inventory-2 (MMPI-2): Manual for administration and scoring.* Minneapolis, MN: University of Minnesota Press.

Callahan, L., Kaplan, M., & Pincus, T. (1991). The Beck Depression Inventory, Center for Epidemiological Studies Depression Scale (CES-D), and General Well-Being Schedule Depression Subscale in rheumatoid arthritis. *Arthritis Care and Research, 4,* 3–11.

Caplan, B., & Reidy, K. (1996). Staff–patient–family conflicts in rehabilitation: Sources and solutions. *Topics in Spinal Cord Injury, 2,* 21–33.

Caplan, B., & Shechter, J. (1993). Reflections on the "depressed," "unrealistic," "inappropriate," "manipulative," "unmotivated," "noncompliant," "denying," "maladjusted," "regressed," etc. patient. *Archives of Physical Medicine and Rehabilitation, 74,* 1123–1124.

Carson, A. J., MacHale, S., Allen, K., Lawrie, S. M., Dennis, M., House, A., et al. (2000). Depression after stroke and lesion location: A systematic review. *The Lancet, 356,* 122–126.

Castillo, C. S., Starkstein, S. E., Fedoroff, J. P., Price, T. R., & Robinson, R. G. (1993). Generalized anxiety disorder after stroke. *Journal of Nervous and Mental Disease, 181,* 100–106.

Costa, P. T., & McCrae, R. R. (1992). Four ways five factors are basic. *Personality and Individual Differences, 13,* 653–665.

Creed, A., Swanwick, G., & O'Neill, D. (2004). Screening for post stroke depression in patients with acute stroke including those with communication disorders. *International Journal of Geriatric Psychiatry, 19,* 595–597.

Davidoff, G. N., Roth, E. J., & Richards, J. S. (1992). Cognitive deficits in spinal cord injury: Epidemiology and outcome. *Archives of Physical Medicine and Rehabilitation, 73,* 275–284.

Demakis, G., Hammond, F., Knotts, A., Cooper, D., Clement, P., Kennedy, J., et al. (2007). The Personality Assessment Inventory in individuals with traumatic brain injury. *Archives of Clinical Neuropsychology, 22,* 123–130.

Dembo, T., Leviton, G. L., & Wright, B. A. (1956). Adjustment to misfortune: A problem of social–psychological rehabilitation. *Artificial Limbs, 3*(2), 4–62.

Derogatis, L. R. (1992). *SCL-90-R. Administration, scoring and procedures manual II.* Baltimore: Clinical Psychometric Research.

Derogatis, L. R. (1993). *The Brief Symptom Inventory (BSI): Administration, scoring, and procedures manual* (3rd ed.). Minneapolis, MN: National Computer Systems.

Derogatis, L. R., Lipman, R. S., & Covi, L. (1973). SCL-90, an outpatient psychiatric rating scale-preliminary report. *Psychopharmacology Bulletin, 9,* 13–28.

Derogatis, L. R., & Melisaratos, N. (1983). The Brief Symptom Inventory: An introductory report. *Psychological Medicine, 13,* 595–605.

Desmond, D. W., Moroney, J. T., Sano, M., & Stern, Y. (2002). Incidence of dementia after ischemic stroke: Results of a longitudinal study. *Stroke, 33,* 2254–2260.

Dodwell, D. (1988). The heterogeneity of social outcome following head injury. *Journal of Neurology, Neurosurgery, and Psychiatry, 51,* 833–838.

Dunn, D., & Dougherty, S. (2005). Prospects for a positive psychology of rehabilitation. *Rehabilitation Psychology, 50,* 305–311.

Elliott, T. (2002). Defining our common ground to reach new horizons. *Rehabilitation Psychology, 47,* 131–143.

Elliott, T., Bush, B., & Chen, Y. (2006). Social problem-solving abilities predict pressure sore occurrence in the first 3 years of spinal cord injury. *Rehabilitation Psychology, 51,* 69–77.

Elliott, T. R., & Frank, R. G. (1996). Depression following spinal cord injury. *Archives of Physical Medicine and Rehabilitation, 77,* 816–823.

Elliott, T., Kurylo, M., & Rivera, P. (2002). Positive growth following acquired physical disability. In C. R. Snyder & S. Lopez (Eds.), *Handbook of positive psychology* (pp. 687–699). Oxford, England: Oxford University Press.

Elliott, T. R., Witty, T. E., Herrick, S., & Hoffman, J. T. (1991). Negotiating reality after physical loss: Hope, depression, and disability. *Journal of Personality and Social Psychology, 61,* 608–613.

Fann, J. R., Burington, B., Leonetti, A., Jaffe, K., Katon, W. J., & Thompson, R. S. (2004). Psychiatric illness following traumatic brain injury in an adult health maintenance organization population. *Archives of General Psychiatry, 61,* 53–61.

Fauerbach, J., Lawrence, J., Bryant, A., & Smith, J. (2002). The relationship of ambivalent coping to depression symptoms and adjustment. *Rehabilitation Psychology, 47,* 387–401.

Fishbain, D., Cole, B., Cutler, R., Lewis, J., Rosomoff, H., & Rosomoff, R. (2006). Chronic pain and the measurement of personality: Do states influence traits? *Pain Medicine, 7,* 509–529.

Frank, R. G., Elliott, T. R., Corcoran, J., & Wonderlich, S. (1987). Depression after spinal cord injury: Is it necessary? *Clinical Psychology Review, 7,* 611–630.

Fullerton, D. T., Harvey, R. F., Klein, M. H., & Howell, T. (1981). Psychiatric disorders in patients with spinal cord injuries. *Archives of General Psychiatry, 38,* 1369–1371.

Gans, J. S. (1981). Depression diagnosis in a rehabilitation hospital. *Archives of Physical Medicine and Rehabilitation, 62,* 386–389.

Gass, C. S. (1996). MMPI-2 interpretation and stroke: Cross-validation of a correction factor. *Journal of Clinical Psychology, 52,* 569–572.

Geisser, M., Perna, R., Kirsch, N., & Bachman, J. E. (1998). Classification of chronic pain patients with the Brief Symptom Inventory: Patient characteristics of cluster profiles. *Rehabilitation Psychology, 43,* 313–326.

Gillen, R., Tennen, H., McKee, T. E., Gernert-Dott, P., & Affleck, G. (2001). Depressive symptoms and history of depression predict rehabilitation efficiency in stroke patients. *Archives of Physical Medicine and Rehabilitation, 82,* 1645–1649.

Green, P., Iverson, G., & Allen, L. (1999). Detecting malingering in head injury litigation with the Word Memory Test. *Brain Injury, 13,* 813–819.

Gromov, S. A., Eroshina, E. S., & Mikhailov, V. A. (2006). Medical rehabilitation and quality of life in patients with temporal lobe epilepsy. *International Journal of Mental Health, 34,* 19–30.

Guze, S., Woodruff, R., & Clayton, P. (1971). A study of conversion symptoms in psychiatric outpatients. *American Journal of Psychiatry, 128,* 643–346.

Hamilton, M. (1960). A rating scale for depression. *Journal of Neurology, Neurosurgery, and Psychiatry, 23,* 56–62.

Hanson, S., Buckelew, S. P., Hewett, J., & O'Neal, G. (1993). The relationship between coping and adjustment after spinal cord injury: A 5-year follow-up study. *Rehabilitation Psychology, 7,* 41–52.

Heckhausen, J., & Schulz, R. (1995). A life-span theory of control. *Psychological Review, 102,* 284–304.

Heinemann, A. W., Schnoll, S., Brandt, M., Maltz, R., & Keen, M. (1988). Toxicology screening in acute spinal cord injury. *Alcoholism Clinical and Experimental Research, 12,* 815–819.

Hunt, M., Auriemma, J., & Cashara, A. C. (2003). Self-report bias and underreporting of depression on the BDI-II. *Journal of Personality Assessment, 80,* 26–30.

Jacomb, P. A., Jorm, A. F., Korten, A. E., Christensen, H., Rodgers, B., & Henderson, A. S. (2000). Factors associated with informant-related personality problems in an elderly population. *Aging and Mental Health, 4,* 36–42.

Jamison, C., & Scogin, F. (1992). Development of an interview-based geriatric depression rating scale. *International Journal of Aging and Human Development, 35,* 193–204.

Jorge, R. E., Robinson, R. G., Moser, D., Tateno, A., Crespo-Facorro, B., & Arndt, S. (2004). Major depression following traumatic brain injury. *Archives of General Psychiatry, 61,* 42–50.

Karlin, B., Creech, S., Grimes, J., Clark, T., Meagher, M., & Morey, L. (2005). The Personality Assessment Inventory with chronic pain patients: Psychometric properties and clinical utility. *Journal of Clinical Psychology, 61,* 1571–1585.

Kashani, J. H., Frank, R. G., Kashani, S. R., Wonderlich, S. A., & Reid, J. C. (1983). Depression among amputees. *Journal of Clinical Psychiatry, 44,* 256–258.

Kazdin, A. E. (2000). *Behavior modification in applied settings* (6th ed.). Belmont, CA: Wadsworth.

Kendell, K., Saxby, B., Farrow, M., & Naisby, C. (2001). Psychological factors associated with short-term recovery from total knee replacement. *British Journal of Health Psychology, 6,* 41–52.

Kennedy, P. C., Marsh, N., Lowe, R., Grey, N., Short, E., & Rogers, B. (2000). A longitudinal analysis of psychological impact and coping strategies following spinal cord injury. *British Journal of Health Psychology, 34,* 627–639.

Kennedy, P., & Rogers, B. A. (2000). Anxiety and depression after spinal cord injury: A longitudinal analysis. *Archives of Physical Medicine and Rehabilitation, 81,* 932–937.

King, C., & Kennedy, P. (1999). Coping effectiveness training for people with spinal cord injury: Preliminary results of a controlled trial. *British Journal of Clinical Psychology, 38,* 5–14.

Kotila, M., Numminen, H., Waltimo, O., & Kaste, M. (1998). Depression after stroke. Results of the Finnstroke study. *Stroke, 29,* 368–372.

Krause, J., & Rohe, D. (1998). Personality and life adjustment after spinal cord injury: An exploratory study. *Rehabilitation Psychology, 43,* 118–130.

Kurtz, J., & Putnam, S. (2006). Patient–informant agreement on personality ratings and self-awareness after head injury. *The Clinical Neuropsychologist, 20,* 453–468.

Lachapelle, D., & Alfano, D. (2005). Revised Neurobehavioral Scales of the MMPI: Sensitivity and specificity in traumatic brain injury. *Applied Neuropsychology, 12,* 143–150.

Lazare, A. (1981). Current concepts in psychiatry: Conversion symptoms. *New England Journal of Medicine, 305,* 745–748.

Lindemann, E. (1994). Symptomatology and management of acute grief. *American Journal of Psychiatry, 151*(Suppl. 6), 155–160.

Lipowski, Z. J. (1987). Somatization: Medicine's unsolved problem. *Psychosomatics, 28,* 296–297.

Lipowski, Z. J. (1990). Somatization and depression. *Psychosomatics, 31,* 13–21.

Mace, C. J., & Trimble, M. R. (1996). Ten-year prognosis of conversion disorder. *British Journal of Psychiatry, 169,* 282–288.

Malec, J., Brown, A., & Moessner, A. (2004). Personality factors and injury severity in the prediction of early and late traumatic brain injury outcomes. *Rehabilitation Psychology, 49,* 55–61.

Martens, M., Parker, J., Smarr, K., Hewett, J., Ge, B., Slaughter, J., et al. (2006). Development of a shortened Center for Epidemiological Studies Depression Scale for assessment of depression in rheumatoid arthritis. *Rehabilitation Psychology, 51,* 135–139.

McCauley, S., Pedroza, C., Brown, S., Boake, C., Levin, H., Goodman, H., et al. (2006). Confirmatory factor structure of the Center for Epidemiologic Studies Depression scale (CES-D) in mild-to-moderate traumatic brain injury. *Brain Injury, 20,* 519–527.

McCrae, R. R., & Costa, P. T. (1990). *Personality in adulthood.* New York: Guilford Press.

McCrae, R. R., & Costa, P. T. (1995). Positive and negative valence within the five-factor model. *Journal of Research in Personality, 29*, 443–460.

McCrae, R. R., & Costa, P. T. (1999). The five factor theory of personality. In L. A. Pervin & O. P. John (Eds.), *The five factor model of personality across cultures* (pp. 105–125). New York: Kluwer Academic.

Millon, T., Millon, C., & Davis, R. D. (1997). *Millon Clinical Multiaxial Inventory-III manual*. Minneapolis, MN: National Computer Systems.

Morey, L. C. (1991). *Personality Assessment Inventory professional manual*. Odessa, FL: Psychological Assessment Resources.

Mossey, J., & Gallagher, R. (2004). The longitudinal occurrence and impact of comorbid chronic pain and chronic depression over two years in continuing care retirement community residents. *Pain Medicine, 5*, 335–348.

Nelson, L., Elder, J., Tehrani, P., & Groot, J. (2003). Measuring personality and emotional functioning in multiple sclerosis: A cautionary note. *Archives of Clinical Neuropsychology, 18*, 419–429.

Nyenhuis, D. L., Rao, S. M., Zajecka, J. M., Luchetta, T., Bernardin, L., & Garron, D. C. (1995). Mood disturbance versus other symptoms of depression in multiple sclerosis. *Journal of the International Neuropsychological Society, 36*, 390–395.

Olkin, R. (1999). *What psychotherapists should know about disability*. New York: Guilford Press.

Olkin, R., & Pledger, C. (2003). Can disability studies and psychology join hands? *American Psychologist, 58*, 296–304.

Palav, O., & McCaffrey, R. (2001). Incremental validity of the MMPI-2 content scales: A preliminary study with brain-injured patients. *Journal of Head Trauma Rehabilitation, 16*, 275–283.

Poole, H., Bramwell, R., & Murphy, P. (2006). Factor structure of the Beck Depression Inventory-II in patients with chronic pain. *Clinical Journal of Pain, 22*, 790–798.

Prigatano, G. (1992). Personality disturbances associated with traumatic brain injury. *Journal of Consulting and Clinical Psychology, 60*, 360–368.

Prigatano, G. P., & Klonoff, P. S. (1998). A clinician's rating scale for evaluating impaired self-awareness and denial of disability after brain injury. *The Clinical Neuropsychologist, 12*, 56–67.

Radloff, L. S. (1977). The CES-D scale: A self-report depression scale for research in the general population. *Applied Psychological Measurement, 1*, 385–401.

Roche, N. L., Fleming, J. M., & Shum, D. (2002). Self-awareness of prospective memory failure in adults with traumatic brain injury. *Brain Injury, 16*, 931–945.

Roth, E., Davidoff, G., Thomas, P., Doljanac, R., Dijkers, M., Berent, S., et al. (1989). A controlled study of neuropsychological deficits in acute spinal cord injury patients. *Paraplegia, 27*, 480–489.

Rush, B., Malec, J., Brown, A., & Moessner, A. (2006). Personality and functional outcome following traumatic brain injury. *Rehabilitation Psychology, 51*, 257–264.

Rush, B., Malec, J., Moessner, A., & Brown, A. (2004). Preinjury personality traits and the prediction of early neurobehavioral symptoms following mild traumatic brain injury. *Rehabilitation Psychology, 49*, 275–281.

Rybarczyk, B. D., Nyenhuis, D. L., Nicholas, J. J., Schulz, R., Alioto, R. J., & Blair, C. (1992). Social discomfort and depression in a sample of adults with leg amputations. *Archives of Physical Medicine and Rehabilitation, 73*, 1169–1173.

Rybarczyk, B., Winemiller, D., Lazarus, L., Haut, A., & Hartman, C. (1996). Validation of a depression screening measure for stroke inpatients. *The American Journal of Geriatric Psychiatry, 4*, 131–139.

Schafer, A. B. (2006). Meta-analyses of the factor structures of four depression questionnaires: Beck, CES-D, Hamilton, and Zung. *Journal of Clinical Psychology, 62*, 123–146.

Scherer, M., & Cushman, L. (2001). Measuring subjective quality of life following spinal cord injury: A validation study of the assistive technology device predisposition assessment. *Disability and Rehabilitation: An International, Multidisciplinary Journal, 23*, 387–393.

Schubert, D., Burns, R., Paras, W., & Sioson, E. (1992). Increase of medical hospital length of stay by depression in stroke and amputation patients: A pilot study. *Psychotherapy and Psychosomatics, 57*, 61–66.

Seligman, M. E. P., Abramson, L. Y., Semmel, A., & von Baeyer, C. (1979). Depressive attributional style. *Journal of Abnormal Psychology, 88*, 242–247.

Skodol, A. E., Gunderson, J. G., Shea, M. T., McGlashan, T. H., Morey, L. C., & Sanislow, C. A. (2005). The Collaborative Longitudinal Personality Disorders Study (CLPS): Overview and implications. *Journal of Personality Disorders, 19*, 487–504.

Slick, D. J., Hopp, G., Strauss, E., & Spellacy, F. J. (1996). Victoria symptom validity test: Efficiency for detecting feigned memory impairment and relationship to neuropsychological tests and MMPI-2 validity scales. *Journal of Clinical and Experimental Neuropsychology, 18*, 911–922.

Snyder, C., Lehman, K., Kluck, B., & Monsson, Y. (2006). Hope for rehabilitation and vice versa. *Rehabilitation Psychology, 51*, 89–112.

Snyder, C. R., Irving, L. M., & Anderson, J. R. (1991). Hope and health: Measuring the will and the way. In C. R. Snyder & D. R. Forsyth (Eds.), *The handbook of social and clinical psychology: The health perspective* (pp. 285–305). Elmsford, NY: Pergamon Press.

Stone, J., Townend, E., Kwan, J., Haga, K., Dennis, M. S., & Sharpe, M. (2004). Personality change after stroke: Some preliminary observations. *Journal of Neurology Neurosurgery and Psychiatry, 75,* 1708–1713.

Storor, D., & Byrne, G. (2006). Premorbid personality and depression following stroke. *International Psychogeriatrics, 18,* 1–13.

Tate, D., Kewman, D., & Maynard, F. (1990). The Brief Symptom Inventory: Measuring psychological distress in spinal cord injury. *Rehabilitation Psychology, 35,* 211–216.

Tate, R. (1998). "It is not only the kind of injury that matters, but the kind of head": The contribution of premorbid psychosocial factors to rehabilitation outcomes after severe traumatic brain injury. *Neuropsychological Rehabilitation, 8,* 1–18.

Taylor, S. E., & Armor, D. A. (1996). Positive illusions and coping with adversity. *Journal of Personality, 64,* 873–898.

Tennen, H., & Affleck, G. (2002). Benefit finding and benefit reminding. In C. R. Snyder & S. J. Lopez (Eds.), *Handbook of positive psychology* (pp. 584–597). Oxford, England: Oxford University Press.

Tombaugh, T. N. (1996). *Test of Memory Malingering (TOMM).* Toronto, Ontario: Multi-Health Systems.

Trieschmann, R. B. (1980). *Spinal cord injuries: Psychological, social, and vocational adjustment.* New York: Pergamon Press.

Turk, D., & Okifuji, A. (1994). Detecting depression in chronic pain patients: Adequacy of self-reports. *Behavior Research and Therapy, 32,* 9–16.

Turner, J. A., Jensen, M. P., Warms, C. A., & Cardenas, D. D. (2002). Catastrophizing is associated with pain intensity, psychological distress, and pain-related disability among individuals with chronic pain after spinal cord injury. *Pain, 98*(1–2), 127–134.

Victorson, D., Farmer, L., Burnett, K., Ouellette, A., & Barocas, J. (2005). Maladaptive coping strategies and injury-related distress following traumatic physical injury. *Rehabilitation Psychology, 50,* 408–415.

Warlow, C. P., Dennis, M. S., van Gijn, J., Hankey, G. J., Sandercock, P. A. G., Bamford, J. M., et al. (2001). *Stroke: A practical guide to management* (2nd ed.). London: Blackwell Science.

Weinryb, R., Gustavsson, J., & Barber, J. (2003). Personality traits predicting long-term adjustment after surgery for ulcerative colitis. *Journal of Clinical Psychology, 59,* 1015–1029.

Widiger, T., & Simonsen, E. (2005). Alternative dimensional models of personality disorder: Finding a common ground. *Journal of Personality Disorders, 19,* 110–130.

Widiger, T. A., & Samuel, D. B. (2005). Diagnostic categories or dimensions: A question for *DSM-V. Journal of Abnormal Psychology, 114,* 494–504.

Widiger, T. A., & Trull, T. J. (2007). Plate tectonics in the classification of personality disorder. *American Psychologist, 62,* 71–83.

Woessner, R., & Caplan, B. (1996). Emotional distress following stroke: Does the SCL-90-R diagnose or mislead? *Assessment, 3,* 291–305.

Wortman, C. B., & Silver, R. C. (1989). The myths of coping with loss. *Journal of Consulting and Clinical Psychology, 57,* 349–357.

Wright, B. A. (1983). *Physical disability: A psychological approach.* New York: Harper & Row.

Youngjohn, J., Davis, D., & Wolf, I. (1997). Head injury and the MMPI-2: Paradoxical severity effects and the influence of litigation. *Psychological Assessment, 9,* 177–184.

Zanarini, M. C., Frankenburg, F. R., Hennen, R., Reich, D. B., & Silk, K. R. (2005). The McClean Study of Adult Development (MSAD): Overview and implications of the first six years of prospective follow-up. *Journal of Personality Disorders, 19,* 505–523.

Zung, W. W. (1965). A self-rating depression scale. *Archives of General Psychiatry, 12,* 63–70.

CHAPTER 13

NEUROIMAGING

Erin D. Bigler

Neuroimaging has revolutionized how the brain and spinal cord can be visualized, with technological advances that inform the rehabilitation process in ways not previously available to the clinician. Only within the last 2 decades have neuroimaging studies become readily available for clinicians to use in their assessment, treatment, and follow-up with patients in need of rehabilitation services. This chapter focuses on the latest neuroimaging technology that may assist rehabilitation clinicians in how to best use this information. By far, traumatic brain injury (TBI) and cerebrovascular accidents (CVA), along with degenerative disorders, have been the most studied from a neuroimaging perspective and are relied on in this chapter as prototypes for establishing brain–behavior relationships in a rehabilitation setting.

A primary goal of this chapter is to familiarize rehabilitation clinicians and researchers with neuroimaging such that neuroimaging becomes a routine part of rehabilitation. Most patients with neurological disease or disorder requiring rehabilitation care and treatment will have neuroimaging, often multiple scans and procedures, during their treatment and that information should be routinely incorporated into a patient's treatment, monitoring and follow-up. However, just presence or absence of abnormalities on a scan, without any other clinical information, has minimal value for prediction of rehabilitation outcome, except for brainstem lesions (Bigler, Ryser, Gandhi, Kimball, & Wilde, 2006).

There are four main approaches to assessing neuroimaging that can now be taken in addition to the standard radiological report. One is *qualitative,* in which clinical ratings of a scan are done in an attempt to describe a particular brain structure or region. For example, visual inspection of the various lobes as to whether atrophy is present, ratings of the size of the hippocampus, and clinical ratings concerning the integrity of the white matter (WM) of the brain (important in understanding cerebrovascular sequelae) can all be done by the clinician working with a neuroradiologist (see Kurth & Bigler, 2008). The second approach is *quantitative,* including rapid fully automated methods that provide surface area, volumetric or specific tissue measurements that quantify a particular region of interest. The third approach is *functional,* which can be integrated with quantitative methods to show regions of activation, blood flow, or radiotracer uptake. The availability of such information has obvious relevance for the rehabilitation clinician as is discussed throughout this chapter. An example of this application in a patient with anoxic injury and stroke secondary to septic shock is shown in Figure 13.1. In this patient, understanding the damage to the temporal lobe, in particular the medial temporal lobe including the hippocampus, helped explain the memory and cognitive impairment, and the presence of basal ganglia involvement helped explain the patient's lack of motivation and lethargy (see

Appreciation is expressed to the following researchers at Baylor College of Medicine and Brigham Young University for providing the images for Figures 13.14 and 13.15 used in this chapter: Elisabeth A. Wilde, Tracy A. Abildskov, Ragini Yallampalli, Harvey S. Leven, Jill V. Hunter, Zili Chu, and Jon M. Chia; for Figure 13.2 to David F. Tate, at Harvard University.

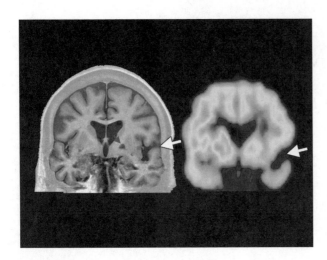

FIGURE 13.1.   The MRI scan on the left, in coronal plane is from a 58 year old individual who suffered an anoxic brain injury and stroke following and episode of septic shock. The scan shows dilated ventricular size, reflective on some generalized atrophy, with the red arrow pointing to the location of one of the strokes that had occurred in the region of the left globus pallidus, and the white arrow points to the left Sylvian fissure. On the image on the right is a positron emission tomography scan performed at the same time as the MRI, showing abnormal uptake of the radiotracer throughout the left temporal lobe and also note the difference in the basal ganglia region between the two hemispheres. Quantitative image analysis also showed that the left hippocampus had significantly atrophied. Qualitative analysis also demonstrated left temporal lobe atrophy. Clinically, this patient exhibited significant memory and motivational problems secondary to these neurological deficits.

Bruen, McGeown, Shanks, & Venneri, 2008). Finally, the fourth approach is *structural. Structural imaging* refers to the ability to identify the structural or anatomical features of a brain scan. Generally, structural imaging refers to computerized tomography (CT) and magnetic resonance imaging (MRI) scans, which reflect the gross anatomy of the brain. In addition, with MRI, there are certain sequences where the definition of WM, gray matter (GM), and cerebrospinal fluid (CSF) are the most distinctly differentiated, which enhances the ability to define brain anatomy, particularly subcortical structures. Being able to visualize and quantify the underlying structural damage and functional impairment assists the rehabilitation clinician in more thoroughly understanding a patient's neurological status.

Before proceeding further with an explanation of the neuroimaging technology as it applies to rehabil-itation, it is important for the rehabilitation clinician to understand how contemporary neuroimaging has advanced our understanding of brain structure and function, particularly showing the interdependence and complexity of cerebral networks and how they can be imaged. One of the remarkable advances in MRI is *diffusion tensor imaging* (DTI), a method that permits identification of aggregate WM pathways. This is discussed in greater detail later in the chapter, but as shown in Figure 13.2, aggregate tracts, their trajectory and orientation can now be readily visualized and quantified. Figure 13.2 demonstrates the complexity of structural brain organization and why a lesion or abnormality in one region can affect or disrupt function elsewhere in the brain. As these types of brain imaging studies become more available, the rehabilitation clinician will have a metric to examine the integrity of pathways and systems in the brain that have been damaged.

BACKGROUND

In the past, most radiological data were stored in what has been referred to as *hardcopy* films that are not very accessible to clinicians. That is no longer the case, as the medium for storage and data transfer now is digital. This also means that clinicians may have ready access to neuroimaging data so that they can actually review the neuroimaging information, not just the radiological report. This is important because radiological reports are typically brief and focused specifically on the medical interpretation of the scan, which may not specifically address many rehabilitation psychology issues. For example, the MRI scan sequence presented in Figure 13.3 is from a teenager who sustained a severe TBI (i.e., Glasgow Coma Score = 5 on admission) in a high-speed rollover accident. She was treated in an extended rehabilitation program, and the scan shown in Figure 13.3 was obtained at approximately 6 months postinjury. The radiological report stated the following as its conclusion: "Right focal frontal lesion consistent with site of old hemorrhagic contusion." There is, of course, far more information in the imaging findings than presented in the report. Although the contusion is localized in the frontal region, the WM just outside of the lesion is compromised, and

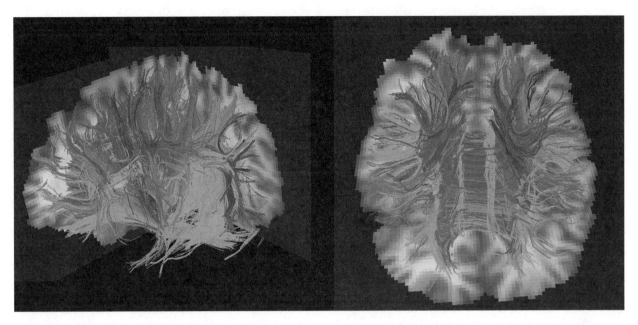

FIGURE 13.2.   (Left) Lateral view of the aggregate white matter pathways of the brain as revealed by diffusion tensor imaging (DTI). (Right) Dorsal view shows the corpus callosum in the middle and the hemispheric projections. DTI represents an amazing technology that illustrates the interconnectiveness of the brain. Courtesy of David Tate, Center for Neurologic Imaging, Harvard University.

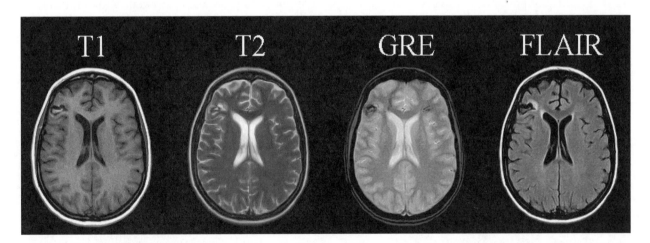

FIGURE 13.3.   Selected axial MRI views at identical levels but with different imaging sequences (as listed above) of the brain of a teenager injured extensively in a high-speed roll-over accident (see also Figure 13.11). In all cases, radiological perspective is present, where the patient's left side is presented on the viewer's right. T1 is often referred to as the anatomical scan, because excellent approximation of gross brain anatomy can be achieved. However, each of the other imaging sequences better defines the trauma-induced neuropathological changes. T2 better shows cerebrospinal fluid and presence of a white matter hyperintensity surrounding the right frontal focal lesion. The gradient recall echo (GRE) sequence is most sensitive to presence of blood-byproducts from shearing, specifically hemosiderin, that shows up as dark splotches. Note that some of the GRE abnormalities are simply not observed in some of the other sequences. The fluid attenuated inversion recovery (FLAIR) sequence further shows white matter damage surrounding the lesion and by the 'capping' evident around the anterior horn of the lateral ventricle. Also, it is evident that the right lateral ventricle is larger than the left, most likely reflecting greater damage to the right hemisphere. What is important about this illustration is that unless the clinician knows what to look for or to ask the radiologist to point out, much of the pathology is never presented in the standard clinical report.

there is some generalized volume loss affecting the entire hemisphere and scattered hemorrhagic lesions present throughout the frontal region, several in the genu region of the corpus callosum.

These types of lesions reflect prior shearing and presence of diffuse axonal injury (DAI; Scheid, Preul, Gruber, Wiggins, & von Cramon, 2003; Scheid, Walther, Guthke, Preul, & von Cramon, 2006), where the degree of lesion burden (i.e., total number or volume of lesions) is negatively associated with cognitive outcome (Scheid et al., 2006). From the neuropsychological standpoint, such deficits would likely affect speed of processing, a variety of executive functions and nonverbal perceptual motor functions, but this would not be fully appreciated by simply reading the radiological report. Furthermore, the extensiveness of the DAI and shearing in the frontal regions bilaterally likely related to the personality and behavioral changes seen in this patient but would not have been understood by just reading the report. If the rehabilitation clinician had relied solely on the radiological report and had not actually viewed the images, considerable information that may have been of critical importance to understanding the patient's rehabilitation potential might have never been known. Rehabilitation clinicians need to understand (a) basic neuropathological principles as they apply to neuroimaging, (b) what such findings may mean for a given patient, and (c) how to directly use neuroimaging data in the evaluation, care, and treatment of their patients.

The traditional challenge in radiology was that the data were always two-dimensional (2-D) but taken from three-dimensional (3-D) space, such as the brain as shown in Figure 13.4. In the past, the clinician had to imagine what a lesion or abnormality looked like by making inferences from flat-surface views of a slice of the brain, as was shown in Figure 13.3. However, now thin slices (i.e., 1 mm) can be made and by stacking each slice on top of the other (i.e., with no gap between slices) a true 3-D reconstruction of the brain can be generated from 2-D image data as shown in Figure 13.5. Figure 13.5 also demonstrates the various sensitivities of different image sequences in the detection of abnormalities found in brain imaging. It is beyond the scope of this chapter to provide much of the details concerning

the advantage of each MRI sequence in the study of brain pathology, but the interested reader can refer to Bigler (2005) for a comprehensive review of this topic. Three-dimensional image representation and ways to highlight abnormalities are becoming more commonplace and are used throughout this chapter. Increased 3-D image presentation means that the clinician does not necessarily need to be a specialist in neuroanatomy or neuropathology to appreciate where atrophy, damage, or a lesion may be located that could be clinically significant. Furthermore, having the imaging data in 3-D provides the clinician with an additional method for presenting the information to the patient and family. Radiological reports are beginning to incorporate the actual images where abnormalities are identified and include those images in the report, some in 3-D image displays. An example of this is presented next.

The scan images shown in Figure 13.6 are from a patient who suffered a severe TBI in a car versus semitrailer truck head-on collision. Of particular interest in this case is that the patient had been seen several years before the head injury for evaluation of chronic headaches and underwent MRI of the brain (shown in the upper left in Figure 13.6), which was interpreted as within normal limits. A calculation can be made that is informative as to the structural normalcy of the brain: the ventricle-to-brain ratio, or VBR. The VBR is calculated by the volume of the entire ventricular system divided by total brain volume (TBV). A typical total ventricular volume (TVV) for an adult is around 20cc (see Blatter et al., 1995), with brain volume between 1,300 and 1,500 cc. The small value of the ventricle means that the uncorrected VBR would be just a fraction of total brain volume, so a correction of 100 is used to generate whole numbers (VBR = TBV ÷ TVV × 100). The typical VBR is approximately 1.5 ($SD = 0.40$).

In the normal brain, the ventricle is small and filled with CSF that is under pressure (i.e., the outward internal pressure gradient keeps the brain buoyant within the cranium and from collapsing in on itself because brain parenchyma is very soft). However, when the brain atrophies, the ventricle passively expands to fill the void left by the loss of cerebral tissue. Thus, as the brain reduces in volume, the ventricle expands. This means that cerebral

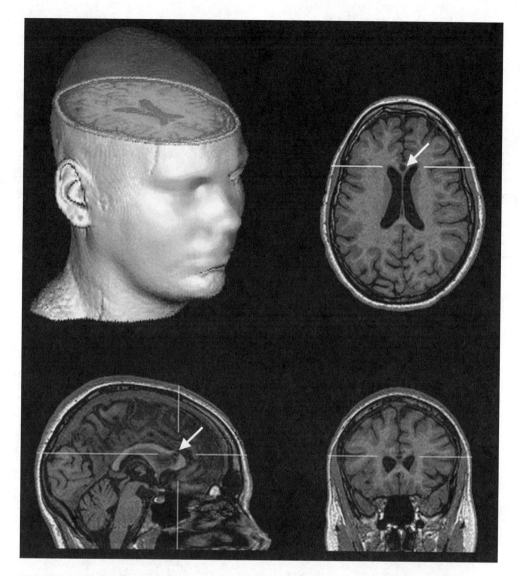

FIGURE 13.4.   3-D reconstruction of the head and face is based on individual slices as shown in the 3-D depiction of the head of this patient who had sustained a severe traumatic brain injury. The level of slice extraction in the upper right is shown on the left, with a faded skull caput, merely to show the level of this slice. When MRI data are acquired in 3-D, the other benefit is to be able to examine any region with great preciseness. For example, in this case there is prominent shearing of the posterior part of the genu of the corpus callosum. The arrow points to the shear injury in the upper right, but the sagittal and coronal views also show this lesion from these different perspectives.

volume loss is reflected in increased VBR, and therefore increased VBR is a measure of the degree of cerebral atrophy (see Carmichael et al., 2007; Nestor et al., 2008). The advantage of using the VBR measure is that, as a ratio, it automatically corrects for differences in head size. Because in both CT and MRI scans there are excellent visualizations of the ventricular system, VBR can be readily calculated with either imaging method. This important metric is easy to

compute and relates to rehabilitation outcome, where the greater the cerebral atrophy, the worse the overall cognitive outcome (Bigler et al., 2006; Wilde, Bigler, Pedroza, & Ryser, 2006).

Returning to Figure 13.6, this patient's preinjury VBR was 1.6, clearly within the normal range. However, when he first arrived at the emergency room and the first CT scan was taken, his VBR dropped to 0.66, a clear sign of generalized cerebral

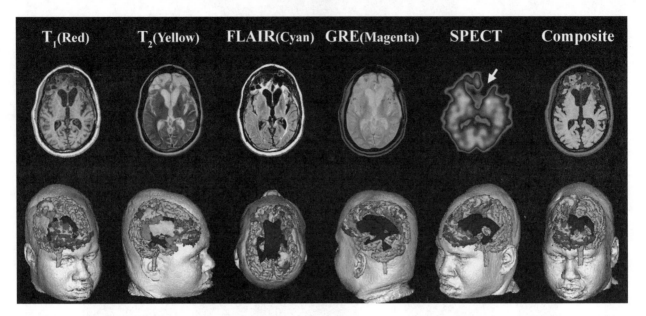

FIGURE 13.5. This patient sustained a severe traumatic brain injury in a high-speed motor vehicle accident. Each MRI sequence is listed with each scan and the lesions identified are color coded. Note the ease with which a 'gestalt' of the patient's area of damage can be identified.

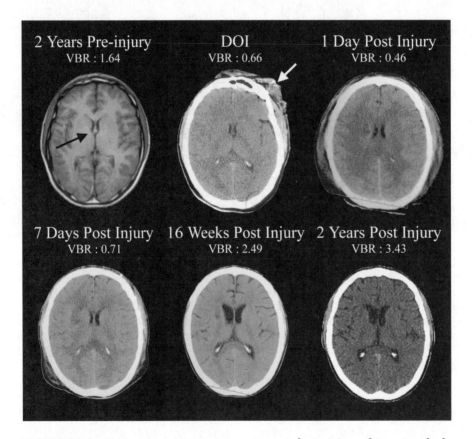

FIGURE 13.6. Prior to sustaining a severe traumatic brain injury, this patient had undergone an MRI 2 years prior representing the perfect baseline. The arrow points to what the ventricular system should appear like. The next five images are in sequence from the first done on admission to the emergency room, through critical care and then at follow-up 2 years later. At the top of each scan is the ventricle-to-brain ratio (VBR) value, normal at pre-injury, significantly reduced on the day-of-injury and day 1 scan because of cerebral edema, then gradually increases reflecting cerebral atrophy (see Figure 13.7). Increased VBR is associated with worse rehabilitation outcome and can be readily appreciated by the rehabilitation clinician by simply viewing the size of the ventricle and prominence of cortical cerebrospinal fluid.

edema. Note in the figure how small the anterior horns appear as well as the lack of any definition of the cerebral sulci, a clear indication of generalized cerebral edema. As shown in Figure 13.6, after reaching its peak on the second day of injury, brain swelling gradually recedes but gives way to generalized cerebral atrophy, evidenced by increasing VBR. Increased VBR is associated with generalized atrophy and, as shown in the patient presented in Figure 13.6, this is best appreciated in 3-D, as illustrated in Figure 13.7. Neuropsychologically, the global nature of brain impairment induced by this TBI resulted in impaired cognitive abilities, particularly memory along with emotional lability, to the point that the patient could not live independently. This kind of information in the hands of the clinician, in particular being able to track abnormalities over time and how the brain atrophies, provides important visual information about the severity of the brain damage.

Although the VBR represents a general marker of brain integrity, as does the 3-D representation of the ventricle in comparison with the brain (shown in Figure 13.7), contemporary neuroimaging has the ability to highlight any brain structure and show the morphology of the structure in 3-D. For example, Figure 13.8 is from a child who suffered a severe brain injury in a motor vehicle accident (MVA) in which he not only sustained a head injury but,

because of a crush injury to the chest, also had an anoxic brain injury (ABI) superimposed on the TBI. This child's imaging studies performed approximately 2 years post-MVA revealed severe atrophy of the hippocampus, readily appreciated on conventional 2-D image display as shown in Figure 13.8, but the 3-D image of the hippocampus demonstrates even more impressive atrophic changes of this structure when compared with an age-matched control. The hippocampus is critical for normal short-term memory function (Squire, 2004) and is particularly susceptible to TBI and ABI (Hopkins, Tate, & Bigler, 2005). Although the child's intellectual functioning was in the average range, testing demonstrated short-term memory impairments. This type of 3-D visualization of the abnormalities can greatly assist the rehabilitation clinician in understanding the underlying neuropathology associated with the memory impairment.

The next section provides useful methods for the clinician, with practical recommendations on how to directly use neuroimaging information and scan data to improve evaluative work with rehabilitation patients.

USING NEUROIMAGING FOR ASSESSMENT WITH REHABILITATION PATIENTS

Given the type and quality of neuroimaging studies that can be done to assist the clinician in assessing any neurological or neuropsychiatric problems, neuroimaging techniques will become even more commonplace. This next section offers some basic guidelines on how to apply neuroimaging to rehabilitation.

Quantitative Image Analysis
Region of interest quantitative magnetic resonance imaging. Despite the near infinite complexity of the human brain, from a gross morphology perspective there are essentially six general categories of intracranial tissue or structures: WM, GM, CSF-filled spaces, blood vessels, choroid plexi, and meninges, each with a characteristic appearance on MRI. However, just three of these represent the major features relevant to most of rehabilitation

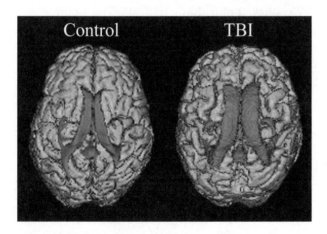

FIGURE 13.7. The 2-year follow-up scan of the patient presented in Figure 13.4 was used to generate a 3-D depiction of the brain and ventricle, as shown on the right. In comparison to an age-matched control shown on the left, the traumatic brain injury patient has generalized cerebral atrophy, quickly appreciated by viewing the 3-D images.

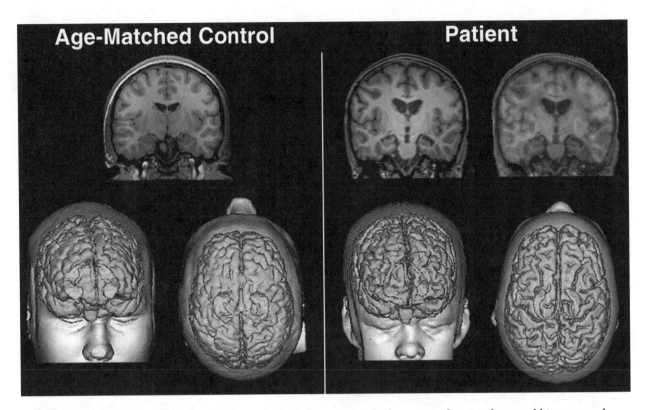

Age-Matched Control   **Patient**

FIGURE 13.8.   The coronal view (left, top centered) is of an age-matched teenage subject with normal hippocampal volume and normal appearing brain. Reconstructing the brain in 3-D in flesh-tones permits visualization of the surface gyri and sulci in their normal configuration, with the visualization of the in situ location of the hippocampus. The patient on the right is from a teenager who sustained a severe injury 2 years previous. Comparing the patient's coronal MRI shows prominent dilation of the temporal horns and a very withered hippocampus. Depicting the hippocampus in 3-D provides even more graphic detail of the degree of atrophy present. In the upper right the coronal MRI image is fused with the positron emission tomography image to show regions of decreased uptake (blue) of the radiotracer in the medial temporal lobe, bilaterally. These findings help the rehabilitation clinician relate structure-to-function deficits.

psychology's questions concerning brain imaging: WM, GM, and CSF. Because of the ease in differentiating these tissue types, region of interest (ROI) quantitative analyses can target essentially any major brain structure. For example, in the case presented earlier as shown in Figure 13.8, this child's hippocampal volume was less than 40% of what would be considered normal for that age. More automated and rapid methods for ROI quantitative image analysis are becoming available (Goldszal et al., 1998; Hahn et al., 2004; Khan, Wang, & Beg, 2008; Kim et al., 2005; Klauschen, Goldman, Barra, Meyer-Lindenberg, & Lundervold, 2008; McDonald et al., 2008). What this means for the clinician is that at some future point, the 3-D presentation as shown in Figure 13.8, along with quantitative information, will be routinely available for every rehabilitation clinician.

Voxel-based morphometry.   When a brain image is segmented into WM, GM, and CSF, an algorithm determines the classification of each pixel into one of these tissue types. A *pixel* is an acronym for the picture element that represents a single point in a graphic image on the computer screen. So, in standard MRI brain imaging, if each pixel has a specified dimension, typically a cubic millimeter, and each pixel is classified by one of the tissue types within any voxel (a *voxel* is an acronym for "VOlume piXEL," or an array of pixels), the density of WM, GM, and CSF pixels within a designated voxel can be determined. Comparing the relative density of WM, GM, or CSF pixels per specified voxel permits comparison with an individual patient or patient group and controls, as shown in Figure 13.9. This is referred to as *voxel-based morphometry* (VBM). The advantage of VBM is that the results come from an

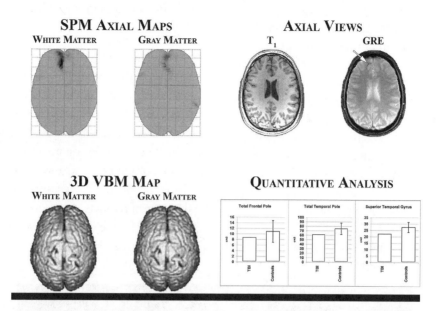

FIGURE 13.9.   This teenager sustained a significant traumatic brain injury in a T-bone crash where he lost consciousness. He had relatively good recovery but was still plagued by some deficits in short-term memory and executive function. The clinical MRI findings presented in the upper right, demonstrated presence of hemosiderin (arrow) in the left frontal region (scans are not in radiological perspective) and a more prominent anterior interhemispheric fissure than would be expected for age, likely reflecting atrophy. However, both of these clinical features are difficult to appreciate by just 'looking' at the images. Applying statistical parametric mapping, which depicts the differences in density of white matter or gray matter pixels within a given voxel compared to a large group of age-matched controls, shows considerable differences that can then be plotted on a conventional brain model for the voxel-based morphometry (VBM) map (lower left). Actual quantification of the volume of the frontal pole, the temporal pole, and the superior temporal gyrus show that there is brain tissue volume loss in this patient's brain in these regions.

automated method that compares the target group with a reference group.

VBM techniques are just beginning to be used in rehabilitation (Gauthier et al., 2008; Gorno-Tempini et al., 2004; Wagner et al., 2006), can be applied individually or in group data, and can also measure changes in brain structure over time. VBM techniques have even been shown to be sensitive to tracking brain changes in new skill learning in noninjured individuals (Gaser & Schlaug, 2003). VBM is rapid, requires a good normative base, and is readily available now (Gale, Baxter, Roundy, & Johnson, 2005). One limitation of this method is that no specific volumetric analysis of an actual anatomical structure or region is accomplished because the method is based on the relative density of WM, GM, or CSF pixels within certain specified voxels. Nonetheless, it is entirely possible that future rehabilitation clinicians will see application of VBM technology that informs the clinician about the brain's capacity to respond to therapies and may even help guide what therapies are selected and their effectiveness in patients being treated after some acquired brain injury (Gauthier et al., 2008).

Qualitative Image Analysis

The advantage of qualitative neuroimaging ratings is that they can typically be established using whatever clinical neuroimaging data are available and do not rely on such rigidly applied research scanning methods to perform the various quantitative analyses discussed earlier. Often, the radiological report will be too general for the specific purposes of the clinician, especially if the report merely states that the findings were "within normal limits" or of "unknown clinical significance." The rehabilitation clinician should always work closely with radiology in any interpretive analysis with qualitative ratings of brain anatomy, but the advantage of using such rating scales is that they can be customized to the clinician's need. In fact, radiologists could incorporate such ratings into any routine work done in conjunction with the rehabilitation clinician. Two ratings are discussed as follows, details of which are contained in Bigler (2005, 2007). There are numerous other clinical rating methods available as well;

the two that follow are merely presented because of the author's experience with them.

Atrophy rating. Atrophy of the frontal or temporal lobes is associated with greater cognitive deficits regardless of the etiology (Bakshi, Benedict, Bermel, & Jacobs, 2001; Benedict et al., 2005; de Mendonca, Ribeiro, Guerreiro, & Garcia, 2004; Mok et al., 2005). Using clinical rating scales with individuals with TBI, Bergeson et al. (2004) demonstrated that the degree of frontal or temporal atrophy was associated with impaired memory and executive function. An example of this type of rating is shown in Figure 13.10. Clinical application of these rating methods was outlined in detail by Kurth and Bigler (2008).

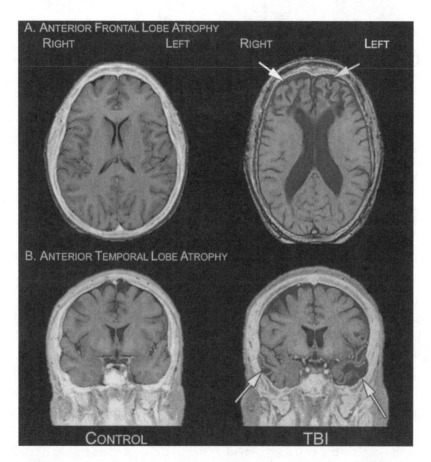

FIGURE 13.10. These images illustrate severe frontal atrophy in the upper right scan, compared with the normal brain in the upper left. The coronal images at the bottom show significant temporal lobe atrophy (lower right) in the patient with traumatic brain injury compared with the control participant (lower left). Note how these differences can be qualitatively determined and that such rating scales have relevance to predicting rehabilitation outcome. From "Clinical Rating of Cortical Atrophy and Cognitive Correlates Following Traumatic Brain Injury," by A. G. Bergeson et al., 2004, *The Clinical Neuropsychologist, 18*(4), pp. 509–520. Copyright 2004 by Taylor & Francis. Reprinted with permission.

White matter hyperintensity or lesion ratings. In viewing the "normal" appearance of an MRI of the brain, the typical pattern of WM and GM is to have relatively homogenous and uniform signal intensity within WM that is different from GM and, depending on the MRI sequence, typically a distinct boundary between the two. As shown in Figure 13.8, WM has a uniform appearance across all WM pixels that can be differentiated from GM and, in this case, no white matter lesions (WMLs) could be identified at the level depicted. WM, representing the myelinated axons and therefore the "connectivity" of the brain, should have at every level a uniform appearance in its healthiest state. Many neurological diseases and disorders, however, affect WM, resulting in cognitive effects (Jorm et al., 2005; Kapeller, Schmidt, Enzinger, Ropele, & Fazekas,

2002; Ovbiagele & Saver, 2006a; van Straaten et al., 2006), as readily observed in MRI scans such as are shown in Figures 13.3 and 13.11. Any disruption in the integrity of WM may disconnect brain regions and block or slow neural transmission.

In the normal brain, until the 6th decade of life, WMLs are infrequent (Hopkins et al., 2006). Thus, the presence of any WMLs may be clinically significant, depending on the disorder. For example, increased presence of white matter hyperintensities (WMHs) or WMLs has been reported in diverse neurological and neuropsychiatric disorders, including multiple sclerosis (Bakshi et al., 2001); anoxia (Parkinson et al., 2002); TBI (Bigler, 2005; Bigler et al., 2006); vascular disease, especially associated with hypertension and diabetes (Ovbiagele & Saver, 2006b); sleep apnea (Gale & Hopkins, 2004); and

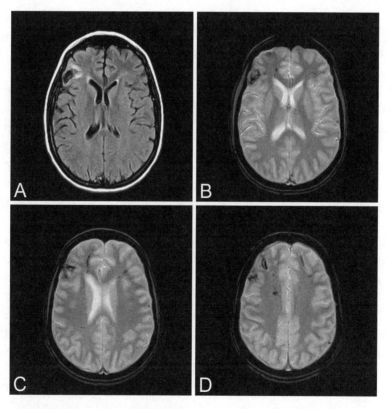

FIGURE 13.11. These images are from the same patient shown in Figure 13.3, just at different levels. (A) Depicts the fluid attenuated inversion recovery sequence showing white matter hyperintensities in the frontal region. (B), (C), and (D) are all gradient recall echo sequences showing how widespread the shearing was in this patient's brain, where extensive hemosiderin deposits are present, particularly involving the frontal lobes. Being able to visualize this allows the rehabilitation clinician to better appreciate the biological basis of the patient's memory and executive deficits.

aging (Bigler et al., 2003). The presence of an abnormal number of WMHs or WMLs is associated with reduced speed of processing, memory and executive impairment (van den Heuvel, ten Dam, de Craen, Admiraal-Behloul, van Es, et al., 2006; van Straaten et al., 2006), and poorer rehabilitation outcome (Sachdev, Wen, Christensen, & Jorm, 2005), particularly in poststroke patients (Burton et al., 2004) but also in aging (van den Heuvel, ten Dam, de Craen, Admiraal-Behloul, Olofsen, et al., 2006). As with the qualitative atrophy ratings described earlier, various clinical ratings of WMHs or WMLs have been reported in the literature and can be used by the rehabilitation clinician in rating either the MRI report or actual imaging studies. This can be done via simple visual rating of the scan or simple image threshold methods if digital data are available (see Davis Garrett et al., 2004). Figure 13.11 is from the same patient as shown in Figure 13.3 and demonstrates numerous WMLs scattered throughout the frontal lobes. The patient also had deficits in executive and short-term memory function along with change in personality and temperament, representing a clinical correlation between the neuroimaging findings and the rehabilitation outcome after severe TBI on the basis of just the clinical ratings of scan data. Multiple sclerosis is the prototype WML degenerative disorder, wherein the degree of WMHs represents lesion burden and overall lesion burden related to rehabilitation potential and outcome, as discussed in chapter 8, this volume.

Functional Neuroimaging

Functional neuroimaging refers to various brain imaging techniques that offer a more dynamic measure of in vivo brain function beyond standard structural MRI or CT imaging (Munoz-Cespedes, Rios-Lago, Paul, & Maestu, 2005). To date, functional neuroimaging has been mostly experimental, but this is likely to change in the next decade because of the promise that these techniques will provide additional clinical information that will be helpful in the rehabilitation setting.

The most common functional neuroimaging methods are functional MRI (fMRI), positron emission tomography (PET), single photon emission computed tomography (SPECT), and magneto-

encephalography (MEG). The basics of these methods and their interpretation were discussed in the first edition of this volume (Bigler, 2000) and elsewhere (see Ricker & Arenth, 2007, 2008), and the basic techniques remain the same (more in-depth information is available from Papanicolaou, 1998). Often, traditional structural 3-D MRI is integrated with functional neuroimaging so that the activation patterns indicative of underlying neural function can be mapped on the 3-D reconstruction of the brain. An example of this is shown in Figure 13.12, which is from an individual first examined as a child. She had been born with an occipital encephalocele that was surgically removed in infancy. Because the occipital area was malformed and contained in the encephalocele sack, the neurosurgeon simply excised the encephalocele at the back of the head, leaving a marked structural defect of both occipital lobes, with no identifiable primary visual cortex, as shown in Figure 13.12. Unexpectedly, as an infant, the child had demonstrated some visual processing abilities, which as an older child included normal reading ability.

This was an intriguing case because, by structural imaging accounts, there was no visual cortex, and higher level visual processing such as reading should have been impossible. So this represented an ideal case for functional imaging to be integrated with structural neuroimaging to determine which brain areas had adapted and were carrying out visual function, in particular the letter processing necessary for reading, because visual cortex was absent. In this case we applied the integrated technique referred to as *magnetic source imaging* (MSI; Halgren et al., 2002; Lewine, Davis, Sloan, Kodituwakku, & Orrison, 1999), which incorporates standard 3-D structural MRI with fMRI and MEG where the activation patterns are superimposed on the structural 3-D image (Papanicolaou, Castillo, Billingsley-Marshall, Pataraia, & Simos, 2005). MSI applied in this manner demonstrated that regions of traditional activation that would have been parietal cortex were now involved in primary visual process, acting very much like striate cortex. Furthermore, traditional areas of inferior temporal cortex, well-documented regions activated by reading stimuli (Cutting et al., 2006), simply were not activated, but a robust

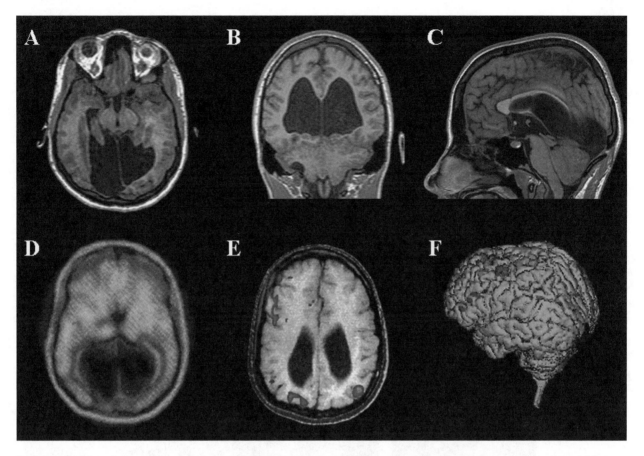

FIGURE 13.12.   As an infant, this patient had an occipital encephalocele removed; the structural imaging on the top row (A = axial, B = coronal, C = sagittal) all show marked structural defects, with absence of visual cortex. However, this individual eventually could actually read at a college level and, by applying functional imaging, it was possible to determine how the brain adapted to accomplish such a function. D is an image of the single photon emission computed tomography scan, showing profound perfusion defect of the radiotracer at the back of the brain. Functional magnetic resonance imaging, however, shows prominent frontal activation in response to reading and the 3-D brain localizes that activity to the left frontal lobe. Note that there is only activation in the posterior parietal area, which likely represents the adaptation of "visual cortex" from this congenital defect.

region of activation was evident in the left inferior and lateral frontal area, including Broca's area. This case demonstrates how rehabilitation specialists could use this information to understand brain reorganization after injury, but what about monitoring recovery of function?

The same type of methods can be applied to monitoring functional activation patterns in the brain over time following some types of acquired injury and their treatment. This work is just beginning but may hold considerable promise in following patients with acquired brain injury needing rehabilitation services. For example, Figure 13.13 shows the changes over time in recovery of language function over the first year after stroke (Fernandez

et al., 2004). It is conceivable that these methods will be used to titrate treatments during rehabilitation and monitoring recovery over time (Dobkin, 2005), eventually becoming standard practices in rehabilitation. Experimentation is now occurring in which functional neuroimaging is being used in important issues for the rehabilitation clinician, such as psychotherapeutic interventions to document brain changes in response to therapy (Cahn & Polich, 2006; Siegle, Carter, & Thase, 2006) and regulation of pain (deCharms et al., 2005).

For example, Toole, Flowers, Burdette, and Absher (2007) provided an excellent case example of the future for structural and functional neuroimaging in rehabilitation. In this case, they examined

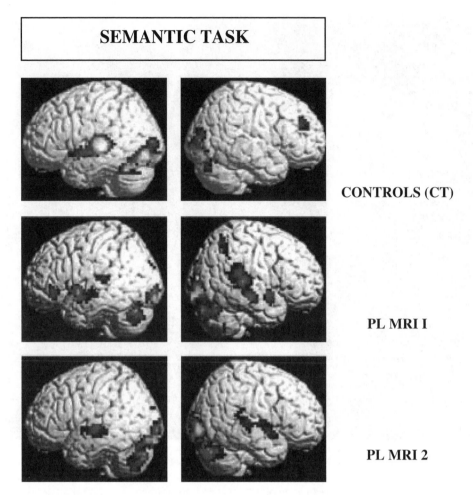

SEMANTIC TASK

CONTROLS (CT)

PL MRI I

PL MRI 2

FIGURE 13.13.   Functional magnetic resonance imaging findings demonstrating "recovery" of function after left hemisphere stroke at 1 month (MRI 1) and 1 year. Note that these images show prominent activation of the left superior temporal area that houses primary auditory cortex in the control participant, yet no activation of the homologue right temporal area. In the patient, however, after the stroke, the initial activation is substantially less and not in the primary auditory cortex. However, the nondominant right hemisphere is activated. Over time, more primary auditory cortex activation takes places in the left hemisphere with concomitant reduction of right hemisphere activation. This is a demonstration of how functional neuroimaging can inform the rehabilitation clinician. Data from Fernandez et al., 2004.

a 63-year-old right-handed man who was a professional pianist and who had experienced a stroke involving the right internal capsule, resulting in left-side hemiplegia. He was eventually able to recover hand dexterity to the degree of returning to play the piano, helped by the combination of structural MRI documenting and tracking the focal lesion coupled with fMRI. This demonstrated that functional brain reorganization during the recovery process involved some regions that would not have been traditionally activated under normal circumstances of hand-

movement or piano playing. It is likely that, in the future when structural damage is identified, the effectiveness of functional recovery will be determined, in part, by functional neuroimaging techniques that show recruitment or activation of other unaffected or less-affected regions, some of which were not primary participants in the affected cognitive function before the injury or disease that damaged that particular part of the brain.

In a larger study that examined patients with chronic stroke, Cramer et al. (2007) used fMRI to identify areas of functional integrity at baseline that were predictive of better response to rehabilitation therapies. Likewise, Cherney and Small (2006) demonstrated that better recovery from aphasia would be associated with fMRI findings more closely resembling "normal" activation patterns in left hemisphere language areas (see also Siekierka et al., 2007). Therefore, combining traditional methods of treatment with better knowledge of what neuroimaging studies indicate about brain integrity should improve overall rehabilitation outcome (see Jang, You, & Ahn, 2007; Mark, Taub, & Morris, 2006). Obviously, large-scale prospective studies are needed on this most important topic of linking neuroimaging with facilitating neurorehabilitation outcome, but what is clear at this time is that the technology to perform these kinds of studies and their relevance to rehabilitation has reached an appropriate scientific standard to pursue these kinds of clinical trials.

When available, the integration of functional imaging with structural imaging also helps the clinician better understand how compromised the brain may be. For example, returning to Figure 13.6, there is clearly hippocampal atrophy, as shown by the MRI, but PET imaging shows that the entire mesial temporal lobe is underactive, even where MRI does not show abnormalities. Functional imaging may be particularly helpful when there is no underlying structural abnormality identified. Mild TBI is a good example and represents clinical cases seen by rehabilitation clinicians where structural imaging is often reported to be "within normal limits." Lewine et al. (1999, 2007) have shown that by using the magnetic source imaging approach, subtle abnormalities in brain function can be detected where persistence of functional neuroimaging abnormalities relates to persistence of mild TBI symptomatology.

Another common area in which subjective patient complaints are sometimes difficult to associate with objective neuropsychological findings is in relation to pain. Although it is well known that pain alters cognitive and emotional functioning, objectively demonstrating that with psychological and neuropsychological testing is problematic. However, functional neuroimaging of pain may provide a much more direct and objective way to assess such

associations (Davis, Taylor, Crawley, Wood, & Mikulis, 1997; Filippi et al., 2002; Kong et al., 2006; Wood, 2005). The same is true for fatigue (de Lange et al., 2005). Indeed, functional neuroimaging is beginning to study how psychotherapeutic techniques alter brain function (Linden, 2006; Roffman, Marci, Glick, Dougherty, & Rauch, 2005). Thus, functional neuroimaging methods may provide additional information that cannot be seen or determined from standard structural neuroimaging that can assist the rehabilitation clinician in understanding how the brain has been compromised and/or is responding to therapy (Linden, 2006; Roffman et al., 2005).

An example of this in the laboratory setting is the use of fMRI to assess changes in cognitive and emotional processing during cognitive tasks (see Herwig et al., 2007); these functional neuroimaging tools are now being used to examine the efficacy of psychotherapeutic treatment, such as positive improvement following cognitive behavior therapy (CBT; Andrasik & Rime, 2007; Felmingham et al., 2007). Indeed, Siegle et al. (2007) used fMRI to predict recovery from unipolar depression in patients treated with CBT. Their findings were straightforward: As the patient improved, predictable activation patterns in the subgenual cingulate cortex and amygdala changed. Specific to rehabilitation in those with TBI, Strangman and colleagues (2008) showed the utility of fMRI methods to predict memory outcome during cognitive rehabilitation following TBI. The implication here is that by monitoring functional neuroimaging, the clinician is literally viewing an aspect of the brain's adaptation or change in response to the therapy. The obvious disadvantage of these procedures thus far is their dependence on the expensive and sophisticated hardware and software required to perform the studies and the limited availability of the studies.

Contributions of Neuroimaging to Cognitive Neuroscience and Clinical Rehabilitation Practice

The term *cognitive neuroscience* became commonplace with the introduction of Gazzaniga's textbook, *The Cognitive Neurosciences*, first published in 1995. Cognitive psychology predated this term and, of course, was the experimental field focused on studying so-called mental or cognitive processes, particularly in the areas of memory and learning. Until the advent of modern neuroimaging, cognitive psychology inferred various neural states and processes but was limited in directly studying them. This has all changed with the advent of neuroimaging. Although the early field of cognitive psychology was once dominated by animal work, neural correlates of human cognition are now effectively and directly studied with neuroimaging. Simultaneous with these developments in cognitive neuroscience came the term *clinical neuroscience,* again first discussed mostly in terms of animal models of human neurological diseases but now a thriving discipline with the objective of applying basic neuroscience techniques (e.g., molecular, genetic) to understand human neurological and neuropsychiatric disorders, including the cognitive neuroscience of rehabilitation (Stuss, 1999).

Within clinical neuroscience, various neuroimaging modalities are being used to investigate neurotransmitters (Pimlott, 2005), underlying genetics (McAllister et al., 2005), and a host of other neurobiological features that should ultimately improve our understanding of how the brain recovers from injury. Clinical neuroscience models integrated with neuroimaging are even being used to construct novel psychotherapeutic and cognitive rehabilitation interventions (Evans, Dougherty, Pollack, & Rauch, 2006; Raedt, 2006; Siegle et al., 2006; Straube, Glauer, Dilger, Mentzel, & Miltner, 2006). As mentioned in the previous section, a less expensive way of performing functional neuroimaging is needed to monitor these changes in brain function in the rehabilitation patient, along with the development of a best practice approach on how these methods should be used in treatment.

Although not a neuroimaging technique per se, transcranial magnetic stimulation may also be integrated with neuroimaging to provide methods of treatment (Brown, Lutsep, Weinand, & Cramer, 2006; Hamzei, Liepert, Dettmers, Weiller, & Rijntjes, 2006; Kim, et al., 2006; Meister et al., 2006), which has the potential of opening exciting new therapy options in rehabilitation. Robertson (2005) and others have begun the dialogue on how cognitive neuroscience will affect rehabilitation.

Given these developments, it is this author's opinion that cognitive and clinical neuroscience will achieve major breakthroughs using neuroimaging technology that will predict and guide the rehabilitation clinician in the future and this, in turn, will greatly modify rehabilitation psychology and clinical neuropsychology. Several techniques with great promise are discussed next.

Important research has demonstrated that in some with minimal conscious state, functional neuroimaging such as fMRI shows changes in response to familiar voices (e.g., the patient's own name spoken by a family member's voice) or simple cognitive challenges (e.g., auditory stimulation) where expected areas of cortical activation demonstrate higher levels of cortical processing (Di et al., 2007; Giacino, Hirsch, Schiff, & Laureys, 2006). Prior to the advent of functional neuroimaging, the rehabilitation clinician could only infer what might be occurring in any patient's brain by his or her behavioral response; because most of these patients are motorically compromised, it was often impossible for the clinician to conclude much about the patient's level of cognitive processing. Functional neuroimaging has the potential to greatly aid the clinician in assessing vegetative and minimally conscious states and tracking patients over time as to whether any progress is being made in response to therapies.

Diffusion tensor imaging. As already noted, DTI examines the diffusion of water molecules in a way that permits assessing the integrity, organization, and directionality of brain WM (Lainhart, Lazar, Bigler, & Alexander, 2006). Such indices are important because WM represents the "connectivity" of the brain: the myelinated fiber pathways as shown in Figure 13.2. Optimal WM integrity is associated with normal speed of neural processing and therein DTI provides a measure to assess the "health" of the brain. The advance that DTI may provide for the rehabilitation clinician is that it is a direct index of WM integrity, particularly within motor pathways (Lee, Choi, & Chun, 2006) and large coursing WM pathways such as the corpus callosum (Lainhart et al., 2006) that relate to neuropsychological and rehabilitation measures. This is visualized in

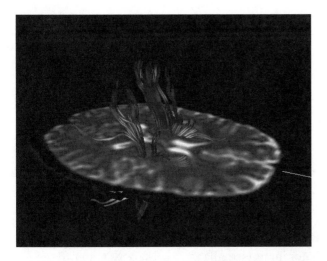

FIGURE 13.14a.   Diffusion tensor imaging is used to isolate tracts within the internal capsule, identifying a loss in the left hemisphere associated with right hemiplegia.

Figure 13.14a, showing atrophy of projecting fibers through the right internal capsule in a child with left hemiplegia. Bilateral projecting pathways should be symmetric but, as readily appreciated in this illustration, the affected side has far fewer pathways, and the DTI technology permits the clinician to directly observe this reduction. In Figure 13.14b, DTI shows a disruption in the tracts across the corpus callosum following TBI. Simply looking at the traditional mid-sagittal section of the MRI, the rehabilitation clinician would not be able to fully appreciate the loss of fiber tracts. All of this information can then be inte-

grated into a 3-D display which highlights the disrupted pathways across the corpus callosum with a backdrop of the brain cutaway to show other anatomical regions as shown in Figure 13.15. Intuitively, this type of information will greatly assist the clinician in understanding the underlying damage but will also provide useful tools to show the patient and family the nature and extent of damage that has occurred.

Although Figures 13.14a and 13.14b are impressive and have straightforward implications for understanding motor (see Figure 13.14a) and inter-hemispheric impairments (see Figure 13.14b), DTI probably will have much wider application in better understanding neuropsychological outcome. For example, Alexander et al. (2007) and Wilde et al. (2006) have shown how DTI methods can be used to show relations with slow speed of information processing in otherwise "normal" appearing WM where the degree of radial diffusion of water relates to speed of processing (Alexander et al., 2007; Goetz et al., 2004; Kumar et al., 2003). Specific to TBI, Salmond et al. (2006) used various DTI coefficients to show the diffuse nature of WM damage in TBI and its relation to cognitive and neurobehavioral sequelae. It is likely that as DTI neuropathology and its functional significance is better understood, this imaging tool will play an increasingly important role in predicting and monitoring rehabilitation outcome

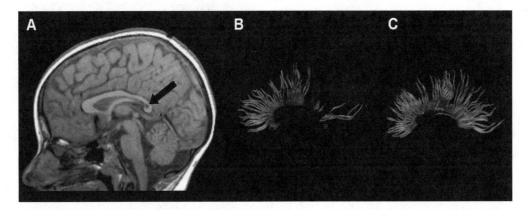

FIGURE 13.14b.   Diffusion tensor imaging tractography is used to show the projections across the corpus callosum and the significant dropout of projecting fibers associated with the posterior thinning of the corpus callosum. In both illustrations, the color refers to directionality of the fiber tracts, with blue indicating vertical orientation, "warm" colors (i.e., orange to red) indicating lateral direction, and green reflecting anterior–posterior orientation. From "Diffusion Tensor Imaging in the Corpus Callosum in Children After Moderate to Severe Traumatic Brain Injury," by E. A. Wilde et al., 2006, *Journal of Neurotrauma*, 23(10), pp. 1412–1426. Copyright 2006 by Mary Ann Liebert, Inc. Reprinted with permission.

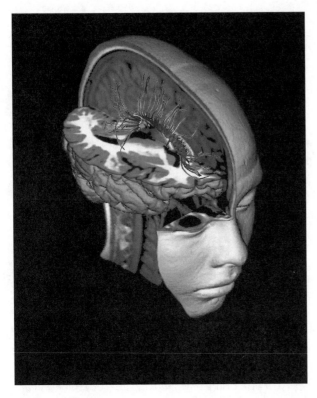

FIGURE 13.15. This 3-D cutaway of a magnetic resonance imaging scan shows major gaps in the corpus callosum in this child with severe traumatic brain injury, with major loss of fiber tracking across the corpus callosum. Note the clarity with which anatomical structures can be displayed with current methods.

(Han, Ahn, & Jang, 2008; Levin et al., 2008; Nguyen et al., 2005).

Magnetic resonance spectroscopy. *Magnetic resonance spectroscopy* (MRS) permits an assessment of the chemical environment of the brain where understanding regional levels of MRS abnormalities has potential in monitoring the functional status of patients' recovery from TBI and stroke (Yoon, Lee, Kim, & Chun, 2005). Several studies have now examined MRS findings in regard to rehabilitation potential, cognitive, and neuropsychiatric outcome (Ashwal et al., 2006; Brooks et al., 2000; Kobayashi, Takayama, Suga, & Mihara, 2001; Yoon et al., 2005); these have shown that MRS findings may be useful in monitoring and predicting recovery in patients with acquired neurological impairment. As a result, rehabilitation patients are now being examined for MRS abnormalities and used as ROI "markers" in the detection of neuronal injury by-products

(Yoon et al., 2005); however, there is not enough data yet to analyze its effectiveness.

Automated magnetic resonance imaging analysis. MRI-based quantitative image analysis largely had to be accomplished by hand tracing of ROIs. However, since the previous version of this chapter was published in the first edition of this handbook in 2000, the automation of image analysis has improved dramatically, as has already been mentioned. VBM has already been discussed, but there are now fully automated structural image analysis programs that can analyze volume and morphology with minimal operator input (see Aljabar, Rueckert, & Crum, 2008; Makris et al., 2006). For example, Figure 13.16 is from an automated image analysis where the ROI identified in the figure is the ventricle. Once the MRI scan data were properly formatted for this analysis, there was no other operator interface required to run the analysis and all images, including the 3-D image of the ventricle, were completely automated. What this means for the clinician is that detailed quantitative data can now be easily extracted from MRI digital data with these automated image analysis methods. This can also be done inexpensively but does require a special type of volume MRI scan to be performed. Because this technology is so new, there are no prospective studies examining how best to use this information in a rehabilitation setting, but it seems intuitive that clinicians could benefit by specifically knowing the integrity, or lack thereof, of critical brain structures on the basis of their morphometry.

CONCLUSION

The traditional rehabilitation psychological and/or clinical neuropsychological assessment has always relied on an inferential process as to how the patient's deficits may relate to underlying abnormal brain function. Until the advent of contemporary neuroimaging, the psychological examiner could not observe behavior with a direct measure of brain function that yielded much useful information. However, this has greatly changed over the last 2 decades. The functional imaging methods of fMRI, MEG, quantitative electroencephalography, and PET

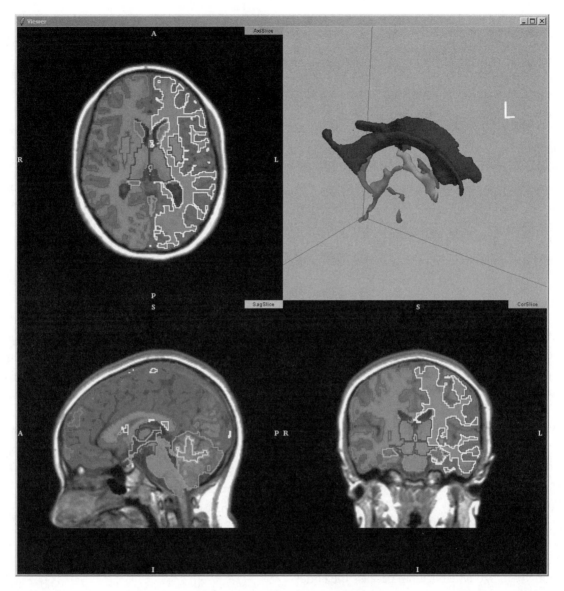

FIGURE 13.16. A completely automated magnetic resonance imaging segmentation showing various regions of interest (ROIs), including the axial (top, left), sagittal (bottom, left), and coronal (bottom, right) slices. In this case, the ROI was the ventricle; it was necessary to calculate its volume and illustrate it in 3-D, as depicted in the upper right. The other images show how white matter is segregated from gray matter and cerebrospinal fluid, and how the ventricle is isolated.

are becoming more widely used in rehabilitation research and clinical work; with faster processing methods for image analysis, more practical in vivo application of these methods is likely to occur (Munson, Schroth, & Ernst, 2006). With the major advances in image analysis in the last decade (see Cabeza, 2006), the rehabilitation clinician will undoubtedly be using neuroimaging methods more routinely (see Butefisch, Kleiser, & Seitz, 2006).

For example, as this chapter is being written, attempts are being made to standardize fMRI procedures to assess language, memory (including working memory), various motor functions, and perceptual and sensory ability. These procedures could have application in rehabilitation psychology (Arenth, Ricker, & Schultheis, 2007). What once had to be inferred from rehabilitation or neuropsychological assessment may ultimately be directly observed via functional neuroimaging methods.

One example from Fernandez et al. (2004) was presented in Figure 13.13 of an individual with a conduction aphasia following a CVA. The figure shows a semantic and rhyming task that in controls brings about prominent left hemisphere activation. At 1 month poststroke, minimal activation was observed in this patient's left hemisphere, but there were large areas of activation of the homologous temporal–parietal regions of the right hemisphere. As the patient progressed through rehabilitation and speech and language therapy, a more normal pattern of left hemisphere activation emerged and could be documented by fMRI techniques. More studies are showing how training, even in the noninjured brain, can be monitored by fMRI, thereby providing a window into the brain's response during learning (Ross, Schomer, Chappell, & Enzmann, 1994). Unquestionably, the application of such methods as applied to rehabilitation will only increase.

As discussed earlier, current functional neuroimaging methods have a number of practical limitations for their widespread use in rehabilitation; however, innovative neuroscientists have been exploring noninvasive methods, such as infrared spectroscopy and functional ultrasonography techniques, to functionally assess the brain (Cannestra, Wartenburger, Obrig, Villringer, & Toga, 2003; Krach, Chen, & Hartje, 2006; Obrig & Villringer, 2003). The near infrared technologies permit the detection of oxygen use by utilizing the ratio of oxyhemoglobin/deoxyhemoglobin because the optics of light absorption differ slightly depending on the level of oxygen concentration to hemoglobin molecules. In some respects this is the same feature that fMRI relies on, but fMRI requires a dedicated MRI machine with special hardware and software to determine blood oxygen level differences. Such methods have the potential for widespread, lower cost and practical use in rehabilitation (Suzuki, Miyai, Ono, & Kubota, 2008; Ward, Soraghan, Matthews, & Markham, 2007). Arenth et al. (2007) published an excellent review of these potential methods in neurorehabilitation.

If these technologies demonstrate clinical effectiveness, the traditional neuropsychological evaluation can be shortened, with some aspects eliminated altogether (Bhambhani, Maikala, Farag, & Rowland, 2006). This would allow additional time for the clinicians to engage in "face-to-face" therapy with the patient. In this model, there is more time to educate the patient and family about their condition and expected outcomes. Instead of assessment roles restricted to traditional psychometric methods (i.e., paper and pencil), the rehabilitation and neuropsychological clinician of the future will become central to the administration of cognitive and behavioral measures contemporaneous with neuroimaging studies of brain structure and function, charting improved underlying cerebral function and/or potentially adaptive brain processes in response to rehabilitation.

The message is clear: The future rehabilitation psychologist must rely on neuroimaging that will be connected with cognitive and neurobehavioral assessment and used to track outcome and prescribe treatments. Over the next decade, it will undoubtedly take considerably more research, but imaging will allow the rehabilitation clinician a more direct route to assessing brain function. Such approaches will incorporate both structural and functional neuroimaging into rehabilitation assessment and will result in improved understanding of neurobehavioral deficits, enhancing the recovery as well as the outcome of the rehabilitation patient.

References

Alexander, A. L., Lee, J. E., Lazar, M., Boudos, R., Dubray, M. B., Oakes, T. R., et al. (2007). Diffusion tensor imaging of the corpus callosum in autism. *Neuroimage, 34,* 61–73.

Aljabar, P., Rueckert, D., & Crum, W. R. (2008). Automated morphological analysis of magnetic resonance brain imaging using spectral analysis. *Neuroimage, 43,* 225–235.

Andrasik, F., & Rime, C. (2007). Can behavioral therapy influence neuromodulation? *Neurological Sciences, 28*(Suppl. 2), S124–129.

Arenth, P. M., Ricker, J. H., & Schultheis, M. T. (2007). Applications of functional near infrared spectroscopy (fNIRS) to neurorehabilitation of cognitive disabilities. *Clinical Neuropsychologist, 21,* 38–57.

Ashwal, S., Babikian, T., Gardner-Nichols, J., Freier, M. C., Tong, K. A., & Holshouser, B. A. (2006). Susceptibility-weighted imaging and proton magnetic resonance spectroscopy in assessment of outcome after pediatric traumatic brain injury. *Archives of*

Physical Medicine and Rehabilitation, 87(12, Suppl. 2), S50–58.

Bakshi, R., Benedict, R. H., Bermel, R. A., & Jacobs, L. (2001). Regional brain atrophy is associated with physical disability in multiple sclerosis: Semiquantitative magnetic resonance imaging and relationship to clinical findings. *Journal of Neuroimaging, 11,* 129–136.

Benedict, R. H., Zivadinov, R., Carone, D. A., Weinstock-Guttman, B., Gaines, J., Maggiore, C., et al. (2005). Regional lobar atrophy predicts memory impairment in multiple sclerosis. *American Journal of Neuroradiology, 26,* 1824–1831.

Bergeson, A. G., Lundin, R., Parkinson, R. B., Tate, D. F., Victoroff, J., Hopkins, R. O., et al. (2004). Clinical rating of cortical atrophy and cognitive correlates following traumatic brain injury. *Clinical Neuropsychologist, 18,* 509–520.

Bhambhani, Y., Maikala, R., Farag, M., & Rowland, G. (2006). Reliability of near infrared spectroscopy measures of cerebral oxygenation and blood volume during handgrip exercise in nondisabled and traumatic brain-injured subjects. *Journal of Rehabilitation Research and Development, 43,* 845–856.

Bigler, E. D. (2000). Neuroimaging and outcome. In R. G. Frank & T. R. Elliott (Eds.), *Handbook of rehabilitation psychology.* Washington, DC: American Psychological Association.

Bigler, E. D. (2005). Structural imaging. In T. W. Silver, T. W. McAllister, & S. C. Yudofsky (Eds.), *Textbook of traumatic brain injury* (pp. 79–105). Washington, DC: American Psychiatric Publishing.

Bigler, E. D. (2007). Neuroimaging correlates in functional outcome. In N. D. Zasler, D. I. Katz, & R. D. Zafonte (Eds.), *Brain injury medicine: Principles and practice* (pp. 201–224). New York: Demos Medical Publishing.

Bigler, E. D., Lowry, C. M., Kerr, B., Tate, D. F., Hessel, C. D., Earl, H. D., et al. (2003). Role of white matter lesions, cerebral atrophy, and APOE on cognition in older persons with and without dementia: The Cache County, Utah, study of memory and aging. *Neuropsychology, 17,* 339–352.

Bigler, E. D., Ryser, D. K., Gandhi, P., Kimball, J., & Wilde, E. (2006). Day-of-injury computerized tomography, rehabilitation status, and development of cerebral atrophy in persons with traumatic brain injury. *American Journal of Physical and Medical Rehabilitation, 85,* 793–806.

Blatter, D. D., Bigler, E. D., Gale, S. D., Johnson, S. C., Anderson, C. V., Burnett, B. M., et al. (1995). Quantitative volumetric analysis of brain MR: Normative database spanning 5 decades of life. *American Journal of Neuroradiology, 16,* 241–251.

Brooks, W. M., Stidley, C. A., Petropoulos, H., Jung, R. E., Weers, D. C., Friedman, S. D., et al. (2000).

Metabolic and cognitive response to human traumatic brain injury: A quantitative proton magnetic resonance study. *Journal of Neurotrauma, 17,* 629–640.

Brown, J. A., Lutsep, H. L., Weinand, M., & Cramer, S. C. (2006). Motor cortex stimulation for the enhancement of recovery from stroke: A prospective, multicenter safety study. *Neurosurgery, 58,* 464–473.

Bruen, P. D., McGeown, W. J., Shanks, M. F., & Venneri, A. (2008). Neuroanatomical correlates of neuropsychiatric symptoms in Alzheimer's disease. *Brain, 131,* 2455–2463.

Burton, E. J., Kenny, R. A., O'Brien, J., Stephens, S., Bradbury, M., Rowan, E., et al. (2004). White matter hyperintensities are associated with impairment of memory, attention, and global cognitive performance in older stroke patients. *Stroke, 35,* 1270–1275.

Butefisch, C. M., Kleiser, R., & Seitz, R. J. (2006). Postlesional cerebral reorganization: Evidence from functional neuroimaging and transcranial magnetic stimulation. *Journal of Physiology–Paris, 99*(4–6), 437–454.

Cabeza, R. K. A. (2006). *Handbook of functional neuroimaging of cognition* (2nd ed.). Cambridge, MA: MIT Press.

Cahn, B. R., & Polich, J. (2006). Meditation states and traits: EEG, ERP, and neuroimaging studies. *Psychological Bulletin, 132,* 180–211.

Cannestra, A. F., Wartenburger, I., Obrig, H., Villringer, A., & Toga, A. W. (2003). Functional assessment of Broca's area using near infrared spectroscopy in humans. *Neuroreport, 14,* 1961–1965.

Carmichael, O., Kuller, L., Lopez, O., Thompson, P., Dutton, R., Lu, A., et al. (2007). Cerebral ventricular changes associated with transitions between normal cognitive function, mild cognitive impairment, and dementia. *Alzheimer Diseases and Associated Disorders, 21,* 14–24.

Cherney, L. R., & Small, S. L. (2006). Task-dependent changes in brain activation following therapy for nonfluent aphasia: Discussion of two individual cases. *Journal of the International Neuropsychological Society, 12,* 828–842.

Cramer, S. C., Parrish, T. B., Levy, R. M., Stebbins, G. T., Ruland, S. D., Lowry, D. W., et al. (2007). Predicting functional gains in a stroke trial. *Stroke, 38,* 2108–2114.

Cutting, L. E., Clements, A. M., Courtney, S., Rimrodt, S. L., Schafer, J. G., Bisesi, J., et al. (2006). Differential components of sentence comprehension: Beyond single word reading and memory. *Neuroimage, 29,* 429–438.

Davis Garrett, K., Cohen, R. A., Paul, R. H., Moser, D. J., Malloy, P. F., Shah, P., et al. (2004). Computer-mediated measurement and subjective ratings of white matter hyperintensities in vascular dementia: Relationships to neuropsychological performance. *Clinical Neuropsychologist, 18,* 50–62.

Davis, K. D., Taylor, S. J., Crawley, A. P., Wood, M. L., & Mikulis, D. J. (1997). Functional MRI of pain- and attention-related activations in the human cingulate cortex. *Journal of Neurophysiology, 77,* 3370–3380.

deCharms, R. C., Maeda, F., Glover, G. H., Ludlow, D., Pauly, J. M., Soneji, D., et al. (2005). Control over brain activation and pain learned by using real-time functional MRI. *Proceedings of the National Academy of Sciences of the United States of America, 102,* 18626–18631.

de Lange, F. P., Kalkman, J. S., Bleijenberg, G., Hagoort, P., van der Meer, J. W., & Toni, I. (2005). Gray matter volume reduction in the chronic fatigue syndrome. *Neuroimage, 26,* 777–781.

de Mendonca, A., Ribeiro, F., Guerreiro, M., & Garcia, C. (2004). Frontotemporal mild cognitive impairment. *Journal of Alzheimer's Disease, 6,* 1–9.

Di, H. B., Yu, S. M., Weng, X. C., Laureys, S., Yu, D., Li, J. Q., et al. (2007). Cerebral response to patient's own name in the vegetative and minimally conscious states. *Neurology, 68,* 895–899.

Dobkin, B. H. (2005). Rehabilitation and functional neuroimaging dose-response trajectories for clinical trials. *Neurorehabilitation & Neural Repair, 19,* 276–282.

Evans, K. C., Dougherty, D. D., Pollack, M. H., & Rauch, S. L. (2006). Using neuroimaging to predict treatment response in mood and anxiety disorders. *Annals of Clinical Psychiatry, 18,* 33–42.

Felmingham, K., Kemp, A., Williams, L., Das, P., Hughes, G., Peduto, A., & Bryant, R. (2007). Changes in anterior cingulate and amygdala after cognitive behavior therapy of posttraumatic stress disorder. *Psychological Science, 18,* 127–129.

Fernandez, B., Cardebat, D., Demonet, J. F., Joseph, P. A., Mazaux, J. M., Barat, M., et al. (2004). Functional MRI follow-up study of language processes in healthy subjects and during recovery in a case of aphasia. *Stroke, 35,* 2171–2176.

Filippi, M., Rocca, M. A., Colombo, B., Falini, A., Codella, M., Scotti, G., et al. (2002). Functional magnetic resonance imaging correlates of fatigue in multiple sclerosis. *Neuroimage, 15,* 559–567.

Gale, S. D., Baxter, L., Roundy, N., & Johnson, S. C. (2005). Traumatic brain injury and grey matter concentration: A preliminary voxel based morphometry study. *Journal of Neurology, Neurosurgery, and Psychiatry, 76,* 984–988.

Gale, S. D., & Hopkins, R. O. (2004). Effects of hypoxia on the brain: Neuroimaging and neuropsychological findings following carbon monoxide poisoning and obstructive sleep apnea. *Journal of the International Neuropsychological Society, 10,* 60–71.

Gaser, C., & Schlaug, G. (2003). Gray matter differences between musicians and nonmusicians. *Annals of the New York Academy of Sciences, 999,* 514–517.

Gauthier, L. V., Taub, E., Perkins, C., Ortmann, M., Mark, V. W., & Uswatte, G. (2008). Remodeling the brain: Plastic structural brain changes produced by different motor therapies after stroke. *Stroke, 39,* 1520–1525.

Gazzaniga, M. S. (1995). *The cognitive neurosciences.* Cambridge, MA: MIT Press.

Giacino, J. T., Hirsch, J., Schiff, N., & Laureys, S. (2006). Functional neuroimaging applications for assessment and rehabilitation planning in patients with disorders of consciousness. *Archives of Physical Medicine and Rehabilitation, 87*(12, Suppl. 2), S67–S76.

Goetz, P., Blamire, A., Rajagopalan, B., Cadoux-Hudson, T., Young, D., & Styles, P. (2004). Increase in apparent diffusion coefficient in normal appearing white matter following human traumatic brain injury correlates with injury severity. *Journal of Neurotrauma, 21,* 645–654.

Goldszal, A. F., Davatzikos, C., Pham, D. L., Yan, M. X., Bryan, R. N., & Resnick, S. M. (1998). An image-processing system for qualitative and quantitative volumetric analysis of brain images. *Journal of Computer Assisted Tomography, 22,* 827–837.

Gorno-Tempini, M. L., Rankin, K. P., Woolley, J. D., Rosen, H. J., Phengrasamy, L., & Miller, B. L. (2004). Cognitive and behavioral profile in a case of right anterior temporal lobe neurodegeneration. *Cortex, 40*(4–5), 631–644.

Hahn, H. K., Millar, W. S., Klinghammer, O., Durkin, M. S., Tulipano, P. K., & Peitgen, H. O. (2004). A reliable and efficient method for cerebral ventricular volumetry in pediatric neuroimaging. *Methods of Information in Medicine, 43,* 376–382.

Halgren, E., Dhond, R. P., Christensen, N., Van Petten, C., Marinkovic, K., Lewine, J. D., et al. (2002). N400-like magnetoencephalography responses modulated by semantic context, word frequency, and lexical class in sentences. *Neuroimage, 17,* 1101–1116.

Hamzei, F., Liepert, J., Dettmers, C., Weiller, C., & Rijntjes, M. (2006). Two different reorganization patterns after rehabilitative therapy: An exploratory study with fMRI and TMS. *Neuroimage, 31,* 710–720.

Han, B. S., Ahn, S. H., & Jang, S. H. (2008). Cortical reorganization demonstrated by diffusion tensor tractography analyzed using functional MRI activation. *NeuroRehabilitation, 23,* 171–174.

Herwig, U., Baumgartner, T., Kaffenberger, T., Bruhl, A., Kottlow, M., Schreiter-Gasser, U., et al. (2007). Modulation of anticipatory emotion and perception processing by cognitive control. *Neuroimage, 37,* 652–662.

Hopkins, R. O., Beck, C. J., Burnett, D. L., Weaver, L. K., Victoroff, J., & Bigler, E. D. (2006). Prevalence of white matter hyperintensities in a young healthy population. *Journal of Neuroimaging, 16,* 243–251.

Hopkins, R. O., Tate, D. F., & Bigler, E. D. (2005). Anoxic versus traumatic brain injury: Amount of tissue loss, not etiology, alters cognitive and emotional function. *Neuropsychology, 19,* 233–242.

Jang, S. H., You, S. H., & Ahn, S. H. (2007). Neurorehabilitation-induced cortical reorganization in brain injury: A 14-month longitudinal follow-up study. *NeuroRehabilitation, 22,* 117–122.

Jorm, A. F., Anstey, K. J., Christensen, H., de Plater, G., Kumar, R., Wen, W., et al. (2005). MRI hyperintensities and depressive symptoms in a community sample of individuals 60–64 years old. *American Journal of Psychiatry, 162,* 699–705.

Kapeller, P., Schmidt, R., Enzinger, C., Ropele, S., & Fazekas, F. (2002). CT and MRI rating of white matter changes. *Journal of Neural Transmission, 62*(Suppl.), 41–45.

Khan, A. R., Wang, L., & Beg, M. F. (2008). FreeSurfer-initiated fully-automated subcortical brain segmentation in MRI using large deformation diffeomorphic metric mapping. *Neuroimage, 41,* 735–746.

Kim, J. S., Singh, V., Lee, J. K., Lerch, J., Ad-Dab'bagh, Y., MacDonald, D., et al. (2005). Automated 3-D extraction and evaluation of the inner and outer cortical surfaces using a Laplacian map and partial volume effect classification. *Neuroimage, 27,* 210–221.

Kim, Y. H., You, S. H., Ko, M. H., Park, J. W., Lee, K. H., Jang, S. H., et al. (2006). Repetitive transcranial magnetic stimulation-induced corticomotor excitability and associated motor skill acquisition in chronic stroke. *Stroke, 37,* 1471–1476.

Klauschen, F., Goldman, A., Barra, V., Meyer-Lindenberg, A., & Lundervold, A. (2008, June 6). Evaluation of automated brain MR image segmentation and volumetry methods. *Human Brain Mapping.* Retrieved August 12, 2008, from http://www3.interscience.wiley.com/cgi-bin/fulltext/119816778/HTMLSTART

Kobayashi, M., Takayama, H., Suga, S., & Mihara, B. (2001). Longitudinal changes of metabolites in frontal lobes after hemorrhagic stroke of basal ganglia: A proton magnetic resonance spectroscopy study. *Stroke, 32,* 2237–2245.

Kong, J., White, N. S., Kwong, K. K., Vangel, M. G., Rosman, I. S., Gracely, R. H., et al. (2006). Using fMRI to dissociate sensory encoding from cognitive evaluation of heat pain intensity. *Human Brain Mapping, 27,* 715–721.

Krach, S., Chen, L. M., & Hartje, W. (2006). Comparison between visual half-field performance and cerebral blood flow changes as indicators of language dominance. *Laterality, 11,* 122–140.

Kumar, R., Gupta, R. K., Rao, S. B., Chawla, S., Husain, M., & Rathore, R. K. (2003). Magnetization transfer and T2 quantitation in normal appearing cortical gray matter and white matter adjacent to focal abnormality in patients with traumatic brain injury. *Magnetic Resonance Imaging, 21,* 893–899.

Kurth, S., & Bigler, E. D. (2008). Structural neuroimaging in clinical neuropsychology. In J. E. Morgan & J. H. Ricker (Eds.), *Textbook of clinical neuropsychology* (pp. 783–839). Lisse, Holland: Swets & Zeitlinger.

Lainhart, J. E., Lazar, M., Bigler, E. D., & Alexander, A. (2006). *The brain during life in autism: Advances in neuroimaging research.* Hauppauge, NY: NOVA Science Publishers.

Lee, J. W., Choi, C. G., & Chun, M. H. (2006). Usefulness of diffusion tensor imaging for evaluation of motor function in patients with traumatic brain injury: Three case studies. *Journal of Head Trauma Rehabilitation, 21,* 272–278.

Levin, H. S., Wilde, E. A., Chu, Z., Yallampalli, R., Hanten, G. R., Li, X., et al. (2008). Diffusion tensor imaging in relation to cognitive and functional outcome of traumatic brain injury in children. *Journal of Head Trauma Rehabilitation, 23,* 197–208.

Lewine, J. D., Davis, J. T., Bigler, E. D., Thoma, R., Hill, D., Funke, M., et al. (2007). Objective documentation of traumatic brain injury subsequent to mild head trauma: Multimodal brain imaging with MEG, SPECT, and MRI. *Journal of Head Trauma Rehabilitation, 22,* 141–155.

Lewine, J. D., Davis, J. T., Sloan, J. H., Kodituwakku, P. W., & Orrison, W. W., Jr. (1999). Neuromagnetic assessment of pathophysiologic brain activity induced by minor head trauma. *American Journal of Neuroradiology, 20,* 857–866.

Linden, D. E. (2006). How psychotherapy changes the brain: The contribution of functional neuroimaging. *Molecular Psychiatry, 11,* 528–538.

Makris, N., Kaiser, J., Haselgrove, C., Seidman, L. J., Biederman, J., Boriel, D., et al. (2006). Human cerebral cortex: A system for the integration of volume- and surface-based representations. *Neuroimage, 33,* 139–153.

Mark, V. W., Taub, E., & Morris, D. M. (2006). Neuroplasticity and constraint-induced movement therapy. *Europa Medicophysica, 42,* 269–284.

McAllister, T. W., Rhodes, C. H., Flashman, L. A., McDonald, B. C., Belloni, D., & Saykin, A. J. (2005). Effect of the dopamine D2 receptor T allele on response latency after mild traumatic brain injury. *American Journal of Psychiatry, 162,* 1749–1751.

McDonald, C. R., Hagler, D. J., Jr., Ahmadi, M. E., Tecoma, E., Iragui, V., Dale, A. M., et al. (2008). Subcortical and cerebellar atrophy in mesial temporal lobe epilepsy revealed by automatic segmentation. *Epilepsy Research, 79,* 130–138.

Meister, I. G., Sparing, R., Foltys, H., Gebert, D., Huber, W., Topper, R., et al. (2006). Functional connectivity between cortical hand motor and language areas during recovery from aphasia. *Journal of the Neurological Sciences, 247,* 165–168.

Mok, V., Chang, C., Wong, A., Lam, W. W., Richards, P. S., Wong, K. T., et al. (2005). Neuroimaging determinants of cognitive performances in stroke associated with small vessel disease. *Journal of Neuroimaging, 15,* 129–137.

Munoz-Cespedes, J. M., Rios-Lago, M., Paul, N., & Maestu, F. (2005). Functional neuroimaging studies of cognitive recovery after acquired brain damage in adults. *Neuropsychology Review, 15,* 169–183.

Munson, S., Schroth, E., & Ernst, M. (2006). The role of functional neuroimaging in pediatric brain injury. *Pediatrics, 117,* 1372–1381.

Nestor, S., Rupsingh, R., Borrie, M., Smith, M., Accomazzi, V., Wells, J., et al. (2008). Ventricular enlargement as a possible measure of Alzheimer's disease progression validated using the Alzheimer's disease neuroimaging initiative database. *Brain and Cognition, 131,* 2443–2454.

Nguyen, T. H., Yoshida, M., Stievenart, J. L., Iba-Zizen, M. T., Bellinger, L., Abanou, A., et al. (2005). MR tractography with diffusion tensor imaging in clinical routine. *Neuroradiology, 47,* 334–343.

Obrig, H., & Villringer, A. (2003). Beyond the visible: Imaging the human brain with light. *Journal of Cerebral Blood Flow and Metabolism, 23,* 1–18.

Ovbiagele, B., & Saver, J. L. (2006a). Cerebral white matter hyperintensities on MRI: Current concepts and therapeutic implications. *Cerebrovascular Diseases, 22,* 83–90.

Ovbiagele, B., & Saver, J. L. (2006b). Ensuring management of vascular risk factors after stroke. *Reviews in Neurological Diseases, 3,* 93–100.

Papanicolaou, A. C. (1998). *Fundamentals of functional brain imaging: A guide to the methods and their applications to psychology and behavioral neuroscience.* Lisse, Holland: Swets & Zeittlinger.

Papanicolaou, A. C., Castillo, E. M., Billingsley-Marshall, R., Pataraia, E., & Simos, P. G. (2005). A review of clinical applications of magnetoencephalography. *International Review of Neurobiology, 68,* 223–247.

Parkinson, R. B., Hopkins, R. O., Cleavinger, H. B., Weaver, L. K., Victoroff, J., Foley, J. F., et al. (2002). White matter hyperintensities and neuropsychological outcome following carbon monoxide poisoning. *Neurology, 58,* 1525–1532.

Pimlott, S. L. (2005). Radiotracer development in psychiatry. *Nuclear Medicine Communications, 26,* 183–188.

Raedt, R. E. (2006). Does neuroscience hold promise for the further development of behavior therapy? The case of emotional change after exposure in anxiety and depression. *Scandinavian Journal of Psychology, 47,* 225–236.

Ricker, J. H., & Arenth, P. M. (2007). Functional neuroimaging in traumatic brain injury. In N. D. Zasler, D. I. Katz, & R. D. Zafonte (Eds.), *Brain injury medicine: Principles and practices* (pp. 149–165). New York: Demos.

Ricker, J. H., & Arenth, P. M. (2008). Functional neuroimaging in clinical neuropsychology. In J. Morgan & J. H. Ricker (Eds.), *Textbook of clinical neuropsychology* (pp. 840–847). Hove, England: Taylor & Francis.

Robertson, I. H. (2005). Science is the search for generalizable processes—clinicians solve complex problems: A reply to Wilson on the importance of not confusing these two things. *Journal of the International Neuropsychological Society, 11,* 494–497.

Roffman, J. L., Marci, C. D., Glick, D. M., Dougherty, D. D., & Rauch, S. L. (2005). Neuroimaging and the functional neuroanatomy of psychotherapy. *Psychological Medicine, 35,* 1385–1398.

Ross, M. R., Schomer, D. F., Chappell, P., & Enzmann, D. R. (1994). MR imaging of head and neck tumors: Comparison of T1-weighted contrast-enhanced fat-suppressed images with conventional T2-weighted and fast spin-echo T2-weighted images. *American Journal of Roentgenology, 163,* 173–178.

Sachdev, P. S., Wen, W., Christensen, H., & Jorm, A. F. (2005). White matter hyperintensities are related to physical disability and poor motor function. *Journal of Neurology, Neurosurgery, and Psychiatry, 76,* 362–367.

Salmond, C. H., Menon, D. K., Chatfield, D. A., Williams, G. B., Pena, A., Sahakian, B. J., et al. (2006). Diffusion tensor imaging in chronic head injury survivors: Correlations with learning and memory indices. *Neuroimage, 29,* 117–124.

Scheid, R., Preul, C., Gruber, O., Wiggins, C., & von Cramon, D. Y. (2003). Diffuse axonal injury associated with chronic traumatic brain injury: Evidence from T2*-weighted gradient-echo imaging at 3 T. *American Journal of Neuroradiology, 24,* 1049–1056.

Scheid, R., Walther, K., Guthke, T., Preul, C., & von Cramon, D. Y. (2006). Cognitive sequelae of diffuse axonal injury. *Archives of Neurology, 63,* 418–424.

Siegle, G. J., Carter, C. S., & Thase, M. E. (2006). Use of FMRI to predict recovery from unipolar depression with cognitive behavior therapy. *American Journal of Psychiatry, 163,* 735–738.

Siekierka, E. M., Eng, K., Bassetti, C., Blickenstorfer, A., Cameirao, M. S., Dietz, V., et al. (2007). New technologies and concepts for rehabilitation in the acute phase of stroke: A collaborative matrix. *Neurodegenerative Diseases, 4,* 57–69.

Squire, L. R. (2004). Memory systems of the brain: A brief history and current perspective. *Neurobiology of Learning and Memory, 82,* 171–177.

Strangman, G. E., O'Neil-Pirozzi, T. M., Goldstein, R., Kelkar, K., Katz, D. I., Burke, D., et al. (2008). Prediction of memory rehabilitation outcomes in traumatic brain injury by using functional magnetic resonance imaging. *Archives of Physical Medicine and Rehabilitation, 89,* 974–981.

Straube, T., Glauer, M., Dilger, S., Mentzel, H. J., & Miltner, W. H. (2006). Effects of cognitive–behavioral therapy on brain activation in specific phobia. *Neuroimage, 29,* 125–135.

Stuss, D. T., Winocur, G., & Robertson, I. H. (Eds.). (1999). *Cognitive neurorehabilitation.* London: Cambridge University Press.

Suzuki, M., Miyai, I., Ono, T., & Kubota, K. (2008). Activities in the frontal cortex and gait performance are modulated by preparation. An fNIRS study. *Neuroimage, 39,* 600–607.

Toole, J. F., Flowers, D. L., Burdette, J. H., & Absher, J. R. (2007). A pianist's recovery from stroke. *Archives of Neurology, 64,* 1184–1188.

van den Heuvel, D. M., ten Dam, V. H., de Craen, A. J., Admiraal-Behloul, F., Olofsen, H., Bollen, E. L., et al. (2006). Increase in periventricular white matter hyperintensities parallels decline in mental processing speed in a nondemented elderly population. *Journal of Neurology, Neurosurgery, & Psychiatry, 77,* 149–153.

van den Heuvel, D. M., ten Dam, V. H., de Craen, A. J., Admiraal-Behloul, F., van Es, A. C., Palm, W. M., et al. (2006). Measuring longitudinal white matter changes: Comparison of a visual rating scale with a volumetric measurement. *American Journal of Neuroradiology, 27,* 875–878.

van Straaten, E. C., Fazekas, F., Rostrup, E., Scheltens, P., Schmidt, R., Pantoni, L., et al. (2006). Impact of white matter hyperintensities scoring method on correlations with clinical data: The LADIS study. *Stroke, 37,* 836–840.

Wagner, A., Greer, P., Bailer, U. F., Frank, G. K., Henry, S. E., Putnam, K., et al. (2006). Normal brain tissue volumes after long-term recovery in anorexia and bulimia nervosa. *Biological Psychiatry, 59,* 291–293.

Ward, T. E., Soraghan, C. J., Matthews, F., & Markham, C. (2007). A concept for extending the applicability of constraint-induced movement therapy through motor cortex activity feedback using a neural prosthesis. *Computational Intelligence and Neuroscience,* 1–9.

Wilde, E. A., Bigler, E. D., Pedroza, C., & Ryser, D. K. (2006). Posttraumatic amnesia predicts long-term cerebral atrophy in traumatic brain injury. *Brain Injury, 20,* 695–699.

Wilde, E. A., Chu, Z., Bigler, E. D., Hunter, J. V., Fearing, M. A., Hanten, G., et al. (2006). Diffusion tensor imaging in the corpus callosum in children after moderate to severe traumatic brain injury. *Journal of Neurotrauma, 23,* 1412–1426.

Wood, P. B. (2005). Neuroimaging in functional somatic syndromes. *International Review of Neurobiology, 67,* 119–163.

Yoon, S. J., Lee, J. H., Kim, S. T., & Chun, M. H. (2005). Evaluation of traumatic brain injured patients in correlation with functional status by localized 1H-MR spectroscopy. *Clinical Rehabilitation, 19,* 209–215.

PART III

CLINICAL INTERVENTIONS

CHAPTER 14

ALCOHOL AND OTHER DRUG USE IN TRAUMATIC DISABILITY

Charles H. Bombardier and Aaron P. Turner

Alcohol and other drug use disorders are global public health issues, but they are of special concern among people with traumatic disabilities. Alcohol is arguably the most used and abused drug in the United States. Although many people use alcohol normally, the 12-month prevalence of alcohol use disorders in the United States is substantial at 8.5% (Stinson et al., 2005). Hazardous alcohol use remains the third leading cause of preventable death (Mokdad, Marks, Stroup, & Gerberding, 2004). The 1-year prevalence of other drug use disorders is 2.0%. A total of 9.4% of the population have either an alcohol or drug use disorder, and nearly 1.1% have both (Stinson et al., 2005).

People with traumatically acquired disabilities have higher rates of substance abuse disorders than the general population. Because rehabilitation psychologists aspire to treat the "whole person," this chapter emphasizes that in many cases this kind of comprehensive care includes addressing substance abuse problems. Although rehabilitation psychologists report they are often not prepared to treat substance abuse problems (Cardoso, Pruett, Chan, & Tansey, 2006), we will show that substance use problems are not that different from other psychological disorders and that nonspecialists can and should learn to provide evidence-based forms of screening, assessment, and treatment within rehabilitation.

For the purposes of this chapter, traumatic brain injury (TBI) and spinal cord injury (SCI) are used as examples of disabling conditions in which alcohol- or drug-related problems play a significant role. The links between alcohol and other drug problems and these two forms of acquired disability are described in terms of the prevalence and effects on outcome. The terminology used to describe types of substance use or abuse varies by study and may be imprecise. Nevertheless, in general, *substance dependence* refers to a maladaptive pattern of substance use within the past 12 months leading to clinically significant impairment or distress and characterized by at least three of seven problems: tolerance; withdrawal; escalating use; persistent desire or unsuccessful attempts to control use; much time spend associated with obtaining substances, use, or recovery; associated psychosocial impairment; and use despite significant use-related problems (American Psychiatric Association, 1994). *Substance abuse* is similar except that only one or more of the following problems associated with recurrent substance use needs to occur within the past year: failure to fulfill major role obligations, exposure to physically hazardous situations, legal problems, or persistent or recurrent interpersonal problems related to substance use (American Psychiatric Association, 1994).

The writing of this chapter was supported by the National Institute on Disability and Rehabilitation Research (NIDRR), Department of Education (Northwest Regional Spinal Cord Injury System, Grant No. H133N000003, Charles Bombardier, P. I.; and the University of Washington Traumatic Brain Injury Model System, Grant No. H133A980023, Kathleen Bell, P. I.), and the Department of Veterans Affairs (VA Center of Excellence in Substance Abuse Treatment and Education and VA RR&D, Grant No. B3319VA, Aaron Turner, P. I.). The contents of this chapter are solely the responsibility of the authors and do not necessarily represent the official views of NIDRR.

The chapter describes the major ways substance use problems and models of treatment are conceptualized. Practical strategies for screening, assessing, and intervening in substance-related problems are discussed, with an emphasis on promoting improved access to treatment for people with disabilities. In the chapter, we show that rehabilitation psychologists are in a good position to assess alcohol and other drug-related problems and intervene when problems are present.

PREVALENCE AND IMPACT OF ALCOHOL AND DRUG PROBLEMS AMONG PERSONS WITH TRAUMATIC BRAIN INJURY AND SPINAL CORD INJURY

There are two major reasons why alcohol and drug problems merit special attention among people with TBI and SCI. The first reason is the sheer prevalence of substance use disorders in these populations. The second is the potential that alcohol or other drugs may contribute to poor recovery or secondary complications. In the following section, prevalence is described in terms of preinjury substance use problems, use of alcohol or drugs at the time of injury, and postinjury alcohol or drug use and associated problems.

Preinjury Alcohol and Drug Problems

Corrigan, Rust, and Lamb-Hart (1995) reviewed the literature on alcohol and TBI and found that the prevalence of preinjury alcohol abuse or dependence ranged from 16% to 66%. The most rigorous studies, and those conducted in rehabilitation settings, produced the highest prevalence rates, with between 44% and 66% reporting abuse, dependence or high-risk drinking (Bombardier, Rimmele, Zintel, 2002; Jorge et al., 2005). Persons with SCI reported greater than average preinjury alcohol consumption, and 35% to 49% reported a history of significant alcohol problems (Bombardier & Rimmele, 1999).

Much larger studies of preinjury alcohol problems have been conducted on general trauma patients. Rivara et al. (1993) found that 44% of consecutive trauma admissions scored in the "alcoholic" range on a brief screening measure. A similar study found that 24% of all admissions met diagnostic criteria for current alcohol dependence (i.e., 28% for males, 15% for females), whereas 17.7% met criteria for drug dependence (Soderstrom et al., 1997).

Substance Use at the Time of Injury

Toxicology data obtained near the time of injury can also provide insight into alcohol and drug problems among people with TBI or SCI. Corrigan (1995) found that rates of alcohol intoxication among patients with TBI (i.e., with a blood alcohol level greater than 100 mg/dL) ranged from 36% to 51% in the seven studies he reviewed. Subsequent studies have produced similar findings (Alexander, Kerr, Yonas, & Marion, 2004; Bombardier et al., 2002; Cunningham, Maio, Hill, & Zink, 2002; Esselman, Dikmen, Bell, & Temkin, 2004; Wilde et al., 2004). Regarding drug use, Bombardier et al. (2002) reported that toxicology data on 114 of 137 consecutive patients with TBI revealed 23.7% were positive for marijuana, 13.2% for cocaine, and 8.8% for amphetamine. A total of 37.7% were positive for one or more illicit drugs (there was some overlap between groups). In the SCI literature, rates of alcohol intoxication at the time of injury range from 29% to 40% (Heinemann, Schnoll, Brandt, Maltz, & Keen, 1988; Levy et al., 2002). Among general trauma patients, Rivara and colleagues (1993) found that 47% had a positive blood alcohol level whereas 36% were intoxicated. Toxicology assays from a large sample of general trauma patients revealed 15.6% were positive for opiates, 14.0% for cocaine, 10.9% for marijuana, 1.0% for phencyclidine and 0.1% were positive for amphetamine (Soderstrom et al., 1997). Data on toxicology assays for opiates should be interpreted cautiously because opiates are commonly used in emergency medical management of trauma.

Postinjury Substance Abuse and Problems

Longitudinal surveys of alcohol use and alcohol problems among persons with TBI and SCI show that drinking declines substantially during the months immediately following injury but then later increases somewhat during the 1st and 2nd years after injury (Dikmen, Machamer, Donovan, Winn, & Temkin, 1995; Heinemann, Keen, Donohue, & Schnoll, 1988). Greater reductions in drinking postinjury are typically seen among the heaviest drinking individuals; nonetheless, a sizeable minority of individuals with TBI retain a pattern of heavy consumption and associated problems (Bombardier, Dikmen, Temkin, & Machamer, 2003). In most cases, drinking problems after injury represent a continuation of a preinjury pattern, although a small minority develop alcohol problems for the first time following their injury (Bombardier et al., 2003; Corrigan et al., 1995; Heinemann, Doll, & Schnoll, 1989; Kolakowsky-Hayner et al., 2002). Extended follow-up data are limited, but in one retrospective study of individuals with TBI, alcohol use disorders remained the second most common lifetime psychiatric diagnoses 30 years following injury (Koponen et al., 2002). Alcohol consumption after TBI and SCI may be somewhat higher than in the general population (Kolakowsky-Hayner et al.; Kreutzer, Witol, & Marwitz, 1996; Young, Rintala, Rossi, Hart, & Fuhrer, 1995). In a large community survey comparing people with TBI and those without TBI, a history of lifetime drug abuse or dependence was 1.8 times greater and a history of alcohol abuse or dependence was 2.2 times greater among those with TBI (Silver, Kramer, Greenwald, & Weissman, 2001). Drinking rates may be particularly high among selected groups such as vocational rehabilitation clients (Kreutzer, Wehman, Harris, Burns, & Young, 1991), those in postacute rehabilitation programs (National Head Injury Foundation, 1988), and among veterans with SCI (Kirubakaran, Kumar, Powell, Tyler, & Armatas, 1986).

Taken together, these studies provide considerable support for the idea that a prior history of illicit drug use or alcohol problems is common among people who sustain an SCI or TBI. Rates of lifetime alcohol abuse or dependence approach 50%, whereas current dependence is nearly 25%, or about three times, higher than the general population (Stinson et al., 2005). Drinking declines soon after injury, but increases over time, probably as the person resumes greater independence and has greater access to alcohol. Little is known about what triggers relapse into problem drinking or drug use after injury. Nevertheless, after-injury rates of substance use problems seem to remain higher than in the general population. People in postacute and vocational rehabilitation settings may have especially high rates of

alcohol abuse, possibly because alcohol problems interfere with achievement of community integration goals and necessitate additional psychosocial services. These settings may represent important opportunities for interventions.

Effects of Alcohol-Related Factors on Outcome

There is considerable evidence to suggest that alcohol use in traumatic injury is associated with a host of poor medical, functional, and psychosocial outcomes. Although the evidence is not always consistent, alcohol use may play an important role at all phases of the injury and recovery cycle.

Alcohol intoxication. Studies of the effects of alcohol intoxication on neurological outcomes have had mixed results. Some studies have shown that alcohol intoxication at the time of TBI is associated with poorer short-term outcomes, such as greater initial injury severity (Cunningham et al., 2002), longer length of coma, longer period of agitation (Corrigan, 1995; Turner, Kivlahan, Rimmele, & Bombardier, 2006), less cerebral blood flow (Alexander et al., 2004), greater cerebral atrophy 3 months postinjury (Wilde et al., 2004), and greater cognitive impairment 1 to 2 months postinjury (Bombardier & Thurber, 1998; Brooks et al., 1989; Kelly, Johnson, Knoller, Drubach, & Winslow, 1997; Tate, Freed, Bombardier, Harter, & Brinkman, 1999). Other studies of persons with TBI have found no relationship between blood alcohol level and neurological outcome (Alexander et al., 2004) or cognitive impairment (Kaplan & Corrigan, 1992; Turner et al., 2006). Alcohol may have both neuroprotective and neurotoxic effects in the context of acute TBI (Kelly, 1995). However, both animal (Halt, Swanson, & Faden, 1992) and human studies (Kiwerski & Krauski, 1992) suggest that alcohol intoxication may be associated with more severe SCI and higher rates of cervical SCI (Garrison et al., 2004).

Preinjury alcohol problems. A preinjury pattern of chronic alcohol abuse or dependence is predictive of numerous negative outcomes after TBI and SCI. Preinjury alcohol abuse is associated with increased risk of mortality and more severe brain lesions (Corrigan, 1995). Patients with a history of alcohol abuse are at higher risk of emotional and behavioral problems, are less likely to successfully integrate back into the community or return to productive activity, have poorer vocational outcomes, and are at higher risk of recurrent TBI (Corrigan, 1995; Jorge et al., 2005). Because many of these studies were not able to completely control for potential confounding factors, such as education, legal difficulties, other substance use, and social support, the precise role alcohol plays in poorer outcomes merits further study (Cherner, Temkin, Machamer, & Dikmen, 2001; Dikmen, Donovan, Loberg, Machamer, & Temkin, 1993).

Persons with SCI who had premorbid alcohol problems were found to spend less time in productive activities such as rehabilitation therapies (Heinemann, Goranson, Ginsberg, & Schnoll, 1989) and have increased risk of pressure sores during the first 3 years after SCI (Elliott, Kurylo, Chen, & Hicken, 2002). In addition, people with SCI and a history of significant alcohol problems have higher rates of depression (Dryden et al., 2005) and suicide (Charlifue & Gerhart, 1991).

Postinjury alcohol use or abuse.   It is widely suspected that even moderate alcohol consumption after TBI may dampen neurological recovery and magnify cognitive impairments (National Head Injury Foundation, 1988). Yet, there is surprisingly little empirical research in this area. Clearly, chronic heavy alcohol consumption can cause cognitive impairment, including permanent brain damage (Rourke & Loberg, 1996). Cognitive impairment also can develop in heavy "social drinkers," and the effects are roughly dose dependent (Parsons & Nixon, 1998). Limited evidence suggests that hazardous alcohol use may have deleterious effects on brain functioning after TBI, as shown by impaired event-related potentials (Baguley et al., 1997) and brain structure, demonstrated by reduced brain volume as shown by magnetic resonance imaging (MRI; Jorge et al., 2005). Support for the idea that TBI magnifies the acute neurocognitive effects of alcohol comes from self-reports of increased sensitivity to alcohol (Oddy, Coughlin, & Tyerman, 1985) and the finding that alcohol intoxication and TBI produce similar neuropsychological impairments (Peterson, Rothfleisch, Zelazo, & Pihl, 1990).

Findings in the existing literature on postinjury alcohol use and neuropsychological outcomes in people with TBI are inconsistent. One study found a positive relation between a history of preinjury alcohol problems and worse postinjury cognitive functioning (Dikmen et al., 1993). Three studies found minimal or no evidence for such a relation (Brooks et al., 1989; Tate, Freed, Bombardier, Harter, & Brinkman, 1999; Turner et al., 2006). It is likely that discrepant findings are due, in part, to a failure to account for postinjury drinking. To date, only one study has examined the contribution of both preinjury and postinjury drinking on neurological and neuropsychological outcomes. Jorge et al. (2005) prospectively examined a cohort of individuals with new TBI. At 3-month follow-up, individuals with a history of alcohol abuse or dependence at baseline had reduced frontal gray matter volumes compared with those with no history of alcohol problems, but there were no differences in neuropsychological functioning between the two groups. However, those individuals with TBI and a history of alcohol abuse or dependence who had resumed drinking following injury displayed not only greater reductions in frontal gray matter but also poorer performance on executive functioning tasks.

In people with SCI, alcohol use after injury is also associated with negative outcomes. People with SCI who report alcohol or drug treatment after injury are more likely to be hospitalized for a pressure ulcer (Krause, Vines, Farley, Sniezek, & Coker, 2001). Heavy drinking after SCI is associated with greater likelihood of sustaining injuries after SCI that are severe enough to require medical treatment (Krause, 2004). Alcohol abuse after SCI is thought to interfere with health maintenance behaviors that are dependent on judgment, coordination, and memory (Krause, 1992); however, this has never been documented empirically.

Taken together, the relevant literature suggests that alcohol intoxication at the time of injury is most likely to affect early indicators of cognitive function but that, with time and physical recovery, the influence of intoxication on cognitive functioning diminishes unless there is a return to drinking. The effect of preinjury alcohol abuse on postinjury outcomes is the most well-established finding.

However, even this relationship remains controversial because of the potential confounding effects of numerous variables, including education level, preinjury socioeconomic status, and postinjury drinking. Less is known about the effects of substance use after injury. Studies are needed that examine the effect of postinjury alcohol and other drug use on outcomes such as cognition, behavior, neurological complications (e.g., seizures), and neuropsychological recovery among people with TBI. Similar research is needed to examine the effect of postinjury substance use on immune functioning, sexual functioning, depression and self-care after SCI. Studies should control for the effects of preinjury substance use, abuse, or dependence.

HISTORICAL PERSPECTIVE AND COMPETING MODELS OF ALCOHOLISM

As is the case with many medical and psychological disorders, our understanding of alcohol and other substance use problems has changed considerably in recent decades. A good understanding of the state of current treatment options requires a background in the theoretical dialogue that has shaped clinical practices over time.

Competing Models of Alcoholism

Alcoholism can be conceptualized in categorical terms as a disease or as a continuum of alcohol-related problems. The disease model views alcoholism as a discrete disease state that is either present or absent, rendering persons with alcoholism qualitatively different from typical individuals who consume alcohol. Specifically, persons with alcoholism are thought to have a medical or psychological defect resulting in a constellation of behaviors including excessive consumption and a loss of control over drinking despite physical and psychosocial consequences. Alcoholism is believed to be chronic and progressive and can only be put in remission through abstinence. The prevailing disease model is most closely represented by the *Diagnostic and Statistical Manual of Mental Disorders* ([*DSM–IV*]; 4th ed.; American Psychiatric Association, 1994) definition of alcohol dependence.

The emphasis on alcoholism as a disease follows a historical pattern similar to that of other medical conditions:

> The historical record also suggests that treatment for any problem tends to originate as a result of attention being drawn to severe cases. Initially, treatment consists of applying to these cases the existing remedies that are available when the problem is first recognized. As time passes, however, it becomes increasingly clear that *(a) cases other than severe cases exist and (b) other methods can be used to deal with them* [italics added]. . . . Thus, it is not surprising to find the same progression in the treatment of persons with alcohol problems. (Institute of Medicine [IOM], 1990, p. 59).

Much contemporary theory and research on alcoholism has moved away from the categorical disease model and toward a continuum model that holds that alcohol-related problems occur along a spectrum of severity (Miller & Brown, 1997). Although it is predicated on the disease model, the *DSM–IV* recognizes gradations of alcoholism other than dependence through the diagnosis of alcohol abuse (American Psychiatric Association, 1994). The IOM (1990) report is notable for moving even further from the disease model by explicitly adopting a continuum of "alcohol problems" that are expressed along numerous dimensions.

In the IOM (1990) report, a triangle diagram was developed to represent this continuum of alcohol problems (see Figure 14.1). The area of the triangle depicts the entire United States population with regard to alcohol consumption and alcohol-related problems. The figure illustrates a number of important conceptual shifts that are relevant to the issue of alcohol and disability.

First, prototypical alcoholics represent a minority of Americans with alcohol problems. A large proportion of Americans consume hazardous amounts of alcohol and incur significant harm from alcohol use without meeting criteria for alcohol dependence or seeking help. Second, the IOM (1990) model emphasizes that there are no clear boundaries between normal

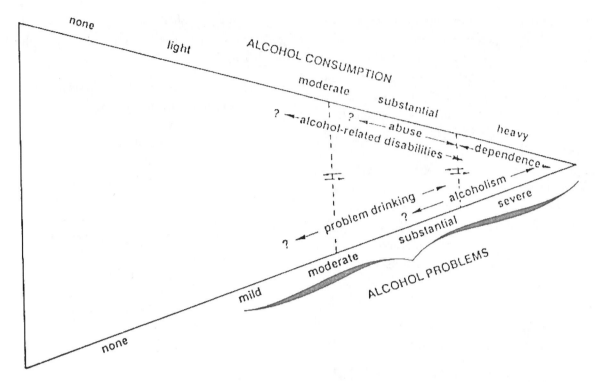

FIGURE 14.1. A terminological map. From *Broadening the Base of Treatment for Alcohol Problems,* by the Institute of Medicine, 1990, Washington, DC: National Academies Press. Copyright 1990 by National Academies Press. Reprinted with permission.

use and abuse of alcohol or between alcohol abuse and dependence. Third, individuals often shift back and forth along the continuum. Among persons with some history of alcohol use disorder, consumption and the degree of alcohol-related problems vary significantly over the course of the person's lifetime (Valliant, 1983). Moreover, the majority of the shifting that occurs is probably not attributable to treatment (Sobell, Cunningham, & Sobell, 1996). Finally, the continuum model provides a more appropriate framework through which to view the modal person whom rehabilitation psychologists will encounter: someone with mild to moderate problems with alcohol.

Common Assumptions Associated With the Disease Model

A number of persistent assumptions about alcohol use disorders appear to conflict with the contemporary literature on addictive behaviors and could interfere with potential innovations in clinical care (see Table 14.1). In contrast with popular conceptions, people with substance use disorders typically acknowledge problems when asked in a nonjudgmen-

tal and empathic manner. In rehabilitation settings, patients with substance abuse problems report the desire to change. They often want to try to change on their own, but many will accept treatment or support from Alcoholics Anonymous (AA; Bombardier et al., 2002). Changing on one's own is the way most people with alcohol problems achieve sobriety (Sobell et al., 1996). Among people with primary alcohol abuse and dependence, brief interventions of one to three sessions are generally as effective as standard treatment (Bien, Miller, & Tonigan, 1993). In many cases, substance use problems may be more treatable than is typically assumed. Moreover, a variety of treatments may be effective, and nonspecialists may be able to provide valuable interventions within the context of comprehensive rehabilitation.

SUBSTANCE ABUSE SCREENING

Accurate identification of alcohol and substance use disorders is an essential first step toward providing effective treatment. Fortunately, a substantial body of research has examined the screening and assessment

TABLE 14.1

Common Beliefs About Substance Abuse: Myths Versus Research Findings

Substance abuse myth	Research findings
Patients must admit they are an "alcoholic" to recover.	▪ Acceptance of the label *alcoholic* is unrelated to treatment outcomes (Trice, 1957).
Alcoholism is a disease of denial.	▪ Alcoholics exhibit no more denial than do nonalcoholics (Donovan, Rohsenow, Schau, & O'Leary, 1977; Skinner & Allen, 1983). ▪ In people with traumatic brain injury and spinal cord injury, more severe alcohol problems are associated with greater readiness to change (Bombardier & Rimmele, 1998; Bombardier, Rimmele, & Zintel, 2002). ▪ Therapist behaviors significantly influence patient resistance and denial (Miller & Sovereign, 1989; Patterson & Forgatch, 1985).
Denial must be confronted.	▪ Confrontation increases resistance to change; empathy increases motivation to change (Miller & Sovereign, 1989; Patterson & Forgatch, 1985).
Not wanting formal treatment is a sign of denial.	▪ Most people with psychological problems do not seek professional help (Prochaska, DiClemente, & Norcross, 1992). ▪ In people with traumatic brain injury, 70% of at-risk drinkers wanted to change their drinking on their own, whereas less than 20% wanted to attend Alcoholics Anonymous or treatment (Bombardier et al., 2002).
Substance abuse treatment is the only route to recovery.	▪ 77% of alcoholics who recover do so without professional help or Alcoholics Anonymous (Sobell, Cunningham, & Sobell, 1996). ▪ Brief interventions of one to three sessions are as effective as more intensive treatment (Bien, Miller, & Tonigan, 1993).
Lifetime abstinence is the only legitimate goal of treatment.	▪ Requiring commitment to abstinence excludes individuals who could make other meaningful changes in their drinking (Dimeff & Marlatt, 1995). ▪ Giving choices regarding treatment goals enhances treatment adherence (Sanchez-Craig & Lei, 1986). ▪ Some problem drinkers achieve good long-term outcomes through moderate drinking (Sanchez-Craig, Wilkinson, & Davila, 1995).

of these disorders in medical and general populations, and a growing body of evidence supports their validity and reliability in rehabilitation populations.

General Considerations

There are several reasons to advocate for universal screening for substance abuse problems in the context of rehabilitation. Substance abuse is prevalent and influences important outcomes relevant to rehabilitation. Yet, health care providers are notoriously poor at detecting substance abuse problems without the systematic use of valid screening measures. Clinical detection has not been well-studied in rehabilitation settings; however, a survey of rehabilitation staff indicated they believe that, on average, 22% of rehabilitation patients have substance abuse problems (Basford, Rohe, Barnes, & DePompolo, 2002), whereas screening studies suggest the actual rate is two to three times higher (Corrigan, 1995;

Heinemann, Keene, et al., 1988). Research in acute trauma care showed that 23% of acutely intoxicated patients were not detected by their physicians, and staff identified less than half of patients with chronic alcohol problems (Gentilello et al., 1999). In the same study, staff also falsely labeled 26% of patients as alcoholic. Clinical judgment in primary care settings also tends to have poor sensitivity for alcohol abuse or dependence (18%–44%) but good specificity (96%–99%; Fiellin, Reid, & O'Connor, 2000). Clinical judgment regarding the presence or absence of substance abuse is subject to systematic biases based on sex, appearance, insurance status, and socioeconomic status (Gentilello et al., 1999). Biases may enter into clinical judgment to the extent that nonevidence-based screening approaches are relied on (Bombardier, Kilmer, & Ehde, 1997). As will be seen as follows, a number of evidence-based screening approaches with good sensitivity and specificity for identifying alcohol abuse and dependence are available.

Accurate identification of people with preinjury problem drinking is an excellent way of predicting those at risk of problem drinking 1 year postinjury (Bombardier et al., 2002). Identification of problem drinkers also may identify people at risk of slower rate of functional improvement within inpatient rehabilitation (Bombardier, Stroud, Esselman, & Rimmele, 2004). Blood alcohol and other toxicology screening can help identify those with substance abuse (Gentilello et al., 1999); however, simple self-report measures tend to be more sensitive and specific (Fiellin et al., 2000). A number of studies show that it is feasible to administer self-report screening measures even within acute medical, surgical, and rehabilitation settings (Bombardier et al., 2002; Gentilello et al., 1999; Soderstrom et al., 1997). Perhaps the most important reason to implement universal screening, however, is to identify people in need of interventions aimed at preventing return to substance abuse.

Some clinicians may be reluctant to institute alcohol screening and assessment procedures because of concerns about federal confidentiality laws and insurance coverage. Before undertaking alcohol screening, staff should become familiar with federal law (United States Public Health Service, 1989) that describes rules regarding protection of health information related to alcohol and drug abuse. Laws regarding potential exclusion of coverage for alcohol or drug related injuries vary by state. A thorough discussion of these laws is beyond the scope of this chapter; however, Rivara et al. (2000) provide an excellent review as well as practical advice for managing substance abuse-related confidentiality and insurance coverage issues.

Another potential barrier to systematic screening is clinician doubt about the validity of self-reported alcohol screening or assessment data. Considerable attention has been paid to this issue in the substance abuse literature, and extensive reviews have concluded that persons with alcohol problems generally provide reliable and valid reports if proper measures and procedures are used (Cooney, Zweben, & Fleming, 1995). With regard to people with TBI, where the validity of alcohol screening measures

may be even more controversial, Sander, Witol, and Kreutzer (1997) demonstrated good agreement (i.e., greater than 90%) between self-reported and independent observer ratings of alcohol use.

Numerous procedures for maximizing the validity of self-reports have been described (Babor, Brown, & Del Boca, 1990; Sobell & Sobell, 1990). Generally, interviews should be conducted in clinical settings when the subject is not under the influence of drugs or alcohol and given reassurances of confidentiality. Alcohol or drug abuse screening measures should be embedded within the context of a larger battery of health-related assessments, and emphasis should be placed on substance use as one of several behavioral risk factors that might impact health or well-being. Adjunctive biomedical data, such as blood alcohol levels or liver function tests, can enhance validity. Any substance use-related assessments should be conducted in a nonjudgmental fashion, avoiding terms such as *alcoholism* or similar labels. Screening batteries that include a measure of recent substance use have the advantage of being able to distinguish patients with current versus lifetime substance-related problems.

Practical Screening Measures

A number of brief screening measures have been found to be reliable and valid indicators of significant alcohol-related problems (see Table 14.2 and Table 14.3). One valid tool for identifying people with alcohol dependence in rehabilitation settings is the CAGE questionnaire (Ewing, 1984). The CAGE acronym stands for four questions: Have you ever felt you should Cut down on your drinking? Have you ever felt Annoyed by someone criticizing your drinking? Have you ever felt bad or Guilty about your drinking? Have you ever had a drink first thing in the morning to steady your nerves or to get rid of a hangover (Eye opener)? Each affirmative response is scored 1, and a total score of 2 or more is considered clinically significant. The sensitivity and specificity of the CAGE for detecting current alcohol abuse among people with TBI also appears to be better than longer measures such as the Short Michigan Alcoholism Screening Test and the Substance Abuse Subtle Screening Inventory (SASSI-3; Ashman, Schwartz, Cantor, Hibbard, & Gordon, 2004).

TABLE 14.2

Commonly Used Alcohol-Screening Measures

Measure	Items	Cutoff score	Time	Comments
CAGE	4	>2	1–2 minutes	Easy to administer; more specific for alcohol dependence; however, no consumption items
AUDIT	10	>8	2–5 minutes	Measures consumption, consequences, and dependence; more sensitive to alcohol abuse
AUDIT-C	3		1 minute	Measures quantity, frequency, and binge drinking, not problems; valid for both men and women using separate cutoff scores
Men		>4		
Women		>3		
SMAST	13	>3	5–7 minutes	Measures consequences, not consumption
RAPS	5	>1	1–2 minutes	Valid screen for alcohol dependence among women and minority persons; no consumption items
SASSI-3	93	Multiple scales	15 minutes	Proprietary measure designed to identify substance use disorders regardless of the respondent's honesty; however, claim has been challenged

Note. CAGE stands for four questions: Have you ever felt you should Cut down on your drinking? Have you ever felt Annoyed by someone criticizing your drinking? Have you ever felt bad or Guilty about your drinking? Have you ever had a drink first thing in the morning to steady your nerves or to get rid of a hangover (Eye opener)? AUDIT = Alcohol Use Disorders Identification Test; AUDIT-C = the three consumption items of the AUDIT; RAPS = Rapid Alcohol Problems Screen; SASSI = Substance Abuse Subtle Screening Inventory; SMAST = Short Michigan Alcoholism Screening Test.

There are also well-validated instruments designed to detect hazardous alcohol use at the lower end of the alcohol use disorder spectrum. The Alcohol Use Disorders Identification Test (AUDIT) was developed by the World Health Organization to promote early identification of problem drinking in primary care medical settings (Allen, Litten, Fertig, & Babor, 1997). The AUDIT consists of 10 items: 3 questions on alcohol consumption, 4 questions on alcohol-related life problems, and 3 questions on alcohol

TABLE 14.3

Clinical Utility of Alcohol Related Screening Measures

	Criterion category			
	Current abuse or at-risk drinking		Current alcohol dependence	
Measure	Sensitivity	Specificity	Sensitivity	Specificity
AUDIT	74%	88%	74%	89%
AUDIT-C				
Men	86%*	89%*	88%*	75%*
Women	73%*	91%*	87%*	85%*
CAGE	54%	91%	84%	90%
RAPS	55%	79%	93%	87%
SMAST	68%*	92%*	100%*	85%*
SASSI			70%	62%

Note. Data from Bradley et al. (2007), and Cherpitel (2000).

dependence symptoms. In recent years, the three consumption items of the AUDIT, known as the AUDIT-C, have been shown to be a practical and valid way of screening for hazardous alcohol use, as well as abuse and dependence, in health care settings (Bradley et al., 2007). In addition, separate cutoffs for men and women have helped optimize screening accuracy.

Fewer options are available for drug use screening. A validity study comparing drug abuse screeners to a Structured Clinical Interview for the *DSM–IV* (SCID; First, Gibbon, Spitzer, & Williams, 1996) diagnosis in people with TBI found that the face-valid drug scale from the SASSI-3 performed better than the CAGE adapted for drug abuse (Ashman et al., 2004). Other options for drug abuse screening include the Alcohol, Smoking and Substance Involvement Screening Test (ASSIST; WHO ASSIST Working Group, 2002). The ASSIST is a reliable instrument designed for use in medical settings. It covers lifetime and current drug use as well as symptoms of dependence and drug-related problems. The measure currently takes 15 minutes to administer; however, a shorter version is under development. Another brief screening test is the Two-Item Conjoint Screening (TICS; Brown, Leonard, Saunders, & Papasouliotis, 2001). The two questions are "In the last year have you ever drank or used drugs more than you meant to?" and "Have you felt you wanted or needed to cut down on your drinking or drug use in the last year?" At least one positive response had a sensitivity and specificity of 81% for an independently diagnosed substance abuse disorder in a primary care medical population (Brown et al., 2001).

In summary, universal screening for alcohol and other drug-related problems is recommended, can be conducted with little investment in clinical time, and can be used to predict a variety of clinical outcomes among people with recent TBI and SCI. For alcohol use disorders, the AUDIT-C seems to be an especially promising tool because it is brief, has strong psychometric properties, and can identify persons at the lower end of problem severity. For other substance use disorders, clinicians must choose between brief but nonsubstance-specific instruments such as the TICS or richer but much longer tools such as the SASSI-3 or the ASSIST.

When recommended screening procedures are followed, they produce valid results and can be conducted with nearly every person who can be interviewed. Screening is the basis for more detailed assessment and brief interventions or treatment.

Assessing Substance Use Patterns

More detailed assessment of substance-related factors may be useful to make appropriate diagnoses, to elicit motivation to change, and to match treatment plans to the specific needs of the individual. Assessment should include at least three dimensions: alcohol or drug use patterns, symptoms of dependence, and alcohol- or drug-related life problems (IOM, 1990; see Table 14.4). Assessment frequently covers diagnosis and readiness to change. Turner, Bombardier, and Rimmele (2003) showed that inpatients with TBI or SCI fell into four general groups: 18% appeared alcohol dependent, perhaps requiring more intensive treatment and follow-up to achieve abstinence; 21% were characterized by heavy consumption but with few symptoms of dependence and the possibility of responding well to brief interventions; 15% were alcohol-dependent persons who were in remission or relapsed and who could benefit from relapse-prevention types of interventions; and 46% were normal drinkers and nondrinkers who may have needed only brief education.

A wide range of measures exists to assess substance use disorders. Choice of measures will depend on clinical needs, time constraints, who can perform the assessments, and their level of training. Attention should be paid to the time frame referred to in the measure (typically lifetime or recent). In persons with TBI, memory impairment may complicate recall depending on the time frame (Corrigan, 1995). Unfortunately, most measures have no psychometric data to support their use among persons with cognitive impairment. Research is needed in this area.

MODELS OF SERVICE DELIVERY

There are at least four broad approaches to providing substance abuse treatment in health care settings. One approach is to develop expertise in a single effective treatment modality and treat all at-risk patients with that model. Another approach is

TABLE 14.4

Commonly Used Substance Abuse Measures

Domain/Measures	Description
Drinking patterns	
Quantity/Frequency/Variability Index (Cahalan & Cisin, 1969)	Measures the approximate number of drinking occasions per time interval and the number of drinks consumed on a typical drinking occasion
Grid Method (Jacobson, 1989)	Typical drinking week reconstructed by assessing alcohol consumption during the morning, afternoon and evening of each day
Timeline Follow-back (Jacobson, 1989)	Actual drinking assessed during a specific time period using calendar and memory anchor points to cue recall
Drinking Diary (Jacobson, 1989)	Alcohol consumption recorded on daily basis
Alcohol dependence	
The Alcohol Dependence Scale (Skinner & Horn, 1984)	25 items measuring symptoms of dependence over the past year; most psychometrically sound dependence measure (Miller, Westerberg, & Waldron, 1995)
Severity of Alcohol Dependence Questionnaire (Stockwell, Hodgson, Edwards, Taylor, & Rankin, 1979)	20 items measuring frequency of dependence symptoms over a 30 day period of heavy drinking
Short Alcohol Dependence Data (Davidson & Raistrick, 1986)	15-item measure sensitive to early signs of dependence (Heather, 1995)
Alcohol-related problems	
Drinker's Inventory of Consequences (Miller, Tonigan, & Longabaugh, 1994)	50-item scale designed to assess negative life events that are specifically attributable to alcohol; five subscales physical, interpersonal, intrapersonal, impulse control, and social responsibility, plus a control scale to check on unreliable reporting
Alcohol Diagnosis	
Structured Clinical for *DSM–IV* (First, Gibbon, Spitzer, & Williams, 1996)	Interview permits diagnosis of alcohol abuse versus mild, moderate or severe dependence
Drug Use	
Drug Abuse Screening Test 28-item version (Gavin, Ross, & Skinner, 1989) 10-item version (French, Roebuck, McGeary, Chitwood, & McCoy, 2001)	The 28-item version demonstrated an overall accuracy of 85% when compared to a *DSM–III* diagnosis of drug abuse or dependence
Readiness to Change	
Readiness to Change Questionnaire (Bombardier & Heinemann, 2000; Rollnick, Heather, Gold, & Hall, 1992)	The original 12-item measure reduced to 10 items and rescaled via Rasch analysis; readiness is more of a continuum than series of stages
Readiness Ruler (LaBrie, Quinlan, Schiffman, & Earleywine, 2005)	Single question readiness rulers (scaled from 0 = "I never think about my drinking" to 10 = "My drinking has changed. I now drink less than before.") may be at least as effective at predicting outcomes as longer stage-based measures
Comprehensive Measures	
Alcohol Use Inventory (Horn, Wanberg, & Foster, 1987)	228-item measure yielding 17 scales on dimensions such as drinking style, physical dependence, loss of control, and readiness to change
Addiction Severity Index (McLellan, Luborsky, O'Brien, & Woody, 1980)	40-minute structured interview covering life problems, medical, legal, employment/support, alcohol, other drugs, family/social, and psychiatric status

to attempt to match patients to different levels or types of treatment depending on the severity of their problem. A third approach is to screen all patients for substance abuse and refer all those with substance abuse or dependence to outside treatment programs (Gentilello et al., 1988). Finally, the use of stepped care models is growing. Stepped care involves providing a small dose of therapy (e.g., brief intervention) to all at-risk patients, followed by reassessment and more intensive treatment only if the person fails to meet a predetermined clinical goal (Marlatt & Tapert, 1993).

In the United States, treatment for alcoholism has developed largely independent of scientific scrutiny. As a result, the most commonly used therapies are often the ones with the least empirical support, and effectiveness is inversely related to cost (Miller et al., 1995). Fortunately, empirical reviews and meta-analyses (Miller et al., 1995) are available as a rational guide to clinical care. In the following sections, several effective alcohol interventions are described with an emphasis on how they may be used in rehabilitation settings. Therapies with the highest cumulative evidence for their efficacy are (in rank order): brief interventions, social skills training, motivational enhancement, and the community reinforcement approach (Miller et al., 1995). It is worth noting that these reviewers have identified a number of therapies that have documented ineffectiveness. These include educational lectures or films, general psychotherapy, general alcohol counseling, relaxation therapy, and antianxiety medications. A growing number of medications can be useful as part of a comprehensive substance abuse treatment plan (Williams, 2005). However, this topic is beyond the scope of this chapter.

In the context of discussing substance abuse treatment, AA merits special mention. AA has not been studied in a way that permits firm conclusions about its efficacy as a stand-alone treatment (Miller et al., 1995). Nevertheless, a large multisite study showed that AA plus 12 sessions of supportive therapy was as effective as 4 sessions of motivation enhancement therapy or 12 sessions of cognitive–behavioral therapy (Project MATCH Research Group, 1997). AA is widely available and provides an element of ongoing social support. When the patient is interested in attending AA or other 12-step programs, it seems prudent to support this plan. Whenever possible, psychologists should educate AA sponsors about disability (e.g., TBI) and provide services aimed at maximizing the patient's ability to benefit from 12-step programs.

Advice

Giving at-risk patients brief advice to abstain or reduce drinking or drug use is possible for any physi-

cian who works with these patient populations. Numerous controlled studies in medical settings have shown that brief physician advice results in significant, lasting decreases in drinking (Cooney et al., 1995). For example, a randomized, controlled study showed that two 10- to 15-minute interactions with a primary care physician resulted in a 40% reduction in alcohol consumption among problem drinkers measured 1 year later (Fleming, Barry, Manwell, Johnson, & London, 1997). Advice may be more effective when it is combined with self-help materials or personalized feedback and information about the adverse health effects of alcohol (Cooney et al., 1995). Several self-help guides have been published (Kishline, 1994; Miller & Munoz, 1982), including one written specifically for persons with TBI (Karol & Sparadeo, 1991). A guide to physicians who want to provide their patients with advice regarding alcohol problems is available on the Web (http://pubs.niaaa.nih.gov/publications/Practitioner/CliniciansGuide2005/clinicians_guide.htm). This model uses a simple four-step approach: Ask about alcohol use, assess for alcohol related problems, advise appropriate action based on risk, and monitor patient progress.

Brief Interventions

Brief interventions have been used in a variety of settings, as a stand-alone treatment, as a way of enhancing the effects of subsequent treatments, and as a means of effecting referral to specialized treatment (Heather, 1995). The effective elements of brief interventions have been summarized by the acronym FRAMES (Bien et al., 1993): Feedback, Responsibility, Advice, a Menu of options, Empathy, and Self-efficacy. Typically, on the basis of the results of an assessment, the patient is provided with personally relevant feedback that includes the impairment or risks associated with past and future drinking. The therapist emphasizes the patient's personal responsibility for change, provides clear advice to make a change in drinking, and gives a menu of alternative strategies for changing problem drinking. This information is provided with empathy and understanding, not confrontation, and reinforces the patient's hope, self-efficacy, or optimism.

The most widely researched model of brief interventions is motivational interviewing (Miller &

Rollnick, 1991, 2002). Motivational interviewing is described as a "client-centered, directive method for enhancing intrinsic motivation to change by exploring and resolving ambivalence" (Miller & Rollnick, 2007). The key therapeutic strategies in motivational interviewing are open-ended questions, reflective listening, affirmations, summarizations, and eliciting change talk from the client. Reviews and meta-analyses of interventions based on motivational interviewing support the efficacy and applicability of this intervention (Burke, Arkowitz, & Menchola, 2003; Dunn, Deroo, & Rivara, 2001; Noonan & Moyers, 1997). Numerous authors have recommended motivational interviewing as a potentially effective intervention among rehabilitation patients (Bombardier & Rimmele, 1999; Cardoso et al., 2006; Jones, 1992; Langley & Kiley, 1992), and two studies have described adaptations of this method in people with TBI (Bombardier & Rimmelle, 1999). In another relevant study, Gentilello et al. (1999) randomized 366 general trauma patients to a 30-minute motivational interview whereas 396 control participants received usual care during their acute medical or surgical hospital stay. At 12-months postinjury, the intervention group not only reduced their alcohol consumption significantly more than the control group (21.8 drinks/week vs. 6.7 drinks/week) but also showed a significantly greater reduction in rates of reinjury and rehospitalization than did the control group.

Coping and Social-Skills Training

This approach to alcohol treatment has evolved out of a social learning perspective on alcohol-use disorders (Monti, Rohsenow, Colby, & Abrams, 1995). The underlying assumption is that persons with alcohol problems lack adequate skills to regulate positive and negative mood and to cope with social and interpersonal situations such as work, marriage, and parenting. Core interpersonal treatment modules include drink refusal skills, giving positive feedback, giving criticism, receiving criticism about substance use, listening skills, conversation skills, developing sober supports, and conflict resolution. Core mood regulation topics include managing negative thinking and coping with drinking-related beliefs, triggers, and craving. Coping and social-skills training has

been adapted for persons with TBI and is highly recommended for those with significant alcohol dependence (Langley & Kiley, 1992). A nonrandomized comparison trial conducted with 40 people with TBI showed that 12 sessions of systematic motivational counseling (Cox et al., 2003) focused on participants' personal goals and concerns in various areas of their lives; helping them to formulate and execute concrete and realistic plans for resolving their concerns was associated with significant reductions in substance use and negative affect as well as improvements in motivational structure. There were no significant pre–post changes in the comparison group (Cox et al., 2003).

Community Reinforcement Approach

The community reinforcement approach (CRA) is a behaviorally based intervention that emphasizes the use of natural reinforcers in the patient's environment (e.g., family, spouse, friends, work, leisure activities) to facilitate change in drinking behavior (Smith & Meyers, 1995). The CRA begins with a traditional functional analysis of drinking and nondrinking behaviors. Rather than requiring clients to make a commitment to lifelong abstinence, CRA therapists negotiate a period of "time out" from drinking that may include the use of Disulfiram (Antabuse). The CRA includes special procedures to address marital or relationship issues, vocational training, lack of social support, and the absence of nondrinking recreational alternatives. This approach has been shown to be effective in four out of four outcome studies (Miller et al., 1995).

A promising application of CRA is when it is used with the concerned friends or family members of a person with an alcohol use disorder who refuses to seek treatment (Meyers, Dominguez, & Smith, 1997). Concerned others are trained to use behavior-management skills, communication skills, and assertiveness to help the person with alcoholism seek treatment. Studies show a dramatic increase in treatment participation and decreased drinking before treatment as well as decreased distress among the concerned others with this treatment (Meyers et al., 1997).

Relapse Prevention

Relapse prevention is an influential cognitive–behavioral self-management program originally designed to complement traditional treatments by anticipating and planning to cope with relapse (Dimeff & Marlatt, 1995). The relapse prevention model includes three major components: behavioral-skills training, cognitive interventions, and lifestyle change. Problem alcohol use is reconceptualized as a commonly occurring link in a chain of maladaptive behavior that can be both anticipated and modified. As noted earlier, relapse prevention is relevant for a significant fraction of rehabilitation patients with a history of substance abuse; however, this model involves the use of abstract and metaphorical content that may need to be adapted for persons with cognitive impairment.

Other Disability-Specific Interventions

Corrigan, Bogner, Lamb-Hart, Heinemann, and Moore (2005) studied ways of improving participation in substance abuse treatment programs. They randomly assigned subjects to motivational interviewing, reduction of logistical barriers to participation, financial incentives, or attention control. Participation rates associated with barrier reduction (74%) and financial incentives (83%) were significantly better than motivational interviewing (45%) or attention control (45%).

In summary, recent innovations in theory and treatment should make it possible for every rehabilitation program to provide on-site interventions. The types and intensity of interventions, as well as the staff who provide treatment, will vary depending on the individual site or program. Legitimate, potentially efficacious interventions range from brief advice provided by a rehabilitation psychologist or physician to intensive interdisciplinary coping skills treatment specifically tailored for persons with neurological impairments. Substance abuse interventions will likely be more effective to the extent they are woven into the daily fabric of a given rehabilitation program and to the extent that the substance abuse intervention focuses on enhancing rehabilitation outcomes, general health, and well-being, rather than solely on reducing alcohol or drug use. As demonstrated by Corrigan and colleagues (2005), providing financial incentives and mitigating barriers to treatment may enhance participation in whatever substance abuse treatments are available.

CONCLUSIONS

Substance abuse is a major cause underlying traumatically induced disability, and rehabilitation represents a window of opportunity to intervene in substance abuse problems for people with TBI and SCI. Although rehabilitation programs report improved attention to substance abuse issues, more can be done (Basford et al., 2002). Currently, only 66% of surveyed programs support universal screening, 53% provide substance abuse education to their patients, and 69% report they provide easy access to substance abuse counselors (Basford et al., 2002).

A key to providing better alcohol-related services for persons with disabilities is improving access to effective treatment. Psychologists can improve participation in substance abuse treatment by reducing barriers to treatment and providing incentives (Corrigan et al., 2005). Psychologists can also promote access to treatment by providing empirically based treatment within medical, rehabilitation, vocational, and independent living settings where people with disabilities are usually seen. Rehabilitation psychologists can facilitate this process in several ways. We can become more familiar with current thinking in the area of addictive behavior. In doing so we can help dispel myths and shed new light on these problems for our colleagues as well. We can expand our clinical expertise to include alcohol and drug-related problems. Psychologists frequently have had little training in the area of substance abuse and tend to think that treating addictions requires unique skills and experiences (Cardoso et al., 2006; Miller & Brown, 1997). However, current theory and practice emphasize that alcohol and drug problems are behaviors that respond to the same psychological principles as other disorders, such as anxiety and depression. Using empirically validated treatments, we can tailor treatment programs to meet the needs of persons with disabilities physically, cognitively, and motivationally. Finally, we can conduct research to determine whether the treatment approaches we have tailored are effective.

References

Alexander, S., Kerr, M. E., Yonas, H., & Marion, D. W. (2004). The effects of admission alcohol level on cerebral blood flow and outcomes after severe traumatic brain injury. *Journal of Neurotrauma, 21,* 575–583.

Allen, J., Litten, R., Fertig, J., & Babor, T. (1997). A review of research on the Alcohol Use Disorders Identification Test (AUDIT). *Alcoholism: Clinical and Experimental Research, 21,* 613–619.

American Psychiatric Association. (1994). *Diagnostic and statistical manual of mental disorders* (4th ed.). Washington, DC: Author.

Ashman, T. A., Schwartz, M. E., Cantor, J. B., Hibbard, M. R., & Gordon, W. A. (2004). Screening for substance abuse in individuals with traumatic brain injury. *Brain Injury, 18,* 191–202.

Babor, T. F., Brown, J., & Del Boca, F. K. (1990). Validity of self-reports in applied research on addictive behaviors: Fact or fiction? *Addictive Behaviors, 12,* 5–32.

Baguley, I., Felmingham, K., Lahz, S., Grodon, E., Lazzarl, H., & Schote, D. (1997). Alcohol abuse and traumatic brain injury: Effect on event-related potentials. *Archives of Physical Medicine and Rehabilitation, 78,* 1248–1253.

Basford, J. R., Rohe, D. E., Barnes, C. P., & DePompolo, R. W. (2002). Substance abuse attitudes and policies in US rehabilitation training programs: A comparison of 1985 and 2000. *Archives of Physical Medicine and Rehabilitation, 83,* 517–522.

Bien, T., Miller, W., & Tonigan, J. (1993). Brief interventions for alcohol problems: A review. *Addiction, 88,* 315–335.

Bombardier, C. H., Dikmen, S., Temkin, N., & Machamer, J. (2003). The natural history of drinking and alcohol-related problems after traumatic brain injury. *Archives of Physical Medicine and Rehabilitation, 84,* 185–191.

Bombardier, C. H., Ehde, D., & Kilmer, J. (1997). Readiness to change alcohol drinking habits after traumatic brain injury. *Archives of Physical Medicine and Rehabilitation, 78,* 592–596.

Bombardier, C. H., Kilmer, J., & Ehde, D. (1997). Screening for alcoholism among persons with recent traumatic brain injury. *Rehabilitation Psychology, 42,* 259–271.

Bombardier, C. H., & Rimmele, C. (1998). Alcohol use and readiness to change after spinal cord injury. *Archives of Physical Medicine and Rehabilitation, 79,* 1110–1115.

Bombardier, C. H., & Rimmele, C. (1999). Motivational interviewing to prevent alcohol abuse after traumatic brain injury: A case series. *Rehabilitation Psychology, 44,* 52–67.

Bombardier, C. H., Rimmele, C. T., & Zintel, H. (2002). The magnitude and correlates of alcohol and drug use before traumatic brain injury. *Archives of Physical Medicine and Rehabilitation, 83,* 1765–1773.

Bombardier, C. H., Stroud, M., Esselman, P., & Rimmele, C. T. (2004). Do preinjury alcohol problems predict poorer rehabilitation progress in persons with spinal cord injury? *Archives of Physical Medicine and Rehabilitation, 85,* 1488–1492.

Bombardier, C. H., & Thurber, C. (1998). Blood alcohol level and early cognitive status after traumatic brain injury. *Brain Injury, 12,* 725–734.

Bradley, K. A., DeBenedetti, A. F., Volk, R. J., Williams, E. C., Frank, D., & Kivlahan, D. R. (2007). AUDIT-C as a brief screen for alcohol misuse in primary care. *Alcoholism: Clinical and Experimental Research, 31,* 1208–1217.

Brooks, N., Symington, C., Beattie, A., Campsie, L., Bryden, J., & McKinlay, W. (1989). Alcohol and other predictors of cognitive recovery after severe head injury. *Brain Injury, 3,* 235–246.

Brown, R. L., Leonard, T., Saunders, L. A., & Papasouliotis, O. (2001). A two-item conjoint screen for alcohol and other drug problems. *Journal of the American Board of Family Practitioners, 14,* 95–106.

Burke, B. L., Arkowitz, H., & Menchola, M. (2003). The efficacy of motivational interviewing: A meta-analysis of controlled clinical trials. *Journal of Consulting and Clinical Psychology, 71,* 843–861.

Cardoso, E., Pruett, S., Chan, F., & Tansey, T. (2006). Substance abuse assessment and treatment: The current training and practice of APA Division 22 members. *Rehabilitation Psychology, 51,* 175–178.

Charlifue, S., & Gerhart, K. (1991). Behavioral and demographic predictors of suicide after spinal cord injury. *Archives of Physical Medicine and Rehabilitation, 72,* 488–492.

Cherner, M., Temkin, N. R., Machamer, J. E., & Dikmen, S. S. (2001). Utility of a composite measure to detect problematic alcohol use in persons with traumatic brain injury. *Archives of Physical Medicine and Rehabilitation, 82,* 780–786.

Cherpitel, C. J. (2000). A brief screening instrument for problem drinking in the emergency room: The RAPS4. Rapid Alcohol Problems Screen. *Journal of Studies on Alcohol, 61,* 447–449.

Cooney, N. L., Zweben, A., & Fleming, M. (1995). Screening for alcohol problems and at-risk drinking in health care settings. In R. Hester & W. Miller (Eds.), *Handbook of alcoholism treatment approaches: Effective alternatives* (pp. 45–60). Boston: Allyn & Bacon.

Corrigan, J. D. (1995). Substance abuse as a mediating factor in outcome from traumatic brain injury. *Archives of Physical and Medical Rehabilitation, 76,* 302–309.

Corrigan, J. D., Bogner, J. A., Lamb-Hart, G. L., Heinemann, A., & Moore, D. (2005). Increasing substance abuse treatment compliance for persons with traumatic brain injury. *Psychology of Addictive Behaviors, 19,* 131–139.

Corrigan, J. D., Rust, E., & Lamb-Hart, G. L. (1995). The nature and extent of substance abuse problems in persons with traumatic brain injury. *Journal of Head Trauma Rehabilitation, 10,* 29–46.

Cox, W., Heinemann, A., Miranti, S., Schmidt, M., Klinger, E., & Blount, J. (2003). Outcomes of systematic motivational counseling for substance use following traumatic brain injury. *Journal of Addictive Diseases, 22,* 93–110.

Cunningham, R. M., Maio, R. F., Hill, E. M., & Zink, B. J. (2002). The effects of alcohol on head injury in the motor vehicle crash victim. *Alcohol and Alcoholism, 37,* 236–240.

Dikmen, S. S., Donovan, D., Loberg, T., Machamer, J., & Temkin, N. R. (1993). Alcohol use and its effects on neuropsychological outcome in head injury. *Neuropsychology, 7,* 296–305.

Dikmen, S. S., Machamer, J. E., Donovan, D. M., Winn, H. R., & Temkin, N. R. (1995). Alcohol use before and after traumatic head injury. *Annals of Emergency Medicine, 26,* 167–176.

Dimeff, L., & Marlatt, A. (1995). Relapse prevention. In R. Hester & W. Miller (Eds.), *Handbook of alcoholism treatment approaches: Effective alternatives* (pp. 148–159). Boston: Allyn & Bacon.

Donovan, D., Rohsenow, D., Schau, E., & O'Leary, M. (1977). Defensive style in alcoholics and nonalcoholics. *Journal of Studies on Alcohol, 38,* 465–470.

Dryden, D. M., Saunders, L. D., Rowe, B. H., May, L. A., Yiannakoulias, N., Svenson, L. W., et al. (2005). Depression following traumatic spinal cord injury. *Neuroepidemiology, 25,* 55–61.

Dunn, C., Deroo, L., & Rivara, F. P. (2001). The use of brief interventions adapted from motivational interviewing across behavioral domains: A systematic review. *Addiction, 96,* 1725–1742.

Elliott, T. R., Kurylo, M., Chen, Y., & Hicken, B. (2002). Alcohol abuse history and adjustment following spinal cord injury. *Rehabilitation Psychology, 47,* 278–290.

Esselman, P. C., Dikmen, S. S., Bell, K., & Temkin, N. R. (2004). Access to inpatient rehabilitation after violence-related traumatic brain injury. *Archives of Physical Medicine and Rehabilitation, 85,* 1445–1449.

Ewing, J. (1984). Detecting alcoholism: The CAGE questionnaire. *JAMA, 252,* 1905–1907.

Feldstein, S. W., & Miller, W. R. (2007). Does subtle screening for substance abuse work? A review of the Substance Abuse Subtle Screening Inventory (SASSI). *Addiction, 102,* 41–50.

Fiellin, D. A., Reid, M. C., & O'Connor, P. G. (2000). Screening for alcohol problems in primary care: A systematic review. *Archives of Internal Medicine, 160,* 1977–1989.

First, M., Gibbon, M., Spitzer, R., & Williams, J. (1996). *User's guide for the Structured Clinical Interview for DSM IV Axis I Disorders.* New York: Biometrics Research Department, New York State Psychiatric Institute.

Fleming, M., Barry, K., Manwell, L., Johnson, J., & London, R. (1997). Brief physician advice for problem alcohol drinkers. *JAMA, 277,* 1039–1045.

Garrison, A., Clifford, K., Gleason, S. F., Tun, C. G., Brown, R., & Garshick, E. (2004). Alcohol use associated with cervical spinal cord injury. *Journal of Spinal Cord Medicine, 27,* 111–115.

Gentilello, L., Duggan, P., Drummond, D., Tonnensen, A., Degner, E., Fischer, R., et al. (1988). Major injury as a unique opportunity to initiate treatment in the alcoholic. *Journal of Surgery, 156,* 558–561.

Gentilello, L., Rivara, F., Donovan, D., Jurkovich, G., Daranciang, E., Dunn, C., et al. (1999). Alcohol interventions in a trauma center as a means of reducing the risk of injury recurrence. *Annals of Surgery, 230,* 473–483.

Halt, P., Swanson, R., & Faden, A. (1992). Alcohol exacerbates behavioral and neurochemical effects of rat spinal cord trauma. *Archives of Neurology, 49,* 1178–1184.

Heather, N. (1995). Brief intervention strategies. In R. Hester & W. Miller (Eds.), *Handbook of alcoholism treatment approaches: Effective alternatives* (pp. 105–122). Boston: Allyn & Bacon.

Heinemann, A., Doll, M., & Schnoll, S. (1989). Treatment of alcohol abuse in persons with recent spinal cord injuries. *Alcohol Health and Research World, 13,* 1110–1117.

Heinemann, A., Goranson, N., Ginsberg, K., & Schnoll, S. (1989). Alcohol use and activity patterns following spinal cord injury. *Rehabilitation Psychology, 34,* 191–206.

Heinemann, A., Keen, M., Donohue, R., & Schnoll, S. (1988). Alcohol use in persons with recent spinal cord injuries. *Archives of Physical Medicine and Rehabilitation, 69,* 619–624.

Heinemann, A., Schnoll, S., Brandt, M., Maltz, R., & Keen, M. (1988). Toxicology screening in acute spinal cord injury. *Alcoholism: Clinical and Experimental Research, 12,* 815–819.

Institute of Medicine. (1990). *Broadening the base of treatment for alcohol problems.* Washington, DC: National Academies Press.

Jones, G. (1992). Substance abuse treatment for persons with brain injuries. *NeuroRehabilitation, 2,* 27–34.

Jorge, R. E., Starkstein, S. E., Arndt, S., Moser, D., Crespo-Facorro, B., & Robinson, R. G. (2005). Alcohol misuse and mood disorders following traumatic brain injury. *Archives of General Psychiatry, 62,* 742–749.

Kaplan, C. P., & Corrigan, J. D. (1992). Effect of blood alcohol level on recovery from severe closed head injury. *Brain Injury, 6,* 337–349.

Karol, R., & Sparadeo, F. (1991). *Alcohol, drugs, and brain injury: A survivor's workbook.* Alberta, Canada: Alcohol and Drug Abuse Commission.

Kelly, D. (1995). Alcohol and head injury: An issue revisited. *Journal of Neurotrauma, 12,* 883–890.

Kelly, M., Johnson, C. T., Knoller, N., Drubach, D. A., & Winslow, M. M. (1997). Substance abuse, traumatic brain injury and neuropsychological outcome. *Brain Injury, 11,* 391–402.

Kirubakaran, V., Kumar, V., Powell, B., Tyler, A., & Armatas, P. (1986). Survey of alcohol and drug misuse in spinal cord injured veterans. *Journal of Studies on Alcohol, 47,* 223–227.

Kishline, A. (1994). *Moderate drinking: The moderation management guide for people who want to reduce their drinking.* New York: Crown House Publishing.

Kiwerski, J., & Krauski, M. (1992). Influence of alcohol intake on the course and consequences of spinal cord injury. *International Journal of Rehabilitation Research, 15,* 240–245.

Kolakowsky-Hayner, S. A., Gourley, E. V., III, Kreutzer, J. S., Marwitz, J. H., Meade, M. A., & Cifu, D. X. (2002). Postinjury substance abuse among persons with brain injury and persons with spinal cord injury. *Brain Injury, 16,* 583–592.

Koponen, S., Taiminen, T., Portin, R., Himanen, L., Isoniemi, H., Heinonen, H., et al. (2002). Axis I and II psychiatric disorders after traumatic brain injury: A 30-year follow-up study. *American Journal of Psychiatry, 159,* 1315–1321.

Krause, J. (1992). Delivery of substance abuse services during spinal cord injury rehabilitation. *NeuroRehabilitation, 2,* 45–51.

Krause, J. S., Vines, C. L., Farley, T. L., Sniezek, J., & Coker, J. (2004). An exploratory study of pressure ulcers after spinal cord injury: Relationship to protective behaviors and risk factors. *Archives of Physical Medicine and Rehabilitation, 82,* 107–113.

Krause, J. S. (2004). Factors associated with risk for subsequent injuries after traumatic spinal cord injury. *Archives of Physical Medicine and Rehabilitation, 85,* 1503–1508.

Kreutzer, J., Wehman, P., Harris, J., Burns, C., & Young, H. (1991). Substance abuse and crime patterns among persons with traumatic brain injury referred for supported employment. *Brain Injury, 5,* 177–187.

Kreutzer, J., Witol, A., & Marwitz, J. (1996). Alcohol and drug use among young persons with traumatic brain injury. *Journal of Learning Disabilities, 29,* 643–651.

Langley, M., & Kiley, D. (1992). Prevention of substance abuse in persons with neurological disabilities. *NeuroRehabilitation, 2,* 52–64.

Levy, D. T., Miller, T. R., Mallonee, S., Spicer, R. S., Romano, E. O., Fisher, D. A., et al. (2002). Blood alcohol content (BAC)-negative victims in alcohol-involved injury incidents. *Addiction, 97,* 909–914.

Marlatt, A., & Tapert, S. (1993). Harm reduction: Reducing the risk of addictive behaviors. In J. Baer & A. Marlatt (Eds.), *Addictive behaviors across the life span: Prevention, treatment, and policy issues* (pp. 243–273). Newbury Park, CA: Sage.

Meyers, R. J., Dominguez, T. P., & Smith, J. E. (1997). Community reinforcement training with concerned others. In V. B. Van Hasselt & M. Hersen (Eds.), *Sourcebook of psychological treatment manuals for adult disorders* (pp. 257–294). New York: Plenum Press.

Miller, W. R., & Brown, S. (1997). Why psychologists should treat alcohol and drug problems. *American Psychologist, 52,* 1269–1279.

Miller, W. R., Brown, J., Simpson, T., Handmaker, N., Bein, T., Luckie, L., et al. (1995). What works? A methodological analysis of the alcohol treatment outcome literature. In R. Hester & W. R. Miller (Eds.), *Handbook of alcoholism treatment approaches: Effective alternatives* (pp. 12–44). Boston: Allyn & Bacon.

Miller, W. R., & Munoz, R. (1982). *How to control your drinking* (Rev. ed.). Albuquerque, NM: University of New Mexico Press.

Miller, W. R., & Rollnick, S. (1991). *Motivational interviewing: Preparing people to change addictive behavior.* New York: Guilford Press.

Miller, W. R., & Rollnick, S. (2002). *Motivational interviewing: Preparing people for change* (2nd ed.). New York: Guilford Press.

Miller, W. R., & Rollnick, S. (2007). Motivational Interviewing Network of Trainers. Retrieved September 6, 2007, from http://www.motivationalinterview.org

Miller, W. R., & Sovereign, R. G. (1989). The check-up: A model for early intervention in addictive behaviors. In P. Loberg, W. R. Miller, P. Nathan, & G. Marlatt (Eds.), *Addictive behaviors, prevention and early intervention* (pp. 219–227). Amsterdam: Swets & Zeitlinger.

Mokdad, A. H., Marks, J. S., Stroup, D. F., & Gerberding, J. L. (2004). Actual causes of death in the United States, 2000. *JAMA, 291,* 1238–1245.

Monti, P. M., Rohsenow, D. J., Colby, S. M., & Abrams, D. B. (1995). Coping and social skills training. In *Handbook of alcoholism treatment approaches: Effective alternatives* (pp. 221–241). Boston: Allyn & Bacon.

National Head Injury Foundation. (1988). *Substance abuse task force white paper.* Southborough, MA: Author.

Noonan, W. C., & Moyers, T. B. (1997). Motivational interviewing: A review. *Journal of Substance Misuse, 2,* 8–16.

Oddy, M., Coughlin, T., & Tyerman, A. (1985). Social adjustment after closed head injury. *Journal of Neurology Neurosurgery and Psychiatry, 48,* 564–568.

Parsons, O., & Nixon, S. (1998). Cognitive functioning in sober social drinkers: A review of the research since 1986. *Journal of Studies on Alcohol, 59,* 180–190.

Patterson, G. R., & Forgatch, M. S. (1985). Therapist behavior as a determinant for patient noncompliance: A paradox for the behavior modifier. *Journal of Consulting and Clinical Psychology, 53,* 846–851.

Peterson, J., Rothfleisch, J., Zelazo, P., & Pihl, R. (1990). Acute alcohol intoxication and cognitive functioning. *Journal of Studies on Alcohol, 51,* 114–122.

Prochaska, J., DiClemente, C., & Norcross, J. (1992). In search of how people change. *American Psychologist, 47,* 1102–1114.

Project MATCH Research Group. (1997). Matching alcoholism to client heterogeneity: Project MATCH posttreatment drinking outcomes. *Journal of Studies on Alcohol, 58,* 7–29.

Rivara, F. P., Jurkovich, G. J., Gurney, J. G., Seguin, D., Fligner, C. L., Ries, R., et al. (1993). The magnitude of acute and chronic alcohol abuse in trauma patients. *Archives of Surgery, 128,* 907–912.

Rivara, F. P., Tollefson, S., Tesh, E., & Gentilello, L. M. (2000). Screening trauma patients for alcohol problems: Are insurance companies barriers? *Journal of Trauma, 48,* 115–118.

Rourke, S., & Loberg, T. (1996). The neurobehavioral correlates of alcoholism. In I. Grant & K. Adams (Eds.), *Neuropsychological assessment of neuropsychiatric disorders* (pp. 423–485). New York: Oxford University Press.

Sanchez-Craig, M., & Lei, H. (1986). Disadvantages to imposing the goal of abstinence on problem drinkers: An empirical study. *British Journal of Addiction, 81,* 505–512.

Sanchez-Craig, M., Wilkinson, D. A., & Davila, R. (1995). Empirically based guidelines for moderate drinking: 1-year results from three studies with problem drinkers. *American Journal of Public Health, 85,* 823–828.

Sander, A., Witol, A., & Kreutzer, J. (1997). Concordance of patients' and caregivers' reports of alcohol use after traumatic brain injury. *Archives of Physical Medicine and Rehabilitation, 78,* 138–142.

Silver, J., Kramer, R., Greenwald, S., & Weissman, M. (2001). The association between head injuries and psychiatric disorders: Findings from the New Haven Epidemiologic Catchment Area Study. *Brain Injury, 15,* 935–945.

Skinner, H. A., & Allen, B. A. (1983). Differential assessment of alcoholism. *Journal of Studies on Alcohol, 44,* 852–862.

Smith, J., & Meyers, R. (1995). The community reinforcement approach. In R. Hester & W. Miller (Eds.), *Handbook of alcoholism treatment approaches: Effective alternatives* (pp. 251–266). Boston: Allyn & Bacon.

Sobell, L. C., Cunningham, J., & Sobell, M. B. (1996). Recovery from alcohol problems with and without treatment: Prevalence in two population surveys. *American Journal of Public Health, 86,* 966–972.

Sobell, L. C., & Sobell, M. B. (1990). Self report issues in alcohol abuse: State of the art and future directions. *Behavior Assessment, 12,* 77–90.

Soderstrom, C. A., Smith, G. S., Dischinger, P. C., McDuff, D. R., Hebel, J. R., Gorelick, D. A., et al. (1997). Psychoactive substance use disorders among seriously injured trauma center patients. *JAMA, 277,* 1769–1774.

Stinson, F. S., Grant, B. F., Dawson, D. A., Ruan, W. J., Huang, B., & Saha, T. (2005). Comorbidity between *DSM–IV* alcohol and specific drug use disorders in the United States: Results from the National Epidemiologic Survey on Alcohol and Related Conditions. *Drug and Alcohol Dependence, 80,* 105–116.

Tate, P. S., Freed, D. M., Bombardier, C. H., Harter, S. L., & Brinkman, S. (1999). Traumatic brain injury: Influence of blood alcohol level on postacute cognitive function. *Brain Injury, 13,* 767–784.

Trice, H. M. (1957). A study of the process of affiliation with Alcoholics Anonymous. *Quarterly Journal of Studies on Alcohol, 18,* 39–54.

Turner, A. P., Bombardier, C. H., & Rimmele, C. T. (2003). A typology of alcohol use patterns among persons with recent TBI or SCI: Implications for treatment matching. *Archives of Physical Medicine and Rehabilitation, 84,* 358–364.

Turner, A. P., Kivlahan, D. R., Rimmele, C. T., & Bombardier, C. H. (2006). Does preinjury alcohol use or blood alcohol level influence cognitive functioning after traumatic brain injury? *Rehabilitation Psychology, 51,* 78–86.

United States Public Health Service. (1989). *Code of federal regulations. Part II: Confidentiality of alcohol and drug abuse patient records.* Washington, DC: Author.

Valliant, G. (1983). *The natural history of alcoholism: Causes, patterns, and paths to recovery.* Cambridge, MA: Harvard University Press.

WHO ASSIST Working Group. (2002). The Alcohol, Smoking and Substance Involvement Screening Test (ASSIST): Development, reliability, and feasibility. *Addiction, 97,* 1183–1194.

Wilde, E. A., Bigler, E. D., Gandhi, P. V., Lowry, C. M., Blatter, D. D., Brooks, J., et al. (2004). Alcohol abuse and traumatic brain injury: Quantitative magnetic resonance imaging and neuropsychological outcome. *Journal of Neurotrauma, 21,* 137–147.

Williams, S. H. (2005). Medications for treating alcohol dependence. *American Family Physician, 72,* 1775–1780.

Young, M., Rintala, D., Rossi, C., Hart, K., & Fuhrer, M. (1995). Alcohol and marijuana use in a community-based sample with spinal cord injury. *Archives of Physical Medicine and Rehabilitation, 76,* 525–532.

CHAPTER 15

PSYCHOTHERAPEUTIC INTERVENTIONS

Michele J. Rusin and Jay M. Uomoto

Psychotherapy is an integral component of the practice of rehabilitation psychology. Training in psychotherapy is required in rehabilitation psychology postdoctoral programs (Patterson & Hanson, 1995), and candidates for certification in rehabilitation psychology by the American Board of Professional Psychology (ABPP) must demonstrate intervention skills to manage the patient's and family's adjustment to disability (ABPP, n.d.).

Unlike most clinical psychologists, whose clients identify problems for which they actively seek help, the rehabilitation psychologist often treats patients who are psychologically naive and sometimes unwilling to participate. An additional obstacle is that patients with neurological disabilities often have cognitive and linguistic impairments that can hamper development of a therapeutic relationship. Furthermore, the distress displayed by rehabilitation patients may be due, at least in part, to societal or environmental factors over which they have limited control. Their issues may include highly personal, human concerns about their goals and aspirations, the meaning of their lives, and other existential matters.

This chapter focuses on psychotherapeutic issues of adults with disabilities. We highlight the commonly occurring clinical needs of this population, discuss the unique challenges faced by psychologists working in rehabilitation settings, review the scientific literature supporting interventions, and offer practical recommendations. Pediatric issues and caregiver concerns are addressed elsewhere in this volume (see chaps. 18, 19, 20, 21, 22).

THEORETICAL FRAMEWORK

Central to contemporary rehabilitation practice are the biopsychosocial model and a psychological coping perspective. Both tend to be nonpathologizing and provide structured ways to deal with change. They implicitly foster a sense of continuity and hope by bringing strengths to bear on current challenges. These approaches transcend medical diagnoses; the extent of distress that follows an injury or illness is better explained by coping style and strategies than by the nature of the condition (Curran, Ponsford, & Crowe, 2000). They define a broad scope of practice for the rehabilitation psychologist, encompassing medical, emotional, cognitive, relational, social, and legal matters (Rusin & Jongsma, 2001).

CONCEPTUAL ISSUES: HEALTH AND BEHAVIOR AND PSYCHOTHERAPY INTERVENTIONS

In January 2002, a new set of procedural codes was introduced by the American Medical Association (2005) under the Current Procedural Terminology that provides options for describing and billing for services (including psychology) to persons who have a primary physical health diagnosis.

The distinction between traditional psychotherapy and health and behavior interventions lies in the presumed source of the problem and the focus of the psychological intervention. When emotional or behavioral disorders precede the disabling event, a psychotherapeutic code may be most appropriate, but those emotional, behavioral, or social problems with onset after the disabling event may be classified under either heading. Similarly, a psychotherapeutic intervention such as cognitive behavior therapy (CBT) can be applied for preexisting psychiatric disorders but is also an evidenced-based intervention for persons with physical health diagnoses. The same psychological intervention can be applied to either a mental or physical health diagnosis; the conceptualization determines whether it would be considered a form of "psychotherapy" or a "health and behavior intervention." In this chapter, the term *psychotherapy* is used for all interventions targeted toward the amelioration of emotional, behavioral, or psychosocial problems, regardless of the procedure code used to describe the service.

ADJUSTMENT TO DISABILITY AND COMMON CLINICAL PROBLEMS

The rehabilitation psychologist's work is broadly conceptualized as facilitating the patient's and family's adjustment to the many changes associated with a disability. The many aspects of this adjustment and the types of clinical problems that the psychologist will address with patients during this process are explored in this section.

Adjustment to Disability

Adjustment to disability describes a process in which persons acknowledge the functional consequences of their illness or injury, incorporating them into the substance and story of their lives. In this process, patients sometimes need to confront preexisting pathology, amend lifelong coping styles, and re-examine spiritual and existential perspectives. Changes patients experience in their bodies may alter their internal worlds, affecting nearly everything they do. Functional changes may challenge long-held beliefs about their identities. Adjustment to disability may require that individuals learn new emotional and cognitive self-management skills, integrate them into existing relationship patterns, or modify relationships to accommodate changed abilities. Those with whom the patient interacts will also have to accommodate these changes; family members, friends, and employers may need to work through their emotional reactions to the patient's

disability, make logistical adjustments, and perhaps alter habitual ways of communicating and spending time together. The patient may be required to take the lead in educating others about changed needs and may even have to use legal means to achieve access to work or community venues. After a disabling event, individuals must often build new linkages with physical, psychological, and social environments. Adjustment to disability is achieved when medical and functional changes are integrated into their identities, and relationships with family, friends, and community are mutually reconfigured to allow for meaningful and satisfying social roles. Or, as one person living with a disability put it, "I acknowledged the disability and went on with my life" (Pfeiffer, 2000, p. 98).

Although general work on coping (e.g., Snyder, 1999) is applicable to persons who have disabling conditions, a psychological paradigm alone is too narrow to adequately address the multiple concerns faced by persons having disabilities (Olkin & Pledger, 2003), which may include environmental, legal, cultural, and sociopolitical issues in addition to psychological and social ones. Therefore, approaches to adjustment for persons having disabilities typically consider socioenvironmental issues as well as individual ones (e.g., Orto & Power, 2007).

Common Clinical Problems

In this section, we outline those clinical problems that are most frequently seen in rehabilitation settings. Some of these problems represent a spectrum of ways in which individuals respond to threat and loss and some are direct results of changes in brain functioning. Other problems predispose persons to disabling injuries or medical events, leading persons with these disorders to be disproportionately represented in rehabilitation settings.

Bereavement. Although it is presumed that the onset of disability elicits bereavement, little is known about the true incidence of bereavement and its implications for rehabilitation. Some physical losses, such as an amputation of a painful limb, may not provoke grief if the "loss" enhances comfort and quality of life (Rybarczyk, Szymanski, & Nicholas, 2000). Some have even reported "positive by-products" of disabilities (e.g., McMillen & Cook, 2003). Contrary to clinical lore, bereavement does not necessarily follow stages (Elliott & Frank, 1996) or require that emotions be openly expressed (Niemeier & Burnett, 2001). Furthermore, manifestations of loss vary according to gender and cultural identity (Niemeier, Kennedy, McKinley, & Cifu, 2004).

Depression. Depression is prevalent among persons in rehabilitation centers, occurring in as many as one third of persons after amputations (Rybarczyk et al., 2000) and half of persons after stroke (Starkstein & Manes, 2000). Major depressive disorders are present in 11% to 30% of persons following spinal cord injury (SCI; Bombardier, Richards, Krause, Tulsky, & Tate, 2004; Elliott & Kennedy, 2004). In addition to exacerbating emotional and physical suffering, depression slows rehabilitation progress, lowers functional outcome, and impedes social recovery (Rosenthal, Christensen, & Ross, 1998; van Wijk, Algra, van de Port, Bevaart, & Lindeman, 2006). Depression is associated with higher mortality rates among persons who have experienced a stroke, and patients' survival rates improve with the use of antidepressant medication (Jorge, Robinson, Arndt, & Starkstein, 2003). Depression is also associated with poor outcomes in cardiac disease (Barth, Schumacher, & Herrmann-Lingen, 2004; Van Melle et al., 2004), cancer (Onitilo, Nietert, & Egede, 2006), and possibly other medical disorders. The data point toward depression as a serious medical as well as emotional problem.

Anxiety. Disabling events are powerful precipitants of anxiety. About one-quarter of patients experience significant anxiety after stroke (Astrom, 1996), SCI (Hancock, Craig, Dickson, Chang, & Martin, 1993), and mild traumatic brain injury (TBI; Epstein & Ursano, 1994). These rates are similar to the estimated lifetime prevalence of anxiety in the general population (Kessler, Berglund, Demler, Jin, & Walters, 2005). Acute stress reactions that progress to posttraumatic stress disorder (PTSD) are commonly seen in candidates for rehabilitation, with 3% to 27% of persons who sustained TBIs (Hiott & Labbate, 2002) and 7% to 17% of those with SCIs (Nielsen, 2003; Radnitz et al., 1995) having PTSD. Rehabilitation patients may experience anxiety and

avoidance reactions to signals reminiscent of their own life-threatening event, be these obvious reminders of automobile accidents, or physical sensations (e.g., wooziness, headache) that recall the onset of a stroke or other disabling medical event.

Denial. Reduced awareness of illness and its implications has been observed in many medical populations. Psychologically based denial and neurologically based anosognosia are two commonly observed presentations of impaired awareness seen in rehabilitation settings. Denial may impede recovery (i.e., if patients do not acknowledge limitations that require therapeutic intervention) or may help to maintain motivation (i.e., by warding off demoralization and despair; see Kortte & Wegener, 2004, for a more detailed discussion). The rehabilitation psychologist often has to collaborate with the team and family in explaining the denial and managing it to promote the patient's recovery.

Neurobehavioral and cognitive disorders. Among persons admitted to rehabilitation following an insult to the brain (e.g., TBI, stroke), the prevalence of cognitive impairments and dementia is high. For example, one study found that 72% of persons had cognitive impairments and 28% had dementia a year after experiencing a stroke (Linden, Skoog, Fagerberg, Steen, & Blomstrand, 2004); the prevalence during inpatient rehabilitation would almost certainly be higher because of acute factors affecting concentration and overall level of alertness. Persons whose injuries have resulted from nonbrain trauma (e.g., SCI) are also at risk of cognitive impairment; in one study, 55% of persons with SCI had impaired performance on at least 25% of the cognitive measures used (Hess, Marwitz, & Kreutzer, 2003).

Cognitive disorders can compromise the validity of the assessment process by limiting the patient's ability to complete questionnaires or participate in psychometric testing. Communication is often challenging and time-consuming. Cognitive disorders can impair participation in psychotherapeutic interventions because of reduced insight, limited attention span, and poor retention of information, among other factors. Implementation of compensatory strategies is spotty when patients fail to realize the need for a strategy or to remember which strategy to use.

Neurobehavioral symptoms such as apathy and emotional lability, which mimic depression, complicate the assessment of affective states. Neurologically based agitation, such as seen in some phases of brain injury recovery, can be misinterpreted as evidence of emotional pain. Familiarity with these conditions and skill in distinguishing one from the other are parts of the rehabilitation psychologist's "toolkit."

Personality disturbances. Personality is a salient factor in the provision of rehabilitation services. Personality factors may put people at risk of injuries; for example, patients with TBIs have high preinjury rates of antisocial and obsessive–compulsive personality disorders (Hibbard et al., 2000), and persons with extroverted, thrill-seeking personalities may be at greater risk of injury, especially when combined with substance use (Rohe, 1996). Brain injuries may result in personality changes; Axis II pathology was detected in 23% (Koponen et al., 2002) to 66% (Hibbard et al., 2000) of persons following TBI, far exceeding rates in the general population. Complaints of lowered self-confidence, cognitive and relationship failures, and problems modulating negative affect are frequent in TBI survivors (Hibbard et al., 2000). However, the occurrence of SCI appears to have no significant impact on personality functioning (Hollick et al., 2001).

Because personality affects how patients relate to their health care providers (Harper, 2004) and perhaps how limited they are by medical problems, it is likely that personality disorders also affect the course of rehabilitation, and this should be taken into account in providing rehabilitation services. For example, action-oriented persons with acquired SCI who do not enjoy intellectual pursuits may learn better from doing than reading and may have a limited tolerance for discussing feelings in psychotherapy. Identifying vocations that suit both the person's physical abilities after SCI and his or her personality style can be a challenge (Rohe, 1996). Personality variables also help to explain why persons with mild TBI rate their injuries as being more severe and as affecting more areas of their lives than do persons with moderate to severe TBI (Uomoto & Fann, 2004).

Substance use disorders. Substance abuse is a major consideration in the rehabilitation of traumat-

ically induced disorders. As many as half of persons who are hospitalized following a TBI (Corrigan, 1995) and about 40% of persons hospitalized with spinal cord (Heinemann, Schnoll, Brandt, Maltz, & Keen, 1988) or other traumatic injuries (Rivara et al., 1993) are intoxicated at the time of injury. Overall, 40% to 80% of persons admitted for TBIs have evidence of recent use of drugs or alcohol (Bombardier, Rimmele, & Zintel, 2002; see chap. 14, this volume, for further information on substance abuse and disability). One year following TBI, 30% of patients in one community study continued moderate to heavy use of alcohol, with young males having fair to moderate mental health, depression, and good physical functioning being at highest risk of heavy drinking (Horner et al., 2005).

Family stress and burden. Often after a disabling event, families must solve novel problems and family members must function in new roles while demands on their time increase and their access to social support and recreation may shrink (see chap. 18, this volume, for discussion of caregiver issues). The family structure is altered in significant ways (e.g., changes in emotional support, changes in management of pragmatic tasks; Palmer & Glass, 2003). Although high levels of distress occur in family caregivers, caregiver characteristics modulate the type and degree of this distress. The caregiver's family role (Perlesz, Kinsella, & Crowe, 1999), access to social support, and social problem-solving skills affect the type and degree of distress (Grant et al., 2006). Patient characteristics, such as memory impairment and comprehension difficulties, also affect caregiver distress (Cameron, Cheung, Streiner, Coyte, & Stewart, 2006).

Patients' disorders affect families, but families also affect patients' recoveries. For example, Palmer and Glass (2003) reported that families of stroke patients who provide emotional support and suitable levels of instrumental support (i.e., avoiding excessive caregiving) facilitate patients' functional and emotional recovery, regardless of stroke-symptom severity.

Existential questions. Losses experienced in rehabilitation provoke questions about justice, meaning, mortality, and identity. These matters can carry a special poignancy when the patient was not responsible for the event and can result in more externalized blame and greater depression, persisting long after the injury (Hart, Hanks, Bogner, Millis, & Esselman, 2007). Existential issues are difficult to quantify and to study empirically. Nevertheless, resolving them is important in achieving a sense of continuity and acceptance.

EVIDENCE-BASED RESEARCH ON PSYCHOTHERAPEUTIC INTERVENTIONS

A number of studies have examined the efficacy of psychotherapeutic interventions in various clinical populations with disability, largely focusing on the modification of mood, emotion, cognitions, and physiological concomitants that add excess disability (e.g., improving depression or chronic pain in a person with a TBI). The interested reader can consult several sources for guidelines on psychotherapeutic interventions grounded in the general psychotherapy literature (e.g., Kaplan-Solms & Solms, 2002; Langer, Laatsch, & Lewis, 1999; Olkin, 1999; Rusin & Jongsma, 2001).

Effectiveness of Psychotherapeutic Interventions in Rehabilitation Settings

One way of determining the benefit of psychotherapy is to compare outcomes from rehabilitation programs that include psychotherapy with those that do not. Patients with TBI who received milieu-based comprehensive rehabilitation in which psychotherapy was a significant part demonstrated better vocational productivity and emotional adjustment than those who were in programs that did not include psychotherapy (Prigatano et al., 1994). Intensity of psychological interventions during inpatient rehabilitation was related to cognitive gains for persons who have experienced a TBI (Heinemann, Hamilton, Linacre, Wright, & Granger, 1995).

Few studies have examined the impact of psychotherapeutic interventions on the main symptoms of the disease or condition. Tesar, Baumhackl, Kopp, and Gunther (2003) found that a 7-week group psychotherapy intervention for patients with multiple sclerosis produced improvements in depressive symptoms and in perceived "vitality and body dynamics" in comparison with a control group.

Psychotherapeutic interventions have had a significant and direct impact on disability in those with acute and chronic pain. In a randomized controlled trial with persons having chronic temporomandibular disorder pain, brief cognitive–behavioral interventions significantly reduced activity interference, pain intensity, and depression and improved jaw function (Turner, Manci, & Aaron, 2006). A recent meta-analysis of psychological interventions for persons with chronic low-back pain provided evidence for positive effects on reduced pain intensity levels, pain-related interference, health quality of life, and depression in this population (Hoffman, Papas, Chatkoff, & Kerns, 2007).

Though not all studies demonstrate a connection between psychotherapy and functional outcomes, there may be disease-specific responses to such treatments that require further investigation. Furthermore, a host of moderating and mediating factors likely contribute to psychotherapy efficacy. One clear example of a mediating effect is seen in a study by Howard, Turner, Olkin, and Mohr (2006), who found a mediating influence of therapeutic alliance between interpersonal problems and depression treatment outcomes in individuals with multiple sclerosis.

Individual psychotherapy with rehabilitation patients has proved challenging to study because it is highly individualized to patient needs, including co-occurring conditions that may interfere with rehabilitation outcomes or foster excess disability. A prime example is in the area of stroke, where depression is a frequent co-occurring condition and is associated with reduced recovery in activities of daily living (Parikh, Robinson, & Lypsey, 1990) and poor long-term functional outcomes (Nannetti, Paci, Pasquini, Lombardi, & Taiti, 2005; van de Weg, Kuik, & Lankhorst, 1999). Therefore, psychologically based interventions may improve outcomes by reducing the negative impact of comorbid depression. Much rehabilitation psychotherapy research focuses on behavioral and cognitive–behavioral interventions. These techniques have demonstrated effectiveness in treating depression and anxiety disorders and may be well suited to rehabilitation patients because their educational tone is less stigmatizing, they foster self-efficacy, and they possess a certain face validity. The structure and concrete goals of CBT may be helpful to those with brain injury; written notes can be easily incorporated to compensate for memory deficits. Cognitive–behavioral group interventions may have unique benefits. Semistructured groups may be less threatening to those who do not like to talk about feelings, and peers may be more credible to patients than professionals (Anson & Ponsford, 2006a). Group interaction can provide a warmth that is diminished in cognitive therapies (Malik, Beutler, Alimohamed, Gallagher-Thompson, & Thompson, 2003). That said, psychotherapy research with older patients reminds us that therapeutic benefit (at least for depression) can be achieved by multiple therapeutic modalities (Thompson, Gallagher, & Breckenridge, 1987).

CBT may not be the most useful technique for addressing bereavement, identity issues, or existential issues. As Hyer, Kramer, and Sohnle (2004) discuss, a strict CBT approach, with its emphasis on defined problems, could interfere with "seeing the big picture" or with addressing the changed sense of self. CBT is suited to disorders involving cognitive distortions but perhaps not to situations in which a patient is grappling realistically with poignant issues concerning identity, love, and meaning. Group CBT has been used effectively with persons who had SCIs to reduce depression and anxiety, with gains maintained over time (Craig, Hancock, Chang, & Dickson, 1998). Individuals with TBI had improved mood after participating in a CBT group; awareness of injury-related deficits was related to improvement (Anson & Ponsford, 2006b).

Consistent with a coping model, psychoeducational activities enhance emotional well-being by building skills. Women with physical disabilities who participated in a self-esteem workshop had lowered levels of depression and increased self-esteem (Hughes, Robinson-Whelen, Taylor, Swedlund, & Nosek, 2004). Psychoeducational interventions also show promise in addressing substance abuse problems (see Bombardier, 2000). Advice, brief interventions, such as motivational interviewing, coping and social skills training, and linkage with community supports all show promise.

Inclusion of family members in psychotherapeutic interventions may also be of benefit, both to patients and the family system. For example, a manualized family intervention program developed by Kreutzer and Taylor (2004) includes education about TBI sequelae, teaches problem solving and coping strategies, instills hope, and builds communication skills such that families can strengthen and sustain their support network. Palmer, Glass, Palmer, Loo, and Wegener (2004) developed a one-session inpatient intervention with the patient and family, covering such topics as defining stroke as a family crisis, identifying coping resources, encouraging caregivers to avoid burnout, problem-solving, and encouraging participation in social, spiritual, and recreational activities. The efficacy of this inoculation and education is certainly appealing and deserves further attention. However, the use of systemic interventions with families of stroke patients has not yet been demonstrated to be efficacious (Palmer & Glass, 2003). These findings suggest that families may benefit most from interventions with a clear linkage to the problems they are experiencing.

Telehealth and Psychotherapy

Technology is creating opportunities to offer rehabilitation psychology services to patients living in rural areas and others for whom psychological services are otherwise inaccessible. Evidence is accumulating for the efficacy of interventions delivered over telephone, computers, or videoconferencing (i.e., *telehealth*). For example, telephone-administered CBT reduced depression and increased positive affect in those with multiple sclerosis (Mohr et al., 2005). Persons with TBI who received telephone counseling and psychoeducational interventions showed improved functional status and quality of life (Bell et al., 2005). Speakerphone functions allow for the implementation of such techniques as relaxation training. Implementation of telehealth interventions requires only that patients with disabilities have access to their own telephone or computer, have the capacity to interact with the clinician, and use of a private space to facilitate confidentiality of communication. Scheduling of appointments may be easier, given the elimination of the need to plan for transportation, commute time, and mobility within a health care setting.

CANDIDACY FOR PSYCHOTHERAPY

Disabling events occur to those who were psychologically healthy as well as to those with histories of significant psychiatric disorders. Some persons have the initial onset of a psychiatric disorder after a disabling event, whereas, for others, a preexisting psychiatric condition can complicate the implementation of the rehabilitation plan. Many persons undergoing rehabilitation appreciate psychosocial support and information that helps place into context changes they are undergoing and facilitates coping. The high incidence of co-occurring psychiatric disorders in rehabilitation populations argues for routine screening for substance abuse, depression, anxiety, and personality disorders. Persons who have sustained TBI may benefit from individual or group psychotherapy as part of their program of care, yet the approach to psychotherapy may need to be modified because of the cognitive impairments that are common in this population.

The deleterious effect of depression on health and functional outcomes is well supported. Depression should clearly be treated, but well-controlled clinical trials to guide the selection of treatments with rehabilitation patients are sparse. Elliott and Kennedy (2004) noted the potential negative side effects of medication, a serious consideration with rehabilitation patients, many of who have sustained central nervous system damage. Studies with primary care patients (Mynors-Wallis, Garth, Lloyd-Thomas, & Tomlinson, 1995) and geriatric patients (Pinquart, Duberstein, & Lyness, 2006) show that psychotherapy and pharmacotherapy are equally effective in treating depression. Until well-controlled treatment studies are completed with patients having various medical diagnoses, decisions about the best treatment for particular individuals will be made on a case-by-case basis, with careful monitoring of treatment response.

A psychoeducational approach shows promise in enhancing coping capabilities as persons with disabilities face new challenges. Psychoeducation is well suited to group formats, which are both economical and appealing to many patients and family members. Psychoeducation regarding depression and disease-specific topics should perhaps be a standard part of rehabilitation.

The rehabilitation psychologist will be challenged to establish rapport with a wide range of persons, most of whom may be unfamiliar with the role of the psychologist in the rehabilitation setting. It is important to align expectations regarding therapeutic goals among the psychologist, treatment team, patient, and family members. The psychologist may also need to be mindful of the possibility of the patient having cognitive deficits prior to engaging in a psychotherapeutic intervention and adjust the approach accordingly. Skill may also be required in a wide range of communication modalities (e.g., facial expressions, yes/no's, artwork, analogies) to compensate for a patient's cognitive changes.

Candidacy also depends on the theoretical model guiding the intervention. The coping model conceptualizes patients' medical conditions and associated changes as stressors, and psychoeducational and psychotherapeutic interventions as resources that enhance coping effectiveness. Using this model, a wide array of patients is likely to benefit from psychological interventions. If the psychologist uses a pathology model, however, only patients with identifiable conditions based on the *Diagnostic and Statistical Manual of Mental Disorders* ([DSM–IV]; 4th ed.; American Psychiatric Association, 1994) would be eligible: depression, anxiety, cognitive changes, substance abuse, PTSD, and other disorders.

Regardless of model, some patients may be poorer candidates for psychotherapy. Competent patients who refuse psychological interventions, those with diminished mental capacity whose proxy decision-maker refuses, patients who cannot maintain attention or comprehend basic language, or patients having other factors that preclude effective participation in psychotherapy should not be treated. The inclusion criteria are broad and the exclusion criteria narrow. This is based both on clinical practice and on what the literature indicates about the benefits of psychotherapy for rehabilitation outcome and the damage done by untreated disorders.

SPECIAL ISSUES

Rehabilitation psychologists need to manage problems that are related to the ways in which patients are referred and to the ways in which their disabilities affect information processing, communication, and relationships. These special problems can often be managed successfully by the strategies described in this section.

Psychotherapy With Reluctant Patients

The rehabilitation psychologist often must initiate a psychotherapeutic relationship with patients who are not requesting it. If there is clinical justification for the service and no ethical or legal contraindications, the psychologist might approach the patient in the following ways:

- *Explaining clinical protocol.* The psychologist can explain that referral for psychotherapy is routine for rehabilitation patients. It may be helpful to have the physician mention this casually to the patient in advance of the psychologist's arrival.
- *Discussing symptom amelioration.* Psychologists can create a convincing rationale for psychotherapy by using conversational English rather than professional terminology. Describing the problems that will be addressed rather than offering diagnoses will often enhance patients' motivation to participate by clarifying how they will benefit from psychotherapeutic work.
- *Using the medical model.* Couching psychological interventions as a component of medical care can put patients more at ease by "normalizing" psychological interventions. Psychologists can allay patients' fears about being "crazy" or "weak" by using medical explanations of psychopathology, and emphasizing one's role as a rehabilitation psychologist who works with medical patients dealing with understandably stressful circumstances. It may be helpful to describe base rates and natural history of depression and anxiety in rehabilitation and to explain the negative impact mood or anxiety disorders can have on outcome.
- *Accepting "no" as an answer.* Psychologists can inadvertently create reactance by pressuring patients to initiate psychological care. Give patients time to think about the decision.
- *Using the psychoeducational approach.* Interventions can be embedded in psychoeducational group or individual offerings. Once patients learn what psychological interventions consist of,

they are better positioned to make informed choices about accepting or declining them.
- *Offering psychotherapy groups.* Patients sometimes find it easier to learn from their peers; groups help to break down the sense of isolation that often follows a disabling event.

Denial

Patients who apparently lack awareness of functional changes present a challenge to the rehabilitation team and the family. Psychologists may find themselves managing not only the behaviors of the patient but also those of persons (staff and family alike) who want the patient to "be realistic." The psychologist might respond as follows:

- *Differentiate psychological denial from anosognosia.* Provide education about the sources of deficit unawareness, and provide plans to help the patient become aware of deficits, to the degree possible, while bolstering hope for improvement.
- *Monitor cognitive and behavioral denial, and foster rehabilitation participation.* Denial becomes problematic when patients refuse to participate in therapies, reducing the chance of a favorable outcome. Behavioral strategies, bargaining, and reframing may keep patients participating, regardless of their professed belief in the need for treatment.
- *Use hope as a motivator.* Remind families and teams that hope provides motivation for the patient to undertake grueling rehabilitation work. Persons with high levels of hope have better outcomes in a variety of situations, including rehabilitation, and there are no documented drawbacks to "false hope" (Snyder, Lehman, Kluck, & Monsson, 2006). The philosophy of "planning for the worst and hoping for the best" is palatable to almost everyone.

Cognitive and Linguistic Impairments

Cognitive impairments can alter communication in both obvious and subtle ways that demand creativity and thoughtfulness on the part of the rehabilitation psychologist. This may involve such tactics as adjusting session length to suit the patient's attentional capacities or using written notes to facilitate carryover. Remain aware of concrete thinking and how this might affect the patient's reaction to subtleties, nuance, jokes, and humor. Analogies drawn from the patient's life experience may help illustrate psychological points. When working with persons having aphasia or speech disorders, remember that speech is only one communication channel; seek alternative ways (e.g., yes/no signals, facial expressions, gestures, music, art) to convey meaning.

Environmental Interventions

In accomplishing a good person–environment fit, the psychologist will sometimes concentrate on the world with which the patient interacts.

Significant others. It is helpful for significant others and the rehabilitation team to have a shared understanding of the disability and the overall treatment plan. Education can be helpful in achieving this. However, persons who have viewpoints discrepant from the rest of the group should be encouraged to discuss these perspectives; often this information is helpful in tailoring the treatment plan to that person's needs. Families and significant others must work through their own losses, fears, and other emotional reactions while learning to reinforce the patient's abilities, to foster maximal independence.

Immediate environment. Attention to the cognitive (e.g., distractions) and physical (e.g., accessibility) environment will help patients function at their best. Education about the effect of different environments on the expression of the disability will enhance self-regulatory skills.

Social environment. Patients must rebuild confidence in their ability to navigate the world with their new abilities. At times, patients may need to demand rights, and it is within the scope of rehabilitation psychology practice to provide general guidance about legal rights, such as those granted by the Americans with Disabilities Act (1990). Psychologists may provide guidance about communicating with employers, educational institutions, and so forth, to implement accommodations and may take an active role in these discussions. They may also provide information about how to seek appropriate legal counsel and support. It is also within the realm of rehabilitation psychology to advocate for legislation to create a more inclusive social environment for those having a broad range of physical and cognitive abilities.

INPATIENT VERSUS OUTPATIENT PSYCHOTHERAPY

The psychological issues that are dealt with in various phases of rehabilitation are determined by resource allocation as well as the time course of psychological processes. The relatively short length of contemporary rehabilitation stays means that the inpatient psychologist will deal with those emotional issues seen at the beginning of a coping process. Denial may be prominent at this point, but denial can foster hope that provides motivation to do the hard work of rehabilitation; forced confrontations with reality may therefore be counterproductive. During inpatient rehabilitation, the psychologist typically supports coping processes and treats depression and anxiety. Psychologists also develop strategies to manage behavioral problems that interfere with the persons ability to participate in rehabilitation. Psychoeducational interventions enhance coping by preparing patients and families for experiences they may face, and by identifying resources that will help patients address issues that might arise after discharge.

"The rubber hits the road" in outpatient rehabilitation psychology. Denial diminishes as more time elapses since the disabling event and patients see how their condition affects their ability to resume activities in their own homes and communities. In this phase, as patients realize that significant adaptations may be required to live with the changes in physical and cognitive capacities, grieving often ensues. It is in this phase that problems such as PTSD can be diagnosed. Patients will now be involved in intense work for depression, anxiety disorders, substance abuse, persistent behavioral problems, and personality disorders. They will continue to confront existential issues. Patients will also work to build linkages between the pre- and post-event selves, integrating functional changes into their identities, appreciating the continuities, but incorporating the differences.

The attention paid to environmental and social issues typically increases as patients move to the outpatient setting. Evaluating the impact of the environment on patients' functioning will fall increasingly in the psychologist's domain. The psychologist may use time in psychotherapy sessions to identify environmental barriers and brainstorm about ways to limit their impact. The psychologist may serve a case management function, ferreting out resources, educating patients about legal rights, and referring patients to others who can help achieve the optimal person–environment fit.

PRACTICAL RECOMMENDATIONS

It is clear that further research is needed in developing evidence-based psychotherapeutic interventions for persons with disabilities. Besides the traditional quantitative approaches, qualitative research designs, such as participatory action research, may offer particularly important routes to understanding the unique features of psychotherapy in populations with disabilities. Such research designs, according to Tate (2006), are congruent with rehabilitation psychology philosophy in being collaborative, multidimensional, and empowering.

Although each rehabilitation psychologist will implement his or her own particular system of psychotherapy, the following recommendations may be generally beneficial in delivering psychotherapeutic services in rehabilitation psychology:

- A consideration of "adjustment to disability" should include a review of the patient's coping resources, coping history, substance use history, comorbid psychiatric conditions, cognition, personality, family functioning, stressors, social support, and environment.
- Psychological interventions should be guided, but not inevitably determined, by evidence-based literature. Empirically supported therapies may be helpful in alleviating symptoms of depression, anxiety, and PTSD, but there is insufficient research to know what works best for bereavement, identity issues, family system changes, existential questions, and other poignant psychological issues triggered by the life-changing

events that bring people to rehabilitation systems. Although specific literature on the psychological treatment with the condition of the patient in question may not be available, modifications to traditionally validated approaches may need to be implemented to generalize the findings of the empirically based literature.

- Maintain a broad perspective. Consider no issue too small or too large to merit concern. Become fluent in multiple treatment approaches and be alert to the variety of influences on health and well-being. To the degree possible, address environmental, social, and even public policy issues affecting a person's functioning.
- Build on continuity and strengths. More has likely remained the same in the individual's life than has changed. "Positive psychology" interventions that enhance optimism and instill hope (e.g., Snyder, Rand, & Sigmon, 2002; chap. 29, this volume) may serve as buffers to stressors and lead to improved psychotherapy outcomes. A balance between reduction of suffering and facilitation of hope may be critical in all therapeutic encounters by rehabilitation psychologists.

CONCLUSIONS

In this chapter, we have discussed clinical problems to be anticipated in the practice of rehabilitation psychology, reviewed relevant research, and offered recommendations for special problems. We have not, however, overtly identified what makes the practice of psychotherapy in rehabilitation different from psychotherapy in other settings. We are a field with a rich tradition, going back to the early 20th century, but with a new identity, with the ABPP certification in rehabilitation psychology dating back only to 1997. We are distinguished by our interest in function (broadly construed), the breadth of issues that concern us, and the integration of medical, personal, social, and environmental factors in treatment planning. We are distinguished by the team approach, whether other team members are across the hall or across the country (see chap. 32, this volume). We are acutely aware that behavioral competence is influenced not only by "person factors" but also by the physical and social environment.

The interventions discussed in this chapter are heavily focused on the person, with some attention to family and environment. As our sophistication in measuring spiritual, social, and environmental influences improves, we can anticipate clinical models that will reflect the interrelatedness of these multiple factors. It is, and will remain, a fascinating journey.

References

American Board of Professional Psychology. (n.d.). *Rehabilitation exam manual.* Retrieved November 1, 2006, from http://www.abpp.org/certification/abpp_certification_rehabilitation.htm

American Medical Association. (2005). *Current procedural terminology: Professional edition* (2006). Chicago: Author.

American Psychiatric Association. (1994). *Diagnostic and statistical manual of mental disorders* (4th ed.). Washington, DC: Author.

Americans With Disabilities Act of 1990, 42 U.S.C.A. § 12101 *et seq.* (West 1993).

Anson, K., & Ponsford, J. (2006a). Evaluation of a coping skills group following traumatic brain injury. *Brain Injury, 20,* 167–178.

Anson, K., & Ponsford, J. (2006b). Who benefits? Outcome following a coping skills group intervention for traumatically brain injured individuals. *Brain Injury, 20,* 1–13.

Astrom, M. (1996). Generalized anxiety disorder in stroke patients: A 3-year longitudinal study. *Stroke, 27,* 270–275.

Barth, J., Schumacher, M., & Herrmann-Lingen, C. (2004). Depression as a risk factor for mortality in patients with coronary heart disease: A meta-analysis. *Psychosomatic Medicine, 66,* 802–813.

Bell, K. R., Temkin, N. R., Esselman, P. C., Doctor, J. N., Bombardier, C. H., Fraser, R. T., et al. (2005). The effect of a scheduled telephone intervention on outcome after moderate to severe traumatic brain injury: A randomized trial. *Archives of Physical Medicine and Rehabilitation, 86,* 851–856.

Bombardier, C. H. (2000). Alcohol and traumatic disability. In R. G. Frank & T. R. Elliott (Eds.), *Handbook of rehabilitation psychology* (pp. 399–416). Washington, DC: American Psychological Association.

Bombardier, C. H., Richards, J. S., Krause, J. S., Tulsky, D., & Tate, D. G. (2004). Symptoms of major depression in people with spinal cord injury: Implications for screening. *Archives of Physical Medicine and Rehabilitation, 85,* 1749–1756.

Bombardier, C. H., Rimmele, C. T., & Zintel, H. (2002). The magnitude and correlates of alcohol and drug use before traumatic brain injury. *Archives of Physical Medicine & Rehabilitation, 83,* 1765–1773.

Cameron, J. I., Cheung, A. M., Streiner, D. L., Coyte, P. C., & Stewart, D. E. (2006). Stroke survivors' behavioral and psychologic symptoms are associated with informal caregivers' experiences of depression. *Archives of Physical Medicine and Rehabilitation, 87,* 177–183.

Corrigan, J. D. (1995). Substance abuse as a mediating factor in outcome from traumatic brain injury. *Archives of Physical Medicine and Rehabilitation, 76,* 302–309.

Craig, A., Hancock, K., Chang, E., & Dickson, H. (1998). The effectiveness of group psychological intervention in enhancing perceptions of control following spinal cord injury. *Australian and New Zealand Journal of Psychiatry, 32,* 112–118.

Curran, C. A., Ponsford, J. L., & Crowe, S. (2000). Coping strategies and emotional outcome following traumatic brain injury: A comparison with orthopedic patients. *Journal of Head Trauma Rehabilitation, 15,* 1256–1274.

Elliott, T. R., & Frank, R. G. (1996). Depression following spinal cord injury. *Archives of Physical Medicine and Rehabilitation, 77,* 816–823.

Elliott, T. R., & Kennedy, P. (2004). Treatment of depression following spinal cord injury: An evidence-based review. *Rehabilitation Psychology, 49,* 134–139.

Epstein, R. S., & Ursano, R. J. (1994). Anxiety disorders. In J. M. Silver, S. C. Yudofsky, & R. E. Hales (Eds.), *Neuropsychiatry of traumatic brain injury* (pp. 3–41). Washington, DC: American Psychiatric Publishing.

Grant, J. S., Elliott, T. R., Weaver, M., Glandon, G. L., Raper, J. L., & Giger, J. N. (2006). Social support, social problem-solving abilities, and adjustment of family caregivers of stroke survivors. *Archives of Physical Medicine and Rehabilitation, 87,* 343–350.

Hancock, F. M., Craig, A. R., Dickson, H. G., Chang, E., & Martin, J. (1993). Anxiety and depression over the first year of spinal cord injury: A longitudinal study. *Paraplegia, 31,* 349–357.

Harper, R. G. (2004). *Personality-guided therapy in behavioral medicine.* Washington, DC: American Psychological Association.

Hart, T., Hanks, R., Bogner, J. A., Millis, S., & Esselman, P. (2007). Blame attribution in intentional and unintentional traumatic brain injury: Longitudinal changes and impact on subjective well-being. *Rehabilitation Psychology, 52,* 152–161.

Heinemann, A. W., Hamilton, B., Linacre, J. M., Wright, B. D., & Granger, C. (1995). Functional status and therapeutic intensity during inpatient rehabilitation. *American Journal of Physical Medicine & Rehabilitation, 74,* 315–326.

Heinemann, A., Schnoll, S., Brandt, M., Maltz, R., & Keen, M. (1988). Toxicology screening in acute spinal cord injury. *Alcoholism: Clinical and Experimental Research, 12,* 815–819.

Hess, D. W., Marwitz, J. H., & Kreutzer, J. S. (2003). Neuropsychological impairments after spinal cord injury: A comparative study with mild traumatic brain injury. *Rehabilitation Psychology, 48,* 151–156.

Hibbard, M. R., Bogdany, J., Uysal, S., Kepler, K., Silver, J. M., Gordon, W. A., et al. (2000). Axis II psychopathology in individuals with traumatic brain injury. *Brain Injury, 14,* 45–61.

Hiott, D. W., & Labbate, L. (2002). Anxiety disorders associated with traumatic brain injuries. *Neuro-Rehabilitation, 17,* 345–355.

Hoffman, B. M., Papas, R. K., Chatkoff, D. K., & Kerns, R. D. (2007). Meta-analysis of psychological interventions for chronic low-back pain. *Health Psychology, 26,* 1–9.

Hollick, C., Radnitz, C. L., Silverman, J., Tirch, D., Birstein, S., & Bauman, W. A. (2001). Does spinal cord injury affect personality? A study of monozygotic twins. *Rehabilitation Psychology, 46,* 58–67.

Horner, M. D., Ferguson, P. L., Selassie, A. W., Labbate, L. A., Kniele, K., & Corrigan, J. D. (2005). Patterns of alcohol use 1 year after traumatic brain injury: A population-based, epidemiological study. *Journal of the International Neuropsychological Society, 11,* 322–330.

Howard, I., Turner, R., Olkin, R., & Mohr, D. C. (2006). Therapeutic alliance mediates the relationship between interpersonal problems and depression outcome in a cohort of multiple sclerosis patients. *Journal of Clinical Psychology, 62,* 1197–1204.

Hughes, R. B., Robinson-Whelen, S., Taylor, H. B., Swedlund, N., & Nosek, M. A. (2004). Enhancing self-esteem in women with physical disabilities. *Rehabilitation Psychology, 49,* 295–302.

Hyer, L., Kramer, D., & Sohnle, S. (2004). CBT with older people: Alterations and the value of the therapeutic alliance. *Psychotherapy: Theory, Research, Practice, Training, 41,* 276–291.

Jorge, R. E., Robinson, R. G., Arndt, S., & Starkstein, S. (2003). Mortality and poststroke depression: A placebo-controlled trial of antidepressants. *American Journal of Psychiatry, 160,* 1823–1829.

Kaplan-Solms, K., & Solms, M. (2002). *Clinical studies in neuropsychoanalysis.* New York: Karnac.

Kessler, R. C., Berglund, P., Demler, O., Jin, R., & Walters, E. E. (2005). Lifetime prevalence and age-of-onset distributions of *DSM–V* disorders in the national comorbidity survey replication. *Archives of General Psychiatry, 62,* 593–602.

Koponen, S., Taiminen, T., Portin, R., Himanen, L., Isoniemi, H., Heinonen, H., et al. (2002). Axis I and II psychiatric disorders after traumatic brain injury: A 30-year follow-up study. *American Journal of Psychiatry, 159,* 1315–1321.

Kortte, K. B., & Wegener, S. T. (2004). Denial of illness in medical rehabilitation populations: Theory, research, and definition. *Rehabilitation Psychology, 49,* 187–199.

Kreutzer, J., & Taylor, L. (2004). *Brain injury family intervention implementation manual.* Richmond, VA: The National Resource Center for Traumatic Brain Injury.

Langer, K. G., Laatsch, L., & Lewis, L. (Eds.). (1999). *Psychotherapeutic interventions for adults with brain injury or stroke: A clinician's treatment resource.* Madison, CT: Psychosocial Press.

Linden, T., Skoog, I., Fagerberg, B., Steen, B., & Blomstrand, C. (2004). Cognitive impairment and dementia 20 months after stroke. *Neuroepidemiology, 23,* 45–52.

Malik, M. L., Beutler, L. E., Alimohamed, S., Gallagher-Thompson, D., & Thompson, L. (2003). Are all cognitive therapies alike? A comparison of cognitive and noncognitive therapy process and implications for the application of empirically supported treatments. *Journal of Consulting and Clinical Psychology, 71,* 150–158.

McMillen, J. C., & Cook, C. L. (2003). The positive by-products of spinal cord injury and their correlates. *Rehabilitation Psychology, 48,* 77–85.

Mohr, D. C., Hart, S. L., Julian, L., Catledge, C., Honos-Webb, L., Vella, L., et al. (2005). Telephone-administered psychotherapy for depression. *Archives of General Psychiatry, 62,* 1007–1014.

Mynors-Wallis, L., Garth, D., Lloyd-Thomas, A., & Tomlinson, D. (1995). Randomised controlled trial comparing problem solving treatment with amitriptyline and placebo for major depression in primary care. *British Medical Journal, 310,* 441–445.

Nannetti, L., Paci, M., Pasquini, J., Lombardi, B., & Taiti, P. G. (2005). Motor and functional recovery in patients with poststroke depression. *Disability and Rehabilitation, 27,* 170–175.

Nielsen, M. S. (2003). Prevalence of posttraumatic stress disorder in persons with spinal cord injuries: The mediating effect of social support. *Rehabilitation Psychology, 48,* 289–295.

Niemeier, J. P., & Burnett, D. M. (2001). No such thing as "uncomplicated bereavement" for patients in rehabilitation. *Disability and Rehabilitation, 23,* 645–653.

Niemeier, J. P., Kennedy, R. E., McKinley, W. O., & Cifu, D. X. (2004). The Loss Inventory: Preliminary reliability and validity data for a new measure of emotional and cognitive responses to disability. *Disability and Rehabilitation, 26,* 614–623.

Olkin, R. (1999). *What psychotherapists should know about disability.* New York: Guilford Press.

Olkin, R., & Pledger, C. (2003). Can disability studies and psychology join hands? *American Psychologist, 58,* 296–304.

Onitilo, A. A., Nietert, P. J., & Egede, L. E. (2006). Effect of depression on all-cause mortality in adults with cancer and differential effects by cancer site. *General Hospital Psychiatry, 28,* 396–402.

Orto, A. E. D., & Power, P. W. (Eds.). (2007). *The psychological and social impact of illness and disability* (5th ed.). New York: Springer Publishing Company.

Palmer, S., & Glass, T. A. (2003). Family function and stroke recovery: A review. *Rehabilitation Psychology, 48,* 255–265.

Palmer, S., Glass, T. A., Palmer, J. B., Loo, S., & Wegener, S. T. (2004). Crisis intervention with individuals and their families following stroke: A model for psychosocial service during inpatient rehabilitation. *Rehabilitation Psychology, 49,* 338–343.

Parikh, R. M., Robinson, R. G., & Lypsey, J. R. (1990). The impact of poststroke depression on recovery in ADL over a two year follow up. *Archives of Neurology, 47,* 785–789.

Patterson, D. R., & Hanson, S. L. (1995). Joint Division 22 and ACRM Guidelines for postdoctoral training in rehabilitation psychology. *Rehabilitation Psychology, 40,* 299–310.

Perlesz, A., Kinsella, G., & Crowe, S. (1999). Impact of traumatic brain injury on the family: A critical review. *Rehabilitation Psychology, 44,* 6–35.

Pfeiffer, D. (2000). The disability paradigm. *Journal of Disability Policy Studies, 11,* 98–99.

Pinquart, M., Duberstein, P. R., & Lyness, J. M. (2006). Treatments for later-life depressive conditions: A meta-analytic comparison of pharmacotherapy and psychotherapy. *American Journal of Psychiatry, 163,* 1493–1501.

Prigatano, G. P., Klonoff, P. S., O'Brien, K. P., Altman, I., Amin, K., Chiapello, D. A., et al. (1994). Productivity after neuropsychologically oriented, milieu rehabilitation. *Journal of Head Trauma Rehabilitation, 9,* 91–102.

Radnitz, C. L., Schlein, I. S., Walczak, S., Broderick, C. P., Binks, M., Tirch, D. D., et al. (1995). The prevalence of posttraumatic stress disorder in veterans with spinal cord injury. *SCI Psychological Process, 8,* 145–149.

Rivara, F., Jukovich, G., Gurney, J., Seguin, D., Flinger, C., Ries, R., et al. (1993). The magnitude of acute and chronic alcohol abuse in trauma patients. *Archives of Surgery, 128,* 907–913.

Rohe, D. E. (1996). Personality and spinal cord injury. *Topics in Spinal Cord Injury Rehabilitation, 2,* 1–10.

Rosenthal, M., Christensen, B. K., & Ross, T. P. (1998). Depression following traumatic brain injury. *Archives of Physical Medicine and Rehabilitation, 79,* 90–103.

Rusin, M. J., & Jongsma, A. E., Jr. (2001). *The rehabilitation psychology treatment planner.* New York: Wiley.

Rybarczyk, B., Szymanski, L., & Nicholas, J. J. (2000). Limb amputation. In R. G. Frank & T. R. Elliott (Eds.), *Handbook of rehabilitation psychology* (pp. 29–47). Washington, DC: American Psychological Association.

Snyder, C. R. (1999). *Coping: The psychology of what works.* New York: Oxford University Press.

Snyder, C. R., Lehman, K. A., Kluck, B., & Monsson, Y. (2006). Hope for rehabilitation and vice versa. *Rehabilitation Psychology, 51,* 89–112.

Snyder, C. R., Rand, K. L., & Sigmon, D. R. (2002). Hope theory: A member of the positive psychology family. In C. R. Snyder & S. J. Lopez (Eds.), *Handbook of positive psychology* (pp. 257–276). New York: Oxford University Press.

Starkstein, S. E., & Manes, F. (2000). Apathy and depression following stroke. *CNS Spectrums, 5,* 43–50.

Tate, D. G. (2006). The John Stanley Coulter Memorial Lecture: The state of rehabilitation research: Art or science? *Archives of Physical Medicine and Rehabilitation, 87,* 160–166.

Tesar, N., Baumhackl, U., Kopp, M., & Gunther, V. (2003). Effects of psychological group therapy in patients with multiple sclerosis. *Acta Neurologica Scandinavica, 107,* 394–399.

Thompson, L. W., Gallagher, D., & Breckenridge, J. S. (1987). Comparative effectiveness of psychotherapy for depressed elders. *Journal of Consulting and Clinical Psychology, 55,* 385–390.

Turner, J. A., Manci, L, & Aaron, L. A. (2006). Short- and long-term efficacy of brief cognitive–behavioral therapy for patients with chronic temporomandibular disorder pain: A randomized, controlled trial. *Pain, 121,* 181–194.

Uomoto, J. M., & Fann, J. R. (2004). Explanatory style and perception of recovery in symptomatic mild traumatic brain injury. *Rehabilitation Psychology, 49,* 334–337.

van de Weg, F. B., Kuik, D. J., & Lankhorst, G. J. (1999). Poststroke depression and functional outcome: A cohort study investigating the influence of depression on functional recovery from stroke. *Clinical Rehabilitation, 13,* 268–272.

Van Melle, J. P., De Jonge, P., Spijkeran, T. A., Tijssen, J. G. P., Ormel, J., Van Veldhuisen, D. J., et al. (2004). Prognostic association of depression following myocardial infaction with mortality and cardiovascular events: A meta-analysis. *Psychosomatic Medicine, 66,* 814–822.

van Wijk, I., Algra, A., van de Port, I., Bevaart, B., & Lindeman, E. (2006). Change in mobility activity in the second year after stroke in a rehabilitation population: Who is at risk for decline? *Archives of Physical Medicine and Rehabilitation, 87,* 45–50.

CHAPTER 16

ASSISTIVE TECHNOLOGY FOR COGNITION AND BEHAVIOR

Ned L. Kirsch and Marcia J. Scherer

Assistive technology for cognition and behavior (ATCB) is a class of interventions that uses electronic devices to facilitate performance of functional tasks. Computerized devices and systems are central to ATCB applications because they provide a method for interacting with users automatically and for monitoring the user's behavior. For several reasons, the reach and applicability of ATCB has broadened considerably in recent years. First, local area wireless technologies have become increasingly common, both at home and in community settings. These networks can be used to design interventions that interact with a user dynamically, rather than requiring that the user be dependent on off-line, static, device specific systems. Second, geographically dispersed, wide area wireless networks are becoming available that permit continuous use of ATCB systems in locations far beyond the clinic, supporting efforts to promote generalization of desired behaviors across community settings. Third, there have been significant advances in the miniaturization and power of environmental sensors that can automatically detect environmental changes so that interventions can be implemented and adjusted based on feedback about the user's performance.

Several key approaches to clinical application have been emphasized for ATCB applications. Most common are those that use devices or systems in an orthotic or augmentative capacity. These interventions use both off-the-shelf and customized tools to prompt users about when or how to perform a task. They are typically recommended for individuals with cognitive impairments but who are able to interact reliably with a device. A second area of interest involves interventions that transfer to the device supervisory duties typically assumed by caregivers, such as monitoring behavioral status or quality of task performance; this permits interventions to be modified in light of feedback from the monitoring system. Such systems are of particular interest because they can function without requiring that the user interact with the technology. A third class of interventions, developed more recently, uses interactive cueing to promote positive neurobehavioral change.

This chapter focuses on several critical issues concerning ATCB. First, we review applications for ATCB, including (a) characteristics of the interventions, (b) major issues in regard to their use, and (c) primary clinical targets to which they have been applied. Second, we discuss the process of matching persons with technology, including issues of user satisfaction and factors that influence sustained use over time. This section provides a conceptual framework for making decisions about when and how ATCB should be prescribed, on the basis of relevant characteristics of the interventions, users, and the milieu in which the user operates. Third, we offer a "how-to" section discussing practical clinical issues in the development of ATCB interventions based on iterative design principles. This section does not address technical matters (e.g., programming, hardware development) but instead provides a useful framework for determining when an intervention should be modified or, if necessary, abandoned. We conclude with a discussion of some potential limitations of ATCB interventions and issues that must be addressed by future research.

WHAT IS AN ASSISTIVE TECHNOLOGY FOR COGNITION AND BEHAVIOR INTERVENTION?

A variety of ATCB approaches have been presented in the literature. In this section, we discuss the following: (a) the general attributes of ATCB interventions, (b) major issues that have been reported in regard to their use, and (c) primary clinical targets to which they have been applied.

What Are the General Attributes of Assistive Technology for Cognition and Behavior?

As noted by Kirsch, Shenton, Spirl, Rowan, et al. (2004) and LoPresti, Mihailidis, and Kirsch (2004), ATCB is a technologically oriented approach to cognitive rehabilitation whose purpose is to facilitate performance of functional activities that would typically require human guidance and support. To address the individual needs of users, design decisions include the degree to which the ATCB application (a) is considered intrusive (i.e., actively calling itself to the user's attention vs. being "transparent"), (b) requires technological competence of the user, (c) is accepted by users because it is directly applicable to their problems (Louise-Bender Pape, Kim, & Weiner, 2003), and (d) is modifiable over time and across settings.

Early reports described simple alarm clocks, calendars, and buzzers (Harris, 1978; Jones & Adams, 1979; Klein & Fowler, 1981) to facilitate prospective task performance. Although still of clinical use, there are several reasons why these applications are of less interest. First, newer, increasingly sophisticated technologies can be used to intervene with activities that are more complex than simply remembering to perform a task at a specific time. These technologies include wireless networks and Internet-based approaches that allow extended data about task state to be maintained on a server, rather than only on the user's device. In addition, for some users, more sophisticated technologies are often less challenging. For example, features such as automated cueing, controlled through a central computer system (Evans, Emslie, & Wilson, 1999), may be more challenging to implement but easier for a person with cognitive

impairments to use (e.g., because there are fewer operating procedures to learn).

What Clinical Approaches to Cognitive Impairment Are Supported by Assistive Technology for Cognition and Behavior?

Typically, an ATCB intervention is one that supports compensatory strategies (Cole, Dehdashti, Petti, & Angert, 1994; Levine, Horstmann, & Kirsch, 1992). There are two major classes of compensatory interventions: person-oriented and environment-oriented (Kirsch, Shenton, Spirl, Rowan, et al., 2004).

Person-oriented interventions emphasize either (a) strategies that are initiated by a person when needed or (b) the recruitment of alternate neurological systems or pathways to achieve a desired outcome. Many intervention strategies in this area have been explored within the more general context of cognitive rehabilitation and are reviewed in another chapter of this book (see chap. 17, this volume). A comprehensive review of approaches to cognitive rehabilitation can also be found in Cicerone et al. (2005).

As an example of a person-oriented intervention, Davis and Coltheart (1999) described a mnemonic technique to teach street names and locations to a person with topographical disorientation. As an example of the *recruitment* approach, Glisky and colleagues (Glisky, 1992; Glisky & Delaney, 1996; Schachter & Glisky, 1986) reported that patients with persisting memory impairments can benefit from verbal priming techniques such as the "method of vanishing cues." Wilson and Evans (1996) described a more general technique using error-free learning to improve performance of a spatial route-finding task. As examples of interventions that appear to induce plastic neurological reorganization, Morris and Taub (2001) and McDonald et al. (2002) suggested it may be possible to therapeutically induce alternative neurological pathways for movement through counterintuitive interventions (e.g., constraining an unaffected limb) or repetitive functional exercises.

In contrast to person-oriented interventions, ATCB interventions are *environment-oriented* and best suited for individuals who require use of external compensatory strategies where support from others may not be available. As examples of this approach, Cole and colleagues (Cole, 1999; Cole et al., 1994) and Bergman (2000, 2002) developed specialized software and communication interventions, such as adapted word processors and personal information managers. Similarly, Sohlberg and Fickas (2005) described an adapted e-mail program for users with acquired cognitive impairments and increased social isolation. Four participants maintained use of the adapted system for at least 9 months posttraining, with increased social interaction by e-mail despite severe cognitive impairments.

A number of other studies also reported interventions based on cueing (Flannery, Butterbaugh, Rice, & Rice, 1997; Goldstein, Beers, Shemansky, & Longmore, 1998; Kim, Burke, Dowds, Boone, & Parks, 2000; LoPresti, Friedman, & Hages, 1997; Wade & Troy, 2001). In early work, Kirsch and colleagues (Kirsch, Levine, Fallon-Krueger, & Jaros, 1987; Kirsch, Levine, Lajiness, Mossaro, & Schneider, 1992) reported that interactive activity guidance facilitated the performance of multistep activities by presenting the user with sequential cues. The most compelling work in this area has been reported by Wilson and colleagues (Evans et al., 1998; Kime, Lamb, & Wilson, 1995; Wilson, Emslie, Quirk, & Evans 1999; Wilson, Evans, Emslie, & Malinek, 1997) who have used an alphanumeric paging system to facilitate performance of functional activities.

What Types of Functional Problems Lend Themselves to Assistive Technology for Cognition and Behavior Intervention?

ATCB interventions are of greatest interest when they are applied to performance of a functional task. These tasks share a number of characteristics.

First, activities suitable to ATCB intervention often require management or tracking of information. For example, Levinson (1997) described a personal digital assistant (PDA)–based system called the planning and execution assistant and training system (PEAT) that can reorganize or postpone items on a daily schedule. Similarly, software applications such as PocketCoach (see http://www.ablelinktech.com/%5Fhandhelds), and ISAAC (Gordon, Dale, Hood, & Rumrell, 2003) running on PDAs, have been used to present users

with sequential prompts that facilitate performance of complex tasks requiring both sequencing and decision-based branching. Pollack et al. (2003) developed a system called Autominder that intelligently manages a user's schedule, shifting tasks to different hours or days based on parameters such as a preferred time block for task performance or task priority. Autominder can be used over wireless networks so data can be maintained on a server.

In addition to fairly routine prospective tasks, ATCB has also been applied to social and behavioral skills. Hart, Hawkey, and Whyte (2002) used a hand-held voice recorder to assist people whose therapy goals required that they implement or refrain from therapeutically identified behaviors. Because the cueing system offered time-specified prompts, the findings suggest that it may not be necessary for an ATCB intervention to be "aware" that a targeted behavior has actually occurred to facilitate change. Similarly, Kirsch, Shenton, Spirl, Simpson, et al. (2004) demonstrated that pragmatic communication patterns could be modified using fixed interval cues about a desirable targeted behavior. In this study, a single subject with marked verbosity successfully modified his behavior in response to the cue "be brief." However, the subject reverted to precueing behavior once the intervention was withdrawn. As the authors noted, intervention and patient parameters that promote persisting change are not well understood, so for many users, long-term use of an effective ATCB strategy may be necessary.

Second, ATCB interventions are applicable to tasks that require a person to make decisions based on relatively complex information or choice branching (e.g., if it is already 6 p.m., the post office is closed, so skip it). For example, Mihailidis, Fernie, and Cleghorn (2000) developed a special sink adaptation that provided sequential cues, based on sophisticated sensing technology that detects task status, to assist a person with Alzheimer's disease complete hand washing. Kirsch, Shenton, Spirl, Rowan, et al. (2004) reported an intervention for topographical orientation. By presenting colored circles on a PDA screen that matched colored circles mounted throughout a therapy facility, sequential prompts successfully guided a user from one location to another.

Third, there has been a growing interest in the use of ATCB interventions for tasks that can be used in the community and are responsive to user input or changing environmental demands. Patterson et al. (2004) described Opportunity Knocks, a global positioning system that guides users through the community. The system uses machine learning techniques that "acquire" a user's typical routes and provide assistance if it appears that an error has been made. Sohlberg, Todis, Fikas, Hung, and Lemoncello (2005) also described a prototype navigation system that can provide cueing in multiple modalities. For example, street level or bird's eye mapping can be presented on the basis of user preference. Alternatively, auditory cueing can be used for individuals who would be distracted by pictures from visual inspection of the environment. Using this system, individuals with cognitive or perceptual impairments were able to traverse community routes (e.g., to a bus stop) without getting lost.

More generally, given a community-wide wireless infrastructure, any ATCB system that incorporates wireless interaction with a centrally maintained (i.e., "server-side") database can be deployed across multiple behavioral settings. There are a number of reasons why this is critical. First, for users who must rely on a caregiver to maintain or examine information, a wireless system allows the caregiver to assist with tasks that are performed in remote locations. Second, wireless systems can be used to assess the generalizability of response to intervention by offering prompts for the same behavioral target in different contexts. Modifications to the intervention can then be easily made on the basis of analysis of error patterns that appear to impede performance. Third, a server-side database can also maintain information about real-time user responses (e.g., the latency between prompt and response). This information can then be analyzed on the basis of specific study hypotheses or intervention objectives.

There has been growing interest in use of "smart" sensing technology, which can determine the status of an activity without requiring user input, including whether the task is being performed correctly. There are many approaches to sensing that are beyond the scope of this chapter, and most have not yet been incorporated into typical rehabilitation practice. However, these technologies offer significant clinical and research opportunities. By way of example, two sensing technologies offer particular promise. The first, developed collaboratively by the Department of Electrical Engineering and Computer Science at the University of California at Berkeley (see http://webs.cs.berkeley.edu) and the Intel Berkeley Research Laboratory (see http://techresearch. intel.com/articles/Exploratory/1501.htm), focuses on small sensors, managed with an operating system called TinyOS (see http://www.tinyos.net). Base units, called *motes,* can be equipped with specific sensors (see http://www.xbow.com/Products/ Wireless_Sensor_Networks.htm) that communicate wirelessly with a server-side database, or even with each other, so that machine-based decisions can be made about the user's or the task's status. For example, a mote equipped with an accelerometer can detect when an oven door has been opened. By sensing patterns of object use relative to a comprehensive task analysis, interventions can be designed that both support completion of complex tasks (e.g., through prompts chosen based on sensor generated information) and also monitor safety (e.g., by sensing that the oven is still on even though the roast is done).

A second major approach to sensing attempts to recognize the specific activity a user is performing (e.g., making a pot of coffee) using passive radio frequency identification (RFID) tags that transmit a unique ID number induced by an RFID reader that is sufficiently close to the tag. Philipose et al. (2004) described an extremely small RFID reader, with wireless capabilities, worn as a lightweight bracelet. The bracelet only detects RFID tags within 4 inches and can therefore determine when any object, such as a coffee can or spoon, has been touched. By examining the duration and sequence of object "touches," machine inferences can be made about what activity is being performed and how accurately or efficiently.

These emerging technologies are particularly important for ATCB applications because they support assessment of a user's functional accuracy or reliability, without necessarily requiring that the user respond to a query. In this way, interventions can be designed even for users whose cognitive limitations limit effective interaction with a prompting device.

More generally, ATCB interventions are relevant to the psychological well-being of users because they promote participation in the day-to-day activities that are required by family, community, and workplace. There are several specific ways in which this aspect of ATCB intervention is critical to rehabilitation psychology. First, apart from the primary benefit of facilitating independence, the functional benefits associated with ATCB interventions may promote improved mood and the adoption of new behavioral routines that ameliorate the personal impact of disability. However, there is as yet little empirical evidence to support a firm conclusion about this possibility. In fact, for some users, the need for an ATCB device (similar to, for example, the need for a cane) may promote a sense of self as "never being the same again" or being "impaired." Rehabilitation psychologists can provide critical counseling that assists a potential ATCB user whose adoption of an otherwise helpful ATCB application is impeded by altered self-concept or self-worth. The individual contextual differences that account for these varied responses also constitute an area that deserves further research.

Second, as noted earlier, ATCB interventions, when directed at behavioral targets, simply represent a new type of clinical tool for interventions that are otherwise quite familiar to rehabilitation psychologists. Specifically, ATCB interventions can be used as components of behavioral treatment plans for various neurologically based symptoms (most notably those that affect interpersonal relationships) by providing (a) real-time reinforcements for the user and for monitoring and (b) a recording of behavioral data for the rehabilitation psychologist. As such, ATCB interventions can also be thought of as a critical tool for assessing the effectiveness of behavioral intervention strategies. More generally, rehabilitation psychologists are concerned with the promotion of independence through improved function and accessibility. ATCB interventions can, in theory, achieve these goals. The following section addresses key issues such as the acceptance of technology, its consistent use, and its impact on long-term psychological adaptation.

ACHIEVING AN APPROPRIATE MATCH OF USER AND ASSISTIVE TECHNOLOGY FOR COGNITION AND BEHAVIOR

Given the range of choices available within the ATCB product line, how can clinicians best decide which ATCB application is most appropriate for any given individual? One recommended approach is to conduct a comprehensive assessment that considers three primary areas: (a) milieu or environmental factors influencing use; (b) consumer personal and psychosocial characteristics, needs, and preferences; and (c) functions and features of the most desirable and appropriate ATCB.

What Milieu, Personal, and Technology Factors Most Influence Assistive Technology for Cognition and Behavior Selection and Use?

By addressing the milieu, personal, and technology (MPT) factors influencing ATCB selection and use, desirable interventions can be identified that (a) help reduce premature or inappropriate device recommendations by the clinical team and (b) minimize device abandonment by the user. Documenting a person's functioning and behavior before and after the device is used can (a) help provide a rationale for securing funding for a device; (b) provide guidance to the clinical team about how best to train for the use of the device, including sustained use over time; (c) demonstrate an individual's improvement in functioning over time; and (d) help organize information typifying the needs of an organization's consumers.

These MPT components are the primary areas in the matching person and technology model (Scherer, 2004, 2005; Scherer, Sax, Vanbiervliet, Cushman & Scherer, 2005). To operationalize the model and theory, an assessment process consisting of several instruments was developed through participatory action research addressing differences between technology users and nonusers. The assessments are clinical measures that identify barriers to technology use for a particular individual and then assess outcomes of use when readministered as follow-up assessments. The measures have been validated for use by persons with disabilities ages 15 and up. Milieu and environmental features influencing ATCB use go beyond architectural and physical barriers and include the variety of attitudes and values of the people in those environments, such as culture, language, lifestyle (e.g., Parette, Huer, & Scherer, 2004; Parette & Scherer, 2004), traditional family structure, and linguistic heritages. Sample considerations regarding the characteristics and requirements of the milieu or environment are listed in Exhibit 16.1, Section A.

What Are Some Key Characteristics of the Individual Who Will Use Assistive Technology for Cognition and Behavior?

It can at times appear that a particular ATCB is perfect for a given user, but then later it is discovered that the person stopped using it, never used it, or uses it only in limited situations. Several factors appear to influence these poor outcomes. When device use interferes with other activities or need satisfaction, it may be abandoned or viewed as ineffective (e.g., Scherer, 2005). In addition, consumers may be unwilling to request training or other assistance for fear that it may appear they "are not doing well" or simply because they are not assertive. Exhibit 16.1, Section B, lists sample questions to ask to better understand the personal needs and aspirations of those for whom an ATCB is being considered.

What Are Key Characteristics and Features of the Assistive Technology for Cognition and Behavior Device and Assistive Technology for Cognition and Behavior Services That Best Meet the Needs and Preferences of a Particular User?

Exhibit 16.1, Section C, lists sample questions to ask to better understand the ATCB needs and features most appropriate for any given individual. To summarize, achieving a good match between person and technology is critical to the development of effective ATCB interventions. This requires a thorough

---

Exhibit 16.1
Considerations for Matching Persons and Assistive Technology for Cognition and Behavior

Section A
Sample milieu or environment areas to review when assistive technology for cognition and behavior (ATCB) is being considered

- What are the perspectives of family members and caregivers regarding the prescribed technology?
- Will family members encourage and support both use and maintenance?
- Is assistance available for user training?
- Will the user feel alienated, stigmatized, or disparaged?
- Will the user feel frustrated by the ATCB?
- Will the ATCB/environment interaction promote community integration?

Section B
Sample personal areas to address when ATCB is being considered

- Is the user in agreement that the proposed technology will result in a gain?
- What are the user's strengths, interests, and learning style?
- Does the user have the requisite skills to operate the technology effectively?
- Will the ATCB require a major interruption in accustomed ways of doing things?

Section C
Sample device and service considerations to address

- What are the initial costs and maintenance costs of the device?
- Is affordable remote or in-home service available?
- Is the ATCB compatible with other prescribed interventions?
- Is the ATCB easily modifiable based on changing clinical status?

assessment of user, milieu or environments, and technology features. After training and a trial period of use, including in natural settings, feedback should be sought on how well the technology is performing for that person and how the user's ability and performance patterns have changed. This evidence-based process is discussed in the next section.

HOW ARE ASSISTIVE TECHNOLOGY FOR COGNITION AND BEHAVIOR INTERVENTIONS DESIGNED?

Choice, design, and implementation of an ATCB intervention involves many decisions, informed by assessment of the patient's cognitive status, the activities both the user and clinical team would like the user to perform, and the resources available to support sustained use over time. In this section, specific issues of intervention design are discussed.

Most critically, an ATCB intervention is one that must interact with a user to facilitate functional change. It must therefore be a system that is "usable" (Hornbaek, 2005; Sutcliffe, Ficas, & Sohlberg, 2003). Careful design is critical because a user experiencing difficulty manipulating the device or comprehending a prompt may fail to perform the target activity competently, even if that user would be able to perform the task with a better designed intervention.

Because interaction is such a critical component of these interventions, decisions must be made about the interface that best suits a user's needs. Interface features must be considered regarding the device or system that will be used, as well as the task that is to be performed. The designs of device and task interfaces are distinguishable operations and should be considered separately. We review some of the distinctions and caveats raised by Scherer, Hart, Kirsch, and Schultheis (2005) in regard to these two aspects of intervention design.

Device Interface Design

Device interface design typically concerns itself with software and hardware features that are necessary for a user to interact with the device or system. As noted by Scherer et al. (2005), designers may consider the following:

- how many buttons can optimally be presented by a device,
- whether the buttons are labeled with words or icons,
- whether only one or alternative operations are available for achieving the same result (e.g., pressing a physical button or tapping an icon with a stylus), and
- how many steps are required to locate a needed feature.

Device design requires attention to both physical and cognitive factors and is often best accomplished using iterative design techniques. As an example, in the study by Kirsch, Shenton, Spirl, Simpson, et al. (2004), the intervention presented a cue to the user at fixed intervals. The cue was recorded in the user's voice and presented by a PDA through an earphone. However, several features of the intervention were repeatedly changed according to user preference, including the cue-interval duration, the placement of the PDA (i.e., table vs. pocket), and the wording of the prompt. The final intervention represented the culmination of a protracted negotiation, resulting in a method that was acceptable for use in a group setting and that minimized frustration and potential embarrassment.

Task Interface Design

In contrast to device interface design, tasks must be analyzed and assessed in much the same way as the device to be used. As noted by Scherer et al. (2005), tasks can be simplified by, for example, modifying the sequence of steps to be performed, simplifying the objects required for the task, using verbal labeling or color coding, modifying spatial arrangements, reducing environmental clutter, or minimizing environmental distraction.

Task interface requirements will often be determined by the user's specific error patterns during task performance. Often, a user's error pattern will be unpredictable so (as for device interface design) an iterative sequence of changes to the task itself must often be made until variability has been minimized and accurate performance consistently achieved. As an example, Kirsch, Shenton, Spirl, Rowan, et al. (2004) reported an intervention using a sequence of pictures on a laptop computer that instructed an elderly woman with severe cognitive impairments how to set her alarm clock. During pilot trials, she made unexpected errors, including misreading the labels on alarm clock buttons. The final ATCB intervention used color-coded buttons on the alarm clock, matched by color-coded pictures, interactively presented on a computer screen. By directing her attention to the colors (rather than verbal labels), she was able to complete the alarm clock setting task.

Clinical experience suggests that as symptom severity increases, the number of iterations required to achieve successful task completion also increases. However, for some users, successful task completion using an ATCB intervention may never be achieved, often because the same cognitive difficulties that demand ATCB also interfere with acquisition of necessary skills for task performance. For these users, error variability, primary cognitive difficulties, or factors such as distractibility and mood change, may be so severe that efforts to match them with appropriate technology will simply not be successful.

ASSISTIVE TECHNOLOGY FOR COGNITION AND BEHAVIOR INTERVENTIONS REQUIRE THE SKILLS OF THE ENTIRE CLINICAL TEAM

As described earlier, ATCB appears to offer promise for individuals with neurocognitive impairments that are not responsive to other therapeutic interventions. In other words, ATCB is (and has typically been used as) a compensatory intervention. As technological tools become pervasively embedded in personal and community functional behavioral contexts, interventions will become possible that address complex activities, across a broader range of contexts. Having noted this, there are many issues that must be addressed concerning the effectiveness of these interventions and their conceptual place in broader rehabilitation programs. In the remainder of this chapter, we briefly summarize some of these issues.

Assistive Technology for Cognition and Behavior and the Clinical Team

As noted earlier, effective ATCB interventions are based on a clinically sound understanding of the

impact a user's impairments have on functional performance. However, ATCB interventions also require familiarity with available technological tools and, in some cases, advanced skills such as wireless network management, Web page construction, database design, and use of environmental sensors and controls.

The complex array of skills that ATCB applications require suggests that they are best implemented by a multidisciplinary team. Clinical assessment, technological implementation, and development of assessment metrics may all be represented by different team members who must work together to develop an effective approach to a user's targeted need. Review of team skills will often be necessary so that those not represented can be trained or recruited. Rehabilitation psychologists will often contribute critical skills in a number of these areas, including the long-term assessment of user satisfaction and the impact of ATCB use on mood and interpersonal relationships.

Assistive Technology for Cognition and Behavior Interventions Have Limited Generalizability

Ideally, an intervention designed to facilitate cognitive performance or behavioral adaptation will promote change across of broad range of behavioral settings. However, this clinical ideal has been difficult to achieve (van den Broek, 2005). ATCB is no different from other interventions in this regard. An intervention that promotes behavior change in one context may not necessarily result in change in another. Similarly, an intervention that promotes specific behavioral change may not affect a highly related behavior, unless the alternate behavioral target is also specifically addressed.

Having noted this, one advantage of ATCB is that carefully chosen technologies can be easily adapted to the changing environmental demands faced by users. Once an ATCB intervention has been designed, modifications can be easily implemented, such as changing text and pictures to facilitate performance of behavioral variations or changing cue content to accommodate the social demands of different situations. For example, the same behavioral target (e.g., verbosity) can be discouraged in some settings (e.g., a classroom) and encouraged in others (e.g., a party or family gathering), simply by modifying prompts. The approach to generalization promoted by ATCB is to utilize "programmability" to adapt a compensatory intervention to contextual demands, in contrast to static interventions that fail to achieve independent functioning across behaviors or contexts.

Assistive Technology for Cognition and Behavior Interventions Are Atheoretical

ATCB interventions are clinical tools. ATCB, as an approach to intervention, does not promote or support a specific theoretical perspective on cognitive rehabilitation, other than the implicit assertion that adaptive behaviors can be facilitated through prompting, despite persisting cognitive impairments. However, ATCB technologies are highly replicable and are particularly well suited to interventions that must be systematically controlled, such as might be required for studies examining the impact that theoretically driven intervention variations have on outcome (Whyte, 2006). For example, ATCB interventions are particularly well-suited to interventions for complex tasks that a user encounters in daily life. Chen, Abrams, and D'Esposito (2006) recommended an approach to cognitive intervention based on a model of prefrontal cortical functioning. They note that a "top-down" rather than a "bottom-up" approach to therapy may be most effective by facilitating specific cognitive skills through the performance of tasks for which those skills are fundamental components. One such therapy model might require, for example, the development of a systematically designed range of interventions for the performance of a functional task, such as a vocational activity requiring management of multiple subtasks simultaneously. By systematically varying the cues provided using ATCB-type technology, theoretical concerns can be tested systematically and with a high degree of replicability.

Assistive Technology for Cognition and Behavior Interventions Can Be Expensive

More technological sophistication and greater therapist time and skill are typically associated with increased cost. In contrast, off-the-shelf devices, such as PDAs, are relatively inexpensive (many less than $100). In our estimation, the clinical team is responsible for developing interventions that minimize cost without sacrificing clinical utility. The tradeoff between these two goals can sometimes be challenging, particularly for interventions that are designed to manage complex activities.

Assistive Technology for Cognition and Behavior Interventions Are Often Abandoned

In the previous sections, we discussed some variables that affect sustained use and abandonment. Other critical variables that affect the success of an ATCB intervention include cost, reliability, availability of interpersonal support, availability of technical support, the degree to which the "prescriber" is well-trained in the use of the intervention, the user's perception that the intervention addresses his or her changing clinical status, and the meaning or significance that the user ascribes to the device (Louise-Bender Pape et al., 2002). Understanding the variable impact of these factors and their interaction remains a goal for future research.

However, clinical experience also suggests that devices are often abandoned for reasons that reflect the same cognitive difficulties that led to the need for the intervention. For example, problems with memory may lead to a device being lost, and problems with executive dysfunction may lead to misapplication or neglect of an intervention strategy that would otherwise be helpful. It is both a challenge and a responsibility for the clinical team to develop interventions that address a user's functional concern without requiring cognitive skills the user cannot recruit. For example, users with attentional problems may require frequent fixed interval cues that remind them to use an intervention, whereas users with memory problems may require that an ATCB device issue alarms whenever the user and device become separated. It is not possible for a clinical team to anticipate every user performance error or every changing environmental contingency. However, ongoing clinical and technical support, including an iterative approach to intervention design that incorporates modifications based on error patterns, may reduce abandonment by maintaining the user's perception that the intervention is relevant and responsive to his or her daily needs.

CONCLUSIONS

ATCB interventions are technological tools that can be used to facilitate the performance of functional activities in the home, community, and workplace. As described in this chapter, these interventions are typically used to facilitate compensation for unremitting cognitive changes but can also be used to promote behavioral change after neurological insult. Rehabilitation psychologists are critical to all stages of development, intervention, and assessment of these interventions, particularly in settings in which rehabilitation psychologists participate in the direct treatment of cognitive impairments. However, apart from treatment of cognitive impairments themselves, ATCB interventions must be developed with an understanding of (a) the user's individual characteristics, including his or her attitudes toward the use of technological compensatory strategies; and (b) the milieu or context in which the user interacts with others. ATCB interventions, however sophisticated or powerful their technology, will only be effective if individuals with cognitive impairments use them on a sustained basis and are willing to interact consistently with the rehabilitation team so that the interventions can be modified in response to changing needs. ATCB interventions may also incidentally affect areas of clinical concern such as a user's mood, family coping patterns, and the reacceptance of the user in the workplace. All these areas of clinical concern are central to the role of rehabilitation psychologists who are, therefore, critical to both the implementation and assessment of ATCB intervention strategies.

References

Bergman, M. M. (2000). Successful mastery with a cognitive orthotic in people with traumatic brain injury. *Applied Neuropsychology, 7,* 76–82.

Bergman, M. M. (2002). The benefits of a cognitive orthotic in brain injury rehabilitation. *Journal of Head Trauma Rehabilitation, 17,* 432–445.

Chen, A. J., Abrams, G. M., & D'Esposito, M. (2006). Functional reintegration of prefrontal neural networks for enhancing recovery after brain injury. *Journal of Head Trauma Rehabilitation, 21,* 107–118.

Cicerone, K. D., Dahlberg, C., Malec, J. F., Langenbahn, D. M., Felicetti, T., Kneipp, S., et al. (2005). Evidence-based cognitive rehabilitation: Updated review of the literature from 1998 through 2002. *Archives of Physical Medicine and Rehabilitation, 86,* 1681–1692.

Cole, E. (1999). Cognitive prosthetics: An overview to two methods of treatment. *Neurorehabilitation, 12,* 39–51.

Cole, E., Dehdashti, P., Petti, L., & Angert, M. (1994). Design and outcomes of computer-based cognitive prosthetics for brain injury: A field study of three subjects. *Neurorehabilitation, 4,* 174–186.

Davis, S. J., & Coltheart, M. (1999). Rehabilitation of topographical disorientation: An experimental single case study. *Neuropsychological Rehabilitation, 9,* 1–30.

Evans, J. J., Emslie, H., & Wilson, B. A. (1998). External cueing systems in the rehabilitation of executive impairments of action. *Journal of the International Neuropsychological Society, 4,* 399–408.

Flannery, M. A., Butterbaugh, G. J., Rice, D. A., & Rice, J. C. (1997). Reminding technology for prospective memory disability: A case study. *Pediatric Rehabilitation, 1,* 239–244.

Glisky, E. B. (1992). Computer-assisted instruction for patients with traumatic brain injury: Teaching of domain-specific knowledge. *Journal of Head Trauma Rehabilitation, 7,* 1–12.

Glisky, E., & Delaney, S. (1996). Implicit memory and new semantic learning in posttraumatic amnesia. *Journal of Head Trauma Rehabilitation, 11,* 31–42.

Goldstein, G., Beers, S. R., Shemansky, W. J., & Longmore, S. (1998). An assistive device for persons with severe amnesia. *Journal of Rehabilitation Research and Development, 35,* 238–244.

Gordon, P., Dayle, R., Hood, C., & Rumrell, L. (2003). Effectiveness of the ISAAC cognitive prosthetic system for improving rehabilitation outcomes with neurofunctional impairment. *Neurorehabilitation, 18,* 57–67.

Harris, J. (1978). External memory aids. In M. Gruneberg, P. Morris, & R. Sykes (Eds.), *Practical aspects of memory* (pp. 172–179). London: Academic Press.

Hart, T., Hawkey, K., & Whyte, J. (2002). Use of a portable voice organizer to remember therapy goals in traumatic brain injury rehabilitation: A within-subjects trial. *Journal of Head Trauma Rehabilitation, 17,* 556–570.

Hornbaek, K. (2005). Current practice in measuring usability: Challenges to usability studies and research. *International Journal of Human–Computer Studies, 64,* 79–102,

Jones, M., & Adams, J. (1979). Toward a prosthetic memory. *Bulletin of the British Psychological Society, 3,* 165–167.

Kim, H., Burke, D., Dowds, M., Boone, K. A., Parks, G. J. (2000). Electronic memory aids for outpatient brain injury: Follow-up findings. *Brain Injury, 14,* 187–196.

Kime, S., Lamb, D., & Wilson, B. A. (1995). Use of a comprehensive program of external cueing to enhance procedural memory in a patient with dense amnesia. *Brain Injury, 10,* 17–25.

Kirsch, N. L., Levine, S. P., Fallon-Krueger, M., & Jaros, L. (1987). The microcomputer as an "orthotic" device for patients with cognitive deficits. *Journal of Head Trauma Rehabilitation, 2,* 77–86.

Kirsch, N. L., Levine, S. P., Lajiness, R., Mossaro, M., & Schneider, M. (1992). Computer-assisted interactive task guidance: Facilitating the performance of a simulated vocational task. *Journal of Head Trauma Rehabilitation, 7,* 13–25.

Kirsch, N. L., Shenton, M., Spirl, E., Rowan, J., Simpson, R., Schreckenghost, D., & LoPresti, E. (2004). Web-based assistive technology interventions for cognitive impairments after traumatic brain injury: A selective review and two cases studies. *Rehabilitation Psychology, 49,* 200–212.

Kirsch, N. L., Shenton, M., Spirl, E., Simpson, R., LoPresti, E., & Schreckenghost, D. (2004). Modifying verbose speech after traumatic brain injury with an assistive technology system for coordinated behavior-change cueing and monitoring. *Journal of Head Trauma Rehabilitation, 19,* 366–377.

Klein, R., & Fowler, R. (1981). Pressure relief training device: The microcalculator. *Archives of Physical Medicine and Rehabilitation, 62,* 500–501.

Levine, S. P., Horstmann, H. M., & Kirsch, N. L. (1992). Performance considerations for people with cognitive impairments in accessing assistive technologies. *Journal of Head Trauma Rehabilitation, 7,* 46–58.

Levinson, R. (1997). PEAT: The planning and execution assistant and training system. *Journal of Head Trauma Rehabilitation, 12,* 85–91.

LoPresti, E. F., Friedman, M. B., & Hages, D. (1997). Electronic vocational aid for people with cognitive disabilities. *Proceedings of the RESNA Annual Conference,* 514–516.

LoPresti, E. F., Mihailidis, A., & Kirsch, N. L. (2004). Assistive technology for cognitive rehabilitation: State of the art. *Neuropsychological Rehabilitation, 14*(1–2), 5–39.

Louise-Bender Pape, T., Kim, J., & Weiner, B. (2002). The shaping of individual meanings assigned to assistive technology: A review of personal factors. *Disability and Rehabilitation, 24*(1–3), 5–20.

McDonald, J. W., Becker, D., Sadowsky, C. L., Jane, J. A., Conturo, T. E., & Schultz, L. M. (2002). Late recovery following spinal cord injury: Case report and review of the literature. *Journal of Neurosurgery, 97,* 252–265.

Mihailidis, A., Fernie, G. R., & Cleghorn, W. L. (2000). The development of a computerized cueing device to help people with dementia be more independent. *Technology and Disability, 12,* 23–40.

Morris, D. M, & Taub, E. (2001). Constraint-induced therapy approach to restoring function after neurological injury. *Topics in Stroke Rehabilitation, 8*(3), 16–30.

Parette, H. P., Huer, M. B., & Scherer, M. (2004). Effects of acculturation on assistive technology service delivery. *Journal of Special Education Technology, 19*(2), 31–41.

Parette, P., & Scherer, M. J. (2004). Assistive technology use and stigma. *Education and Training in Developmental Disabilities, 39,* 217–226.

Patterson, D., Liao, L., Gajos, K., Collier, M., Livic, N., Olson, K., et al. (2004). Opportunity Knocks: A system to provide cognitive assistance with transportation services. In I. Siio, N. Davies, & E. Mynatt (Eds.), *Proceedings of UBICOMP 2004: The Sixth International Conference on Ubiquitous Computing.* Berlin: Springer Publishing Company.

Philipose, M., Fishkin, K. P., Perkowitz, M., Patterson, D. J., Fox, D., Kautz, H, & Hähnel, D. (2004). Inferring activities from interactions with objects. *IEEE Pervasive Computing, 3*(4), 50–57.

Pollack, M. E., Brown, L., Colbry, D., McCarthy, C. E., Orosz, C., Peintner, B., et al. (2003). Autominder: An intelligent cognitive orthotic system for people with memory impairment. *Robotics and Autonomous Systems, 44,* 273–282.

Schacter, D. L., & Glisky, E. L. (1986). Memory remediation: Restoration, alleviation, and the acquisition of domain-specific knowledge. In B. P. Uzzell & Y. Gross (Eds.), *Clinical neuropsychology of intervention* (pp. 257–282). Boston: Martinus Nijhoff.

Scherer, M. J. (2004). *Connecting to learn: Educational and assistive technology for people with disabilities.* Washington, DC: American Psychological Association.

Scherer, M. J. (2005). *Living in the state of stuck: How technology impacts the lives of people with disabilities* (4th ed.). Cambridge: Brookline.

Scherer, M. J., Hart, T., Kirsch, N., & Schultheis, M. (2005). Assistive technologies for cognitive disabilities. *Critical Reviews in Physical and Rehabilitation Medicine, 17,* 195–215.

Scherer, M. J., Sax, C., Vanbeirvliet, A., Cushman, L. A., & Scherer, J. V. (2005). Predictors of assistive technology use: The importance of personal and psychosocial factors. *Disability & Rehabilitation, 27,* 1321–1331.

Sohlberg, M. M., & Fickas, S. (2005). The longitudinal effects of accessible e-mail for individuals with severe cognitive impairments. *Aphasiology, 19,* 651–681.

Sohlberg, M. M., Todis, B., Fickas, S., Hung, P., & Lemoncello, R. (2005). A profile of community navigation in adults with chronic cognitive impairments. *Brain Injury, 19,* 1249–1259.

Sutcliffe, A., Fickas, S., & Sohlberg, M. M. (2003). Investigating the usability of assistive user interfaces. *Interacting With Computers, 15,* 577–602.

van den Broek, M. D. (2005). Why does neurorehabilitation fail? *Journal of Head Trauma Rehabilitation, 20,* 464–473.

Wade, T. K., & Troy, J. C., (2001). Mobile phones as a new memory aid: A preliminary investigation using case studies. *Brain Injury, 15,* 305–320.

Whyte, J. (2006). Using treatment theories to refine the designs of brain injury rehabilitation treatment effectiveness studies. *Journal of Head Trauma Rehabilitation, 21,* 99–106.

Wilson, B. A., Emslie, H., Quirk, K., & Evans, J. J., (1999). George: Learning to live independently with NeuroPage. *Rehabilitation Psychology, 44,* 284–296.

Wilson, B. A., & Evans, J. J. (1996). Error-free learning in the rehabilitation of people with memory impairments. *Journal of Head Trauma Rehabilitation, 11,* 54–64.

Wilson, B. A., Evans, J. J., Emslie, H., & Malinek, V. (1997). Evaluation of NeuroPage: A new memory aid. *Journal of Neurology, Neurosurgery & Psychiatry, 63,* 113–115.

CHAPTER 17

COGNITIVE REHABILITATION

Tessa Hart

Cognitive rehabilitation is a field with a colorful past, a vigorous present, and a promising future. This chapter presents definitions and general models of cognitive rehabilitation followed by an overview of cognitive rehabilitation methods organized by the cognitive functions described in the clinical research literature: attention, memory, executive function, visuospatial function (including hemispatial neglect), and language. A section on comprehensive and holistic cognitive rehabilitation is included in recognition of important treatment models that seek to address multiple cognitive functions along with emotional, psychosocial, and community outcomes. The chapter closes with a discussion of the challenges and opportunities for the future of cognitive rehabilitation, as its practitioners seek to develop a sound, theoretically motivated evidence base.

DEFINITION AND CONCEPTS

To use the singular term *field* for an enterprise as diverse as cognitive rehabilitation may be a misnomer because cognitive rehabilitation does not have a sole professional home. Cognitive rehabilitation is practiced by speech pathologists, occupational therapists, and psychologists from diverse specialties. Neuroscientists, linguists, physicians, and behaviorists, among others, struggle to contribute to its evidence base. This eclecticism enriches the field but also lends itself to a certain theoretical incoherence and a multiplicity of definitions. In one of the more

comprehensive attempts to define cognitive rehabilitation, a Task Force of the Brain Injury Special Interest Group of the American Congress of Rehabilitation Medicine (ACRM) proposed that it could be defined as follows:

> A systematic, functionally oriented service of therapeutic activities that is based on assessment and understanding of the patient's brain-behavioral deficits. Specific interventions may have various approaches, including (1) reinforcing, strengthening, or reestablishing previously learned patterns of behavior; (2) establishing new patterns of cognitive activity through compensatory cognitive mechanisms for impaired neurological systems; (3) establishing new patterns of activity through external compensatory mechanisms such as personal orthoses or environmental structuring and support; and (4) enabling persons to adapt to their cognitive disability, even though it may not be possible to directly modify or compensate for cognitive impairments, in order to improve their overall level of functioning and quality of life. (Cicerone et al., 2000, pp. 1596–1597)

Several important concepts are embedded in this definition, reflecting themes that weave through the

This work was supported by the Neuro-Cognitive Rehabilitation Research Network, Grant No. R24 HD050836, sponsored by the National Institutes of Health (National Institute of Child Health and Human Development). Rebecca Hardin provided able assistance with reference management.

field from its earliest history to the present day. The first is the notion that cognitive rehabilitation operates at multiple levels of human function. To use the terminology of the International Classification of Function (ICF; World Health Organization, 2001), cognitive rehabilitation may be intended to improve cognitive functions such as attention, memory, language, visual perception, or executive function; but may also be focused on redressing limitations in activities or participation in societal roles that are due at least in part to cognitive impairments (Wade, 2005). At yet another level, cognitive rehabilitation may be practiced to help people adapt to cognitive impairments that cannot be changed. The breadth of the definition captures the richness and complexity of research and clinical activities that fall under the umbrella of cognitive rehabilitation.

Second, the ACRM definition includes one of the important organizing concepts of cognitive rehabilitation, namely, the distinction between restorative and compensatory approaches to remediation. This distinction dates at least to the seminal article by Oliver Zangwill, published in 1947, on these two major classes of methods for "re-education" of persons with brain injury (for a discussion of this article and other landmarks in the history of cognitive rehabilitation, see Boake, 2003). As the name implies, *restorative* approaches are meant to restore a lost or damaged function to the preinjury state, usually through direct retraining and often using repetitive activities, such as drills. By analogy to repetitive muscle exercise, these activities are supposed to stimulate and/or strengthen the lost or damaged function. By contrast, *compensatory* approaches avoid or circumvent the damaged functions, seeking instead to encourage the use of intact functions or external strategies to accomplish tasks. Using a checklist to organize a multistep activity and learning to ask questions to double-check one's comprehension of oral language and/or to slow down the speaker are both examples of compensatory approaches to cognitive rehabilitation. Note that, in these examples, the underlying cognitive deficit is not assumed to change. Rather, the functional goals (i.e., completing the activity, following the conversation) are met using an alternative route or substi-

tuted set of behaviors. Compensatory approaches may be further conceptualized as those based on changes focused on the person (e.g., when a patient is taught to use a compensatory strategy or device) versus those based on environmental modifications. For example, the physical environment may be simplified by removing extraneous objects to help compensate for visual impairments; the social environment may be structured by stipulating that only one person speak to the patient at any given time to compensate for attention or comprehension problems.

Restorative approaches fell somewhat out of favor when computerized exercises for attention, memory, and problem solving, enthusiastically adopted in the 1980s with the arrival of the personal computer, showed mostly disappointing results in efficacy studies (Tate, 1997). However, restorative methods are gaining new attention as the result of the success of forced-use rehabilitation techniques. Developed to treat chronic hemiparesis, *forced-use* techniques are based on the theory that chronic deficits are caused at least in part by learned disuse. Forcing use of the function by, for example, restraining the intact arm in a mitt, which forces the patient to use the impaired arm, has resulted in remarkable gains even years after stroke (Taub & Uswatte, 2000). The forced-use concept has already been used in rehabilitation of chronic aphasia, with promising results (Pulvermuller et al., 2001), and may have other applications to cognitive rehabilitation (Lillie & Mateer, 2006). The success of these methods calls into question the conventional wisdom that substantial gains cannot be made after natural recovery has "plateaued," and challenges the common clinical assumption that restoration should be attempted first, followed by compensatory strategies when restoration meets with diminishing returns. It must now be considered that some compensatory training could even be harmful by contributing to learned disuse of both physical and cognitive functions.

Robertson (1999) has proposed criteria for selecting restorative versus compensatory approaches on the basis of the degree of sparing in the affected neuronal system. Very severe disruption would indicate the need for a compensatory approach because there would not be enough neuronal circuitry recruited to benefit from practice. Moderate disruption should be treated with an aggressive restorative or forced-use approach, whereas mild disruption may enjoy enough spontaneous recovery that neither approach would be necessary. Until further research has clarified these issues, it should be remembered that it is seldom possible to reverse cognitive deficits altogether. Therefore, it is necessary to include compensatory methods in the armamentarium of practical therapeutic techniques (Prigatano, 2005). Compensatory approaches also lend themselves well to the targeting of "real world" outcomes of importance to the client and family (Wilson, 2000).

Aside from the distinction between restoration and compensation, few conceptual models provide organizing frameworks for research and practice in cognitive rehabilitation. One that bears mention, however, is the concept of contextualized cognitive rehabilitation (Ylvisaker, Hanks, & Johnson-Greene, 2002). As noted earlier, cognitive rehabilitation may be targeted to conceptually separate cognitive functions or impairments of functions, such as attention or memory. Moreover, cognitive rehabilitation may involve working on these functions or impairments outside of a meaningful context, such as when patients perform attention or comprehension tasks, using standardized stimuli, in the quiet confines of a therapist's office. The underlying assumption is that when the cognitive skill is strengthened, the person's performance will then improve on a range of real-world tasks and activities that are affected by that skill. This assumption tends to apply more to restorative approaches, although compensatory techniques may also be applied outside of a realistic context. For example, a patient may be taught to practice taking notes during a television show on the assumption that the ability to take notes (a compensatory skill) will transfer to a classroom lecture situation.

In the contextualized cognitive rehabilitation model, cognitive functions are conceptualized not as isolated modules but as interactive with one another, with other aspects of intrapersonal function (e.g., emotions) and with the social and physical environments. The primary focus is not on improving function but on helping the person to attain or regain meaningful activities and societal roles. Cognitive limitations are addressed with restorative or compensatory techniques, if appropriate, but are primarily managed with natural supports that allow successful participation to take place. These supports may include creative modification of the job or other role, and coaching, strategy development, or other assistance from people on-site. Support people may include a mixture of professionals and "everyday people" such as supervisors, teachers, friends, family, and coworkers. As the person with cognitive limitations develops new habits in personally meaningful activities, independence may improve and the supports may be faded over time. However, generalization of cognitive skills from one situation to another is neither assumed nor required by this approach.

Although contextualized interventions are targeted to the activity or participation level, they may have unexpected benefits at the level of cognitive function. For example, a controlled study of family training in home-based rehabilitation versus standard clinic rehabilitation for children with traumatic brain injury (TBI) showed that those who were trained by family members improved more on intellectual tests (Braga, Da Paz, & Ylvisaker, 2005). It also appears that people with serious mental illness who participate in aggressive supported work programs may show improvements in cognitive function (McGurk & Mueser, 2004). It is reasonable to consider that enabling people with cognitive limitations to act and interact in more normal environments provides stimulation and learning—perhaps even "forced use" of stale cognitive abilities—that would otherwise not be available to them.

METHODS OF COGNITIVE REHABILITATION

A brief and highly selective discussion of specific methods used in cognitive rehabilitation is presented in the following sections. Both restorative and compensatory approaches as well as "hybrids" are included with an attempt to include those that have garnered the most empirical support. For much more detailed presentations of the evidence base of cognitive rehabilitation, see the comprehensive reviews of Cicerone et al. (2000, 2005) and the edited volume by Halligan and Wade (2005), and the series of systematic reviews by the traumatic brain injury Practice Guidelines Subcommittee of the Academy of Neurologic Communication Disorders and Sciences (e.g., Kennedy et al., 2008).

Attention

The remediation of attention has attracted a great deal of study, including several recent evidence syntheses. This may be because attention deficits are so common in a variety of neurological disorders and because they are presumed to have widespread impact on functional status. It is appealing to think that, if basic functions of attention could be improved, there would be a positive impact on a diverse range of performances in the real world. In a widely cited meta-analysis, Park and Ingles (2001) combined results from 30 studies on the efficacy of attention retraining, using a total of 359 participants. Separate analyses examined the effects of direct retraining of attention, commonly using neuropsychological test scores as outcome measures, and training in functional skills demanding of attention, such as driving, reading, and performing activities of daily living. In brief, no effects of direct attention training were found over and above the effects of practice or pretesting on the outcome measures. Significant treatment effects were found, however, in the group of studies focusing on functional skills training with gradually increasing demands on attention. Park and Ingles recommended that attention deficits be addressed by breaking down functional tasks into structured training activities with graduated challenges to attention, a process they termed "neuropsychological scaffolding." This article also underscored the critical importance of controlling for practice effects on the measures used to assess outcomes in studies of cognitive rehabilitation.

Similar conclusions about the limited real-world usefulness of direct training of attention were drawn by Cicerone and colleagues (2000) in their first synthetic review of cognitive rehabilitation for TBI and stroke. By the time of the updated review (Cicerone et al., 2005), several studies had tested interventions for attention that were both better controlled and more sophisticated, offering participants the oppor-

tunity to learn strategies for managing incoming information and testing efficacy on outcomes other than psychometric test scores. Two examples are noted here. Sohlberg and colleagues (Sohlberg, McLaughlin, Pavese, Heidrich, & Posner, 2000) tested the effects of a cognitive training program called Attention Process Training (APT), which consists of a hierarchy of exercises requiring attention skills that are hypothesized to be successively more difficult: sustained, selective, alternating, and divided attention. Outcomes were measured on a set of neuropsychological tests and self- and other-report questionnaires evaluating everyday cognitive function. Structured interviews were also conducted with study participants and their significant others to examine subjective experiences related to treatment effects. Participants were people with acquired brain injury who had stable (i.e., chronic) complaints in the area of attention.

Ten weeks of APT were compared with the same duration of a control condition offering general brain injury education and emotional support. Both treatments were effective but in different ways. As expected, the APT condition resulted in more gains on attention tasks (including tasks quite different from those used in treatment) and more subjective improvements in attention-related functions. Brain injury education showed slight superiority for improving self-reported psychosocial function. The authors acknowledged that, although the results were promising, they shed little light on the mechanisms of apparent improvement in cognitive function. It is possible that programs such as APT, which systematically vary the level of challenge to the impaired system, encourage implicit learning of new internal strategies for managing more difficult tasks, strategies that may then be used spontaneously in real-world, attention-demanding situations.

In the other example, Fasotti, Kovacs, Eling, and Brouwer (2000) studied the effects of an intervention called *time pressure management* for speed of processing disorders after acquired brain injury compared with a more generic concentration training method. Rather than subjecting participants to gradually increasing demands on attention, time pressure management teaches alternative strategies to compensate for cognitive slowing in real-world activities. These strategies include becoming more self-aware of one's vulnerability to time pressure, planning ahead to prevent pressure, and creating emergency plans to deal with "information overload." The *concentration training* group received generic instructions during therapy tasks such as "try not to get distracted." As in the Sohlberg et al. (2000) study, participants in both treatment conditions improved. However, the time pressure management group improved more, and appeared to show more generalization of treatment to a diverse set of outcome measures.

These examples and others mentioned in recent reviews suggest that cognitive strategies for improved attention may be learned (or relearned) by people with attention disorders due to brain injury. However, simply practicing repetitive attention exercises cannot be expected to improve attention performance aside from the performance on the practiced tasks. Rather, functional gains may be achieved by learning to compensate for attention disturbances in real life, by practicing tasks that systematically challenge specific aspects of attention, and/or by engaging in a structured progression of real-world tasks that are analyzed with respect to their attention demands (Park & Ingles, 2001). The latter strategy may be particularly effective because it encourages gradual reautomatization of cognitive and motor operations that have become harder to perform—that is, more dependent on conscious or effortful processing—after brain injury.

Memory

Like attention, memory can be affected by a wide variety of nervous system insults. Unlike attention, however, memory deficits have a number of compensatory solutions with high face value. Many people in the general population are in the habit of using lists, calendars, planner books, personal digital assistants (PDAs), and even cell phones to help them keep up with appointments and tasks to be done. Although compensating for acquired memory impairment is not a simple matter of using these devices more often, they are at least familiar and acceptable to many people, and may require less new learning compared with other strategies.

Also, in contrast to some of the literature on attention retraining that suggests that some forms of practice on attention tasks may be generally benefi-

cial and transfer to other tasks, it appears that memory functions cannot be restored through practice. A restorative model of memory rehabilitation would claim that performing memory drills, such as learning gradually longer lists of words or playing "Concentration" on a computer, would improve memory by exercising or "stretching" memory capacity. Some patients are still offered this form of treatment, but the evidence is clear that it does nothing to affect memory other than (possibly) improving recall of the practiced material (Glisky, 2005; Malec & Cicerone, 2006). Some improvement on closely related tasks may be observed if the repetition is accompanied by teaching of a mnemonic strategy, such as visual imagery, to help the person organize the material in memory. The evidence for the latter approach is mixed, but seems to favor those who have mild memory deficits to begin with (Kaschel et al., 2002). The apparent failure of restorative approaches to memory function does not mean, however, that people with severe memory deficits cannot learn new material. On the contrary, the work of Glisky and colleagues (e.g., Glisky, 1995) shows clearly that by using structured, supported rehearsal along with avoidance of error (i.e., the method of *vanishing cues*), even patients who are densely amnestic can learn fairly complex, novel task routines and new semantic information. As with the "memory drills" approach, this specialized training does not generalize to other tasks or domains, supporting the interpretation that memory capacity itself has been unchanged by the new learning.

A similar training method known as *errorless learning* has been widely studied for its potential application to cognitive rehabilitation (for a meta-analysis see Kessels & de Haan, 2003). Like the method of vanishing cues, errorless learning provides maximal cues and support during the learning process, and is intended not to change memory capacity but to enhance learning of specific novel information or task routines. Although it is seldom possible to prevent all errors during learning, errorless learning techniques minimize the interference from errors that can occur when the explicit memory system is impaired (i.e., when there is significant impairment of episodic recall). Errorless learning has been used to help people with brain injury to learn practical material such as new face-name associations (Evans et al., 2000), and the effective use of memory notebooks (Squires, Hunkin, & Parkin, 1996). Perhaps most impressively, errorless learning has been used to promote long-lasting improvement in the everyday memory function of people with progressive cognitive decline due to Alzheimer's disease (Clare, Wilson, Carter, Hodges, & Adams, 2001). The challenges of using errorless learning in the clinical setting are to prevent errors while still allowing for active engagement in the task, and to know when to fade cueing even though an error may occur. Findings from errorless learning research have implications for typical clinical practice. For example, a procedure commonly used by clinicians and family members with patients who are memory impaired—"quizzing" them on orientation items and other information in short term memory—may actually be detrimental because of the probability that errors will be reinforced.

Compensatory strategies for improving performance of everyday memory activities have been widely investigated, producing strong evidence for the effectiveness of external memory aids such as notebooks or portable electronic reminder devices even for those with severe, chronic memory deficit (Cicerone et al., 2005; Glisky, 2005). For example, Schmitter-Edgecombe, Fahy, Whelan, and Long (1995) showed that a 16-session training regimen for teaching individuals with severe TBI how to use specially structured memory notebooks was more effective than group problem-solving discussions for reducing the impact of everyday memory problems. However, no differences were found on standard memory tests, suggesting that underlying memory function, which was not targeted by the intervention, was indeed unaffected. Wilson and colleagues (Wilson, Emslie, Quirk, & Evans, 2001) showed in a large, randomized cross-over trial that a programmable paging device, the NeuroPage, enabled people with brain injury to keep appointments and complete other prospective assignments more independently. The effects were so robust that, in Britain, the NeuroPage service is now covered as part of the national health benefit. Similar findings have been reported for specially programmed cell phones and portable voice recording devices (see Scherer,

Hart, Kirsch, & Schultheis, 2005, for a review of research on electronic reminding systems for cognitive disabilities).

External reminder systems, including notebooks and, increasingly, PDAs, are among the most widely used clinical strategies in cognitive rehabilitation. Even with their face validity and empirical support, these systems are harder to use effectively than they might appear, leading to several important caveats for the practitioner wishing to guide their use in the clinic. First, people with cognitive deficits frequently have difficulty with the metacognitive demands of using external strategies (i.e., particularly the executive and memory skills involved in knowing *what* to record in a notebook *when*), remembering or figuring out how to program a device, remembering to do it consistently, and using recorded information prospectively. Too often, clinicians assume that patients will use external strategies appropriately on their own and fail to provide the kind of intensive, systematic training and practice that have been demonstrated to be effective in research protocols (e.g., Schmitter-Edgecombe et al., 1995).

Second, the success of any reminder system depends partly on an individual's awareness of memory deficits and acceptance of the need to use external strategies, both of which may need to be addressed before any system is introduced. It is important to ask for details as to what strategies have been used by the person both before and after disability and how well those strategies have worked, as well as exploring attitudes toward external aids. Younger, more educated people who used memory devices before brain injury are likely to use them after injury as well (Evans, Wilson, Needham, & Brentnall, 2003). However, paper reminder systems such as notebooks and clipboards may be resisted postinjury as stigmatizing (Tate, 1997). Compensatory strategies should be developed collaboratively with the user and practiced in the context of what the person is doing in everyday life to be effective.

Executive Function

Interventions for executive function deficits, once described almost exclusively in case reports, have received more controlled and systematic study in recent years. As aptly noted by Evans (2005), progress in the treatment of executive functions has been constrained by ongoing confusion about how to conceptualize and define these complex cognitive operations. For current purposes, executive functions refer to the cognitive–affective regulatory processes that enable purposeful, goal-directed behavior in complex social environments. In the normal state, behavior is continually adjusted toward the achievement of both long-term goals and short-term goals that are nested within them, each requiring scores or hundreds of individual actions and decisions. At any point, behavior may need to be adjusted if the "plan" goes awry or unexpected factors intrude. The processes by which human beings manage these complicated routines are not completely understood, but it is clear that we would not be able to accomplish so much simultaneous behavior, nor rapid adjustment to changes in the environment, if all of our behavior were consciously controlled.

One influential model posits a *supervisory attention system* (SAS) that monitors the need for conscious control over action (see Shallice & Burgess, 1996). The SAS forces awareness and conscious decision-making if an error is made, the routines are novel, or something in the environment requires immediate decision-making. A damaged SAS, however, results in dysexecutive behavior: the person fails to recognize problem situations and/or to mobilize behavior to meet them, or is unable to organize the behaviors necessary to perform, particularly in novel situations. Clinically, executive dysfunction is manifested as behavior that is disorganized or contradictory with respect to one's stated goals. There is often defective judgment and decision-making and poor self-monitoring and self-awareness as well as a limited ability to profit from error feedback. There may also be difficulties indicative of poor regulation of emotions and drive states, such as apathy, irritability, or impulsivity. Executive dysfunction in varying degrees is common after brain injury, particularly after diffuse injuries or those involving anterior (i.e., frontotemporal) cerebral systems.

The severity of the deficits may dictate whether interventions should be targeted at the environment versus a model that attempts to use relearning or strategy training. At the extreme, deficits of executive function may be managed using environmental

modifications that provide external structure to the individual's behavior. These may include basic strategies that simplify the environment and keep the person "on task," such as the repetitive schedules and routines that are found in residential and day treatment facilities for people with severe brain injury. Environmental modifications may also include efforts to change stimulus control over behavior (Worthington, 2005). In particular, analyzing and changing the antecedent conditions that appear to trigger dysexecutive behavior problems may lead to positive outcomes. Giles and Manchester (2006) describe a comprehensive approach to managing behavior dyscontrol after brain injury that incorporates motivational interviewing and other nonaversive methods along with traditional operant learning techniques.

Several approaches to the rehabilitation of executive function have sought to teach the explicit steps involved in solving problems or reaching goals, on the assumption that this will help to replace the lost ability to organize goal-directed behavior. As noted by Evans (2005), this approach is not strictly restorative; although at first glance it appears to retrain a preinjury skill, the person is actually using a new, externalized way of dealing with life situations. Several controlled investigations have demonstrated the effectiveness of teaching problem-solving algorithms. Von Cramon and colleagues (1991) reported positive results in a randomized controlled trial of a 6-week, 25-session *Problem-Solving Training* intervention administered to small groups of participants. The intervention consisted of training in how to focus on information relevant to a problem solving situation, how to generate alternative solutions and decide on one, and how to verify that the chosen solution was or was not effective.

A similar method known as *Goal Management Training* was evaluated by Levine and colleagues (2000). The intervention teaches the steps involved in defining tasks, breaking them into steps, and checking one's performance. In comparison with a sham treatment condition (i.e., a motor-skills training procedure), Goal Management Training resulted in faster and more accurate performance on cognitively demanding, multistep tasks. Problem-solving training has been implemented with positive results for both adults (Rath, Simon, Langenbahn, Sherr, & Diller, 2003) and children (Suzman, Morris, Morris, & Milan, 1997) with acquired brain injury. In the Rath et al. study, emotional self-regulation was integrated with the cognitive aspects of executive function, and the program included extensive role-playing and homework to enhance generalization. Thus far, these intensive programs have been tested primarily in persons with relatively milder levels of cognitive impairment; it is not clear whether there is a minimal level of remaining executive function that is necessary for retraining to succeed. However, a meta-analysis of studies using step-by-step metacognitive strategy instruction concluded that there was sufficient evidence to recommend such training with persons with TBI when everyday problem-solving was the goal of treatment (Kennedy et al., 2008).

In a related vein, rehabilitation of executive function may benefit from a family of theories derived from social–cognitive theory (Bandura, 1986) which posits, in brief, that human behavior is self-regulated to meet personal standards or goals. Self-regulation and goal theories have been tested in hundreds of studies in domains as diverse as organizational science, sports, and health management, documenting the factors and manipulations that lead to improved goal attainment in both the short- and long-term. These factors include the specificity of goals, their challenge or difficulty level, the effects of incentives and feedback, and whether goals are focused on outcomes or processes (e.g., learning strategies). There is some evidence that people with brain injury respond to the same goal manipulations as do uninjured people and that the effects are not significantly distorted by cognitive impairment (Gauggel & Billino, 2002).

A relatively recent trend in health care management combines many of these findings and techniques into a comprehensive and well-tested treatment "package" known as *Self-Management Training* (SMT; Lorig & Holman, 2003). Influenced strongly by social–cognitive theory, SMT emphasizes patient autonomy and active participation in treatment through training in goal-setting, which is embedded in training on how to identify problems and their causes, how to select and set goals for solving those problems, and how to monitor and

self-reward one's success. In controlled studies, SMT has been shown to be superior to traditional patient education programs for enhancing disease-related knowledge and positive health behaviors and for decreasing symptom severity and health care resource use (Lorig et al., 1999; Newman, Steed, & Mulligan, 2004). Goal and self-management interventions are worthy of further study for their potential application to brain injury rehabilitation (for a review, see Hart & Evans, 2006).

Even if the person with executive dysfunction learns an algorithm or routine for problem-solving, the same question arises as for memory compensation: How will he or she know when to use it? Recognition of everyday problem situations is compromised after brain injury, partly because of impaired self-awareness of deficit (Hart, Whyte, Kim, & Vaccaro, 2005). Ownsworth, McFarland, and Young (2000) designed a 16-week group treatment that targeted a broad range of executive skills including problem-solving and self-awareness. The authors reported that one effect of this treatment was to improve so-called emergent and anticipatory awareness. Based on the model of self-awareness posited by Crosson and colleagues (1989), *emergent self-awareness* refers to recognizing situations in which one's limitations are causing problems; *anticipatory awareness* allows one to preplan preventive or compensatory strategies for situations that are likely to be problematic. Treatment models such as this are valuable, because the ultimate success of any cognitive rehabilitation method will depend on the application of learned strategies being "triggered" in real time.

Another approach to the idea of triggering executive control is found in the work of Manly and colleagues on the "electronic knot in the handkerchief," a series of randomly spaced tones that appear to improve performance on complex multistep tasks (Manly, Hawkins, Evans, Woldt, & Robertson, 2002). The alerts contain no reminding content, although the patient is told at the outset that she or he will hear random tones that might be helpful in reminding them to think about what they are doing. Manly et al. theorize that the tones interrupt a "stuck-in-set" approach to tasks. The tone is a cue to interrupt one's behavior, take stock of the needs of the task, and evaluate whether one's behavior is filling the bill—all functions that are carried out at least semiautomatically by a normally working executive control system. There is some evidence that these "content-free" cues do help people with brain injury to carry out intended, but previously neglected, real-world activities over a span of several weeks (Fish et al., 2006).

Self-monitoring and self-awareness are important aspects of executive function that afford human behavior its flexibility and adaptability to different task demands and social environments. Self-awareness treatments have been somewhat elusive, partly because it is difficult to conceptualize treatment of this construct outside of specific content (i.e., self-awareness of what?), and partly because we still lack comprehensive theories that tie together the complex behavioral, neuropsychological, and psychological determinants of impaired awareness. A review and discussion of awareness interventions by Fleming and Ownsworth (2006) highlights the value of selecting key tasks and environments; providing clear feedback and structured learning experiences, including peer feedback via group therapy; and carefully considering the emotional consequences of improving self-awareness. For very severe cases of inappropriate behavior of which the patient seems to be unaware, several controlled single-case studies have shown benefit of self-monitoring training, in which patients are taught systematically to monitor specific aspects of their behavior in comparison with the observations of other people. It is of interest that self-monitoring training has led to a reduction in target undesirable behaviors, even when there is no instruction to reduce the behavior nor reinforcement for doing so (Dayus & van den Broek, 2000; Knight, Rutterford, Alderman, & Swan, 2002). This strategy would work best with individuals who "know" that certain behaviors are not appropriate but lack the ability to evaluate or inhibit their behavior as it is occurring.

Hemispatial Attention and Visuospatial Function

Disorders of hemispatial attention, referred to collectively as neglect (most commonly, left neglect), affect a substantial proportion of people with right hemispheric stroke and have widespread effects on functional outcomes (Katz, Harman-Maeir, Ring, & Soroker, 1999). In a comprehensive review, Pierce

and Buxbaum (2002) organized their discussion around the theoretical models of hemispatial neglect underlying the many treatment approaches that have been attempted. Perhaps the most widely studied approaches rest on the assumption that neglect is primarily a disorder of visual attention, which might be overcome by teaching explicit strategies to direct visual attention toward left hemispace. In a now classic study, Weinberg, Diller, Gordon, and Stubbs (1977) constructed a large horizontal apparatus around whose perimeter moved an attention-getting target. Patients with left neglect were instructed to scan to the left so as not to let the target out of their sight. Systematic training on this and other scanning tasks led to improvements on scanning tests and on functional tasks that require scanning, such as reading. Several other studies have replicated these basic findings with similar interventions (e.g., Antonucci et al., 1995). The few negative findings appear to be due to using too small a training display to engage effective scanning behaviors. Notably, using a computer screen-sized display to train scanning does not appear to be effective for left neglect (Robertson, Gray, Pentland, & Waite, 1990). Although scanning training in a wider field does lead to measurable effects, the long-term effects of such training have not been established, nor is it clear that the effects generalize to functional activities beyond paper-and-pencil, academic-type tasks (Pierce & Buxbaum, 2002).

Other methods for treating neglect are based on evidence that the disorder is caused by defective representation of space at the level of the neural substrate. The Limb Activation Training method developed by Robertson, McMillan, MacLeod, and Brock (2002) is an example. Limb activation, which involves inducing active movements of the left limb in left hemispace, theoretically ameliorates neglect because it activates overlapping neural circuits that represent both left-sided personal and extrapersonal space. Limb activation has been shown to be effective in randomized clinical trials and is even claimed to result in significantly shorter lengths of hospital stay (Kalra, Perez, Gupta, & Wittink, 1997). A limitation of this treatment modality is that many people with left neglect also have dense left hemiparesis, which precludes active movement (Pierce & Buxbaum, 2002).

A promising treatment method that could be used more routinely and that also claims to change internal spatial representation is the prism adaptation method. In this method, developed by Rossetti and colleagues (1998), the patient wears lenses that shift the visual display toward the right field. With time and practice the user adapts to the shift and is able to override it to reach for objects and interact with the environment correctly. Training in how to use the prisms has led to marked reduction in left neglect in several controlled studies (see Redding & Wallace, 2006). Prism adaptation is sometimes incorrectly described as a purely compensatory approach (i.e., that it overcomes neglect by simply shifting the left visual field into right space). However, on the contrary, it is not wearing the prisms but adapting to them that causes a reduction in neglect. This finding is reinforced by the observation that the beneficial effects can persist for weeks after the prisms are removed (Frassinetti, Angeli, Meneghello, Avanzi, & Ladavas, 2002), and that the effects are seen on tasks different from those used in training, even including haptic as well as visual stimuli (Redding & Wallace, 2006). A few treatments have been evaluated for visuospatial functions other than neglect (e.g., exercises to address visual organization, size estimation). There is some suggestion that these activities could benefit patients with visuospatial deficits who do not have neglect, but the evidence is not compelling (Cicerone et al., 2005).

Language and Communication

Over more than a century, highly specialized practitioners and researchers—speech and language pathologists and aphasiologists—have developed rich traditions and sophisticated research methods to apply to the treatment of language and communication disorders. As entire textbooks are devoted to these methods, only a few brief comments will be offered here. Both restorative and compensatory methods are used in language therapy, and both have been investigated in controlled studies. Language tests are the typical measure of outcome, with real-world outcomes included only rarely (Marshall, 2005). Restorative treatments typically include various forms of practice or stimulation, such as object naming or sentence production. The evidence from meta-analyses (e.g., Robey, 1998) indicates that language therapies can produce strong treatment effects and that these effects are often dose-dependent; that is, the effects are stronger for more intensive and/or longer lasting treatments. As noted earlier, recent work with intensive massed practice (i.e., constraint-induced therapy) has highlighted the possibility of substantial and persistent improvement from chronic aphasia (Meinzer, Djundja, Barthel, Elbert, & Rockstroh, 2005; Pulvermuller et al., 2001).

Although restorative approaches to language deficits have more empirical support than treatments in most other areas of cognition, it appears once again that improvements tend to be specific to the trained materials. For example, studies of object naming therapy commonly use untrained word lists as control stimuli because of the expectation that therapy will affect only the specific words used in training trials. In addition, no matter how strong is the aggregate evidence for language therapies, the relative effectiveness of specific techniques for specific disorders remains obscure (Cicerone et al., 2005).

Compensatory approaches are traditionally applied later in recovery when spontaneous changes appear to be slowing down and/or direct restorative approaches do not appear to be working. Speech pathologists commonly train patients in compensatory strategies such as circumlocution ("talking around" words that cannot be retrieved) and prescribe the use of picture or alphabet boards or augmentative and assistive communication devices for expressive language deficits. As with any compensatory strategy, effective use of these methods may be hampered by concomitant deficits in learning or executive function. There is empirical support for compensatory communication treatment that is targeted to the dyad of the language-impaired person and a support person such as a spouse or significant other, an approach that has been called "conversational coaching" (Holland, 1991). For example, Kagan, Black, Duchan, Simmons-Mackie, and Square (2001) trained volunteers in "supported conversation," methods designed to facilitate communication with language-impaired conversational partners. Compared with untrained volunteers who spent equivalent time with patients in social or recreational activities, both the conversation coaches and their language-impaired conversational partners drew higher communication ratings from observers blinded to treatment group. Conversational abilities have also been addressed via structured group feedback and modeling to improve *pragmatic skills:* cognitive–behavioral aspects of communication such as taking turns in conversation, maintaining appropriate eye contact, using humor appropriately, modulating voice volume, and staying on topic (Wiseman-Hakes, Stewart, Wasserman, & Schuller, 1998).

Comprehensive–Holistic Cognitive Rehabilitation

Cognitive rehabilitation experienced a phase of expansion and clinical experimentation in the 1970s and 1980s, driven by several factors. First, advances in medical and emergency care made both stroke and TBI more survivable. Second, many survivors of TBI were young adults injured in high-speed motor vehicle collisions. The diffuse pathophysiology of such TBI leads to deficits in diffusely represented cognitive functions such as attention, memory, and executive function; these were discovered in short order to cause widespread deleterious effects on adaptive behavior. In response to the needs of TBI and stroke survivors, Yehuda Ben-Yishay, Leonard Diller, and others pioneered what is now often termed *comprehensive–holistic cognitive rehabilitation.* These programs offered a variety of cognitive rehabilitation methods, including direct retraining of "core" functions such as attention, blended into a therapeutic milieu emphasizing peer support and feedback, group as well as individual therapy, and family interventions. Vocational training was also included, first in "protected" work trials to maximize success.

In a sense, it may be a misnomer to include these approaches in a discussion of cognitive rehabilitation because they also deliberately attend to treatment targets such as emotional, interpersonal, and vocational outcomes. Comprehensive–holistic rehabilitation approaches implicitly reject a reductionistic or modular approach to cognitive rehabilitation,

although modular exercises may be included as an integrated part of treatment. These programs emphasize treating the whole person with his or her complex array of cognitive, emotional, interpersonal, and family difficulties, with the goal of restoring as much independence as possible in productive activities, living situations, and satisfying relationships. This form of rehabilitation depends heavily on a group or milieu treatment model and, in its original form, was structured into classes of people who underwent daily treatment at the same time for several months and "graduated" together. The group milieu was, and still is, considered crucial for developing social skills and a realistic view of oneself based on peer feedback (Ben-Yishay & Prigatano, 1990).

Comprehensive–holistic cognitive rehabilitation programs are generally designed for people with chronic limitations who have derived maximum benefit from discipline-specific therapies and need additional help resuming a productive lifestyle. The programs vary in the exact mix of their ingredients, but they tend to be intensive (e.g., 5 days/week for 5–6 months) and to offer a high staff-to-client ratio (Malec & Cicerone, 2006). These features and others, such as intensive hands-on participation by doctoral level staff, make the cost of such programs high. Empirical validation of the success of these programs would be helpful for maintaining private and public funding sources. Compared with treatments that target cognitive functions in relative isolation, assessing the efficacy and effectiveness of holistic rehabilitation is challenging for several reasons. The diversity in treatment components makes it difficult to define specific "active ingredients" and to compare results across settings. Partly for this reason and also because of ethical concerns about withholding comprehensive treatment from those in obvious need, this treatment model is difficult to test with a randomized controlled trial, although it has been done.

In a study that generated substantial controversy, Salazar and colleagues (2000) randomly assigned military service personnel with TBI to one of two 8-week treatment conditions. One condition was a hospital-based program modeled after the comprehensive milieu programs of Ben-Yishay and

Prigatano (1990). The other was comprised of education about TBI and a home program of physical and mental exercise, supplemented by periodic phone calls from a study nurse. A year after injury, the groups did not differ significantly on return to work (i.e., active duty) status nor on a comprehensive battery measuring neuropsychological and emotional function. Although some have interpreted this result to mean that comprehensive–holistic rehabilitation is neither necessary nor cost-effective for TBI, the people studied in this investigation appeared to differ substantially from those who usually receive intensive postacute rehabilitation in the civilian population. First, Salazar et al. enrolled people within 3 months of TBI, at which point many cognitive and emotional sequelae are still evolving spontaneously. Prigatano (2005) has noted that comprehensive–holistic cognitive rehabilitation may be better suited to people with relatively stable deficits. Second, the extremely high return to work rate in the Salazar study (i.e., 90% and 94% in the two groups) implies that the sample, overall, had milder injuries than do most people typically found in such programs. A subgroup analysis did suggest that the most severely injured participants in the Salazar et al. study showed the most benefit from the hospital-based program compared with the home care condition.

It has been argued that most participants in comprehensive–holistic rehabilitation programs have natural "baselines" of years or months of repeated failure against which treatment effects may be assessed without using a comparison group. Studies have compared participants nonrandomly enrolled into holistic versus traditional therapy programs (Cicerone, Mott, Azulay, & Friel, 2004) or have used quasi-control groups composed of people who were referred for treatment but did not receive it (Prigatano et al., 1984). The accumulated evidence does support the use of this rehabilitation model for enhancing participation level outcomes (e.g., independent living, supported or competitive work) for those with severe limitations. Much additional study will be needed to understand the critical components of these complex treatment models and the best clinical decision-making algorithms for matching patients to treatment components within the mix.

CHALLENGES AND OPPORTUNITIES FOR THE FUTURE OF COGNITIVE REHABILITATION

As discussed earlier, cognitive rehabilitation is practiced and studied by people from diverse disciplines. A resulting challenge to the field is to develop coherent theories that will help to advance both research and practice. To the extent that cognitive rehabilitation is influenced by medical rehabilitation more generally, it has inherited the latter field's pragmatic focus on "whatever works," regardless of why. But it will not be possible ultimately to refine our treatments—especially the complex, experience-based treatments used in cognitive rehabilitation—without generating testable hypotheses as to their primary mechanisms of action (Whyte & Hart, 2003). What kinds of theories will help us meet this challenge? There is by no means universal agreement that theories derived from cognitive neuroscience, explaining how cognitive functions are organized in the brain and how they break down, are necessary and sufficient to guide cognitive rehabilitation (Hillis, 2005; Robertson, 2005; Wilson, 2005). Cognitive rehabilitation needs to develop explanatory links between changes in cognition and behavior, both natural and treatment-induced, with changes in the underlying substrate (Robertson, 1999). No doubt, this quest will be aided by functional neuroimaging techniques to help pinpoint the changes in neural circuitry that correspond to plasticity at the behavioral level (Strangman et al., 2005).

A more coherent theoretical base will enhance not only research efforts but also another challenge facing cognitive rehabilitation: the fragmented communication between scientists and practitioners (Powell, Hunt, & Pepping, 2004). Theories of treatment will produce higher quality evidence for cognitive rehabilitation and will also provide organizing frameworks for the dissemination of proven methods to the clinic, a process increasingly conceptualized not simply as knowledge flow but as knowledge translation, a challenging process for any field. Certainly one challenge for clinicians in cognitive rehabilitation is simply keeping up with, much less critically evaluating, the flood of information about new methods, materials, and devices. Web-based methods of dissemination may help busy clinicians by supplementing their efforts to attend conferences and read print journals. For example, an Australian group (Tate et al., 2004) have launched an open-access website called PsycBITE (Psychological database for Brain Impairment Treatment: www.psycbite.com), which may be searched free of charge for citations on numerous cognitive and behavioral rehabilitation methods rated for methodological quality. This type of effort supplements the established subscription-based sites such as that of the Cochrane Collaboration (http://www.cochrane.org).

Cognitive rehabilitation has made substantial strides in recent years, and is poised for more. Our greatest challenges are to keep high standards for methodological rigor while encouraging more research, to continue to push for methods that are motivated by testable theories of plasticity linking brain and behavior, to develop better ways of disseminating key findings to the clinic, and to harness the opportunities afforded by the technological revolutions in our midst.

References

Antonucci, G., Guariglia, C., Judicia, A., Magnotti, L., Paolucci, S., Pizzamiglio, L., et al. (1995). Effectiveness of neglect rehabilitation in a randomized group study. *Journal of Clinical and Experimental Neuropsychology, 17,* 383–389.

Bandura, A. (1986). *Social foundations of thought and action: A social–cognitive view.* Englewood Cliffs, NJ: Prentice Hall.

Ben-Yishay, Y., & Prigatano, G. (1990). Cognitive remediation. In M. Rosenthal, E. R. Griffith, M. R. Bond, & J. D. Miller (Eds.), *Rehabilitation of the adult and child with traumatic brain injury* (pp. 393–400). Philadelphia: F. A. Davis.

Boake, C. (2003). Stages in the development of neuropsychological rehabilitation. In B. A. Wilson (Ed.), *Neuropsychological rehabilitation: Theory and practice* (pp. 11–21). Lisse, Netherlands: Swets & Zeitlinger.

Braga, L. W., Da Paz, A. C., Jr., & Ylvisaker, M. (2005). Direct clinician-delivered versus indirect family-supported rehabilitation of children with traumatic brain injury: A randomized controlled trial. *Brain Injury, 19,* 819–831.

Cicerone, K. D., Dahlberg, C., Kalmar, K., Langenbahn, D. M., Malec, J., Berquist, T. F., et al. (2000). Evidence-based cognitive rehabilitation: Recommendations for clinical practice. *Archives of Physical Medicine and Rehabilitation, 81,* 1596–1615.

Cicerone, K. D., Dahlberg, C., Malec, J. F., Langenbahn, D., Felicetti, T., Kneipp, S., et al. (2005). Evidence-based cognitive rehabilitation: Updated review of the literature from 1998 through 2002. *Archives of Physical Medicine and Rehabilitation, 86,* 1681–1692.

Cicerone, K. D., Mott, T., Azulay, J., & Friel, J. C. (2004). Community integration and satisfaction with functioning after intensive cognitive rehabilitation for traumatic brain injury. *Archives of Physical Medicine and Rehabilitation, 85,* 943–950.

Clare, L., Wilson, B. A., Carter, G., Hodges, J. R., & Adams, M. (2001). Long-term maintenance of treatment gains following a cognitive rehabilitation intervention in early dementia of Alzheimer type: A single case study. *Neuropsychological Rehabilitation, 11*(3/4), 474–494.

Crosson, B., Barco, P. P., Velozo, C. A., Bolesta, M. M., Cooper, P. V., Werts, D., & Brobeck, T. C. (1989). Awareness and compensation in postacute head injury rehabilitation. *Journal of Head Trauma Rehabilitation, 4*(3), 46–54.

Dayus, B., & van den Broek, M. D. (2000). Treatment of stable delusional confabulations using self-monitoring training. *Neuropsychological Rehabilitation, 10,* 415–427.

Evans, J. (2005). Can executive impairments be effectively treated? In P. W. Halligan & D. T. Wade (Eds.), *The effectiveness of rehabilitation for cognitive deficits* (pp. 247–256). New York: Oxford University Press.

Evans, J., Wilson, B., Needham, P., & Brentnall, S. (2003). Who makes good use of memory aids? Results of a survey of people with acquired brain injury. *Journal of the International Neuropsychological Society, 9,* 925–935.

Evans, J. J., Wilson, B. A., Schuri, U., Andrade, J., Baddeley, A., Bruna, O., et al. (2000). A comparison of "errorless" and "trial-and error" learning methods for teaching individuals with acquired memory deficits. *Neuropsychological Rehabilitation, 10,* 67–101.

Fasotti, L., Kovacs, F., Eling, P., & Brouwer, W. H. (2000). Time pressure management as a compensatory strategy training after closed head injury. *Neuropsychological Rehabilitation, 10,* 47–65.

Fish, J., Evans, J. J., Nimmo, M., Martin, E., Kersel, D., Bateman, A., et al. (2006). Rehabilitation of executive dysfunction following brain injury: "Content-free" cueing improves everyday prospective memory performance. *Neuropsychologia, 45,* 1318–1330.

Fleming, J. M., & Ownsworth, T. (2006). A review of awareness interventions in brain injury rehabilitation. *Neuropsychological Rehabilitation, 16,* 474–500.

Frassinetti, F., Angeli, V., Meneghello, F., Avanzi, S., & Ladavas, E. (2002). Long-lasting amelioration of visuospatial neglect by prism adaptation. *Brain, 125,* 608–623.

Gauggel, S., & Billino, J. (2002). The effects of goal setting on the arithmetic performance of brain damaged patients. *Archives of Clinical Neuropsychology, 17,* 283–294.

Giles, G. M., & Manchester, D. (2006). Two approaches to behavior disorder after traumatic brain injury. *Journal of Head Trauma Rehabilitation, 21,* 168–178.

Glisky, E. L. (1995). Acquisition and transfer of word processing skill by an amnesic patient. *Neuropsychological Rehabilitation, 5,* 299–318.

Glisky, E. L. (2005). Can memory impairment be effectively treated? In P. W. Halligan & D. T. Wade (Eds.), *The effectiveness of rehabilitation for cognitive deficits* (pp. 135–142). New York: Oxford University Press.

Halligan, P. W., & Wade, D. T. (Eds.). (2005). *The effectiveness of rehabilitation for cognitive deficits.* New York: Oxford University Press.

Hart, T., & Evans, J. (2006). Self-regulation and goal theories in brain injury rehabilitation. *Journal of Head Trauma Rehabilitation, 21,* 142–155.

Hart, T., Whyte, J., Kim, J., & Vaccaro, M. (2005). Executive function and self-awareness of "real-world" behavior and attention deficits following traumatic brain injury. *Journal of Head Trauma Rehabilitation, 20,* 333–347.

Hillis, A. E. (2005). For a theory of cognitive rehabilitation: Progress in the decade of the brain. In P. W. Halligan & D. T. Wade (Eds.), *The effectiveness of rehabilitation for cognitive deficits* (pp. 271–280). New York: Oxford University Press.

Holland, A. (1991). Pragmatic aspects of intervention in aphasia. *Journal of Neurolinguistics, 6,* 197–211.

Kagan, A., Black, S., Duchan, J., Simmons-Mackie, N., & Square, P. (2001). Training volunteers as conversational partners using "supported conversation for adults with aphasia" (SCA): A controlled trial. *Journal of Speech and Hearing Research, 44,* 624–638.

Kalra, L., Perez, I., Gupta, S., & Wittink, M. (1997). The influence of visual neglect on stroke rehabilitation. *Stroke, 28,* 1386–391.

Kaschel, R., Della Sala, S., Cantagallo, A., Fahlbock, A., Laaksonen, R., & Kazen, M. (2002). Imagery mnemonics for the rehabilitation of memory: A randomised group controlled trial. *Neuropsychological Rehabilitation, 12,* 127–153.

Katz, N., Harman-Maeir, A., Ring, H., & Soroker, N. (1999). Functional disability and rehabilitation outcome in right hemisphere damaged patients with and without unilateral spatial neglect. *Archives of Physical Medicine & Rehabilitation, 80,* 379–384.

Kennedy, M. R. T., Coelho, C., Turkstra, L., Ylvisaker, M. Sohlberg, M. M., Yorkston, K., et al. (2008). Intervention for executive functions after traumatic brain injury: A systematic review, meta-analysis and clinical recommendations. *Neuropsychological Rehabilitation, 18,* 257–299.

Kessels, R. P. C., & de Haan, E. H. F. (2003). Implicit learning in memory rehabilitation: A meta-analysis on errorless learning and vanishing cues methods. *Journal of Clinical and Experimental Neuropsychology, 25,* 805–814.

Knight, C., Rutterford, N. A., Alderman, N., & Swan, L. J. (2002). Is accurate self-monitoring necessary for people with acquired neurological problems to benefit from the use of differential reinforcement methods? *Brain Injury, 16,* 75–87.

Levine, B., Robertson, I. H., Clare, L., Carter, G., Hong, J., Wilson, B. A., et al. (2000). Rehabilitation of executive functioning: An experimental–clinical validation of Goal Management Training. *Journal of the International Neuropsychological Society, 6,* 299–312.

Lillie, R., & Mateer, C. A. (2006). Constraint-based therapies as a proposed model for cognitive rehabilitation. *Journal of Head Trauma Rehabilitation, 21,* 119–130.

Lorig, K., & Holman, H. (2003). Self-management education: History, definition, outcomes, and mechanisms. *Annals of Behavioral Medicine, 26,* 1–7.

Lorig, K., Sobel, D., Stewart, A., Brown, B., Bandura, A., Ritter, P., et al. (1999). Evidence suggesting that a chronic disease self-management program can improve health status while reducing hospitalization: A randomized trial. *Medical Care, 37,* 5–14.

Malec, J. F., & Cicerone, K. D. (2006). Cognitive rehabilitation. In R. Evans (Ed.), *Neurology and trauma* (2nd ed., pp. 238–261). New York: Oxford University Press.

Manly, T., Hawkins, K., Evans, J., Woldt, K., & Robertson, I. H. (2002). Rehabilitation of executive function: Facilitation of effective goal management on complex tasks using periodic auditory alerts. *Neuropsychologia, 40,* 271–281.

Marshall, J. (2005). Can speech and language therapy with aphasic people affect activity and participation levels? A review of the literature. In P. W. Halligan & D. T. Wade (Eds.), *The effectiveness of rehabilitation for cognitive deficits* (pp. 195–207). New York: Oxford University Press.

McGurk, S. R., & Mueser, K. T. (2004). Cognitive functioning, symptoms, and work in supported employment: A review and heuristic model. *Schizophrenia Research, 70,* 147–173.

Meinzer, M., Djundja, D., Barthel, G., Elbert, T., & Rockstroh, B. (2005). Long-term stability of improved language functions in chronic aphasia after constraint-induced aphasia therapy. *Stroke, 36,* 1462–6.

Newman, S., Steed, L., & Mulligan, K. (2004). Self-management interventions for chronic illness. *The Lancet, 364,* 1523–1537.

Ownsworth, T., McFarland, K., & Young, R. M. (2000). Self-awareness and psychosocial functioning following acquired brain injury: An evaluation of a group support programme. *Neuropsychological Rehabilitation, 10,* 465–484.

Park, N. W., & Ingles, J. L. (2001). Effectiveness of attention rehabilitation after an acquired brain injury: A meta-analysis. *Neuropsychology, 15,* 199–210.

Pierce, S., & Buxbaum, L. J. (2002). Treatments of unilateral neglect: A review. *Archives of Physical Medicine and Rehabilitation, 83,* 256–268.

Powell, J. M., Hunt, E., & Pepping, M. (2004). Collaboration between cognitive science and cognitive rehabilitation: A call for action. *Journal of Head Trauma Rehabilitation, 19,* 266–276.

Prigatano, G. (2005). A history of cognitive rehabilitation. In P. W. Halligan & D. T. Wade (Eds.), *The effectiveness of rehabilitation for cognitive deficits* (pp. 3–10). New York: Oxford University Press.

Prigatano, G. P., Fordyce, D. J., Zeiner, H. K., Roueche, J. R., Pepping, M., & Wood, B. C. (1984). Neuropsychological rehabilitation after closed head injury in young adults. *Journal of Neurology, Neurosurgery, and Psychiatry, 47,* 505–513.

Pulvermuller, F., Neininger, B., Elbert, T., Mohr, B., Rockstroh, B., Koebbel, M. A., et al. (2001). Constraint-induced therapy of chronic aphasia after stroke. *Stroke, 32,* 1621–1626.

Rath, J., Simon, D., Langenbahn, D., Sherr, R. L., & Diller, L. (2003). Group treatment of problem solving deficits in outpatients with traumatic brain injury: A randomized outcomes study. *Neuropsychological Rehabilitation, 13,* 461–488.

Redding, G. M., & Wallace, B. (2006). Prism adaptation and unilateral neglect: Review and analysis. *Neuropsychologia, 44,* 1–20.

Robertson, I. H. (1999). Setting goals for cognitive rehabilitation. *Current Opinion in Neurology, 12,* 705–708.

Robertson, I. H. (2005). The neural basis for a theory of cognitive rehabilitation. In P. W. Halligan & D. T. Wade (Eds.), *The effectiveness of rehabilitation for cognitive deficits* (pp. 281–291). New York: Oxford University Press.

Robertson, I. H., Gray, J. M., Pentland, B., & Waite, L. J. (1990). Microcomputer-based rehabilitation for unilateral visual neglect: A randomized controlled trial. *Archives of Physical Medicine and Rehabilitation, 71,* 663–668.

Robertson, I. H., McMillan, T. M., MacLeod, E., & Brock, D. (2002). Rehabilitation by Limb Activation Training (LAT) reduces impairment in unilateral neglect patients: A single-blind randomised control trial. *Neuropsychological Rehabilitation, 12,* 439–454.

Robey, R. R. (1998). A meta-analysis of clinical outcomes in the treatment of aphasia. *Journal of Speech, Language and Hearing Research, 41,* 172–187.

Rossetti, Y., Rode, G., Pisella, L., Farne, A., Li, L., Boisson, D., et al. (1998). Prism adaptation to a rightward optical deviation rehabilitates left-hemispatial neglect. *Nature, 395,* 166–169.

Salazar, A. M., Warden, D. L., Schwarb, K., Spector, J., Braverman, S., & Walter, J. (2000). Cognitive rehabilitation for traumatic brain injury: A randomized trial. *JAMA, 283,* 3075–3081.

Scherer, M. J., Hart, T., Kirsch, N., & Schultheis, M. (2005). Assistive technologies for cognitive disabilities. *Critical Reviews in Physical and Rehabilitation Medicine, 17,* 195–215.

Schmitter-Edgecombe, M., Fahy, J. F., Whelan, J. P., & Long, C. J. (1995). Memory remediation after severe closed head injury: Notebook training versus supportive therapy. *Journal of Consulting and Clinical Psychology, 63,* 484–489.

Shallice, T., & Burgess, P. (1996). The domain of supervisory processes and temporal organization of behaviour. *Philosophical Transactions of the Royal Society of London Series B: Biological Sciences, 351,* 1405–1411.

Sohlberg, M. M., McLaughlin, K. A., Pavese, A., Heidrich, A., & Posner, M. (2000). Evaluation of attention process training and brain injury education in persons with acquired brain injury. *Journal of Clinical and Experimental Neuropsychology, 22,* 656–676.

Squires, E. J., Hunkin, N. M., & Parkin, A. J. (1996). Memory notebook training in a case of severe amnesia: Generalising from paired associate learning to real life. *Neuropsychological Rehabilitation, 6,* 55–65.

Strangman, G., O'Neil-Pirozzi, T. M., Burke, D., Cristina, D., Goldstein, R., Rauch, S. L., et al. (2005). Functional Neuroimaging and cognitive rehabilitation for people with traumatic brain injury. *American Journal of Physical Medicine and Rehabilitation, 84,* 62–75.

Suzman, K., Morris, R., Morris, M., & Milan, M. (1997). Cognitive–behavioral remediation of problem solving deficits in children with acquired brain injury. *Journal of Behavior Therapy and Experimental Psychiatry, 28,* 203–212.

Tate, R. L. (1997). Beyond one-bun, two-shoe: Recent advances in the psychological rehabilitation of memory disorders after acquired brain injury. *Brain Injury, 11,* 907–918.

Tate, R. L, Perdices, M., McDonald, S., Togher, L., Moseley, A., Winders, K., et al. (2004). Development of a database of rehabilitation therapies for the psychological consequences of acquired brain impairment. *Neuropsychological Rehabilitation, 14,* 517–534.

Taub, E., & Uswatte, G. (2000). Constraint-induced (CI) movement therapy based on behavioral neuroscience. In R. G. Frank & T. R. Elliot (Eds.), *Handbook of rehabilitation psychology* (pp. 475–496). Washington, DC: American Psychological Association.

von Cramon, D., Matthes-von Cramon, G., & Mai, N. (1991). Problem-solving deficits in brain injured patients: A therapeutic approach. *Neuropsychological Rehabilitation, 1,* 45–64.

Wade, D. T. (2005). Applying the WHO ICF framework to the rehabilitation of patients with cognitive deficits. In P. W. Halligan & D. T. Wade (Eds.), *The effectiveness of rehabilitation for cognitive deficits* (pp. 31–42). New York: Oxford University Press.

Weinberg, J., Diller, L., Gordon, W., & Stubbs, K. (1977). Visual scanning training effect on reading-related tasks in acquired right brain damage. *Archives of Physical Medicine and Rehabilitation, 58,* 479–486.

Whyte, J., & Hart, T. (2003). It's more than a black box; it's a Russian doll: Defining rehabilitation treatments. *American Journal of Physical Medicine and Rehabilitation, 82*(8), 639–652.

Wilson, B. A. (2000). Compensating for cognitive deficits following brain injury. *Neuropsychology Review, 10,* 233–243.

Wilson, B. A. (2005). The clinical neuropsychologist's dilemma. *Journal of the International Neuropsychological Society, 11,* 488–493.

Wilson, B., Emslie, H., Quirk, K., & Evans, J. (2001). Reducing everyday memory and planning problems by means of a paging system: A randomised control crossover study. *Journal of Neurology, Neurosurgery, and Psychiatry, 70,* 477–482.

Wiseman-Hakes, C., Stewart, M. L., Wasserman, R., & Schuller, R. (1998). Peer group training of pragmatic skills in adolescents with acquired brain injury. *Journal of Head Trauma Rehabilitation, 13,* 23–36.

World Health Organization (2001). *The international classification of function (ICF).* Geneva: Author.

Worthington, A. (2005). Rehabilitation of executive deficits: Effective treatment of related disabilities. In P. W. Halligan & D. T. Wade (Eds.), *The effectiveness of rehabilitation for cognitive deficits* (pp. 257–267). New York: Oxford University Press.

Ylvisaker, M., Hanks, R., & Johnson-Greene, D. (2002). Perspectives on rehabilitation of individuals with cognitive impairment after brain injury: Rationale for reconsideration of theoretical paradigms. *Journal of Head Trauma Rehabilitation, 17,* 191–209.

Zangwill, O. L. (1947). Psychological aspects of rehabilitation in cases of brain injury. *British Journal of Psychology, 37,* 60–69.

CHAPTER 18

EVIDENCE-BASED PRACTICE WITH FAMILY CAREGIVERS: DECISION-MAKING STRATEGIES BASED ON RESEARCH AND CLINICAL DATA

Kathleen Chwalisz and Stephanie Clancy Dollinger

An estimated 44.4 million Americans provide informal care for a person age 18 or older (National Alliance for Caregiving & American Association for Retired Persons [NAC & AARP], 2004), and informal caregiving has an estimated value of $257 billion annually in the United States (Arno, 2002). The majority of family caregivers are women (72%), with spouses accounting for almost half of the caregivers. Based on a recent report from the U.S. Bureau of Labor Statistics, 9% of women 45 to 56 years of age provide care to both their children and their aging parents (Pierret, 2006). Often, one family member serves as the primary source of care, although others in the family and friend networks may serve as "secondary caregivers." When available, a spouse provides the majority of care, followed by a daughter. The person designated to be the primary caregiver tends to be the person with the fewest competing family or work obligations. Caregivers provide assistance with instrumental activities of daily living (e.g., transportation, shopping, housework, arranging services) and/or activities of daily living (e.g., dressing, bathing, mobility). According to Horowitz (1985), caregivers also provide emotional care (e.g., social support, encouragement), mediation care (i.e., negotiating on behalf of the care recipient), and financial care (e.g., managing finances). A national survey on caregiving revealed that 79% of care recipients were age 50 or older and receiving care primarily from adult children or grandchildren for aging-related and/or physical illnesses (NAC & AARP, 2004).

Caregivers are diverse in the manner in which they provide care and the consequences that they experience. Caregiving stress has often been associated with negative physical and mental health consequences such as decreased well-being, depression, anxiety, health problems (e.g., headaches, cardiac and respiratory problems, ulcers) and social isolation, as well as negative career consequences and financial loss (e.g., Bodnar & Kiecolt-Glaser, 1994; Metlife, 1999; NAC & AARP, 2004; Rose-Rego, Strauss, & Smyth, 1998; Schulz & Beach, 1999). Caregivers also exhibit reduced immune function, hypertension, blood chemistry disruption, cardiac arrhythmias (Ory, Yee, Tennstedt, & Schulz, 2000); they tend to get less sleep, report less physical activity, and engage in problematic health-related behaviors (e.g., using alcohol, smoking, poor diet) at a higher rate than noncaregivers. Thus, it is becoming increasingly important to create and implement programs designed to assist informal caregivers.

Effective intervention with caregivers is critical to the well-being of caregivers, care recipients, and the overall health care system. It is imperative that rehabilitation psychologists attend to the needs of caregivers as well as to those of their patients. The caregiver intervention literature is an invaluable resource for rehabilitation psychologists. A summary of existing caregiver interventions is beyond the scope of this chapter and appears elsewhere (e.g., Cooke, McNally, Mulligan, Harrison, & Newman, 2001; Mittelman, 2005). Instead, we highlight clinical and research issues and summarize

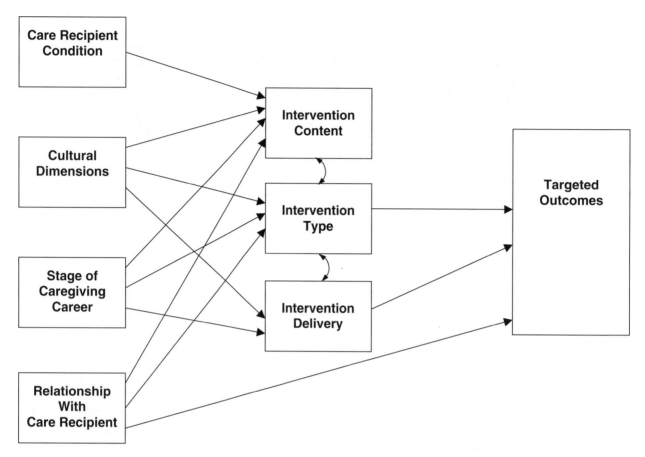

FIGURE 18.1.   Dimensions and relations to consider in developing caregiver interventions.

treatment recommendations that can be extrapolated from the intervention research literature. It is important to assess each caregiving situation and make treatment decisions considering intervention domains and available evidence. Figure 18.1 presents the dimensions of caregiver intervention and relations among them that rehabilitation psychologists should consider in developing and implementing caregiver interventions. The utility of this decision-making framework is discussed and illustrated throughout the chapter.

DESIGN AND METHODOLOGICAL ISSUES IN CAREGIVER INTERVENTION AND INTERVENTION RESEARCH

Researchers and practitioners have developed and tested a wide variety of intervention programs for family caregivers that vary in effectiveness (e.g., Sörensen, Pinquart, & Duberstein, 2002; Toseland & McCallion, 1997). Findings from these studies

can be used to guide the development and implementation of interventions with caregivers. However, caregiver intervention research has not yet reached the point where one can consider findings in the traditional levels of evidence sense that has characterized developments in evidence-based practice (e.g., Nathan & Gorman, 2002), because few traditional randomized controlled trial studies currently exist. Although some researchers have used randomized designs, most of the research has been conducted in real-world caregiving settings, placing it in the realm of effectiveness research (Sörensen et al., 2002). Although the range of evidence may not be as broad as it is for other types of psychological interventions, in some ways one might consider this literature to be a better guide for rehabilitation psychologists' activities, given that it reflects the complexities of real-world caregivers and caregiving situations. We recommend that future research, rather than being concerned with generating efficacy data, be focused on identifying the constituent change processes involved in caregiver interventions (see Chwalisz, Dollinger, O'Neill, & Tamkin, 2005; Henry, 1998) and improving the design and implementation of caregiver intervention effectiveness research (see Leichsenring, 2004).

In spite of widely reported client satisfaction, effect sizes for caregiver interventions have ranged from small to moderate. Sörensen and colleagues' (2002) meta-analysis of 78 caregiver intervention studies revealed effect sizes of 0.14 to 0.41 standard deviation units across different types of interventions (e.g., psychoeducational, supportive, psychotherapy) and outcomes (e.g., caregiver burden, depressed mood, caregiving satisfaction, knowledge). Caregiver interventions have often lacked a theoretical basis (e.g., Bourgeois, Schulz, & Burgio, 1996; Coon, Ory, & Schulz, 2003) and have been conducted with convenience samples (e.g., White urban) and select populations (e.g., dementia). Rural, ethnic minority, intergenerational, overwhelmed caregivers and a broader range of rehabilitation issues need to be included in future caregiver research (National Institute of Nursing Research, 2001).

Research Methods

Outcome measures in caregiver intervention research have often not been sensitive to change, yielding small or no postintervention effects. Baseline and follow-up data at longer intervals postintervention are needed (e.g., Cooke et al., 2001). Outcome measures should be more closely linked to proximal outcomes (i.e., targets of the intervention), tap into caregiver well-being, and be more practice friendly (e.g., Coon, Ory, & Schulz, 2003). Caregiving circumstances must also be assessed. Greater objective burden (e.g., number of hours of care provided) was associated with less improvement in burden, depression, and subjective well-being, but greater improvement in ability and knowledge. Higher levels of subjective caregiver burden, in contrast, were associated with greater improvements in burden, depression, and well-being, but smaller improvements in ability and knowledge and care recipient symptoms (Sörensen et al., 2002). Study logistics are also a factor in outcomes. Random assignment to treatment and control conditions significantly predicted treatment

effect sizes for caregiver depression, well-being, ability and knowledge, and care recipient symptoms with smaller effect sizes for randomized studies. Longer treatments have been associated with greater effects on caregiver depression but relatively smaller effects on caregivers' knowledge and ability (Sörensen et al., 2002).

Intervention Delivery Methods

Rehabilitation psychologists must also consider how best to deliver a caregiver intervention. Available research can be used to guide such decisions. Rehabilitation setting resources and consumer preferences should also be taken into account.

Individual versus group intervention. Reviews of caregiver interventions indicate that individual services are more effective than group interventions (Cooke et al., 2001; Knight, Lutzky, & Macofsky-Urban, 1993; Sörensen et al., 2002). Lack of focus on strategies to improve life quality and problem-solving is often cited as a limitation of caregiver support groups (Gallagher-Thompson, Coon, Rivera, Powers, & Zeiss, 1998). Thus, it is not clear whether the small effect sizes associated with group interventions are due to the group modality or simply that poorly designed interventions are more likely to be presented in a group format and be peer led. Toseland, Rossiter, Peak, and Hill (1990) found that peer-led groups were more effective in terms of social processes (e.g., amount of social interaction, discussion of community resources, leader as role model), and professionally led groups were more effective in terms of therapeutic processes (e.g., discussing specific problems, gaining insight, development of coping skills).

In-person versus telehealth interventions. Positive aspects of telehealth services include reduced long-term costs, increased accessibility for those who are not willing or able to travel, privacy, and increased comfort because of being able to receive services in one's own home (Wright, Bennett, Gramling, & Daley, 1999). These benefits are especially evident in rural areas (e.g., Schopp, Demiris, & Glueckauf, 2006). No difference has been found on key therapeutic variables (e.g., therapeutic alliance, client satisfaction) between in-person, audio-only, and audio-video modalities (Day & Schneider, 2000). In our own randomized clinical trial of an eight-session multicomponent telephone-based intervention with rural caregivers of older adults, caregivers have shown significant improvement in physical health, mental health, and psychosocial functioning; these improvements continue to be maintained at a 6-month follow-up (Clancy Dollinger, Chwalisz, & Zerth, 2006). Moderate effect sizes have also been reported for an online cognitive–behavioral intervention for caregivers of persons with Alzheimer's disease (Glueckauf, Ketterson, Loomis, & Dages, 2004) and for telephone-based support groups for ethnically diverse groups of caregivers (Bank, Argüelles, Rubert, Eisdorfer, & Czaja, 2006).

Another dimension to consider in choosing an in-person versus telehealth intervention is whether the in-person intervention occurs in the home. The intervention program conducted by Gitlin, Corcoran, Winter, Boyce, and Hauck (2001) involved home visits by occupational therapists to assist caregivers in modifying their living space to address specific care problems. The in-home intervention had modest but significant effects on caregiver and care recipient outcomes and greater improvements were evident in minority caregivers. Telehealth interventions with rural caregivers have also incorporated sophisticated technologies such as videoconferencing to make them more analogous to an in-home service (e.g., Buckwalter, Davis, Wakefield, Kienzle, & Murray, 2002).

Standardized versus tailored interventions. Bourgeois and colleagues (1996) recommended attending to specific caregiver characteristics and tailoring interventions to the individual. Whereas multicomponent interventions appear to be superior to specific interventions (e.g., Sörensen et al., 2002), the nature and appropriateness of specific interventions included in those comparisons were typically not investigated. One important research question that has yet to be answered is whether a specific intervention, tailored to unique caregiver characteristics, is more effective than a standardized multicomponent caregiver intervention. Rehabilitation psychologists in clinical settings are in an excellent position to assess caregiving situations and deliver and test such tailored interventions.

EVIDENCE-BASED CAREGIVER INTERVENTION: CONTENT AND PROCESS

Available theoretical and empirical literature on caregiving and caregiver interventions provides guidance and specific treatment recommendations. Figure 18.1 is an overview of caregiver intervention dimensions and the relations among those dimensions that have been established. A logical consideration of these dimensions can guide development and implementation of caregiver interventions.

Caregivers and caregiving situations should be assessed according to cultural dimensions, relationship with the care recipient, and stage in the caregiving process (see Figure 18.1). Such assessment should occur early in the rehabilitation process (e.g., before discharge for inpatients, initial outpatient visit). These important background and context dimensions, as well as the care recipient's condition, will determine both the content and type of intervention that will be most relevant for a given caregiver. As previously noted, intervention delivery approach is determined by resources and consumer preferences and can be guided by research. It is also important to consider the desired caregiver and care recipient outcomes, as particular types of interventions have been associated with particular caregiver outcomes.

Cultural Dimensions in Caregiving

Culture influences an individual's concept of health and disease (Mulatu & Berry, 2001). A culturally competent psychologist needs to understand and appreciate other cultures, recognize and address one's own values and biases, intervene in a way that is appropriate to a given client's culture and worldview, and, most important, behave in a manner consistent with principles and ethics of multicultural counseling (Baruth & Manning, 1999). Cultural dimensions including age, race and ethnicity, gender, and sexual orientation have been examined and vary according to illness concepts, caregiving experiences, health, resources, intervention recruitment and retention. Intervention needs may vary based on culture, and cultural variations of caregiver interventions have been implemented (e.g., Gallagher-Thompson, Hargrave, et al., 2003), but few culturally specific interventions have been developed and assessed.

Race and ethnicity.   Minority caregivers are likely to have lower socioeconomic status, be younger, be a spouse, rely on informal support, provide more caregiving hours, have a stronger sense of filial obligation, and experience poor physical health (Pinquart & Sörensen, 2005). Especially salient issues for racial and ethnic minority caregivers are the role of religiosity and the church, greater emphasis on family and community, experiences of discrimination and mistrust of the majority community and professionals, language barriers, intergenerational conflict, stigma surrounding the care recipient's condition, and health disparities. Racial and ethnic minority caregivers are more likely to seek support from family, church, and community-based support programs rather than from traditional services (e.g., Gallagher-Thompson, Hargrave, et al., 2003; Pinquart & Sörensen, 2005).

Gender.   Meta-analyses of studies examining gender in caregiving often indicate small differences. Pinquart and Sörensen's (2006) meta-analysis revealed that women exhibited more burden, depression, behavioral problems, hours of care, and less subjective well-being and poorer physical health relative to men. Yee and Schulz (2000) found a higher rate of psychiatric morbidity in women caregivers relative to noncaregivers. Kaye (2002), for example, found that gender differences in caregiving are often based on emphasis differences (e.g., knowledge and skills more salient for male caregivers), use of formal services, instrumental versus personal care (varying by caregiving relationship), and social isolation (greater in male caregivers). Pinquart and Sörensen (2006) proposed that gender differences in caregiving should be further examined within a stress and coping theoretical framework.

Sexual orientation.   One's sexual orientation also influences the caregiving experience. Gay and lesbian caregivers, with caregiving relationships varying by gender, provide higher levels of care. There are greater health risks for gay and lesbian care-

givers, however, complicated by discrimination and mistrust of professionals. Discrimination, legal issues, and potentially lower levels of support from family and friends are a few of the challenges that gay and lesbian caregivers encounter (e.g., Coon & Zeiss, 2003).

Rural versus urban.   The stresses of living in poverty, inadequate housing, social isolation, and a lack of health care and social services often contribute to poor outcomes for rural caregivers and their families (Lishner, Richardson, Levine, & Patrick, 1996). Family caregivers in rural areas especially view the use of community-based services as a sign of personal weakness or failure (e.g., Glasglow, 2000). Rural caregivers have a strong commitment to family and caregiving, attitudes that impede help-seeking (e.g., individualism), stigma regarding care recipient's illness and caregiver help-seeking, and fewer resources (e.g., financial, interpersonal) and services (Chwalisz, Buckwalter, & Tally, in press).

Relationship With the Care Recipient

The relationship between the caregiver and the care recipient (e.g., spouse, adult child, parent) has important implications for the caregiving experience. A meta-analysis of caregiver intervention studies by Sörensen and colleagues (2002) indicated that treatment effects were greater for caregiver burden, depression, well-being, and ability or knowledge when a high proportion of caregivers in the study were adult children. Greater improvements in care recipient symptoms were found in studies with a greater proportion of spouse caregivers. Caregiving may be less emotionally demanding for parents or spouses who functioned in a more nurturing manner toward the care recipient prior to the illness or injury.

Care recipient condition.   The specific nature of the care recipient's condition may be a factor, to some extent, in determining the nature of the intervention with the caregiver. The care recipient's condition obviously dictates the content of psycho-educational and skills-based interventions with caregivers and care recipients. However, there is mounting evidence that many aspects of the caregiving situation and caregiver adjustment are consistent across care recipient populations. For instance, a review of the caregiver burden literature and a measurement study revealed that caregiver-perceived stress, a universal indicator of subjective caregiver burden, was a better predictor of caregiver outcomes than objective burden and burden measures that are based on more objective aspects of the caregiving situation (Chwalisz & Kisler, 1995). More evidence for universal caregiving experiences can be found as the same intervention is applied to different caregiving subpopulations (e.g., Elliott, Shewchuk, & Richards, 1999; Grant, Elliott, Giger, & Bartolucci, 2001). Additional attention should be directed toward identifying the universal versus specific aspects of caregiving for different caregiving subpopulations.

Stage of caregiving career.   Understanding the natural progression of caregiving can facilitate caregiver coping and help rehabilitation psychologists identify a caregiver's needs by his or her stage in the process (e.g., Skaff, Pearlin, & Mullan, 1996). Being new to the caregiving role is characterized by shock, confusion, and a health care crisis. New caregivers are most in need of crisis intervention and support and are likely to interact with a rehabilitation psychologist in abrupt caregiving situations. The period of learning new skills is characterized by striving to gain caregiving competence, seeking specific information or skills, gaining competence with various caregiving demands, and learning to navigate legal and health care systems. Psychoeducational and skills training programs are particularly helpful for caregivers at this stage in the caregiving role.

Caregivers move into the maintenance and survival stage with the realization their caregiving role may be long-term and that changes will be necessary to survive this period of their lives. Maintenance caregivers may benefit most from psychotherapeutic interventions to manage stress and balance responsibilities, set limits, or seek respite care. The next stage of active caregiving involves adapting to changes in the caregiver and care recipient. Changes in the care recipient may include health status and social isolation. Caregiver changes may include exhaustion, depression, attitude changes, and social pressures. Caregivers may benefit from various types of inter-

ventions (e.g., psychotherapy, psychoeducation, support) as they respond to these changes.

The final stage of active caregiving is the end of direct caregiving, which typically occurs when the care recipient's living situation changes (e.g., a move to assisted living or nursing home) or a major aspect of the caregiving situation changes (e.g., health decline, death). Caregivers in this last phase of the caregiving process might need additional knowledge about nursing homes, hospitals, and hospice programs and benefit from material on stress, grief, and loss (including anticipatory grief). Psychotherapy or support services, directed toward the emotional aspects experienced during the last phase of caregiving and planning for the future, may be beneficial.

Intervention content.   Although caregiving is a common role that individuals naturally take on, it is also a demanding one. Caregivers require unique knowledge, skills, and resources to be effective and healthy in the role. Intervention content is determined by cultural dimensions, stage of caregiving, relationship with the care recipient, and the care recipient's condition.

Knowledge. Caregivers may need knowledge about the caregiving process and role to prepare them for demands at different points in their caregiving career. Caregivers also need knowledge of the care recipient's condition and treatment options. It is obviously impossible to know everything there is to know about every care recipient condition that one might encounter in a rehabilitation setting. Thus, beyond knowledge of the most commonly encountered care recipient conditions, rehabilitation psychologists should focus on developing excellent information-seeking skills in caregivers. Caregivers should be taught about the types of information that are important to know (e.g., course or prognosis, related sequelae, effects of comorbidity), general information seeking strategies, and potential sources of such information (e.g., professionals, books, internet, agencies). Information about available resources and services is also critical for successful caregiving.

Skills. Caregivers may require specific care-related skills such as lifting, use of medical equipment or assistive devices, or daily medical maintenance (e.g., changing dressings, testing blood sugar). Behavior management skills (e.g., managing impulsivity after TBI) may also be needed (Carnevale, Anselmi, Busichio, & Millis, 2002). Caregivers often require a variety of communication skills. For example, Done and Thomas (2001) found caregivers could be trained to structure questions for more successful communication with patients with Alzheimer's disease. Assertiveness training might be used with caregivers who are having difficulty getting information from professionals or assistance from family members.

Perhaps the most far-reaching and well-researched of the general caregiving skills are social problem-solving skills. Problem solving involves self-efficacy, ability to gather relevant information, creativity in generating possible solutions, effective choice among solutions, and the ability to evaluate the results of one's efforts. Social problem-solving ability is an important predictor of physical and emotional health among both urban and rural caregivers (e.g., Grant et al., 2001). Caregiver problem-solving may also affect care recipient outcomes such as acceptance of disability and health complications over time (Elliott et al., 1999).

Affect. Caregivers experience a wide variety of negative emotions (e.g., guilt, frustration, anger, sadness, grief). Intervention programs should include strategies to manage negative emotions, as these negative emotions can directly impact psychological difficulties in caregivers (e.g., depression, anxiety). Cognitive behavior therapy (CBT) is particularly useful in helping caregivers combat irrational beliefs (e.g., not believing one has time or deserves to make time for self-care) and manage negative affect. Interventions based on CBT have been widely implemented, with demonstrated effectiveness (e.g., Thompson & Gallagher-Thompson, 1996). Specific techniques related to stress management (e.g., relaxation training) and anger management might also be included in affect-oriented interventions with caregivers.

Social support. Social support-oriented interventions tend to involve support groups, with the assumption that putting caregivers together in a group will enhance support. Outcomes measured in support group research have tended to be global physical or mental health outcomes. Such studies have yielded small effect sizes (Knight et al., 1993), indicating that more specific considerations regarding support intervention are warranted. Development of skills related to increasing the size and range of the support network (e.g., identifying potential supporters, strategies to find and engage supporters, social skills training) may be important to some caregivers. Caregivers may also have inaccurate perceptions of available support (e.g., not recognizing supporters who already exist), and professionals may help caregivers develop more realistic perceptions and expectations. Still other caregivers need help maintaining existing support. Caregivers often report that they lose touch with their support network, or that supporters drift away because of discomfort surrounding the caregiving situation (e.g., Chwalisz & Stark-Wroblewski, 1996). Some caregivers may have adequate support systems but need assistance in getting more help from the network. Asking for help is particularly challenging for caregivers, who are in the role because they are high functioning individuals.

Intervention type. Given the widely varied needs of different types of caregivers, it is not surprising that a broad range of interventions have been developed and tested. Sörensen and colleagues (2002), in perhaps the most comprehensive meta-analysis of caregiver intervention literature to date, identified six types of interventions that have been developed to assist caregivers: (a) psychoeducation, (b) psychotherapy, (c) supportive interventions, (d) care recipient training, (e) respite or adult day care, and (f) multicomponent interventions. Six types of outcomes have been considered: (a) caregiver burden, (b) caregiver depression, (c) caregiver well-being, (d) caregiver knowledge, (e) caregiver physical health, and (f) care recipient symptoms. It is interesting that caregiver physical health was not significantly affected by caregiver intervention.

Psychoeducational interventions. Psycho-educational interventions are designed to increase caregivers' knowledge or skills and typically involve a structured program by a trained leader. Programs may include lectures, discussion, worksheets or handouts, and audiovisual materials. The goal is to provide information about the care recipient's condition and/or build skills to handle problems related to the care recipient's condition. Sörensen et al. (2002) reported that psychoeducational interventions had small effects on care recipients' symptoms (–.24) and caregiver burden (–.12) and moderate effects on caregiver knowledge and ability (.53), caregiver well-being (.50), and caregiver depression (–.43). Psychoeducational interventions have also been found effective with Latino caregivers (Gallagher-Thompson, Coon, Solano, et al., 2003).

Psychotherapy interventions. Psychotherapy interventions involve a formal helping relationship between a caregiver and a professional. Psychotherapy interventions, in contrast to supportive interventions, are more likely to be theoretically derived, evidence-based, standardized, and/or manualized. Nine of 10 studies reviewed by Sörensen and colleagues (2002) involved cognitive–behavioral approaches. Interventions may target caregivers' irrational thoughts, help them learn new skills (e.g., managing emotions, time), or increase caregiver participation in pleasant activities. Psychotherapy interventions were found to have significant effects on all caregiving outcomes with small effects on care recipient symptoms (–.19) and moderate effects on caregivers' ability and knowledge (–42), caregiver well-being (–.37), caregiver burden (–.31), and caregiver depression (–.29).

Supportive interventions. Supportive interventions are those designed to increase caregivers' experience of social support and the sense that they are not alone in their difficulties with the role. Support groups have typically been unstructured opportunities for caregivers to discuss their challenges and concerns, rather than using group dynamics to address deeper psychological processes. Sörensen and colleagues (2002) noted that support group interventionists have not provided much detail about the exact nature of their interventions, and such interventions tend not to be standardized or manualized. They found significant effects for supportive interventions for caregiver burden (–.35) and caregivers' ability and knowledge (–.29).

Care recipient training. A few published studies have involved care recipient training programs, conducted primarily for patients with dementia. Such interventions have included memory clinics or activity therapy programs. Care recipient training interventions yielded a moderate effect on care recipient symptoms (–.51) and a fairly large (.74) effect on caregiver well-being (Sörensen et al., 2002). Although such interventions did not affect other psychological outcomes for caregivers, such as perceived burden or depression, care recipient training interventions may be quite valuable, particularly when care recipient aberrant behavior is a primary stressor. Such interventions should be implemented and assessed with additional rehabilitation populations.

Respite or adult day care. Respite and adult day care programs are designed to give caregivers a break from their caregiving duties. Assistance is provided to the care recipient either in the home or in another setting and varies in length and amount of engagement. Sörensen and colleagues (2002) found that respite or day care programs had significant but relatively small effects on caregiver burden (–.30), caregiver depression (–.23), and caregiver well-being (–.20).

Multicomponent interventions. Multicomponent interventions involve combinations of the intervention types (e.g., psychoeducational, supportive, psychotherapy, respite). There is theoretical and empirical support that multicomponent interventions are more effective than targeted interventions (Thompson & Gallagher-Thompson, 1996), as are interventions with greater frequency and intensity (Kennet, Burgio, & Schulz, 2000). Sörensen and colleagues (2002) found some of the strongest effects for multicomponent interventions, although significant effects were only in the outcome domains of caregivers' ability and knowledge (.86), caregiver well-being (.75), and caregiver burden (–.62). Targeted multicomponent interventions have also yielded sustained effects on caregiver well-being. For example, a counseling and support intervention was superior to treatment as usual in decreasing depression in spouse caregivers of patients with Alzheimer's disease, and the effects were sustained for more than 3 years. Furthermore, the full benefits of the treatment were realized only after all treatment components had been received (Mittelman, Roth, Coon, & Haley, 2004).

CONCLUSIONS

A comprehensive rehabilitation treatment program should include treatment for the patient and family caregiver. Available theoretical and empirical literature on caregiving and caregiver interventions provides guidance and specific treatment recommendations that can be selected based on patient and caregiver assessment data and treatment preferences. Although the most promising caregiver interventions appear to be multicomponent interventions, more targeted interventions, if carefully matched with patient and caregiver characteristics, may be equally as effective, depending on the desired patient and caregiver outcomes. Specific questions raised in this review can be systematically investigated. Increasing attention given to these questions by both practitioners and researchers is encouraging as we look to the country's future caregiving needs.

Caregiving needs and support for family caregivers can only be expected to increase as the caregiver crisis grows (e.g., Schmieding, 2006). Rehabilitation psychologists can, and should, direct their attention to this growing health care population. Rehabilitation settings truly provide a unique and exciting opportunity to test evidence-based interventions with diverse patient and caregiver populations.

References

Arno, P. S. (2002, February). *Economic value of informal caregiving*. Paper presented at the meeting of the American Association of Geriatric Psychiatry, Orlando, FL.

Bank, A. L., Argüelles, S., Rubert, M., Eisdorfer, C., & Czaja, S. J. (2006). The value of telephone support groups among ethnically diverse caregivers of persons with dementia. *The Gerontologist, 46,* 134–138.

Baruth, L. G., & Manning, M. L. (1999). *Multicultural counseling and psychotherapy: A lifespan perspective* (2nd ed.). Columbus, OH: Merrill.

Bodnar, J. C., & Kiecolt-Glaser, J. K. (1994). Caregiver depression after bereavement: Chronic stress isn't over when it's over. *Psychology and Aging, 9,* 372–380.

Bourgeois, M. S., Schulz, R., & Burgio, L. (1996). Interventions for caregivers of patients with Alzheimer's disease: A review and analysis of content, process, and outcomes. *International Journal of Aging and Human Development, 43,* 35–92.

Buckwalter, K. C., Davis, L. L., Wakefield, B. J., Kienzle, M. G., & Murray, M. A. (2002). Telehealth for elders and their caregivers in rural communities. *Family & Community Health, 25,* 31–40.

Carnevale, G. J., Anselmi, V., Busichio, K., & Millis, S. R. (2002). Changes in ratings of caregiver burden following a community-based behavior management program for persons with traumatic brain injury. *Journal of Head Trauma Rehabilitation, 17,* 83–95.

Chwalisz, K., Buckwalter, K. C., & Tally, R. C. (in press). Rural caregiving: A matter of culture. In R. C. Tally, K. Chwalisz, & K. C. Buckwalter (Eds.), *Rural caregiving: Practice, education, research, and policy issues.* New York: Oxford University Press.

Chwalisz, K., Dollinger, S. M. C., O'Neill, E., & Tamkin, V. L. (2005, August). *Manualized treatment in real-world psychotherapy settings.* Paper presented at the meeting of the American Psychological Association, Washington, DC.

Chwalisz, K., & Kisler, V. (1995). Perceived stress: A better measure of caregiver burden. *Measurement and Evaluation in Counseling and Development, 28,* 88–98.

Chwalisz, K., & Stark-Wroblewski, K. (1996). The subjective experience of spouse caregivers of persons with brain injuries: A qualitative analysis. *Applied Neuropsychology, 3,* 28–40.

Clancy Dollinger, S., Chwalisz, K., & Zerth, E. O. (2006). Tele-help Line for Caregivers (TLC): A comprehensive telehealth intervention for rural family caregivers. *Clinical Gerontologist, 30,* 51–64.

Cooke, D. D., McNally, L., Mulligan, K. T., Harrison, M. J. G., & Newman, S. P. (2001). Psychosocial interventions for caregivers of people with dementia: A systematic review. *Aging and Mental Health, 5,* 120–135.

Coon, D. W., & Zeiss, L. M. (2003). The families we choose: Intervention issues with LGBT caregivers. In D. W. Coon, D. Gallagher-Thompson, & L. W. Thompson (Eds.), *Innovative interventions to reduce dementia caregiver distress: A clinical guide* (pp. 267–295). New York: Springer.

Coon, D. W., Ory, M. G., & Schulz, R. (2003). Family caregivers: Enduring and emergent themes. In D. W.

Coon, D. Gallagher-Thompson, & L. W. Thompson (Eds.), *Innovative interventions to reduce dementia caregiver distress: A clinical guide* (pp. 3–27). New York: Springer.

Day, S. X., & Schneider, P. (2000). The subjective experiences of therapists in face-to-face, video, and audio sessions. In J. W. Bloom & G. R. Walz (Eds.), *Cybercounseling and cyberlearning: Strategies and resources for the millennium* (pp. 203–218). Alexandria, VA: American Counseling Association.

Done, D. J., & Thomas, J. A. (2001). Training in communication skills for informal carers of people suffering from dementia: A cluster randomized clinical trial comparing a therapist led workshop and a booklet. *International Journal of Geriatric Psychiatry, 16,* 816–821.

Elliott, T. R., Shewchuk, R. M., & Richards, J. S. (1999). Caregiver social problem-solving abilities and family member adjustment to recent onset physical disability. *Rehabilitation Psychology, 44,* 104–123.

Gallagher-Thompson, D., Coon, D. W., Rivera, P., Powers, D., & Zeiss, A. M. (1998). Family caregiving: Stress, coping and intervention. In M. Hersen & V. B. Van Hasselt (Eds.), *Handbook of clinical geropsychology* (pp. 469–493). New York: Plenum Press.

Gallagher-Thompson, D., Coon, D. W., Solano, N., Ambler, C., Rabinowitz, Y., & Thompson, L. W. (2003). Change in indices of distress among Latino and Anglo female caregivers of elderly relatives with dementia: Site-specific results from the REACH national collaborative study. *The Gerontologist, 43,* 580–591.

Gallagher-Thompson, D., Hargrave, R., Hinton, L., Árean, P., Iwamasa, G., & Zeiss, L. M. (2003). Interventions for a multicultural society. In D. W. Coon, D. Gallagher-Thompson, & L. W. Thompson (Eds.), *Innovative interventions to reduce dementia caregiver distress: A clinical guide* (pp. 50–73). New York: Springer.

Gitlin, L., Corcoran, M., Winter, L., Boyce, A., & Hauck, W. W. (2001). A randomized controlled trial of a home environmental intervention: Effect on efficacy and upset in caregivers and on daily function of persons with dementia. *The Gerontologist, 26,* 253–259.

Glasglow, N. (2000). Rural/urban patterns of aging and caregiving in the United States. *Journal of Family Issues, 21,* 611–631.

Glueckauf, R. L., Ketterson, T. U., Loomis, J. S., & Dages, P. (2004). Online support and education for dementia caregivers: Overview, utilization, and initial program evaluation. *Telemedicine Journal and e-Health, 10,* 223–232.

Grant, J. S., Elliott, T. R., Giger, J. N., & Bartolucci, A. A. (2001). Social problem-solving abilities, social support, and adjustment among family caregivers of

individuals with a stroke. *Rehabilitation Psychology, 46,* 44–57.

Henry, W. P. (1998). Science, politics, and the politics of science: The use and misuse of empirically validated treatment research. *Psychotherapy Research, 8,* 126–140.

Horowitz, A. (1985). Family caregiving to the frail elderly. In M. P. Lawton & G. Maddox (Eds.), *Annual review of gerontology and geriatrics* (pp. 194–246). New York: Springer Publishing Co.

Kaye, L. W. (2002). Service utilization and support provision of caregiving men. In B. J. Kramer & E. H. Thompson (Eds.), *Men as caregivers: Theory, research, and service implications* (pp. 359–378). New York: Springer.

Kennet, J., Burgio, L., & Schulz, R. (2000). Interventions for in-home caregivers: A review of research 1990 to present. In R. Schulz (Ed.), *Handbook on dementia caregiving: Evidence-based interventions for family caregivers* (pp. 61–125). New York: Springer.

Knight, B. G., Lutzky, S. M., & Macofsky-Urban, F. (1993). A meta-analytic review of interventions for caregiver distress: Recommendations for future research. *The Gerontologist, 33,* 240–248.

Leichsenring, F. (2004). Randomized controlled versus naturalistic studies: A new research agenda. *Bulletin of the Menninger Clinic, 68,* 137–151.

Lishner, D. M., Richardson, M., Levine, P., & Patrick, D. (1996). Access to primary health care among persons with disabilities in rural areas: A summary of the literature. *Journal of Rural Health, 12,* 445–53.

MetLife. (1999). *The MetLife juggling act study: Balancing caregiving with work and the costs involved.* Westport, CT: Metropolitan Life Insurance Company.

Mittelman, M. (2005). Taking care of the caregivers. *Current Opinion in Psychiatry, 18,* 633–639.

Mittelman, M. S., Roth, D. L., Coon, D. W., & Haley, W. E. (2004). Sustained benefit of supportive intervention for depressive symptoms in caregivers of patient's with Alzheimer's disease. *American Journal of Psychiatry, 161,* 850–856.

Mulatu, M. S., & Berry, J. W. (2001). Cultivating health through multiculturalism. In M. MacLachlan (Ed.), *Cultivating health: Cultural perspectives on promoting health* (pp. 15–35). New York: Wiley.

Nathan, P., & Gorman, J. M. (Eds.). (2002). *A guide to treatments that work* (2nd ed.). New York: Oxford University Press.

National Alliance for Caregiving & American Association of Retired Persons. (2004). *Caregiving in the United States.* Retrieved April 5, 2006, from http://www.caregiving.org/data/04finalreport.pdf

National Institute of Nursing Research. (2001). *Research in informal caregiving: State of the science workgroup meeting executive summary.* Retrieved December 15, 2008, from http://www.ninr.nih.gov/NR/rdonlyres/5B7C2DB8-9C63-4F26-A26B-13D1F947FFCB/4868/WorkingGrouponInformalCaregiving.pdf

Ory, M. G., Yee, J. L., Tennstedt, S. L., & Schulz, R. (2000). The extent and impact of dementia care: Unique challenges experienced by family caregivers. In R. Schulz (Ed.), *Handbook of dementia caregiving: Evidence-based interventions for family caregivers* (pp. 1–32). New York: Springer.

Pinquart, M., & Sörensen, S. (2005). Ethnic differences in stressors, resources, and psychological outcomes of family caregiving: A meta-analysis. *The Gerontologist, 45,* 90–106.

Pinquart, M., & Sörensen, S. (2006). Gender differences in caregiver stressors, social resources, and health: An updated meta-analysis. *Journal of Gerontology: Psychological Sciences, 61B,* P33–P45.

Pierret, C. R. (2006, September). The "sandwich generation": Women caring for parents and children. *Monthly Labor Review,* 3–9.

Rose-Rego, S. K., Strauss, M. F., & Smyth, K. A. (1998). Differences in the perceived well-being of wives and husbands caring for persons with Alzheimer's disease. *The Gerontologist, 38,* 224–230.

Schmieding, L. (2006). *Caregiving in America.* New York: International Longevity Center and Springdale, AK: Schmeiding Center for Senior Health and Education of Northwest Arkansas.

Schopp, L. H., Demiris, G., & Glueckauf, R. L. (2006). Rural backwaters or front-runners? Rural telehealth in the vanguard of psychology practice. *Professional Psychology: Research and Practice, 37,* 165–173.

Schulz, R., & Beach, S. (1999). Caregiving as a risk factor for mortality: The Caregiver Health Effects Study. *JAMA, 282,* 2215–2219.

Skaff, M., Pearlin, L. I., & Mullan, J. T. (1996). Transitions in the caregiving career: Effects on sense of mastery. *Psychology & Aging, 11,* 247–257.

Sörensen, S., Pinquart, M., & Duberstein, P. (2002). How effective are interventions with caregivers? An updated meta-analysis. *The Gerontologist, 42,* 356–372.

Thompson, L. W., & Gallagher-Thompson, D. (1996). Practical issues related to maintenance of mental health and positive well-being in family caregivers. In L. L. Carstensen & B. A. Edelstein (Eds.), *The practical handbook of clinical gerontology* (pp. 129–150). Thousand Oaks, CA: Sage.

Toseland, R. W., & McCallion, P. (1997). Trends in caregiving intervention research. *Social Work Research, 21,* 154–164.

Toseland, R. W., Rossiter, C. M., Peak, T., & Hill, P. (1990). Therapeutic processes in peer led and professionally led support groups for caregivers. *International Journal of Group Psychotherapy, 40,* 279–303.

Wright, L. K., Bennett, G., Gramling, L., & Daley, L. (1999). Family caregiver evaluation of telehealth interventions [Special issue 1]. *Gerontologist, 39,* 67.

Yee, J. L., & Schulz, R. (2000). Gender differences in psychiatric morbidity among family caregivers: A review and analysis. *The Gerontologist, 40,* 147–16.

PART IV

PEDIATRICS

CHAPTER 19

PEDIATRIC NEUROPSYCHOLOGY IN MEDICAL REHABILITATION SETTINGS

Janet E. Farmer, Stephen M. Kanne, Maureen O. Grissom, and Sally Kemp

The number of children who survive life-threatening illnesses, injuries, and congenital disorders has increased steadily with advances in medical technology (Farmer & Deidrick, 2006; Wallander & Thompson, 1995). Neurological impairments are common among survivors and can result in physical, cognitive, and behavioral disabilities. These children and their families often require medical rehabilitation services to optimize functional outcomes and improve quality of life. The primary role of the pediatric neuropsychologist on the rehabilitation team is to assess each child's level of cognitive and behavioral functioning to assist with treatment planning.

Children treated in medical rehabilitation vary widely in the nature and complexity of their presenting problems. From a neuropsychological perspective, children can be classified into four main groups. First, many children experience sudden onset, acquired brain injury due to events such as head trauma, stroke, viral and infectious diseases, and hypoxic injuries. Second, there are youngsters who experience more gradual, insidious declines in functioning due to diseases affecting the central nervous system, such as brain tumors, leukemia, and other forms of cancer. These children often receive rehabilitation services following debilitating treatment regimens. Third, others have neurodevelopmental disorders with primary physical dysfunction and increased risk of cognitive deficits, including those with cerebral palsy and spina bifida. Finally, among children receiving rehabilitation services for injury- or illness-related physical disabilities that are not typically associated with cerebral damage (e.g.,

burns, amputees, juvenile rheumatoid arthritis), there exists a subgroup of children with learning problems that occur in the general population, including developmental delays and learning disabilities.

The purpose of this chapter is to discuss the application of pediatric neuropsychology to meet the various needs of these children during the rehabilitation process. Children may be referred during the course of an inpatient hospitalization or as the result of concerns raised during outpatient clinic visits or therapies. Because most young people with disabilities and chronic illnesses return to school, questions for the pediatric neuropsychologist are often raised by educators as well. Interactions with both rehabilitation and educational treatment teams allow a unique opportunity to support continuity of care across systems.

HISTORICAL PERSPECTIVE

Contributions to the assessment and understanding of brain–behavior relationships in children have come from many disciplines, including child clinical psychology, school psychology, adult neuropsychology, developmental psychology, cognitive psychology, neurolinguistics, special education, psychobiology, and neurology (Baron, 2004; Bigler, 1996). However, research on brain–behavior relationships in children has lagged behind such study in adults for several reasons. First, many clinicians have been influenced heavily by early evidence that "a young brain" offered protection against the negative effects of brain injury (Ryan, LaMarche, Barth, & Boll, 1996). This belief was driven by research that examined brain plasticity during development and found a remarkable potential for cerebral reorganization and recovery of function in the immature brain (e.g., Kennard, 1940). In addition, subsequent studies such as those of Bruce and colleagues (Bruce et al., 1979) suggested a relatively low mortality rate of children with serious neurological injury compared with adults. These studies provided important insights into the resilient aspects of the developing brain, but they did not capture the full scope of morbidity associated with childhood brain injury (Kolb, 2004; Taylor & Alden, 1997) and may have inadvertently discouraged examination of brain-based changes in child functioning.

A second reason that pediatric neuropsychology has developed more slowly is the lack of adequate measurement strategies for assessment of cognition in youth at varying stages of development. Early measures were often downward extensions of adult neuropsychological tests that were not normed by age and that did not capture key areas of vulnerability such as memory and learning (e.g., Halstead-Reitan Neuropsychological Battery for Children 9 to 14; Reitan & Davison, 1974). Finally, the complex relationship between brain structure and function was poorly understood in the normally developing brain, making it difficult to document changes associated with neurological insult during childhood and adolescence.

Several factors have worked synergistically to create contemporary patterns of growth in the field of pediatric neuropsychology. A growing number of studies began to document the link between neurologic aberrations and childhood disorders of learning and behavior (e.g., Rutter, Chadwick, Shaffer, & Brown, 1980). Neuropsychological batteries and related tests for children became more widely available in the 1970s and 1980s (e.g., Golden, 1986; Reitan & Davison, 1974), and better-standardized measures began to appear in the 1990s. At the same time, rapid developments in allied neuroscience fields produced new neurodiagnostic imaging techniques and advanced methodology for understanding microanatomical changes at the cellular level (Bigler, 1997). These refinements have led to greater knowledge about normal brain growth and development, more specific questions about developmental

pathology following brain injury, expansion of the instrumentation used by clinicians to assess neurodevelopmental functioning, and accumulating evidence of the impact of physical disease, injury, and congenital brain abnormalities on children's learning and behavioral adaptation (Baron, 2004; Farmer, Donders, & Warschausky, 2006; Wilde et al., 2005; Yeates, Ris, & Taylor, 2000). Furthermore, evidence of the potential to enhance brain development and recovery through enriching and supportive environments has fueled the growth of pediatric rehabilitation and educational interventions for children with neurological disorders (Farmer et al., 2006).

FUNDAMENTAL CONCEPTS IN PEDIATRIC REHABILITATION NEUROPSYCHOLOGY

Pediatric neuropsychologists in rehabilitation settings adhere to the basic premises of general neuropsychological assessment: Brain functioning and behavior are causally related, and cognitive or behavioral deficits resulting from cerebral damage can be identified and treated. However, three unique factors shape service provision by pediatric neuropsychologists in rehabilitation settings: (a) the importance of development as a determinant of brain–behavior relationships in children; (b) the emphasis in rehabilitation on treatment goals and functional outcomes, as opposed to diagnosis; and (c) the interdisciplinary team approach to assessment, including the family, school, and other personnel beyond the traditional rehabilitation treatment team.

The Role of Development

A fundamental concept in pediatric neuropsychology is that children are not simply small adults (Baron, 2004; Yeates et al., 2000). Instead, they have a developing central nervous system and a constantly changing level of skills. Behaviors that are normal and expected at one age level can be abnormal and unexpected at subsequent ages (e.g., falling on the floor in a temper tantrum is normal in a 2-year-old but is unusual in a 12-year-old). Furthermore, developmental milestones typically emerge unevenly, with substantial variability in rate of skills acquisition both within and across children.

Assessment of children with neurological impairments must take into account two parallel processes that influence behavior: normal maturational changes and adaptations associated with recovery from cerebral damage. The task of the child neuropsychologist is to tease out the impact of known or suspected cerebral injury on an already complex and changing system. This can be a daunting assignment for a number of reasons. The behavioral expression of brain injury in young people varies greatly, depending not only on the location and extent of neurologic damage but also on the age at injury. Like adults, children can show full or partial recovery of functioning after loss of ability due to neurological insults. However, children are unique because cerebral damage can also lead to delayed emergence of new skills or the failure of such skills to emerge at all. A child may exhibit generally age-appropriate functioning shortly after injury followed by the late onset of impairments as more mature abilities fail to develop. Although brain plasticity and the capacity for cerebral reorganization may be greater in children than adults, a growing body of literature documents that younger age at injury may be associated with poorer developmental outcomes (Kolb, 2004; Taylor & Alden, 1997; Thomson & Kerns, 2000). Early brain injury can exact a toll on new learning abilities and developing cognitive skills, which in turn interferes with subsequent maturation.

Other factors also make the process of child assessment challenging. For instance, test interpretation may be confounded by factors such as the lack of premorbid baseline data in young injured children; error variance due to children's easy fatigability, limited attention span, and motivational fluctuations; and the increased influence of social and environmental factors on rate of early development. Thus, maturational level is a central concept because it shapes the biological response to injury, the presenting problems, the methods of assessment, the interpretation of test performance, and treatment options.

The focus on treatment goals and functional outcomes. Neuropsychology as a field developed out of a tradition of diagnostic assessments aimed at localizing lesions and describing structure–function relationships. Tests were designed to accurately

measure central nervous system integrity and emphasized *neurological validity* (Taylor & Schatschneider, 1992). Pediatric neuropsychologists in rehabilitation settings may focus on diagnosis at times, such as when they are asked to determine whether a child's learning problems are related to his or her early history of brain injury. However, neuropsychological assessment in rehabilitation settings is primarily treatment-oriented (Johnstone & Farmer, 1997). That is, the ultimate purpose of assessment during rehabilitation is to determine ways to increase everyday functioning in real world settings. The assessment process must provide data that have *ecological validity,* or the ability to describe the child's capabilities, predict level of functioning in daily activities, and define a treatment plan (Sbordone & Long, 1996). Specific assessment goals during rehabilitation treatment may be to do the following:

- determine the child's cognitive, behavioral, social, and emotional competencies;
- document changes in functioning over time;
- indicate to what extent presenting problems are related to neurological dysfunction;
- make prescriptive statements regarding the child's ability to engage in daily activities;
- identify the types of intervention strategies that are most likely to be effective;
- help plan child-focused rehabilitation and/or educational programs;
- describe environmental and social factors that influence everyday functioning; and
- recommend interventions that optimize environmental and social supports.

Assessment that contributes to treatment planning involves more than interpretation of standardized tests. This approach requires ecological assessment of children and their families in a context of multiple systems or levels of influence (Farmer & Drewel, 2006; Fletcher, Levin, & Butler, 1995; Kazak, 1997; Teeter, 1997). Cognitive ability as measured by neuropsychological tests remains a central aspect of assessment and an important indicator of central nervous system integrity. However, as Taylor and Fletcher (1990) pointed out, impairments identified on such tests only estimate the upper limits of the child's basic behavioral competencies. The actual level of disability and handicap is more broadly determined over time by interactions between child characteristics and the social–environmental context. Because functional outcomes are multiply determined, both child and contextual variables must be assessed to identify a range of treatment options. Exhibit 19.1 depicts variables that influence treatment planning and child outcomes following neurological injury.

To illustrate, neuropsychological assessment of an 8-year-old girl with a history of myelomenigocele, hydrocephalus, and multiple ventriculoperitoneal shunt revisions may identify cognitive impairments in nonverbal processing and oral discourse as well as significant sensorimotor problems (Fletcher, Dennis, & Northrup, 2000; Warschausky, 2006). Without a doubt, this child needs specialized, child-focused interventions to maximize learning, social integration, and long-term level of independence. However, the extent of her disability may vary considerably depending on social and environmental circumstances, such as whether she lives with an uninsured single mother in an isolated rural town or with an insured, middle-class family in an area rich with medical, rehabilitation, and educational resources. Specific treatment recommendations by the neuropsychologist must take such circumstances in account.

The interdisciplinary team approach. A third principle shaping assessment strategies in rehabilitation settings is a philosophical commitment to teamwork and interdisciplinary collaboration. Children treated in rehabilitation typically have complex needs that extend beyond the expertise of any single discipline. Furthermore, cognitive assessments are conducted by several disciplines, including the neuropsychologist, the speech/language pathologist, the occupational therapist, and sometimes by an educational specialist. Poor communication among these specialists can result in extensive testing with either an incorrect or incomplete picture of the child's abilities, inadequate treatment goals, and less than optimal child outcomes (Ylvisaker, Chorazy, Feeny, & Russell, 1999). Coordinated team assessments are often more efficient and effective, resulting in treatment recommendations that are made on the

Exhibit 19.1
Factors Influencing Outcomes in Children With Neurological Disorders

Child characteristics
- Age at the time of neurologic injury
- Severity of injury
- Type and persistence of impairments
- Time since onset
- General health
- Premorbid functioning
- Postinjury adjustment

Family characteristics
- Socioeconomic status
- Family size and structure
- Level of education
- Cultural background
- Stage of family life cycle
- Premorbid functioning
- Postinjury adjustment
- Coping resources
- Social supports
- Other life stressors
- Advocacy skills

Community characteristics
- Educational services
- Teacher knowledge about neurologic injury
- Support from school administrators
- Availability of ancillary services
- Formal community support services
- Medical and rehabilitation services
- Mental health services
- Social services (i.e., housing, transportation, financial assistance)
- Vocational rehabilitation
- Support groups
- Interagency service coordination
- Public and private funding resources
- Informal support networks (e.g., relatives, friends, co-workers, church and service groups)
- Attitudes toward disability
- Public policy

Note. From *Handbook of Rehabilitation Psychology* (p. 382), edited by R. G. Frank and T. R. Elliott, 2000, Washington, DC: American Psychological Association. Copyright 2000 by the American Psychological Association.

basis of pooled expertise. Another aspect of this team model of service delivery is the importance of including input from family members, school personnel, and other community-based professionals in the assessment process. This greatly extends knowledge about the child's presenting problems, behaviors in real life settings, and the social–environmental context for treatment.

Professional Skills

The pediatric neuropsychologist requires a broad range of clinical knowledge and skills to function effectively in rehabilitation settings. The clinician must have a fund of knowledge about normal child development and brain maturation, understand common changes in child functioning associated with various neurological problems, identify strategies to measure factors that affect child outcomes, integrate multiple viewpoints about the child's abilities and concerns, help to plan treatment strategies, and communicate these plans to other professionals and family members (see Exhibit 19.2).

The skills needed to work in rehabilitation overlap considerably with those needed to practice child neuropsychology in other medical and educational settings. However, during rehabilitation, cognitive deficits are rarely the only concern. Children seen are often physically impaired because of illness, injury, or congenital motor dysfunction. Stressors such as hospitalization, pain, changes in medication, new onset of disability, disfigurement, and disruption of normal routines can tax the coping resources of even the most well-adjusted child and family. The following sections address assessment procedures and treatment considerations that are particularly applicable to children treated in rehabilitation settings.

Assessment procedures. An individualized, flexible approach to child neuropsychological assessment is needed during rehabilitation (Farmer,

---

Exhibit 19.2
Core Competencies for the Pediatric Neuropsychologist in Rehabilitation Settings

Assessment procedures
- Strategies for obtaining background information from parents, therapists, and educators.
- Selection and administration of children's standardized tests coordinated with other testing conducted by cognitive therapists or educators.
- Qualitative assessment strategies.
- Methods of test interpretation, including integration of neuropsychological results with other team members' assessments.

Communication skills
- Report writing, with inclusion of data needed for educational diagnosis and treatment.
- Feedback to child, family, and professionals.

Intervention skills for children with neurological disorders
- Cognitive, behavioral, and multisystem treatment strategies.
- Consultation with health and educational professionals.
- Interdisciplinary and interagency collaboration skills.
- Child and family advocacy.

Knowledge base
- Normal child development.
- Neuroanatomy of the developing brain.
- Neuroimaging techniques.
- The effect of neurological insults on brain development and behavior.
- Common cognitive and behavioral sequelae of childhood central nervous system disorders.
- Child and family coping with brain-based disorders.
- Educational policies and procedures and special education service delivery options.
- Other state agencies and local community resources for children and their families.
- Ethical and legal concerns (e.g., child abuse reporting).
- Disability mandates and concepts (e.g., inclusive education).

Note. From *Handbook of Rehabilitation Psychology* (p. 384), edited by R. G. Frank and T. R. Elliott, 2000, Washington, DC: American Psychological Association. Copyright 2000 by the American Psychological Association.

Clippard, Luehr-Wiemann, Wright, & Owings, 1997; Ylvisaker et al., 1999). The first step is to formulate an assessment plan based on the unique characteristics of the child. Important child variables to consider are age and general developmental level; the nature of the injury or illness, including time since onset and course; the presenting problems; the child's ability to participate in standardized testing (e.g., limited response modalities); the length of time the child will be available for testing (e.g., shortened by decreased child endurance or by plans for rapid discharge from an inpatient rehabilitation setting); recent testing by other therapists and educators; and whether the child needs to participate in serial assessments to track change. Valuable sources of such background information include medical and school records, the child, family members, teachers, and other rehabilitation specialists.

Test selection is the next step in assessment planning. Specified domains of functioning ranging from aspects of cognition to emotional and adaptive skills are often affected in children with known neurological disorders and must be evaluated. Within these domains, clinicians must select assessment instruments from a "menu" of tests available in each domain, taking into account child characteristics and utilizing as many standardized tests as possible (for sample menus, see Baron, 2004; D'Amato & Rothlisberg, 1997). Tests and subtests should be chosen with consideration given to level of orientation, attention, and fatigue, and to the specific question that must be answered to assist with rehabilitation goals. Tests that have historically met these needs in a rehabilitation setting include the Children's Orientation and Amnesia Test (COAT; Ewing-Cobbs, Levin, Fletcher, Miner, & Eisenberg, 1990), Expressive One-Word Picture Vocabulary Test-III (Gardner, 2000), and the Peabody Picture Vocabulary Test-III (Dunn & Dunn, 1997). These tests have been successful because of a combination of factors, including ease of administration, capability to be given bedside, results that easily translate into meaningful recommendations for the treatment.

The difficulty with this menu approach is that selected assessment tools are likely to be derived from many different reference groups. Therefore,

what may appear to be real differences in a child's performance might be due only to differences in normative groups from one test to another. One instrument that assesses multiple domains using one normative base is the Developmental Neuropsychological Assessment (NEPSY; Korkman, Kirk, & Kemp, 1997), based on the flexible model and diagnostic principles of Luria (Baron, 2004; Korkman, 1999). A recent revision made it even more useful for quantitative assessment in rehabilitation settings (NEPSY-II; Korkman, Kirk, & Kemp, 2007). The developmental model of NEPSY-II may provide the flexibility needed in rehabilitation settings to tailor the assessment to the child's needs, to be more effective in treatment planning, and to facilitate recommendations for teaching the child in a particular setting.

Both quantitative, standardized measures and qualitative clinical data contribute to a comprehensive assessment of child functioning during rehabilitation (Batchelor, 1996; Ylvisaker et al., 1990). Each approach has advantages and disadvantages. Standardized measures have the advantage of offering normative age-based comparisons, uniformity of procedure, and the ability to track performance over time. However, children seen in rehabilitation settings often have such significant cognitive and physical impairments that they cannot participate in standardized tests, and the results of these tests may overestimate or underestimate the functional skills of children, depending on their needs for support.

Qualitative or nonstandardized measures of child functioning continue to be particularly important during rehabilitation. Such assessments might be as simple as altering nonessential features on a standardized test (e.g., the response modality) so that a child with sensory or motor limitations can respond to its content or essential features (Sattler, 1992). However, most qualitative testing relies heavily on the examiner's knowledge about normal brain development and behavior and about common sequelae of specific neurological disorders. Given a broad fund of such knowledge, the examiner can formulate hypotheses about expected competencies at the child's developmental level and then devise diagnostic tasks to assess the child's ability to meet the expectations (see Ylvisaker, Hartwick, Ross, &

Nussbaum, 1994, for a listing of informal probes to use during cognitive assessments).

Using informal assessments, clinicians can examine the process or how a task is performed, as well as the product or what is achieved, in both controlled and real-life situations. In addition to noting basic skill levels, the examiner can observe the child's endurance and stamina, ability to initiate and sustain goal-directed behavior, rate of processing complex or lengthy material, retention and generalization of new learning, and awareness of deficits. Aspects of the learning environment can be manipulated to determine their effect on performance (e.g., length of training session, number of distracters). Data may be collected by directly observing the child and/or by consulting with other rehabilitation staff, family members, and teachers to obtain their observations. These informal assessments provide rich opportunities to identify functional deficits and/or effective use of compensatory strategies and thus have strong implications for treatment. Drawbacks to qualitative assessment include subjectivity and potential examiner bias that can interfere with the reliability and validity of results. Interdisciplinary team assessments may offset some of these drawbacks, as this practice draws on the observations of multiple professionals and may decrease the likelihood of error.

To illustrate this assessment approach using a case example, a neuropsychologist was asked to evaluate an 8-year-old inpatient boy following a pedestrian versus bicycle injury that resulted in severe diffuse axonal injury and a 4-week coma. Three weeks after admission to rehabilitation, at the time of consultation, the child had recovered many basic language skills and was dressing and feeding himself with setup and standby assist. He was still dependent in mobility because of right-side hemiparesis, and he had toileting accidents throughout the day that were without known medical cause. His parents were frustrated because they thought he was not trying hard enough to achieve toileting goals. They noted that he could tell them whether he needed to use the toilet when they asked. The nursing staff expressed concern that the child might simply be using toileting accidents to gain adult attention, as the family visited him infrequently during the course of his hospital stay.

Although the parents and nurses identified behavioral and psychosocial concerns, the neuropsychologist raised questions about attention, orientation, and general level of cognitive functioning at this early stage of recovery. Cognitive screening tests combined with observation and informal mental status testing (e.g., COAT; Ewing-Cobbs et al., 1990) revealed that the child showed a 10- to 15-minute attention span under highly structured conditions. In addition, he displayed marked impairments in orientation to place and time, memory functioning, oral word fluency, speed of processing, motor dexterity, planning and problem solving, and initiation. His strengths were in one-word receptive language, conversational speech, and visual perception. Interactions with therapists confirmed these observations across treatment settings.

The neuropsychologist provided feedback about the child's cognitive functioning to the parents and rehabilitation team. During the feedback session, the parents expressed distress over their child's slow rate of recovery, their uncertainty about how to help him, and their problems juggling the demands of work and their other children. In response, additional family supports were arranged through the team social worker. An orientation notebook was devised for the child by the rehabilitation team, and the parents were instructed in its use. Finally, the nursing staff was educated about this child's cognitive limits, and an externally structured toileting program was successfully implemented. Rehabilitation staff contacted school personnel to provide an update about this child's cognitive status and to discuss the need to meet closer to the time of discharge to design a school reentry plan. Thus, the assessment process led directly to multidimensional treatment strategies.

Treatment strategies. Young people with disabilities remain at greatly increased risk of poor educational and vocational outcomes (Donders, 2006; Farmer & Clippard, 1995; Hornby & Kidd, 2001; Taylor et al., 2003; Yeates & Taylor, 2006). They are much more likely to live with their parents, less likely to participate in postsecondary education, and have lower employment rates compared with nondisabled peers. Recent research has increased our understanding of these poor functional outcomes among children with acquired and congenital brain impairments, identifying persistent cognitive, emotional, and behavioral deficits (Ganesalingam, Sanson, Anderson, & Yeates, 2006; Yeates & Enrile, 2005; Yeates et al., 2005) and family factors that influence recovery (e.g., Swift et al., 2003; Wade et al., 2003; Yeates et al., 2004).

Assessment results should lead directly to formulations about how to improve the child's level of functioning and prevent secondary disability (e.g., school failure, maladaptive emotional and social adjustment). The goals of treatment will vary depending on the child's specific needs. However, as a guideline, Blosser and DePompei (1994) proposed that child treatment should be designed to achieve four major long-term outcomes: maximum participation in the learning process; development of independent living skills; competence in social skills needed for communication at home, school, and work; and development of vocational skills. To accomplish these broad objectives, the pediatric neuropsychologist may act as a consultant to rehabilitation and educational teams or may provide direct treatment interventions. Regardless of the exact treatment role, the clinician must be aware of a range of cognitive, behavioral, and systemic interventions to promote well-being in children with neurological impairments.

Cognitive interventions. There is a small, but growing, body of literature about the use of cognitive rehabilitation strategies with children (for reviews, see Butler, 2006; Ylvisaker et al., 2005; chap. 17, this volume). Ylvisaker, Szekeres, Hartwick, and Tworek (1994) identified six goals of cognitive rehabilitation in those with acute brain injuries including: (a) improving spontaneous recovery through general stimulation, (b) remediating impaired cognitive processes through direct retraining, (c) developing compensatory strategies for residual deficit areas, (d) devising environmental accommodations that promote adequate performance, (e) using instructional procedures that use cognitive strengths, and (f) increasing metacognitive awareness.

These goals reflect three broad approaches to cognitive rehabilitation (Mateer, Kerns, & Eso, 1997):

(a) remediation, (b) compensation, and (c) environmental supports. The first two approaches are child focused, whereas the third approach is externally focused.

Remediation involves interventions that attempt to restore or build the child's cognitive processing capabilities in areas of deficit. Although restorative techniques are often used to support spontaneous recovery immediately following acquired brain injury, such process-training approaches are not generally accepted for children with stable cognitive deficits (Reynolds & Fletcher-Janzen, 1997; Ylvisaker & Szekeres, 1998). Mental-muscle building strategies, such as rote memory drills, typically are not effective, and improvements do not generalize to functional applications of the skill.

There may be some exceptions to this rule. For example, Thomson and Kerns (2000) reported evidence of improved attentional abilities following a pediatric adaptation of Sohlberg and Mateer's (1989) Attention Process Training. In contrast, Light et al. (1996) did not find similar effects for an attention-training module in the Neurocognitive Reeducation Project, a comprehensive program for children with head injuries that provided remediation in attention, memory, behavior, and executive functioning. They did, however, identify significant improvements in children's overall functional skills. Research on cognitive remediation remains inconclusive. More data from methodologically sound intervention studies are needed to identify cognitive rehabilitation strategies that benefit children under various conditions.

Compensation, the second child-focused intervention, teaches the child strategies that increase performance on cognitively effortful tasks, without attempting to change the underlying cognitive deficit. For example, the child may be taught to use external aids (e.g., daily schedules, memory notebook, calculator), behavioral strategies (e.g., asking for clarification, using paraphrasing to improve memory and comprehension in social interactions), or metacognitive procedures (e.g., mental self-cuing about steps for problem solving, organizational procedures, mnemonic strategies). However, Ylvisaker and Szekeres (1998) noted that the dichotomy that has developed between restorative and compensatory approaches is unfortunate because both are generally necessary aspects of the cognitive rehabilitation process.

Finally, externally focused interventions can be used to improve the child's cognitive functioning (Mateer et al., 1997). These include modifying the environment (e.g., removing distractors, increasing the size of print for a child with visual deficits), changing others' expectations regarding the child's performance, and using specialized instructional strategies (e.g., Glang, Singer, Cooley, & Tish, 1992). This approach sets up procedures that use the child's cognitive strengths to achieve therapeutic goals (Reynolds & Fletcher-Janzen, 1997).

Neuropsychological assessments can be especially helpful in defining external supports for cognitive remediation. For example, an 11-year-old boy with severe burns to the face and arms and hypoxia due to inhalation injury was referred by the outpatient occupational therapist and physical therapist because of concerns over the child's memory problems during therapies. Neuropsychological screening revealed significant verbal memory and language processing problems but also identified generally intact nonverbal functioning. After sharing these findings with the therapists, the neuropsychologist helped the team develop a plan to reach rehabilitation goals by relying primarily on the child's visual processing strengths (e.g., through visual cuing, pictorial directions, and modeling of new skills). The child's participation and cooperation in therapies improved, as did his learning and level of independence.

For these interventions to be effective for the individual, and for maintenance over time, those involved in the rehabilitation process must take an approach that involves many facets (Ylvisaker & Szekeres, 1998). These include (a) taking into account the typical progressions in cognitive development; (b) assisting in the child's recovery of previously learned information as well as in acquiring new information; (c) using a balance between restorative, compensatory, and environmental structuring approaches; (d) supporting generalization to everyday activities; (e) providing services in a meaningful environments to support adaptive functioning; (f) providing an initial high level of support with gradual reduction as the child demonstrates success; and (g) ensuring that adults (e.g., teachers, parents) appreciate the connection between cognitive impairments and behavior problems.

Behavioral interventions. Children with brain-based disorders are at increased risk of both cognitive and behavioral problems, including internalizing and externalizing problems and decreased social competence (Butler, Rourke, Fuerst, & Fisk, 1997; Fletcher et al., 1995; Horton, 1997). Pediatric neuropsychologists in rehabilitation settings must be keenly aware of the association between cognition and behavioral concerns, as there will be opportunities to recommend behavioral treatments for children referred for cognitive concerns and cognitive treatments for those referred for behavioral problems. Children with neurological impairments are often seen as noncompliant or unmotivated when, in fact, their cognitive deficits interfere with task completion or work production. Cognitive problems may be underestimated, especially when basic language abilities are intact, or executive functioning problems may interfere with the child's ability to access intact abilities. Cognitive interventions can improve behavioral problems. For instance, Glang et al. (1992) demonstrated that teaching a child with brain injury a metacognitive problem-solving strategy increased frustration tolerance and on-task behavior during math instruction and generalized to other instructional periods.

In other cases, the rehabilitation staff may assume that the behavioral problems of a child with severe cognitive impairments cannot be treated. For example, a 5-year-old boy with a genetic syndrome that caused severe growth delays and mental retardation was admitted to rehabilitation after physical abuse by his mother. The youngster was so inattentive and overactive that it was difficult for therapists to assess his level of functioning, even during one-to-one interactions in quiet settings. The neuropsychologist recognized that this level of hyperactivity was not typical for children at his estimated level of cognitive functioning, pharmacological treatment was instituted, and the child's behavior and ability to interact with others improved substantially.

Ylvisaker and colleagues (2005) reviewed the last 2 decades of rehabilitation research in pediatric traumatic brain injury. Among other findings, these authors advocated for comprehensive intervention programs and found that the use of positive behavioral supports may be more effective than traditional applied behavior analysis. Whereas traditional applied behavior analysis targets specific behaviors via specific consequences or rewards, positive behavioral supports focus on the modifying the context and setting to achieve the desired behavioral outcome. These interventions were found to be effective in supporting and maintaining improvements across settings.

Systemic interventions. Outcomes for children with neurological impairments are multiply determined, and the pediatric neuropsychologist is often in the unique position of consulting with others in many systems that influence child outcomes. Therefore, treatment recommendations should be considered in the following domains: medical (e.g., review of pharmacological treatment), rehabilitation (e.g., cognitive–behavioral treatments to be implemented by the rehabilitation staff), education (e.g., goals and interventions for academic programming), family (e.g., information about ways to manage behavioral problems), and community (e.g., referrals for additional services from public agencies). These can be communicated either directly through face-to-face feedback and team meetings, or indirectly through a written report.

An example of a systemic intervention occurs when a child transitions from the rehabilitation hospital to school following a moderate to severe brain injury. This time of transition is a prime opportunity for the pediatric neuropsychologist and other rehabilitation team members to provide information to educators about the child's strengths and needs, as well as to work with representatives from the school to devise optimal strategies for school reentry. Protocols have been developed to aid communication across the rehabilitation and educational systems (e.g., Ylvisaker & Feeney, 1998).

Despite the strong rationale for exchange of information, there are substantial barriers to interdisciplinary and interagency interactions. Team members often lack a common vocabulary and a unified conceptual framework for evaluation and planning. Schedules must be coordinated and time set aside for collaboration. Professional turf issues may impede interactions. Such barriers must be addressed systematically if a team is to become truly efficient and effective. Improvements in team functioning involve adopting a philosophy of collaboration, increasing awareness and appreciation of other members' knowledge and roles, improving communication through decreased use of professional jargon, structuring time for interactions, and engaging in joint problem solving efforts (DePompei & Blosser, 1993; Holland, Hogg, & Farmer, 1997). It is particularly important to include family members in team planning efforts, as they often provide continuity for the child across settings and systems of care.

Recently, researchers have recognized the impact of family functioning on child outcomes following neurological insults and have turned their attention to family-level interventions (Farmer & Drewel, 2006; Naar-King & Donders, 2006; Wade, 2006). In a series of studies that examined a family-level problem-solving intervention, Wade, Michaud, and Brown (2006) found that children in the treatment group showed more improvement in numerous behavioral symptoms than those in the untreated group.

SUMMARY AND FUTURE DIRECTIONS

Pediatric neuropsychological assessment in rehabilitation settings must be developmentally sensitive, treatment-oriented, and integrated into the continuum of interdisciplinary and interagency services for children with neurodevelopmental disorders. Its conceptual roots are in the understanding of brain–behavior relationships in children, but its branches have extended into applications of that knowledge to treatments involving the child, the rehabilitation team, the family, the school, and the community. This type of assessment is designed not only to diagnose brain-based disorders but also to produce a positive change in the child's level of functioning and to prevent secondary disability.

However, the need for additional research remains acute. Efforts must continue to develop and test psychometrically sound and ecologically valid measures of children's cognitive and behavioral functioning, particularly for children who are young, multiply handicapped, or in the early stages of recovery from brain insult. Studies must continue to investigate methods of increasing understanding of patterns of behavior in real-world settings that result from specific types of brain injury and identifying biologically based prognostic indicators for long-term outcome. Others must focus more on treatment of the outward manifestations of neurological impairments, carefully defining how best to individualize treatment strategies and support caregivers. Research methodology challenges, including heterogeneity within similar disorders, small sample sizes, nonrepresentative samples, and difficulties establishing an appropriate control group, must be overcome (see Taylor & Fletcher, 1995).

In parallel to these efforts, models of service delivery must be created and evaluated to ensure that they are efficient, cost-effective, and family centered. National efforts have attempted to increase the numbers of children who receive rehabilitation services after acute hospitalization (Christopher, 1997) and to integrate rehabilitation and education services using blended funding from public and private sources (Savage, 1997). However, progress toward adequate service delivery in school settings for many children with rehabilitation needs has been slow (e.g., Hibbard, Martin, Cantor, & Moran, 2006). Pediatric neuropsychologists must be aware of such trends so they can encourage and participate in a continuum of care for children with neurological disorders and advocate for treatment and service delivery strategies that improve long-term outcomes.

References

Baron, I. S. (2004). *Neuropsychological evaluation of the child.* New York: Oxford University Press.

Batchelor, E. S. (1996). Neuropsychological assessment of children. In E. S. Batchelor & R. S. Dean (Eds.), *Pediatric neuropsychology: Interfacing assessment and treatment for rehabilitation* (pp. 9–26). Boston: Allyn & Bacon.

Bigler, E. D. (1996). Bridging the gap between psychology and neurology: Future trends in pediatric neuropsychology. In E. S. Batchelor & R. S. Dean (Eds.), *Pediatric neuropsychology: Interfacing assessment and treatment for rehabilitation* (pp. 27–54). Boston: Allyn & Bacon.

Bigler, E. D. (1997). Brain imaging and behavioral outcome in traumatic brain injury. In E. D. Bigler, E. Clark, & J. E. Farmer (Eds.), *Childhood traumatic brain injury* (pp. 7–29). Austin, TX: PRO-ED.

Blosser, J., & DePompei, R. (1994). *Pediatric traumatic brain injury: Proactive intervention.* San Diego, CA: Singular Publishing Group.

Bruce, D. A., Raphaely, R. C., Goldberg, A. I., Zimmerman, R. A., Bilaniuk, L. T., Schut, L., & Kuhl, D. E. (1979). Pathophysiology, treatment, and outcome following severe head injury in children. *Child's Brain, 2,* 174–191.

Butler, K., Rourke, B. P., Fuerst, D. R., & Fisk, J. L. (1997). A typology of psychosocial functioning in pediatric closed-head injury. *Child Neuropsychology, 3,* 98–133.

Butler, R. W. (2006). Cognitive and behavioral rehabilitation. In J. E. Farmer, J. Donders, & S. Warschausky (Eds.), *Treating neurodevelopmental disabilities* (pp. 186–207). New York: Guilford Press.

Christopher, R. P. (1997). Emergency medical services for children: Early referral to physical medicine and rehabilitation. *Archives of Physical Medicine and Rehabilitation, 78,* 339.

D'Amato, R. C., & Rothlisberg, B. A. (1997). How education should respond to students with traumatic brain injury. In E. D. Bigler, E. Clark, & J. E. Farmer (Eds.), *Childhood traumatic brain injury* (pp. 213–237). Austin, TX: PRO-ED.

DePompei, R., & Blosser, J. L. (1993). Professional training and development for pediatric rehabilitation. In C. J. Durgin, M. D. Schmidt, & L. J. Fryer (Eds.), *Staff development and clinical intervention in brain injury rehabilitation* (pp. 229–253). Gaithersburg, MD: Aspen Publishers.

Donders, J. (2006). Traumatic brain injury. In J. E. Farmer, J. Donders, & S. Warschausky (Eds.), Treating neurodevelopmental disabilities (pp. 23–41). New York: Guilford Press.

Dunn, L. M., & Dunn, L. M. (1997). *Examiner's manual for the Peabody Picture Vocabulary Test* (3rd ed.). Circle Pines, MN: American Guidance Service.

Ewing-Cobbs, L., Levin, H. S., Fletcher, J. M., Miner, M. E., & Eisenberg, H. M. (1990). The Children's Orientation and Amnesia Test: Relationship to severity of acute head injury and to recovery of memory. *Neurosurgery, 27,* 683–691.

Farmer, J. E., & Clippard, D. S. (1995). Educational outcomes in children with disabilities: Linking hospitals and schools. *NeuroRehabilitation, 5,* 49–56.

Farmer, J. E., Clippard, D. S., Luehr-Wiemann, Y., Wright, E., & Owings, S. (1997). Assessing children with traumatic brain injury during rehabilitation: Promoting school and community reentry. In E. D. Bigler, E. Clarke, & J. E. Farmer (Eds.), *Childhood traumatic brain injury* (pp. 33–61). Austin, TX: PRO-ED.

Farmer, J. E., & Deidrick, K. K. (2006). Introduction to childhood disability. In J. E. Farmer, J. Donders, & S. Warschausky (Eds.), *Treating neurodevelopmental disabilities* (pp. 3–20). New York: Guilford Press.

Farmer, J. E., Donders, J., & Warschausky, S. (Eds.). (2006). *Treating neurodevelopmental disabilities.* New York: Guilford Press.

Farmer, J. E., & Drewel, E. (2006). Systems intervention for comprehensive care. In J. E. Farmer, J. Donders, & S. Warschausky (Eds.), *Treating neurodevelopmental disabilities* (pp. 269–288). New York: Guilford Press.

Fletcher, J. M., Dennis, M., & Northrup, H. (2000). Hydrocephalus. In K. M. Yeates, M. D. Ris, & H. G. Taylor (Eds.), *Pediatric neuropsychology: Research, theory, and practice* (pp. 25–46). New York: Guilford Press.

Fletcher, J. M., Levin, H. S., & Butler, I. J. (1995). Neurobehavioral effects of brain injury in children: Hydrocephalus, traumatic brain injury, and cerebral palsy. In M. C. Roberts (Ed.), *Handbook of pediatric psychology* (2nd ed., pp. 362–383). New York: Guilford Press.

Ganesalingam, K., Sanson, A., Anderson, V., & Yeates, K. O. (2006). Self-regulation and social and behavioral functioning following childhood traumatic brain injury. *Journal of the International Neuropsychological Society, 12,* 609–621.

Gardner, M. F. (2000). *Expressive One-Word Picture Vocabulary Test—2000 Edition.* Novato, CA: Academic Therapy Publications.

Glang, A., Singer, G., Cooley, E., & Tish, N. (1992). Tailoring direct instruction techniques for use with elementary students with brain injury. *Journal of Head Trauma Rehabilitation, 7,* 93–108.

Golden, C. J. (1986). *Manual for the Luria-Nebraska Neuropsychological Battery: Children's revision.* Los Angeles: Western Psychological Services.

Hibbard, M. R., Martin, T., Cantor, J., & Moran, A. I. (2006). Students with acquired brain injury: Identification, accommodations, and transactions in the schools. In J. E. Farmer, J. Donders, & S. Warschausky (Eds.), *Treating neurodevelopmental disabilities* (pp. 208–233). New York: Guilford Press.

Holland, D. C., Hogg, J. R., & Farmer, J. E. (1997). Fostering effective team communication: Developing community standards within interdisciplinary cognitive rehabilitation settings. *NeuroRehabilitation, 8,* 21–29.

Hornby, G., & Kidd, R. (2001). Transfer from special to mainstream: Ten years later. *British Journal of Special Education, 28*(1), 10–17.

Horton, A. M. (1997). Child behavioral neuropsychology: Update and further considerations. In C. R. Reynolds & E. Fletcher-Janzen (Eds.), *Handbook of clinical child neuropsychology* (2nd ed., pp. 651–662). New York: Plenum Press.

Johnstone, B., & Farmer, J. E. (1997). Preparing neuropsychologists for the future: The need for additional training guidelines. *Archives of Clinical Neuropsychology, 12,* 523–530.

Kazak, A. E. (1997). A contextual family/systems approach to pediatric psychology: Introduction to the special issue. *Journal of Pediatric Psychology, 22,* 141–148.

Kennard, M. A. (1940). Relation of age to motor impairment in man and in subhuman primates. *Archives of Neurology and Psychiatry, 44,* 377–397.

Kolb, B. (2004). Mechanisms of cortical plasticity after neuronal injury. In J. Ponsford (Ed.), *Cognitive and behavioral rehabilitation: From neurobiology to clinical practices* (pp. 30–58). New York: Guilford Press.

Korkman, M. (1999). Applying Luria's diagnostic principles in the neuropsychological assessment of children. *Neuropsychology Review, 9,* 89–105.

Korkman, M., Kirk, U., & Kemp, S. (1997). *NEPSY Developmental Neuropsychological Assessment.* San Antonio, TX: Psychological Corporation.

Korkman, M., Kirk, U., & Kemp, S. (2007). *NEPSY: Developmental Neuropsychological Assessment* (2nd ed.). San Antonio, TX: Psychological Corporation.

Light, R., Satz, P., Asarnow, R. F., Lewis, R., Ribbler, A., & Neumann, E. (1996). Disorders of attention. In E. S. Batchelor & R. S. Dean (Eds.), *Pediatric neuropsychology: Interfacing assessment and treatment for rehabilitation* (pp. 269–302). Boston: Allyn & Bacon.

Mateer, C. A., Kerns, K. A., & Eso, K. L. (1997). Management of attention and memory disorders following traumatic brain injury. In E. D. Bigler, E. Clark, & J. E. Farmer (Eds.), *Childhood traumatic brain injury* (pp. 153–175). Austin, TX: PRO-ED.

Naar-King, S., & Donders, J. (2006). Pediatric family-centered rehabilitation. In J. E. Farmer, J. Donders, & S. Warschausky (Eds.), *Treating neurodevelopmental disabilities* (pp. 149–169). New York: Guilford Press.

Reitan, R. M., & Davison, L. A. (Eds.). (1974). *Clinical neuropsychology: Current status and applications.* Washington, DC: Winston.

Reynolds, C. R., & Fletcher-Janzen, E. (Eds.). (1997). *Handbook of clinical child neuropsychology* (2nd ed.). New York: Plenum Press.

Rutter, M., Chadwick, O., Shaffer, D., & Brown, C. (1980). A prospective study of children with head injuries. I: Description and methods. *Psychological Medicine, 10,* 633–645.

Ryan, T. B., LaMarche, J. A., Barth, J. T., & Boll, T. J. (1996). Neuropsychological consequences in treatment of pediatric head trauma. In E. S. Batchelor &

R. S. Dean (Eds.), *Pediatric neuropsychology: Interfacing assessment and treatment for rehabilitation,* (pp. 117–138). Boston: Allyn & Bacon.

Sattler, J. M. (1992). *Assessment of children* (3rd ed., rev.). San Diego, CA: Sattler.

Savage, R. C. (1997). Integrating rehabilitation and education services for school-age children with brain injuries. *Journal of Head Trauma Rehabilitation, 12*(2), 11–20.

Sbordone, R. J., & Long, C. (Eds.). (1996). *Ecological validity of neuropsychological testing.* Delray Beach, FL: St. Lucie Press.

Sohlberg, M. M., & Mateer, C. A. (1989). *Introduction to cognitive rehabilitation: Theory and practice.* London: Guilford Press.

Swift, E. E., Taylor, H. G., Kaugars, A. S., Drotar, D., Yeates, K. O., Wade, S. L., & Stancin, T. (2003). Sibling relationship and behavior after pediatric traumatic brain injury. *Journal of Developmental and Behavioral Pediatrics, 24(1),* 24–31.

Taylor, H. G., & Alden, J. (1997). Age-related differences in outcomes following childhood brain insults: An introduction and overview. *Journal of the International Neuropsychological Society, 3,* 555–567.

Taylor, H. G., & Fletcher, J. M. (1990). Neuropsychological assessment of children. In. M. Hersen & G. Goldstein (Eds.), *Handbook of psychological assessment* (2nd ed., pp. 228–255). New York: Plenum Press.

Taylor, H. G., & Fletcher, J. M. (1995). Editorial: Progress in pediatric neuropsychology. *Journal of Pediatric Psychology, 20,* 695–701.

Taylor, H. G., & Schatschneider, C. (1992). Child neuropsychological assessment: A test of basic assumptions. *The Clinical Neuropsychologist, 6,* 259–275.

Taylor, H. G., Yeates, K. O., Wade, S. L., Drotar, D., Stancin, T., & Montpetite, M. (2003). Long-term educational interventions after traumatic brain injury in children. *Rehabilitation Psychology, 48,* 227–236.

Teeter, P. A. (1997). Neurocognitive interventions for childhood and adolescent disorders: A transactional model. In C. R. Reynolds & E. Fletcher-Janzen (Eds.), *Handbook of clinical child neuropsychology* (2nd ed., pp. 387–417). New York: Plenum Press.

Thomson, J. B., & Kerns, K. A. (2000). Cognitive rehabilitation of the child with mild traumatic brain injury. In S. Raskin & C. Mateer (Eds.), *Neuropsychological management of mild traumatic brain injury.* New York: Oxford University Press.

Wade, S. L. (2006). Intervention to support families of children with traumatic brain injuries. In J. Farmer, J. Donders, & S. Warschausky (Eds.), *Treating neurodevelopmental disabilities* (pp. 170–185). New York: Guilford Press.

Wade, S. L., Michaud, L. M., & Brown, T. M. (2006). Putting the pieces together: Family intervention to improve child outcomes following traumatic brain injury (TBI). *Journal of Head Trauma Rehabilitation, 21,* 57–67.

Wade, S. L., Taylor, H. G., Drotar, D., Stancin, T., Yeates, K. O., & Minich, N. M. (2003). Parent-adolescent interactions after traumatic brain injury: Their relationship to family adaptation and adolescent adjustment. *Journal of Head Trauma Rehabilitation, 18,* 164–76.

Wallander, J. L., & Thompson, R. J. (1995). Psychosocial adjustment of children with chronic physical conditions. In M. C. Roberts (Ed.), *Handbook of pediatric psychology* (2nd ed., pp. 124–141). New York: Guilford Press.

Warschausky, S. (2006). Physical impairments and disability. In J. E. Farmer, J. Donders, & S. Warschausky (Eds.), *Treating neurodevelopmental disabilities* (pp. 81–97). New York: Guilford Press.

Wilde, E. A., Hunter, J. V., Newsome, M. R., Scheibel, R. S., Bigler, E. D., Johnson, J. L., et al. (2005). Frontal and temporal morphometric findings on MRI in children after moderate to severe traumatic brain injury. *Journal of Neurotrauma, 22,* 333–344.

Yeates, K. O., Armstrong, K., Janusz, J., Taylor, H. G., Wade, S., Stancin, T., & Drotar, D. (2005). Long-term attention problems in children with traumatic brain injury. *Journal of the American Academy of Child & Adolescent Psychiatry, 44,* 574–584.

Yeates, K. O., & Enrile, B. (2005). Implicit and explicit memory in children with congenital and acquired brain disorder. *Neuropsychology, 19,* 618–628.

Yeates, K. O., Ris, D., & Taylor, H. G. (Eds.). (2000). *Pediatric neuropsychology: Research, theory, and practice.* New York: Guilford Press.

Yeates, K. O., Swift, E., Taylor, H. G., Wade, S., Drotar, D., Stancin, T., & Minich, N. (2004). Short- and long-term social outcomes following pediatric traumatic brain injury. *Journal of the International Neuropsychological Society, 10,* 412–426.

Yeates, K. O., & Taylor, H. G. (2006). Behavior problems in school and their educational correlates among children with traumatic brain injury. *Exceptionality, 14,* 141–154.

Ylvisaker, M., Adelson, P. D., Braga, L. W., Burnett, S. M., Glang, A., Feeney, T., et al. (2005). Rehabilitation and ongoing support after pediatric TBI: 20 years of progress. *Journal of Head Trauma Rehabilitation, 20,* 95–109.

Ylvisaker, M., Chorazy, A. J. L., Cohen, S. B., Mastrilli, J. P., Molitor, C. B., Nelson, J., et al. (1990). Rehabilitative assessment following head injury in children.

In M. Rosenthal, E. R. Griffith, M. R. Bond, & J. D. Miller (Eds.), *Rehabilitation of the adult and child with traumatic brain injury* (2nd ed., pp. 558–592). Philadelphia: F. A. Davis.

Ylvisaker, M., Chorazy, A. J. L., Feeny, T. J., & Russell, M. L. (1999). Traumatic brain injury in children and adolescents: Assessment and rehabilitation. In M. Rosenthal, E. R. Griffith, J. S. Kreutzer, & B. Pentland (Eds.), *Rehabilitation of the adult and child with traumatic brain injury* (pp. 356–392). Philadelphia: F. A. Davis.

Ylvisaker, M., & Feeney, T. (1998). School reentry after traumatic brain injury. In M. Ylvisaker (Ed.), *Traumatic brain injury rehabilitation: Children and adolescents* (pp. 369–387). Boston: Butterworth-Heineman.

Ylvisaker, M., Hartwick, P., Ross, B., & Nussbaum, N. (1994). Cognitive assessment. In R. C. Savage & G. F. Wolcott (Eds.), *Educational dimensions of acquired brain injury* (pp. 69–119). Austin, TX: PRO-ED.

Ylvisaker, M., & Szekeres, S. F. (1998). A framework for cognitive rehabilitation. In M. Ylvisaker (Ed.), *Traumatic brain injury rehabilitation* (pp. 125–158). Newton, MA: Butterworth-Heineman.

Ylvisaker, M., Szekeres, S. F., Hartwick, P., & Tworek, P. (1994). Cognitive intervention. In R. C. Savage & G. F. Wolcott (Eds.), *Educational dimensions of acquired brain injury* (pp. 121–184). Austin, TX: PRO-ED.

Chapter 20

NEURODEVELOPMENTAL CONDITIONS IN CHILDREN

Seth Warschausky and Jacqueline Kaufman

Children with neurodevelopmental conditions (NDCs) have congenital or acquired central nervous system abnormalities that can affect cognitive, behavioral, and motoric development. As Farmer and Deidrick (2006) noted in a recent superb review, this is a heterogeneous set of conditions that can be categorized in a number of ways, including the nature of the pathophysiology, functional status, and program eligibility. The pediatric rehabilitation psychologist specializes in serving populations with both cognitive and motoric impairments. This includes children with cerebral palsy (CP), the most common type of childhood physical disability, and children with spina bifida (SB). This chapter largely draws on research with these two populations of children with congenital NDCs.

Other NDCs commonly encountered in pediatric rehabilitation psychology settings include sensory impairments, communicative disorders, and neuropathological conditions such as epilepsy, brain tumors, and hydrocephalus. Although they are not typical target populations in rehabilitation psychology settings, the pediatric rehabilitation psychologist must have expertise in common NDCs such as mental retardation, attention-deficit/hyperactivity disorder, learning disabilities, and autism. These latter conditions are not unusual comorbidities to many of the typical target populations seen in rehabilitation psychology settings.

As described by Harper and Peterson (2000) in the previous edition of this handbook, the psycho-social development of children with NDCs is affected by a multitude of factors that include the nature of the child's condition and impairments; socio-environmental factors, such as family functioning and parenting; socioeconomic status; and physical and attitudinal barriers to participation. Initial research with these populations focused largely on characterizing the nature of the children's impairments. Recent multifactorial work has focused on moderating and mediating effects on the relations between disability and psychosocial outcomes by using developmental–biosocial frameworks (Harper, 1997) that recognize the changing nature of disability throughout the life span. This chapter begins with a description of neurocognitive risks associated with congenital NDCs commonly seen in pediatric rehabilitation psychology, continues with comments on factors associated with psychological and social development and risks, and concludes with a discussion of the importance of community participation.

NEUROCOGNITIVE RISKS

The neurocognitive risks associated with congenital NDCs are complex, given the significant neurological heterogeneities both across and within conditions. The underlying etiologies are quite varied, and the phenotypic presentation can range from severe impairment to minimally detectable deficits. Nevertheless, CP and SB, as two of the most frequently encountered congenital NDCs in rehabilitation

Completion of this chapter was supported by U.S. Department of Education, Office of Special Education Programs (OSEP) Model Demonstration Project (H234M020077), and National Institutes of Health (1 R21 HD052592-01A1) awards to Seth Warschausky.

psychology, involve white matter tract abnormalities including risk of general projection fiber and specific corpus callosal neuropathologies associated with risk of impairments in visual perception, attention, and executive functions. There is a paucity of research on the neuropsychology of the CPs but a significant literature that focuses on specific types of SB.

There is high risk of mental retardation in children with CP, ranging from 30% to 77%, with children with hemiplegic or diplegic conditions having better cognitive outcomes (Warschausky, 2006). What is largely unknown is the degree to which limits to educational access and assumption of low cognitive status negatively affect cognitive development in this population. Much of the information regarding specific neuropsychological risks associated with CP comes from studies of individuals with periventricular leukomalacia (PVL), a frequent preterm injury that can result in CP, particularly the spastic types. Extent of PVL and parenchymal abnormalities has been associated with degree of motoric and cognitive impairment (Serdaroglu et al., 2004). PVL is associated with risk of visuoperceptual and navigational impairments (Ito et al., 1996; Pavlova, Sokolov, & Krageloh-Mann, 2006), though the impact of oculomotor control and/or vision loss on visuoperceptual test performance is not known. High functioning children with bilateral spastic CP were also shown to have impaired inhibitory control and processing speed (Christ, White, Brunstrom, & Abrams, 2003).

With regard to the acquisition of academic skills, there is some concern that the associations between phonological processing and reading acquisition may be different in children with CP versus typically developing children, but there is no strong empirical evidence to date (Sandberg, 2006). Acquisition of mathematics skills appears to include early risk of difficulty learning to perceive small numerosities or the ability to accurately count a small number of items (Arp, Taranne, & Fagard, 2006).

Of the neural tube defects, including the SBs and types of cephalocaudal dysgenesis, the rehabilitation psychologist is most likely to see children with myelomeningocele (MM). This form of SB carries significant risk of various orthopedic abnormalities as well as high risks of hydrocephalus, Chiari malformations, and other brain abnormalities (Del

Bigio, 1993). The presence of hydrocephalus in MM is a strong predictor of cognitive impairment (Iddon, Morgan, Loveday, Sahakian, & Pickard, 2004), as is higher level lesion (Shaffer, Friedrich, Shurtleff, & Wolf, 1985). Overall IQ scores tend to fall in the average to borderline range (Mirzai, Ersahin, Mutluer, & Kayahan, 1998) and have increased over past decades with improvements in shunting. There is a risk in this population of impairments in visuoperceptual functions (Donders, Rourke, & Canady, 1991). Fletcher, Francis, Thompson, Davidson, and Miner (1992) found that perceptual skill deficits were more evident in children with hydrocephalic MM as opposed to nonhydrocephalic MM. In the language domain, although children with MM typically develop adequate form and content of language, there is risk of "cocktail chatter" and difficulties with pragmatic aspects of speech (Fletcher, Barnes, & Dennis, 2002).

Studies of academic skill development suggest that children with SB with hydrocephalus are at an increased risk of impairments in arithmetic, though incidence figures are not known (Barnes et al., 2006). There is also evidence of reading comprehension deficiencies and writing deficiencies in the presence of relatively better word decoding skills (Barnes, Dennis, & Hetherington, 2004). The presence of increased risk of deficits in multiple academic domains underscores the importance of neuropsychological management of children with this condition at the first indication of academic delays. Although school personnel typically are somewhat familiar with language-associated dyslexias, they tend to be less familiar with visuoperceptual and visuospatial deficits and executive dysfunction, For example, there is no special education categorization for a nonverbal learning disorder. It can be particularly helpful in school planning to provide education regarding the nature of a student's difficulties in these domains as well as recommendations regarding organizational strategies. Webbing or mapping strategies, for example, used in note taking and organization of writing, may be particularly difficult for students with impairments in the nonverbal domains; traditional outlining strategies, with emphasis on sequential steps, can be more productive.

Clearly, there are significant risks for cognitive impairments in these populations. The terrible irony of pediatric neuropsychological assessment, however, is that many of the traditional instruments are not accessible to children with significant communicative, sensory, or motoric impairments. Most pediatric neuropsychological studies exclude participants who cannot be administered traditional measures. There have been efforts to create accessible assessments. For example, Sabbadini, Bonanni, Carlesimo, and Caltagirone (2001) provided participants with three response option methods to participate in modified traditional testing, including multiple-choice, dichotomous yes/no responses, and sensor pointer techniques. To date, however, it is not known whether such modifications alter the construct validity of those instruments. It falls to rehabilitation neuropsychologists to highlight the need to address these issues in the laboratory, clinic, and school settings, given the general mission of improving the lives of those with disabilities.

PSYCHOSOCIAL RISKS

Children with congenital NDCs are at risk of psychological and behavioral difficulties, but surprisingly few studies examine psychopathology per se. Symptoms, such as pain, associated with the child's physical condition have been shown to predict depression and lower health-related quality of life. Some findings suggest that specific acquired conditions, such as stroke and traumatic brain injury and congenital conditions with milder cognitive comorbidities, entail greater long-term risk of depression than more severe congenital conditions (McDermott et al., 2005). At this point it is not clear to what extent these findings stem from differences in the experience of loss, social experience, self-awareness, neuropathology, and other factors.

There is some evidence that self-worth in children and young adults with physical impairments may be associated with age, that is, with lower self-worth in older children and young adults. Ability to walk has not been linked with sense of self-worth in children; rather, a key correlate is perceived social support from parents and close friends. Varni and colleagues (2005) recently showed that approximately 50% of children with CP can provide self-report regarding health-related quality of life. Parent–child concor-

dance was lowest for emotional functioning. These findings highlight the importance of obtaining multi-informant ratings of the child's psychological status. Although there is no evidence that low self-concept is a pervasive problem among children with NDCs who have significant physical impairments, some evidence suggests increased risk among adolescent females with disabilities in general and specifically those with CP (Antle, 2004; Shields, Murdoch, Loy, Dodd, & Taylor, 2006).

RISKS OF ABUSE

The rehabilitation psychologist must be attentive to the risks of abuse and neglect in children with disabilities. The extent of maltreatment of children with disabilities is not definitively known, although an epidemiological study in the United States in 2000 reported that children with disabilities are 3.4 times more likely to be maltreated than typically developing children (Sullivan & Knutson, 2000). Children with disabilities have many barriers to reporting maltreatment, including but not limited to communication deficits, dependence on a caregiver who may abuse or neglect (e.g., disclosure may mean loss of known caregiver), intellectual deficits that may preclude awareness of maltreatment, and lack of access to other individuals necessary for reporting maltreatment (e.g., isolation due to disability). Maltreatment can take many forms, including neglect. In a study of children with extremely low birth weight referred to child protective services for suspected maltreatment, neglect was the most frequent type of maltreatment observed. The authors suggested possible cognitive consequences in a population that is already at considerable risk of cognitive deficits (Strathearn, Gray, & Wood, 2001). Parents with a pattern of maltreatment are less likely to take their child for medical or mental health care, thus reducing the opportunity for intervention (Jonson-Reid, Drake, Kim, Porterfield, & Han, 2004).

All children require sexual education training related to protection of self, and this may be overlooked in children with disabilities and cognitive impairments. Adolescents in particular require developmental sexual education training that may need to be provided in an alternative and accessible manner if their condition includes significant cognitive, sensory, and/or physical impairments. Of note, schools typically do not have access to adapted sexuality education materials. This places children at additional risk of both sexual abuse and uninformed sexual decision-making because of lack of instruction about sexual contact.

ACCESSIBLE PSYCHOLOGICAL TREATMENT

The strong emphasis on empirically supported psychological interventions has led to a bourgeoning outcome study literature; however, given the complexity of the treatment–condition–person matrix, it is unlikely that treatments will be entirely grounded in empirical findings. This can create dilemmas for rehabilitation psychologists, as outcome studies of treatments for common psychological disorders such as depression and anxiety typically do not include samples with physical or cognitive impairments. Some rehabilitation psychologists have argued that this largely is a nonissue but that there are two unavoidable concerns: (a) accessibility of treatment techniques, and (b) treatment implications of population-specific intervening variable differences.

Clearly, children with NDCs can exhibit a depressogenic cognition that is amenable to treatment with techniques such as CBTs. However, specific types of cognitive impairments such as deficits in attention, executive functions, and academic skill deficits require modifications of CBT procedures. For example, types of executive dysfunction adversely affect ability to generate alternative solutions to problems, and written language deficits preclude access to written information and writing assignments. Regarding population-specific moderating factors, Rose, Holmbeck, Coakley, and Franks (2004) showed important differences between families of children with and without SB in the extent to which IQ moderates the effects of early parenting on later childhood depression. In the comparison sample, low IQ increased the strength of association, but in the SB sample, moderating effects were not significant.

Social Risks

Childhood social competence is a critical predictor of success and happiness in adulthood (Parker & Asher, 1987), and this is no less important in children with NDCs, who are already at risk of limited peer relations, social skills deficits, and social rejection. Social developmental difficulties in these populations have multifactorial etiologies and change with development. Among children with CP, cognitive impairments, social stigma because of physical impairments, and comorbid behavioral difficulties have been associated with social risks (Warschausky, 2006). Children with SB have similar social risks (Holmbeck, Coakley, Hommeyer, Shapera, & Westhoven, 2002), and previously described risks of impairments in social pragmatics further exacerbate overall social risk in this population.

Although social skills interventions typically target externalizing behaviors such as aggression, research suggests that children with NDCs are instead at greatest risk of passivity, including specific difficulties joining into peer activities, termed *peer-entry situations* (Warschausky, Argento, & Hurvitz, 2003). Children with CP have difficulty initiating social interactions (Dallas, Stevenson, & McGurk, 1993), and children with SB have an increased risk of exhibiting significant social passivity (Holmbeck, Johnson, et al., 2002). Studies of social information processing (SIP) have shown that children with both congenital and acquired NDCs exhibit situation specific deficits in ability to generate prosocial solutions to peer-entry situations. At this point, it is not clear whether this difficulty stems primarily from the complexity and sophistication of this type of problem solving or whether it is a symptom of a general passivity, a difficulty that Weymeyer recently referred to as *causal agency* (Weymeyer, 2004). In typically developing children, SIP skills clearly predict aspects of social behavior (Dodge, Laird, Lochman, & Zelli, 2002), but these ties have been surprisingly elusive in studies of children with NDCs (Yeates et al., 2004); SIP profiles have not been strong intervening variables in the social competence of children with NDCs.

Similarly, the search for specific cognitive predictors of social functioning in these populations has proven complex. Holmbeck, Johnson, et al. (2002) showed that, in children with SB, verbal intellect mediated parental overprotectiveness in family interactions, which in turn was associated with child passivity. In this population, level of cognition is a key correlate of child passivity and parental over-protectiveness. Given that parental overprotectiveness predicts lower levels of adolescent autonomous decision making in this population, an understanding of the contributions of intellect becomes critical to the development of an informed intervention.

SOCIOENVIRONMENTAL FACTORS AND COMMUNITY PARTICIPATION

There is long-standing emphasis in rehabilitation psychology on socioenvironmental contexts in psychological understanding and intervention for children (and adults) with disabilities; however, the nature and salience of contextual factors may differ depending on the degree and nature of disability present. For example, physical environmental accessibility is not necessarily a salient issue in the development of children with depression. Social stigmatization may differ with the nature and visibility of conditions.

Research that examines the nature and effects of community participation for children is just coming into its own. Recent empirical work has been driven by the development of accessible measures of participation, quality of life, and social and academic inclusion. Current survey methods suffer from variable nomenclature for concepts of "participation" and "quality of life," and many commonly used surveys, such as the Child Health Questionnaire (Landgraf, Abetz, & Ware, 1996), include language that is more appropriate for typically developing children. Clearly, current measures of participation will require modification and revision to include complex factors such as the individual–environment interface (Hammal, Jarvis, & Colver, 2004; Morris, Kurinczuk, & Fitzpatrick, 2005).

For children with musculoskeletal and/or neuromuscular conditions, there are a number of potential environmental barriers to participation. For example, children with CP or myelomeningocele may have limited access to common social activities for youth, which often involve more physical activity than they can manage (e.g., camping trips, ballet class, tree climbing). In addition, disability-related needs may limit spontaneity (e.g., planning for catheterization or tube feed schedule, having necessary transportation immediately available). Although there are increasing opportunities for children with disabilities to participate in activities such as organized sports, resources remain limited (Jackson & Davis, 1983; Patel & Greydanus, 2002).

In the school setting, levels of participation are inversely associated with severity and complexity of motor disability (Mancini, Coster, Trombly, & Heeren, 2000; Schenker, Coster, & Parush, 2005). Although there is considerable debate about the benefits and problems associated with inclusion programs in schools for children with disabilities, there is evidence of a positive association between degree of participation in school activities and quality of life (Simeonsson, Carlsonoe, Huntington, McMillen, & Brent, 2001). Nadeau and Tessier (2006) suggested early (i.e., preschool age) interventions to reduce social exclusion, with a goal of turning the focus away from physical differences and redirecting it toward social and behavioral similarities. Interventions are targeted toward prosocial behavior skill building and the importance of friendship reciprocity.

CONCLUSIONS

The pediatric rehabilitation psychologist has a unique role in providing psychological services for, and conducting research with, children with NDCs. Regarding assessment, the risk of neurocognitive impairments that affect skill acquisition and needs currently is not met with accessible neuropsychological instrumentation; thus, parents and educators often have lingering questions about a child's learning potential and targeted educational needs. Psychological and behavioral rating forms commonly used to screen for difficulties focus largely on psychopathology and rarely on the more relevant domains of assertiveness and passivity. As participation is critical to children's psychological, cognitive, and physical development, advocacy and collaboration remain bedrock activities for the clinician.

References

Antle, B. J. (2004). Factors associated with self-worth in young people with physical disabilities. *Health & Social Work, 29,* 167–175.

Arp, S., Taranne, P., & Fagard, J. (2006). Global perception of small numerosities (subitizing) in cerebral-palsied children. *Journal of Clinical and Experimental Neuropsychology, 28,* 405–419.

Barnes, M., Dennis, M., & Hetherington, R. (2004). Reading and writing skills in young adults with spina bifida and hydrocephalus. *Journal of the International Neuropsychological Society, 10,* 655–663.

Barnes, M. A., Wilkinson, M., Khemani, E., Boudesquie, A., Dennis, M., & Fletcher, J. M. (2006). Arithmetic processing in children with spina bifida: Calculation accuracy, strategy use, and fact retrieval fluency. *Journal of Learning Disabilities, 39,* 174–187.

Christ, S. E., White, D. A., Brunstrom, J. E., & Abrams, R. A. (2003). Inhibitory control following perinatal brain injury. *Neuropsychology, 17,* 171–8.

Dallas, E., Stevenson, J., & McGurk, H. (1993). Cerebral-palsied children's interactions with siblings-II. Interactional structure. *Journal of Child Psychology and Psychiatry, 34,* 649–671.

Del Bigio, M. R. (1993). Neuropathological changes caused by hydrocephalus. *Acta Neuropathologica, 85,* 573–85.

Dodge, K. A., Laird, R., Lochman, J. E., & Zelli, A. (2002). Multidimensional latent-construct analysis of children's social information processing patterns: Correlations with aggressive behavior problems. *Psychological Assessment, 14,* 60–73.

Donders. J., Rourke, B. P., & Canady, A. (1991). Neuropsychological functioning of hydrocephalic children. *Journal of Clinical and Experimental Neuropsychology, 13,* 607–13.

Farmer, J. E., & Deidrick, K. K. (2006). Introduction to childhood disability. In J. Farmer, J. Donders, & S. Warschausky (Eds.), *Neurodevelopmental Disabilities: Clinical research and practice* (pp. 3–20). New York: Guilford Press.

Fletcher, J. M., Barnes, M., & Dennis, M. (2002). Language development in children with spina bifida. *Seminars in Pediatric Neurology, 9,* 201–208.

Fletcher, J. M., Francis, D. J., Thompson, N. M., Davidson, K. C., & Miner, M. E. (1992). Verbal and nonverbal skill discrepancies in hydrocephalic children. *Journal of Clinical and Experimental Neuropsychology, 14,* 593–609.

Hammal, D., Jarvis, S. N., & Colver, A. F. (2004). Participation of children with cerebral palsy is influenced by where they live. *Developmental Medicine and Child Neurology, 4,* 292–298.

Harper, D. C. (1997). Pediatric psychology: Child health in the next century. *Journal of Clinical Psychology and Medical Settings, 4,* 179–190.

Harper, D. C., & Peterson, D. B. (2000). Neuromuscular and musculoskeletal disorders in children. In R. G. Frank & T. R. Elliot (Eds.), *Handbook of rehabilitation psychology* (pp. 123–144). Washington, DC: American Psychological Association.

Holmbeck, G. N., Coakley, R. M., Hommeyer, J. S., Shapera, W. E., & Westhoven, V. C. (2002). Observed and perceived dyadic and systemic functioning in families of preadolescents with spina bifida. *Journal of Pediatric Psychology, 27,* 177–189.

Holmbeck, G. N., Johnson, S. Z., Wills, K. E., McKernon, W., Rose, B., Erklin, S., & Kemper, T. (2002). Observed and perceived parental overprotection in relation to psychosocial adjustment in preadolesents with a physical disability: The mediational role of behavioral autonomy. *Journal of Consulting and Clinical Psychology, 70,* 96–110.

Iddon, J. L., Morgan, D. J., Loveday, C., Sahakian, B. J., & Pickard, J. D. (2004). Neuropsychological profile of young adults with spina bifida with or without hydrocephalus. *Journal of Neurology, Neurosurgery, and Psychiatry, 75,* 1112–1118.

Ito, J., Saijo, H., Araki, A., Tanaka, H., Tasaki, T., Cho, K., & Miyamoto, A. (1996). Assessment of visuoperceptual disturbance in children with spastic diplegia using measurements of the lateral ventricles on cerebral MRI. *Developmental Medicine and Child Neurology, 38,* 496–502.

Jackson, R. W., & Davis, G. M. (1983). The value of sports and recreation for the physically disabled. *Orthopedic Clinics of North America, 14,* 301–315.

Jonson-Reid, M., Drake, B., Kim, J., Porterfield, S., & Han, L. (2004). A prospective analysis of the relationship between reported child maltreatment and special education eligibility among poor children. *Child Maltreatment, 9,* 382–394.

Landgraf, J. M., Abetz, L., & Ware, J. E. (1996). *The CHQ User's Manual.* Boston: The Health Institute, New England Medical Center.

Mancini, M. C., Coster, W. J., Trombly, C. A., & Heeren, T. C. (2000). Predicting elementary school participation in children with disabilities. *Archives of Physical Medicine and Rehabilitation, 81,* 339–347.

McDermott, S., Moran, R., Platt, T., Issac, T., Wood, H., & Dasari, S. (2005). Depression in adults with disabilities, in primary care. *Disability and Rehabilitation, 27,* 117–123.

Mirzai, H., Ersahin, Y., Mutluer, S., & Kayahan, A. (1998). Outcome of patients with meningomyelocele: The Ege University experience. *Child Nervous System, 14(3),* 120–123.

Morris, C., Kurinczuk, J. J., & Fitzpatrick, R. (2005). Child or family assessed measures of activity performance and participation for children with cerebral palsy: A structured review. *Child Care, Health and Development, 31,* 397–407.

Nadeau, L., & Tessier, R. (2006). Social adjustment of children with cerebral palsy in mainstream classes:

Peer perception. *Developmental Medicine and Child Neurology, 48,* 331–336.

Parker, J. G., & Asher, S. R. (1987). Peer relations and later personal adjustment: Are low-accepted children at risk? *Psychological Bulletin, 102,* 357–389.

Patel, D. R., & Greydanus, D. E. (2002). The pediatric athlete with disabilities. *Pediatric Clinics of North America, 49,* 803–827.

Pavlova, M., Sokolov, A., & Krageloh-Mann, I. (2007). Visual navigation in adolescents with early periventricular lesions: Knowing where, but not getting there. *Cerebral Cortex, 17,* 363–369.

Rose, B. M., Holmbeck, G. N., Coakley, R. M., & Franks, E. A. (2004). Mediator and moderator effects in developmental and behavioral pediatric research. *Developmental and Behavioral Pediatrics, 25,* 58–67.

Sabbadini, M., Bonanni, R., Carlesimo, G. A., & Caltagirone, C. (2001). Neuropsychological assessment of patients with severe neuromotor and verbal disabilities. *Journal of Intellectual Disability Research, 45,* 169–79.

Sandberg, D. A. (2006). Reading and spelling abilities in children with severe speech impairments and cerebral palsy at 6, 9, and 12 years of age in relation to cognitive development: A longitudinal study. *Developmental Medicine and Child Neurology, 48,* 629–634.

Schenker, R., Coster, W., & Parush, S. (2005). Participation and activity performance of students with cerebral palsy within the school environment. *Disability and Rehabilitation, 27,* 539–552.

Serdaroglu, G., Tekgul, H., Kitis, O., Serdaroglu, E., & Gokben, S. (2004). Correlative value of magnetic resonance imaging for neurodevelopmental outcome in periventricular leukomalacia. *Developmental Medicine and Child Neurology, 46,* 733–739.

Shaffer, J., Friedrich, W. N., Shurtleff, D. B., & Wolf, L. (1985). Cognitive and achievement status of children with myelomeningocele. *Journal of Pediatric Psychology, 10,* 325–336.

Shields, N., Murdoch, A., Loy, Y., Dodd, K. J., & Taylor, N. F. (2006). A systematic review of the self-concept of children with cerebral palsy compared with children without disability. *Developmental Medicine & Child Neurology, 48,* 151–157.

Simeonsson, R. J., Carlsonoe, D., Huntington, G. S., McMillen, J. S., & Brent, J. L. (2001). Students with disabilities: A national survey of participation in school activities. *Disabilities and Rehabilitation, 23,* 49–63.

Strathearn, L., Gray, P. H., Wood, & D. O. (2001). Childhood neglect and cognitive development in extremely low birth weight infants: A prospective study. *Pediatrics, 108,* 142–151.

Sullivan, P. M., & Knutson, J. F. (2000). Maltreatment and disabilities: A population-based epidemiological study. *Child Abuse and Neglect, 24,* 1257–1273.

Varni, J. W., Burwinkel, T. M., Sherman, S. A., Hanna, K., Berrin, S. J., Malcarne, V. L., & Chambers, H. G. (2005). Health-related quality of life of children and adolescents with cerebral palsy: Hearing the voices of the children. *Developmental Medicine & Child Neurology, 47,* 592–597.

Warschausky, S. (2006). Social development and adjustment of children with neurodevelopmental conditions. In K. J. Hagglund & A. Heinemann (Eds.), *Handbook of applied disability and rehabilitation research* (pp. 103–116). Springer Publishing Company.

Warschausky, S., Argento, A. G., & Hurvitz, E. B. M. (2003). Neuropsychological status and social problem-solving in children with congenital or acquired brain dysfunction. *Rehabilitation Psychology, 48,* 250–254.

Weymeyer, M. L. (2004). Beyond self-determination: Causal agency theory. *Journal of Developmental and Physical Disabilities, 16,* 337–359.

Yeates, K. O., Swift, E., Taylor, H. G., Wade, S. L., Drotar, D., Stancin, T., et al. (2004). Short- and long-term social outcomes following pediatric traumatic brain injury. *Journal of the International Neuropsychological Society, 10,* 412–426.

CHAPTER 21

REHABILITATION IN PEDIATRIC CHRONIC ILLNESS: JUVENILE RHEUMATIC DISEASES AS AN EXEMPLAR

Janelle Wagner, Kevin A. Hommel, Larry L. Mullins, and John M. Chaney

In the past 30 years, dramatic advances in medical care and health-related technology have resulted in significant increases in both the incidence and prevalence of pediatric chronic health conditions. Improvements in early diagnosis and detection, development of life-saving medicines and surgical procedures, and the increased prevalence of new conditions (e.g., HIV, AIDS) have resulted in a doubling of the prevalence of children with chronic health conditions (Gortmaker & Sappenfield, 1984; Thompson & Gustafson, 1996). Children who would have previously died in early childhood or adolescence now may live well into adulthood. However, many of these children continue to face physical, cognitive, psychosocial, and academic challenges over the course of their life span.

The nature of these chronic health conditions is heterogeneous and diverse. Many of these children face relatively minor disability; however, others experience problems in daily living that warrant comprehensive treatment and, more specifically, interdisciplinary intervention involving outpatient or inpatient rehabilitation. These children often contend with various sensory and mobility impairments, endure recurrent hospitalizations and medical procedures, and are required to adhere to complex therapy regimens. The nature of their impairment also impacts interpersonal relationships by reducing social contacts and the number of individuals in their social network (Lyons, Sullivan, Ritvo, & Coyne, 1995). Finally, children with disabilities also experience stigma, difficulty adjusting to their disease or condition and associated challenges, and anxiety about their future (Austin,

Dunn, Perkins, & Shen, 2006). Clearly, many pediatric health conditions lend themselves to rehabilitation psychology interventions.

Several of these conditions, in particular, warrant the expertise of pediatric rehabilitation psychologists. For example, children with sickle cell disease, who now may live well into their 50s and 60s, are at high risk of both silent and classic stroke, which may result in various deficits and subsequent academic and vocational challenges. Many will also experience significant vaso-occlusive pain crises. Children with hemophilia are at risk of significant deterioration in joint function after bleeding episodes, particularly if they are nonadherent with factor prophylaxis. Musculoskeletal disorders, which affect primarily the joints and bones (e.g., arthritis), muscles (e.g., lupus), or other soft tissues (e.g., fibromyalgia), are associated with immune system dysfunction, chronic pain, movement limitations, and diminished involvement in life activities.

A review of all childhood chronic illnesses warranting rehabilitation is well beyond the scope of this chapter. As an exemplar, we have chosen one class of the musculoskeletal disorders, the juvenile rheumatic diseases (JRDs), to illustrate the complex psychosocial challenges that face these children and their families and to provide a framework for pediatric rehabilitation within this context.

JUVENILE RHEUMATIC DISEASES

The JRDs represent a heterogeneous group of autoimmune disorders, yet they are characterized by similar symptoms, including intermittent and sometimes chronic episodes of joint swelling, pain, and restricted functional ability. JRDs have many disease manifestations similar to adult rheumatoid arthritis; however, the degree of skeletal immaturity remains one of the most important, yet poorly understood, differences between adult and child rheumatic diseases. The most prevalent JRDs include juvenile idiopathic arthritis (JIA; formerly known as juvenile rheumatoid arthritis), systemic lupus erythematosus, juvenile ankylosing spondylitis, and juvenile dermatomyositis (Cassidy & Petty, 2001). Similar clinical manifestations and lack of definitive medical indices often pose particular diagnostic challenges for physicians in making clear distinctions between symptoms of rheumatic disease and other common childhood conditions. The hallmark features of JRD also make distinguishing specific subclasses of rheumatic disease somewhat challenging. Consequently, JRD symptoms may persist for months or even years before a definitive diagnosis is given, suggesting that JRDs are possibly diagnoses of exclusion (Cassidy & Petty, 2001; Miller-Hoover, 2005).

In terms of treatments for JRD, pharmacological interventions such as nonsteroidal anti-inflammatory drugs, corticosteroids, and disease-modifying antirheumatic drugs are routinely used. Newer therapies such as biological response modifiers, including bone marrow transplants, require continued research to determine their safety and effectiveness (Reiff, 2004). Orthopedic surgery may be an option for progressive disease. Patients with JRD should be followed by ophthalmology, and dietary intervention may be necessary for patients who have difficulty maintaining appropriate caloric and protein intake. Physical and occupational therapies are also crucial to the treatment of JRD, and psychological interventions that target pain management and improvement of coping skills can be effective at symptom reduction (e.g., Walco, Varni, & Ilowite, 1992). Provision of these therapies in childhood is critical to disease outcomes, as symptoms of JRD often persist into adult life. Research has shown that 36% to 50% of patients with JRD have active arthritis in adulthood and require further rheumatological care (Minden et al., 2000; Zak & Pederson, 2000). Thus, a multidisciplinary approach to the treatment of JRD across the life span is considered to be the optimal standard of care.

PSYCHOLOGICAL ADJUSTMENT

Children with JIA may experience pain, stiffness, and fatigue almost daily, with significant associations between pain experience, mood, stress, and participation in social activities (Schanberg, Gil, Anthony, Yow, & Rochon, 2005). Not surprisingly, then, disease manifestations of JRD can be associated with poorer quality of life (Brunner et al., 2004) and psychological (LeBovidge, Lavigne, Donenberg, & Miller, 2003), social (Reiter-Purtill, Gerhardt, Vannatta, Passo, & Noll, 2003), and family difficulties (Gerhardt et al., 2003). Indeed, the uncertainty associated with JRD and the essential readjustment in coping with various stressors produced by disease fluctuation may be the underlying context through which psychosocial functioning and quality of life of patients and their families is determined. Thus, the JRDs, with their unpredictable and variable course and illness-associated concomitants (e.g., pain, disability, functional limitations) are a relevant prototype for a discussion of psychosocial adjustment to disability and the role of pediatric rehabilitation psychologists in treatment. Psychosocial factors in JRD are summarized next. Specific social and familial correlates of pediatric chronic health conditions are reviewed in other chapters of this volume (see chaps. 18, 22, 27, this volume) and will not be detailed here, but they are nonetheless critical to treatment outcome in a child with JRD or other chronic illness.

Psychological Comorbidity

Psychosocial adjustment in JIA has been widely examined; however, there have been far fewer studies examining adjustment in children with other JRDs. Therefore, studies examining adjustment in children with JIA as well as those including samples of youth with JIA and other JRDs are briefly reviewed here.

Several studies in the late 1980s and early 1990s indicated significant psychological maladjustment in children with JIA (Billings, Moos, Miller, &

Gottlieb, 1987; David et al., 1994; Vandvik, 1990). In contrast, a meta-analysis of more recent studies revealed that parents reported greater overall child maladjustment and internalizing behaviors compared with study-recruited control participants but not to normative values. Further, higher levels of overall adjustment difficulties were found among children in samples of various JRDs compared with children in arthritis-only groups, suggesting greater adjustment difficulties in children with rheumatic disease other than JIA. Unfortunately, no analyses were performed on child-report measures because only two studies in the meta-analysis included them (LeBovidge et al., 2003).

In one of the studies included in LeBovidge et al.'s (2003) meta-analysis, Noll and colleagues (2000) found that mothers rated their children with JIA as being less adaptive and having less positive affect than control participants. However, they did not find significant differences on child-report measures of overall adjustment. Other studies found non-significant differences between children with JRD and control participants on measures of depression, anxiety, number of missed school days, self-esteem, and parent-reported behavior problems (Brace, Smith, McCauley, & Sherry, 2000; Huygen, Kuis, & Sinnema, 2000).

Since the publication of LeBovidge et al.'s (2003) meta-analysis, several other studies on adjustment have been published. A small study of youth with JIA in Bangladesh, reported prevalence rates of 35% for psychiatric diagnoses in general and 15% for a depressive disorder (Mullick, Nahar, & Haq, 2005). Conversely, Rangel et al. (2003) found that children with JIA experienced fewer psychiatric symptoms than children with chronic fatigue syndrome.

Thus, findings regarding psychological adjustment outcomes in children with rheumatic disease are mixed. A possible reason for this discrepancy is the use of different methodologies (i.e., parent vs. child report, questionnaire vs. interview, examination of symptoms vs. clinical disorder) and use of different diagnostic guidelines. In light of these findings, Dahlquist (2003) recommended that future research focus on specific adaptation processes (e.g.,

coping strategies, cognitive appraisals) instead of global adjustment outcomes.

Cognitive appraisals. Given the often lengthy and ambiguous diagnostic process as well as the unpredictable and variable course of chronic conditions such as JRD, cognitive appraisal mechanisms are salient to youths' experience of their illness. Examination of self-report cognitive appraisal variables, such as causal attributions, perceived control, and attitudes allows for insight into children's perceptions of outcomes in general and, more specifically, of their illness.

To illustrate, LeBovidge, Lavigne, and Miller (2005) revealed that more positive attitudes toward illness protected against the impact of psychosocial stress on depressive symptoms in youth with JRD. In addition, they found that higher levels of both illness-related and nonillness-related stress were associated with greater child-reported depressive and anxiety symptoms as well as parent-reported adjustment. Barlow and colleagues (Barlow, Shaw, & Wright, 2000, 2001) found that higher self-efficacy for managing arthritis symptoms was associated with lower anxiety and depressive symptoms.

Several studies of youth with JRD have shown that the relationship between parent distress and child adjustment is moderated by child cognitive appraisal variables. For example, illness intrusiveness, or "illness-induced barriers" across a variety of life domains (Devins et al., 1983), has been shown to moderate the relationship between parental distress and child depressive symptoms (Wagner et al., 2003). More specifically, parent distress was shown to impact child depressive symptoms to a greater extent when children perceived their illness as restricting their activities across a range of nonillness-related life domains (e.g., social, school, leisure). In a similar study, children's perceived illness uncertainty moderated the parent distress/child depressive symptom relationship (White et al., 2005). It is plausible, on the basis of these findings, that perceptions of illness intrusiveness and illness uncertainty create an emotional vulnerability (i.e., diathesis) to the influence of parent distress.

Other cognitive appraisal factors that appear particularly relevant to the illness experience in JRD are attributional style and perceived illness control, which are central to the reformulated learned helplessness theory of depression (Abramson et al., 1989). Indeed, Wagner et al. (2007) found that disease-unrelated global and stable attributions for negative events were associated with greater depressive symptoms when children perceived less control over their JRD symptoms. Similar findings have been observed in the adult arthritis literature (e.g., Chaney et al., 1996, 2004).

In a related study, Hommel, Chaney, Wagner, and Jarvis (2006) randomized children with JRD to learned helplessness and control conditions using contingent and noncontingent computerized experimental feedback. Results revealed that noncontingent feedback (i.e., learned helplessness) resulted in poorer internalization of success for problem-solving, whereas contingent feedback produced greater internalization of success for problem-solving and greater self-efficacy for functional ability. The authors concluded from this laboratory study that perceptions of contingency in a child's environment might translate into greater perceptions of control over functional ability and thereby enhance cognitive appraisals associated with favorable disease outcome.

Collectively, these studies support the importance of examining the relationships between cognitive appraisal variables and psychological adjustment in youth with JRD. Whereas the majority of children in these studies demonstrated subclinical anxiety and depressive symptoms (i.e., LeBovidge et al., 2005; Wagner et al., 2003; White et al., 2005), taken together, the results suggest that cognitive appraisal variables contribute significantly to adjustment outcomes in at least a significant portion of the JRD population and may serve as salient risk factors for these children and adolescents.

Disease-related factors associated with adjustment. Some studies have revealed a significant relationship between child distress and pain (i.e., Benestad, Vinje, Veierod, & Vandvik, 1996; Ross et al., 1993). However, more recent studies have indicated that the relationship between pain

and psychological adjustment is quite complex, as pain does not appear to be a direct indicator of disease activity (Rapoff & Lindsley, 2000). Disease severity and functional disability are two other disease features that have complicated associations with psychological adjustment in JRD, with inconsistent findings (Brunner et al., 2004; Reiter-Purtill et al., 2003; Wagner et al., 2003). In a recent study, Hoff, Palermo, Schluchter, Zebracki, and Drotar (2006) examined the complexity of these relationships in a longitudinal design. They found that greater initial depressive symptoms significantly predicted increased future pain symptoms but only when initial pain symptoms were mild to moderate. Hoff et al. also demonstrated that initial depressive symptoms predicted future child-reported disability only when initial disability was reported to be low. Thus, it appears that the relationships between pain, disability, and psychosocial adjustment are multifaceted and require further investigation.

Quality of life.   Children with JIA have reported poorer health-related quality of life (HRQL) compared with healthy children but higher general and arthritis specific HRQL than parents reported for these children (Sawyer et al., 2005). According to child participants, HRQL was negatively correlated with pain experiences (Sawyer et al., 2005) and increased disability (Brunner et al., 2004). Similarly, in a large study in the United Kingdom, Shaw, Southwood, and McDonagh (2006) found that adolescents reported the lowest ratings for gross motor and systemic functioning and that one third of adolescents reported frustration with their JRD symptoms. Pharmacological interventions impact arthritis-specific HRQL, with children who receive steroidal intervention demonstrating the greatest improvement in HRQL over 4 months, despite more severe side effects compared with nonsteroidal anti-inflammatory drugs or methotrexate (Riddle et al., 2006).

PSYCHOLOGICAL INTERVENTIONS

This literature summary highlighting the relationships between HRQL, cognitive appraisal variables, disease-related variables, social adaptation, family functioning, and psychological adjustment in children with JRD clearly indicates the role of psychological interventions in the treatment of children with JRD and their families. Unfortunately, there is a paucity of research examining behavioral treatments for dysfunction associated with chronic illnesses such as JRD. Studies have shown that behavioral pain management techniques can equip children with skills to control their pain experiences (Lavigne, Ross, Berry, & Hayford, 1992; Walco et al., 1992). Furthermore, arthritis camps have been effective in helping families adjust to JRD and empowering them to develop realistic goals for aspects of the disease over which they can have control (e.g., Hagglund et al., 1996). Despite the empirically supported relevance of cognitive appraisal variables in adjustment to JRD and the success of cognitive–behavioral therapy (CBT) in other chronic illness populations, no studies have examined the effects of CBT in JRD maladjustment. The absence of randomized clinical trials evaluating this treatment approach in JRD is perhaps the most significant gap in the current literature. Systematic development and evaluation of psychological treatments that target control and self-efficacy over daily illness management, attributional style, and attitudes toward illness are a necessary and logical next step in improving both psychological and physical outcome in this population.

CLINICAL IMPLICATIONS FOR THE REHABILITATION PSYCHOLOGIST

As mentioned at the beginning of this chapter, a multidisciplinary approach to chronic physical conditions such as JRD provides best chance for optimal outcomes. Thus, it is important for the rehabilitation psychologist to be a key player in treating children with JRD and other similar physical conditions. Communication with other health care providers is critical. For example, it will be important for psychologists to consult with a child's physical therapist and assist with motivation, adherence to physical therapy regimen, and pain management. Children with JRD should be encouraged to remain as physically active as possible and to be independent and responsible for adhering to the treatment if age-appropriate (Lovell, 1997; Singsen, 1993). Klepper (1999) demonstrated that children and adolescents

with JRA could improve their aerobic endurance through an 8-week physical conditioning program, without increased pain. However, simply explaining the necessities of therapy to a child or adolescent is not sufficient. Instead, they must become an active partner in self-management (Kroll, Barlow, & Shaw, 1999). Parental involvement is important and may involve massage therapy, which lowers anxiety, cortisol levels, and pain, even in small increments of 15 minutes daily (Field et al., 1997).

Pain management is salient to treatment of chronic physical conditions such as JRD, as pain has been identified as a hallmark symptom and daily challenge for these children. Rehabilitation psychologists may use behavioral pain management techniques to provide children with skills to alleviate their pain experiences (Lavigne et al., 1992; Walco et al., 1992). Indeed, Schanberg, Lefebvre, Keefe, Kredich, and Gil (1997) demonstrated that adaptive coping skills are related to lower ratings of pain intensity. Given the importance of a child's social and familial support network to overall functioning, these domains should be assessed and available resources enhanced and used to ensure success of rehabilitation therapeutic efforts. Further, as parents of children with JIA may be more directive (e.g., they provide more clues, prompts, structure) when interacting with their children compared with parents of healthy children (Power, Dahlquist, Thompson, & Warren, 2003) and may perceive their children as more vulnerable (Anthony, Gil, & Schanberg, 2003), parenting behaviors should be addressed in the context of the child's rehabilitation program to include attainment of physical and psychological goals.

The rehabilitation psychologist should also be aware of agencies, organizations, and resources for children with physical disabilities such as JRD. The Arthritis Foundation sponsors activities of the American Juvenile Arthritis Organization (AJAO) to facilitate adjustment to the academic, emotional, and physical challenges associated with rheumatic disease. The AJAO has also developed written materials and training workshops for parents and health care professionals to provide specific recommendations for optimal school and social functioning.

CONCLUSION

The extant literature suggests that, in general, children with chronic physical conditions such as JRD evidence levels of clinical distress similar to that of other pediatric chronic illness populations. Moreover, there is clearly a subpopulation of patients and families that are at higher risk of psychological maladjustment, poor quality of life, social dysfunction, and parent and family distress. In addition to increased disease severity, cognitive appraisal mechanisms, including perceived control and causal attributions of behavior-outcome contingency, illness uncertainty, and illness intrusiveness appear to be particularly salient predictors of poor adjustment outcomes.

Future research efforts should be directed toward three areas. First, multisite prospective studies examining models of patient and family adjustment, quality of life, and potential mediators, such as cognitive appraisal mechanisms, should be conducted to advance health care providers' understanding of psychosocial adjustment trajectories and identify risk factors for maladjustment (see Beale, 2006). Second, randomized clinical trials using cognitive–behavioral or family-based interventions to reduce patient and family distress and improve physical outcomes and quality of life for patients and families are needed. Finally, domains of biopsychosocial functioning requiring substantial investigation include psychoneuroimmunological processes, child and family decision making, and adherence to medical and physical therapy regimens.

References

Abramson, L. Y., Metalsky, G. I., & Alloy, L. B. (1989). Hopelessness depression: A theory-based subtype of depression. *Psychological Review, 96,* 358–372.

Anthony, K. K., Gil, K. M., & Schanberg, L. E. (2003). Brief report: Parental perceptions of child vulnerability in children with chronic illness. *Journal of Pediatric Psychology, 28,* 185–190.

Austin, J. K., Dunn, D. W., Perkins, S. M., & Shen, J. (2006). Youth with epilepsy: Development of a model of children's attitudes toward their condition. *Children's Health Care, 35,* 2, 123–140.

Barlow, J. H., Shaw, K. L., & Wright, C. C. (2000). Development and preliminary validation of a self-efficacy measure for use among parents of children with juvenile idiopathic arthritis. *Arthritis Care & Research, 13,* 227–236.

Barlow, J. H., Shaw, K. L., & Wright, C. C. (2001). Development and preliminary validation of a children's arthritis self-efficacy scale. *Arthritis Care & Research, 45,* 159–166.

Beale, I. L. (2006). Efficacy of psychological interventions for pediatric chronic illnesses. *Journal of Pediatric Psychology, 31,* 437–451.

Benestad, B., Vinje, O., Veierod, M. B., & Vandvik, I. H. (1996). Quantitative and qualitative assessments of pain in children with juvenile chronic arthritis based on the Norwegian version of the pediatric pain questionnaire. *British Journal of Rheumatology, 25,* 293–299.

Billings, A. G., Moos, R. H., Miller, J. J., & Gottlieb, J. E. (1987). Psychosocial adaptation in juvenile rheumatic disease: A controlled evaluation. *Health Psychology, 6,* 343–359.

Brace, M. J., Smith, M. S., McCauley, E., & Sherry, D. D. (2000). Family reinforcement of illness behavior: A comparison of adolescents with chronic fatigue syndrome, juvenile arthritis, and healthy controls. *Developmental and Behavioral Pediatrics, 21,* 332–339.

Brunner, H. I., Klein-Gitelman, M. S., Miller, M. J., Trombley, M., Baldwin, N., Kress, A., et al. (2004). Health of children with chronic arthritis: Relationship of different measures and the quality of parent proxy reporting. *Arthritis & Rheumatism, 51,* 763–773.

Cassidy, J. T., & Petty, R. E. (2001). *The textbook of pediatric rheumatology* (4th ed.). Philadelphia: W. B. Saunders.

Chaney, J. M., Mullins, L. L., Urtesky, D. L., Doppler, M. J., Palmer, W. R., Wees, S. J., et al. (1996). Attributional style and depression in rheumatoid arthritis: The moderating role of perceived illness control. *Rehabilitation Psychology, 41,* 205–223.

Chaney, J. M., Mullins, L. L., Wagner, J. L., Hommel, K. A., Page, M. C., Doppler, M. J. (2004). A longitudinal examination of causal attributions and depression in rheumatoid arthritis. *Rehabilitation Psychology, 49,* 126–133.

Dahlquist, L. M. (2003). Commentary: Are children with JRA and their families at risk or resilient? *Journal of Pediatric Psychology, 28,* 45–46.

David, J., Cooper, C., Hickey, L., Lloyd, J., Dore, C., McCullough, C., & Woo, P. (1994). The functional and psychological outcomes of juvenile chronic arthritis in young adulthood. *British Journal of Rheumatology, 33,* 876–881.

Devins, G. M., Binik, Y. M., Hutchinson, T. A., Hollomby, D. J., Barre, P. E., & Guttmann, R. D. (1983–84). The emotional impact of end-stage renal disease:

Importance of patients' perception of intrusiveness and control. *International Journal of Psychiatry in Medicine, 13,* 327–343.

Field, T., Hernandez-Reif, M., Seilgman, S., Krasnegor, J., Sunshine, W., Rivas-Chacon, et al. (1997). Juvenile rheumatoid arthritis: Benefits from massage therapy. *Journal of Pediatric Psychology, 22,* 607–617.

Gerhardt, C. A., Vannatta, K., McKellop, M., Zeller, M., Taylor, J., Passo, M. et al. (2003). Comparing parental distress, family functioning, and the role of social support for caregivers with and without a child with juvenile rheumatoid arthritis. *Journal of Pediatric Psychology, 28,* 5–16.

Gortmaker, S. L., & Sappenfield, W. (1984). Chronic childhood disorders: Prevalence and impact. *Pediatric Clinics of North America, 31,* 3–18.

Hagglund, K. J., Doyle, N. M., Clay, D. L., Frank, R. G., Johnson, J. C., & Pressly, T. A. (1996). A family retreat as a comprehensive intervention for children with arthritis and their families. *Arthritis Care and Research, 9,* 35–41.

Hoff, A. L., Palermo, T. M., Schluchter, M., Zebracki, K., & Drotar, D. (2006). Longitudinal relationships of depressive symptoms to pain intensity and functional disability among children with disease-related pain. *Journal of Pediatric Psychology, 31,* 1046–1056.

Hommel, K. A., Chaney, J. M., Wagner, J. L., & Jarvis, J. N. (2006). Learned helplessness in children and adolescents with juvenile rheumatic disease. *Journal of Psychosomatic Research, 60,* 73–81.

Huygen, A. C. J., Kuis, W., & Sinnema, G. (2000). Psychological, behavioral, and social adjustment in children and adolescents with juvenile chronic arthritis. *Annuals of Rheumatic Disease, 59,* 276–282.

Klepper, S. E. (1999). Effects of an 8-week physical conditioning program on disease signs and symptoms in children with chronic arthritis. *Arthritis Care and Research, 12,* 52–60.

Kroll, T., Barlow, J. H., & Shaw, K. (1999). Treatment adherence in juvenile rheumatoid arthritis: A review. *Scandinavian Journal of Rheumatology, 28,* 10–18.

Lavigne, J. V., Ross, C. K., Berry, S. L., & Hayford, J. R. (1992). Evaluation of a psychological treatment package for treating pain in juvenile rheumatoid arthritis. *Arthritis Care and Research, 5,* 101–110.

LeBovidge, J. S., Lavigne, J. V., Donenberg, G. R., & Miller, M. (2003). Psychological adjustment of children and adolescents with chronic arthritis: A meta-analytic review. *Journal of Pediatric Psychology, 28,* 29–40.

LeBovidge, J. S., Lavigne, J. V., & Miller, M. L. (2005). Adjustment to chronic arthritis of childhood: The roles of illness-related stress and attitude towards illness. *Journal of Pediatric Psychology, 30,* 273–286.

Lovell, D. J. (1997). Juvenile rheumatoid arthritis and juvenile spondyloarthropathies. In J. H. Klippel (Ed.), *Primer on the rheumatic diseases* (11th ed., pp. 393–398). Atlanta, GA: Arthritis Foundation.

Lyons, R. F., Sullivan, M. J. L., Ritvo, P. G., & Coyne, J. C. (1995). *Relationships in chronic illness and disability.* Thousand Oaks, CA: Sage.

Miller-Hoover, S. (2005). Juvenile idiopathic arthritis: Why do I have to hurt so much? *Journal of Infusion Nursing, 28,* 385–391.

Minden, K., Kiessling, U., Listing, J., Niewerth, M., Doring, E., Meincke, J., et al. (2000). Prognosis of patients with juvenile chronic arthritis and juvenile spondyloarthropathy. *The Journal of Rheumatology, 27,* 2256–2263.

Mullick, M. S. I., Nahar, J. S., & Haq, S. A. (2005). Psychiatric morbidity, stressors, impact, and burden in juvenile idiopathic arthritis. *Journal of Health, Population, & Nutrition, 23,* 142–9.

Noll, R. B., Kozloqski, K., Gerhardt, C., Vannatta, K., Taylor, J., & Passo, M. (2000). Social, emotional, and behavioral functioning in children with juvenile rheumatoid arthritis. *Arthritis and Rheumatism, 43,* 1387–1396.

Power, T. J., Dahlquist, L. M., Thompson, S. M., & Warren, R. (2003). Interactions between children with juvenile rheumatoid arthritis and their mothers. *Journal of Pediatric Psychology, 28,* 213–221.

Rangel, L., Garralda, M. W., Hall, A., & Woodham, S. (2003). Psychiatric adjustment in chronic fatigue syndrome of childhood and in juvenile idiopathic arthritis. *Psychological Medicine, 33,* 289–297.

Rapoff, M. A., & Lindsley, C. B. (2000). The paint puzzle: A visual and conceptual metaphor for understanding and treating pain in pediatric rheumatic disease. *Journal of Rheumatology, 58*(Suppl.), 29–33.

Reiff, A. O. (2004). Developments in the treatment of juvenile arthritis. *Expert Opinion in Pharmacotherapy, 5,* 1485–1496.

Reiter-Purtill, J., Gerhardt, C. A., Vannatta, K., Passo, M. H., & Noll, R. B. (2003). A controlled longitudinal study of the social functioning of children with juvenile rheumatoid arthritis. *Journal of Pediatric Psychology, 28,* 17–28.

Riddle, R., Ryset, C. N., Morton, A. A., Sampson, J. D., Browne, R. H., Punaro, M. G., & Gatchel, R. J. (2006). The impact on health-related quality of life from nonsteroidal anti-inflammatory drugs, methotrexate, or steroids in treatment for juvenile idiopathic arthritis. *Journal of Pediatric Psychology, 31,* 262–271.

Ross, C. K., Lavigne, J. V., Hayford, J. R., Berry, S. L., Sinacore, J. M., & Pachman, L. M. (1993). Psychological factors affecting reported pain in juvenile rheumatoid arthritis. *Journal of Pediatric Psychology, 18*, 561–573.

Sawyer, M. G., Carbone, J. A., Whitham, J. N., Roberton, D. M., Taplin, J. E., Varni, J. W., & Baghurst, P. A. (2005). The relationship between health-related quality of life, pain, and coping strategies in juvenile arthritis: A 1-year prospective study. *Quality of Life Research, 14*, 1585–1598.

Schanberg, L. E., Gil, K. M., Anthony, K. K., Yow, E., & Rochon, J. (2005). Pain, stiffness, and fatigue in juvenile polyarticular arthritis: Contemporaneous stressful events and mood as predictors. *Arthritis and Rheumatism, 52*, 1196–1204.

Schanberg, L. E., Lefebvre, J. C., Keefe, F. J., Kredich, D. W., & Gil, K. M. (1997). Pain coping and the pain experience in children with juvenile chronic arthritis. *Pain, 73*, 181–189.

Shaw, K. L., Southwood, T. R., Duffy, C. M., & McDonagh, J. E. (2006). Health-related quality of life in adolescents with juvenile idiopathic arthritis. *Arthritis & Rheumatism, 55*, 199–207.

Singsen, B. H. (1993). Pediatric rheumatic diseases. In H. R. Schumacher Jr., J. H. Klippel, & W. J. Koopman (Eds.), *Primer on the rheumatic diseases* (10th ed. pp. 171–174). Atlanta, GA: Arthritis Foundation.

Thompson, R. J., & Gustafson, K. E. (1996). *Adaptation to chronic childhood illness*. Washington, DC: American Psychological Association.

Vandvik, I. H. (1990). Mental health and psychosocial functioning in children with recent onset of rheumatic disease. *Journal of Child Psychology and Psychiatry, 31*, 961–971.

Wagner, J. L., Chaney, J. M., Hommel, K. A., & Felts, N. (2007). A cognitive diathesis–stress model of depressive symptoms in children and adolescents with juvenile rheumatic disease. *Children's Health Care, 36*, 45–62.

Wagner, J. L., Chaney, J. M., Hommel, K. A., Page, M. C., Mullins, L. L., White, M. M., et al. (2003). The influence of parental distress on child depressive symptoms in juvenile rheumatic diseases: The moderating effect of illness intrusiveness. *Journal of Pediatric Psychology, 28*, 453–462.

Walco, G. A., Varni, J. W., & Ilowite, N. T. (1992). Cognitive–behavioral pain management in children with juvenile rheumatoid arthritis. *Pediatrics, 89*, 1975–1077.

White, M. M., Chaney, J. M., Mullins, L. L., Wagner, J. L., Hommel, K. A., Andrews, N. R., & Jarvis, J. N. (2005). Children's perceived illness uncertainty as a moderator in the parent–child distress relationship in juvenile rheumatic diseases. *Rehabilitation Psychology, 50*, 224–231.

Zak, M., & Pederson, F. K. (2000). Juvenile chronic arthritis into adulthood: A long-term follow-up study. *Paediatric Rheumatology, 39*, 198–204.

CHAPTER 22

FAMILY, SCHOOL, AND COMMUNITY: THEIR ROLE IN THE REHABILITATION OF CHILDREN

Shari L. Wade and Nicolay Chertkoff Walz

The child's family, school, and community are central to the role of the rehabilitation psychologist from two distinct and interrelated perspectives. First, the child's condition often places additional, and, at times, novel, demands on each of these systems, resulting in increased burden, distress, and dysfunction. Family adaptation can be a key determinant of child recovery, thus making healthy parent and family functioning even more important to the child's rehabilitation (Taylor et al., 1999; Yeates et al., 1997). Moreover, facilitation of successful child adaptation necessitates involvement of these key aspects of the child's life in the rehabilitation program. As inpatient rehabilitation stays become shorter, parents and educators must assume a more central role in the child's acute and chronic rehabilitation. This chapter addresses the following issues: (a) the impact of various pediatric conditions on family functioning and school performance; (b) the relationship of parent and family functioning to child adaptation and recovery; (c) interventions to reduce family burden and distress or to improve educational outcomes; and (d) strategies for involving the family, school, and community in the child's rehabilitation.

CAREGIVER, FAMILY, AND SCHOOL BURDEN AND DISTRESS: A FAMILY SYSTEMS ILLNESS MODEL PERSPECTIVE

Rehabilitation psychologists in pediatric settings assess and treat children with a wide range of conditions (e.g., traumatic brain injury [TBI], spinal cord injury [SCI], severe burns, spina bifida, cerebral

palsy [CP], muscular dystrophy) that may impact their medical, physical, cognitive, behavioral, and social functioning in the family and school settings. According to Rolland (1999), these disabilities vary in terms of age of onset (i.e., birth, later childhood), degree of cognitive–behavioral involvement, level of uncertainty regarding the course of recovery, and the likely longer term outcome (i.e., recovery versus deterioration or death). A child's condition may be chronic, short-term, evolving, or variable (e.g., increased needs corresponding with medical treatment, exacerbation of medical condition). Whether the child's disability was present at birth or acquired at a later point in time, ongoing social, emotional, and cognitive development require continual consideration of the child's age and current developmental level. The family-systems illness model developed by Rolland provides a useful framework for understanding how such condition-specific factors interact with individual and family development to determine the impact of the child's condition on the family, school, and community. See Figure 22.1 for an illustration of this model.

Nature of the Condition

With respect to onset, families of children with developmental disabilities such as CP and spina bifida begin the process of adapting to the child's condition at birth, and, by school entry, both parents and educators are likely to have a grasp on the child's adaptive functioning and need for accommodations. Conversely, traumatic injuries such as TBI, SCI, and burns force parents and educators to reevaluate the physical, emotional, and cognitive

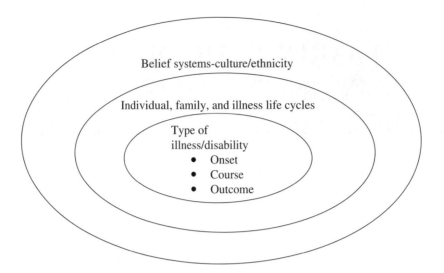

FIGURE 22.1.   The family systems-illness model. From *Families, Illness, and Disability: An Integrative Treatment Model,* by J. S. Rolland, 1994, New York: Basic Books. Copyright 2002 by Basic Books. Adapted with permission.

needs of a previously healthy and typically developing child. Likewise, when the onset is sudden (e.g., TBI, SCI), parents and educators must mobilize resources and crisis management skills rapidly, whereas when the onset is gradual (e.g., Duchenne's muscular dystrophy), families and educators have the possibility of anticipating and accommodating to emerging changes over time.

Families often face the additional burden of serving as the primary advocate for their child's new and emerging educational needs at a time when they are also coping with novel medical needs and additional burdens and stressors on the home environment. Whereas parents of children with a neurodevelopmental disorder present from birth have typically familiarized themselves with special education services starting with early intervention, acquired conditions often burden the family with learning to navigate a confusing and overwhelming special education system. Unfortunately, many parents are forced to do this with little support or guidance. Thus, rehabilitation psychologists can play an important role by providing support and guidance as the family attempts to meet the educational needs of their child.

Research suggests that conditions that are associated with cognitive and behavioral impairments arising from CNS involvement (e.g., TBI) result in greater family distress and burden than do conditions that primarily affect physical functioning. Emotional volatility, impulsivity, and acting out behaviors may be difficult for parents and educators to anticipate and respond to effectively. Such behaviors are more likely to create problems with peers, neighbors, and classmates, thereby potentially contributing to social isolation for the child and family. Moreover, families and educators often have difficulty distinguishing behaviors resulting from brain insult from the emotional effects of the injury or condition or the additional attention that the child may be receiving.

Finally, the course and likely outcome of the condition over time (i.e., recovery, stability, fluctuations in functioning, deterioration, or death), as well as where the child is in the course of the condition, also influence the family's and educators' responses. The time of initial diagnosis can be a particularly stressful time for families, particularly in conditions with acute onset. However, stress may persist for months and even years after onset (Holmbeck et al., 1997; Rivara et al., 1996). Conditions such as Duchenne's muscular dystrophy require families and educators to accommodate to deteriorating functioning over time while coping with the emotional issues of what this physical deterioration means in terms of the child's mortality.

Certain conditions, such as TBI, may be more stressful for family members and educators because of the ambiguous nature of their symptoms (e.g., emotional outbursts) and uncertainty regarding the likely outcome. Research suggests that such illness uncertainty contributes to increased distress for the individual with the illness as well as for his or her caregivers (Carpentier, Mullins, Chaney, & Wagner, 2006; Mishel, 1984). Thus, TBI poses a particular challenge because the course and recovery trajectory may be uncertain and extremely variable, with rapid initial recovery followed by plateaus, fluctuations in abilities, and in some cases, emerging deficits as new skills are required. As a result, parents and educators often express frustration at medical professionals' inability to predict long-term outcome and functioning.

Role of the Child's and Family's Developmental Stage

In addition to condition-specific factors, Rolland (1994) pointed to the need to consider both the child's and the family's stage of development. The stresses and challenges that the family is facing will vary substantially depending on whether the child is a preschooler getting ready to enter kindergarten or an adolescent facing issues of increasing autonomy and transitioning into adulthood. For example, Macias, Saylor, Rowe, and Bell (2003) found that parents of school-aged children with spina bifida reported significantly higher stress regarding concerns for their child than did parents of younger children. Likewise, the family's stage of development (e.g., whether the couple has only been married a few years with young children or is middle-aged with children leaving the home and aging parents to care for) will influence the impact of the child's condition on the family and their resources to cope and adapt. For example, maternal age was found to be related to parenting stress in mothers of children with spina bifida, with older mothers reporting greater stress (Macias, Clifford, Saylor, & Kreh, 2001; Macias et al., 2003). Parents are also presented with the ongoing challenge of continued monitoring and advocacy for a changing child in a changing school environment. That is, the child may require more organizational supports as he or she fails to

meet expected developmental milestones and the school environment places more demands on self-management and executive functioning skills such as changing classes throughout the day and tracking multiple assignments (Savage, DePompei, Tyler, & Lash, 2005; Savage, Pearson, McDonald, Potoczny-Gray, & Marchese, 2001).

EMPIRICAL FINDINGS REGARDING CAREGIVER AND FAMILY ADAPTATION

The research literature regarding family adaptation to pediatric conditions requiring ongoing rehabilitation has grown considerably over the past decade. However, research on some conditions, such as SCI or muscular dystrophy, continues to be lacking in part because of their relative infrequency. This section considers what is known regarding caregiver and family adaptation to various conditions and the illness and social environmental factors that have been shown to influence adaptation over time.

Family Burden and Distress

Empirical findings on family adaptation and burden are largely condition-specific, with considerable research on some conditions (i.e., spina bifida, TBI, developmental disability) and less on others (i.e., SCI). Taken together, these studies suggest that pediatric conditions such as TBI and spina bifida contribute to elevated parental burden and distress (Holmbeck et al., 1997; Rivara et al., 1992; Wade et al., 2002). Research on various conditions suggests that stress levels are most closely linked to concerns regarding the child's behavioral adjustment and future prospects (Stores, Stores, Fellows, & Buckley, 1998; Wade et al., 2002). However, pediatric conditions and disabilities have also been linked to increased stress in relationships with spouses, other children, and extended family (Wade et al., 2002).

Parents of children with certain conditions (i.e., brain injury, spina bifida) also report increased marital strain and deteriorating family functioning (Holmbeck, Coakley, Hommeyer, Shapera, & Westhoven, 2002; Rivara et al., 1992; Wade et al., 2002). Healthy siblings may also be negatively affected (McMahon, Noll, Michaud, & Johnson,

2001; Swift et al., 2003). However, adverse family outcomes are not universal. Studies of families of children with CP found virtually no differences in family functioning relative to normative comparison groups (Britner, Morog, Pianta, & Marvin, 2003; Magill-Evans, Darrah, Pain, Adkins, & Kratochvil, 2001). In fact, the partners of mothers of children with severe CP appear to provide more primary care and support than partners of children with moderate CP or no disability (Button, Pianta, & Marvin, 2001). Clinically, parents often report that the child's condition has brought them closer together as a couple and a family. These findings point again to the need for a more complex model of influences on family adaptation that takes into account condition-specific factors such as the degree of behavioral involvement as well as intra- and interpersonal resources that contribute to enhanced family resiliency (see Exhibit 22.1).

Moderators of Family Adaptation

Although a significant minority of parents experience persistent burden and distress, many families adapt successfully to the increased demands of their

---

Exhibit 22.1
Influences on Family Adaptation

Condition-specific factors
- Age of onset
- Degree of associated behavior problems or impairment
- Course
- Likely outcome

Family and child development
- Child's age or developmental expectations
- Parent's age
- Family's developmental expectations (i.e., parenting young children vs. transitioning to empty nest)

Intrapersonal and intrafamilial resources
- Premorbid functioning
- Coping skills
- Socioeconomic status and financial resources

Interpersonal resources and risk factors
- Social support
- Community integration
- Chronic relationship strains and other life stresses

---

child's condition (Wade, Taylor, Drotar, Stancin, & Yeates, 1998; Wade et al., 2002). Beyond the condition-specific factors outlined earlier, demographic and family characteristics, such as socioeconomic status, ethnicity, pre-injury family resources and stresses, and initial response to the diagnosis or injury, appear to moderate the impact on caregivers, placing some families at greater risk of long-term difficulties (Wade et al., 2001, 2004; Yeates et al., 2002). For example, parents of children with severe TBI who had high levels of family stress and conflict and low levels of family support at the time of the injury reported significantly more injury-related stress during the initial year postinjury than parents of children with severe injuries who had low levels of stress and high levels of support (Wade et al., 2004). Perhaps more important is that parents with low levels of stress coupled with high levels of support did not report the elevated injury-related stress and burden typically associated with severe TBI, underscoring the potential of a supportive environment to buffer stress. Similarly, individual differences in initial coping responses to the child's condition have been shown to contribute to parental distress, with the efficacy of specific coping strategies varying by condition (Wade et al., 2002). Considered together, these findings suggest that it may be possible to identify families at risk of long-term problems with adaptation.

BURDEN ON TEACHERS AND THE SCHOOL SYSTEM

Coping with children with disabilities places increased burden and distress on educators and the school system. Despite the heterogeneity of children seen in rehabilitation settings described earlier, most of the children have long-term educational needs that may be evolving and unpredictable over time (Farmer & Peterson, 1995; Savage et al., 2005). In addition to academic assistance, many of these children have social, psychological, or behavioral problems that require intervention by educators (Clark, Russman, & Orme, 1999; Dykmen, 2003). The school environment and culture are likely to be different from the hospital or family environment, making assessment of the child's performance in the school setting vital to appropriate accommodations. Children who do require hospitalization are likely to stay for shorter periods of time than in the past and return to school with more complex medical and academic needs (Savage et al., 2005; Ylvisaker et al., 2005). This complexity can place significant demands and stress on educators and school systems that are attempting to educate all children in the most appropriate and least restrictive environment despite limited budgets (Glang, Tyler, Pearson, Todis, & Morvant, 2004; Savage et al., 2005; Ylvisaker et al., 2001). Most surveys of rehabilitation populations indicate that children are underidentified and underserved in schools (Clark, 1996; Glang et al., 2004; Savage et al., 2005; Ylvisaker et al., 2001). For example, experts in the field of educational needs of children following TBI have identified the following school system needs: information and knowledge and training for educators, state level resources, support from administration, availability of ancillary services, and better documentation and identification of children with persistent disabilities that impact school performance (Glang et al., 2004; Ylvisaker et al., 2005). In summary, most school systems and educators face multiple challenges as they attempt to develop and implement proper educational programming for children with disabilities.

RELATIONSHIP BETWEEN FAMILY ADAPTATION AND CHILD ADJUSTMENT

Several prospective studies have demonstrated a relationship between the family environment and cognitive and behavioral outcomes among school-aged children with TBI and spina bifida (Ammerman, et al., 1998; Friedman, Holmbeck, Jandasek, Zukerman, & Abad, 2004; Kinsella, Ong, Murtagh, Prior, & Sawyer, 1999; Max et al., 1998; Taylor et al., 1999; Yeates et al., 1997). These studies suggest that child adjustment and family adaptation exert reciprocal influences on one another over time, with family conflict and dysfunction contributing to adverse child outcomes and child behavior problems, resulting in mounting family conflict. Although reciprocal relationships between child adjustment and family functioning are found for typically developing children, parental behavior and family func-

tioning may have a greater impact on children at biological risk, with positive family environment contributing to better child development over time (Landry, Smith, Miller-Loncar, Swank, 1997, 1998; Taylor et al., 1999; Yeates et al., 1997). Thus, family-centered interventions may provide a viable means for improving both child and family outcomes.

Empirically supported interventions to reduce family burden and facilitate long-term adaptation have received relatively little attention in the rehabilitation literature. However, existing studies shed light on potentially efficacious strategies for working with families while suggesting future avenues for research and development. A major thrust of family-centered rehabilitation programs is responding to identified family needs (Naar-King & Donders, 2006); however, evidence suggests that families have difficulty expressing and meeting their emotional and personal needs, despite obvious distress (Meade, Taylor, Kreutzer, Marwitz, & Thomas, 2004; Wade et al., 1996). Moreover, there have been few randomized studies of the efficacy of providing information and support following pediatric TBI. In one such study, Ponsford et al. (2001) examined the efficacy of providing an informational pamphlet regarding the symptoms of mild TBI and strategies for coping with these symptoms to children with mild TBI. The authors found that children receiving the informational pamphlet were less stressed and had fewer behavioral and postconcussive symptoms overall than children with mild TBI not receiving the pamphlet. In a small, randomized clinical trial (RCT), Singer and colleagues (1994) compared an informational support group, comparable with the type provided on many rehabilitation units, to a structured stress management program involving self-monitoring, relaxation training, and cognitive modification. Findings indicated that parents in the stress management group experienced a substantial reduction in both anxiety and depression following the intervention, whereas those in the informational support group actually reported an increase in anxiety and depression. Although the study sample was limited to nine families, the results suggest that identifying and addressing family needs alone is unlikely to be sufficient for families with significant risk factors or other stressors.

Another approach to family intervention as part of pediatric rehabilitation is to target the interaction between the parent and child. Family therapy approaches such as that described by Robin and Foster (1989) explicitly have the goal of reducing family conflicts by improving communication and eliminating dysfunctional interaction patterns. Likewise, the "positive everyday routines" outlined by Ylvisaker and Feeney (1998) emphasize clear communications between parent and child and structuring the environment to reduce problem situations. Although this approach has not been examined in controlled studies, it holds promise for reducing problem behaviors and family stress. However, truly changing the interaction requires some level of participation from the child, which may not be possible with very young or very impaired children.

Given the multidimensional nature of family stress associated with developmental disabilities and chronic conditions, and the range of factors influencing family adaptation, comprehensive approaches targeting multiple risks, moderators, and/or outcomes might have the greatest efficacy, particularly with families at heightened risk. An individualized or tailored approach may be warranted because family stress is likely to vary as a function of the nature of the condition, intra- and interpersonal risks and resources, as well as the child's and family's developmental stage. Wade, Michaud, and Brown (2006) tested a family-centered skill-building intervention emphasizing problem solving, communication, and behavior management skills with families of children with moderate to severe TBI. In an RCT with 32 families, they found significant improvements in internalizing child behavior problems in the treatment group relative to the usual care comparison. However, they did not find corresponding improvements in parental distress.

Based on the findings from this initial study, Wade, Carey, and Wolfe (2006a) developed and tested an online version of the family-centered intervention (i.e., online family problem solving; OFPS). An RCT with 20 families per group testing the efficacy of this intervention relative to an Internet resource comparison group revealed significantly greater reductions in parental depression, anxiety, and distress in the OFPS group relative to the com-

parison group. These initial studies of family interventions with pediatric TBI suggest that a variety of approaches may effective in reducing family distress and burden and, in turn, improving child adaptation. However, further study is needed to identify families who are likely to benefit from more limited support and those who require more intensive intervention.

INTERVENTIONS TO REDUCE SCHOOL BURDEN AND IMPROVE EDUCATIONAL OUTCOMES

Models and research on school interventions for children with the complex disabilities seen in medical rehabilitation are limited; in comparison with the literature on other disabilities that impact school functioning, such as learning disabilities or attention-deficit/hyperactivity disorder (ADHD). However, some models specific for TBI have been proposed. For example, Glang and colleagues (2004) developed a model for educational consulting teams to adequately address the needs and challenges of educating children with TBI. The goal of the model is to "make available to schools statewide a group of well-trained peer consultants who can provide in-service training and ongoing consultation" (Glang et al., 2004, p. 222). It is important that because research has shown that brief workshops without follow-up are rarely successful in helping educators use the new skills presented to them, the model focuses on on-site, ongoing, situation-specific assistance for educators. The components of this model include surveys of parents and educators regarding training needs; recruitment of team members; training of team members including intensive workshop training, mentorship, and ongoing support; and evaluation of implementation and outcomes. Initial efficacy and cost effectiveness evaluation offers preliminary support for this model (Glang et al., 2004).

In addition to the model by Glang et al. (2004), which has received some empirical support, others have developed models based on theory and clinical experience. As a whole, the literature on school intervention emphasizes the need for a comprehensive, interdisciplinary, ongoing approach to evaluation and intervention. The process of planning for return to school should begin as soon as the child's medical condition is identified. For children who require hospitalization, "school reintegration checklists" have been developed (e.g., Clark, 1996). An interdisciplinary team approach is considered crucial. Necessary school personnel, family, child, and relevant outside consultants (e.g., therapists and physicians) should work collaboratively in developing an individualized educational plan (Clark et al., 1999; Farmer et al., 1996). New "context-sensitive" approaches are emerging, in which specialists such as rehabilitation psychologists serve as consultants to parents, schools, and communities in facilitating successful integration of the child into activities of daily living (Braga et al., 2005; Ylvisaker et al., 2005). A child's adjustment and performance in the school setting is an interaction between the child and the school environment. Thus, according to Clark et al. (1999) and Farmer and Peterson (1995), appropriate assessment and intervention requires not only gaining an understanding of the child's strengths and weaknesses but also assessment of the school context, including variables such as teacher qualities (e.g., management style), peers, and the classroom setting (e.g., structure, physical environment).

Current models of educational assessment and intervention of children with disabilities emphasize the individuality of needs and outcomes. That is, although there may be some "common" outcomes of specific childhood disabilities (e.g., TBI), there are also significant individual differences that require careful individualized educational programming. The trend in education to address a child's individualized functional needs rather than their classification category is positive for children with all types of disabilities, including children followed by rehabilitation services (Savage et al., 2001; Savage et al., 2005; Ylvisaker et al., 2001; Ylvisaker et al., 2005). For example, educators should be encouraged to use behavioral strategies known to be effective for poor sustained attention, regardless of the underlying etiology (e.g., ADHD, TBI, CP). Finally, inherent in these individualized programs is the need to be flexible, communicate closely and frequently with family members, reassess needs frequently, and develop a plan for long-term monitoring that includes evalu-

ation of educational needs throughout the school years and as the child transitions to work (Farmer et al., 1995; Savage et al., 2005; Ylvisaker et al., 2001).

INVOLVING THE FAMILY, SCHOOL, AND COMMUNITY IN THE CHILD'S REHABILITATION

The community and the individuals within it constitute the broader context in which the child's rehabilitation and development occur. Community members include extended family, friends, neighbors, employers and colleagues, health care professionals, and school personnel. Each of these individuals has the potential to facilitate child and family adjustment through the provision of instrumental and/or emotional support or to increase family stress and risk of dysfunction through perceived nonunderstanding, insensitivity, and criticism. Although time intensive, community-based interdisciplinary assessments, as promoted by the Maternal and Child Health Leadership Education in Neurodevelopmental Disabilities program, may serve to engage and educate key community members in the rehabilitation process (O'Rourke & Dennis, 2004). Even in the absence of a community-based assessment, it may be useful to diagram the number and quality (i.e., close vs. conflicted) of the family's relationships with others in their community to determine areas of support and stress.

As inpatient rehabilitation stays become shorter, parents and educators have been forced to assume an increasingly central role in the child's rehabilitation. However, there is some evidence that parents, if provided with proper training and support, can serve as effective therapists for their children, resulting in better outcomes than clinic-based therapies (Braga et al., 2005). In a study conducted in Brazil, 87 children with TBI were randomly assigned to standard clinic-based therapies delivered by professionals or to a home-based program in which parents were trained to provide cognitive and physical therapy to their children. These investigators found superior cognitive and motor outcomes among the children receiving treatment from their parents at home relative to the clinic-based treatment group. These findings suggest that parents with proper supports can provide effective rehabilitation services for their children. A central part of the role of the rehabilitation psychologist is to support parents in serving as effective advocates and "therapists" for their children. Rehabilitation psychologists can also provide critical education and support to school staff thereby enabling them to develop effective, empirically based educational and behavioral programming for children with a variety of conditions.

CONCLUSIONS AND IMPLICATIONS FOR PRACTICE

Taken together, the existing literature suggests that many of the conditions evaluated and treated by rehabilitation psychologists, including TBI and spina bifida, place additional burdens on families and schools. Moreover, factors such as the nature of the condition, the child's and family's developmental stage, a lack of supports, and the presence of other stressors may place certain families at increased risk of long-term distress and dysfunction. It is important for rehabilitation psychologists to actively identify and treat families who are having difficulties with adaptation given that their functioning is a key predictor of child recovery and adjustment.

Although evidence-based treatments for pediatric rehabilitation populations are in their infancy, several recent studies of TBI suggest that multifaceted, cognitive–behavioral skill approaches may be effective in reducing parental distress and improving child outcomes (Singer et al., 1994; Wade et al., 2006a, 2006b). Likewise, although there have been few studies of effective school interventions, the work of Glang and colleagues (2004) has underscored the potential promise of ongoing consultation teams. In addition, best practices have increasingly emphasized the importance of an interdisciplinary, context-sensitive approach that accounts for both the child's and the school's strengths. Rehabilitation professionals are also increasingly drawing on strategies shown to be effective for a particular problem or symptom (e.g., disruptive behavior) regardless of the presenting diagnosis (Ylvisaker et al., 2005). As inpatient rehabilitation stays continue to shorten, parents and teachers will play an ever-larger role in the child's rehabilitation, and, thus, facilitating their

ability to do so will be a key role for rehabilitation psychologists. Additional research, including multisite and multicondition studies, will be essential to further our knowledge regarding effective family and school interventions. However, there is also much to be learned from other interrelated fields, including developmental psychology, child health psychology, and family therapy theory and practice, among others. By expanding our evidence base and drawing on the conceptual models of our colleagues in other fields and disciplines, we can more effectively meet the needs of families and schools in the future.

References

Ammerman, R. T., Kane, V. R., Slomka, G. T., Reigel, D. H., Franzen, M. D., & Gadow, K. D. (1998). Psychiatric symptomatology and family function in children and adolescents with spina bifida. *Journal of Clinical Psychology in Medical Settings, 5,* 449–465.

Braga, L. W., Da Paz, A. C., & Ylvisaker, M. (2005). Direct clinician versus indirect family-supported rehabilitation of children with traumatic brain injury: A randomized clinical trial. *Brain Injury, 19,* 819–831.

Britner, P. A., Morog, M. C., Pianta, R. C., & Marvin, R. S. (2003). Stress and coping: A comparison of self-report measures of functioning in families of young children with cerebral palsy or no medical diagnosis. *Journal of Child and Family Studies, 12,* 335–348.

Button, S., Pianta, R. C., & Marvin, R. S. (2001). Partner support and maternal stress in families raising young children with cerebral palsy. *Journal of Developmental and Physical Disabilities, 13,* 61–81.

Carpentier, M. Y., Mullins, L. L., Chaney, J. M., & Wagner, J. L. (2006). The relationship of illness uncertainty and attributional style to long-term psychological distress in parents of children with type 1 diabetes. *Children's Health Care, 36,* 141–154.

Clark, E. (1996). Children with adolescents with traumatic brain injury: Reintegration challenges in educational settings. *Journal of Learning Disabilities, 29,* 549–560.

Clark, E., Russman, S., & Orme, S. (1999). Traumatic brain injury: Effects on school functioning and intervention strategies. *School Psychology Review, 28,* 242–250.

Dykmen, B. F. (2003). School-based interventions for treating social adjustment difficulties in children with traumatic brain injury. *Journal of Instructional Psychology, 30,* 225–230.

Farmer, J. E., Clippard, D. S., Luehr-Wiemann, Y., Wright, E., & Owings, S. (1996). Assessing children with traumatic brain injury during rehabilitation:

Promoting school and community reentry. *Journal of Learning Disabilities, 29,* 532–548.

Farmer, J. E., & Peterson, L. (1995). Pediatric traumatic brain injury: Promoting successful school reentry. *School Psychology Review, 24,* 230–245.

Friedman, D., Holmbeck, G. N., Jandasek, B., Zukerman, J., & Abad, M. (2004). Parent functioning in families of preadolescents with spina bifida: Longitudinal implications for child adjustment. *Journal of Family Psychology, 18,* 609–619.

Glang, A., Tyler, J., Pearson, S., Todis, B., & Morvant, M. (2004). Improving educational services for students with TBI through statewide consulting teams. *NeuroRehabilitation, 19,* 219–231.

Holmbeck, G. N., Coakley, R. M., Hommeyer, J. S., Shapera, W. E., & Westhoven, V. C. (2002). Observed and perceived dyadic and systemic functioning in families of preadolescents with spina bifida. *Journal of Pediatric Psychology, 27,* 177–189.

Holmbeck, G. N., Gorey-Ferguson, L., Hudson, T., Seefeldt, T., Shapera, W., Turner, T., & Uhler, J. (1997). Maternal, paternal, and marital functioning in families of preadolescents with spin bifida. *Journal of Pediatric Psychology, 22,* 167–181.

Kinsella, G. J., Ong, B., Murtagh, D., Prior, M., & Sawyer, M. (1999). The role of the family for behavioral outcome in children and adolescents following traumatic brain injury. *Journal of Consulting and Clinical Psychology, 67,* 166–123.

Landry, S. H., Smith, K. E., Miller-Loncar, C. L., & Swank, P. (1997). Predicting cognitive-language and social growth curves from early maternal behaviors in children at varying degrees of biological risk. *Developmental Psychology, 33,* 1040–1053.

Landry, S. H., Smith, K. E., Miller-Loncar, C. L., & Swank, P. (1998). The relation of change in maternal interactive styles to the developing social competence of full-term and preterm children. *Child Development, 69,* 105–123.

Macias, M. M., Clifford, S. C., Saylor, C. F., & Kreh, S. M. (2001). Predictors of parenting stress in families of children with spina bifida. *Children's Health Care, 30,* 57–65.

Macias, M. M., Saylor, C. F., Rowe, B. P., & Bell, N. L. (2003). Age-related parenting stress differences in mothers of children with spina bifida. *Psychological Reports, 93,* 1223–1232.

Magill-Evans, J., Darrah, H., Pain, K., Adkins, R., & Kratochvil, M. (2001). Are families with adolescents and young adults with cerebral palsy the same as other families? *Developmental Medicine & Child Neurology, 43,* 466–472.

Max, J. E., Castillo, C. S., Robin, D. A., Lindgren, S. D., Smith, W. L., Sata, Y., et al. (1998). Predictors of family functioning following traumatic brain injury in children and adolescents. *Journal of the American Academy of Child and Adolescent Psychiatry, 37,* 83–90.

McMahon, M. A., Noll, R. B., Michaud, L. J., & Johnson, J. C. (2001). Sibling adjustment to pediatric traumatic brain injury: A case-controlled study. *Journal of Head Trauma Rehabilitation, 16,* 587–594.

Meade, M. A., Taylor, L. A., Kreutzer, J. S., Marwitz, J. H., & Thomas, V. (2004). A preliminary study of acute family needs after spinal cord injury: Analysis and implications. *Rehabilitation Psychology, 49,* 150–155.

Mischel, M. H. (1984). Perceived uncertainty and stress in illness. *Research in Nursing and Health, 7,* 163–171.

Naar-King, S., & Donders, J. (2006). Pediatric family centered rehabilitation. In J. E. Farmer, J. Donders, & S. Warchausky (Eds.), *Treating neurodevelopmental disabilities.* New York: Guilford Press.

O'Rourke, D. A., & Dennis, R. (2004). Community-based, interdisciplinary assessment: Considering the context for a child with spina bifida. In C. M. Vargas & P. A. Prelock (Eds.), *Caring for children with neurodevelopmental disabilities and their families: An innovative approach to interdisciplinary practice.* Mahwah, NJ: Erlbaum.

Ponsford, J., Willmott, C., Rothwell, A., Cameron, P., Ayton, G., Nelms, R., et al. (2001). Impact of early intervention after mild traumatic brain injury in children. *Pediatrics, 108,* 1297–1303.

Rivara, J. B., Fay, G., Jaffe, K., Polissar, N., Shurtleff, H., & Martin, K. (1992). Predictors of family functioning one year following traumatic brain injury in children. *Archives of Physical Medicine and Rehabilitation, 73,* 899–910.

Rivara, J. B., Jaffe, K. M., Polissar, N. L., Fay, G. C., Liao, S., & Martin, K. M. (1996). Predictors of family functioning and change 3 years after traumatic brain injury in children. *Archives of Physical Medicine and Rehabilitation, 77,* 754–764.

Robin, A. L., & Foster, S. L. (1989). *Negotiating parent–adolescent conflict: A behavioral-family systems approach.* New York: Guilford Press.

Rolland, J. S. (1994). *Families, illness, and disability: An integrative treatment model.* New York: Basic Books.

Rolland, J. S. (1999). Parental illness and disability: A family systems framework. *Journal of Family Therapy, 21,* 242–266.

Savage, R. C., DePompei, R., Tyler, J., & Lash, M. (2005). Paediatric traumatic brain injury: A review of pertinent issues. *Pediatric Rehabilitation, 8,* 92–103.

Savage, R. C., Pearson, S., McDonald, H., Potoczny-Gray, A., & Marchese, N. (2001). After hospital: Working with schools and families to support the long-term needs of children with brain injuries. *NeuroRehabilitation, 16,* 49–58.

Singer, G. H. S., Glang, A., Nixon, C., Cooley, E., Kerns, K. A., Williams, D., & Powers, L. E. (1994). A comparison of two psychosocial interventions for parents of children with acquired brain injury: An exploratory study. *Journal of Head Trauma Rehabilitation, 9,* 38–49.

Stores, R., Stores, G., Fellows, B., & Buckley, S. (1998). Daytime behaviour problems and maternal stress in children with Down's syndrome, their siblings, and nonintellectually disabled and other intellectually disabled peers. *Journal of Intellectual Disability Research, 42,* 228–237.

Swift, E. E., Taylor, H. G., Kaugars, A. S., Drotar, D., Yeates, K. O., Wade, S. L., & Stancin, T. (2003). Sibling relationship and behavior after pediatric traumatic brain injury. *Journal of Developmental and Behavioral Pediatrics, 24,* 24–31.

Taylor, H. G., Yeates, K. O., Wade, S. L., Drotar, D., Klein, S., & Stancin, T. (1999). Influences on first-year recovery from traumatic brain injury in children. *Neuropsychology,* 76–89.

Taylor, H. G., Yeates, K. O., Wade, S. L., Drotar, D., Stancin, T., & Burant, C. (2001). Bidirectional child–family influences on outcomes of traumatic brain injury in children. *Journal of the International Neuropsychological Society, 7,* 755–767.

Wade, S. L., Borawski, E. A., Taylor, H. G., Drotar, D., Yeates, K. O., & Stancin, T. (2001). The relationship of caregiver coping to family outcomes during the initial year following pediatric traumatic injury. *Journal of Consulting and Clinical Psychology, 69,* 406–415.

Wade, S. L., Carey, J., & Wolfe, C. R. (2006a). The efficacy of an online cognitive–behavioral, family intervention in improving child behavior and social competence following pediatric brain injury. *Rehabilitation Psychology, 51,* 179–189.

Wade, S. L., Carrey, J., & Wolfe, C. R. (2006b). The efficacy of an online family intervention to reduce parental distress following pediatric brain injury. *Journal of Consulting and Clinical Psychology, 74,* 445–454.

Wade, S. L., Michaud, L., & Brown, T. M. (2006). Putting the pieces together: A family problem-solving intervention for pediatric TBI. *Journal of Head Trauma Rehabilitation, 21,* 57–67.

Wade, S. L., Taylor, H. G., Drotar, D., Stancin, T., & Yeates, K. O. (1996). Childhood traumatic brain injury: Initial impact on the family. *Journal of Learning Disabilities, 29,* 652–661.

Wade, S. L., Taylor, H. G., Drotar, D., Stancin, T., & Yeates, K. O. (1998). Family burden and adaptation during the initial year following traumatic brain injury (TBI) in children. *Pediatrics, 102,* 110–116.

Wade, S. L., Taylor, H. G., Drotar, D., Stancin, T., Yeates, K. O., & Minich, M. (2002). A prospective study of long-term caregiver and family adaptation following brain injury in children. *Journal of Head Trauma Rehabilitation, 17,* 96–111.

Wade, S. L., Taylor, H. G., Drotar, D., Yeates, K. O., Stancin, T., & Minich (2004). Interpersonal stressors and resources as predictors of caregiver adaptation following pediatric traumatic injury. *Journal of Consulting and Clinical Psychology, 72,* 776–784.

Yeates, K. O., Taylor, H. G., Drotar, D., Wade, S. L., Klein, S., Stancin, T., & Schatschneider, C. (1997). Preinjury family environment as a determinant of recovery from traumatic brain injuries in school-age children. *Journal of the International Neuropsychological Society, 3,* 617–630.

Yeates, K. O., Taylor, H. G., Woodrome, S. E., Wade, S. L., Stancin, T., & Drotar, D. (2002). Race as a moderator of parent and family outcomes following pediatric traumatic brain injury. *Journal of Pediatric Psychology, 27,* 393–404.

Ylvisaker, M., Adelson, D., Braga, L. W., Burnett, S. M., Glang, A., Feeney, T., et al. (2005). Rehabilitation and ongoing support after pediatric TBI: Twenty years of progress. *Journal of Head Trauma Rehabilitation, 20,* 95–109.

Ylvisaker, M., & Feeney, T. (1998). *Collaborative brain injury intervention: Positive everyday routines.* San Diego, CA: Singular Publishing Group.

Ylvisaker, M., Todis, B., Glang, A., Urbanczyk, B., Franklin, C., DePompei, R., et al. (2001). Educating students with TBI: Themes and recommendations. *Journal of Head Trauma Rehabilitation, 16,* 76–93.

PART V

EMERGING TOPICS FOR REHABILITATION PSYCHOLOGY

CHAPTER 23

VOCATIONAL REHABILITATION

Robert T. Fraser and Kurt Johnson

The rehabilitation psychologist is an integral part of the interdisciplinary vocational rehabilitation (VR) process for individuals with disabilities. Important services provided by the rehabilitation psychologist can include cognitive and psychosocial assessment, individual and family psychotherapy, behavioral intervention and consultation, pain management, and so forth, all of which enhance the client's vocational functioning. A rehabilitation psychologist is a licensed psychologist with the appropriate doctoral training, internship, and postdoctoral training, in some cases. The VR counselor, however, is usually an individual with a master's degree in rehabilitation counseling. Typically, a rehabilitation facility outpatient or inpatient team VR counselor provides targeted vocational services including initial vocational evaluation, situational assessment, return to work or work access planning, and liaison with state VR agencies in securing funding for diverse services important to a patient's work access or return to work. When a rehabilitation counselor is not on staff, the rehabilitation psychologist may play a more prominent role in the VR process. This chapter reviews the VR process, profiles VR counselor characteristics, discusses access to state agency services and their components, and offers advice for working with the state agency. By so doing, we intend to equip rehabilitation psychologists with the requisite knowledge to promote the VR process in their customary role.

THE VOCATIONAL REHABILITATION PROCESS

The federal/state VR program is the largest resource for clients with disabilities as they attempt to engage in work or reenter the workforce following injury or disability onset. Over the years, a significant private sector VR presence has emerged, largely serving those injured on the job within workers' compensation systems or providing services for veterans. Nonetheless, federal funding authorized by the Rehabilitation Act of 1973 and subsequent amendments and reauthorizations is the most significant source of support for VR efforts. The underpinning for this system is a large federal–state match from the Rehabilitation Services Administration (RSA). The federal match can be withdrawn if state agencies do not meet performance standards. States use differing administrative mechanisms for VR services provision ranging from a general agency or combined model to a specific agency for those with a discrete disability such as blindness.

VR counseling and one-to-one planning with consumers is the foundation of the state–federal VR program (Lewis & Johnson, 2003). This approach relies on a partnership between the person with the disability and the counselor who work together to identify the client's vocational interests and corresponding abilities, establish a suitable employment goal (or goals), and develop an action plan, traditionally known as an *individualized written rehabilitation plan*. The viability of this plan is generally based on the VR counselor's personal expertise and knowledge of the employment market.

The VR counselor must complete a comprehensive review of a client's strengths and vocational barriers (including possible accommodations that take into account the client's physical, mental, or emotional challenges) and then work with the client to identify discrete objectives to reach the goal (Rubin & Roessler, 2001). Specialized placement staff or other health professionals (e.g., a speech/language pathologist, assistive technology specialist, or occupational therapist) may become part of the treatment team as well. The VR process should be a dynamic one in which differing health care professionals collaborate in pursuit of the client's vocational goal.

PROFILE OF A STATE VOCATIONAL REHABILITATION COUNSELOR

State rehabilitation agencies are mandated to have master's level employees trained in VR. These individuals are eligible for the certification process as *certified rehabilitation counselors* (CRCs). Unfortunately, there are shortages of qualified counselors in a number of states. An individual with a master's degree in rehabilitation counseling should be trained in the VR process and eligibility determination, case finding, understanding medical and psychosocial aspects of disability, vocational evaluation and assessment, individual and group counseling, career information, assistive technology, and direct provision of vocational services such as job development (Flowers, Strong, Turner, Moore, & Edwards, 1998).

Froehlich and Linkowski (2002) surveyed perceived competencies of 413 rehabilitation counselors in three states and found significant discrepancies between training and the demands of their job. Counselors without graduate work and the CRC designation indicated needs for training in vocational services, case management, workers' compensation and employer services (to include technology), and assessment. Counselors, even at the advanced CRC level, cited continuing needs for training in vocational services and workers' compensation and employer service needs. Consequently, there may

not be a VR counselor with true vocational expertise working with clients referred for VR, but more of a "case manager." This can be problematic if the assigned counselor does not know a good community placement services vendor. The counselor, however, still may be a good case manager and guide to vocational and other funded services within the community.

It is important that the rehabilitation psychologist, whether a member of an inpatient/outpatient rehabilitation team or in other practice, know whether the liaison state VR counselor has a master's degree in rehabilitation counseling or has otherwise developed a considerable base of vocational expertise. Having met the CRC certification requirements (i.e., passing the CRC national test and credentials review) is a reasonable indication of professional competence in this field. Nonetheless, if one is referring a client with severe disability, no established viable vocational goal, and who is in need of intensive VR intervention, it is important to talk with the liaison counselor to establish how suitable services can be financed and a vocational goal achieved. In some cases, the rehabilitation psychologist's goal is to advocate effectively for the client with the state VR counselor.

State agency counselor education and skill level are not necessarily functions of an urban geographical location in the United States. For many years, some rural states, such as Alaska and Idaho, have hired state agency counselors trained at the master's level. Individuals in these largely rural states need to be particularly creative in services provision because often there are no community vendors from whom to purchase services. These counselors can be inventive in the provision of services in unique rural situations (e.g., development of home employment options, on-the-job training).

ACCESS TO THE STATE VOCATIONAL REHABILITATION AGENCY

Clients, particularly those with cognitive difficulties, should be directed to the state agency office nearest their residence and also told (in writing) the day and time for intake, as many state offices will take new referrals only on designated days. Clients should be sent to the agency with a specific referral letter from the rehabilitation psychologist, unit social worker, or other coordinator with any information about relevant history, potential vocational goals, and the types of services that may be necessary to achieve the goals (e.g., vocational evaluation, situational assessment, assistive technology, job coaching). Second, with the client's authorization, copies of pertinent medical, psychological, and other background information (e.g., relevant functional limitations) should accompany the referral letter. In some cases, the client will bring this information to the meeting. Having this information in place can expedite eligibility, establishing the level of severity that is needed to establish eligibility for services.

When agencies have more clients than they have resources to serve, federal regulations permit them to invoke an "order of selection" where clients with the most severe disabilities receive the highest priority. Severity is determined by the number of domains with significant functional limitations. Under these circumstances it is important that the referring source clearly document these functional limitations. The client, if able, rehabilitation psychologist, or other staff member should periodically contact the local agency to determine the client's placement on a "wait list" if services are not immediately available. Clients can move, or in the case of those with cognitive impairments, forget, or misinterpret that an appointment has been scheduled. One of our clients works at a private health club with the benefit of supported employment. His case had been terminated twice by the state agency because of his failure to respond to a letter for appointment because of his severe memory deficits. He had to be contacted and personally transported to the meeting with the state VR counselor to have his services reinstated.

ONE-STOP STATE EMPLOYMENT CENTERS

The Workforce Investment Act of 1998 instituted a standard expectation to locate state VR agencies (or at least counselors of the agency) within one-stop state employment service centers containing all relevant employment services. This center may help clients use computer software training programs. It can also provide access to other short-term programs

(e.g., job-seeking skills training). Service specialists worry that the specialized needs of employment seekers with disabilities may be lost in the hustle and bustle of general job seeking activity and service provision occurring at these one-stop employment centers.

SERVICES THAT CAN BE PROVIDED THROUGH STATE VOCATIONAL REHABILITATION

Many services are available through the state VR agency, and others are funded through approved community vendors. Specific services include the following:

- *Basic counseling, guidance, and case management.* State agency rehabilitation counselors often have large caseloads but can be effective in these roles during the VR process.
- *Vocational evaluation services for vocational goal clarification.* Initially this involves a comprehensive clinical interview and review of all available medical and psychosocial data. Transferability of skills to other potential jobs is also assessed. Additional testing can evaluate vocational interests, work values, personality and emotional functioning, academic ability, and other specific aptitudes. Psychological or neuropsychological data is generally integrated into the assessment effort. Identification of barriers to employment as well as specific areas of vocational strength and weakness relative to employment goals are functions of the evaluation. A good vocational evaluation should result in several specific viable occupational goals that are achievable and/or short- or long-term training necessary to attain the job goals. Other health and psychosocial needs should be addressed in the recommendations section of this report. If a job goal is not deemed viable, a community-based situational assessment can be recommended that will be provided by a community vendor.
- *Community-based situational assessment.* Transitional assessment or tryout as a volunteer at nonprofit educational institutions, hospitals, and other facilities which have an established volunteer program is a common service. Under

the U.S. Department of Labor (1993) waiver, a situational assessment can also be developed within the private sector for individuals with disabilities to explore their interests, assess current skill level, and provide training. Labor and Industry insurance is provided by the rehabilitation vendor who has established and is monitoring the assessment. The time limit for this nonpaid community assessment experience is 215 hours, on either a full-time or part-time basis. Whether public or private, it is extremely helpful to establish these "try-outs" where jobs are available. Many situational assessments, in addition to providing excellent data as to a job's viability for a given client, can provide a transition to paid work. They can also assist in determining accommodations that will be necessary for successful competitive employment.

- *Individual job-site consultation.* This is often requested for an individual whose job status is in question because of lack of proficiency. It involves an accommodation review as to whether a change in procedure, a workstation modification, or some type of assistive equipment may help a client stabilize on the job. Consistent with the provision for technical assistance under the Americans With Disabilities Act of 1990, this can be done by a vendor who is a private rehabilitation counselor, an occupational therapist, an assistive technologist, or some other pertinent health care provider, such as a neuropsychologist.

- *Job development, job placement follow-up (retention) services.* This involves targeted job development for a client and assistance in the actual job placement activity. In some cases, the client is supported with job leads, job-seeking skill training, resume revision, and so forth, whereas in other cases, the client is directly brokered by the rehabilitation provider to the company. State agencies vary on how these services are funded. It is ideal to have funding for follow-up, but given current funding limitations, state agencies may not fund follow-up activity by rehabilitation providers and have their own counselors assume this activity.

- *Job site supports or stabilization services.* This includes diverse forms of support to stabilize a client at a job site. Over the past 15 years, supported employment has become an important strategy (Gilbride, 2000). Wehman et al. (1990) and Wehman, Bricout, & Targett (1999) provided detailed descriptions of supported employment in traumatic brain injury. This process can involve a job coach using specific instructional techniques, prompts, accommodations, and so forth. A rehabilitation vendor might also use some other type of natural support or a paid coworker as trainer, using the model by Curl et al. (1996), as an example with traumatic brain injury. There are also different models of supported employment that include an enclave in which one job coach supports several individuals within a company that has a mix of workers with and without disability (Wehman et al., 1999). Unfortunately, state VR agencies often cannot pay for long-term supported employment services and cannot even provide preliminary services unless there is a plan in place to provide the needed long-term supports.

- *Benefits counseling.* Clients seeking employment may not grasp the impact of competitive employment on the benefits that they are receiving, which also can include important medical coverage. A benefits counselor can review an individual's Supplemental Security Income (SSI) and Social Security Disability Income (SSDI), workers' compensation, short-term or long-term disability, or other funding profile and establish what can be earned without losing current benefits, if this is a concern. A plan for achieving self-sufficiency, or individual work-related expense plan, can reduce income because of costs associated with work (e.g., auto costs, caregiver costs, job coaching). These plans relate to those on SSI or SSDI, respectively.

- *Transportation.* This can include a range of services such as a paid bus pass, taxi script, gas mileage, parking costs, a paid driver, and so forth. In sum, if it is required to allow a client's work access or return to work plan, transportation subsidy can often be provided.

- *Short- or long-term training.* The training provided may be relatively short certifications, such as forklift training, driver training, grocery clerk, nurse's aide, phlebotomist, and so forth. In other cases, it can be for 1 to 4 year technical or college programs, although 4-year support is quite infrequent.

■ *Other health services.* Specialty medical and health professions referral for diverse services (e.g., physiatrist consultation, neuro-opthalmology, pain management, neuropsychological evaluation, psychological, and other services) can be made. The state agency will generally fund these services when other client financial resources (i.e., first resources) including Medicaid are exhausted or unavailable, but this certainly can be an option.

■ *Assistive technology services.* When assistive technology is necessary either to clarify vocational or educational potential or to achieve employment, the state agency can either conduct or pay for an assistive technology evaluation, purchase devices, and provide training in device use. (For more information on assistive technology, see chap. 16, this volume.)

The rehabilitation psychologist should also be aware that psychological evaluation, neuropsychological evaluation, psychological or behavioral management consultation, or short-term psychotherapy (i.e., generally involving between 8 and 16 sessions) can be supported by state agency funding. This request should certainly be part of the client's referral letter to the state agency. In some cases, a legitimate service will be denied by a client's state agency counselor. If advocacy efforts are insufficient, it is important to note that every state has a Client Assistance Program (CAP) to help people who are applying for or receiving services funded by the federal Rehabilitation Act of 1973 (as amended). This can include not only client service issues with a state VR agency but also independent living centers and, which is discussed next. If a client has a valid concern, the CAP advocate will work with the state agency counselor or supervisor to resolve areas of disagreement.

THE PROJECTS WITH INDUSTRY PROGRAM

The Projects With Industry (PWI) program is a discretionary program funded by the RSA specifically to develop rehabilitation or employment sector part-

nerships within the community to assist clients with disabilities in gaining access to employment. RSA funding for 2006 was $19.5 million supporting 74 programs nationally. Projects of this type are funded throughout the country, some serving a specific disability group (e.g., multiple sclerosis), whereas others serve a general disability population. The availability of these PWIs is not uniform, but local state VR agencies will know whether any such programs are available in a particular (chiefly urban) area. Each rehabilitation placement program has an employer business advisory board, often with commitments from employers within the community to hire a specific number of employees with disabilities annually and yet requires no service fee from clients because of the RSA grant funding. As a caveat, however, the client must be as "job ready" as possible and have one or more viable job goals. This is an exciting federally sponsored program that requires a strong rehabilitation community/ employer partnership. Evaluation data (2003–2005) relating to the success of this PWI effort nationally have been encouraging relative to the percentages of those with severe disability who were placed (88%–90%; overall placement rate, 52%–62%), weekly increase in wages ($242–$253), and other indicators of rehabilitation placement success (U.S. Department of Education, Office of Special Education and Rehabilitation Services, 2007). The benefit of these programs is that if disability can be established with a viable job goal for the client, "no-cost" direct placement services can begin immediately.

WORKING SUCCESSFULLY WITH VOCATIONAL REHABILITATION

There are a number of considerations, or perhaps "tips," for working more effectively with a state VR agency. A simple referral may not evolve into timely services because of both client and agency issues. Some important considerations are as follows:

■ Develop a good working relationship with one or more rehabilitation counselors related to the disabilities you serve. Some medical and mental health centers have a liaison state VR counselor who comes weekly to do intake and work with new referrals. In other cases, this liaison relationship needs to be established and nurtured. It will be helpful to identify, through local consumer groups, state agency counselors who have an interest in the disabilities with which you are concerned as a rehabilitation psychologist. Over time, you may develop a liaison relationship or know when your counselor contact is doing intake work at the state agency. Having that personal contact with a trusted counselor with expertise relating to your disability group or groups is invaluable.

■ Once the client is referred to the state agency for VR services, it is important that the rehabilitation psychologist periodically follow up with the client or with the local agency, as necessary, to ensure that the client has made contact with the agency and is receiving services or is on the waiting list.

■ With authorization from the client, the VR counselor should be updated about any significant changes in the client's psychosocial status. To be successful, particularly with clients who have a severe disability, open communication is as important as the intervention being conducted. It can be helpful to maintain a weekly in-person or phone conference schedule. Over time, this can involve succinct information exchange about several mutual clients.

■ Be available to the local state agency VR personnel. This can involve in-service training, participation in annual training conferences or open rehabilitation forum discussions, and so forth. The more trust that state agency counselors have in the rehabilitation psychologist, the better attention will be paid to the needs of client referrals. This bond will also foster a flow of referrals to the rehabilitation psychologist's practice and/or service center.

Although some texts are specific to VR practices with particular groups such as those with traumatic brain injury (Fraser & Clemmons, 1999) or multiple sclerosis (Fraser, Clemmons, & Bennett, 2002), the comprehensive text by Brodwin, Tellez, and Brodwin (2002) provides VR practices information across all major disability groups. Being privy to

this type of information can be helpful in dealing with state VR counselors and requesting services.

CONCLUSION

This chapter has reviewed diverse aspects of the structure of the VR process, state agency VR, the VR services provided, and suggestions for working with the agency and its personnel. There are many effective state agency VR counselors who can provide critical services for VR clients and markedly improve their outcome. As in many states, the local agencies can be underfunded and overworked, with counselors having 150 or more client cases. When rehabilitation psychologists can serve as a resource for these individuals, their ability to work effectively and efficiently in achieving optimal outcomes for clients with disabilities is enhanced.

References

Brodwin, M. C., Tellez, F. A., & Brodwin, S. K. (Eds.). (2002). Medical, psychosocial, and vocational aspects of disability (2nd ed.). Athens, GA: Elliot & Fitzpatrick.

Curl, R. M., Fraser, R. T., Cook, R. G., & Clemmons, D. C. (1996). Traumatic brain injury rehabilitation: Preliminary findings for the coworker as trainer project. *Journal of Head Trauma Rehabilitation, 11,* 75–85.

Flowers, C., Strong, R., Turner, T., Moore, C., & Edwards, D. (1998). State vocational rehabilitation agency and preservice educational programs: Are complimentary needs being met? *Rehabilitation Counseling Bulletin, 41,* 217–230.

Fraser, R. T., & Clemmons, D. C. (Eds.). (1999). *Traumatic brain injury rehabilitation: Practical, vocational, neuropsychological, and psychotherapy interventions.* Boca Raton, FL: CRC Press.

Fraser, R. T., Clemmons, D. C., & Bennett, F. (2002). *Multiple sclerosis: Psychosocial and vocational interventions.* New York: Demos.

Froehlich, R., & Linkowski, D. (2002). An assessment of the training needs of state vocational rehabilitation counselors. *Rehabilitation Counseling Bulletin, 46,* 42–50.

Gilbride, D. (2000). Going to work: Placement trends in public rehabilitation. *Journal of Vocational Rehabilitation, 14,* 89–94.

Lewis, D., & Johnson, D. (2003). Assessing state vocational rehabilitation performance in serving individuals with disability. *Journal of Intellectual & Developmental Disability, 28,* 24–39.

Rubin, S., & Roessler, R. (2001). Foundations of the vocational rehabilitation process (5th ed.). Austin, TX: PRO-ED.

Wehman, P., Bricout, J. B., & Targett, P. (1999). Supported employment for persons with traumatic brain injury: A guide for implementation. In R. T. Fraser & D. C. Clemmons (Eds.), *Traumatic brain injury rehabilitation: Practical, vocational neuro-psychological, and psychotherapy interventions* (pp. 201–240). Boca Raton, FL: CRC Press.

Wehman, P., Kreutzer, J., West, M., Sherron, P., Zasler, N. D., Groah, C. H., et al. (1990). Return to work for persons with traumatic brain injury: A supported employment approach. *Archives of Physical Medicine and Rehabilitation, 71,* 1047–1052.

U.S. Department of Education, Office of Special Education and Rehabilitation Services. *Projects With Industry: Performance.* Retrieved April 20, 2007, from http://www.ed.gov/programs/rsapwi/performance.html

CHAPTER 24

SPIRITUALITY AND REHABILITATION

Kathie J. Albright, Martin Forchheimer, and Denise G. Tate

Tonya (a fictitious name) sustained a traumatic spinal cord injury in a motor vehicle accident at 22 years of age. Viewing herself as a religious and "good" person who devoted herself to community service, her initial framework for making sense of her injury was that it was "going to be a test from God," which she "assumed" she would pass and, thereby, she would be "up and walking in no time." Her focus at first was outward and other-centered; she concentrated her energies on trying to make her family "comfortable" by putting on a "smiley face." Initially, she did not experience a disruption in how she regarded herself, her place in the world, or her relationship with God. She read the Bible daily. Although she recognized that health care providers in the context of acute rehabilitation tried to help her achieve a "good enough mental state to be able to overcome this adversity," she was confused by feedback about her manner of coping: "I mean, they thought I was crazy talking about all this God stuff." It was further communicated to her that she was "not dealing with the reality" of her accident. About her generalized experience of rehabilitation professionals, she stated, "They don't want you to be suicidal, but they don't want you to be too hopeful. And I couldn't; I literally had trouble understanding that, because to me it was pick one. One or the other, but not both." About her rehabilitation stay, she recounted, "I didn't find it to be an encouraging atmosphere or anything." For over 3 years after her return to living in the community, Tonya found solace in her belief that she would be cured through an act of God. Later on, however, she confronted a spiritual crisis and, along with this, a marked dis-

ruption in her identity and her sense of self-worth. She became haunted by suicidal ideation, despite her belief that suicide is a sin. She reflected on this change in her life trajectory: "At first, you know, I was really upbeat, hopeful, thinking that this was going to be temporary—kind of like the story of Job. But then the reality, I guess, set in and then I got really upset, and I was mad at God because I know that He is all-powerful; He could snap His finger and I could be up and walking. Does it mean I'm not worth it? What does it say about me that God would allow me to suffer through something like this?" For Tonya, spiritual crisis cycles viciously with feelings of guilt: "What makes you [referring to herself] so important over others that are asking for miracles, that your miracles should be granted? And that's what makes this really, really hard for me, because I understand the selfishness that I have for wanting to be healed and wanting to walk again." [Story as told during an audiotaped interview in which Tonya reflected on her experience in coping with spinal cord injury.]

Tonya's story exemplifies the importance of considering spirituality in the overall health assessment and treatment of patients. Rehabilitation psychology is a health profession with expertise centering on psychosocial factors associated with chronic health conditions and disability (Frank & Elliott, 2000). Yet the field's literature is scant in its focus on an important dimension: spirituality. This is surprising, given the ascendance of spirituality as a construct in the wider psychological literature and, with this, more careful attention to its conceptualization and measurement (Hill et al., 2000). Spirituality is identified as an important factor in health (Plante & Sherman, 2001) and as a mechanism for coping with health-related adversity (Miller & Thoresen, 2003). Still, "at best it has received broad brush strokes on the canvas of holistic treatment and rehabilitation" (Webb, 2003, p. 16). This chapter acknowledges the importance of spirituality in rehabilitation and, in doing so, reviews: (a) defining the construct of spirituality, (b) measuring spiritual well-being, (c) empirical research, and (d) the clinical relevance of spirituality for rehabilitation psychologists.

DEFINING THE CONSTRUCT OF SPIRITUALITY

The English word *spirit* derives from the Latin *spiritus,* meaning "breath," and evolved to refer to the essence of something (Harper, 2001), although the term *spirituality* defies consensual definition. The task of defining spirituality is thorny because of its intrinsically intangible nature. Also, from a cultural and historical perspective, what it means to be spiritual is highly variable from individual to individual and context-dependent. However, a distinctive characteristic of spirituality, in all forms, is considered to be transcendence or a sense of connection to a greater whole that provides ultimate meaning (Ellison, 1983; Martsolf & Mickley, 1998). This connection may or may not involve a relationship with a higher power or a belief that God or gods exist (i.e., theism). In the context of this chapter, spirituality refers broadly to that which is core to a human sense of being, meaning, and purpose, and encompasses the search for life's meaning (Frankl, 1992).

In the attempt to define spirituality, many authors discriminate it from religion for varying philosophical and conceptual purposes (Ellison, 1983; Frankl, 1969; Hill et al., 2000). Others have sought to specify its dimensional character (Miller, 1999; Webb, 2003). Still others maintain that distinguishing between the constructs of spirituality and religiosity, or elucidating what they share in common, is an empirical matter, as is the discovery of how they, alone or together, impact other factors, such as health and resilience (Hill & Pargament, 2003). Although the construct of spirituality continues to evolve within the psychological literature

(Hill et al., 2000), it remains elusive and controversial, with its mainstream integration thwarted by the prevailing scientific paradigm requiring rigorous operational definitions.

MEASURING SPIRITUAL WELL-BEING

Coinciding with the recent expanded interest in spirituality, especially within the realm of health research (Miller & Thoresen, 2003), the number of measures assessing spirituality has grown. Historically, most measures have focused on religious spirituality or religiosity, generally Christian beliefs and with this, on religious observance, practice, or cohesion within a "faith community." Although religiously oriented measures are beyond this chapter's scope, excellent reviews can be found (Hill & Hood, 1999; Koenig, McCullough, & Larson, 2001). Nonreligious measures are fewer in number, with only a few having well-established psychometrics. A main reason for this is the lack of accessible, objective criteria for nonreligious, spiritual well-being.

Reviewed as follows are two scales designed to measure the construct of spiritual well-being. These measures, the Spiritual Well-Being Scale (Paloutzian & Ellison, 1982) and the Functional Assessment of Chronic Illness Therapies-Spiritual (Brady, Peterman, Fitchett, Mo, & Cella, 1999), could be considered when conducting research in this area. Their value as clinical tools is not well established, however, and norms are not available for rehabilitation populations. Reflecting different underlying conceptualizations, the two measures are quite different but share two important characteristics for which they were selected: (a) being part of a small group of primarily nontheistic measures demonstrating solid psychometrics and (b) enjoying extensive use with patient populations. Two other psychometrically promising measures developed with patient populations in mind, are the Spiritual Index of Well-Being (Daaleman & Frey, 2002) and the Spiritual Transcendence Scale (Piedmont, 2001). These instruments, with unique development using a motivational/trait approach, are not reviewed here for they have not enjoyed extensive field-testing.

The *Spiritual Well-Being Scale* (SWBS; Paloutzian & Ellison, 1982) is the most widely used measure for assessing spiritual well-being. Comprising two 10-item subscales, Existential Well-Being (EWB) and Religious Well-Being (RWB), it also yields a total score of Spiritual Well-Being (SWB). The EWB assesses sense of life satisfaction, direction, and purpose, whereas the RWB addresses the quality of one's relationship with God. Although nondenominational by design, the RWB's references to God and prayer limit its applicability somewhat. Psychometrically, the SWBS has good reliability (Paloutzian & Ellison, 1982), with coefficient alpha for the SWB, EWB, and RWB being .89, .78, and .82, respectively. Test–retest coefficients are .91, .86, and .94. Validity is suggested by the EWB's relatively high, negative correlation with depression (−0.43) and low correlations with frequency of religious worship (.22) and measures of religious fundamentalism (.08). Similarly, the RWB has a nominal association with depression (−.05) and high correlations with fundamentalism (.63) and religious worship (.56). The SWBS has been used extensively with various chronic illness and disability populations, with good results (Chiu, Emblen, Van Hofwegen, Sawatzky, & Meyerhoff, 2004), but it is problematic in terms of having significant ceiling effects among Protestants and Catholics (Genia, 2001).

The *Functional Assessment of Chronic Illness Therapies–Spiritual* (FACIT–SP; Brady et al., 1999) was first used in oncology and has been used extensively in spinal cord injury research. It has 12 items and two scales: Meaning and Faith. None of the items have any theistic attributes. An example of one of its items is: "I find comfort in my faith." Good internal consistency has been demonstrated for the FACIT–SP Total and scale scores, with Cronbach's alpha ranging from .81 to .88 and convergent/discriminant validity demonstrated with numerous scales of mood, life satisfaction, and religiosity in multiple patient populations (Peterman, Fitchett, Brady, Hernandez, & Cella, 2002). In a rehabilitation sample, the FACIT–SP was a significant predictor of global quality of life, controlling for physical, functional, and social well-being (Tate & Forchheimer, 2002).

In sum, a few measures assessing nontheistic, spiritual well-being are promising given evidence of their psychometric soundness and their patient applicability. Significant challenges remain, however, with the most fundamental concerning the absence of conceptual uniformity across measures. Lacking consistent definitions, validation of spiritual well-being measures is, at best, a daunting task. The lack of valid measures serves as a major barrier to spirituality's widespread incorporation into rehabilitation research; findings may be criticized as being artifacts of particular instruments and operational definitions, instead of providing insight into spirituality's dynamics as a whole or into its relationship with other important constructs. Although the constructs of spirituality and spiritual well-being elude consensual definition, the measures reviewed here, through consistent empirical use, may be the best tools available. A proliferation of measures could hinder progress because of the added diversity of conceptualizations this would entail.

EMPIRICAL RESEARCH

Spirituality has not sustained attention within the field of rehabilitation research, in contrast with its growing examination in the field of health research (Miller & Thoresen, 2003). The comparatively few researchers addressing it empirically have focused on spirituality in relationship with coping and/or quality of life (QoL), some linking it with rehabilitation outcomes (e.g., Fitchett, Rybarczyk, DeMarco, & Nicholas, 1999; Kim, Heinemann, Bode, Sliwa, & King, 2000; Matheis, Tulsky, & Matheis, 2006; McColl et al., 2000; Reily et al., 1998). Findings are consistent across the cited studies concerning the positive correlation between nontheistic or existential spirituality and self-reported, high QoL, in various aspects. In a recent meta-analysis of the relationship between spirituality and QoL pertaining to health, including most of the rehabilitation research cited earlier, the researchers concluded that their set of findings "support the conceptualization of spirituality as a distinct concept that *relates* [italics added] to quality of life" instead of a concept subsumed by QoL (Sawatzky, Ratner, & Chiu, 2005, p. 180). This meta-analysis underlines the significant relationship between the constructs of spirituality and QoL. With the caveat of the need for enhanced methodological rigor, the researchers call for further primary research detailing the nature and direction of this relationship. This also has intuitive appeal for rehabilitation populations.

Although little exists in terms of evidence-based knowledge in this area, continuing research is warranted on how one's spirituality may affect overall outcomes and QoL after disability through illness or injury. As expressed in the model of disability by the World Health Organization (WHO, 2001), the International Classification of Functioning, Disability, and Health, a number of factors should be considered in best addressing the needs of persons with disabilities and, therefore, in designing interventions for addressing these needs in a holistic manner. Systematic research is required to clarify how spirituality is implicated in the rehabilitation process and how it impacts the experience of living with disability and/or illness. Applied research is needed to examine how rehabilitation professionals, including psychologists, can adequately assess spiritual needs, identify spiritual factors predictive of community participation, and specify spiritually related interventions to improve outcomes. Careful analyses of spiritually oriented coping strategies at intrapersonal, interpersonal, and transpersonal levels are also needed to tease out naturally occurring connections as a basis for fostering the development of new forms of intervention. Methodological advances in specifying such conceptually and empirically derived intervention approaches are also needed to then conduct outcome studies using them (Kim et al., 2000).

CLINICAL RELEVANCE OF SPIRITUALITY FOR REHABILITATION PSYCHOLOGISTS

Clinical neglect of spirituality in medical rehabilitation is tied, in part, to health care providers feeling unprepared to address issues of spirituality given their scope of training and practice (Kilpatrick & McCullough, 1999). Other likely factors interfering with systematic attention to spiritual needs include the following: skepticism about the appropriateness of spiritually oriented interventions in health care, the nebulousness of spirituality, and the perceived risk of intrusiveness or inadvertent offense of individual values or beliefs. Reimbursement procedures and health care policies requiring documentation of

concrete, if not quantifiable, interventions and outcomes also pose obstacles to the integration of spirituality into medical rehabilitation.

Barriers aside, spirituality is clinically relevant for rehabilitation psychologists; they tread in the borderland containing spirituality and psychology when supporting the search for meaning in the face of adversity (Vash, 1994). As expressed by Shafranske (2001):

> Psychology shares with religion the focus on the personal heuristics that people use to make sense of their lives. These heuristics derive from beliefs concerning the fundamental nature of human existence. From this perspective, it may be found that psychological treatment necessarily involves *religious sentiment as broadly defined* [italics added]. (p. 315)

Spiritual crisis and existential tumult are often experienced in tandem in connection with serious physical disability or illness, making it difficult to distinguish between the need for spiritual counsel and the need for assistance in adjusting from a psychological perspective. In fixing attention within their scope of responsibilities, rehabilitation psychologists may view spirituality from the clinically pragmatic perspective of a basic will to meaning (Frankl, 1969), instead of through the lens of a particular spiritual orientation. Culturally diverse competency requires being prepared to provide support to persons with varying belief systems; utter respect and tolerance for personal beliefs empowers patients to discuss their innermost feelings and spiritual values, to find effective ways to process and cope with trauma and loss, and to establish a balance between asserting and letting go of control in the process of rebuilding their lives.

The role spirituality plays during rehabilitation for any given individual will reflect internal, dynamic fluctuations, making it important for the practitioner to attend to subtle shifts in what a patient may be communicating so as to respond appropriately. For example, a patient may dismiss spirituality as an issue initially but later experience a loss of faith. Another patient may start out as optimistic but lose motivation to engage in rehabilitation when functional gains stall. Yet other patients, such as those with a history of heavy substance abuse, may experience a spiritual awakening and, in concert, realize personal transformation. A patient's sense of personal meaning and spirituality, and struggles and successes in finding them, form a unique scaffold for providing psychological help. Key interventions may perhaps include encouraging patients to foster acceptance, forgiveness, motivation, serenity, or courage to embrace the future.

Certain traditions of applied research and practice located at the interface of psychology and spirituality are especially relevant for medical rehabilitation, with the psychology of forgiveness (Worthington, 2005) being a particularly good example. With their cognitive–motivational underpinnings, psychotherapeutic developments from a positive psychology perspective, such as hope psychology, hold considerable promise for rehabilitation psychologists as well (Dunn & Dougherty, 2005; Snyder, Lehman, Kluck, & Monsson, 2006). Many excellent resources (e.g., Miller, 1999; Sperry & Shafranske, 2004) examining the integration of spirituality in psychotherapeutic intervention exist for practitioners wanting to expand their competence.

CONCLUDING REMARKS

The risk is great that seriously injured or ill people will encounter a crisis of meaning, spiritual crisis, threatened identity, foreshortened sense of future, hopelessness, and even despair. However, confronting circumstances leading to disability or illness, and making sense of resultant change, can give rise to posttraumatic growth, newfound meaning, and positive identity transformation (Faull & Hills, 2006; Tate et al., 2006). A central aim of psychological practice in this context is to assist the individual in restoring a sense of integrity, meaning, purpose, and, ultimately, a future worth the taxing journey of rehabilitation. Rehabilitation psychologists can, in dialectical fashion, sensitively attend to personal meanings of trauma, loss, illness, and disability while, at the same time, assisting in mobilizing resources contributing to a sense of spiritual well-being, high QoL, and purpose in life. Although medical rehabilitation programs primarily target the restoration of physical function and independence, with rapidly advancing technologies further promoting a biomedical focus, advances are needed on another plane, too. Spirituality remains a relatively unexplored dimension warranting further empirical investigation and clinical consideration.

References

Brady, M. J., Peterman, A. H., Fitchett, G., Mo, M., & Cella, D. (1999). A case for including spirituality in quality of life measurement in oncology. *Psycho-Oncology, 8,* 417–428.

Chiu, L., Emblen, J. D., Van Hofwegen, L., Sawatzky, R., & Meyerhoff, H. (2004). An integrative review of the concept of spirituality in the health sciences. *Western Journal of Nursing Research, 26,* 405–28.

Daaleman, T. P., & Frey, B. B. (2004). The Spirituality Index of Well-Being: A new instrument for health-related quality-of-life research. *Annals of Family Medicine, 2,* 499–503.

Dunn, D. S., & Dougherty, S. B. (2005). Prospects for a positive psychology of rehabilitation. *Rehabilitation Psychology, 50,* 305–311.

Ellison, C. W. (1983). Spiritual well-being: Conceptualization and measurement. *Journal of Psychology and Theology, 11,* 330–340.

Faull, K., & Hills, M. D. (2006). The role of the spiritual dimension of the self as the prime determinant of health. *Disability and Rehabilitation, 28,* 729–740.

Fitchett, G. E., Rybarczyk, B. D., DeMarco, G. A., & Nicholas, J. J. (1999). The role of religion in medical rehabilitation outcomes: A longitudinal study. *Rehabilitation Psychology, 44,* 333–353.

Frank, R. G., & Elliot, T. R. (Eds.). (2000). *Handbook of rehabilitation psychology.* Washington, DC: American Psychological Association.

Frankl, V. E. (1969). *The will to meaning.* New York: New American Library.

Frankl, V. E. (1992). *Man's search for meaning: An introduction to logotherapy* (I. Lasch, Trans., 4th ed.). Boston: Beacon Press.

Genia, V. (2001). Evaluation of the Spiritual Well-Being Scale in a sample of college students. *The International Journal for the Psychology of Religion, 11*(1), 25–33.

Harper, D. (2001). *Online Etymology Dictionary.* Retrieved July 28, 2006, from http://www.etymonline.com

Hill, P. C., & Hood, R. W. (Eds.). (1999). *Measures of religiosity.* Birmingham, AL: Religious Education Press.

Hill, P. C., & Pargament, K. I. (2003). Advances in the conception and measurement of religion and spirituality: Implications for physical and mental health research. *American Psychologist, 58,* 64–74.

Hill, P. C., Pargament, K. I., Hood, R. W., Jr., McCullough, M. E., Swyers, J. P., Larson, D. B., & Zinnbauer, B. J. (2000). Conceptualizing religion and spirituality: Points of commonality, points of departure. *Journal for the Theory of Social Behavior, 30,* 51–77.

Kilpatrick, S. D., & McCullough, M. E. (1999). Religion and spirituality in rehabilitation psychology. *Rehabilitation Psychology, 44,* 388–402.

Kim, J., Heinemann, A. W., Bode, R. K., Sliwa, J., & King, R. B. (2000). Spirituality, quality of life, and functional recovery after medical rehabilitation. *Rehabilitation Psychology, 45,* 365–385.

Koenig, H. G., McCullough, M. E., & Larson, D. B. (2001). *Handbook of religion and health: A century of research reviewed.* Oxford, England: Oxford University Press.

Martsolf, D. S., & Mickley, J. R. (1998). The concept of spirituality in nursing theories: Differing worldviews and extent of focus. *Journal of Advanced Nursing, 27,* 294–303.

Matheis, E. N., Tulsky, D. S., & Matheis, R. J. (2006). The relation between spirituality and quality of life among individuals with spinal cord injury. *Rehabilitation Psychology, 51,* 265–261.

McColl, M. A., Bichenbach, J., Johnson, J., Nishihama, S., Schumaker, M., Smith, K., et al. (2000). Spiritual issues associated with traumatic-onset disability. *Disability and Rehabilitation, 22,* 555–564.

Miller, W. R. (Ed.). (1999). *Integrating spirituality into treatment: Resources for practitioners.* Washington, DC: American Psychological Association.

Miller, W. R., & Thoresen, C. E. (2003). Spirituality, religion, and health: An emerging research field. *American Psychologist, 58,* 24–35.

Paloutzian, R. F., & Ellison, C. W. (1982). Loneliness, spiritual well-being and the quality of life. In L. A. Peplau, & D. Perlman, (Eds.), *Loneliness: A sourcebook of current theory, research, and therapy* (pp. 224–237). New York: Wiley.

Piedmont, R. L. (2001). Spiritual transcendence and the scientific study of spirituality. *Journal of Rehabilitation, 67,* 4–14.

Peterman, A. H., Fitchett, G., Brady, M. J., Hernandez, L., & Cella, D. (2002). Measuring spiritual well-being in people with cancer: The Functional Assessment of Chronic Illness Therapy-Spiritual Well-Being Scale (FACIT-Sp). *Annals of Behavioral Medicine, 24,* 49–58.

Plante, T. G., & Sherman, A. C. (Eds.). (2001). *Faith and health: Psychological perspectives.* New York: Guilford Press.

Riley, B. B., Perna, R., Tate, D. G., Forchheimer, M., Anderson, C., & Luera, G. (1998). Types of spiritual well-being among persons with chronic illness: Their relation to various forms of quality of life. *Archives of Physical Medicine and Rehabilitation, 79,* 258–264.

Sawatzky, R., Ratner, P. A., & Chiu, L. (2005). A meta-analysis of the relationship between spirituality and quality of life. *Social Indicators Research, 72,* 153–188.

Shafranske, E. (2001). The religious dimension of patient care within rehabilitation medicine. In T. G. Plante & A. C. Sherman (Eds.), *Faith and health: Psychological perspectives* (pp. 311–335). New York: Guilford Press.

Snyder, C. R., Lehman, K. A., Kluck, B., & Monsson, Y. (2006). Hope for rehabilitation and vice versa. *Rehabilitation Psychology, 51,* 89–112.

Sperry, L., & Shafranske, E. P. (Eds.). (2004). *Spiritually oriented psychotherapy.* Washington, DC: American Psychological Association.

Tate, D. G., Duggan, C. H., Albright, K. J., Epstein, M. J., Jeji, T., Lequerica, A., et al. (2006). *Stress and coping over the life course: A perspective on women with spinal cord injury. Final report to the National Institute on Disability and Rehabilitation Research.* Ann Arbor, MI: University of Michigan Department of Physical Medicine and Rehabilitation.

Tate, D. G., & Forchheimer, M. (2002). Quality of life, life satisfaction, and spirituality: Comparing outcomes between rehabilitation and cancer patients. *American Journal of Physical Medicine & Rehabilitation, 81,* 400–410.

Vash, C. (1994). *Personality and adversity: Psychospiritual aspects of rehabilitation.* New York: Springer.

Webb, J. R. (2003). Spiritual factors and adjustment in medical rehabilitation: Understanding forgiveness as a means of coping. *Journal of Applied Rehabilitation Counseling, 34,* 16–23.

World Health Organization. (2001). *International classification of functioning and disability.* Geneva: Author.

Worthington, E. L., Jr. (Ed.). (2005). *Handbook of forgiveness.* New York: Routledge.

CHAPTER 25

WOMEN'S EXPERIENCE
OF DISABILITY

Margaret A. Nosek

The path to positive outcomes in counseling women with disabilities is best illuminated by an understanding of some of the many psychosocial challenges they face. This chapter provides a brief overview of the life context of women with disabilities, followed by a discussion of the physical and mental health issues they often confront, concluding with recommendations for rehabilitation psychologists working with this population.

PREVALENCE

Women with disabilities represent 15.4% of the 137 million noninstitutionalized, civilian women over age 5, compared with 14.3% of 130 million men (U.S. Census Bureau, 2005). They are significantly more likely than women with no limitations to live alone, be divorced, have less education, be unemployed, and live in poverty (Chevarley, Thierry, Gill, Ryerson, & Nosek, 2006). The demographic characteristics of this population will change substantially in the coming years because of the improved survival rate of low-birth-weight newborns, resulting in higher rates of children with activity limitation and permanent disability (National Center for Health Statistics, 2005) as well as the aging and functional decline of baby boomers. The combination of longer life expectancy and increased disability rates is expected to more than triple the number of persons over age 65 with severe or moderate disabilities in the next 50 years (Siegel, 1996). Our society does not seem prepared for the rapidly expanding population of women with disabilities across the life span who will face serious and possibly worsening social disadvantages (Nosek, 2006).

Population-based studies show that more than a quarter of women with disabilities live below the poverty level (American Community Survey, 2003a; Chevarley et al., 2006; Iezzoni, McCarthy, Davis, Harris-David, & O'Day, 2001). For women with disabilities age 21 to 64, two and one half times as many live in poverty, as do women with no disability in the same age group (26.4% vs. 10.5%). In every age group, more women than men with disabilities live in poverty (American Community Survey, 2003a).

ATTITUDINAL AND
ENVIRONMENTAL CONTEXT

Persistent negative stereotypes about disability have a serious effect on girls and women who are born with or acquire functional limitations. Viewed as "damaged goods" (Gill, 1996; Phillips, 1990), their sexuality is either devalued or overlooked altogether. Because they are not expected to seek or achieve satisfying intimate relationships, they are often not prepared to develop socially, to understand their sexuality or reproductive potential, or to recognize when they are being treated inappropriately or are in an abusive relationship (Nosek, Foley, Hughes, & Howland, 2001; Nosek, Howland, Rintala, Young, & Chanpong, 2001). This stereotype even penetrates the health care system, where primary physicians and obstetricians/gynecologists may forgo well-woman care if it is too difficult or time-consuming to perform the exams (Nosek & Howland, 1997; Nosek et al., 1996).

It can also be seen in law enforcement, where reports of abuse against women with disabilities are often not viewed as serious or credible, particularly in cases of abuse against women with mental impairments or those living in institutional settings (Nosek, Howland, & Young, 1997). Environmental barriers can be seen in restricted access to education, which is correlated with extremely low employment rates for women with disabilities. Women with disabilities and high educational attainment are less than half as likely to be employed as women in general (American Community Survey, 2003b). The combination of being unemployed and unmarried deprives many women with disabilities of access to private health insurance or retirement benefits. The accumulated effect of overt and subtle messages of being inadequate as well as being literally being excluded from the social mainstream may account for some of the significant psychological and social health problems that many women with disabilities experience, as described as follows.

Physical Health Issues

The functional limitations that define disability affect women at higher rates as they age, increasing from 6% of women ages 18 to 44 to 40% of those age 65 or older (Chevarley et al., 2006). In addition to their primary disabling condition, women also tend to experience secondary conditions such as skin breakdown, respiratory and urinary tract infections, as well as menstrual problems or diabetes. Pain, fatigue, and weakness are almost universally associated with physical disability in women but are often inadequately acknowledged or treated by health care professionals (Nosek, Hughes, Petersen, et al., 2006). Nearly a third of women with extensive functional limitations rate their overall health as poor compared with less than 1% of women with no limitations (Chevarley et al., 2006).

Women with physical disabilities are much less likely than women without disabilities to report regular moderate physical activity or regular vigorous activity (U.S. Department of Health and Human Services, 2000), particularly African American women with mobility impairments (Rimmer & Braddock, 2002). Women with a longer duration of disability, and those with greater pain, tended to report less physical activity, but those with greater self-efficacy for physical activity tended to engage in more of it

(Nosek, Hughes, Robinson-Whelen, Taylor, & Howland, 2006).

An unfortunate by-product of inadequate disability-related health-promotion information and environmental barriers experienced by many women with functional limitations is poor nutritional behaviors, a problem that is more severe among those who have greater self-care and mobility impairments and inadequate personal assistance (Nosek, Hughes, Robinson-Whelen, et al., 2006). Nearly half of women with physical disabilities are obese (Chevarley et al., 2006) compared with one fifth of women in the general population (U.S. Department of Health and Human Services, 2004). Better nutritional behaviors are strongly associated with better general mental health, more vitality, and higher levels of emotional role functioning in women with disabilities (Nosek, Hughes, Robinson-Whelen, et al., 2006).

Higher rates of smoking have been documented in women with physical disabilities compared with women without disabilities, especially among 18- to 44-year-olds (Chevarley et al., 2006), exacerbating their already high risk of breathing problems, poor circulation, osteoporosis, and skin problems. Some women with physical limitations indicate that they smoke to deal with depression and stress (Chappell, 1995).

Social Health Issues

Women with disabilities typically experience extraordinary problems with dating and establishing intimate relationships. Interviews with 31 women who had a range of physical disabilities revealed that they perceive themselves to be older than their nondisabled peers at the time of their first date and first serious relationship (Rintala et al., 1997). Some women with early onset of disability reported lacking age-appropriate social skills associated with dating, but even those who appeared to be socially outgoing and have strong social skills reported that friendships were less likely to evolve into romantic relationships than they were for their nondisabled friends. Potential dating partners experienced negative peer pressure or mistakenly believed that the woman was physically unable to have sex. Practical barriers including dependence on parents for personal assistance, the use of an assistive devices or medical equipment, such as a wheelchair or urinary catheter, were often factors affecting intimacy. Women whose disabilities were largely invisible reported frustration with partners who expected them to function normally. Women with adult onset disability told of having difficulty reestablishing trust and being willing to take risks. Many problems in pursuing positive relationships, especially dealing with the expectations of others and establishing a positive self-identity, are even more difficult for women with disabilities who come from minority cultures (Parkin & Nosek, 2002).

Violence, insecurity, and fear of rejection or abandonment, plus a lack of awareness among helping professionals and the architectural and program inaccessibility of most battered women's resources, result in many women with disabilities staying in destructive relationships (Nosek et al., 1997). A national study of approximately 1,000 women showed that women with disabilities are more likely to experience abuse at the hands of a greater number of perpetrators, both intimate partners and strangers, and for longer periods than are women without disabilities (Young, Nosek, Howland, Chanpong, & Rintala, 1997). Women with disabilities encounter risks unique to their disabling conditions, including refusal to provide assistance with essential personal needs and the withholding of assistive devices or medications (Nosek, Foley, et al., 2001). Another investigation of women with physical disabilities revealed a 10% rate of physical, sexual, or disability-related violence in the past year (McFarlane et al., 2001). A later analysis revealed that women who were less mobile, either because of impairment or lack of assistive devices, who were younger, who experienced greater social isolation, and who had higher levels of depression were more likely to report abuse within the past year (Nosek, Taylor, Hughes, & Taylor, 2006). According to the National Institute of Mental Health (National Institute of Mental Health, 2005), abuse may lead to depression by fostering low self-esteem, a sense of helplessness, self-blame, and social isolation. Not surprisingly, then, depression and experience with abuse have been linked in research on women with disabilities (Hughes, Swedlund, Petersen, & Nosek, 2001; Nosek, Taylor, et al., 2006).

Mental Health Issues

The impact of disability on the mental health of women can be even more significant than the physical impact. Measures of independent-mindedness, perceived control, self-esteem, or depression, to name a few, are often not associated with level of physical impairment or functional limitation. A mild case of arthritis can be emotionally devastating and incapacitating to one woman whereas a serious injury may have the effect of giving another woman purpose in life and a drive to succeed. Many factors related to personal history, personality traits, life context, demographic characteristics, educational and work opportunities, and social support can mediate the effect of disability on mental health.

Self-esteem.   Diminished self-esteem in people with disabilities and chronic illnesses has been associated with depression (Harter, 1993), increased pain and fatigue (Cornwell & Schmitt, 1990; Krol et al., 1994), and greater functional limitation (Burckhardt, 1985; Taal, Rasker, & Wiegman, 1997). In a national study of women with physical disabilities (Nosek, Howland, et al., 2001), more than three quarters of the women had high self-esteem and a positive body image, regardless of the severity of disability. For the remainder, however, factors such as unemployment, social isolation, abuse, and limited opportunities to establish satisfying intimate relationships were correlated with low self-esteem (Nosek, Hughes, Swedlund, Taylor, & Swank, 2003). Women with more severe disabilities tended to perceive that others saw them less favorably and, thus, were significantly less likely to have positive intimate relationships (Nosek et al., 2003).

Sexuality.   Conventional social opinion is that women with disabilities are asexual (Adcock & Newbigging, 1990; Danek, 1992; Lesh & Marshall, 1984), have no need for intimacy or sexual expression, and are incapable of being a sexual partner (Hanna & Rogovsky, 1992). Prior to the last decade, sexuality was rarely examined from the perspective of women with disabilities (Nosek, 1996).

The association of physical disability in women with physiological, psychological, emotional, and interpersonal problems with sexuality is well documented. The national comparative study of women with and without physical disabilities (Nosek et al., 1996) found that both groups had equivalent sexual desire, but women without disabilities tended to have sexual activity less often and reported lower levels of sexual satisfaction. Difficulties with sexual response are especially prevalent in women who have central nervous system disorders, such as spinal cord injury, multiple sclerosis, brain injury, or stroke (Ferreiro-Velasco et al., 2005; Sipski, 2001; Sipski & Arenas, 2006; Zorzon et al., 1999).

Both men and women with more severe and shorter duration of disability experienced lower levels of sexual self-esteem and sexual satisfaction and significantly higher levels of what the authors refer to as *sexual depression* when compared with people who reported mild or no impairments (McCabe & Taleporos, 2003). Greater intrusiveness of rheumatoid arthritis on sexuality was related to greater physical disability, pain, and depression in both men and women (Kraaimaat, Bakker, Janssen, & Bijlsma, 1996). Higher depression scores were among the characteristics that distinguished persons with multiple sclerosis who had sexual dysfunction from those who did not (Demirkiran, Sarica, Uguz, Yerdelen, & Aslan, 2006; Zorzon et al., 1999).

Stress. Women with physical disabilities report elevated perceived stress (Hughes, Taylor, Robinson-Whelen, & Nosek, 2005; Rintala, Hart, & Fuhrer, 1996), which reflects the extent to which they view their lives as unpredictable, uncontrollable, and overloading (Cohen & Williamson, 1988). One study found that those with three or more functional limitations are 10 times more likely to report having difficulty with day-to-day stress than are women with no limitations (21% vs. 2%) when age was adjusted (Chevarley et al., 2006). Greater perceived stress in a sample of women with physical disabilities was linked with lower levels of social support, greater pain limitations, and recent experience with abuse (Hughes, Taylor, et al., 2005). A stress management intervention designed to enhance self-efficacy and social connectedness in women with physical disabilities was found to reduce stress and pain limitations and improve mental health (Hughes, Robinson-Whelen, Taylor, & Hall, 2006).

Depression. Women with disabilities are at least twice as likely to report depressive symptomotology as men and women in general (McGrath et al., 1990; U.S. Department of Health and Human Services, 1999), with prevalence estimates ranging from 30% to 59% (Chevarley et al., 2006; Ferguson & Cotton, 1996; Hughes et al., 2001; U.S. Department of Health and Human Services, 2000; Ward et al., 1999). Some common disability-related symptoms (e.g., fatigue, sleep disturbance) can mask psychological distress (Hughes, Robinson-Whelen, Taylor, Petersen, & Nosek, 2005) and leave depression in women with disabilities underdetected and undertreated. A study of a large sample of predominantly minority and low income women with physical disabilities found that half scored in the mildly depressed range or higher, and less than half of those had received recent treatment (Hughes, Robinson-Whelen, Taylor, Petersen, & Nosek, 2005). Those identified as Hispanic were the least likely to have received treatment. Women classified as depressed were significantly younger, had shorter duration of disability, and had more secondary conditions than the nondepressed women, but did not differ on any demographic characteristic or level of functional limitation. The Center for Research on Women with Disabilities has developed a depression self-management intervention for women with disabilities that incorporates the following five elements: (a) monitoring of daily mood and activities, (b) self-management skill-building exercises, (c) self-efficacy training, (d) a buddy system designed to enhance connectedness and offer mutual support for weekly action planning, and (e) disability awareness.

RECOMMENDATIONS FOR THE PRACTICE OF REHABILITATION PSYCHOLOGY

A growing movement of women with disabilities is advocating for their rightful position in society and sharing their successful strategies with others in the same situation. The proliferation of Web-based resources for women's health, information on disability rights advocacy, and personal stories by women thriving with disability are helping many women strengthen their survival skills and assert their self-worth.

There is much that rehabilitation psychologists can do to counteract the damaging effects of social stereotypes and insensitive, inaccessible social and health care systems and to promote healthy living among women with disabilities. The following five recommendations may improve the provision of services to women with disabilities:

- *Reinforce intrinsic value.* Cognitive behavior therapy and psychoeducational interventions can teach women to reject stereotypic and limiting perceptions about their self-worth and deal with their fears about survival and rejection. Skills for enhancing self-esteem, managing depression, and reducing stress have been successfully taught in workshops that use peer facilitators (Hughes et al., 2006; Hughes, Robinson-Whelen, Taylor, Hall, & Rehm, 2008; Hughes, Taylor, Robinson-Whelen, Swedlund, & Nosek, 2004).

- *Encourage health-promoting behaviors.* The development and maintenance of behaviors, such as physical activity and good nutrition can result in significantly improved physical and mental health. Some women may assume that their disability exempts them from exercise and healthy eating, that smoking is an acceptable means of self-managing depression and pain, and that abusive relationships are better than no relationships at all. Mental health professionals may help to undermine these assumptions and connect women with disabilities with resources that could support and assist them in achieving a healthier lifestyle.

- *Focus on connections.* There is much to be gained by applying to women with disabilities the Relational Cultural Model, which focuses on the power of caregiving and relationships in women's lives (Jordan, 1994, 2002; Jordan & Hartling, 2002; Miller, 1988). To counteract the isolation that characterizes the lives of women with disabilities, encouragement and information should be offered about how they can improve their levels of social integration and seek out opportunities for connecting with others.

- *Work with other health providers.* Insurance reimbursement restrictions, privacy requirements, and barriers to interdisciplinary communication can prevent rehabilitation psychologists from

obtaining important information about their clients' physical health as it relates to their mental health, but this type of communication is essential for developing appropriate therapeutic protocols. Changing one medication, authorizing the purchase of one assistive device, or obtaining a referral to a therapeutic recreation program may be the key ingredient for obtaining a successful rehabilitation outcome.

- *Teach empowerment.* By increasing the visibility of disability issues and providing peer role models, the disability rights movement and its service arm, the national network of centers for independent living, have made significant differences in the lives of many people overwhelmed by the realities of living with disability who have been unable to obtain needed services. Referral to these organizations can help women with disabilities improve their self-advocacy skills and connect with others who share their struggle.

Appreciation of one's worth, understanding of one's disability and its potential for physical and mental wellness, recognition of violent or discriminatory treatment, assertive communication, self-management of health conditions, partnerships with health care providers, and the ability to seek and obtain assistance in all areas of need are perceptions that can be changed and skills that can be taught. The challenge and privilege for rehabilitation psychologists is to increase their awareness of the numerous issues that are relevant for women with disabilities, to become competent in teaching empowerment skills, and to learn to judge when the timing is right for intervention.

References

Adcock, C., & Newbigging, K. (1990). Women in the shadows: Women, feminism, and clinical psychology. In E. Burman (Ed.), *Feminists and psychological practice* (pp. 132–188). London: Sage.

American Community Survey. (2003a). *Sex by age by disability status by poverty status for the civilian noninstitutionalized population 5 years and over. Summary Table P060.* Retrieved July 31, 2006 from http://factfinder.census.gov/servlet/DTTable?_bm=y &-state=dt&-context=dt&-ds_name=ACS_2004_ EST_G00_&-mt_name=ACS_2004_EST_G2000_ B18030&-tree_id=304&-all_geo_types=N&-_caller=

geoselect&-geo_id=05000US48201&-search_
results=01000US&-format=&-_lang=en

American Community Survey. (2003b). *Sex by age by physical disability by employment status for the civilian noninstitutionalized population 5 years and over, Summary Table PCT041.* Retrieved July 31, 2006, from http://www.census.gov/hhes/www/disability/data_title.html#2000

Burckhardt, C. S. (1985). The impact of arthritis on quality of life. *Nursing Research, 34,* 11–16.

Chappell, M. (1995). *Relief at what cost: Women with disabilities and substance use/misuse: tobacco, alcohol and other drugs, lessons from the research.* Montréal, Québec: DisAbled Women's Network Canada.

Chevarley, F., Thierry, J. M., Gill, C. J., Ryerson, A. B., & Nosek, M. A. (2006). Health, preventive health care, and health care access among women with disabilities in the 1994–1995 National Health Interview Survey. *Women's Health Issues, 16,* 297–312.

Cohen, S., & Williamson, G. M. (1988). Perceived stress in a probability sample of the United States. In S. Spacapan & S. Oskamp (Eds.), *The social psychology of health: Claremont symposium on applied social psychology* (pp. 31–67). Newbury Park, CA: Sage.

Cornwell, C. J., & Schmitt, M. H. (1990). Perceived health status, self-esteem, and body image in women with rheumatoid arthritis or systemic lupus erythematosus. *Research in Nursing and Health, 13,* 99–107.

Danek, M. M. (1992). The status of women with disabilities revisited. *Journal of Applied Rehabilitation Counseling, 23,* 7–13.

Demirkiran, M., Sarica, Y., Uguz, S., Yerdelen, D., & Aslan, K. (2006). Multiple sclerosis patients with and without sexual dysfunction: Are there any differences? *Multiple Sclerosis, 12,* 209–214.

Ferguson, S. J., & Cotton, S. (1996). Broken sleep, pain, disability, social activity, and depressive symptoms in rheumatoid arthritis. *Australian Journal of Psychology, 48,* 9–14.

Ferreiro-Velasco, M. E., Barca-Buyo, A., de la Barrera, S. S., Montoto-Marques, A., Vazquez, X. M., & Rodriguez-Sotillo, A. (2005). Sexual issues in a sample of women with spinal cord injury. *Spinal Cord, 43,* 51–55.

Gill, C. (1996). Becoming visible: Personal health experiences of women with disabilities. In D. M. Krotoski, M. A. Nosek, & M. A. Turk (Eds.), *Women with physical disabilities: Achieving and maintaining health and well-being* (pp. 5–15). Baltimore: Brookes Publishing.

Hanna, W. J., & Rogovsky, E. (1992). On the situation of African-American women with disabilities. *Journal of Applied Rehabilitation Counseling, 23*(4), 39–45.

Harter, S. (1993). Causes and consequences of low self-esteem in children and adolescents. In R. Baumeister (Ed.), *Self-esteem: The puzzle of low self-regard* (pp. 87–111). New York: Plenum Press.

Hughes, R. B., Robinson-Whelen, S., Taylor, H. B., Petersen, N., & Nosek, M. A. (2005). Characteristics of depressed and non-depressed women with physical disabilities. *Archives of Physical Medicine and Rehabilitation, 86,* 473–479.

Hughes, R. B., Robinson-Whelen, S., Taylor, H. B., & Hall, J. W. (2006). Stress self-management: An intervention for women with physical disabilities. *Women's Health Issues, 16,* 389–399.

Hughes, R. B., Robinson-Whelen, S., Taylor, H. B., Hall, J. W., & Rehm, L. P. (2008). *A group depression intervention for rural women with physical disabilities.* Unpublished manuscript.

Hughes, R. B., Robinson-Whelen, S., Taylor, H. B., Petersen, N., & Nosek, M. A. (2005). Characteristics of depressed and nondepressed women with physical disabilities. *Archives of Physical Medicine and Rehabilitation, 86,* 473–479.

Hughes, R. B., Swedlund, N., Petersen, N., & Nosek, M. A. (2001). Depression and women with spinal cord injury. *Topics in Spinal Cord Injury Rehabilitation, 7*(1), 16–24.

Hughes, R. B., Taylor, H. B., Robinson-Whelen, S., & Nosek, M. A. (2005). Perceived stress in women with physical disabilities: Identifying psychosocial correlates. *Womens Health Issues, 15,* 14–20.

Hughes, R. B., Taylor, H. B., Robinson-Whelen, S., Swedlund, N., & Nosek, M. A. (2004). Enhancing self-esteem in women with physical disabilities. *Rehabilitation Psychology, 19,* 295–302.

Iezzoni, L. I., McCarthy, E. P., Davis, R. B., Harris-David, L., & O'Day, B. (2001). Use of screening and preventive services among women with disabilities. *American Journal of Medical Quality, 16*(4), 135–144.

Jordan, J. V. (1994). *A relational perspective on self-esteem: Work in progress.* Wellesley, MA: Stone Center Working Paper Series.

Jordan, J. V. (2002). *Learning at the margin: New models of strength.* Wellesley, MA: Stone Center Working Paper Series.

Jordan, J. V., & Hartling, L. M. (2002). New developments in relational-cultural theory. In M. Ballou & L. S. Brown (Eds.), *Rethinking mental health and disorders: Feminist perspectives* (pp. 48–70). New York: Guilford Press.

Kraaimaat, F. W., Bakker, A. H., Janssen, E., & Bijlsma, J. W. (1996). Intrusiveness of rheumatoid arthritis on sexuality in male and female patients living with a spouse. *Arthritis Care and Research, 9,* 120–125.

Krol, B., Sanderman, R., Suurmeijer, T. P. B. M., Doeglas, D. M., van Rijswijk, M., & van Leeuwen, M. (1994). Disease characteristics, level of self-esteem and psychological well-being in rheumatoid arthritis patients. *Scandinavian Journal of Rheumatology, 23,* 8–12.

Lesh, K., & Marshall, C. (1984). Rehabilitation: Focus on women with disabilities. *Journal of Applied Rehabilitation Counseling, 15*(1), 18–21.

McCabe, M. P., & Taleporos, G. (2003). Sexual esteem, sexual satisfaction, and sexual behavior among people with physical disability. *Archives of Sexual Behavior, 32,* 359–369.

McFarlane, J., Hughes, R. B., Nosek, M. A., Groff, J. Y., Swedlund, N., & Mullen, P. D. (2001). Abuse assessment screen-disability (AAS-D): Measuring frequency, type, and perpetrator of abuse towards women with physical disabilities. *Journal of Women's Health and Gender-Based Medicine, 10,* 861–866.

McGrath, E., Keita, G. P., Strickland, B. R., Russo, N. F., McGrath, E., Keita, G. P., et al. (1990). *Women and depression: Risk factors and treatment issues. Final report.* Washington, DC: American Psychological Association's National Task Force on Women and Depression.

Miller, J. B. (1988). *Connections, disconnections, and violations.* Wellesley, MA: Stone Center Working Paper Series.

National Center for Health Statistics. (2005). *Health, United States, 2005, with Chartbook on Trends in the Health of Americans. Table 58: Limitation of activity caused by chronic conditions, according to selected characteristics. United States, selected years 1997–2003.* Retrieved August 28, 2006, from www.cdc.gov/nchs/data/hus/hus05.pdf

National Institute of Mental Health. (2005). *Depression: What every woman should know.* Retrieved November 23, 2006 from http://www.nimh.nih.gov/publicat/depwomenknows.cfm

Nosek, M. A. (1996). Wellness among women with physical disabilities. *Sexuality and Disability, 14,* 165–182.

Nosek, M. A. (2006). The changing face of women with disabilities: Are we ready? *Journal of Women's Health and Gender-Based Medicine, 15,* 996–999.

Nosek, M. A., Foley, C. C., Hughes, R. B., & Howland, C. A. (2001). Vulnerabilities for abuse among women with disabilities. *Sexuality and Disability, 19,* 177–190.

Nosek, M. A., & Howland, C. A. (1997). Breast and cervical cancer screening among women with physical disabilities. *Archives of Physical Medicine and Rehabilitation, 78*(12, Suppl. 5), S39–S44.

Nosek, M. A., Howland, C. A., Rintala, D. H., Young, M. E., & Chanpong, G. F. (2001). National study of women with physical disabilities: Final report. *Sexuality and Disability, 19*(1), 5–39.

Nosek, M. A., Howland, C. A., & Young, M. E. (1997). Abuse of women with disabilities: Policy implications. *Journal of Disabilities Policy Studies, 8,* 157–176.

Nosek, M. A., Hughes, R. B., Petersen, N. J., Taylor, H. B., Robinson-Whelen, S., Byrne, M., et al. (2006). Secondary conditions in a community-based sample of women with physical disabilities over a 1-year period. *Archives of Physical Medicine and Rehabilitation, 87,* 320–327.

Nosek, M. A., Hughes, R. B., Robinson-Whelen, S., Taylor, H. B., & Howland, C. A. (2006). Physical activity and nutritional behaviors of women with physical disabilities: Physical, psychological, social, and environmental influences. *Women's Health Issues, 16,* 323–333.

Nosek, M. A., Hughes, R. B., Swedlund, N., Taylor, H. B., & Swank, P. (2003). Self-esteem and women with disabilities. *Social Science and Medicine, 56,* 1737–1747.

Nosek, M. A., Rintala, D. H., Young, M. E., Howland, C. A., Foley, C. C., Rossi, C. D., et al. (1996). Sexual functioning among women with physical disabilities. *Archives of Physical Medicine and Rehabilitation, 77,* 107–115.

Nosek, M. A., Taylor, H. B., Hughes, R. B., & Taylor, P. (2006). Disability, psychosocial, and demographic characteristics of abused women with physical disabilities. *Violence Against Women, 12,* 838–850.

Parkin, E. F., & Nosek, M. A. (2002). Collectivism versus independence: Perceptions of independent living and independent living services by Hispanic Americans and Asian Americans with disabilities. *Rehabilitation Education, 14,* 375–394.

Phillips, M. J. (1990). Damaged goods: Oral narratives of the experience of disability in American culture. *Social Science and Medicine, 30,* 849–857.

Rimmer, J. H., & Braddock, D. (2002). Health promotion for people with physical, cognitive and sensory disabilities: An emerging national priority. *American Journal of Health Promotion, 16,* 220–224.

Rintala, D. H., Hart, K. A., & Fuhrer, M. J. (1996). Perceived stress in individuals with spinal cord injury. In D. Krotoski, M. A. Nosek, & M. A. Turk (Eds.), *Women with physical disabilities: Achieving and maintaining health and well-being* (pp. 223–242). Baltimore: Brookes Publishing.

Rintala, D. H., Howland, C. A., Nosek, M. A., Bennett, J. L., Young, M. E., Foley, C. C., et al. (1997). Dating issues for women with physical disabilities. *Sexuality and Disability, 15,* 219–242.

Siegel, J. (1996). Aging into the 21st century. Bethesda, MD: Administration on Aging, U.S. Department of Health and Human Services.

Sipski, M. L. (2001). Sexual function in women with neurologic disorders. *Physical Medicine and Rehabilitation Clinics of North America, 12,* 79–90.

Sipski, M. L., & Arenas, A. (2006). Female sexual function after spinal cord injury. *Progress in Brain Research, 152,* 441–447.

Taal, E., Rasker, J. J., & Wiegman, O. (1997). Group education for rheumatoid arthritis patients. *Seminars in Arthritis and Rheumatism, 26,* 805–816.

U.S. Census Bureau. (2005). *2005 American community survey S1801. Disability characteristics.* Retrieved January 24, 2007, from http://factfinder.census.gov/servlet/STTable?_bm=y&-qr_name=ACS_2005_EST_G00_S1801&-geo_id=01000US&-ds_name=ACS_2005_EST_G00_&-_lang=en&-format=&-CONTEXT=st

U.S. Department of Health and Human Services. (1999). *Executive summary mental health: Culture, race, and ethnicity. A supplement to mental health: A report of the Surgeon General.* Retrieved November 21, 2006, from http://www.surgeongeneral.gov/library/mentalhealth/cre/execsummary-1.html

U.S. Department of Health and Human Services. (2000). *Healthy people 2010: Understanding and improving health and objectives for improving health* (2nd. ed.). Bethesda, MD: U.S. Government Printing Office.

U.S. Department of Health and Human Services. (2004). *Women's health USA.* Retrieved December 30, 2006, from http://mchb.hrsa.gov/whusa04/pages/ch2.htm#obesity

Ward, M. M., Lotstein, D. S., Bush, T. M., Lambert, R. E., van Vollenhoven, R., & Neuwelt, C. M. (1999). Psychosocial correlates of morbidity in women with systemic lupus erythematosus. *Journal of Rheumatology, 26,* 2153–2158.

Young, M. E., Nosek, M. A., Howland, C. A., Chanpong, G., & Rintala, D. H. (1997). Prevalence of abuse of women with physical disabilities. *Archives of Physical Medicine and Rehabilitation, 78* (12, Suppl. 5), S34–S38.

Zorzon, M., Zivadinov, R., Bosco, A., Bragadin, L. M., Moretti, R., Bonfigli, L., et al. (1999). Sexual dysfunction in multiple sclerosis: A case-control study: I. Frequency and comparison of groups. *Multiple Sclerosis, 5,* 418–427.

CHAPTER 26

THE SOCIAL PSYCHOLOGY
OF DISABILITY

Dana S. Dunn

There is general consensus in the literature on physical disability that the
problems of the handicapped are not
physical, but social and psychological.
—*Meyerson* (1948a, p. 2)

Because the world sets people with con-
spicuous disabilities apart as different,
we become objects of fascination, curiosity, and analysis . . . avatars of misfortune and misery, stock figures
in melodramas about courage and
determination . . . Instead of letting the
world turn me into a disability object,
I have insisted on being a subject in the
grammatical sense: not the passive "me"
who is acted on, but the active "I" who
does things.
—*Johnson* (2005, pp. 2–3)

As these epigraphs—one old, one recent—amply
illustrate, the social world affects the experiences of
people with spinal cord injuries, amputations, brain
injuries, mental illness, multiple sclerosis, and other
disabilities now as it did almost 60 years ago. The
social psychology of disability involves social perception, judgment, affect, and behavior on the part
of the perceiver and the perceived. Social psychological processes are undeniable and influential,
impinging on people with disabilities, individuals

receiving rehabilitative services, and nondisabled
caregivers and casual observers.

The social psychology of disability should be a
pressing concern if only because people with disabilities represent close to 20% of the population of
the United States (LaPlante & Carlson, 1996). Yet
people with disabilities are not a special community within the larger citizenry (Gill, Kewman, &
Brannon, 2003); they share in, contribute to, and are
bound up with the wider social milieu. To that end,
I review some social psychological theories and key
factors identified within them that inform the rehabilitative process and the understanding of the experience of disability. Although social psychology and
rehabilitation psychology share some assumptions
about human psychology, regrettably, scholarly
communication between the two subdisciplines is
limited, so that research efforts progress along separate, if generally parallel, pathways. Still, hope for a
constructive rapprochement remains (Asch & Fine,
1988; Dunn, 1994; Leary & Maddux, 1987; see also
Olkin & Pledger, 2003), especially with the renewed
focus on broader frameworks for disability research
(e.g., Tate & Pledger, 2003) that embrace established values of practice and science in rehabilitation psychology (e.g., Dembo, 1982; Frank &
Elliott, 2000; Meyerson, 1948a) and the subfield
known as positive psychology (Dunn & Dougherty,
2005; Seligman & Csikszentmihalyi, 2000).

This chapter is dedicated to the memory of two fine psychologists who cared deeply about the social worlds and well-being of others: Harold E. Yuker
and C. R. Snyder. Portions of this chapter are based on the version appearing in the first edition of this handbook. I thank the editors for their helpful
suggestions and constructive comments.

OVERVIEW

Social psychology is the scientific study of social behavior, and it entails the critical examination of how we think and feel about, influence, and relate to the actual, imagined, or assumed presence of other people (e.g., Allport, 1985; see also Jones, 1998). To study social behavior, social psychologists systematically examine personal or situational factors affecting social perception, expectation, and interaction when two or more persons gather together. Personal factors include people's physical or dispositional qualities, their emotional states, and the role of individuals as perceivers or as the targets of others' perceptions. Situational factors—variables or constants outside people—can be tangible (e.g., friends, acquaintances, strangers) or intangible (e.g., cultural norms, social roles), stable (e.g., physical boundaries, organizational rules) or transient (e.g., temperature, crowding).

Social psychology is not limited to the study of individual actions and reactions to the personal and the situational. Group dynamics matter, as social life occurs within groups or in response to group processes (e.g., Levine & Moreland, 1998). Groups, especially small ones, pass on and maintain social norms and cultural knowledge. Socialization processes, majority–minority relations, roles and social status, stereotyping, prejudice and discrimination, stigma and group inequality are also social psychological topics.

Rehabilitation psychology examines behavior through a narrower lens than does social psychology, one focused on personal and situational factors that promote the assessment, amelioration, and treatment of chronic physical, cognitive, or mental disabilities. Whether these disabilities are congenital or induced by trauma or disease, many of the same factors examined by social psychologists come into play, but these factors are usually evaluated from primarily clinical or therapeutic points of view. Thus, psychosocial research in rehabilitation psychology is aimed at reducing or eliminating societal barriers preventing people with disabilities from achieving life goals—whether major (e.g., employment) or minor (e.g., access to public recreation facilities)— often creating an amalgam of knowledge from

psychology, medicine, physical therapy, social policy, and education in the process (Fenderson, 1984). Similarly, aside from research dealing with disability as stigma or attitudes toward people with disabilities, broader questions concerning groups and group processes are generally ignored by contemporary rehabilitation psychology (but see Dunn & Dougherty, 2005; Wright, 1983).

Although rehabilitation psychology and social psychology represent different, if adjacent, branches of the wider discipline, they nonetheless share common roots. Both areas are predicated on the idea that personal and situational factors have profound effects on behavior, which is broadly construed as referring to cognition and emotion as well as action. These roots are embodied in the work of the social–personality psychologist Kurt A. Lewin (1890–1947) and his colleagues and students, some of whom studied questions incorporating these disciplinary foci in some seminal works in rehabilitation psychology (e.g., Barker, Wright, Meyerson, & Gonick, 1953; Dembo, 1982; Dembo, Leviton, & Wright, 1956; G. Lewin, 1957; Meyerson, 1948a, 1948b, 1988; Wright, 1980). K. A. Lewin (1935) argued for a field theory where behavior is a function of both the person and the environment—his or her phenomenal situation or "life space." Lewin expressed this relation as $B = f(P, E)$, an oft-cited formula in social psychology whose reciprocal wisdom has influenced related theoretical and empirical formulations in rehabilitation (e.g., Brandt & Pope, 1997; Pope & Tarlov, 1991).

Social psychologists assume that social behavior is best understood by examining how people and situations mutually affect one another. In practice, traditional social psychological research occurs in controlled laboratory settings, which affords experimental clarity and interpretive precision but can inhibit the dynamic interplay of social forces touted by K. A. Lewin (1935); real-world vigor is sometimes sacrificed for scientific rigor.

Rehabilitation researchers work more in the field and clinic than in the lab, and their research is usually practice-based and pragmatic: How can knowledge about a person (e.g., personality, health, psychological strengths) and his or her life space (e.g., work, family, community) inform the rehabilitative process? Vigor and rigor are mutually dependent, but a rehabilitation researcher's motivation is to first identify treatments to enhance a client's physical and mental well-being. Though important, refining or extending theory is a secondary focus. Rehabilitation psychologists also tend to work in interdisciplinary settings (Stubbins, 1989), routinely crossing disciplinary boundaries, as disability is as much a social construction as it is a psychological and physical process.

Lewin's legacy is represented in the research and philosophy of rehabilitation psychology, especially where the interplay of the situational forces and perceived dispositions are concerned. Rehabilitation psychologists have long recognized that constraints imposed by the environment—the absence of ramps or elevators in buildings, for example—lead to greater behavioral restrictions than do most disabilities (Dembo, 1982; Wright, 1983). K. A. Lewin (1935) recognized, however, that observers downplay the power of situations and instead presume that qualities of the person (i.e., personality traits, physical or cognitive disabilities) cause behavior. People's actions (or inactions) draw perceivers' attention—after all, behavior engulfs the field—and the resulting attributions provide perceivers with a sense of predictability and control, however erroneous it can sometimes be (e.g., Heider, 1958; Ross, 1977). Such attributions are more problematic still when a disability in one area (e.g., speech production following stroke) is mistakenly presumed to "spread" to related areas (e.g., speech comprehension, memory; Dembo et al., 1956).

HISTORY, THEORIES, AND BACKGROUND

The social–clinical interface between social psychology and rehabilitation psychology promotes research focused on two main areas: attitudes toward people with disabilities and the processes of coping with disability. A third area, the normative experience of disability, is gradually emerging. In this section, I introduce the scope of each area and highlight representative research.

Attitudes Toward People With Disabilities

The attitude literatures in social psychology and rehabilitation psychology are extensive. The attitude construct has been an essential tool for the American psychological community since the 1920s (e.g., Albarracin, Johnson, & Zanna, 2005; Eagly & Chaiken, 1993). Most research explores variations on a theme: the conditions under which an expressed attitude predicts future behavior. Avenues of empirical inquiry derived from this theme include attitude formation, stability, accessibility, and change; measurement issues; and attitude structure.

Social psychologists treat attitudes as individual tendencies toward favorable or unfavorable evaluations of an entity (Eagly & Chaiken, 1993). Attitudes have cognitive, affective, and behavioral components (e.g., Breckler, 1984), that is, collections of beliefs, feelings, and actions that guide approach toward or avoidance of some entity (in social psychology's parlance, the "attitude object"). Knowing that one person likes liberal politicians or another dislikes spicy food, for example, allows for prediction of a probable vote and meal choice, respectively. Considerable research attention has focused on the nature and consequences of prejudiced attitudes and their link to discriminatory behavior (e.g., Allport, 1954; Sidanius & Pratto, 1999).

The attitude literature concerning disability developed independently of research in social psychology, as it focuses largely on identifying variables influencing attitudes toward people with disabilities (for reviews, see Yuker, 1988, 1994). Various direct attitude measures demonstrate whether these attitudes are positive or negative, and include adjective checklists, social distance scales, ranking measures, semantic differential scales, and instruments aimed at assessing reactions to real or imagined interactions with persons with disabilities (e.g., Antonak & Livneh, 2000; Yuker & Block, 1986; Yuker, Block, & Young, 1966). Nonreactive or indirect attitude measures also exist. Designed to reduce or eliminate attitude distorting influences (e.g., social desirability biases), this category of research tools includes physiological methods (e.g., arousal), unobtrusive behavioral measures (e.g., physical distance), disguised techniques (e.g., bogus pipeline methods), and projective tests (e.g., evaluation of response to ambiguous stimuli; for a review, see Antonak & Livneh, 2000).

Regrettably, disability attitude research is rarely acknowledged by mainstream social psychology.

Examination of recent social psychological works on attitudes revealed no entries concerning disability or rehabilitation in the subject indexes (e.g., Albarracin et al., 2005; Oskamp & Schultz, 2005). Exceptions to this pattern are few in number, presumably because social and rehabilitation psychologists are apt to read and publish in different journals. The explanation for the lack of scholarly exchange may be that the focus of attitudinal research follows the aforementioned, distinct paths within the literatures of the respective disciplines.

The study of attitudes toward people with disabilities generally emphasizes nondisabled people's reactions to people with disabilities. The reason for a primary emphasis on the reactions of people without disabilities is the stigmatized role that individuals with disabilities are assumed to hold in society. Nondisabled people tend to hold unfavorable attitudes toward those with disabilities (e.g., Yuker, 1988), although some authors have suggested that societal opinion is more ambivalent than prejudicial (Soder, 1990). The sources of these stigmatizing attitudes range from curiosity to simple ignorance about the nature of disability, but psychological investigations naturally consider affective and cognitive explanations. Many people without disabilities intentionally ignore those with disabilities for emotional reasons. They may fear saying the wrong thing or drawing attention to a disability, for example, or they may experience anxiety, tension, or general unease when encountering people with disabilities (Heinemann, 1990). Unfortunately, ignoring people or characteristics that they possess only creates a climate for rejection, isolation, and limited contact.

When interpersonal contact does occur, the affective states of people with disabilities can influence the perceptions and subsequent reactions of nondisabled individuals. Frank et al. (1986) had college students and rehabilitation staff members listen to an audiotape of an actor portraying someone with a spinal cord injury (SCI). When the actor exhibited depressive reactions, a common disorder following SCI, both groups responded negatively. The students, who reported dysphoria, rated the actor as low in competence, attractiveness, and desirability. Although clinically experienced and professionally dispassionate, the staff members eval-

uated the supposedly depressed person with SCI as low in attractiveness and reported greater levels of hostile mood than did those who heard the nondepressed version of the tape. Desire for additional contact with the individual, too, was lower in the experimental than in the control condition (for related research, see Corcoran, Frank, & Elliott, 1988; Elliott & Frank, 1989; Frank et al., 1987).

A prominent social psychological theory used to explain negative reactions to people with disabilities is the *just-world hypothesis* (Lerner, 1980); people believe that good things should happen to good people and, consequently, when bad events—including disability—befall individuals, they must somehow be deserving of them. To maintain a consistent worldview and to preserve their place in it, nondisabled people must devalue, even derogate, people with disabilities. In a related vein, competence and other desirable personal traits are linked to ascriptions of interpersonal attractiveness, so that differences in physique (e.g., missing a limb, facial disfigurement) can influence perceptions negatively (Hahn, 1988). Perceived responsibility for one's condition, too, is a relevant factor influencing social judgments (Weiner, 2006).

Not all attitudes regarding disability are negative in content, nor are they the result of social stigma. Some perceivers attribute highly favorable traits to people with disabilities because they view coping with a cognitive, physical, or psychiatric impairment as somehow ennobling or otherwise indicative of outstanding personal success (e.g., Wright, 1983). Such attitudes also miss the mark, however; they are merely the mirror-image distortion, again placing undue emphasis on people's disabilities rather than on their abilities (Yuker, 1994) and assuming that a particular quality (albeit a positive one) necessarily accompanies disability. Nondisabled perceivers rarely recognize that disability is merely one aspect of an individual's experience or personality and that people with disabilities do not wish to be seen as either saints or victims (Fine & Asch, 1988; Wright, 1983).

Other research points to several interpersonal behaviors that can ameliorate negative social reactions to disability and modify accompanying attitudes. People with disabilities can establish positive social interactions by casually explaining a disability

(Hastorf, Wildfogel, & Cassman, 1979), being assertive when requesting assistance (Mills, Belgrave, & Boyer, 1984), and displaying adaptive emotional adjustment to a disability (Elliott & Frank, 1990). Each strategy promotes social encounters; in turn, people without disabilities may come to evaluate people with disabilities (and perhaps disability generally) in more positive ways (for broader discussion of theories of intergroup contact, see Pettigrew, 1998).

Coping With Disability

Historically, research on coping processes (i.e., the reactions of people with disabilities to their conditions and social worlds) has undergone a variety of shifts in perspective and received substantial criticism on social, psychological, and even political grounds (e.g., Fine & Asch, 1988; Olkin & Pledger, 2003; Vash, 1981). In Vash's view, for example, the idea of accepting disability was understood in different ways across the past 60 or so years, from functionally acknowledging the reality of disability (i.e., absence of psychological denial) and accepting one's "limitations," to an activist orientation portraying disability as one facet of many in the lives of people with disabilities. As Fine and Asch succinctly noted, "What needs to be stated is that disability—although never wished for—may simply not be as wholly disastrous as imagined" (p. 11).

Considered from the latter perspective, terms such as *coping, adjustment,* and *adaptation* sometimes take on a pejorative tinge because they intimate that people with disabilities are never wholly satisfied with their situations and that, in any case, "rational" people would never see their circumstances as positive. Such views are naïve at best and prejudiced at worst. In fact, dissatisfaction is more often apt to be directed at the aforementioned environmental and social constraints, not the self (e.g., Wright, 1983), and tends to be a judgment of observers (including well-meaning researchers) and not people with disabilities themselves (e.g., Cole, 2004; Dunn, 2005; Johnson, 2005; Vash & Crewe, 2004).

Both social and rehabilitation psychologists have shown a great deal of interest in subjective reactions to disability. For instance, there is substantial overlap between the literatures concerning the search for meaning in disability (Dunn, 1994). Rehabilitation

psychologists have been interested in how individual reactions to disability affect well-being in the context of rehabilitative experiences (e.g., Dembo et al., 1956; Elliott, Witty, Herrick, & Hoffman, 1991). Social psychologists study disability as a negative or threatening event, how it is integrated into people's lives and thoughts, and the affective consequences (if any) of that integration (e.g., Tait & Silver, 1989).

Conceptual agreement diverges, however, regarding the portrayal of people with disabilities within the respective literatures. Some social psychological approaches apply the terms *victim* and *victimization* to people who experience traumas, including the onset of disability (e.g., Janoff-Bulman & Frieze, 1983). Practitioners and researchers in the rehabilitation tradition are quick to criticize this nomenclature on the grounds that it implies that people with disabilities are helpless and dependent, objects instead of actors where their fate is concerned (Fine & Asch, 1988; Shontz, 1982).

The paradigm example of this conceptual disagreement is a well-intentioned study by Bulman and Wortman (1977) on adjustment to spinal cord injury (for related discussions, see Dunn, 1996; Janoff-Bulman & Frieze, 1983). These researchers noted that many people in their sample reevaluated an injury as positive after asking "Why me?" questions (for a conceptual replication, see Heinemann, Bulka, & Smetak, 1988). Bulman and Wortman (1977) concluded that such defensive attributions were adaptive under the circumstances, but at least one rehabilitation researcher noted that the term *reevaluation* elicited notions of rationalizations that did not accurately reflect the real situation (Schontz, 1982). Besides highlighting sensitivity in semantics, an important issue emerging from this dispute is the status of self-report: Are the self-reports of people with disabilities trustworthy, reflective accounts of the experience of disability, or are they simply biased, self-serving attributions? Debate over the status of such self-insight is not new in the context of disability (Dunn, 1994, 2005) and more research on its salutary implications is clearly needed.

A potentially fruitful approach to the study of salutary effects integrating social and rehabilitation psychology is *reality negotiation* (Snyder, 1989; see also Dunn, 1994, 1996, 2005; Elliott et al., 1991). Reality negotiation is contextual, occurring when individuals rely on cognitive strategies that promote favorable beliefs about the self in situations that threaten self-esteem and well-being (Elliott et al., 1991; Snyder, 1989). To manage negative events, individuals seek out and assimilate positive views of themselves (Barone, Maddux, & Snyder, 1997). When people negotiate their realities, they engage in two activities: protective behaviors and self-enhancing behaviors (Snyder, 1989). Protective behaviors, such as making an excuse for the inability to perform some action, lead people away from situations that threaten their self-image. In contrast, self-enhancing behaviors direct people to situations that are positive in content or outcome. Reality negotiation may be conceptually and semantically acceptable to rehabilitation researchers precisely because it does not deny the perspectives of people with disabilities (Dunn, 1994, 2005).

The Experience of Disability

Attitudes toward people with disabilities and the study of coping with disability are well-established research areas. The study of disability experiences, personal and self-focused, however, is new and represents a decided departure from reliance on self-versus-able-bodied other sets of comparisons. This emerging area is relevant to social psychology, where one of the rarely acknowledged goals of research is to characterize subjective human experience, not just social interaction; some suggest this may be the subdiscipline's raison d'être (Wegner & Gilbert, 2000). Indeed, the study of subjective states (i.e., emotion, self-reflection) is as much a disciplinary force as is the examination of objective social processes. Within rehabilitation psychology, there is a tradition of considering the subjective: what it means to have and to live with, for example, chronic pain or a central nervous system disorder (e.g., Wright, 1983).

Part of the impetus for the interest in the experience of disability comes from disability studies, an interdisciplinary field whose purpose is to "legitimize the study of disability as a universal human condition" (Olkin & Pledger, 2003, p. 296). To further this goal while properly characterizing the disability

experience, disability studies advocate providing ample opportunity for persons with disabilities, their families, and significant others to help create and shape a research agenda in collaboration with practitioners and researchers (Tate & Pledger, 2003). Such collaboration promotes participant action research while breaking down the "we–they" barrier present in traditional disability research. In part, this approach requires professionals to give serious credence to subjective accounts while rejecting the strict and pathology-oriented medical model of disability in favor of a socioecological model (Olkin & Pledger). Beyond incorporating subjective perspectives, the socioecological model portrays disability systemically, involving political, economic, societal, and legal dimensions, not exclusively the social constraints of having or not having a disability.

Beyond this activist-based approach to the experience of disability, there is also a call to examine disability identity. How does the presence of disability shape or create a positive identity? How can (or do) parents help their children develop a positive disability identity (Olkin, 1997)? An intriguing question is whether an established, optimistic character can act as a psychological cushion promoting resilience against the hassles of daily life and psychosocial well-being across the life span. Related work in the new discipline of positive psychology suggests that such positive qualities of character are psychologically and even physically beneficial (e.g., Peterson & Seligman, 2004).

Prospects for the positive study of self or personality and its connection to the social experience of disability can be approached in another way: through narratives. Narrative approaches critically evaluate the stories people tell about themselves to make sense of their individual experience and development. These "life stories" lend structure and coherence to experience and allow one's growth to be shared with others. McAdams (1993) suggested that people know themselves by reflecting on their own narratives (see also McAdams, Josselson, & Lieblich, 2001, 2006). Where disability is concerned, narrative approaches can capture significant moments with important psychological consequences (e.g., the onset of disability) as well as the normality of much of daily living. Relevant works in this emerging genre include Johnson (2005) and Cole (2004; see also Rybarczyk & Bellg, 1997). Psychologists interested in developing a new research agenda for rehabilitation psychology should consider adopting a narrative approach.

FUNDAMENTAL PSYCHOSOCIAL CONCEPTS

Rehabilitation psychologists rely on particular psychosocial concepts for understanding and characterizing the experience of individuals with disabilities. These concepts are integral to the theory, research, and practice associated with the rehabilitative process (Dunn & Dougherty, 2005; see also Dunn & Elliott, 2005).

The Somatopsychological Relation

Simply put, the *somatopsychological relation* posits that a person's physique is fundamentally tied to his or her self-image, the nature and quality of social interactions, and performance of daily activities. Rehabilitation psychology affirms that a person's ability to perform daily routines, to move about in familiar and unfamiliar terrain, and to engage others while handling their curiosity about one's physical or mental condition supersede the need for one's body to meet some standard of performance. The somatopsychological relation affects an individual's psychology far more than any psychosomatic connection between other physical or organic disorders (Barker et al., 1953; Wright, 1983). Psychosocial adjustment, whether smooth or difficult, should not be attributed solely to disability per se; rather, it should be viewed as influenced by individuals and their physical, social, and psychological environment (see K. A. Lewin, 1935).

The Insider–Outsider Distinction

One's perspective matters: Experiencing disability is phenomenally distinct and different from imagining what having a disability is or, more to the point, must be like. Rehabilitation psychology distinguishes between the experience of those who have a disability or undergo rehabilitation (*insiders*) and the able-bodies who witness and speculate on the nature of disability (*outsiders;* Dembo, 1969; Shontz, 1982;

Wright, 1991). Outsiders tend to believe that disability is all-encompassing, that insiders are preoccupied with their physical states and that living normally is impossible. Insiders know that disability is not central to their identities and, in any case, prefer to emphasize what they can do. The problems associated with disability are largely external and situational (e.g., the environment; well-intentioned, but misguided, social judgments), not personal. These divergent attributions may result from outsiders' cognitive confusing of the experience of becoming disabled (i.e., a salient, acute event) with being a person with a disability (i.e., a chronic, but not necessarily comprehensive, condition; e.g., Kahneman, 1999).

Individuation and Labeling

Where social judgments are concerned, we usually paint with a broad brush: People are readily perceived as part of homogeneous groups (e.g., "stroke patients") and not as individuals (e.g., "Jack, who had a stroke"). To counteract this tendency, rehabilitation psychology adopted a "person-first" platform promoting *individuation* over group membership (Wright, 1983, 1991). Thus, researcher–practitioners speak and write of "persons with disabilities" and never "the disabled" or "the handicapped." People should not be equated with labels based on physical states or medical diagnoses or prognoses; one is not an amputee but rather a person with an amputation. Negative information stands out (e.g., "Megan is quadriplegic"), affecting perceiver–listeners more than positive information (e.g., "Megan passed the bar exam"). Thus, monolithic language and labels are eschewed in favor of linguistic approaches promoting dignity, worth, self-reliance, and collaboration in the rehabilitative process. To emphasize the rising importance of collaboration in rehabilitation, people with disabilities are increasingly referred to by rehabilitation professionals as active *consumers* or *clients,* not as passive patients or worse, victims (Dunn & Elliott, 2005).

Existing or Potential Assets

Regardless of the severity of a disability, every person is anticipated to either possess or to have a chance to develop some *assets*. This term refers to a broad array of resources that are unique to every individual, including personal qualities or strengths; intellectual, physical, social, or professional skills; self-concept; and work-related talents. Assets can be real (e.g., social support, income), imagined (e.g., goals), achieved or achievable (e.g., education), and, of course, psychological (e.g., sense of humor, tenacity). Whether real or perceived, actual or potential, there is little doubt that assets contribute to the development and maintenance of identity and social role, that they promote connections with others, and perhaps motivate individuals to thrive within their unique situations. Conversely, emphasizing the loss of assets (i.e., never being able to do *x* again) can be dispiriting and counterproductive. Disability is neither a beginning nor an end-point in any person's development; it is one frame of reference among many. As such, the rehabilitative focus must be positive, aimed at what a person with a disability can do or can learn to do (e.g., Keany & Glueckauf, 1993).

Construing Well-Being

Well-being should not be equated with absence of disability, nor should chronic disability be misconstrued as "permanent illness or loss." The negative presumption, of course, is outsider-based: the onset of disability irrevocably alters well-being, so that subsequent experience is forever compared with life in "before" and "after" terms. Ample evidence from social and rehabilitation psychology, as well as from the testaments of insiders, illustrates such characterizations of well-being are erroneous (e.g., Brickman, Coates, & Janoff-Bulman, 1978; Bulman & Wortman, 1977; Dunn, 1996; Fine & Asch, 1988; Heinemann et al., 1988). Just as material well-being does not ensure happiness (e.g., Kasser, 2002), the presence of disability—chronic or acute—does not guarantee its absence. In fact, the onset of disability can promote a search for meaning that affects well-being in beneficial ways (Dunn, 1996; see also Dunn, 2005). Where disability is concerned, well-being is contextual and in the eye of the insider–beholder.

There is compelling evidence that people with disabilities can maintain a sense of well-being by comparing their physical, cognitive, or social states with those of real or imagined others. Taylor (1985; Taylor & Lobel, 1989), for example, found that patients with breast cancer often made downward

social comparisons—thinking of or identifying someone whose experience was considerably worse than their own—as a means to ward off depression and despair. The perspective that "things could be worse" is not a form of denial but a constructive form of coping that is routinely relied on following the onset of disability and the rehabilitative process.

FUTURE DIRECTIONS: INTEGRATING SOCIAL AND REHABILITATIVE PERSPECTIVES

Opportunities abound for researchers interested in exploring the social psychology of disability. A well-established, person-first foundation of scholarship can be extended in new directions. Beyond the issues and areas already reviewed in this chapter, two other promising avenues for research are introduced in this section.

Exploring Social–Cognitive Opportunities

Insights from recent research in social cognition can be fruitfully used to explore the social psychology of disability. For instance, studies examining *affective forecasting* (Wilson & Gilbert, 2003), that is, how well people can predict their future emotional states linked to specific events, might have implications for rehabilitation research on so-called positive byproducts following the onset of disability (McMillen & Cook, 2003). People do not predict their own future feelings accurately (e.g., expecting to be happier following a gain or sadder after a loss), nor do they fully anticipate their abilities to cope with or adjust to life's vagaries (Kahneman, 2000; Wilson & Gilbert, 2003). Perhaps some forms of affective forecasting can be used to assist insiders during rehabilitation, to validate their positive self-reports following disability, and to persuade outsiders that psychosocial adjustment is not a defense mechanism.

In contrast to the positive implications of affective forecasting, research on *stereotype threat* suggests that the resilience of some people with disabilities could be cognitively undermined. Studies now amply demonstrate that group membership coupled with individual-based anxiety associated with the possibility of fulfilling group-based stereotypes (e.g., "Black people are not expected to do well on standardized tests") demonstrably affects intellectual performance (e.g., Steele, 1997). In a similar manner, can insiders' efforts to cope with the challenges of rehabilitation and living with disability be affected by threatening stereotypes that the formerly-outsider-now-insider may have shared (e.g., "People in wheelchairs cannot care for themselves")? Future efforts should explore whether such stereotype threat can undermine positive disability identities and successful rehabilitation.

A Need to Adopt Broader Models for Theory and Practice

As noted in this chapter's opening, social psychological processes affect all aspects of disability, and any person with a disability is always a part of his or her wider situation. Whether focused on theory or therapy, however, too many research efforts to characterize disability and rehabilitation rely on discrete questions or narrow issues. A wider lens is need for viewing disability as a social—and a social psychological—problem. Instead of only producing piecemeal studies, rehabilitation researchers need to conduct research based on larger, broader models that incorporate a variety of variables pertaining to the person and the situation, everything from personality and demographic factors to social and environmental constraints. These ideas, like this observation, are not new (e.g., Meyerson, 1948a, 1948b), but increasingly sophisticated, integrative models and methods for exploring them are now available (e.g., Elliott, Kurylo, & Rivera, 2002; Olkin & Pledger, 2003; see also Lopez & Snyder, 2003). Although interesting in their own right, findings from the social psychology of disability are most likely to have constructive, dynamic, and helpful effects on the lives of people with disabilities when properly placed in new models for theory and practice.

CODA

"Research that produces nothing but books will not suffice"
—*Kurt A. Lewin, 1948, p. 144*

Although theoretically and empirically grounded, social psychological research on disability and rehabilitation must be more than intellectually com-

pelling. Researchers, practitioners, and consumers will benefit by remembering how perceptions of people and their situations can augment or inhibit understanding of social psychological issues in disability and rehabilitation. Ultimately, knowledge gained from study of the social psychology of disability must be used to improve the lives of people with disabilities and to promote understanding among people who have, do not have, or will have a disability.

References

Albarracin, D., Johnson, B. T., & Zanna, M. P. (Eds.). (2005). *The handbook of attitudes.* Mahwah, NJ: Erlbaum.

Allport, G. W. (1954). *The nature of prejudice.* Cambridge: Perseus.

Allport, G. W. (1985). The historical background of social psychology. In G. Lindzey & E. Aronson (Eds.), *Handbook of social psychology: Vol. 1. Theory and methods* (3rd ed., pp. 1–46). New York: Random House.

Antonak, R. F., & Livneh, H. (2000). Measurement of attitudes towards persons with disabilities. *Disability and Rehabilitation, 22,* 211–224.

Asch, A., & Fine, M. (1988). Introduction: Beyond pedestals. In M. Fine & A. Asch (Eds.), *Women with disabilities: Essays in psychology, culture, and politics* (p. 1–37). Philadelphia: Temple University Press.

Barker, R. G., Wright, B. A., Meyerson, L., & Gonick, M. R. (1953). *Adjustment to physical handicap and illness: A survey of the social psychology of physique and disability* (2nd ed.). New York: Social Science Research Council.

Barone, D. F., Maddux, J. E., & Snyder, C. R. (1997). *Social cognitive psychology: History and current domains.* New York: Plenum Press.

Brandt, E. N., & Pope, A. M. (Eds.). (1997). *Enabling America: Assessing the role of rehabilitation science and engineering.* Washington, DC: National Academy Press.

Breckler, S. J. (1984). Empirical validation of affect, behavior, and cognition as distinct components of attitude. *Journal of Personality and Social Psychology, 47,* 1191–1205.

Brickman, P., Coates, D., & Janoff-Bulman, R. (1978). Lottery winners and accident victims: Is happiness relative? *Journal of Personality and Social Psychology, 37,* 917–927.

Bulman, R. J., & Wortman, C. B. (1977). Attributions of blame and coping in the "real world": Severe accident victims react to their lot. *Journal of Personality and Social Psychology, 35,* 351–363.

Cole, J. (2004). *Still lives: Narratives of spinal cord injury.* Cambridge: MIT Press.

Corcoran, J. R., Frank, R. G., & Elliott, T. R. (1988). The interpersonal influence of depression following spinal cord injury: A methodological study. *Journal of the Multihandicapped Person, 1,* 161–174.

Dembo, T. (1969). Rehabilitation psychology and its immediate future: A problem of utilization of psychological knowledge. *Rehabilitation Psychology, 16,* 63–72.

Dembo, T. (1982). Some problems in rehabilitation as seen by a Lewinian. *Journal of Social Issues, 38,* 131–139.

Dembo, T., Leviton, G. L., & Wright, B. A. (1956). Adjustment to misfortune: A problem of social-psychological rehabilitation. *Artificial Limbs, 3,* 4–62.

Dunn, D. S. (1994). Positive meaning and illusions following disability: Reality negotiation, normative interpretation, and value change. *Journal of Social Behavior and Personality, 9,* 123–138.

Dunn, D. S. (1996). Well-being following amputation: Salutary effects of positive meaning, optimism, and control. *Rehabilitation Psychology, 41,* 285–302.

Dunn, D. S. (2005). Negotiating realities to understand others: Teaching about meaning and well-being. *Journal of Social and Clinical Psychology, 24,* 30–40.

Dunn, D. S., & Dougherty, S. B. (2005). Prospects for a positive psychology of rehabilitation. *Rehabilitation Psychology, 50,* 305–311.

Dunn, D. S., & Elliott, T. R. (2005). Revisiting a constructive classic: Wright's *Physical disability: A psychosocial approach. Rehabilitation Psychology, 50,* 183–189.

Eagly, A. H., & Chaiken, S. (1993). *The psychology of attitudes.* Fort Worth, TX: Harcourt.

Elliott, T. R., & Frank, R. G. (1989). Social–cognitive responses to depression and physical stigma. *Journal of the Multihandicapped Person, 2,* 211–223.

Elliott, T. R., & Frank, R. G. (1990). Social and interpersonal responses to depression and disability. *Rehabilitation Psychology, 35,* 135–147.

Elliott, T. R., Kurylo, M. & Rivera, P. (2002). Positive growth following acquired physical disability. In C. R. Snyder & S. J. Lopez (Eds.), *Handbook of positive psychology* (pp. 687–699). New York: Oxford University Press.

Elliott, T. R., Witty, T. E., Herrick, S. M., & Hoffman, J. T. (1991). Negotiating reality after physical loss: Hope, depression, and disability. *Journal of Personality and Social Psychology, 61,* 608–613.

Fenderson, D. A. (1984). Opportunities for psychologists in disability research. *American Psychologist, 39,* 524–528.

Fine, M., & Asch, A. (1988). Disability beyond stigma: Social interaction, discrimination, and activism. *Journal of Social Issues, 44,* 3–21.

Frank, R. G., & Elliott, T. R. (Eds.). (2000). *Handbook of rehabilitation psychology.* Washington, DC: American Psychological Association.

Frank, R. G., Elliott, T. R., Wonderlich, S. A., Corcoran, J. R., Umlauf, R. L., & Ashkanazi, G. S. (1987). Gender differences in the interpersonal response to depression and spinal cord injury. *Cognitive Therapy and Research, 11,* 437–448.

Frank, R. G., Wonderlich, S. A., Corcoran, J. R., Umlauf, R. L., Ashkanazi, G. H., Brownlee-Duffeck, M., & Wilson, R. (1986). Interpersonal response to spinal cord injury. *Journal of Social and Clinical Psychology, 4,* 447–460.

Gill, C. J., Kewman, D. G., & Brannon, R. W. (2003). Transforming psychological practice and society: Policies that reflect the new paradigm. *American Psychologist, 58,* 305–312.

Hahn, H. (1988). The politics of physical differences: Disability and discrimination. *Journal of Social Issues, 44,* 39–48.

Hastorf, A. H., Wildfogel, J., & Cassman, T. (1979). Acknowledgement of handicap as a tactic on social interaction. *Journal of Personality and Social Psychology, 37,* 1790–1797.

Heider, F. (1958). *The psychology of interpersonal relations.* New York: Wiley.

Heinemann, A. W. (1990). Meeting the handicapped: A case of affective–cognitive inconsistency. In W. Stroebe & M. Hewstone (Eds.), *European Review of Social Psychology* (Vol. 1, pp. 323–338). Chichester, England: Wiley.

Heinemann, A. W., Bulka, M., & Smetak, S. (1988). Attributions and disability acceptance following traumatic injury: A replication and extension. *Rehabilitation Psychology, 33,* 195–206.

Janoff-Bulman, R., & Frieze, I. H. (1983). A theoretical perspective for understanding reactions to victimization. *Journal of Social Issues, 39,* 1–17.

Johnson, H. M. (2005). *Too late to die young: Nearly true tales from a life.* New York: Holt.

Jones, E. E. (1998). Major developments in five decades of social psychology. In D. T. Gilbert, S. T. Fiske, & G. Lindzey (Eds.), *The handbook of social psychology* (4th ed., pp. 3–57). New York: McGraw-Hill.

Kahneman, D. (1999). Objective happiness. In D. Kahneman, E. Diener, & N. Schwartz (Eds.), *Well-being: The foundations of hedonic psychology* (pp. 3–25). New York: Russell Sage Foundation.

Kahneman, D. (2000). Experienced utility and objective happiness: A moment-based approach. In D. Kahneman

& A. Tversky (Eds.), *Choices, values, and frames* (pp. 673–692). New York: Russell Sage Foundation and Cambridge University Press.

Kasser, T. (2002). *The high price of materialism.* Cambridge: MIT Press.

Keany, K. M. H., & Glueckauf, R. L. (1993). Disability and value change: An overview and reanalysis of acceptance of loss theory. *Rehabilitation Psychology, 38,* 199–210.

LaPlante, M. P., & Carlson, D. (1996). *Disability in the United States: Prevalence and causes,* 1992 (Disability Statistics Rep. No. 7). Washington, DC: U.S. Department of Education, National Institute on Disability and Rehabilitation Research.

Leary, M. R., & Maddux, J. F. (1987). Progress toward a viable interface between social and clinical-counseling psychology. *American Psychologist, 42,* 904–911.

Lerner, M. J. (1980). *The belief in a just world: A fundamental delusion.* New York: Plenum Press.

Levine, J. M., & Moreland, R. L. (1998). Small groups. In D. T. Gilbert, S. T. Fiske, & G. Lindzey (Eds.), *The handbook of social psychology* (4th ed., pp. 415–469). New York: McGraw-Hill.

Lewin, G. W. (1957). Some characteristics of the socio-psychological life space of the epileptic patient. *Human Relations, 10,* 249–256.

Lewin, K. A. (1935). *A dynamic theory of personality.* New York: McGraw-Hill.

Lewin, K. A. (1948/1997). *Resolving social conflicts: Field theory in social science.* Washington, DC: American Psychological Association.

Lopez, S. J., & Snyder, C. R. (Eds.). (2003). *Positive psychological assessment: A handbook of models and measures.* Washington, DC: American Psychological Association.

McAdams, D. P. (1993). *The stories we live by: Personal myths and the making of the self.* New York: Morrow.

McAdams, D. P., Josselson, R., & Lieblich, A. (Eds.). (2001). *Turns in the road: Narrative studies of lives in transition.* Washington, DC: American Psychological Association.

McAdams, D. P., Josselson, R., & Lieblich, A. (Eds.). (2006). *Identity and story: Creating self in narrative.* Washington, DC: American Psychological Association.

McMillen, J. C., & Cook, C. L. (2003). The positive by-products of spinal cord injury and their correlates. *Rehabilitation Psychology, 48,* 77–85.

Meyerson, L. (1948a). Physical disability as a social psychological problem. *Journal of Social Issues, 4,* 2–10.

Meyerson, L. (Ed.). (1948b). The social psychology of physical disability. *Journal of Social Issues, 4*(4), 1–115.

Meyerson, L. (1988). The social psychology of physical disability: 1948 and 1988. *Journal of Social Issues, 44,* 173–188.

Mills, J., Belgrave, F. Z., & Boyer, K. M. (1984). Reducing avoidance of social interaction with a physically disabled person by mentioning the disability following a request for aid. *Journal of Applied Social Psychology, 14,* 1–11.

Olkin, R. (1997). Human rights of children with disabilities. *Women and Therapy, 20,* 29–42.

Olkin, R., & Pledger, C. (2003). Can disability studies and psychology join hands? *American Psychologist, 58,* 296–304.

Oskamp, S., & Schultz, P. W. (2005). *Attitudes and opinions* (3rd ed.). Mahwah, NJ: Erlbaum.

Peterson, C., & Seligman, M. E. P. (2004). *Character strengths and virtues: A handbook and classification.* New York: Oxford University Press.

Pettigrew, T. F. (1998). Intergroup contact theory. *Annual Review of Psychology, 49,* 65–85.

Pope, A. M., & Tarlov, A. R. (Eds.). (1991). *Disability in America: Toward a national agenda for prevention.* Washington, DC: National Academy Press.

Ross, L. (1977). The intuitive psychologist and his shortcomings: Distortions in the attribution process. In L. Berkowitz (Ed.), *Advances in experimental social psychology* (Vol. 10, pp. 174–221). New York: Academic Press.

Rybarczyk, B., & Bellg, A. (1997). *Listening to life stories: A new approach to stress intervention in health care.* New York: Springer.

Seligman, M. E. P., & Csikszentmihalyi, M. (2000). Positive psychology: An introduction. *American Psychologist, 55,* 5–14.

Shontz, F. C. (1982). Adaptation to chronic illness and disability. In T. Millon, C. Green, & R. Meagher (Eds.), *Handbook of clinical health psychology* (pp. 153–172). New York: Plenum Press.

Sidanius, J., & Pratto, F. (1999). *Social dominance theory: An intergroup theory of social hierarchy and oppression.* New York: Cambridge University Press.

Snyder, C. R. (1989). Reality negotiation: From excuses to hope and beyond. *Journal of Social and Clinical Psychology, 8,* 130–157.

Soder, M. (1990). Prejudice or ambivalence? Attitudes toward people with disabilities. *Disability, Handicap, and Society, 5,* 227–241.

Steele, C. M. (1997). A threat in the air: How stereotypes shape intellectual identity and performance. *American Psychologist, 52,* 613–629.

Stubbins, J. (1989). The interdisciplinary status of rehabilitation psychology. *Rehabilitation Psychology, 34,* 207–215.

Tait, R., & Silver, R. C. (1989). Coming to terms with major negative events. In J. S. Uleman & J. A. Bargh (Eds.), *Unintended thought* (pp. 351–382). New York: Guilford Press.

Tate, D. G., & Pledger, C. (2003). An integrative conceptual framework of disability: New directions for research. *American Psychologist, 58,* 289–295.

Taylor, S. E. (1985). Adjustment to threatening events: A theory of cognitive adaptation. *American Psychologist, 38,* 1161–1173.

Taylor, S. E., & Lobel, M. (1989). Social comparison activity under threat: Downward evaluation and upward contacts. *Psychological Review, 96,* 569–575.

Vash, C. L. (1981). *The psychology of disability.* New York: Springer Publishing Company.

Vash, C. L., & Crewe, N. M. (2004). *Psychology of disability* (2nd ed.). New York: Springer.

Wegner, D. M., & Gilbert, D. T. (2000). Social psychology—the science of human experience. In H. Bless & J. P. Forgas (Eds.), *The message within: The role of subjective experience in social cognition and behavior* (pp. 1–9). Philadelphia: Psychology Press.

Weiner, B. (2006). *Social motivation, justice, and the moral emotions: An attributional approach.* Mahwah, NJ: Erlbaum.

Wilson, T. D., & Gilbert, D. T. (2003). Affective forecasting. In M. P. Zanna (Ed.), *Advances in experimental social psychology* (Vol. 35, pp. 345–511). San Diego, CA: Academic Press.

Wright, B. A. (1980). Person and situation: Adjusting the rehabilitative focus. *Archives of Physical and Medical Rehabilitation, 61,* 59–64.

Wright, B. A. (1983). *Physical disability: A psychosocial approach* (2nd ed.). New York: Harper Collins.

Wright, B. A. (1991). Labeling: The need for greater person–environment individuation. In C. R. Snyder & D. R Forsyth (Eds.), *Handbook of social and clinical psychology: The health perspective* (pp. 469–487). New York: Pergamon Press.

Yuker, H. E. (Ed.). (1988). *Attitudes toward persons with disabilities.* New York: Springer.

Yuker, H. E. (1994). Variables that influence attitudes toward people with disabilities: Conclusions from the data. *Journal of Social Behavior and Personality, 9,* 3–22.

Yuker, H. E., & Block, J. R. (1986). *Research with the Attitude Toward Disabled People Scales: 1960–1985.* West Hempstead, NY: Hofstra University Center for the Study of Attitudes Toward People With Disabilities.

Yuker, H. E., Block, J. R., & Young, J. H. (1966). *The measurement of attitudes toward disabled persons.* Albertson, NY: Human Resources Center.

CHAPTER 27

CENTRAL NERVOUS SYSTEM
PLASTICITY AND REHABILITATION

Gitendra Uswatte, Edward Taub, Victor W. Mark, Christi Perkins, and Lynne Gauthier

The dominant view in neuroscience for most of the
20th century was that the central nervous system
(CNS) had little capacity to reorganize and repair
itself in response to injury. This view extends well
back into the 19th century, when it was influenced
in part by Broca's (1861) seminal studies that localized specific functions to specific brain areas. Though
contrary views were expressed (e.g., Fleurens, 1842;
Fritsch & Hitzig, 1870; Lashley, 1938; Munk, 1881),
the mature CNS was generally believed (Kaas, 1995)
to exhibit little or no plasticity (e.g., Hubel & Wiesel,
1970; Ruch, 1960).

Hughlings Jackson's hierarchical view that lower
centers of the brain assumed functions of damaged
higher centers after CNS insult (Jackson, 1873, 1884),
and other related formulations, strongly influenced
thought concerning the neurophysiological substrate
for recovery of sensory, motor, and cognitive function for most of the last century. However, the
phenomenon of spontaneous recovery of function
after CNS injury was never fully explained and
received little experimental attention. Beginning in
the 1970s, animal studies from a number of laboratories (e.g., Kaas, Merzenich, & Killackey, 1983;
Merzenich et al., 1984; Wall & Egger, 1971)
showed that contrary to established belief, the
adult mammalian nervous system does have some
capacity to reorganize itself functionally after

injury. Studies in humans from the 1990s
(reviewed in Taub, Uswatte, & Elbert, 2002)
showed not only that brain reorganization occurs
after disuse or abolition of a function following
nervous system injury but also that brain reorganization can be produced by intense, concentrated
use of a function, as Merzenich's laboratory had
first demonstrated in new world monkeys (e.g.,
Jenkins, Merzenich, Ochs, Allard, & Guic-Robles,
1990). In the first decade of this century, animal
and human research began to suggest ways that
such experience-dependent CNS plasticity can be
harnessed to enhance the rehabilitation of CNS
injury survivors (Taub, 2004; Taub et al., 2002).

This chapter reviews this revolutionary work
with an emphasis on its import for rehabilitation. We
summarize basic research establishing the remarkable degree of plasticity possessed by the adult
CNS, briefly describe work on spontaneous recovery
from neurological injury and CNS plasticity, and in
greater depth discuss research on rehabilitation-
induced CNS plasticity. Research on constraint-
induced movement therapy (Taub et al., 1993), which
is a physical rehabilitation method derived from
behavioral neuroscience studies of deafferented
monkeys (Taub, 1977, 1980), is presented as a model
for translating findings from neuroscience to the
clinical arena.

Portions of this chapter are adapted from "Harnessing Brain Plasticity Through Behavioral Techniques to Produce New Treatments in Neurorehabilitation" by E. Taub, 2004, *American Psychologist, 59,* 692–704. Copyright 2004 by the American Psychological Association.

Work on this chapter was supported by National Institutes of Health Grant HD34273 and National Institute of Disability and Rehabilitation Research Grant H133G050222.

BASIC RESEARCH ON CENTRAL NERVOUS SYSTEM PLASTICITY

Animal Studies

Changes in how particular motor or sensory functions are represented in the CNS were observed by several investigators in the first third of the 20th century. By repeatedly stimulating the motor cortex, Brown and Sherrington (1912) found that the movement evoked could change from flexion to extension and even occur in areas of the body other than the initial evoked movement. This demonstrated that a cortical change could result in a change in the periphery. In the middle of the 20th century, Gellhorn and Hyde (1953) discovered that simply repositioning a limb could change which part of the cortex controlled its movement, suggesting that a change in the periphery could also alter the cortex.

This dynamic relationship between cortex and periphery was not generally understood as plasticity in the currently accepted sense, nor did the authors discuss it as such. The work of Michael Merzenich, Jan Kaas, and others in the 1980s demonstrated with clarity the phenomenon of injury-related brain plasticity, the idea that a physically induced change in afferent input from an extremity affects its representation in the brain. The first study in this line of research involved the removal of afferent inputs from an extremity in adult owl and squirrel monkeys by cutting the median nerve, which innervates the second and third digit. After 2 to 9 months, the portion of cortical area 3b that originally received input from the skin surface of digit 3 was encroached on by inputs from surrounding intact skin fields (Merzenich et al., 1983). The cortical areas representing the surrounding fingers "invaded" the original cortical area of the deafferented third digit. A subsequent study involved removing input from a digit by amputation instead of cutting the median nerve. Cortical representations for the hand area were identified using microelectrode mapping 2 to 8 months after surgical amputation of either digit 3 only or both digits 2 and 3. In both types of surgery, the cortical representation field of the intact digits expanded to occupy most of the original cortical territory of the now amputated fingers (Merzenich et al., 1984).

Both studies showed that inputs could cross borders of the representation zones of separate digits to invade nearby cortical representations. They also suggested that the extent of reorganization did not extend beyond 2 mm from the original representational boundary of the digit.

Jenkins et al. (1990) determined that reorganization could happen without injury. If elimination of afferent inputs could produce a change in cortical representation, perhaps a modification of behavior that increased input could result in similar changes, that is, what has come to be known as *use-dependent* or *skill-related reorganization*. In their study, microelectrode maps were obtained of the hand representation in cortical area 3b before, immediately after, and 3 weeks after monkeys underwent behavioral training. The monkeys were conditioned to keep the fingertips of one or more of the longest digits in contact with a rotating disc to receive a reward. This "behaviorally relevant" stimulation of the fingers produced an expansion of their cortical areas and shifting of some representation borders. Passive stimulation of the fingers, in which reward was not contingent on keeping digits in contact with the disc, did not result in cortical reorganization.

The work of Pons et al. (1991) challenged the idea of a 2 mm limit in the amount of reorganization that could occur. Fingers, palm, upper limb, and neck of monkeys were deafferented so that their cortex was deprived of inputs from these areas. Tactile evoked responses recorded from the cortex 12 years after the deafferentation indicated that the area representing the face had invaded the deafferentation zone (i.e., the cortical area that had once received input from the deafferented parts of the body). The expansion of the border of the representation zone of the face greatly exceeded 2 mm. It was observed to take place over the entire representation of the arm (i.e., 10–14 mm) and was designated "massive" cortical reorganization (Pons et al., 1991).

Thus, by the middle of the 1990s, the view that adult brain had substantial capacity for plasticity gained a strong foothold. CNS reorganization was shown to occur in adult animals following a variety of interventions, including nerve dissection, amputation, and behavioral modification. The concept that borders between the receptive fields of individual digits were fixed gave way to the idea of borders that were dynamically determined by the amount of sensory input to each receptive field. An upper limit to the expansion of the cortical representation of discrete somatic areas has yet to be identified. The importance of the behavioral relevance of any changes in sensory input for stimulating plastic changes was also established.

Human Studies

Modern neuroimaging methods have permitted researchers to test whether the remarkable plastic brain changes observed in animals have parallels in humans. Magnetic source imaging studies by Elbert, Flor, Taub and coworkers have shown that when the amount of sensory input to a particular brain region increases with increased use of a body part, this region expands. Blind individuals who used three fingers on both hands simultaneously to read Braille showed substantial enlargement of the hand area compared with sighted non-Braille-reading persons (Sterr et al., 1998). In addition, the medial to lateral order of the representations of the three "reading" fingers on the convexity of the cortex was altered or "smeared" in the three-finger Braille readers. This alteration in topography correlated with impaired ability to detect which finger was being touched. It appears that a "smearing" of cortical representations may be adaptive for Braille readers because it facilitates integrating sensory information from all three reading fingers, which would help in the perception of words. Consistent with the findings from blind readers of Braille, string instrument players also have an increased cortical representation for the left hand, which performs the complex task of fingering the strings, but not the right hand, which has the less dexterity-demanding task of bowing the strings (Elbert, Pantev, Wienbruch, Rockstroh, & Taub, 1995).

An increase in cortical representation areas has been observed in the auditory cortex of blind persons and is thought to be due to increased reliance on audition for information about their environment (Elbert et al., 2002). Blind persons receive the same amount of auditory stimulation as those who are sighted. Therefore, this result suggests again that cortical reorganization is not merely a passive response

to increases in sensory stimulation but rather depends on the behavioral relevance of input into the neural system and the attention devoted to it. This property would appear to permit the brain to adapt itself to the functional demands placed on an individual.

Recent studies using structural magnetic resonance imaging (MRI) have shown that brain plasticity in humans involves not only reorganization (i.e., one region of the brain representing a function it had not previously) but also the growth of new tissue. Maguire and coworkers (2000) showed that London taxi cab drivers, compared with people who do not drive taxis, have increased posterior hippocampal volume and decreased anterior hippocampal volume. Furthermore, the amount of time spent driving a taxi was associated with the extent of these structural differences (Maguire et al., 2000). The posterior hippocampus is thought to be preferentially involved in accessing previously learned spatial information, whereas the anterior hippocampus is preferentially involved in encoding new spatial information. Draganski et al. (2004) showed that training to juggle increased the density of cortical tissue in anterior occipital regions over the course of 3 months.

In addition to such "input increase" driven expansion of cortical representations or increases in gray matter density, "input decrease" cortical reorganization has been observed subsequent to the abolition of sensation from a body part or its decreased use (Weiss, Miltner, Liepert, Meissner, & Taub, 2004). Elbert et al. (1994) demonstrated that in upper extremity amputees the topographic representation for the face shifted an average of 1.5 cm into the cortical space normally receiving input from the lost hand and fingers. Reorganization of primary somatomotor cortex also been observed within an hour of abolishing sensation from the radial and medial three quarters of the hand by pharmacological blockage of the radial and median nerves (Weiss et al., 2004). Casting the ankle joint has been shown to lead to a decrease in its motor representation (Liepert, Tegenthoff, & Malin, 1995). This reduction in cortical area was related to the duration of time spent in the cast and could be reversed by removing the cast and permitting striate muscle contraction.

This body of work established that CNS plasticity is a rapidly occurring, bidirectional process in adult humans. Increases in the area of cortex representing a function, as well as increases in brain tissue density or volume, were shown to accompany increased use of the function. Shrinking cortical representations were shown to accompany decreased use of a function or sensory input. Plasticity thus emerged as a mechanism by which the brain can respond to changes in functional demands placed on an individual.

BRAIN PLASTICITY AND RECOVERY AFTER CENTRAL NERVOUS SYSTEM INJURY

Animal Studies

To now, we have only discussed brain plasticity subsequent to a change in behavior or injury in the periphery. Plasticity also occurs after direct damage to the CNS, and it has been studied in animal models of stroke, traumatic brain injury (TBI), and spinal cord injury (SCI; Brant Zawadzki, Atkinson, Detrick, Bradley, & Scidmore, 1996). Nudo and Milliken (1996) mapped the cortical representation in Brodmann area 4 of distal forelimb movement after creating focal ischemic infarcts by surgically occluding arteries. The infarcts generated a deficit in coordinated movements of the digits of the contralateral hand. Five months after the initial damage the representation of the digits decreased in areas adjacent to the lesion, whereas the representation of the proximal arm and shoulder increased. Studies involving rat models of TBI have discovered that the hippocampus can actually restore synaptic connections that were lost because of injuries. Scheff et al. (2005) produced cortical contusion injuries in rats in which there was a 60% loss of synapses in the CA1 region of the hippocampus. Sixty days after injury, the total number of synapses approached normal levels, and there was an improvement in spatial memory (Scheff et al., 2005). In animal models of SCI, inhibitory gamma-aminobutyric acid (GABA) signaling is increased as well as the number of astroglial cells around the injury site. Weight-bearing or step training returns these levels to near normal (Edgerton et al., 2001; Tillakaratne et al., 2000).

Human Studies

Brain plasticity after CNS injury in humans has been best studied in stroke survivors (Schaechter, 2004). During the first 8 months after the stroke, there appear to be two shifts in cortical activation. The first shift occurs as soon as 1 week after stroke in which activation from the ipsilesional cortex decreases and activation from the contralesional cortex increases. In 3 to 6 months, this shift reverses to favor the ipsilesional hemisphere (Marshall et al., 2000). By the end of this 8-month time frame, the activation of the two hemispheres seems to normalize. This normalization is associated with gains in the functional abilities of patients, which suggests that plastic brain changes are occurring during spontaneous recovery that are related to functional motor recovery (Calautti, Leroy, Guincestre, & Baron, 2001) and could possibly involve a compensatory role of uncrossed motor pathways (Cramer et al., 2001). Studies in TBI have produced evidence that although the areas of activation are similar in persons with TBI when compared with controls, the former show more diffuse activation during working memory tasks. Christodoulou et al. (2001) suggested that this might indicate a recruitment of additional cerebral areas to help perform tasks that stress working memory.

REHABILITATION-INDUCED CENTRAL NERVOUS SYSTEM PLASTICITY

Animal Studies

The evidence that intensive use of a function is associated with changes in its cortical representation leads naturally to the question of whether this phenomenon can be harnessed to treat deficits in function after neurological injury. Using the squirrel monkey model of ischemic stroke described previously, Nudo's laboratory has shown that postinfarction training of the impaired hand on a task that requires skilled movements (a) improves hand movement substantially and (b) in spared cortical areas adjacent to the infarct, prevents the invasion of this territory by other functions that occur after infarction in the absence of rehabilitation (Nudo, Wise, SiFuentes, & Milliken, 1996). Other animal models that have strongly influenced neurorehabilitation research include work from the laboratories of Edgerton (Edgerton, Tillakaratne, Bigbee, de Leon, & Roy, 2004) and Schallert (Woodlee & Schallert, 2006). In cats whose spinal cord has been transected surgically, Edgerton's group has shown that training stepping on a treadmill with support of the body weight results in successful weight-bearing stepping and plasticity in the spinal cord, although the precise nature of the plastic changes has yet to be determined (Edgerton et al., 2004). In rats that have had a neurotoxin injected into the contralateral medial forebrain bundle to simulate Parkinson's disease, Schallert's research group has shown that forced use of the impaired forelimb protects against the decline in use of the impaired forelimb and reduction in dopamine levels that takes place spontaneously after this type of insult (Tillerson et al., 2002).

Although animal studies have contributed important knowledge about effective techniques for rehabilitating function and driving plasticity, relatively little is known about the neural mechanisms that underlie the physiological changes observed in the injured brain after training. Three possible mechanisms are the following: (a) strengthening of existing connections between neurons, (b) growth of new connections (e.g., axonal sprouting), and (c) growth of new neurons or supporting cells, such as glia (Taub et al., 2002). Furthermore, the evidence that CNS plasticity is essential for behavioral recovery after CNS injury, rather than being an epiphenomenon or a correlate of some other underlying process, is mostly indirect. Among exceptions are studies involving manipulation of noradrenergic systems; noradrenaline is required for several forms of experience-dependent plasticity (Kasamatsu, Pettigrew, & Ary, 1979). Kolb, Stewart, and Sutherland (1997) have shown that rats given large frontal lesions after depleting their forebrains of noradrelanine do not display functional recovery and exhibit a decrease in dendritic arborization in pyramidal cells throughout the remaining neocortex. Rats given only the forebrain lesion show functional recovery, a decrease in dendritic arborization, and an apparently compensatory increase in spine density. These results suggest that brain plasticity, in this case, an increase in spine density, is necessary for recovery of function.

A general criticism of animal models in the neurorehabilitation literature has been that the models do not capture important elements of CNS injuries in humans (Duncan, 2002). For example, actual stroke infarcts do not have the neat topography exhibited by the surgically induced infarcts used by Nudo's lab, and subjects in animal studies are typically young and healthy rather than old and in poor general health, such as several neurorehabilitation populations. Some recent studies have attempted to address these shortcomings (e.g., Li & Carmichael, 2006).

Human Studies

Brain plasticity and overcoming disability. Few rehabilitative methods for chronic CNS disease have actually been shown in a controlled manner to benefit real-world behaviors. The approach with the most substantiation of treatment efficacy is constraint-induced movement therapy (CI therapy) for poststroke chronic upper extremity hemiparesis (Ottawa Panel et al., 2006). The treatment, which is provided over 10 or 15 consecutive weekdays, involves (a) intensive task practice with the more-involved upper extremity, (b) restraint of the less-involved upper extremity for 90% of waking hours, and (c) a "transfer package" of behavioral techniques to reinforce adherence to treatment and adapt training tasks to the home environment (Taub et al., 1993, 2006). In two separate single-site, controlled trials, CI therapy, compared with two types of placebo interventions, produced prolonged improvement in use of the hemiparetic arm in daily life in individuals more than 1 year after stroke (Taub et al., 1993, 2006). In addition, CI therapy has been shown to be superior to customary care in a blinded, randomized, multisite clinical trial of CI therapy for mild to moderate upper extremity hemiparesis in individuals 3 to 9 months after stroke (Wolf et al., 2006). Participants in the CI therapy group ($n = 106$) showed significantly larger gains in real-world use of the more-impaired arm up to 1 year after treatment than did participants who were permitted access to any care available on a clinical basis ($n = 116$).

This treatment has attracted considerable attention from laboratories interested in determining whether it would provoke neurophysiologic changes that would suggest plastic brain changes. Mark, Taub, and Morris (2006) recently identified 20 studies thus far that have evaluated CI therapy effects on cerebral physiology. These have shown in nearly every instance substantial evidence for brain reorganization based on a wide range of investigational modalities, including transcranial magnetic stimulation (TMS), electroencephalography, dipole source localization, functional MRI (fMRI), positron emission tomography, and near-infrared spectroscopy. The first and best-known study showed a doubling in the cortical region from which electromyography responses of a muscle in the paretic hand can be elicited by TMS after CI therapy (Liepert et al., 2000). However, findings overall have been inconsistent with respect to the localization of regional brain activation changes from pre- to posttreatment. Lack of control over therapy administration, evaluation methods, and participant recruitment are likely to account for these neurophysiologic inconsistencies. Nonetheless, despite inconclusive findings concerning the localization of associated brain physiologic changes, the studies agree in showing improvements in both neurologic impairment and disability.

Structural MRI is free from some of the methodological challenges faced by fMRI and other neurophysiological measures, such as whether the behavior used to elicit brain activation during imaging changes from one testing occasion to another and how to interpret changes in activation. Voxel-wise analysis of structural MRI scans obtained before and after CI therapy from 16 chronic stroke survivors showed widespread increases in gray matter in sensorimotor cortices both contralateral and ipsilateral to the hemiparetic arm, as well as in the hippocampi bilaterally (Gauthier et al., 2008). The aforementioned sensorimotor clusters were bilaterally symmetrical and encompassed the hand and arm regions of primary sensory and motor cortices as well as the anterior supplementary motor area and portions of Brodmann's area 6. Scans from 20 stroke survivors who received a comparison therapy did not show such changes. Moreover, the gray matter changes, across all participants, were correlated with changes in use of the hemiparetic arm in daily life ($rs > .05$, $ps < .05$). The demonstration of these neuroanatomical

changes supports a true remodeling of the brain after CI therapy.

Other treatments for disability with evidence for central nervous system reorganization. Several studies have evaluated real-world effects of other specific forms of physical therapy for chronic CNS impairments. These interventions have not been studied as fully as CI therapy; thus, determining their efficacy will require substantial additional investigation. We review here two interventions with real-world benefits that have been evaluated for their effects on CNS physiology.

Following years of practice, musicians may manifest focal hand dystonia on their specialty musical instrument, in which loss of finger control occurs during performance. An extension of CI therapy techniques termed *sensorimotor retuning* (SMR; Candia et al., 2002) has been found to alleviate focal hand dystonia in string players. In SMR, patients wear a specially designed splint on the hand that restricts movements of one or more fingers on the dystonic hand (but not the main dystonic finger) while practicing multiple exercises involving sequential movement of the fingers on the dystonic hand at varying tempi for many consecutive days. During practice, the musicians are prompted to gradually change the way in which the keys are struck. Thus, the technique involves the three major components of CI therapy: restraint, massed practice, and shaping. Initial trials of SMR for focal hand dystonia in musicians demonstrated not only reduced dystonia during formal laboratory evaluation but also resumption of concert performances or at least self-reported improvement in performance quality that persisted for months after completing the treatment program (Candia et al., 1999, 2002). A subsequent study of 10 dystonic musicians used magnetoencephalography to evaluate the cortical representations of the digits based on evoked responses to controlled tactile stimulation (Candia, Wienbruch, Elbert, Rockstroh, & Ray, 2003). The study demonstrated significant increases in the interdigital distances in the cortical representation of the dystonic hand from pre- to posttreatment, resulting in interdigital distances approximating those of the nondystonic hand at both pre- and posttreatment.

Complex regional pain syndrome (CPRS; formerly termed *reflex sympathetic dystrophy* or *causalgia*) is an uncommon, chronic consequence of focal bodily injury that is most often described after upper extremity fracture (de Mos et al., 2007). It is typified by severe pain in a limb (i.e., most often the upper extremity) and less consistently by various soft tissue changes in the affected limb (i.e., skin temperature or color changes, edema). CRPS may also follow stroke, particularly when there is accompanying motor deficit (Daviet et al., 2002; Petchkrua, Weiss, & Patel, 2000).

Patients with CRPS have been shown to have a smaller representation of the involved hand in the contralateral primary sensory cortex following nonpainful peripheral somatosensory evoked potential mapping or magnetic source imaging (Maihöfner, Handwerker, Neundörfer, & Birklein, 2004; Pleger et al., 2006). Moreover, the degree of hemispheric asymmetry of somatosensory representations has been correlated with the severity of pain. Accordingly, therapy that is directed at altering the somatosensory representation of the involved limb would appear to have the potential to improve the pain disorder. In a study of six patients with CRPS from limb trauma, Pleger et al. (2006) provided a form of CI therapy as an extended desensitization procedure in which skin contact by the affected hand was progressively increased with firmer (hence, initially more painful) objects over 1 to 6 months. Over the same period, patients were required to progressively increase their active movement with the affected hand. The results indicated a significant correlation between reduction in general pain perception from the preceding 4 months and increase in the area of the contralateral somatosensory cortex showing activity in response to tactile stimulation of the affected hand as measured by fMRI. Although Pleger et al. treated patients who had incurred CRPS following peripheral injury, it would be reasonable to predict that the poststroke form of CRPS would respond similarly.

Brain plasticity and ameliorating impairment. In addition, numerous studies in recent years have probed the neurophysiologic changes that follow interventions to improve a broad array of specific

chronic impairments that follow CNS disease in children and adults. (*Impairment* here refers to inability to perform a specific function when asked to do so in the laboratory setting, as opposed to a limitation in actual everyday functioning.) Table 27.1 summarizes the treatment approaches and neurophysiologic findings of contemporary, representative studies (Barker, Brauer, & Carson, 2006; Forrester, Hanley, & Macko, 2006; Fridriksson, Morrow-Odom, Moser, Fridriksson, & Baylis, 2006; Hoffman & Field-Fote, 2006; Luft, Macko, Forrester, Villagra, & Hanley, 2005; Luft et al., 2004; Sturm et al., 2004; Temple et al., 2003). The findings indicate that across a wide variety of interventions, the resulting neurophysiologic changes were consistent with physiologic brain plasticity. Thus, it appears that chronic neurologic impairments are generally physiologically responsive to training interventions.

Methodologic concerns about evaluating neuroplasticity in rehabilitation. Mapping the outcomes from the patient's performance of specific activities during scanning is complicated by the lack of complete control over the patient's behavior. Practice effects, fatigue effects, differences in attention, and changes in strategy may develop and thus significantly affect the physiologic outcomes but without truly reflecting changes in synaptic or axonal physiology (Buonomano & Merzenich, 1998). Thus, it is not clear from such performance-based imaging studies to what extent behavioral plasticity rather than neurophysiologic plasticity had been measured (Rosenberger & Rottenberg, 2002).

In contrast, physiologic studies that involve passive stimulation of the patient without specific task performance appear to have less risk of such effects. Baseline changes in TMS motor mapping outcomes because of stimulus repetition in the absence of a training intervention have not been found (Liepert et al., 2000). However, prolonged TMS stimulation over auditory cortex has been associated with significant increases in the underlying gray matter volume and auditory evoked potentials in healthy participants who did not undergo specific training (May, Hajak, & Gansbauer, 2007). Thus, the neurophysiologic evaluation does not,

TABLE 27.1

Summary of Physiologic Studies of Treatment Responses for Specific Impairments Following Central Nervous System Disease

Reference	Intervention	Disease	N	Clinical evaluations	Physiologic evaluations	Results
Upper extremity hemiparesis						
Hummel & Cohen, 2005	tDCS versus sham treatment	Stroke	1	JT, pinch force, reaction time	TMS	Experimental patients: improved JT time, pinch force, reaction time; increased cortical excitability; reduced intracortical inhibition
Barker, Brauer, & Carson, 2006	Reaching training versus control therapy	Stroke	33	Unspecified assessment of reaching	TMS	Experimental patients: improved reaching; more normal contralateral MEPs
Hoffman & Field-Fote, 2006	Unilateral versus bilateral somatosensory training	Cervical spinal cord injury	12	Tactile function, pinch grip, JT, Chedoke-McMaster Inventory	TMS	Both groups: improved tactile function, pinch; increased area, volume of UE muscles on TMS
Kim, You, et al., 2006	Finger exercises plus rTMS versus sham rTMS	Stroke	15	Movement accuracy and time	TMS	Experimental patients: improved motor measures; increased MEP
Jang et al., 2003	Task practice with more-affected arm	Stroke	4	Purdue Pegboard, grip strength	fMRI	Tendency for improved motor measures to be correlated with activation shift toward lesioned cortex
Luft et al., 2004	Bilateral arm training versus standard therapy	Stroke	21	FM, WMFT performance time	fMRI	Experimental patients: increased FM score; increased lesioned cerebral hemisphere and contralateral cerebellum activity
Henderson et al., 2006	Pointing practice in virtual reality environment	Stroke	NI	Kinematic limb analysis	fMRI	Increased active ROM associated with decreased activation of motor cortices and cerebellum
Kim, Ohn, et al., 2006	rTMS plus finger exercises	Stroke	6	Movement accuracy and time	fMRI	Improved motor measures; increased activity in ipsilateral cerebellum and contralateral cortex
Gait Disorder						
Luft, Macko, Forrester, Villagra, & Hanley, 2005	AEX versus standard therapy	Stroke	18	30-ft walk time, 6-min walk distance	fMRI	Clinical effects not indicated; AEX increased red nucleus activity
Forrester, Hanley, & Macko, 2006	Treadmill training	Stroke	11	30-ft walk time	TMS	Clinical effects not indicated; contralateral MEPs increased in patients who had had more training

	Intervention	Population	N	Outcome measure	Imaging	Results
Dyslexia						
Simos et al., 2002	Two different reading training programs	Developmental dyslexia	8	Phonological decoding tests	Magnetic source imaging	Differential effects of interventions not indicated; improved reading; increased activation left superior temporal gyrus
Temple et al., 2003	Fast ForWord	Developmental dyslexia	20	Phonological decoding, reading comprehension	fMRI	Normalized reading scores; increased activation in left temporoparietal and inferior frontal areas
Aphasia						
Cornelissen et al., 2003	Picture naming practice	Stroke	3	Picture naming	MEG	Improved naming; increased activation left inferior parietal lobe
Crosson et al., 2005	Picture naming practice	Stroke	2	Picture naming	fMRI	Improved naming; increased posterior perisylvian activity
Fridriksson, Morrow-Odom, Moser, Fridriksson, & Baylis, 2006	Picture naming practice	Stroke	3	Picture naming	fMRI	Variable changes across patients pre- to posttreatment; amount of bilateral cerebral hemispheric activation related to clinical gain
Inattention and Unilateral Neglect						
Sturm et al., 2004	Alertness versus memory training	Stroke	8	TAP	fMRI, PET	Alertness scores improved more in alertness group than memory group; right frontal increased activity greater in alertness group
Thimm, Fink, Küst, Karbe, & Sturm, 2006	Alertness training	Stroke	7	TAP, German BIT	fMRI	Greater improvement in neglect than alertness scores; diffuse bilateral cerebral hemispheric activity increases
Luauté et al., 2006	Prism adaptation training	Stroke	5	BIT	PET	Improved neglect; increased rCBF right parietal and cerebellar and left temporal areas

Note. AEX = aerobic treadmill exercise training; BIT = Behavioural Inattention Test; JT = Jebsen-Taylor Test; MEG = magnetoencephalography; MEP = motor endplate potentials; NI = not indicated; PET = positron emission tomography; rCBF = regional cerebral blood flow; ROM = range of motion; rTMS = repetitive transcranial magnetic stimulation; TAP = Test Battery of Attentional Performance; tDCS = transcranial direct current stimulation; TMS = transcranial magnetic stimulation; UE = upper extremity; WMFT = Wolf Motor Function Test.

in principle, preclude inducing significant plastic changes in the neurophysiology itself. Consequently, studies to evaluate neurophysiologic plasticity following rehabilitation that incorporate passive stimulation would do best to compare an experimental subject group with a control intervention group.

Constraint-Induced Movement Therapy: A General Method for Harnessing Brain Plasticity to Enhance Rehabilitation

CI therapy, as noted, is a well-validated, behavioral approach to rehabilitation derived by Taub and coworkers from basic research using a deafferented monkey model (reviewed in Taub, 1977, 1980). When a single forelimb is deafferented in a monkey by surgically severing the sensory nerves that innervate that limb as they enter the spinal cord, the animal does not use the forelimb in the free situation (Knapp, Taub, & Berman, 1963; Mott & Sherrington, 1895). Several converging lines of evidence suggest that nonuse of a single deafferented limb is a learning phenomenon involving a conditioned suppression of movement. (For a description of the experimental analysis leading to this conclusion, see Taub, 1977, 1980.) As a background for this explanation, one should note that substantial neurological injury usually leads to a depression in motor and/or perceptual function. Recovery processes then come into operation so that after a period of time movements can once again, at least potentially, be expressed. In monkeys, the initial period of depressed function lasts from 2 to 6 months following forelimb deafferentation (Taub, 1977; Taub & Berman, 1968). Thus, immediately after operation, the monkeys cannot use a deafferented limb; recovery from the initial depression of function requires considerable time. An animal with one deafferented limb tries to use that extremity in the immediate postoperative situation, but it cannot. It gets along quite well in the laboratory environment on three limbs and is therefore positively reinforced for this pattern of behavior, which, as a result, is strengthened. Moreover, continued attempts to use the impaired limb often lead to painful and otherwise aversive consequences, such as incoordination and falling, as well as to loss of food objects, and, in general, failure of any activity attempted with the deafferented limb. These aversive consequences condition the animal to avoid using that limb. Many learning experiments have demonstrated that punishment results in the suppression of behavior (Azrin & Holz, 1966; Catania, 1998; Estes, 1944). This response tendency persists, and consequently the monkey does not learn that several months after operation the limb has become potentially useful. In addition, following stroke (Liepert et al., 2000), and presumably after extremity deafferentation, there is a marked contraction in the size of the cortical representation of the affected limb; this phenomenon is probably related to the reports of persons with stroke that movement of that extremity is effortful. These three processes (i.e., punishment for use of the deafferented limb, reinforcement of use of the intact limb only, and plastic brain reorganization; see Figure 27.1) interact to produce a vicious downward spiral that results in a learned nonuse of the affected extremity that is normally permanent (Taub et al., 2002).

Learned nonuse of a deafferented limb can be overcome by either intensive training of that extremity, particularly by the operant conditioning technique termed *shaping,* or by continuous restraint of the intact limb over a period of a week or more. Both procedures have the effect of changing the contingencies of reinforcement for the use of the affected extremity. For example, when the movements of the intact limb are restricted several months after unilateral deafferentation, the animal either uses the deafferented limb or it cannot with any degree of efficiency feed itself, walk, or carry out a large portion of its normal activities of daily life. This dramatic change in motivation overcomes the learned nonuse of the deafferented limb. If the movement restriction device is left on for several days or longer, use of the affected limb acquires strength and is then able to compete successfully with the well-learned habit of learned nonuse of that limb in the free situation. The conditioned response and shaping techniques, just like the restriction of the intact limb, also involve major alterations in the contingencies of reinforcement; the animal must use its compromised limb or forgo food or other reinforcers. Increased use of the more-impaired limb after CI therapy in stroke, and presumably also after

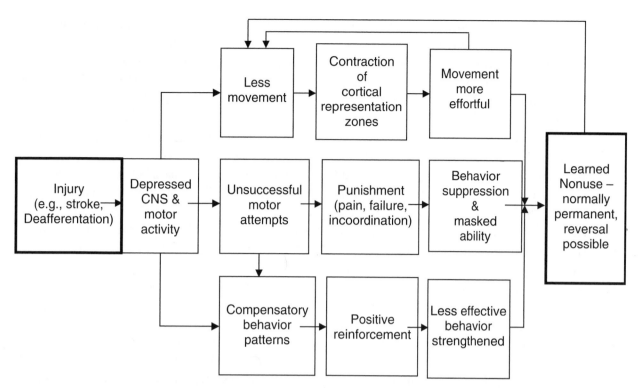

FIGURE 27.1. Model of the development of learned nonuse. CNS = central nervous system. From "Implications of the Learned Nonuse Formulation for Measuring Rehabilitation Outcomes: Lessons from Constraint-Induced Movement Therapy" by G. Uswatte and E. Taub, 2005, *Rehabilitation Psychology, 50*, p. 36. Copyright 2005 by the American Psychological Association.

forced used and shaping in deafferented monkeys, stimulates an expansion in the cortical representation of the more-impaired limb (Liepert et al., 2000) and other changes in the brain (see previous section). One might speculate that such CNS changes support movement that is less effortful and more skillful, in turn encouraging even greater use of the deafferented limb and setting up a virtuous cycle.

A noteworthy aspect of this research and its translation into a rehabilitation method is the generality of the learned nonuse formulation. Learned nonuse was conceptualized as occurring whenever (a) an injury results in an initial reduced ability to use a function so that an animal is punished for attempts to use that function by failure and rewarded for use of other functions and (b) there is slow recovery from the injury so that the animal recovers the physical ability to use that function, but the conditioned suppression of use that developed in the acute phase remains in force. Therefore, even though the type of nervous system injury in the deafferented monkey model was different from that in stroke

(i.e., peripheral vs. central, sensory vs. sensory and motor), it was plausible to hypothesize that the techniques used to overcome nonuse of deafferented forelimb in monkeys (i.e., restraint of the unimpaired limb and shaping of the impaired limb) would also be effective for rehabilitating hemiparetic arm use in human stroke survivors (Taub, 1980). After stroke, many survivors experience a marked reduction in motor ability of the hemiparetic arm followed by a gradual recovery. Furthermore, a large number of activities can be accomplished using the less-impaired arm alone, and many survivors are encouraged to do so in traditional therapy soon after their stroke.

Other disorders that meet conditions (a) and (b) that have been shown to be amenable to CI therapy include paresis of the more impaired arm after TBI and cerebral palsy, aphasia after stroke, and maladaptive patterns of ambulation after stroke and SCI (Taub & Uswatte, 2003). The interventions for upper extremity impairment after TBI (Shaw et al., 2005) and cerebral palsy (Taub, Ramey, DeLuca, &

Echols, 2004) are modeled closely on the protocol for upper extremity hemiparesis after stroke. CI therapy for aphasia "constrains" patients to speak by (a) reinforcing patients for making progressively more articulate responses during a therapeutic language game (i.e., shaping verbal output) that is "played" for 3 to 4 hours per day for 10 consecutive weekdays, (b) withdrawing reinforcement of any nonverbal forms of expression during training, and (c) monitoring and reinforcing speech outside of the training setting (Pulvermüller et al., 2001). Because stroke survivors who recover the capacity to walk at least a short distance must use both of their legs to do so, the primary target of intervention for these individuals is not learned nonuse but "learned misuse," that is, persisting use of maladaptive patterns of ambulation adopted during the acute phase when motor recovery was poor even in later phases of injury after substantial additional motor recovery has taken place (Taub, Uswatte, & Pidikiti, 1999).

CI therapy for lower extremity motor impairment constrains patients to ambulate using more adaptive movement patterns by (a) shaping ambulatory movement during overground walking, treadmill training, and transfers for 6 hours per day for 15 consecutive weekdays; (b) withdrawing reinforcement of maladaptive patterns of ambulation whenever possible during training; and (c) monitoring and reinforcing the amount and quality of ambulatory activity outside of the training setting. Unlike CI therapy for the upper extremity, treatment does not include physically restraining movement of the less-affected lower extremity (Taub et al., 1999). Principles from CI therapy also have been used to derive treatments for disorders associated with maladaptive changes in the cortical representation of a body part, such as focal hand dystonia (see previous section).

The successful application of CI therapy, or derivations thereof, to a wide array of neurological disorders provides several signposts for rehabilitation research. First, the development of CI therapy indicates the value of basic research for informing new rehabilitation treatments. Even though an animal model might not have a direct parallel in humans, the principles derived from the animal model, if they are sufficiently general, may have value for formulating an effective therapy. As noted, the shaping

and restraint components of CI therapy for upper extremity hemiparesis after stroke, which is of course a CNS injury, were borrowed directly from the studies of monkeys after forelimb deafferentation, a peripheral injury. Second, there may be mechanisms, such as learned nonuse, that influence impairment after several different types of CNS injury so that techniques that are effective with one type of injury may also be effective with others (e.g., upper extremity CI therapy for stroke and TBI). Finally, the elements shared by the CI therapy family of interventions suggest four general principles for harnessing brain plasticity to ameliorate impaired function after CNS injury. They are (a) providing extended and concentrated practice in using the function by scheduling intensive training; (b) increasing use of the impaired function in the treatment and home setting by providing reinforcement for its use, forcing its use by preventing the use of compensatory functions, or both; (c) emphasizing training on tasks rather than small components of the task such as individual movements; and (d) implementing methods for transferring gains made in the treatment setting to daily life. It is hoped that these pointers give some guidance for the considerable work still needed on how to fully exploit the degree of brain plasticity now known to be present in the adult and even aging brain to the advantage of survivors of CNS injury.

References

Azrin, N. H., & Holz, W. C. (1966). Punishment. In W. K. Honig (Ed.), *Operant behavior: Areas of research and application* (pp. 380–447). New York: Appleton-Century-Crofts.

Barker, R. M., Brauer, S. G., & Carson, R. G. (2006). Training-induced brain plasticity in stroke survivors with severe and chronic upper limb paresis as revealed with TMS [Abstract]. *Society for Neuroscience* (Vol. Program No. 559.6 2006 Neuroscience Meeting Planner Online). Retrieved December 11, 2008, from http://www.abstractsonline.com/viewer/?mkey={D197 4E76-28AF-4C1C-8AE8-4F73B56247A7

Brant Zawadzki, M., Atkinson, D., Detrick, M., Bradley, W. G., & Scidmore, G. (1996). Fluid-attenuated inversion recovery (FLAIR) for assessment of cerebral infarction. Initial clinical experience in 50 patients. *Stroke, 27,* 1187–1191.

Broca, P. (1861). Nouvelle observation d'aphemie produite par une lesion de la motie posterieure des deuxieme et troisieme circonvulutions frontales [New observations on aphasia produced by a lesion of the posterior portion of the second and third frontal gyri]. *Bullet de la Societe Anatomique de Paris, 6,* 398–407.

Brown, T., & Sherrington, C. (1912). On the instability of a cortical point. *Proceedings of the Royal Society of London: Series B, 85,* 585–602.

Buonomano, D., & Merzenich, M. M. (1998). Cortical plasticity: From synapses to maps. *Annual Review of Neuroscience, 21,* 149–186.

Calautti, C., Leroy, F., Guincestre, J. Y., & Baron, J. C. (2001). Dynamics of motor network overactivation after striatocapsular stroke: A longitudinal PET study using a fixed-performance paradigm. *Stroke, 32,* 2534–2542.

Candia, V., Elbert, T., Altenmüller, E., Rau, H., Schäfer, T., & Taub, E. (1999). Constraint-Induced Movement therapy for focal hand dystonia in musicians. *The Lancet, 353,* 42.

Candia, V., Schafer, T., Taub, E., Rau, H., Altenmuller, E., Rockstroh, B., et al. (2002). Sensory motor retuning: A behavioral treatment for focal hand dystonia of pianists and guitarists. *Archives of Physical Medicine and Rehabilitation, 83,* 1342–1348.

Candia, V., Wienbruch, C., Elbert, T., Rockstroh, B., & Ray, W. (2003). Effective behavioral treatment of focal hand dystonia in musicians alters somatosensory cortical organization. *Proceedings of the National Academy of Sciences of the United States, 100,* 7942–7946.

Catania, A. C. (1998). *Learning* (4th ed.). Upper Saddle River, NJ: Prentice Hall.

Christodoulou, C., DeLuca, J., Ricker, J. H., Madigan, N. K., Bly, B. M., Lange, G., et al. (2001). Functional magnetic resonance imaging of working memory impairment after traumatic brain injury. *Journal of Neurology, Neurosurgery, and Psychiatry, 71,* 161–168.

Cornelissen, K., Laine, M., Tarkiainen, A., Järvensivu, T., Martin, N., & Salmelin, R. (2003). Adult brain plasticity elicited by anomia treatment. *Journal of Cognitive Neuroscience, 15,* 444–461.

Cramer, S. C., Nelles, G., Schaechter, J. D., Kaplan, J. D., Finklestein, S. P., & Rosen, B. R. (2001). A functional MRI study of three motor tasks in the evaluation of stroke recovery. *Neurorehabilitation and Neural Repair, 15,* 1–8.

Crosson, B., Moore, A. B., Gopinath, K., White, K. D., Wierenga, C. E., Gaiefsky, M. E., et al. (2005). Role of the right and left hemispheres in recovery of function during treatment of intention in aphasia. *Journal of Cognitive Neuroscience, 17,* 392–406.

Daviet, J. C., Preux, P. M., Salle, J. Y., Lebreton, F., Munoz, M., Dudognon, P., et al. (2002). Clinical factors in the prognosis of complex regional pain syndrome Type I after stroke: A prospective study.

American Journal of Physical Medicine and Rehabilitation, 81, 34–39.

de Mos, M., de Bruijn, A., Huygen, F., Dieleman, J. P., Stricker, B., & Sturkenboom, M. (2007). The incidence of complex regional pain syndrome: A population-based study. *Pain, 129,* 12–20.

Draganski, B., Gaser, C., Busch, V., Schuierer, G., Bogdahn, U., & May, A. (2004). Changes in grey matter induced by training. *Nature, 427,* 311–312.

Duncan, P. W. (2002). Stroke recovery and rehabilitation research. *Journal of Rehabilitation Research & Development, 39,* IX–XI.

Edgerton, V. R., Leon, R. D., Harkema, S. J., Hodgson, J. A., London, N., Reinkensmeyer, D. J., et al. (2001). Retraining the injured spinal cord. *The Journal of Physiology, 533,* 15–22.

Edgerton, V. R., Tillakaratne, N. J. K., Bigbee, A. J., de Leon, R. D., & Roy, R. R. (2004). Plasticity of the spinal neural circuitry after injury. *Annual Review of Neuroscience, 27,* 145–167.

Elbert, T., Flor, H., Birbaumer, N., Knecht, S., Hampson, S., Larbig, W., et al. (1994). Extensive reorganization of the somatosensory cortex in adult humans after nervous system injury. *Neuroreport, 5,* 2593–2597.

Elbert, T., Pantev, C., Wienbruch, C., Rockstroh, B., & Taub, E. (1995). Increased cortical representation of the fingers of the left hand in string players. *Science, 270,* 305–307.

Elbert, T., Sterr, A., Rockstroh, B., Pantev, C., Muller, M. M., & Taub, E. (2002). Expansion of the tonotopic area in the auditory cortex of the blind. *The Journal of Neuroscience, 22,* 9941–9944.

Estes, W. K. (1944). An experimental study of punishment. *Psychological Monographs, 57*(263), 1–40.

Fleurens, P. (1842). *Recherches experimentales sur les propietes et les functions du systeme neurveux dans les animaux* [Experiments on the properties and functions of the nervous system of animals] (2nd ed.). Paris: Belliere.

Forrester, L. W., Hanley, D. F., & Macko, R. F. (2006). Effects of treadmill exercise on transcranial magnetic stimulation-induced excitability to quadriceps after stroke. *Archives of Physical Medicine and Rehabilitation, 87,* 229–234.

Fridriksson, J., Morrow-Odom, L., Moser, D., Fridriksson, A., & Baylis, G. (2006). Neural recruitment associated with anomia treatment in aphasia. *Neuroimage, 32,* 1403–1412.

Fritsch, G., & Hitzig, E. (1870). Uber die electrische erregbarkeit des grosshirns [On the electrical excitability of the cerebral cortex]. *Archiv fuer Anatomie und Physiologie, 37,* 300–332.

Gauthier, L. V., Taub, E., Perkins, C., Ortmann, M., Mark, V. W., & Uswatte, G. (2008). Remodeling the brain: Plastic structural brain changes produced by different motor therapies after stroke. *Stroke, 39,* 1520–1525.

Gellhorn, E., & Hyde, J. (1953). Influence of proprioception on map of cortical responses. *The Journal of Physiology, 122,* 371–385.

Henderson, A. K., Subramanian, S., Knaut, L. A., Pitto, A., Doyon, J., & Levin, M. F. (2006). fMRI study of training-induced cortical reorganization in individuals with hemiparesis [Abstract]. *Society for Neuroscience* (Vol. Program No. 451.9 2006 Neuroscience Meeting Planner Online). Retrieved December 11, 2008, from http://www.abstractsonline.com/viewer/?mkey={D19 74E76-28AF-4C1C-8AE8-4F73B56247A7

Hoffman, L. R., & Field-Fote, E. C. (2006). Cortical reorganization in individuals with cervical spinal cord injury following two different hand training interventions [Abstract]. *Society for Neuroscience* (Vol. Program No. 228.29 2006 Neuroscience Meeting Planner Online). Retrieved December 11, 2008, from http://www.abstractsonline.com/viewer/?mkey= {D1974E76-28AF-4C1C-8AE8-4F73B56247A7

Hubel, D. H., & Wiesel, T. N. J. (1970). The period of susceptibility to the physiological effects of unilateral eye closure in kittens. *Journal of Physiology, 206,* 419–436.

Hummel, F., & Cohen, L. G. (2005). Improvement of motor function with noninvasive cortical stimulation in a patient with chronic stroke. *Neurorehabilitation and Neural Repair, 19,* 14–19.

Jackson, J. H. (1873). On the anatomical and physiological localization of movements in the brain. *The Lancet, 1,* 84–85, 162–164, 232–234.

Jackson, J. H. (1884). Evolution and dissolution of the nervous system. *British Medical Journal, 1,* 591–754.

Jang, S. H., Kim, Y. H., Cho, S. H., Lee, J. H., Park, J. W., & Kwon, Y. H. (2003). Cortical reorganization induced by task-oriented training in chronic hemiplegic stroke patients. *Neuroreport, 14,* 137–141.

Jenkins, W. M., Merzenich, M. M., Ochs, M. T., Allard, T., & Guic-Robles, E. (1990). Functional reorganization of primary somatosensory cortex in adult owl monkeys after behaviorally controlled tactile stimulation. *Journal of Neurophysiology, 63,* 82–104.

Kaas, J. H. (1995). Neurobiology. How cortex reorganizes. *Nature, 375,* 735–736.

Kaas, J. H., Merzenich, M. M., & Killackey, H. P. (1983). The reorganization of somatosensory cortex following peripheral nerve damage in adult and developing mammals. *Annual Review of Neuroscience, 6,* 325–356.

Kasamatsu, T., Pettigrew, J. D., & Ary, M. (1979). Restoration of visual cortical plasticity by local microperfusion of norepinephrine. *Journal of Comparative Neurology, 185,* 163–181.

Kim, Y. H., Ohn, S. H., Park, S. J., Yoo, W. K., Kim, S. T., & Lee, K. H. (2006). Reorganization of motor cortical activity induced by high-frequency repetitive transcranial magnetic stimulation in chronic stroke patients [Abstract]. *Archives of Physical Medicine and Rehabilitation, 87,* e51–e52.

Kim, Y. H., You, S. H., Ko, M. H., Park, J. W., Lee, K. H., Jang, S. H., et al. (2006). Repetitive transcranial magnetic induced stimulation-corticomotor excitability and associated motor skill acquisition in chronic stroke. *Stroke, 37,* 1471–1476.

Knapp, H. D., Taub, E., & Berman, A. J. (1963). Movements in monkeys with deafferented forelimbs. *Experimental Neurology, 7,* 305–315.

Kolb, B., Stewart, J., & Sutherland, R. J. (1997). Recovery of function is associated with increased spine density in cortical pyramidal cells after frontal lesions and/or noradrenaline depletion in neonatal rats. *Behavioral Brain Research, 89,* 61–70.

Lashley, K. S. (1938). Factors limiting recovery after central nervous lesions. *Journal of Nervous and Mental Diseases, 88,* 733–755.

Li, S., & Carmichael, S. T. (2006). Growth-associated gene and protein expression in the region of axonal sprouting in the aged brain after stroke. *Neurobiology of Disease, 23,* 362–373.

Liepert, J., Bauder, H., Wolfgang, H. R., Miltner, W. H., Taub, E., & Weiller, C. (2000). Treatment-induced cortical reorganization after stroke in humans. *Stroke, 31,* 1210–1216.

Liepert, J., Tegenthoff, M., & Malin, J. P. (1995). Changes of cortical motor area size during immobilization. *Electroencephalography and Clinical Neurophysiology, 97,* 382–386.

Luauté, J., Michel, C., Rode, G., Pisella, L., Jacquin-Courtois, S., Costes, N., et al. (2006). Functional anatomy of the therapeutic effects of prism adaptation on left neglect. *Neurology, 66,* 1859–1867.

Luft, A. R., Macko, R., Forrester, L., Villagra, F., & Hanley, D. (2005). Subcortical reorganization induced by aerobic locomotor training in chronic stroke survivors [Abstract]. *Society for Neuroscience* (Vol. Program No. 865.8 2005 Neuroscience Meeting Planner Online). Retrieved December 11, 2008, from http://www.abstractsonline.com/viewer/?mkey={D19 74E76-28AF-4C1C-8AE8-4F73B56247A7

Luft, A. R., McCombe-Waller, S., Whitall, J., Forrester, L. W., Macko, R., Sorkin, J. D., et al. (2004). Repetitive bilateral arm training and motor cortex activation in chronic stroke: A randomized controlled trial. *JAMA, 292,* 1853–1861.

Maguire, E. A., Gadian, D. G., Johnsrude, I. S., Good, C. D., Ashburner, J., Frackowiak, R. S. J., et al. (2000). Navigation-related structural change in the hippocampi of taxi drivers. *Proceedings of the National Academy of Sciences USA, 97,* 4398–4403.

Maihöfner, C., Handwerker, H. O., Neundörfer, B., & Birklein, F. (2004). Cortical reorganization during recovery from complex regional pain syndrome. *Neurology, 63,* 693–701.

Mark, V., Taub, E., & Morris, D. M. (2006). Neuroplasticity and Constraint-Induced Movement Therapy. *Europa Medicophysica, 42,* 269–284.

Marshall, R. S., Perera, G. M., Lazar, R. M., Krakauer, J. W., Constantine, R. C., & DeLaPaz, R. L. (2000). Evolution of cortical activation during recovery from corticospinal tract infarction. *Stroke, 31,* 656–661.

May, A., Hajak, G., & Gansbauer, S. (2007). Structural brain alterations following 5 days of interventionL dynamic aspects of neuroplasticity. *Cerebral Cortex, 17,* 205–210.

Merzenich, M. M., Kaas, J. H., Wall, J., Nelson, R. J., Sur, M., & Felleman, D. (1983). Topographic reorganization of somatosensory cortical areas 3b and 1 in adult monkeys following restricted deafferentation. *Neuroscience, 8,* 33–55.

Merzenich, M. M., Nelson, R. J., Stryker, M. P., Cynader, M. S., Schoppmann, A., & Zook, J. M. (1984). Somatosensory cortical map changes following digit amputation in adult monkeys. *Journal of Comparative Neurology, 224,* 591–605.

Mott, F. W., & Sherrington, C. S. (1895). Experiments upon the influence of sensory nerves upon movement and nutrition of the limbs. *Proceedings of the Royal Society of London, 57,* 481–488.

Munk, H. (1881). *Ueber die funktionen der grosshirnrinde, gesammelte mitteilungen aus den jahren 1877–1880* [On the functions of the cerebral cortex, collected writing from the years 1877–1880]. Berlin: Hirshwald.

Nudo, R. J., & Milliken, G. W. (1996). Reorganization of movement representations in primary motor cortex following focal ischemic infarcts in adult squirrel monkeys. *Journal of Neurophysiology, 75,* 2144–2149.

Nudo, R. J., Wise, B. M., SiFuentes, F., & Milliken, G. W. (1996). Neural substrates for the effects of rehabilitative training on motor recovery after ischemic infarct. *Science, 272,* 1791–1794.

Ottawa Panel, Khadilkar, A., Phillips, K., Jean, N., Lamothe, C., Milner, S., et al. (2006). Ottawa Panel evidence-based clinical practice guidelines for post-stroke rehabilitation. *Topics in Stroke Rehabilitation, 2006,* 1–269.

Petchkrua, W., Weiss, D. J., & Patel, R. R. (2000). Reassessment of the incidence of complex regional pain syndrome type 1 following stroke. *Neurorehabilitation and Neural Repair, 14,* 59–63.

Pleger, B., Ragert, P., Schwenkreis, P., Forster, A. F., Wilimzig, C., Dinse, H., et al. (2006). Patterns of cortical reorganization parallel impaired tactile discrimination and pain intensity in complex regional pain syndrome. *Neuroimage, 32,* 503–510.

Pons, T. P., Garraghty, P. E., Ommaya, A. K., Kaas, J. H., Taub, E., & Mishkin, M. (1991). Massive cortical reorganization after sensory deafferentation in adult macaques. *Science, 252,* 1857–1860.

Pulvermüller, F., Neininger, B., Elbert, T., Mohr, B., Rockstroh, B., Kaas, J. H., et al. (2001). Constraint-induced therapy of chronic aphasia after stroke. *Stroke, 32,* 1621–1626.

Rosenberger, P. B., & Rottenberg, D. A. (2002). Does training change the brain? [Editorial]. *Neurology, 58,* 1139–1140.

Ruch, T. C. (1960). The cerebral cortex: Its structure and motor functions. In T. C. Ruch & J. F. Fulton (Eds.), *Medical physiology and biophysics* (18th ed., pp. 249–276). Philadelphia: W. B. Saunders Company.

Schaechter, J. D. (2004). Motor rehabilitation and brain plasticity after hemiparetic stroke. *Progress in Neurobiology, 73,* 61–72.

Scheff, S. W., Price, D. A., Hicks, R. R., Baldwin, S. A., Robinson, S., & Brackney, C. (2005). Synaptogenesis in the hippocampal CA1 field following traumatic brain injury. *Journal of Neurotrauma, 22,* 719–732.

Shaw, S. E., Morris, D. M., Uswatte, G., McKay, S., Meythaler, J. M., & Taub, E. (2005). Constraint-induced movement therapy for recovery of upper-limb function following traumatic brain injury. *Journal of Rehabilitation Research and Development, 42,* 769–778.

Simos, P. G., Fletcher, J. M., Bergman, E., Breier, J. I., Foorman, B. R., Castillo, E. M., et al. (2002). Dyslexia-specific brain activation profile becomes normal following successful remedial training. *Neurology, 58,* 1203–1213.

Sterr, A., Muller, M. M., Elbert, T., Rockstroh, B., Pantev, C., & Taub, E. (1998). Changed perceptions in Braille readers. *Nature, 391,* 134–135.

Sturm, W., Longoni, F., Weis, S., Specht, K., Herzog, H., Vohn, R., et al. (2004). Functional reorganization in patients with right hemisphere stroke after training of alertness: A longitudinal PET and fMRI study in eight cases. *Neuropsychologia, 42,* 434–450.

Taub, E. (1977). Movement in nonhuman primates deprived of somatosensory feedback. *Exercise and Sports Sciences Reviews, 4,* 335–374.

Taub, E. (1980). Somatosensory deafferentation research with monkeys: Implications for rehabilitation medicine. In L. P. Ince (Ed.), *Behavioral psychology in rehabilitation medicine: Clinical applications* (pp. 371–401). New York: Williams & Wilkins.

Taub, E. (2004). Harnessing brain plasticity through behavioral techniques to produce new treatments in neurorehabilitation. *American Psychologist, 59,* 692–704.

Taub, E., & Berman, A. J. (1968). Movement and learning in the absence of sensory feedback. In S. J. Freedman (Ed.), *The neuropsychology of spatially oriented behavior* (pp. 173–192). Homewood, IL: Dorsey Press.

Taub, E., Miller, N. E., Novack, T. A., Cook, E. W., III, Fleming, W. C., Nepomuceno, C. S., et al. (1993). Technique to improve chronic motor deficit after stroke. *Archives of Physical Medicine and Rehabilitation, 74,* 347–354.

Taub, E., Ramey, S. L., DeLuca, S., & Echols, K. (2004). Efficacy of Constraint-Induced Movement Therapy for children with cerebral palsy with asymmetric motor impairment. *Pediatrics, 113,* 305–312.

Taub, E., & Uswatte, G. (2003). Constraint-Induced Movement therapy: Bridging from the primate laboratory to the stroke rehabilitation laboratory. *Journal of Rehabilitation Medicine* (Suppl. 41), 34–40.

Taub, E., Uswatte, G., & Elbert, T. (2002). New treatments in neurorehabilitation founded on basic research. *Nature Reviews Neuroscience, 3,* 228–236.

Taub, E., Uswatte, G., King, D. K., Morris, D., Crago, J., & Chatterjee, A. (2006). A placebo controlled trial of Constraint-Induced Movement Therapy for upper extremity after stroke. *Stroke, 37,* 1045–1049.

Taub, E., Uswatte, G., & Pidikiti, R. (1999). Constraint-Induced Movement Therapy: A new family of techniques with broad application to physical rehabilitation—a clinical review. *Journal of Rehabilitation Research and Development, 36,* 237–251.

Temple, E., Deutsch, G. K., Poldrack, R. A., Miller, S. L., Tallal, P., Merzenich, M. M., et al. (2003). Neural deficits in children with dyslexia ameliorated by behavioral remediation: Evidence from functional MRI. *Proceedings of the National Academy of Science of the United States, 100,* 2860–2865.

Thimm, M., Fink, G. R., Küst, J., Karbe, H., & Sturm, W. (2006). Impact of alertness training on spatial neglect: A behavioural and fMRI study. *Neuropsychologia, 44,* 1230–1246.

Tillakaratne, N. J. K., Mouria, M., Ziv, N. B., Roy, R. R., Edgerton, V. R., & Tobin, A. (2000). Increased expression of glutamate decarboxylase (GAD67) in feline lumbar spinal cord after complete thoracic spinal cord transection. *Journal of Neuroscience Research, 60,* 219–230.

Tillerson, J. L., Cohen, A. D., Caudle, W. M., Zigmond, M. J., Schallert, T., & Miller, G. W. (2002). Forced nonuse in unilateral parkinsonian rats exacerbates injury. *Journal of Neuroscience, 22,* 6790–6799.

Wall, P. D., & Egger, M. D. (1971). Formation of new connections in adult rat brains following partial deafferentation. *Nature, 232,* 542–545.

Weiss, T., Miltner, W., Liepert, J., Meissner, W., & Taub, E. (2004). Rapid functional plasticity in the primary somatomotor cortex and perceptual changes after nerve block. *European Journal of Neuroscience, 20,* 3413–3423.

Wolf, S. L., Winstein, C., Miller, J. P., Taub, E., Uswatte, G., Morris, D. M., et al. (2006). Effect of Constraint Induced Movement Therapy on upper extremity function among patients 3–9 months following stroke: The EXCITE randomized clinical trial. *JAMA, 296,* 2095–2104.

Woodlee, M. T., & Schallert, T. (2006). The impact of motor activity and inactivity on the brain. *Current Directions in Psychological Science, 15,* 203–206.

CHAPTER 28

PREVENTION, ASSESSMENT, AND MANAGEMENT OF WORK-RELATED INJURY AND DISABILITY

Stephen T. Wegener and William Stiers

This chapter focuses on the psychological aspects of the etiology, assessment, and treatment of work-related injury, and the prevention of long-term disability. However, the provision of clinical services is only one role for rehabilitation psychologists in the care of injured workers. Psychologists can offer expertise at multiple levels, including human factors in ergonomic interventions, injury prevention, management of disability compensation programs, and development of policies that promote inclusive work environments.

Work-related disability can involve psychological and physiological stresses that can be either traumatic or repetitive. Although the primary examples in this chapter are from the literature and practice in the area of physical impairments, the concepts are applicable to the entire range of impairments experienced by workers.

PREVALENCE AND COSTS OF WORK-RELATED INJURY AND DISABILITY

Occupational risk factors are responsible for 8.8% of global mortality—approximately 2 million deaths—and 8.1% of disability-adjusted life years (DALY—with 1 DALY being equal to the loss of 1 healthy life year; Eijkemans & Takala, 2005). In the United States, approximately 6,500 job-related deaths from injury and 13.2 million nonfatal injuries occur annually in the civilian workforce, as well as 60,300 deaths from disease and 862,200 nonfatal illnesses (Leigh, Markowitz, Fahs, Shin, & Landrigan, 1997) with immense direct ($65 billion) and indirect ($106 billion) costs. Common work-related conditions include circulatory diseases, cancer due to carcinogenic expo-

sure, chronic obstructive pulmonary disease and asthma due to airborne particulates, and musculoskeletal disorders related to injury and ergonomic trauma (Leigh et al., 1997). These estimates are certainly low, as they ignore costs associated with pain and suffering, as well as costs of care provided by family members, and also because the numbers of occupational injuries and illnesses are probably underreported.

Musculoskeletal injuries and disorders (MSID) have a major impact on the health and quality of life of the workforce population and on work productivity. This is particularly true for those under age 45, for whom low back pain is the most common cause of disability (Leigh et al., 1997). MSIDs account for 33% to 40% of the workers' compensation claims in the United States (Tanaka et al., 1995; U.S. Bureau of Labor Statistics, 1998a, 1998b), and the number of lost workdays per MSID (25 days per case) far exceeds the 5 lost workdays for the average work injury (U.S. Bureau of Labor Statistics, 1998a, 1998b). The majority of persons with MSIDs return to work relatively quickly (Reid, 1997), and only a minority develops persistent functional problems (Nachemson, 1992). However, this minority accounts for most of the costs associated with MSIDs (Linton, Hellsing, & Hallden, 1998; Nachemson, 1992).

WORKERS' COMPENSATION SYSTEMS

Currently, state law requires most employers to provide their employees with workers' compensation insurance, which pays for medical care and wage replacement of those with work-related injuries or illnesses. Employers pay premiums into the system on the basis of their claims record. Each state legislature determines what injuries and illnesses will be covered, what benefits will be awarded, how much will be paid for medical and legal fees, and how the appeals process is established and administered. In general, benefits are limited to wage replacement and medical costs, without compensation for pain or suffering and without punitive damages. According to Rischitelli (1999), final settlement payments are determined according to medical loss (i.e., bodily function or structure) and wage loss (i.e., diminution of wage earning capacity). In 2003, approximately 125 million persons were covered by workers compensation insurance (Social Security Administration, 2005), or about 98% of the total U.S. workforce (U.S. Department of Labor, 2003), with workers' compensation costs including $26 billion for medical care and $29 billion for disability payments (Social Security Administration, 2005).

Although the current system in the United States is a no-fault system, meaning that injured workers do not need to prove the employer is at fault, there is an increasing tendency for injured workers to litigate. Litigation often arises around disputes about the severity of the condition or whether it is work related (Hirsch, 1997). In 1995, approximately 44% of all cases were being litigated, with a usual time to settlement of 5 to 6 years (Pye & Orris, 2000). Disputes are initially resolved at administrative hearings before a commissioner or administrative law judge, but outcomes can be appealed to the courts (Rischitelli, 1999).

AMERICANS WITH DISABILITIES ACT AND FAMILY AND MEDICAL LEAVE ACT

Laws related to workers' compensation claims may interact with laws related to the Americans With Disabilities Act (ADA) and the Family and Medical Leave Act (FMLA). Psychologists should be aware of these implications in both clinical work and work-related program development (Bruyere & O'Keefe, 1994).

The ADA prohibits discrimination against qualified individuals with disabilities in hiring, employment, promotion, and termination (ADA, 1990), and requires "reasonable accommodations" to allow

persons with disabilities to work. A worker who is injured on the job and has a residual permanent impairment would be covered under the ADA if the impairment substantially limits one or more major life activities, but the ADA does not cover temporary conditions (Geaneh, 2004). Reasonable accommodations include job restructuring, modified work schedules, and making facilities accessible, that is, changing the marginal aspects of the job. However, workers who cannot perform the essential functions of a job are not required to be employed in that job, and the employer does not have to create a new job to accommodate a worker. Injured workers can be reassigned to a vacant position that better suits them at equivalent pay, but if no such job is available they can be reassigned to a lower paying position. In addition, employers do not need to allow indefinite leave, and if an injured worker cannot return to work for an extended period of time, the employer can terminate him or her (but not discontinue his or her workers' compensation benefits).

The FMLA allows up to 12 weeks of job-protected leave in a 12-month period for serious personal or family medical conditions; employers must continue medical insurance benefits and return the employee to the same position or an equivalent position at equivalent pay. However, employers have the right to count the time an injured worker is out of work and covered under workers' compensation as FMLA leave.

Workers' compensation, ADA, and FLMA all include the right of the employer to ask the employee to submit to an examination to obtain a health care provider's certification for fitness for duty. Employers are not obligated to allow an individual to work who might be harmed by work activities, nor are they required to create "light-duty" positions for injured employees. If they do so, these can be limited to a temporary basis.

RISK AND PROTECTIVE FACTORS FOR WORK-RELATED MUSCULOSKELETAL INJURIES AND DISORDERS AND DISABILITY

A number of factors have important effects on work-related MSID and subsequent disability. These include demographic factors, workplace factors, psychosocial factors, environmental factors, and treatment factors.

Demographic Factors
Those with occupational low-back injuries, African Americans, and those with lower socioeconomic status (SES) have poorer outcomes than Caucasians and those with higher SES (Bellamy, 1997). This is certainly related to the fact that, because of inequalities in opportunity, African Americans and persons with lower SES are more likely to work in jobs that are lower paying, less satisfying, less autonomous, and more physically stressful and to have poor access to health care (Chibnall, Tait, Andresen, & Hadler, 2005). Those with greater education and income tend to work in safer environments and have lower workers' compensation claim rates, tend to work in less physically demanding occupations, and have higher return-to-work rates. In addition, because a typical formula for disability wage replacement is two thirds of predisability before-tax wage, capped at a maximum of 67% to 150% of the average state weekly wage (Hirsch, 1997), this provides significantly limited income replacement for higher-earning workers; thus, the cost of missing work is higher for those individuals. Older age and lower education are associated with poorer work-injury outcomes (DeBerard, Masters, Colledge, & Holmes, 2003; DeBerard, Masters, Colledge, Schleusener, & Schlegel, 2001; Turner et al., 2006). Finally, higher local-sector unemployment rates are also related to a larger numbers of workers' compensation claims (McIntosh, Frank, Hogg-Johnson, Bombardier, & Hall, 2000) because marginalized workers are more at-risk in tight job markets.

Workplace Factors
A comprehensive review of 22 studies of acute low-back pain identified several work-related factors associated with developing chronic disability: physical factors, such as manual material handling and physically heavy work; and social factors, such as poor social support at work, high perceived stress and job demands, and job tenure less than 2 years (Shaw, Pransky, & Fitzgerald, 2001). Other studies have also found that chronic work disability is related

to lower satisfaction with job and with coworkers (Turner et al., 2006).

Psychosocial Factors
Multiple studies have identified psychological factors associated with developing chronic disability after acute low-back pain, including greater emotional distress, poor coping patterns (especially avoidant problem solving and catastrophizing), and greater self-reported pain and functional limitations at onset, but not objective measures of injury (Gauthier, Sullivan, Adams, Stanish, & Thibault, 2006; Shaw et al., 2001; Sullivan et al., 2005). Vlaeyen, Kole-Snijders, Boeren, and van Eek (1995) and others (e.g., Turner et al., 2006) have suggested a model wherein individuals with high psychosocial dysfunction respond to injury and pain with catastrophizing cognitive distortions, fear and avoidance of activity, lowered self-efficacy and lower expectations for recovery, and subsequent work disability.

Environmental Factors
Environmental contingencies are known to affect behavior. As benefit levels increase, claims frequency and severity do so as well (Butler, Hartwig, & Gardner, 1997). Also, for a given condition, the higher the percentage of income replacement, the longer the period of disability (Hirsch, 1997). States where workers are compensated until they have reached maximum medical improvement and then receive a settlement for percentage impairment have higher rates of return to work and lower costs than states that compensate injured workers until they return to preinjury functional status or until alternative work at equal pay is achieved (Bednar, Baesher-Griffith, & Osterman, 1998). Numerous studies have shown that individuals with injuries covered under workers' compensation have poorer treatment outcomes than individuals with injuries not covered under workers' compensation. These include focal back injuries (Chibnall et al., 2005; Coste, Lefrancois, Guillemin, & Pouchot, 2004; Pransky et al., 2000; Rainville, Sobel, Hartigan, & Wright, 1997), shoulder injuries (Harris, Mulford, Solomon, van Gelder, & Young, 2005), and head injuries (Binder & Rohling, 1996), as well as multiple-trauma injuries (Zelle et al., 2005).

Treatment Factors

It is important that providers who operate in work-injury contexts be aware of factors that may affect their judgment. Practitioners who treat chronic pain often have negative attitudes about such patients (Merskey & Teasell, 2000; Rohling, Binder, & Langhinrichsen-Rohling, 1995), especially when compensation is involved (May, Doyle, & Chew-Graham, 1999). This may interact with class- and race-based stereotypes (Smedley, Stith, & Nelson, 2003) to affect provider judgments and decisions (van Ryn & Burke, 2000). For example, studies have shown that health care providers are likely to underestimate pain intensity for individuals who report high levels of pain (Todd, Lee, & Hoffman, 1994; van Dulmen, Fennis, Mokkink, van der Velden, & Bleijenberg, 1994), who are older (Davitz & Pendleton, 1969), who are non-White (Todd, Samaroo, & Hoffman, 1993), and who are female (McDonald & Bridge, 1991). In addition, observers tend to underestimate the pain of patients with emotional distress or other life stresses (Swartzman & McDermid, 1993). However, some factors lead to overestimation of symptoms, including the presence of medical evidence consistent with reported symptoms (Chibnall & Tait, 1995). Thus, clinicians conducting disability examinations should be aware of a range of contextual factors that may influence their judgments.

Patients also have unique issues when embroiled in the workers' compensation environment. Like other social welfare programs, there is stigma attached to being a beneficiary. Injured workers may encounter suspicion and disbelief, antagonism, and delays or denials of benefits when interacting with workers' compensation personnel. Many injured workers in the United States, Canada, and Australia describe their experience as demeaning and dehumanizing, and report feeling mistreated, frustrated, and helpless (Strunin & Boden, 2004).

The risk of chronic disability rises with increased time off work. For example, most workers with musculoskeletal low-back pain return to work within 3 months, but those who do not often have long-term disability (McIntosh et al., 2000). Injured workers who reported a less favorable treatment experience were 3.5 times more likely to be off work

and receiving compensation at 6 and 12 months postinjury compared with workers reporting a more favorable treatment experience (Wickizer et al., 2004). Workers who were less satisfied with the administration of their claim are more than three times as likely to retain an attorney or file an appeal. In comparisons of countries with and without no-fault insurance coverage (Carron, DeGood, & Tait, 1985), and of countries before and after the introduction of a no-fault system (Cassidy et al., 2000), litigation was related to worse functional outcomes (Harris et al., 2005). Thus, worker satisfaction with claims management and medical treatment is a crucial factor in the risk of long-term disability.

PREVENTION OF SECONDARY DISABILITY

A number of secondary prevention efforts have used early interventions to prevent complications of chronic pain, disability, reduced quality of life and lost productivity after work injury. Several studies have used self-management based on cognitive–behavior therapy (CBT) in persons with acute back pain with a secondary prevention model. These interventions have been shown to reduce days of sick leave and health care use (Linton & Andersson, 2000) as well as to decrease fear-avoidance beliefs, number of days with pain, time off work, and long-term sick leave (Linton & Ryberg, 2001). Thus, despite the strong natural recovery rate for back pain, cognitive–behavioral interventions have a significant preventive effect with regard to disability. Furthermore, the addition of a CBT intervention to physical therapy improved return to work rates by 25% over physical therapy alone for individuals following whiplash injury (Sullivan, Adams, Rhodenizer, & Stanish, 2006). These studies and others provide evidence that CBT-based self-management interventions reduce chronic disability in persons at risk.

A novel approach to improving outcomes following MSID delivers health and rehabilitation services to injured workers in the work environment. These programs are based on the premise that early assessment and easy access to treatment in the work environment can lead to improved outcomes. A survey of 400 major U.S. corporations revealed that although a majority (81%) included health and rehabilitation services in their benefit package, only a small number (7%) offered on-site physical therapy or vocational rehabilitation services. Two studies with relatively small samples suggested that these on-site programs improved outcomes following MSID (Grayzel, Finegan, & Ponchak, 1997; Hochanadel & Conrad, 1993). More recently, a larger study at a major manufacturer compared the outcomes of workers seen at on-site rehabilitation centers with those seen in community care (Wegener, Kuhlemeier, & Mitchell, 2002). The effects of age, gender, body part injured, diagnosis, and plant location were statistically controlled. Workers treated at on-site centers had significantly fewer days away from work, fewer restricted workdays and reduced workers' compensation costs compared with workers treated by community rehabilitation providers. Thus, prevention efforts that focus on both individual and health system changes have the potential to reduce the impact and costs of work-related injury.

PSYCHOLOGICAL ASSESSMENT AND TREATMENT

Psychologists may provide clinical services to injured workers in multiple settings and roles, often in traditional mental health settings but increasingly in the context of medical and rehabilitative care. Psychologists' activities may also include disability determination assessment and impairment ratings, which require specialized knowledge and expertise in addition to those skills needed to operate effectively in traditional clinical contexts.

Clinical Assessment and Treatment

In cases of work-related injury or illness, psychological assessment may be part of the evaluation to determine whether employment caused or substantially contributed to the development or aggravation of the worker's disease and whether there is sufficient evidence to support a causal connection between an identifiable exposure or event and a specific injury or illness (Rischitelli, 1999). In addition, psychologists may be asked whether there are problems that predate the injury and are related to cur-

rent work disability. Determination is based on the preponderance of evidence that is, a determination that it is probable, or more likely than not (Pye & Orris, 2000). The psychologist may function either as a clinician who provides evaluation and on-going care or as an independent medical evaluator who provides only evaluation services. Evaluations may occur at the request of the employee, the employer, the insurer, or the state (Pye & Orris, 2000). In all cases, it is important to make clear to patients that information will be transmitted to their employer.

An independent medical examination is usually requested to obtain a second opinion to document the condition, its cause, the appropriate treatments, and the level of functional impairment. There is no doctor–patient relationship, and examinations are usually limited to one encounter. The psychologist needs to ensure that the examinee understands that the evaluation's purpose is assessment, not treatment. However, if new diagnoses are discovered, the psychologist has an obligation to inform the requesting party and the individual about the condition and recommend further assessment (Andersson, Cocchiarella, & Association, 2001).

Evaluation should determine whether the patient has reached maximum medical improvement (MMI). MMI is the state at which the condition is considered stable and further treatment is not expected to substantially alter it. If MMI has not been reached, the disability is considered temporary, and employees may be categorized as having temporary total disability, temporary partial disability (i.e., able to work with restrictions), or no work disability. Once MMI has been reached, the condition is considered permanent and is categorized as permanent total disability, permanent partial disability, or no work disability. Exhibit 28.1 lists key components of the work-related disability evaluation report.

When receiving treatment from a psychologist, the employee expects that his or her health will be the most important concern and that he or she will receive fair and appropriate evaluation and treatment. The treating psychologist should be an advocate for reasonable, necessary, and appropriate care of the employee's condition, with an emphasis on returning to work as soon as feasible (Pye & Orris, 2000; Rischitelli, 1999). The employer expects that

---

Exhibit 28.1
Key Components of a Work-Related Disability Evaluation Report

---

1. Chief complaints: onset and course, treatment and response, current status
2. Review of records
3. Personal history: social, psychological, medical, vocational
4. Current situation: living environment, daily activities (i.e., activities of daily living [ADLs], instrumental activities of daily living [IADLs]), work (i.e., type, intensity, frequency, duration), social and recreational participation, financial situation
5. Examinations performed (i.e., interviews, tests)
6. Examination findings: cognition (i.e., attitudes, beliefs), mood (i.e., depression, anxiety), personality (i.e., adjustment, coping), motivation (i.e., primary and secondary gain, fictitious disorders, malingering), social factors, behavioral factors, differentiation of preexisting findings versus work-related findings
7. Discussion of differential diagnoses
8. Diagnosis and conclusions
9. Determination that the person is at maximum medical improvement, or undergoing recommended treatment; estimation of the expected date of full or partial recovery
10. Statement of the impairment rating criteria used
11. Impairment rating, discussing specific examination findings in relation to the rating criteria, with a summary list of impairments and percentage ratings
12. Job-specific disability (i.e., correlation of impairments with specific job requirements)

---

the provider will render appropriate and timely care, communicate in a timely manner, and be sensitive to cost and expeditious return to work. Medical or psychological services for issues not relevant to the work-related injury or illness should not be billed to the employer or compensation carrier (Pye & Orris, 2000).

Research indicates that psychological interventions can improve treatment outcomes and reduce costs (Friedman, Sobel, Myers, Caudill, & Benson, 1995; Sobel, 1995). Psychological interventions should focus on increasing normal activities. For patients who have medical clearance to engage in rehabilitation activities, the benefits of activity should be described and appropriate self-care, social, work, and recreational activities prescribed. Stepwise goal setting and activity monitoring to improve self-management and self-efficacy are important (Lorig & Holman, 1993), as graded exposure to activities can decrease fear and improve function (Turner et al., 2006). Physical therapy combined with CBT can significantly reduce pain catastrophizing and fear avoidance (Smeets, Vlaeyen, Kester, & Knottnerus, 2006). Psychotherapy addressing accommodation and coping with functional difficulties is also often important.

Disability Determination and Impairment Ratings

The treating psychologist's role when performing an impairment evaluation is complicated by an already established relationship with the patient. It is likely to be a major challenge to provide a fair and unbiased assessment of an individual with whom the clinician has a well-established therapeutic relationship; the treating psychologist may wish to refer the evaluation to another clinician to avoid complicating the therapeutic relationship.

The psychologist may also be asked to apportion or distribute a permanent impairment rating between the effect of a current injury or illness and a prior condition. In cases in which impairment from a work-related injury or disease is increased (i.e., aggravated) because of the effects of a preexisting impairment, the employer is liable only for the disability from the injury or occupational disease. Because causation, apportionment, and aggravation have unique legal definitions within specific systems, psychologists must familiarize themselves with these terms in their local jurisdictions (Andersson et al., 2001).

Different states require the use of different systems for rating of impairments, but many use the

Guides to the Evaluation of Permanent Impairment (Andersson et al., 2001). Impairment percentages or ratings are assigned on the basis of specialist consensus to indicate the severity of the condition and the extent to which the impairment reduces the individual's ability to perform common activities excluding work: self-care, communication, mobility, sensory function, nonspecialized hand activities, travel, sexual function, and sleep. However, the determination of impairments alone is not sufficient for identifying work disability (Andersson et al., 2001). Impairments are not related to work disability in a linear fashion: An individual with an impairment may have no disability for some occupations yet be disabled for others. Disability is context-specific: It is not inherent in the individual but is a function of the interaction of the individual, the task, and the environment. If the individual can adapt to the environment, he or she may not be disabled from performing that activity (Andersson et al., 2001).

Work is highly individualized, and impairments interact with work environments, the worker's age, education, skills, job duties, and job environment to determine the extent of work disability (Pye & Orris, 2000). Work-specific impairment must be considered in relation to the individual's healthy preinjury or preillness state, and in relation to usual age- and gender-specific states. The employer can provide a detailed job analysis and review of the work environment, and the psychologist can determine the extent to which the individual's abilities match the job demands (Andersson et al., 2001) or might match other potential jobs.

References

Andersson, G., Cocchiarella, L., & Association, A. M. (2001). *Guides to the evaluation of permanent impairment* (5th ed.). Chicago: American Medical Association.

Bednar, J. M., Baesher-Griffith, P., & Osterman, A. L. (1998). Workers compensation. Effect of state law on treatment cost and work status. *Clinical Orthopaedics and Related Research, 351,* 74–77.

Bellamy, R. (1997). Compensation neurosis: Financial reward for illness as nocebo. *Clinical Orthopaedics and Related Research, 336,* 94–106.

Binder, L. M., & Rohling, M. L. (1996). Money matters: A meta-analytic review of the effects of financial incen-

tives on recovery after closed-head injury. *American Journal of Psychiatry, 153*(1), 7–10.

Bruyere, S. M., & O'Keefe, J. (Eds.). (1994). *Implications of the Americans with Disabilities Act for psychology.* New York: Springer Publishing Company.

Butler, R. J., Hartwig, R. P., & Gardner, H. (1997). HMOs, moral hazard, and cost shifting in workers' compensation. *Journal of Health Economics, 16,* 191–206.

Carron, H., DeGood, D. E., & Tait, R. (1985). A comparison of low-back pain patients in the United States and New Zealand: Psychosocial and economic factors affecting severity of disability. *Pain, 21*(1), 77–89.

Cassidy, J. D., Carroll, L. J., Cote, P., Lemstra, M., Berglund, A., & Nygren, A. (2000). Effect of eliminating compensation for pain and suffering on the outcome of insurance claims for whiplash injury. *New England Journal of Medicine, 342,* 1179–1186.

Chibnall, J., & Tait, R. (1995). Observer perceptions of low-back pain: Effects of pain report and other contextual factors. *Journal of Applied Social Psychology, 25,* 418.

Chibnall, J. T., Tait, R. C., Andresen, E. M., & Hadler, N. M. (2005). Race and socioeconomic differences in postsettlement outcomes for African American and Caucasian Workers' Compensation claimants with low back injuries. *Pain, 114,* 462–472.

Coste, J., Lefrancois, G., Guillemin, F., & Pouchot, J. (2004). Prognosis and quality of life in patients with acute low back pain: Insights from a comprehensive inception cohort study. *Arthritis and Rheumatism, 51,* 168–176.

Davitz, L. J., & Pendleton, S. H. (1969). Nurses' inferences of suffering. *Nursing Research, 18,* 100–107.

DeBerard, M. S., Masters, K. S., Colledge, A. L., & Holmes, E. B. (2003). Presurgical biopsychosocial variables predict medical and compensation costs of lumbar fusion in Utah workers' compensation patients. *Spine, 3,* 420–429.

DeBerard, M. S., Masters, K. S., Colledge, A. L., Schleusener, R. L., & Schlegel, J. D. (2001). Outcomes of posterolateral lumbar fusion in Utah patients receiving workers' compensation: A retrospective cohort study. *Spine, 26,* 738–746.

Eijkemans, G. J., & Takala, J. (2005). Moving knowledge of global burden into preventive action. *American Journal of Industrial Medicine, 48,* 395–399.

Friedman, R., Sobel, D., Myers, P., Caudill, M., & Benson, H. (1995). Behavioral medicine, clinical health psychology, and cost offset. *Health Psychology, 14,* 509–518.

Gauthier, N., Sullivan, M. J., Adams, H., Stanish, W. D., & Thibault, P. (2006). Investigating risk factors for chronicity: The importance of distinguishing between return-to-work status and self-report measures of disability. *Journal of Occupational and Environmental Medicine, 48,* 312–318.

Geaneh, J. (2004). The relationship of workers' compensation to the Americans with Disabilities Act and Family and Medical Leave Act. *Clinics in Occupational and Environmental Medicine, 4,* 273–293.

Grayzel, E. F., Finegan, A. M., & Ponchak, R. E. (1997). The value of in-house physical therapy. *Journal of Occupational and Environmental Medicine, 39,* 344–346.

Harris, I., Mulford, J., Solomon, M., van Gelder, J. M., & Young, J. (2005). Association between compensation status and outcome after surgery: A meta-analysis. *JAMA, 293,* 1644–1652.

Hirsch, B. T. (1997). Incentive effects of workers' compensation. *Clinical Orthopaedics and Related Research, 336,* 33–41.

Hochanadel, C. D., & Conrad, D. E. (1993). Evolution of an on-site industrial physical therapy program. *Journal of Occupational Medicine, 35,* 1011–1016.

Leigh, J. P., Markowitz, S. B., Fahs, M., Shin, C., & Landrigan, P. J. (1997). Occupational injury and illness in the United States. Estimates of costs, morbidity, and mortality. *Archives of Internal Medicine, 157,* 1557–1568.

Linton, S. J., & Andersson, T. (2000). Can chronic disability be prevented? A randomized trial of a cognitive–behavior intervention and two forms of information for patients with spinal pain. *Spine, 25,* 2825–2831.

Linton, S. J., Hellsing, A. L., & Hallden, K. (1998). A population-based study of spinal pain among 35–45-year-old individuals. Prevalence, sick leave, and health care use. *Spine, 23,* 1457–1463.

Linton, S. J., & Ryberg, M. (2001). A cognitive–behavioral group intervention as prevention for persistent neck and back pain in a nonpatient population: A randomized controlled trial. *Pain, 90*(1–2), 83–90.

Lorig, K., & Holman, H. (1993). Arthritis self-management studies: A 12-year review. *Health Education Quarterly, 20*(1), 17–28.

May, C., Doyle, H., & Chew-Graham, C. (1999). Medical knowledge and the intractable patient: The case of chronic low back-pain. *Social Science and Medicine, 48,* 523–534.

McDonald, D. D., & Bridge, R. G. (1991). Gender stereotyping and nursing care. *Research in Nursing and Health, 14,* 373–378.

McIntosh, G., Frank, J., Hogg-Johnson, S., Bombardier, C., & Hall, H. (2000). Prognostic factors for time receiving workers' compensation benefits in a cohort of patients with low back pain. *Spine, 25,* 147–157.

Merskey, H., & Teasell, R. W. (2000). The disparagement of pain: Social influences on medical thinking. *Pain Research and Management, 5,* 259–270.

Nachemson, A. L. (1992). Newest knowledge of low back pain. A critical look. *Clinical Orthopedics, 279,* 8–20.

Pransky, G., Benjamin, K., Hill-Fotouhi, C., Himmelstein, J., Fletcher, K. E., Katz, J. N., & Johnson, W. G. (2000). Outcomes in work-related upper extremity and low back injuries: Results of a retrospective study. *American Journal of Industrial Medicine, 37,* 400–409.

Pye, H., & Orris, P. (2000). Workers' compensation in the United States and the role of the primary care physician. *Primary Care, 27,* 831–844.

Rainville, J., Sobel, J. B., Hartigan, C., & Wright, A. (1997). The effect of compensation involvement on the reporting of pain and disability by patients referred for rehabilitation of chronic low back pain. *Spine, 22,* 2016–2024.

Reid, S., Haugh, L. D., Hazard, R. G., & Tripathi, M. (1997). Occupational low back pain: Recovery curves and factors associated with disability. *Journal of Occupational Rehabilitation, 7,* 1–14.

Rischitelli, D. G. (1999). A workers' compensation primer. *Annals of Allergy, Asthma, and Immunology, 8,* 614–617.

Rohling, M. L., Binder, L. M., & Langhinrichsen-Rohling, J. (1995). Money matters: A meta–analytic review of the association between financial compensation and the experience and treatment of chronic pain. *Health Psychology, 14,* 537–547.

Shaw, W. S., Pransky, G., & Fitzgerald, T. E. (2001). Early prognosis for low back disability: Intervention strategies for health care providers. *Disability and Rehabilitation, 23,* 815–828.

Smedley, B. D., Stith, A. Y., & Nelson, A. R. (2003). *Unequal treatment: Confronting racial and ethnic disparities in health care.* Washington, DC: National Academy Press.

Smeets, R. J., Vlaeyen, J. W., Kester, A. D., & Knottnerus, J. A. (2006). Reduction of pain catastrophizing mediates the outcome of both physical and cognitive–behavioral treatment in chronic low back pain. *Journal of Pain, 7,* 261–271.

Sobel, D. S. (1995). Rethinking medicine: Improving health outcomes with cost-effective psychosocial interventions. *Psychosomatic Medicine, 57,* 234–244.

Social Security Administration. (2005). *Annual statistical supplement to the Social Security Bulletin* (Publication No. 13-117). Washington, DC: Social Security Administration.

Strunin, L., & Boden, L. I. (2004). The workers' compensation system: Worker friend or foe? *American Journal of Industrial Medicine, 45,* 338–345.

Sullivan, M. J., Adams, H., Rhodenizer, T., & Stanish, W. D. (2006). A psychosocial risk factor-targeted intervention for the prevention of chronic pain and disability following whiplash injury. *Physical Therapy, 86*(1), 8–18.

Sullivan, M. J., Ward, L. C., Tripp, D., French, D. J., Adams, H., & Stanish, W. D. (2005). Secondary prevention of work disability: Community-based psychosocial intervention for musculoskeletal disorders. *Journal of Occupational Rehabilitation, 15,* 377–392.

Swartzman, L. C., & McDermid, A. J. (1993). The impact of contextual cues on the interpretation of and response to physical symptoms: A vignette approach. *Journal of Behavioral Medicine, 16,* 183–198.

Tanaka, S., Wild, D. K., Seligman, P. J., Halperin, W. E., Behrens, V. J., & Putz-Anderson, V. (1995). Prevalence and work-relatedness of self-reported carpal tunnel syndrome among U.S. workers: Analysis of the Occupational Health Supplement data of 1988 National Health Interview Survey. *American Journal of Industrial Medicine, 27,* 451–470.

Todd, K. H., Lee, T., & Hoffman, J. R. (1994). The effect of ethnicity on physician estimates of pain severity in patients with isolated extremity trauma. *JAMA, 271,* 925–928.

Todd, K. H., Samaroo, N., & Hoffman, J. R. (1993). Ethnicity as a risk factor for inadequate emergency department analgesia. *JAMA, 269,* 1537–1539.

Turner, J. A., Franklin, G., Fulton-Kehoe, D., Sheppard, L., Wickizer, T. M., Wu, R., et al. (2006). Worker recovery expectations and fear-avoidance predict work disability in a population-based workers' compensation back pain sample. *Spine, 31,* 682–689.

U.S. Bureau of Labor Statistics. (1998a). *BLS issues 1998: Lost-worktime injuries and illnesses survey.*

U.S. Bureau of Labor Statistics. (1998b). *Lost worktime injuries and illnesses: Characteristics and resulting days.* New York: Cambridge University Press

van Dulmen, A. M., Fennis, J. F., Mokkink, H. G., van der Velden, H. G., & Bleijenberg, G. (1994). Doctors' perception of patients' cognitions and complaints in irritable bowel syndrome at an outpatient clinic. *Journal of Psychosomatic Research, 38,* 581–590.

van Ryn, M., & Burke, J. (2000). The effect of patient race and socioeconomic status on physicians' perceptions of patients. *Social Science and Medicine, 50,* 813–828.

Vlaeyen, J. W., Kole-Snijders, A. M., Boeren, R. G., & van Eek, H. (1995). Fear of movement/(re)injury in chronic low-back pain and its relation to behavioral performance. *Pain, 62,* 363–372.

Wegener, S. T., Kuhlemeier, K. V., & Mitchell, C. (2002). Principles and practices of on-site rehabilitation. Paper presented at the meeting of the American College of Occupational and Environmental Medicine, Chicago, IL.

Wickizer, T. M., Franklin, G., Turner, J., Fulton-Kehoe, D., Mootz, R., & Smith-Weller, T. (2004). Use of attorneys and appeal filing in the Washington State workers' compensation program: Does patient satisfaction matter? *Journal of Occupational and Environmental Medicine, 46,* 331–339.

Zelle, B. A., Panzica, M., Vogt, M. T., Sittaro, N. A., Krettek, C., & Pape, H. C. (2005). Influence of workers' compensation eligibility upon functional recovery 10 to 28 years after polytrauma. *American Journal of Surgery, 190,* 30–36.

CHAPTER 29

APPLICATION OF POSITIVE PSYCHOLOGY TO REHABILITATION PSYCHOLOGY

Dawn M. Ehde

Since having my amputation, I don't worry about the past like I used to; I look forward to my future without my leg . . . I am grateful for the people in my life in ways I didn't think of before my surgery. (53-year-old man 6 months after an above-knee amputation)

After my diagnosis, people treated me like I was going to have a nervous breakdown . . . I knew I wouldn't, though. Sure, I wish that I didn't have MS, but most days I focus not on what I've lost but instead on what I've gained. MS has given me permission to try things I never would have dared do before, such as singing in my chorale group and painting. (33-year-old woman with multiple sclerosis)

Over the past 10 years, a positive psychology movement has emerged in the field of psychology, resulting in increased theorizing, basic science, and applied research on the positive dimensions and processes of human functioning (Snyder & Lopez, 2002). The field of clinical psychology has been criticized for its predominant focus on the diagnosis and treatment of psychopathology at the cost of our understanding of psychological health (Sheldon & King, 2001). However, the last decade has seen considerably more attention in research and practice on understanding and describing psychological well-being, including among individuals who have faced traumatic events (e.g., terrorism, interpersonal violence) as well as health crises (e.g., cancer diagnosis, HIV/AIDS).

Psychologists, researchers, and writers in the field of rehabilitation have long recognized that many persons with disabilities are psychologically healthy (e.g., Dembo, Leviton, & Wright, 1956; Trieschmann, 1988; Wright, 1983). Despite this history, the science of rehabilitation has focused more on the negative consequences of disability, including psychopathological reactions to disability. For example, a PubMed search of the terms *spinal cord injury* and *depression* revealed 281 citations (limited to English and humans). In contrast, the terms *spinal cord injury* and *resilience* revealed no citations, as did a search of *spinal cord injury* and *posttraumatic growth*. Psychological states such as resilience or posttraumatic growth following acquired disability have received scant empirical attention. This tendency to focus on "negative" emotional reactions to disability and the attitudinal, social, and cultural biases leading to such viewpoints has previously been described (Livneh & Antonak, 1997; Trieschmann; Wright, 1988). Our current empirical understanding of psychological functioning and disability is constrained by this restrictive focus.

The field of rehabilitation psychology has considerable potential to not only join the positive psychology movement but also to play an important role in its quest to broaden our understanding of human functioning beyond negative, pathological conditions. This chapter begins with a review of one aspect of psychological functioning in disability, psychological distress after acquired disability, to provide context for the remainder of the chapter. The chapter then provides an overview of three specific constructs from the positive psychology movement that have received considerable study in nondisabled populations: resilience, posttraumatic growth, and positive emotions. After discussing several potential implications of positive psychology for intervention within rehabilitation, the chapter concludes with a discussion of future directions for integrating positive psychology and rehabilitation psychology. Spirituality, another important but previously overlooked dimension of human functioning relevant to our understanding of the disability experience, is reviewed elsewhere in this text (see chap. 25, this volume).

PSYCHOLOGICAL DISTRESS AFTER ACQUIRED DISABILITY

The literature's focus on psychopathology after acquired disability may stem, in part, from the knowledge that psychological disorders such as depressive and anxiety disorders are indeed more common in rehabilitation populations relative to the general population. For example, the lifetime prevalence of depressive symptoms and disorders in persons with multiple sclerosis is approximately three times that of the general population (Ehde & Bombardier, 2006). Depressive disorders are also prevalent in other disability groups, including amputation (Darnall et al., 2005), spinal cord injury (SCI; Elliott & Frank, 1996), stroke (Dafer, Rao, Shareef, & Sharma, 2008), and traumatic brain injury (Rosenthal, Christensen, & Ross, 1998). In general, these rates are two to three times higher than rates of depressive disorders found in the general population (Kessler et al., 2003) or primary care populations (Coyne, Fechner-Bates, & Schwenk, 1994). Posttraumatic stress disorder also occurs in a sizable proportion of persons with traumatically acquired disabilities, such as burn (Difede et al., 2002) and SCIs (Nielsen, 2003). Given that persons with disability may be at increased risk of mood or anxiety disorders, it is prudent for rehabilitation psychologists to attend to such disorders.

In a recent review, Ehde and Williams (2006) indicated that in most studies of psychological responses to traumatic disability, half or more of the survivors did not have clinically significant levels of depressive and posttraumatic stress symptoms immediately following as well as 1 to 2 years after the onset of disability. Unfortunately, little is known about this majority, that is, those persons who do not experience significant emotional distress following the onset of disability. It is quite likely that many individuals respond over time with a variety of nonpathological responses, such as positive emotions, resilience, and posttraumatic growth. Gaps exist in our knowledge of these and other nonpathological dimensions of psychological functioning in rehabilitation populations. An overview of these three positive psychology constructs—resilience, posttraumatic growth, and positive emotions—follows in the hope of catalyzing their application to rehabilitation psychology.

RESILIENCE

Research has repeatedly shown that many individuals not only persevere but also thrive when confronted with adversity, trauma, tragedy, or loss. This phenomenon of a human capacity to bounce back from or flourish after aversive events is often referred to as *resilience*. In the broader psychology literature, resilience is increasingly recognized as common after loss and trauma (Bonanno, 2004). For example, prospective studies have repeatedly shown that the majority of bereaved individuals experience few or no symptoms of psychopathology after loss (Bonanno & Kaltman, 2001). Resilience appears to be the norm, rather than the exception, in survivors of violent and life-threatening events such as assault (Resnick, Kilpatrick, Dansky, Saunders, & Best, 1993), terrorism (Bonanno, Galea, Bucciarelli, & Vlahov, 2006), and natural disasters (McMillen, Smith, & Fisher, 1997). Being resilient does not mean that the individual never experiences any negative emotions, thoughts, or actions in response to adversity or loss. Such experiences are common and may in fact be part of the resilience process (Bonanno, 2004). However, in resilient individuals, they are typically transient, co-occur with positive emotions, and do not significantly interfere with functioning (Bonanno, Wortman, & Nesse, 2004).

Although certain personality traits may predispose some individuals to resilience (Florian, Mikulincer, & Taubman, 1995), resilience is currently thought to be a process and a set of cognitive, behavioral, and interpersonal skills, many of which may be learned, encouraged, and practiced. A number of factors are likely contribute to resilience, including (a) supportive relationships, (b) the ability to solve difficulties with realistic plans, (c) good interpersonal skills, (d) the ability to cope with strong negative emotions, and (e) self-efficacy (American Psychological Association, 2004). Finally, as Bonanno (2004) observed in his review, there are likely multiple paths or strategies to resilience after adversity.

Throughout its history, rehabilitation psychology has recognized that many people bounce back from and/or thrive while living with a disability (Elliott, Kurylo, & Rivera, 2002). Studies have repeatedly documented that the majority of persons with acquired disability do not experience psychopathology. However, resilience as an important or primary focus in its own right has generally been neglected in the empirical literature on psychosocial functioning and disability. Resilience has been examined more specifically in a few samples, including adolescents with mobility disability (Alriksson-Schmidt, Wallander, & Biasini, 2007), preadolescents with spina bifida (Holmbeck et al., 2003), adults with amyotrophiclateral sclerosis (ALS; Rabkin, Wagner, & Del Bene, 2000), and adults with chronic pain (Karoly & Ruehlman, 2006). These studies varied in their definition and measurement of resilience. For example, in one study of adults with chronic pain (Karoly & Ruehlman), resilience was defined as "high pain severity in the context of low interference (with activities) and low emotional burden" (p. 91). Resilience included the absence of psychopathology as well as active engagement in social, recreational, and intellectual activities despite progressive illness (ALS) in another (Rabkin et al., 2000). These findings as well as the broader literature suggest that resilience is most likely the norm rather than the exception in persons with disabilities. Clearly more theoretically driven investigations of resilience, including its measurement, prevalence, characteristics, pre-

dictors, and influence on health, are needed in the rehabilitation field.

POSTTRAUMATIC GROWTH

The literature on psychological functioning after traumatic stress has increasingly shown that individuals have "the capacity not just for resilience but also . . . to use aversive events as a springboard for further growth and development" (Linley & Joseph, 2005, pp. 262–263). *Posttraumatic growth* may be defined as positive psychological changes resulting from or in response to a challenging circumstance such as a traumatic event or loss (Tedeschi & Calhoun, 2004). It is thought to involve more than resilience, that is, growth and improved functioning beyond a return to a pre-event level of psychological functioning. Posttraumatic growth can be manifested in a variety of ways, including, but not limited to, having an increased appreciation for life, feeling increased personal strength, experiencing improved interpersonal relationships, changing life priorities, gaining positive spiritual changes, or finding new meaning and purpose in life. Other terms for such positive changes exist in the literature and include *stress-related growth* (Park, Cohen, & Murch, 1996), benefit-finding (McMillen & Cook, 2003), *thriving,* and *adversarial growth* (Linley & Joseph, 2004). These all share the belief that positive changes can, and do, occur after an adverse life experience, an idea of significant relevance to rehabilitation psychology.

The concept of posttraumatic growth has received considerable attention in the psychology literature in the past decade, with a number of studies supporting its utility as a construct for understanding positive changes that occur following adversity (Linley & Joseph, 2004). Well before the positive psychology movement gained momentum, rehabilitation psychologists were describing the potential for positive growth as a result of disability (e.g., Vash, 1981; Wright, 1983). Despite this tradition, only a few studies have specifically examined the construct of posttraumatic growth in disability samples. In a small (*N* = 21) cross-sectional study of adults with severe acquired brain injury, McGrath & Linley (2006) found that growth occurred following brain injury, particularly for persons who had been living with brain injury for some time ($M = 118$ months). This "late" group had posttraumatic growth scores higher than most survivor groups previously studied (Linley & Joseph, 2004) on a widely used measure of posttraumatic growth, the Posttraumatic Growth Inventory (PTGI: Tedeschi & Calhoun, 1996). The PTGI asks respondents rate the degree to which 21 positive changes have occurred as a result of their traumatic experience on a six-point scale from 0 (*I did not experience this change*) to 5 (*I experienced this change to a very great degree*). A total PTGI score is tabulated, as are five scales, labeled New Possibilities (5 items), Relating to Others (7 items), Personal Strength (4 items), Spiritual Change (2 items), and Appreciation of Life (3 items).

McMillen and Cook (2003) examined the "positive by-products" of SCI using the Perceived Benefits Scale (PBS; McMillen, Howard, Nower, & Chung, 2001). The PBS asks respondents to rate 30 items that are delineated into eight subscales: increased self-efficacy, increased faith in people, increased compassion, increased spirituality, increased community closeness, increased family closeness, positive lifestyle changes, and material gain. Respondents (42 persons between 18–36 months post-SCI) were also asked whether they had experienced other benefits as a result of SCI. A majority (79%) of participants reported at least one positive by-product; the average number of positive benefits was 2.28 ($SD = 1.83$). The most frequently reported positive by-products were increased family closeness and compassion, whereas the least frequently reported were material gain and community closeness. Additional by-products of SCI included gaining new attitudes and perspectives, improved views of self, improved views of persons with disabilities, increased gratitude, and increased helping of others. In a survey of adults with limb loss ($N = 138$), Dunn (1996) reported that 77% reported that something positive had happened as a result of their amputation. Other less rigorous studies have described positive benefits in other disability groups, such as amputation (Oaksford, Frude, & Cuddihy, 2005) and brain injury (Adams, 1996). Clearly the construct of growth is applicable to persons with acquired disability and merits further consideration and research.

POSITIVE EMOTIONS

Positive emotions can be defined as positive feelings or affective states, which may include subjective feelings, physiological changes, and observable expressions. Although positive emotions may be by-products or signals of optimal psychological functioning, research suggests that they may also play important causal roles in promoting optimal psychological functioning (Folkman & Moskowitz, 2000; Fredrickson & Losada, 2005). Positive emotions have been theorized to provide psychological "respite" from negative emotions, sustain continued coping efforts, and replenish personal resources that have been exhausted by stressful events (Folkman & Moskowitz, 2000). In Fredrickson's (1998) broaden-and-build theory, positive emotions broaden individuals' momentary attentional focus, thoughts, and behaviors such that they facilitate and build personal resources such as creativity, flexibility, problem-solving, coping strategies, and social connections. Both of these theories have support in the empirical literature in a variety of populations (Folkman & Moskowitz, 2000; Fredrickson & Losada, 2005) and are appealing in their potential applications to the experience of disability.

A number of benefits of positive emotions have been described in the literature (for a review, see Lyubomirsky, King, & Diener, 2005), including benefits to health, such as reductions in pain (Gil et al., 2004), improved immune functioning (Davidson et al., 2003), and reduced inflammatory response to stress (Steptoe, Wardle, & Marmot, 2005). Positive emotions have also been shown to play a mediating role in effective emotion regulation and in finding positive meaning in negative circumstances (Tugade & Fredrickson, 2004). Prospective studies have shown that frequent positive emotions predict resilience to adversity and posttraumatic growth (Fredrickson, Tugade, Waugh, & Larkin, 2003). It is important to note that in the context of stressful events, positive emotions and negative emotions are not mutually exclusive but instead frequently co-occur, even under severe stressors such as severe illness and bereavement (Folkman & Moskowitz, 2000). In addition, the amount of time experiencing positive affect appears to be more beneficial than the intensity of the positive emotions (Lyubomirsky et al., 2005). Given these findings, the field of rehabilitation psychology could benefit from further study of the experience and benefits of positive emotions after acquired disability.

IMPLICATIONS FOR INTERVENTION

The positive psychology movement is just beginning to examine interventions for promoting human resilience, posttraumatic growth, and positive emotions (e.g., Seligman, Steen, Park, & Peterson, 2005). Within rehabilitation, there appears to be the potential for interventions to promote psychological well-being in addition to treating psychological distress when it occurs. Although perhaps not typically conceptualized as an intervention for promoting resilience, physical rehabilitation hypothetically has the potential to encourage, increase, or maintain resilience in at least several ways. Rehabilitation often emphasizes and teaches individuals to solve existing and potential challenges from the disability as well as the physical, social, and cultural environment. Consistent with this idea, social problem-solving abilities have been associated with positive adaptation to health problems and caregiving (Elliott, Grant, & Miller, 2004). Self-efficacy may increase through realistic goal-setting and attainment during rehabilitation. Rehabilitation provides opportunities for new supportive social relationships with rehabilitation professionals and other individuals with disabilities. Rehabilitation activities promoting participation in social, recreational, and community activities may provide opportunities for positive emotions, leisure skill acquisition, and development of support and social contacts. A commonly accepted strategy for treating mood disorders, pleasant events scheduling, is another example of an intervention rehabilitation professionals can provide to promote positive emotions and resilience.

Rehabilitation psychologists have long recognized the importance of recognizing individual strengths and environmental resources in promoting psychological well-being following acquired disability (Elliott et al., 2002). By virtue of our health care system, however, our clinical practice is typically focused on treating distress. Nonetheless, rehabilitation psychologists are encouraged to consider how to translate emerging findings from the positive psychology movement to the practice of rehabilitation psychology. For example, brief interventions such as teaching individuals to identify and use their particular strengths, or regularly writing down good things that occurred and why have been shown to increase happiness and decrease depressive symptoms for 6 months (Seligman et al., 2005). Similar interventions or others that promote positive affect, growth, and resilience warrant development and investigation.

FUTURE DIRECTIONS

The paucity of rehabilitation research on resilience, posttraumatic growth, positive emotions, and other nonpathological dimensions of psychological functioning suggests that there is much to be done to advance our understanding of psychological functioning in the context of disability. A positive psychology research agenda should include not only exploration of the constructs of resilience, posttraumatic growth, and positive emotions but also their potential relationships to other important dimensions of human functioning, including social relationships and participation. What follows are several additional considerations for future rehabilitation research in positive psychology.

Need for Conceptual Clarity

The field lacks a commonly accepted operational definition of what is meant by, or constitutes, "adjustment," let alone a "good adjustment." Across studies, *adjustment* has been defined and/or conceptualized in a variety of ways, including, but not limited to, the following: (a) the absence of psychopathology, most commonly the absence of depressive disorders; (b) general emotional well-being; (c) global satisfaction with or quality of life; or (d) participation in important life situations. Although these dimensions are important to our understanding of outcomes following disability, they do not provide the wealth of information needed for a more complete understanding of the phenomenology of experience after acquired disability.

The operational definition of resilience has been the subject of considerable debate (see Masten & Reed, 2002). For example, some authors (e.g., Bonanno, 2004) have defined resilience as the absence of psychopathology, whereas others view it as a process or family of phenomena involving adaptation in the face of adversity (Roisman, 2005). Likewise, the constructs of posttraumatic growth and positive emotions also vary in their operational definitions. Although it is valuable to report the number of persons without a condition such as posttraumatic stress disorder, researchers are encouraged to also examine other dimensions of positive change and to provide clear operational definitions of the constructs being studied. A volume consisting of measures from the positive psychology field may be helpful in this regard (Lopez & Snyder, 2003).

Theoretically Driven Models of Positive Psychological Functioning in Disability

Much of the research on psychological health in persons with acquired disability has been conducted from a medical model of human functioning that focuses primarily on the prevalence or absence of psychopathological reactions to disability. Future research and practice should be conducted using theoretically driven models of psychosocial functioning that take into account not only what goes "wrong" after the onset of disability but also, perhaps more important, on what goes "right," and the risk and protective factors predicting both. Several existing theoretical models already exist and warrant testing (Dunn & Dougherty, 2005; Elliott et al., 2002). Rehabilitation psychology has long recognized the importance not only of intrapersonal factors but also the environment in human functioning, particularly after disability (Wright, 1983). The positive psychology movement, however, has generally focused on individual factors, with some attention to social resources but focused to a lesser extent on other environmental factors that may play a role in an individual's responses to adversity and stress. As such, rehabilitation psychology can be on the forefront of examining more complex models that include not only intrapersonal variables but also environmental variables, both in terms of protective, as well as risk, factors.

Longitudinal Research

Although a variety of research designs examining positive psychology constructs would benefit the rehabilitation field, prospective, longitudinal research in particular is needed to increase our understanding of psychological functioning after acquired disability. Many rehabilitation psychologists are in the unique position of regularly working with persons with a newly acquired disability, which provides an opportunity to study over time psychological functioning in the aftermath of disability. Such research, particularly if informed by theory, will extend to not only the rehabilitation field but also to the broader field of psychology. For example, most of the research on posttraumatic growth in nondisabled populations has been cross-sectional; therefore, increased understanding of posttraumatic growth after an acquired disability could inform the broader posttraumatic growth literature. Longitudinal research should examine not only positive outcomes but also the potentially variable paths or trajectories by which individuals attain such outcomes. Such information could lead to strategies for identifying persons and environments at risk and subsequent interventions for promoting positive outcomes such as resilience, growth, and positive emotions.

CONCLUSION

The study of positive psychological responses to, and functioning after, acquired disability, including positive emotions, resilience, and posttraumatic growth, is long overdue. Research on these phenomena has the potential to not only close gaps in our knowledge but also to inform the broader trauma, loss, growth, and resilience literatures. Theoretically driven, longitudinal studies of the broad range of responses as well as potential risk and protective factors may lead to greater recognition of, and interventions for, promoting psychological well-being, the prevention of suffering, and treatment of distress when it exists. It will be important for rehabilitation psychology to honor our roots and advance the overall positive psychology movement by promoting the inclusion of environmental factors in addition to intrapersonal factors.

References

Adams, N. (1996). Positive outcomes in families following traumatic brain injury. *Australian and New Zealand Family Therapy, 17,* 75–84.

Alriksson-Schmidt, A. I., Wallander, J., & Biasini, F. (2007). Quality of life and resilience in adolescents with a mobility disability. *Journal of Pediatric Psychology, 32,* 370–379.

American Psychological Association. (2004). *The road to resilience.* Retrieved October 6, 2006, from http://www.apahelpcenter.org/featuredtopics/feature.php?id=6&ch=2

Bonanno, G. A. (2004). Loss, trauma, and human resilience: Have we underestimated the human capacity to thrive after extremely aversive events? *American Psychologist, 59,* 20–28.

Bonanno, G. A., Galea, S., Bucciarelli, A., & Vlahov, D. (2006). Psychological resilience after disaster: New York City in the aftermath of the September 11th terrorist attack. *Psychological Science, 17,* 181–186.

Bonanno, G. A., & Kaltman, S. (2001). The varieties of grief experience. *Clinical Psychology Review, 21,* 705–734.

Bonanno, G. A., Wortman, C. B., & Nesse, R. M. (2004). Prospective patterns of resilience and maladjustment during widowhood. *Psychology of Aging, 19,* 260–271.

Coyne, J. C., Fechner-Bates, S., & Schwenk, T. L. (1994). Prevalence, nature, and comorbidity of depressive disorders in primary care. *General Hospital Psychiatry, 16,* 267–276.

Dafer, R. M., Rao, M., Shareef, A., & Sharma, A. (2008). Poststroke depression. *Top Stroke Rehabilitation, 15,* 13–21.

Darnall, B. D., Ephraim, P., Wegener, S. T., Dillingham, T., Pezzin, L., Rossbach, P., & MacKenzie, E. J. (2005). Depressive symptoms and mental health service utilization among persons with limb loss: Results of a national survey. *Archives of Physical Medicine and Rehabilitation, 86,* 650–658.

Davidson, R. J., Kabat-Zinn, J., Schumacher, J., Rosenkranz, M., Muller, D., Santorelli, S. F., Urbanowski, F., et al. (2003). Alterations in brain and immune function produced by mindfulness meditation. *Psychosomatic Medicine, 65,* 564–570.

Dembo, T., Leviton, G. L., & Wright, B. A. (1956). Adjustment to misfortune: A problem of social–psychological rehabilitation. *Artificial Limbs, 3*(2), 4–62.

Difede, J., Ptacek, J. T., Roberts, J., Barocas, D., Rives, W., Apfeldorf, W., et al. (2002). Acute stress disorder after burn injury: A predictor of posttraumatic stress disorder? *Psychosomatic Medicine, 64,* 826–834.

Dunn, D. S. (1996). Well-being following amputation: Salutary effects of positive meaning, optimism, and control. *Rehabilitation Psychology, 41,* 285–302.

Dunn, D. S., & Dougherty, S. B. (2005). Prospects for a positive psychology of rehabilitation. *Rehabilitation Psychology, 50,* 305–311.

Ehde, D. M., & Bombardier, C. H. (2005). Depression in persons with multiple sclerosis. *Physical Medicine Rehabilitation Clinics of North America, 16,* 437–448.

Ehde, D. M., & Williams, R. M. (2006). Adjustment to trauma. In L. R. Robinson (Ed.), *Trauma rehabilitation* (pp. 245–72). Philadelphia: Lippincott Williams & Wilkins.

Elliott, T. R., & Frank, R. G. (1996). Depression following spinal cord injury. *Archives of Physical Medicine and Rehabilitation, 77,* 816–823.

Elliott, T. R., Grant, J., & Miller, D. M. (2004). Social problem-solving abilities and behavioral health. In E. C. Chang, T. J. D'Zurilla, & L. J. Sanna (Eds.), *Social problem-solving: Theory, research, and training* (pp. 117–33). Washington, DC: American Psychological Association.

Elliott, T. R., Kurylo, M., & Rivera, P. (2002). Positive growth following acquired disability. In C. R. Snyder & S. J. Lopez (Eds.), *Handbook of positive psychology* (pp. 687–699). New York: Oxford University Press.

Florian, V., Mikulincer, M., & Taubman, O. (1995). Does hardiness contribute to mental health during a stressful real-life situation? The roles of appraisal and coping. *Journal of Personality and Social Psychology, 68,* 687–695.

Folkman, S., & Moskowitz, J. T. (2000). Positive affect and the other side of coping. *American Psychologist, 55,* 647–654.

Fredrickson, B. L. (1998). What good are positive emotions? *Review of General Psychology, 2,* 300–319.

Fredrickson, B. L., & Losada, M. F. (2005). Positive affect and the complex dynamics of human flourishing. *American Psychologist, 60,* 678–686.

Fredrickson, B. L., Tugade, M. M., Waugh, C. E., & Larkin, G. R. (2003). What good are positive emotions in crises? A prospective study of resilience and emotions following the terrorist attacks on the United States on September 11th, 2001. *Journal of Personality and Social Psychology, 84,* 365–76.

Gil, K. M., Carson, J. W., Porter, L. S., Scipio, C., Bediako, S. M., & Orringer, E. (2004). Daily mood and stress predict pain, health care use, and work activity in African American adults with sickle-cell disease. *Health Psychology, 23,* 267–274.

Holmbeck, G. N., Westhoven, V. C., Phillips, W. S., Bowers, R., Gruse, C., Nikolopoulos, T., et al. (2003). A multimethod, multi-informant, and multi-dimensional perspective on psychosocial adjustment in preadolescents with spina bifida. *Journal of Consulting and Clinical Psychology, 71,* 782–96.

Karoly, P., & Ruehlman, L. S. (2006). Psychological "resilience" and its correlates in chronic pain: Findings from a national community sample. *Pain, 123,* 90–97.

Kessler, R. C., Berglund, P., Demler, O., Jin, R., Koretz, D., Merikangas, K., et al. (2003). The epidemiology of major depressive disorder: Results from the National Comorbidity Survey Replication (NCS-R). *JAMA, 289,* 3095–105.

Linley, P. A., & Joseph, S. (2004). Positive change following trauma and adversity: A review. *Journal of Traumatic Stress, 17,* 11–21.

Linley, P. A., & Joseph, S. (2005). The human capacity for growth through adversity. *American Psychologist, 60,* 262–264.

Livneh, H., & Antonak, R. (1997). *Psychosocial adaptation to chronic illness and disability.* Gaithersburg, MD: Aspen Publishers.

Lopez, S. J., & Snyder, C. R. (Eds.). (2003). *Positive psychological assessment: A handbook of models and measures.* Washington, DC: American Psychological Association.

Lyubomirsky, S., King, L., & Diener, E. (2005). The benefits of frequent positive affect: Does happiness lead to success? *Psychological Bulletin, 131,* 803–855.

Masten, A. S., & Reed, M. G. J. (2002). Resilience in development. In C. R. Snyder & S. J. Lopez (Ed.), *Handbook of positive psychology* (pp. 74–88). New York: Oxford University Press.

McGrath, J. C., & Linley, P. A. (2006). Posttraumatic growth in acquired brain injury: A preliminary small scale study. *Brain Injury, 20,* 767–773.

McMillen, J. C., & Cook, C. L. (2003). The positive by-products of spinal cord injury and their correlates. *Rehabilitation Psychology, 48,* 77–85.

McMillen, J. C., Howard, M. O., Nower, L., & Chung, S. (2001). The Perceived Benefits Scales: Measuring perceived positive life changes following negative life events. *Social Work Research, 22,* 173–187.

McMillen, J. C., Smith, E. M., & Fisher, R. (1997). Perceived benefit and mental health after three types of disaster. *Journal of Consulting and Clinical Psychology, 65,* 733–739.

Nielsen, M. S. (2003). Posttraumatic stress disorder and emotional distress in persons with spinal cord lesions. *Spinal Cord, 41,* 296–302.

Oaksford, K., Frude, N., & Cuddihy, R. (2005). Positive coping and stress-related psychological growth following lower limb amputation. *Rehabilitation Psychology, 50,* 266–277.

Park, C. L., Cohen, L. H., & Murch, R. L. (1996). Assessment and prediction of stress-related growth. *Journal of Personality, 64,* 71–105.

Rabkin, J. G., Wagner, G. J., & Del Bene, M. (2000). Resilience and distress among amyotrophic lateral sclerosis patients and caregivers. *Psychosomatic Medicine, 62,* 271–279.

Resnick, H. S., Kilpatrick, D. G., Dansky, B. S., Saunders, B. E., & Best, C. L. (1993). Prevalence of civilian trauma and posttraumatic stress disorder in a representative national sample of women. *Journal of Consulting and Clinical Psychology, 61,* 984–991.

Roisman, G. I. (2005). Conceptual clarifications in the study of resilience. *American Psychologist, 60,* 264–265.

Rosenthal, M., Christensen, B. K., & Ross, T. P. (1998). Depression following traumatic brain injury. *Archives of Physical Medicine and Rehabilitation, 79,* 90–103.

Seligman, M. E. P., Steen, T. A., Park, N., & Peterson, C. (2005). Positive psychology progress: Empirical validation of interventions. *American Psychologist, 60,* 410–421.

Sheldon, K. M., & King, L. (2001). Why positive psychology is necessary. *American Psychologist, 56,* 216–217.

Snyder, C. R., & Lopez, S. J. (2002). *Handbook of positive psychology.* Oxford, England: Oxford University Press.

Steptoe, A., Wardle, J., & Marmot, M. (2005). Positive affect and health-related neuroendocrine, cardiovascular, and inflammatory processes. *Proceedings of the National Academy of Sciences of the United States of America, 102,* 6508–6512.

Tedeschi, R. G., & Calhoun, L. G. (2004). Posttraumatic growth: Conceptual foundations and empirical evidence. *Psychological Inquiry, 15,* 1–18.

Trieschmann, R. B. (1988). *Spinal cord injuries: Psychological, social, and vocational rehabilitation.* New York: Demos.

Tugade, M. M., & Fredrickson, B. L. (2004). Resilient individuals use positive emotions to bounce back form negative emotional experiences. *Journal of Personality and Social Psychology, 86,* 320–333.

Vash, C. L. (1981). The psychology of disability. New York: Springer Publishing Company.

Wright, B. A. (1983). Physical disability: A psychosocial approach. New York: HarperCollins.

Wright, B. A. (1988). Attitudes and the fundamental negative bias. In H. E. Yuker (Ed.), *Attitudes towards persons with disabilities* (pp. 3–21). New York: Springer Publishing Company.

PART VI

PROFESSIONAL ISSUES

CHAPTER 30

ETHICS

Stephanie L. Hanson and Thomas R. Kerkhoff

An attorney defending the driver responsible for causing a patient's traumatic brain injury (TBI) subpoenas the rehabilitation psychologist. The subpoena is for the test protocol and notes regarding patient behavior on a nonstandardized functional assessment measure. The rehabilitation psychologist is uncomfortable releasing the information because it has not been reviewed with the patient and family and it may be inappropriate to do so, given the patient's current emotional lability and history of depression, the symptoms of which are typically manifested following significant stress.

This case, which is briefly revisited later in the chapter, illustrates three points: (a) rehabilitation psychology practice is embedded in a broad health care system that is influenced by multiple factors, such as patient's needs, available social and economic resources, institutional policies, and legal mandates; (b) because of competing professional demands, all psychologists will face situations in which they need to consider ethical concepts as these are applied to everyday practice; and (c) ethical decision making requires a choice and a rationale for valuing, and thus choosing, one course of action over another (Behnke, 2005). Using an ethics framework can help psychologists sort through competing information, recognize values impacting the evaluative process, and make informed choices toward resolving a particular situation.

Professional codes of conduct, when developed and used effectively, provide part of the moral framework for ethical analysis and decision making. The relevance of a discipline-specific ethics code lies largely in its ability to (a) express the core, consensual values of the profession; (b) offer guidance regarding ethical conduct; and (c) provide a structure within which to regulate the actions of the profession's individual members without undue influence from outside entities.

Although professional ethics codes are ultimately designed to protect the welfare of those served by the discipline, these codes must capture the principles underpinning practice to encourage a proactive and systematic analysis of moral dilemmas rather than simply encouraging corrective or idiosyncratic response after the fact. For example, embracing the moral position that the bioethical principle of beneficence (i.e., preventing harm or facilitating good) carries more weight than respect for autonomy when significant risk of harm is evident directly supports the broad practice of disclosing suicidal intent. It would also support the position that unsafe drivers should not return to driving despite their legal right to do so. The ability to engage in ethical analysis is integral to sound professional practice, and understanding one's professional ethics code can contribute to one's development as an ethical professional. In this chapter, we therefore focus on the American Psychological Association (APA) "Ethical Principles of Psychologists and Code of Conduct" (APA, 2002a; henceforth the APA Ethics Code). We consider substantive changes from the 1992 APA Ethics Code (APA, 1992) and their potential implications for rehabilitation psychology practice. We also include a brief discussion of the ethical decision-making process and provide examples of decision-making models.

REVISING THE AMERICAN PSYCHOLOGICAL ASSOCIATION'S ETHICS CODE

The ninth revision of the APA Ethics Code was ratified in 2002 by the APA Council of Representatives and took effect on June 1, 2003. Ethics code revisions must reflect the evolution of professional values (i.e., principles), offer reasonable practical applications of these values (i.e., standards) that enhance or confirm professional judgment, and take into account the contemporary societal context within which the discipline operates. The revisions to the 2002 APA Ethics Code embody these basic premises. The APA Ethics Code Task Force, charged with revising the code (Jones, 2001), deliberated for 5 years and provided multiple opportunities for psychologists to offer opinions on working drafts. (See Clay [2000] and Behnke [2004a] for examples of changes considered and/or incorporated based on feedback received. See also 1992 and 2002 Ethics Code text comparisons at http://www.apa.org/ethics.) The field-driven spirit of the revisions incorporated into the 2002 Ethics Code captures the evolving voice of the membership in values and application. The substantive changes to the code were also influenced by the sociocultural climate, which has become increasingly regulated, although not uniquely toward psychology as a profession. This is briefly discussed in this chapter in the context of specific changes adopted.

REVISED GENERAL PRINCIPLES

The *General Principles* of the APA Ethics Code represent professional values psychologists strive to uphold. The principles serve to inform psychologists regarding reasonable ethical decisions in morally ambiguous circumstances. In the 2002 Ethics Code, the framework for considering ethical issues was revised. In addition to the Preamble, Introduction, and Ethical Standards, the 1992 Ethics Code had six principles; the 2002 Ethics Code includes only five principles: (a) Beneficence and Nonmaleficence (originally "Concern for Others' Welfare"); (b) Fidelity and Responsibility (originally "Professional and Scientific Responsibility"); (c) Integrity; (d) Justice; and (e) Respect for People's Rights and Dignity. The

principles of Competence and Social Responsibility were eliminated, and the principle of Justice was added. In general, the changes to the principles appear organizational or offer clarifications rather than reflecting a major shift in our core professional values. For example, the concepts of recognizing boundaries of competence and protecting the rights of others, originally embodied in the principle of Competence, now rest in the principles of Justice and Beneficence and Nonmaleficence. Key elements of Social Responsibility, such as consumers' access to services and pro bono work, are captured within Justice and Fidelity and Responsibility, respectively. Renaming the principles is also more consistent with common parlance in other contemporary principle-based approaches toward ethics (e.g., Beauchamp & Childress, 2001). In addition, in the Ethics Code's Introduction, APA has placed more emphasis on the distinction between the principles and standards such that the aspirational nature of the principles are unlikely to be misconstrued as enforceable rules that could place psychologists at risk of sanction (Behnke, 2004a). Instead, the principles are what they are meant to represent: the ideals of the profession.

Two specific changes in Principle E (previously Principle D), Respect for People's Rights and Dignity, are of particular note for rehabilitation psychologists. First, culture has been added to the list of factors to consider in respecting a person's rights and dignity. This change reflects not only the shifting demographics of the United States but also APA's increased emphasis on cultural competence as reflected in the cultural competence guidelines (APA, 2002b). Lomay and Hinkebein (2006) argued that developing cultural competence is particularly important for rehabilitation psychologists because we address multiple psychosocial issues affected by cultural factors; Hanson and Kerkhoff (2007) linked specific cultural issues to ethical decision-making in rehabilitation practice. The second change to Principle E is the addition, "special safeguards may be necessary to protect the rights and welfare of persons or communities whose vulnerabilities impair autonomous decision making" (APA, 2002a, p. 7). Clearly, a hallmark of rehabilitation practice is the inclusion and treatment of individuals with compromised decision-making capacity resulting from traumatic injury.

Therefore, rehabilitation psychologists should already be sensitized to this guiding principle, which now more adequately applies to the broad scope of contemporary psychology practice.

REVISED ETHICAL STANDARDS

Martin (2002) and Smith (2003) have summarized the substantive changes to the APA *Ethical Standards*. In addition, Stephen Behnke, the director of the APA ethics office, has discussed individual sections of the Ethics Code in a series of *APA Monitor on Psychology* articles. Examples of significant changes these authors highlighted include new standards or subsections on test data release (Standard 9.04); student privacy protection, particularly related to personal disclosures and mandatory psychotherapy (Standards 7.04, 7.05); delineating what must be covered in acquiring informed consent for (a) assessment or use of interpreters (Standard 9.03), (b) new therapies (Standard 10.01), or (c) clinical research (Standard 8.02); distinguishing abandonment from therapy termination (Standard 10.10); and including an explicit definition of *multiple relationships* (Standard 3.05). We discuss three of these topics—test data release, informed consent, and multiple relationships—and their relevance to rehabilitation psychology practice.

Release of Test Data

A particularly noteworthy change in the standards is the new requirement for psychologists to release test data to patients (9.04). The 1992 APA Ethics Code prevented the release of test data to "unqualified individuals." The new standard has removed this prohibition, allowing psychologists to provide test data to the person or entity identified in the release of information. Embedded in the new language are two key elements: (a) the distinction between test data and test materials and (b) the impact of the Health Insurance Portability and Accountability Act (HIPAA; U.S. Department of Health and Human Services, 2006) of 1996 on how we differentially weigh the bioethical principles of beneficence and respect for autonomy.

The distinction between test data and test materials is critical, given that it defines the scope of what

can be released with consent. *Test data* are defined not only as raw and scaled scores and patient's responses to test items but also as the psychologist's notes concerning what the patient said or did during the evaluation. Therefore, if a psychologist writes notes on a test protocol, such as when a rehabilitation psychologist records behavioral observations directly on either a standardized or nonstandardized measure, that portion of the protocol is subject to release. By contrast, and as defined in Standard 9.11, *test materials* include protocols (without notes), questions, manuals, and test instruments and are not subject to release under the Ethics Code. However, legal obligations limit the psychologist's right to withhold information. In addition, psychologists may be ordered to comply with subpoena requests. In the case example presented at the beginning of the chapter, the psychologist must balance the subpoena request to release test data and materials with his concerns for patient welfare and his responsibilities to his profession. One reasonable action for the psychologist to consider is to consult the judge regarding risk of harm to the patient (and to the profession) and discuss specific contingencies, such as limited release and viewing of data, blacking out test questions to protect test security, and delaying the release to allow further patient recovery and more appropriate engagement with the attorney. In addition, if the rehabilitation psychologist decides to provide the patient with information on release by subpoena, it would be equally important to inform the primary team of this action to increase their sensitivity to possible depressive symptoms and to mobilize constructive family support. Family support reflects sound practice generally when patients have compromised cognitive or behavioral function that limits autonomous information processing.

If there had been no legal considerations in the case presented, the psychologist would not have been obligated under the 2002 Ethical Standards to release the test protocol if the notes existed independently of the test protocol itself. By contrast, he or she would have been obligated in most circumstances to release the nonstandardized measure if performance data and clinical observations were written on the assessment instrument. Behavioral commentary is so critical to understanding the evolving recovery of patients in rehabilitation that documentation of behavioral change is routine. Therefore, it would not have been unusual for the psychologist in the case scenario to create such notations during the assessment process. Rehabilitation psychologists must be vigilant in weighing the potential benefit or harm that could be caused by release of behavioral data documented on test materials. This deliberation should necessarily incorporate consideration of what and where data are recorded (with serious thought given to separating data collection from assessment design elements), the timing of test data release, and familial support in the test data review process. A potential exception to release of data should also be considered. In the case example, if there had been no subpoena and the psychologist could document that probable and significant harm would result by releasing the test data, he or she could make an ethically driven decision to refrain from release at the specific point in time requested by an informed party. The psychologist would be ethically obligated to reconsider this decision with improvement in the patient's functional abilities and family stability.

Behnke (2004b) briefly reviewed the new test data standard (9.04), describing it as an attempt to reconcile the principles of Beneficence and Respect for People's Rights and Dignity. Clearly, however, the new requirement is a significant move toward weighing respect for autonomy more heavily than beneficence (i.e., people's right of access is the rule rather than the exception). A strong influence has been exerted by the implementation of HIPAA, a federal law designed to protect patient privacy and access to health information, as well as to improve the overall fabric of our society's health care information system (U.S. Department of Health and Human Services, 2006). However, HIPAA's influence on the Ethics Code and/or perhaps psychologists' discussions regarding how privacy risk is considered is more far reaching than test data release.

The sensitivity throughout the Ethics Code to the electronic transmission of information (i.e., 3.10 Informed Consent, 5.04 Media Presentations, 5.01 Avoidance of False or Deceptive Statements) and the addition of subsection 4.02, specifically on privacy risk, reflect the cultural context in which

HIPAA was established. Implementation of HIPAA has resulted in significant change in the business of health care; for example, modified informed consent procedures to include HIPAA and increased demands on secure data storage. The practical upshot for psychologists is that HIPAA violations, such as failure to protect records from unauthorized access, are also likely to be APA Ethics Code violations.

Informed Consent

Access to health information and other data is, to a great extent, controlled by informed consent. There are four primary informed consent standards in the 2002 APA Ethics Code: general Informed Consent (3.10), Informed Consent to Research (8.02), Informed Consent to Therapy (10.01), and the new Standard of Informed Consent in Assessments (9.03). In addition, other code subsections, notably Psychological Services Delivered to or Through Organizations (3.11), Discussing the Limits of Confidentiality (4.02), Dispensing with Informed Consent for Research (8.05), and the new Standard on Group Therapy (10.03), include informed consent components. We discuss the scope of changes to the primary informed consent standards next.

General issues in informed consent and informed consent in assessment. The changes to the informed consent standards reflect a more balanced application of the bioethical principles of Respect for Autonomy and Beneficence and Nonmaleficence than does that concerning test data release. The changes focus on increased specificity of content, the intention of which is to contribute to the protection of both patients' rights (i.e., to be better informed) and welfare (i.e., to understand the risks and benefits). These protections can be seen in language added across consent for assessment, therapy, and research that delineates specific content to be covered in the consent process. For example, fees, involved third parties, and confidentiality limits are topics that must be covered in soliciting consent for assessment. The new subsection, Use of Assessments (Standard 9.02), also reminds rehabilitation psychologists of the importance of including information on nonstandardized procedures, a common rehabilitation practice, during consent solicitation. This might include a description of the modification(s) used, the rationale for its use, and any limitations on interpretation because of that modification.

In general, the increased informed consent specificity in the code helps ensure that an adequate explanation for services has been provided and that the patient is involved in the decision-making process. This latter point is illustrated by the assessment standard (9.03), which includes the requirement that the patient (and, as appropriate, family members) be able to ask and receive answers to their questions. Similarly, this standard also specifies that psychologists must obtain the consent of the patient to use the services of an interpreter. By including more specific and comprehensive language in the 2002 Ethics Code, the threshold for adequate coverage and patient participation has, we hope, been brought into clearer focus.

In practice, rehabilitation psychologists work with patients whose compromised cognitive and behavioral function make it challenging to provide what might be considered appropriate coverage of planned services or adequate patient participation in informed consent procedures. In working with patients with limited capacity, rehabilitation psychologists should take steps to ensure their consumers understand critical information. Elsewhere, we have delineated several steps to enable consent or assent (Hanson & Kerkhoff, 2004). For example, presenting basic information across multiple sessions and linking material to personal experience with concrete examples may facilitate patient understanding. In addition, family assistance can be invaluable in helping the patient process material relevant to consent. One word of caution is in order, however. Psychologists must not assume that the person providing assistance is the person who can also give consent on behalf of the patient. Rehabilitation psychologists typically work with an array of family members, most of whom do not have the designated legal authority to speak for the patient. Standard 4.02 (Disclosing Limits of Confidentiality) heightens the sensitivity psychologists must have toward acquiring "appropriate" legally recognized consent prior to initiation of services. State statute commonly dictates the hierarchy of others' authority on behalf of the patient (e.g., spouse, adult child, parent), and

psychologists need to be familiar with statutes relevant to their practice.

Conversely, the generic standard of Informed Consent (3.10) now recognizes that consent is not required when provision of services occurs under legal or regulatory mandate. This qualifying statement appears again in Informed Consent in Assessments (9.03). Rehabilitation psychologists should also keep in mind that disclosure of information is allowed without consent of the legally recognized authority if the disclosure is critical to the purposes of the consultation. The Disclosure Standard (4.05), along with Standard 3.09, Cooperation with Other Professionals, provides coverage to rehabilitation psychologists on an interdisciplinary team, all members of which benefit from information sharing in treatment plan development. However, psychologists must use discretion in determining what is necessary to release. They also need to recognize that the patient's rights to access and control release of health information can be bolstered by statute in many states (Romano, 2006), potentially overriding the Ethics Code. Other aspects of the Ethics Code also reinforce patient protection. Language has been added to the 2002 APA Ethics Code emphasizing the psychologist's obligation to protect the rights and welfare of those from whom consent is not required (e.g., 3.10b), for whom capacity is in question (10.03), or for those who are legally incompetent (3.10). Regardless of whether consent is required, consent solicitation should be the rule rather than the exception. Patients and families typically benefit from understanding the utility and potential impact of evaluation and information sharing on the rehabilitation process (Standard 9.02a), including implications for the home and community.

Informed consent to therapy.   Cognitive, behavioral, and emotional changes in patients needing rehabilitation are typically related to the precipitating physical illness or injury that altered their daily living baseline, and are not necessarily characterized by psychopathology (Adcock, Goldberg, Patterson, & Brown, 2000). Therefore, one obvious challenge in the therapy consenting process is to provide a rationale for psychological intervention in the context of the rehabilitation team treatment milieu. Informed consent to therapy needs to link the patient's diagnosis and resulting presentation with rehabilitation treatment goals and daily life. By providing a rationale that relates the team's goals for intervention to the patient's everyday experience, psychologists attempt to increase the salience of therapeutic benefit to the patient. Because of the comprehensiveness of psychological interventions in the rehabilitation setting, a detailed explanation of applicable individualized interventions should be provided to help the patient understand the overall process.

An interesting conundrum implicit in this consenting process is defining which treatments are viewed as established and which are not (see Informed Consent to Therapy, 10.01b). Ragnarsson (2006) argued that much work remains to be done to determine TBI rehabilitation interventions that are empirically supported. Hence, clinical practice remains a primary guiding factor in addition to evolving research knowledge in following ethical standards relevant to informed consent to intervention.

Adequate informed consent also requires that patients and family members have the opportunity to ask questions regarding applicable services and clarify their roles in the rehabilitation process (Standard 10.02). Examples are often played out in cross-disciplinary interactions during family conferences, medicine–psychology daily rounds, and individual treatment sessions. The patient's and family's questions regarding sharing of treatment performance data among team members, limits of confidentiality, and the relevance of specific therapeutic interventions to their home environment must be fielded in the spirit of openness and reinforcement of participation in the rehabilitation process.

Finally, any expected interruptions in treatment as the patient moves throughout the health care continuum should be addressed during explanation of the treatment process (Standard 10.09). For instance, medical complications in patients who have multitraumatic injuries frequently require transfer from inpatient rehabilitation centers to acute hospitals until stabilization occurs. This can be a frustrating process, requiring patient understanding of health care system complexities and consistent patient support during times of transition (Standard 10.09). The transitional nature of the continuum demands that psychologists communicate treatment-related information to colleagues across treatment settings and organizational boundaries (Standard 10.04). The consumer's incremental understanding of the process of rehabilitation within the larger health care system will likely require serial inquiry and clarification by the psychologist throughout the duration of treatment.

Informed consent to research. Similar to consent standards regarding assessment and therapy, the demand for detailed explanations and the opportunity for patients to be active participants in the informed consent process (e.g., question and answer sessions, receiving research contact) are also apparent in Standard 8.02, Informed Consent for Research. For example, the new subsection on experimental treatment (8.02b) requires coverage of how groups are assigned, services available to the control group, alternative treatments available, costs, and reimbursements. Perhaps more interesting to rehabilitation psychologists, however, is the requirement to clearly identify when treatment used in research is considered experimental. Purtilo (2005) stated that almost every experimental procedure in health care necessitates some infringement on a person's physical and psychological independence. She cautioned that if conservative policy makers consider the rehabilitation patient population as "vulnerable" (p. 227), implying questions of irrevocably compromised capacity or dependency to the point of easy coercion, applied research could be considered ethically prohibited.

The rehabilitation psychology researcher who honors the following will, it is hoped, minimize the likelihood of ethical reproach and preserve the societal value inherent in experimental inquiry: (a) use a "model experimental participants' bill of rights" (Pozgar, 2005, p. 57); (b) clearly define measurable potential benefits of the proposed research to patient and family (Pence, 2007); (c) adequately accommodate study-pertinent special needs of participants; (d) seek guidance from the APA Ethics Code and available guidelines for research; and (e) incorporate procedural safeguards recommended by an institutional review board with the intent to prevent adverse effects in the design of experiments.

Multiple Relationships and Conflict of Interest

The standard on Multiple Relationships (3.05) includes two new elements: (a) an explicit definition of what constitutes a multiple relationship, and (b) clarification that not all multiple relationships are unethical. Only relationships that "could reasonably be expected to impair the psychologist's objectivity, competence, or effectiveness in performing his or her functions as a psychologist, or otherwise risks exploitation or harm to the person with whom the professional relationship exists" would be considered unethical (APA, 2002a, p. 1065). The definition incorporates having multiple roles with the same person (e.g., therapist/friend, teacher/therapist) or the patient being closely related to, or associated with, someone else with whom the psychologist has a professional relationship. For example, in the former case, a patient might be receiving inpatient care in a rural rehabilitation center that employs only one psychologist who also happens to be the patient's neighbor. In the latter case, the patient might be a relative of the psychologist's business partner. The challenge in the first example is that the patient's care cannot be reassigned because no other psychologist is immediately available. If it is deemed unreasonable to transfer the patient's care to a psychologist in another location, then several steps are critical to protect the patient's welfare. These include clarifying role expectations and the limits of confidentiality with specific acknowledgement of the boundaries regarding the personal relationship. Additional steps include reinforcement of these boundaries at appropriate points during the rehabilitation process and heightened sensitivity to potential loss of objectivity and potential patient harm. Critical self-analysis of decision-making and collegial consultation regarding patient concerns and clinical decisions can help minimize the risk of unethical conduct.

The second example may not be inherently unethical depending on the frequency and type of contact occurring among the patient, psychologist, and business partner. To ensure the relationship between the psychologist and patient is not exploited, the psychologist should define appropriate boundaries. Limits to consider include no discussion of the business with the patient and no coercive actions toward the patient to influence the partner's business decisions in support of the psychologist's point of view. In addition, it may be reasonable to expect the business partner to inquire about the patient's health status. Anticipating such an event, the psychologist must focus on preserving patient privacy. Overall, psychologists have a responsibility to ensure the safety and well-being of individuals with whom they have entered into a professional relationship. Therefore, the determination of whether a multiple relationship is harmful should be directly focused on the potential risk of patient care being compromised. (See Anderson & Kitchener [1998] and Schank & Skovholt [1997] for further commentary on multiple relationships and recommendations for managing these during and after treatment cessation.)

Standard 3.06, Conflict of Interest, also addresses the importance of avoiding exploitative and harmful professional relationships. In the rehabilitation environment, psychologists commonly have multiple professional responsibilities that are layered within the larger context of the health care organization (Pozgar, 2005). The breadth of these responsibilities can increase the risk of role conflict. For example, rehabilitation psychologists may find themselves advocating for services at one level and restricting privileges at another. It is understandable that a patient or family member might confuse the psychologist's varied professional roles (e.g., team member, therapist) as potentially compromising the therapeutic relationship, especially if routine lines of communication among team members are misunderstood. As each may pertain to a specific activity, it is important that these multiple roles (e.g., patient advocate, contracted employee, organizational consultant) be made explicit to the consumer to avoid misinterpreting routine team or organizational communication as broken confidentiality or conflict of interest. In addition, careful explanation of the treatment team process from the perspective of both the recipient of treatment and the team members is important in avoiding misunderstanding.

Simultaneously, potentially conflicting influences linked to these multiple roles must be carefully parsed out as the rehabilitation psychologist establishes necessary ethical and professional boundaries. This is best exemplified by a patient, naïve to the complexities of the health care system, who expects to receive pro bono care (i.e., in light of state Medicaid not funding psychological services) from a contracted psychology consultant within an ongoing rehabilitation program. Explaining professional boundaries, potentially conflicting organizational policies and ethical requirements (see Commission on Accreditation of Rehabilitation Facilities [CARF], 2005; Joint Commission on Accreditation of Health Care Organizations, 2004; Weber, 2001), and governmental and private managed care procedures regarding allocation of funding resources, all the while trying to maintain an adaptive working relationship with the patient, might well be perceived as a daunting challenge. Fortunately, the ethical standards published by rehabilitation facility accreditation agencies, which focus primarily on the operation of the health care organization, are complementary to the APA Ethics Code as applied to psychologists working in accredited facilities.

Multiple roles can certainly be carried out within appropriate bounds of ethical practice and, in fact, may be necessary for patient goal attainment. However, careful delineation of these roles is a sine qua non for ethical practice and is critical to dispelling perceived conflicts of interest. In addition, how one defines professional boundaries should hold up to professional scrutiny. That is, the actions of the psychologist across these roles and the boundaries the psychologist uses should be recognized as reasonable by one's professional peers.

Ethical Decision Making

Although the APA Ethics Code represents the values and wisdom of the psychology profession, the code is insufficient to guarantee ethical conduct (i.e., no code violations) because it cannot possibly cover all foreseeable ethical challenges. In addition, ethical dilemmas require the psychologist to weigh competing values when the General Principles conflict (Behnke, 2005). Therefore, it is ultimately the moral compass of the individual that drives the ethics decision-making process, and each decision a professional makes reflects on the discipline as a whole. Moral character is shaped by the experience, knowledge, and values of the individual psychologist, and decision making is driven by how these characteris-

tics intersect with the circumstances posed by the ethical dilemmas the psychologist faces.

Rehabilitation is rich with ethical dilemmas to which to apply one's ethics philosophy. Kirschner, Stocking, Wagner, Foye, and Siegler (2001) found the most common ethical concerns reported by rehabilitation professionals in an open-ended survey were in the areas of reimbursement, team goal setting, patient decision-making capacity, and confidentiality of patient information. As we discussed in the previous edition (Hanson, Guenther, Kerkhoff, & Liss, 2000), the principles of Beneficence and Respect for People's Rights and Dignity often conflict in the rehabilitation milieu when staff attempt to balance patients' rights with their safety. Elsewhere, we have offered extensive discussion on how to balance these rights (Hanson & Kerkhoff, 2004). An important component of this balance is to determine whether the patient has the ability to protect his or her own welfare in the specific situation being considered (i.e., even if the team disagrees with the patient's decision). If the patient lacks this skill, the provider must then determine whether risk of significant harm outweighs respect for autonomy, thus tilting the decision toward the patient's safety. However, safeguards that clearly identify criteria for terminating restrictive, albeit beneficent, actions are also required ethical practice. For example, the CARF Facility Standards require monitoring and identifying mitigating factors in restraint use. In this situation, the team's recommendations and rationale for safety enhancement, as well as termination of the beneficent restrictive procedures, should be provided to the patient and family.

If the patient does have autonomous choice and makes a risky decision, the team is obligated to discuss that risk with the patient. For example, a patient or family member might elect an unsafe discharge placement (e.g., risk of fire or physical injury). The social worker might assist in identifying alternative placements, or the occupational therapist might review potential modifications to ensure a safer environment. In addition, the team might identify significant risk of harm that demands alerting a governmental agency that has responsibility for monitoring community-based patient safety. The team's risk assessment and intention to alert such an agency would typically be shared with the patient and family prior to discharge to allow further discussion of potential decisional consequences.

Maintaining confidentiality on an interdisciplinary team, team treatment planning to maximize patient benefit, and involving the family in decision making and patient care also pose challenges. Being proactive rather than reactive in each case is important to sound ethical practice. We strongly advise that all professionals articulate and internalize a systematic approach to ethical decision making. Otherwise, providers are at substantial risk of inadvertently being excessively influenced by the emotional valences of the situation based on patient, family, and health care provider reactions or by secondary minutiae rather than by the core ethical issues that should be the focus of case resolution.

There are a variety of decision-making models to guide the psychologist. These typically represent one of two schemas: (a) overarching guidelines to sound ethical practice or (b) steps to follow when working through a specific ethical concern. The global view of ethical decision making is designed to help the psychologist avoid common mistakes and is oriented toward risk management. Canter, Bennett, Jones, and Nagy (1994) offered the following recommendations: know the discipline's ethics code, the law, and regulations at work; engage in continuing education; identify potential ethical problems; learn an ethical analysis method; and consult with colleagues about ethical issues. Nagy (2005) offered a list of questions to determine whether one's conduct requires increased vigilance. For example, "Do I find myself changing my usual and customary practices in dealing with a particular individual or situation?" (p. 15). This type of questioning can lead to increased insight regarding one's own patterns of behavior requiring attention.

Specific decision-making models typically have several common features, including the following: (a) identify the affected parties, (b) identify the ethically relevant principles, (c) develop alternative courses of action, (d) consider possible risks and benefits, (e) choose and implement a course of action, and (f) evaluate the results (Doverspike, 1999). Four models illustrating these types of problem-solving components are presented in Table 30.1.

Although each model has its unique emphases, all include careful informational analyses (e.g., evaluating available data and competing values) and incorporate an action plan with accountability. Any of these models could readily be adopted by an institutional ethics consultation team.

CONCLUSIONS

The APA Ethics Code revisions reflect the current sociocultural context in the following ways: (a) a broader acknowledgment of our diverse society (e.g., the addition of the terms *culture* and *gender identity* to Principle E and throughout the standards); (b) an increased emphasis on patient autonomy related to decision making, access to data, and disclosure; (c) increased patient and student protections (e.g., clarifying boundaries of competence, including Standards 2.01 and 2.02; minimizing harm in research, Standards 8.05 and 8.08; protecting students' publication credit, Standard 8.12; avoiding multiple relationships with students, Standard 7.05); and (d) ensuring psychologists are law abiding citizens (i.e., the need to follow the law when an unresolved conflict exists, explicitly delineated in the Introduction). More specificity has been provided within some standards to clarify the psychologist's obligations and to provide enhanced guidance about specific actions, such as the importance of early and effective explanation of the rehabilitation process, the integrative communication characterizing the interdisciplinary team, and the patient's active role on this team. The usefulness of this type of specificity is perhaps reflected in the continued reduction in the number of ethics complaints investigated by the APA Ethics Committee (APA Ethics Committee, 2004).

Nevertheless, well-intentioned people can sink into the murky soup of ethical dilemmas and make poor choices, particularly when under significant personal or professional stress. During these times, it is especially important to use a systematic and consultative process to wade through ethical quagmires. By incorporating a planned, reasoned approach to decision making, the psychologist can reduce the sometimes compelling emotional valence and avoid the pitfalls that ethical dilemmas create.

TABLE 30.1

Comparison of Ethical Decision-Making Models

Canadian Psychological Association (1991)	Koocher & Keith-Spiegel (1998)	Kitchener (2000)	Hanson, Kerkhoff, & Bush (2005)
Identify ethically relevant issues.	Determine that the matter is an ethical one.	Pause and think about the response.	Identify relevant ethical principles and standards and conflicts among them.
Develop alternative courses of action.	Consult guidelines available that might apply to identifying and resolving the issue.	Review available information.	Identify institutional and legal concepts that are relevant.
Analyze risks and benefits of potential actions on all parties affected.	Consider all sources that might influence the decision (e.g., prejudices, personal needs).	Identify possible options.	Identify the context in which the dilemma has occurred (i.e., the events leading up to and surrounding the dilemma).
Choose a course of action.	Consult with a trusted colleague.	Consult the Ethics Code.	Identify key stakeholders (i.e., roles, potential biases, contributions to the solution).
Act with a commitment to assume responsibility for consequences.	Evaluate the rights, responsibilities, and vulnerabilities of all affected parties.	Assess the foundational ethical issues (i.e., balance the principles in each option).	Resolve case (i.e., weigh alternatives and choose a course of action).
Evaluate results of the action.	Enumerate consequences of possible decisions.	Identify legal concerns.	Understand the case disposition (i.e., the result and could it have been better).
Assume responsibility for consequences of the action.	Make the decision.	Reassess options and identify a plan.	
	Implement the decision.	Implement the plan and document the process.	
		Reflect on the outcome of the decision.	

Clearly, the APA Ethics Code offers significant guidance as part of this process.

References

Adcock, R., Goldberg, M., Patterson, D., & Brown, P. (2000). Staff perceptions of emotional distress in patients with burn trauma. *Rehabilitation Psychology, 45,* 179–192.

American Psychological Association (1992). Ethical principles of psychologists and code of conduct. *American Psychologist, 47,* 1597–1611.

American Psychological Association. (2002a). Ethical principles of psychologists and code of conduct. *American Psychologist, 57,* 1060–1073.

American Psychological Association. (2002b). Guidelines on multicultural education, training, research, prac- tice, and organizational change for psychologists. Retrieved May 4, 2006, from http://www.apa.org

American Psychological Association, Ethics Committee. (2004). Report of the Ethics Committee, 2003. *American Psychologist, 59,* 434–411.

Anderson, S. K., & Kitchener, K. S. (1998). Nonsexual posttherapy relationships: A conceptual framework to assess ethical risks. *Professional Psychology, Research, and Practice, 29,* 91–99.

Beauchamp, T., & Childress, J. (2001). *Principles of biomedical ethics* (5th ed.). New York: Oxford University Press.

Behnke, S. (2004a). APA's new ethics code from a practitioner's perspective. *Monitor on Psychology, 35,* 54–55.

Behnke, S. (2004b). Release of test data and the new ethics code. *Monitor on Psychology, 35,* 90–91.

Behnke, S. H. (2005). On being an ethical psychologist. *Monitor on Psychology, 36,* 114–115.

Canadian Psychological Association. (1991). *Canadian code of ethics for psychologists.* Ottawa, Ontario, Canada: Author.

Canter, M., Bennett, B., Jones, S., & Nagy, T. (1994). *Ethics for psychologists: A commentary on the APA Ethics Code.* Washington, DC: American Psychological Association.

Clay, R. A. (2000). APA task force considers changes to proposed ethics code. *Monitor on Psychology, 31*(7), 86–87.

Commission on Accreditation of Rehabilitation Facilities. (2005). *Medical rehabilitation standards manual.* Tucson, AZ: Author.

Doverspike, W. (1999). *Ethical risk management: Guidelines for practice.* Sarasota, FL: Professional Resource Press.

Hanson, S., Guenther, R., Kerhoff, T., & Liss, M. (2000). Ethics: Historical foundations, basic principles, and contemporary issues. In R. G. Frank & T. Elliott (Eds.), *Handbook of rehabilitation psychology* (pp. 629–643.). Washington, DC: American Psychological Association.

Hanson, S., & Kerkhoff, T. (2004). The implications of bioethical principles in traumatic brain injury rehabilitation. In M. Ashley & D. Krych (Eds.), *Traumatic brain injury: Rehabilitative treatment and case management* (pp. 685–721). Boca Raton, FL: CRC Press.

Hanson, S. L., & Kerkhoff, T. R. (2007). Ethical decision making in rehabilitation: Consideration of Latino cultural factors. *Rehabilitation Psychology, 52,* 409–420.

Hanson, S., Kerkhoff, T., & Bush, S. (2005). Health care ethics for psychologists: A casebook. Washington, DC: American Psychological Association.

Joint Commission on Accreditation of Health Care Organizations. (2004). *Comprehensive accreditation manual for hospitals: The official handbook.* Oakbrook, IL: Joint Commission Resources.

Jones, S. (2001). Ethics code draft published for comment. *Monitor on Psychology, 32*(2), 76–89.

Kirschner, K. L., Stocking, C., Wagner, L. B., Foye, S. J., & Siegler, M. (2001). Ethical issues identified by rehabilitation clinicians. *Archives of Physical Medicine and Rehabilitation, 82*(Suppl. 2), S2–S8.

Kitchener, K. S. (2000). *Foundations of ethical practice, research, and teaching in psychology.* Mahawah, NJ: Erlbaum.

Koocher, G., & Keith-Spiegel, P. (1998). *Ethics in psychology: Professional standards and cases* (2nd ed.). New York: Oxford University Press.

Lomay, V. T., & Hinkebein, J. H. (2006). Cultural considerations when providing rehabilitation services to American Indians. *Rehabilitation Psychology, 51,* 36–42.

Martin, S. (2002). APA's council adopts a new ethics code. *Monitor on Psychology, 33*(10). Retrieved September 7, 2006, from http://apa.org/monitor/nov02/ethicscode.html

Nagy, T. F. (2005). *Ethics in plain English: An illustrative casebook for psychologists* (2nd ed.). Washington, DC: American Psychological Association.

Pence, G. (2007). *The elements of bioethics.* New York: McGraw-Hill.

Pozgar, G. (2005). *Legal and ethical issues for health professionals.* Sudbury, MA: Jones and Bartlett Publishers.

Purtilo, R. (2005). *Ethical dimensions in the health professions* (2nd ed.). Philadelphia: Elsevier.

Ragnarsson, K. T. (2006). Traumatic brain injury research since the 1998 NIH Consensus Conference: Accomplishments and unmet goals. *Journal of Head Trauma Rehabilitation, 21,* 379–387.

Romano, J. (2006). *Legal rights of the catastrophically ill and injured: A family guide.* Norristown, PA: Author.

Schank, J. A., & Skovholt, T. M. (1997). Dual-relationship dilemmas of rural and small-community psychologists. *Professional Psychology, Research, and Practice, 28,* 44–49.

Smith, D. (2003). What you need to know about the new code: The chair of APA's Ethics Code Task Force highlights changes to the 2002 Ethics Code. *Monitor on Psychology, 34*(1), 62–65.

U.S. Department of Health and Human Services. (2006). *Health Insurance Portability and Accountability Act of 1996.* Retrieved June 6, 2006, from http://www.hhs.gov/ocr/hipaa

Weber, L. (2001). *Business ethics in health care.* Bloomington, IN: Indiana University Press.

CHAPTER 31

HEALTH POLICY 101: FUNDAMENTAL ISSUES IN HEALTH CARE REFORM

Glenn S. Ashkanazi, Kristofer J. Hagglund, Andrea Lee, Zoe Swaine, and Robert G. Frank

Health services have become a global enterprise (Frank, Farmer, & Klapow, 2003) employing more than 23 of every 1,000 employed persons (Reinhardt, Hussey, & Anderson, 2002). Data from the Organization for Economic Cooperation and Development (OECD) reveal that all developed countries spend more than 8% of their gross domestic product (GDP) on health services (Frank, Farmer, & Klapow, 2003). In most industrialized countries, the proportion of spending dedicated to health services now exceeds 9% of the GDP. The United Kingdom, for many years among the most frugal developed nations in terms of health care spending, now spends 9% of its GDP on health. Canada, another long-time model of balanced health spending, exceeded 10% in 2006 (OECD, 2008).

HISTORY OF HEALTH CARE FINANCING IN THE UNITED STATES

The United States has experienced a relentless, upward spiral of health care spending for more than 4 decades. In 1970, the United States spent about $75 billion on health care, or about $356 per resident, accounting for 7.6% of the country's GDP. Since that point, health spending has exceeded growth in the GDP by 2.5%. The only exception in the growth of health spending was a period during the last decade of the 20th century. The Centers for Medicare and Medicaid Services (CMS) projected that health care spending will exceed $4.1 trillion by 2016, or about $12,782 per resident, an alarming 19.6% of the GDP (Kaiser Commission on Medicaid and the Uninsured, 2007).

Americans have long been ambivalent regarding public financing of health care, a system enacted by virtually all other developed nations. In the United States, over the last 100 years, increasingly frequent national debates have arisen regarding the roles of individuals, employers, and the government in financing health care. Until World War II, most individuals paid directly for health care services. The antecedents of the current health insurance system date to 1929, when schoolteachers and the Baylor University Hospital in Dallas, Texas, agreed to an insurance arrangement in which teachers received hospital room and board and ancillary services at a predetermined rate in return for a monthly premium of $6. During the Great Depression, other hospitals copied this model and the American Hospital Association promoted the development of group hospitalization to Blue Cross plans across the nation. The model became widespread.

During World War II, employers faced with federally mandated wage freezes increasingly offered health insurance to attract employees (Starr, 1982). After World War II, employers offered health insurance as an employment benefit in a tight job market and as a result of collective bargaining by unions (Starr, 1982). The private health insurance markets, funded by employers, created a health care system that served the country from the late 1940s until the late 1980s (Enthoven & Fuchs, 2006). Growth of the privately funded, employer-supported market was enhanced by the exemption of employer health insurance payments from the employees' taxable income (Enthoven & Fuchs, 2006). Employer-based coverage peaked during the 1980s. Between 1987 and 1999, coverage for workers age 18 to 64 declined 2.8 percentage points. From 1999 to 2004, the Employee Benefit Research Institute (EBRI) reported another 3.5% decline (EBRI Issue Brief 287, as cited in Enthoven & Fuchs, 2006). Overall, there has been a stunning 15% decline in employer-based coverage in the last 15 years (Enthoven & Fuchs, 2006).

Erosion in the employer-based insurance system has paralleled increases in the number of Americans lacking health insurance. The ambivalence that has marked the United States' approach to comprehensive health coverage has led to surprising tolerance for a lack of health coverage for many Americans. Approximately 12.3% of the population under age 65 lacked health insurance in 1978. As coverage by employer-based systems has declined, the number of Americans lacking health coverage from any source has soared. In 2006, 18% of those younger than 65 years—46.5 million people—lacked health insurance (Kaiser Commission on Medicaid and the Uninsured, 2007). The Kaiser Commission on Medicaid and the Uninsured (2007) reported that about half of all Americans with private health insurance receive health insurance through their own employers and half (49%) as an employee's dependent. Most individuals have difficulty affording health insurance coverage in the nongroup market; only 5% purchase health insurance in this manner. In the private nongroup market, rates are based on individual health risk rather than group risk, the basis for employer/group based-policies. Those with chronic conditions and/or disabilities are virtually uninsurable in the individual health insurance market (Kaiser Commission on Medicaid and the Uninsured, 2007).

Medicaid, the federal–state social insurance program, provides health insurance to more Americans (13%) than any other single health insurer. Medicaid provides coverage to certain low income and other categorically defined groups according to legislative mandates, including four groups of nonelderly individuals: children, their parents, pregnant women, and individuals with disabilities (Kaiser Commission on Medicaid and the Uninsured, 2007). As the Kaiser Commission noted, 40% of the poor receive public coverage, but 37% of individuals below poverty level remain uninsured because they do not meet income or categorical requirements for eligibility. It is impor-

tant that Medicaid is a significant source of health coverage for individuals with disabilities, providing health and long-term care coverage for eight million nonelderly, low income individuals with disability. Even with Medicaid, almost half of the uninsured have one or more chronic health conditions (Kaiser Commission on Medicaid and the Uninsured, 2007).

HOW MODERN INSURANCE WORKS IN THE UNITED STATES

In the United States, health insurance has become the major source of health care financing. Insurance is designed to spread risk of infrequent events across a broad group. Through a contractual relationship, the insurer establishes a premium for the policy. The premium covers anticipated losses for the individual or group purchasing the policy (i.e., the risk adjustment function of insurance). The premium also includes payment for administration of the policy. Policy administration includes risk assessment, management of the policy, marketing, claim processing, and profit. Insurers assess the risk of an event through underwriting. Actuaries assess the likelihood of events occurring in specific populations and adjust risk to create outcomes matching the insurer's policies. Prior claims create a basis for experience ratings, which allows the prediction of further use or claims.

Cream-skimming or *cherry-picking* is the process by which insurers manipulate the likelihood the healthiest individuals will select their plans; these individuals are less likely to use services or make health claims, thereby enhancing the insurer's profit. Selection bias may also work against an insurer. When an insurer offers a richer benefit plan, attracting a disproportionate number of sicker individuals who use more services, this is called *adverse selection* (Barton, 2003). The adjustment of risk occurs through *risk pooling,* in which pools of individuals or groups are created to spread risk. Prediction of future health services use is fundamental to all parties involved in the insurance process. Insurers attempt to achieve a favorable loss ratio (i.e., premiums received are more than losses claimed). A favorable loss ratio creates greater profit for the insurance company (i.e., retention rate).

Moral hazard, a term derived from the economic literature, has become an important concept in health policy. Economists believe moral hazard arises when an individual does not bear the full consequences of his or her actions. It follows then, that the lack of consequence for health care spending for individuals with health insurance leads to moral hazard. Despite the fact that there has been no clear proof that moral hazard applies to health services, it is the basis for the application of a variety of cost-sharing practices by insurance companies. Insurance policies, guided by the moral hazard model, typically include several cost-sharing elements for which the insured is responsible. These deductibles, co-payments, and co-insurance decrease the insurance function encouraging the insured to appreciate the financial consequences of health care use. All of these are designed to make consumers more sensitive to health costs and to reduce costs to the insurance company (or to the employer financing the plan). Deductibles arose from the Rand Health Insurance Experiments, the first large-scale health intervention trial. In the Rand study, 2,005 families were assigned to different health coverage conditions ranging from full-coverage to varying co-pays. All types of services were used less with consumer cost-sharing. The only exception to the effects of cost-sharing was hospital admissions for children. Mental health services were found to be extremely sensitive to cost-sharing effects. This experiment profoundly influenced health services reimbursement, deductibles, and copays (Newhouse, 1993).

In 1974, the United States faced a pension crisis because many pension plans were inadequately funded and failing to meet their contractual obligations. To address this problem, Congress modified pension requirements. A small change inserted into the 1974 Employee Retirement Income and Security Act during the conference between the House of Representatives and the Senate exempted self-insured or self-funded programs from having to offer benefits mandated by state insurance commissions. Self-insured funds are not required to pay state insurance taxes and are exempt from "any willing provider" laws (Barton, 2003).

Employers funding their own insurance program must reserve funds to cover expenses. Self-insured employers may contract with a third party for administrative services (i.e., so-called administrative services only [ASO] agreements). ASO plans may look to an outsider like an insurance plan providing actuarial estimates, plan design, and claims processing. A firm may wish to buffer, or limit, the financial risk to which they expose the company by purchasing reinsurance from another insurer. Reinsurance allows the employer to establish a *stop-loss* level that caps their risk. For example, an employer may purchase reinsurance establishing a stop-loss level at $25,000 per covered individual. The employer's risk is then limited to $25,000 for each insured person (Barton, 2003).

UNSUCCESSFUL ATTEMPTS AT HEALTH CARE REFORM

Despite periodic, intense debates, the United States has been unable to implement comprehensive health care reform (Bingaman, Frank, & Billy 1993). During the 1990s President Bill Clinton proposed comprehensive reform of the health care system, engaging virtually every health care stakeholder group, but several key interest groups, including health insurance companies and business groups, lobbied against the reform proposal. The ensuing debate demonstrated the complexity of implementing broad reform affecting many constituencies. Although comprehensive reform presents significant political challenges, increases in the cost of health coverage and lack of health coverage for many Americans suggests that reform of the health care system will be an important continuing political topic.

The persistence of American's concern with quality, coverage, and cost of health services ensures ongoing discussions about how the system should be reformed. In 1994, the failure of the ambitious Clinton health system proposal, which proposed broad changes, made most politicians and policymakers leery of comprehensive reform models. Future discussions of health reform will likely focus on modification of specific areas of the health system, rather than reform of the entire system. Such initiatives, labeled *incremental reform,* characterize the history of major health policy changes in the United States over the last 100 years. Although comprehensive change is needed addressing the uninsured, cost escalation, quality lapses and even-handed implementation of new technology, incremental reform, addressing smaller aspects of the health system, is more likely to occur (Fuchs, 2007).

Even incremental changes in health policy rarely happen quickly. Etheredge (2007) stated that changes in national health policy require sustained development across several election cycles. Indeed, keen observers of changes in health policy over the last 50 years will note that most innovations were heralded more than 10 years prior to implementation. For example, Medicare's prospective payment program, implemented in the 1980s, had early support in the 1972 Social Security Amendments (Etheredge, 2007). HMOs, created by legislation during the Nixon administration, were the foundation for managed care initiatives modifying the insurance market (Etheredge, 2007).

The long percolation period for most changes in health policy is often obscured by the drama of change associated with new policy initiatives. For example, the national debate on reform of the health system that occurred during the 102nd Congress (1993–1994) resulted in little health legislation. The debate, however, fueled a shift by private and public health payers toward prospective payment models specifying the quantity of care provided by insurance benefits (i.e., managed care; Johnstone et al., 1995). This shift represented 30 years of discussion and research among health policy experts (Etheredge, 2007). Psychologists, however, rarely participated in these conversations. Increasing the psychologist's understanding of the basic tenets of health policy is critical to the integration of the discipline into broader discussions on health services and prospective changes.

Chronic and disabling conditions engender significant cost (Frank, Hagglund, & Farmer, 2004). Kronick, Gilmer, Dreyfus, and Lee (2000) stated: "Among people with disabilities, health care expenditures are strongly related to recent diagnoses, and health plans are well aware that attracting too many people with costly problems can lead to large financial losses" (p. 29). The magnitude of health expenditures associated with disabling conditions enhances the importance of rehabilitation psychologists

appreciating health policy implication. Because of the long incubation of health policy innovations, it is relatively easy to learn the fundamental elements of health reform and remain informed for several iterations of the conversation. The range of options for reform is relatively limited. Few totally new ideas are considered (Roper, 2007). Most clinical practitioners focus attention on reimbursement issues because of the immediate impact on clinical revenue. Reimbursement is, however, only a part of a broader, interconnected, health system. For example, an individual's health insurance coverage is directly affected by insurance regulations. These regulations influence costs because they specify how insurance companies are allowed to band individuals into groups. Understanding health reform requires understanding the insurance system and implications for change.

SUCCESSFUL ATTEMPTS AT HEALTH CARE REFORM

Over the past 2 decades, the decline of employer-sponsored insurance has spawned a steady increase in insurance products, vastly diversifying offerings beyond the "one-size-fits-all" products common during the managed care era. Newer approaches stress cost-conscious purchasing, including passing discounts provided by physicians and hospitals to the insured individual (Robinson, 2004). In the next 10 years, many of these innovations will become common insurance vehicles. Understanding the structure and function of these new practices provides insight into the types of health access policy initiatives likely to appear in Congress and state legislatures.

Health Savings Accounts

Health savings accounts (HSAs), which were first discussed during the 108th Congress (2003–2005), have proven enduringly popular with the Republican members of Congress. HSAs combine high-deductible policies with employee-managed, employer-financed savings accounts. HSAs cover medical costs exceeding the deductibles. Balances can be rolled over and accumulated, encouraging cost-conscious purchasing (Robinson, 2004). HSAs are designed to minimize unnecessary health costs, unlike traditional insurance, which is often seen as encouraging the use of health services. HSAs function as traditional insurance coverage for events exceeding the high deductible. HSAs can also serve as savings accounts, allowing the enrollees to retain unspent allocations as long as they remain with the same employer. HSAs and similar products mark an important transition in the insurance market. Historically, collective insurance has transferred coverage from low users of health care to high users. In HSAs, the savings accounts principle guides the retention of unspent balances by the insured. In HSAs, discounts provided by hospitals, physicians, and other ancillary service providers are passed on to consumers (Robinson). This pattern reflects the trend toward discounted rates for medical and psychological services not covered by insurance.

Consumer-Directed Care

The shift of risk from insurers to consumers has increased interest in high-deductible plans such as HSAs. High-deductible plans emphasize moral hazard; when the insured is responsible for "first dollar" costs, he or she will, theoretically, become an active evaluator of the quality and value of care. One drawback of this model, however, is that quality of health care services is not transparent, hampering consumers' ability to make informed decisions. High-deductible plans give consumers more freedom in the selection of benefits; however, most often they pay directly for the benefit.

The increased emphasis on consumer selection parallels a movement led by individuals with disability. During the past 2 decades, there has been a steady increase in publicly funded (i.e., Medicaid waivers to states) programs allowing home- and community-based services for individuals with disability and the choice of more flexible benefits, including attendants. These efforts have occurred in response to strong advocacy by individuals with disability for more control of their own care and for the "demedicalization" of many basic services, such as personal assistants. The policy implications of this movement are intriguing. In particular, the funding of these services is challenging. As insurers, employers, and governments have pushed for leaner benefit packages, these self-directed plans appear more

costly and difficult to regulate. Some European countries have experimented with direct cash payments to consumers for these services. Although these models challenge national trends within health care, the potential to improve access to health services, along with the strong advocacy of individuals with disability, has encouraged experimentation. One such model that reflects the new interest in consumer-directed care is the cardinal symptom model.

Cardinal Symptom Model

Frank, Hagglund, and Farmer (2004) noted that one in three Americans is affected by a chronic health condition, and that these individuals incur disproportionate health costs. The U.S. health care system functions best in the treatment of acute disorders. Chronic and disabling conditions most often require preventive and routine care. Such services fare poorly in a system focused on acute management. Chronic and disabling conditions require comprehensive, coordinated care focusing on the individual's needs. This approach, which is akin to consumer-directed care, allows the individual to determine the most important aspects of health care and direct the use of health benefits to reflect these decisions.

Individuals with chronic health conditions use more health care services and are therefore more sensitive to cost increases in the health care system and to changes in private or social insurance. Individuals with disabilities need primary care systems that can respond to the chronic nature of disability and invite them to be active in their own health care. The wraparound services needed by individuals with disabilities include, for example, responsive scheduling of appointments, telephone consultation, remote monitoring of health status, and/or nontraditional transportation. Frank, Hagglund, and Farmer (2004) labeled systems able to provide consumers the ability to manage their health care in concordance with their own perceptions of health services needs as *cardinal symptom management*. Cardinal symptom management encourages consumers to become knowledgeable participants in their own health care management. Cardinal symptom management also recognizes the impact of the information economy on health care. With increasing access to health information, consumers are likely to become more educated and involved in choosing different services from different providers.

The advent of the educated health consumer has significant implications for rehabilitation psychology. Over the past 50 years, the influence of national health policy decisions has increased. Government's roles in health care financing and in economic programs that increase wealth demonstrate the importance of understanding health policy (Frank, Farmer, & Klapow, 2003). Government's role in health policy is a driving force in health care financing, health insurance regulations, and health care delivery methods, especially for older people, persons with low incomes, and veterans. National health policy influences nearly every aspect of health care, including psychology. Rehabilitation psychology has begun to recognize the implications of federal and state health policies and their effects on rehabilitation psychology practice and research and on the health and well-being of its constituents. In the remainder of the chapter, we provide an overview of health policy and how changes in health policy are implemented.

RECENT EFFORTS TO IMPROVE HEALTH CARE QUALITY

Improving health care quality has been an elusive goal for the U.S. health care system. The largest barrier to improved quality is the system's complexity, especially the discontinuities in financing, payment, and delivery systems created by a dual private–public system.

The Institute of Medicine's (IOM) reports *To Err is Human* (2000) and *Crossing the Quality Chasm* (2001) brought health care quality problems to the attention of the nation. *To Err is Human* first documented the often-cited statistic that health care errors account for 98,000 deaths per year. *Crossing the Quality Chasm* emphasized the importance of interorganizational cooperation and health system redesign to improve the quality of care. Several specific recommendations made by this report pertain directly to persons with chronic illness and/or disability. For example, the IOM recommended that

care be based on "continuous healing relationships" that follow patients' needs and values, and that the health care system anticipate these needs. Rehabilitation and health psychologists are critical to implementing these (and many other) changes to the health care system to improve quality of care. These reports remain the seminal works in the field of quality improvement and have spawned other quality initiatives, including the 5 Million Lives campaign (Institute for Healthcare Improvement [IHI], 2007).

The 5 Million Lives campaign, sponsored by the IHI, follows its successful 100,000 Lives campaign (IHI, 2007). The latter campaign involved 3,100 hospitals and surrounding communities to implement six basic interventions designed to prevent errors of omission and commission (e.g., establishing rapid response teams to react to patients in distress). Because the six interventions were based on empirical evidence, the changes in practice established a "community" standard of care. If hospitals ignore such standards, they could be legally, if not morally, liable for injuries or deaths that could have been prevented (Gosfield & Reinertsen, 2005). The 5 Million Lives campaign added an additional six interventions (e.g., preventing pressure ulcers) that require interdisciplinary teams for implementation.

Another promising trend in improving quality is the Pay for Performance (P4P) approach to reimbursement. In contrast to the usual method of reimbursing by the quantity of service, P4P is designed to reimburse providers (broadly defined) by their adherence to quality processes and/or success in improving the health outcomes of their patients. Traditional methods of payment that reward for quantity of services have contributed to substantial practice variations that are not supported by evidence and wide geographic variations in use of services (Weinstein, Bronner, Morgan, & Wennberg, 2004; Wennberg, Fisher, Skinner, & Bronner, 2007).

P4P initiatives are promoting participation in health information technology systems (e.g., electronic health records), following quality processes (e.g., percentage of patients with myocardial infarction receiving recommended beta-blockers; Wennberg, Fisher, & Skinner, 2002) and implementing care management for persons with chronic illnesses (Wennberg, O'Conner, Collins, & Weinstein,

2007). The majority of health insurance plans and Medicare have implemented P4P programs focused on specific populations (e.g., geriatric primary care), conditions (e.g., asthma), or services (e.g., surgery protocols). These initiatives involve physician groups, hospitals, and clinics. P4P is also being used by more than half of state Medicaid programs and rapid growth is expected during the next several years (Kuhmerker & Hartman, 2007). Although promising, implementation and evaluation of most P4P programs has just begun.

Implementation of these procedures is not without challenges. Payers and participants have to negotiate critical components, such as the reimbursement model. For example, should providers who fail to meet goals be penalized or those who do meet goals given bonuses (Kuhmerker & Hartman, 2007)? Also, there is significant discussion about the use of process or structural outcome measures (e.g., adopting health information technology) versus health outcome measures (e.g., infection rates; Kuhmerker & Hartman, 2007). In the field of psychology, P4P may be initially difficult to implement because of the variability in accepted practices and potential difficulty in establishing appropriate outcome measures. Indeed, the American Psychological Association (APA) only recently officially endorsed evidence-based practice, and there was substantial controversy about this endorsement (APA Presidential Task Force on Evidence-Based Practice, 2006).

Other quality improvement initiatives focus on expanding health information technology. The Department of Veterans Affairs, for example, implemented *computerized physician order entry* (CPOE), which removes misinterpretations and similar mistakes associated with handwritten orders for medications and other treatments. Although CPOE has been repeatedly shown to substantially reduce medication errors (e.g., Bates et al., 1998), it has not been widely implemented because of funding barriers, physician resistance, and complexities associated with the conversion to CPOE (Poon et al., 2004). Nevertheless, health information technology has been promoted as an important vehicle to improve safety and quality in health care. In fact, legislation promoting health information technology passed the U.S. Senate Health, Education, Labor, and

Pensions Committee, specifically, Senate Bill 1693, the Wired for Health Care Quality Act (Office of Senator Hillary Rodham Clinton, 2007).

REHABILITATION-SPECIFIC LEGISLATIVE INITIATIVES

Since 1983, classification of a facility as an inpatient rehabilitation facility (IRF) has required the hospital to comply with the *75% rule,* that is, to document that 75% of admissions or discharges fell into 1 of 10 diagnostic categories: stroke, spinal cord injury, congenital deformity, amputation, major multiple trauma, femur fracture (i.e., hip fracture), brain injury, neurological disorders (e.g., Parkinson's disease, muscular dystrophy, polyneuropathy), burns, or polyarthritis. To meet this regulation, IRFs submitted an annual affidavit showing how they met the 75% rule. Fiscal intermediaries (FIs), independent third parties contracted by Medicare to administrate billing, had little oversight over IRFs. CMS began to question the level of accountability in the annual affidavit, as rumors of facilities overstating their compliance became common.

In July 2004, CMS enacted Federal Rule 42 (42 CFR Part 412) requiring 75% of IRF patients to be included in one of 13 diagnostic categories, as opposed to the previous 10 diagnostic categories. Polyarthritis was expanded to include three separate arthritis disease states: polyarthricular rheumatoid arthritis, systemic vasculidities, and advanced osteoarthritis. In addition, certain knee or hip replacements in an acute setting immediately preceding an inpatient rehabilitation stay were added to make the final 13 categories. CMS instructed rehabilitation hospitals that failure to meet the new 75% criterion would mean loss of the higher payments from Medicare associated with an intensive rehabilitation setting. The policy was originally intended to cut down on inappropriate admissions to inpatient facilities and required FIs to conduct routine, targeted reviews for medical necessity. The new rule encouraged research into the effectiveness of intensive rehabilitation and the factors that predict patient need for intensive rehabilitation services. Combined with the FI's reviews of medical necessity, it was hoped the new rule would identify subgroups of patients that are appropriate for IRFs rather than other settings.

Federal Rule 42 was only partially implemented in 2004. The first phase of the implementation iterated the expectation that 50% of admissions would include the 13 diagnostic groups. The thresholds were to increase during 2005 and 2006 to 65% (Phase 2) with the final 75% (Phase 3) threshold becoming effective in 2008. On December 19, 2007, Congress passed the Medicare, Medicaid, and State Children's Health Insurance Program Extension Act of 2007 that halted the 2008 implementation of the full 75% and has lessened it permanently to 60% of the inpatient rehabilitation hospitals patient population in the categories described later. In addition, the bill requires that the U.S. Department of Health and Human Services study beneficiary access to inpatient rehabilitation services and make recommendations for classifying inpatient rehabilitation hospitals and units.

Proponents of the rule change argue that during the period of nonimplementation of the rule, IRFs treated patients who could have received the same quality of care in a more cost-effective setting such as a skilled nursing facility (SNF). They propose that the 75% rule differentiates the patients who truly need high-acuity settings and intensive rehabilitation from those who could be served in settings such as SNFs that deliver high quality, but less expensive, care, saving the Medicare system millions of dollars. CMS previously estimated that failure to fully implement the 75% rule would cost the taxpayers an additional $370 million annually in new Medicare spending. Critics of the rule argue that the FIs do not have the necessary resources or clinical expertise in their medical review process to appropriately refine the rule, as was CMS's original hope. Further, they criticize CMS's use of "arbitrary" criteria specified by the 75% rule to determine an individual patient's admission eligibility rather than medical necessity and functional deficits. These critics claim that it creates a system in which rehabilitation hospitals are forced to manage their patient mix on the basis of a payment system rather than clinical judgment or rehabilitation need. Further, they claim that the rule can cause access to inpatient care to be partly determined by the time at which the patient is referred. So, for example, a patient referred later in the fiscal year may not be admitted to an IRF.

Critics argue that the rule fails to consider that many patients outside the 13 diagnostic groups are able to benefit from inpatient rehabilitation and have better outcomes than if treated in SNFs with a lower intensity of care. They have characterized this as a "quota" system for people with disabilities seeking inpatient rehabilitation. These opponents question why patients with cancer undergoing chemotherapy, people who have undergone extensive cardiac surgery, or those requiring pulmonary rehabilitation who have documented needs should not be allowed to benefit from more intensive therapies than what can normally be found in skilled nursing facilities. They speculate that the rule itself may be responsible for increasing the rate of morbidities and mortality in these populations because, they claim, nursing homes cannot adequately manage the medical and physical needs of these patients in the early stages of their recovery.

Rehabilitation providers need a strategy to identify patients' rehabilitation needs and determine the most appropriate level of care, such as inpatient rehabilitation, skilled nursing, home health, extended care, or outpatient care. To meet both patients' needs and the regulatory requirements, providers may need to examine and modify some of their processes. For example, examination of discharge planning will be necessary so that when physicians order a transfer of a patient to one level of care who is better suited at a different level of care, the mismatch is recognized. In addition, hospitals may want to consider centralizing their postacute care intake process to lessen conflict between managers of the various levels of care who may be competing for patients to meet census and budget projections. Other management plans will need to include excellent documentation, referral source education, and assessment of the fit of one's current continuum of services to their geographic market.

ADVOCACY

Advocacy is an important activity that brings issues to the awareness of members of Congress, possibly prompting political action. To effectively advocate for an issue, one must have a basic understanding of the legislative process, the factors that influence Congress to take action, and the ways one can be involved with advocacy efforts.

The particulars of the structure and functions of the U.S. Congress are often forgotten. In this section, we provide a brief, basic overview of the U.S. Congress. (Readers well-versed on the Congress may want to skip this section.) The U.S. Congress has two branches or chambers, consisting of 100 members in the Senate and 435 members in the House of Representatives (Evans & Degutis, 2003). Both chambers of Congress are organized into committees and subcommittees and each member of Congress is assigned to serve on various committees and subcommittees. Any member of the House or Senate may introduce a bill at any time during the congressional session. The bill is referred to the appropriate committee or subcommittee for consideration. During committee consideration, changes (i.e., amendments) may be made to the bill. If a bill is referred to a subcommittee once the bill is approved, the bill is forwarded to the full committee where more amendments may take place. The full committee subsequently votes whether the bill will be reported to the full chamber of the legislative body for consideration. Once the bill reaches the full chamber, interested legislators debate it. The bill may be further amended and voted on, either passing or failing to pass out of the respective chamber of the legislature to the other chamber. That is, if a bill passes in the House first, it is later sent to the Senate for a similar process of debate, amendments, and voting. After the bill is voted on by both chambers and passed, the bill is referred to a conference committee that reconciles any differences between the two versions of the bill from the House and Senate and one version of the bill is created. This consolidated bill is then sent to both chambers for final approval. Once both chambers have passed this legislation, it is sent to the President to be signed. The president may sign the bill enacting it into law or veto the bill, returning it to the Congress.

The legislative process enacting a piece of legislation into law may take several months to several years. Those knowledgeable about the actions of the Congress understand that hearings on a topic, or even introducing a bill may not create adequate interest in the topic of the bill to yield passed legislation. A bill, once introduced, is valid for the length of a Congress (i.e., a biennial, for which members of the House of Representatives are elected).

There are a number of ways to interest a member of Congress in an issue. A member may be personally affected by an issue or a situational crisis may arise that creates public support for action (APA Education Directorate, 2004). Another factor that prompts a member of Congress to act is his or her perception that the issue negatively affects a large number of constituents. Members of Congress may introduce a bill when they appreciate that the problem can be solved through federal legislation. Thus, it is important for advocates to communicate the message that the problem affects a significant number of people and the solution lies in legislation.

The member of Congress may need education on an issue and, through education, support may be gained or opposition toward an issue may be avoided or eliminated (APA Public Policy Office, 2005). The ways in which advocates may communicate are through indirect, one-way, or two-way communications. Indirect communication can involve writing letters to newspapers to express an opinion (e.g., op-ed letters, letters to the editor), press releases, or demonstrations. One-way communication may involve phone messages, letters, or e-mails to members. However, the best way to communicate with Congress is through two-way communication that involves meetings with members or staff. This can be achieved by visiting Capitol Hill or the member's district office or attending events such as fundraisers or town-hall meetings. When an advocate meets with a member of Congress or their staff, it is important to present a clear and concise message. Local examples, anecdotes, or data illustrate the importance of an issue and demonstrate real implications. Although it may be assumed that research data is the most influential piece of evidence, personal anecdotes often play a larger role in motivating a member to act. Other essential elements of a two-way communication include an explicit request for support from the member. Be sure to indicate how the member can show their support (e.g., introducing a bill, cosponsoring a bill, supporting funding). If appropriate, an advocate may discuss follow-up communication and in all cases, an advocate should express appreciation for the meeting.

Advocacy is only one way that constituents may get involved in the political process. A good way to gain access to members of Congress is to become involved in their political campaigns. Early involvement assures the best people get elected and the member hears your voice. Participating in, or organizing, fundraisers that benefit members are other ways to build a mutually beneficial relationship with members. Finally, joining a political action committee, which is a private group that raises funds for federal elections, can be another way to get involved.

CONCLUSION

Rehabilitation psychologists need to understand basic concepts affecting health insurance and access to care for people with disabling and chronic health conditions. Rehabilitation incurs significant costs for health payers. Consequently, payment for rehabilitation involves unique factors important to rehabilitation psychology. Lastly, rehabilitation psychologists need to appreciate how to influence health policy through advocacy and effective communication with members of Congress.

References

American Psychological Association Education Directorate. (2004). *Advancing psychology education and training: A psychologist's guide to federal advocacy* [Brochure]. Washington, DC: American Psychological Association.

American Psychological Association Presidential Task Force on Evidence-Based Practice. (2006). Evidenced-based practice in psychology. *American Psychologist, 61,* 271–285.

American Psychological Association Public Policy Office. (2005). *Influencing the congressional process: Garnering federal support.* Workshop conducted at the annual meeting of the American Psychological Association, Washington, DC.

Barton, P. L. (2003). *Understanding the U.S. health services system* (2nd ed.). Chicago: Health Administration Press.

Bates, D. W., Leape, L. L., Cullen, D. J., Laird, N., Petersen, L. A., Teich, J. M., et al. (1998). Effect of computerized physician order entry and a team inter-vention on prevention of serious medication errors. *JAMA, 280,* 1311–1316.

Bingaman, J., Frank, R. G., & Billy, C. L. (1993). Combining a global budget with a market driven system: Can it be done? *American Psychologist, 48,* 270–276.

Enthoven, A. C., & Fuchs, V. R. (2006). Employer-based health insurance: Past, present, and future. *Health Affairs, 25,* 1538–1547.

Etheredge, L. M. (2007). Technologies of health policy. *Health Affairs, 26,* 1537–1539. Retrieved January 8, 2009, from http://content.healthaffairs.org/cgi/content/full/26/6/1537?maxtoshow=&HITS=10&hits=10&RESULTFORMAT=&author1=Etheredge%2C+L.+M.&andorexactfulltext=and&searchid=1&FIRSTINDEX=0&resourcetype=HWCIT

Evans, C. H., & Degutis, L. C. (2003). What it takes for congress to act. *American Journal of Health Promotion, 18,* 177–181.

Frank, R. G., Farmer, J. E., & Klapow, J. C. (2003). The relevance of health policy to the future of clinical health psychology. In S. Llewely & P. Kennedy (Eds.), *Handbook of clinical health psychology* (pp. 547–561). Sussex, England: Wiley.

Frank, R. G., Hagglund, K. J., & Farmer, J. E. (2004). Chronic illness management in primary care: The Cardinal Symptoms Model. In R. G. Frank, S. H. McDaniel, J. H. Bray, & M. Heldring (Eds.), *Primary care psychology* (pp. 259–275). Washington, DC: American Psychological Association.

Fuchs, V. R. (2007). What are the prospects for enduing comprehensive health care reform? *Health Affairs, 26,* 1542–1544. Retrieved January 8, 2009, from http://content.healthaffairs.org/cgi/content/full/26/6/1542?maxtoshow=&HITS=10&hits=10&RESULTFORMAT=&author1=V.+R.+Fuchs&andorexactfulltext=and&searchid=1&FIRSTINDEX=0&volume=26&firstpage=1542&resourcetype=

Gosfield, A. G., & Reinertsen, J. L. (2005). The 100,000 lives campaign: Crystallizing standards of care for hospitals. *Health Affairs, 24,* 1560–1570. Retrieved January 8, 2009, from http://content.healthaffairs.org/cgi/content/full/24/6/1560?maxtoshow=&HITS=10&hits=10&RESULTFORMAT=&author1=Gosfield%2C+A.+G.%2C+%26+Reinertsen%2C+J.+L.&andorexactfulltext=and&searchid=1&FIRSTINDEX=0&volume=24&firstpage=1560&resourcetype=HWCIT

Greenwald, L. M. (2000). Medicare risk-adjusted capitation payments: From research to implementation. *Health Care Financing Review, 21*(3), 1–5.

Institute of Medicine. (2000). *To err is human: Building a safer health system.* Washington, DC: National Academy Press.

Institute of Medicine. (2001). *Crossing the quality chasm: A new health delivery system for the twenty-first century.* Washington, DC: National Academy Press.

Institute for Healthcare Improvement. (2007). Overview of the 100,000 Lives Campaign. Retrieved December 22, 2008, from http://www.ihi.org/IHI/Programs/Campaign/100KCampaignOverviewArchive.htm

Institute for Healthcare Improvement. (2007, December). Protecting 5 million lives from harm. Retrieved December 22, 2008, from http://www.ihi.org/NR/rdonlyres/BE0083C9-1CCC-46BB-A826-A5D6BDB16950/5557/IHI5MillionLivesCampaignBrochure.pdf

Johnstone, B., Frank, R. G., Belar, C., Berk, S., Bieliauskas, L. A., Bigler, E. D., et al. (1995). Psychology in health care: Future directions. *Professional Psychology: Research and Practice, 26,* 341–365.

Kaiser Commission on Medicaid and the Uninsured. (2007). *The uninsured: A primer.* Retrieved December 22, 2008, from www.kff.org/uninsured/7451.cfm

Kronick, R. Gilmer, T., Dreyfus, T., & Lee, L. (2000). Improving health-based payment for Medicaid beneficiaries: CDPS. *Health Care Financing Review, 21*(3), 29–64.

Kuhmerker, K., & Hartman, T. (2007). *Pay-for-performance in state Medicaid programs: A survey of state Medicaid directors and programs.* Washington, DC: The Commonwealth Fund.

Newhouse, J. P. (1993). *Free for all? Lessons from the RAND health insurance experiment.* Cambridge: Harvard University Press.

Office of Senator Hillary Rodham Clinton. (2007). *Health IT passes senate committee.* Retrieved December 18, 2007, from http://www.senate.gov/~clinton/news/statements/record.cfm?id=277936

Organization for Economic Cooperation and Development. (2008). *OECD Health Data 2008.* Retrieved December 22, 2008, from http://www.oecd.org/health/healthdata

Poon, E. G., Blumenthal, D., Jaggi, T., Honour, M. M., Bates, D. W., & Kaushal, R. (2004). Overcoming the barriers to adopting and implementing computerized physician order entry systems in U.S. hospitals. *Health Affairs, 23,* 184–190. Retrieved December 22, 2008, from http://content.healthaffairs.org/cgi/content/full/23/4/184

Reinhardt, U. E., Hussey, P. S., & Anderson, G. F. (2002). Cross-national comparisons of health systems using OECD data, 1999. *Health Affairs, 21,* 169–181. Retrieved December 22, 2008, from http://content.healthaffairs.org/cgi/content/full/21/3/169

Robinson, J. C. (2004). Reinvention of health insurance in the consumer era. *JAMA, 291,* 1880–1886.

Roper, W. L. (2007). Here we go again: Lessons on health reform. *Health Affairs, 26,* 1551–1552. Retrieved January 8, 2009, from http://content.healthaffairs.org/cgi/content/full/26/6/1551?maxtoshow=&HITS=10&hits=10&RESULTFORMAT=&author1=w+l+roper&andorexactfulltext=and&searchid=1&FIRSTINDEX=0&firstpage=1551&resourcetype=HWCIT

Starr, P. (1982). *The social transformation of American medicine.* New York: Basic Books.

Weinstein, J. N., Bronner, K. K., Morgan, T. S., & Wennberg, J. E. (2004). Trends and geographic variations in major surgery for degenerative diseases of the hip, knee, and spine. *Health Affairs, 23,* VAR-81-VAR-89. Retrieved December 22, 2008, from http://content.healthaffairs.org/cgi/content/full/hlthaff.var.81/DC3

Wennberg, J. E., Fisher, E. S., & Skinner, J. S. (2002). Geography and the debate over Medicare reform. *Health Affairs, 10,* W96–W114. Retrieved December 22, 2008, from http://content.healthaffairs.org/cgi/content/full/hlthaff.w2.96v1/DC1

Wennberg, J. E., Fisher, E. S., Skinner, J. S., & Bronner, K. K. (2007). Extending the P4P agenda: Part 2. How Medicare can reduce waste and improve the care of the chronically ill. *Health Affairs, 26,* 1575–1585.

Wennberg, J. E., O'Conner, A. M., Collins, E. D., & Weinstein, J. N. (2007). Extending the P4P agenda: Part 1. How Medicare can improve patient decision-making and reduce unnecessary care. *Health Affairs, 26,* 1564–1574.

CHAPTER 32

THE REHABILITATION TEAM

Lester Butt and Bruce Caplan

Rehabilitation has historically been a team enterprise, in recognition of the multifaceted needs of most patients requiring treatment, and psychologists have often, albeit not always, been considered "core" team members. "Regardless of setting or area of specialization, the rehabilitation psychologist is consistently involved in interdisciplinary teamwork" (Scherer et al., in press). However, there is a paucity of research that substantiates the benefit of the team concept, perhaps an understandable fact given the complexity, diversity, and idiosyncrasies of rehabilitation teams and the consequent difficulty of studying them empirically. (However, see Sander & Constantinidou, 2008, for a discussion of team functioning in treatment of traumatic brain injury.) Nonetheless, teams of various shapes and sizes are the rule in many rehabilitation centers.

This chapter briefly reviews the history of the team concept; describes differences among three theoretical models of team functioning; discusses some potential conflicts between and challenges to hospital administrators, staff, patients, and families; offers a review of the rehabilitation team literature; and considers the multiplicity of roles the rehabilitation psychologist can play to promote optimal team functioning. The chapter concludes with a discussion of factors believed to constitute the foundation of a high-level rehabilitation team, a multidisciplinary cadre of professionals working to assist an injured individual's transition from acute rehabilitation to a constructive and satisfying posthospital life.

BRIEF HISTORY OF THE TREATMENT TEAM

The team concept is not unique to rehabilitation, having been endorsed in primary care medicine (Dingwall, 1980), psychiatry (Ovretviet, 1986; Royal College of Psychiatrists, 1984), pain management (Flor, Fydrich, & Turk, 1992), and in health care in general (Furnell, Flett, & Clarke, 1987). Brown (1982) conceptualized several distinct periods in the evolution of medical treatment teams in the United States. Before World War II, treatment teams were rare, but medicine's increasing complexity, expanding scientific knowledge base, development of new technologies, and creation of new specialties virtually mandated coordinated multidisciplinary care. Howard Rusk, considered the father of comprehensive rehabilitation medicine, was a pioneer of the multidisciplinary approach in the postwar period (Rusk, 1969).

In the 1960s and 1970s in the United States, the intuitive value of teams attracted a wide array of health professionals' interest. Some institutions created diagnosis-specific teams for conditions such as traumatic brain injury or spinal cord injury (e.g., Dunn, Sommer, & Gambina, 1992). Although certifying agencies such as the Joint Commission on Accreditation of Healthcare Organizations and the Commission on Accreditation of Rehabilitation Facilities generally do not define specific treatment team composition, physicians, nurses, physical and occupational therapists, psychologists, and social workers are typically considered to form the core of the team.

TEAM MODELS: STRENGTHS AND CHALLENGES

According to Furnell et al. (1987), clinical teams possess the following characteristics: Professionals from different disciplines regularly convene, team objectives are pursued by all team members, there is agreement regarding explicit shared objectives that determine the team's structure and function, adequate clinical and administrative coordination to support the work of the team are present, and there is a clear differentiation and respect for unique skills and roles played by individual team members. Nijhuis et al. (2007) reviewed the pediatric literature and identified five key elements of good team functioning: communication, decision making, goal setting, organization, and team process. Research has demonstrated the importance of these factors for team functioning (Wageman, 2001).

Contemporary rehabilitation has witnessed the emergence of several models of treatment teams: the multidisciplinary, interdisciplinary, and transdisciplinary approaches, each with advantages and disadvantages. Members of the differing disciplines on multidisciplinary teams work collaboratively, but with separate roles and distinct rehabilitation goals, conducting independent evaluations. Mullins, Keller, and Chaney (1994) and Woodruff and McGonigle (1988) noted that this approach could lead to fragmented care, especially if team communication is faulty. Additionally, Linder (1983) argued that the multidisciplinary approach could lead to divergent and antithetical goals and expectations from different team members.

The interdisciplinary model is predicated on the alternate assumption of overlap of roles and functions across team members. Eames (1989) referred to this concept as the "blurring and sharing of roles," which may require staff to "learn and develop new skills, which may be outside their normal professional requirements and experience" (p. 52). This model's inherent challenges include the mandate for team members to communicate collaboratively and openly, negotiate priorities, reconcile potential role conflicts, and resolve differences about treatment decisions. The interdisciplinary model places a premium on sharing of assessment findings, development of communal goals, negotiation of responsibilities, and interdisciplinary collaboration while maintaining one's unique discipline identity.

The further extension of the interdisciplinary model is the transdisciplinary approach, in which each team member assumes roles and responsibilities that significantly overlap with those of other disciplines. Mullins et al. (1994) labeled this concept *role release,* implying the virtual elimination of disciplinary lines. This model's ultimate goal is the promotion of a unified treatment plan implemented by all members, regardless of training and discipline. The challenges of this approach are vast, including, but not limited to, reimbursement concerns, communication demands, personalities of team members, the mandate to share one's expertise and skills, and the ability to divest from one's discipline-specific training.

Critiques of, and cautions about, the treatment team models are plentiful. For example, Diller (1990) opined that rehabilitation professionals "have not developed an adequate theory of teams and the logic under which they operate" (p. 277). Wood (2003) stated,

> Instead of providing a clinical utopia, attempts to establish and implement rehabilitation teams often flounder on the rocks of personality conflict, role ambiguity, status problems, or the lack of a clinical model that will provide a framework for team activities and direct efforts in a way that unifies clinical staff rather than fragments them. (p. 49)

Certain dilemmas exist as consequences of the treatment team structure. Gans (1987) listed five domains that are catalysts for conflict: intrinsic differences between staff and patients, the institutional nature of the rehabilitation hospital setting, the phenomenology of catastrophic illness, staff's insufficient psychological training, and the goal-oriented nature of rehabilitation. Noting the few scientific studies on team effectiveness, Strasser and Falconer (1997a) held that "the team approach is more an act of faith than a proven strategy in inpatient medical rehabilitation" (p. 15). Nonetheless, rehabilitation teams appear to have "kept the faith," despite abundant countervailing forces in contemporary health care.

TREATMENT TEAM LITERATURE REVIEW

In 1976, Halstead surveyed the 1950 to 1975 literature on team care in chronic illness and disability and discerned three major categories of support for its value: the *opinion base* solely reflected faith in the efficacy of the team approach, the *descriptive base* contained personal testimony of programs using the team concept, and the *study base* included empirical endeavors evaluating team effectiveness. Only 10 studies qualified for the study base designation, of which just five involved comprehensive rehabilitation. Halstead concluded,

> The concept of team care has become an integral part of health delivery for persons with chronic illness. The accumulated material of the past quarter century relating to team care can best be described as a literature explosion as opposed to an information explosion. This should not obscure the fact, however, that there are a few good solid studies concerning the effectiveness of team care, which demonstrates that research is indeed possible and suggests that the overall effects are beneficial. (pp. 510–511)

Studies since the mid-1980s reached diverse conclusions regarding the efficacy of coordinated team treatment. For example, equivocal findings were obtained in a comparison of traditional and coordinated team care during acute stroke rehabilitation (Wood-Dauphinee et al., 1984) and in a study of treatment of rheumatoid arthritis (Ahlmen, Sullivan, & Bjelle, 1988). In contrast, reports from geriatrics (Applegate et al., 1990), the intensive care unit (Shortell et al., 1995), and the emergency room (Georgopoulos, 1986) found that organizational structures and processes associated with teams (e.g., effective communication, constructive leadership, conflict-resolution skills) led to improved outcomes. Also contrasting with the findings of Wood-Dauphinee et al. are the positions of Dombovy,

Sandok, and Basford (1986) and Ottenbacher and Jannell (1993), whose reviews noted the superiority of specialized stroke rehabilitation units (presumably using a team approach) over services delivered within general hospitals where care is less likely to be team-based. Furthermore, the effectiveness of a coordinated team approach to pain management was shown by the reviews of Flor et al. (1992), Turk and Okifuji (2002), and Guzman, Esmail, and Karjalainen (2001).

Cifu and Stewart (1999) concluded from their review of 16 studies of stroke rehabilitation that interdisciplinary team treatment produced shorter lengths of stay, better functional outcomes, reduced costs, and improved quality of life compared with treatment by a multidisciplinary team. Lincoln, Walker, Dixon, and Knights (2004) reported that stroke survivors who received care from a community stroke team were more satisfied with their emotional support, and their caregivers less distressed and better-informed about stroke than those who were given routine care.

Strasser, Falconer, and Martino-Saltzmann (1994) examined interprofessional relationships within the rehabilitation treatment team. They concluded,

> Despite the philosophical importance of the team approach in rehabilitation, work-related identity and authority reside in the profession. When conflict arises between the interests of various reference groups, one aligns with the most powerful reference group, which is usually the profession. The interprofessional discord expressed by team members may reflect the tension between one's professional identity and other reference groups where overlapping or conflicting authority exists. (p. 180)

In a subsequent report, Strasser, Smits, Falconer, Herrin, and Bowen (2002) studied the impact of hospital culture on team functioning in 50 Veterans Administration Hospitals. They found that those hospitals characterized as personal and dynamic, in contrast to formal and bureaucratic, had higher ratings of team effectiveness. Strasser and his colleagues (2008) recently demonstrated that a structured training program can effectively educate staff about team processes and structures. Equally important, they found greater functional improvement in patients treated by staff who had participated in the training than in patients under the care of staff in an "information only" condition. Their 6-month program included a workshop, development of action plans to improve teamwork, and use of telephone and video consultations.

Evans, Sherer, Nakase-Richardson, Mani, and Irby (2008) evaluated the impact of a training program designed to improve rehabilitation staff members' skills in such techniques as building rapport, effective listening, and managing difficult patients, all in the service of improving the therapeutic alliance between staff and patients. Although ratings of the alliance did not differ between the experimental participants and historical controls, those in the former group had superior function at discharge. Given the complexity and heterogeneity of the pertinent research, including diversity of patient populations, team composition, leadership styles, team processes, and team communication skills, it is difficult to cogently integrate the empirical data. Nonetheless, given the ever-mounting stress on efficiency, economy, and accountability, it is unlikely that team treatment approaches would have persisted if they did not achieve these aims.

REHABILITATION PSYCHOLOGIST ROLES ON THE TEAM

The rehabilitation psychologist can fulfill many roles in the service of improving rehabilitation team functioning. He or she can serve as an advocate to administration and departmental chairs regarding the importance of quality psychosocial care. The rehabilitation psychologist can also be an educator, attuning colleagues to deleterious patterns of interaction, assisting in conflict resolution techniques, and modeling supportive team behaviors. The rehabilitation psychologist can help staff appreciate individual differences and integrate these elements into well-defined treatment plans. Assisting colleagues to understand and manage noncompliant patient behaviors is instrumental for effective team

functioning. Additional roles embraced by the rehabilitation psychologist may include, but are not limited to, team leader (Brown & Folen, 2005), researcher, patient and family advocate, consensus builder, problem-solver, risk manager, system analyzer, mediator, negotiator, modeler of self-care and reflection, sounding board, debriefer, and treatment team visionary.

CHARACTERISTICS OF THE OPTIMAL REHABILITATIVE TREATMENT TEAM

We now briefly consider what we believe to be the fundamental structural features and process elements of effective teams. For other (partially related) views, see Brown and Bishop (1980); Dunn, Sommer, and Gambina (1992); and Strasser and Falconer (1997b).

Team Structure

The essential structural component is a consistent cadre of clinicians comprising a specific treatment team and a structure that ensures transmission of requisite clinical information to all shifts in the service of continuity of care. This promotes consistency of treatment goals and minimizes potential fragmentation of care. There must be a collective commitment to a common set of values, mission, beliefs, and norms that forms the basis for the institutional culture. Discipline-specific roles and skills that are clearly defined promote cohesion and solidarity. Furthermore, administrators endeavor to minimize distracting bureaucratic demands on the team, as they appreciate the priority of the clinical imperative. There is an understanding that by providing the highest quality rehabilitation (i.e., even if some activities, such as case conferences and retreats, are not directly billable) all parties benefit. This includes insurers who, because of reduced recidivism and secondary complications, have reduced costs. More effective teams are characterized by fluid leadership, depending on the unique demands of the clinical situation. Although there is usually a titular head, this vertical approach yields to a horizontal one when specific patient-related circumstances dictate. Most important, the whole of the team far surpasses the sum of its parts.

Team Process

Contributions of specific disciplines are not static, but vary from case to case. Furthermore, the team recognizes that patients tend preferentially to embrace disciplines (e.g., physical therapy) whose treatments symbolize hope, change, and potential cure while eschewing those (e.g., occupational therapy, psychology) that focus on management of the consequences of the disability. Grasping this dynamic, the team strives to prevent interdisciplinary rivalries, educating patients and families on the dual foci of rehabilitation, to contend with current realities while striving for an improved tomorrow. The team knows that hope should never be abandoned, as it can be a motivator for involvement in rehabilitation and life afterward. The team appreciates that patient resistance should be gently challenged but its genesis and purposes understood. Reality of a disability and its consequences cannot be "force-fed." Patients' styles and schedules for accommodating their disabilities vary, and these differences must be expected and accepted.

The superior team is not tied to one treatment model or paradigm but is patient-centered and lets unique patient features drive the treatment approach; this entails consideration of both their premorbid background and current status. Although recognizing the deficits of the patient, the team is also aware of the patient's strengths, skills, and competencies and goals, even if these bring them into conflict with the team. Using a flexible treatment algorithm, therapy aims to maximize positive outcome and heighten motivation. The team focuses on the person, not the patient, reducing the propensity for pathological labeling (Caplan & Shechter, 1993). Treatment is performed with, not to, the person, as the team knows that quality rehabilitation results from the alliance between clinicians and those they serve. One feature of this successful alliance is the congruence between treatment philosophy and treatments that are mutually derived. In contrast to acute care medicine, where the patient is the passive recipient of care, rehabilitation decision making is collaborative, collegial, and mutual.

The effective rehabilitation team learns from experience, profiting from discussion about both good and lesser outcomes. Such on-the-job education is necessary because, as Sander and Constantinidou (2008) noted, most training programs do not include exposure to interdisciplinary teamwork. Patient complaints regarding specific disciplines are objectively assessed without staff splitting or team fragmentation. When confronted by problematic patient behaviors, the team understands that "the goal of rehabilitation is adequate preparation for life in the community, not in the hospital. In the real world, it is often productive to be strong willed, even stubborn, and to question authority" (Caplan & Reidy, 1996, p. 31). The team strives to understand, not simply label and criticize.

CONCLUSION

The team concept has an honorable pedigree in rehabilitation despite the relative paucity of empirical support for its effectiveness. Given the profoundly catastrophic nature of many of the injuries and conditions encountered in rehabilitation and the emotional toll this can take on treating staff, the importance of the availability of support from similarly stressed colleagues should not be minimized. The structural, organizational, and functional complexity of the rehabilitation treatment team is self-evident. As a result, a successful team does not emerge without commitment, risk taking, energy, and focus, the cultivation of which is the responsibility of all team members. Exemplary team functioning is a major determinant in the transition from a system of care to a system that cares. Herein, all components of the treatment system—patients, families, and rehabilitation professionals—are treated with respect, support, and sensitivity, and all parts of this highly interdependent system consequently benefit.

References

Ahlmen, M., Sullivan, M., & Bjelle, A. (1988). Team versus nonteam outpatient care in rheumatoid arthritis: A comprehensive outcome evaluation including an overall health measure. *Arthritis and Rheumatism, 31,* 471–479.

Applegate, W. B., Miller, S. T., Grancy, M. J., Elam, J. T., Burns, R., & Akins, D. E. (1990). A randomized, controlled trial of a geriatric assessment unit in a community rehabilitation hospital. *New England Journal of Medicine, 322,* 1572–1578.

Brown J. A., & Bishop, D. (1980). Team functioning: A professional versus lay perspective. In D. Bishop (Ed.), *Behavioral problems and the disabled: Assessment and management* (pp. 378–400). Baltimore: Williams & Wilkins.

Brown, K. S., & Folen, R. A. (2005). Psychologists as leaders of multidisciplinary chronic pain management teams: A model for health care delivery. *Professional Psychology: Research and Practice, 36,* 587–594.

Brown, T. M. (1982). An historical view of health care teams. In G. J. Agich (Ed.), *Responsibility in health care* (pp. 3–21). Dordrecht, the Netherlands: D. Reidel.

Caplan, B., & Reidy, K. (1996). Staff–patient–family conflicts in rehabilitation: Sources and solutions. *Topics in Spinal Cord Injury Rehabilitation, 2*(2), 21–33.

Caplan, B., & Shechter, J. (1993). Reflections on the "depressed," "unrealistic," "inappropriate," "manipulative," "unmotivated," "noncompliant," "denying," "maladjusted," "regressed," etc. patient. *Archives of Physical Medicine and Rehabilitation, 74,* 1123–1124.

Cifu, D., & Stewart, D. (1999). Factors affecting functional outcome after stroke: A critical review of rehabilitation interventions. *Archives of Physical Medicine and Rehabilitation, 80,* S35–S39.

Diller, L. (1990). Fostering the interdisciplinary team: Fostering research in a society in transition. *Archives of Physical Medicine and Rehabilitation, 71,* 275–278.

Dingwall, R. (1980). Problems of team work in primary care. In S. Londale, A. Webb, & T. Briggs (Eds.), *Team work in the personal social services and health care.* London: Croom Helm.

Dombovy, M. L., Sandok, B. A., & Basford, J. R. (1986). Rehabilitation for stroke: A review. *Stroke, 17,* 363–369.

Dunn, M., Sommer, N., & Gambina, H. (1992). A practical guide to team functioning in spinal cord injury rehabilitation. In C. P. Zejdlik (Ed.), *Management of spinal cord injury* (2nd ed., pp. 229–239). Boston: Jones and Bartlett Publishers.

Eames, P. G. (1989). Head injury rehabilitation: Towards a "model" service. In R. L. I. Wood & P. G. Eames (Eds.), *Models of brain injury rehabilitation.* London: Croom Helm.

Evans, C., Sherer, M., Nakase-Richardson, R., Mani, T., & Irby, J. (2008). Evaluation of an interdisciplinary team intervention to improve therapeutic alliance in postacute brain injury rehabilitation. *Journal of Head Trauma Rehabilitation, 23,* 329–338.

Flor, H., Fydrich, T., & Turk, D. C., (1992). Efficacy of multidisciplinary pain treatment centers: A meta-analytic review. *Pain, 49,* 221–230.

Furnell, J., Flett, S., & Clarke, D. F. (1987, January). Multidisciplinary clinical teams: Some issues in establishment and function. *Hospital and Health Services Review,* 15–18.

Gans, J. (1987). Facilitating patient-staff interactions in rehabilitation. In B. Caplan (Ed.), *Rehabilitation psychology desk reference* (pp. 185–218). Rockville, MD: Aspen Publishers.

Georgopoulos, B. S. (1986). *Organizational structure, problem solving, and effectiveness.* San Francisco: Jossey-Bass.

Guzman, J., Esmail, R., & Karjalainen, K. (2001). Multidisciplinary rehabilitation for chronic low back pain: Systematic review. *British Medical Journal, 322,* 1511–1516.

Halstead, L. S. (1976). Team care in chronic illness: A critical review of the literature of the past 25 years. *Archives of Physical Medicine and Rehabilitation, 58,* 507–511.

Halstead, L. S., Rintala, D. H., Kanellos, M., Griffin, B., Higgins, L., Rheinecker, S., et al. (1986). The innovative rehabilitation team: An experiment in team building. *Archives of Physical Medicine and Rehabilitation, 67,* 357–361.

Lincoln, N. B., Walker, M. F., Dixon, A., & Knights, P. (2004). Evaluation of a multiprofessional community stroke team: A randomized controlled trial. *Clinical Rehabilitation, 18,* 40–47.

Linder, T. (1983). *Early childhood special education: Program development and administration.* Baltimore: Brookes Publishing.

Mullins, L. L., Keller, J. R., & Chaney, J. M. (1994). A systems and social cognitive approach to team functioning in physical rehabilitation settings. *Rehabilitation Psychology, 39,* 161–178.

Nijhuis, B. J., Reinders-Messelink, H. A., de Blecourt, A. C., Olijve, W. G., Groothoof, J. W., Nakken, H., & Postema, K. (2007). A review of salient elements defining team collaboration in paediatric rehabilitation. *Clinical Rehabilitation, 21,* 195–211.

Ottenbacher, K. J., & Jannell, S. (1993). The results of clinical trials in stroke rehabilitation research. *Archives of Neurology, 50,* 37–44.

Ovretveit, J. (1986). *Organisation of multidisciplinary community teams.* Uxbridge, England: Health Services Centre, Brunel University.

Royal College of Psychiatrists. (1984). The responsibility of consultants in psychiatry. *Bulletin of the Royal College of Psychiatrists, 8,* 123–126.

Rusk, H. A. (1969). The growth and development of rehabilitation medicine. *Archives of Physical Medicine and Rehabilitation, 50,* 463–466.

Sander, A., & Constantinidou, F. (2008). Preface to special issue: The interdisciplinary team. *Journal of Head Trauma Rehabilitation, 23,* 271–272.

Scherer, M., Blair, K., Bost, R., Hanson, S., Hough, S., Kurylo, M., et al. (in press). Rehabilitation psychology. In I. B. Weiner & W. E. Craighead (Eds.), *The concise Corsini encyclopedia of psychology and behavioral science* (4th ed.). Hoboken, NJ: Wiley.

Shortell, S. M., O'Brien, J. L., Carman, J. M., Foster, R. W., Hughes, E. F. X., Boerstler, H., & O'Connor, E. J. (1995). Assessing the impact of continuous quality improvement/total quality management: Concept versus implementation. *Health Services Research, 30,* 377–401.

Strasser, D. C., & Falconer, J. A. (1997a). Linking treatment to outcomes through teams: Building a conceptual model of rehabilitation effectiveness. *Topics in Stroke Rehabilitation, 4,* 15–27.

Strasser, D. C., & Falconer, J. A. (1997b). Rehabilitation team process. *Topics in Stroke Rehabilitation, 4,* 34–39.

Strasser, D. C., Falconer, J. A., & Martino-Saltzmann, D. (1994). The rehabilitation team: Staff perceptions of the hospital environment, the interdisciplinary team environment, and interprofessional relations. *Archives of Physical Medicine and Rehabilitation, 75,* 177–182.

Strasser, D. C., Falconer, J. A., Stevens, A. B., Uomoto, J. M., Herrin, J. S., Bowen, S. E., & Burridge, A. B. (2008). Team training and stroke rehabilitation outcomes: A cluster randomized trial. *Archives of Physical Medicine and Rehabilitation,* 89, 10–15.

Strasser, D. C., Smits, S. S., Falconer, J. A., Herrin, J. S., & Bowen, S. E. (2002). The influence of hospital culture on rehabilitation team functioning in VA hospitals. *Journal of Rehabilitation Research and Development, 39,* 115–125.

Turk, D. C., & Okifuji, A., (2002). Psychological factors in chronic pain: Evolution and revolution. *Journal of Counseling and Clinical Psychology, 70,* 678–690.

Wageman, R. (2001). How leaders foster self-managing team effectiveness: Design choice versus hands-on coaching. *Organizational Science, 12,* 559–577.

Wood, R. L. I. (2003). The rehabilitation team. In R. J. Greenwood, M. P. Barnes, T. M. McMillan, & C. D. Ward (Eds.), *Handbook of neurological rehabilitation* (pp. 41–51). New York: Psychology Press.

Wood-Dauphinee, S., Shapiro, S., Bass E., Fletcher, C., Georges, P., Hensby, V., & Mendelsohn, B. (1984). A randomized trial of team care following stroke. *Stroke, 15,* 864–872.

Woodruff, G., & McGonigle, J. J. (1988). Early intervention team approaches: The transdisciplinary model. In J. B. Jordon (Ed.), *Early childhood special education.* Reston, VA: Council for Exceptional Children.

CHAPTER 33

REHABILITATING THE HEALTH CARE ORGANIZATION: ADMINISTERING PSYCHOLOGY'S OPPORTUNITY

Charles D. Callahan

It has been nearly 2 decades since rehabilitation was boldly declared as "psychology's greatest opportunity" (Frank, Gluck, & Buckelew, 1990). In many ways, time has shown this to have been a credible assertion. Today, approximately 33 million Americans (10% of the population) have daily life activity limitations stemming from a chronic health condition (Robert Wood Johnson Foundation, 2004). Since 1990, membership in the American Psychological Association's (APA's) clinical health-related divisions (i.e., rehabilitation, neuropsychology, health) grew at five times the rate of overall APA membership, indicative of professional interest in applying scientist–practitioner methods to facilitate participation outcomes among those with physical health concerns (APA, 2006a). Specialized billing codes for both behavioral interventions and cognitive assessment with medical patients are now available (APA, 2006b; see also chap. 15, this volume). Finally, median salaries for rehabilitation and other clinical health psychologists exceed those of other doctoral psychologists, providing another indication that the opportunity has to some extent been realized (Medical Group Management Association, 2005; U.S. Department of Labor, 2003).

Yet, rehabilitation psychology's opportunity does not lie exclusively in direct clinical service provision but also in the application of psychological principles and methods in the exercise of health care organizational leadership (Callahan, 2005). Frank and Elliott (2000) suggested this potential in their assertion that doctoral rehabilitation psychologists are "best suited for roles in research, treatment planning/

development, and *administration* [italics added]" (p. 647). This chapter makes the case that significant leadership needs exist in the nation's health care organizations and that rehabilitation psychologists possess specialized competencies well-matched to these needs. Through advancement by some of its members to health care executive leadership roles, rehabilitation psychology can capitalize on the foretold professional opportunity in the pursuit of effective advocacy for our clients and our profession.

A HEALTH CARE SYSTEM IN NEED OF REHABILITATION

Despite amazing technological and procedural advances that allow dramatic reductions in mortality, morbidity, and suffering, many signs point to a health care system in need of rehabilitation. The Institute of Medicine (1999) reported that more than 1 million injuries and nearly 100,000 deaths occur annually in the U.S. health care system due to medical errors. This places medical error as the eighth leading cause of adult death, with heart disease and stroke being the first and third, respectively (Herzlinger, 2006). Despite spending proportionally more on health care than any other industrialized nation (16% of U.S. gross domestic product in 2006), the United States scores in the bottom third of industrialized nations in life expectancy and other key indicators of health care quality (Bente, 2005; Chernew, Hirth, & Cutler, 2003; Commonwealth Fund, 2004).

Shortages of essential professional health care staff appear to be a chronic condition. By 2020, demand for registered nurses will exceed supply by more then 800,000 workers, and double-digit vacancy rates are common for many other health care professions, including rehabilitation therapists (American Hospital Association, 2002; Herman, Olivo, & Gioia, 2002; U.S. Department of Health and Human Services, 2002). Although community hospital profit margins improved to an average return of approximately 5% in 2004, this level is barely sufficient to maintain current clinical technology and facility infrastructure, much less afford the significant new information technology required to achieve the safety benefits of a truly electronic medical record (Hoppszallern, 2003; Institute of Medicine, 2001).

Add a simultaneously increasing demand for health care services driven in part by an aging population (U.S. General Accounting Office, 2003), and the fact that more than 40 million Americans lack health insurance and associated access to care (Herzlinger, 2006), and a troubling portrait emerges. Clearly, an industry balancing tremendous opportunities and challenges requires strong leadership to be successful. Unfortunately, health care currently faces a daunting leadership void and impending experience gap: Industry analysts lament an even deeper void in the near future as increasing numbers of senior executives retire from a field with an insufficient pool of successor talent because of chronic undervaluing of leadership development activities (Burt, 2005; Dye, 2000; Thrall, 2001) and the expansion of viable career options outside of health care. This leadership void represents an opportunity for rehabilitation psychology.

THE EFFECTIVE HEALTH CARE EXECUTIVE

Whereas management can be said to focus on the completion of tasks through defining and controlling how things are done, leadership involves persuading others to set aside their individual concerns to pursue a common goal that is important for the welfare of the team or group (Hogan, Curphy, & Hogan, 1994). O'Neal (2003) concluded that effective leaders manifest four characteristics: an unwavering vision of what needs to be done, a commitment to

making the vision a reality, an understanding of people, and the persuasiveness to convince or inspire them to follow. Importantly, effective leaders are able to facilitate empirically superior results by their teams or organizations (Collins, 2001) and achieve higher employee satisfaction and retention, thus reducing the huge costs and operational disruption of staff turnover (Herman et al., 2002).

Hamm (2006) extended this logic to argue that effective leaders "understand that their role is to bring out the answers in others. They do this by clearly and explicitly seeking contributions, challenges, and collaboration from the people who report to them, using their positional power not to dominate but rather to drive the decision-making process" (p. 120). Thus, the effective health care executive is a senior organizational leader with the charge of inspiring the organization to take responsibility for creating a future of improved health for its constituents and for effecting meaningful outcomes through the actions of committed team members (Butler & Waldroop, 2004; Drucker, 2004).

COMPETENCIES OF THE ORGANIZATIONAL/REHABILITATION PSYCHOLOGIST

By virtue of training and experience, competent doctoral level rehabilitation psychologists have much to offer as health care executives. In fact, given the aforementioned challenges in modern health care and the features of the effective executive, it is argued that rehabilitation psychologists possess five specific competencies well-matched to the role demands of executive leadership: clinical, analytical, relational, interventional, and ethical.

Clinical Competency

The mission of health care is to provide clinical services that improve people's health status. Rehabilitation psychologists have internalized the shared values and process knowledge of clinical providers who have served patients on the front lines of care. These values and experiences form vital bedrock on which the successful health care executive can grow. Sometimes referred to as "industry human capital" (Groysberg, McLean, &

Nohria, 2006), this is a sector-specific values and experience base that is lacking in the business executive transplanted from other industries.

The presence of such an informed clinical sense is invaluable in executing the duties of health care leadership. To begin with, it assists in establishing one's credibility and dedication to mission with physicians and staff members who are by nature suspicious of "suits" and "bean-counters." There is real strategic advantage in being perceived as the expert patient-care colleague who now offers administrative assistance as an executive with responsibility and authority. Further, a sound clinical sense will assist the executive in asking needed questions, balancing competing priorities, and setting organizational strategy in a manner that maintains focus on the health care organization's unique mission, vision, and values.

Analytical Competency

The current quality movement in health care demands "management by fact" (Institute of Medicine, 2001). Rehabilitation psychologists come from a rich psychometric assessment tradition allowing integration of discrete measurements into a meaningful holistic portrait that serves as the basis for action. This tradition provides reasonable levels of confidence and skepticism regarding the reliability, validity, and utility of applied data. Rehabilitation psychologists are experts in the measurement of present state and are among the few health care professionals able to empirically distinguish change from random variation. Further, applied statistical methods exist that can be effectively applied to a great variety of health care organizational issues (i.e., statistical process control; Callahan & Barisa, 2005; Callahan & Griffen, 2003). The analytical competency places rehabilitation psychologists in a unique and valuable position in an era dominated by calls for evidence-based practice and pay-for-performance reimbursement contingencies (Pfeffer & Sutton, 2006).

Relational Competency

Much of health care leadership is people management, in which an understanding of interpersonal transactions among staff, patients, and other stakeholders is the key to differentiating the successful versus

unsuccessful manager (Butler & Waldroop, 2004). Topics such as conflict management, increasing desired work behaviors, overcoming resistance to change, staff selection and development, and differentiating state versus trait behaviors are of keen interest to health care managers and parallel the kinds of issues that rehabilitation psychologists deal with every day in their clinical practices. Rehabilitation psychologists' historically close integration as dedicated interdisciplinary team members (i.e., vs. independent consultant–liaison) yields great potential for impact in a business model increasingly reliant on the success of work teams (Fischer & Boynton, 2005; Katzenbach & Smith, 1993).

Rehabilitation psychologist executives can deploy their relational competence toward recruitment and selection of managers on behalf of their organizations, in the process reducing significant external consultant fee expenditures while improving outcome. Hogan et al. (1994) reported that a leader's personality has predictable effects on team performance and can be used for both leadership selection and development purposes. Personality traits aligning to the so-called Big Five model of normal personality (McCrae & Costa, 1997) were shown to predict effective performance. Thus, leaders high on traits of extroversion (or surgency), emotional stability (i.e., low in neurotic or anxiety-prone tendencies), conscientiousness, agreeableness, and openness to new experience (i.e., who have a range of interests) were significantly more "effective" in terms of compensation, advancement, and peer ratings across a number of studies in industry.

Conversely, personality features predictive of "executive derailment" (i.e., job failure rates reported by the authors to be as high as 50% of all executive hires) included being perceived by others as arrogant, vindictive, untrustworthy, emotional, compulsive, overcontrolling, insensitive, abrasive, aloof, too ambitious, and/or unable to delegate or make decisions (Hogan et al., 1994). It is important that the Big Five model of normal personality has been validated in over 70 years of research and performs comparably across geographic, language, and cultural boundaries (McCrae & Costa, 1997), with stability of one's core personality style established by early adulthood and persisting with little

461

change through the geriatric years (Costa & McCrae, 1988).

Even in these challenging times of critical staff shortages and declining levels of reimbursement for services, it must be remembered that people per se are not the answer; the "right" people are the answer (Collins, 2001), and these right people must further be mentored into the right roles so they may best contribute. Thus, the relational competency is largely an assessment competency based on the organizational or rehabilitation psychologist's depth of knowledge in a variety of interrelated disciplines.

In applying the relational competency, it is helpful for the new administrative or team leader to heed Ellis and Harper's (1961) advice on the cognitive fallacy of seeking to be liked by almost everyone for almost everything that one does. Managers motivated by appeasement or conflict avoidance invariably create discord in their teams. Effective leaders select the right people for their teams, set expectations of the outcomes to be achieved, provide honest feedback regarding progress, and work to help team members find the roles in which they perform best, even to the point of helping them find other teams to be part of for mutual success (Buckingham & Coffman, 1999).

Finally, in today's increasingly culturally diverse workplace, the rehabilitation psychologist's understanding of the damaging effects of stereotype, misunderstanding, and deindividuation gleaned from disability studies can foster more effective ways of leveraging team members' uniqueness into important differential business advantage.

Interventional Competency

Rehabilitation psychologists are experts in the methods of behavior change. Clinical practice is based on the ability to develop, implement, and monitor a treatment intervention plan. These are precisely the same methods required for successful executive management. The ability to develop a strategic (i.e., action) plan, comprising discrete steps or components, and to deploy and modify that plan to achieve organizational goals is the basis for modern "management by objectives" performance appraisal systems and pay-for-performance reimbursement models.

The mechanisms (specific and nonspecific) for effective behavior change have been established, refined, and affirmed over the past century (Seligman, 1995). The good news is that these same mechanisms appear as applicable for personal growth interventions in the "normal" organizational setting as they are for emotional and behavioral disorder remediation in the clinical setting (Seligman, Steen, Park, & Peterson, 2005). Specific interventions designed to produce high-functioning (i.e., high reliability) interdisciplinary teams now exist and are beginning to be applied to health care (Wilson, Burke, Priest, & Salas, 2005). The interventional competency makes the organizational or rehabilitation psychologist–executive a dynamic change agent at a time when dynamic change is an operational necessity.

Ethical Competency

Recent well-publicized allegations of ethical violations committed by senior business leadership and the resultant criminal investigations make plain that a solid ethical compass is needed in the executive boardroom if the organization is going to sustain long-term adherence to its customer-focused and financial missions (Gardner, 2007). Consideration of ethical behavior has historically been prominent in professional psychology (e.g., in the ongoing evolution of a detailed ethical code of conduct, in the education curriculum of APA-approved doctoral training programs, in the licensing examination allowing applied clinical practice, in the board certification process). Such prominence is not yet achieved in even the most vaunted health or business administration graduate programs. APA's "Ethical Principles of Psychologists and Code of Conduct" (APA, 2002) provides a well-defined and evolving road map for professional behavior well-matched to today's business and regulatory climate.

Financial Competency

An important competency that is arguably not addressed by traditional rehabilitation psychology training and experience is the financial one. Health care is an increasingly "no margin, no mission" enterprise, and considerable administrative talent and effort is expended to keep abreast of ever-changing reimbursement and compliance regulations. Within the rehabilitation field, the controversy over the so-called 75% rule is an illustrative example. Originally implemented in 1983, this rule states that at least 75% of the annual admissions to a qualifying inpatient rehabilitation facility (IRF) must come from a list of 13 specific diagnoses deemed to require such intensive rehabilitation. Unfortunately, a 2003 RAND Corporation study commissioned by the Centers for Medicare and Medicaid (CMS) found that only 13% of IRFs across the nation were in compliance with this regulation, suggesting that IRFs had earned increased payments from Medicare by admitting large numbers of patients who did not require such intensive acute rehab services (i.e., orthopedic total joint replacements) while reducing services to patients with more intensive needs (i.e., brain injury).

CMS responded by promising staunch enforcement of the 75% rule beginning in July 2008, with penalties for noncompliance going as far as removal from the Medicare payment program. To aid in transition, CMS offered a stair step compliance threshold of 50% until June 30, 2005, and 65% until July 30, 2007, as a means for IRFs to undertake procedural changes to comply with the rule. At this writing, major rehabilitation constituencies (e.g., American Hospital Association, American Academy of Physical Medicine and Rehabilitation) are actively lobbying for abolition of the 75% rule entirely, lest its enforcement significantly threaten the financial viability of individual IRF provider organizations and/or access by persons who need such services. This example highlights the sensitive balance between regulatory compliance, reimbursement, patient and staff selection, operations and financial management. Those who aspire to senior administrative roles are well-advised to include financial management studies in their self-development plan.

AN EIGHT-POINT PROFESSIONAL DEVELOPMENT PLAN

Today's effective health care executive has three primary objectives: (a) to provide for the care of dependent people at the most vulnerable points in their lives, (b) to maintain the moral and social order of their organization through advocacy and mediation among competing values and interests, and (c) to increase the operational efficiency and financial stability of their organization (Haddock, McLean, & Chapman, 2002). Toward this end, some within our profession may seek to redefine themselves as organizational/rehabilitation psychologists in the pursuit of health care executive leadership roles. This chapter has attempted to demonstrate that core doctoral rehabilitation psychologist competencies translate exceedingly well into areas of need and that the skillful application of our particular assets could significantly enhance the work cultures and performance characteristics of the health care organizations in which we serve. Despite this goodness of fit, the pathway to the executive suite must not be intuitive or natural for rehabilitation psychologists; otherwise it would be more common. Certainly, there are areas of content knowledge (e.g., those related to financial management and business law) that are not addressed within our training curriculum. However, these are readily accessible through formal and informal avenues. Rather, the apparent novelty of the organizational/rehabilitation psychology approach may be because of other more dynamic forces. If necessity is the mother of invention, and dissatisfaction its father, then perhaps now is the time for some rehabilitation psychologists to thoughtfully consider applying their skills in new ways as executives to address unmet needs among the medical populations and organizations they serve. Such a path likewise offers unique avenues for personal growth and development (Callahan, 2005).

In this vein, the following eight-point professional development plan is offered as an initial behavioral prescription for developing ourselves as health care executives:

1. *Learn Microsoft Excel.* This ubiquitous computer spreadsheet package has become the medium for information exchange in almost all business environments. Compiling clinical and financial data, analyzing trends, trying "what if" scenarios and reporting with graphical output are core activities of those who influence others. Likewise, proficiency in Microsoft PowerPoint allows one to cogently present analyses and recommendations for maximal impact to senior decision makers.

2. *Improve your business literacy.* Explore readings such as Collins's (2001) *Good to Great* or the *Harvard Business Review* to improve your business IQ and to quickly gain appreciation for the value business leaders place on psychological research and applications.

3. *Become a data repository.* If knowledge is power, a database is the "extension cord." Offer to compile a database of key operational information and periodically provide graphical summary of interesting trends. Leaders will begin plugging into you as a prime contact.

4. *Volunteer to interview prospective employees.* Sharpen your diagnostic and prognostic skills in a new way. Expressing your opinion professionally can invite new opportunities for progressive responsibility and impact.

5. *Seek choppy waters.* Calm seas do not make for a skilled mariner. Selectively and progressively seek involvements in challenging staff behavior matters. Offer to accept a difficult staff member onto your team, or offer constructive feedback to managers on ways to address operational difficulties. You will gain self-knowledge and inform others about your potential as a health care executive.

6. *Ask about the budget.* Begin developing financial management skills through an understanding of your department's operating budget, charge versus cost structure, and payer mix. Supplement this with seminars or formal coursework in financial management concepts.

7. *Practice doctoral modesty.* Respect among decision makers will be gained by what you do, not what you are. The days of psychologists' sole claim to "the other doctor" on the health care team are gone. Doctoral physical therapists are becoming the new norm, with occupational therapists in close pursuit. Interesting questions about differential productivity and compensation standards among rehabilitation professionals cannot be far behind.

8. *Model change adaptation.* The extent to which you visibly demonstrate the ability to flexibly take the long and broad view, stay cool under fire, and change adaptively in response to evolving conditions, the more likely people will see you as a leader they will follow into the future. If

you cannot manage yourself, why would anyone allow you to manage others?

CONCLUSION

Over the past 20 years, rehabilitation psychology has in many ways acted on its opportunity to formalize and extend its scope as a specialty. The emergence of dedicated textbooks, board certification procedures, annual educational conference, and specialized billing codes tailored for our practice during this interval support the predictions made by Frank et al. (1990). An aging general population, increased individual life span, and the increasing proportion of Americans with participation limitations because of health issues combine to suggest continued opportunity for clinical service provision and health policy consultation.

A new avenue of opportunity is seen in organizational/rehabilitation psychology: the application of our core competencies in executive or administrative roles to refine, reengineer, and expand health care organizations to meet the challenges of today and tomorrow. Rehabilitation psychologist competencies in five domains (i.e., clinical, analytical, relational, interventional, and ethical) are congruent with the elements of effective executive leadership. The development and innovative application of these competencies to an evolving health care system is offered as an additional avenue for rehabilitation psychology to administer its potential for the benefit of its members and constituents.

References

American Hospital Association. (2002). *Cracks in the foundation: Averting a crisis in America's hospitals.* Chicago: Author.

American Psychological Association. (2002). Ethical principles of psychologists and code of conduct. Retrieved February 19, 2009, from http://www.apa.org/ethics/code2002.html

American Psychological Association. (2006a). *Division profiles.* Retrieved June 16, 2006, from http://www.apa.org/about/division/profiles.html

American Psychological Association. (2006b). *FAQs on the Health and Behavior CPT Codes.* Retrieved June 18, 2006, from http://www.apa.org/practice/cpt_faq.html

Bente, J. R. (2005). Performance measurement, health care policy, and implications for rehabilitation services. *Rehabilitation Psychology, 50,* 87–93.

Buckingham, M., & Coffman, C. (1999). *First, break all the rules: What the world's greatest managers do differently.* New York: Simon & Schuster.

Burt, T. (2005, November/December). Leadership development as corporate strategy: Using talent reviews to improve senior management. *Health Executive, 20,* 14–18.

Butler, T., & Waldroop, J. (2004). Understanding "people" people. *Harvard Business Review, 82,* 78–86.

Callahan, C. D. (2005). Rehabilitation psychologist as health care executive: A platform for professional diversification. *Rehabilitation Psychology, 50,* 177–182.

Callahan, C. D., & Barisa, M. T. (2005). Statistical process control and rehabilitation: The single-subject design reconsidered. *Rehabilitation Psychology, 50,* 24–33.

Callahan, C. D., & Griffen, D. L. (2003). Applying statistical process control techniques to emergency medicine: A primer for providers. *Academic Emergency Medicine, 10,* 883–890.

Chernew, M. E., Hirth, R. A., & Cutler, D. M. (2003). Increased spending on health care: How much can the United States afford? *Health Affairs, 22,* 15–25.

Collins, J. (2001). *Good to great: Why some companies make the leap and others don't.* New York: Harper-Business.

Commonwealth Fund. (2004). *Mirror, mirror on the wall? Looking at the quality of American health care through the patient's lens.* Retrieved May 20, 2006, from http://www.cmwf.org/Publications/Publications_show.htm?doc_id=364436

Costa, P. T., & McCrae, R. R. (1988). Personality in adulthood: A 6-year longitudinal study of self-reports and spouse ratings on the NEO Personality Inventory. *Journal of Personality and Social Psychology, 54,* 853–863.

Drucker, P. F. (2004). What makes an effective executive. *Harvard Business Review, 82,* 58–63.

Dye, C. F. (2000). *Leadership in health care: Values at the top.* Chicago: Health Administration Press.

Ellis, A., & Harper, R. A. (1961). *A new guide to rational living.* Chatworth, CA: Wilshire Book Company.

Fischer, B., & Boynton, A. (2005). Virtuoso teams. *Harvard Business Review, 83,* 117–123.

Frank, R. G., & Elliott, T. R. (Eds.). (2000). *Handbook of rehabilitation psychology.* Washington, DC: American Psychological Association.

Frank, R. G., Gluck, J. P., & Buckelew, S. P. (1990). Rehabilitation: Psychology's greatest opportunity? *American Psychologist, 45,* 757–761.

Gardner, H. (2007). The ethical mind. *Harvard Business Review, 85,* 51–56.

Groysberg, B., McLean, A. N., & Nohria, N. (2006). Are leaders portable? *Harvard Business Review, 84,* 92–100.

Haddock, C. C., McLean, R. A., & Chapman, R. C. (2002). *Careers in health management: How to find your path and follow it.* Chicago: Health Administration Press.

Hamm, J. (2006). The five messages leaders must manage. *Harvard Business Review, 84,* 115–123.

Herman, R. E., Olivo, T. G., & Gioia, J. L. (2002). *Impending crisis: Too many jobs, too few people.* Winchester, VA: Oakhill Press.

Herzlinger, R. E. (2006). Why innovation in health care is so hard. *Harvard Business Review, 84,* 58–66.

Hogan, R., Curphy, G. J., & Hogan, J. (1994). What we know about leadership: Effectiveness and personality. *American Psychologist, 49,* 493–504.

Hoppszallern, S. (2003). *Health care benchmarking guide 2003* (No. 084026). Chicago: Hospitals and Health Networks.

Institute of Medicine. (1999). *To err is human: Building a safer health system.* Washington, DC: National Academy Press.

Institute of Medicine. (2001). *Crossing the quality chasm: A new health system for the twenty-first century.* Washington, DC: National Academy Press.

Katzenbach, J. R., & Smith, D. K. (1993). The discipline of teams. *Harvard Business Review, 71,* 111–120.

McCrae, R. R., & Costa, P. T. (1997). Personality trait structure as a human universal. *American Psychologist, 52,* 509–516.

Medical Group Management Association. (2005). *Physician Compensation and Production Survey.* Englewood, CO: Author.

O'Neal, D. (2003). *Managing strategically for superior performance.* Boston: American Press.

Pfeffer, J., & Sutton, R. I. (2006). Evidence-based management. *Harvard Business Review, 84,* 63–74.

Rand Corporation. (2003). Case mix certification rule for inpatient rehabilitation facilities (Report DRU-2981-CMS), Retrieved March 3, 2007, from http://www.rand.org/pubs/drafts/DRU2981

Robert Wood Johnson Foundation. (2004, September). *Chronic conditions: Making the case for ongoing care.* Retrieved June 16, 2006, from http://www.rwjf.org/research/researchdetail.jsp?id=1502&ia=142&gsa=1

Seligman, M. E. P. (1995). The effectiveness of psychotherapy. *American Psychologist, 50,* 965–974.

Seligman, M. E. P., Steen, T. A., Park, N., & Peterson, C. (2005). Positive psychology progress: Empirical validation of interventions. *American Psychologist, 60,* 410–421.

Thrall, T. H. (2001, September). A leadership vacuum. *Hospitals and Health Networks, 75,* 44–47.

U.S. Department of Health and Human Services. (2002). *Projected supply, demand, and shortages of registered nurses: 2000–2020.* Washington, DC: Author.

U.S. Department of Labor. (2003). *Occupational employment and wages, 2003.* Retrieved June 23, 2006, from http://www.bls.gov/oes/release_archive.htm

U.S. General Accounting Office. (2003). *Hospital emergency departments: Crowded conditions vary among hospitals and communities* (No. GAO–03–460). Washington, DC: Author.

Wilson, K. A., Burke, C. S., Priest, H. A., & Salas, E. (2005). Promoting health care safety through training high reliability teams. *Quality and Safety in Health Care, 14,* 303–309.

CHAPTER 34

COMPETENCIES OF
A REHABILITATION PSYCHOLOGIST

Mary R. Hibbard and David R. Cox

All health disciplines have sought to define *competence*. Efforts to assess competence by third parties such as the Joint Commission on Accreditation in Healthcare have increased pressure to identify meaningful ways to evaluate competence (Joint Commission on Accreditation of Healthcare Organizations, 2000). Competence is defined as "the habitual and judicious use of communication, knowledge, technical skills, clinical reasoning, emotions, values, and reflection in daily practice for the benefit of the individual and the community being served" (Epstein & Hundert, 2002, p. 227). Competence assessment strategies facilitate the determination of what one knows, if one knows how, if one shows how, and how one does (Miller, 1990). As in other health care professions, psychologists have a responsibility to promote high quality and safe psychological services (American Psychological Association [APA], 2006). Competence also sets the standard for professional development of future clinicians in the field, provides guidelines for development of lifelong competence evaluations of practicing clinicians, and more important, serves to protect and inform the public (APA).

A recent APA task force examined the issue of competence in professional psychology (Roberts, Borden, & Christiansen, 2005) in anticipation of a shift within the profession toward an emphasis on the acquisition and maintenance of competence

through all phases of the professional life span, from the beginning practitioner to the established professional planning retirement. The task force defined competence in the field of psychology as the

> capability of critical thinking and analysis, the successful exercise of professional judgment in assessing a situation and making decisions about what to do or not do based on that assessment, and the ability to evaluate and modify one's decisions, as appropriate through reflective practice. (APA, 2006, p. 10)

Competent actions are executed in accord with ethical principles, standards, guidelines, and values of the profession of psychology (Rodolfa et al., 2005). As noted by APA, three concepts are implicit in the core definition of professional competence:

- Competence is *developmental* (i.e., competencies will differ depending on the individual's stage of professional development);
- competence is *incremental* (i.e., competencies are expected to increase as the professional matures, which in turn effect subsequent functioning); and
- competence is *context dependent* (i.e., competencies, aspects of competencies, and execution of competencies will vary depending on the setting of professional practice).

Although the first author (MRH) is an officer of the American Board of Rehabilitation Psychology (ABRP) and the second author (DRC) is the executive officer of the American Board of Professional Psychology (ABPP), it is to be noted that the information provided herein is intended to be a general interpretation of the competence areas as identified by the ABRP and the ABPP. The authors have taken liberty to reframe competence areas of the ABRP within guidelines of Foundational and Functional Competence as suggested by the American Psychological Association (2006). These reframes do not represent a formal opinion or statement of either board. Information is subject to change at the sole discretion of the respective boards.

The APA Task Force recommended that competence in professional psychology be organized around two domains: *Foundational Competence* and *Functional Competence*. Foundational Competence is organized into the areas of ethics and legal foundations, individual and cultural diversity, interpersonal interactions, and professional identification. Functional Competence is organized into areas of assessment, intervention, consultation, science base and application, supervision, and management and teaching. In response to APA Task Force recommendations, the 13 current specialty boards of the American Board of Professional Psychology (ABPP) are restructuring their specialty specific advanced competencies to adhere to these competence domains (see http://www.abpp.org/abpp_public_directory.php). This restructuring, when complete for all individual boards, will retain all prior competency areas of a given specialty board placed within the structure of the Foundational Competence and Functional Competence areas. With these recent and expected developments in mind, we consider their applicability to rehabilitation psychology. First, however, we glance back at some pertinent historical landmarks.

REHABILITATION PSYCHOLOGY: A HISTORICAL PERSPECTIVE

Although a full historical treatment is beyond the scope of this chapter, a brief overview provides insight into the competencies expected of a rehabilitation psychologist. In 1949, a group of psychologists under the auspices of APA formed a special interest group, the National Council on Psychological Aspects of Physical Disability (NCPAPD), to address the needs of returning World War II veterans (Larson & Sacks, 2000). Federal funding from state and federal partnerships supported these psychologists in the development of vocational rehabilitation services for veterans. Thus, the initial emphasis of rehabilitation psychology was vocational, and vocational counseling remains a core competency of today's rehabilitation psychologist.

In 1958, rehabilitation psychology was designated a clinical specialty of APA, one of the first applied psychology specialties to be recognized by the association (Frank & Elliot, 2000). During that same year, members of the newly organized Division 22 (Division of Rehabilitation Psychology, which replaced the NCPAPD) met to discuss issues related to preparation of future psychologists for work in rehabilitation. Proceedings from the "Princeton Institute" (Wright, 1959) set forth guidelines that have become core to the practice of rehabilitation psychology:

- The scope of rehabilitation requires psychological training at the doctoral level.
- The needs of rehabilitation are best served by psychologists educated as psychologists who are well-prepared in the basic principles and methods of science and the profession through study of a wide variety of behavior.
- The roles and functions of psychologists in rehabilitation do not require the creation of a specialized doctoral program but rather expansion of existing clinical and counseling doctoral programs to incorporate an introduction to rehabilitation psychology and community resources.
- There is no single path to competence as a psychologist in rehabilitation because many branches of psychology have contributed to rehabilitation.
- Rehabilitation psychology has made contributions to psychology in general.
- It is important to have a specialized internship in the area of rehabilitation psychology.

These early guidelines have shaped both the educational preparation and the professional practices of rehabilitation psychologists today.

In 1959, a second conference was held at Clark University to discuss the importance of research in rehabilitation psychology. Sustained programs of research by investigators in the field were strongly encouraged (Leviton, 1959). Knowledge of relevant research and its application to clinical interventions remain expected competencies of today's rehabilitation psychologist.

During the 1960s and 1970s, the field continued to expand within the context of major social change. The civil rights movement of the 1960s and disability right movements of the 1970s, which culminated in 1973 with the passage of the Rehabilitation Act and in 1990 with the passage of Americans With Disabilities Act, directly promoted normalization, empowerment, and maximal community integration of individuals with disabilities. Advocacy for individuals with disability remains an expected area of competence for today's rehabilitation psychologist (Larson & Sacks, 2000).

The guidelines initially proposed by Division 22 founding psychologists have expanded over the past 5 decades. Doctoral preparation remains the minimal competency expectation of today's rehabilitation psychologist. Clinical and counseling doctoral programs offer electives on topics germane to rehabilitation psychology such as geropsychology, health psychology, and/or neuropsychology (Glueckfauf, 2000). A continuum of rehabilitation psychology experiences exists at the externship, internship, and postdoctoral levels of training, with APA now accrediting specialized postdoctoral fellowships in rehabilitation psychology.

There continues to be no single path to competence as a rehabilitation psychologist, as rehabilitation psychologists emerge from clinical, counseling, school, neuropsychology, and health psychology backgrounds. Because of the scope of disabilities currently addressed by rehabilitation psychologists, today's practitioners cull clinical skills from prior training in clinical and counseling psychology, developmental psychology, school psychology, educational psychology, neuropsychology, social psychology, medical psychology, health psychology, knowledge of individual and family systems, and community/public health policy.

Within rehabilitation psychology, today's clinicians are likely to be specialists rather than generalists. Some practitioners will specialize in pediatric disabilities (e.g., Asperger's syndrome, attention-deficit/hyperactivity disorder, asthma, cerebral palsy, cystic fibrosis, spina bifida, juvenile rheumatoid arthritis, pediatric traumatic brain injury, learning disorders) and work closely with families and education systems. Others focus on conditions associated with aging (e.g., stroke, dementia, cardiovascular disease, degenerative disc disease), whereas still others work with disabilities affecting individuals across the life span (e.g., acquired spinal cord injury, brain injury, burn, chronic pain, cancer, cardiac conditions, amputation).

Across specializations, however, rehabilitation psychologists address generic disability-related issues in assessment, intervention, and consultation. Rehabilitation psychologists, regardless of clinical emphasis, evaluate and treat individuals with disabling conditions as a part of a larger system, inclusive of the bidirectional (and often multidirectional) interactions that arise as one adjusts to a lifelong illness or injury. As these activities demand multifaceted knowledge and skills, assessment of competence in rehabilitation psychology is, of necessity, complex and multifactorial. Advanced competence in the field of rehabilitation psychology is recognized by *board certification* (also referred to as a *diplomate* or *specialty certification*) by the American Board of Rehabilitation Psychology (ABRP; see http://www.abpp.org/certification/abpp_certification_rehabilitation.htm).

In keeping with the recent focus on assessment of competence in professional psychology put forth by the APA (2006), we address issues of psychologists-in-training and foundational and functional competence expected of practitioners within the specialty field of rehabilitation psychology.

DOCTORAL AND POSTDOCTORAL PREPARATION OF STUDENTS IN REHABILITATION PSYCHOLOGY

Predoctoral practica offer psychology graduate students their first clinical training experiences. Traditionally, practica involve a sequence of 2 years of supervised training that meet a requirement for licensing (Farberman, 2000). Practica experiences progress to an internship and postdoctoral work en route to licensure for independent practice (Lewis, Hatcher, & Pate, 2005). APA has recommended more substantial practica training, with the internship considered the second year of the 2-year expectation for organized, sequential supervised training necessary to ensure competence for independent practice at the "journeyman level" (Farberman). It is currently the responsibility of individual states to consider APA's recommendations and determine whether they wish to realign their respective practice acts accordingly. The Association of State and Provincial Psychology Boards has taken APA's recommendations under advisement and is reviewing model legislative language and the implications of implementing this change.

Predoctoral training of future rehabilitation psychologists typically is generic, drawing heavily from practica experiences involving traditional clinical or counseling psychology assessment and intervention (Parker & Chan, 1990). In a recent study (Lewis et al., 2005), the majority of practica sites (35%) were located in hospital settings and medical centers in military hospitals, Veterans Administration hospitals, and private and state psychiatric settings; however, it remains uncertain what proportion of these practica sites provide relevant clinical experiences in rehabilitation settings. In reviewing the Division 22 Education and Training Web page (http://www.div22.org/educ_train.php), eight current specialized doctoral training programs and four practica sites are identified. Thus, it can be assumed that most clinical and counseling psychology students' first exposure to the principles and practice of rehabilitation psychology occurs not during practica but during their internship or postdoctoral training experiences.

Glueckauf (2000) noted an increase in the number of APA-approved internships offering rehabilitation rotations in stroke, traumatic brain injury, renal dialysis, and pain units, with a particular increase in these types of programs located in hospital settings. On the Division 22 Web site (http://www.div22.org/educ_train.php), 19 internship programs with a focus on rehabilitation psychology were identified. In these clinical settings, it is likely that psychologists-in-training are exposed to rehabilitation assessment and interventions as well as the multidisciplinary team approach (Glueckauf, 2000). Patterson and Hanson (1995) argued that it is at the postdoctoral level that systematic and comprehensive training in rehabilitation psychology occurs. In 1997, 19 postdoctoral programs were identified that offered comprehensive training in rehabilitation psychology (Patterson, 1997). On the Division 22 Web site (http://www.div22.org/educ_train.php), the number of postdoctoral training sites recently listed had increased to 32, suggesting substantial growth of postdoctoral opportunities over the past decade. APA has begun to accredit specialized postdoctoral fellowships in rehabilitation psychology. As more programs seek APA accreditation, it can be expected that successful completion of a rehabilitation psychology postdoctoral training program will become an expec-

tation in the field. Specialized postdoctoral training in rehabilitation psychology will also serve as evidence of competency as an advanced clinician in the area of rehabilitation psychology.

FOUNDATIONAL COMPETENCE OF A REHABILITATION PSYCHOLOGIST

APA has established areas of competence expected of an individual functioning independently as a psychologist, regardless of area of specialization. These are generally completed developmentally, establishing attainment of foundational competence as defined by the APA Task Force (APA, 2006). Demonstration of foundational competence as well as educational, training, and licensure requirements are viewed as the essential minimal requirements for all health-service provider specialty boards of the ABPP, including the ABRP (http://www.abpp.org/abpp_public_directory.php). As credentialing in specialty areas becomes more widely expected within the profession of psychology, it is anticipated that board certification by a given specialty board of the ABPP will be viewed as part of a natural progression of education, training, licensure, and certification. The movement toward expectation of specialty credentialing represents a shift professionally from a time when board certification (i.e., credentialing) was viewed as "only for the cream of the crop" (Bent, Packard, & Goldberg, 1999); indeed, it is increasingly becoming an expectation for demonstration of essential competency in a specialty area.

As is typical of other specialty boards of the ABPP, the ABRP, the clinical specialty board for rehabilitation psychologists, demands the minimal requirements suggested by the APA Task Force as necessary for foundational competence. However, these requirements are expected to have been accrued within the context of rehabilitation psychology and focused on professional activities expected of a candidate seeking specialty certification in that field. These requirements are found on the ABPP Web site (http://www.abpp.org/certification/abpp_certification_rehabilitation.htm) and are summarized as follows. A candidate seeking specialty certification should possess the following qualifications:

1. An earned doctoral degree in psychology from a regionally accredited university. This is a generic

requirement of all ABPP specialty boards, including the ABRP.

2. A licensure or certification at independent practice level. Although there are state-to-state variations in requirements for psychologist licensure and/or certification, rehabilitation psychologists must be certified at an independent practice level. This requirement is generic to all ABPP specialty boards, including ABRP.

3. Three years of experience in rehabilitation psychology, 2 years of which must be supervised. Although a number of years of clinical experience and duration of supervision is generic to all ABPP specialty boards, the focus of experience and supervision for ABRP specialization must be in the field of rehabilitation psychology. These experiences should have resulted in competence reflective of a rehabilitation psychologist in the areas historically referred to as assessment, intervention, consultation, supervision, research and inquiry, consumer protection, and professional development. Training experiences can be met in two ways: (a) 3 years of experience, 1 of which may be predoctoral internship with an emphasis in rehabilitation psychology; and (b) 1 year of pre- and/or post-doctoral experience and successful completion of a recognized postdoctoral program in rehabilitation psychology. Given that the number of APA-accredited postdoctoral programs in rehabilitation psychology is limited (although expanding), most rehabilitation psychologists currently meet this competency through the minimum 3 years of related and supervised rehabilitation experience. As the number of accredited postdoctoral programs in rehabilitation psychology increases, it is anticipated that there will be a shift in the number of rehabilitation psychologists meeting this advanced competency requirement via completion of a specialized postdoctoral fellowship.

4. A minimum of 2 years of supervised experience in rehabilitation psychology. Although 2 years of supervision is required of all ABPP candidates, the ABRP requires that these 2 years of supervision specifically occur within the practice of rehabilitation psychology. These hours can be

satisfied in three ways: (a) 2 years of postdoctoral supervision, (b) 1 year of predoctoral and 1 year of postdoctoral supervision, or (c) completion of a recognized 2-year postdoctoral program in rehabilitation psychology.

5. Membership in professional psychological organizations that have identifiable purposes and policies that are congruent with psychology. Although involvement in professional organizations is a generic competency within the ABPP process, the ABRP requires that the psychologist maintain active involvement in professional organizations with identifiable purposes and policies congruent with those of rehabilitation psychology. Such organizations may include the Division of Rehabilitation Psychology of the APA, American Congress of Rehabilitation Medicine, American Association of Spinal Cord Injury Psychologists and Social Workers, National Rehabilitation Association, International Association of Rehabilitation Professionals, and Brain Injury Association.

Candidates who meet these requirements for ABRP certification are presumed to have demonstrated the ABRP specialty-specific requirements pertaining to education, training, and experience. Developmentally, such an individual would be expected to have had ample opportunity to establish competence in the foundational and functional skills expected of a rehabilitation psychologist.

FUNCTIONAL COMPETENCE OF A REHABILITATION PSYCHOLOGIST

In addition to possessing foundational competencies, a candidate for board certification in rehabilitation psychology must demonstrate functional competence within the specialty area, that is, those more specialty-specific, or advanced, clinical skills of a rehabilitation psychologist. Functional competence assumes continued incremental development of advanced skills while emphasizing the context in which the competence is developed. As previously noted, the ABRP required competencies for advanced practice in the area of rehabilitation psychology are currently being restructured to adhere to APA Task Force recommendations of foundational and functional competence (APA, 2006). Once completed, traditional competency areas of the ABRP will be reorganized into domains of assessment, intervention, consultation, science base and application, supervision, and management and teaching as recommended by the APA Task Force (APA).

The competency areas evaluated by the ABRP are specific to the scope and practice of rehabilitation psychology at the advanced clinician level. The ABRP recognizes a professional as having achieved advanced competences in rehabilitation psychology by granting of a board certification (or diplomate) in rehabilitation psychology. As traditionally evaluated, select competency areas in rehabilitation practice are deemed essential or required. Because of the diverse nature of rehabilitation psychology and the roles that rehabilitation psychologists have in various clinical, research, administrative, and public policy settings, it was assumed that professionals would present with varying areas of relative strength and weakness across areas of rehabilitation practice. As a result, select competence areas, although significant areas of expertise, are viewed as supplemental because not all clinicians will be involved in a work setting allowing for development of these particular competencies. A brief listing of both required and supplemental competency domains appears in Table 34.1, with an overview of each of these expected competencies described as follows:

1. *Assessment competence.* Assessment competence refers to the rehabilitation psychologist's ability to select, use, and interpret suitable psychometric tests and measures, complete a comprehensive psychosocial history via clinical interview, medical record review, and collateral interviews with family and other rehabilitation staff. Assessment should be focused or broad-based, depending on the scope of the referral question. At a minimum, most assessments include evaluation of emotional state and personality, adjustment to disability by individual and family, and the individual's overall functioning in the broader community. More comprehensive assessments evaluate multiple domains of functioning, including cognitive, social and behavioral, sexual, and educational or vocational functioning. When indicated, sub-

stance use, pain, and competency may be assessed. The advanced clinician is expected to be able to integrate data from all sources, identify the extent and nature of the individual's disability as well as areas of preserved abilities. The advanced clinician is expected to address the impact of assessment findings on the person's overall functioning within his or her home, vocational and community setting, and plan needed interventions to enhance overall quality of life for the individual and family members.

2. *Intervention competence.* Intervention competence refers to the rehabilitation psychologist's ability to provide and/or coordinate individualized psychological services for an individual as well as for the individual's family or significant others. Clinical intervention may be provided directly to the individual, a couple, the extended family member, or within a group format. Interventions may include provision of therapeutic services as part of an ongoing rehabilitation program, in consultation or during supervision of other rehabilitation team members.

3. *Consultation competence.* Rehabilitation psychologists typically work collaboratively with other members of the rehabilitation team, other health care providers, and diverse professionals in the community. Consultation competence refers to the rehabilitation psychologist's ability to engage other professionals in these diverse health care and service arenas and provide input about a patient's overall functioning after disability.

4. *Consumer protection competence.* The rehabilitation psychologist typically engages in activities that safeguard the well-being of consumers of psychological care. Rehabilitation psychologists are expected to be cognizant of, and abide by, APA ethical guidelines; patient confidentiality and privacy laws; and licensing laws, rules, and regulations of the state in which they practice. Consumer protection may involve direct advocacy for a consumer, for example, to ensure adequate accommodations under the Americans with Disabilities Act, or to advocate for an individualized approach given the diversity background of a given client. Consumer protection may encompass indirect advocacy for consumers, such as

TABLE 34.1

Competence Domains: American Board of Professional Psychology

Domain	Core competencies	Required	Supplemental
Assessment	Adjustment to disability: Patient	X	
	Adjustment to disability: Family	X	
	Identification of extent and nature of disability and preserved abilities	X	
	Assessment as it relates to education and/or vocational capacities	X	
	Personality and emotional assessment	X	
	Cognitive testing	X	
	Competency evaluation	X	
	Sexual functioning assessment	X	
	Pain assessment	X	
	Substance use or abuse identification and assessment	X	
	Social and behavioral functioning assessment	X	
Intervention	Individual psychotherapy related to adjustment to disability	X	
	Family or couples therapeutic interventions related to disability	X	
	Behavioral management	X	
	Sexual counseling with disabled population(s)	X	
	Pain management		X
	Cognitive retraining		X
	Group therapy related to adjustment to disability		X
Consultation	Behavioral functioning improvements	X	
	Cognitive functioning	X	
	Vocational and/or educational considerations	X	
	Personality and emotional factors	X	
	Substance abuse identification and management	X	
	Improvement in physical functioning		X
	Sexual therapy and disability	X	
	Integration of assistive technology to enhance functioning		X
Consumer protection	State laws of practice	X	
	Laws related to and including ADA	X	
	APA Ethical Principles	X	
	Awareness and sensitivity to multicultural and diversity factors	X	
	Issues related to patient confidentiality and privacy	X	
	Advance directives or wish to die		X
	Abuse or exploitation (e.g., sexual, financial, physical, psychological)		X
	Prevention (e.g., advocacy of legislative policy changes, education)		X
	Establishment of Standards of Care and Practice in Rehabilitation		X
Professional development	Continuing education in area of rehabilitation psychology	X	
	Professional presentation (i.e., at local, state, national levels)		X
	Publications		X
	Teaching		X
	Involvement in advocacy groups		X
	Expertise in related subspecialty areas (e.g., supervision, workshops)		X
Supervision	Students, interns, postdoctoral students		X
	Psychologists		X
	Other professionals		X
	Programs		X
Research and inquiry	Psychological, emotional, and behavioral factors; social psychology of disability; ethnic and gender issues in disability		X
	Intervention efficacy		X
	Individual and/or family acute and long-term adjustment to disability		X
	Assessment and measurement of rehabilitation outcomes		X
	Adaptive or assistive technology		X
	Life span issues as related to disability		X
	Injury prevention		X
	Sexuality and disability		X
	Substance abuse and disability		X

Note. Competence of the American Board of Professional Psychology (http://www.abpp.org/certification/abpp_certification_rehabilitation.htm) will be restructured to meet guidelines for Foundational and Functional Competence areas as requested by the American Psychological Association (2006).

involvement in medical ethics reviews related to such matters as advance directives and end of life issues. Consumer protection may focus on primary prevention activities such as providing community-based education on the use of helmets or reduction of tobacco, drugs, and alcohol. Consumer protection can also involve a role in ensuring standards of psychological or medical care in the area of rehabilitation are maintained and could entail participation in accreditation reviews under the auspices of oversight agencies such as the APA Committee on Accreditation, or the Committee on Accreditation of Rehabilitation Facilities.

5. *Professional development competency.* Psychologists are expected to engage in continuing professional development such as continuing education, additional training, participation in activities such as professional presentation, teaching, and the like. Professional development competency refers to the rehabilitation psychologist's involvement in ongoing educational activities related specifically to expanding knowledge and expertise in the area of rehabilitation psychology.

6. *Supervision competence.* Rehabilitation psychologists are often involved in supervising others in the process of rehabilitation. At the advanced rehabilitation psychologist level, experiences typically focus on clinical supervision (i.e., the overseeing of actual clinical care provided by other professionals from both psychology and nonpsychology backgrounds, junior psychologists, and/or students in training). Rehabilitation psychologists may also be responsible for supervision of programs and/or other professionals involved in the delivery of care within the program. Such roles may include administrative supervision such as might occur with a psychologist who is a department head or team leader. In these situations, the psychologist is cognizant not to expand supervision beyond their areas of clinical training and scope of psychological expertise. Supervision competency refers to the rehabilitation psychologist's ability to supervise professionals both in training and in other rehabilitation service arenas.

7. *Competence in research and inquiry.* Competence in research and inquiry refers to the psychologist's knowledge of research relevant to the specialty of rehabilitation psychology and their ability to integrate this body of knowledge into their daily practice. Although the ABRP diploma is a clinical credential (as are all ABPP diplomas) and not all rehabilitation psychologists are actively engaged in scientific research, many have been or are. Psychologists working in clinical, applied settings are expected to demonstrate this competence in their ability to adequately judge the merits of research and discuss relevant findings knowledgably with their patients and others as needed.

SUMMARY

Over the past 50 years, rehabilitation psychology has expanded its role as a unique and respected specialty within psychology. The ABPP has created clear and consistent guidelines for training of future professionals in the field of psychology at the predoctoral, doctoral, and postdoctoral level with its specialty board of rehabilitation psychology establishing guidelines for training of professionals in rehabilitation psychology. As a result, the field has a well-established set of competencies expected of an advanced clinician in the field. Although the ABRP is currently restructuring its competence domains to align with Foundational and Functional Competence domains outlined by APA (2006), the competencies initially outlined by ABRP and discussed in this chapter will continue to be essential areas of expertise expected of rehabilitation psychologists. As a specialty field, rehabilitation psychology stands ready for its next challenge, that is, establishing guidelines for ongoing maintenance of clinical competence of future practitioners as they provide quality assessments, interventions, consultations, and advocacy.

References

American Board of Professional Psychology Certification of Rehabilitation Psychology. (n.d.). Retrieved December 2, 2008, from http://www.abpp.org/certification/abpp_certification_rehabilitation.htm

American Board of Professional Psychology Directory of Specialties. (n.d.). Retrieved December 2, 2008, from http://www.abpp.org/abpp_public_directory.php

American Psychological Association. (2006, March). Task force on the assessment of competence in professional psychology: Final Report. Washington, DC: Author.

Bent, R. J., Packard, R. E., & Goldberg, R. W. (1999). The American Board of Professional Psychology, 1947–1997: A historical perspective. *Professional Psychology: Research and Practice, 30,* 65–73.

Epstein R. M., & Hundert, E. M. (2002). Defining and assessing professional competence. *JAMA, 287,* 226–235

Farberman, R. K. (2000). *When is a new psychologist ready for independent practice?* Retrieved December 15, 2008, from http://www.apa.org/monitor/sep00/independent.html

Frank, R. G., & Elliot, T. R. (2000) Rehabilitation psychology: Hope for a psychology of chronic conditions. In R. G. Frank & T. R. Elliot (Eds.), *Handbook of rehabilitation psychology* (pp. 3–8). Washington, DC: American Psychological Association.

Glueckauf, R. L. (2000) Doctoral education in rehabilitation and health care psychology: Principles and strategies for unifying subspecialty training. In R. G. Frank & T. Elliot (Eds.), *Handbook of rehabilitation psychology* (pp. 615–627). Washington, DC: American Psychological Association.

Joint Commission on Accreditation of Healthcare Organizations. (2000). *Meeting the competency challenge in behavioral healthcare: The resource tool for behavioral healthcare human resource professionals who must meet the rigorous requirements of JCAHO.* Washington DC: C & R Publications.

Larson, P., & Sachs, P. (2000). A history of Division 22: Rehabilitation psychology. In D. A. Dewsbury (Ed.), *Unification through division: Histories of the American Psychological Association: Vol. 5* (pp. 33–58). Washington, DC: American Psychological Association.

Lewis B. L., Hatcher, R. L., & Pate, W. E. (2005). The practicum experience: A survey of practicum site coordinators. *Professional Psychology: Research and Practice, 36,* 291–298.

Leviton, G. L. (1959, June). *The relationship between rehabilitation and psychology.* Proceedings of a conference sponsored by the Office of Vocational Rehabilitation, Worchester, MA.

Miller, G. E. (1990). *Assessment of clinical skills/competence/performance. Academic Medicine, 65*(Suppl.), S63–S67.

Parker, H. J., & Chan, F. (1990). Psychologists in rehabilitation: Preparation and experience. *Rehabilitation Psychology, 35,* 239–248.

Patterson, D. R. (1997). Training programs in psychology. *Rehabilitation Psychology News, 24*(2), 7.

Patterson, D. R., & Hanson, S. (1995). Joint Division 22 and American Congress of Rehabilitation Medicine guidelines for postdoctoral training in rehabilitation psychology. *Rehabilitation Psychology, 40,* 299–310.

Roberts, M. C., Borden, K. A., & Christiansen, M. (2005). Towards a culture of competence: Assessment of competence in the education and careers of professional psychologists. *Professional Psychology: Research and Practice, 36,* 355–361.

Rodolfa, E., Bent R. J., Eisman, E., Nelson, P. D., Rehm L., & Ritchie, P. (2005). A cube model for competency development: Implications for psychology educators and regulators. *Professional Psychology: Research and Practice, 36,* 347–354.

Wright, B. A. (1959). *Psychology and rehabilitation.* Washington, DC: American Psychological Association.

AFTERWORD:
OF BINS AND ARROWS

John D. Corrigan

Reality is no more than a collective
hunch.

—*Lily Tomlin* (Wagner, 1986)

My premise is simple: We are heading for a paradigm
shift in how we think about disability and chronic
illness because our overarching theoretical models
are not directing us to the most fruitful sources of
new discoveries. Rehabilitation psychology has previously been dominated by self-contained models
that rely little—if at all—on other theories. These
clearly bounded "bins" of theory did not inform
each other, but rather sat side-by-side as competing
models. The bins are less interesting than the spaces
between them.

When George Engel (1977) proposed a biopsychosocial model of human functioning, his intent
was to add psychological and social factors into the
treatment considerations for psychiatric illnesses,
arguing against a strictly medical model. In the more
than 3 decades since, his proposal has had significant
impact across much of medicine and has certainly
spurred the field of health psychology. Before a
biopsychosocial model was posited, there was only
one bin of interest, the biological one. Research and
treatment since have raised the importance of psychological and social factors, not just with respect to
psychiatric disorders but also for all health conditions, including wellness. Specific theoretical models
spawned by the biopsychosocial premise have been
productive, and, as a result, outcome for a chronic
health condition is assumed to be the product of
genetic predispositions, disease manifestation, biological mediators, individual attitudes, and health

care management. (The reader is welcome to expand
on this list of bins and sub-bins.) However, the
emphasis in research has been disproportionately
about phenomena within the bins, rather than how
the bins interact. Treatment too has tended to be
bin-specific, and, of course, health policy has been
bin-myopic.

The biopsychosocial model was not revolutionary in the field of rehabilitation psychology because
the very foundation of the specialty posited the
importance of social and other environmental factors
for functional outcome and psychological adaptation
(Wright, 1960). Rehabilitation psychology not only
had multiple bins, but there were also theoretical
postulations about how at least some of the bins
interacted—physical impairment and social attitude
interact to affect psychological adjustment (Kutner,
1971; Shontz, 1971); psychological adjustment and
physical impairment interact to affect functional
outcome (Diller, 1971; Fordyce, 1971). Thus, in the
1960s when Saad Nagi proposed his schema for
conceptualizing disability (see Appendix A of the
Institute of Medicine [IOM] report *Disability in
America*, 1990), it may have resonated with rehabilitation psychologists not so much because all the
needed bins were labeled but because his underlying
rationale acknowledged what rehabilitation psychologists well knew: that multiple influences, not just
bodily function, affect disability. The 1980 World
Health Organization's *International Classification of
Impairment, Disability, and Handicap* (ICIDH; World
Health Organization [WHO], 1980) and the IOM's
Disability in America proposed categorization systems with different nuances given to the labels and

definitions of bins; however, it was not until the successor to the WHO's ICIDH, the *International Classifications of Functioning, Disability, and Health* (ICF; WHO, 2001), that some of the most important bins for rehabilitation psychology were explicitly included in the model of health and function.

The individual (i.e., personal factors) and the environment were merely implicit in previous models of disability; they were not explicit sources of influence. The ICIDH was criticized for localizing disability at the level of the person (Chapireau & Colvez, 1998), in contrast to the social models of disablement (Oliver, 1990) that asserted that the political, social, and physical environments in which people function are what limit their full participation. In response, the ICF posited that functional independence and participation in society occur within the context of the environment in which the individual lives. While not ignoring impairments of bodily structure and function, inclusion of environmental influences shifted the locus of disability from being the sole province of either the individual or the society, and instead focused on the interaction between the individual's capabilities and the impact of the environment. The ICF also allowed that personal factors provide context for understanding health conditions, including demographic characteristics,

attitudes, lifestyle, and coping strategies, although a taxonomy of these influences was not attempted.

Changes incorporated into the ICF, though limited, resonated well with much of the underpinnings of rehabilitation psychology. Perhaps most important, the ICF took a first step in integrating the earlier self-contained models into a larger-picture model that considers many factors. Conceptually, they added "arrows" to connect the bins. Thus, as shown in Figure 1, the schematic for the ICF allowed that inter-bin influences could manifest in multiple ways; indeed, it would appear that any bin could conceivably influence any other. However, I believe, that although we have embraced the multi-influenced nature of disability and chronic illness, we have not attended enough to the interactions between the bins. If our current status were a multiple regression model, we might say that we have been inclusive in allowing independent variables to demonstrate their utility for contributing main effects to model-building but have not tested the potential for true interaction terms. Examples from other areas of science may be helpful for illuminating the difference between multiple bins and true interactions.

Psychology has moved beyond the nature versus nurture argument by acknowledging the complexity of genetic and environmental influences on human

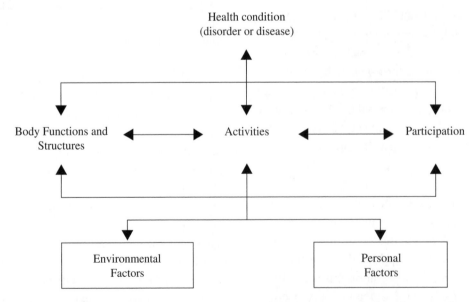

FIGURE 1.   Interactions between components of the International Classification of Functioning, Disability, and Health. From *International Classification of Functioning, Disability, and Health,* by the World Health Organization, 2001, p. 18. Copyright 2001 by the World Health Organization. Reprinted with permission.

development. However, we have not fully appreciated the potentially critical interaction between these bins of factors affecting behavior. In biology, *phenotypic plasticity* is the differential expression of genotypic variance as a function of environmental influences. And, most important, this plasticity can occur within the lifetime of a single organism. Although we readily accept that environment may determine where within the range of a gene's variation a particular trait will be expressed (i.e., the norm of reaction), we are less likely to anticipate that the phenotypic expression may not be along a continuum and could include a qualitatively different manifestation of the trait. For example, the differences among social insects (e.g., worker bees vs. queen bees) are environmental and not genetic; yet the phenotypes differ in more than just degree. The genome of each bee contains the instructions to develop into either type, but early environmental exposure determines which genes are activated. While social insects may be remote from human experience (or maybe not), the point is that environment and genetics are not just vectors for which the net result is the combination of magnitude and direction (i.e., the Lewinian model).

An example closer to home comes from the study of brain structures and functions that mediate decision-making. *Neuroeconomics* is a relatively new field that brings together researchers from neuroscience and economics with a common interest in how people make decisions (Glimcher & Rustichini, 2004; Sanfey, Loewenstein, McClure, & Cohen, 2006). The economists contributing to this field are particularly interested in decisions people make that seem illogical because they run counter to the theory of expected utility (Schoemaker, 1982). Insight into these decisions could benefit understanding of behaviors such as saving money, retirement planning, or investing. Neuroscientists in this field are interested in how different systems of the brain are involved in decisions that involve trade-offs, especially those choices that include both cognitive and emotional factors.

Functional magnetic resonance imaging has been used in neuroeconomics research to visualize areas of brain activation during decision making. Studies have begun to identify brain systems that appear

central to decisions such as delaying gratification, choosing in the face of ambiguity, and altering decisions on the basis of expected gains or losses. Research has identified different brain systems that are involved not only in evaluation of the magnitude and probability of a potential reward (i.e., expected value) but also in the ambiguity of the information used to make this judgment (i.e., uncertainty; Glimcher, Dorris, & Bayer, 2005; Sanfey et al., 2006). Furthermore, multiple studies have revealed that when determining expected value, both animals and humans judge the potential for gain differently than they judge the potential for loss (Novemsky & Kahneman, 2005; Rabin, 2000; Tversky & Kahneman, 1992). A person who stands to gain from an action takes fewer risks, thus ensuring at least some benefit accrued. However, when judging loss, more risks are taken to try to minimize the damage. This differential approach to judging expected value has been called *risk aversion* for gain and *risk taking* for loss.

Neuroeconomics is uncovering interesting interactions among the bodily structure, brain function, and person factors bins. Basic precepts about decision making have been found to manifest in unique ways with persons who have neurological lesions. For instance, people with lesions to the orbitofrontal cortex are less sensitive to uncertainty, essentially willing to make judgments about expected value, ignoring the adequacy of the information on which they base those judgments (Hsu, Bhatt, Adolphs, Tranel, & Camerer, 2005). A considerable body of research stimulated by the work of Antoine Bechara and colleagues has shown that people with impaired ventromedial prefrontal cortex appear less risk averse when judging gains and thus are willing to incur substantial losses in the pursuit of immediate rewards, even if in the long run they gain less (Bechara, 2005; Bechara & Damasio, 2002; Rogers et al., 1999). Although these examples of interactions between bodily structure and personal factors are evident in instances of known brain impairment, it is not far-fetched to anticipate a neuroanatomy of personality differences or a neurochemical basis of attitudinal proclivities. These arrows would certainly be of more interest than the respective bins from which they emanate.

A final example of the shift from bins to arrows comes from the field of public health. Significant advances in the magnitude, quality, and accessibility of data tied to geographic location have spawned new and innovative investigations of environmental influences on all levels of societal functioning. Public health research has begun using data available via geographic information systems to study associations between social aspects of neighborhoods or communities and health issues observed in these geographic locations. Whereas early work focused primarily on proximity to toxins and the relation to disease prevalence, recent studies have greatly expanded the concept of environmental influence. Public health researchers are giving increasing attention to the role of communities in mediating disease and injury. A number of recent studies have found community factors to have important influences on social as well as behavioral variations in health states. Furthermore, it appears that characteristics of neighborhoods and communities can have effects on health independent of the individual's socio-demographic characteristics. While these effects tend to be relatively small when compared with individual factors, the contribution to predicting health outcomes is significant nonetheless (Kawachi & Berkman, 2003; Pickett & Pearl, 2001).

There is considerable heterogeneity in the types of community factors that have been investigated. One area of study has examined social disparities and such aspects as social capital (Baum & Palmer, 2002; Pearce & Davey Smith, 2003), social inequality (Barnett, Pearce, & Moon, 2005), residential segregation (Collins & Williams, 1999), area deprivation (Breeze et al., 2005), and sense of neighborhood (Young, Russell, & Powers, 2004). Other researchers have studied the effect of accessibility to community resources (e.g., health care facilities, public transport, parks, recreation facilities) on various health outcomes. Studies have shown that reduced access to retail outlets selling healthy and affordable food is associated with increased rates of obesity, diabetes, and cardiovascular disease (Cummins & Macintyre, 2002a, 2002b). A recent study examined how neighborhood concentration of outlets for recreation affected levels of adolescent physical activity (Jago, Baranowski, & Baranowski, 2006). Relevant to dis-

ability, Culham and colleagues (2002) examined the correspondence between the residence for people with low vision and accessibility of services for them.

New areas of study have also investigated the contribution of community influences to discreet behaviors. For instance, Moss and colleagues examined neighborhood patterns of functional disability and the impact of chronic disease among American Indians and Alaskan Natives (Moss, Schell, & Goins, 2006). Mason and colleagues studied adolescents from low-income neighborhoods who did and did not consume alcohol regularly (Mason, Cheung, & Walker, 2004). They examined the distance between each participant's home and places where alcohol was consumed as part of social or recreational activities (i.e., risky places) and those where alcohol-free socialization occurred (i.e., safe places). On average, the distance between the homes of regular users and safe places was three times greater than that for risky places. Jennifer Bogner and I recently reported that neighborhood characteristics improve the prediction of subjective well-being among individuals with traumatic brain injury over and above that predicted by demographic characteristics, injury-related parameters, current functioning, and the individual's perception of their environment (Corrigan & Bogner, 2008). Despite the field of rehabilitation's fundamental interest in the contribution of the environment to disability, research in rehabilitation has not attended to the full array of possible environmental influences.

Paradigm shifts change the perspective of a field when a field is ripe for a new perspective. Myopic conformance to the medical model spawned the biopsychosocial paradigm. It may be time to look beyond disability and chronic illness as complex conditions with multiple influences and attend to the ways these influences interact and influence each other in their own right. Our current theories do not have the heuristic power needed to explore the new ways we are coming to understand human behavior. While I am not farsighted enough to envision the next paradigm, I feel the wear on the current one. On what basis would we hypothesize that adjustment to disability has a genetic factor? Are individual differences in neural pathways person factors or bodily functions? What are all the mechanisms by which a neighborhood characteristic shapes a person's participation in life? We need to be able to conceive of possibilities that are as unthinkable as "disability is not just a medical condition" would have been half a century ago. We need to posit interventions as unimaginable as "restrain the unaffected extremity" would have been a quarter of a century ago. Our preoccupation with the bins may be distracting us from the arrows. And in the end, it is not the arrows with which we should be concerned; it is the new, so far nameless, bins that cannot be defined by the existing schema.

References

Barnett, R., Pearce, J., & Moon, G. (2005). Does social inequality matter? Assessing the effects of changing ethnic socio–economic disparities on Maori smoking in New Zealand, 1981–96. *Social Science & Medicine, 60,* 1515–1526.

Baum, F., & Palmer, C. (2002). Opportunity structure: Urban landscape, social capital, and health promotion in Australia. *Health Promotion International, 17,* 351–361.

Bechara, A. (2005). Decision-making, impulse control and loss of willpower to resist drugs: A neurocognitive perspective. *Nature Neuroscience, 8,* 1458–1463.

Bechara, A., & Damasio, H. (2002). Decision-making and addiction: Part 1. Impaired activation of somatic states in substance dependent individuals when pondering decisions with negative future consequences. *Neuropsychologia, 40,* 1675–1689.

Breeze, E., Jones, D., Wilkinson, P., Bulpitt, C. J., Grundy, C., Latif, A. M., et al. (2005). Area deprivation, social class, and quality of life among people aged 75 years and over in Britain. *International Journal of Epidemiology, 34,* 276–283.

Chapireau, F., & Colvez, A. (1998). Social disadvantage in the international classification of impairments, disabilities, and handicap. *Social Science and Medicine, 47,* 59–66.

Collins, C., & Williams, D. (1999). Segregation and mortality: The deadly effects of racism. *Sociological Forum, 14,* 495–523.

Corrigan, J. D., & Bogner, J. A. (2008). Neighborhood characteristics and outcomes following traumatic brain injury. *Archives of Physical Medicine and Rehabilitation. 89,* 912–921.

Culham, L. E., Ryan, B., Jackson, A. J., Hill, A. R., Jones, B., Miles, C., et al. (2002). Low vision services for vision rehabilitation in the United Kingdom. *British Journal of Ophthalmology, 86,* 743–747.

Cummins, S., & Macintyre, S. (2002a). A systematic study of an urban foodscape: The price and availability of food in greater Glasgow. *Urban Studies, 39,* 2115–2130.

Cummins, S., & Macintyre, S. (2002b). Food deserts: Evidence and assumption in health policy making. *British Medical Journal, 325,* 436–439.

Diller, L. (1971). Cognitive and motor aspects of handicapping conditions in the neurologically impaired. In W. S. Neff (Ed.), *Rehabilitation psychology* (pp. 1–32). Washington, DC: American Psychological Association.

Engel, G. L. (1977). The need for a new medical model: A challenge for biomedicine. *Science, 196,* 129–136.

Fordyce, W. E. (1971). Behavioral methods in rehabilitation. In W. S. Neff (Ed.), *Rehabilitation psychology* (pp. 74–108). Washington, DC: American Psychological Association.

Glimcher, P. W., Dorris, M. C., & Bayer, H. M. (2005). Physiological utility theory and the neuroeconomics of choice. *Games and Economic Behavior, 52,* 213–256.

Glimcher, P. W., & Rustichini, A. (2004). Neuroeconomics: The consilience of brain and decision. *Science, 306,* 447–452.

Hsu, M., Bhatt, M., Adolphs, R., Tranel, D., & Camerer, C. F. (2005). Neural systems responding to degrees of uncertainty in human decision-making. *Science, 310,* 1680–1683.

Institute of Medicine. (1991). *Disability in America: Toward a national agenda for prevention.* Washington, DC: National Academy Press.

Jago, R., Baranowski, T., & Baranowski, J. C. (2006). Observed, GIS, and self-reported environmental features and adolescent physical activity. *American Journal of Health Promotion, 20,* 422–428.

Kawachi, I., & Berkman, L. (2003). Introduction. In I. Kawachi, & L. Berkman (Eds.), *Neighbourhoods and health* (pp. 4–19). Oxford, England: Oxford University Press.

Kutner, B. (1971). The social psychology of disability. In W. S. Neff (Ed.), *Rehabilitation psychology* (pp. 143–167). Washington, DC: American Psychological Association.

Mason, M., Cheung, I., & Walker, L. (2004). Substance use, social networks, and the geography of urban adolescents. *Substance Use and Misuse, 39,* 1751–1778.

Moss, M. P., Schell, M. C., & Goins, R. T. (2006). Using GIS in a first national mapping of functional disability among older American Indians and Alaska Natives from the 2000 census. *International Journal of Health Geographics, 1*(5), 37.

Novemsky, N., & Kahneman, D. (2005). The boundaries of loss aversion. *Journal of Marketing Research, 42,* 119–128.

Oliver, M. (1990). *The politics of disablement: Critical texts in social work and the welfare state.* London: Macmillan.

Pearce, N., & Davey Smith, G. (2003). Is social capital the key to inequalities in health? *American Journal of Public Health, 93,* 122–129.

Pickett, K., & Pearl, M. (2001). Multilevel analyses of neighborhood socioeconomic context and health outcomes: A critical review. *Journal of Epidemiology and Community Health, 55,* 111–122.

Rabin, M. (2000). Risk aversion and expected-utility theory: A calibration theorem. *Econometrica, 68*(5), 1281–1292.

Rogers, R. D., Owen, A. M., Middleton, H. C., Williams, E. J., Pickard, J. D., Sahakian, B. J., et al. (1999). Choosing between small, likely rewards and large, unlikely rewards activates inferior and orbital prefrontal cortex. *Journal of Neuroscience, 19,* 9029–9038.

Sanfey, A. G., Loewenstein, G., McClure, S. M., & Cohen, J. D. (2006). Neuroeconomics: Cross-currents in research on decision-making. *Trends in Cognitive Sciences, 10,* 108–116.

Schoemaker, P. J. (1982). The expected utility model: Its variants, purposes, evidence and limitations. *Journal of Economic Literature, 20,* 529–563.

Shontz, F. C. (1971). Physical disability and personality. In W. S. Neff (Ed.), *Rehabilitation psychology* (pp. 33–73). Washington, DC: American Psychological Association.

Tversky, A. D., & Kahneman, D. (1992). Advances in prospect theory: Cumulative representation of uncertainty. *Journal of Risk and Uncertainty, 5,* 297–323.

Wagner, J. (1986). The search for signs of intelligent life in the universe. New York: HarperCollins.

World Health Organization. (1980). *International classification of impairments, disabilities and handicaps: A manual of classification relating to the consequences of disease.* Geneva, Switzerland: Author.

World Health Organization. (2001). *International classification of functioning, disability, and health.* Geneva: Author.

Wright, B. (1960). *Physical disability: A psychological approach.* New York: Harper & Row.

Young, A., Russell, A., & Powers, J. (2004). The sense of belonging to a neighborhood: Can it be measured and is it related to health and well being in older women? *Social Science and Medicine, 59,* 2627–2637.

Index

AA. *See* Alcoholics Anonymous

Abnormal personality functioning, 196–197

ABPP. *See* American Board of Professional Psychology

ABRP. *See* American Board of Rehabilitation Psychology

ABS (Agitated Behavior Scale), 167

Abstinence, from substance use, 247

Abuse
  of children with neurodevelopmental conditions, 331–332
  of women with disabilities, 373

ACA (Amputation Coalition of America), 37

Academic reintegration
  of children, 324, 351
  after spinal cord injury, 20
  after traumatic brain injury, 53–54

Academy of Rehabilitation Psychology, 4

Acalculia, 71

ACA (anterior cerebral artery) stroke, 67

Acceleration, brain injury due to, 44

Acceptance, of pain, 124

Access, to community resources, 480

Accessibility, of psychological treatment, 332–333

Accommodations
  psychologist's guidance about, 267
  reasonable, 408
  in schools, 349
  workplace, 82, 358, 408

ACRM. *See* American Congress of Rehabilitation Medicine

Active coping, 124

Activist-based approach, 384

Activities of daily living (ADLs), 97, 149, 153

Activity limitations, 148

Activity limitation theory, 100

Activity Measure for PostAcute Care (AM-PAC), 152, 154

ADA. *See* Americans With Disabilities Act of 1990

Addiction Severity Index, 251

Adjustment
  to disability, 260
  need for clarification of term, 421
  to spinal cord injury, 11–14

Adjustment domain, of personality, 196

ADLs. *See* Activities of daily living

Administrative services only (ASO) agreements, 441

Adolescents, 33–34

Adult day care, 308

Adversarial growth, 419

Adverse selection, 440

Advice, giving, 115, 252

Advocacy
  for children with chronic illnesses, 346, 347
  for health care reform, 446–448

Aerobic exercise, 97

Affective forecasting, 386

African Americans, 65, 372, 409

Age differences
  with burn injuries, 107
  with stroke, 63–65

Agency for Health Care Policy and Research (AHCPR), 68, 70, 79

Agitated Behavior Scale (ABS), 167

Agitation, 50, 51, 167

Agnosia, 71

Agoraphobia, 77

Agraphia, 71

AHCPR. *See* Agency for Health Care Policy and Research

AJAO. *See* American Juvenile Arthritis Organization

Alcohol, Smoking and Substance Involvement Screening Test (ASSIST), 250

Alcohol abuse
  among elderly, 102
  and proximity to places of consumption, 480
  with spinal cord injury, 16
  after traumatic brain injury, 54

Alcohol dependence, 245

Alcohol Dependence Scale, 251

Alcoholics Anonymous (AA), 246, 252

Alcoholism
  continuum model of, 245–246
  disease model of, 245, 246
  myths about, 247

Alcohol use disorders
  effects of, on rehabilitation outcome, 243–245
  intoxication, 243
  postinjury, 242–245
  preinjury, 242–244
  prevalence of, 241

Alcohol Use Disorders Identification Test (AUDIT), 249, 250

Alcohol Use Inventory, 251

Alexia, 71, 72

Alphabet boards, 294

Alphanumeric paging system, 275

Alzheimer's disease, 98, 275, 290

Amantadine, 50, 139

Ambivalent coping, 198

American Board of Forensic Psychology, 180

American Board of Professional Psychology (ABPP), 4, 259, 468

American Board of Rehabilitation Psychology (ABRP), 4, 469–472

American Burn Association, 108

American Congress of Rehabilitation Medicine (ACRM), 54, 285

American Hospital Association, 439

American Juvenile Arthritis Organization (AJAO), 341

American Medical Association, 259

American Pain Society, 121

American Psychological Association (APA), 179, 445, 470

American Psychology-Law Society, 180

American Stroke Association, 83

Americans With Disabilities Act (ADA) of 1990, 83, 267, 360, 408, 468

Amitriptyline, 77

Amnesia
    posttraumatic, 46, 47, 51
    with spinal cord injury, 14

Amnestic syndromes, 72

AM-PAC. *See* Activity Measure for PostAcute Care

Amphetamines, 242

AMPS. *See* Assessment of Motor and Process Skills

Amputation. *See* Limb amputation

Amputation Coalition of America (ACA), 37

Analgesics, 17

Analytical competency, of rehabilitation psychologist, 461

Anatomical scan, 215

Aneurysm, 66

Animal studies
    on central nervous system plasticity, 392–393
    on plasticity after CNS injury, 394
    on rehabilitation-induced CNS plasticity, 394–395

Anomic aphasia, 71

Anosognosia, 67, 72, 74–75, 261, 266

Anoxia, 14

Anoxic injury, 213, 214, 219

Antabuse, 253

Anterior cerebral artery (ACA) stroke, 67

Anterior left hemisphere injury, 70

Anticipatory awareness, 292

Antidepressants, 12, 77, 100, 116

Antihistamines, 116

Antipsychotic medications, 51

Antiseizure medications, 16, 50–51

Anxiety
    assessment of, 170, 206
    with burn injuries, 110, 111
    measures of, 204
    with multiple sclerosis, 134–135
    psychotherapeutic interventions for, 261

among rehabilitation clients, 261
    with spinal cord injury, 12–13
    with stroke, 77–78, 201

APA. *See* American Psychological Association

APA Division 22, 4, 468, 470

APA Division 40, 180

APA Ethics Code, 427, 428

APA Ethics Code Task Force, 428

APA Monitor on Psychology, 429

APA Task Force, 467–468

Apathetic syndromes, 72

Apathy, 78

Aphasia
    and alternative communication methods, 267
    and assessing decision-making capacity, 171
    neuroimaging studies of, 227
    and stroke, 67, 70, 71, 76
    therapies for, 294, 399, 402

Appeasement, 462

Applied behavioral analysis, 323

Apraxia, 71, 72

Aprosodia, 67, 78

Aprosodic speech, 76

Aprosody, 72

APT (Attention Process Training), 288

Archives of Clinical Neuropsychology, 185

Arithmetic skills, 330

Arm amputation, 36

Army Individual Test Battery, 184

"Arrows," 478–481

Arthritis, 96, 97, 445

Arthritis camps, 341

Arthritis Foundation, 341

Arthroplasty, 121

ASO (administrative services only) agreements, 441

Assertiveness training, 54, 307

Assessment competency, 472, 473

Assessment of Motor and Process Skills (AMPS), 151, 153–154

Assessment phase (of trial), 183

Assessment Systems Corp., 161

Asset and Health Dynamics, 152

Assets, existing and potential, 385–386

ASSIST (Alcohol, Smoking and Substance Involvement Screening Test), 250

Assistive technology for cognition and behavior (ATCB), 273
    attributes of, 274
    clinical approaches supported by, 274–275

for functional problems, 275–277
    interventions using, 279–281
    matching users with, 277–279
    on-the-job, 21

Assistive technology services, 361

Association of State and Provincial Psychology Boards, 469

ATCB. *See* Assistive technology for cognition and behavior

ATCB interventions, 279–281
    atheoretical, 281
    cost of, 281
    design of, 279–280
    device interface design, 280
    issues with, 280–281
    limited generalizability of, 280–281
    task interface design, 280–281
    team approach to, 280
    user abandonment of, 281

Atherosclerosis, 66, 155

Atrophy, 216–219, 221

Atrophy rating, 222

Attention
    and ATCB devices, 280
    hemispatial, 293–294
    remediation of, 288–289

Attention Process Training (APT), 288

Attitudes
    toward people with disabilities, 381–383
    toward women with disabilities, 371–374

Attributional style, 198

AUDIT. *See* Alcohol Use Disorders Identification Test

AUDIT-C, 249, 250

Auditory agnosia, 71

Auditory cortex, 393

Australian Council for Educational Research, 161

Automated MRI analysis, 230, 231

Autominder, 275

Autotopagnosia, 71

Avoidant coping
    with burn injuries, 112–113
    and personality, 197
    with spinal cord injury, 14

Avonex, 139

Awareness. *See also* Impaired awareness
    of bias toward amputees, 35
    of cognitive deficits, 99
    self-, 292–293

Axonal injuries, 45

Axonal pathways, 45

Back pain. *See also* Low-back pain
  and arthroplasty, 121
  cognitive–behavioral therapy with,
    410
  multidisciplinary treatments for, 127
  radiofrequency denervation for, 126
BAI. *See* Beck Anxiety Inventory
Barona Index, 185
Barrier reduction, 254
Barthel Index, 153
BDI-II. *See* Beck Depression Inventory-II
Beauticians, stroke awareness program
    with, 64
Bechara, Antoine, 479
Beck Anxiety Inventory (BAI), 204, 206
Beck Depression Inventory-II (BDI-II),
    204–206
Behavioral assessment, 167, 170–171
Behavioral data, 430
Behaviorally relevant stimulation, 392
Behavioral model of disability, 198
Behavioral observation, 202
Behavioral pain management, 341
Behavioral therapy
  with children, 323–324
  for pain, 126
Behavior management, 50
Beliefs
  in control over pain, 127
  pain, 102
Benefits counseling, 360
Ben-Yishay, Yehuda, 4, 295
Bereavement, 260–261
Betaseron, 139
Bias
  perceived clinician, 186
  toward amputees, 35
Bilateral spastic CP, 330
"Bins" of theory, 477–481
Biopsychosocial model, 195, 477
Birth control, 18
Blind people, 393
Blue Cross plans, 439
Body image dissatisfaction
  and amputation, 33–34
  in burn patients, 113, 114
Body perception disturbances, 71
Borderline personality disorder, 114
Border-zone regions, 67
Boundaries, 433, 434
Braille readers, 393
Brain Injury Special Interest Group, 54
Brain plasticity
  and ameliorating impairment, 397–399
  and overcoming disability, 395–396

and pediatric neuropsychology, 315–316
  and recovery after CNS injury, 394
Brain reorganization, 138, 225, 226,
    316, 391
Brief Symptom Inventory (BSI), 204, 206
Broca, P., 391
Broca's aphasia, 71
Bromocriptine, 50
Brown-Sequard's syndrome, 9–10
BSI. *See* Brief Symptom Inventory
Budgets, 464
Burn care with pain management, 4
Burn injuries, 107–117
  acute phase of recovery from, 111–112
  and body image dissatisfaction, 113, 114
  classification of, 107
  coping strategies for, 112–113
  critical phase of recovery from, 111
  demographics/trends of, 107–108
  motivational issues with, 114–116
  nonpharmacological pain management
    for, 112
  outpatient phase of recovery from, 112
  physical rehabilitation problems
    with, 108
  preinjury factors in psychological
    recovery from, 109–110
  pruritus problem with, 116
  psychological rehabilitation problems
    with, 108–109
  rehabilitation phases with, 110–112
  self-inflicted, 114
  and sleep, 116
Burn size, 108–109
Bush, S., 436
Business literacy, 464

CAGE questionnaire, 248, 249
California Verbal Learning Test
    (CVLT-II), 185
Cambridge Examination for Mental
    Disorders in the Elderly
    (CAMCOG), 99
Canada, 439
Canadian Psychological Association, 436
CAP (Client Assistance Program), 361
Capacity to Consent to Treatment
    Instrument, 172
Cardinal symptom management, 443–444
Caregiver adaptation, pediatric rehabilita-
    tion and, 347–348
Caregiver burden
  and education, 170
  negative health consequences with,
    301
  with stroke, 81

Caregiver interventions, 301–309
  for affect, 307
  cultural dimensions in, 304–305
  delivery methods for, 303–304
  design/methodological issues in,
    302–304
  importance of, 301
  individual *vs.* group, 303
  in-person *vs.* telehealth, 303–304
  for knowledge, 306
  and relationship with care recipient,
    305–309
  research methods on, 303
  for skills, 306–307
  for social support, 307
  standardized *vs.* tailored, 304
Caregivers, family, 301
Caregiving career, stage of, 306
Care recipient
  caregiver's relationship with, 305
  condition of, 305–306
Care recipient training, 308
CARF. *See* Commission on Accreditation
    of Rehabilitation Facilities
CARF Facility Standards, 434
Case management, 359
Case managers, 358
CAT (computer adaptive testing), 152
Catastrophizing, 122–123, 197
Categorical model, of personality, 196
Causal agency, 332
Causalgia, 397
CBTs. *See* Cognitive–behavioral therapies
Ceiling effect, 160
Center for Epidemiological Studies
    Depression Scale (CES-D),
    204–206
Center for Research on Women with
    Disabilities, 374
Centers for Medicare and Medicaid
    Services (CMS), 153, 158, 439,
    445, 463
Central cord syndrome, 10
Central nervous system (CNS)
  personality disturbance and injury
    to, 199
  recovery after injury to, 394
  reorganization of, 396–397
Central nervous system plasticity
  basic research on, 392–394
  and constraint-induced movement
    therapy, 400–402
  methodologic concerns about
    evaluating, 397, 400

Central nervous system plasticity
  (*continued*)
    and recovery after CNS injury, 394
    rehabilitation-induced, 394–402
Central poststroke pain, 120
Central sensitization, 128
Cerebral atrophy, 216–219
Cerebral infarction. *See* Ischemic stroke
Cerebral palsy (CP), 329–333, 345, 348
Cerebrospinal fluid (CSF), 214, 231
Cerebrovascular accidents (CVAs), 213
Certification
    in forensic psychology, 180
    in rehabilitation counseling, 358
    in rehabilitation psychology, 259,
      268, 469
    in specialties, 470–471
Certified rehabilitation counselors
    (CRCs), 358
Certifying agencies, 451
Cervicobrachial pain, 126
CES-D. *See* Center for Epidemiological
    Studies Depression Scale
Change adaptation, 464
Changing Faces program, 114
Chapple v. Ganger, 181–182, 184
Cherry-picking, 440
Children
    adjustment by, 349–350
    amputations among, 33
    neuropsychological classification
      of, 315
    with spinal cord injuries, 21–22
    testimony in cases involving, 186
Children with neurodevelopmental
    conditions, 329–333
    abuse risks of, 331–332
    accessible psychological treatment
      of, 332–333
    and community participation, 333
    neurocognitive risks of, 329–331
    psychosocial risks of, 331
    social risks of, 332–333
    socioenvironmental context of, 333
Chronic illness, children with. *See*
    Pediatric chronic illness,
    rehabilitation with
Chronic pain, 119–128
    assessment of, 121–124
    central sensitization for, 128
    measurement of, 121–122
    medication for, 124–125
    multidimensional nature of, 119–120
    negative affect with, 122–124
    with orthopedic/musculoskeletal
      conditions, 121

and placebos, 127–128
    prolotherapy for, 126
    psychological interventions for,
      126–127
    radiofrequency denervation for, 126
    with spinal cord injury, 120
    spinal cord stimulation for, 125–126
    with stroke, 120–121
    transcutaneous electrical nerve
      stimulation for, 126
    with traumatic brain injury, 120
    treatment of, 124–128
Chronic Pain Acceptance
    Questionnaire, 124
Chronic pain management, 4
Cicerone, K. D., 285
CIQ (Community Integration
    Questionnaire), 48
Circumlocution, 294
CI therapy. *See* Constraint-induced
    movement therapy
Civil cases, 184
Clark University, 468
Claudication, 155
Client Assistance Program (CAP), 361
Clients (term), 385
Clinical competency, of rehabilitation
    psychologist, 460–461
Clinical neuroscience, 228
Clinical team approach, 280
Clinton, Bill, 441
CMS. *See* Centers for Medicare and
    Medicaid Services
CNS. *See* Central nervous system
Cocaine, 242
Cochrane Collaboration, 296
Cognistat, 68, 167
Cognitive assessment
    with juvenile rheumatic diseases,
      339–340
    with multiple sclerosis, 136
    neuropsychologist's role in, 166–167
Cognitive–behavioral therapies (CBTs)
    with back pain, 410
    with caregivers, 307
    effectiveness of, 263–264
    with elderly, 102
    for pain, 126–127
    with spinal cord injury, 19
Cognitive disorders, 261
Cognitive impairment
    and geriatric rehabilitation, 98–100
    and linguistic impairment, 266–267
    with multiple sclerosis, 133–134
    with spinal cord injury, 14–15
    with stroke, 201

Cognitive interventions, with children,
      322–323
Cognitive Log, 166
Cognitive neuroscience, 227–230
The Cognitive Neurosciences
    (Gazzaniga), 227
Cognitive processing, 227
Cognitive psychology, 227–228
Cognitive rehabilitation, 285–297
    for attention, 288–289
    comprehensive–holistic, 295–296
    for executive function, 290–293
    future of, 296–297
    for hemispatial attention/visuospatial
      function, 293–294
    for language/communication, 294–295
    for memory, 289–290
    methods of, 287–296
    terminology/concepts, 285–287
    after traumatic brain injury, 51
Cognitive remediation, 167
Cognitive Screening Test, 100
Collins, J., 464
Coma
    length of, 51
    with traumatic brain injury, 45–46
Commission on Accreditation of
    Rehabilitation Facilities (CARF),
    52, 54, 121, 157, 158, 451
Committee on Ethical Guidelines for
    Forensic Psychologists, 179, 182
Communication
    ATCB interventions for aiding, 275
    remediation of, 294–295
Communication skills, 307
Community
    and children with neurodevelopmen-
      tal conditions, 333
    involving, in pediatric rehabilitation,
      351–352
    role of, 480
Community-based situational assessment,
    359–360
Community-integrated programs, 52
Community Integration Questionnaire
    (CIQ), 48
Community-integrative standards, 55
Community reinforcement approach
    (CRA), 253
Community standard of care, 444
Comorbidity
    in geriatric population, 96–97
    with pediatric chronic illness,
      338–340

Compensatory interventions, 274, 280, 286–287, 322
Competency(-ies), of rehabilitation psychologist, 460–463, 467–474
  analytical, 461
  clinical, 460–461
  context-dependent, 467
  defined, 467
  developmental, 467
  ethical, 462
  financial, 462–463
  foundational, 470–471
  functional, 471–474
  incremental, 467
  interventional, 462
  and practica, 469–470
  relational, 461–462
Competency (legal decision), 171
Complete spinal cord injuries, 9
Complex regional pain syndrome (CPRS), 125, 397
Complex regional pain syndrome type 1 (CRPS 1), 125–126
Complicated mild brain injuries, 48
Comprehensive healthcare reform, 441
Comprehensive–holistic cognitive rehabilitation, 295–296
Computer adaptive testing (CAT), 152
Computerized physician order entry (CPOE), 445
Computerized tomography (CT), 214, 217
Concentration training, 289
Conduction aphasia, 71
Confidentiality, 433, 435
Conflicts of interest, 433–434
Confusional state, 166, 167
Confusion Assessment Protocol, 167
Consciousness, loss of
  with spinal cord injury, 14
  with traumatic brain injury, 45–46
Constraint-induced movement therapy (CI therapy), 395–396, 400–402
Constructional apraxia, 71, 72
Construct validity, of assessment instrument, 159
Consultation competency, 472, 473
Consumer-directed health care, 443
Consumer protection, 55, 472–474
Consumers (term), 385
Contextualized cognitive rehabilitation, 287
Continuum model of alcoholism, 245–246
Contralesional cortex, 394
Control, perceptions of, 340
Control coping continuum, 113

Conversational coaching, 294
Conversion disorder, 201
Copaxone, 139
Coping
  after amputation, 35–36
  with burn injuries, 110, 112–113
  with disability, 383–384
  and personality, 198
  with spinal cord injury, 13–14, 19
Coping and social skills training, 253
Coping Strategies Questionnaire (CSQ), 124
Cortical reorganization, 31
Couples counseling, 54
Courtroom testimony, 181–184
CP. *See* Cerebral palsy
CPOE (computerized physician order entry), 445
CRA (community reinforcement approach), 253
CRCs (certified rehabilitation counselors), 358
Cream-skimming, 440
Credentialing, 470
Criminal records, 44
Crisis coping, 198
Criterion validity, of assessment instrument, 159
Critical pathway, 68
Cross-examination, 181, 183–184
Crossing the Quality Chasm (IOM), 444
CRPS. *See* Complex regional pain syndrome
CRPS 1. *See* Complex regional pain syndrome type 1
CSF. *See* Cerebrospinal fluid
CSQ (Coping Strategies Questionnaire), 124
CT. *See* Computerized tomography
Cueing, 273, 275, 276
Cultural competency, 428
Culture, caregiving and, 304–305
CVAs (cerebrovascular accidents), 213
CVLT-II (California Verbal Learning Test), 185

DAI. *See* Diffuse axonal injury
DALY (disability-adjusted life years), 407
Daubert standard, 181, 185
Day treatment, for traumatic brain injury, 52
Debriding burned skin, 108
Deceleration, brain injury due to, 44
Decision making
  ATCB interventions for aiding, 275

  ethical, 434–436
  mediators of, 479
  models of, 436
Decision-making capacity
  ethics related to, 428
  evaluation of, 171–172
Deductibles, 441, 443
Degenerative disorders, 213
Degenerative spinal conditions, 121
Delirium, 46, 166
Demedicalization of services, 443
Dementia
  assessing, 167
  caregiving for patients with, 308
  and disability, 97
  in geriatric population, 98
  and personality changes, 199
  and stroke, 69
Dementia Rating Scale (DRS), 99
Dementia Rating Scale-2, 167
Demographic prediction equations, 185
Denial. *See also* Impaired awareness
  anosognosia *vs.* psychological, 266
  benefits of, 267
  of illness/injury, 261
  psychotherapeutic interventions with, 261, 266
  of substance abuse, 247
  of symptoms, 74–75
Deposition ("discovery") phase (of trial), 183
Depression
  and amputation, 30–33, 201
  assessment of, 170, 205–206
  with burn injuries, 110, 112
  effectiveness of psychotherapeutic interventions with, 263
  among elderly, 100–101
  fMRI for predicting recovery from, 227
  measures of, 204
  with multiple sclerosis, 134
  psychotherapeutic interventions for, 261
  among rehabilitation clients, 261
  with spinal cord injury, 11–12, 201
  and stroke, 72, 75–77, 199, 201
  in women with disabilities, 373, 374
Descriptive base, 453
Developmental level (of measurement instrument), 160
Developmental Neuropsychological Assessment (NEPSY), 320
Developmental stages
  and amputation, 33–34
  forensic testimony about, 186

Developmental stages (*continued*)
  and pediatric neuropsychology,
    316–318
  and pediatric rehabilitation, 347
  and spinal cord injury, 22
Device interface design, for ATCB
  interventions, 280
Diabetes, 29
*Diagnostic and Statistical Manual of Mental
  Disorders* (4th ed.) (*DSM–IV*), 245
*Diagnostic and Statistical Manual of Mental
  Disorders* (4th ed., text rev.)
  (*DSM–IV–TR*), 196, 200
Diffuse axonal injury (DAI), 45, 216
Diffusion tensor imaging (DTI), 214, 215,
  228–230
Diller, Leonard, 4, 295
Dimensional models, of personality, 196
Diplomates, 4, 469
Direct examination, 183
Disability(-ies)
  and amputation, 33
  attitudes toward people with, 381–383
  brain plasticity and overcoming,
    395–396
  context-specific, 413
  coping with, 383–384
  defined, 96
  determination of, 412–413
  and existing/potential assets, 385–386
  experience of, 384–385
  in geriatric population, 96–97
  prevalence of people with, 379
  psychological distress with, 418
  social–cognitive opportunities with,
    386–387
Disability-adjusted life years (DALY),
  407
Disability identity, 384
Disability in America (IOM), 477
Disability-induced emotional turmoil, 3
Disability Rating Scale (DRS), 47
Disability rights movement, 375
Disability wage replacement, 409
Disablement model, 147–148
Discharge planning, 165, 446
Disclosure, of information, 431
Discrimination, 408
Disease model of alcoholism, 245, 246
Disease-specific instruments, 152
Disease-specific QoL instruments, 150
Disfigurement, 108
Disinhibition syndrome, 72
Dispositional domain, of personality, 196
Distress. *See also* Caregiver burden;
    Family burden

  with burn injuries, 108–109
  with disabilities, 418
  parental, 339
  psychotherapy for, 167–168
District of Columbia Court of Appeals, 180
Disulfram, 253
Doctoral modesty, 464
Donepezil, 139
Downward social comparisons, 36, 386
Drinker's Inventory of Consequences, 251
Drinking Diary, 251
Driving, return to, 79–80, 173
Driving ability, 134
DRS (Dementia Rating Scale), 99
Drug Abuse Screening Test, 251
Drug dependence, 242
Drug use disorders
  preinjury, 242
  prevalence of, 241
*DSM–IV. See Diagnostic and Statistical
    Manual of Mental Disorders*
DTI. *See* Diffusion tensor imaging
Duchenne's muscular dystrophy, 346
Dyslexia, 399
Dysphoria, 170

EBRI (Employee Benefit Research
    Institute), 440
Ecological validity, 317
ED. *See* Executive dysfunction
Edema, 45
Education. *See also* Academic reintegration
  about brain injury, 288
  about traumatic brain injury, 50
  family. *See* Family education
  patient. *See* Patient education
  of staff, 168
Education levels, 185, 409
Ejaculation, 17
Elderly persons
  alcohol abuse among, 102
  depression among, 100–101
  memory disturbances among, 98
  personality changes in, 199
"Electronic knot in the handkerchief,"
    292
E-mail programs, 275
Embolic stroke, 65, 66
Emergent self-self-awareness, 292
Emic/cultural perspective, 151
Emotional assessment, 167, 170–171
Emotional disorders, 72, 75–79
Emotional functioning, disturbances of, 72
Emotional processing, 227

Emotions
  and multiple sclerosis, 134–135
  positive, 420–421
Empathy, 115
Employee Benefit Research Institute
    (EBRI), 440
Employee Retirement Income and
    Security Act of 1974, 441
Employer-based health insurance,
    439–440
Employment centers, 359
Empowerment, 375
Engel, George, 477
Environmental context
  of driving ability, 173
  immediate, 267
  social, 267
  of women with disabilities, 371–374
  of work-related injury and disability, 409
Environmental influences, on disabilities,
    478, 480
Environmental interventions, 267,
    274–275, 291
Environmental supports, 322–323
Epidural injections, of steroids, 125
Episodic memory, 134
Erections, male
  and spinal cord injury, 17
  and stroke, 80
eRehabData, 157
Errorless learning, 289–290
Error patterns, 279–280
Ethical competency, of rehabilitation
    psychologist, 462
Ethical Standards (APA), 429–436
Ethics, 427–436
  APA *Ethical Standards* revised,
    429–436
  APA Ethics Code revisions, 428
  APA *General Principles* revised,
    428–429
  and decision making, 434–436
  and informed consent, 430–432
  and multiple relationships/conflicts of
    interest, 433–434
  and test data release, 429–430
Ethnicity
  and caregiving, 305
  of spinal cord injuries, 10
Etic/universal perspective, 151–152
Everyday life functioning, 134–135
Executive dysfunction (ED)
  effects of, 167
  remediation of, 290–293
  and stroke, 72–73

Executive function syndrome, 72
Existential questions, 262–263
Expectancies, for successful treatment outcome, 127
Expectations, 128
Experience of disability, 384–385
Expert testimony, 180, 182
Exposure therapy, 112
Extended Glasgow Outcome Scale (GOS-E), 47
Externally-focused interventions, 322–323
External reminder systems, 290

FACIT (Functional Assessment of Chronic Illness Therapy), 154
FACIT Measurement System, 155
FACIT-SP (Functional Assessment of Chronic Illness Therapies–Spiritual), 367
FACT-G (Functional Assessment of Cancer Therapy-General), 155
Failed back surgery syndrome (FBSS), 125–126
Falconer, J. A., 453
Falls
    risk of, 173
    spinal cord injuries from, 10
FAM. *See* Functional Assessment Measure
Family
    and burn critical phase, 111
    involving, in pediatric rehabilitation, 351–352
    in psychotherapeutic interventions, 264
    and stroke, 78–79
    TBI-patient reintegration into, 53
Family adaptation, child adjustment and, 349–350
Family and Medical Leave Act (FMLA), 408
Family burden. *See also* Caregiver burden
    and pediatric rehabilitation, 347–348
    with rehabilitation, 262
    after traumatic brain injury, 53
Family-centered interventions, 349–350
Family counseling, 69
Family education
    about neuropsychological rehabilitation, 170
    about spinal cord injury, 19
    about stroke, 69–70, 81
    about traumatic brain injury, 50
Family systems illness model, 345–347

Family therapy, 350
Fatigue, 135, 138, 227
FBS. *See* MMPI-2 Fake Bad Scale
FBSS. *See* Failed back surgery syndrome
Fear avoidance, 123
Federal Rule 42, 445–446
Federal Rules of Evidence, 181, 182
Feedback, 115
Fertility, 17
FFM (five-factor personality model), 197
FIM. *See* Functional Independence Measure
Financial competency, of rehabilitation psychologist, 462–463
Financial incentives, 254
Finger agnosia, 71
First degree burns, 107
Fiscal intermediaries (FIs), 445
5 Million Lives campaign, 444
Five-factor personality model (FFM), 197
Fixed batteries, 168–169, 181–182, 184
FLAIR (fluid attenuated inversion recovery), 215
Flexible batteries, 169, 184–185
Floor effect, 160
Florida Appellate Court, 182
Fluid attenuated inversion recovery (FLAIR), 215
FMLA (Family and Medical Leave Act), 408
fMRI. *See* Functional MRI
Focal hand dystonia, 396
Follow-up assessment, 168–169
Forced-choice testing, 187
Forced-use techniques, 286
Fordyce, Wilbert, 4
Forensic rehabilitation psychology, 179–189
    admissibility of testimony from, 181–182
    assessment measures in, 184–185
    and courtroom testimony, 182–184
    developmental issues/injury outcome in, 186
    growth of, 179–180
    and history of psychology in legal system, 180
    malingering detection in, 186–188
    overdiagnosis of impairment in, 188–189
    and perceived clinician bias, 186
    premorbid functioning estimation in, 185
Foundational competency, of rehabilitation psychologist, 468, 470–471
Foundation of Accountability, 157

Frailty, 96–97
FRAMES, 115, 252
Frontal-lobe syndromes, 72
Frye standard, 181
Frye v. United States, 181
Fuhrer, Marcus, 149
Full thickness burns, 107
Functional assessment, 149–154
    dimensions of, 151–154
    generic vs. disease-specific instruments for, 152
    instruments for, 150–151
    mode of administration of, 151–152
    rehabilitation psychologist's role in, 149
    research directions for, 160–161
    technology for, 152–153
    type of, 151
Functional Assessment Measure (FAM), 47–48
Functional Assessment of Cancer Therapy-General (FACT-G), 155
Functional Assessment of Chronic Illness Therapies–Spiritual (FACIT-SP), 367
Functional Assessment of Chronic Illness Therapy (FACIT), 154
Functional competency, of rehabilitation psychologist, 468, 471–474
Functional imaging, 213
Functional independence, 478
Functional Independence Measure (FIM), 47–48, 151
Functional Independence Measure-Pediatric (Wee-FIM), 160
Functional magnetic resonance imaging, 479
Functional MRI (fMRI), 137–138, 224
Functional neuroimaging, 224–227
Functional status
    conceptualization of, 149
    and health-care-quality measures, 156–157
    measurement of, 149–154
    terminology used with, 147–149

Gabapentin, 16
GABA (gamma-aminobutyric acid) signaling, 394
GAD (generalized anxiety disorder), 77
Gait disorder, 398
Galveston Orientation and Amnesia Test (GOAT), 47, 166
Gamma-aminobutyric acid (GABA) signaling, 394

Index

Gazzaniga, M. S., 227
GCS. *See* Glasgow Coma Scale
GDS. *See* Geriatric Depression Scale
Gender differences, in caregiving, 305
Generalized anxiety disorder (GAD), 77
General Principles (APA Ethics Code),
    428–429
Generic instruments, 152
Generic QoL instruments, 150
Geriatric Depression Scale (GDS),
    204–206
Geriatric rehabilitation, 95–104
    demographics of, 95
    and depression, 100–101
    and disability/cormorbidity/frailty
        concepts, 96–97
    and pain, 101–102
    psychologist's role in, 101–103
    and sleep disturbance, 102
    and substance abuse, 102–103
Glasgow Coma Scale (GCS), 45, 47
Glasgow-Liege Score, 47
Glasgow Outcome Scale (GOS), 47
Global aphasia, 71
Global positioning system, 276
GM. *See* Gray matter
Goal Management Training, 291–292
Goal-setting, 292
GOAT. *See* Galveston Orientation and
    Amnesia Test
Good to Great (Collins), 464
GOS (Glasgow Outcome Scale), 47
GOS-E (Extended Glasgow Outcome
    Scale), 47
Gradient recall echo (GRE), 215
Gradual-decline brain diseases, 315
Gray matter (GM), 214, 231, 244
GRE (gradient recall echo), 215
Grid Method, 251
Grief, 101
Group dynamics, 380
Group interventions
    for amputees, 37
    for caregivers, 303
    effectiveness of, 264
    neuropsychologist's role in, 167
    peer-led, 303
    for reluctant patients, 266
    with spinal cord injury, 18–19
    for stress management, 349
Growth, posttraumatic, 419–420
*Guides to the Evaluation of Permanent
    Impairment* (Andersson), 413
Gunshot injuries, 15

Halstead, L. S., 453
Halstead-Reitan Neuropsychological
    Battery (HRB or HRNB), 168–169,
    182, 185
Hamm, J., 460
Hand amputation, 36
Hand washing, 275
Hanson, S., 436
Hardcopy films, 214
Harvard Business Review, 464
Health care
    attitudes within, 371
    modern U.S. insurance for, 440–441
    quality of, 444–445
    spending worldwide on, 439
    U.S. history of financing for, 439–440
Health care financing, 439–440
Health Care Financing Administration,
    157
Health care leadership, 460–464
    analytical competency of, 461
    characteristics of effective, 460
    clinical competency of, 460–461
    ethical competency of, 462
    financial competency of, 462–463
    interventional competency of, 462
    professional development plan for,
        463–464
    rehabilitation psychologist as
        candidate for, 460–463
    relational competency of, 461–462
Health care policy, government's role
    in, 444
Health care quality
    functional status as measure of,
        156–157
    quality of life as measure of, 156–157
Health-care-quality measures, 156–160
    administrative requirements for,
        158–159
    applications of, 158
    instruments for, 157–160
    interpretability of, 159
    issues with, 158
    level of measurement in, 159–160
    quality of life/functional status as,
        156–157
    reliability of, 159
    selection of, 158–160
    sensitivity to change by, 160
    target-audience considerations with, 160
Health care reform, 439–448
    advocacy for, 446–448
    and cardinal symptom model, 443–444

and consumer-directed care, 443
    and health savings accounts, 442–443
    recent efforts at, 444–445
    rehabilitation-specific legislative
        initiatives on, 445–446
    unsuccessful attempts at, 441–442
Health care system
    annual deaths in U.S., 459
    leadership gaps in, 460
    need for reform of, 459–460
    staff shortages in, 459–460
Health information, access to, 444
Health Information Portability and
    Accountability Act (HIPAA) of
    2006, 429, 430
Health information technology, 445
Health insurance, 439–441
Health Insurance Study
    Experiment/Medical Outcomes
    Study, 154
Health maintenance organizations
    (HMOs), 442
Health Outcomes Institute, 154
Health Pages, 157–158
Health Plan Employer Data and
    Information Set (HEDIS), 157
Health-promoting behaviors, 375
Health-related QoL, 148
Health-related quality of life (HRQL or
    HRQoL)
    in children with chronic illnesses, 340
    and ICF classifications, 149
    and juvenile rheumatic diseases, 340
Health savings accounts (HSAs), 442–443
Health services, 361
Health Status Questionnaire, 154
Heart disease, 96
HEDIS (Health Plan Employer Data and
    Information Set), 157
Helplessness, learned. *See* Learned
    helplessness
Hemiparesis, 398
Hemiplegia, 226, 229
Hemiplegic shoulder pain, 120
Hemispatial attention, 293–294
Hemophilia, 337
Hemorrhagic stroke, 65–66
High-deductible plans, 443
HIPAA. *See* Health Information
    Portability and Accountability Act
    of 2006
Hippocampus, 219, 220, 227, 393, 394
Hip replacement, 445
Hiscock Digit Recognition Test, 187, 188

490

Hispanics, 374
HMOs (health maintenance organizations), 442
Holistic rehabilitation, 52
Home Health Compare, 158
Hope, 455
Hopelessness, 198, 266
Horne v. Goodson Logging Company, 180
HRB. *See* Halstead-Reitan Neuropsychological Battery
HRNB. *See* Halstead-Reitan Neuropsychological Battery
HRQL. *See* Health-related quality of life
HRQoL. *See* Health-related quality of life
HSAs. *See* Health savings accounts
Human studies
    on central nervous system plasticity, 393–394
    on plasticity after CNS injury, 394
    on rehabilitation-induced CNS plasticity, 395–400
Humor, 36
Hydrocephalus, 330
Hyperalgesia, 128
Hypertension, 96
Hypnosis, 111, 116

IADLs. *See* Instrumental activities of daily living
ICA (internal carotid artery) stroke, 67
ICF. *See* International Classification of Functioning, Disability, and Health
ICH. *See* Intracerebral hemorrhage
ICIDH. *See* International Classification of Impairment, Disability, and Handicap
ICUs (intensive care units), 111
Ideational apraxia, 71
Ideomotor apraxia, 71
Idiographic criterion approaches, to personality, 196
IHI (Institute for Healthcare Improvement), 444
Illness burden, 97
Illness-induced barriers, 339
Imaging. *See* Neuroimaging
Imipramine, 77
Impaired awareness, 74–75, 167, 170, 261
Impairment
    defined, 148
    determination of, 412–413
Impairment ratings, 413
Impulse control, 54

Impulsivity, 114
Inattention, 399
Incomplete spinal cord injuries, 9
Incremental healthcare reform, 441–442
Independence, 168, 172–173, 277
Indiana Court of Appeals, 180
Indianapolis Union Railway v. Walker, 180
Indifference reaction, 78
Indirect interventions, 19
Individual caregiver interventions, 303
Individualized education plan, 54
Individualized functional needs, 351
Individualized programs, 351
Individualized written rehabilitation plan, 53, 358
Individuals with Disabilities Education Act of 2006, 54
Individuation, 385
Industry human capital, 460
Infection, 45
Information processing speed, 133–134
Information Technology for the Social and Behavioral Sciences, 161
Information tracking, 275
Informed consent, 430–432
    general issues in, 430–431
    to research, 432
    to therapy, 431–432
    to treatment, 172
Inpatient rehabilitation facility (IRF), 445–446, 463
Inpatient setting
    psychotherapy in, 267
    rehabilitation neuropsychology in, 165–168
    stroke treatment in, 79
In-person caregiver interventions, 303–304
Insiders, outsiders *vs.,* 385
Institute for Healthcare Improvement (IHI), 444
Institute for Objective Measurement, 160
Institute of Medicine (IOM), 245, 246, 444, 477, 478
Instrumental activities of daily living (IADLs), 149, 153
Insurance regulations, 442
Intensive care units (ICUs), 111
Intensive massed practice, 294
Interdisciplinary teams, 452, 453
Internal carotid artery (ICA) stroke, 67
International Association for the Study of Pain, 119

International Classification of Functioning, Disability, and Health (ICF), 148, 368, 478
International Classification of Impairment, Disability, and Handicap (ICIDH), 477, 478
International Society for Quality of Life Research, 154
Internships, 469, 470
Interpretability, of assessment instrument, 159
Interpreters, 431
Interval level of measurement, 160
Intervention competency, 462, 472, 473
Intimate relationships, 54, 372–373
Intoxication, 242, 243, 262
Intracerebral hemorrhage (ICH), 65, 66
Intracranial hemorrhage, 65
Intramuscular injections, 125
Intrapsychic domain, of personality, 196
Intraspinal narcotics, 125
Intrinsic value, of women, 375
IOM. *See* Institute of Medicine
Ipsilesional cortex, 394
Iraq war, 29
IRF. *See* Inpatient rehabilitation facility
ISAAC, 275
Ischemic penumbra, 66
Ischemic stroke, 65, 66
Itching, 116
Iterative design, 279

Jackson, Hughlings, 391
Jean Piaget Society, 161
Jenkins v. United States, 180
JIA. *See* Juvenile idiopathic arthritis
Job coaching, 53
Job development, 360
Job markets, 409
Job placement follow-up, 360
Job retention services, 21
Job-site consultation, 360
Job site supports, 360
Job stabilization services, 360
Job "try-outs," 360
Johnson, H. M., 379
Joint Commission on Accreditation of Health Care Organizations, 121, 157, 451
Joint conditions, 121
Joint pain, 121, 126
Joint replacement, 121
JRDs. *See* Juvenile rheumatic diseases

Just-world hypothesis, 382
Juvenile court, 180
Juvenile idiopathic arthritis (JIA), 338–340
Juvenile rheumatic diseases (JRDs),
    337–341
  cognitive appraisals with, 339–340
  disease-related factors in adjustment
      to, 340
  psychological adjustment to, 338–340
  psychological comorbidity with,
      338–340
  psychological interventions for,
      340–341
  psychologist's role in, 341
  and quality of life, 340

Kaas, Jan, 392
Keith-Spiegel, P., 436
Kerkhoff, T., 436
Kitchener, K. S., 436
Knee replacement, 445
Koocher, G., 436

Labeling, 385
Lacunar stroke, 66
Language
  and myelomeningocele, 330
  neuroimaging of functional, 225–227
  and poststroke return to driving, 79
  remediation of, 294–295
Language therapies, 294
Lateral cord syndrome, 9–10
Lateralized lesions, 70
Law enforcement, 371–372
Learned helplessness, 114–115, 198, 340
Learned nonuse, 400–402
Learning disabilities, 44
Learning problems, 315
Left hemiparesis, 293
Left hemisphere lesions, 70, 72
Left hemisphere stroke, 173
Left neglect, 293–294
Legal rights, 267
Legal system, psychology in, 180
Legislation and legislative initiatives
  on rehabilitation-specific health care
      reform, 445–446
  on work-related-injury and -disability,
      408
Lewin, Kurt A., 380, 381, 387
Lewinsohnian theory, 101
Lexapro, 77
Lidocaine, 125

"Life space," 380
Ligaments, 126
Limb Activation Training, 293
Limb amputation, 29–39
  amputation-related factors in
      adjustment to, 30–32
  of arm/hand, 36
  body-image factors in adjustment to, 34
  brain reorganization after, 392, 393
  coping-strategy factors in adjustment
      to, 35–36
  and depression, 31, 201
  developmental factors in adjustment
      to, 33–34
  disability factors in adjustment to, 33
  interpersonal factors in adjustment to,
      34–35
  intervention issues with, 36–38
  pain factors in adjustment to, 32–33
  phantom limb pain with, 38
  prevalence of, 29
  psychological adjustment to, 30–36
  research directions on, 38–39
  and sexual functioning, 38
Limited data sets, 149
Linguistic impairments, 266–267
Listening, reflective. *See* Reflective listening
Litigation, 179, 183, 199, 408, 410
Local anesthetic, 125
Low-back pain
  effectiveness of psychotherapeutic
      interventions with, 263
  medications for, 125
  prolotherapy for, 126
  work-related, 407, 409, 410
Lower limb amputation, 29
Luria-Nebraska Neuropsychological
    Battery, 184–185

MacArthur Competence Assessment
    Tool, 172
MACFIMS (Minimal Assessment of
    Cognitive Functioning in Multiple
    Sclerosis), 136
MacNeill-Lichtenberg Decision Tree
    (MLDT), 99
Magnetic resonance imaging (MRI),
    214–218, 221
Magnetic resonance spectroscopy
    (MRS), 230
Magnetic source imaging (MSI), 224
Magnetoencephalography (MEG), 224
Maladaptive coping, 197
Malingering detection, 168, 186–188

Malingering of neurocognitive
    dysfunction (MND), 188
Maltreatment (of children), 331–332
Management by fact, 461
Marijuana, 242
Marital strain, 347
Martino-Saltzmann, D., 453
Maryland Hospital Association, 157
Massage therapy, 341
MAST (Mississippi Aphasia Screening
    Test), 166
Matching users
  with assistive technology for cognition
      and behavior, 277–279
  with substance treatments, 251
Maternal age, 347
Maternal and Child Health Leadership
    Education in Neurodevelopmental
    Disabilities program, 351
Mathematics skills, 330
Maximum medical improvement (MMI),
    411
MCA (middle cerebral artery) stroke, 67
McGill Pain Questionnaire (MPQ), 122
MCID (minimally clinically important
    difference), 160
MCMI-III. *See* Millon Clinical Multiaxial
    Inventory-III
MDS (Minimum Data Set), 153
Measurement level, 159–160
Measures of effort, 187
Mechanical neck pain, 125
Medicaid, 440
Medical model, 265
Medical Outcomes Trust of the Health
    Institute, 154
Medical Outcome System, 157
Medicare, 153, 158, 442, 445, 446, 463
Medicare, Medicaid, and SCHIP
    Extension Act of 2007, 446
Medication, assessing impact of, 169–170
MEG (magnetoencephalography), 224
Memory and memory disturbances
  and ATCB devices, 280
  in elderly population, 98
  with multiple sclerosis, 134
  remediation of, 289–290
  with stroke, 69, 72
Memory notebooks, 290
Mental health issues, 373–374
Mental retardation, 330
Menu of options, 115
Merzenich, Michael, 392
Metacognition, 98–99
Methylphenidate, 50

Meyerson, L., 379
MI. *See* Motivational interviewing
Microsoft Excel, 463
Microsoft PowerPoint, 463
Middle cerebral artery (MCA) stroke, 67
Mild brain injuries, 48–49
Milieu, personal, and technology (MPT) factors, 277–279
Military personnel, 3, 4, 29, 39
Millon Clinical Multiaxial Inventory-III (MCMI-III), 203, 204
Minimal Assessment of Cognitive Functioning in Multiple Sclerosis (MACFIMS), 136
Minimal conscious state, 228
Minimally clinically important difference (MCID), 160
Mini-Mental State Examination (MMSE), 68, 99, 166–167
Minimum Data Set (MDS), 153
Minnesota Multiphasic Personality Inventory (MMPI), 184
Minnesota Multiphasic Personality Inventory-2 (MMPI-2), 184, 187–188, 203–205
Mirror box techniques, 38
Misidentification syndromes, 168
Mississippi Aphasia Screening Test (MAST), 166
MLDT (MacNeill-Lichtenberg Decision Tree), 99
MM. *See* Myelomeningocele
MMI (maximum medical improvement), 411
MMPI (Minnesota Multiphasic Personality Inventory), 184
MMPI-2. *See* Minnesota Multiphasic Personality Inventory-2
MMPI-2 Fake Bad Scale (FBS), 187, 188
MMPI-2 F-K ratio, 187, 188
MMSE. *See* Mini-Mental State Examination
MND (malingering of neurocognitive dysfunction), 188
Mnemonic techniques, 274
Modafinil, 139
Model Systems of Care, 4, 10, 49, 51, 55, 83
Modesty, 464
Modified MMSE (3MS), 68
Moral hazard, 441
Motivation
    assessing, 202
    in burn patients, 114–116

Motivational interviewing (MI)
    with burn injuries, 115
    for substance abuse, 16, 252–253
Motor skills, 153
Motor vehicle crashes
    spinal cord injuries from, 10, 21
    TBI and alcohol-related, 44
Mourning, 109
Movement therapy, constraint-induced, 400–402
MPQ (McGill Pain Questionnaire), 122
MPT factors. *See* Milieu, personal, and technology factors
MRI. *See* Magnetic resonance imaging
MRS (magnetic resonance spectroscopy), 230
MS. *See* Multiple sclerosis
MSI (magnetic source imaging), 224
MSID. *See* Musculoskeletal injuries and disorders
MSNQ (Multiple Sclerosis Neuropsychology Questionnaire), 136
Multi-component interventions, 308–309
Multidisciplinary teams, 452
Multidisciplinary treatments, 127
Multifactorial model of adjustment, 3–4
Multiple relationships, 433–434
Multiple sclerosis (MS), 133–139
    assessment of effects of, 136–137
    cognitive assessment with, 136
    effectiveness of psychotherapeutic interventions with, 263
    and everyday life functioning/ emotions, 134–135
    and fatigue, 135
    and functional neuroimaging, 137–138
    neuroimaging assessment of, 137–138
    prevalence of cognitive impairment with, 133–134
    and quality of life, 135
    quality-of-life assessment with, 136, 137
    research directions for, 139
    and sexuality, 374
    and structural neuroimaging, 137
    symptoms of, 133
    treatment of cognitive impairment in, 138–139
    white matter degeneration in, 224
Multiple Sclerosis Neuropsychology Questionnaire (MSNQ), 136
Multiple Sclerosis Quality of Life Inventory (MSQLI), 137
Multisystem war injuries, 4

Mundt interview, 98
Muscle relaxants, 125
Musculoskeletal injuries and disorders (MSID)
    in children, 337
    chronic pain with, 121
    work-related, 407–410
Musicians, 393, 396
Myelomeningocele (MM), 330, 333

Nagi, Saad, 477
NAN (National Academy of Neuropsychology), 180
Narcotics, 17
Narrative approaches, 384–385
National Academy of Neuropsychology (NAN), 180
National Commission for Quality Assurance (NCQA), 157
National Council on Psychological Aspects of Physical Disability (NCPAPD), 468
National Institute of Aging Toolbox for Assessment of Neurological and Behavioral Function, 152–153
National Institute of Disability and Rehabilitation Research (NIDRR), 4, 49, 55, 108
National Institute of Neurological Disorders and Stroke Neurology Quality of Life project, 152
National Institutes of Health (NIH), 155
National Spinal Cord Injury Statistical Center (NSCISC), 10
Navigation systems, 276
NCPAPD (National Council on Psychological Aspects of Physical Disability), 468
NCQA (National Commission for Quality Assurance), 157
NCSE. *See* Neurobehavioral Cognitive Status Examination
NDCs (neurodevelopmental conditions), 315
Neck pain, 126
Negative affect, 119, 122–124
Negative emotions, 197
Neglect (disorder), 71, 293–294, 399
Neglect, childhood, 331–332
Neighborhoods, 480
NEO-PI. *See* Neuroticism, Extroversion, and Openness Personality Inventory

NEPSY (Developmental Neuropsychological Assessment), 320
NEPSY-II, 320
Neural tube defects, 330
Neurobehavioral Cognitive Status Examination (NCSE), 68, 99
Neurobehavioral disorders, 262
Neurobehavioral residential treatment, 53
Neurocognitive Reeducation Project, 322
Neurocognitive risks, of children with neurodevelopmental conditions, 329–331
Neurodevelopmental conditions (NDCs), 315. *See also* Children with neurodevelopmental conditions
Neuroeconomics, 479
Neuroimaging, 213–232
    background of, 214–220
    contributions of, 227–231
    functional, 224–227
    MS assessment with, 137–138
    of pain, 122
    qualitative image analysis, 221–224
    quantitative image analysis, 219–221
    on rehabilitation patients, 219–231
    for stroke, 83
Neurological validity, 317
NeuroPage, 290
Neuropsychological assessment, 49–50
Neuropsychological disorders, 70–74
Neuropsychological rehabilitation, 52
Neuropsychological scaffolding, 288
Neuropsychology, 165. *See also* Rehabilitation neuropsychology
Neuroticism, 197, 199
Neuroticism, Extroversion, and Openness Personality Inventory (NEO-PI), 204, 205
Neurotransmitter model, 100
New England Medical Center, 154
New England Rehabilitation Hospital, 82
NIDRR. *See* National Institute of Disability and Rehabilitation Research
NIH (National Institutes of Health), 155
NIH PROMIS, 161
Nociceptive information, 122
No-fault insurance coverage, 410
Nominal scales, 159
Nomothetic criterion approaches, to personality, 196
Nontricyclic antidepressants, 12
Nonverbal learning disorder, 330
Noradrenaline, 395

Norming, 169
Nortriptyline, 77, 78
"No work disability," 411
NRS (numerical rating scale), 122
NSCISC (National Spinal Cord Injury Statistical Center), 10
NSQLI (Multiple Sclerosis Quality of Life Inventory), 137
Numerical rating scale (NRS), 122
Nursing Home Compare, 158
Nutritional behaviors, 372

Objective QoL, 148
Object naming therapy, 294
OECD (Organization for Economic Cooperation and Development), 439
Ohio Appellate Court, 182
Oklahoma Premorbid Intelligence Estimate, 185
O-LOG. *See* Orientation Log
100,000 Lives campaign, 444
One-stop state employment centers, 359
Online family problem solving, 350
Opiates, 242
Opinion base, 453
Opioid analgesics, 124
Opioid medications, 124–125
Opportunity Knocks, 276
Ordinal scales, 159–160
Organization for Economic Cooperation and Development (OECD), 439
Orgasm, 17–18
Orientation Log (O-LOG), 47, 166
Orthopedic conditions, 121
Osteoarthritis, 97
Outcome and Assessment Information Set, 153
Outcome-focused instruments, 151
Outcome measurement, 156–157
Outpatient setting
    psychotherapy in, 267–268
    rehabilitation neuropsychology in, 168–171
    therapy for TBI patients in, 52
Outsiders, insiders *vs.*, 385
Overdiagnosis of impairment, 188–189

P4P. *See* Pay for performance
PADLs (personal activities of daily living), 149
PAI. *See* Personality Assessment Inventory

Pain
    and amputation, 32–33
    chronic. *See* Chronic pain
    classifications of, 15
    defined, 119
    functional neuroimaging of, 227
    and geriatric rehabilitation, 101–102
    quality of, 122
    and spinal cord injury, 15–16
    and stroke, 79
"Pain: The Fifth Vital Sign" (phrase), 121
Pain behaviors, 123
Pain beliefs, 102
Pain coping, 123–124
Pain intensity, 121–122, 410
Pain management
    with burn injuries, 110, 111
    in children with chronic illnesses, 341
PALS (Promoting Amputee Life Skills) program, 37
Paraplegia, 9
Parental distress, 339
Parental involvement, 341
Parental overprotectiveness, 333
Parenting behaviors, 341
Parents, as therapists, 351–352
Parkinson's Disease Activities of Daily Living Scale, 152
Partial thickness burns, 107
Participants' bill of rights, 432
Participation in society, 478
Participation restrictions, 148
Passive coping with pain, 124
Passivity, 332, 333
Patient Assessment Instrument, 153
Patient education
    about neuropsychological rehabilitation, 170
    about stroke, 69–70
    about traumatic brain injury, 50, 349
Patient Evaluation Conference System (PECS), 152
Patient history, 166, 169, 201–202
Patient interview, 169, 201–202
Patient privacy, 248, 429, 430, 433
Patient protection, 431
Patient-Reported Outcomes Measurement Information System (PROMIS), 155–156, 161
Pay for performance (P4P), 147, 444–445
PBS (Perceived Benefits Scale), 420
PCA stroke. *See* Posterior cerebral artery stroke
PDAs. *See* Personal digital assistants

PEAT (planning and execution assistant and training system), 275
PECS (Patient Evaluation Conference System), 152
Pediatric chronic illness, rehabilitation with, 337–342
cognitive appraisals for, 339–340
and comorbidity, 338–340
disease-related factors in, 340
and psychological adjustment, 338–340
psychological interventions in, 340–341
psychologist's role in, 341
Pediatric Evaluation of Disability Inventory, 160
Pediatric neuropsychology, 315–325
assessment procedures in, 319–321
and child development, 316–318
factors affecting outcomes with, 318
future of, 324–325
historical perspective on, 315–316
professional skills in, 319–324
treatment strategies in, 321–324
Pediatric rehabilitation, 345–352
and child adjustment, 349–350
and developmental stages, 347
and family/caregiver adaptation, 347–350
and family systems illness model, 345–347
involving family/community in, 351–352
and nature of condition, 345–347
and teachers/school system, 348–352
Peer-coping intervention, 19
Peer counseling
for burn injuries, 112
with spinal cord injury, 20
Peer-entry situations, 332
Peer-led groups, 303
Pension plans, 441
People management, 461
Perceived Benefits Scale (PBS), 420
Perception, disorders of, 71
Performance measures, 157–158
Peripheral vascular disease (PVD), 29
Periventricular leukomalacia (PVL), 330
Permanent partial disability, 411
Permanent total disability, 411
Permission, Limited Information, Specific Suggestions, and Intensive Therapy (PLISSIT), 80
Persistent vegetative state (PVS), 45–46

Personal activities of daily living (PADLs), 149
Personal digital assistants (PDAs), 275, 290
Personality, 195–200
assessment measures for, 203–206
assessment of personality functioning, 201–202
and interpersonal interactions/rehabilitation services, 199–200
interpretive issues of, 202–203
leadership, 461–462
and neurologically-based changes in, 198–199
and rehabilitation, 197–198
terminology, 196
theoretical dimensions of, 196–197
Personality Assessment Inventory (PAI), 204, 205
Personality disorders
DSM–IV–TR definition of, 200
as preinjury burn factors, 110
Personality disturbances, 262
Personality measures, 203–205
Personality theory, 196
Personality traits, 197
Person-oriented interventions, 274
PET (positron emission tomography), 224
PF-10 (10 physical function) items, 155
PGI (Posttraumatic Growth Inventory), 420
Phantom limb pain (PLP), 31, 34, 36, 38
Pharmacotherapy
changes in, 170
for depression with spinal cord injury, 12
for juvenile rheumatic diseases, 338
for poststroke anxiety, 78
for poststroke depression, 77
Phencyclidine, 242
Phenotypic plasticity, 479
Physical activity, 77, 97, 372
Physical conditioning, 341
Physical health issues, 372
Picture boards, 294
Pixel, 220
Placebos, 127–128
Place–train model, 53
Planning and execution assistant and training system (PEAT), 275
Plasticity, 479. See also Brain plasticity; Central nervous system plasticity
PLISSIT (Permission, Limited Information, Specific Suggestions, and Intensive Therapy), 80
PLP. See Phantom limb pain

PocketCoach, 275
Polyarthritis, 445
Polythetic criterion approaches, to personality, 196
Polytrauma, 39
Portland Digit Recognition Test, 187, 188
Positive behavioral supports, 323–324
Positive emotions, 420–421
Positive health behaviors, 97
Positive psychology, 198, 417–422
and amputation, 35–36
future research on, 421–422
interventions with, 421
and positive emotions, 420–421
and posttraumatic growth, 419–420
and psychological distress with disability, 418
and resilience, 418–419
theoretical models of, 422
Positron emission tomography (PET), 224
Post-acute rehabilitation services, for traumatic brain injury, 51–53
Postconcussion syndrome, 189
Postdoctoral programs, 470
Posterior cerebral artery (PCA) stroke, 67–68
Posterior left hemisphere lesions, 70, 72
Poststroke depression (PSD), 72, 75–77
Post-Stroke Rehabilitation Guideline, 68
Posttraumatic amnesia (PTA), 46, 47, 51
Posttraumatic growth, 419–420
Posttraumatic Growth Inventory (PGI), 420
Posttraumatic headache (PTHA), 120
Posttraumatic stress disorder (PTSD), 170
after acquired disability, 418
and amputation, 31, 36
with burn injuries, 110, 112
and malingering, 186
with spinal cord injury, 13
Post-World War II, 3–4
Poverty, 371, 440
Practica training, 469–470
"Practice effects," 168
Preassessment phase (of trial), 183
Predoctoral training, 470
Pregabalin, 16
Pregnancy, 18
Premorbid functioning estimation, 185
Present Pain Intensity index, 122
Pressure ulcers, 244
Primary injuries, with traumatic brain injury, 44
Primary intracerebral hemorrhage, 66
Princeton Institute, 468

Prism adaptation method, 293–294
Privacy, patient. *See* Patient privacy
Privacy laws, 248. *See also* Health Information Portability and Accountability Act of 2006
Problem solving, 350
Problem-solving skills, 307
Problem-solving therapy, 77
Problem-Solving Training, 291–292
Procedural codes, 259–260
Process skills, 153
Professional development competency, 473, 474
Professional development plan, 463–464
Professional psychological organizations, 471
Prognostication of long-term outcome, 51
Projects With Industry (PWI) program, 361
Prolotherapy, 126
PROMIS. *See* Patient-Reported Outcomes Measurement Information System
Promoting Amputee Life Skills (PALS) program, 37
Prospective payment systems, 147, 442
Prostheses, 34, 36
Prosthetic clinics, 37
Protective behaviors, 384
Pruritus (itching), 116
PSD. *See* Poststroke depression
PsycBITE, 296
Psychoeducation
  candidacy for, 265
  for caregivers, 307–308
  effectiveness of, 264
Psychopathology
  assessment measures for, 203–206
  assessment of, 201–202
  interpretive issues of, 202–203
  and rehabilitation, 200–201
  theoretical dimensions of, 196–197
Psychopharmacological management, 50–51
Psychostimulants, 50
Psychotherapeutic interventions, 259–269
  for adjustment to disability, 260
  and anxiety, 261
  and bereavement, 260–261
  candidacy for, 265
  for caregivers, 308
  for cognitive/linguistic impairments, 266–267
  and denial, 261, 266
  and depression, 261
  effectiveness of, 263–264

for emotional distress, 167–168
  environmental, 267
  and existential questions, 262–263
  and family stress/burden, 262
  and health/behavior, 259–260
  inpatient *vs.* outpatient, 267–268
  and neurobehavioral/cognitive disorders, 261–262
  and personality disturbances, 262
  recommendations for, 268
  in rehabilitation settings, 263–264
  with reluctant patients, 266
  and substance use disorders, 262
  telephone-based, 264
  theoretical framework for, 259
Psychotherapy groups, 266
PTA. *See* Posttraumatic amnesia
PTHA (posttraumatic headache), 120
PTSD. *See* Posttraumatic stress disorder
Public health, 480
Puente, Antonio, 180
Pure alexia, 71
PVD (peripheral vascular disease), 29
PVL (periventricular leukomalacia), 330
PVS. *See* Persistent vegetative state
PWI (Projects With Industry) program, 361

Qol. *See* Quality of life
Qualitative image analysis, 213, 221–224
QualityMetric, Inc., 161
Quality of life (QoL)
  conceptualization of, 150
  defined, 148
  domains of, 150
  and health-care-quality measures, 156–157
  and juvenile rheumatic diseases, 340
  with multiple sclerosis, 135
  with spinal cord injury, 13
  and spirituality, 367–368
  terminology used with, 147–149
Quality-of-life assessment
  instruments for, 154–156
  with multiple sclerosis, 136, 137
  rehabilitation psychologist's role in, 149
  research directions for, 160–161
Quality of Life Research, 154
Quantitative image analysis, 213, 219–221
Quantity/Frequency/Variability Index, 251
Quota system, 115–116

Race, 305
Radiofrequency denervation, 126
Radio frequency identification (RFID) tags, 276
Rancho Los Amigos Levels of Cognitive Functioning Scale (RLAS), 47
Rand 36-Item Health Survey, 154
Rand Corporation, 154, 463
Rand Health Insurance Experiments, 441
Rapid Alcohol Problems Screen (RAPS), 250
Rasch analysis, 158
Rating scale analysis, 158
Ratio level measurement (ratio level of measurement), 122, 160
RBANS. *See* Repeatable Battery for Assessment of Neuropsychological Status
Readiness Ruler, 251
Readiness to Change Questionnaire, 251
Reading ability, 72, 185, 224
Reading acquisition, 330
Reality negotiation, 383–384
"Reasonable accommodations," 408
"Reasonable certainty" standard, 184
Re-cross-examination phase (of trial), 184
Recruitment approach, 274
Redirect phase (of trial), 184
Referral letters, 359, 361
Referred pain, 15
Reflective listening, 115
Reflex erections, 17
Reflex sympathetic dystrophy, 397
Regional stroke syndromes, 67–68, 70, 72
Region of interest (ROI), 220, 230, 231
Rehabilitation Act of 1973, 357, 361, 468
Rehabilitation Institute of Chicago, 82
Rehabilitation neuropsychology, 165–174
  and behavioral/emotional assessment, 167, 170–171
  and cognitive assessment, 166–167
  and decision-making capacity, 171–172
  and follow-up assessment, 168–169
  in inpatient setting, 165–168
  and interventions, 167–168
  in outpatient setting, 168–171
  and patient/family education, 170
  and patient history, 166, 169
  and return to driving, 173
  and return to work, 172
  sensitivity in, 170
  and supervision of patients, 172–173
  testing in, 168–171

and treatment planning, 169–170
and treatment team, 165–166
Rehabilitation psychologist, competencies
of. *See* Competency(-ies), of
rehabilitation psychologist
Rehabilitation psychology
defined, 3
history of, 3–4, 468
increasing demand for, 3
multiple influences on, 477
practica in, 469–470
Rehabilitation services, in workplace,
410–411
Rehabilitation Services Administration
(RSA), 357
Rehabilitation team(s), 451–455
and ATCB interventions, 280
characteristics of optimal, 454–455
elements of successful, 452
history of the, 451
literature on, 453–454
models of, 452–453
and neuropsychology, 165–166
and pediatric neuropsychology,
318, 324
process of, 455
psychologist's role on, 454
structure of, 454
Reimbursement systems, 147, 444–445
Reinsurance, 441
Reitan, Ralph, 180
Relapse prevention, 253–254
Relational competency, of rehabilitation
psychologist, 461–462
Relational Cultural Model, 375
Relaxation, 111
Reliability
of assessment instrument, 159
of patient, 201
Reluctant patients
psychotherapy with, 266
with spinal cord injuries, 18
Remediation interventions, 322
Reminder systems, 290
Repeatable Battery for Assessment of
Neuropsychological Status
(RBANS), 68–69, 99, 167
"Requirement for of mourning," 109
Research, informed consent to, 432
Research competency, 473, 474
Resilience, 198, 418–419, 422
Respite care, 308
Responsibility, for change, 115
Restorative interventions, 286

Return to driving, 79–80, 173
Return to work, 51, 172
Reversible ischemic neurologic deficits
(RINDs), 64
RFID (radio frequency identification)
tags, 276
Rheumatoid arthritis, 374
Right hemisphere lesions, 72
Right hemisphere stroke, 172, 293
Right-left disorientation, 71
RINDs (reversible ischemic neurologic
deficits), 64
Risk aversion, 479
Risk pooling, 440
Risk taking, 479
RLAS (Rancho Los Amigos Levels of
Cognitive Functioning Scale), 47
Road tests, 173
ROI. *See* Region of interest
ROI quantitative image analysis, 219–220
Role release, 452
RSA (Rehabilitation Services
Administration), 357
Rural setting, caregiving in, 305
Rusk, Howard, 451
Rusk Institute of Rehabilitation
Medicine, 4

Safety monitoring, 276
SAH. *See* Subarachnoid hemorrhage
SAS (supervisory attention system), 291
SASSI-3. *See* Substance Abuse Subtle
Screening Inventory
SB. *See* Spina bifida
SCHIP (State Children's Health Insurance
Program), 446
School systems. *See also* Academic
reintegration
children with neurodevelopmental
conditions in, 333
and pediatric rehabilitation, 348–352
SCI. *See* Spinal cord injury
SCID. *See* Structured Clinical Interview
for the *DSM—IV*
SCI Model System of Care, 10, 55
SCL-90-R. *See* Symptom Check List-90-R
SCS. *See* Spinal cord stimulation
Secondary caregivers, 301
Secondary disability
in children with neurodevelopmental
conditions, 322
prevention of, 410–411
Secondary injuries, with traumatic brain
injury, 45

Seizures, 45, 50
Selective serotonin reuptake inhibitors
(SSRIs.), 12, 77, 100
Self-awareness, 167, 292–293
Self-directed plans, 443
Self-efficacy, 115, 421
Self-enhancing behaviors, 384
Self-esteem, 373
Self-esteem workshops, 264
Self-generation, 139
Self-image, 54, 385
Self-inflicted burns, 114
Self-insight, 383
Self-insured funds, 441
Self-management, 341
Self-Management Training (SMT), 292
Self-medication, 15
Self-monitoring training, 293
Self-regulation, 292
Self-worth, 331, 375
Sensing technologies, 276
Sensitivity
of assessment instrument, 159
to change, 160
to evolving difficulties, 170
Sensorimotor retuning (SMR), 396
SensorPain Rating Index, 122
Sensory neglect, 71
Septic shock, 213, 214
SES (socioeconomic status), 409
75% rule, 445–446, 463
Severe brain injury, 48
Severity of Alcohol Dependence
Questionnaire, 251
Sexual depression, 374
Sexual education, 54, 331–332
Sexuality
and amputation, 38
and spinal cord injury, 17–18
and stroke, 80–81
and traumatic brain injury, 54
of women with disabilities, 373–374
Sexually transmitted diseases (STDs), 18
Sexual orientation, 305
Sexual response, 374
SF-36 (Short form-36) health survey, 154
Shafranske, E., 368
Shaping, 400
Short Alcohol Dependence Data, 251
Short form-36 health survey (SF-36), 154
Short Michigan Alcoholism Screening
Test (SMAST), 248, 249
Shunting, 330
Siblings, 347
Sickle cell disease, 337

SIDI. *See* Stroke Inpatient Depression Inventory
Significant others, 267
Silent strokes, 64
Single photon emission computed tomography (SPECT), 224
SIP (social information processing), 332
16PF. *See* Sixteen Personality Factor Questionnaire
Sixteen Personality Factor Questionnaire (16PF), 204, 205
Skilled nursing facility (SNF), 446
Skill-related reorganization, 392
Skin grafts, 108
Sleep disturbance
    in burn patients, 116
    and geriatric rehabilitation, 102
Sleep restriction, 102
"Smart" sensing technology, 276
SMAST. *See* Short Michigan Alcoholism Screening Test
"Smearing," 393
Smoking, 372
SMR (sensorimotor retuning), 396
SMT (Self-Management Training), 292
SNF (skilled nursing facility), 446
Social anxiety, 13
Social–cognitive opportunities, 386–387
Social environment, 267
Social health issues, 372–373
Social information processing (SIP), 332
Social model of disability, 198
Social passivity, 332
Social phobia, 13
Social problem-solving skills, 307
Social psychology of disability, 379–387
    about, 380–381
    and attitudes toward people with disabilities, 381–383
    and coping with disability, 383–384
    existing/potential assets in, 385–386
    and experience of disability, 384–385
    future of, 386–387
    individuation/labeling in, 385
    insider–outsider distinction in, 385
    need for broader models of, 387
    and social–cognitive opportunities, 386–387
    somatopsychological relation in, 385
    and well-being, 386
Social risks, of children with neurodevelopmental conditions, 332–333
Social role participation, 156
Social Security Amendments of 1972, 442
Social Security assistance, 179

Social Security Disability Income (SSDI), 360
Social skills, 22, 372
Social skills training, 253
Social support
    and amputation, 31
    for caregivers of stroke victims, 81
    for children with neurodevelopmental conditions, 331
    and personality, 200
Socioeconomic status (SES), 409
Socioenvironmental context, 333
Soldiers, 3, 4, 29, 39
Somatic functioning, 204, 206
Somatoform disorders, 201
Somatomotor cortex, 393
Somatopsychological relation, 385
Somatosensory agnosia, 71
Spatial neglect, 71
Spatial route-finding tasks, 274–275
Specialization, 469
Specialty certification, 469–471
Specificity, of assessment instrument, 159
SPECT (single photon emission computed tomography), 224
Speech, 70–72, 76, 267, 294, 330
Speech Sounds Perception Test, 188
Speed-of-processing disorders, 288
Spina bifida (SB), 329, 330, 332–333, 345, 347, 349
Spinal cord injury (SCI), 9–23
    assessment/treatment issues with, 10–18
    characteristics of, 9–10
    classification of, 9
    cognitive deficits from, 14–15
    cognitive impairment with, 201
    coping/cognitive–behavioral interventions with, 19
    depression after, 201
    etiology and demographics of, 10
    intervention strategies for, 18–20
    pain with, 15–16, 120
    pediatric, 21–22
    peer counseling with, 20
    psychoeducational interventions with, 18–19
    psychological adjustment to, 11–14
    and sexuality, 17–18
    and substance abuse, 16–17, 201, 242–245
    vocational/educational issues with, 20–21
Spinal cord stimulation (SCS), 125–126
Spirituality, 365–369

defined, 366
    measuring spiritual well-being, 366–367
    and quality of life, 367–368
    and rehabilitation psychologists, 368–369
Spiritual well-being, 366–367
Spiritual Well-Being Scale (SWBS), 366–367
Sport-related concussions, 48–49
Sports activities, 10
Spouses, 53, 267
SR (subacute rehabilitation), 52
SSDI (Social Security Disability Income), 360
SSI (Supplemental Security Income), 360
SSRIs. *See* Selective serotonin reuptake inhibitors
Staff concerns, 78–79, 464
Standardized caregiver interventions, 304
State Children's Health Insurance Program (SCHIP), 446
State employment centers, 359
State–federal VR programs, 357
State v. Driver, 180
State vocational rehabilitation agencies
    access to, 358–359
    referral to, 53
    services provided through, 359–361
    working with, 361–362
State vocational rehabilitation counselors, 358
STDs (sexually transmitted diseases), 18
Stepped care models, 251–252
Stereotypes, 410
Stereotype threat, 386–387
Steroids, 125
Stigma, 382, 410
Stimulus conditioning, 116
Stimulus control, 102
Stop-loss levels, 441
Strasser, D. C., 453
Strategic Outcome Initiative (of CARF), 157
Stress, 374. *See also* Caregiver burden; Family burden
Stress management, 374
Stress management groups, 349
Stress-related growth, 419
String instrument players, 393
Stroke, 63–84
    about, 64–65
    acute medical assessment/treatment for, 68–70

acute rehabilitation assessment/
treatment for, 70–72
anterior cerebral artery, 67
anxiety with, 77–78
apathy with, 78
brain plasticity after, 394
and brain reorganization, 226
and caregiver burden, 81
chronic pain with, 120–121
cognitive impairment with, 201
defined, 64
and depression, 75–77, 101
economic impact of, 65
effectiveness of psychotherapeutic
interventions with, 263
emotional disorders with, 75–79
epidemiology of, 65
family/staff concerns about, 78–79
hemorrhagic, 66
impaired awareness with, 74–75
internal carotid artery, 67
ischemic, 66
middle cerebral artery, 67
neuropsychological disorders with,
70–74
and personality changes, 199
postacute assessment/treatment
for, 79–82
posterior cerebral artery, 67–68
psychological assessment/
interventions for, 68–82
psychologist's role in treatment of,
68–70, 73, 78–80, 82–84
regional, 67–68
research directions with, 82–84
risk factors for, 65
and sexual functioning, 80–81
types of, 65–68
and vocational functioning, 81–82
warning signs of, 64
Stroke Inpatient Depression Inventory
(SIDI), 204–206
Stroke psychologists, 63, 68
Stroke screening programs, 64
Stroke secondary to septic shock,
213, 214
Stroke units, 68
Structural imaging, 137, 214
Structured Clinical Interview for the
DSM–IV (SCID), 250, 251
Study base, 453
Stump pain, 36
Subacute rehabilitation (SR), 52
Subarachnoid hemorrhage (SAH), 65, 66

Subjective perspectives, 384
Subjective QoL, 148
Substance abuse, 241–254
alcoholism models, 245–247
brief interventions for, 252–253
and burn injuries, 110
community reinforcement approach to
treating, 253
coping and social skills training for
treating, 253
defined, 241
disability-specific interventions
for, 254
and geriatric rehabilitation, 102–103
myths about, 247
postinjury, 242–243
and relapse prevention, 253–254
screening for, 246–251
service delivery models for treating,
250–254
and spinal cord injury, 15–17,
242–245
and traumatic brain injury, 54, 201,
242–245
Substance abuse screening, 246–251
considerations in, 247–248
for patterns of substance use, 250
practical measures for, 248–250
Substance Abuse Subtle Screening
Inventory (SASSI-3), 248–250
Substance dependence, 241
Substance use, at time of injury, 242
Substance use disorders, 262
Sudden-onset brain injury, 315
Suicide, 12, 76
Superficial burn injuries, 107
Supervised experience, 471
Supervision, need for, 172–173
Supervision competency, 473, 474
Supervisory attention system (SAS), 291
Supplemental Security Income (SSI), 360
Supported conversation, 294
Supported employment, 21, 53, 82,
287, 360
Support groups
for amputees, 37
for burn injuries, 112
for caregivers, 307, 308
for families, 349
Support people, 287
SWBS. *See* Spiritual Well-Being Scale
Symptom Check List-90-R (SCL-90-R),
204, 206
Symptom validity testing, 187
Systemic interventions, 324

Tailored caregiver interventions, 304
Task Force of the Brain Injury Special
Interest Group, 285
Task interface design, for ATCB interven-
tions, 280–281
TBI. *See* Traumatic brain injury
TBI Model System of Care, 49, 51, 55
TBV (total brain volume), 216
Teachers, pediatric rehabilitation and,
348–352
Team, rehabilitation. *See* Rehabilitation
team(s)
Technical assistance, 360
Telehealth caregiver interventions,
303–304
Telephone-based psychotherapy, 264
Temporal summation, 128
Temporary partial disability, 411
Temporary total disability, 411
Temporomandibular disorder pain, 263
10 physical function (PF-10) items, 155
TENS (transcutaneous electrical nerve
stimulation), 126
Test data release, 429–430
Testimony, courtroom, 181–184
Test materials, 429
Test of Memory Malingering (TOMM), 187
Tetraplegia, 9, 14
Therapeutic exercise, 77
Third degree burns, 107
3MS (Modified MMSE), 68
Three-dimensional image representation,
216, 217
Threshold levels, of pain, 122
Thrombotic stroke, 65, 66
TIAs (transient ischemic attacks), 64
TICS (Two-Item Conjoint Screening), 250
Timeline Follow-back, 251
Time pressure management, 288–289
TinyOS, 276
TMS. *See* Transcranial magnetic stimulation
To Err is Human (IOM), 444
Tomlin, Lily, 477
TOMM (Test of Memory Malingering),
187
Total brain volume (TBV), 216
Total ventricular volume (TVV), 216
Trail Making Test, 184, 185
Training
in rehabilitation psychology, 471
for rehabilitation staff, 454
vocational, 360–361
Transcranial magnetic stimulation (TMS),
228, 396, 397

Transcutaneous electrical nerve stimulation (TENS), 126
Transdisciplinary teams, 452
Transient ischemic attacks (TIAs), 64
Transitional living programs, 52–53
Transportation, 360
Traumatic axonal injury, 45
Traumatic brain injury (TBI), 43–57
    academic reintegration after, 53–54
    acute stage of, 49
    assessment/interventions for, 49–54
    behavioral disturbance after, 201
    behavior management with, 50
    chronic pain with, 120
    cognitive rehabilitation after, 51
    complications, 45
    consciousness/coma with, 45–46
    defined, 43
    economic issues after, 56
    effectiveness of psychotherapeutic interventions with, 263
    efficacy of rehabilitation for, 56
    epidemiology of, 43–44
    and family reintegration, 53
    litigation over, 179
    models/standards of care for, 54–55
    nature/pathology of, 44–46
    neuropsychological assessment of, 49–50
    patient/family education and support for, 50
    postacute stage of, 49–54
    primary injuries with, 44
    prognostication of long-term outcome for, 51
    psychologist's role with, 49–54
    psychopharmacological management of, 50–51
    recovery/medical complications with, 46
    rehabilitation measurement with, 46–48
    secondary injuries with, 45
    and sexuality, 54
    and spinal cord injury, 14–15
    stages of, 48–49
    and substance abuse, 54, 201, 242–245
    vocational reintegration after, 53
Traumatic Brain Injury Model Systems of Care National Database, 43
Trazadone, 116
Treatment planning, 169–170
Trends, knowledge of, 464

Tricyclic antidepressants, 12, 77, 100, 116
Tunnel vision, 68
TVV (total ventricular volume), 216
Two-Item Conjoint Screening (TICS), 250
Type 2 diabetes, 29

"Ultimate issue" questions, 182
Unawareness. *See* Impaired awareness
Uniform Data System for Medical Rehabilitation, 157
Unilateral neglect, 399
United Kingdom, health-care spending in, 439
United States, health-care spending in, 439
Upper extremity amputation, 36
Urban setting, caregiving in, 305
U.S. Congress, 447–448
U.S. Department of Defense, 83
U.S. Department of Health and Human Services, 446
U.S. Department of Veterans Affairs, 83, 445
Use-dependent reorganization, 392

Validity
    of assessment instrument, 159
    ecological, 317
    neurological, 317
Valium, 17
Vanderbilt Multidimensional Pain Coping Inventory, 124
Vanderbilt Pain Management Inventory, 124
Vanishing cues, 289
VAS. *See* Visual analog scales
Vascular cognitive impairment (VCI), 69
Vascular dementia, 69
Vascular depression hypothesis, 100–101
VBM. *See* Voxel-based morphometry
VBR. *See* Ventricle-to-brain ratio
VCI (vascular cognitive impairment), 69
Ventral (anterior) cord syndrome, 9
Ventricle-to-brain ratio (VBR), 216–219
Ventromedial prefrontal cortex, 479
Verbal intellect, 332–333
Verbal priming, 274
Veterans, 29, 39
Veterans Administration Hospitals, 453
Victimization, 35
Violence, 10, 373
Virtual reality programs, 173

Visual agnosia, 71
Visual analog scales (VAS), 121–122
Visuoperceptual deficits, 330
Visuospatial deficits, 330
Visuospatial function, 293–294
Vocational evaluation services, 359
Vocational functioning, 81–82
Vocational goal clarification, 359
Vocational rehabilitation (VR), 357–362
    access to state agencies for, 358–359
    certified rehabilitation counselors in, 358
    considerations for, 361–362
    and one-stop state employment centers, 359
    process of, 357–358
    Projects With Industry program for, 361
    services provided for, 359–361
Vocational rehabilitation agencies
    access to, 358–359
    services provided through, 359–361
    working with, 361–362
Vocational reintegration
    after spinal cord injury, 20–21
    after traumatic brain injury, 53
Vocational training, 360–361
Voice recorders, 275
Voxel, 220
Voxel-based morphometry (VBM), 220–221
VR. *See* Vocational rehabilitation
VR counselors, 357, 358

WAIS-III. *See* Wechsler Adult Intelligence Scale-III
WAIS-R. *See* Wechsler Adult Intelligence Scale-Revised
Ware, John, 154
War injuries, 3, 4
Wechsler Adult Intelligence Scale-III (WAIS-III), 169, 185
Wechsler Adult Intelligence Scale-Revised (WAIS-R), 184, 188
Wechsler Intelligence Scale for Children-III (WISC-III), 185
Wechsler Memory Scale-III (WMS-III), 169, 185
Wechsler Memory Scale-Revised, 184
Wee-FIM (Functional Independence Measure-Pediatric), 160
Weinberg, Joseph, 4
Well-being
    construct of, 386
    spiritual, 366–367

Wernicke's aphasia, 71
Western Ontario and McMaster
    Osteoarthritis Index
    (WOMAC 3.1), 152
Whispering strokes, 64
White matter (WM), 213–215, 228–229,
    231, 330
White matter hyperintensity (WMH),
    215, 223–224
White matter hyperintensity (WMH)
    ratings, 223–224
White matter lesion ratings, 223–224
White matter lesions (WMLs), 223–224
WHO. *See* World Health Organization
Widowhood, 101
Wilson, Barbara, 169
Windup, 128
Wired for Health Care Quality Act of
    2007, 445
WISC-III (Wechsler Intelligence Scale for
    Children-III), 185
WMH. *See* White matter hyperintensity
WMLs. *See* White matter lesions

WMS-III. *See* Wechsler Memory Scale-III
WOMAC 3.1 (Western Ontario and
    McMaster Osteoarthritis Index),
    152
Women with disabilities, 371–375
    attitudinal/environmental context of,
        371–374
    mental health issues of, 373–374
    physical health issues of, 372
    prevalence of, 371
    recommendations for rehabilitation
        psychology with, 374–375
    social health issues of, 372–373
Wood, R. L. I., 452
Work, return to, 51, 172
Workers' compensation claims, 407
Workers' compensation systems,
    407–409
Workforce Investment Act of 1998, 359
Working memory disturbance, 72
Workplace, rehabilitation services in, 408
Work-related injury and disability,
    407–413

demographic factors in, 409
environmental factors in, 409
legislation related to, 408
musculoskeletal, 408–410
prevalence/costs of, 407
psychological assessment/treatment of,
    411–413
psychosocial factors in, 409
and secondary disability, 410–411
treatment factors in, 410
and workers' compensation systems,
    407–408
workplace factors in, 409
World Health Organization (WHO), 147,
    477, 478
World War II veterans, 468
Wraparound services, 443

Zaliplon, 116
Zangwill, Oliver, 286
Zoloft, 77
Zolpidem, 116
Zygapophyseal joint pain, 126

About the Editors

Robert G. Frank, PhD, is senior vice president for academic affairs and provost at Kent State University in Ohio. Previously, he was the dean of the College of Public Health and Health Professions at the University of Florida, where he also served as a professor in the Department of Clinical and Health Psychology. His first appointment was at the University of Missouri–Columbia School of Medicine, Department of Physical Medicine and Rehabilitation, where he established the Division of Clinical Health Psychology and Neuropsychology. He was a Robert Wood Johnson Health Policy Fellow in 1991–1992 and worked with Senator Jeff Bingaman (D-NM). After completing the fellowship, Dr. Frank returned to the University of Missouri, where, as assistant to the dean for health policy, he continued to work on federal and state health policy. He continued to work with Senator Bingaman and managed Missouri's state health reform effort, the ShowMe Health Reform Initiative. Dr. Frank holds a doctorate in clinical psychology from the University of New Mexico. He is a diplomate in clinical psychology from the American Board of Professional Psychology. He is past president and current fellow of Division 22 (Rehabilitation Psychology) of the American Psychological Association and a fellow of Division 12 (Society of Clinical Psychology) and Division 38 (Health Psychology).

At the time of his death in May 2007, **Mitchell Rosenthal, PhD,** was the chief operating officer at the Kessler Medical Rehabilitation Research and Education Corporation in West Orange, New Jersey and professor of physical medicine and rehabilitation at the New Jersey Medical School of the University of Medicine and Dentistry of New Jersey. He previously held faculty appointments at Wayne State University in Detroit, Rush Medical College in Chicago, Tufts University School of Medicine in Boston, and Virginia Commonwealth University in Richmond.

Dr. Rosenthal published the first comprehensive textbook on brain injury rehabilitation in 1993 (*Rehabilitation of the Adult and Child with Traumatic Brain Injury*), now in its third edition (1999). He cofounded the first scientific journal solely dedicated to traumatic brain injury, the *Journal of Head Trauma Rehabilitation*. Dr. Rosenthal was one of the original cofounders of the Brain Injury Association (formerly known as the National Head Injury Foundation) in 1980. He published over 100 peer-reviewed articles.

Dr. Rosenthal served as president of Division 22 (Rehabilitation Psychology) of the American Psychological Association (1992–1993), president of the American Board of Rehabilitation Psychology (1999–2001), president of the American Congress of Rehabilitation Medicine (2005–2006), and was a member of the board of trustees of the Commission on the Accreditation of Rehabilitation Facilities (1993–1998) and the American Board of Professional Psychology (2005–2007).

He received the first Annual Sheldon Berrol, MD, Clinical Services Award from the Brain Injury Association in 1988 for contributions to the advancement of the field of brain injury rehabilitation and the 2002 Robert L. Moody Prize for Distinguished Contributions to Brain Injury Rehabilitation from the University of Texas, as well as the American Congress of Rehabilitation Medicine Gold Key Award in 2002.

Bruce Caplan, PhD, ABPP, FACRM, is board certified in rehabilitation psychology and clinical neuropsychology by the American Board of Professional Psychology and is a fellow of the American Psychological Association (APA), National Academy of Neuropsychology, and American Congress of Rehabilitation Medicine. Dr. Caplan serves as associate editor of the *Journal of Head Trauma Rehabilitation* and is a member of the editorial boards of the *Archives of Physical Medicine and Rehabilitation, Topics in Stroke Rehabilitation,* and *Rehabilitation Psychology.* He previously served as editor of *Rehabilitation Psychology.* In 1987, Dr. Caplan edited the first comprehensive rehabilitation psychology textbook (*Rehabilitation Psychology Desk Reference*), and he is a coeditor of the forthcoming *Encyclopedia of Clinical Neuropsychology.* He is past president of the Philadelphia Neuropsychology Society and of Division 22 (Rehabilitation Psychology) of the APA. He is the recipient of 2 Distinguished Service Awards and the Lifetime Achievement Award from Division 22. Dr. Caplan was a founding member of the American Board of Rehabilitation Psychology. Currently in independent practice, he was formerly professor and chief psychologist in the Department of Rehabilitation Medicine at Jefferson Medical College.